EXPERT SYSTEMS

Principles and Programming

Fourth Edition

Joseph Giarratano
University of Houston-Clear Lake

Gary Riley
PeopleSoft, Inc.

THOMSON
COURSE TECHNOLOGY

Australia • Canada • Mexico • Singapore • Spain • United Kingdom • United States

Expert Systems
Principles and Programming
by Joseph Giarratano and Gary Riley

Senior Acquisitions Editor: Amy Yarnevich
Senior Product Manager: Alyssa Pratt
Editorial Assistant: Jennifer Smith
Production Editor: Jennifer Harvey

Designer: Pre-Press Company, Inc.
Cover Design: Laura Rickenbach
Compositor: Pre-Press Company, Inc.
Printer: Transcontinental, Louiseville

Printed in Canada

1 2 3 4 5 6 7 8 9 BM 06 05 04 03 02

For more information, contact Course Technology,
25 Thomson Place, Boston, Massachusetts, 02210.
Or find us on the World Wide Web at: www.course.com

ISBN 0-534-38447-1

Contents

PREFACE

OR HOW TO USE THIS BOOK EFFECTIVELY

This 4th edition is a major revision of the internationally used textbook on expert systems and programming in the CLIPS expert system tool. Expert systems have experienced tremendous growth and popularity since their commercial introduction in the 1980s. Today, expert systems are widely used in business, science, engineering, agriculture, manufacturing, medicine, video games, and virtually every other field. In fact, it's difficult to think of a field in which expert systems are not used today.

This book is meant to educate students about expert systems theory and programming. The material is written at the upper-division/graduate level suitable for majors in computer science, management information systems, software engineering, and other fields who are interested in expert systems. New terminology is shown in boldface and immediately explained and indexed. Numerous examples and references help clarify the meaning of the text and provide guidance for supplementary reading. In this new 4th edition, links to many new free and trial versions of software tools that can serve as the basis of additional exercise and learning materials are also in Appendix G.

The discussion of new material is generally treated in the historical context so that students can appreciate why the material was developed, not just how to use it. It is this focus on *why* new techniques have to be invented to solve problems that is at the heart of education, rather than training courses which focus simply on how to use an application.

Expert Systems: Principles and Programming is divided into two parts: theory in Chapters 1–6, and programming in the CLIPS expert systems tool in Chapters 7–12. The first part comprises the theory behind expert systems and how expert systems fit into the scope of computer science.

While a previous course in Artificial Intelligence (AI) is helpful, this book provides a self-contained introduction to AI topics in Chapter 1 that are appropriate for expert systems. Naturally a single chapter cannot cover what is contained in entire books on AI. However it is adequate for a broad survey of AI and the role expert systems was developed for. The first part of the book covers the logic, probability, data structures, AI concepts, and other topics that form the theory of expert systems.

We have tried to explain the theory behind expert systems so that a student may make an informed decision regarding the appropriate use of expert system technology. The important point we emphasize is that like any other tool, expert systems have advantages and disadvantages. The theory also explains how expert systems relate to other programming methods such as conventional programming. Another reason for discussing theory is that the student can read current research papers in expert systems, but, because expert systems draw from so many diverse fields, it is difficult for a beginner to just start reading papers with comprehension.

The second part of this book is an introduction to the CLIPS expert system tool. This part is a practical introduction to expert system programming that serves to reinforce and clarify the theoretical concepts developed in the first part. As with the theory part of the book, the programming part can be understood by students with some programming experience in a high-level language. Students learn the practical problems associated with expert system development using CLIPS, a modern, powerful expert system tool.

A new feature discussed in this 4th edition is COOL, the CLIPS Object-Oriented Language. COOL allows expert systems to be developed entirely using objects, or with both rules and objects in a hybrid approach. The advantage of an object-oriented approach is that sets of knowledge can be conveniently grouped in larger collections than individual rules. All the normal properties of objects–such as multiple inheritance–make it easy to extend objects with more specialized knowledge rather than "reinventing the wheel" and coding from scratch each time as in the case of a pure rule system. The 4th edition also discusses the procedural programming capabilities of CLIPS, including global variables, functions, and generic functions.

The first versions of CLIPS were developed by NASA at the Johnson Space Center where Gary Riley was the lead programmer in developing its rule-based components. Joseph C. Giarratano served as consultant and wrote the official NASA CLIPS User Guides. Today, CLIPS is used for real-world projects in government, business, and industry, and virtually everywhere. A search using any Internet search engine will turn up hundreds or thousands of references to expert systems written in CLIPS, and courses at many universities around the world that use CLIPS.

Because the CLIPS source code is portable, it can be run on virtually any computer or operating system that supports an ANSI C or C++ compiler. The CD-ROM included with this book contains: CLIPS executables for Windows, and MacOS; the CLIPS Reference Manual and CLIPS Users Guide; and the well-documented complete C source code for CLIPS.

Some expert systems courses have a term project associated with them. A project is an excellent way to develop skills in expert systems. Students usually complete small expert systems of 50–150 rules in a semester project of their choice. Thousands of projects and hundreds of courses based on this book have been done including medical, automobile diagnosis, taxi scheduling, personnel scheduling, computer network management, weather forecasting, stock market prediction, consumer buying advice, and many others. A search using an Internet search engine will reveal many courses and resources such as PowerPoint slides, syllabi, and assignments developed by universities around the world.

The suggested plan for a one-semester course is as follows:

1. Cover Chapter 1 to provide a quick introduction to expert systems. In particular, assign Problems 1, 2, and 3.
2. Cover Chapters 7–10 to introduce the basic programming in CLIPS. It is helpful for students to recode Problem 2 of Chapter 1 to contrast the expert system approach with the language they originally used in Chapter 1.

This contrast is very useful in pointing out the differences between a rule-based language such as CLIPS, and LISP, PROLOG, or whatever the original language used for Problem 2. Alternatively, after Chapter 10, the instructor may return to the theory section. If students have a strong background in logic and PROLOG, most of Chapters 2 and 3 may be skipped. Students who have had a LISP-based introductory AI course or none at all will benefit from Chapters 2 and 3 if a strong emphasis on logic and the fundamental theory of expert systems is desired. If students have a strong background in probability and statistics, the material in Chapter 4 up to Section 4.11 can be skipped.

3. Chapters 4 and 5 discuss the topic of dealing with uncertainty. This is very important since human beings deal with uncertainty all the time and without it, expert systems would be no more than simple decision trees. Uncertainty topics include probabilistic and Bayesian inference, certainty factors, Dempster-Shafer theory, and fuzzy theory. Students will gain an understanding of these methods in sufficient detail so that they can read current papers in the field and start doing research, if desired.
4. Chapter 6 discusses knowledge acquisition and the software engineering of expert systems; it is meant for those students planning to work on large expert systems. It is not necessary to discuss this chapter before assigning term projects. In fact, it would be best to cover this chapter last so that the student can appreciate all the factors that go into building a quality expert system.

SUPPLEMENTAL RESOURCES

A manual with solutions to the odd-numbered problems and selected even-numbered programs, as well as a complete PowerPoint presentation, are available for download from the publisher's website, http://www.course.com. In addition, many Web links to software and other resources have been added throughout the text. These resources have been chosen so that students can gain a better hands-on understanding of the topics, such as logic and probability, by using software to experiment with non-trivial problems instead of doing problems only be hand. A large number of resources on AI, logic, probability, Bayesian inference, fuzzy logic, and other topics have also been included so that students will have a broader knowledge of the AI and expert systems community worldwide.

CONTRIBUTORS TO CLIPS

We would like to thank all of the people who contributed to the success of CLIPS. As with any large project, CLIPS is the result of the efforts of numerous people. The primary contributors have been: Robert Savely, Chief Scientist of Advanced Software Technology at JSC, who conceived the project and provided overall direction and support; Chris Culbert, Branch Chief of the Software Technology Branch, who managed the project and wrote the original CLIPS

Reference Manual; Gary Riley, who designed and developed the rule-based portion of CLIPS, co-authored the CLIPS Reference Manual and CLIPS Architecture Manual, developed the Macintosh interface for CLIPS, and maintains CLIPS as well as the official CLIPS website at http://www.ghg.net/clips/CLIPS.html; Brian Donnell, who developed the CLIPS Object Oriented Language (COOL), co-authored the CLIPS Reference Manual and CLIPS Architecture Manual; Bebe Ly, who developed the X Window interface for CLIPS; Chris Ortiz, who developed the Windows 3.1 interface for CLIPS; Dr. Joseph Giarratano of the University of Houston Clear Lake, who wrote the official NASA CLIPS User Guide for each release of CLIPS by NASA; and especially Frank Lopez, who wrote the original prototype version of CLIPS.

ACKNOWLEDGEMENTS

In writing this book, a number of people have made very helpful comments: Ted Leibfried, Jeanne Leslie, Mac Umphrey, Terry Feagin, Dennis Murphy, Jenna Giarratano, and Melissa Giarratano. We would also like to acknowldge the feedback of the 4th edition reviewers: Chien-Chung Chan, University of Akron; Constantine Vassiliadis, Ohio University: Jenny Scott, Concordia University—Canada; and Anthony Zygmont, Villanova University.

We also wish to thank the many people who have added enhancements to CLIPS over the 20 years since its first release in 1985. By providing the complete source code for CLIPS available free, the open source community has greatly expanded the power and popularity of CLIPS to a degree we did not dream of back in 1985 when we were just developing CLIPS. At that time expert systems was still a new and untested technology and no one knew if it would stand the test of time. Over the last 20 years CLIPS has grown from a modest beginning at NASA to being used by thousands of people in a worldwide community proving the benefits of CLIPS in virtually every area. We particularly want to thank all these developers who have expanded the power and capabilities of CLIPS, turning what was once a small and risky project meant only as a simple trial of AI technology at NASA into to a worldwide phenomenon.

One person who has contributed to the spread of expert systems in a significant way is Ernest Friedman-Hill who independently wrote a version of CLIPS in Java called JESS with new features. He has also written a book on JESS, *Jess in Action: Rule-Based Systems in Java*, with a number of interesting projects.

JESS: (http://herzberg.ca.sandia.gov/jess/) that complement CLIPS, and

KAPICLIPS 1.0: (http://www.cs.umbc.edu/kqml/software/kapiclips.shtml)

Other descendants of CLIPS:

PerlCLIPS (http://www.discomsys.com/~mps/dnld/clips-stuff/)
Protégé is an ontology editor and a knowledge-base editor for CLIPS (http://protege.stanford.edu/index.html)
Python-CLIPS interface (http://www.yodanet.com/portal/Products/download/clips-python.tar.gz/view)
TixClips is an Integrated Development Environment for the CLIPS expert system using the Tix (http://tix.sourceford.net)/
TclClips (www.eolas.net/tcl/clips), SWIG (http://www.swig.org/) wrapping (http://starship.python.net/crew/mike/TixClips/)

WebCLIPS is an implementation of CLIPS as a CGI application.
WebCLIPS: (http://www.monmouth.com/~km2580/wchome.htm)
wxCLIPS, an environment for developing knowledge base systems applications with graphical user interfaces: (http://www.anthemion.co.uk/wxclips/wxclips2.htm)
ZClips 0.1allows Zope to interact with CLIPS:
(http://www.zope.org/Members/raystream/zZCLIPS0.1)

CLIPS/R2 from Production Systems Technologies: (http://www.pst.com/clips_r2.htm)

Other versions of CLIPS are available such as the FuzzyClips from the National Research Council of Canada: (http://ai.iit.nrc.ca/IR_public/fuzzy/fuzzyClips/fuzzyCLIPSIndex.html)

Togai InfraLogic, Inc. FuzzyClips: (http://www.ortech-engr.com/fuzzy/fzyclips.html)

AdaCLIPS: (http://www.telepath.com/~dennison/Ted/AdaClips/AdaClips.html)

CLIPS and Perl with extensions: (http://cape.sourceforge.net/)

Many other versions of CLIPS-based tools are listed at (http://www.ghg.net/clips/OtherWeb.html).

CHAPTER 1
Introduction to Expert Systems

1.1 INTRODUCTION

This chapter is a broad introduction to expert systems. The fundamental principles of expert systems are introduced. The advantages and disadvantages of expert systems are discussed and the appropriate areas of application for expert systems are described. The relationship of expert systems to other methods of programming are also discussed.

1.2 WHAT IS AN EXPERT SYSTEM?

During the 20th Century, a number of definitions of **artificial intelligence** (AI) were proposed. One of the earliest popular definitions of AI was, and still is: "making computers think like people," as evident by the large number of science fiction movies that promote this view. Actually this definition has its roots in the British mathematician and computer pioneer Alan Turing's famous Turing Test in which a human would try to determine if the "person" they were talking to via a remote keyboard was a human or computer program. Passing such a test is considered to be **strong AI**. The term *strong AI* is promoted by the people who believe AI should be based on a strong logical foundation rather than what they call the **weak AI** based on artificial neural networks, genetic algorithms, and evolutionary methods. Today it is evident that no one technique of AI can successfully deal with all problems; a combination of methods works best.

The first program to pass the Turing Test was written as an experiment in psychology by Steven Weizenbaum in 1967; since then the knowledge and interaction with people has greatly increased and a $100,000 competition called the **Loebner Prize** is held to see which is best (http://www.loebner.net/Prizef/loebner-prize.html). Of course, today communication is often by speech recognition rather than the old-style teletype or keyboard. So if you are ever frustrated thinking you're talking to a person on the phone and they just don't understand what you're saying, ask if they've passed the Turing test.

Expert systems were developed as research tools in the 1960s as a special type of AI to successfully deal with complex problems in a narrow domain such as medical disease diagnosis. The classic problem of building a general-purpose AI program that can solve any problem has been too difficult without specific knowledge of the problem domain, i.e., medical disease diagnosis. Expert systems have greatly increased in popularity since their commercial introduction in the early 1980s. Today, expert systems are used in business, science, engineering, manufacturing, and many other fields in which there exists a well-defined problem domain. In fact if you are selected to get audited by the IRS or turned down for a credit card, an expert system made that decision.

The keyword mentioned in the previous sentence is "well-defined," and will be discussed in more detail later. The basic idea is that if a human expert can specify the steps of reasoning by which a problem may be solved, so too can an expert system. If a person cannot explain their reasoning, they may have better luck in Las Vegas.

As a counterexample, many people have attempted to write expert systems to predict the stock market; in fact Wall Street uses these systems all the time. However, if you look at all the ups and downs of Wall Street, no obvious trend occurs and the systems are no better than their creator. The big advantage of these systems is in real-time trading in which delays in purchasing of a millisecond are critical since a competitor's expert system may notice the same trend as yours and be placing buy or sell orders for hundreds of millions of dollars worth of stock, far faster than any human being can do. How well does it work? The infamous stock market crash of 1987 brought a host of new restrictions to trading to prevent computers selling hundreds of millions of shares to make a profit of a few hundred dollars and potentially cause a crash.

Expert systems is a very successful application of artificial intelligence technology. Many hybrid approaches exist to combine expert systems with other techniques such as genetic algorithms and artificial neural networks. The common term for a system that uses AI is **intelligent system** or automated system (Hopgood 01).

In general, the first step in solving any problem is defining the problem area or **domain** to be solved. This consideration is just as true in AI as in conventional programming. However, because of the mystique associated with AI by the general public, there is a lingering tendency to still believe the old adage: "It's an AI problem if it ain't been solved yet." Another popular definition believed by most people is that "AI is making computers act like they do in the movies." This type of mindset may have been popular in the 1970s when AI was entirely in a research stage. Today there are many real-world problems that are being solved by AI and many commercial applications, as discussed in online magazines such as *PCAI.com*, conferences such as the AAAI (http://aaii.org/conferences/conferences.htm), and books (Luger 02). For more details, see Appendix G.

Before discussing AI in more detail, it is worthwhile to step back and look at the big picture of how AI fits into the scheme of life itself. This leads us to the first question: What is life? There are many definitions of life as described in

(Adami 98) ranging from physiological, metabolic, biochemical, genetic, and thermodynamic depending on how you view it. Which definition is correct? It all depends on what aspect of life you are interested in. Perhaps the simplest is Shakespeare's, "Life is a tale told by an idiot, full of sound and fury, signifying nothing."

From a computer perspective, *life* can be represented as software. In fact there is software on the CD in the Adami book that allows the user to create artificial lifeforms and experiment with them. There is also the metaphysical definition of life as so aptly described in movies like *The Matrix* in which people "line" inside some giant computer program. Other aspects of artificial life as created in the digital computer are described in (Helmreich 98), which discusses in more detail the philosophical and even spiritual aspects of computer artificial life.

From a biological point of view, we are no longer limited to computer systems in the quest to create artificial lifeforms. Starting in the 1990s it was possible to clone mammals such as Dolly the Sheep, and companies now sell cows to business as well as cloned pets such as cats to bereaved pet owners. But cloning to make a close copy of a living creature, i.e., artificial life, is only the first step in "improving" life. For example, one group of researchers has created a bunny with an extra gene from fireflies to make it glow in the dark. Such forms of artificial life have no single natural ancestors from which to descend and are truly artificial life. At the same time, since these creatures are intelligent, they can also be considered to have artificial intelligence, although not the kind it has been customary to represent using digital computers.

Extending on artificial life is the new field of *creative evolutionary systems* in which artificial life systems are allowed to change their own programming in response to evolutionary pressure as described in (Bentley 02). Many different techniques such as genetic algorithms are described with practical applications to music, art, circuit design, architecture, and fighter aircraft maneuvering. Also included with the Bentley book is a CD that allows the user to experiment with creative evolutionary systems. Note that the book is concerned with the computer representation of these systems, not the new biological lifeforms which in the future will be purposely grown to achieve the designer's dreams—e.g., a glowing bunny (already created) to comfort children in the dark, or a monkey that is a better aircraft pilot than any human being.

In (de Silva 00) another definition of intelligence is given as: "Intelligence is the capacity to learn, the capacity to acquire, adapt, modify, and extend knowledge in order to solve problems." In this case, the desire is to build intelligent machines that interact with the real world through robotics, factories, appliances, and other hardware. The challenge is to incorporate into machines the complex human mechanisms in dealing with the real world such as ambiguity, vagueness, generality, imprecision, uncertainty, fuzziness, belief, and plausibility. Many of these topics are discussed later in this book in Chapters 4 and 5 on Uncertainty. Note that the previous sentence is itself vague. Does "this book" refer to the de Silva book or *Expert Systems Principles and Programming*? As living creatures we are used to dealing with problems like this all the time but robots and computers have a difficult time with ambiguity if only classical logic is used.

An even more challenging problem is to develop artificial intelligence systems that are also conscious. While much is known about the brain (Cotterill

98), we still do not know where is the screen on which consciousness is played or what makes you the person you are. However with new tools such as functional magnetic resonance imaging (fMRI), the brain is being mapped dynamically to see which areas are activated during metal activities. Of course if we use the artificially cloned animal's model, then we have already succeeded because the sheep and cats are certainly conscious. Nevertheless, we still do not know how to imbue a machine with consciousness. Even more important, after seeing the *Terminator* or the *Matrix* movies, it may not be wise to even want a conscious machine intelligence. After all, no one likes to be unplugged, people or machines.

Although perfect solutions to classic AI problems such as natural language translation, speech understanding, and vision have not been found, restricting the problem domain produces a useful solution. For example, it is not difficult today to build simple natural language systems if the input is restricted to sentences of the form: noun, verb, and object. Currently, systems of this type work very well in providing a user-friendly interface to many software products such as database systems and spreadsheets. Speaker-independent voice recognition systems are also now available with a high degree of accuracy that do not require training on a particular user's voice as was the case with early systems. Coupled with expert systems, such intelligent systems will eventually replace many telephone call centers that take orders from customers once these systems pass the Turing Test (Luger 02).

A number of commercial versions of speech recognition systems that work with standard PC programs are available and quite reasonably priced. Voice recognition systems are also widely available for hands-free cell phone operation in automobiles and have excellent recognition if the problem domain is limited to digits rather than all words. In fact, the parsers associated with popular computer text-adventure games today exhibit an amazing degree of ability in understanding natural language, which is a necessity with multiplayer LAN-party games in which typing would slow down the game.

Expert systems have been combined with databases for human-like pattern recognition and automated decision systems to yield knowledge discovery through **data mining** and thus produce an **intelligent database** (Bramer 99). One important application is in airport security systems that use face recognition of suspects as a front-end to an expert system, which then determines if there is justification in proceeding with further notification of authorities.

Another exciting area of artificial intelligence has to do with artificial **discovery systems.** These are computer programs that can actually discover knowledge in certain problem domains. For example, the Automatic Mathematician (AM) program discovers new mathematical theorems and rediscovers knowledge made by humans such as the significance of prime numbers. The BACON 3 discovery system discovers new scientific knowledge such as a version of Kepler's third law of planetary motion, and a number of discovery systems are summarized in (Wagman 99).

While AI was originally defined as a branch of Computer Science in the 20th Century, it is now a standalone discipline that draws on many fields such as computer science, psychology, biology, neuroscience, and many others. In fact there are a growing number of universities that offer degrees in AI.

Figure 1.1 shows some areas of interest for AI. The area of expert systems is a very successful approximate solution to the classic AI problem of programming intelligence. Professor Edward Feigenbaum of Stanford University, an early pioneer of expert systems technology, has defined an **expert system** as ". . . an intelligent computer program that uses knowledge and inference procedures to solve problems that are difficult enough to require significant human expertise for their solution". That is, an expert system is a computer system that emulates the decision-making ability of a human expert. The term **emulate** means that the expert system is intended to act in all respects like a human expert. An emulation is much stronger than a *simulation* which is required to act like the real thing in only some respects.

Although a general-purpose problem solver still eludes us, expert systems function very well in their restricted domains. As proof of their success, you need only observe the many applications of expert systems today in business, medicine, science, and engineering as well as all the books, journals, conferences, and products devoted to expert systems shown in Appendix G.

Expert systems makes extensive use of specialized knowledge to solve problems at the level of a human expert. An **expert** is a person who has *expertise* in a certain area. That is, the expert has knowledge or special skills that are not known or available to most people. An expert can solve problems that most people cannot solve at all or solve them much more efficiently (but not necessarily

Figure 1.1 Some Areas of Artificial Intelligence

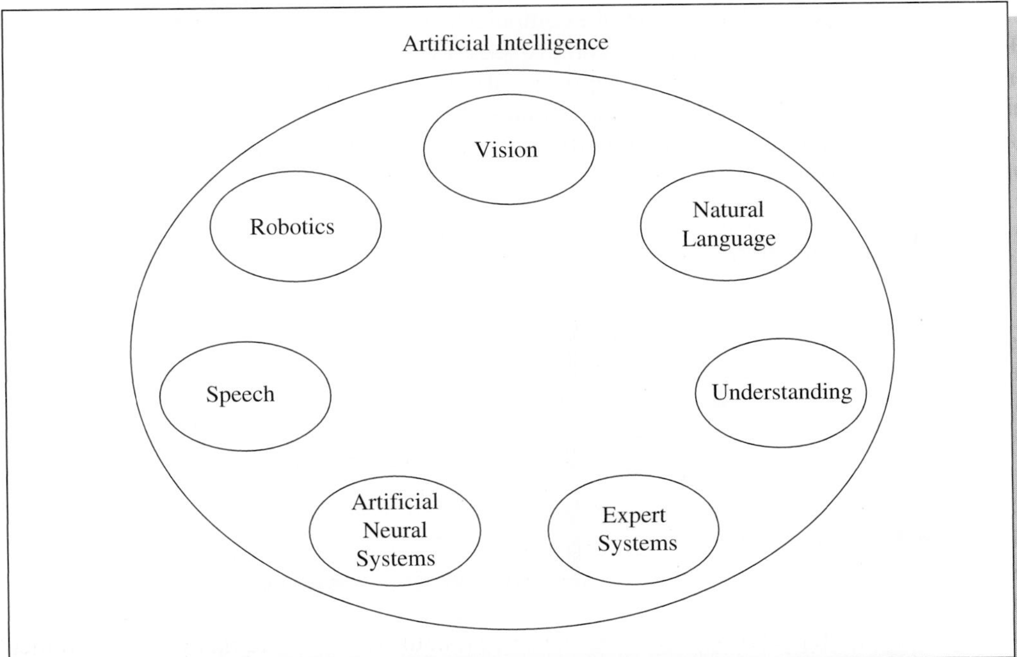

as inexpensively.) When expert systems were first developed they contained expert knowledge exclusively. However, the term expert system is often applied today to any system that uses expert system technology. Expert system technology may include special expert system languages, programs, and hardware designed to aid in the development and execution of expert systems.

The knowledge in expert systems may be either expertise, or knowledge that is generally available from books, magazines, and knowledgeable persons. In this sense, *knowledge* is considered to be at a lower level than the more rare expertise. The terms **expert system**, **knowledge-based system,** and **knowledge-based expert system** are often used synonymously. Most people use expert system simply because it's shorter, even though there may be no expertise in their expert system, only knowledge.

Figure 1.2 illustrates the basic concept of a knowledge-based expert system. The user supplies facts or other information to the expert system and receives expert advice or expertise in response. Internally, the expert system consists of two main components. The knowledge base contains the knowledge with which the **inference engine** draws conclusions. These conclusions are the expert system's responses to the user's queries for expertise.

Useful knowledge-based systems also have been designed to act as an intelligent assistant to a human expert. These intelligent assistants are designed with expert systems technology because of the development advantages. As more knowledge is added to the intelligent assistant, it acts more like an expert. Developing an intelligent assistant may be a useful milestone in producing a complete expert system. In addition, it may free up more of the expert's time by speeding up the solution of problems. Intelligent tutors are another application of artificial intelligence. Unlike the old computer-assisted instruction systems, intelligent tutor systems can provide context-sensitive instruction (Giarratano 91a).

An expert's knowledge is specific to one **problem domain** as opposed to general problem-solving techniques. A problem domain is the special problem area such as medicine, finance, science, or engineering that an expert can solve problems in very well. Expert systems, like human experts, are generally

Figure 1.2 Basic Function of an Expert System

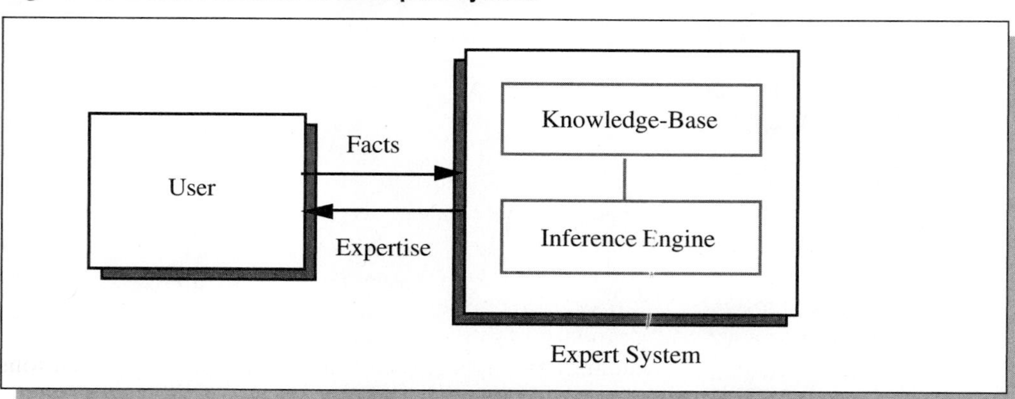

Figure 1.3 Problem and Knowledge Domain Relationship

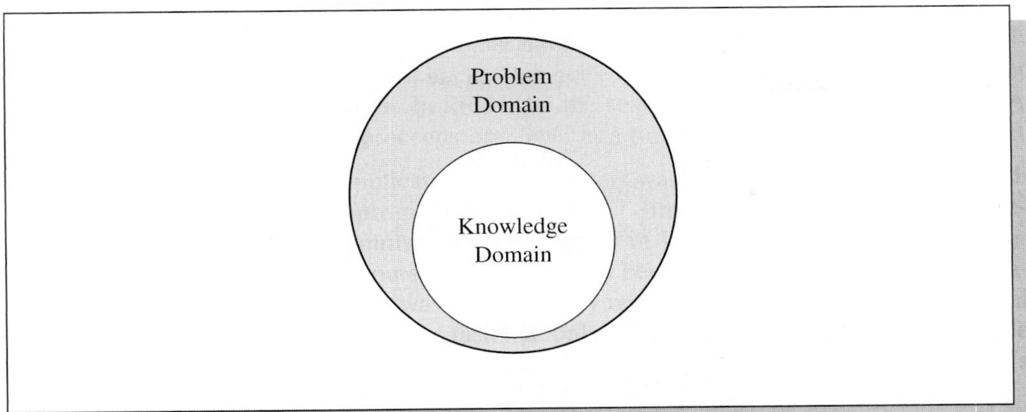

designed to be experts in one problem domain. For example, you would not normally expect a chess expert to have expert knowledge about medicine. Expertise in one problem domain does not automatically carry over to another.

The expert's knowledge about solving specific problems is called the **knowledge domain** of the expert. For example, a medical expert system designed to diagnose infectious diseases will have a great deal of knowledge about certain symptoms caused by infectious diseases. In this case the knowledge domain is medicine and consists of knowledge about diseases, symptoms, and treatments. Figure 1.3 illustrates the relationship between the problem and knowledge domain. Notice that this knowledge domain is entirely included within the problem domain. The portion outside the knowledge domain symbolizes the area in which there is not knowledge about all the problems within the problem domain.

One expert system, such as an infectious diseases diagnostic system, usually does not have knowledge about other branches of medicine such as surgery or pediatrics. Although its knowledge of infectious disease is equivalent to or greater than a human expert, the expert system would not know anything about other knowledge domains unless it was programmed with that domain knowledge.

In the knowledge domain that it knows about, the expert system reasons or makes **inferences** in the same way that a human expert would reason or infer the solution of a problem. That is, given some facts, a logical, possible conclusion that follows is inferred by reason. For example, if your spouse hasn't spoken to you in a month, you may infer that he or she had nothing worthwhile to say. However, this is only one of several possible inferences.

As with any technology, there are many ways of viewing its utility. Table 1.1 summarizes the differing views of the participants in a technology. In this table, the technologist may be an engineer or software designer and the technology may be hardware or software. In solving any problem, there are questions that need to be answered or the technology will not be successfully used. Like any other tool, expert systems have appropriate and inappropriate applications. Chapter 6 discussed choosing appropriate applications in more detail.

Table 1.1 Differing Views of Technology

Person	Question
Manager	What can I use it for?
Technologist	How can I best implement it?
Researcher	How can I extend it?
Consumer	Will it save me time or money?
Business owner	Can I cut labor?
Stockbroker	How will it affect quarterly profits?

1.3 ADVANTAGES OF EXPERT SYSTEMS

Expert systems have a number of attractive features:

- *Increased availability.* Expertise is available on any suitable computer hardware. In a very real sense, an expert system is the mass production of expertise.
- *Reduced cost.* The cost of providing expertise per user is greatly lowered.
- *Reduced danger.* Expert systems can be used in environments that might be hazardous for a human.
- *Permanence.* The expertise is permanent. Unlike human experts who may retire, quit, or die, the expert system's knowledge will last indefinitely.
- *Multiple expertise.* The knowledge of multiple experts can be made available to work simultaneously and continuously on a problem at any time of day or night. The level of expertise combined from several experts may exceed that of a single human expert.
- *Increased reliability.* Expert systems increase confidence that the correct decision was made by providing a second opinion to a human expert or a tie-breaker in disagreements among multiple human experts. (Of course, this method probably won't work if the expert system was programmed by one of the experts.) The expert system should always agree with the expert, unless a mistake was made by the expert, which may happen if the human expert is tired or under stress.
- *Explanation.* The expert system can explain in detail the reasoning that led to a conclusion. A human may be too tired, unwilling, or unable to do this all the time. This increases the confidence that the correct decision is made.
- *Fast response.* Fast or real-time response may be necessary for some applications. Depending on the software and hardware used, an expert system may respond faster and be more available than a human expert. Some emergency situations may require responses faster than a human; in this case a real-time expert system is a good choice.
- *Steady, unemotional, and complete response at all times.* This may be very important in real-time and emergency situations when a human expert may not operate at peak efficiency because of stress or fatigue.
- *Intelligent tutor.* The expert system may act as an intelligent tutor by letting the student run sample programs and explaining the system's reasoning.

- *Intelligent database.* Expert systems can be used to access a database in an intelligent manner. Data mining is an example.

The process of developing an expert system has an indirect benefit also since the knowledge of human experts must be put into an explicit form for entering in the computer. Because the knowledge is then explicitly known instead of being implicit in the expert's mind, it can be examined for correctness, consistency, and completeness. The knowledge may then have to be adjusted (which is not appreciated by the expert!)

1.4 GENERAL CONCEPTS OF EXPERT SYSTEMS

The knowledge of an expert system may be represented in a number of ways. One common method of representing knowledge is in the form of IF THEN type **rules**, such as:

```
IF the light is red THEN stop
```

If a fact exists that the light is red, this matches the pattern "the light is red." The rule is satisfied and performs its action of "stop." Although this is a very simple example, many significant expert systems have been built by expressing the knowledge of experts in rules. In fact, the knowledge-based approach to developing expert systems has completely supplanted the early AI approach of the 1950s and 1960s which tried to use sophisticated reasoning techniques with no reliance on knowledge. Some types of expert systems tools such as CLIPS allow **objects** as well as rules. Knowledge can be encapsulated in rules and objects. Rules can pattern match on objects as well as facts. Alternatively, objects can operate independently of the rules.

Since their first successful commercial use in the XCON/R1 system of Digital Equipment Corporation, which knew much more than any single human expert on how to configure computer systems, expert systems have demonstrated their value and usefulness over and over again. Many small systems for specialized tasks have been constructed with several hundred rules. These small systems may not operate at the level of an expert but are designed to take advantage of expert systems technology to perform knowledge-intensive tasks. For these small systems, the knowledge may be in books, journals, or other publicly available documentation.

In contrast, a classic expert system embodies unwritten knowledge that must be extracted from an expert by extensive interviews with a **knowledge engineer** over a long period of time. The process of building an expert system is called **knowledge engineering** and is done by a knowledge engineer. Knowledge engineering refers to the acquisition of knowledge from a human expert or other source and its coding in the expert system.

The general stages in the development of an expert system are illustrated in Figure 1.4. The knowledge engineer first establishes a dialog with the human expert in order to elicit the expert's knowledge. This stage is analogous to a system designer in conventional programming discussing the system requirements with

Figure 1.4 Development of an Expert System

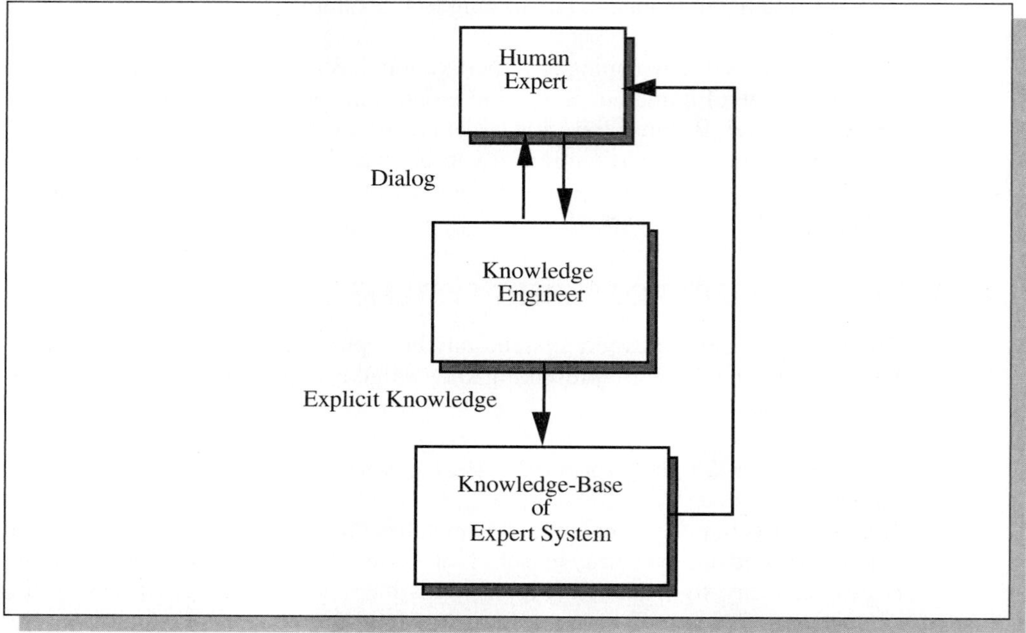

a client for whom the program will be constructed. The knowledge engineer then codes the knowledge explicitly in the knowledge base. The expert then evaluates the expert system and gives a critique to the knowledge engineer. This process iterates until the system's performance is judged to be satisfactory by the expert.

The expression **knowledge-based system** is a better term for the application of knowledge-based technology because it may be used for the creation of either expert systems or knowledge-based systems. However, like the term *artificial intelligence*, it is common practice today to use the term *expert systems* when referring to both expert systems and knowledge-based systems, even when the knowledge is not at the level of a human expert.

Expert systems are generally designed very differently from conventional programs because the problems have no satisfactory algorithmic solution and rely on inferences to achieve a reasonable solution. An algorithm is the ideal solution to a problem because it is guaranteed to yield an answer in finite time (Berlinski 00). However an algorithm may not be satisfactory and the problem scales up in size, and that is why AI is used. Note that a reasonable solution is about the best we can expect if no algorithm is available to help us achieve the optimum solution. Since the expert system relies on inference, it must be able to explain its reasoning so that its reasoning can be checked. An **explanation facility** is an integral part of sophisticated expert systems. In fact, elaborate explanation facilities may be designed to allow the user to explore multiple lines of "What if" type questions, called **hypothetical reasoning.**

Some expert systems even allow the system to learn rules by example, through **rule induction**, in which the system creates rules from data. Formalizing the knowledge of experts into rules is not simple, especially when the expert's knowledge has never been systematically explored. There may be inconsistencies, ambiguities, duplications, or other problems with the expert's knowledge that are not apparent until attempts are made to formally represent the knowledge in an expert system.

Human experts should also know the extent of their knowledge and qualify their advice as the problem reaches their **limits of ignorance**. A human expert also knows when to "break the rules." Unless expert systems are explicitly designed to deal with uncertainty, they will make recommendations with the same confidence even if the data they are dealing with is inaccurate or incomplete. An expert system's advice, like a human expert's, should degrade gracefully at the boundaries of ignorance rather than abruptly.

A practical limitation of many expert systems today is lack of **causal knowledge**. That is, the expert systems do not really have an understanding of the underlying causes and effects in a system. It is much easier to program expert systems with **shallow knowledge** based on empirical and heuristic knowledge than **deep knowledge** based on the basic structure, function, and behavior of objects. For example, it is much easier to program an expert system to prescribe an aspirin for a person's headache than program all the underlying biochemical, physiological, anatomical, and neurological knowledge about the human body. The programming of a causal model of the human body would be an enormous task and even if successful, the response time of the system would probably be extremely slow because of all the information that the system would have to process.

One type of shallow knowledge is **heuristic knowledge;** the term *heuristic* comes from the Greek and means *to discover*. Heuristic solutions are not guaranteed to succeed in the same way that an algorithm is a guaranteed solution to a problem. Instead, heuristics are rules of thumb or empirical knowledge gained from experience that may aid in the solution but are not guaranteed to work. However, in many fields such as medicine and engineering, heuristics play an essential role in some types of problem solving. Even if an exact solution is known, it may be impractical to use because of cost or time constraints. Heuristics can provide valuable shortcuts that can reduce time and cost.

Another problem with expert systems today is that their expertise is limited to the knowledge domain contained in the systems. Typical expert systems cannot generalize their knowledge by using **analogy** to reason about new situations the way people can. Although rule induction helps, only limited types of knowledge can be put into an expert system this way. The customary way of building an expert system by having the knowledge engineer repeat the cycle of interviewing the expert, constructing a prototype, testing, interviewing, and so on is a very time-consuming and labor intensive task. In fact, this problem of transferring human knowledge into an expert system is so major that it is called the **knowledge acquisition bottleneck**. This is a descriptive term because the knowledge acquisition bottleneck constricts the building of an expert system like an ordinary bottleneck constricts fluid flow from a bottle.

In spite of their present limitations, expert systems have been very successful in dealing with real-world problems that conventional programming methodologies have been unable to solve, especially those dealing with uncertain or incomplete information. The important point is to be aware of the advantages and limitations of any technology so that it can be appropriately utilized.

1.5 CHARACTERISTICS OF AN EXPERT SYSTEM

An expert system is usually designed to have the following general characteristics:

- *High performance.* The system must be capable of responding at a level of competency equal to or better than an expert in the field. That is, the quality of the advice given by the system must have high integrity.
- *Adequate response time.* The system must perform in a reasonable time, comparable to or better than the time required by an expert to reach a decision. An expert system that takes a year to reach a decision compared to a human expert's time of one hour would not be useful. The **time constraints** placed on the performance of an expert system may be especially severe in the case of real-time systems, when a response must be made within a certain time interval such as landing an aircraft in fog.
- *Good reliability.* The expert system must be reliable and not prone to crashes or else it will not be used.
- *Understandable.* The system should be able to explain the steps of its reasoning while executing so that it is understandable. Rather than being just a "black box" that produces a miraculous answer, the system should have an explanation capability in the same way that human experts can explain their reasoning. This feature is important for several reasons:

One reason is that human life and property may depend on the answers of the expert system. Because of the great potential for harm, an expert system must be able to justify its conclusions in the same way a human expert can explain why a certain conclusion was reached. Thus, an explanation facility provides a sanity check of the reasoning for humans.

A second reason for having an explanation facility occurs in the development phase of an expert system to confirm that the knowledge has been correctly acquired and is being correctly used by the system. This is critical in debugging since the knowledge may be incorrectly entered due to typos or be incorrect due to misunderstandings between the knowledge engineer and the expert. A good explanation facility allows the expert and knowledge engineer to validate the accuracy of the knowledge. Also, because of the way that typical expert systems are constructed, it is very difficult to read a long program listing and understand its operation.

An additional source of error may be unforeseen interactions in the expert system, which may be detected by running test cases with known reasoning that the system should follow. As we will discuss in more detail later, multiple rules may apply to a given situation about which the system is reasoning. The flow of execution is not sequential in an expert system; i.e., you cannot just read its code line by line and understand how the system operates. The order in which rules have been entered in the system is not necessarily the order in which they will be executed. The expert system acts much like a parallel program in which the rules are independent knowledge processors.

- *Flexibility.* Because of the large amount of knowledge that an expert system may have, it is important to have an efficient mechanism for adding, changing, and deleting knowledge. One reason for the popularity of rule-based systems is the efficient and modular storage capability of rules.

Depending on the system, an explanation facility may be simple or elaborate. A simple explanation facility in a rule-based system may simply list all the facts that caused the latest rule to execute. More elaborate systems may do the following:

- *List all the reasons for and against a particular hypothesis.* A **hypothesis** is a **goal** which is to be proved; e.g., in a medical diagnostic expert system the hypothesis might be "The patient has a tetanus infection." In a real problem, there may be multiple hypotheses, or the patient may really have several diseases at once. A hypothesis is an assertion whose truth is in doubt and must be proved. Once a goal has been assumed, **subgoals** are generated that are simpler, and so on until simple enough subgoals may be solved. This method of solving a problem is the classic **divide-and-conquer** method that is the basis of backward chaining discussed in a later chapter.
- List all the hypotheses that may explain the observed evidence.
- Explain all the consequences of a hypothesis. For example, assuming that the patient does have tetanus, there should also be evidence of fever as the infection runs its course. If this symptom is then observed, it adds credibility that the hypothesis is true. If the symptom is not observed, it reduces the credibility of the hypothesis.
- Give a **prognosis** or prediction of what will occur if the hypothesis is true.
- Justify the questions that the program asks of the user for further information. These questions may be used to direct the line of reasoning to likely diagnostic paths. In most real problems, it is too expensive or time consuming to explore all possibilities, and some way must be provided to guide the search for the correct solution. For example, consider the cost, time, and effect of administering all possible medical tests to a patient complaining of a sore throat (very profitable to the medical business, very bad for the patient).
- *Justify the knowledge of the program.* For example, if the program claims that the hypothesis "The patient has a tetanus infection" is true, the user could ask for an explanation. The program might justify this conclusion on the basis of a rule that says that if the patient has a positive blood test for tetanus, the patient has tetanus. Now the user could ask the program to justify this rule. The program could respond by stating that a positive blood test for a disease is proof of the disease. Unfortunately this ignores false positives, as discussed in a later chapter.

In this case, the program is actually quoting a **metarule**, which is knowledge about rules. The prefix *meta* means "above or beyond." Programs have been explicitly created to infer new rules using the process of **machine learning**. A hypothesis is justified by knowledge and the knowledge is justified by a **warrant** that it is correct. A warrant is essentially a meta-explanation that explains the expert system's explanation of its reasoning.

Knowledge can easily grow **incrementally** in a rule-based system, which is one of the reasons why these systems have proven so successful. That is, the knowledge base can grow little by little as rules are added so that the performance and validity of the system can be continually verified. This is analogous to the way a child learns new knowledge every day and checks that the new knowledge is correct. If the rules are properly designed, the interactions between rules will be minimized or eliminated to protect against unforeseen effects. The incremental growth of knowledge facilitates **rapid prototyping** so that the knowledge engineer can quickly show a working prototype of the expert system. This is an important feature because it maintains the expert's and management's interest in the project. Rapid prototyping also quickly exposes any gaps, inconsistencies, or errors in the expert's knowledge or the system so that corrections can be made immediately.

1.6 THE DEVELOPMENT OF EXPERT SYSTEMS TECHNOLOGY

The roots of expert systems lie in many disciplines; in particular, the area of psychology that is concerned with human information processing, **cognitive science**. Cognition is the study of how humans know or process information. In other words, cognition is the study of how people think, especially when solving problems. A variety of cognitive tools have been developed to provide better teaching (Lajoie 00).

Another important concept that AI machines must have is the ability to recognize signs, which forms the basis of the field named **semiotics** (Fetzer 01). In semiotics, we do not mean simple written signs such as a Stop sign, but the whole concept of signs in general. A sign is something that represents something else. For example, if you watch a movie that also has music playing, a common sign that something exciting is going to happen is a rise in pitch and faster rhythm of the music. Likewise when something suspenseful is about to happen, the music becomes slower and deeper. Many different nonverbal signs exist in music, movies, television, and ordinary life. For example, if a person is lying or uncomfortable about a question, they will usually drop their eyes. This has vast bearing on intelligent machines designed to exist in the real world. Simple programming to understand words is not enough; the machines must also recognize the underlying meaning of signs.

The study of cognition is very important if we want to make computers emulate human experts. Often, experts can't explain how they solve problems—the solution just comes to them. If the expert can't explain how a problem is solved, it's not possible to encode the knowledge in an expert system based on explicit knowledge. In this case, the only possibility is programs that learn by themselves to emulate the expert. These are programs based on induction, artificial neural systems, and other soft computing methods to be discussed later.

Human Problem Solving and Productions

The development of expert systems technology draws on a wide background. Table 1.2 is a brief summary of some important developments that have led to CLIPS. Whenever possible, the starting dates of projects are used. Many projects extend over many years. These developments are covered in more detail in this chapter and others. A number of expert systems tools and modern expert systems are described in Appendix G.

Table 1.2 Some Important Events Leading to the First Release of CLIPS

Year	Events
1943	Post production rules; McCulloch and Pitts Neuron Model
1954	Markov Algorithm for controlling rule execution
1956	Dartmouth Conference; Logic Theorist; Heuristic Search; term "AI" coined
1957	Perceptron invented by Rosenblatt; GPS (General Problem Solver) started (Newell, Shaw, and Simon)
1958	LISP AI language (McCarthy)
1962	Rosenblatt's *Principles of Neurodynamics* on Perceptions
1965	Resolution Method of automatic theorem proving (Robinson) Fuzzy Logic for reasoning about fuzzy objects (Zadeh) Work begun on DENDRAL, the first expert system (Feigenbaum, Buchanan)
1968	Semantic nets, associative memory model (Quillian)
1969	MACSYMA math expert system (Martin and Moses)
1970	Work begins on PROLOG (Colmerauer, Roussell)
1971	HEARSAY I for speech recognition *Human Problem Solving* popularizes rules (Newell and Simon)
1973	MYCIN expert system for medical diagnosis (Shortliffe) leading to GUIDON, intelligent tutoring (Clancey) and TEIRESIAS, explanation facility concept (Davis) and EMYCIN, first shell (Van Melle, Shortliffe, and Buchanan) HEARSAY II, blackboard model of multiple cooperating experts
1975	Frames, knowledge representation (Minsky)
1976	AM (Artificial Mathematician) creative discovery of math concepts (Lenat); Dempster-Shafer Theory of Evidence for reasoning under uncertainty; Work begun on PROSPECTOR expert system for mineral exploration (Duda, Hart)
1977	OPS expert system shell (Forgy), an ancestor of CLIPS
1978	Work started on XCON/R1 (McDermott, DEC) to configure DEC computer systems Meta-DENDRAL, metarules, and rule induction (Buchanan)
1979	Rete algorithm for fast pattern matching (Forgy) Commercialization of AI begins Inference Corp. formed (releases ART expert system tool in 1985)
1980	Symbolics, LMI founded to manufacture LISP machines
1982	SMP math expert system; Hopfield Neural Net; Japanese Fifth Generation Project to develop intelligent computers
1983	KEE expert system tool (IntelliCorp)
1985	CLIPS version 1 expert system tool (NASA). Freely available on all computers, not just special purpose and expensive LISP machines.

In the late 1950s and 1960s, a number of programs were written with the goal of general problem solving. The most famous of these was the **General Problem Solver** created by Newell and Simon. This caused a huge sensation because the press termed the big computers then that filled a whole room, "Giant Brains." People became afraid that they would lose their jobs until companies such as IBM claimed the machines would only do the work that thousands of mathematicians would take a million years to accomplish. In those days when the machines cost a million dollars and CPU time was charged at $1 a microsecond, it never seemed possible that people would someday have inexpensive personal computers in their homes or at work.

One of the most significant results demonstrated by Newell and Simon was that much of human understanding or **cognition** could be expressed by IF-THEN **production rules**. For example, IF it looks like it's going to rain THEN carry an umbrella, or IF your spouse is in a bad mood THEN don't appear happy. A rule corresponds to a small, modular collection of knowledge called a **chunk**. The chunks are organized in a loose arrangement with links to related chunks of knowledge. One theory is that all human memory is organized in chunks. Here is an example of a rule representing a chunk of knowledge:

```
IF the car doesn't run and
   the fuel gauge reads empty
THEN fill the gas tank
```

Newell and Simon popularized the use of rules to represent human knowledge and showed how standard reasoning could be done with rules. Cognitive psychologists have used rules as a model to explain human information processing. The basic idea is that sensory input provides stimuli to the brain. The stimuli trigger the appropriate rules of **long-term memory,** which produces the appropriate response. Long-term memory is where our permanent knowledge is stored. For example, we all have rules such as:

```
IF there is flame THEN there is a fire
IF there is smoke THEN there may be a fire
IF there is a siren THEN there may be a fire
```

Notice that the last two rules are not expressed with complete certainty. The fire may be out, but there may still be smoke in the air. Likewise, a siren does not prove that there is a fire since it may be a false alarm. The stimuli of seeing flames, smelling smoke, and hearing a siren will trigger these and similar types of rules.

Long-term memory consists of many rules having the simple IF THEN structure. In fact, a Grand Master chess expert may know 50,000 or more chunks of knowledge about chess patterns. In contrast to the long-term memory, the **short-term memory** is used for the temporary storage of knowledge during problem solving. Although long-term memory can hold hundreds of thousands or more chunks, the capacity of working memory is surprisingly small—four to seven chunks. As a simple example of this, try visualizing some numbers in your mind. Most people can only see four to seven numbers at once. Of course we can memorize many more than four to seven numbers. However, those numbers are kept in long-term memory and it takes a while to make them permanent.

One theory proposes that short-term memory represents the number of chunks that simultaneously can be active and considers human problem solving as a spreading of these activated chunks in the mind. Eventually, a chunk may be activated with such intensity that a conscious thought is generated and you say to yourself, "Hmm ... something's burning. Wonder if my pants are on fire?"

The other element necessary for human problem solving is a **cognitive processor**. The cognitive processor tries to find the rules that will be **activated** by the appropriate stimuli. Not just any rule will do. For example, you wouldn't want to fill your gas tank every time you heard a siren. Only a rule that matched the stimuli would be activated. If there are multiple rules that are activated at once, the cognitive processor must perform a **conflict resolution** to decide which rule has highest priority. The rule with highest priority will be executed. For example, if both of the following rules are activated:

```
IF there is a fire THEN leave
IF my clothes are burning THEN put out the fire
```

then the actions of one rule will be executed before the other. The **inference engine** of modern expert systems corresponds to the cognitive processor.

The Newell and Simon model of human problem solving in terms of long-term memory (rules), short-term memory (working memory), and a cognitive processor (inference engine) is the basis of modern rule-based expert systems.

Rules like these are a type of **production system**. Rule-based production systems are a popular method of implementing expert systems today. The individual rules that compose a production system are the **production rules**. In designing an expert system, an important factor is the amount of knowledge or **granularity** of the rules. Too little granularity makes it difficult to understand a rule without reference to other rules. Too much granularity makes the expert system difficult to modify since several chunks of knowledge are intermingled in one rule. The ability of CLIPS to use objects as well as rules is a major asset.

Until the mid-1960s, a major quest of AI was to produce intelligent systems that relied little on domain knowledge and greatly on powerful methods of reasoning. Even the name *General Problem Solver* illustrates the concentration on machines that were not designed for one specific domain but were intended to solve many types of problems. Although the methods of reasoning used by general problem solvers were very powerful, the machines were eternal beginners. When presented with a new domain, they had to discover everything from first principles and were not as good as human experts who relied on domain knowledge for high performance.

An example of the power of knowledge is playing chess. Although computers now rival humans, people play well despite the fact that computers can do calculations millions of times faster. Studies have shown that human expert chess players do not have super powers of reasoning but instead rely on knowledge of chesspiece patterns built up over years of play. As mentioned previously, one estimate places an expert chess player's knowledge at about 50,000 patterns.

Humans are very good at recognizing patterns such as pieces on a chessboard. Instead of trying to reason ahead 50, 100 or more possible moves for every piece, the best human chessplayers analyze the game in terms of patterns that reveal long-term threats while remaining alert for short-term surprise moves. This strategy rather than the bruteforce look-ahead method of anticipating moves is what has enabled computer chess programs like IBM's Big Blue to beat all the human chess champions.

While domain knowledge is very powerful, it is generally limited to the particular domain. For example, a person who becomes an expert chess player does not automatically become an expert at solving math problems or even a checkers expert. While some knowledge may carry over to another domain, such as careful planning of moves, this is a skill rather than genuine expertise.

By the early 1970s, it became apparent that domain knowledge was the key to building machine problem solvers that could function at the level of human experts. Although methods of reasoning are important, studies have shown that experts do not primarily rely on reasoning for problem solving. In fact, reasoning may play a minor role in an expert's problem solving. Instead, experts rely on a vast knowledge of heuristics and experience that they have built up over the years. If an expert cannot solve a problem based on expertise, then it is necessary for the expert to reason from first principles and theory (or more likely ask another expert.) The reasoning ability of an expert is generally no better than that of an average person in dealing with a totally unfamiliar situation. The early attempts at building powerful problem solvers based only on reasoning have shown that a problem solver is crippled if it must rely solely on reasoning.

The insight that domain knowledge was the key to building real-world problem solvers led to the success of expert systems. The successful expert systems today are thus knowledge-based expert systems rather than general problem solvers. The same technology that led to the development of expert systems led to the development of knowledge-based systems that do not necessarily contain human expertise.

While expertise is considered knowledge that is specialized and known to only a few, knowledge is generally found in books, the Web, periodicals, and other widely available resources. For example, the knowledge of how to solve a quadratic equation or perform integration and differentiation is widely available. Knowledge-based computer programs such as Mathematica and MATLAB are available to automatically perform these and many other mathematical operations on either numeric or symbolic operands. Other knowledge-based programs may perform process control of manufacturing plants. Today the terms *knowledge-based systems* and *expert systems* are often used synonymously. In fact, expert systems is now considered an alternative programming model or **paradigm** to conventional algorithmic programming.

The Rise of Knowledge-Based Systems

With the acceptance of the knowledge-based paradigm in the 1970s, a number of successful expert systems were created. These systems are described here in more detail since they are all well documented with many papers and books devoted to their workings and knowledge base. The general problem with modern expert systems that you will read about is that their knowledge is proprietary and secret. Companies use expert systems to encapsulate the knowledge of human experts who work for them. They do not want this knowledge available to competitors and especially not to lawyers. Consider a medical expert system that gives a diagnosis from which the patient dies or claims injury. In fact the plaintiff need not even have suffered personal injury but simply be in a class action suit with others who claim injury. Both the software as well as the knowledge base in an expert system will be subject to inspection by other experts. As shown in many trials, you can always find one expert to refute another.

These classic expert systems could interpret mass spectrograms to identify chemical constituents (DENDRAL), diagnose illness (MYCIN), analyze geologic data for oil (DIPMETER) and minerals (PROSPECTOR), and configure computer systems (XCON/R1). The news that PROSPECTOR had discovered a mineral deposit worth $100 million dollars and that XCON/R1 was saving Digital Equipment Corporation (DEC) millions of dollars a year triggered a sensational interest in the new expert systems technology by 1980. The branch of AI that had started off in the 1950s as a study of human information processing had now grown to achieve commercial success by the development of practical programs for real-world use.

The MYCIN expert system was important for several reasons. First, it demonstrated that AI could be used for medical diagnosis. Second, MYCIN was the testbed of new concepts such as the explanation facility, automatic acquisition of knowledge, and intelligent tutoring that are found in a number of expert systems today. The third reason that MYCIN was important is that it demonstrated the feasibility of the expert system **shell** in which the program software is separate from the data. In other words, the data or knowledge is not hard-coded in with the software program. In fact a shell allows easy replacement of one knowledge-base domain with another.

Previous expert systems such as DENDRAL were one-of-a-kind systems in which the knowledge base was intermingled with the software that applied the knowledge, the inference engine. MYCIN explicitly separated the knowledge base from the inference engine. This was extremely important to the development of expert system technology since it meant that the essential core of the expert system could be reused. That is, a new expert system could be built much more rapidly than a DENDRAL-type system by emptying out the old knowledge and putting in knowledge about the new domain. The part of MYCIN that dealt with inference and explanation, the shell, could then be refilled with knowledge about the new system. The shell produced by removing the medical knowledge of MYCIN was called EMYCIN (essential or empty MYCIN).

By the late 1970s, the three concepts that are basic to most expert systems today had converged, as shown in Figure 1.5. These concepts are rules, the shell, and knowledge.

By 1980 new companies started to bring expert systems out of the university laboratory and produce commercial products. Powerful new software and specialized software written directly in LISP for expert system development were introduced. Unfortunately the high cost and significant training time ultimately

Figure 1.5 Convergence of Three Important Factors to Create the Modern Rule-Based Expert Systems

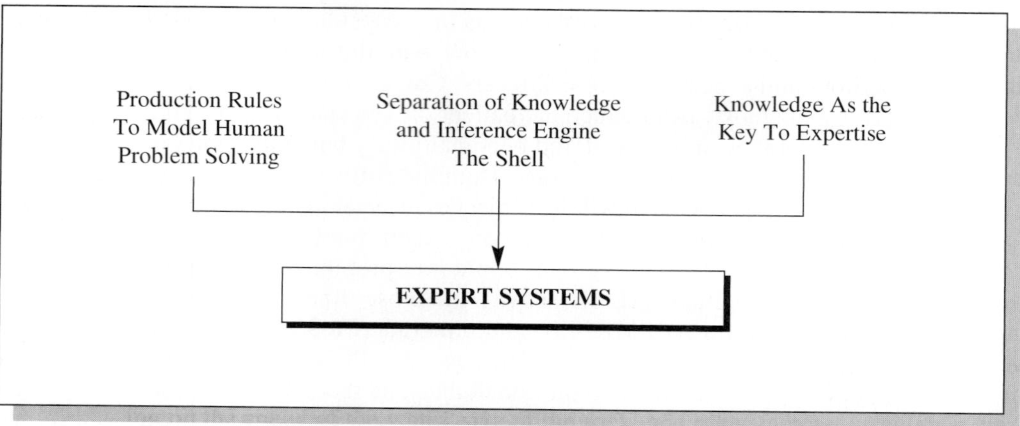

spelled the demise of these systems as PCs grew more powerful and expert systems tools such as CLIPS were introduced. In LISP machines, the native assembly language, operating system, and all other fundamental code were done in LISP so a great deal of maintenance was required.

CLIPS was originally written in C for speed and portability, and uses powerful pattern matching called the Rete Algorithm. Also unlike any other expert system tool, CLIPS is not only free, but the source code is well documented and comes with it. CLIPS can be installed on any C compiler that supports the standard Kernigan and Richie C language and has been installed on all makes of computers. A number of CLIPS-descended languages have been developed with advanced features such as fuzzy logic, and backward chaining, they have even been coded in Java, called Jess, as mentioned in the Preface.

1.7 EXPERT SYSTEMS APPLICATIONS AND DOMAINS

Conventional computer programs are used to solve many types of problems. Generally, these problems have algorithmic solutions that lend themselves well to conventional programs and programming languages such as C, C++, Java, C#, and so on. In many application areas such as industry and engineering, numeric calculations are of primary importance. By contrast, expert systems are primarily designed for symbolic reasoning.

While classic AI languages such as LISP and PROLOG are also used for symbolic manipulation, they are more general purpose than expert system shells. This does not mean that it is not possible to build expert systems in LISP and PROLOG. The term **logic programming** is generally applied today to programming that is done in PROLOG although a number of other languages have also been developed for this purpose. Many expert systems have been built with PROLOG and LISP. PROLOG especially has a number of advantages for diagnostic systems because of its built-in backward chaining. It is more convenient and efficient to build large expert systems with shells and utility programs specifically designed for expert system building. Instead of "reinventing the wheel" every time a new expert system is to be built, it is more efficient to use specialized tools designed for expert system building than general-purpose tools.

Applications of Expert Systems

Expert systems have been applied to virtually every field of knowledge. Some have been designed as research tools while others fulfill important business and industrial functions. The first major commercial success of an expert system in routine business use in the 1970s was the XCON system of DEC. The XCON system (originally called R1) was developed in conjunction with John McDermott of Carnegie-Mellon University. XCON was an expert configuring system for DEC computer systems.

The **configuration** of a system means that when a customer places an order, all the right parts—software, hardware, and documentation—are supplied. This is still a topic of major importance especially when people order computers, cars, and other products over the Internet by filling in forms. It would be extremely inefficient for a computer maker or automobile manufacturing plant to check each order for availability of parts and determine whether a special order can be delivered. Today, for any system that must be configured and delivered in a timely fashion, an expert system is a logical and financial necessity.

Thousands of expert systems have been built and reported in computer journals, the Internet, books, and conferences. This undoubtedly represents only the tip of the iceberg since many companies and government will not report details of their systems because of proprietary or secret knowledge contained in the systems. Based on the systems described in the open literature, certain broad classes of expert systems applications can be discerned, as shown in Table 1.3. Tables 1.4–1.9 list well known classic systems because they are well-documented, and modern systems have similar applications.

Table 1.3 Broad Classes of Expert Systems

Class	General Area
Configuration	Assemble proper components of a system in the proper way.
Diagnosis	Infer underlying problems based on observed evidence.
Instruction	Intelligent teaching so that a student can ask *why*, *how*, and *what if* questions just as if a human were teaching.
Interpretation	Explain observed data.
Monitoring	Compares observed data to expected data to judge performance.
Planning	Devise actions to yield a desired outcome.
Prognosis	Predict the outcome of a given situation.
Remedy	Prescribe treatment for a problem.
Control	Regulate a process. May require interpretation, diagnosis, monitoring, planning, prognosis, and remedies.

Table 1.4 Classic Chemistry Expert Systems

Name	Chemistry
CRYSALIS	Interpret a protein's 3-D structure.
DENDRAL	Interpret molecular structure.
TQMSTUNE	Remedy Triple Quadruple Mass Spectrometer (keep it tuned).
CLONER	Design new biological molecules.
MOLGEN	Design gene-cloning experiments.
SECS	Design complex organic molecules.
SPEX	Plan molecular biology experiments.

Table 1.5 Classic Electronics Expert Systems

Name	Electronics
ACE	Diagnose telephone network faults.
IN-ATE	Diagnose oscilloscope faults.
NDS	Diagnose national communication net.
EURISKO	Design 3-D microelectronics.
PALLADIO	Design and test new VLSI circuits.
REDESIGN	Redesign digital circuits to new.
CADHELP	Instruct for computer-aided design.
SOPHIE	Instruct circuit fault diagnosis.

Table 1.6 Classic Medical Expert Systems

Name	Medicine
PUFF	Diagnose lung disease.
VM	Monitors intensive-care patients.
ABEL	Diagnose acid-base/electrolytes.
AI/COAG	Diagnose blood disease.
AI/RHEUM	Diagnose rheumatoid disease.
CADUCEUS	Diagnose internal medicine disease.
ANNA	Monitor digitalis therapy.
BLUE BOX	Diagnose/remedy depression.
MYCIN	Diagnose/remedy bacterial infections.
ONCOCIN	Remedy/manage chemotherapy patients.
ATTENDING	Instruct in anesthetic management.
GUIDON	Instruct in bacterial infections.

Table 1.7 Classic Engineering Expert Systems

Name	Engineering
REACTOR	Diagnose/remedy reactor accidents.
DELTA	Diagnose/remedy GE locomotives.
STEAMER	Instruct operation of steam powerplant.

Table 1.8 Classic Geology Expert Systems

Name	Geology
DIPMETER	Interpret dipmeter logs.
LITHO	Interpret oil well log data.
MUD	Diagnose/remedy drilling problems.
PROSPECTOR	Interpret geological data for minerals.

Table 1.9 Classic Computer Expert Systems

Name	Computer Systems
PTRANS	Give prognosis for managing DEC computers.
BDS	Diagnose bad parts in switching net.
XCON	Configure DEC computer systems.
XSEL	Configure DEC computer sales order.
XSITE	Configure customer site for DEC computers.
YES/MVS	Monitor/control IBM MVS operating system.
TIMM	Diagnose DEC computers.

Appropriate Domains for Expert Systems

Before starting to build an expert system, it is essential to decide if an expert system is the appropriate paradigm. For example, one concern is whether an expert system should be used instead of an alternative paradigm such as conventional programming. The appropriate domain for an expert system depends on a number of factors:

- *Can the problem be solved effectively by conventional programming?* If the answer is yes, then an expert system is not the best choice. For example, consider the problem of diagnosing some equipment. If all the symptoms for all malfunctions are known in advance, then a simple table lookup or decision tree of the fault is adequate. Expert systems are best suited for situations in which there is no efficient algorithmic solution. Such cases are called **ill-structured problems** and reasoning may offer the only hope of a good solution.

As an example of an ill-structured problem, consider the case of a person who cannot decide where to book a vacation online and decides to see a travel agent. Table 1.10 lists some characteristics of an **ill-structured problem** as indicated by the person's responses to the travel agent's questions.

Although this is an extreme case, it does illustrate the basic concept of an ill-structured problem. As you can see, an ill-structured problem would not lend itself well to an algorithmic solution because there are so many possibilities. In this case, a default option should be exercised when all else fails. For example, the travel agent could say, "Ah ha! I have the perfect trip for you: a round-the-world cruise. Please fill out the following credit card application and everything will be taken care of."

Table 1.10 Example of an Ill-Structured Problem

Travel Agent's Questions	Responses
Can I help you?	I'm not sure.
Where do you want to go?	Somewhere.
Any particular destination?	Here and there.
How much can you afford?	I don't know.
Can you get some money?	I don't know.
When do you want to go?	Sooner or later.

In dealing with ill-structured problems, there is a danger that the expert system design may accidentally develop into an algorithmic solution. If there is a good algorithm, there is no need for an expert system. A clue that this has happened occurs if a solution is found that requires a rigid **control structure**. That is, the rules are forced to execute in a certain sequence by the knowledge engineer explicitly setting the priorities of many rules. Forcing a rigid control structure on the expert system cancels a major advantage of expert systems technology, which is dealing with unexpected input that does not follow a predetermined pattern. That is, expert systems react opportunistically to their input, whatever it is. Conventional programs generally expect input to follow a certain sequence. An expert system with a lot of control often indicates a disguised algorithm and may be a good candidate for recoding as a conventional program.

- *Is the domain well bounded?* It is very important to have well-defined limits on what the expert system is expected to know and what its capabilities should be. For example, suppose you wanted to create an expert system to diagnose headaches. Certainly medical knowledge of a physician would be put in the knowledge base. However, for a deep understanding of headaches, you might also put in knowledge about neurochemistry, then its parent area of biochemistry, then chemistry, molecular biophysics, and so forth, perhaps down to subnuclear physics. Other domains such as biofeedback, psychology, psychiatry, physiology, exercise, yoga, and stress management may also have pertinent knowledge about headaches. The point of all this is—when do you stop adding domains? The more domains, the more complex the expert system becomes.

In particular, the task of coordinating all the expertise becomes a major task. In the real world, we know from experience how difficult it is to have coordinated teams of experts working on problems, especially when they come up with conflicting recommendations. If we knew how to program well the coordination of expertise, then we could try programming an expert system to have the knowledge of multiple experts. The first attempts made to coordinate multiple expert systems were the HEARSAY II and HEARSAY III systems. These projects demonstrated the complexity of the task. As a familiar example, try bringing your car into multiple service centers when you have a problem and note how many disparate diagnoses you get. As expertise becomes more scarce, so do the number of opinions, which makes it very difficult to decide on a course of action.

- *Is there a need and a desire for an expert system?* Although it's great experience to build an expert system, it's rather pointless if no one is willing to use it. If there already are many human experts, it's difficult to justify an expert system based on the reason of scarce human expertise. Also, if the experts or users don't want the system, it will not be accepted even if there is a need for it. For example, many simulations have shown AI-controlled traffic lights can cut gas consumption by 50 percent, but it would also reduce gasoline tax revenues to city, state, and Federal governments by 50 percent.

Management especially must be willing to support the system. This is even more critical for expert systems than conventional programs because deployment of expert systems is sometimes viewed as a precursor to downsizing the workforce. Workers must be reassured that the expert system will not lead to job loss but to increased profitability as expertise becomes more widely available at a lower cost. The area of expert systems deserves more support because it attempts to solve the problems that cannot be done by conventional programming. The risks are greater but so are the rewards.

- *Is there at least one human expert who is willing to cooperate?* There must be an expert who is willing, and preferably enthusiastic, about the project. Not all experts are willing to have their knowledge examined for faults and then put into a computer. Even if there are multiple experts willing to cooperate in the development, it might be wise to limit the number of experts involved in development. Different experts may have different ways of solving a problem, such as requesting different diagnostic tests. Sometimes they may even reach different conclusions. Trying to code multiple methods of problem-solving in one knowledge base may create internal conflicts and incompatibilities.
- *Can the expert explain the knowledge so that it is understandable by the knowledge engineer?* Even if the expert is willing to cooperate, there may be difficulty in expressing the knowledge in explicit terms. As a simple example of this difficulty, can you explain in words how you move a finger? Although you could say it's done by contracting a muscle in the finger, the next question is—how do you contract a finger muscle? The other difficulty in communication between expert and knowledge engineer is that the knowledge engineer doesn't know the technical terms of the expert. This problem is particularly acute with medical terminology. It may take a year or longer for the knowledge engineer to even understand what the expert is talking about, let alone translate that knowledge into explicit computer code.
- *Is the problem-solving knowledge mainly heuristic and uncertain?* Expert systems *are* appropriate when the expert's knowledge is largely heuristic and uncertain. That is, the knowledge may be based on experience, called

experiential knowledge, and the expert may have to try various approaches in case one doesn't work. In other words, the expert's knowledge may be a trial-and-error approach, rather than one based on logic and algorithms. However, the expert can still solve the problem faster than someone who is not an expert. This is a good application for expert systems. If the problem can be solved simply by logic and algorithms, it is better solved by a conventional program.

1.8 LANGUAGES, SHELLS, AND TOOLS

A fundamental decision in defining a problem is deciding how best to model it. Sometimes experience is available to aid in choosing the best paradigm. For example, experience suggests that a payroll is best done using conventional procedural programming. Experience also suggests that it is preferable to use a commercial package, if available, rather than writing one from scratch. A general guide to selecting a paradigm is to consider the most traditional one first—conventional programming. The reason for doing this is because of the vast amount of experience we have with conventional programming and the wide variety of commercial packages available. If a problem cannot be effectively solved by conventional programming, then turn to nonconventional paradigms such as AI, which requires knowledge of theory, rather than a single course in C.

Like the standard relational database language SQL, an expert system language is a higher-order language than third-generation languages like LISP or C because it is easier to do certain things; but there is also a smaller range of problems that can be addressed. That is, the specialized nature of expert systems languages makes them very suitable for writing expert systems but not for general-purpose programming. In many situations, it is even necessary to exit temporarily from an expert systems language to perform a function in a procedural language. CLIPS is designed to make this easy.

The primary functional difference between expert systems languages and procedural languages is the focus of representation. Procedural languages focus on providing flexible and robust techniques to represent data. For example, data structures such as arrays, records, linked lists, stacks, queues, and trees are easily created and manipulated. Modern languages such as Java and C# are designed to aid in **data abstraction** by providing structures for encapsulation such as objects, methods, and packages. This provides a level of abstraction that is then implemented in the program. The data and methods to manipulate the data are tightly interwoven in objects. In contrast, expert system languages focus on providing flexible and robust ways to represent knowledge. The expert system paradigm allows two levels of abstraction: data abstraction and **knowledge abstraction**. Expert system languages specifically separate the data from the methods of manipulating the data. An example of this separation is that of facts (data abstraction) and rules (knowledge abstraction) in a rule-based expert system language. In addition, CLIPS provides objects and all the features of a true object-oriented language.

This difference in focus also leads to a difference in program design methodology. Because of the tight interweaving of data and knowledge in procedural languages, programmers must carefully describe the sequence of execution. However, the explicit separation of data from knowledge in expert system languages requires considerably less rigid control of execution sequence. Typically, an entirely separate piece of code, the inference engine, is used to apply the knowledge to the data. This separation of knowledge and data allows a higher degree of parallelism and modularity.

The customary way of defining the need for an expert system program is to decide if you want to program the expertise of a human expert. If such an expert exists and will cooperate, then an expert system approach may be successful. Likewise, a very knowledge-intensive tasks with uncertainty may best be solved with an expert system tool.

The road to selecting an expert system tool is paved with confusion since there is such a rich variety to choose from today. While CLIPS does not have all the features of other languages, it is simpler to learn and is thus a good choice for an introductory textbook. In addition, CLIPS still maintains its original advantages of small program size and fast execution where real-time response is critical.

Besides the confusing choice of the many languages available today, the terminology used to describe the languages is confusing. Some vendors refer to their products as "tools," while others refer to "shells" and still others talk about "integrated environments." For clarity in this book, the terms are defined as follows:

- **language**—A translator of commands written in a specific syntax. An expert system language will also provide an inference engine to execute the statements of the language. Depending on the implementation, the inference engine may provide forward chaining, backward chaining, or both. Under this language definition, LISP is not an expert system language while PROLOG is. However, it is possible to write an expert system language using LISP, and write AI in PROLOG. For that matter you can even write an expert system or AI language in assembly language. Questions of development time, convenience, maintainability, efficiency, and speed determine what language software is written in.
- **tool**—A language plus associated utility programs to facilitate the development, debugging, and delivery of application programs. Utility programs may include text and graphics editors, debuggers, file management, and even code generators. Some tools may even allow the use of different paradigms such as forward and backward chaining in one application.

In some cases, a tool may be integrated with all its utility programs in one environment to present a common interface to the user. This approach minimizes the need for the user to leave the environment to perform a task. For example, a simple tool may not provide facilities for file management and so a user would have to exit the tool to give conventional commands in a C host language, for example. An integrated environment allows easy exchange of data between utility programs in the environment. Some tools do not even require the user to write any code. Instead, the tool allows a user to enter knowledge by examples from tables or spreadsheets and generates the appropriate code itself.

- **shell**—A special-purpose tool designed for certain types of applications in which the user must supply only the knowledge base. The classic example of this is the EMYCIN (empty MYCIN) shell. This shell was made by removing the medical knowledge base of the MYCIN expert system.

MYCIN was designed as a backward-chaining system to diagnose disease. By simply removing the medical knowledge, EMYCIN was created as a shell containing knowledge about other kinds of consultative systems that use backward chaining. The EMYCIN shell demonstrated the reusability of the essential MYCIN software such as the inference engine and user interface. This was a very important step in the development of modern expert system technology because it meant that an expert system would not have to be built from scratch for each new application. Today the field of expert systems tools is quite competitive with many features and GUIs available.

There are many ways of characterizing expert systems such as representation of knowledge, forward or backward chaining, support of uncertainty, hypothetical reasoning, explanation facilities, and so forth. Unless a person has built a number of expert systems, it is difficult to appreciate all of these features, especially those found in the more expensive tools. The best way to learn expert systems technology is to develop a number of systems with an easy-to-learn language and then invest in a more sophisticated tool if you need its features.

1.9 ELEMENTS OF AN EXPERT SYSTEM

The elements of a typical expert system are shown in Figure 1.6. In a rule-based system, the knowledge base contains the domain knowledge needed to solve problems coded in the form of rules. While rules are a popular paradigm for representing knowledge, other types of expert systems use different representations, as discussed in Chapter 2.

An expert system consists of the following components:

- **user interface**—the mechanism by which the user and the expert system communicate.
- **explanation facility**—explains the reasoning of the system to a user.
- **working memory**—a **global database** of facts used by the rules.
- **inference engine**—makes inferences by deciding which rules are satisfied by facts or objects, prioritizes the satisfied rules, and executes the rule with the highest priority.
- **agenda**—a prioritized list of rules created by the inference engine, whose patterns are satisfied by facts or objects in working memory.
- **knowledge acquisition facility**—an automatic way for the user to enter knowledge in the system rather than by having the knowledge engineer explicitly code the knowledge.

Figure 1.6 Structure of a Rule-Based Expert System

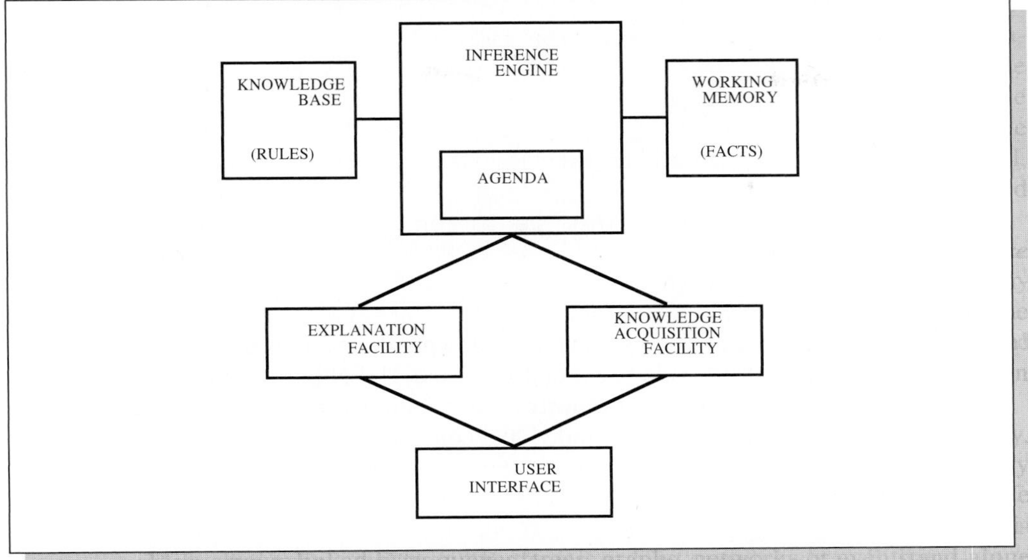

The knowledge acquisition facility is an optional feature on many systems. In some expert systems tools, the tool can learn by rule induction through examples and automatically generate rules. Other methods such as ID3, C 4.5, C 5.1, artificial neural networks, and genetic algorithms have been used in machine learning to generate rules. The major problem with machine learning to generate rules is that there is no explanation as to why this was created. Unlike a human who can explain the reason for a rule, machine learning systems have never been able to explain their actions and so unpredictable results may occur. However, the examples are generally from tabular- or spreadsheet-type data better suited to decision trees. General rules constructed by a knowledge engineer can be much more complex than the simple rules from rule induction.

Depending on the implementation of the system, the user interface may be a simple text-oriented display or a sophisticated high-resolution, bit-mapped display. High-resolution displays are commonly used to simulate a control panel with dials and displays.

The knowledge base is also called the **production memory** in a rule-based expert system. As a very simple example, consider the problem of deciding to cross a street. The productions for the two rules are as follows, where the arrows mean that the system will perform the actions on the right of the arrow if the conditions on the left are true:

```
the light is red → stop
the light is green → go
```

The production rules can be expressed in an equivalent pseudocode IF-THEN format as:

```
Rule: Red_light
IF
      the light is red
THEN
      stop

Rule: Green_light
IF
       the light is green
THEN
       go
```

Each rule is identified by a name. Following the name is the IF part of the rule. The section of the rule between the IF and THEN part of the rule is called by various names such as the **antecedent**, **conditional part**, **pattern part,** or **left-hand-side** (**LHS**). The individual condition:

```
the light is green
```

is called a **conditional element** or a **pattern**.

The following are some examples of rules from the classic systems:

```
MYCIN system for diagnosis of meningitis and
  bacteremia (bacterial infections)
IF
     The site of the culture is blood, and
     The identity of the organism is not known with
        certainty, and
     The stain of the organism is gramneg, and
     The morphology of the organism is rod, and
     The patient has been seriously burned
THEN
     There is weakly suggestive evidence (.4) that
        the identity of the organism is
        pseudomonas

XCON/R1 for configuring DEC VAX computer systems
IF
     The current context is assigning devices to
       Unibus modules and
     There is an unassigned dual-port disk drive
       and
     The type of controller it requires is known
       and
     There are two such controllers, neither of
       which has any devices assigned to it, and
```

```
        The number of devices that these controllers
           can support is known
    THEN
        Assign the disk drive to each of the
           controllers, and
        Note that the two controllers have been
           associated and each supports one drive
```

In a rule-based system, the inference engine determines which rule antecedents, if any, are satisfied by the facts. Two general methods of inferencing are commonly used as the problem-solving strategies of expert systems: **forward chaining** and **backward chaining**. Other methods used for more specific needs may include means-ends analysis, problem reduction, backtracking, plan-generate-test, hierarchical planning and the least commitment principle, and constraint handling.

Forward chaining is reasoning from facts to the conclusions resulting from those facts. For example, if you see that it is raining before leaving home (the fact), then you should take an umbrella (the conclusion).

Backward chaining involves reasoning in reverse from a hypothesis, a potential conclusion to be proved, to the facts that support the hypothesis. For example, if you have not looked outside and someone enters with wet shoes and an umbrella, your hypothesis is that it is raining. In order to support this hypothesis, you could ask the person if it was raining. If the response is yes, then the hypothesis is proven true and becomes a fact. As mentioned before, a hypothesis can be viewed as a fact whose truth is in doubt and needs to be established. The hypothesis can then be interpreted as a goal to be proven.

Depending on the design, an inference engine will do either forward or backward chaining or both. For example, CLIPS is designed for forward chaining, PROLOG performs backward chaining, and the version of CLIPS called Eclipse developed by Paul Haley does both forward and backward chaining. The choice of inference engine depends on the type of problem. Diagnostic problems are better solved with backward chaining while prognosis, monitoring, and control are better done by forward chaining. However, there is a memory size and execution speed penalty involved in using a more enhanced tool since more code is involved in creating the tool. CLIPS was designed to be "lean and mean" so that it would execute as fast as possible and be suitable for deployed applications in small memory devices such as ROM. Although people who use desktop computers with 512 megs of RAM don't normally think about this, developing a product such as an intelligent remote control or microwave oven requires ROM for cheap permanent memory. The cost of memory goes down with size so it is desirable to use as little memory as possible in consumer devices to be competitive. CLIPS can actually generate a C code executable that is small and easily burnt into a small ROM.

The working memory may contain facts regarding the current status of the traffic light such as "the light is green" or "the light is red." Either or both of these facts may be in working memory at the same time. If the traffic light is working normally, only one fact will be in memory. However, it is possible that both facts may be in working memory if there is a malfunction in the light. Notice the difference between the knowledge base and working memory. Facts do not interact with one another. The fact "the light is green" has no effect on the fact "the light is red." Instead, our knowledge of traffic lights says that if both facts are simultaneously present, then there is a malfunction in the light.

If there is a fact "the light is green" in working memory, the inference engine will notice that this fact satisfies the conditional part of the green light rule and put this rule on the agenda. If a rule has multiple patterns, then all of its patterns must be simultaneously satisfied for the rule to be placed on the agenda. Some patterns may even be satisfied by specifying the absence of certain facts in working memory.

A rule whose patterns are all satisfied is said to be **activated** or **instantiated**. Multiple activated rules may be on the agenda at the same time. In this case, the inference engine must select one rule for **firing**. The term *firing* comes from neurophysiology, the study of the way the nervous system works. An individual nerve cell or **neuron** emits an electrical signal when stimulated. No amount of further stimulation can cause the neuron to fire again for a short time period. This phenomenon is called **refraction**. Rule-based expert systems are built using refraction in order to prevent trivial loops. That is, if the green light rule kept firing on the same fact over and over again, the expert system would never accomplish any useful work.

Various methods have been invented to provide refraction. In one type of expert system language, OPS5, each fact is given a unique identifier called a **timetag** when it is entered in working memory. After a rule has fired on a fact, the inference engine will not fire on that fact again because its time stamp has been used too recently.

Following the THEN part of a rule is a list of **actions** to be executed when the rule fires. This part of the rule is known as the **consequent** or **right-hand side** (**RHS**). When the red light rule fires, its action "stop" is executed. Likewise, when the green light rule fires, its action is "go." Specific actions usually include the addition or removal of facts from working memory or printing results. The format of these actions depends on the syntax of the expert system language. For example, in CLIPS, the action to add a new fact called "stop" to working memory would be (assert stop). Because of the LISP ancestry of CLIPS, parentheses are required around patterns and actions.

The inference engine operates in **recognize-act cycles**. Various names have been given to describe this such as **select-execute cycle**, **situation-response cycle**, and **situation-action cycle**. By any name for a cycle, the inference engine will repeatedly execute a group of tasks until certain criteria cause execution to cease. The general tasks are shown in the following pseudocode as **conflict resolution**, **act**, **match**, and **check for halt**:

```
WHILE not done
```

Conflict Resolution: If there are activations, then select the one with highest priority, else done.

Act: Sequentially perform the actions on the RHS of the selected activation. Those that change working memory have immediate effect in this cycle. Remove the activation that has just fired from the agenda.

Match: Update the agenda by checking if the LHS of any rules are satisfied. If so, activate them. Remove activations if the LHS of their rules are no longer satisfied.

Check for Halt: If a halt action is performed or break command given, then done.

```
END-WHILE
```

Accept a new user command

Multiple rules may be activated and put on the agenda during one cycle. Also, activations will be left on the agenda from previous cycles unless they are deactivated because their LHS is no longer satisfied. Thus the number of activations on the agenda will vary as execution proceeds. Depending on the program, an activation may always be on the agenda but never selected for firing. Likewise some rules may never become activated. In these cases, the purpose of these rules should be reexamined because the rules are either unnecessary or their patterns were not correctly designed.

The inference engine executes the actions of the highest priority activation on the agenda, then the next highest priority activation, and so on until no activations are left. Various priority schemes have been designed into expert system tools. Generally, all tools let the knowledge engineer define the priority of rules.

Agenda conflicts occur when different activations have the same priority and the inference engine must decide on one rule to fire. Different shells have different ways of dealing with this problem. In the original Newell and Simon paradigm, those rules entered first in the system had the highest default priority. In OPS5, rules with more complex patterns automatically have a higher priority. In CLIPS, rules have the same default priority unless assigned different ones by the knowledge engineer.

At this time, control is returned to the **top-level** command interpreter for the user to give further instructions to the expert system shell. The top-level is the default mode in which the user communicates with the expert system, and is indicated by the task "Accept a new user command." It is the top-level that accepts the new command.

The top-level is the user interface to the shell while an expert system application is under development. More sophisticated user interfaces are usually designed for the expert system to facilitate its operation. For example, the expert system may have a user interface for control of a manufacturing plant that shows a block diagram of the plant. Warnings and status messages may appear in flashing colors with simulated dials and gauges. In fact, more effort may go into the design and implementation of the user interface than in the expert system knowledge base, especially in a prototype. Depending on the capabilities of the expert system shell, the user interface may be implemented by rules or in another language called by the expert system. For example, the Java version of CLIPS, called Jess, created by Ernest Friedman-Hill (Friedman-Hill 03), makes it easy to call Java classes to easily display a GUI since Java has many objects designed for this purpose.

A key feature of an expert system is an explanation facility that allows the user to ask how the system came to a certain conclusion and why certain information is needed. The question of how the system came to a certain conclusion is easy to answer in a rule-based system since a history of the activated rules and contents of working memory can be maintained in a stack. This is not readily available in artificial neural networks, genetic algorithms, or other systems that evolve. Although attempts have been made to provide an explanation capability is some systems, they cannot match the clarity of a human-design expert system. Sophisticated explanation facilities may allow the user to ask *what if* questions to explore alternate reasoning paths through hypothetical reasoning.

1.10 PRODUCTION SYSTEMS

The most popular type of expert system today is the rule-based system. Instead of representing knowledge in a relatively declarative, static way (as a number of things that are true), rule-based systems represent knowledge in terms of multiple rules that specify what should or should not be concluded in different situations. A rule-based system consists of IF-THEN *rules*, *facts*, and an *interpreter* that controls which rule is invoked depending on the facts in working memory.

There are two broad kinds of rule systems: forward chaining and backward chaining. A forward-chaining system starts with the known initial facts and keep using the rules to draw new conclusions or take certain actions. A backward-chaining system starts with some hypothesis or goal you are trying to prove, and keeps looking for rules that would allow the hypothesis to be proven true. New subgoals may be created to break up the large problem into smaller pieces that can be more easily proved. Forward-chaining systems are primarily data-driven, while backward-chaining systems are goal-driven (Debenham 98). There will be more extensive discussion of chaining in a later chapter and a complete example of how backward-chaining can be done in CLIPS.

Rules are popular for a number of reasons:

- *Modular nature*. This makes it easy to encapsulate knowledge and expand the expert system by incremental development.
- *Explanation facilities*. It is easy to build explanation facilities with rules since the antecedents of a rule specify exactly what is necessary to activate the rule. By keeping track of which rules have fired, an explanation facility can present the chain of reasoning that led to a certain conclusion.
- *Similarity to the human cognitive process*. Based on the work of Newell and Simon, rules appear to be a natural way of modeling how humans solve problems. The simple IF-THEN representation of rules make it easy to explain to experts the structure of the knowledge that you are trying to elicit from them.

Rules are a type of production whose origins go back to the 1940s. Because of the importance of rule-based systems, it is worthwhile to examine the development of the rule concept. This will give you a better idea of why rule-based systems are so useful for expert systems.

Post Production Systems

Production systems were first used in symbolic logic by Post who originated the name. He proved the important and amazing result that any system of mathematics or logic could be written as a certain type of production rule system. This result established the great capability of production rules for representing major classes of knowledge rather than being limited to a few types. Under the term **rewrite rules**, they are also used in linguistics as a way of defining the grammar of a language. Computer languages are commonly defined using the Backus-Naur Form (BNF) of production rules, like CLIPS in Appendix D.

The basic idea of Post was that any mathematical or logic system is simply a set of rules specifying how to change one string of symbols into another set of symbols. That is, given an input string, the antecedent, a production rule could produce a new string, the consequent. This idea is also valid with programs and expert systems where the initial string of symbols is the input data and the output string is some transformation of the input.

As a very simple case, if the input string is "patient has fever" the output string might be "take an aspirin." Note that there is no meaning attached to these strings. That is, the manipulations of the strings are based on syntax and not any semantics or understanding of what a fever, aspirin, and patient represent. A human knows what these strings mean in terms of the real world mean but a Post production system is just a way of transforming one string into another. A production rule for this example could be:

```
Antecedent → Consequent
person has fever → take aspirin
```

where the arrow indicates the transformation of one string into another. We can interpret this rule in terms of the more familiar IF-THEN notation as:

```
IF person has fever THEN take aspirin
```

The production rules can also have multiple antecedents. For example:

```
person has fever AND
      fever is greater than 102 → see doctor
```

Note that the special connective AND is not part of the string. The AND indicates that the rule has multiple antecedents.

A Post production system consists of a group of production rules, such as the following (where the numbers in parentheses are for our discussion):

```
(1)   car won't start → check battery
(2)   car won't start → check gas
(3)   check battery AND battery bad → replace
       battery
(4)   check gas AND no gas → fill gas tank
```

If there is a string "car won't start," the rules (1) and (2) may be used to generate the strings "check battery" and "check gas." However, there is no control mechanism that applies both these rules to the string. Only one rule may be applied, both or none. If there is another string "battery bad" and a string "check battery," then rule (3) may be applied to generate the string "replace battery."

Unlike a conventional programming language such as C or C+, there is no special significance to the order in which rules are written. The rules of our example could have been written in the following order and it would still be the same system:

```
(4)  check gas AND no gas → fill gas tank
(2)  car won't start → check gas
(1)  car won't start → check battery
(3)  check battery AND battery bad → replace
      battery
```

Although Post production rules were useful in laying part of the foundation of expert systems, they are not adequate for writing practical programs. The basic limitation of Post production rules for programming is lack of a **control strategy** to guide the application of the rules. A Post system permits the rules to be applied on the strings in any manner because there is no specification given on how the rules should be applied.

As an analogy, suppose you go to the library to find a certain book on expert systems. At the library, you start randomly looking at books on the shelves for the one you want. If the library is fairly large, it may take a long time to find the book you need. Even if you find the section of books on expert systems, your next random choice could take you to an entirely different section, such as French cooking. The situation becomes even worse if you need material from the first book to help you determine the second book that you need to find. A random search for the second book will also take a long time.

Markov Algorithms

The next advance in applying production rules was made by Markov, who specified a control structure for production systems. A **Markov algorithm** is an ordered group of productions that are applied in order of priority to an input string. If the highest priority rule is not applicable, then the next one is applied, and so forth. The Markov algorithm terminates if either, (1) the last production is not applicable to a string or, (2) a production that ends with a period is applied.

Markov algorithms can also be applied to substrings of a string, starting from the left. For example, the production system consisting of the single rule:

```
AB → HIJ
```

when applied to the input string GABKAB produces the new string GHIJKAB. Since the production now applies to the new string, the final result is GHIJKHIJ.

The special character $\wedge$ represents the **null string** of no characters. For example, the production:

```
A → ∧
```

deletes all occurrences of the character A in a string.

Other special symbols represent any single character and are indicated by lowercase letters a, b, c, ... x, y, z. These symbols represent single-character variables and are an important part of modern expert system languages. For example, the rule:

```
AxB → BxA
```

will reverse the characters A and B, where *x* is any single character.

The Greek letters α, β, and so forth are used for special punctuation of strings. The Greek letters are used because they are distinct from the alphabet of ordinary letters.

An example of a Markov algorithm that moves the first letter of an input string to the end is shown following. The rules are ordered in terms of highest priority (1), next highest (2), and so forth. The rules are prioritized in the order that they are entered:

```
(1)   αxy → yαx
(2)   α → ∧
(3)   ∧ → α
```

For the input string ABC, the execution trace is shown in Table 1.11.

Table 1.11 Execution Trace of a Markov Algorithm

Rule	Success or Failure	String
1	F	ABC
2	F	ABC
3	S	αABC
1	S	BαAC
1	S	BCαA
1	S	BCAα
2	S	BCA

Notice that the α symbol acts analogously to a temporary variable in a conventional programming language. However, instead of holding a value, the α is used as a place holder to mark the progression of changes in the input string. Once its job is done, the α is eliminated by rule 2. Hidden Markov Models (HMM) are widely used in pattern recognition applications, most notably speech recognition.

The Rete Algorithm

Notice that there is a definite control strategy to Markov algorithms with higher-priority rules ordered first. As long as the highest priority rule applies, it is used.

If not, the Markov algorithm tries lower-priority ones. Although the Markov algorithm can be used as the basis of an expert system, it is very inefficient for systems with many rules. The problem of efficiency becomes of major importance if we want to create expert systems for real problems containing hundreds or thousands of rules. No matter how good everything else is about a system, if a user has to wait a long time for a response, the system will not be used. What we really need is an algorithm that knows about all the rules and can apply any rule without having to try each rule sequentially.

A solution to this problem is the **Rete Algorithm** developed by Charles L. Forgy at Carnegie-Mellon University in 1979 for his Ph.D. dissertation on the OPS (Official Production System) expert system shell. The term *Rete* comes from the Latin word *rete,* which means net. The Rete Algorithm functions like a net in holding a lot of information so that much faster response times and rule firings can occur compared to a large group of IF-THEN rules which must be checked one by one in a conventional program. The Rete Algorithm is a dynamic data structure like a standard B+ tree which reorganizes itself to optimize search.

The Rete Algorithm is a very fast pattern-matcher that obtains its speed by storing information about the rules in a network in memory. The Rete Algorithm is intended to improve the speed of forward-chained rule systems by limiting the effort required to recompute the conflict set after a rule is fired. Its drawback is that it has high memory space requirements, but this is not a problem these days in which memory is so cheap. The Rete takes advantage of two empirical observations that were used to come up with its data structure:

Temporal Redundancy—The firing of a rule usually changes only a few facts, and only a few rules are affected by each of those changes.
Structural Similarity—The same pattern often appears in the left-hand side of more than one rule.

If you have hundreds or thousands of rules, it would be very inefficient for the computer to sequentially check whether each rule is likely to fire. The Rete Algorithm made expert system tools practical on the slow computers of the 1970s. Today the Rete network is still important for fast execution when many rules are involved in an expert system.

Instead of having to match facts against every rule on every recognize-act cycle, the Rete algorithm looks only for changes in matches on every cycle. This greatly speeds up the matching of facts to antecedents since the static data that doesn't change from cycle to cycle can be ignored. This topic will be discussed further in the chapters on CLIPS. Fast pattern matching algorithms such as the Rete completed the foundation for the practical application of expert systems. Figure 1.7 summarizes the foundations of modern rule-based expert system technologies.

1.11 PROCEDURAL PARADIGMS

Programming paradigms can be classified as procedural and nonprocedural. Figure 1.8 shows a **taxonomy** or classification of the procedural paradigms in terms of languages. Figure 1.9 shows a taxonomy for nonprocedural paradigms.

Figure 1.7 Foundations of Modern Rule-Based Expert Systems

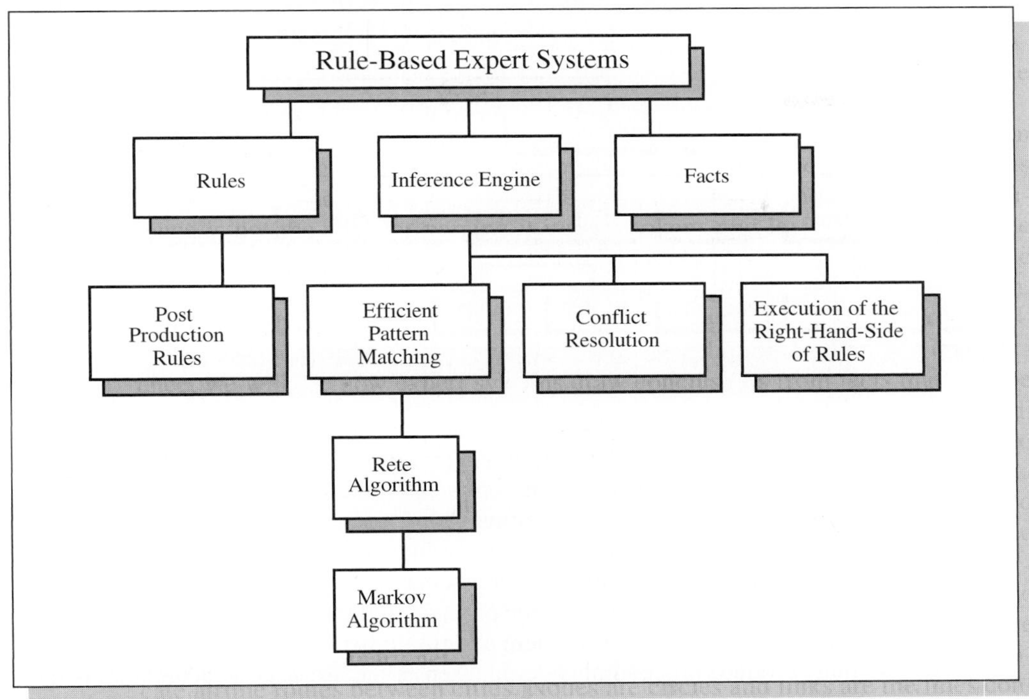

These figures illustrate the relationship of expert systems to other paradigms and should be considered a general guide rather than strict definitions. In particular, although CLIPS is shown as rule-based, it is possible to write an entirely object-oriented expert system in CLIPS, or a hybrid system using both rules and objects. Some of the paradigms and languages have characteristics that may place them in more than one class. For example, some consider functional programming procedural, while others consider it declarative.

An **algorithm** is a method of solving a problem in a finite number of steps. The implementation of an algorithm in a program is a **procedural program**. The terms *algorithmic programming*, *procedural programming*, and *conventional*

Figure 1.8 Procedural Languages

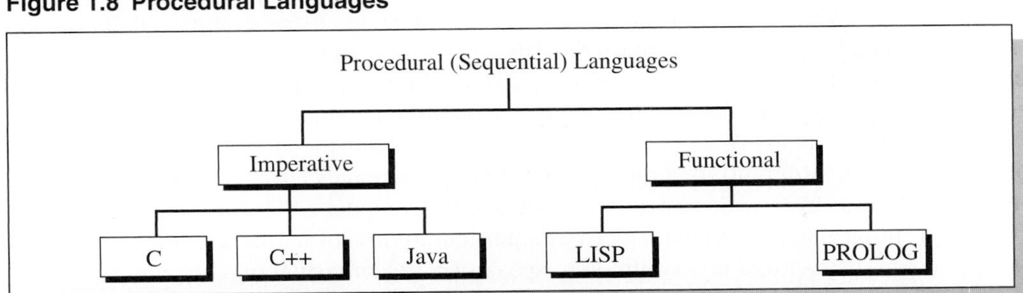

Figure 1.9 Nonprocedural Languages

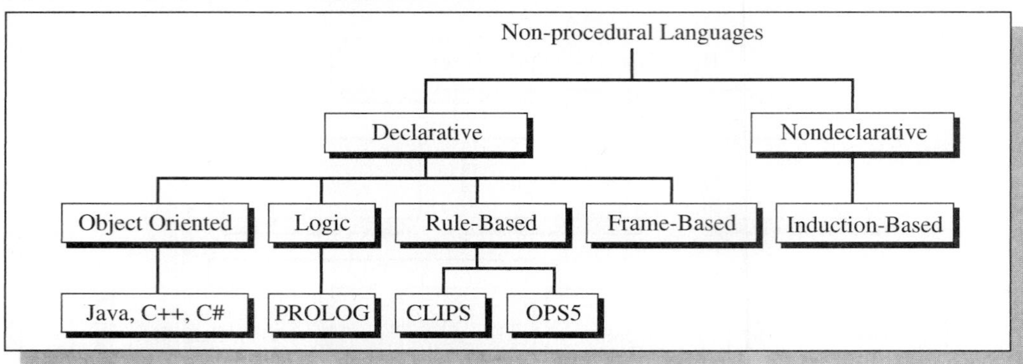

programming are often used synonymously to mean *non-AI programs*. A common conception of a procedural program is that it proceeds sequentially, statement by statement, unless a branch instruction is encountered. Another often used synonym for procedural program is **sequential program**. However, the term sequential programming implies too much constraint since all modern programming languages support recursion and so programs may not be strictly sequential.

The distinguishing feature of the procedural paradigm is that the programmer must specify exactly *how* a problem solution must be coded. Even code generators must produce procedural code. In a sense, the use of code generators is **nonprocedural** programming because it removes most or all of the procedural code writing from the programmer. The goal of nonprocedural programming is to have the programmer specify *what* the goal is and let the system determine *how to* accomplish it.

Imperative Programming

The terms *imperative* and *statement-oriented* are used synonymously. A language such as C has the dominant characteristic that statements are imperatives or commands to the computer telling it what to do. Note that in an object-oriented version C++, objects may also be used and the general concept is that of objects passing messages to each other. Thus the execution of an object-oriented program is more similar to an event-driven system rather than an imperative one in which program flow is assumed to execute sequentially from beginning to end.

The imperative programming paradigm is an abstraction of real computers which in turn are based on the Turing machine and the von Neumann machine with its registers and store (memory). At the heart of these machines is the concept of a modifiable store. Variables and assignments are the programming language analog of the modifiable **store**. The *store* is the object that is manipulated by the program. Imperative programming languages have a rich variety of commands to provide structure to code and to manipulate the store. Each imperative programming language defines a particular view of hardware. These views are so distinct that it is common to speak of a Pascal virtual machine, or a Java virtual machine that executes bytecodes that will execute on any hardware platform. This feature of bytecode portability accounted for much of the success of Pascal in the 1970s and 80s until Java used the same system. In fact, a compiler implements the virtual machine defined by the programming language in the language supported by the actual hardware and operating system.

In imperative programming, a name may be assigned to a value and later reassigned to another value. The collection of names and the associated values and the location of control in the program constitute the **state**. The state is a logical model of storage that is an association between memory locations and values. During execution, a program can be characterized as making a transition from the initial state to a final state by passing through a sequence of intermediate states. The transition from one state to the next is determined by assignment operations, input, and sequencing commands.

Imperative languages developed as a way of freeing the programmer from coding assembly language in the von Neumann architecture. Consequently, imperative languages offer great support to variables, assignment operations, and repetition. These are all low-level operations that modern languages attempt to hide by providing features such as recursion, procedures, modules, packages, and so forth. Imperative languages are also characterized by their emphasis on rigid control structure and their associated **top-down** program designs.

A serious problem with all languages is the difficulty of proving the correctness of programs which means the program is valid (discussed more in Chapter 2). From the AI standpoint, another serious problem is that imperative languages are not very efficient symbol manipulators. Because the imperative language architecture was molded to fit the von Neumann computer architecture, we have languages that can support number-crunching very well but not symbolic manipulation. However, imperative languages such as C and object-oriented languages such as C++ and Java have been used as the underlying base language to write expert system shells. These languages and the shells built from them run more efficiently and quickly on common general-purpose computers than the early shells built using LISP that required special hardware expressly designed for LISP.

Because of their sequential nature, imperative languages are not very efficient for directly implementing expert systems, especially rule-based ones. As an illustration of this problem, consider the task of encoding the information of a real-world problem with hundreds or thousands of rules. For example, the classic XCON system used to configure computer systems had about 7000 rules in its knowledge base. Early unsuccessful attempts were made to code this program in FORTRAN and BASIC before settling on the successful expert systems approach. An expert system tool like CLIPS makes it much easier to create such a large rule base than programming in a 3rd generation language or object-oriented language like Java, C++, or C#. To fully appreciate the advantages of an expert system language, you need to try coding in it. Programming in CLIPS is covered in the second part of this book.

The direct way of coding this knowledge in an imperative language would require 7000 IF-THEN statements or a very, very long CASE. This style of coding would present major efficiency problems since all 7000 rules would need to be searched for matching patterns on every recognize–act cycle. Note that the inference engine and its recognize–act cycle would also have to be coded in the imperative language. However the situation is much more complex than merely writing 7000 rules since many of the rules are triggered by other rules. For example, in the case of stopping for a red light, this would only apply if you were approaching the light; not if you had passed it. Many other interactions are possible in a rule-based system. Some rules assert facts, some may retract facts, some may modify facts. More sophisticated rules may create new rules or delete rules in the case of machine learning.

The efficiency of the program could be improved if rules were ordered so that those most likely to be executed were put at the beginning. However, this would require considerable tuning of the system and would change as new rules are added, or old ones deleted and modified. A better method for improving efficiency would be to build a dynamic network in memory of the rule patterns to reduce search time in determining which rules should be activated. Rather than making the programmer manually construct the tree, it should preferably be built automatically by the computer, based on the pattern and action syntax of the IF-THEN rules. It would also be helpful to have an IF-THEN syntax that was more conducive to representing knowledge and had powerful pattern matching tests. This requires the development of a parser to analyze input structure and an interpreter or compiler to execute the new IF-THEN syntax.

When all of these techniques for improving efficiency are implemented, the result is a dedicated expert system. If the inference engine, parser, and interpreter are removed to provide easy development of other expert systems, they compose an expert system shell. Of course, instead of doing all of this development from scratch, today it is much easier to use an existing tool like CLIPS, that is well-documented and extensively tested.

Functional Programming

The nature of **functional programming**, as exemplified by languages such as LISP, is very different from statement-oriented languages with their heavy reliance on elaborate control structures and top-down design. Conventional languages place conceptual limits on the way problems can be modularized. Functional languages push those limits back. Two features of functional languages in particular, higher-order functions and lazy evaluation, can contribute greatly to modularity. The fundamental idea of functional programming is to combine simple functions to yield more powerful functions. This is essentially a **bottom-up** design in contrast to the common **top-down** designs of imperative languages.

Functional programming is centered around **functions**. Mathematically, a function is an **association** or rule that maps members of one set, the **domain**, into another set, the **codomain**. The following is an example of a function definition:

```
cube(x) ≡ x*x*x, where x is a real number and
cube is a function with real values
```

The three parts of the function definition are:

(1) the association, $x*x*x$
(2) the domain, real numbers
(3) codomain, real numbers

of the cube function. The symbol ≡ means "is equivalent to" or "is defined as." The following notation is a shorthand way of writing that the cube mapping is from the domain of real numbers, symbolized as $\Re$, to the codomain of real numbers:

$$\text{cube}: \Re \rightarrow \Re$$

A general notation for a function f that maps from a domain S to a domain T is $f{:}S \rightarrow T$. The **range** of the function f is the set of all **images** $f(s)$ where s is an element of S. For the case of the cube function, the images of s are $s*s*s$ and the range is the set of all real numbers. The range and codomain are the same for the cube function. However, this may not be true for other functions such as the square function, $x*x$, with domain and codomain of real numbers. Since the range of the square function is only nonnegative real numbers, the range and codomain are not the same.

Using set notation, the range of a function can be written as:

```
R ≡ {f(s) | s ∈ S}
```

The **curly braces { }** denote a **set**. The **bar**, |, is read as "where." The previous statement can be read that the range R is equivalent to the set of values $f(s)$ where every element s is in the set S. The association is a set of ordered pairs (s,t), where $s \in S$, $t \in T$, and $t=f(s)$. Every member of S must have one and only one element of T associated with it. However, multiple t values may be associated with a single s. As a simple example, every positive number n has two square roots, $\pm\sqrt{n}$.

Functions may also be defined recursively as in:

```
factorial(n) ≡ n*factorial(n-1)
        where n is an integer and
        factorial is an integer function
```

Recursive functions are commonly used in functional languages such as LISP.

Mathematical concepts and expressions are **referentially transparent** because the meaning of the whole is completely determined from its parts. No synergism is involved between the parts. For example, consider the functional expression $x+(2*x)$. The result is obviously $3*x$. Both $x+(2*x)$ and $3*x$ give the same result no matter what values are substituted for x. Even other functions can be substituted for x and the result is the same. For example, let $h(y)$ be some arbitrary function. Then $h(y) + (2 * h(y))$ would still be equivalent to $3*h(y)$.

Now consider the following assignment statement in an imperative computer language such as C:

```
sum = f(x) + x
```

If the parameter *x* is passed by reference and its value is changed in the function call, *f(x)*, what value will be used for *x*? Depending on how the compiler is written, the value of *x* might be the original value if it was saved on a stack, or the new value if *x* was not saved. Another source of confusion occurs if one compiler evaluates expressions right-to-left while another evaluates left-to-right. In this case, *f(x)+x* would not evaluate the same as *x+f(x)* on different compilers even if the same language was used. Other side effects may occur due to global variables. Thus, unlike mathematical functions, program functions are not referentially transparent.

Functional programming languages were created to be referentially transparent. Five parts make up a functional language:

- **data objects** for the language functions to operate on
- **primitive functions** to operate on the data objects
- **functional forms** to synthesize new functions from other functions
- **application operations** on functions that return a value and
- **naming procedures** to identify new functions.

Functional languages are generally implemented as interpreters for ease of construction and immediate user response.

In LISP (LISt Processing), data objects are **symbolic expressions** (S-expressions) that are either **lists** or **atoms**. The following are examples of lists and are shown because the style is similar to how patterns are programmed in CLIPS:

```
    (milk eggs cheese)
    (shopping (groceries (milk eggs cheese) clothes
(pants)))
    ()
```

Patterns like this may be programmed in the conditional or **left-hand-side** (**LHS**) of a rule and represent facts or lists within lists as is the case of the "shopping" example. If the conditional is true, the **right-hand-side** (**RHS**) of the rule is executed and new lists made. Other things may be programmed to occur on the right-hand-side of rules such as retracting facts. Lists are always enclosed in matching parentheses with spaces separating the elements. The elements of lists can be atoms, such as milk, eggs, and cheese, or embedded lists such as (milk eggs cheese) and (pants). Lists can be split up but atoms cannot. The **empty list**, (), contains no elements and is called **nil**.

The original version of LISP was called *pure LISP* because it was purely functional. However, it was also not very efficient for writing programs. Non-functional additions have been made to LISP to increase the efficiency of writing programs. For example, SET acts as the assignment operator, while LET and PROG can be used to create local variables and execute a sequence of S-expressions. Although they act like functions, they are not functional in the original mathematical sense.

Since its creation, LISP has been the leading AI language in the United States. Many of the original expert system shells were written in LISP because it is so easy to experiment with LISP. However, conventional computers do not execute LISP very efficiently and execute the shells built using LISP even more inefficiently. Of course, as processors and clock rates have improved, so has the performance of LISP.

This problem of high cost has an impact on both the development and the **delivery problem**. It is not enough just to develop a great program if it cannot be delivered for use because of high cost. A good development workstation is not necessarily a good delivery vehicle due to speed, power, size, weight, environmental, or cost constraints. Some applications may even require that the final code be placed in ROM for reasons of cost and nonvolatility. Putting code into ROM can be a problem with some AI and expert systems tools that require special hardware to run. It's better to consider this possibility in advance rather than have to recode a program later.

An additional problem is that of embedding AI with conventional programming languages such as C, C++, C#, and Java to create intelligent systems. Applications that require extensive number crunching are best done in conventional languages rather than in an expert systems tool. This is why CLIPS makes it easy for you to write your own functions in the host language. For more details on this and other advanced topics, see the *CLIPS Reference Manual* available online at (http://www.ghgcorp.com/clips/CLIPS.html).

Unless special provisions are made, expert systems that are written in LISP are generally difficult to embed in anything other than LISP programs. One major consideration in selecting an AI language should be the language in which the tool is written. For reasons of portability, efficiency, and speed, many expert systems tools are now being written in or converted to C. This also eliminates the problem of requiring expensive special hardware for LISP-based applications.

1.12 NONPROCEDURAL PARADIGMS

Nonprocedural paradigms do not depend on the programmer giving exact details for how a problem is to be solved. This is the opposite of the procedural paradigms which specify *how* a function or statement sequence computes. In nonprocedural paradigms, the emphasis is on specifying *what* is to be accomplished and letting the system determine how to accomplish it.

Declarative Programming

The **declarative paradigm** separates the **goal** from the methods used to achieve the goal. The user specifies the goal while the underlying mechanism of the implementation tries to satisfy the goal. A number of paradigms and associated programming languages have been created to implement the declarative model.

Object-Oriented Programming

The **object-oriented** paradigm is another case of a paradigm that can be considered partly imperative and partly declarative. Today, the term *object-oriented* is used programming languages such as C++, Java, and C#. The basic idea is to design a program by considering the data used in the program as objects and then implementing operations on those objects. This is the opposite of top-down design which proceeds by stepwise refinement of a program's control structure. The Unified Modeling Language (UML) is a popular method for object-oriented design.

As an example of object-oriented design, consider the task of writing a program to manage a charge account with an interactive menu. The important data objects are current balance, amount of charge, and amount of payment. Various methods can be defined to act on the data objects once the appropriate classes have been defined. These operations would be add charge, make payment, and add monthly interest. Once all data objects, operations, and the menu interface are defined, coding can begin. This object-oriented design methodology is well-suited to a program that has a weak control structure. It would not be as suitable in a program that requires a strong control structure such as a payroll application. However OOP is popular today because of maintenances and code reuse of objects.

The term **object-oriented programming** was originally used for languages such as Smalltalk, which was specifically designed for objects. Sometimes the term is used to mean programming of an object-oriented design even in a language that has no true object support.

Modern object-oriented languages such as C++, Java, and C# have features to support objects built into the language. Smalltalk is descended from SIMULA 67, a language developed for simulation. SIMULA 67 introduced the concept of **class** which led to the concept of information hiding so that a programmer need only know how to use an object and not the inner details of how it was programmed. A class is not a type. An **instance** of a class is a data object that can be manipulated. The term *instance* has carried over to expert systems where it denotes a fact that matches a pattern. Likewise, a rule is said to be instantiated if its LHS is satisfied. The terms *activated* and *instantiated* in rule-based systems are synonymous.

Another significant concept that came from SIMULA 67 is **inheritance** in which a **subclass** could be defined to inherit the properties of classes. For example, one class may be defined to consist of objects that can be used in a stack and another class defined to be complex numbers. Now a subclass can be easily defined as objects that are complex numbers used in a stack. That is, these objects have inherited properties from both classes above them, called **superclasses**. The concept of inheritance can be extended to organize objects in a hierarchy where objects can inherit from their classes, which can inherit from their classes, and so on. Inheritance is very useful since objects can inherit properties from their classes without the programmer having to specify every property. Implementing multiple inheritance is not easy which is why Java and C# do not have it. However since CLIPS is written in C++ it takes advantage of multiple inheritance. The full object-oriented language embedded within CLIPS is called **COOL** (**Common Object-Oriented Language**). The operation of COOL is transparent to the user so you just have to understand the features of object-oriented programming.

Logic Programming

One of the first AI applications of computers was in proving logic theorems with the Logic Theorist program of Newell and Simon. This program was first reported at the Dartmouth Conference on AI in 1956 and caused a sensation because electronic computers previously had been used only for numeric calculations. Now a computer was mechanically reasoning the proofs of mathematical theorems, which had been a task that only mathematicians were thought capable of doing. The term *mechanical* means automated and dates back to Babbage's Mechanical computer of the nineteenth century.

In the Logic Theorist and its successor, the General Problem Solver (GPS), Newell and Simon concentrated on trying to implement powerful algorithms that could solve any problem. While the Logic Theorist was meant only for mathematical theorem proving, GPS was designed to solve any kind of logic problem, including games and puzzles such as chess, Tower of Hanoi, Missionaries and Cannibals, and cryptarithmetic. An example of their famous cryptarithmetic (secret arithmetic) puzzle is:

```
   DONALD
 + GERALD
   ROBERT
```

and it is known that D=5. The object is to figure out the arithmetic values of the other letters in the range 0–9.

GPS was the first problem solving program to clearly separate the problem-solving knowledge from the domain knowledge. This paradigm of explicitly separating the problem-solving knowledge from the domain knowledge is now used as the basis of expert systems. In expert systems today, the inference engine decides what knowledge should be used and how it should be applied.

Efforts continued to improve mechanical theorem proving. By the early 1970s, it had been discovered that computation is a special case of mechanical, logical deduction. When backward chaining was applied to sentences of the form "conclusion if conditions," it was powerful enough for significant theorem proving. The conditions can be thought of as representing patterns to be matched as in production rules discussed earlier. Sentences expressed in this form are called **Horn clauses** after Alfred Horn, who first investigated them. In 1972, the language PROLOG was created by Kowalski, Colmerauer, and Roussel to implement logic programming by backward chaining using Horn clauses.

Backward chaining can be used both to express the knowledge in a declarative representation and also control the reasoning process. Typically, backward chaining proceeds by defining smaller **subgoals** that must be satisfied if the initial goal is to be satisfied. These subgoals are then further broken down into smaller subgoals and so forth.

An example of declarative knowledge is the following classic example:

```
All men are mortal
Socrates is a man
```

which can be expressed in the Horn clauses:

```
someone is mortal
  if someone is a man
Socrates is a man
  if (in all cases)
```

For the sentence about Socrates, the IF condition is true in all cases. In other words, the knowledge about Socrates does not require any pattern to match. Contrast this with the mortal case in which someone must be a man for the pattern of the IF condition to be satisfied.

Notice that a Horn clause can be interpreted as a procedure that tells how to satisfy a goal. That is, to determine if someone is mortal, it is necessary to determine if someone is a man. As a slightly more complex example:

```
A car needs gas, oil, and inflated tires to run
```

which can be expressed in a Horn clause as:

```
x is a car and runs
  if x has gas and
  if x has oil and
  if x has inflated tires
```

Notice how the problem of determining if a car will run has been reduced to three simpler subproblems or subgoals. Now suppose there is some additional declarative knowledge as follows:

```
The fuel gauge shows not-empty if a car has gas
The dipstick shows not-empty if a car has oil
The air pressure gauge shows at least 20 if a car
  has inflated tires
The fuel gauge shows not-empty
The dipstick reads empty
The air pressure gauge shows 15
```

These can be translated into the following Horn clauses:

```
x has gas
  if the fuel gauge shows not-empty
x has oil
  if the dipstick shows not-empty
x has inflated tires
  if the air pressure gauge shows at least 20
```

```
Fuel gauge is not empty
  if (in all cases)
Dipstick reads empty
Air pressure is 15
  if (in all cases)
```

From these clauses, a mechanical theorem prover can prove that the car will not run because there is no oil and insufficient air pressure.

One of the advantages of backward-chaining systems is that execution can proceed in parallel. That is, if multiple processors were available, they could work on satisfying subgoals simultaneously. PROLOG is more than just a language since it incorporates a backward-chaining inference engine. At a minimum, PROLOG is a shell since it requires:

- an interpreter or inference engine
- a database (facts and rules)
- a form of pattern matching called **unification**
- a **backtracking** mechanism to pursue alternate subgoals if a search to satisfy a goal is unsuccessful.

As an example of backward chaining, suppose you can pay for the oil to make the car run if you have cash or a credit card. One subgoal is checked to see if you have cash. If there is no fact that you do have cash, the backtracking mechanism will then explore the other subgoal to see if you have a credit card. If you have a credit card, the goal of paying for oil can be satisfied. Notice that the absence of a fact to prove a goal is just as effective, although perhaps less efficient, than a negative fact such as "Dipstick reads empty." Either negative facts or missing facts can cause a goal to be unsatisfied (except in political logic.)

If the backtracking and pattern-matching mechanisms are not needed by the problem, then the programmer must work around them or code in a different language. One of the advantages of logic programming is executable specifications. That is, specifying the requirements of a problem by Horn clauses produces an executable program. This is very different from conventional programming in which the requirements document does not look at all like the final executable code.

Unlike production rule systems, the order in which subgoals, facts, and rules are entered in a PROLOG program has significant effects. Efficiency, and therefore speed, are affected by the way that PROLOG searches its database. Furthermore, there are programs that execute correctly if subgoals, facts, and rules are entered one way but go into an infinite loop or have a run-time error if the order changes.

Expert Systems

Expert systems can be considered **declarative programming** because the programmer does not specify how a program is to achieve its goal at the level of an algorithm. For example, in a rule-based expert system, any of the rules may become activated and put on the agenda if its LHS matches the facts. The order that the rules were entered does not affect which rules are activated. Thus, the program statement order does not specify a rigid control flow. Other types of expert systems are based on **frames**, discussed in Chapter 2, and **inference nets** discussed in Chapter 4.

There are a number of differences between expert systems and conventional programs. Table 1.12 lists some differences.

Table 1.12 Some Differences Between Conventional Programs and Expert Systems

Characteristic	Conventional Program	Expert System
Control by . . .	Statement order	Inference engine
Control and data	Implicit integration	Explicit separation
Control Strength	Strong	Weak
Solution by . . .	Algorithm	Rules and inference
Solution search	Small or none	Large
Problem solving	Algorithm is correct	Rules
Input	Assumed correct	Incomplete, incorrect
Unexpected input	Difficult to deal with	Very responsive
Output	Always correct	Varies with problem
Explanation	None	Usually
Applications	Numeric, file, and text	Symbolic reasoning
Execution	Generally sequential	Opportunistic rules
Program design	Structured design	Little or no structure
Modifiability	Difficult	Reasonable
Expansion	Done in major jumps	Incremental

Expert systems are normally used to deal with uncertainty. The uncertainty may arise in the input data to the expert system and even the knowledge base itself. At first this may seem surprising to people used to conventional programming. However, much of human knowledge is heuristic, which means that it may only work correctly part of the time so we try something else. In addition, the input data may be incorrect, incomplete, inconsistent, and have other errors. Algorithmic solutions are not capable of dealing with situations like this because an algorithm guarantees the solution of a problem in a finite series of steps.

Depending on the input data and the knowledge base, an expert system may come up with the correct answer, a good answer, a bad answer, or no answer at all. While this may seem shocking at first, the alternative is to have *no* answer all of the time. Again, the important thing to keep in mind is that a good expert system will perform no worse than the best problem solver for problems like this—a human expert—and may do better. If we knew an efficient algorithmic method that was better than an expert system, we would use it. The important thing is to use the best, and perhaps only, tool for the job.

Nondeclarative Programming

Nondeclarative paradigms are very popular in PROLOG and SQL. New versions of PROLOG have been developed for AI_1 and SQL is the standard for relational databases. They are used for a wide variety of applications, from standalone applications or in conjunction with other paradigms.

Induction-Based Programming

An application of AI that has attracted a great deal of interest is **induction-based** programming such as the classic ID3 Algorithm for machine learning and the newer C4.5 and C5.1. In this paradigm, the program learns by generalizing from a sample, just like a person would from the sequence 2,4,6,"?". One application to which this paradigm has been applied is database access. Instead of the user having to type in the specific values for one or more fields for a search, it is necessary to select only one or more appropriate example fields with those characteristics. The database program infers the characteristics of the data and searches the database for a match. Oracle and other relational database management systems which use the structured English query language (SQL) are good examples of using pattern recognition in searches.

Some expert systems tools offer induction learning by which they accept examples and case studies and automatically generate rules (see Appendix G.)

1.13 ARTIFICIAL NEURAL SYSTEMS

In the 1980s, a new development in programming paradigms arose called **artificial neural systems** (**ANS**), which is based on one way the brain processes information. This paradigm is sometimes called **connectionism** because it models solutions to problems by training simulated neurons connected in a network. Today ANS are found in many applications ranging from face recognition, medical diagnosis, games, speech recognition to car engines.

Connectionist researchers conjecture that thinking about computation in terms of the brain metaphor rather than the digital computer metaphor will lead to insights into the nature of intelligent behavior. The idea behind connectionism, then, is that we may see significant advances in AI if we approach problems from the point of view of brain-style computation rather than rule-based symbol manipulation. Neural networks are an information processing technique based on the way biological nervous systems, such as the brain, process information. The fundamental concept of neural networks is the structure of the information processing system. Composed of a large number of highly interconnected processing elements or neurons, a neural network system uses the human-like technique of learning by example to resolve problems. The neural network is configured for a specific application, such as data classification or pattern recognition, through a learning process called **training**. Just as in biological systems, learning involves adjustments to the synaptic connections that exist between the neurons.

There are many ways to classify the types of ANS but a useful distinction is whether a training set of input and output data is provided or not. If a training set is provided, the ANS is called a supervised model. If it has to learn to classify input without knowing any output, it is called unsupervised. A good example of supervised ANS is in face recognition. In contrast, if you do not know what the output should be, an ANS serves as a good classifier to group input as in the case of identifying outbreaks of disease.

Neural networks can differ on the way their neurons are connected, the specific kinds of computations their neurons do, the way they transmit patterns of activity throughout the network, and the way and rate at which they learn. Neural networks have been applied to all kinds of real-world problems. Their primary advantage is that they can solve problems that are too complex for conventional technologies—problems that do not have an algorithmic solution or for which an algorithmic solution is too complex to be defined. In general, neural networks are well suited to problems that people are good at solving, but cannot explain how they do it. These problems include pattern recognition and forecasting which require the recognition of trends in data. Today the field of **data mining** makes extensive use of AI to seek patterns in historical data that may serve to guide a company in the future. For example, data mining could be used to show a company when to stock certain kinds of items because of a seasonal variation.

Neural nets are also used as the front end of expert systems that require massive amounts of input from sensors as well as real-time response. Over 50 free ANS are available for download from the FAQ of the newsgroup comp.ai.neural-nets, and other resources mentioned in Appendix G.

The Traveling Salesman Problem

ANS has had remarkable success in providing real-time response to complex pattern recognition problems. In the 1980s, a neural net running on an ordinary microcomputer obtained a very good solution to the Traveling Salesman problem in 0.1 seconds compared to the optimum solution that required an hour of CPU time on a mainframe. The Traveling Salesman problem is important because it is the classic problem faced in optimizing the routing of signals in a telecommunications system. Optimizing routing is important in minimizing the travel time, and thus efficiency and speed whether it is routing packets through the Internet or delivering parcels in the mail to many locations

The basic Traveling Salesman problem is to compute the shortest route through a given list of cities. Table 1.13 shows the possible routes for one to four cities. Notice that the number of routes is proportional to the factorial of the number of cities minus one, $(N - 1)!$.

Table 1.13 Traveling Salesman Problem Routes

Number of Cities	Routes
1	1
2	1–2–1
3	1–2–3–1
	1–3–2–1
4	1–2–3–4–1
	1–2–4–3–1
	1–3–2–4–1
	1–3–4–2–1
	1–4–2–3–1
	1–4–3–2–1

While there are $9! = 362880$ routes for 10 cities, there are $29! = 8.8E30$ possible routes for thirty cities. The Traveling Salesman problem is a classic example of **combinatorial explosion** because the number of possible routes increases so rapidly that there are no practical solutions for realistic numbers of cities. If it takes one hour of CPU time to solve for 30 cities, it will take 30 hours for 31 cities, and 330 hours for 32 cities. These are actually very small numbers when compared to the thousands of telecommunications switches and cities that are used in routing of data packets and real items.

A neural net can solve the 10-city case just as fast as the 30-city case while a conventional computer takes much longer. For the 10-city case, the neural net came up with one of the two best routes and for the 30-city case, it came up with one of the best 100,000,000 routes. This is more impressive if it is realized that this route is in the top 1E-22 of the best solutions. Although neural nets may not always give the optimum answer, they can provide a best guess in real time. In many cases, a 99.9999999999999999999% correct answer in 0.1 second is better than a 100% correct answer in 30 hours. Other techniques to solve the problem have used genetic algorithms, as shown in Appendix G, and the Evolutionary Art Algorithm (Dorigo 04). Another approach is real DNA (Sipper 02).

Elements of an ANS

An **ANS** can be thought of as an analog computer that uses simple processing elements connected in a highly parallel manner. The processing elements perform very simple Boolean or arithmetic functions on their inputs. The key to the functioning of an ANS is the **weights** associated with each element. The weights represent the information stored in the system.

A typical artificial neuron is shown in Figure 1.10. The neuron may have multiple inputs but only one output. The human brain contains about 10^{11} neurons and one neuron may have thousands of connections to another. The input signals to the neuron are multiplied by the weights and are summed to yield the total neuron input, I. The weights can be represented as a matrix and identified by subscripts.

The neuron output is often taken as a **sigmoid function** of the input. The sigmoid is representative of real neurons, which approach limits for very small and very large inputs. The sigmoid is called an **activation function** and a commonly used function is $(1 + e^{-X})^{-1}$. Each neuron also has an associated **threshold value**, θ, which is subtracted from the total input, I. Figure 1.11 shows an ANS that can compute the **exclusive-OR** (**XOR**) of its inputs using a technique called **back propagation**. The XOR gives a true output only when its inputs are not all true or not all false. The number of nodes in the hidden layer will vary depending on the application and design.

Neural nets are not programmed in the conventional sense. There are many neural net learning algorithms, such as **counter propagation** and back propagation, to train nets. The programmer "programs" the net by simply supplying the input and corresponding output data. The net learns by automatically adjusting weights in the network which connect the neurons. The weights and the threshold

Figure 1.10 Neuron Processing Element

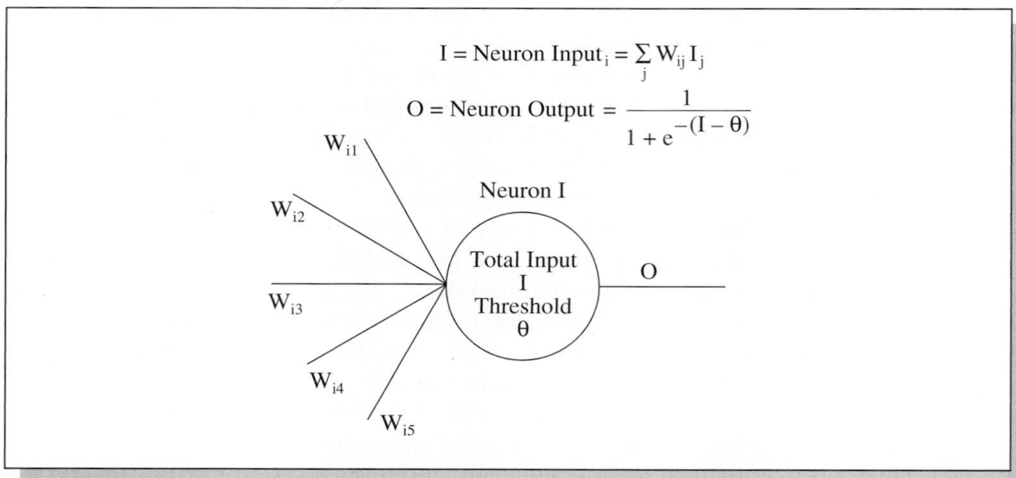

values of neurons determine the propagation of data through the net and so its correct response to the training data. Training the net to the correct responses may take hours or days, depending on the number of patterns that the net must learn and the necessary hardware and software. However, once the learning is accomplished, the net responds very quickly.

If software simulation is not fast enough, ANS can be fabricated in chips for real-time response. Once the network has been trained and the weights determined, a chip can be constructed.

Figure 1.11 A Back-Propagation Net

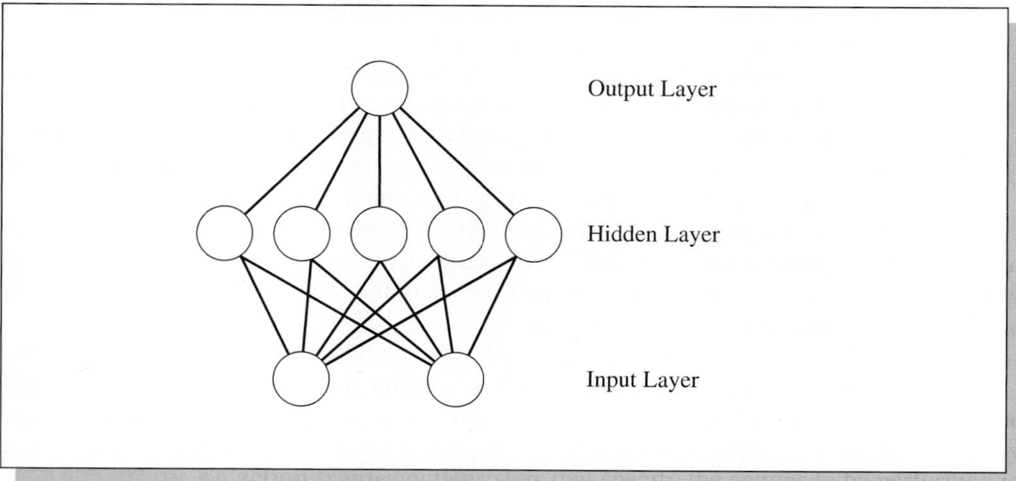

Characteristics of ANS

ANS architecture is very different from conventional computer architecture. In a conventional computer it is possible to correlate discrete information with memory cells. For example, a Social Security number could be stored as ASCII code in a contiguous group of memory cells. By examining the contents of this contiguous group the Social Security number could be directly reconstructed. This reconstruction is possible because there is a one-to-one relationship between each character of the Social Security number and the memory cell that contains the ASCII code of that character.

ANSs are modeled after current brain theories, in which information is represented by the weights. However, there is no direct correlation between a specific weight and a specific item of stored information. This distributed representation of information is similar to that of a hologram in which the lines of the hologram act as a diffraction grating to reconstruct the stored image when laser light is passed through.

A neural net is a good choice when there is much empirical data and no algorithm exists that provides sufficient accuracy and speed. ANS offers several advantages compared to the storage of conventional computers:

- *Storage is* ***fault tolerant***. Portions of the net can be removed and there is only a degradation in quality of the stored data. This occurs because the information is stored in a distributed manner.
- *The quality of the stored image degrades gracefully in proportion to the amount of net removed.* There is no catastrophic loss of information. The storage and quality features are also characteristic of holograms.
- *Data is stored naturally in the form of* ***associative memory***. An associative memory is one in which partial data is sufficient to recall all of the complete stored information. This contrasts with conventional memory in which data is recalled by specifying the address of the data to be recalled. A partial or noisy input may still elicit the complete original information.
- *Nets can extrapolate and interpolate from their stored information.* Training teaches a net to look for significant features or relationships in the data. Afterwards, the net can extrapolate to suggest relationships on new data. In one experiment a neural net was trained on the family relationships of 24 hypothetical people. Afterwards, the net could also answer correctly relationships about which it had not been trained.
- *Nets have* ***plasticity***. Even if a number of neurons are removed, the net can be retrained to its original skill level if enough neurons remain. This is also a characteristic of the brain, in which portions can be destroyed and the original skill levels can be relearned in time.

These characteristics make ANS very attractive for robot spacecraft, oil field equipment, underwater devices, process control, and other applications that need to function a long time without repair in a hostile environment. Besides the issue of reliability, ANS offers the potential of low maintenance costs because of plasticity. Even if hardware repair can be done, it will probably be more cost effective to reprogram the neural net than to replace it.

ANSs are generally not well suited for applications that require number crunching or an optimum solution. Also, if a practical algorithmic solution exists, an ANS is not a good choice unless the ANS is cheaper to implement than a chip.

Developments in ANS Technology

A central concern for connectionists is the idea that we must "take the brain seriously" in our psychological theorizing. This idea, of course, dates to ancient Greek speculations concerning the action of animal spirits in the nervous system. Later, notable speculations may be found in Rene Descartes' *Treatise of Man*. The origins of ANS started with the mathematical modeling of neurons by McCulloch and Pitts in 1943. An explanation of learning by neurons was given by Hebb in 1949. In Hebbian learning, a neuron's efficiency in triggering another neuron increases with firing. The term **firing** means that a neuron emits an electrochemical impulse which can stimulate other neurons connected to it. There is evidence that the conductivity of connections between neurons at their connections, called **synapses**, increases with firing. In ANS, the weight of connections between neurons is changed to simulate the changing conductance of natural neurons (Swingler 96).

In 1961, Rosenblatt published an influential book dealing with a new type of artificial neuron system he had been investigating called a **perceptron**. The perceptron was a remarkable device that showed capabilities for learning and pattern recognition. It basically consisted of two layers of neurons and a simple learning algorithm. The weights had to be manually set, in contrast to modern ANS, that set the weights themselves based on training. Many researchers entered the field of ANS and began studying perceptrons during the 1960s.

The early perceptron era came to an end in 1969 when Minsky and Papert published a book, called *Perceptrons*, that showed the theoretical limitations of perceptrons as a general computing machine. They pointed out a deficiency of the perceptron in being able to compute only 14 of the 16 basic logic functions, which means that a perceptron is not a general-purpose computing device. In particular, they proved a perceptron could not recognize the exclusive-OR. Although they had not seriously investigated multiple layer ANS, they gave the pessimistic view that multiple layers would probably not be able to solve the XOR problem. Government funding of ANS research ceased in favor of the symbolic approach to AI using languages such as LISP and algorithms. New methods of representing symbolic AI information by frames, invented by Minsky, became popular during the 1970s. Frames have evolved to modern scripts. Because of their simplicity, perceptrons and other ANSs are easy to construct with modern integrated circuit technology.

ANS research continued on a small scale in the 1970s. During the late 1970s, Geoffrey Hinton, James McClelland, David Rumelhart, Paul Smolensky, and other members of the Parallel Distributed Processing Research Group became interested in neural network theories of cognition. Their landmark book published in 1986, *Parallel Distributed Processing: Explorations in the Microstructure of Cognition,* marked the return of connectionism as a significant theory of cognition. Hopfield put ANS on a firm theoretical foundation with the Hopfield Net and demonstrated how ANS could solve a wide variety of problems. The general structure of a Hopfield Net is shown in Figure 1.12. In particular, he showed how an ANS could solve the Traveling Salesman problem in constant time as compared to the combinatorial explosion encountered by conventional algorithmic solutions. An electronic circuit form of an ANS could solve the Traveling Salesman problem in 1 μ second or less. Other combinatorial optimization problems can easily be done by ANS such as the four-color map, the Euclidean match, and the transposition code.

An ANS that can easily solve the XOR problem is the **back-propagation** net, also known as the **generalized delta rule**. The back-propagation net is commonly implemented as a three-layer net, although additional layers can be specified. The layers between the input and output layers are called **hidden layers** because only the input and output layers are visible to the external world. Another popular type of ANS is counterpropagation, invented by Hecht-Nielsen in 1986. An important theoretical result from mathematics, the Kolmogorov Theorem, can be interpreted as proving that a three-layer network with n inputs and 2n + 1 neurons in the hidden layer can map any continuous function.

Applications of ANS Technology

A significant example of learning by back propagation was demonstrated by a neural net that learned correct pronunciation of words from text. The ANS was trained by correcting its output using a text-to-speech device called DECTalk. It required 20 years of linguistic research to devise rules for correct pronunciation used by DECTalk. The ANS taught itself equivalent pronunciation skills overnight by simply listening to the correct pronunciation of speech from text. No linguistic skills were programmed into the ANS.

ANSs are used for recognition of radar targets by electronic and optical computers. New implementations of neural nets using optical components promise optical computers with speeds millions of times faster than electronic ones. Optical implementation of ANS is attractive because of the inherent parallelism

Figure 1.12 Hopfield Artificial Neural Net

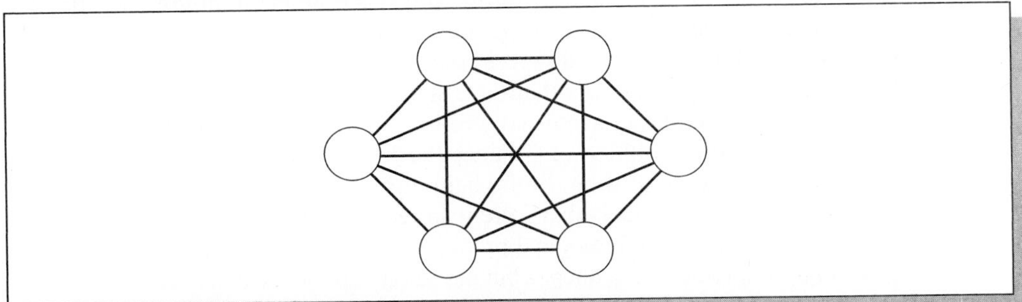

of light. That is, light rays do not interfere with one another as they travel. Huge numbers of photons can easily be generated and manipulated by optical components such as mirrors, lenses, high-speed programmable spatial light modulators, arrays of optical bistable devices that can function as optical neurons, and diffraction gratings. Optical computers designed as ANS appear to be complementary to one another.

Classic ANS applications are discussed in (Giarratano 90a). In particular, ANSs are useful in control systems where conventional approaches are not satisfactory (Giarratano 91b). In fact, ANSs are widely used in a variety of industrial control systems (Hrycej 97) and in the links in Appendix G.

1.14 CONNECTIONIST EXPERT SYSTEMS AND INDUCTIVE LEARNING

It is possible to build expert systems using ANS. In one system the ANS is the knowledge base constructed by training examples from medicine for diagnosis. This expert system tries to classify a disease from its symptoms into one of the known diseases that the system has been trained on. An inference engine called MACIE (Matrix Controlled Inference Engine) was designed that uses the ANS knowledge base. The system uses forward chaining to make inferences and backward chaining to query the user for any additional data needed to produce a solution. Although an ANS by itself cannot explain why its weights are set to certain values, MACIE can interpret the ANS and generate IF-THEN rules to explain its knowledge.

An ANS expert system such as this uses **inductive learning**. That is, the system **induces** the information in its knowledge base by example. Induction is the process of inferring the general case from the specific. Besides ANS, there are a number of commercially available decision software as discussed in Appendix G that explicitly generate rules from examples. The goal of inductive learning is to reduce or eliminate the knowledge acquisition bottleneck. By placing the burden of knowledge acquisition on the expert system, the development time may be reduced and the reliability may be increased if the system induces rules that were not known by a human. Expert systems have been combined with ANS (Giarratano 90b).

1.15 THE STATE OF THE ART IN ARTIFICIAL INTELLIGENCE

Many advances were made in AI during the 1990s and continuing on in the 21st Century. The strong AI view that the only good AI is that produced by logic and reasoning has had very limited success outside the closed world of the laboratory. Successful AI-based systems that have withstood the harsh reality of a tough, competitive marketplace have usually relied on biologically-based systems. Figure 1.13 shows the evolution of AI since the 1950s where the vertical scaledown indicates the passage of time. In the beginning, AI was divided into two broad paradigms based on models that were inspired by symbolic logic, with the other main branch inspired by biological processes. There has always been fierce competition between the two branches but based on experience constructing AI-based solutions, we can now say that no one approach will generally give the right

Figure 1.13 Evolution of Artificial Intelligence

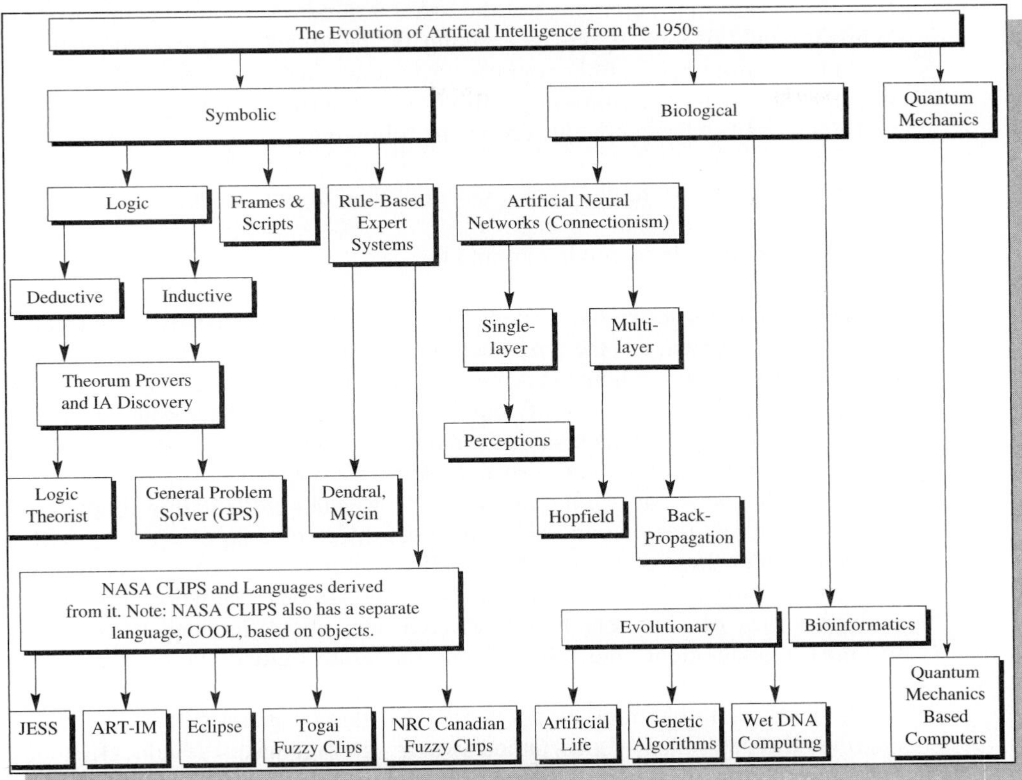

answer to a hard problem. The best we should hope for is an optimum solution, and be satisfied with a merely good solution.

The right part of the diagram in Figure 1.13 shows newer approaches based on physics, especially using quantum computers. While today we are thinking of using quantum computers to speed up searches only by many orders of magnitudes, that is a simplistic way of using these devices. When quantum mechanics was discovered in the 20th Century through Schroedinger's Equation and its equivalent formalism, Heisenberg's Matrix Mechanics, many people including Albert Einstein would not accept it. As Einstein was fond of saying, "God does not play dice with the Universe." Yet quantum mechanics is inextricably intertwined with probability and so unlike classical Newtonian theory, now nothing is certain. In fact, there is a theory that suggests consciousness is a quantum mechanical phenomena (Satinover 01).

A number of authors have speculated that the mind and consciousness itself may be an emergent property of the brain, which itself is built from neurons that in the final analysis are built from atoms and subatomic particles right on down to the quantum foam underlying all existence at distances so small, 10^{-60} meters, that space itself is grainy, not smooth as mathematics and classical

Newtonian physicists assume. At such small-distance scales, physicists have speculated that space contains not the usual 3 dimensions, but 11 dimensions. While it would be nice to think everything can be solved in terms of human reasoning and thinking, as philosophers have done since the time of the ancient Greeks 2500 years ago, thinking without real experimentation ignores the real world and leads to such conclusions as the following:

Premise: I am not moving because I don't feel myself moving.
Premise: I see the sun rise and set.
Therefore the sun is moving around me.

The term **emergence** has a special meaning when discussing evolutionary algorithms. Emergence is the term used for an unexpected behavior to arise that could not have been predicted in advance. For example, running water in a creek may appear to flow very smoothly until a rock is dropped in the water. Depending on the speed of the water, size of the rock, and other factors, turbulence may occur. The water exhibits nonlinear behavior with whitewater, rip currents, and other dynamic behavior coming into play that was not predicted by simple fluid dynamics but requires second- or higher-order differential equations to describe. The solution of these equations analytically is often not possible; therefore, approximate numerical solutions are the best that can be obtained. Many important examples of emergent behavior have been identified and applications to cities, management, and other widely disparate fields have been obtained (Johnson 01).

A classic example of emergent behavior is that of an ant colony in which a distributed type of intelligence, called **swarm intelligence,** is at work (Kennedy 01). This is in contrast to the centralized intelligence that humans and other mammals exhibit but which works well with colony type insects. The application of swarm intelligence is being studied for establishing robust robot colonies on other planets where each individual robot may not have much capacity for intelligence, thus saving cost and power, but the colony as a whole may prosper. Other applications to factories, networks, and distribution systems appear promising. In fact the Internet itself can be viewed as a swarm intelligence which uses the distributed low-level intelligence of packet switches to route packets with a high degree of survivability. This has met well one of the original goals of the Internet (or Arpanet as it was originally called) when started in the 1960s.

The major new player that has arisen in AI is Evolutionary algorithms (Fogel 03). These are generally used with other AI techniques such as ANS to increase the reliability of the result. The problem with ANN, Genetic algorithms, and other schemes is that the final solutions may become trapped in a local minimum rather than converging to the true solution of a global maximum. For this reason, some techniques purposely keep in some "unfit" solutions for reproduction rather than only the most fit since the unfit ones may wander farther from the local minimum and stumble across the global maximum.

Evolving connectionist systems is a powerful way to optimize the ANN architecture while making little or no presumptions as to what it might be (Kasabov 02). These parallel processing techniques take a lot of computer power but are more feasible as computers become more powerful and the Internet Grid and private companies provide access to many computers for computation (Foster 03).

Strictly speaking, the type of evolutionary algorithms used in computers are not based on Darwin's Theory of Evolution, which proceeds in small gradual steps over many thousands or millions of years, but on a competitive theory by Lamarck. He was a contemporary of Darwin's in the 19th Century who believed that if an animal gained extra strength in a limb through exercise, the offspring of that animal would have a stronger limb. Using computers, we force evolution to proceed as in the Lamarckian case by selecting for reproduction only those that come closest to our fitness criteria.

Evolutionary algorithms have also been applied to creating artificial life forms as part of a computer program. These are not just genetic algorithms or neural nets used to solve a particular problem; they are used in the broader context of fields such as ecology and economics to study predator-prey relationships in the wild, or more domestically, any environment such as a manufacturer-consumer in the global economy. Video games also make heavy use of environmental algorithms in defining new virtual creatures for the user to compete with. A classic example is the immensely powerful game *The Sims,* and the online version which people can play interactively with others all around the world.

When using evolutionary techniques with connectionist systems, surprising things may occur that were not planned on. This only adds to the criticism of connectionist systems by those who support logic-based AI since ANN cannot explain how their rules of connection and weights were achieved. Although many people have devised ANSs that purport to "explain" their rules, the fact remains that the rules and weights were not designed by a human but were formed as a "reflex" to the inputs and desired output of the system. In a sense, an ANN or evolutionary algorithm grows the correct solution or it does not survive.

With the decoding of the Human Genome, the field of **bioinformatics** has achieved increasing importance as it applies computer techniques to deal with a truly massive amount of information. Many jobs are open in this field to people with a background in artificial intelligence. Also the new fields of **genomics** and **proteomics** have appeared. The human genome is made up of about 30,000 genes. Each gene is basically a living factory that produces proteins to carry out the functions of the body either by acting in cells or sending messages to cells. The great challenge now is to determine what each of these genes and proteins does; not only in healthy genes but also in genetic diseases. These tasks require huge amounts of computing power because of the immense data and possible solutions. Artificial intelligence is a vital tool.

AI has also proven its worth in defense. At the end of the first Gulf War in 1990, it was stated that the savings from the use of AI in military logistics planning had repaid many times over all the money the Defense Advanced Research Projects Agency (DARPA) had put into AI research since the 1950s (http://www.au.af.mil/au/aul/school/acsc/ai02.htm). Today, AI saves many billions in computer games for military training as opposed to live war games where fuel and ammunition are used.

It would have been very difficult in the 1950s to imagine how commercially successful AI has become. At that time and for the next quarter century, the emphasis of AI researchers was on finding noble, serious applications such as theorem proving and automated discoveries. Although using AI programs to play checkers, chess, and other board games was also undertaken, AI programs were developed with serious goals in mind of understanding how humans reason, not for their entertainment value.

Today the commercial success of AI in video gaming and special effects in movies would be a great surprise to those early researchers. The video gaming industry now competes on an equal footing with movies and music for the consumer's money. People enjoy interactive games, especially when coupled with playing other people in other countries, cities, or states. Advanced video games rely heavily on AI to make creatures behave in realistic ways, not in a simple predictable pattern.

In fact a growing number of universities are now offering not only courses but degrees in video games, recognizing that a multibillion dollar industry is here to stay and there are good job opportunities in it. AI is also found in business, most notably as knowledge-based screening assistants to weed out the easy 90% of problems. Expert systems with real expertise are also used in many businesses. The only problem is that these business systems are based on the company's proprietary information and so the companies generally do not publish details about the systems lest their competitors get an advantage.

However there are still many examples of expert systems described in Appendix G on the Internet, many on the World Wide Web, some in papers located at sites like CiteSeer, and others discussed in newsgroups such as comp.ai.shells, which has much discussion of CLIPS expert systems. The advantage of a newsgroup is that you can post questions and hopefully someone will reply.

Besides job opportunities in AI and expert systems, a new job is that of **ontological engineer**. This can be considered a branch of philosophical engineering (in fact the only commercially viable branch to date.) In AI and expert systems, the term *ontology* has a different meaning than in the traditional philosophical sense of an ontology.

An ontology is the explicit formal specifications of the terms in the domain and relations among them (Gruber 93). Although the average Web user does not realize this, ontologies are common on the Web behind the scenes. These range from large ontologies organized as taxonomies, i.e., as a hierarchical top-down collection of related information in sites such as Yahoo, to sites like Amazon.com, eBay, and others that categorize items by sale price or time of auction and starting bid. Basically an ontology is a standard, agreed upon set of terms used to describe a domain, whether it be books, auction items, or something else. Without a common vocabulary, a Tower of Babel scenario would develop where no one knew what was being discussed in the domain. Many organizations are developing their own ontologies to better clarify what is being discussed in an unequivocal manner.

One of the biggest advantages of a standardized ontology is that it can become machine readable and thus computers can then aid humans in searching for the desired item. A similar effort is being made in specifying the Extensible Markup Language (XML) for different fields. Today there is a real need for people with a background in AI who are interested in becoming ontological engineers and classifying huge amounts of knowledge. Ontological engineering is also used in setting up and maintaining a database used by an expert system. This is not a trivial task, especially as the knowledge base becomes bigger and the user is allowed to enter in new knowledge for the expert system to use.

1.16 SUMMARY

In this chapter we have reviewed the problems and developments that have led to expert systems. The problems that expert systems are used to solve are generally not solvable by conventional programs because they lack a known or efficient algorithm. Since expert systems are knowledge-based, they can be effectively used for real-world problems that are ill-structured and difficult to solve by other means. A number of different paradigms for representing knowledge have been discussed, along with their pros and cons. For a more detailed discussion see (Giarratano 04).

The advantages and disadvantages of expert systems were also discussed in the context of selecting an appropriate problem domain for an expert systems application. Criteria for selecting appropriate applications were given.

The essentials of an expert system shell were discussed with reference to rule-based expert systems. The basic recognize-act inference engine cycle was described and illustrated by a simple rule example. Finally, the relationship of expert systems to other programming paradigms was described in terms of the appropriate domain of each paradigm. The important point is the concept that expert systems should be viewed as another programming tool that is suitable for some applications and unsuitable for others. Later chapters will describe the features and suitability of expert systems in much more detail. The advantages and disadvantages of expert systems were also discussed in the context of selecting an appropriate problem domain for an expert.

Future advances in AI will undoubtedly involve revolutionary new quantum computers (Brown 00), as well as computers using massive computation ability by linking up millions of computers on the Internet using the Grid, and biological wetlab using strands of RNA. These two methods can be used to solve a very complex Traveling Salesman problem in only a couple of days, much faster than any single supercomputer.

Appendix G has many links for general current information about artificial intelligence. A huge amount of information and software is available online. Other newsgroups are concerned with fuzzy logic, neural nets, expert system shells, and many other topics. In addition to the information and software, these newsgroups allow you to post questions and receive answers from other people. It is highly recommended you explore the online resources available in Appendix G for online resources by chapter.

PROBLEMS

1.1 Identify a person other than yourself who is considered either an expert or very knowledgeable. Interview this expert and discuss how well this person's expertise would be modeled by an expert system in terms of *each* criterion in the section "Advantages of Expert Systems."

1.2 (a) Write 10 nontrivial rules expressing the knowledge of the expert in Problem 1.1.
(b) Write a program that will give your expert's advice. Include test results to show that each of the 10 rules gives the correct advice. For ease of programming, you may allow the user to provide input from a menu.

1.3 (a) In Newell and Simon's classic book *Human Problem Solving* they mention the Nine-Dot Problem. Given nine dots arranged as follows, how can you draw four lines through all the dots without (a) lifting your pencil from the paper and (b) crossing any dot? (Hint: you can extend the line past the dots.)

• • •
• • •
• • •

(b) Explain your reasoning (if any) in finding the solution and discuss whether an expert system or some other type of program would be a good paradigm to solve this type of problem.

1.4 Write a program that can solve cryptarithmetic problems. Show the result for the following problem, where D=5:

```
  DONALD
+ GERALD
  ------
  ROBERT
```

1.5 Write a set of production rules to extinguish five different types of fire such as oil, chemical, and so forth, given the type of fire.

1.6 (a) Write a set of production rules to diagnose three types of poison based on symptoms.
(b) Modify the program so that it will also recommend a treatment once the poison has been identified.

1.7 Give 10 IF-THEN type heuristic rules for planning a vacation.

1.8 Give 10 IF-THEN type heuristic rules for buying a used car.

1.9 Give 10 IF-THEN type heuristic rules for planning your class schedule.

1.10 Give 10 IF-THEN type heuristic rules for buying an SUV or car.

1.11 Give 10 IF-THEN type heuristic rules for buying stocks or bonds.

1.12 Give 10 IF-THEN type heuristic rules for excuses on a late assignment.

1.13 Write a report on a modern expert system. Good sources are *PCAI*, *IEEE Expert* magazines, and Appendix G.

BIBLIOGRAPHY

(Adami 98). Christoph Adami, *Knowledge Introduction to Artificial Life*, Springer-Verlag, pp. 5, 1998.

(Bentley 02). Peter J. Bentley et al., *Creative Evolutionary Systems*, Academic Press, 2002.

(Berlinski 00). David Berlinski, *The Advent of the Algorithm*, Harcourt, Inc., pp. xvix, 2000.

(Brown 00). Julian Brown, *Minds, Machines, and the Multiverse*, Simon & Schuster, 2000.

(Bramer 99). Ed. by M.A. Bramer, *Knowledge Discovery and Data Mining*, IEEE Press, 1999.

(Cotterill 98). Rodney Cotterill, *Enchanted Looms*, Cambridge University Press, pp. 360, 1998.

(Debenham 98). John Debenham, *Knowledge Engineering: Unifying Knowledge base and Database Design*, Springer-Verlag, 1998.

(de Silva 00). Ed. by Clarence W. de Silva, *Intelligent Machines: Myths and Realities*, CRC Press, pp. 13, 2000.

(Dorigo 04). Marco Dorigo and Thomas Stützle, *Ant Colony Optimization* by MIT Press, 2004. Note the book also has a CD with software for solving the Traveling Salesman Problem using the Ant Evolutionary Algorithm.

(Fetzer 01). James H. Fetzer, *Computers and Cognition: Why Minds Are Not Machines,* Kluwer Academic Publishers, pp. 25-182, 2001.

(Foster 03). Ian Foster, "The Grid: Computing without Bounds" *Scientific American,* Volume 288, Number 4, pp. 78–85, April 2003.

(Friedman-Hill 03), Ernest Friedman-Hill, *Jess in Action: Rule-Based Systems in Java*, Manning Publications, 2003

(Fogel 03). Ed. by Gary B. Fogel and David W. Corne, *Evolutionary Computation in Bioinformatics*, Morgan Kaufmann Publisher, 2003.

(Giarratano 90a). Joseph C. Giarratano, et al., "Future Impacts of Artificial Neural Systems on Industry," *ISA Transactions*, pp. 9-14, Jan. 1990.

(Giarratano 90b). Joseph C. Giarratano, et al., "The State of the Art for Current and Future Expert System Tools," *ISA Transactions*, pp. 17-25, Jan. 1990.

(Giarratano 91a). Joseph C. Giarratano, et al., "An Intelligent SQL Tutor," 1991 Conference on Intelligent Computer-Aided Training (ICAT '91), pp. 309-316, 1991.

(Giarratano 91b). Joseph C. Giarratano, et al.,"Neural Network Techniques in Manufacturing and Automation Systems," in *Control and Dynamic Systems*, Vol. 49, ed. by C.T. Leondes, Academic Press, pp. 37-98, 1991.

(Giarratano 04). Joseph C. Giarratano, (http://www.pcai.com/Paid/Issues/PCAI-Online-Issues/17.4_OL/New_Folder/So&9i2/17.4_PA/PCAI-17.4-Paid-pp.18-Art1.htm).

(Gruber 93). T.R. Gruber, "A Translation Approach to Portable Ontology Specification," *Knowledge Acquisition* 5: 199-220, 1993.

(Hecht-Nielsen 90). Robert Hecht-Nielsen, *Neurocomputing*, Addison-Wesley Publishing Co., pp. 147, 1990.

(Helmreich 98) Stefan Helmreich, *Silicon Second Nature*, University of California Press, pp. 180-202, 1998.

(Hopgood 01). Adrian A. Hopgood, *Intelligent Systems for Engineers and Scientists*, CRC Press, 2001.

(Hrycej 97). Tomas Hrycej, *Neurocontrol*, John Wiley & Sons, Inc., 1997.

(Luger 02). George F. Luger, *Artificial Intelligence,* Fourth Edition, Addison-Wesley, 2002.

(Jackson 99). Peter Jackson, *An Introduction to Expert Systems*, Addison-Wesley Publishing Co., 1999.

(Johnson 01). Steven Johnson, *Emergence: The connected lives of ants, brains, cities, and software*, Scribner, 2001.

(Kantardzic 03). Mehmed Kantardzic, *Data Mining,* IEEE Press, 2003.

(Kasabov 02). Nikola Kasabov, *Evolving Connectionist Systems*, Springer-Verlag, pp. 7-29, 2002.

(Kennedy 01). James Kennedy and Russel C. Eberhart, Swarm Intelligence, Morgan-Kaufmann Publishers, 2001.

(Lajoie 00). Ed. by Susanne P. Lajoie, *Computers As Cognitive Tools, Volume Two: No More Walls*, Lawrence Erlbaum Associates, Publishers, 2000.

(Lakemeyer 03) ed. by Gerhard Lakemeyer and Bernhard Nebel, *Artificial Intelligence in the New Millenium,* Morgan-Kaufmann Publishers, 2003.

(Mendel 01). Jerry M. Mendel, *"Introduction to Rule-Based Fuzzy Logic Systems,"* IEEE Press, 2001.

(Satinover 01). Jeffrey Satinover, *The Quantum Brain*, John Wiley, 2001.

(Sipper 02). Moshe Sipper, *Machine Nature: The Coming Age of Bio-Inspired Computing,* McGraw-Hill, 2002.

(Swingler 96). Kevin Swingler, *"Applying Neural Networks: A Practical Guide,"* 1996.

(Wagman 99). Morton Wagman, *The Human Mind According To Artificial Intelligence*, Praeger Publishers, p. 76, 1999.

CHAPTER 2
The Representation of Knowledge

2.1 INTRODUCTION

This chapter and the next are about **logic**. Most people think of logic as meaning the same as reasonable. That is, if someone is logical, they are reasonable and don't jump to conclusions. However we need to define these terms more closely in order to work with AI and expert systems based on logic. As anyone who's used computers knows, the advantage of computers is that they do exactly as told. And the disadvantage of computers is that they do exactly as told. Since expert systems now determine your credit rating, whether you will be audited by the IRS, the operation of nuclear power plants, and other events of similar importance, it's a good idea to make them very, very logical and not subject to ambiguities. In technical terms, logic is the study of making valid inferences. This means that given a set of true facts, the conclusion will always be true. An invalid inference means that a false conclusion is reached with true facts. (So if you're ever stopped for speeding, simply show this book to the police officer.)

We also want to make clear the distinction between **formal logic** and **informal logic**. Informal logic is the kind of logic people and especially lawyers use when trying to win an argument, i.e., a case. An argument is not necessarily a heated exchange that erupts in gunfire, but a legal argument in a courtroom where emotionally charged words are used to persuade the jury which side has the best lawyer and so win the case. A complex logical argument is a chain of inferences in which one conclusion leads to another and so on. In court this may lead to one of several conclusions until the verdict of Guilty, or Not Guilty, or Not Guilty by Reason of Insanity, or a mistrial is declared, and then the case is appealed.

In **formal logic**, also called **symbolic logic**, the inferences and other factors which enter into proving the final conclusion true or false in a valid way are of utmost importance. If you've ever encountered a bug in a computer program, that is a perfect example of the program making an invalid symbolic inference. (Fortunately, if you have spent hundreds of dollars to upgrade your operating system to the latest version, you can now always get immediate satisfaction by sending an error report to the manufacturer.) Logic also needs **semantics** to give meaning to symbols. In formal logic we choose semantics that are not emotionally charged words like "Do you prefer Pepsi or Coke?" Instead the semantics of formal logic are like choosing meaningful names for variables in ordinary programming.

In addition to introducing logic, this chapter is also an introduction to the commonly used representations of knowledge. Knowledge representation (KR) has long been considered central to AI because it is as significant a factor in determining the success of a system as the software that uses the knowledge. This importance also carries over to computer science in the field of database design. While databases are generally considered as repositories of current data, such as a store's product inventory, accounts payable, accounts due, etc., rather than knowledge, many companies are now actively engaged in **data mining** to extract knowledge.

Data mining is meant to use **archival data** stored in **data warehouses** in order to predict future trends. For example, a company may look at its last five years of sales reports for the month of December to predict what kind and how much of a certain inventory to keep in stock, For example, they may discover through data mining that Christmas cards sell well in December but Valentine's Day cards do not. A slightly more realistic case would be the discovery that red and green clothes sell better in Winter than Spring since red and green are associated with Christmas, while brown, orange and yellow clothes sell better in the Fall. While human managers may be aware of this, data mining can serve to provide quantitative estimates of how much clothes to buy and when to put them on sale once the season is over. Of course the real value of data mining is in discovering patterns that are not obvious to a human but may be discovered by analyzing huge amounts of historical data that is stored in a company's data archive. In addition to classical statistical methods, AI techniques such as ANS, Genetic algorithms, Evolutionary algorithms, and expert systems may all be used with data mining, either singly or in hybrid combinations (Werbos 94).

KR is of major importance in expert systems for two reasons. First, expert systems are designed for a certain type of knowledge representation based on **rules of logic** called **inferences**. Normally we think of **reasoning** as drawing conclusions from facts. Unfortunately people are not very good at this because we tend to mix up the semantics with the reasoning process itself, and so do not always reach a valid conclusion. Good examples of this occur in ads for political races. The method of reasoning that uses no facts, unreliable facts, or the same facts to reach completely opposite conclusions is the basis of political logic.

Making inferences is the formal term for a special type of reasoning that does not rely on semantics; that is the meaning of words. While semantics are indispensable in the real world, an expert system is designed to reason on the basis of logic and not get involved in the emotional entanglements that semantics may bring into reasoning. The object of inferences is to reach a valid conclusion based on the facts and form of the argument. Here again, in Logic, the term *argument* means the formal way that facts and rules of inference are made to justify a valid conclusion. If you've ever watched news shows in which the newscaster engages in a long discussion with someone who is a former general, former ambassador, former juror, or whatever, the purpose is not to reach a valid conclusion but to keep the TV viewer entertained.

Making valid inferences is logical reasoning. While the terms *commonsense* and *probabilistic reasoning* are invaluable in the real world, they involve uncertainty because things in the real world are never 100 percent certain. If someone says, "The sky is blue," a little while later it may be grey or even worse, green! Reasoning under uncertainty is a very important subject that we will discuss in more detail in Chapters 4 and 5.

The second reason KR is important is it affects the development, efficiency, speed, and maintenance of the system. This is just like the situation in ordinary programming where the choice of data structure is of fundamental importance to the program. A good program design must choose from simple named variables, arrays, linked lists, queues, trees, graphs, networks or even stand-alone external databases such as Microsoft Access, SQL Server, or Oracle. In CLIPS, the KR can be rules, deftemplates, objects, and facts.

In the next chapter we will discuss how inferences are made on knowledge to produce valid conclusions, and common fallacies you should watch out for that may appear logical but are not. This is especially important in knowledge acquisition discussed in Chapter 6 when you have to interview a human expert for your expert system. You will have to identify true knowledge from the semantics that can lead to invalid conclusions. On the other hand, if you argue too much with your knowledge expert and don't come up with the conclusions they want, you may get fired!

Many computer programs have been written using AI for reasoning, theorem proving, and even learning logic as shown in Appendix G.

2.2 THE MEANING OF KNOWLEDGE

Knowledge, like love, is one of those words that everyone knows the meaning of, yet finds hard to define or even feel the same way about. In fact, the only true love that all people feel the same about is for their cat or dog (with apologies for those who love snakes and tarantulas.) Like love, knowledge has many meanings depending on the mind of the beholder. Other words such as data, facts, and information are often used interchangeably with knowledge (Russell 03).

People may seek solutions to problems through reasoning and experience. The general term for using experience to solve a problem is **heuristics**. Long, specific examples of heuristic experience are called **case-based reasoning**. This is one of the main types of reasoning used in law, medicine, and repairs where lawyers, doctors, and auto mechanics try to repair a problem using previous similar cases, called **precedents** (Leake 96). While you may feel a case-based solution is expensive since someone's already had your problem, see how much it costs to establish a new medical, legal, or auto repair precedent!

An expert system may have hundreds or thousands of little cases to refer to. Each rule may be thought of as a micro-precedent which may be able to solve the problem or be used in a chain of inference that will hopefully provide a solution.

The study of knowledge is **epistemology**. It is concerned with the nature, structure, and origins of knowledge. Figure 2.1 illustrates some of the categories of epistemology. Besides the philosophical kinds of knowledge expressed by Aristotle, Plato, Descartes, Hume, Kant, and others, there are two special types called **a priori** and **a posteriori**. The Latin term *a priori* means *that which precedes*. A priori knowledge comes before and is independent of knowledge from the senses. For example, the statements "everything has a cause" and "all triangles have 180 degrees in the Euclidean plane" are examples of a priori knowledge. A priori knowledge is considered to be universally true and cannot be denied without contradiction. Logic statements, mathematical laws, and the knowledge possessed by teenagers are examples of a priori knowledge.

The opposite of a priori knowledge is knowledge derived from the senses: *a posteriori* knowledge. The truth or falsity of a posteriori knowledge can be verified using sensory experience, as in the statement "the light is green." However, since sensory experience may not always be reliable, a posteriori knowledge can be denied on the basis of new knowledge without the necessity of contradictions. For example, if you see someone with brown eyes, you would believe that their eyes were brown. However, if you later saw that person removing brown contact lenses to reveal blue eyes, your knowledge would have to be revised.

Knowledge can be further classified into **procedural knowledge**, **declarative knowledge**, and **tacit knowledge**. The procedural and declarative knowledge types correspond to the procedural and declarative paradigms discussed in Chapter 1 and in more depth in (Brewka 97).

Figure 2.1 Some Categories of Epistemology

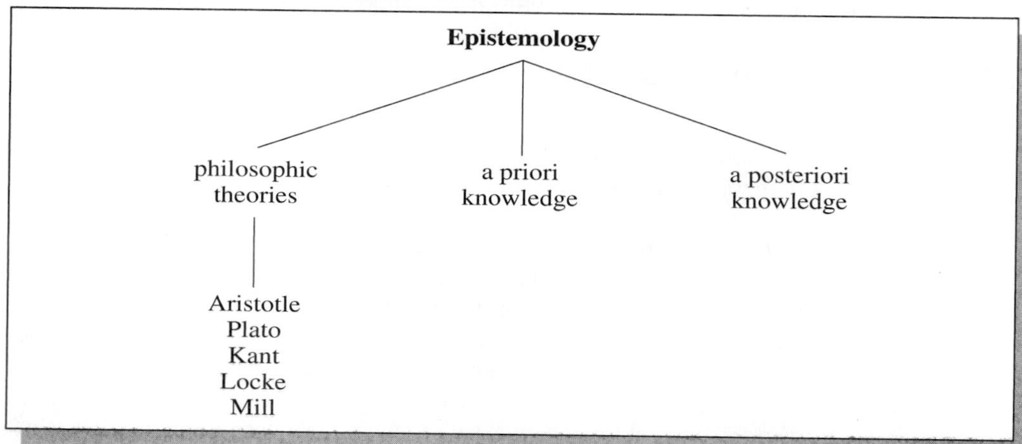

Procedural knowledge is often referred to as knowing how to do something. An example of procedural knowledge is knowing how to boil a pot of water. Thinking you know how to boil water at all elevations can lead to a failure of commonsense reasoning; a true oxymoron since there's no reasoning in commonsense but real world experience (see the problem at the end of the chapter on boiling water). Declarative knowledge refers to knowing that something is true or false. It is concerned with knowledge expressed in the form of declarative statements such as "Don't put your fingers in a pot of boiling water." Many different ways of representing knowledge using logic have been developed, see (Sowa 00)

Tacit knowledge is sometimes called **unconscious knowledge** because it cannot be expressed by language. An example is knowing how to move your hand. On a gross scale, you might say that you move your hand by tightening or relaxing certain muscles and tendons. But at the next lower level, how do you know how to tighten or relax the muscles and tendons? Other examples are walking or riding a bicycle. In computer systems ANS is related to tacit knowledge because normally the neural net cannot directly explain its knowledge, but may be able to if given an appropriate program (see Section 1.14).

Knowledge is of primary importance in expert systems. In fact, an analogy to Nicholas Wirth's classic expression used in his seminal book on Pascal:

```
Algorithms + Data Structures = Programs
```

is the following for expert systems:

```
Knowledge + Inference = Expert Systems
```

As used in this book and illustrated in Figure 2.2, knowledge is part of a hierarchy. At the bottom is noise, consisting of items that are of no interest and may obscure data. The next higher level is raw data, which are items of potential interest. Next higher is information, which is processed data of definite interest. Next up is knowledge, which represents such important information that it should be preserved and acted upon. In Chapter 1, knowledge in rule-based expert systems is defined as the rules that were activated by facts or other rules to produce new facts or conclusions. A conclusion is the end product of a chain of reasoning, called inferencing when done according to formal rules. This process of making inferences is an essential part of an expert system. The term **inferencing** is generally used for mechanical systems such as expert systems. Reasoning is the term used for human thinking.

An ANS does not make inferences. Rather it seeks to find an underlying pattern to data that is not obvious to a human. Basically a ANS is a pattern classifier. For example, your ability to read is based on pattern recognition of a neural net in your brain that has been trained to recognize the pattern of letters. Another part of your brain translates those patterns into the words that people hear in their minds when reading because this is how they were taught to read as children: by sounding out the words in a phonetic manner. As an example, turn this book upside down and try to read it. Most people cannot read upside down at first but it is possible to retrain your reading neural net to recognize letters. In

Figure 2.2 The Pyramid of Knowledge

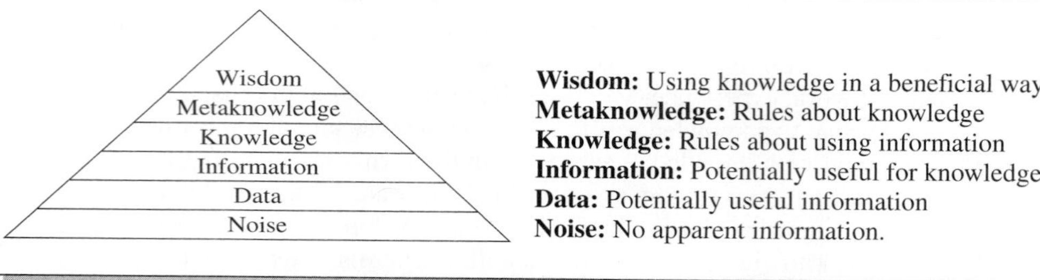
Wisdom
Metaknowledge
Knowledge
Information
Data
Noise
Wisdom: Using knowledge in a beneficial way
Metaknowledge: Rules about knowledge
Knowledge: Rules about using information
Information: Potentially useful for knowledge
Data: Potentially useful information
Noise: No apparent information.

classical psychological experiments, people wore glasses that inverted the image of the world. After a few days their brains adapted and things looked right-side-up again. In fact the lens of our eyes project an image upside down and our brain inverts this to make it seem normal.

Another example of the versatility of neural nets is to rotate the book by an angle, say 30° (Saratchandran 96). You will still be able to read although a bit more slowly. As you rotate the book towards 180°, you will have a harder time reading. With practice, some people can read as well upside down which shows the amazing adaptability of our neural nets. In the same way, a ANS that is trained on letters at different angles will be able to interpolate and read text that is not shown normal. The more rotations that the net is trained on, the faster will be its accuracy. Likewise, training a net on different cursive styles will enable a ANS to read more styles of handwriting just as a person can read different writers' handwriting.

The term **facts** mean information that is considered reliable. Expert systems draw inferences using facts. Facts that are later shown to be false may be retracted using the Truth Maintenance facility of CLIPS and all conclusions, rules, and other facts generated by the false fact are automatically retracted. Expert systems may also (1) separate data from noise, (2) transform data into information, or (3) transform information into knowledge. It is extremely dangerous to use raw data in an expert system that expects facts since the reliability of the resulting conclusions may be highly unreliable. This is, of course, another way of saying the adage, "Garbage in, garbage out." Unless of course someone wants garbage to support a particular agenda.

As an example of these concepts, consider the following sequence of 24 numbers:

```
137178766832525156430015
```

Without knowledge, this entire sequence may appear to be noise. However, if it is suspected or known that this sequence is meaningful, then the sequence is data. Determining what is data and what is noise is like the old saying about gardening: "a weed is anything that grows which isn't what you want."

Certain knowledge may exist to transform data into information. For example, the following algorithm processes the data to yield information:

```
Group the numbers by twos.
Ignore any two-digit numbers less than 32.
Substitute the ASCII characters for the two-digit
numbers.
```

Application of this algorithm to the previous 24 numbers yields the information:

```
GOLD 438+
```

Now knowledge can be applied to this information. For example, there may be a rule:

```
IF gold is less than 500
   and the price is rising (+)
THEN
   buy gold
```

Although not explicitly shown in the figure, **expertise** is a specialized type of knowledge and skill that experts have. It is in the knowledge, metaknowledge, and wisdom sections of Figure 2.2. Although very specialized knowledge may be found in public sources of information such as books and papers, just reading the book does not an expert make. For example, detailed information about surgical procedures may be found in a medical textbook. Yet would you be willing to undergo brain surgery if someone came to your door claiming they had taken an online course and was willing to do it at a cut-rate price? Even if you get a free set of Ginsu knifes (slightly used from your brain surgery?)

Expertise is the implicit knowledge and skills of the expert that must be extracted and made explicit so that it can be encoded in an expert system. The reason the knowledge is implicit is that a true expert knows the knowledge so well that it is second-nature and does not require thinking. As an example, after graduating from medical school, interns serve a year typically working 80 or more hours per week until they can practice medicine without even thinking. While this practice has been criticized, it does embed the knowledge so deeply it becomes second nature. (Of course if you're a patient, it's also a good idea to ask the intern how much sleep they've gotten this week.) Near the top of the hierarchy, above knowledge, is **metaknowledge.** The prefix **meta** means "above."

Metaknowledge is knowledge about knowledge and expertise. Although an expert system may be designed with knowledge about several different domains, this is generally undesirable because the system becomes less well-defined. Experience has shown that the most successful expert systems are restricted to as small a domain as possible. For example, if an expert system was designed to identify bacterial diseases, it would not be good to have it also diagnose car problems. As a real world example, consider that doctors specialize in only one small area, not all of medicine. Even a family physician (who used to be called a general practitioner) refers patients to the appropriate specialist when needed.

In expert systems, an ontology is the metaknowledge that describes everything known about the problem domain. Ideally an ontology should be described in a formal manner so that inconsistencies and inadequacies can be easily identified. A number of free and commercial tools are available to construct ontologies. Constructing an ontology should be done before the expert system is implemented or else the rules may have to be revised as more information is known about the domain, thus increasing the cost, development time and bugs.

For example, an expert system could have knowledge bases about repairing GM cars, GM SUVs, and GM diesel trucks. Depending on which type of vehicle needed repair, the appropriate knowledge base would be used. It would be inefficient in terms of memory and speed for all the knowledge bases to reside in memory at once since the Rete network continuously modifies the network of all rules in memory. In addition, there could be conflicts if the antecedents of a rule for truck and car were the same pattern, yet the conclusion was different. For example, if the fuel gauge read empty, the car expert system might say "Fill tank with gas," while the truck expert system might say, "Fill tank with diesel." It would not be good to fill the car's gas tank with diesel or the truck's with gas. The expert system also slows down as the number of rules in the system increases since the Rete network gets larger. Metaknowledge can be used to decide which knowledge domain should be loaded into memory and also as a general guide to designing and maintaining the expert system and ontology.

In a philosophical sense, **wisdom** is the peak of all knowledge. Wisdom is the metaknowledge of determining the best goals of life and how to obtain them. A rule of wisdom might be expressed as:

```
IF I have enough money to keep my spouse happy
THEN I will retire and enjoy life
```

The subject of AI-based wisdom engineering has been in constant growth. However, while there is a great abundance of wisdom in the world there are few listeners. In this book we shall restrict ourselves to knowledge-based systems and leave wisdom-based systems to politicians and other experts.

2.3 PRODUCTIONS

A number of different knowledge-representation techniques have been devised. These include rules, semantic nets, frames, scripts, logic, conceptual graphs, and others. In particular, many knowledge representation languages have been proposed such as the classic knowledge language one, KL-ONE, and its frame-based descendant, CLASSIC (Brachman 91). Many others have been proposed including visual-based languages.

As described in Chapter 1, rules are commonly used as the knowledge base in expert systems since their advantages greatly outweigh their disadvantages.

One formal notation for defining productions is the Backus-Naurform-(BNF). This notation is a **metalanguage** for defining the **syntax** of a language. Syntax defines the form, while **semantics** refers to meaning. A metalanguage is a language for describing languages. Since the prefix meta means above, a metalanguage is above normal language.

There are many types of languages such as natural languages, logic languages, mathematics, and computer languages. The BNF notation for a simple English language rule that a sentence consists of a noun and a verb followed by ending punctuation is given as the following production rule:

```
<sentence>::= <subject> <verb> <end-mark>
```

where the **angle brackets,** <>, and ::= are symbols of the metalanguage and not of the language being specified. The symbol ::= means "is defined as" and is the BNF equivalent of the arrow, Æ, used in Chapter 1 with production rules.

The terms within angle brackets are called **nonterminal symbols** or simply *nonterminals.* A nonterminal is a variable that represents another term. The other term may be a nonterminal or a **terminal**. A terminal cannot be replaced by anything else and so is a constant.

The nonterminal <sentence> is special because it is the one **start symbol** from which the other symbols are defined. In the definition of programming languages, the start symbol is usually named <program>. The production rule:

```
<sentence> → <subject> <verb> <end-mark>
```

states that a sentence is composed of a subject, followed by a verb, followed by an end-mark. The following rules complete the nonterminals by specifying their possible terminals. The **bar** means "or" in the metalanguage:

```
<subject> →I | You | We
<verb> →left | came
<end-mark> →. | ? | !
```

All possible sentences in the language, i.e., the productions, can be produced by successively replacing each nonterminal by its right-hand-side nonterminals or terminals until all nonterminals are eliminated. The following are some productions:

```
I left.
I left?
I left!
```

```
You left.
You left?
You left!
We left.
We left?
We left!
```

A set of terminals is called a **string** of the language. If the string can be derived from the start symbol by replacing nonterminals with their definition rules, then the string is called a valid **sentence**. For example, "We," "WeWe," and "leftcamecame" are all valid strings of the language, but are not valid sentences.

A **grammar** is a complete set of production rules that defines a language unambiguously. While the previous rules do define a grammar, it is a very restricted one because there are so few possible productions. For example, a more elaborate grammar could also include direct objects, as in the following productions:

```
<sentence> →<subject> <verb> <object> <end-mark>
<object> →home | work | school
```

Although this is a valid grammar, it is too simple for practical use. A more practical grammar is the following where the end-mark has been left out for simplicity:

```
<sentence> →<subject phrase> <verb> <object
  phrase>
<subject phrase> →<determiner> <noun>
<object phrase> →<determiner> <adjective> <noun>
<determiner> →a | an | the | this | these | those
<noun> →man | eater
<verb> → is | was
<adjective> →dessert | heavy
```

The <determiner> is used to indicate a specific item. Using this grammar, we can generate sentences such as:

```
the man was a dessert eater
an eater was the heavy man
```

A **parse tree** or **derivation tree** is a graphic representation of a sentence decomposed into all the terminals and nonterminals used to derive the sentence. Figure 2.3 shows the parse tree for the sentence "the man was a heavy eater." However, the string "man was a heavy eater" is not a valid sentence because it lacks the determiner in the subject phrase. A compiler creates a parse tree when it tries to determine if statements in a program conform to the valid syntax of a language.

Figure 2.3 Parse Tree of a Sentence

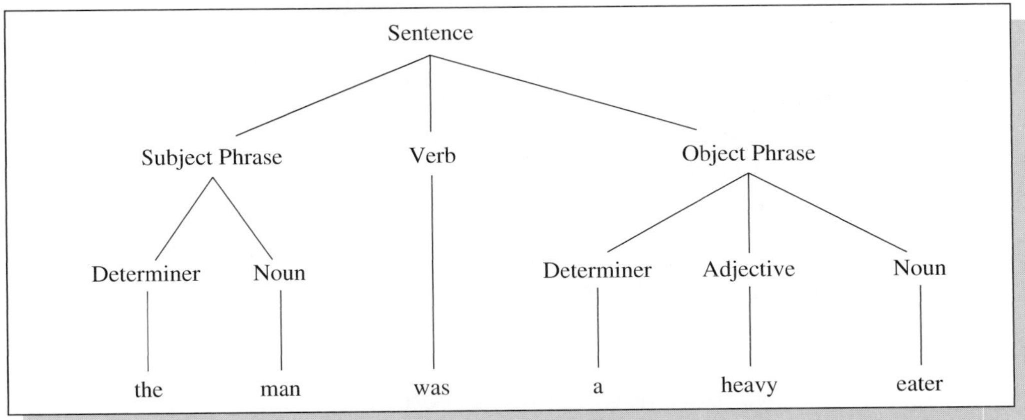

The tree in Figure 2.3 shows that the sentence "the man was a heavy eater" can be derived from the start symbol by applying appropriate productions. The steps in this process are shown following; where the **double arrow, =>**, means apply the productions shown:

```
<sentence> => <subject phrase> <verb>
              <object phrase>
<subject phrase> => <determiner> <noun>
<determiner> => the
<noun> => man
<verb> => was
<object phrase> => <determiner> <adjective> <noun>
<determiner> => a
<adjective> => heavy
<noun> => eater
```

An alternative way of using productions is to generate valid sentences by substituting all the appropriate terminals for nonterminals, as discussed previously. Of course, not all productions, such as "the man was the dessert," make sense (unless you're a cannibal).

Finite state machines (FSMs) are well suited to recognizing sentence structure. For example, compilers that translate source code of computer languages use FSM to **parse** source code into the smallest units of meaning, called **tokens.** FSM and parsing are essential to applications such as compilers to translate source code into assembly language, and accurate speech recogination. The term **compiler** has now been broadened with Java to mean translating source code using the javac compiler into a platform independent bytecode, as was done with the introduction of Pascal in the 1970s, whose bytecode could run on any microprocessor. Pascal's conversion into bytecode was correctly called an interpreter rather than a compiler since the bytecode was not specific machine language instructions like assembly language. However interpreters are slower than compilers and so it makes better advertising to call something a compiler rather than an interpreter.

An online demo of a finite state machine from Xerox is at (http://www.xrce.xerox.com/competencies/content-analysis/fsCompiler/fsinput.html). Links to examples of FSM such as the soft-drink machine is at (http://www.xrce.xerox.com/competencies/content-analysis/fsCompiler/fsexamples.html). A very comprehensive reference to FSM is (http://odur.let.rug.nl/alfa/fsa_stuff/).

Although FSMs are good with a restricted set of symbols, e.g., the numerals 0-9, or the letters of the alphabet, a problem occurs in areas such as speech recognition where ambiguities may occur. For example, in the two sentences:

```
(1) No one has let us read
  or
(2) No one has lettuce red
```

In sentence (1), someone is complaining they have not been able to read. In (2), no one has red lettuce. A good way to disambiguate the words "lettuce," "let us," "read," and "red" uses a **hidden Markov Machine** (HMM) that assigns probabilities to actions in a finite state machine. By looking at the whole sentence structure or additional sentences, the HMM figures out the correct context (either reading a book or searching for a vegetable on a grocery list). While expert systems are not the software of choice for doing HMM, they can be used as a front-end for speech recognition that an expert system like CLIPS can use to trigger an appropriate rule.

In fact, CLIPS has the capability to easily interface C or C++ code so that an HMM written in C or C++ can be called just like any other CLIPS keyword. One of the strengths of CLIPS is that it is an extensible language where the user can easily add keywords at compile time for greatest efficiency. Also with the object-oriented features of COOL, objects can be used to extend CLIPS using all the power of multiple inheritance. Other software such as ANS, genetic algorithms, and other software written in C or C++ can be added either on the left-hand-side to trigger rules or on the right-hand-side of rules for output. For example, a speech synthesizer, robotic effectors, and actuator can be called from CLIPS by defining the appropriate keyword functions. The availability of the source code for CLIPS means that the new keyword calls can be compiled in CLIPS with no loss of speed compared to other expert tools in which the source code is not provided.

2.4 SEMANTIC NETS

A **semantic network**, or net, is a classic AI representation technique used for propositional information. (http://www.pcai.com/web/T6110H2/R6.o1.h8/pcai.htm) A semantic net is sometimes called a **propositional net**. As discussed before, a proposition is a statement that is either true or false, such as "all dogs are mammals" and "a triangle has three sides." Propositions are a form of declarative knowledge because they state facts. In mathematical terms, a semantic net is a labeled, directed graph. A proposition is always true or false and is called **atomic** because its truth value cannot be further divided. Here the term *atomic* is used in the classical Greek sense of an indivisible object. In contrast, the fuzzy propositions discussed in Chapter 5 need not be exactly true or false.

Semantic nets were first developed for AI as a way of representing human memory and language understanding by Quillian in 1968. He used semantic nets to analyze the meanings of words in sentences. Note that the meaning of a sentence is not the same as parsing it into its tokens and lexical structure as the FSM and HMM mentioned in the previous section can do. Since then semantic nets have been applied to many problems involving knowledge representation. Such understanding of meaning is necessary to move beyond simple expert systems or AI software in order to avoid ambiguity. In the next chapter on inference, we will see how expert systems draw conclusions from facts that may be used by other rules in a chain of inference until a valid conclusion is reached. Without semantics, expert systems might fail in the same way that a human who is confused by ambiguity may also fail.

The structure of a semantic net is shown graphically in terms of **nodes** and the **arcs** connecting them. Nodes are sometimes referred to as **objects** and the arcs as **links** or **edges**.

The links of a semantic net are used to express relationships. Nodes are generally used to represent physical objects, concepts, or situations. Figure 2.4a shows an ordinary net, actually a directed graph, in which the links indicate airline routes between cities. Nodes are circles and links are the lines connecting nodes. The arrows show the directions in which planes can fly, hence the term *directed graph.* In Figure 2.4b the links show the relationship between members of a family. Relationships are of primary importance in semantic nets because they provide the basic structure for organizing knowledge. Without relationships, knowledge is simply a collection of unrelated facts. With relationships, knowledge is a cohesive structure about which other knowledge can be inferred. For example, in Figure 2.4b, it can be inferred that Ann and Bill are the grandparents of John even though there is no explicit link labeled "grandfather-of."

Semantic nets are sometimes referred to as **associative nets** because nodes are associated or related to others. In fact, Quillian's original work modeled human memory as an associative net in which concepts were the nodes and links formed the connections between concepts. According to this model, as one concept node is stimulated by reading words in a sentence, its links to other nodes are activated in a spreading pattern. If another node receives sufficient activation, the concept is elevated to the conscious mind. For example, although you know thousands of words, you are thinking of only the specific words in this sentence as you read it.

Certain types of relationships have proven particularly useful in a wide variety of knowledge representations. Rather than defining new relationships for different problems, it is customary to use these types. The use of common types makes it easier for different people to understand an unfamiliar net.

Figure 2.4 Two Types of Nets

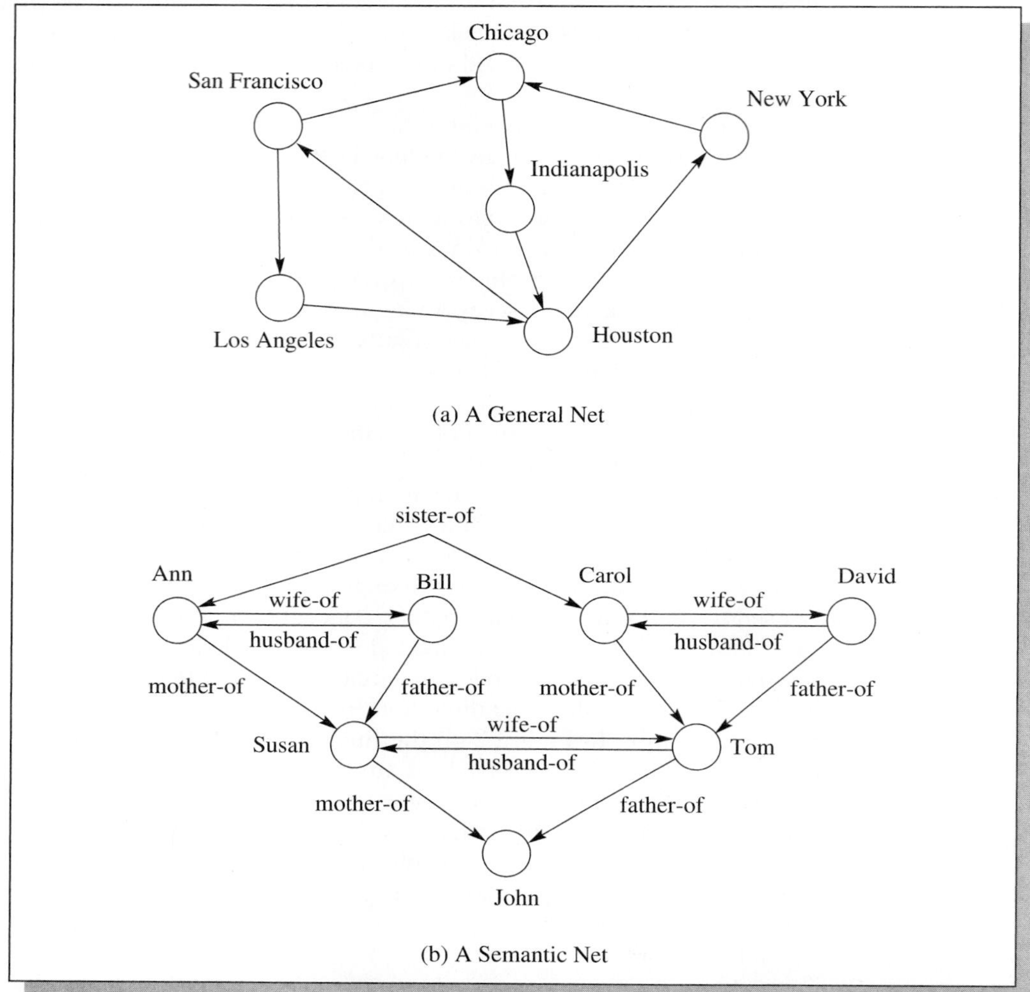

Two types of commonly used links are **IS-A** and **A-KIND-OF**, which are sometimes written as **IS-A** and **AKO**. Figure 2.5 illustrates a semantic net using these links. In this figure the IS-A means "is an instance of" and refers to a specific member of a class. A **class** is related to the mathematical concept of a set in that it refers to a group of objects. While a set can have elements of any type, the objects in a class have some relation to one another. For example, it is possible to define a set consisting of the following elements:

```
{ 3, eggs, blue, tires, art }
```

Figure 2.5 A Semantic Net with IS-A and A-Kind-Of (AKO) Links

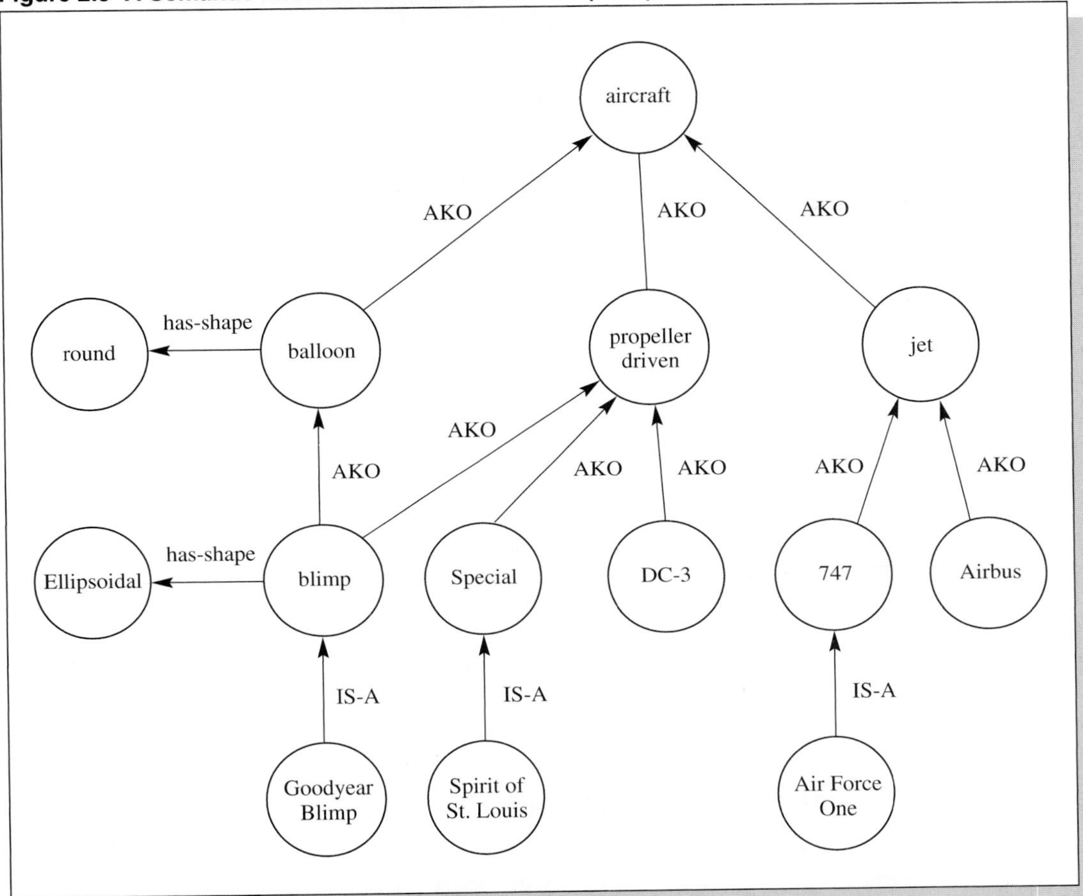

However, members of this set have no common relationship. In contrast, the class consisting of planes, trains, and automobiles are related because they are all types of transportation.

The link AKO is used here to relate one class to another. The AKO is not used to relate a specific individual because that is the function of IS-A. The AKO relates an individual class to a parent class of classes of which the individual is a child class.

From another viewpoint, the AKO relates **generic** nodes to generic nodes while the IS-A relates an instance or **individual** to a generic class. In Figure 2.5 notice that the more general classes are at the top and the more specific classes at the bottom. The more general class that an AKO arrow points to is called a **superclass**. If a superclass has an AKO pointing to another node, then it is also a class of the superclass the AKO points to. Another way of expressing this is that an AKO points from a **subclass** to a class. The link **ARE** is sometimes used for AKO where ARE is read as the ordinary word "are."

The objects in a class have one or more **attributes** in common. Each attribute has a **value**. The combination of attribute and value is a **property**. For example, a blimp has attributes of size, weight, shape, and color. The value of the shape attribute is ellipsoidal. In other words, a blimp has the property of an ellipsoidal shape. Other types of links may also be found in semantic nets. The **IS-A** link defines a value. For example, whatever aircraft the President is on is Air Force One. If the President is on a helicopter, then Air Force One IS -A helicopter. The **CAUSE** link expresses causal knowledge. For example, hot air CAUSES a balloon to rise.

Since the Goodyear Blimp is a blimp and blimps have ellipsoidal shape, it follows that the Goodyear Blimp is ellipsoidal. The duplication of one node's characteristics by a descendent is called **inheritance**. Unless there is more specific evidence to the contrary, it is assumed that all members of a class will inherit all the properties of their superclasses. For example, balloons have a round shape. However, since the blimp class has a link pointing to the ellipsoidal shape, this takes precedence. Inheritance is a useful tool in knowledge representation because it eliminates the need to repeat common characteristics. Links and inheritance provide an efficient means of knowledge representation since many complex relationships can be shown with a few nodes and links. Later on we will discuss the object-oriented capabilities of CLIPS using its embedded language called COOL. You can write expert systems in rules, objects, or a combination of rules and objects with true multiple inheritance.

2.5 OBJECT-ATTRIBUTE-VALUE TRIPLES

One problem with using semantic nets is that there is no standard definition of link names. For example, some books use IS-A for both generic and individual relations. The IS-A is then used in the sense of the ordinary words "is a" and is also used for AKO.

Another common link is HAS-A, which relates a class to a subclass. The HAS-A points opposite to the AKO and is often used to relate an object to a part of the object. For example,

```
car HAS-A engine
car HAS-A tires
car IS-A ford
```

More specifically, the IS-A relates a value to an attribute while a HAS-A relates an object to an attribute.

The three items of object, attribute, and value occur so frequently that it is possible to build a simplified semantic net using just them. An **object-attribute-value triple (OAV)**, or **triplet**, can be used to characterize all the knowledge in a semantic net and was used in the expert system MYCIN for diagnosing infectious diseases. The OAV triple representation is convenient for listing knowledge in the form of a table and thus translating the table into computer code by rule induction. An example of an OAV triple table is shown in Table 2.1. Induction is a powerful tool of logic that is often misused. The classic example is asking someone why they haven't backed up their hard drive. The usual faulty inductive answer is that their hard drive has never crashed and so by induction it never will. (Stockbrokers love this kind of "reasoning.") For more details on inductive logic programming, see (Bergadano 96).

OAV triples are especially useful for representing facts and the patterns to match the facts in the antecedent of a rule. The semantic net for such a system consists of nodes for objects, attributes, and values connected by HAS-A and IS-A links. If only a single object is to be represented and inheritance is not required, then an even simpler representation called **attribute-value (AV) pairs** may suffice.

Table 2.1 An OAV Table

Object	Attribute	Value
apple	color	red
apple	type	mcintosh
apple	quantity	100
grapes	color	red
grapes	type	seedless
grapes	quantity	500

2.6 PROLOG AND SEMANTIC NETS

Semantic nets are easy to translate into PROLOG. For example, the following PROLOG statements express some of the relationships in the semantic net of Figure 2.5:

```
is_a(goodyear_blimp,blimp).
is_a(spirit_of_st_louis,special).
has_shape(blimp,ellipsoidal).
has_shape(balloon,round).
```

Notice that a period marks the end of a PROLOG statement.

Essentials of PROLOG

Each of the statements above is a PROLOG **predicate expression**, or simply a predicate, because it is based on predicate logic. However, PROLOG is not a true predicate logic language because it is a computer language with executable statements. In PROLOG a predicate expression consists of the predicate name, such as is_a, followed by zero or more arguments enclosed in parentheses and separated by commas. The following are some examples of PROLOG predicates. Comments are preceded by semicolons and ignored by the PROLOG engine:

```
color(red).                  ;  red is a color is a
                                fact
mother(pat,ann).             ;  pat is the mother of
                                ann
parents(jim,ann,tom)         ;  jim and ann are
                                parents of tom
surrogatemother(pat,tom). ;  pat is surrogatemother
                                of tom
```

Predicates with two arguments are more easily understood if you consider the predicate name following the first argument. The meanings of predicates with more than two arguments must be explicitly stated, as the parents predicate illustrates. Another difficulty is that semantic nets are primarily useful for representing binary relationships since a drawn line has only two ends. It's not possible to draw the parents predicate as a single directed edge since there are three arguments. The idea of drawing Tom and Susan together in one parent's node and John at the other leads to a new complication. It is then impossible to use the parent's node for other binary relationships, such as mother-of, since it would also involve Tom.

Predicates can also be expressed with relations such as the IS-A and HAS-A:

```
is_a(red,color).
has_a(john,father).
has_a(john,mother).
has_a(john,parents).
```

Notice that the has_a predicates do not express the same meaning as previously because John's father, mother, and parents are not explicitly named. In order to name them, some additional predicates must be added:

```
is_a(tom,father).
is_a(susan,mother).
is_a(tom,parent).
is_a(susan,parent).
```

Even these additional predicates do not express the same meaning as the original predicates. For example, we know that John has a father and that Tom is a father, but this does not provide the information that Tom is the father of John.

All the preceding statements actually describe facts in PROLOG. Programs in PROLOG consist of facts and rules in the general form of **goals**:

```
p:- p1,p2,...pN.
```

where p is called the rule's head and the p_k are the **subgoals**. Normally this expression is a Horn clause which states that the head goal, p, is satisfied if and only if all of the subgoals are satisfied. The exception is when the special predicate for failure is used. A failure predicate is convenient because it's not easy to prove negation in classical logic, and PROLOG is based on classical logic. Negation is viewed as the failure to find a proof and this can be a very long and involved process if there are many potential matches. The **cut** and special failure predicate makes the negation process more efficient by reducing the searching for a proof.

The commas separating the subgoals represent a logical AND. The symbol, **:-** , is interpreted as an IF. If only the head exists and there is no right-hand side, as in:

```
p.
```

then the head is considered true. This is why predicates such as the following are considered facts and thus must be true:

```
color(red).
has_a(john,father).
```

Another way of thinking about facts is that a fact is an unconditional conclusion that does not depend on anything else and so the IF,:- , is not necessary. In contrast, PROLOG rules require the IF because they are conditional conclusions whose truth depends on one or more conditions. As an example, the parent rules are as follows:

```
parent(X,Y):- father(X,Y).
parent(X,Y):- mother(X,Y).
```

which means that X is the parent of Y if X is the father of Y or if X is the mother of Y. Likewise, a grandparent can be defined as:

```
grandparent(X,Y):- parent(X,Z),parent(Z,Y).
```

and an ancestor can be defined as:

```
(1) ancestor(X,Y):- parent(X,Y).
(2) ancestor(X,Y):- ancestor(X,Z),ancestor(Z,Y).
```

where (1) and (2) are used for identification purposes in this book.

Searching in PROLOG

A system for executing PROLOG statements is generally an interpreter, although some systems can generate compiled code. The general form of a PROLOG system is shown in Figure 2.6. The user interacts with PROLOG by entering predicate queries and receiving answers. The **predicate database** contains the rule and fact predicates that have been entered and thus forms the knowledge base. The interpreter tries to determine whether a query predicate that the user enters is in the database. The answer returned is yes if it is in the database and no if it is not. If the

Figure 2.6 General Organization of a PROLOG System

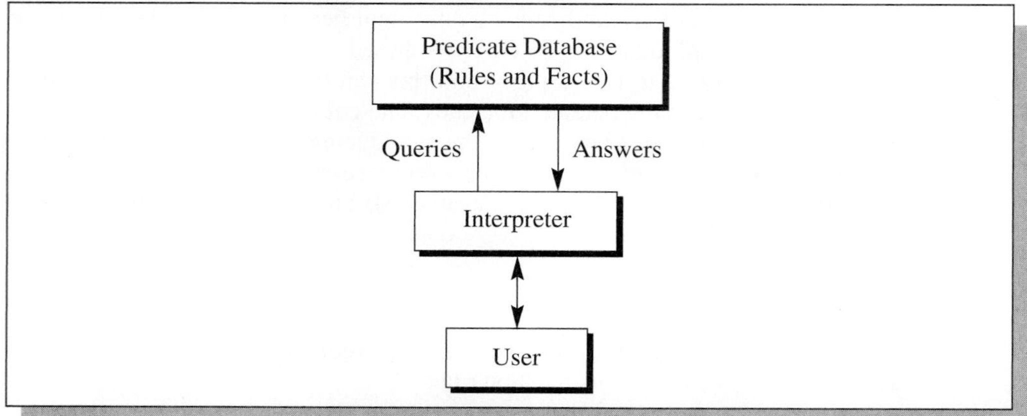

Figure 2.7 Depth-First and Breadth-First Searches for an Arbitrary Tree

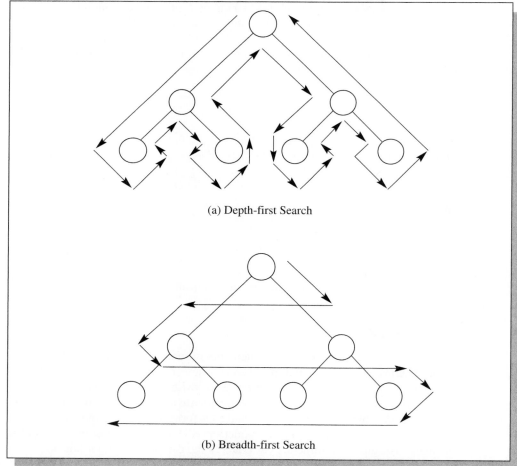

(a) Depth-first Search

(b) Breadth-first Search

query is a rule, the interpreter will try to satisfy the subgoals by conducting a **depth-first search**, as shown in Figure 2.7. For contrast, a **breadth-first search** is also shown, although this is not the normal mode of PROLOG.

In a depth-first search, the search goes down as far as possible from the root and then back up again. In PROLOG the search also goes from left to right. A breadth-first search proceeds one level at a time before descending to the next lower level.

As an example of goal searching in PROLOG, consider the ancestor rules defined as (1) and (2). Assume the following facts are now input:

```
(3) parent(ann,mary).
(4) parent(ann,susan).
(5) parent(mary,bob).
(6) parent(susan,john).
```

Now suppose PROLOG is queried to determine if Ann is the ancestor of Susan:

```
:- ancestor(ann,susan).
```

where the absence of a head indicates a **query**, which is a condition to be proved by PROLOG. Facts, rules, and queries are the three types of Horn clauses of PROLOG. A condition can be proved if it is the conclusion of an instance of a clause. Of course, the clause itself must be provable, and this is done by proving the conditions of the clause.

On receipt of this input PROLOG will start searching for a statement whose head matches the input pattern of `ancestor(ann,susan)`. This is called **pattern matching**, just like the pattern matching to facts in the antecedent of a production rule. The search starts from the first statement that was entered (1), the **top**, and goes to the last statement (6), the **bottom**. There is a possible match with the first ancestor rule (1). The variable `X` matches `ann` and the variable `Y` matches `susan`. Since the head matches, PROLOG will now try to match the body of (1), yielding the subgoal `parent(ann,susan)`. PROLOG now tries to match this subgoal against clauses and eventually matches with the fact (4) `parent(ann,susan)`. There are no more goals to match and PROLOG answers "yes" because the original query is true.

As another example, suppose the query is the following:

```
:- ancestor(ann,john).
```

The first ancestor rule (1) matches and `X` is set to `ann` while `Y` is set to `john`. PROLOG now tries to match the body of (1), `parent(ann,john)` with every parent statement. None match and so the body of (1) cannot be true. Since the body of (1) is not true, the head cannot be true.

Since (1) cannot be true, PROLOG then tries the second ancestor statement (2). `X` is set to `ann` and `Y` is set to `john`. PROLOG tries to prove that the head of (2) is true by proving that the subgoals of (2) are both true. That is, `ancestor(ann,Z)` and `ancestor(Z,john)` must be proven true. PROLOG tries to match the subgoals in a left-to-right manner starting with `ancestor(ann,Z)`. Starting from the top, this first match's statement (1) and so PROLOG tries to prove the body of (1), `parent(ann,Z)`. Starting to search from the top again, this body first matches statement (3) and so PROLOG sets `Z` to `mary`. Now PROLOG tries to match the second subgoal of (2) as `ancestor(mary,john)`. This matches (1) and so PROLOG tries to satisfy its body, `parent(mary,john)`. However, there is no `parent(mary,john)` in the statements (3) through (6) and so this search fails.

PROLOG then reconsiders its guess that `Z` should be `mary`. Since this choice did not work, it tries to find another value that will work. Another possibility arises from (4) by setting `Z` to `susan`. This technique of going back to try a different search path when one path fails is called **backtracking**, and is often used for problem solving.

With the choice of `Z` as `susan`, PROLOG attempts to prove that `ancestor(susan,john)` is true. By (1), the body `parent(susan,john)` must be proven true. Indeed, the fact (3) does match and so the query:

```
:- ancestor(ann,john)
```

is proven true since its conditions have been proven true.

Notice that the control structure of PROLOG is of the Markov algorithm type, where searching for pattern matching is normally determined by the order that the Horn clauses are entered. This contrasts with rule-based expert systems, which normally follow the Post paradigm, in which the order that rules are entered does not affect the search.

PROLOG has many other features and capabilities not mentioned here. From an expert systems point of view, the backtracking and pattern matching are especially relevant. The declarative nature of PROLOG is also useful because a program specification is an executable program.

2.7 DIFFICULTIES WITH SEMANTIC NETS

Although semantic nets can be very useful in representing knowledge, they have limitations, such as the lack of link name standards discussed previously. This makes it difficult to understand what the net is really designed for and whether it was designed in a consistent manner. A complementary problem to naming links is the naming of nodes. If a node is labeled "chair," for example, does it represent:

a specific chair
the class of all chairs
the concept of a chair
the person who is the chair of a meeting

or something else? For a semantic net to represent **definitive knowledge**, that is, knowledge that can be defined, the link and node names must be rigorously defined. Of course, the same problems may occur in programming languages. Fortunately this problem has now been solved with the introduction of **extensible markup language (XML)** and ontologies. XML has proven invaluable in providing a standard way of encoding formal semantics into all kinds of languages. A rule-based version of XML is also available as are markup languages for math, music, the food industry and all other fields that use computers for information processing. XML and ontologies are turning the World Wide Web (WWW or W3) from just data into a collection of machine readable information of much more use. The web is now being referred to as the **Semantic Web** rather than just the web because of its new sense of meaning.

Another problem is the combinatorial explosion of searching nodes, especially if the response to a query is negative. That is, for a query to produce a negative result, many or all of the links in a net may have to be searched. As shown in the Traveling Salesman problem in Chapter 1, the number of links is the factorial of the number of nodes minus one if they are all connected. Although not all representations will require this degree of connectivity, the possibility of a combinatorial explosion exists.

Semantic nets were originally proposed as a model of human associative memory in which one node has links to others and information retrieval occurs due to a spreading activation of nodes. However, other mechanisms must also be available to the human brain since it does not take a long time for a human to answer the query—Is there a football team on Pluto? There are about 10^{11} neurons in the human brain and about 10^{15} links. If all knowledge were represented by a semantic net, it would take a very, very long time to answer negative queries like the football question because of all the searching involved with 10^{15} links.

Semantic nets are logically inadequate because they cannot define knowledge in the way that logic can. A logic representation can specify a certain chair, some chairs, all chairs, no chairs, and so forth, as will be discussed later in this chapter. Another problem is that semantic nets are heuristically inadequate because there is no way to embed heuristic information in the net on how to efficiently search the net. A **heuristic** is a rule of thumb that may help in finding a solution but is not guaranteed, in the way an algorithm is guaranteed, to find a solution. Heuristics are very important in AI because typical AI problems are so hard that an algorithmic solution does not exist or is too inefficient for practical use. The only standard control strategy built into a net that might help is inheritance but not all problems may have this structure.

A number of approaches have been tried to correct the inherent problems of semantic nets. Logic enhancements have been made and heuristic enhancements have been tried by attaching procedures to nodes. The procedures will be executed when the node becomes activated. However, the resulting systems gained little in capability at the expense of the natural expressiveness of semantic nets. The conclusion of all this effort is that like any tool, semantic nets should be used for those things they do best, showing binary relationships, and not be distorted into a universal tool.

2.8 SCHEMATA

A semantic net is an example of a **shallow knowledge structure**. The shallowness occurs because all the knowledge in the semantic net is contained in the links and nodes. **Knowledge structure** is analogous to a data structure in that it represents an ordered collection of knowledge rather than just data. A **deep knowledge structure** has causal knowledge that explains why something occurs. For example, it is possible to build a medical expert system with shallow knowledge as follows:

```
IF a person has a fever
THEN take an aspirin
```

But these systems do not know the fundamental biochemistry of the body and why aspirin decreases fever. The rule could have been defined:

```
IF a person has a pink monkey
THEN take a refrigerator
```

In other words, the expert system's knowledge is shallow because it is based on *syntax* rather than *semantics*, where any two words could be substituted for `X` and `Y` in the following rule:

```
IF a person has a (X)
THEN take a (Y)
```

Note that `(X)` and `(Y)` are not variables in this rule, but represent any two words. Doctors have causal knowledge because they have many years of medical school and have experience treating ill people. If a treatment is not working right, doctors can use reasoning powers to find an alternative to their usual case-based method. In other words, an expert knows when to break the rules.

Many types of real-world knowledge cannot be represented by the simple structure of a semantic net. More complex structures are needed to better represent complex knowledge structures. In AI, the term **schema** (plural schemas or schemata) is used to describe a more complex knowledge structure than the semantic net. The term schema comes from psychology, where it refers to the continual organizing of knowledge or responses by a creature in response to stimuli. That is, as creatures learn the causal relationship between a cause and its outcome, they will try to repeat the cause if pleasurable and avoid the cause if painful.

For example, the acts of eating and drinking are pleasurable **sensorimotor schemata** that involve coordinating information from the senses with the required motor (muscle) movements to eat and drink. A person does not have to think about this tacit knowledge to know to perform these acts, and it is very difficult to explain exactly how it is done down to the level of controlling muscles. An even more difficult schema to explain is how to ride a bicycle. Try explaining a sense of balance!

Another type of schema is the **concept schema** by which we represent concepts. For example, everyone has the concept of animal. If most people were asked to explain what an animal is, they would probably describe it in terms of something that has four legs and fur. Of course, the concept of animal differs depending on whether the person grew up on a farm, in a city, or near a river. However, we all have **stereotypes** in our minds of concepts. While the term stereotype may have a derogatory meaning in casual language, in AI it means a typical example. Thus a stereotype of an animal might be a dog to many people.

A conceptual schema is an abstraction in which specific objects are classified by their general properties. For example, if you see a small red, round object with a green stem under a sign that says Artificial Fruit, you will probably recognize it as an artificial apple. The object has the properties of appleness that you associate with the conceptual schema of apple.

The conceptual schema of a real apple will include general properties of apples such as sizes, colors, tastes, uses, and so forth. The schema will not include details of exactly where the apple was picked, the truck by which it was transported to the supermarket, or the name of the person who put it on the shelf. These details are not important to the properties that comprise your abstract concept of an apple. Also, note that a person who is blind may have a very different concept schema of an apple in which texture is most important.

By focusing on the general properties of an object, it is easier to reason about them without becoming distracted by irrelevant details. Customarily, schemas have internal structure to their nodes while semantic nets do not. The label of a semantic net is all the knowledge about the node. A semantic net is like a data structure in computer science, in which the search key is also the data stored in the node. A schema is like a data structure in which nodes contain records. Each record may contain data, records, or pointers to other nodes.

2.9 FRAMES

One type of schema that has been used in many AI applications is the **frame**. Another type of schema is the **script**, which is essentially a time-ordered sequence of frames. Proposed as a method for understanding vision, natural language, and other areas, frames provide a convenient structure for representing objects that are typical to a given situation such as stereotypes. In particular, frames are useful for simulating commonsense knowledge, which is a very difficult area for computers to master. While semantic nets are basically a two-dimensional representation of knowledge, frames add a third dimension by allowing nodes to have structures. These structures can be simple values or other frames.

The basic characteristic of a frame is that it represents related knowledge about a narrow subject that has much default knowledge. A frame system would be a good choice for describing a mechanical device, for example a car. Components of the car such as the engine, body, brakes, and so forth would be related to give an overall view of their relationships. Further detail about the components could be obtained by examining the structure of the frames. Although individual brands of cars will vary, most cars have common characteristics such as wheels, engine, body, and transmission. The frame contrasts with the semantic net, which is generally used for broad knowledge representation. Just as with semantic nets, there are no standards for defining frame-based systems. A number of special-purpose languages have been designed for frames, such as FRL, SRL, KRL, KEE, HP-RL, and frame enhancement features to LISP such as LOOPS and FLAVORS.

A frame is analogous to a record structure in a high-level language such as C or an atom with its property list in LISP. Corresponding to the fields and values of a record are the **slots** and slot **fillers** of a frame. A frame is basically a group of slots and fillers that defines a stereotypical object. A frame for a car is shown in Figure 2.8. In OAV terms, the car is the object, the slot name is the attribute, and the filler is the value.

Figure 2.8 A Car Frame

Slots	Fillers
manufacturer	General Motors
model	Chevrolet Caprice
year	1979
transmission	automatic
engine	gasoline
tires	4
color	blue

Most frames are not as simple as of the one shown in Figure 2.8. The utility of frames lies in hierarchical frame systems and inheritance. By using frames in the filler slots and inheritance, very powerful knowledge representation systems can be built. In particular, frame-based expert systems are very useful for representing causal knowledge because their information is organized by cause and effect. By contrast, rule-based expert systems generally rely on unorganized knowledge that is not causal.

Some frame-based tools such as KEE allow a wide range of items to be stored in slots. Frame slots may hold rules, graphics, comments, debugging information, questions for users, hypotheses concerning a situation, or other frames.

Frames are generally designed to represent either generic or specific knowledge. Figure 2.9 illustrates a generic frame for the concept of human property.

The fillers may be values, such as property in the name slot, or a range of values, as in the types slot. The slots may also contain procedures attached to the slots, called **procedural attachments**. These are generally of three types. The **if-needed** type is executed when a filler value is needed but none are initially present or the **default** value is not suitable. Defaults are of primary importance in frames because they model some aspects of the brain. Defaults

Figure 2.9 A Generic Frame for Property

Slots	Fillers
name	property
specialization_of	a_kind_of object
types	(car, boat, house) if-added: Procedure ADD_PROPERTY
owner	default: government if-needed: Procedure FIND_OWNER
location	(home, work, mobile)
status	(missing, poor, good)
under_warranty	(yes, no)

correspond to the expectations of a situation that we build up based on experience. When we encounter a new situation, the closest frame is modified to help us adjust to the situation. People do not start from scratch in every new situation. Instead, the defaults or other fillers are modified. Defaults are often used to represent commonsense knowledge. **Commonsense knowledge** can be considered to be the knowledge that is generally known. We use commonsense when no more situation-specific knowledge is available.

The **if-added** type is run for procedures to be executed when a value is to be added to a slot. In the types slot, the if-added procedure executes a procedure called ADD-PROPERTY to add a new type of property, if necessary. For example, this procedure would be run for jewelry, TV, stereo, and so forth since the types slot does not contain these values.

An **if-removal** type is run whenever a value is to be removed from a slot. This type of procedure would be run if a value were obsolete.

Slot fillers may also contain relations, as in the specialization of slots. The a-kind-of and is-a relations are used in Figures 2.9, 2.10, and 2.11 to show how these frames are hierarchically related. The frames of Figures 2.9 and 2.10 are generic frames while that of Figure 2.11 is a specific frame because it is an instance of the car frame. We have adopted the convention here that a-kind-of relations are generic and is-a relations are specific.

Frame systems are designed so that more generic frames are at the top of the hierarchy. It is assumed that frames can be customized for specific cases by modifying the default cases and creating more specific frames. Frames attempt to model real-world objects by using generic knowledge for the majority of an object's attributes and specific knowledge for special cases. For example, we commonly think of birds as creatures that can fly. Yet certain types of birds such as penguins and ostriches cannot fly. These types represent more specific classes

Figure 2.10 Car Frame—A Generic Subframe of Property

Slots	Fillers
name	car
specialization_of	a-kind-of property
types	(sedan, sports, convertible)
manufacturer	(GM, Ford, Toyota)
location	mobile
wheels	4
transmission	(manual, automatic)
engine	(gasoline, hybrid gas/electric)

Figure 2.11 An Instance of a Car Frame

Slots	Fillers
name	John's car
specialization_of	is_a car
manufacturer	GM
owner	John Doe
transmission	automatic
engine	gasoline
status	good
under_warranty	yes

of birds and their characteristics would be found lower in a frame hierarchy than birds like canaries or robins. In other words, the top of the bird frame hierarchy specifies things that are more true of all birds while the lower levels reflect the fuzzy boundaries between real-world objects. The object that has all of the typical characteristics is called a **prototype**, which literally means the *first type*.

Frames may also be classified by their applications. A **situational frame** contains knowledge about what to expect in a given situation, such as a birthday party. An **action frame** contains slots that specify the actions to be performed in a given situation. That is, the fillers are procedures to perform some actions, such as removing a defective part from a conveyer belt. An action frame represents procedural knowledge. The combination of situational and action frames can be used to describe cause-and-effect relationships in the form of **causal knowledge frames**.

Very sophisticated frame systems have been built for a variety of tasks. One of the most impressive systems that demonstrated the power of frames to creatively discover mathematical concepts was the Automated Mathematician (AM) of Doug Lenat. The classic AM system of Lenat made conjectures of interesting new concepts and explored them. It came up with some completely new mathematical proofs of certain theorems. Many other examples of theorem provers and discovery systems are shown in Appendix G for this chapter.

2.10 DIFFICULTIES WITH FRAMES

Frames were originally conceived as a paradigm for representing stereotyped knowledge. The important characteristic of a stereotype is that it has well-defined features so that many of its slots have default values. Mathematical concepts are good examples of stereotypes well suited to frames. The frame paradigm has an intuitive appeal because its organized representation of knowledge is generally easier to understand than either logic or production systems with many rules (Jackson 99).

However, major problems have appeared in frame systems that allow unrestrained alteration or cancellation of slots. The classic example of this problem is illustrated with a frame describing elephants, as shown in Figure 2.12.

Figure 2.12 Elephant Frame

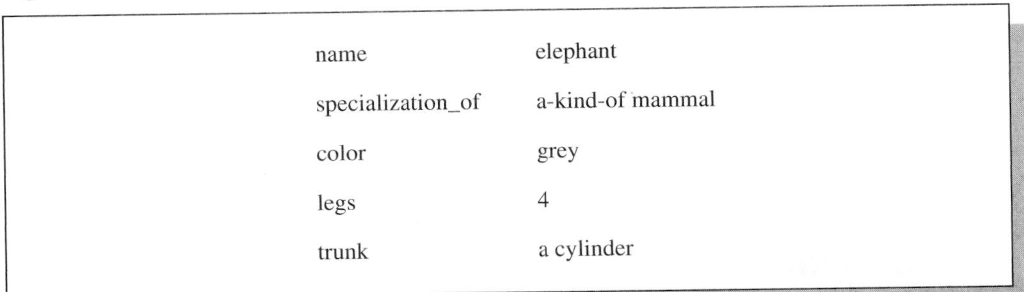

name	elephant
specialization_of	a-kind-of mammal
color	grey
legs	4
trunk	a cylinder

At first sight, the elephant frame seems like a reasonable generic description of elephants. However, suppose there exists a specific, three-legged elephant called Clyde. Clyde may have lost a leg due to a hunting accident or simply lied about losing a leg to get his name in this book. The significant thing is that the elephant frame claims that an elephant has four legs, not three. Thus we cannot consider the elephant frame to be the valid definition of an elephant.

Of course, the frame could be modified to allow three-legged, two-legged, one-legged, or even legless elephants as exceptions. However, this does not provide a very good definition. Additional problems may arise with the other slots. Suppose Clyde gets a bad case of jaundice and his skin turns yellow. Is he then not an elephant?

An alternative to viewing a frame as a definition is to consider it as describing a typical elephant. However, this leads to other problems because of inheritance. Notice that the elephant frame says that an elephant is a-kind-of mammal. Since we are interpreting frames as typical, then our frame system says that a typical elephant is a typical mammal. Although an elephant is a mammal, it is probably not a typical mammal. On the basis of quantity, people, cows, rats, and sheep are probably more representative of typical mammals.

Most frame systems do not provide a way of defining unalterable slots. Since any slot can be changed, the properties that a frame inherits can be altered or cancelled anywhere in the hierarchy. This means that every frame is really a primitive frame because there is no guarantee that properties are common. Each frame makes up its own rules and so each frame is a primitive. Nothing is really certain in such an unrestrained system, and so it is impossible to make universal statements such as those made in defining an elephant. Also, from simpler definitions such as that for an elephant, it is impossible to reliably build composite objects such as elephant-with-three-legs. The same types of problems apply to semantic nets with inheritance. If the properties of any node can be changed, then nothing is certain.

However there is another way to view frames that is very useful. If the concept of frame is extended to include the properties of objects, then an object can be considered a frame. CLIPS has a complete object-oriented language called COOL embedded within it that can be considered as an extension of a frame-based language. All the advantages of objects are now available in CLIPS. Object-oriented expert systems can be constructed in CLIPS that have both the advantages of rules as small chunks of knowledge while providing the capability to organize larger chunks of knowledge into objects for easier maintenance and development. Rules can operate on facts or objects and thus CLIPS has the advantages of both a rule-based and object-based expert system tool. The use of objects in CLIPS makes it easier to organize, execute, and maintain large knowledge bases rather than trying to keep all the knowledge in thousands of separate rules and facts.

2.11 LOGIC AND SETS

In addition to rules, frames, and semantic nets, knowledge can also be represented by the symbols of **logic**, which is the study of the rules of exact reasoning. An important part of reasoning is inferring conclusions from premises. The application of computers to perform reasoning has resulted in **logic programming** and the development of logic-based languages such as PROLOG. Logic is also of primary importance in expert systems in which the inference engine reasons from facts to conclusions. In fact, a descriptive term for logic programming and expert systems is **automated reasoning systems**.

The earliest formal logic was developed by the Greek philosopher Aristotle in the fourth century B.C. Aristotelian logic is based on the **syllogism**, of which he invented fourteen types. Five more were invented in medieval times. Syllogisms have two **premises** and one **conclusion**, which is inferred from the premises. The following is a classic example of a syllogism:

```
Premise:    All men are mortal
Premise:    Socrates is a man
Conclusion: Socrates is mortal
```

In a syllogism the **premises** provide the evidence from which the conclusion must necessarily follow. A syllogism is a way of representing knowledge. Another way is a **Venn diagram**, as shown in Figure 2.13.

Figure 2.13 Venn Diagram

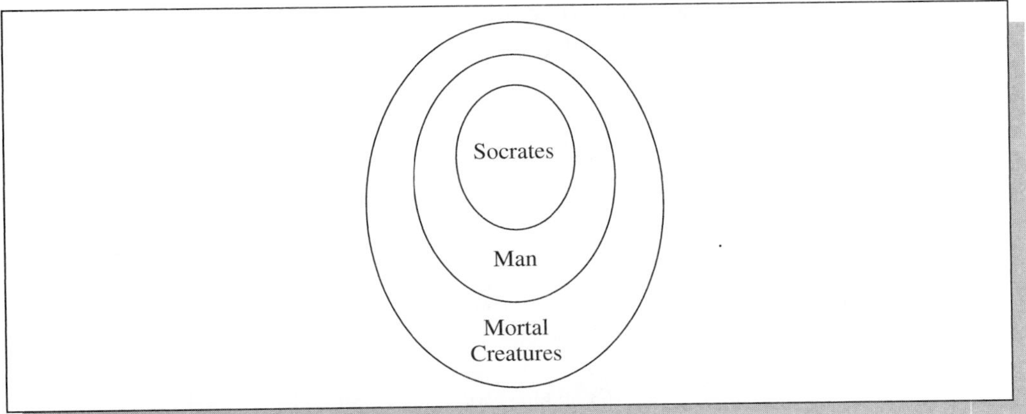

The outer circle represents all mortal creatures. The inner circle representing men is drawn entirely within the mortal circle to indicate that all men are mortal. Since Socrates is a man, the circle representing him is drawn entirely within the human circle. Strictly speaking, the circle representing Socrates should be a point, since a circle implies a class. For readability, we'll use circles for all. The conclusion that Socrates is mortal is a consequence of the fact that his circle is within that of mortal creatures and so he must be mortal.

In mathematical terms, a circle of the Venn diagram represents a **set**, which is a collection of objects. The objects within a set are called its **elements**. Some examples of sets are the following:

```
A = {1,3,5}
B = {1,2,3,4,5}
C = {0,2,4,...}
D = {...,-4,-2,0,2,4,...}
E = {airplanes,balloons,blimps,jets}
F = {airplanes,balloons}
```

where the three dots, ..., called **ellipses**, indicate that the terms continue on indefinitely.

The Greek symbol epsilon, $\in$, indicates an element is a member of a set. For example, $1 \in A$, means that the number 1 is an element of the set A, previously defined. If an element is not a member of a set, the symbol $\notin$ is used, as in $2 \notin A$.

If two arbitrary sets, such as X and Y, are defined such that every element in X is an element of Y, then X is a **subset** of Y and is written in the mathematical form $X \subset Y$ or $Y \supset X$. From the definition of a subset it follows that every set is a subset of itself. A subset that is not the set itself is called a **proper subset**. For example, the set X defined previously is a proper subset of Y. In discussing sets it is useful to consider the sets under discussions as subsets of a **universal set**. The universal set (universe) changes as the topic of discussion change. Figure 2.14 illustrates a subset formed as the **intersection** of two sets in the universe of all cars. In discussing numbers the universe is all numbers. The universe is drawn as a rectangle surrounding its subsets. Universal sets are not used just for convenience. The indiscriminate use of conditions to define sets can result in logical paradoxes.

Figure 2.14 Intersecting Sets

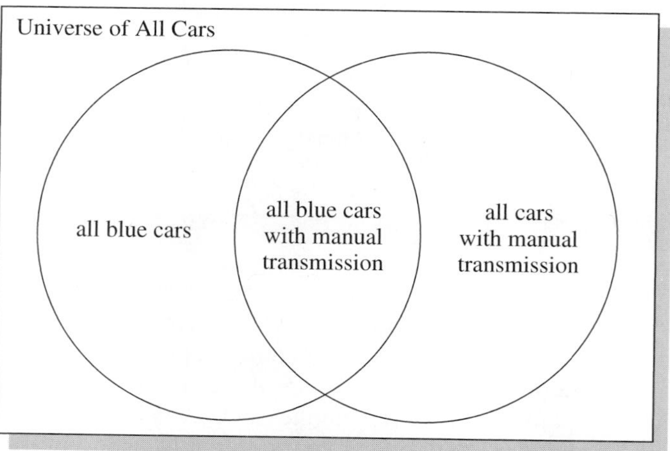

If we let A be the set of all blue cars, B the set of all cars with manual transmissions, and C the set of all blue cars with manual transmissions, we can write:

$$C = A \cap B$$

where the symbol $\cap$ represents the intersection of sets. Another way of writing this is in terms of elements x as follows:

$$C = \{x \in U \mid (x \in A) \wedge (x \in B)\}$$

where:

U represents the universe set.

| is read as "such that." A colon, :, is sometimes used instead of |.

$\wedge$ is the logical AND.

The expression for C is read that C consists of those elements x in the universe such that x is an element of A and x is an element of B. The logical AND comes from Boolean algebra. An expression consisting of two operands connected by the logical AND operator is true if and only if both operands are true. If A and B have no elements in common, then $A \cap B = \emptyset$ where the Greek letter phi, Ø, represents the **empty set** or **null set** { }, which contains no elements. Sometimes the Greek letter lambda, Λ, is used for the null set. Other notations for the universe set are sometimes the numeral 1 and the numeral 0 for the null set. Although the null set has no elements, it is still a set. An analogy is a restaurant with a set of customers. If nobody comes, the set of customers is empty, but the restaurant still exists.

Another set operation is **union**, which is the set of all elements in either A or B:

$$A \cup B = \{x \in U \mid (x \in A) \vee (x \in B)\}$$

where:

$\cup$ is the set operator for **union.**
$\vee$ is the **logical OR** operator.

The **complement** of set A is the set of all elements not in A:

$$A' = \{x \in U \mid \sim(x \in A)\}$$

where:

Prime, ′, means complement of a set.
Tilde, ~, is the **logical NOT** operator.

The Venn diagrams for these basic operations are shown in Figure 2.15 on next page.

2.12 PROPOSITIONAL LOGIC

The oldest and one of the simplest types of **formal logic** is the syllogism. The term *formal* means that the logic is concerned with the form of logical statements rather than their meaning. In other words, formal logic is concerned with the syntax of statements, not their semantics. This is extremely important in building expert systems because you have to separate knowledge from reasoning. What may appear as reasoning could be knowledge. For example, the

Figure 2.15 Venn Diagrams of Basic Set Operations

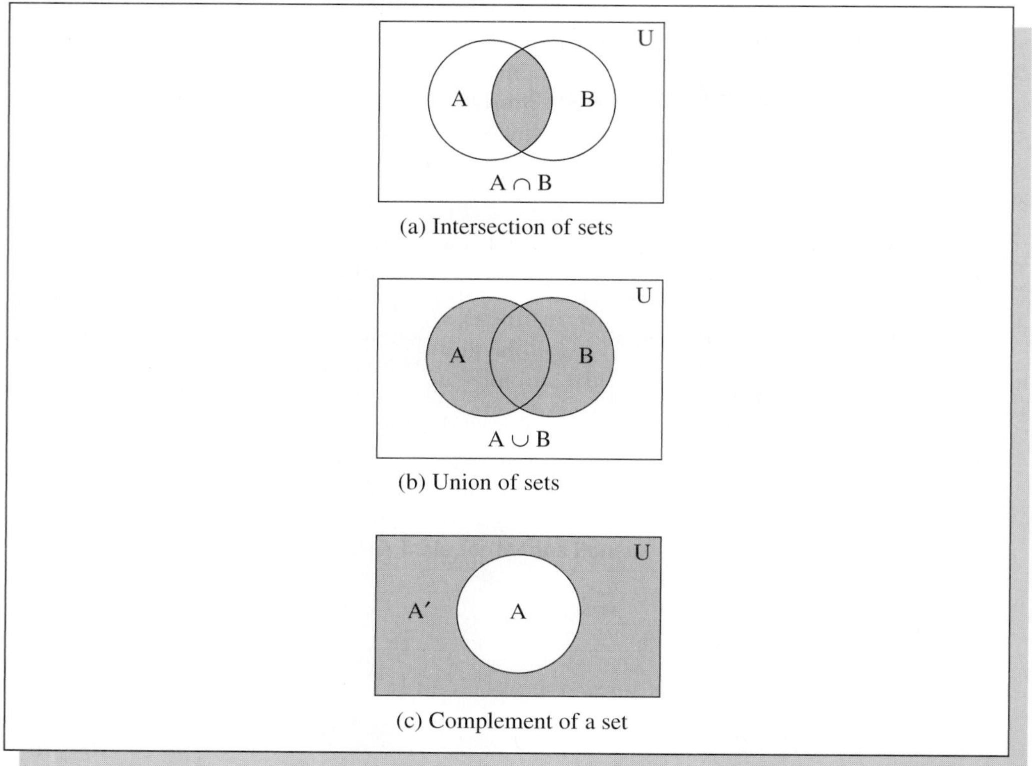

(a) Intersection of sets

(b) Union of sets

(c) Complement of a set

statement, "The President is always right because he is never wrong," has the appearance of reasoning due to the "because" that connects the two parts of the sentence. In fact, an assertion of this type is called a **tautology** because unlike a fact which may or may not be true in the real world, a tautology is always true in a purely logical sense because it refers to itself for proof. It states, "X is X." However if you are not of the same political party as the President, you may disagree based on the semantics rather than the form of the statement, and prefer the tautology, "The President is always wrong because he is never right."

Although the term *formal logic* may sound intimidating, it is no more difficult than algebra. In fact, algebra is really a formal logic of numbers. For example, suppose you were asked to solve the following problem: A school has 25 computers with a total of 60 memory chips. Some of the computers have two memory chips while others have four. How many computers of each type are there? The solution can be written algebraically as follows:

```
25 = X + Y
60 = 2X + 4Y
```

which can easily be solved for X = 20 and Y = 5.

Now consider this problem. There are 25 animals in a barnyard with a total of 60 legs. Some of the animals have two legs, while others have four. (Note: Clyde, our three-legged elephant is in Africa, not the barnyard.) How many animals of each type are there? As you can see, the same algebraic equations apply whether we are talking about computers, animals, or anything else. In the same way that algebraic equations let us concentrate on the mathematical manipulation of symbols without regard to what they represent, formal logic lets us concentrate on the reasoning without becoming confused by what objects we are reasoning about.

As an example of formal logic, consider the syllogism with the nonsense words *squeeg* and *moof*.

```
Premise:     All squeegs are moofs
Premise:     John is a squeeg
Conclusion: John is a moof
```

Although the words squeeg and moof are nonsense and have no meaning, the *form* of this argument is still correct. That is, the argument is **valid** no matter what words are used because the syllogism has a valid form. In fact any syllogism of the form:

```
Premise:     All X are Y
Premise:     Z is a X
Conclusion: Z is a Y
```

is valid no matter what is substituted for X, Y, and Z. This example illustrates that meanings do not matter in formal logic. Only the form or appearance is important. This concept of separating the form from the meaning or semantics is what makes logic such a powerful tool. By separating the form from the semantics, the validity of an argument can be considered objectively, without prejudice caused by the semantics. An analogy to formal logic is algebra, in which the correctness of expressions such as $X + X = 2X$ holds whether X is an integer, apples, or airplanes.

Aristotelian syllogisms were the foundations of logic until 1847, when the English mathematician George Boole published the first book describing **symbolic logic**. Although Leibnitz had developed his own version of symbolic logic in the Seventeenth Century, it never achieved general use. One of the new concepts that Boole proposed was a modification of the Aristotelian view that the subject have existence, called **existential import**. According to the classic Aristotelian view, a proposition such as "all mermaids swim well" could not be used as a premise or conclusion because mermaids don't exist. The Boolean view, now called the modern view, relaxes this restriction. The importance of the modern view is that empty classes can now be reasoned about. For example, a proposition such as "all disks that fail are cheap" could not be used in an Aristotelian syllogism unless there was at least one disk that had failed.

Another contribution by Boole was the definition of a set of **axioms** consisting of symbols to represent objects and classes, and algebraic operations to manipulate the symbols. Axioms are the fundamental definitions from which logical systems such as mathematics and logic itself are built. Using only the axioms, theorems can be constructed. A theorem is a statement that can be proved by showing how it is derived from the axioms. Between 1910 and 1913, Whitehead and Russell published their monumental 2,000-page, three-volume work *Principia Mathematica*, which showed a formal logic as the basis of mathematics. This was hailed as a great milestone because it appeared to put mathematics on a firm foundation—rather than appealing to intuition—by totally eliminating the meaning of arithmetic and instead concentrating on forms and their manipulation. Because of this, mathematics has been described as a collection of meaningless marks on paper.

In 1931 the famous mathematician Gödel proved that formal systems based on axioms could not always be proved internally consistent and free from contradictions. Gödel's proof was a great blow to mathematicians who had hoped that arithmetic could be proved true once and for all. Instead it seems we can't really count on arithmetic (note that any intelligent mathematician reading this pun will think it very funny).

Propositional logic, sometimes called **propositional calculus**, is a symbolic logic for manipulating propositions. In particular, propositional logic deals with the manipulation of **logical variables**, which represent propositions. Although most people think of calculus in terms of the calculus invented by Newton and Leibnitz, the word has a more general meaning. It comes from the Latin word *calculus* and means a little stone used for calculations. The general meaning of calculus is a special system for manipulating symbols. Other terms used for propositional logic are **statement calculus** and **sentential calculus**. Sentences are generally classified as one of four types, as illustrated in Table 2.2.

Table 2.2 Types of Sentences

Type	Example
Imperative	Do what I tell you!
Interrogative	What is that?
Exclamatory	That's great!
Declarative	A square has four equal sides.

Propositional logic is concerned with the subset of declarative sentences that can be classified as either true or false. A sentence such as "A square has four equal sides" has a definite truth value of true, while the sentence "George Washington was the second president" has a truth value of false. A sentence whose truth value can be determined is called a **statement** or **proposition**. A statement is also called a **closed sentence** because its truth value is not open to question.

If I put a preface to this book stating "everything in these pages is a lie" that statement cannot be classified as either true or false. If it is true, then I told the truth in the preface—which I cannot do. If it is untrue, and so every word written must be true, then I lied—which also cannot be true. Statements of this type are known as the **Liar Paradox**. Statements that cannot be answered absolutely are called **open sentences**. The sentence "Spinach tastes wonderful" is also an open sentence because it is true for some people and not true for others. The sentence "He is tall" is called an open sentence because it contains a variable "He." Truth values cannot be assigned to open sentences until we know the specific person or instance referred to by the variable. Another difficulty with this sentence is the meaning of the word "tall." What's tall to some people is not tall to others. While this ambiguity of "tall" cannot be handled in the propositional or predicate calculus, it can be easily dealt with in fuzzy logic, described in Chapter 5.

A **compound statement** is formed by using logical connectives on individual statements. The common logical connectives are shown in Table 2.3.

Table 2.3 Common Logical Connectives

Connective	Meaning
$\wedge$	AND; conjunction
$\vee$	OR; disjunction
~	NOT; negation
$\rightarrow$	if...then; conditional
$\leftrightarrow$	if and only if; biconditional

Strictly speaking, the negation is not a connective because it is a unary operation that applies to the one operand following, so it doesn't really connect anything. The negation has higher precedence than the other operators and so it is not necessary to put parentheses around it. That is, a statement like $\sim p \wedge q$ means the same as $(\sim p) \wedge q$.

The conditional is analogous to the arrow of production rules in that it is expressed as an IF-THEN form. For example:

```
if it is raining then carry an umbrella
```

can be put in the form:

$$p \rightarrow q$$

where:

```
p = it is raining
q = carry an umbrella
```

Sometimes the $\supset$ is used for $\rightarrow$. Another term for the conditional is **material implication**.

The biconditional, $p \leftrightarrow q$, is equivalent to:

$$(p \rightarrow q) \wedge (q \rightarrow p)$$

and is true only when p and q have the same truth values. That is, $p \leftrightarrow q$ is true only when p and q are both true or when they are both false. The biconditional has the following meanings:

```
p if and only if q
q if and only if p
if p then q, and if q then p
```

As mentioned earlier, a tautology is a compound statement that is always true, whether its individual statements are true or false. A **contradiction** is a compound statement that is always false. A **contingent** statement is one that is neither a tautology nor a contradiction. Tautologies and contradictions are called analytically true and analytically false respectively, because their truth values can be determined by their forms alone. For example, the truth table of $p \vee \sim p$ shows it is a tautology, while $p \wedge \sim p$ is a contradiction.

If a conditional is also a tautology, then it is called an **implication** and has the symbol $\Rightarrow$ in place of $\rightarrow$. A biconditional that is also a tautology is called a **logical equivalence** or **material equivalence** and is symbolized by either $\Leftrightarrow$ or $\equiv$. Two statements that are logically equivalent always have the same truth values. For example, $p \equiv \sim \sim p$.

Unfortunately, this is not the only possible definition for implication, since there are sixteen possible truth tables for two variables that can take on true and false values. In early expert systems of the 1980s, 11 different definitions of the implication operator were defined.

The conditional does not mean exactly the same as the IF-THEN in a procedural language or a rule-based expert system. In procedural and expert systems, the IF-THEN means to execute the actions following the THEN if the conditions of the IF are true. In logic, the conditional is defined by its truth table. Its meaning can be translated into natural language in a number of ways. For example, if:

```
p → q
```

where p and q are any statements, this can be translated as:

```
p implies q
if p then q
p, only if q
p is sufficient for q
q if p
q is necessary for p
```

For example, let p represent "you are 18 or older" and q represents "you can vote." The conditional $p \rightarrow q$ can mean any of the following:

```
you are 18 or older implies you can vote
if you are 18 or older then you can vote
you are 18 or older, only if you can vote
```

```
you are 18 or older is sufficient for you can vote
you can vote if you are 18 or older
you can vote is necessary for you are 18 or older
```

In some cases, a change of wording is necessary to make these grammatically correct English sentences. The last example says if q does not occur, then neither will p. It is expressed in proper English as "Being able to vote requires you to be 18 or older."

Values for the binary logical connectives are shown in Table 2.4. These are binary connectives because they require two operands. The negation connective, ~, is a unary operator on the one operand that follows it, as shown in Table 2.5.

A set of logical connectives is **adequate** if every truth function can be represented using only the connectives from the adequate set. Examples of adequate sets are { ~, ∧, ∨ }, { ~, ∧ }, {~, ∨ }, and { ~, → }.

A single element set is called a **singleton**. There are two adequate singleton sets. These are the NOT-OR (**NOR**) and the NOT-AND (**NAND**). The NOR set is { ↓ } and the NAND set is { | }. The " | " operator is called a **stroke** or **alternative denial**. It is used to deny that both p and q are true. That is, p | q affirms that at least one of the statements p or q is true. The **joint denial operator**, "↓", denies that either p or q is true. That is, p ↓ q affirms that both p and q are false.

Table 2.4 Truth Table of the Binary Logical Connectives

p	q	p ∧ q	p ∨ q	p → q	p ↔ q
T	T	T	T	T	T
T	F	F	T	F	F
F	T	F	T	T	F
F	F	F	F	T	T

Table 2.5 Truth Table of Negation Connectives

p	~p
T	F
F	T

2.13 THE FIRST ORDER PREDICATE LOGIC

Although propositional logic is useful, it does have limitations. The major problem is that propositional logic can deal with only complete statements. That is, it cannot examine the internal structure of a statement. Propositional logic cannot even prove the validity of a syllogism such as:

```
All humans are mortal
All women are humans
Therefore, all women are mortal
```

In order to analyze more general cases, the **predicate logic** was developed. Its simplest form is the **first order** predicate logic and is the basis of logic programming languages such as PROLOG. In this section, we will use the term *predicate logic* to refer to first order predicate logic. Propositional logic is a subset of predicate logic.

Predicate logic is concerned with the internal structure of sentences. In particular, it is concerned with the use of special words called **quantifiers**, such as "all," "some," and "no." These words are very important because they explicitly quantify other words and make sentences more exact. All the quantifiers are concerned with "how many" and thus permit a wider scope of expression than does propositional logic.

2.14 THE UNIVERSAL QUANTIFIER

A universally quantified sentence has the same truth value for all replacements in the same domain. The **universal quantifier** is represented by the symbol ∀ followed by one or more arguments for the **domain variable**. The symbol ∀ is interpreted as "for every" or "for all." For example, in the domain of numbers:

```
(∀ x)  (x + x = 2x)
```

states that for every x (where x is a number), the sentence x + x = 2x is true. If we represent this sentence by the symbol p, then it can be expressed even more briefly as:

```
(∀ x)  (p)
```

As another example, let p represent the sentence "all dogs are animals," as in:

```
(∀ x)  (p)  ≡ (∀ x)  (if x is a dog → x is an animal)
```

The opposite statement is "no dogs are animals" and is written as:

```
(∀ x)  (if x is a dog → ~x is an animal)
```

It may also be read as:

```
Every dog is not an animal
All dogs are not animals
```

As another example, "all triangles are polygons" is written as follows:

```
(∀ x)  (x is a triangle → x is a polygon)
```

and is read "for all x, if x is a triangle, then x is a polygon." A shorter way of writing logic statements involving predicates is using **predicate functions** to describe the properties of the subject. The above logic statement can also be written as:

```
(∀ x)  (triangle(x) → polygon(x))
```

Predicate functions are usually written in a briefer notation using uppercase letters to represent the predicates. For example, let T = triangle and P = polygon. Then the triangle statement can be written even more briefly as:

$$(\forall x)\ (T(x) \rightarrow P(x)) \quad \text{or} \quad (\forall y)\ (T(y) \rightarrow P(y))$$

Note that any variables could be used in place of the dummy variables x and y. As another example, let H be the predicate function for human and M be the function for mortal. Then the statement that all humans are mortal can be written as:

$$(\forall x)\ (H(x) \rightarrow M(x))$$

and is read that for all x, if x is human, then x is mortal. This predicate logic sentence can also be represented as a semantic net, as shown in Figure 2.16. It can also be expressed in terms of rules:

```
IF x is human
THEN x is mortal
```

Figure 2.16 Semantic Net Representation of a Predicate Logic Statement

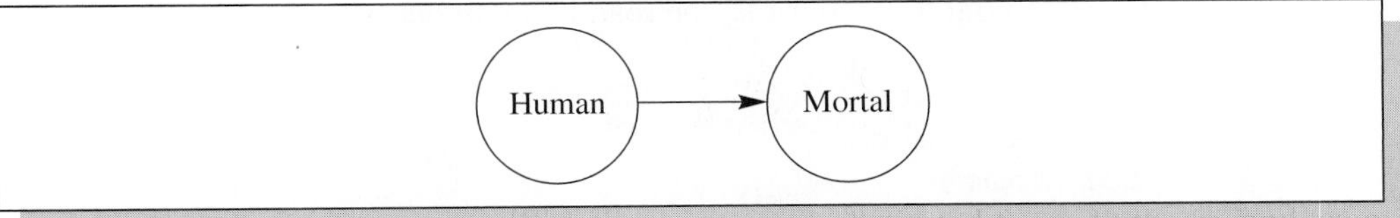

The universal quantifier can also be interpreted as a conjunction of predicates about instances. As mentioned earlier, an instance is a particular case. For example, a dog named Sparkler is a particular instance of the class of dogs, which can be expressed as:

```
Dog(Sparkler)
```

where Dog is the predicate function and Sparkler is an instance.

A predicate logic sentence such as:

$$(\forall x)\ P(x)$$

can be interpreted in terms of instances a_i as:

$$P(a_1) \wedge P(a_2) \wedge P(a_3) \wedge \ldots P(a_N)$$

where the ellipses indicate that the predicates extend to all members of the class. This statement says that the predicate applies to all instances of the class.

Multiple quantifiers can be used. For example, the commutative law of addition for numbers requires two quantifiers, as in:

```
(∀ x) (∀ y) (x + y = y + x)
```

This states that "for every x and for every y, the sum of x and y equals the sum of y and x."

2.15 THE EXISTENTIAL QUANTIFIER

Another type of quantifier is the **existential quantifier**. An existential quantifier describes a statement as being true for at least one member of the domain. This is a restricted form of the universal quantifier, which states that a statement is true for all members of the domain. The existential quantifier is written as ∃ followed by one or more arguments. For example:

```
(∃ x) (x · x = 1)
(∃ x) (elephant(x) ∧ name(Clyde))
```

The first sentence above states that there is some x whose product with itself equals 1. The second statement says there is some elephant with the name Clyde.

The existential quantifier may be read in a number of ways, such as:

```
there exists
at least one
for some
there is one
some
```

As another example,

```
(∀ x) (elephant(x) → four-legged(x))
```

says that all elephants are four-legged. However, the statement that some elephants are three-legged is written with the logical AND and existential quantifier as follows:

```
(∃ x) (elephant(x) ∧ three-legged(x))
```

Just as the universal quantifier can be expressed as a conjunction, the existential quantifier can be expressed as a disjunction of instances, a_i:

$$P(a_1) \lor P(a_2) \lor P(a_3) \lor \ldots P(a_N)$$

Table 2.6 shows quantified statements and their negations for the example in which P represents "elephants are mammals." The numbers in parentheses identify the examples for the following discussion.

Table 2.6 Examples of Negated Quantifiers

Example		Meaning
(1a)	$(\forall x)(P)$	All elephants are mammals.
(1b)	$(\exists x)(\sim P)$	Some elephants are not mammals.
(2a)	$(\exists x)(P)$	Some elephants are mammals.
(2b)	$(\forall x)(\sim P)$	No elephants are mammals.

Examples (1a) and (1b) are negations of each other, as are (2a) and (2b). Notice that the negation of a universally quantified statement of (1a) is an existentially quantified statement of the negation of P as shown by (1b). Likewise, the negation of an existentially quantified statement of (2a) is the universally quantified statement of the negation of P as shown by (2b).

2.16 QUANTIFIERS AND SETS

Quantifiers may be used to define sets over a universe, U, as shown in Table 2.7.

The relation that A is a proper subset of B, written as $A \subset B$, means that while all elements in A are in B, there is at least one element in B that is not in A. Letting E represent elephants and M represent mammals, the set relation:

$$E \subset M$$

states that all elephants are mammals, but not all mammals are elephants. Letting G = grey and F = four-legged, the statement that all grey, four-legged elephants are mammals is written:

$$(E \cap G \cap F) \subset M$$

Table 2.7 Some Set Expressions and Their Logical Equivalents

Set Expression	Logical Equivalent
$A = B$	$\forall x\,(x \in A \leftrightarrow x \in B)$
$A \subseteq B$	$\forall x\,(x \in A \rightarrow x \in B)$
$A \cap B$	$\forall x\,(x \in A \wedge x \in B)$
$A \cup B$	$\forall x\,(x \in A \vee x \in B)$
A'	$\forall x\,(x \in U \mid \sim(x \in A))$
U (Universe)	T (True)
Ø (empty set)	F (False)

Using the following definitions, some examples of quantified sentences are shown:

```
E=elephants
R=reptiles
G=grey
```

```
F=four-legged
D=dogs
M=mammals


No elephants are reptiles
E ∩ R = Ø
Some elephants are grey
E ∩ G ≠ Ø
No elephants are grey
E ∩ G = Ø
Some elephants are not grey
E ∩ G´ ≠ Ø
All elephants are gray and four-legged
E ⊂ (G ∩ F)
All elephants and dogs are mammals
(E ∪ D) ⊂ M
Some elephants are four-legged and are grey
(E ∩ F ∩ G) ≠ Ø
```

As another analogy of sets and logic forms, de Morgan's laws are shown in Table 2.8. The equivalence symbol, ≡, the (biconditional) means that the statement on the left has the same truth value as the statement on the right. That is, the statements are equivalent.

Table 2.8 Set and Logic Forms of de Morgan's Laws

Set	Logic
$(A \cap B)' \equiv A' \cup B'$	$\sim(p \wedge q) \equiv \sim p \vee \sim q$
$(A \cup B)' \equiv A' \cap B'$	$\sim(p \vee q) \equiv \sim p \wedge \sim q$

2.17 LIMITATIONS OF PREDICATE LOGIC

Although predicate logic is useful in many types of situations, there are some types of statements that cannot be expressed in predicate logic using the universal and existential quantifiers. For example, the following statement cannot be expressed in predicate logic:

```
Most of the class received A's
```

In this statement the quantifier *Most* means more than half.

The *Most* quantifier cannot be expressed in terms of the universal and existential quantifiers. To implement *Most*, a logic must provide some predicates for counting, as in fuzzy logic described in Chapter 5. Another limitation of predicate logic is expressing things that are sometimes, but not always true. This problem can also be solved by fuzzy logic. is However, introducing counting also introduces more complications into the logic system and makes it more like mathematics.

2.18 SUMMARY

In this chapter we have discussed the elements of logic, knowledge representation and some methods for representing knowledge. Knowledge representation is of major importance in expert systems. Fallacies were discussed because it is so important for the knowledge engineer to understand the rules of the domain and not confuse the form of knowledge with semantics. Unless formal rules are specified, an expert system may not yield valid conclusions, which could spell disaster in mission-critical systems on which human life and property depend.

From a logical view, knowledge can be classified in a number of ways such as a priori, a posteriori, procedural, declarative, and tacit. Production rules, objects, semantic nets, schemata, frames, and logic are common methods by which knowledge is represented in expert systems. Each of these paradigms has advantages and disadvantages. Before designing an expert system you should decide which is the best paradigm for the problem to be solved. Rather than trying to use one tool for all problems, pick the best tool. The advantage of CLIPS in being able to represent knowledge by both objects as well as rules was covered. Many references to logic, knowledge, and fallacies are given in Appendix G. Appendices A, B, and C contain collections of useful equivalences, quantifiers, and set properties.

PROBLEMS

2.1 Draw a semantic net for computers using AKO and IS-A links. Consider the classes of microcomputer, mainframe, supercomputer, computing system, dedicated, general purpose, board-level, computer-on-a-chip, single processor, and multiprocessor. Include specific instances.

2.2 Draw a semantic net for computer communications using AKO and IS-A links. Consider the classes of local area net, wide area net, token ring, star, centralized, decentralized, distributed, modems, telecommunications, newsgroups, and electronic mail. Include specific instances.

2.3 Draw a frame system for the building in which you are attending classes. Consider offices, classrooms, laboratories, and so forth. Include instances with filled slots for one type of each frame such as office and classroom.

2.4 Draw an action frame system telling what to do in case of hardware failure for your computer system. Consider disk crash, power supply, CPU, and memory problems.

2.5 Draw the Venn diagram and write the set expression for

(a) Exclusive-OR of two sets A and B consists of all elements that are in one, but not both sets. The exclusive-OR is also called the **symmetric set difference** and is symbolized by the / sign. For example:
$\{1,2\} / \{2,3\} = \{1,3\}$
(b) **Set difference** of two sets, symbolized by "–" consists of all the elements in the first set that are not also in the second. For example:
$\{1,2\} - \{2,3\} = \{1\}$
where $\{1,2\}$ is the first set and $\{2,3\}$ is the second.

2.6 Write the truth tables and determine which of the following are tautologies, contradictions, or **contingent statements**, and which are neither. For (a) and (b), first express the statements with logic symbols and connectives.

(a) If I pass this course and make an A then
I pass this course or I make an A.
(b) If I pass this course then I make an A
and
I pass this course and I do not make an A.
(c) $((A \wedge \sim B \rightarrow (C \wedge \sim C)) \rightarrow (A \rightarrow B)$
(d) $(A \rightarrow B) \wedge (\sim B \vee C) \wedge (A \wedge \sim C)$
(e) $A \rightarrow \sim B$ (contingent)

2.7 Two sentences are logically equivalent if and only if they have the same truth value. Thus if A and B are any statements, the biconditional statement,

$A \leftrightarrow B$, or the equivalence, $A \equiv B$

will be true in every case, giving a tautology. Determine if the two sentences below are logically equivalent by writing them using logical symbols and determine if the truth table of their biconditional is a tautology.

If you eat a banana split, then you cannot eat a pie.
If you eat a pie, then you cannot eat a banana split.

2.8 Write the logical equivalent corresponding to set difference and symmetric set difference.

2.9 Show that the following are identities for any sets A, B, and C and Ø as the null set:

(a) $(A \cup B) \equiv (B \cup A)$
(b) $(A \cup B) \cup C \equiv A \cup (B \cup C)$
(c) $A \cup \emptyset \equiv A$
(d) $A \cap B \equiv B \cap A$
(e) $A \cap A' \equiv \emptyset$

2.10 Write the following in quantified form:

(a) All dogs are mammals.
(b) No dog is an elephant.
(c) Some programs have bugs.

(d) None of my programs have bugs.
(e) All of your programs have bugs.

2.11 The **power set**, P(S), of a set S is the set of all elements that are subsets of S. P(S) will always have at least the null set, Ø, and S as members.

(a) Find the power set of A = {2, 4, 6}.

Meaning	Definition
either p or q	$(p \vee q) \wedge \sim(p \wedge q)$
neither p nor q	$\sim(p \vee q)$
p unless q	$\sim q \rightarrow p$
p because q	$(p \wedge q) \wedge (q \rightarrow p)$
no p is q	$p \rightarrow \sim q$

(b) For a set with N elements, how many elements does the power set have?

2.12 (a) Write the truth table for the following:
(b) Show that $(p \vee q) \wedge \sim(p \wedge q) \equiv p/q$ where / is the exclusive OR.

2.13 (a) Write the NOR and NAND truth tables.
(b) Prove that $\{\downarrow\}$ and $\{\mid\}$ are adequate sets by expressing $\sim$, $\wedge$, and $\vee$ in terms of $\downarrow$ and then in terms of $\mid$ by constructing truth tables to show the logical equivalences as follows:

$\sim\sim p \equiv p$

$(p \wedge q) \equiv (p \downarrow p) \downarrow (q \downarrow q)$

$\sim p \equiv p \mid p$

$(p \vee q) \equiv (p \mid p) \mid (q \mid q)$

(c) Since $p \rightarrow q \equiv \sim(p \wedge \sim q)$, express $p \rightarrow q$ in terms of $\downarrow$.
(d) What is the advantage and disadvantage of using adequate singleton sets in terms of (i) notation and (ii) construction of chips for electronic circuits?

2.14 What are the advantages and disadvantages of designing an expert system with knowledge about several domains?

2.15 Explain how you would boil water differently in Denver than in Houston if you were cooking an egg that should be hard-boiled. Is this a problem in logic or physics?

2.16 Given the following PROLOG statements, prove that Tom is his own grandfather:

```
mother(pat,ann).   ; pat is the mother of ann
parents(jim,ann,tom)   ; jim and ann are parents of tom
surrogatemother(pat,tom).  ;   pat is the surrogatemother of tom
```

BIBLIOGRAPHY

(Bergadano 96). *Inductive Logic Programming*, The MIT Press, 1996.

(Brewka 97). Gerhard Brewka, *Principles of Knowledge Representation,* CSLI Publications, 1997.

(Brachman 91). R. Brachman, D. McGuinness, P. Patel-Schneider, A. Borgida, and L. Resnick, Living with CLASSIC: When and How to Use a KL-ONE-Like Language, *Principles of Semantic Networks,* Morgan Kaufman, pp. 401–456, May, 1991.

(Huth 04). Michael Huth and Mark Ryan, Logic in Computer Science, 2nd Edition, Cambridge University Press, 2004. NOTE: Also see software in following list for their book.

(Jackson 99). Peter Jackson, *Introduction to Expert Systems*, Addison-Wesley, Third Edition, 1999.

(Leake 96). Ed. By David Leake et al., *Case-Based Reasoning*, AAAI Press/MIT Press 1996.

(Kahane 03). Howard Kahane & Paul Tidman, *Logic and Philosophy: A Modern Introduction,* 9th edition, Wadsworth, 2003.

(Jacquette 01). Dale Jacquette, *Symbolic Logic,* Wadsworth, 2001.

(Saratchandran 96). P. Saratchandran, et al., *Parallel Implementations of Backpropagation Neural Networks on Transputers: A Study of Training Set Parallelism, Progress in Neural Processing 3,* World Scientific Pub. Co, July 1996

(Sowa 00). J.F. Sowa, *Knowledge Representation: Logical, Philosophical, and Computational Foundations,* Brooks-Cole, 2000.

(Russell 03). Stuart Russell and Peter Norvig, *Artificial Intelligence*, Second Edition, by Pearson Education, 2003.

(Werbos 94). Paul Werbos, *The Roots of Backpropagation: From Ordered Derivatives to Neural Networks and Political Forecasting: Adaptive and Learning Systems for Signal Processing,* Wiley-Interscience, 1994.

CHAPTER 3
Methods of Inference

3.1 INTRODUCTION

This chapter is an introduction to reasoning about knowledge. It is important to separate the meaning of the words used in reasoning from the reasoning itself so we will cover it in a formal way by discussing various methods of inference (Russell 03). In particular we will look at an important type of reasoning in expert systems in which conclusions follow from facts by using rules. It is particularly important in expert systems because making inferences is the fundamental method by which expert systems solve problems (Klir 98).

As mentioned in Chapter 1, expert systems are commonly used when an inadequate algorithm or no algorithmic solution exists. The expert system should make a chain of inferences to come up with a solution just as a person would, especially when faced with incomplete or missing information. A simple computer program that uses an algorithm to solve a problem cannot supply an answer if all the parameters needed are not given.

However an expert system makes a best guess just like a human would when a problem needs to be solved and the optimum solution cannot be determined. The idea is to come up with a solution just as people come up with a (hopefully) good solution rather than none at all. While the solution may only be 95% as efficient as the optimum solution, that's still better than no solution. This type of approach is really nothing new. For example, numeric computations in mathematics such as the Runge-Kutta method of solving differential equations have been used for centuries to solve problems for which no analytic solution is possible.

NOTE: Appendices A, B, and C contain useful reference material for this chapter.

3.2 TREES, LATTICES, AND GRAPHS

A **tree** is a hierarchical data structure consisting of **nodes,** which store information or knowledge and **branches,** which connect the nodes. Branches are sometimes called **links** or **edges** and nodes are sometimes called **vertices**. Figure 3.1 shows a general binary tree which has zero, one, or two branches per node. In an **oriented tree** the **root node** is the highest node in the **hierarchy** and the **leaves** are the lowest. A tree can be considered a special type of semantic net in which every node except the root has exactly one **parent** and zero or more **child** nodes. For the usual type of binary tree there is a maximum of two children per node, and the left and right child nodes are distinguished.

Figure 3.1 Binary Tree

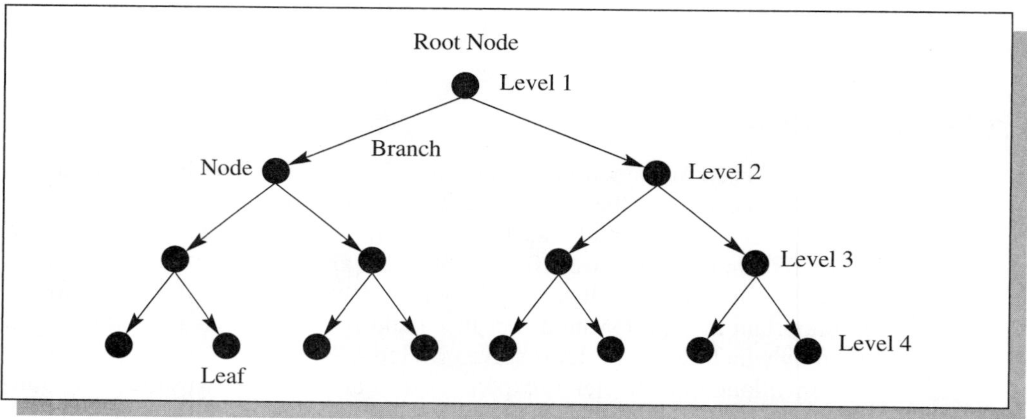

If a node has more than one parent, it is in a network. In Figure 3.1, notice that there is only one sequence of edges or **path** from the root to any node since it is not possible to move against an arrow. In oriented trees the arrows all point downward.

Trees are a special case of a general mathematical structure called a **graph**. The terms *network* or simply *net* are often used synonymously with graph when describing a particular example such as an ethernet network. A graph can have zero or more links between nodes and no distinction between parents and children. A simple example of a graph is a map, where the cities are the nodes and the links are the roads. The links may have arrows or directions associated with them and a **weight** to characterize some aspect of the link. An analogy is one-way streets with limits on how much weight trucks can carry. The weights in a graph can be any type of information. If the graph represents an airline route, the weights can be miles between cities, cost of flying, fuel consumption, and so forth.

A supervised artificial neural network is another example of a graph with cycles since during training there is feedback of information from one layer of the

Figure 3.2 Simple Graphs

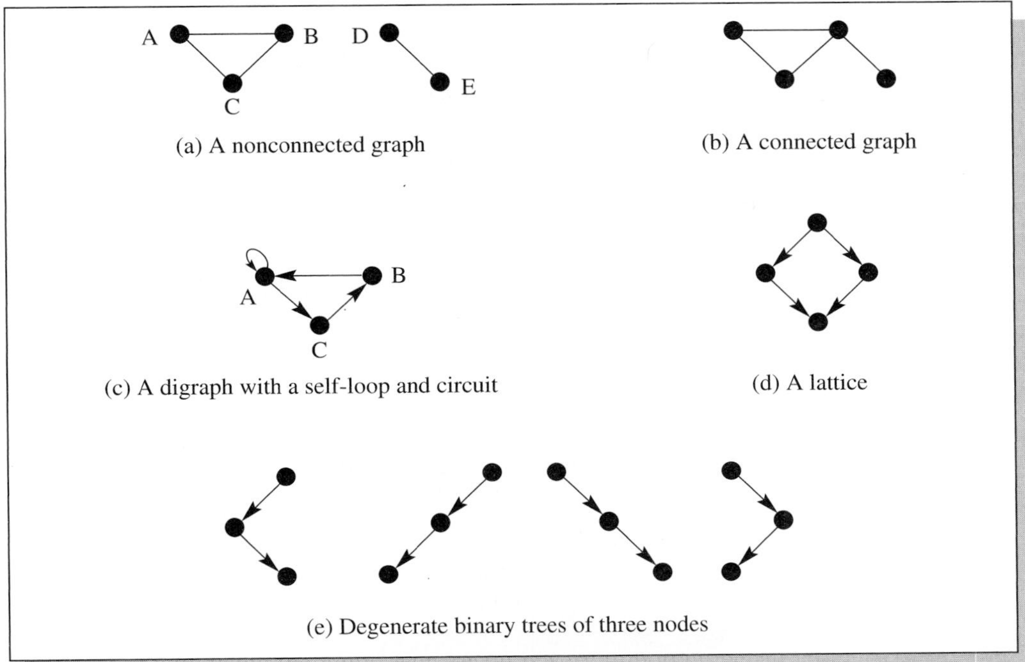

net to another, which modifies the weights. A simple graph has no links that come immediately back on the node itself, as shown in Figure 3.2a. A **circuit** or **cycle** is a path through a graph that begins and ends on the same node, as does the path ABCA in Figure 3.2a An **acyclic graph** has no cycles. A **connected graph** has links to all its nodes as shown in Fig. 3.2b. A graph with directed links, called a **digraph,** and a **self-loop** is shown in Figure 3.2c. A directed acyclic graph is a **lattice**, and an example is shown in Figure 3.2d. A tree with only a single path from the root to its one leaf is a **degenerate tree**. The degenerate binary trees of three nodes are shown in Figure 3.2e. Generally in a tree, the arrows are *not* explicitly shown because they are assumed to be pointing down.

Trees and lattices are useful for classifying objects because of their hierarchical nature, with parents above children. An example is a family tree, which shows the relationships and ancestry of related people. Another application of trees and lattices is making decisions; these are called **decision trees** or **decision lattices** and are very common for simple reasoning. We will use the term **structure** to refer to both trees and lattices. A decision structure is both a knowledge representation scheme and a method of reasoning about its knowledge. An example of a decision tree for classifying animals is shown in Figure 3.3. This example is for the classic game of twenty questions. The nodes contain questions, the branches "yes" or "no" responses to the questions, and the leaves contain the guesses of what the animal is.

Figure 3.3 Decision Tree Showing Knowledge About Animals

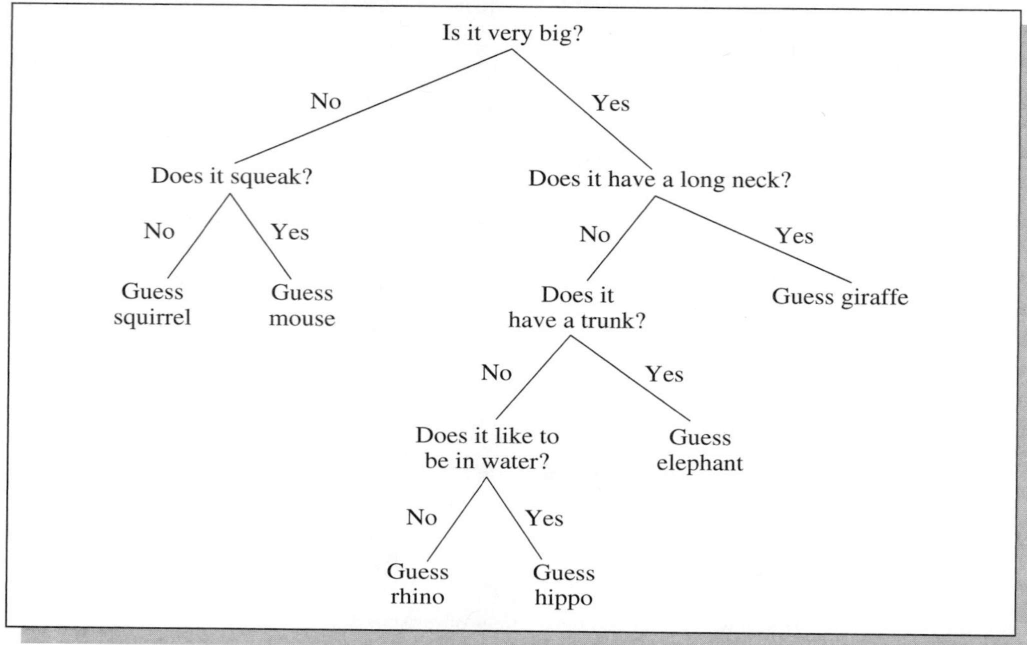

A small portion of a decision tree to classify raspberries is shown in Figure 3.4. Unlike Computer Science trees, classification trees may be drawn with the root down. Not shown is the root which has a branch to the "Leaves Simple" node and another branch to the "Leaves Compound" node. The decision process starts at the bottom by identifying gross features, such as whether the leaves are simple or compound. More specific details requiring closer observation are used as we travel up the tree. That is, larger sets of alternatives are examined first and then the decision process starts narrowing down the possibilities to smaller sets. This is a good way of organizing the decisions in terms of the time and effort to carry out more detailed observations.

If the decisions are binary, then a binary decision tree is easy to construct and is very efficient. Every question goes down one level in the tree. One question can decide one of two possible answers. Two questions can decide one of four possible answers. Three questions can decide one of eight possible answers and so on. If a binary tree is constructed such that all the leaves are answers and all the nodes leading down are questions, there can be a maximum of 2^N answers for N questions. For example, ten questions can classify one of 1,024 animals while twenty questions can classify one of 1,048,576 possible answers.

Another useful feature of decision trees is that they can be made **self-learning**. If the guess is wrong, a procedure can be called to query the user for a new, correct classification question and the answers to the "yes" and "no" responses. A new node, branches, and leaves can then be dynamically created and added to the tree. In the original Animals program written in BASIC, knowledge was stored in DATA statements. When the user taught the program a new animal, automatic

Figure 3.4 Portion of a Decision Tree for Species of Raspberries

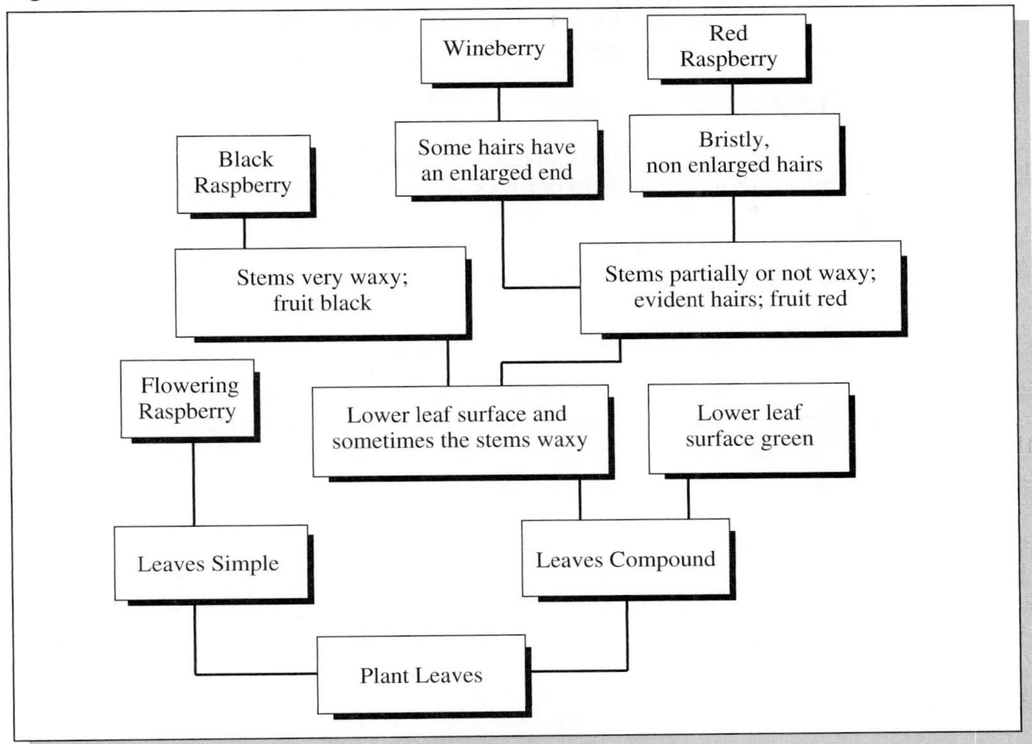

learning took place as the program generated new DATA statements containing information about the new animal. For maximum efficiency, the animal knowledge is stored in trees. Using CLIPS, new rules can be built automatically as the program learns new knowledge using the **build** keyword (Giarratano 93). This **automated knowledge acquisition** is very useful since it can circumvent the knowledge acquisition bottleneck described in Chapter 6 in simple cases.

Decision structures can be mechanically translated into production rules. This can easily be done by a breadth-first search of the tree and generating IF-THEN rules at every node. For example, the decision tree of Figure 3.3 could be translated into rules as follows:

```
IF QUESTION = "IS IT VERY BIG?" AND RESPONSE = "NO"
     THEN  QUESTION := "DOES IT SQUEAK?"

IF QUESTION = "IS IT VERY BIG?" AND RESPONSE = "YES"
     THEN  QUESTION := "DOES IT HAVE A LONG NECK?"
```

and so forth for the other nodes. A leaf node would generate an ANSWER response rather than a question. Appropriate procedures would also query the user for input and construct new nodes if wrong.

Although decision structures are very powerful classification tools, they are limited because they cannot deal with variables as an expert system can. Expert systems are general-purpose tools rather than simply classifiers.

3.3 STATE AND PROBLEM SPACES

Graphs can be applied to many practical problems. A useful method of describing the behavior of an object is to define a graph called the **state space**. A state is a collection of characteristics that can be used to define the status or **state** of an object. The state space is the set of states showing the **transitions** between states that the object can experience. A transition takes an object from one state to another.

Examples of State Spaces

As a simple example of state spaces, consider the purchase of a soft drink from a machine. As you put coins into the machine, it makes a transition from one state to another. Figure 3.5 illustrates the state space assuming that only quarters and nickels are available and 55¢ is required for a drink. Adding other coins such as dimes and fifty-cent pieces makes the diagram more complicated and is not shown here.

Figure 3.5 State Diagram for a Soft Drink Vending Machine Accepting Quarters (Q) and Nickels (N)

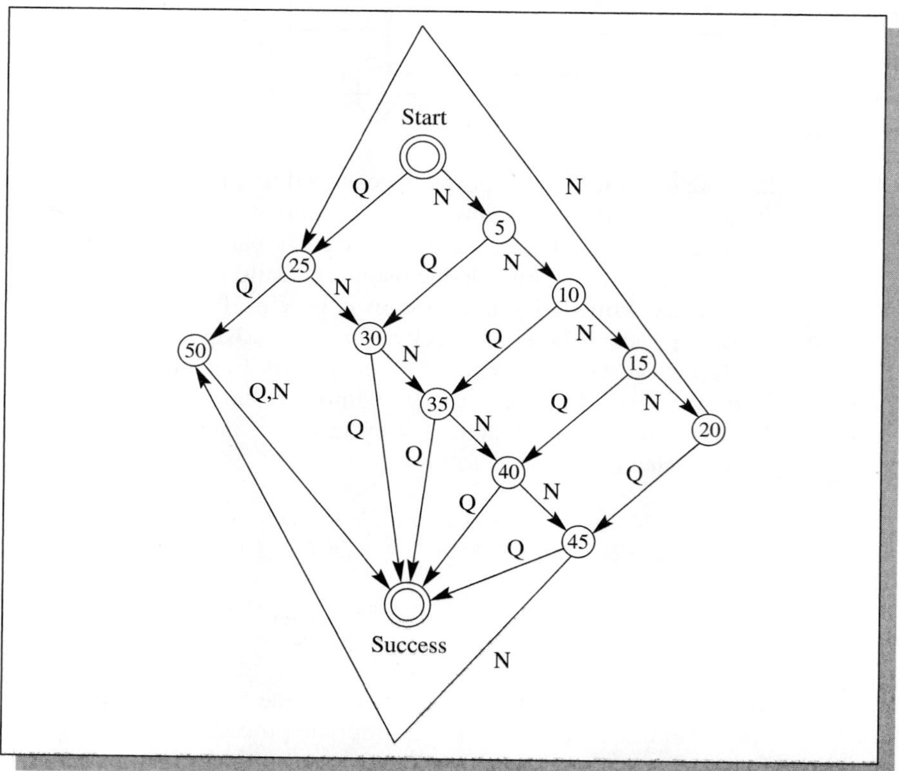

The start and success states are drawn as double circles to make them easier to identify. The states are shown as circles and the possible transitions to other states are drawn as arrows. Notice that this diagram is a weighted digraph, where the weights are the possible coins that can be input to the machine in every state.

This diagram is also called a **finite state machine diagram** because it describes the finite number of states of a machine. The term *machine* is used in a very general sense. The machine can be a real object, an algorithm, a concept, and so forth. Associated with every state are the actions that drive it to another state. At any time, this machine can be in only one state. As the machine accepts input to a state, it progresses from that state to another. If the correct inputs are given, the machine will progress from the start to the success or final state. If a state is not designed to accept a certain input, the machine will become hung up in that state. For example, the soft drink machine has no provision to accept dimes. If someone puts a dime in the machine, the response is undefined. A good design will include the possibility of invalid inputs from every state and provide for transitions to an error state. The error state is designed to give appropriate error messages and take whatever action is necessary.

Finite state machines are often used in compilers and other programs to determine the validity of an input. For example, Figure 3.6 shows part of a finite state machine to test input strings for validity. Characters of the input are examined one at a time. Only the character strings WHILE, WRITE, and BEGIN will be accepted. Arrows are shown from the BEGIN state for successful input and also for erroneous input going to the error state. For efficiency, some states, such as the one pointed to by "L" and "T," are used for testing both WHILE and WRITE.

NOTE: Only some of the error state transitions are shown.

Figure 3.6 Part of a Finite State Machine for Determining Valid Strings WHILE, WRITE, and BEGIN.

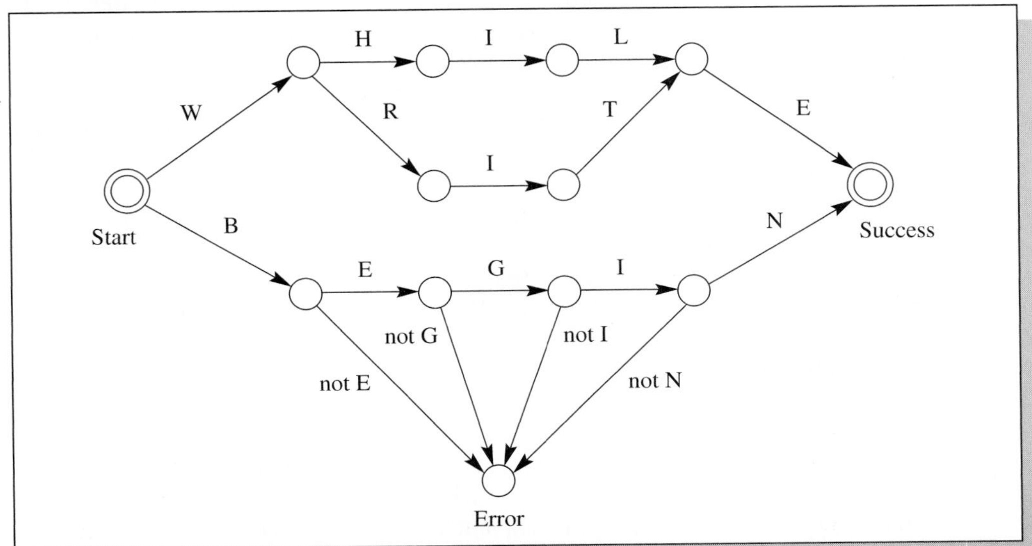

State diagrams are also useful in describing solutions to problems. In these kinds of applications we can think of the state space as a **problem space**, where some states correspond to intermediate stages in problem solving and some states correspond to answers. In a problem space there may be multiple success states corresponding to possible solutions. Finding the solution to a problem in a problem space involves finding a valid path from start (problem statement) to success (answer). The animal decision tree can be viewed as a problem space where the yes/no responses to questions determine the state transition.

Another example of a problem space occurs in the classic Monkey and Bananas problem shown in Figure 3.7. The problem is to give instructions to a monkey telling how to retrieve some bananas hanging from the ceiling. The bananas are out of reach. Inside the room are a couch and a ladder. The initial starting configuration is typically with the monkey on the couch. Instructions might be:

```
jump off couch
move to ladder
move ladder under bananas' position
climb ladder
grab bananas
```

The instructions will vary depending on the initial configuration of monkey, couch, and ladder. Since there are a number of initial start states, the special double circles for the start are not shown. For example, another possible starting state is with the monkey on the couch under the bananas. The monkey will then have to push the couch out of the way before moving the ladder under the bananas. In the simplest starting state, the monkey is already on the ladder under the bananas.

Although this problem seems obvious to a human, it involves a considerable amount of reasoning. A practical application of a reasoning system like this is giving instructions to a robot concerning the solution of a task. Rather than assuming that all objects in the environment are fixed in place, a general solution is a reasoning system that can deal with a variety of situations. A rule-based solution to the Monkey and Bananas problem is distributed with the CLIPS CDROM.

Another useful application of graphs is exploring paths to find a problem's solution. Figure 3.8a shows a simple net for the Traveling Salesman problem. In this example, assume the problem is to find a complete path from node A that visits all other nodes. As usual in the Traveling Salesman problem, no node can be visited twice. Figure 3.8b shows all the possible paths starting from node A in the form of a tree. The correct paths ABDCA and ACDBA are shown as thick lines in this graph.

Depending on the search algorithm, the exploration of paths to find the correct one may involve a considerable amount of backtracking. For example, the path ABA may be first searched unsuccessfully and then backtracked to B. From B, the paths CA, CB, CDB, and CDC will be unsuccessfully searched. Next the path BDB will be unsuccessfully searched until the first correct path ABDCA is found.

Figure 3.7 The State Space for the Monkey and Bananas Problem

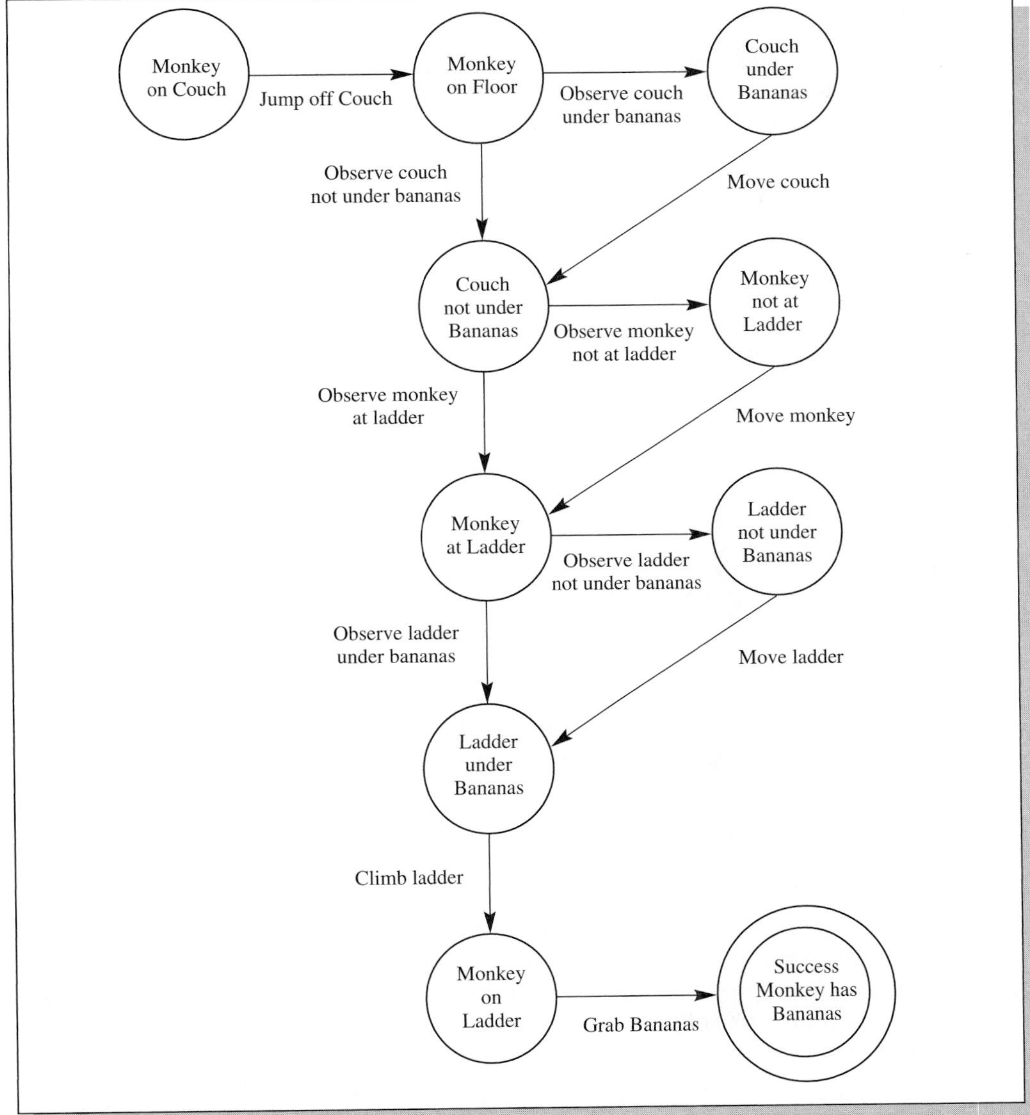

Ill-Structured Problem Spaces

A useful application of state spaces is in characterizing ill-structured problems. In Chapter 1 an ill-structured problem was defined to have uncertainties associated with it. These uncertainties can be specified more precisely by a problem space.

As an example of an ill-structured problem, let's consider again the case of a person who is thinking about traveling and an online search doesn't help, so

Figure 3.8 A Traveling Salesman Problem

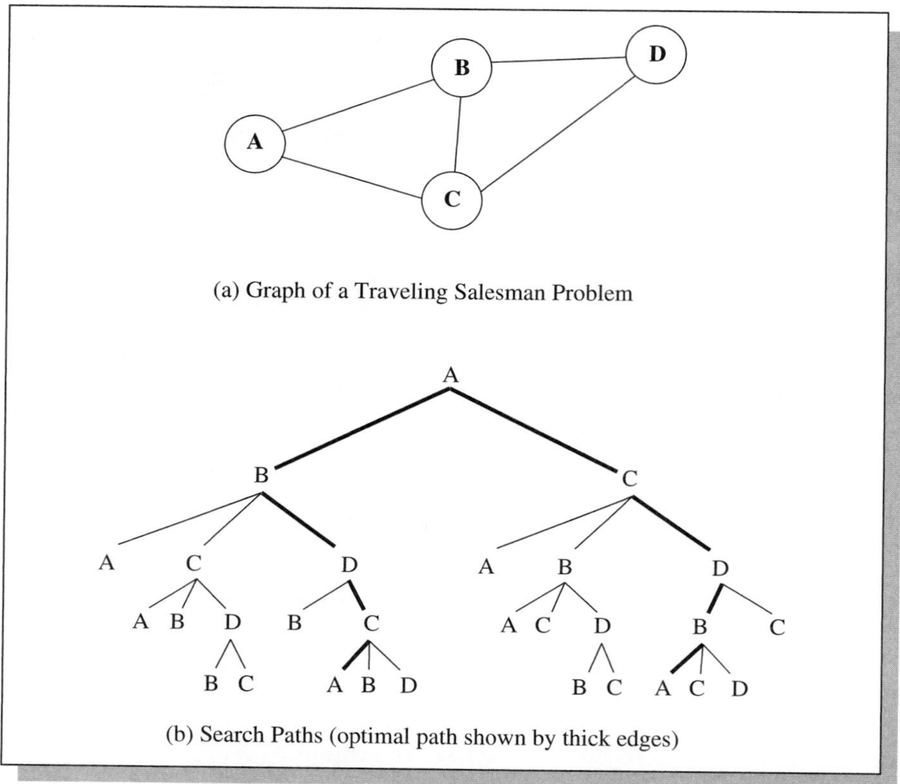

(b) Search Paths (optimal path shown by thick edges)

visits a travel agent as discussed in Chapter 1. Table 3.1 lists some characteristics of this ill-structured problem as a problem space, indicated by the person's responses to the travel agent's questions.

If you compare Table 3.1 to Table 1.10 in Chapter 1, you'll see that the concept of a problem space lets us specify more precisely the characteristics of an ill-structured problem. It is essential to characterize these parameters precisely to determine if a solution is feasible, and if so, what is needed for a solution. A problem is not necessarily ill-structured just because it has one, some, or even all of these characteristics since much depends on the severity. For example, all theorem-proving problems have an infinite number of potential solutions, but this does not make theorem proving an ill-structured problem.

As you can see from Table 3.1, there are many uncertainties and yet travel agents cope with them every day. While not all cases may be as bad as this, it indicates why an algorithmic solution would be very difficult.

A well-formed problem is one in which we know the explicit problem, goal, and operators that can be applied to go from one state to another. A well-formed problem is **deterministic** because when an operator is applied to a state, we are sure of the next state. The problem space is bounded and the states are discrete. This means that there are a finite number of states and each state is well defined.

Table 3.1 Example of an Ill-Structured Problem for Travel

Characteristic	Response
Goal not explicit	I'm thinking about going somewhere
Problem space unbounded	I'm not sure where to go
Problem states not discrete	I just like to travel; the destination is not important
Intermediate states difficult to achieve	I don't have enough money to go
State operators unknown	I don't know how to get the money
Time constraint	I must go soon

In the travel problem, the states are unbounded because there are infinitely many possible destinations that a traveler might go to. An analogous situation occurs with an analog meter, which may indicate an infinite number of possible readings. If we consider each reading of the meter to be a state, then there are an infinite number of states and they are not well defined because they correspond to real numbers. Since there are an infinite number of real numbers between any two real numbers, the states are not discrete because the next state differs only infinitesimally. In contrast, the readings of a digital meter are bounded and discrete.

3.4 AND-OR TREES AND GOALS

Many types of expert systems use backward chaining to find solutions to problems. PROLOG is a good example of a backward-chaining system that tries to solve a problem by breaking it up into smaller subproblems and solving them. During the 1990s PROLOG started to become widely used for commercial applications in business and industry (http://www.ddj.com/documents/s=9064/ddj0212ai004/0212aie004.htm). Solving a problem is considered by optimists as a goal to be achieved. In order to accomplish a significant goal, many subgoals may need to be accomplished.

One type of tree or lattice that is useful in representing backward-chaining problems is the AND-OR tree. Figure 3.9 shows a simple example of an AND-OR lattice to solve the goal of obtaining a college degree. To accomplish this goal, you can either attend a college in person or through correspondence courses. With correspondence courses, work can be performed either by mailing assignments or electronically using a home computer and modem.

In order to satisfy requirements for the degree, three subgoals must be accomplished: (1) apply for admittance, (2) take courses, and (3) apply to graduate. Notice that there is an arc through the edges from the Satisfy Requirements goal to these three subgoals. The arc through the edges indicates that Satisfy Requirements is an AND-node that can be satisfied only if all three of its subgoals are satisfied. Goals without the arc such as Mail, Computer and Modem, and In Person are OR-nodes in which accomplishing any of these subgoals satisfies its parent goal of Get a College Degree.

This diagram is a lattice because the Satisfy Requirements subgoal has three parent nodes: (1) Mail, (2) Computer and Modem, and (3) In Person. Notice that it would be possible to draw this diagram as a tree by simply duplicating the

Figure 3.9 AND-OR Lattice Showing How to Obtain a College Degree

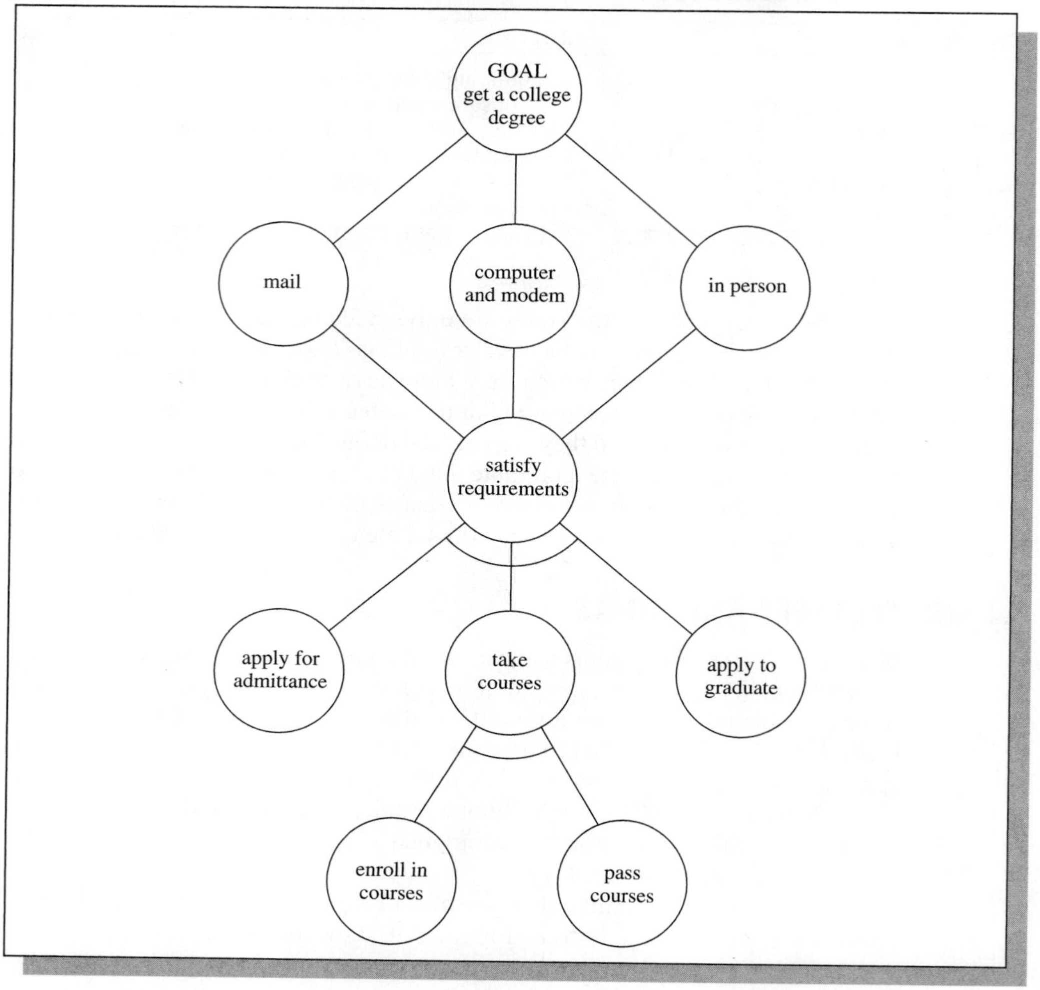

subgoal Satisfy Requirements and its subtree of goals for the Mail, Computer and Modem, and In Person goals. However, since the Satisfy Requirements is the same for each of its parents there is no real advantage, and it uses more paper to draw the tree.

As another simple example, Figure 3.10 shows an AND-OR tree for the problem of getting to work by different possible ways. For completeness, this could also be converted into a lattice. For example, an edge could be added from the node Drive to Train Station to the Car node and from Walk to Train Station to the Walk node. Figure 3.11 shows an AND-exclusive OR type lattice.

Another way of describing problem solutions is an AND-OR-NOT lattice, which uses logic gate symbols instead of the AND-OR tree type notation. The logic gate symbols for AND, OR, and NOT are shown in Figure 3.12. These

Figure 3.10 A Simple AND-OR Tree Showing Methods of Getting to Work

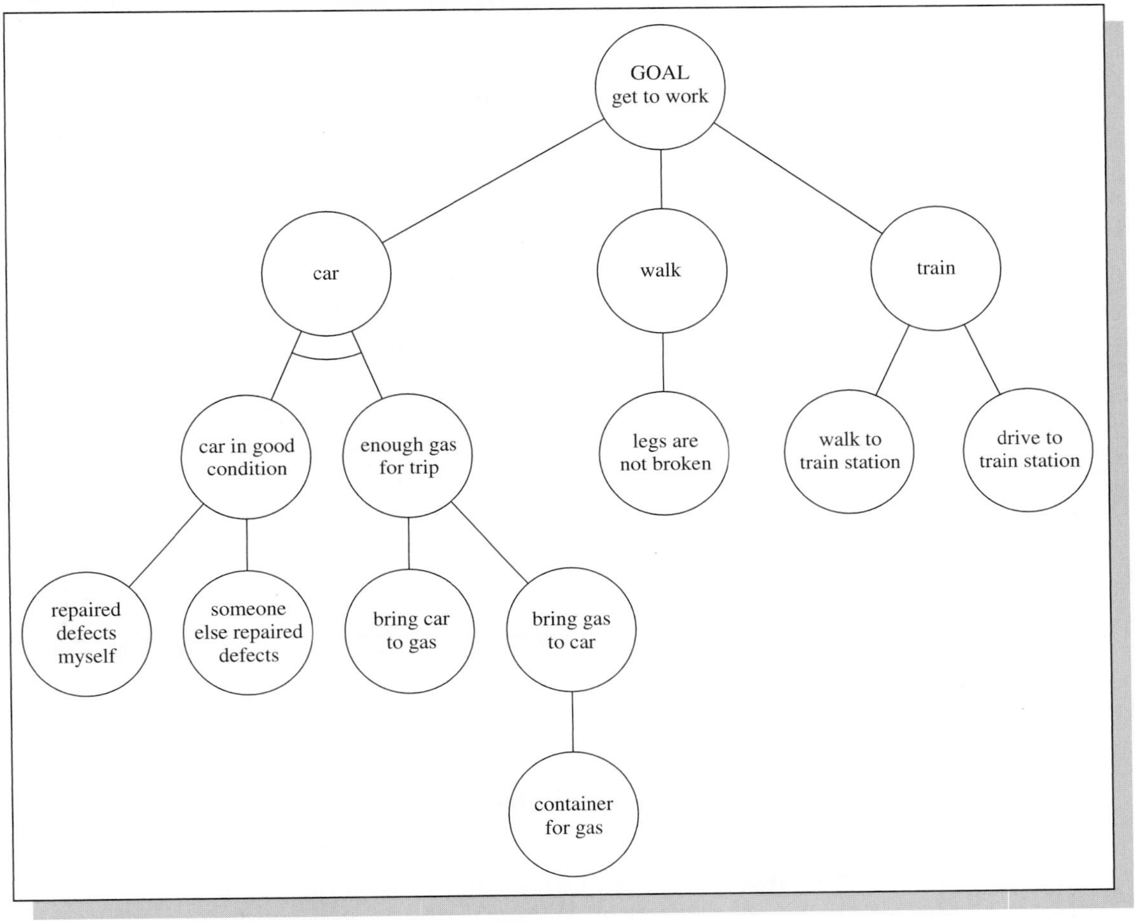

gates implement the truth tables for AND, OR, and NOT discussed in Chapter 2. Figure 3.13 shows Figure 3.9 implemented with AND and OR gates.

AND-OR trees and decision trees have the same basic advantages and disadvantages. The main advantage of AND-OR-NOT lattices is their potential implementation in hardware for fast processing speeds. These lattices can be custom designed for fabrication as integrated circuits. In practice, one type of logic gate such as the NOT-AND or NAND is used for reasons of manufacturing economy rather than separate AND, OR, and NOT gates. From logic it can be proved that any logic function can be implemented by a NAND gate. An integrated circuit with one type of device is cheaper to manufacture than one with multiple types of logic gates.

A chip using forward chaining can compute the answer very quickly as a function of its inputs since processing proceeds in parallel. Chips like this can be used for real-time monitoring of sensor data and make an appropriate response

Figure 3.11 AND-OR Lattice for Car Selling/Repair Decision

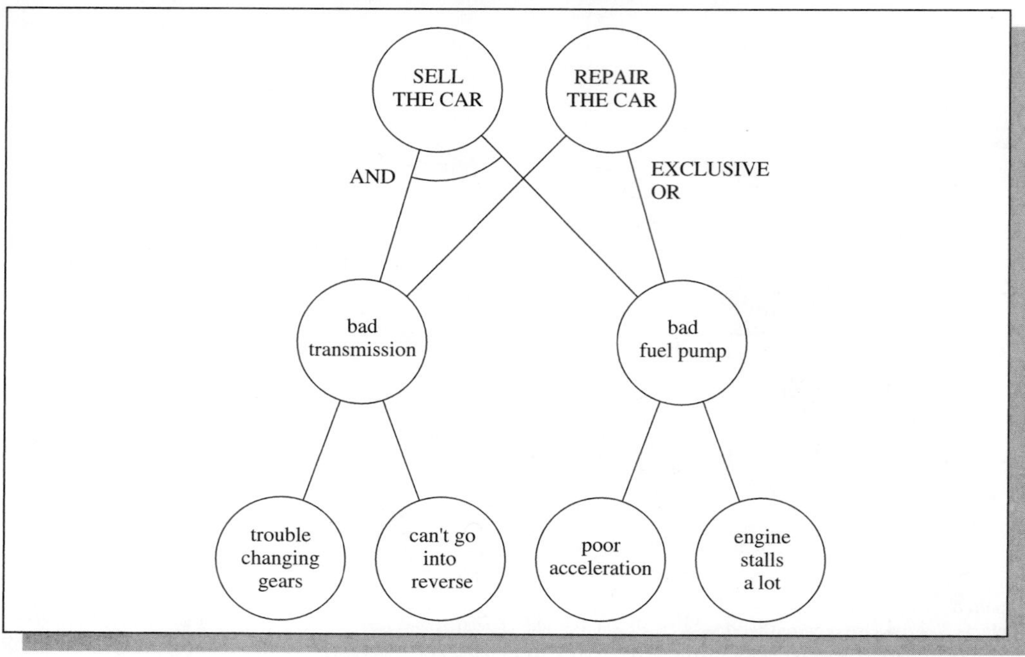

Figure 3.12 AND, OR, and NOT Logic Gate Symbols

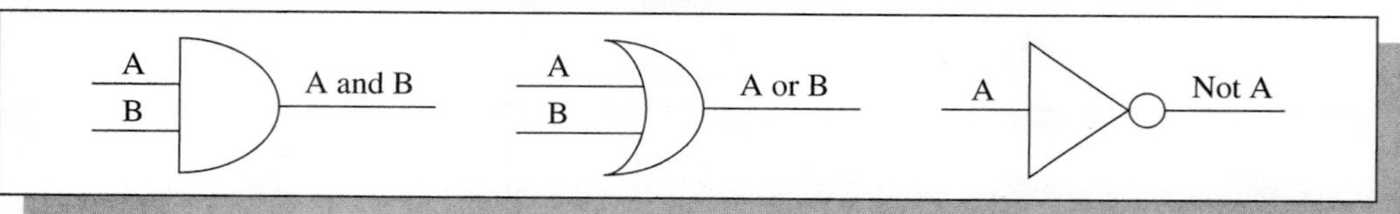

Figure 3.13 AND-OR Logic Gate Representation for Figure 3.9

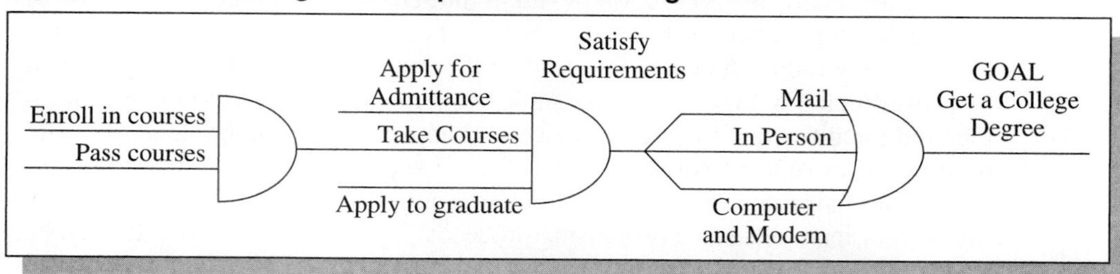

depending on the inputs. The main disadvantage is that like other decision structures, a chip designed for logic cannot handle situations it was not designed for. However, an ANS implemented on a chip can handle unexpected inputs.

3.5 DEDUCTIVE LOGIC AND SYLLOGISMS

In Chapter 2, we discussed the representation of knowledge by logic. Now you will see how inferences are made to derive new knowledge or information. In the remainder of this chapter we will discuss different methods of inference. Figure 3.14 is an overview of the methods of inference. A brief summary is as follows:

- *Deduction.* Logical reasoning in which conclusions must follow from their premises.
- *Induction.* Inference from the specific case to the general. Induction is one of the main methods of machine learning in which computers learn without human intervention. Three popular methods of machine learning are the connectionist Hopfield network, the symbolic ID3/ID5R, and evolution-based genetic algorithms (http://ai.bpa.arizona.edu/papers/mlir93/ mlir93.html).
- *Intuition.* No proven theory. The answer just appears, possibly by unconsciously recognizing an underlying pattern. Expert systems do not implement this type of inference yet. ANS may hold promise for this type of inference since they can extrapolate from their training rather than just provide a conditioned response or interpolation. That is, a neural net will always give its best guess for a solution.
- *Heuristics.* Rules of thumb based on experience.
- *Generate and test.* Trial and error. Often used with planning for efficiency.
- *Abduction.* Reasoning back from a true conclusion to the premises that may have caused the conclusion.
- *Default.* In the absence of specific knowledge, assume general or common knowledge by default.
- *Autoepistemic.* Self-knowledge, such as what color the sky appears to you.
- *Nonmonotonic.* Previous knowledge may be incorrect when new evidence is obtained.
- *Analogy.* Inferring a conclusion based on the similarities to another situation. Neural networks do this by recognizing patterns in the data and then extrapolating to a new situation.

Although not explicitly shown in Figure 3.14, **commonsense knowledge** is a combination of all of these types based on our experience. Commonsense reasoning is the type that people use in ordinary situations, and is very difficult for computers. The major attempt to build a huge database of commonsense knowledge suitable for computer use has been underway by Doug Lenat since the 1980s and practical applications are now being made (http://www.OpenCyc.org). This database consists of many assertions and rules that may be

Figure 3.14 Types of Inference

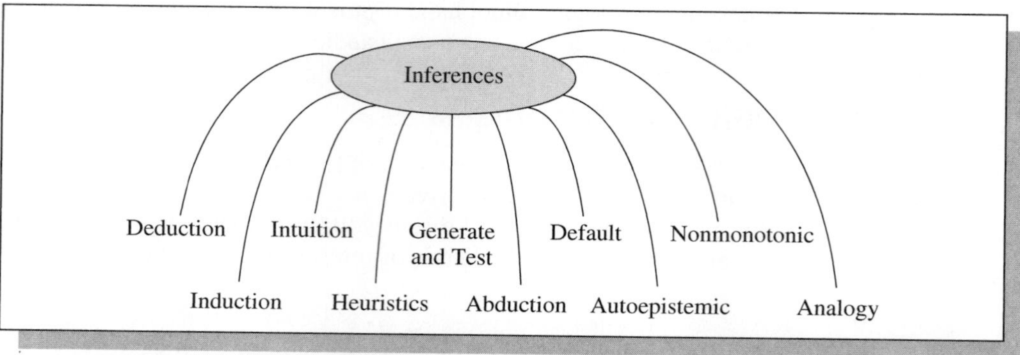

used for applications ranging from better speech understanding to more efficient construction of ontologies. The interesting thing is that the adage, "Bigger is better," does not always hold. In the following communication from Doug Lenat (personal email) he explains why:

> "3 million rules have been entered by hand; through generalization and factoring we have that number down to 1.5 million today. We try to make the number as small as possible, not as large—we could easily expand this into over a billion rules, e.g. Consider 2 types of animals—no rat is also a camel. Knowing 10,000 animals, one could write 100,000,000 rules of that sort. Instead, Cyc has 10,001 rules: Linnaean taxon relationships plus a rule that says that two taxons that aren't known to stand in a genl/spec relationship are disjoint. The "tens of thousands of rules" is talking about a very special type of rule, namely one of a certain level of complexity, through which NONE of the assertions I just mentioned would count as rules at all.
>
> We have a couple million assertions because that's as few as we can get away with for the content. We don't TRY to make the number large, because it would slow things down, but if we WANTED it to be large we could take 10,001 of the (2 million) assertions in the current knowledge base, and equivalently replace them with 100,000,000 only slightly less general-seeming rules. That would be bad."

The application of fuzzy logic to commonsense reasoning is discussed in Chapter 5.

One of the most often-used methods of drawing inferences is **deductive logic**, which has been used since ancient times to determine the validity of an **argument**. Although people commonly use the word argument to describe an angry "exchange of views," it has a very different meaning in logic. A logical argument is a group of statements in which the last is claimed to be justified on the basis of the previous ones in the **chain of reasoning**. One type of logical argument is the syllogism, which was discussed in Chapter 2. As an example of a syllogism:

```
Premise:     Anyone who can program is intelligent
Premise:     John can program
Conclusion: Therefore, John is intelligent
```

In an argument the premises are used as evidence to support the conclusions. The premises are also called the **antecedent** and the conclusion is called the **consequent**. The essential characteristic of deductive logic is that the true conclusion *must* follow from true premises. A line is customarily drawn to separate the premises from the conclusion, as shown above, so that it is not necessary to explicitly label the premises and conclusion.

The argument could have been written more briefly as:

```
Anyone who can program is intelligent
John can program
∴ John is intelligent
```

where the three dots, ∴, mean "therefore."

Let's take a closer look at syllogistic logic now. The main advantage of studying syllogisms is that it is a simple, well-understood branch of logic that can be completely proven. Also, syllogisms are often useful since they can be expressed in terms of IF-THEN rules. For example, the previous syllogism can be rephrased as:

```
IF   Anyone who can program is intelligent and
     John can program
THEN John is intelligent
```

In general, a syllogism is any valid deductive argument having two premises and a conclusion. The classic syllogism is a special type called a **categorical syllogism**. The premises and conclusions are defined as categorical statements of the following four forms, as shown in Table 3.2.

Table 3.2 Categorical Statements

Form	Schema	Meaning
A	All S is P	universal affirmative
E	No S is P	universal negative
I	Some S is P	particular affirmative
O	Some S is not P	particular negative

Note that in logic, the term *schema* specifies the logical form of the statement. This also illustrates another use of the word schema, which is different from its AI use, discussed in Chapter 2. In logic, the word schema is used to show the essential form of an argument. Schemata may also specify the logical form of an entire syllogism as in:

```
All M is P
All S is M
∴ All S is P
```

The subject of the conclusion, S, is called the **minor term** while the predicate of the conclusion, P, is called the **major term**. The premise containing the major term is called the **major premise** and the premise containing the minor term is called the **minor premise**. For example:

```
Major Premise:   All M is P
Minor Premise:   All S is M
Conclusion: All S is P
```

is a syllogism said to be in **standard form**, with its major and minor premises identified. The **subject** is the object that is being described while the **predicate** describes some property of the subject. For example, in the statement:

```
All microcomputers are computers
```

the subject is "microcomputers" and the predicate is "computers." In the statement:

```
All computers with 1 Gigabyte of RAM
are computers with a lot of memory
```

the subject is "computers with 1 Gigabyte" and the predicate is "computers with a lot of memory."

The forms of the categorical statements have been identified since ancient times by the letters A, E, I, and O. The A and I indicate affirmative and are thought to come from the first two vowels of the Latin word *affirmo* (I affirm); while E and O come from *nego* (I negate). The A and I forms are said to be **affirmative in quality** by affirming that the subjects are included in the predicate class. The E and O forms are **negative in quality** because the subjects are excluded from the predicate class.

The verb *is* comes from **copula** in Latin, which means to connect. The copula connects the two parts of the statement. In the standard categorical syllogism, the copula is the present tense form of the verb *to be*. So another version is:

```
All S are P
```

The third term of the syllogism, M, is called the **middle term** and is common to both premises. The middle term is essential because a syllogism is defined such that the conclusion cannot be inferred from either of the premises alone. So the argument:

```
All A is B
All B is C
∴ All A is B
```

is not a valid syllogism since it follows from the first premise alone.

The **quantity** or **quantifier** describes the portion of the class included. The quantifiers *All* and *No* are **universal** because they refer to entire classes. The quantifier *Some* is called **particular** because it refers to just part of the class.

The **mood** of a syllogism is defined by the three letters that give the form of the major premise, minor premise, and conclusion, respectively. For example, the syllogism:

```
All M is P
All S is M
∴ All S is P
```

is an AAA mood.

There are four possible patterns of arranging the S, P, and M terms, as shown in Table 3.3. Each pattern is called a figure, with the number of the **figure** specifying its type.

Table 3.3 Patterns of Categorical Statements

	Figure 1	Figure 2	Figure 3	Figure 4
Major Premise	M P	P M	M P	P M
Minor Premise	S M	S M	M S	M S

So the previous example is completely described as an AAA-1 syllogism type. Just because an argument has a syllogistic form does not mean that it is a valid syllogism. Consider the AEE-1 syllogism form:

```
All M is P
No S is M
∴ No S is P
```

which is not a valid syllogism, as can be seen from the example:

```
All microcomputers are computers
No mainframe is a microcomputer
∴ No mainframe is a computer
```

Rather than trying to think up examples to prove the validity of syllogistic arguments, there is a **decision procedure** that can be used. A decision procedure is a method of proving validity. A decision procedure is some general mechanical method or algorithm by which the process of determining validity can be automated. While there are decision procedures for syllogistic logic and propositional logic, Church showed in 1936 that there is none for predicate logic. Instead, people or computers must apply creativity to generate proofs. In the 1970s, programs such as the Automated Mathematician and Eurisko by Doug Lenat rediscovered mathematical proofs of the Goldbach's Conjecture and the Unique Factorization Theorem. Mathematics journals have not been keen on publishing creative works by computers in the same way literary journals and magazines have not exactly encouraged the submission of poems or novels by computers. (They're only willing to pay a little bit.)

The decision procedure for propositions is simply constructing a truth table and examining it for tautology. The decision procedure for syllogisms can be done using Venn diagrams with three overlapping circles representing S, P, and M, as shown in Figure 3.15a. For the syllogism form AEE-1:

```
All M is P
No S is M
∴ No S is P
```

the major premise is illustrated in Figure 3.15b. The lined section of M indicates that there are no elements in that portion. In Figure 3.15c the minor premise is included by lining its portion with no elements. From Figure 3.15c it can be seen that the conclusion of AEE-1 is false since there are some S in P.

As another example, the following EAE-1 is valid as can be seen from Figure 3.16c:

```
No M is P
All S is M
∴ No S is P
```

Venn diagrams that involve "some" quantifiers are a little more difficult to draw. The general rules for drawing categorical syllogisms under the Boolean view that there may be no members in the A and E statements are:

Figure 3.15 Decision Procedure for Syllogism AEE-1

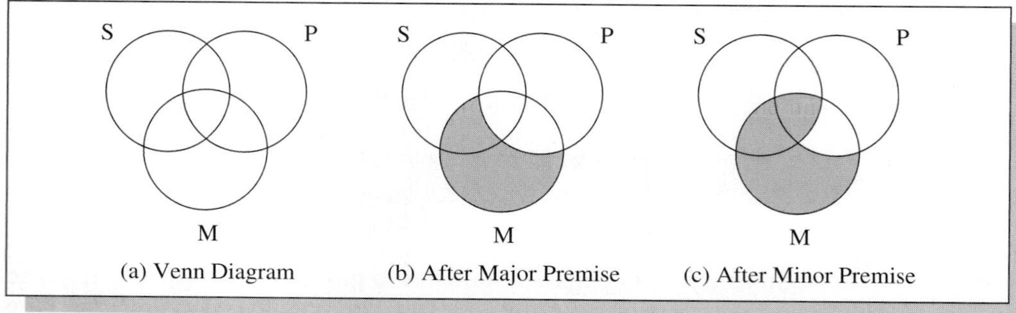

Figure 3.16 Decision Procedure for Syllogism EAE-1

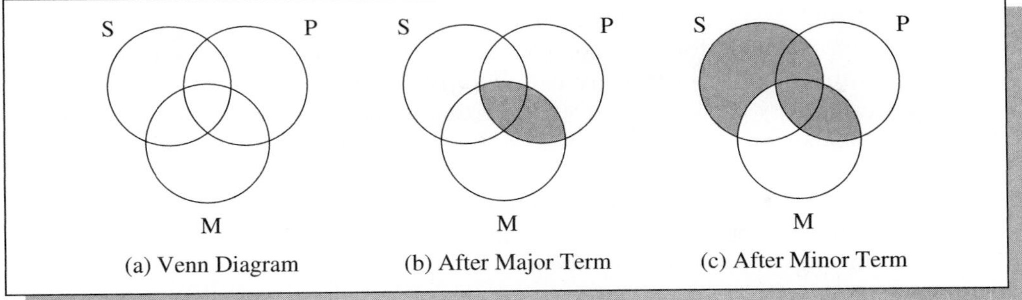

(a) Venn Diagram (b) After Major Term (c) After Minor Term

1. If a class is empty, it is shaded.
2. Universal statements, A and E, are always drawn before particular ones.
3. If a class has at least one member, mark it with an *.
4. If a statement does not specify in which of two adjacent classes an object exists, place an * on the line between the classes.
5. If an area has been shaded, no * can be put in it.

As an example,

```
Some computers are laptops
All laptops are transportable
∴ Some transportables are computers
```

which can be put in IAI-4 type:

```
Some P are M
All M are S
∴ Some S are P
```

Following the rules 2 and 1 for Venn diagrams, we start with the universal statement for the minor premise and shade it, as shown in Figure 3.17a. Next, rule 3 is applied to the particular major premise and a * is drawn, as shown in Figure 3.17b. Since the conclusion "Some transportables are computers" is shown in the diagram, it follows that the argument IAI-4 is a valid syllogism.

Figure 3.17 Syllogism of IAI-4 Type

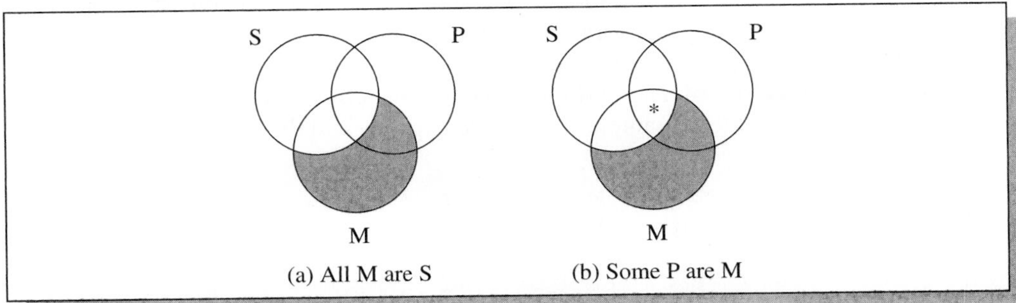

(a) All M are S (b) Some P are M

3.6 RULES OF INFERENCE

Although Venn diagrams are a decision procedure for syllogisms, the diagrams are inconvenient for more complex arguments because they become more difficult to read. However, there is a more fundamental problem with syllogisms because they address only a small portion of the possible logical statements. In particular, categorical syllogisms only address categorical statements of the A, E, I, and O form.

Propositional logic offers another means of describing arguments. In fact, we often use propositional logic without realizing it. For example, consider the following propositional argument:

```
If there is power, the computer will work
There is power
∴ The computer will work
```

This argument can be expressed in a formal way by using letters to represent the propositions as follows:

```
A = There is power
B = The computer will work
```

and so the argument can be written as:

```
A → B
A
∴ B
```

Arguments like this occur often. A general schema for representing arguments of this type is:

```
p → q
p
∴ q
```

where p and q are logical variables that can represent any statements. The use of logical variables in propositional logic allows more complex types of statements than the four syllogistic forms A, E, I, and O. Inference schema of this propositional form is called by a variety of names: **direct reasoning**, **modus ponens**, **law of detachment,** and **assuming the antecedent** (Lakoff 00).

Notice that this example can also be expressed in the syllogistic form:

```
All computers with power will work
This computer has power
∴ This computer will work
```

which demonstrates that *modus ponens* is really a special case of syllogistic logic. Modus ponens is important because it forms the basis of rule-based expert systems.

However, rule-based systems do not rely exclusively on logic because people use more than logic to solve problems. In the real world there may be several competing rules, not just the single rules of syllogisms. The expert system rule-engine must decide which is the appropriate rule to execute just as a person must decide, "Should I eat that last piece of candy and satisfy my craving or not eat it and stay slim?"

It is not enough to just write a bunch of rules in C and have the power of an expert system tool, although this may be all that is required for very simple applications (http://www.ddj.com/documents/s=9064/ddj0301aie001/0301aie001.htm). The real power of an expert systems tool comes into play when there are hundreds or thousands of rules and they conflict. The Rete pattern-matching algorithm is one of the most powerful and yet efficient methods of resolving rule conflicts and is the basis of CLIPS pattern matching (http://www.ddj.com/documents/s=9064/ddj0212ai002/0212aie002.htm).

The compound proposition $p \rightarrow q$ corresponds to the rule while the p corresponds to the pattern that must match the antecedent for the rule to be satisfied. However, as discussed in Chapter 2, the conditional $p \rightarrow q$ is not exactly equivalent to a rule because the conditional is a logical definition defined by a truth table and there are many possible definitions of the conditional.

Generally we will follow the convention of logic theory of using uppercase letters such as A, B, C . . . to represent constant propositions such as "There is power." Small letters such as p, q, r . . . will represent logical variables, which can stand for different constant propositions. Note that this convention is opposite to that of PROLOG, which uses uppercase letters for variables.

This modus ponens schema could also have been written with differently named logical variables as:

$$\begin{array}{l} r \rightarrow s \\ \underline{r \qquad\quad} \\ \therefore\ s \end{array}$$

and the schema would still mean the same.

Another notation for this schema is:

$$r,\ r \rightarrow s;\ \therefore\ s$$

where the comma is used to separate one premise from another and the semicolon indicates the end of the premises. Although so far we have looked at arguments with only two premises, a more general form of an argument is:

$$P_1,\ P_2,\ \ldots\ P_N;\ \therefore\ C$$

where the uppercase letters P_i represent premises such as r, r → s, and C is the conclusion. Notice how this resembles the goal satisfaction statement of PROLOG discussed in Chapter 2.:

```
p :- p1, p2, ... pN.
```

The goal, p, is satisfied if all the subgoals $p_1, p_2, \ldots p_N$ are satisfied. An analogous argument for production rules can be written in the general form:

$$C_1 \wedge C_2 \wedge \ldots C_N \rightarrow A$$

which means that if each condition, C_i, of a rule is satisfied, then the action, A, of the rule is done. As discussed previously, a logical statement of the form above is strictly not equivalent to a rule because the logical definition of the conditional is not the same as a production rule. However, this logical form is a useful intuitive aid in thinking about rules.

The notation of the logic operators AND and OR have different forms in PROLOG compared to the usual ∧ and ∨. The comma between subgoals in PROLOG means a conjunction, ∧, while the disjunction, ∨, is indicated with a semicolon. For example,

```
p :- p1; p2.
```

means that p is satisfied if p_1 or p_2 is satisfied. Conjunctions and disjunctions can be mixed. For example,

```
p :- p1, p2; p3, p4.
```

is the same as the two PROLOG statements:

```
p :- p1, p2.
p :- p3, p4.
```

Although PROLOG has a powerful built-in reasoning strategy, rules created this way are not always suitable for custom use. However it is possible to customize the rule execution using PROLOG so that the knowledge representation and inference strategy can be tuned to the application, such as one that automates pediatric offices (www.visualdatallc.com) and is described in more detail in (Merritt 04).

In general, if the premises and conclusion are all schemata, the argument:

$$P_1, P_2, \ldots P_N; \therefore C$$

is a formally valid deductive argument if and only if:

$$P_1 \wedge P_2 \wedge \ldots P_N \rightarrow C$$

is a tautology. As an example,

$$(p \wedge q) \rightarrow p$$

is a tautology because it is true for any values, T or F, of p and q. You can verify this by constructing the truth table.

The argument of modus ponens,

$$\begin{array}{l} p \rightarrow q \\ \underline{p \quad\quad} \\ \therefore\ q \end{array}$$

is valid because it can be expressed as a tautology:

$$(p \rightarrow q) \wedge p \rightarrow q$$

Note that we are assuming that the arrow has lower precedence than conjunction and disjunction. This saves writing additional parentheses such as:

$$((p \rightarrow q) \wedge p) \rightarrow q$$

The truth table for modus ponens is shown in Table 3.4. It is a tautology because the values of the argument, shown in the rightmost column, are all true no matter what the values of its premises. Notice that in the third, fourth, and fifth columns, the truth values are written under certain operators such as the $\rightarrow$ and $\wedge$. These are called the main connectives because they connect the two main parts of a compound proposition.

Table 3.4 Truth Table for Modus Ponens

p	q	$p \rightarrow q$	$(p \rightarrow q) \wedge p$	$(p \rightarrow q) \wedge p \rightarrow q$
T	T	T	T	T
T	F	F	F	T
F	T	T	F	T
F	F	T	F	T

Although this method of determining valid arguments works, it does require checking every row of the truth table. The number of rows is 2^N, where N is the number of premises and so the rows increase very rapidly with the number of premises. For example, five premises would require 32 rows to be checked while ten premises require 1,024 rows. A shorter method of determining a valid argument is to consider only those rows of the truth table in which the premises are all true. The equivalent definition of a valid argument states that it is valid if and only if the conclusion is true for each of these rows. That is, the conclusion is tautologically implied by the premises. For modus ponens, the $p \rightarrow q$ premise and p premise are both true only in the first row, and so is the conclusion. Hence, modus ponens is a valid argument. If there were any other row in which the premises were all true and the conclusion false, then the argument would be invalid.

The shorter way of expressing the truth table for modus ponens is shown in Table 3.5, where all the rows are explicitly shown. In practice, only those rows that have true premises, such as the first row, need be considered.

Table 3.5 Alternate Short-Form Truth Table for Modus Ponens

		Premises		Conclusion
p	q	$p \rightarrow q$	p	q
T	T	T	T	T
T	F	F	T	F
F	T	T	F	T
F	F	T	F	F

The truth table for modus ponens shows that it is valid because the first row has true premises and a true conclusion, and there are no other rows that have true premises and a false conclusion.

Arguments can be deceptive. To show this, first consider the following valid example of modus ponens:

```
If there are no bugs, then the program compiles
There are no bugs
∴ The program compiles
```

Compare this with the following argument that somewhat resembles modus ponens:

```
If there are no bugs, then the program compiles
The program compiles
∴ There are no bugs
```

Is this a valid argument? The schema for arguments of this type is:

$$\begin{array}{l} p \rightarrow q \\ \underline{q \qquad} \\ \therefore\ p \end{array}$$

and its short-form truth table is shown in Table 3.6.

Table 3.6 Short-Form Truth Table of p → q, q; ∴ p

		Premises		Conclusion
p	q	p → q	q	p
T	T	T	T	T
T	F	F	F	T
F	T	T	T	F
F	F	T	F	F

Notice that this argument is not valid. Although the first row does show that the conclusion is true if all the premises are true, the third row shows that if the premises are true, the conclusion is false. Thus this argument fails the if and only if criteria of a valid argument. Although many programmers wish arguments like this were true, logic (and experience) proves it a fallacy or invalid argument. This particular fallacious argument is called the **fallacy of the converse.** The converse is defined in Table 3.9.

As another example, the argument schema:

$$\begin{array}{l} p \rightarrow q \\ \underline{\sim q \qquad} \\ \therefore\ \sim p \end{array}$$

is valid since Table 3.7 shows the conclusion is true only when the premises are true.

Table 3.7 Short-Form Truth Table of p → q, ~q; ∴ ~p

		Premises		Conclusion
p	q	p → q	~q	~p
T	T	T	F	F
T	F	F	T	F
F	T	T	F	T
F	F	T	T	T

This particular schema is called by a variety of names: **indirect reasoning**, **modus tollens**, and **law of contraposition**.

Modus ponens and modus tollens are rules of inference, sometimes called **laws of inference**. Table 3.8 shows some of the laws of inference.

The Latin name *modus* means "way," while *ponere* means "assert," and *tollere* means to "deny." The real names of the modus rules and their literal meanings are shown in Table 3.9. Modus ponens and modus tollens are short for

Table 3.8 Some Rules of Inference for Propositional Logic

Law of Inference	Schemata	
1. Law of Detachment	$p \rightarrow q$ p $\therefore q$	
2. Law of the Contrapositive	$p \rightarrow q$ $\therefore \sim q \rightarrow \sim p$	
3. Law of Modus Tollens	$p \rightarrow q$ $\sim q$ $\therefore \sim p$	
4. Chain Rule (Law of the Syllogism)	$p \rightarrow q$ $q \rightarrow r$ $\therefore p \rightarrow r$	
5. Law of Disjunctive Inference	$p \vee q$ $\sim p$ $\therefore q$	$p \vee q$ $\sim q$ $\therefore p$
6. Law of the Double Negation	$\sim(\sim p)$ $\therefore p$	
7. De Morgan's Law	$\sim(p \wedge q)$ $\therefore \sim p \vee \sim q$	$\sim(p \vee q)$ $\therefore \sim p \wedge \sim q$
8. Law of Simplification	$p \wedge q$ $\therefore p$	$\sim(p \vee q)$ $\therefore q$
9. Law of Conjunction	p q $\therefore p \wedge q$	
10. Law of Disjunctive Addition	p $\therefore p \vee q$	
11. Law of Conjunctive Argument	$\sim(p \wedge q)$ p $\therefore \sim q$	$\sim(p \wedge q)$ q $\therefore \sim p$

Table 3.9 The Modus Meanings

Rule of Inference Number	Name	Meaning "mood which by..."
1	modus ponendo ponens	affirming, affirms
3	modus tollendo tollens	denying, denies
5	modus tollendo ponens	denying, affirms
11	modus ponendo tollens	affirming, denies

the first two types (Stebbing 50). The Rule of Inference numbers correspond to those in Table 3.8.

The rules of inference can be applied to arguments with more than two premises. For example, consider the following argument:

```
Chip prices rise only if the yen rises.
The yen rises only if the dollar falls and
   if the dollar falls then the yen rises.
Since chip prices have risen,
   the dollar must have fallen.
```

Let the propositions be defined as follows:

```
C = chip prices rise
Y = yen rises
D = dollar falls
```

Recall from Section 2.12 that one of the meanings of the conditional is "p, only if q." A proposition such as "The yen rises only if the dollar falls" has this meaning and so is represented as $C \rightarrow Y$. The entire argument has the following form:

$$
\begin{array}{l}
C \rightarrow Y \\
(Y \rightarrow D) \land (D \rightarrow Y) \\
\underline{C \qquad\quad} \\
\therefore\ D
\end{array}
$$

The second premise has an interesting form, which can be further reduced by using a variant of the conditional. The conditional $p \rightarrow q$ has several variants, which are the converse, **inverse**, and **contrapositive**. These are listed with the conditional, for completeness, in Table 3.10.

Table 3.10 The Conditional and Its Variants

conditional	$p \rightarrow q$
converse	$q \rightarrow p$
inverse	$\sim p \rightarrow \sim q$
contrapositive	$\sim q \rightarrow \sim p$

As usual, it is assumed that the negation operator has a higher priority than the other logical operators and so no parentheses are used around $\sim p$ and $\sim q$.

If the conditional $p \rightarrow q$ and its converse $q \rightarrow p$ are both true, then p and q are equivalent. That is, $p \rightarrow q \land q \rightarrow p$ is equivalent to the **biconditional** $p \leftrightarrow q$ or **equivalence** $p \equiv q$. Notice that the ordinary assignment or equality symbols are written with two short horizontal bars, =, while the equivalence is written with three, ≡. In other words, p and q always take the same truth values. If p is T then q is true and if p is F then q is F. The argument becomes:

```
(1) C → Y
(2) Y ≡ D
(3) C
    ∴ D
```

where numbers are now used to identify the premises. Since Y and D are equivalent from (2), we can substitute D for Y in (1) to yield:

```
(4) C → D
```

where (4) is an inference made on the basis of (1) and (2). Premises (3) and (4) and the conclusion are:

```
(4) C → D
(3) C
    ∴ D
```

which can be recognized as a schema of modus ponens. Hence the argument is valid.

The substitution of one variable that is equivalent to another is a rule of inference called the **rule of substitution**. The rules of modus ponens and substitution are two basic rules of deductive logic.

A formal logic proof is usually written by numbering the premises, conclusion, and inferences as follows:

```
1. C → Y
2. (Y → D) ∧ (D → Y)
3. C                          / ∴ D
4. Y ≡ D                      2 Equivalence
5. C → D                      1 Substitution
6. D                          3,5 Modus Ponens
```

Lines 1, 2, and 3 are the premises and conclusion while 4, 5, and 6 are the inferences obtained. The right-hand column lists the rule of inference and line numbers used to justify the inference.

3.7 LIMITATIONS OF PROPOSITIONAL LOGIC

Consider our familiar classic argument:

```
All men are mortal
Socrates is a man
Therefore, Socrates is mortal
```

We know that this is a valid argument since it is a valid syllogism. Can we prove its validity using propositional logic? To answer this question, let's first write the argument as a schema:

```
p = All men are mortal
q = Socrates is a man
r = Socrates is mortal
```

and so the argument schema is:

```
p
q___
∴ r
```

Notice that there are no logical connectives in the premises or conclusions and so each premise and each conclusion must have a different logical variable. Also, propositional logic has no provision for quantifiers and so there is no way to represent the quantifier "all" in the first premise. The only representation of this argument in propositional logic is thus the schema above of three independent variables.

To determine if this is a valid argument, consider the truth table of three independent variables for all possible combinations of T and F, shown in Table 3.11. The second row of this truth table shows the argument to be invalid because the premises are true while the conclusion is false.

Table 3.11 Truth Table for the Schema p, q; ∴ r

p	q	∴r
T	T	T
T	T	F
T	F	T
T	F	F
F	T	T
F	T	F
F	F	T
F	F	F

The invalidity of this argument should *not* be interpreted as meaning the conclusion is incorrect. Any person would recognize this as a correct argument. The invalidity simply means that *the argument cannot be proven under propositional logic*. The argument can be proven valid if we examine the internal structure of the premises. For example, we would have to attribute some meaning to "all" and recognize "men" as the plural of "man." However, syllogisms and the propositional calculus do not allow the internal structure of propositions to be examined. This limitation is overcome by predicate logic, and this argument is a valid argument under predicate logic. In fact, all of syllogistic logic is a valid subset of first-order predicate logic and can be proven valid under it.

The only valid syllogistic form of the proposition is:

```
If Socrates is a man, then Socrates is mortal
Socrates is a man
Therefore, Socrates is mortal
```

Let:

```
p = Socrates is a man
q = Socrates is mortal
```

The argument becomes:

$$\begin{array}{l} p \rightarrow q \\ \underline{p\quad} \\ \therefore\ q \end{array}$$

which is a valid syllogistic form of modus ponens.

As another example, consider the following classic argument:

```
All horses are animals
Therefore, the head of a horse
   is the head of an animal
```

We know that this argument is correct and yet it cannot be proved under propositional logic, although it can be proven under predicate logic (see Problem 3.12).

3.8 FIRST-ORDER PREDICATE LOGIC

Syllogistic logic can be completely described by predicate logic. Table 3.12 shows the four categorical statements and their representation in predicate logic. In addition to the rules of inference previously discussed, predicate logic has rules that deal with quantifiers.

Table 3.12 Representation of the Four Categorical Syllogisms Using Predicate Logic

Type	Schema	Predicate Representation
A	All S is P	$(\forall x)\ (S(x) \rightarrow P(x))$
E	No S is P	$(\forall x)\ (S(x) \rightarrow \sim P(x))$
I	Some S is P	$(\exists x)\ (S(x) \wedge P(x))$
O	Some S is not P	$(\exists x)\ (S(x) \wedge \sim P(x))$

The Rule of Universal Instantiation essentially states that an individual may be substituted for a universal. For example, if ϕ is any proposition or **propositional function:**

```
(∀ x) ϕ(x)
∴ ϕ(a)
```

is a valid inference, where *a* is an instance. That is, *a* refers to a specific individual while *x* is a variable that ranges over all individuals. For example, this can be used to prove that Socrates is human:

```
(∀ x) H(x)
∴ H(Socrates)
```

where H(x) is the propositional function that says *x* is a human. The above states that for every *x*, that *x* is human, and so by inference Socrates is human.

Other examples of the Rule of Universal Instantiation are:

```
(∀ x) A(x)
∴ A(c)

(∀ y) (B(y) ∨ C(b))
∴ B(a) ∨ C(b)

(∀ x) [A(x) ∧ (∃ x) (B(x) ∨ C(y))]
∴ A(b) ∧ (∃ x) (B(x) ∨ C(y))
```

In the first example, the instance *c* is substituted for x. In the second example, notice that the instance *a* is substituted for *y* but not for *b* since *b* is not included in the **scope** of the quantifier. That is, a quantifier such as ∀ x applies only to x variables. The variables such as x and y used with quantifiers are called **bound** while the others are called **free**. In the third example, the quantifier x has as its scope only A(x). That is, ∀ x does not apply to the existential quantifier ∃ x and its scope over B(x) ∨ C(y). The convention of nested quantifiers such as this is that the scope ends when a new quantifier is used, even if it uses the same variable, such as *x*. The formal proof of the syllogism:

```
All men are mortal
Socrates is a man
∴ Socrates is mortal
```

is shown following, where H = man, M = mortal, and *s* = Socrates:

```
1. (∀ x) (H(x) → M(x))
2. H(s)                    /∴ M(s)
3. H(s) → M(s)             1 Universal Instantiation
4. M(s)                    2,3 Modus Ponens
```

3.9 LOGIC SYSTEMS

A **logic system** is a collection of objects such as rules, axioms, statements, and so forth organized in a consistent manner. The logic system has several goals.

The first goal is to specify the forms of arguments. Since logical arguments are meaningless in a semantic sense, a valid form is essential if the validity of the argument is to be determined. Thus, one important function of a logic system is to determine the **well-formed formulas** (**wffs**) that are used in arguments. Only wffs can be used in logic arguments. For example, in syllogistic logic,

```
All S is P
```

could be a wff, but:

```
All
All is S P
Is S all
```

are not wffs. Although the symbols of the alphabet are meaningless, the sequence of symbols that make up the wff is meaningful.

The second goal of a logic system is to indicate the rules of inference that are valid. The third goal of a logic system is to extend itself by discovering new rules of inference and so extend the range of arguments that can be proven. By extending the range of arguments, new wffs, called **theorems**, can be proven by a logic argument.

When a logic system is well developed it can be used to determine the validity of arguments in a way that is analogous to calculations in systems such as arithmetic, geometry, calculus, physics, and engineering. Logic systems have been developed such as the Sentential or Propositional Calculus, the Predicate Calculus, and so forth. Each system relies on formal definitions of its **axioms** or **postulates**, which are the fundamental definitions of the system. From these axioms people (and sometimes computer programs such as the Automated Mathematician) try to determine what can be proven. Anyone who has studied Euclidian geometry in high school is familiar with axioms and the derivation of geometric theorems. Just as geometric theorems can be derived from geometric axioms, so can logic theorems be derived from logic axioms.

An axiom is simply a fact or **assertion** that cannot be proven from within the system. Sometimes we accept certain axioms because they make "sense" by appealing to commonsense or observation. Other axioms, such as "parallel lines meet at infinity," do not make intuitive sense because they appear to contradict Euclid's axiom of parallel lines as never meeting. However, this axiom about parallel lines meeting at infinity is just as reasonable from a purely logical viewpoint as Euclid's and is the basis of one type of non-Euclidean geometry.

A formal system requires the following:

1. An alphabet of symbols.
2. A set of finite strings of these symbols, the wffs.
3. Axioms, the definitions of the system.

4. Rules of inference, which enable a wff, A, to be deduced as the conclusion of a finite set, G, of other wffs where G= {A1, A2 ... An}. These wffs must be axioms or other theorems of the logic system. For example, a propositional logic system can be defined using only modus ponens to derive new theorems.

If the argument:

$A_1, A_2, \ldots A_N; \therefore A$

is valid, then A is said to be a **theorem** of the formal logic system and is written with the symbol ⊢. For example, Γ ⊢ A means that A is a theorem of the set of wffs, G. A more explicit schema of a proof that A is a theorem is the following:

$A_1, A_2, \ldots A_N \vdash A$

The symbol ⊢, which indicates that the following wff is a theorem, is not a symbol of the system. Instead, ⊢ is a **metasymbol,** because it is used to describe the system itself. An analogy is a computer language such as Java. Although programs can be specified using Java's syntax, there is no syntax in Java for indicating a valid program.

A rule of inference in a formal system specifies exactly how new assertions, the theorems, can be obtained from axioms and previously derived theorems. An example of a theorem is our syllogism about Socrates, written in predicate logic form:

$(\forall x)\ (H(x) \rightarrow M(x)),\ H(s) \vdash M(s)$

where H is the predicate function for man and M is the predicate function for mortal. Since M(s) can be proven from its axioms on the left, it is a theorem of these axioms. However, note that M(Zeus) would not be a theorem since Zeus, the Greek god, is not a man, and there is no alternative way of showing M(Zeus).

If a theorem is a tautology, it follows that Γ is the null set since the wff is always true and so does not depend on any other axioms or theorems. A theorem that is a tautology is written with the symbol ⊨ as in:

$\models A$

For example, if $A \equiv p \vee \sim p$, then:

$\models p \vee \sim p$

states that $p \vee \sim p$ is a theorem, which is a tautology. Notice that whatever values are assigned to p, either T or F, the theorem $p \vee \sim p$ is always true. An assignment of truth values is an **interpretation** of a wff. A **model** is an interpretation in which the wff is true. For example, a model of $p \rightarrow q$ is p = T and q = T. A wff is called **consistent** or **satisfiable** if there is an interpretation that makes it true, and **inconsistent** or **unsatisfiable** if the wff is false in *all* interpretations. An example of an inconsistent wff is $p \land \sim p$.

A wff is **valid** if it is true in all interpretations; else it is **invalid**. For example, the wff $p \lor \sim p$ is valid, while $p \rightarrow q$ is an invalid wff since it is not true for p = T and q = F. A wff is **proved** if it can be shown to be valid. All propositional wffs can be proved by the truth table method since there is only a finite number of interpretations for wffs and so the propositional calculus is **decidable**. However, the predicate calculus is not decidable since there is no general method of proof like truth tables for all predicate calculus wffs.

One example of a valid predicate calculus wff that can be proved is that for any predicate B,

$$(\exists x)\ B(x) \rightarrow \sim [(\forall x) \sim B(x)]$$

which shows how the existential quantifier can be replaced by the universal quantifier. This predicate calculus wff is therefore a theorem.

There is a big difference between an expression like $\vdash A$ and $\models B$. The *A* is a theorem and so can be proven from the axioms by the rules of inference. The *B* is a wff and there may be no known proof to show its derivation. While propositional logic is decidable, predicate logic is not. That is, there is no mechanical procedure or algorithm for finding the proof of a predicate logic theorem in a finite number of steps. In fact, there is a theoretical proof that there is no decision procedure for predicate logic. However, there are decision procedures for subsets of predicate logic like syllogisms and propositional logic. Sometimes predicate logic is referred to as **semidecidable** because of this.

Note that PROLOG is based on predicate logic. In the first rush of enthusiasm toward it in the 1970s, the Japanese announced plans for their 5th Generation ultra-advanced computer system. This system would have allowed natural language input and output and really understood what was being said. However there was not enough computerized commonsense knowledge available nor were the microprocessors of the 1980s sufficiently powerful enough to allow voice recognition with a high degree of accuracy. Now with the Open.Cyc project for commonsense ontologies and good voice recognition with no training, such a system has a stronger chance of success (although not with PROLOG).

As a very simple example of a complete formal system, define the following:

Alphabet : The single symbol "1"
Axiom : The string "1" (which happens to be the same as the symbol 1)
Rule of Inference : If any string $ is a theorem, then so is the string $11. This rule can be written as a Post production rule,

```
$ → $11.
   If $ = 1 then this rule gives $11 = 111.
   If $ = 111 then the rule gives $11 = 11111 and in
      general
      1, 111, 11111, 1111111, ...
```

The strings above are the theorems of this formal system.

Although strings like 11111 do not look like the types of theorems we are used to seeing, they are perfectly valid logic theorems. These particular theorems also have a semantic meaning because they are the odd numbers expressed in a **unary number system** of the single symbol 1. Just as the binary number system has only the alphabet symbols 0 and 1, the unary number system has only the single symbol 1. Numbers in the unary and decimal system are expressed as:

Unary	Decimal
1	1
11	2
111	3
1111	4
11111	5

and so forth.

Notice that because of our rule of inference and axiom, the strings 11, 1111, and so forth cannot be expressed in our formal system. That is, 11 and 1111 are certainly strings from our formal alphabet, but they are not theorems or wffs because they cannot be proven using only the rule of inference and the axiom. This formal system allows only the derivation of the odd numbers, not the even numbers. The axiom "11" must be added in order to be able to derive the even numbers.

Another property of a formal system is **completeness**. A set of axioms is **complete** if every wff can either be proved or **refuted**. The term *refute* means to prove some assertion is false. In a complete system, every logically valid wff is a theorem. However, since predicate logic is not decidable, coming up with a proof depends on our luck and cleverness. Of course, another possibility is writing a computer program that will try to derive proofs and let it grind away.

A further desirable property of a logical system is that it be **sound**. A sound system means that every theorem is a logically valid wff. In other words, a sound system will not allow a conclusion to be inferred that is not a logical consequence of its premises. No invalid arguments will be inferred as valid.

There are different **orders** of logic. A **first-order** language is defined so that the quantifiers operate on objects that are variables such as ∀ x. A **second-order** language would have additional features such as two kinds of variables and quantifiers. In addition to the ordering variables and quantifiers, the second-order logic can have quantifiers that range over function and predicate symbols. An example of second-order logic is the **equality axiom**, which states that two objects are equal if all predicates of them are equal. If P is any predicate of one argument, then:

```
x = y ≡ (∀ P) [P(x) ↔ P(y)]
```

is a statement of the equality axiom using a second-order quantifier, ∀ P, which ranges over all predicates.

3.10 RESOLUTION

The very powerful **resolution** rule of inference introduced by Robinson in 1965 is commonly implemented in theorem-proving AI programs. In fact, resolution is the primary rule of inference in PROLOG. Instead of many different inference rules of limited applicability such as modus ponens, modus tollens, merging, chaining, and so forth, PROLOG uses the one general-purpose inference rule of resolution. This application of resolution makes automatic theorem provers such as PROLOG practical tools for solving problems. Instead of having to try different rules of inference and hoping one succeeds, the single rule of resolution can be applied. This approach can greatly reduce the search space.

As a way of introducing resolution, let's first consider the syllogism about Socrates expressed in PROLOG as follows, where comments are shown with a percent sign:

```
mortal(X) :- man(X).       % All men are mortal
man(socrates).             % Socrates is a man
:- mortal(socrates).       % Query - is Socrates mortal?
yes                        % PROLOG answers yes
```

PROLOG uses a **quantifier-free** notation. Notice that the universal quantifier, ∀, is implied in the statement that all men are mortal.

PROLOG is based on first-order predicate logic. However it also has a number of extensions to make it easier for programming applications. These special programming features violate pure predicate logic and are called **extralogical features**: input/output, cut (which alters the search space), and assert/retract (to alter truth values without any logical justification).

Before resolution can be applied, the wff must be in a **normal** or standard form. The three main types of normal forms are **conjunctive normal form**, clausal form, and its Horn clause subset. The basic idea of normal form is to express wffs in a standard form that uses only the ∧, ∨, and possibly ~. The resolution method is then applied to normal form wffs in which all other connectives and quantifiers have been eliminated. This conversion to normal form is necessary because resolution is an operation on pairs of **disjuncts**, which produces new disjuncts, which simplifies the wff.

The following illustrates a wff in conjunctive normal form, which is defined as the conjunction of disjunctions that are **literals:**

$$(P_1 \lor P_2 \lor \ldots) \land (Q_1 \lor Q_2 \lor \ldots) \land \ldots (Z_1 \lor Z_2 \lor \ldots)$$

Terms such as P_i must be literals, which mean that they contain no logical connectives such as the conditional and **biconditional**, or quantifiers. A literal is an atomic formula or a negated atomic formula. For example, the following wff:

$$(A \lor B) \land (\sim B \lor C)$$

is in conjunctive normal form. The terms within parentheses are clauses:

$A \vee B$ and $\sim B \vee C$

As will be shown later, any predicate logic wff, which includes propositional logic as a special case, can be written as clauses. The full **clausal form** can express any predicate logic formula but may not be as natural or readable for a person. The syntax of PROLOG is the Horn clause subset, which makes mechanical theorem proving by PROLOG much easier and efficient to implement than standard predicate logic notation or full clausal form. As mentioned in Chapter 1, PROLOG allows only one head. A full clausal form expression is generally written in a special form called Kowalski clausal form:

$$A_1, A_2, \ldots A_N \rightarrow B_1, B_2, \ldots B_M$$

which is interpreted as saying that if all the subgoals $A_1, A_2, \ldots A_N$ are true, then one or more of B_1 or $B_2 \ldots$ or B_M are true also. Note that sometimes the direction of the arrow is reversed in this notation. This clause, written in standard predicate notation, is:

$$A_1 \wedge A_2 \ \ldots \ A_N \rightarrow B_1 \vee B_2 \ \ldots \ B_M$$

This can be expressed in **disjunctive form** as the disjunction of literals using the equivalence:

$$p \rightarrow q \equiv \sim p \vee q$$

so:

$$\begin{aligned} A_1 \wedge A_2 \ \ldots \ A_N &\rightarrow B_1 \vee B_2 \ \ldots \ B_M \\ &\equiv \sim(A_1 \wedge A_2 \ \ldots \ A_N) \vee (B_1 \vee B_2 \ \ldots \ B_M) \\ &\equiv \sim A_1 \vee \sim A_2 \ \ldots \ \sim A_N \vee B_1 \vee B_2 \ \ldots \ B_M \end{aligned}$$

where de Morgan's law:

$$\sim(p \wedge q) \equiv \sim p \vee \sim q$$

is used to simplify the last expression.

As discussed in Chapter 1, PROLOG uses a restricted type of clausal form, the Horn clause, in which only one head is allowed:

$$A_1, A_2, \ldots A_N \rightarrow B$$

which is written in PROLOG syntax as:

```
B :- A1, A2, ... AN
```

The problem with trying to prove a theorem directly is the difficulty of deducing it using only the rules of inference and axioms of the system. It may take a very long time to derive a theorem or we may not be clever enough to derive it at all. To prove a theorem is true the classical method of **reductio ad absurdum**, or *method of contradiction*, is used. In this method we try to prove the negated wff is a theorem. If a contradiction results, then the original non-negated wff is a theorem.

The basic goal of resolution is to infer a new clause, the **resolvent**, from two other clauses called **parent clauses**. The resolvent will have fewer terms than the parents. By continuing the process of resolution, eventually a contradiction will be obtained or the process is terminated because no progress is being made. A simple example of resolution is shown in the following argument:

$$\begin{array}{l} A \lor B \\ \underline{A \lor \sim B} \\ \therefore\ A \end{array}$$

One way of seeing how the conclusion follows is by writing the premises as:

$$(A \lor B) \land (A \lor \sim B)$$

One of the Axioms of Distribution is:

$$p \lor (q \land r) \equiv (p \lor q) \land (p \lor r)$$

Applying this to the premises gives:

$$(A \lor B) \land (A \lor \sim B) \equiv A \lor (B \land \sim B) \equiv A$$

where the last step follows since $(B \land \sim B)$ is always false. This follows from the Law of the Excluded Middle, which states that something cannot be both true and false. In fuzzy logic, discussed in Chapter 5, we'll see that this law does not hold. Another way of writing this uses the term **nil** or **null**, which means empty, nothing, or false. For example, a null pointer in C points to nothing, while the Law of the Excluded Middle states

$$(B \land \sim B) \equiv \text{nil}.$$

The example of resolution shows how the parent clauses $(A \lor B)$ and $(A \lor \sim B)$ can be simplified into the resolvent A. Table 3.13 summarizes some basic parent clauses and their resolvents in clause notation, where the comma separating clauses means $\land$.

3.11 RESOLUTION SYSTEMS AND DEDUCTION

Given wffs $A_1, A_2, \ldots A_N$ and a logical conclusion or theorem C, we know:

$$A_1 \land A_2 \ \ldots \ A_N \vdash C$$

Table 3.13 Clauses and Resolvents

Parent Clauses	Resolvent	Meaning
$p \rightarrow q, p$ or $\sim p \vee q, p$	q	Modus Ponens
$p \rightarrow q, q \rightarrow r$ or $\sim p \vee q, \sim q \vee r$	$p \rightarrow r$ or $\sim p \vee r$	Chaining or Hypothetical Syllogism
$\sim p \vee q, p \vee q$	q	Merging
$\sim p \vee \sim q, p \vee q$	$\sim p \vee p$ or $\sim q \vee q$	TRUE (a tautology)
$\sim p, p$	nil	FALSE (a contradiction)

is equivalent to stating that:

$$(1)\quad A_1 \wedge A_2 \ \ldots\ A_N \rightarrow C \equiv \sim(A_1 \wedge A_2 \ \ldots\ A_N) \vee C$$
$$\equiv \sim A_1 \vee \sim A_2 \ \ldots\ \sim A_N \vee C$$

is valid. Suppose we take the negation as follows:

$$\sim[A_1 \wedge A_2 \ \ldots\ A_N \rightarrow C]$$

Now:

$$p \rightarrow q \equiv \sim p \vee q$$

and so the above becomes:

$$\sim[A_1 \wedge A_2 \ \ldots\ A_N \rightarrow C] \equiv \sim[\sim(A_1 \wedge A_2 \ \ldots\ A_N) \vee C]$$

From de Morgan's laws:

$$\sim(p \vee q) \equiv \sim p \wedge \sim q$$

and so the above becomes:

$$(2)\quad \sim[A_1 \wedge A_2 \ \ldots\ A_N \rightarrow C] \equiv [\sim\sim(A_1 \wedge A_2 \ \ldots\ A_N) \wedge \sim C]$$
$$\equiv A_1 \wedge A_2 \ \ldots\ A_N \wedge \sim C$$

Now if (1) is valid, then its negation (2) must be invalid. In other words, if (1) is a tautology then (2) must be a contradiction. Formulas (1) and (2) represent two equivalent ways of proving that a formula C is a theorem. Formula (1) can be used to prove a theorem by checking to see if it is true in all cases. Equivalently, formula (2) can be used to prove a theorem by showing (2) leads to a contradiction.

As mentioned in the previous section, proving a theorem by showing its negation leads to a contradiction is proof by reductio ad absurdum. The primary part of this type of proof is the **refutation**. To refute something means to prove it false. Resolution is a sound rule of inference that is also **refutation complete** because the empty clause will always be the eventual result if there is a contradiction in the set of clauses. Essentially this means that **resolution refutation** will terminate in a finite number of steps if there is a contradiction. Although resolution refutation can't tell us how to *produce* a theorem, it will definitely tell us if a wff *is* a theorem.

As a simple example of proof by resolution refutation, consider the argument:

$$\begin{array}{l} A \rightarrow B \\ B \rightarrow C \\ \underline{C \rightarrow D} \\ \therefore\ A \rightarrow D \end{array}$$

To prove that the conclusion A → D is a theorem by resolution refutation, first convert it to disjunctive form using the equivalence:

$$p \rightarrow q \equiv {\sim}p \lor q$$

So:

$$A \rightarrow D \equiv {\sim}A \lor D$$

and its negation is:

$${\sim}({\sim}A \lor D) \equiv A \land {\sim}D$$

The conjunction of the disjunctive forms of the premises and the negated conclusion gives the conjunctive normal form suitable for resolution refutation.

$$({\sim}A \lor B) \land ({\sim}B \lor C) \land ({\sim}C \lor D) \land A \land {\sim}D$$

The resolution method can now be applied to the premises and conclusion. Figure 3.18 shows a method of representing resolution refutation in the form of a **resolution refutation tree diagram**, where clauses on the same level are

Figure 3.18 Resolution Refutation Tree

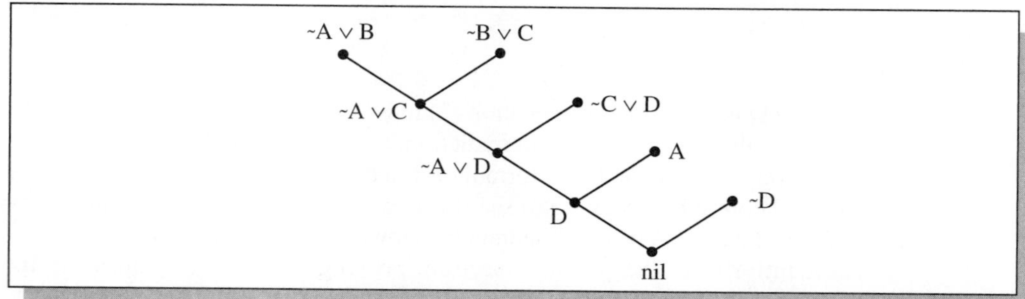

resolved. The root, which is the final resolvent, is nil, as can be verified from the last row of Table 3.13 for ~p, p, and so the original conclusion A → D is a theorem.

3.12 SHALLOW AND CAUSAL REASONING

Resolution systems and production rule systems are two popular paradigms for proving theorems. Although most people think of a theorem in the mathematical sense, we have seen that a theorem is actually the conclusion of a valid logical argument. Now consider an expert system that uses an inference chain. In general, a longer chain represents more causal or deep knowledge, while shallow reasoning commonly uses a single rule or a few inferences. Besides the length of the inference chain, the quality of knowledge in the rules is also a major factor in determining deep and shallow reasoning. Sometimes another definition of shallow knowledge is used, called **experiential knowledge**, which is knowledge based on experience.

The conclusion of an inference chain is a theorem because it is proven by the chain of inference, as demonstrated by the previous example:

$$A \rightarrow B,\ B \rightarrow C,\ C \rightarrow D \vdash A \rightarrow D$$

In fact, expert systems that use an inference chain to establish a conclusion are really using theorems. This result is very important because otherwise we could not use expert systems for causal inference. Instead, expert systems would be restricted to shallow inferences of single rules with no chaining.

Let's look at some rules now in order to better contrast shallow and deep reasoning. As a first example, consider the following rule, where the number in parentheses is for identification purposes only:

```
(1) IF a car has
       a good battery
       good sparkplugs
       gas
       good tires
    THEN the car can move
```

This is a perfectly good rule that could be used in an expert system.

One of the important features of an expert system is the explanation facility, as discussed in Chapter 1. Rule-based expert systems make it easy for the system to explain its reasoning. In this case, if the user asked how the car can move, the expert system could respond by listing its conditional elements:

```
a good battery
good sparkplugs
gas
good tires
```

This is an elementary type of explanation facility since the system lists only the conditional elements of the rule. More sophisticated explanation facilities can be designed to list previous rules that have fired and resulted in the current rule firing. Other explanation facilities may allow the user to ask "What if" type questions to explore alternative reasoning paths.

This rule is also an example of **shallow reasoning**. That is, there is little or no understanding of cause and effect in shallow reasoning because there is little or no inference chain. The previous rule is essentially a heuristic in which all the knowledge is contained in the rule. The rule becomes activated when its conditional elements are satisfied and not because there is any understanding by the expert system of what function the conditional elements perform. In shallow reasoning there is little or no **causal chain** of cause and effect from one rule to another. In the simplest case, the cause and effect are contained in one with no relationship to any other rule. If you think of rules in terms of the chunks of knowledge discussed in Chapter 1, shallow reasoning makes no connections between chunks and so is like a simple reflex reaction.

The advantage of shallow reasoning compared to causal reasoning is the ease of programming. Easier programming means the development time is shorter and the program is smaller, faster, and costs less to develop.

Frame are useful for causal or **deep reasoning**. The term *deep* is often used synonymously for causal reasoning to imply a deep understanding of the subject. However, a deep understanding implies that besides understanding the causal chain by which a process occurs, you also understand the process in an abstract sense.

We can add simple causal reasoning to our rule by defining additional rules such as:

```
(2) IF the battery is good
    THEN there is electricity

(3) IF there is electricity
       and the sparkplugs are good
    THEN the sparkplugs will fire

(4) IF the sparkplugs fire
       and there is gas
    THEN the engine will run

(5) IF the engine runs and
       there are good tires
    THEN the car will move
```

Notice that with causal reasoning, the explanation facility can give a good explanation of what each car component does since each element is specified by a rule. Such a causal system also makes it easier to write a diagnostic system to determine what effect a bad component will have. Causal reasoning may be used for an arbitrary refinement of the operation of a system limited by the speed of execution, memory size, and increasing development cost.

Causal reasoning can be used to construct a **model** of the real system that behaves in all respects like the real system. Such a model can be used for simulation to explore hypothetical reasoning of the "What if" type of queries. However, causal models are neither always necessary nor desirable. For example, the classic MUD expert system serves as a consultant to drilling fluid or mud engineers. Drilling fluid, called mud because of its resemblance to mud, is an important aid in drilling for a number of reasons, such as cooling and lubrication of the bit. MUD diagnoses problems with the mud and suggests treatments.

A causal system would not be of much use because the drilling engineer cannot normally observe the causal chain of events occurring far below the ground. Instead, the engineer can observe only the symptoms on the surface and not the unobservable intermediate events of potential diagnostic significance.

The situation is very different in medicine where physicians have a wide range of diagnostic tests that can be used to verify intermediate events. For example, if a person complains of feeling ill, the physician can check for fever. If there is a fever, there may be an infection and so a blood test may be done. If the blood test reveals a tetanus infection, the physician may check the person for recent cuts from a rusty object. In contrast, if the drilling fluid becomes salty, the drilling engineer may suspect the drill has gone through a salt dome. However, there is no simple way to check this since it's not possible to go into the hole (except by robot), and a seismic test is expensive and not always reliable. Because drilling engineers cannot normally test intermediate hypotheses the way that physicians can, they do not approach diagnostic problems the way that physicians do, and MUD reflects this approach.

Another reason for not using causal reasoning in MUD is that there are a limited number of diagnostic possibilities and symptoms. Most of the relevant tests used by MUD are conducted routinely and input in advance. There is little advantage in an interactive query session with an engineer to explore alternate diagnostic paths if the system knows all the relevant tests and diagnostic paths. If there were many possible diagnostic paths to follow with a verifiable intermediate hypothesis, there would be an advantage to causal knowledge because the engineer could work with the system to prune the search to likely paths.

Because of the increased requirements for causal reasoning, it may become necessary to combine certain rules into a shallow reasoning one. The resolution method with refutation can be used to prove that a single rule is a true conclusion of multiple rules. The single rule is the theorem that will be proved by resolution.

As an example, suppose we want to prove that rule (1) is a logical conclusion of rules (2) – (5). Using the following propositional definitions, the rules can be expressed as follows:

```
B = battery is good          C = car will move
E = there is electricity     F = sparkplugs will fire
G = there is gas             R = engine will run
S = sparkplugs are good      T = there are good tires
```

(1) $B \wedge S \wedge G \wedge T \rightarrow C$
(2) $B \rightarrow E$
(3) $E \wedge S \rightarrow F$
(4) $F \wedge G \rightarrow R$
(5) $R \wedge T \rightarrow C$

The first step in applying resolution refutation is to negate the conclusion or goal rule:

$$(1') \quad \sim(B \wedge S \wedge G \wedge T \rightarrow C) = \sim[\sim(B \wedge S \wedge G \wedge T) \vee C] = \sim[\sim B \vee \sim S \vee \sim G \vee \sim T \vee C]$$

Now each of the other rules is expressed in disjunctive form using equivalences such as:

$$p \rightarrow q \equiv \sim p \vee q \text{ and } \sim(p \wedge q) \equiv \sim p \vee \sim q$$

to yield the following new versions of (2) – (5):

(2') $\sim B \vee E$
(3') $\sim(E \wedge S) \vee F = \sim E \vee \sim S \vee F$
(4') $\sim(F \wedge G) \vee R = \sim F \vee \sim G \vee R$
(5') $\sim(R \wedge T) \vee C = \sim R \vee \sim T \vee C$

As described in the previous section, a convenient way of representing the successive resolvents of (1') – (5') is with a resolution refutation tree, as shown in Figure 3.19. Starting at the top of the tree, the clauses are represented as nodes, which are resolved to produce the resolvent below. For example,

$\sim B \vee E$ and $\sim E \vee \sim S \vee F$

Figure 3.19 Resolution Refutation Tree for the Car Example

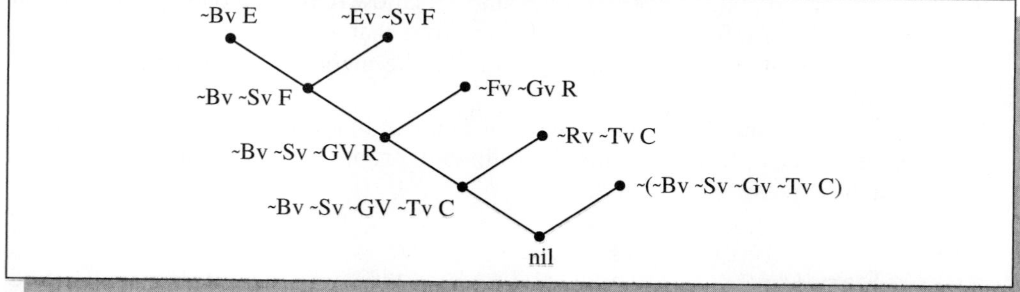

are resolved to infer:

$\sim B \lor \sim S \lor F$

which is then resolved with:

$\sim F \lor \sim G \lor R$

to infer:

$\sim B \lor \sim S \lor \sim G \lor R$

and so forth. For simplicity in drawing, the last resolvents are implied, rather than drawing in every single one.

Since the root of the tree is nil, this is a contradiction. By refutation, the original conclusion:

$B \land S \land G \land T \rightarrow C$

is a theorem since its negation leads to a contradiction. Thus rule (1) does logically follow from rules (2) – (5).

3.13 RESOLUTION AND FIRST-ORDER PREDICATE LOGIC

The resolution method is also used with the first-order predicate logic. In fact, it is the primary inference mechanism of PROLOG. However, before resolution can be applied, a wff must be put in clausal form. As an example,

```
Some programmers hate all failures
No programmer hates any success
∴ No failure is a success
```

Define the following predicates:

```
P(x)   = x is a programmer
F(x)   = x is a failure
S(x)   = x is a success
H(x,y) = x hates y
```

The premises and negated conclusion are written as:

(1) $(\exists x)\ [P(x) \land (\forall y)\ (F(y) \rightarrow H(x,y))]$
(2) $(\forall x)\ [P(x) \rightarrow (\forall y)\ (S(y) \rightarrow \sim H(x,y))]$
(3) $\sim(\forall y)\ (F(y) \rightarrow \sim S(y))$

where the conclusion has been negated in preparation for resolution.

Conversion to Clausal Form

The following nine steps are an algorithm to convert first-order predicate wffs to clausal form. This procedure is illustrated using wff (1) from the previous page.

1. Eliminate conditionals, →, using the equivalence:

   ```
   p → q ≡ ~p ∨ q
   ```

   so the wff (1) becomes:

   ```
   (∃ x) [P(x) ∧ (∀ y) (~F(y) ∨ H(x,y))]
   ```

2. Wherever possible, eliminate negations or reduce the scope of negation to one atom. Use the equivalences shown in Appendix A such as:

   ```
   ~~p ≡ p
   ~(p ∧ q) ≡ ~p ∨ ~q
   ~(∃ x) P(x) ≡ (∀ x) ~P(x)
   ~(∀ x) P(x) ≡ (∃ x) ~P(x)
   ```

3. Standardize variables within a wff so that the bound or dummy variables of each quantifier have unique names. Note that the variable names of a quantifier are dummies. That is,

   ```
   (∀ x) P(x) ≡ (∀ y) P(y) ≡ (∀ z) P(z)
   ```

   and so the standardized form of:

   ```
   (∃ x) ~P(x) ∨ (∀ x) P(x)
   ```

   is:

   ```
   (∃ x) ~P(x) ∨ (∀ y) P(y)
   ```

4. Eliminate existential quantifiers, ∃, by using **Skolem functions**, named after the Norwegian logician, Thoralf Skolem. Consider the wff:

   ```
   (∃ x) L(x)
   ```

   where L(x) is defined as the predicate, which is true if x is < 0. This wff can be replaced by:

   ```
   L(a)
   ```

   where a is a constant such as -1 that makes L(a) true. The a is called a Skolem constant, which is a special case of the Skolem function. For the case in which there is a universal quantifier in front of an existential one,

```
(∀ x) (∃ y) L(x,y)
```

where L(x,y) is true if the integer x is less than the integer y. This wff means that for every integer x there is an integer y that is greater than x. Notice that the formula does not tell how to compute y given a value for x. Assume a function $f(x)$ exists which produces a y greater than x. So the above wff becomes Skolemized as:

```
(∀ x) L(x,f(x))
```

The Skolem function of an existential variable within the scope of a universal quantifier is a function of all the quantifiers on the left. For example,

```
(∃ u) (∀ v) (∀ w) (∃ x) (∀ y) (∃ z) P(u,v,w,x,y,z)
```

is Skolemized as:

```
(∀ v) (∀ w) (∀ y) P(a,v,w,f(v,w),y,g(v,w,y))
```

where a is some constant and the second Skolem function, g, must be different from the first function, f. Our example wff becomes:

```
P(a) ∧ (∀ y) (~F(y) ∨ H(a,y))
```

5. Convert the wff to **prenex form**, which is a sequence of quantifiers, Q, followed by a **matrix** M. In general, the quantifiers can be either ∀ or ∃. However, in this case step 4 has already eliminated all existential quantifiers and so the Q can only be ∀. Also, since each ∀ has its own dummy variable, all the ∀ can be moved to the left of the wff and the scope of each ∀ can be the entire wff.

   Our example becomes:

```
(∀ y) [P(a) ∧ (~F(y) ∨ H(a,y)]
```

   where the matrix is the term in brackets.

6. Convert the matrix to conjunctive normal form, which is a conjunctive of clauses. Each clause is a disjunction. Our example is already in conjunctive normal form where one clause is P(a) and the other is (~F(y) ∨ H(a,y)). If necessary, the following distributive rule can be used as necessary to put the matrix in conjunctive normal form:

```
p ∨ (q ∧ r) ≡ (p ∨ q) ∧ (p ∨ r)
```

7. Drop the universal quantifiers as unnecessary since all the variables in a wff at this stage must be bound. The wff is now the matrix. Our example wff becomes:

```
P(a) ∧ (~F(y) ∨ H(a,y))
```

8. Eliminate the ∧ signs by writing the wff as a set of clauses. Our example is:

```
{ P(a), ~F(y) ∨ H(a,y) }
```

which is usually written without the braces as the clauses:

```
P(a)
~F(y) ∨ H(a,y)
```

9. Rename variables in clauses, if necessary, so that the same variable name is used in only one clause. For example, if we had the clauses:

```
P(x) ∧ Q(x) ∨ L(x,y)
~P(x) ∨ Q(y)
~Q(z) ∨ L(z,y)
```

these could be renamed as:

```
P(x1) ∧ Q(x1) ∨ L(x1,y1)
~P(x2) ∨ Q(y2)
~Q(z) ∨ L(z,y3)
```

If we carry out the procedure to convert to clausal form the second premise and the negated conclusion of our example, we finally obtain the clauses:

```
(1a) P(a)
(1b) ~F(y) ∨ H(a,y)
(2a) ~P(x) ∨ ~S(y) ∨ ~H(x,y)
(3a) F(b)
(3b) S(b)
```

where the numbers refer to the original premises and negated conclusion. Thus, premises (1) and (3) are converted to two clauses with suffixes (a) and (b), while premise (2) is converted to the single clause (2a).

Unification and Rules

Once the wffs have been converted to clausal form, it is usually necessary to find appropriate **substitution instances** for the variables. That is, clauses such as:

```
~F(y) ∨ H(a,y)
F(b)
```

cannot be resolved on the predicate *F* until the arguments of *F* match. The process of finding substitutions for variables to make arguments match is called **unification**.

Unification is one feature that distinguishes expert systems from simple decision trees. Without unification, the conditional elements of rules could match only constants. This means that a specific rule would have to be written for every possible fact. For example, suppose someone wanted to sound a fire alarm if a sensor indicated smoke. If there are N sensors, you would need a rule for each sensor as follows:

```
IF sensor 1 indicates smoke THEN sound fire alarm 1
IF sensor 2 indicates smoke THEN sound fire alarm 2
...
IF sensor N indicates smoke THEN sound fire alarm N
```

However, with unification, a variable called ?N can be used for the sensor identifier so that one rule can be written as follows:

```
IF sensor ?N indicates smoke
THEN sound fire alarm ?N
```

When two complementary literals are unified, they can be eliminated by resolution. For the two preceding clauses, the substitution of *y* by *b* gives:

```
~F(b) ∨ H(a,b)
F(b)
```

The predicate *F* has now been unified and can be resolved into:

```
H(a,b)
```

A substitution is defined as the simultaneous replacement of variables by terms that differentiate from the variables. The terms may be constants, variables, or functions. The substitution of terms for variables is indicated by the set:

$$\{ t_1/v_1,\ t_2/v_2\ \dots\ t_N/v_N \}$$

If θ is such a set and A an argument, then Aθ is defined as the substitution instance of A. For example, if:

$$\theta = \{ a/x,\ f(y)/y,\ x/z \}$$
$$A = P(x) \vee Q(y) \vee R(z)$$

Then:

$$A\theta = P(a) \vee Q(f(y)) \vee R(x)$$

Notice that the substitution is simultaneous, so that we get R(x) and not R(a).

Suppose there are two clauses C_1 and C_2 defined as:

$$C_1 = \sim P(x)$$
$$C_2 = P(f(x))$$

One possible unification of P is:

$$C_1' = C_1 \{ f(x)/x \} = \sim P(f(x))$$

Another possible unification for P is the two substitutions using the constant *a:*

$$C_1'' = C_1 \{ f(a)/x \} = \sim P(f(a))$$
$$C_2' = C_2 \{ a/x \} = P(f(a))$$

Notice that P(f(x)) is more general than P(f(a)) since there are infinitely many instances of P(f(x)) that can be produced by substituting a constant for x. A clause like C_1 is called the **most general clause.**

In general, a substitution θ is called a **unifier** for a set of clauses $\{A_1, A_2, \ldots A_n\}$ if and only if $A_1\theta = A_2\theta = \ldots A_n\theta$. A set that has a unifier is called **unifiable**. The **most general unifier (mgu)** is that from which all the other unifiers are instances. This can be expressed more formally by stating that θ is the most general unifier if and only if for each unifier, α, of a set, there is a substitution β such that:

$$\alpha = \theta\beta$$

where $\theta\beta$ is the compound substitution created by first applying θ and then β. The **Unification Algorithm** is a method of finding the most general unifier for a finite unifiable set of arguments.

For our example with clauses (1a) –(3b), the results of substitution and unification are shown in the resolution refutation tree of Figure 3.20. Since the root is nil, the negated conclusion is false and so the conclusion is valid that "no failure is a success."

Figure 3.20 Resolution Refutation Tree to Prove No Failure Is a Success

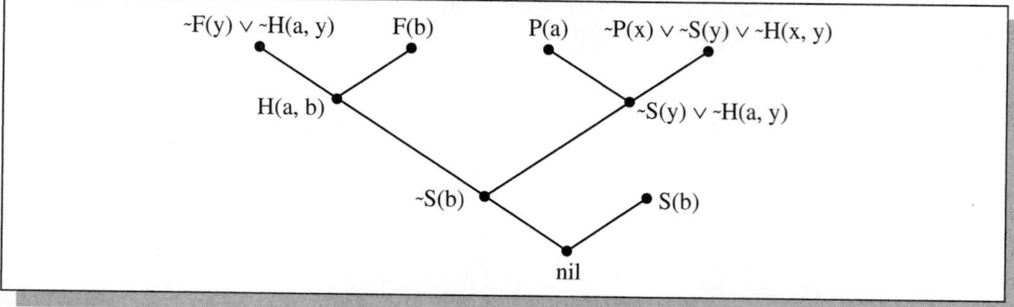

The examples used so far are very simple and their resolution is straightforward, although tedious for a human. However, in many other situations the resolution process may lead to a dead end and so backtracking is necessary to try alternative clauses for resolution. Although resolution is very powerful and is the basis of PROLOG, it may be inefficient for some problems. One of the problems with resolution is that it has no efficient built-in search strategy and so the programmer must supply heuristics, such as the PROLOG cut, for efficient searching.

A number of modified versions of resolution have been investigated, such as unit preference, input resolution, linear resolution, and set of support. The main advantage of resolution is that it is a single powerful technique that is adequate for many cases. This makes it easier to build a mechanical system such as PROLOG than systems that attempt to implement many different rules of inference. Another advantage of resolution is that when successful, resolution automatically provides a proof by showing the sequence of steps to a nil.

3.14 FORWARD AND BACKWARD CHAINING

A group of multiple inferences that connect a problem with its solution is called a **chain**. A chain that is searched or traversed from a problem to its solution is called a forward chain. Another way of describing forward chaining is reasoning from facts to the conclusions that follow from the facts. A chain that is traversed from a hypothesis back to the facts that support the hypothesis is a backward chain. Another way of describing a backward chain is in terms of a goal that can be accomplished by satisfying subgoals. As this shows, the terminology used to describe forward and backward chaining depends on the problem being discussed.

Chaining can be easily expressed in terms of inference. For example, suppose we have rules of the modus ponens type:

$$\begin{array}{l} p \rightarrow q \\ \underline{p \qquad\;} \\ \therefore\ q \end{array}$$

that form a chain of inference, such as the following:

```
elephant(x)  →  mammal(x)
mammal(x)  →  animal(x)
```

These rules may be used in a causal chain of forward inference, which deduces that Clyde is an animal given that Clyde is an elephant. The inference chain is illustrated in Figure 3.21. Notice that the same diagram also illustrates backward chaining.

In Figure 3.21 the causal chain is represented by the sequence of **bars**, **|**, connecting the consequent of one rule to the antecedent of the next. A bar also indicates the unification of variables to facts. For example, the variable x in the predicate elephant(x) must first be unified with the fact elephant(Clyde) before

Figure 3.21 Causal Forward Chain

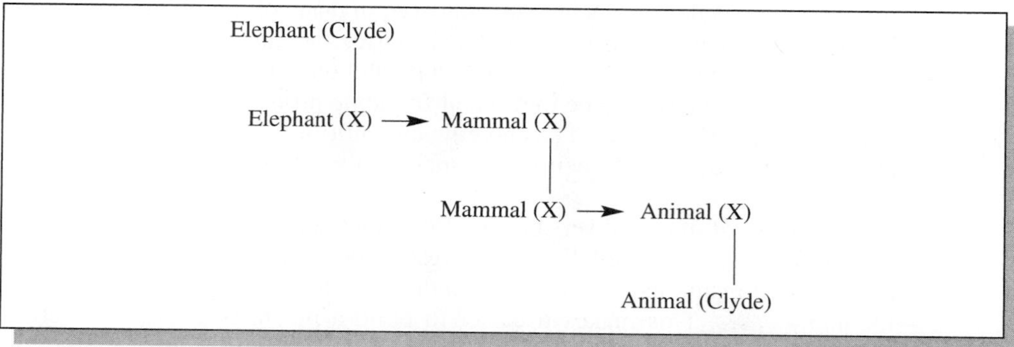

the elephant rule can be applied. The causal chain is really a sequence of implications and unifications, as shown in Figure 3.22.

Backward chaining is the reverse process. Suppose we want to prove the hypothesis animal(Clyde). The central problem of backward chaining is to find a chain linking the evidence to the hypothesis. The fact elephant(Clyde) is called the **evidence** in backward chaining to indicate it is used to support the hypothesis, like the way that evidence in a court is used to prove the guilt or innocence of the defendant.

As a simple example of forward and backward chaining, suppose you are driving and suddenly see a police car with flashing lights and siren. By forward chaining, you may infer that the police want you or someone else to stop. That is, the initial facts support two possible conclusions. If the police car pulls up right in back of you or the police wave at you, a further inference is that they want you rather than someone else. Adopting this as a working hypothesis, you can apply backward chaining to reason why.

Some possible intermediate hypotheses are littering, speeding, malfunctioning equipment, and driving a stolen vehicle. Now you examine the evidence to support these intermediate hypotheses. Was it the beer bottle that you threw out the window, going 100 in a 30 miles per hour speed zone, the broken tail-lights or the license plates identifying the stolen car you're driving? In this case, each

Figure 3.22 Explicit Causal Chain

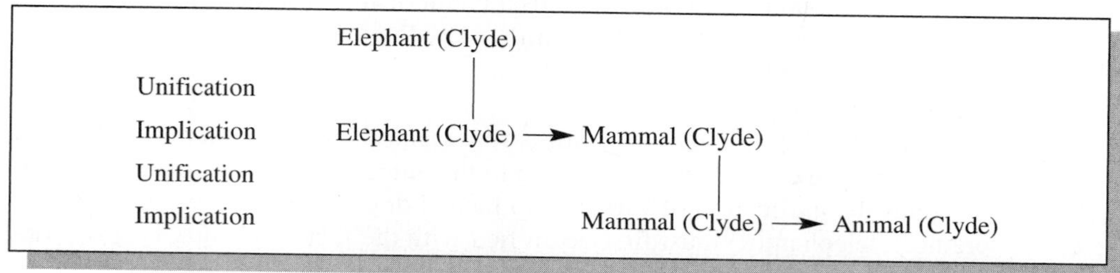

piece of evidence supports an intermediate hypothesis and so they are all true. Any or all of these intermediate hypotheses are possible reasons to prove the working hypothesis that the police want you.

It's helpful to visualize forward and backward chaining in terms of a path through a problem space in which the intermediate states correspond to intermediate hypotheses under backward chaining or intermediate conclusions under forward chaining. Table 3.14 summarizes some of the common characteristics of forward and backward chaining. Note that the characteristics in this table are meant only as a guide. It is certainly possible to do diagnosis in a forward-chaining system and planning in a backward-chaining one. In particular, explanation is facilitated in backward chaining because the system can easily explain exactly what goal it is trying to satisfy. In forward chaining, explanation is not so easily facilitated because the subgoals are not explicitly known until discovered.

Figure 3.23 illustrates the basic concept of forward chaining in a rule-based system. Rules are triggered by the facts that satisfy their antecedent or left-hand-sides (LHS). For example, the rule R_1 must be satisfied by facts B and C for it to be activated. However, only fact C is present, and so R_1 is not activated. Rule R_2 is activated by facts C and D, which are present and so R_2 produces the intermediate fact H. Other satisfied rules are R_3, R_6, R_7, R_8, and R_9. The execution of rules R_8 and R_9 produce the conclusions of the forward-chaining process. These conclusions may be other facts, output, and so forth.

Forward chaining is called **bottom-up reasoning** because it reasons from the low-level evidence, facts, to the top-level conclusions that are based on the facts. Bottom-up reasoning in an expert system is analogous to bottom-up conventional programming, which was discussed in Chapter 1. Facts are the elementary units of the knowledge-based paradigm since they cannot be decomposed into any smaller units that have meaning. For example, the fact "duck" has definite meanings as a noun and as a verb. However, if it is decomposed any further, the result is the letters d, u, c, and k, which have no special meaning. In conventional programs the basic units of meaning are **data**.

By custom, higher-level constructs that are composed of lower-level ones are put at the top. So reasoning from the higher-level constructs such as

Table 3.14 Some Characteristics of Forward and Backward Chaining

Forward Chaining	Backward Chaining
Planning, monitoring, control	Diagnosis
Present to future	Present to past
Antecedent to consequent	Consequent to antecedent
Data driven, bottom-up reasoning	Goal driven, top-down reasoning
Work forward to find what solutions follow from the facts	Work backward to find facts that support the hypothesis
Breadth-first search facilitated	Depth-first search facilitated
Antecedents determine search	Consequents determine search
Explanation not facilitated	Explanation facilitated

Figure 3.23 Forward Chaining

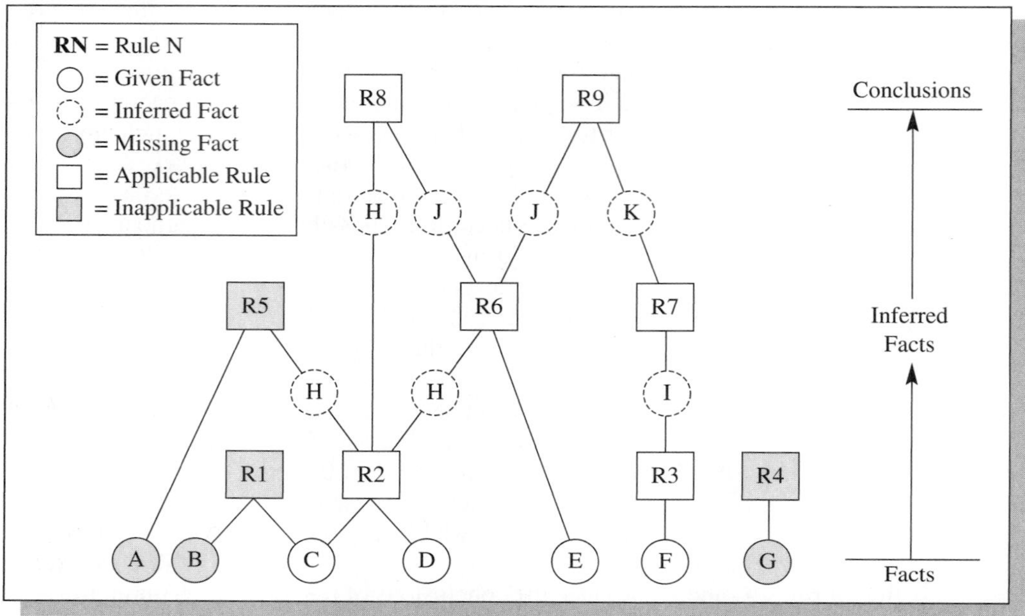

hypotheses down to the lower-level facts that may support the hypotheses is called **top-down reasoning** or backward chaining. Figure 3.24 illustrates the concept of backward chaining. In order to prove or disprove hypotheses H, at least one of the intermediate hypotheses, H_1, H_2, or H_3, must be proven. Notice that this diagram is drawn as an AND-OR tree to indicate that in some cases, such as H_2, all its lower-level hypotheses must be present to support H_2. In other cases, such as the top-level hypotheses, H, only one lower-level hypothesis is necessary. In backward chaining the system will commonly elicit evidence from the user to aid in proving or disproving hypotheses. This contrasts with a forward-chaining system, in which all the relevant facts are usually known in advance.

If you look back at Figure 3.4 in Section 3.2, you will see that the decision net is organized very well for backward chaining. The top-level hypotheses are the different types of raspberries such as flowering raspberry, black raspberry, wineberry, and red raspberry. The evidence to support these hypotheses is lower down. The rules to identify a raspberry can be easily written. For example,

```
IF the leaves are simple THEN flowering raspberry
```

One important aspect of eliciting evidence is asking the right questions. The right questions are those that improve the efficiency in determining the correct answer. One obvious requirement for this is that the expert system should ask questions that deal only with the hypotheses that it is trying to prove. While there may be hundreds or thousands of questions that the system could ask about, there is a cost in time and money to obtain the evidence to answer the

Figure 3.24 Backward Chaining

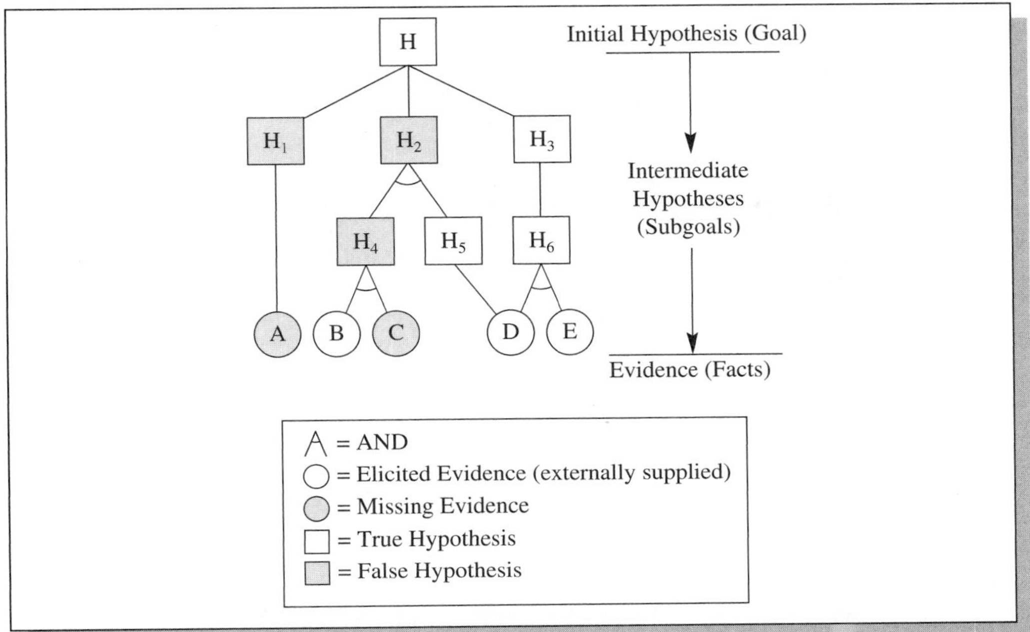

questions. Also, accumulating certain types of evidence such as medical test results may be uncomfortable and possibly hazardous to the patient (in fact, it's difficult to think of a pleasurable medical test).

Ideally the expert system should also allow the user to volunteer evidence even if the system has not asked for it. Allowing the user to volunteer evidence speeds up the backward-chaining process and makes the system more convenient for the user. The volunteered evidence may let the system skip some links in the causal chain or pursue a completely new approach. The disadvantage is that more complex programming of the expert system is involved since the system may not follow a chain link by link.

Good applications for forward and backward chaining are shown in Figure 3.25. For simplicity these diagrams are drawn as trees instead of a general network. A good application for forward chaining occurs if the tree is wide and not very deep. This is because forward chaining facilitates a breadth-first search. That is, forward chaining is good if the search for conclusions proceeds level by level. In contrast, backward chaining facilitates a depth-first search. A good tree for depth-first search is narrow and deep.

Notice that the structure of the rules determines the search for a solution. That is, the activation of a rule depends on the patterns that the rule is designed to match. The patterns on the LHS determine whether a rule can become activated by facts. The actions on the RHS determine the facts that are asserted and deleted and so affect other rules. An analogous situation exists for backward chaining except that hypotheses are used instead of rules. Of course, an intermediate

Figure 3.25 Forward and Backward Chaining

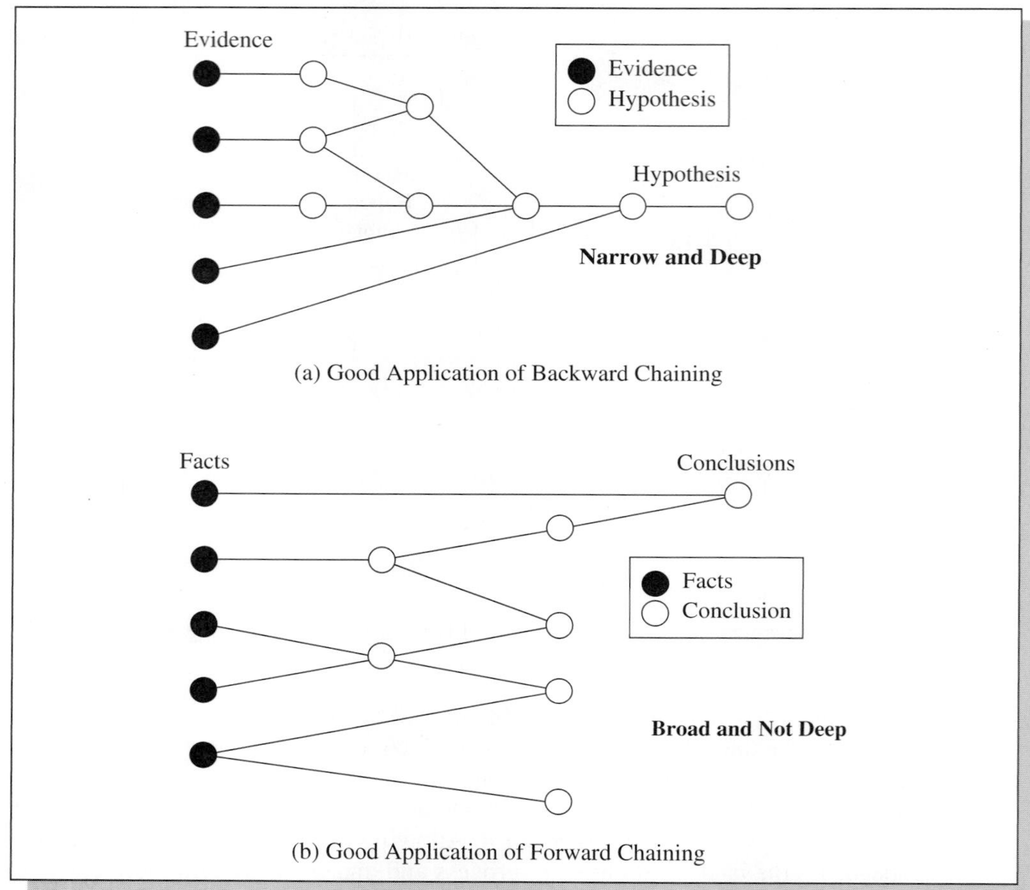

(a) Good Application of Backward Chaining

(b) Good Application of Forward Chaining

hypothesis may be simply a rule that is matched on its consequent instead of its antecedent.

As a very simple example, consider the following IF-THEN type rules:

```
IF A THEN B
IF B THEN C
IF C THEN D
```

If fact A is given and the inference engine is designed to match facts against antecedents, then the intermediate facts B and C will be asserted and conclusion D. This process corresponds to forward chaining. The inference engine is the heart of an expert system.

In contrast, if the fact (actually hypothesis) D is asserted and the inference engine matches facts against consequents, the result corresponds to backward chaining. In systems designed for backward chaining, such as PROLOG, the backward-chaining mechanism includes a number of features, such as automatic backtracking, to facilitate backward chaining.

Backward chaining can be accomplished in a forward-chaining system and vice versa by redesign of the rules. For example, the previous rules for forward chaining can be rewritten as:

```
IF D THEN C
IF C THEN B
IF B THEN A
```

Now C and B are considered as subgoals or intermediate hypotheses that must be satisfied to satisfy the hypothesis D. The evidence A is the fact that indicates the end of the generation of subgoals. If there is a fact A, then D is supported and considered true under this chain of backward inference. If there is no A, then the hypothesis D is unsupported and considered false.

One difficulty with this approach is efficiency. A backward-chaining system facilitates depth-first search while a forward-chaining system facilitates breadth-first search. Although you can write a backward-chaining application in a forward-chaining system and vice versa, the system will not be as efficient in its search for a solution. The second difficulty is a conceptual one. The knowledge elicited from the expert will have to be altered to meet the demands of the inference engine. For example, a forward-chaining inference engine matches the antecedent of rules while a backward-chaining one matches the consequent. That is, if the expert's knowledge is naturally backward chaining, it will have to be totally restructured to cast it in a forward-chaining mode, and vice versa.

3.15 OTHER METHODS OF INFERENCE

A number of other types of inference are sometimes used with expert systems. While these methods are not as general purpose as deduction, they are very useful.

Analogy

Besides deduction and induction, another powerful inference method is **analogy**. The basic idea of reasoning by analogy is to try and relate old situations as a guide to new ones. All living creatures are very good at applying analogical reasoning in their lives, which is essential because of the tremendous number of new situations that are encountered in the real world. Rather than treating every new situation as unique, it's often helpful to try and see the similarities of the new situation to old ones that we know how to deal with. Analogical reasoning is related to induction. While induction makes inferences from the specific to the general of the same situation, analogy tries to make inferences from situations that are not the same. Analogy cannot make formal proofs like deduction. Instead, analogy is a heuristic reasoning tool that may sometimes work and is the primary tool of case-based reasoning in legal arguments and medical diagnosis.

An example of reasoning by analogy is medical diagnosis. When you see a doctor because of a medical problem, the doctor will elicit information from you and note the symptoms of the problem. If your symptoms are identical or strongly similar to those of other people with Problem X, the doctor may infer by analogy that you have Problem X. Analogy is cheap reasoning.

Notice that this diagnosis is not a deduction, because you are unique. Just because someone else with the problem shows certain symptoms doesn't mean that you will exhibit the same symptoms. Instead, the doctor assumes that your symptoms make you analogous to a person with the same symptoms and known problem. This initial diagnosis is a hypothesis that medical tests may either prove or disprove. It's important to have an initial working hypothesis because it narrows down the thousands of potential problems. It would be prohibitively expensive and time consuming to just start giving you every possible test without an initial hypothesis.

As an example of the utility of reasoning by analogy, suppose two people play a game called the 15 Game. They take turns in picking a number from 1 to 9 with the constraint that the same number cannot be used twice. The first person whose numbers add up to 15 wins. Although at first this seems like a strange game that requires some thinking, an analogy can make it very easy to play.

Consider the tic-tac-toe board below with values assigned to each cell as shown:

6	1	8
7	5	3
2	9	4

This is a **magic square** because the sum of the values in the rows, columns, and diagonals is a constant. The tic-tac-toe board with the magic square values can be considered an analogy to the 15 Game. Playing the 15 Game is now very easy if you think in terms of tic-tac-toe and then translate the winning strategy to the 15 Game.

This particular magic square is called the **standard square of order 3**. The term *order* refers to the number of rows or columns of a square. There is only one unique square of order 3. Other magic squares can be created by rotating or reflecting the standard square. Another way to construct magic squares is by adding the same constant to each cell. Knowing this information allows us to deduce the winning strategies for the 18 Game, where the numbers must be selected from the set:

```
{2, 3, 4, 5, 6, 7, 8, 9, 10}
```

or the 21 Game, using the set:

```
{3, 4, 5, 6, 7, 8, 9, 10, 11}
```

We can now use induction to infer the winning strategy for the 15 + 3N Game, where N is any natural number 1, 2, 3, ... by thinking of the game as analogous to a tic-tac-toe board, which is analogous to a magic square of values:

```
{1+N, 2+N, 3+N, 4+N, 5+N, 6+N, 7+N, 8+N, 9+N}
```

Using the analogy of the order 3 square for games of three moves, by induction we can infer that magic squares of higher order can be used for games involving more than three moves. For example, the magic square of order 4:

16	3	2	13
5	10	11	8
9	6	7	12
4	15	14	1

allows you to play the winning strategy of the four-move, 34 game, by thinking of it in terms of tic-tac-toe. In contrast to the one standard order 3 square, there are 880 standard squares of order 4, which allows considerably more games.

Reasoning by analogy is an important part of commonsense reasoning, which is very difficult for computers (and children). Other applications of analogy have been to learning.

Generate-and-Test

Another method of inference is the classic AI strategy of **generate-and-test**, sometimes called generation and test, which involves the generation of a likely solution and then testing it to see if the proposed solution meets all the requirements. If the solution is satisfactory, then quit, else generate a new solution, test again, and so forth. This method was used in the first expert system, DENDRAL, conceived in 1965, to aid in identifying organic molecular structures. Data from an unknown sample are supplied by a mass spectrometer and input to DENDRAL, which generates all the potential molecular structures that could produce the unknown spectrogram. DENDRAL then tests the most likely candidate molecules by simulating their mass spectrograms and comparing the results to the original unknown. Another program that uses generate-and-test is the Artificial Mathematician program to infer new mathematical concepts.

In order to reduce the enormous number of potential solutions, generate-and-test is normally used with a planning program to limit the likely potential solutions for generation. This variation is called **plan-generate-test** and is used for efficiency in many systems. For example, the medical diagnosis expert system MYCIN also has the capability of planning a therapeutic drug treatment after a patient's disease has been diagnosed. A **plan** is essentially finding chains of rules or inferences that connect a problem with a solution, or goal, with the evidence to support it. Planning is most efficiently done by simultaneously searching forward from the facts and backward from the goal.

The MYCIN planner first creates a prioritized list of therapeutic drugs to which the patient is sensitive. In order to reduce undesirable drug interactions, it's best to limit the number of drugs that a patient receives, even if the patient is thought to be suffering from several different infections. The generator takes the prioritized list from the planner and generates sublists of one or two drugs if possible. These sublists are then tested for efficacy against the infections, patient's allergies, and other considerations before a decision is made to administer them to the patient.

Generate-and-test can also be considered the basic inference paradigm of rules. If the conditional elements of a rule are satisfied, it generates some actions such as new facts. The inference engine tests these facts against the conditional elements of rules in the knowledge base. Those rules that are satisfied are put on the agenda and the top-priority rule generates its actions, which are then tested, and so forth. Thus generate-and-test produces an inference chain that may lead to the correct solution.

Abduction

Inference by abduction is another method that is commonly used in diagnostic problem solving. The schema of abduction resembles modus ponens, but is actually very different, as shown in Table 3.15.

Table 3.15 Comparison of Abduction and Modus Ponens

Abduction	Modus ponens
$p \rightarrow q$	$p \rightarrow q$
q	p
$\therefore p$	$\therefore q$

Abduction is another name for a fallacious argument that we discussed in Section 3.6, as the Fallacy of the Converse. Although abduction is not a valid deductive argument, it is a useful method of inference and has been used in expert systems. Like analogy, which also is not a valid deductive argument but is quick and cheap (in reasoning time, not money). Abduction may be useful as a heuristic rule of inference. That is, when we have no deductive method of inference, abduction may prove useful but is not guaranteed to work. Analogy, generate-and-test, and abduction are all methods that are not deductive and are not guaranteed to work all the time. From true premises, these methods cannot prove true conclusions. However, these techniques are useful in reducing the search space by generating reasonable hypotheses, which can then be used with deduction.

Abduction is sometimes referred to as *reasoning from observed facts to the best explanation*. As an example of abduction, consider the following:

```
IF x is an elephant THEN x is an animal
IF x is an animal THEN x is a mammal
```

If we know that Clyde is a mammal, can we conclude that Clyde is an elephant?

The answer to this question depends on whether we are talking about the real world or our expert system. In the real world we could not make this conclusion with any degree of certainty. Clyde could be a dog, cat, cow, or any other kind of animal that was a mammal but not an elephant. In fact, considering how many species of animals there are, the probability of Clyde being an elephant is rather low, without knowing any more information about Clyde.

However, in an expert system with only the preceding rules, we could say by abduction with 100% certainty that if Clyde is a mammal, then Clyde is an elephant. This inference follows from a closed-world-assumption in which we have assumed that nothing else exists outside the closed world of our expert system. Any-thing that cannot be proven is assumed false in a closed world. Under the closed-world assumption, all the possibilities are known. Since the expert system consists of only these two rules and only an elephant can be a mammal, then if Clyde is a mammal, he must be an elephant.

Suppose we add a third rule, as follows:

```
IF x is a dog THEN X is an animal
```

We can still operate our expert system under the closed-world assumption. However, now we cannot conclude with 100 percent certainty that Clyde is an elephant. All we can be sure of is that Clyde is either an elephant or a dog.

In order to decide between the two, more information is needed. For example, if there is another rule,

```
IF x is a dog THEN x barks
```

and evidence that Clyde barks, the rules can be revised as follows:

```
(1) IF x is an animal THEN x is a mammal
(2) IF x barks THEN x is an animal
(3) IF x is a dog THEN x barks
(4) IF x is an elephant THEN x is an animal
```

Now a backward chain of abductive inference using rules (1), (2), and (3) can be made to show that Clyde must be a dog.

A backward chain of abduction is not the same as the customary meaning of backward chaining. The term backward chaining means that we are trying to prove a hypothesis by looking for evidence to support it. Backward chaining would be used in trying to prove that Clyde is a mammal. Of course, for our small system there are no other possibilities. However, other classifications could be added for reptiles, birds, and so forth.

If it's known that Clyde is a mammal, abduction could be used to determine if Clyde is an elephant or a dog. Forward chaining would be used if it is known that Clyde is an elephant and we wanted to know if he is a mammal. As you can see, the choice of inference method depends on what is to be determined. Since forward chaining is deductive, only its conclusions are always guaranteed valid. Table 3.16 summarizes the purpose of each of the three inference techniques.

Table 3.16 Summary of the Purpose of Forward Chaining, Backward Chaining, and Abduction

Inference	Start	Purpose
Forward chaining	Facts	Conclusions that must follow
Backward chaining	Uncertain conclusion	Facts to support the conclusion
Abduction	True conclusion	Facts which may follow

A number of AI and expert systems have used frame-based abduction for diagnostic problem solving. In these systems, the knowledge base contains **causal associations** between disorders and symptoms. Inferences are made using generate-and-test of hypotheses for the disorders.

Nonmonotonic Reasoning

Normally the addition of new axioms to a logic system means that more theorems can be proven since there are more axioms from which theorems can be derived. This property of increasing theorems with increasing axioms is known as **monotonicity** and systems such as deductive logic are called **monotonic systems**.

However, a problem can occur if a newly introduced axiom partially or completely contradicts a previous axiom. In this case, the theorems that had been proven may no longer be valid. Thus, in a **nonmonotonic system**, the theorems do not necessarily increase as the number of axioms increases.

The concept of nonmonotonicity has an important application to expert systems. As new facts are generated—which is analogous to theorems being proved—a monotonic expert system would keep building up facts. A major problem can occur if one or more facts becomes false because a monotonic system cannot deal with changes in the truth of axioms and theorems. As a very simple example, suppose there is a fact that asserts the time. As soon as time changes by one second, the old fact is no longer valid. A monotonic system would not be capable of dealing with this situation. As another example, suppose a fact was asserted by an aircraft identification system that a target was hostile. Later, new evidence proves the target is friendly. In a monotonic system, the original identification of hostile could not be changed. A nonmonotonic system allows the retraction of facts.

As another application, suppose you wanted to write an explanation facility for an expert system that would allow a user to go back to previous inferences and explore alternate inference paths of "What if" type questions. All inferences made after the desired previous one must be retracted from the system. Besides facts, rules may also have been excised from the system and so must be put back in the knowledge base for nonmonotonicity. Further complications arise in systems such as OPS5 in which rules can be created automatically on the right-hand side of rules during execution. For nonmonotonicity, any inferred rules made after the previous desired inference would have to be excised from the system. Keeping track of all inferences made can consume a lot of memory and significantly slow down the system.

In order to provide for nonmonotonicity, it is necessary to attach a justification or dependency to each fact and rule that explains the reason for belief in it. If a nonmonotonic decision is made, then the inference engine can examine the justification of each fact and rule to see if it is still believed, and also to possibly restore excised rules and retracted facts that are believed again.

The problem of justifying facts was first pointed out in the **frame problem**, which is not the same concept as the frames discussed in Chapter 2. The frame problem is a descriptive term named after the problem of identifying what has or has not changed in a movie frame. Motion pictures are photographed as a succession of still pictures, called frames. When played back at 24 frames per second or faster, the human eye cannot distinguish the individual frames and so the illusion of motion results. An AI frame problem is to recognize changes in an environment over time. As an example, consider the Monkey and Bananas problem discussed earlier. Suppose the monkey must step on a red box to reach the bananas and so the action is "push red box under bananas." Now the frame problem is—how do we know the box is still red after the action? Pushing the box should not change the environment. However, other actions such as "paint the box blue" will change the environment. In some expert-system tools an environment is called a **world** and consists of a set of related facts. An expert system may keep track of multiple worlds to do hypothetical reasoning simultaneously. The problem of maintaining the correctness or truth of a system is called **truth maintenance**. Truth maintenance or a variation called **assumption-based truth maintenance,** is essential for keeping each world pure by retracting unjustified facts.

As a simple example of nonmonotonic reasoning, let's consider the classic example of Tweety the bird. In the absence of any other information, we would therefore assume that since Tweety is a bird, then Tweety can fly. This is an example of **default reasoning**, much like the defaults used in frame slots. Default reasoning can be considered as a rule that makes inferences about rules, a **metarule** which states:

```
IF X is not known for certain, and
      there is no evidence contradicting X
THEN tentatively conclude Y
```

Metarules are discussed more extensively in the next section.

In our case the metarule has the more specific form:

```
X is the rule "All birds can fly," and
      fact "Tweety is a bird"
Y is the inference "Tweety can fly"
```

In terms of production rules, this can be expressed as a rule in our knowledge base, which says:

```
IF X is a bird THEN X can fly
```

and the fact that exists in working memory:

```
Tweety is a bird
```

Unifying the fact with the antecedent of the rule gives the inference that Tweety can fly.

Now comes the problem. Suppose an additional fact is added to working memory, which says that Tweety is a penguin. We know that penguins cannot fly and so the inference that Tweety can fly is incorrect. Of course, there must be a rule in the system that also states this knowledge or else the fact will be ignored.

In order to maintain the correctness of our system, the incorrect inference must be removed. However, this may not be sufficient if other inferences were based on the incorrect inference. That is, other rules may have used the incorrect inference as evidence to draw additional inferences, and so on. This is a problem of truth maintenance. The inference that Tweety can fly was a **plausible inference** that is based on default reasoning. The term *plausible* means not impossible and will be discussed further in Chapter 4.

One way of allowing for nonmonotonic inference is by defining a sentential operator M, which can be informally defined as "is consistent." For example,

$$(\forall\ x)\ [\texttt{Bird}(x)\ \wedge \texttt{M}(\texttt{Can\_fly}(x)) \rightarrow \texttt{Can\_fly}(x)]$$

can be stated as "For every x, if x is a bird and it is consistent that a bird can fly, then x can fly." A more informal way of stating this is "Most birds can fly." The term *is consistent* means that there are no contradictions with other knowledge. However, this interpretation has been criticized as really stating that the only birds that cannot fly are those which have been inferred not capable of flying. This is an example of **autoepistemic reasoning**, which literally means reasoning about your own knowledge. Both default and autoepistemic reasoning are used in **commonsense reasoning**, which humans generally do quite well but is very difficult for computers.

Autoepistemic reasoning is reasoning about your own knowledge as distinct from knowledge in general. Generally, you can do this very well because you know the limits of your knowledge. For example, suppose a total stranger came up and stated you were their spouse. You would immediately know (unless you had amnesia) that you were not their spouse because you had no knowledge of that stranger. The general metarule of autoepistemic reasoning is:

```
IF I have no knowledge of X
THEN X is false
```

Notice how autoepistemic reasoning relies on the closed-world assumption. Any fact that is not known is assumed false. In autoepistemic reasoning, the closed world is your self-knowledge.

Autoepistemic and default reasoning are both nonmonotonic. However, the reasons are different. Default reasoning is nonmonotonic because it is **defeasible**. The term defeasible means that any inferences are tentative and may have to be withdrawn as new information becomes available. However, pure autoepistemic reasoning is not defeasible because of the closed-world assumption that declares all true knowledge is already known to you. For example, since married people know who is their spouse (unless they want to forget), a married person would not accept that a total stranger was their spouse if they were told that. Because most people recognize that they have imperfect memories, they do not adhere to pure autoepistemic reasoning. Of course, computers do not have this problem until their hard disk crashes.

Autoepistemic reasoning is nonmonotonic because the meaning of an autoepistemic statement is **context-sensitive**. The term *context-sensitive* means that the meaning changes with the context. As a simple example of context-sensitivity, consider how the word "read" is pronounced in the two sentences:

```
I have read the book
I will read the book
```

The pronunciation of "read" is context sensitive.

Now consider a system consisting of the following two axioms:

```
(∀ x) [Bird(x) ∧ M(Can_fly(x))→ Can_fly(x)]
Bird(Tweety)
```

In this logic system, Can_fly(Tweety) is a theorem derived by unification of Tweety with the variable x and implication.

Now suppose a new axiom is added that states that Tweety cannot fly and thus contradicts the previously derived theorem:

```
~Can_fly(Tweety)
```

The M-operator must change its operation on its argument because now M(Can_fly(Tweety)) is not consistent with the new axiom. In this new context of three axioms, the M-operator would not give a TRUE result for Can_fly(Tweety) because it conflicts with the new axiom. The returned value by the M-operator must be FALSE in this new context, and so the conjunction is FALSE. Thus, there is no implication to produce the theorem Can_fly(Tweety) and no conflict.

One way of implementing this by rules is as follows:

```
IF x is a bird AND x is typical
THEN x can fly
IF x is a bird AND x is nontypical
THEN x cannot fly

Tweety is a bird
Tweety is nontypical
```

Notice that this system does not invalidate the conclusion Can_fly(Tweety), but rather prevents the incorrect rule from firing at all. This is a much more efficient method of truth maintenance than if we had one rule and the special axiom ~Can_fly(Tweety). Now we have a more general system that can easily handle other nonflying birds such as ostriches without our having to continually add new inferences, which is what the system is supposed to do.

3.16 METAKNOWLEDGE

The Classic Meta-DENDRAL program used induction to infer new rules of chemical structure. Meta-DENDRAL was an attempt to overcome the knowledge bottleneck of trying to extract molecular structural rules from human experts. Some expert system tools come with progress to induce rules.

For example, the following classic metarule is taken from the TEIRESIAS knowledge acquisition program for MYCIN, the expert system to diagnose blood infections and meningitis:

```
METARULE 2
IF
The patient is a compromised host, and
There are rules which mention in their premise
   pseudomonas, and
There are rules which mention in their premise
   klebsiellas
THEN
There is suggestive evidence (0.4) that the former
   should be done before the latter
```

The number 0.4 in the action of the rule is a degree of certainty and will be discussed in a later chapter.

TEIRESIAS acquires knowledge interactively from an expert. If a wrong diagnosis has been made by MYCIN, then TEIRESIAS will lead the expert back through the chain of incorrect reasoning until the expert states where the incorrect reasoning started. While going back through the reasoning chain, TEIRESIAS will also interact with the expert to modify incorrect rules or acquire new rules.

Knowledge about new rules is not immediately put into MYCIN. Instead, TEIRESIAS checks to see if the new rule is compatible with similar rules. For example, if the new rule describes how an infection enters the body and other accepted rules have a conditional element stating the portal of entry to the body, then the new rule should also. If the new rule does not state the portal of entry, then TEIRESIAS will query the user about this discrepancy. TEIRESIAS has a **rule model pattern** of similar rules that it knows about, and tries to fit the new rule into its rule model. In other words, the rule model is the knowledge that TEIRESIAS has about its knowledge. An analogous situation for a human would occur if you went to a car dealer to buy a new car and the dealer tried to sell you a car with three wheels.

The metaknowledge of TEIRESIAS is of two types. The METARULE 2, described previously, is a control strategy that tells how rules are to be applied. In contrast, the rule model type of metaknowledge determines if the new rule is in the appropriate form to be entered in the knowledge base. In a rule-based expert system, determining if the new rule is in the correct form is called **verification** of the rule. Determining that a chain of correct inferences leads to the correct answer is called **validation**. Validation and verification are so interdependent that the acronym **V&V** is commonly used to refer to both. A more colloquial definition of the terms from software engineering:

```
Verification: "Am I building the product right?"
Validation: "Am I building the right product?"
```

Basically, verification has to do with internal correctness while validation has to do with external correctness. V&V will be discussed in more detail in Chapter 6.

3.17 HIDDEN MARKOV MODELS

As a modern example of metaknowledge, consider path planning for a robot. If the robot does not have a global positioning system (GPS), or it is not precise enough, which is usually the case for commercial systems that can only determine a location to within 3 meters, other means must be used. A good application to path planning uses a **Markov decision process** (**MDP**) (Kaelbling 98). Other methods use the classic A* algorithm, Kalman Filters, and other techniques (Lakemeyer 03).

In the real world there are always uncertainties and pure logic is not a good guide when there is uncertainty. A MDP is more realistic in the case of partial or hidden information about the state and parameters, and the need for planning. Such processes are not restricted to physical path planning but cover any type of planning in a partially known environment such as oil exploration, transportation logistics, and factory process control where sensors may malfunction and things go wrong. Such process control may be especially important when the process being controlled is a nuclear power plant.

The ultimate example of partial information occurs when a robot is exploring the surface of another planet, such as Mars. If the goal is to get to a certain rock but the path is partially obscured, the robot must try to make optimum decisions on how to reach the goal while subject to constraints such as its limited energy supply and perhaps an inability to retrace the correct path once it has gone into a steep crater.

A MDP can be defined as the tuple {States, Actions, Transitions, Rewards}. More formally we can write MDP≡ {S, A, T, R} where

```
S is a set of states of the environment;
A is a set of actions;
```

T: S x A ≡∏(S); where ∏ is called the **state-transition function** which determines what state a particular action will determine. The "x" is the Cartesian product operator. ∏ is the set of all possible states and actions. Naturally some may not be feasible or desirable but the Cartesian operation does not filter out which are optimum. In order to determine which actions lead to better states, e.g., the robot not stuck in a dead end, a reward is necessary.

R: S x A→R(S) where **R** is the **reward function** which provides the immediate reward gained by the **agent** for taking a certain action. The term agent is used for any entity that acts on behalf of another. Thus the robot is a human agent on another planet. Different states will give different expected rewards. In search for the optimum path to the goal, one way of defining the optimum is by maximizing the expected sum of the rewards. The immediate reward is given right away but the sum of rewards determines whether the agent will succeed or fail in reaching the goal. For example, if the robot takes a right turn it may find a clear path. Unfortunately this clear path may not lead to the goal of getting to the desired rock. This is like the verification discussed earlier while validation in this case means the robot has gone to the correct rock. In the next chapter we will see more examples of rewards in terms of the utility functions and Bayes Theorem for dealing with uncertainty.

In (1) the case of the robot not sure of its location, an unknown state, or (2) which path to take, an unknown parameter, the Hidden Markov Model (HMM) is very useful. Software for HMM is available such as the HTK toolkit (http://htk.eng.cam.ac.uk/). This has been successfully used for speech recognition, speech synthesis, character recognition, and DNA sequencing. Once the biological structure is determined by finding the sequence of its genetic material, it can be synthesized or modified to identify and treat disease. Other software is HMMER, a freely distributable implementation of HMM for protein sequence analysis (http://hmmer.wustl.edu/).

The popular Matlab has a toolkit available for HMM which supports various types of scientific inference especially suited for signal analysis (http://www.ai.mit.edu/~murphyk/Software/HMM/hmm.html). The classic case is to determine the phonemes and thus the words from speech when the user speaks into a microphone to generate an acoustic signal for computer analysis. While broken speech or that enunciated slowly has been solved by many techniques such as ANS, the hard problem is continuous speech recognition by any speaker without training the system (independent speaker recognition.)

Path planning is also essential to many video games where a character has to get from one location to another with walls and obstacles in the way. The popular A* algorithm is often used.

3.18 SUMMARY

In this chapter the commonly used methods of inference for expert systems have been discussed. Inference is particularly important in expert systems because it is the technique by which expert systems solve problems. The application of trees, graphs, and lattices to the representation of knowledge was discussed. The advantages of these structures to inferences were illustrated.

Deductive logic was covered starting with simple syllogistic logic. Next, the propositional and first-order predicate logic was discussed. Truth tables and rules of inference were described as ways of proving theorems and statements. The characteristics of logical systems such as completeness, soundness, and decidability were mentioned.

The resolution method of proving theorems was discussed for propositional logic and first-order predicate logic. The nine steps involved in converting a well-formed formula to clausal form were illustrated by an example. Skolemization, the prenex-normal form, and unification were all discussed in the context of converting a wff to clausal form.

Another powerful method of inferences, analogy, was discussed. Although not widely used in expert systems because of the difficulty in implementing it, analogy is the normal method of doctors and lawyers, and should be considered in the design of expert systems. Generate-and-test was also discussed with an example of its use in MYCIN. The application of metaknowledge in TEIRESAS was described and its relationship to verification and validation of expert systems.

PROBLEMS

3.1 Write a decision tree program that is self-learning. Teach it the animal knowledge of Figure 3.3.

3.2 Write a program that will automatically translate the knowledge stored in a binary decision tree into IF-THEN type rules. Test it with the animal decision tree of Problem 3.1.

3.3 Draw a semantic net containing the raspberries knowledge of Figure 3.4.

3.4 Draw the state diagram showing a solution to the classic problem of the farmer, fox, goat, and cabbage. In this problem a farmer, fox, goat, and cabbage are on one bank of a river. A boat must be used to transport them to the other side. However, the boat can be used to hold only two at a time (and only the farmer can row). If the fox is left with the goat and the farmer is not present, then the fox will eat the goat. If the goat is left alone with the cabbage, the goat will eat the cabbage.

3.5 Draw a state diagram for a well-structured travel problem having:

(a) three methods of payment: cash, check, or charge
(b) traveler's interests: sun, snow
(c) four possible destinations depending on the traveler's interests and money
(d) three types of transportation

Write IF-THEN rules to advise a traveler where to go depending on money and interests. Pick real destinations and find out the costs to get there from your location.

3.6 Determine whether the following are valid or invalid arguments:

(a) $p \rightarrow q, \sim q \rightarrow r, r; \therefore p$
(b) $\sim p \vee q, p \rightarrow (r \wedge s), s \rightarrow q; \therefore q \vee r$
(c) $p \rightarrow (q \rightarrow r), q; \therefore p \rightarrow r$

3.7 Using the Venn diagram decision procedure, determine if the following are valid or invalid syllogisms:

(a) AEE-4
(b) AOO-1
(c) OAO-3
(d) AAI-1
(e) OAI-2

3.8 Prove whether the following are fallacies or rules of inference. Give an example of each.

(a) Complex Constructive Dilemma

$p \rightarrow q$
$r \rightarrow s$
$\underline{p \vee r}$
$\therefore q \vee s$

(b) Complex Destructive Dilemma

$p \rightarrow q$
$r \rightarrow s$
$\underline{\sim q \vee \sim s}$
$\therefore \sim p \vee \sim r$

(c) Simple Destructive Dilemma

$p \rightarrow q$
$p \rightarrow r$
$\underline{\sim q \vee \sim r}$
$\therefore \sim p$

(d) Inverse

$p \rightarrow q$
$\underline{\sim p}$
$\therefore \sim q$

3.9 Draw the conclusion from the following premises, taken from Lewis Carroll, author of the famous *Alice's Adventures in Wonderland*:

(a) All the dated letters in this room are written on blue paper.
(b) None of them are in black ink, except those that are written in the third person.
(c) I have not filed any of them that I can read.
(d) None of them, that are written on one sheet, are undated.
(e) All of them, that are not crossed, are in black ink.
(f) All of them, written by Brown, begin with "Dear Sir,".
(g) All of them, written on blue paper, are filed.
(h) None of them, written on more than one sheet, are crossed.
(i) None of them, that begin with "Dear Sir," are written in the third person.

Hint: Use the law of contrapositives to define the following:

A = beginning with "Dear Sir" | B = crossed | C = dated
D = filed | E = in black ink | F = in third person
G = letters that I can read | H = on blue paper | I = on one sheet
J = written by Brown

3.10 Give a formal proof using predicate logic for the syllogism:

No software is guaranteed
<u>All programs are software</u>
∴ No programs are guaranteed

3.11 Use the following to write quantified first-order predicate logic formulas:

P(x) = x is a programmer

S(x) = x is smart

L(x,y) = x loves y

(a) All programmers are smart.

(b) Some programmers are smart.

(c) No programmers are smart.

(d) Someone is not a programmer.

(e) Not everyone is a programmer.

(f) Everyone is not a programmer.

(g) Everyone is a programmer.

(h) Some programmers are not smart.

(i) There are programmers.

(j) Everyone loves someone.

Hint: Use Appendix B.

3.12 Consider the predicate logic argument:

A horse is an animal

Therefore, the head of a horse is the head of an animal. Define the following:

H(x,y) = x is the head of y

A(x) = x is an animal

S(x) = x is a horse

The premise and conclusion are as follows:

$(\forall x)\ (S(x) \rightarrow A(x))$

$$(\forall x)\ \{[(\exists y)\ (S(y) \wedge H(x,y))] \rightarrow [(\exists z)\ (A(z) \wedge H(x,z))]\}$$

Prove the conclusion using resolution refutation. Show all nine steps in clausal conversion for the conclusion.

3.13 (a) Obtain information from your bank or savings & loan on the criteria for obtaining a car loan. Write a backward-chaining system of rules to determine if an applicant should get a car loan. Be as specific as possible.

(b) Obtain information on qualifying for a home mortgage. Give the modifications of your car loan program to handle home loans as well as car loans.

(c) Obtain information on qualifying for a business loan. Give the modifications to the car-mortgage program to handle business loans as well.

3.14 Write a production system of causal rules to simulate the operation of the fuel system of your car. You may obtain this information from the repair guide for your car. Be as detailed as possible.

3.15 Using the repair guide for your car, write a production system that can diagnose and remedy electrical problems for your car, given symptoms of problems.

3.16 If the conclusion is false and you wanted to determine the facts that followed, would you use abduction or another method of inference? Explain.

3.17 Write IF-THEN rules to identify raspberries using the portion of the decision tree shown in Figure 3.4.

3.18 A parent and two children are on the left bank of a river and wish to cross to the right side. The parent weighs 200 lb and each child weighs 100 lb. One boat is available with a capacity of 200 lb. At least one person is required to row the boat. Draw the decision tree showing all the possibilities for them crossing the river and indicate the successful path through the tree so that they all cross. Assume the following operators in labeling your tree:

SL–Single child crosses from left to right
SR–Single child crosses from right to left
BL–Both children cross from left to right
BR–Both children cross from right to left
PL–Parent crosses from left to right
PR–Parent crosses from right to left

3.19 (a) Draw a logic diagram version of the AND-exclusive-OR car decision of Figure 3.11. Note that you will have to implement the exclusive-OR using standard AND, OR, and NOT elements.
(b) Write forward chaining IF-THEN rules to determine which hypothesis to follow, i.e., sell or repair.

3.20 What type of inference (if any) do the following statements represent?

(a) "The reason I keep insisting that there was a relationship between Iraq and Saddam and al Qaeda is because there was a relationship between Iraq and al Qaeda."
(b) "If it is reasonable to think that a Supreme Court justice can be bought so cheap, the nation is in deeper trouble than I had imagined."

BIBLIOGRAPHY

(Giarratano 93). Joseph Giarratano, *CLIPS User's Guide*, NASA, Version 6.2 of CLIPS, 1993.

(Kaelbling 98). Leslie Pack Kaelbling, Michael L. Littman, and Anthony R. Cassandra, "Planning and Acting in Partially Observable Stochastic Domains," *Artificial Intelligence* 101 pp. 99-134, 1998.

(Klir 98). George J. Klir and Mark J. Weirman, *Uncertainty-Based Information, Physica-Verlag*, 1998.

(Lakemeyer 03). ed. by Gerhard Lakemeyer and Bernhard Nebel, *Exploring Artificial Intelligence in the New Millennium,* Morgan Kaufmann Publishers, 2003.

(Lakoff 00). George Lakoff and Rafael E. Nunez, *Where Mathematics Comes From*, Basic Books, 2000.

(Merritt 04). Dennis Merrit, "Building a Custom Rule Engine with PROLOG," *Dr. Dobb's Journal*, pp. 40-45, March 2004.

(Russell 03). Stuart J. Russell and Peter Norvig, *Artificial Intelligence: A Modern Approach,* 2nd Edition, 2002.

CHAPTER 4
Reasoning under Uncertainty

4.1 INTRODUCTION

This chapter discusses some methods of reasoning under **uncertainty** using **probability theory** and **fuzzy logic**. These topics are very important since one of the main strengths of an expert system is its ability to handle uncertainty just like a real person. If a satisfactory algorithm or decision tree is known, there is no need for the power of an expert system. Dealing with uncertainty is one of the main advantages of an expert system over a simple decision tree in which all the facts must be known to achieve an outcome. Probability theory is the foundation for some theories of uncertainty and so this chapter covers those elements that are relevant to probabilistic uncertainty and fuzzy logic in expert systems.

In the next chapter other theories of dealing with uncertainty will be introduced and fuzzy logic will be studied in more detail under its formal title of Approximate Reasoning. While it would be nice to have to deal with only one theory of uncertainty such as classic probability theory, there are advantages and disadvantages with each theory. This is analogous to the decisions a programmer must face in deciding what algorithm and data structure should be used in an ordinary computer program. By understanding the advantages and disadvantages of each approach to uncertainty, you will create an expert system that is best for the particular expertise being modeled. Some expert system tools have uncertainty built into the language such as two versions of CLIPS that were customized to handle fuzzy logic, the FuzzyClips from the National Research Council of Canada and the Togai InfraLogic, FuzzyClips. Some other customized versions are described in the Preface.

Before using such a customized tool, you should be sure that is the correct method for uncertainty. It may be that all you need are some particular rules in which you can code the method yourself, or define an uncertainty function rather than using a whole special tool. Another possibility is that you may need to have more than one type of uncertainty modeled and there is no one tool that will handle all. Appendix G shows many software tools and other resources for probability. Some of these are complete tools while other resources are special classes, e.g., in C++, to help you modify and recompile CLIPS for ease of adding uncertainty or other features you would like. This again illustrates one of the great advantages in CLIPS being open source so that you can customize the tool to fit your needs rather than try to make your needs fit the tool. Versions of CLIPS, written in other languages such as Java, are also listed at the official CLIPS Website.

4.2 UNCERTAINTY

Uncertainty can be considered as the lack of adequate information to make a decision. Uncertainty is a problem because it may prevent us from making the best decision and may even cause a bad decision to be made. In medicine, uncertainty may overlook the best treatment for a patient or contribute to an incorrect therapy. In business, uncertainty may mean financial loss instead of profit.

A number of theories have been devised to deal with uncertainty. These include classical probability, **Bayesian probability** (Castillo 97), Hartley theory based on classical sets, Shannon theory based on probability, **Dempster-Shafer theory**, Markov Models, and Zadeh's **fuzzy theory**. In particular, Bayesian theory and fuzzy theory have proven very popular in many diverse areas such as biology, psychology, music, and physics. Fuzzy logic is also found in many consumer appliances ranging from washing machines that know how clean clothes are by measuring the cleanliness of the clothes rather than the electrical timer invented in the 19th century, to producing great pictures in cameras. Fuzzy logic, also called Approximate Reasoning, will be discussed in more detail in the next chapter.

All living creatures are experts at dealing with uncertainty or they could not survive in the real world. In particular, human beings are used to uncertainty about traffic, weather, jobs, school, and life in general. After awhile, we all become experts at driving under various traffic conditions, treating a cold, and choosing easy classes. Some people get to be experts in choosing the easy way in all things. Dealing with uncertainty requires reasoning under uncertainty and having a lot of commonsense. The only problem with commonsense is that it doesn't necessarily mean "good sense," but only what is normally done in normal situations. Sometimes the normal way is not the best way which is why reasoning under uncertainty is important. For example, if you've ever played a slot machine and won some money, then started losing, commonsense whispers in your ear that if you play long enough you'll eventually win again. Unfortunately commonsense doesn't tell whether you'll run out of cash, max out your credit cards, sell your car, or pawn your spouse's wedding ring before you win again.

The deductive method of reasoning described in Chapter 3 is called **exact reasoning** because it deals with exact facts and the exact conclusions that follow from those facts. Recall that a deductive argument is so strong that the conclusion *must* be true if the premises are true. Likewise, if the premises are false, then the conclusion *must* be false.

On the other hand, an inductive argument does not guarantee the truth of the conclusion like a deductive one. The premises of an inductive argument give support to the conclusion but are no guarantee. For example, given the sequence of integers, 1, 2, 3, you might use induction to assume that the next number is 4. However, what if you were told the next number is 5? Such would be the case if "1,2,3" was a sequence of three numbers selected from the famous Fibonacci sequence in which each number is the sum of the two previous numbers and the sequence is 0,1,1,2,3,5. In an inductive argument, the more premises that support the conclusion, the more likely we believe the conclusion to be true.

However there is a problem with this interpretation of induction that the more premises support a conclusion the more it is likely to be true. Suppose you are a right-wing raven (they have one more pinion on the right wing) and heard a left-wing raven (they have one more pinion on the left wing; a difference of a pinion) claim that all ravens are black. So you go out counting ravens and after a long time, observe that all the 1,000,000 you have seen are indeed black. Now at this point some right-wingers might give up, but since this theory was advanced by a left-winger you think, "Just because I have not seen a non-black raven does not mean it does not exist. Perhaps they are all in hiding." While this may be true (or they were all removed one night by UFOs), the statement, "All ravens are black," is logically equivalent to the statement, "All non-black-things are non-ravens."

For example, a red apple is certainly not a black raven. So the more red apples you see increase the probability little by little that all ravens are black by adding strength to the premises, i.e., the number of non-black things. This bird-brained story is called the **Raven Paradox** because it shows how applying induction can contradict intuition.

Now this could be a disaster because there are a lot of red apples and that would mean the left-wingers are correct in saying all ravens are black. But this is no time to give up! Consider that there are also a lot of blackberries. So if you keep on counting black things that are not black ravens, this weakens the premise that some will be black ravens. If you go into any grocery store that has blackberries and start counting them, you will find that there are a lot more blackberries in the dozen or so pints the store carries than the number of red apples they carry (not too many apples fit into a pint box). Since there are more blackberries than apples, it means the left-wingers are wrong and there must indeed be a non-black raven, even if you haven't found it yet!

Counting red apples or anything non-black to increase the likelihood that all ravens are black can lead to invalid conclusions. Various solutions to the Raven Paradox have been proposed but the best one seems to be Bayesian theory, discussed later in this chapter.

When uncertain facts are involved, exact reasoning does not apply although people may mistakenly think it does as in the case of the ravens or the gambler discussed previously. Uncertainty increases the number of possible outcomes so that it may become not merely difficult but impossible to find the best solution. Even worse, uncertainty may lead to faulty reasoning and we wind up counting blackberries all day long.

Unfortunately, determining the "best" conclusion may not be easy. A number of different methods have been proposed for dealing with uncertainty and aid in picking the best conclusion. However in dealing with uncertainty we may have to settle not for the best solution but a good solution. On the other hand, a good solution that is 99% achieved in real time may be better than the optimum solution that takes a million years to compute. It is the responsibility of the expert systems designer to pick the most appropriate method, depending on the application. While there are expert systems tools that incorporate mechanisms for reasoning under uncertainty, they are generally not flexible in allowing other methods to be used. There is an adage that if the only tool you have is a hammer, then everything looks like a nail. Choosing a tool that is powerful in only one area is like choosing only a hammer.

While there are many expert systems applications that can be done with exact reasoning, many others require **inexact reasoning** because the facts or knowledge itself is not known precisely. A good example is the medical business. In order to optimize profits, the goal is to find an acceptable treatment with the minimum number of tests because tests cost money. In expert systems, there may be uncertain facts, rules, or both. Classic examples of successful expert systems that dealt with uncertainty are MYCIN for medical diagnosis and PROSPECTOR for mineral exploration.

The main reason these systems are so often quoted in the literature is that they were well-documented and were meant to show the feasibility of expert systems as equivalent or better than human experts, which both systems did. These days you cannot get access to the exact rules by which the credit bureaus' expert systems determine your credit rating, or why you were denied a credit card from the same bank that approved your large mortgage. Also since these are software programs, what are the chances there are no bugs in the code of the program itself? Yet you still can't see the code to determine if the reason you were denied credit or a loan was the program itself.

In the MYCIN and PROSPECTOR systems, conclusions are arrived at even when all the evidence needed to absolutely prove the conclusion is not known. Although it is possible to arrive at a more reliable conclusion by performing more tests, there are problems with the increasing time and cost of performing the tests. These constraints of time and money are particularly important in the case of medical treatment. Delaying treatment for more tests adds considerable cost; in the meantime, the patient may die. In the case of mineral exploration, the cost of additional tests is also a significant factor. It may be more cost effective to start drilling when you are 95 percent certain of success than to spend hundreds of thousands of dollars to be 98 percent certain.

4.3 TYPES OF ERROR

Many different types of **error** can contribute to uncertainty. Different theories of uncertainty attempt to resolve some or all of these to provide the most reliable inference. Figure 4.1 illustrates a simplified classification scheme for errors.

This figure should strictly be drawn as a lattice since there may be interconnections between many of the different types of error. For example, human error could be linked to ambiguity, measurement, reasoning, and so on. Table 4.1 gives examples of these errors.

Figure 4.1 Types of Errors

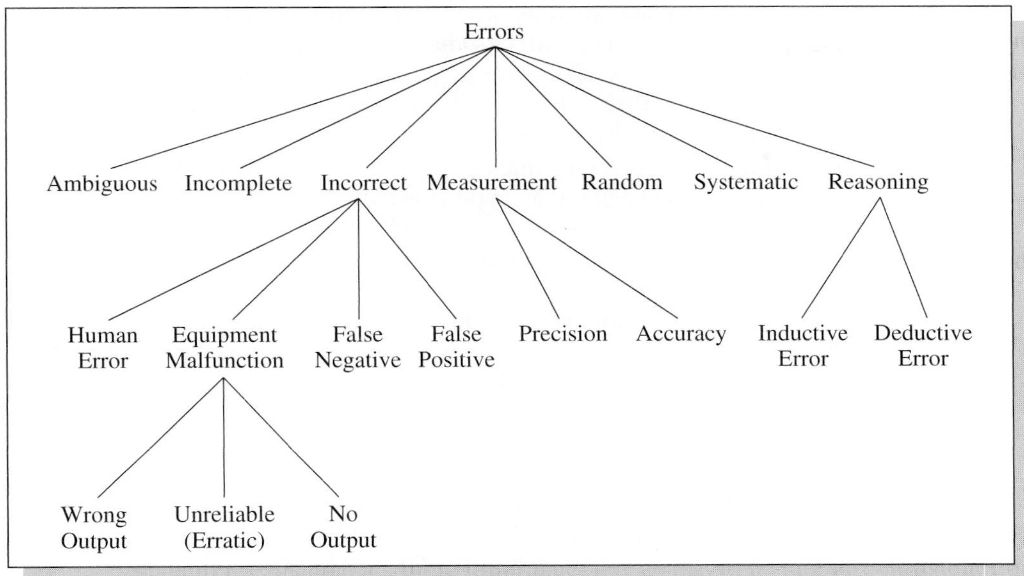

The first type of error shown is **ambiguity**, in which something may be interpreted in more than one way. The second type of error is **incompleteness** where some information is missing. A third type of error is **incorrectness** in which the information is wrong. Possible causes of incorrectness are human error, such as the accidental misreading of a dial or data, lying or misinformation, and malfunctioning equipment.

Table 4.1 Examples of Common Types of Errors

Example	Error	Reason
Turn the valve off	Ambiguous	What valve?
Turn valve-1	Incomplete	Which way?
Turn valve-1 off	Incorrect	Correct is on
Valve is stuck	False positive	Valve is not stuck
Valve is not stuck	False negative	Valve is stuck
Turn valve-1 to 5	Imprecise	Correct is 5.4
Turn valve-1 to 5.4	Inaccurate	Correct is 9.2
Turn valve-1 to 5.4 or 6 or 0	Unreliable	Equipment error
Valve-1 setting is 5.4 or 5.5 or 5.1	Random Error	Statistical Fluctuation
Valve-1 setting is 7.5	Systematic Error	Miscalibration
Valve-1 is not stuck because it has never been stuck before	Invalid Induction	Valve is stuck
Output is normal and so valve-1 is in good condition	Invalid deduction	Valve is stuck in open position

A **hypothesis** is an assumption to be tested. The **null hypothesis** is the assumption initially made, such as "the valve is stuck." One type of incorrect information is called **false positive,** which means acceptance of a hypothesis when it is not true. Likewise, a **false negative** means rejection of a hypothesis when it is true. Thus, if the valve is really not stuck, then accepting the hypothesis that it is stuck is a false positive. In statistics this is called a **Type I error**. Likewise, if the valve is really stuck and the hypothesis "the valve is stuck" is rejected, this is a false negative or **Type II error**.

The next two types of error shown in Table 4.1 are **errors of measurement**. These are errors of **precision** and **accuracy**. Although these terms are sometimes used synonymously, they are very different. Consider two rulers, one of which is graduated in millimeters and the other is graduated in centimeters. Obviously the millimeter ruler is more precise than the centimeter one. However, suppose the graduations of the millimeter ruler were incorrectly made. In that case the millimeter ruler is inaccurate and its measurements cannot be trusted unless a correction factor is known. Thus accuracy corresponds to the truth, while precision corresponds to how well the truth is known. For the two rulers, the millimeter ruler measures precision ten times more precisely than the centimeter one, but its inaccuracy can lead to serious problems.

Another type of error is **unreliability**. If the measuring equipment supplying the facts is unreliable, the data are **erratic**. An erratic reading is one that is not constant but fluctuates. Sometimes it may be correct, and sometimes not.

A reading that fluctuates may be caused by the basic random nature of the system being studied, such as the decay of radioactive atoms. Because the cause of the decay is a quantum mechanics phenomenon, the rate of decay fluctuates randomly about a mean value. The random fluctuations about the mean constitute a **random error** and lead to uncertainty of the mean. Other types of random error may be caused by Brownian motion, electronic noise due to thermal effects, and so forth. However, erratic readings may also be caused by a loose connection.

A **systematic error** is one that is not random but instead is introduced because of some bias. For example, the miscalibration of a ruler so that its graduations are smaller than normal gives a systematic error that indicates readings are higher than normal.

4.4 ERRORS AND INDUCTION

The next type of error is an **invalid induction**: "The valve is not stuck because it's never been stuck before." The process of **induction** is the opposite of deduction. It used to be said that deduction proceeds from the general to the specific, as in:

```
All men are mortal
Socrates is a man
∴ Socrates is mortal
```

to deduce the specific conclusion that Socrates is mortal.

It was also said that induction goes from the specific to the general, as in:

```
My disk has never crashed
∵ My disk will never crash
```

where the upside down triangle symbol, ∵ , stands for the "**inductive therefore**" in contrast to the triangle, ∴, "**deductive therefore**." The above fallacious inductive argument about disks shows the problem in the old-style thinking of considering deduction as reasoning from the specific to the general. The above is really a fallacious deductive argument since it argues from the general case that my disk has never crashed to the specific case that it will not crash even one time.

While you may still see some books which claim that deduction goes from the general to specific and induction goes from the specific to the general, contemporary logic considers that deduction guarantees the truth of the conclusion if the premises are true. An inductive argument simply means that the stronger the premises, the more probable it is for the conclusion to be true.

Consider the following statements:

```
My two pets are Smokey and Boots
Smokey has a tail
Boots has a tail
∴ All my pets have tails
```

This is an example of a valid deductive argument in which the specific premises lead to a general conclusion; the opposite of what was formerly taught as deduction going from the general to the specific, and still found in some old dictionaries. The moral is that even math and logic evolve. This type of argument is also called **sound** because it is both valid and based on true premises. Here we mean true in a semantically valid way; that is, the meaning in the real world is true since both my pets do have tails.

Now consider the following argument:

```
My two pets are Smokey and Boots
Smokey has a trunk
Boots has a trunk
∴ All my pets have trunks
```

This is still a valid argument but no longer sound because Smokey and Boots are not elephants and so do not have trunks. (Well they do have hope chests but that's not the same thing.)

Except for mathematical induction, inductive arguments can never be proven correct. Instead, inductive arguments can only provide some degree of confidence that the conclusion is correct. We would not have much confidence in the preceding inductive argument about hard disk failure. As another example, consider the following argument:

```
The fire alarm goes off
∵ There is a fire
```

An even stronger inductive argument is:

```
The fire alarm goes off
I smell smoke
∵ There is a fire
```

Although this is a stronger argument, it is not proof that there is a fire. The smoke could be coming from hamburgers cooking on a grill and the fire alarm could have been set off accidentally. A deductive proof of a fire is the following:

```
The fire alarm goes off
I smell smoke
My clothes are burning
∴ There is a fire
```

Notice that this is a deductive argument because you can see the flames even though it argues from specific premises, not general ones.

Expert systems may consist of deductive and inductive rules, where the inductive rules are of a heuristic nature. Induction has also been applied to the automatic generation of rules, as you will see in a later chapter on knowledge acquisition.

Besides uncertainty with facts, the rules of an expert system may have uncertainty if they are based on heuristics. A heuristic is commonly called a rule of thumb because it is based on personal experience. (For example, if you would like to learn an important rule about hammering a nail correctly, first hit your thumb. This is called learning by "rule of thumb." This is remarkably effective compared to sitting in a lecture for three hours and sleep learning.)

Sometimes experience is a good guide. However, it may not be applicable to 100 percent of the cases since experience is heuristic. For example, you would expect that everyone who jumps off a fifty-story building would be killed. However, people can jump off a fifty-story building and not be killed—if they wear a parachute.

One of the interesting characteristics of human experts is that they reason well under uncertainty. Even if there is a great deal of uncertainty, experts can usually make good judgments, or they won't be considered experts for long.

Another characteristic is that experts can easily revise their opinions if it turns out that some of the original facts were wrong. This is nonmonotonic reasoning, as discussed in Chapter 3. It is more difficult to program expert systems to backtrack their reasoning process because all the intermediate facts need to be saved and a history kept of rule firings. Human experts appear to revise their reasoning with little effort, especially politicians.

Besides inductive errors, there may also be deductive errors or fallacies, as described in Chapter 3. An example of a fallacious schema discussed in Chapter 3 is:

```
p → q
q
∴ p
```

For example,

```
If the valve is in good condition,
   then the output is normal
The output is normal
∴ The valve is in good condition
```

is a fallacious argument. The valve may be stuck in the open position so that the output is normal. However, if it is necessary to close the valve, the problem will show up. This can be very serious if the valve needs to be closed quickly, as in the case of an emergency shutdown of a nuclear reactor.

In contrast to the previous errors we have discussed, inductive and deductive errors are errors of reasoning. These types of errors lead to the incorrect formulation of rules.

Generally, humans do not seem to process uncertain information in the best possible way. Even experts are not immune to making mistakes, especially under uncertainty. This can be a major problem in knowledge acquisition, when the expert's knowledge must be quantified in rules. Inconsistencies, inaccuracy, and all the other possible errors of uncertainty may show up. Experts will then have to correct their knowledge, which can delay completion of the expert system.

4.5 CLASSICAL PROBABILITY

The oldest tool and still very important tool in AI problem solving is **probability** (Grinstead 97). Probability is a quantitative way of dealing with uncertainty. The concept of probability originated in the 17th century when some French gamblers asked for help from the leading mathematicians such as Pascal, Fermat, and others. Gambling had become very popular; and since large amounts of money were involved, gamblers wanted methods to aid in calculating the odds of winning. In fact, the classic Gambler's Ruin problem is a proof using probability theory of the empirical fact noticed by gamblers: that the house always wins if you play long enough (Ross 02). (Unfortunately it's the gamblers who lose the most who would benefit by studying probability.)

The theory of **classical probability** was first proposed by Pascal and Fermat in 1654. Since then much work has been done with probability and several new branches have been developed. Many applications of probability have been shown in science, engineering, business, economics, and virtually every other field.

The Definition of Classical Probability

Classical probability is also called **a priori probability** because it deals with ideal games or systems. As discussed in Chapter 2, the term *a priori* means "before," that is, without regard to the real world. A priori probability considers games such as dice, cards, coins, or whatever, as ideal systems that do not become worn out.

Ideal systems do not exhibit the real-world characteristics of wear-and-tear because then they would not have precisely reproducible characteristics. That is, a real die (plural dice) may exhibit a bias toward some particular numbers after one side becomes worn down after numerous throws. Likewise, depending on the manufacturer, a real die may exhibit a preference toward higher numbers because more pips (small colored holes) are drilled in higher numbers. This bias was determined by analyzing data from 1,000,000 throws of a real die. A new die was used every 20,000 throws to avoid bias caused by uneven wearing of the faces. The fraction of times different numbers came up is shown in Table 4.2.

Table 4.2 Results of 1,000,000 Throws of a Die

Number	1	2	3	4	5	6
Fraction	0.155	0.159	0.164	0.169	0.174	0.179

In an ideal system all numbers occur equally, which makes analysis much easier.

The fundamental formula of classical probability is defined as the probability:

$$P = \frac{W}{N}$$

where W is the number of wins and N is the number of equally possible **events**, which are the possible outcomes of an experiment or **trial**. For example, if you throw a die once, there are six possible events from this single trial. The die may come to rest with its top showing either a 1, 2, 3, 4, 5, or 6. Under classical probability it is assumed that any of these six events is equally possible and so the probability of rolling a 1, $P(1)$, is:

$$P(1) = \frac{1}{6}$$

Likewise:

$$P(2) = \frac{1}{6}$$

and so forth.

The probability of losing, Q, is:

$$Q = \frac{N - W}{N} = 1 - P$$

The fundamental formula for P is an a priori definition because the probability is calculated *before* the game is played. Because the term *a priori* means "that which precedes" or "before the event" when discussing probabilities, an a priori probability assumes that all possible events are known and that each event is equally likely to happen.

For example, in rolling a die, the possible spots on each face are known as 1, 2, 3, 4, 5, and 6. Also, if the die is *fair*—not loaded—then each side is equally likely to come up. Likewise, in a fair deck of cards, all 52 cards are known and equally likely to be drawn under a fair shuffle. The probability of any one face of the die coming up is 1/6 and for any card it is 1/52.

When repeated trials give exactly the same result, the system is **deterministic**. If it is not deterministic, it is **nondeterministic**. However, nondeterministic is strictly not the same as random. The term *random* may have good or bad connotations. For example, a random event like shooting dice in Las Vegas may make you a millionaire or a pauper depending on the outcome. In contrast, a system that is designed to be nondeterministic simply means that there may be more than one way to meet one or more goals given the same input.

A nondeterministic finite state machine that could go to either state 1 or 2 if a digit is input. If only digits are input, eventually it recognizes integers. If real numbers with a decimal point or using exponential notation are input, it will eventually recognize this and wind up in a different fiinal state. In general, a nondeterministic finite state machine design has fewer states than a deterministic one. It can always be converted to a finite state machine.

People are very familiar with nondeterminism when using a search engine. Given the same input, you will see different output appear first on the list (unless it is a "sponsored" link and always appears first). For example, go to google.com and enter the search words, "giarratano expert systems," and note what results are listed first. Now try, "expert systems giarratano" and you will see different results even though you have supplied the search engine with the same search terms.

Another example is what you do in case of a headache. There are many ways of trying to treat a headache and which one you choose depends on the mood you're in or what's available. In some types of expert system tools such as CLIPS, nondeterminism is used to prevent bias in rule firings. When the patterns of multiple rules are satisfied and there is no explicit preference as to which rule should be executed, the inference engine makes an arbitrary choice of the rule to be executed. This prevents a bias in which one rule, say the first one entered, is fired. This would be the case if all the knowledge were entered in a conventional programming language as IF-THEN rules and the program just kept trying them in the order they were typed in the source code. In fact this is one reason expert systems are not written in a conventional language: to avoid too much determinism! The expert system inference engine operates like a person and does not always make the same decision when rules of equal priority are applicable, such as: should I take an aspirin or a Bloody Mary for my headache?

Sample Spaces

The result of a trial is a **sample point** and the set of all possible sample points defines a **sample space**. For example, if a single die is rolled, any one of the

Figure 4.2 Sample Space and Events

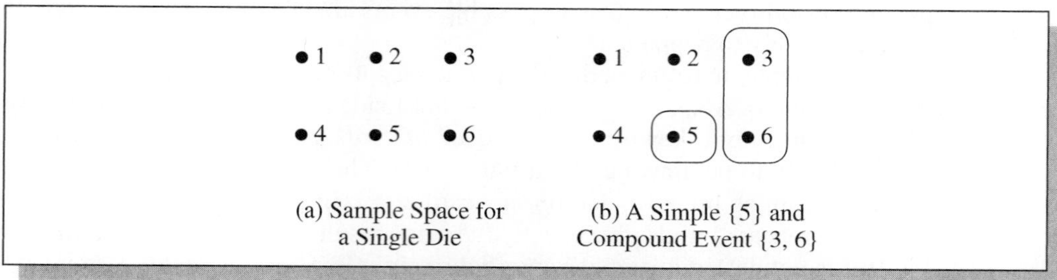

(a) Sample Space for a Single Die

(b) A Simple {5} and Compound Event {3, 6}

sample points 1, 2, 3, 4, 5, or 6 can occur. Figure 4.2(a) shows the sample space for the roll of a single die. The sample space is the set { 1, 2, 3, 4, 5, 6 }.

An **event** is a subset of the sample space. For example, the event { 1 } occurs if the die comes up with a 1. A **simple event** has only one element and a **compound event** has more than one, as shown in Figure 4.2.

A graphical way of determining the sample space is constructing an **event tree**. As a simple example, suppose there are two computers which either work, *W*, or don't work, *D*. Figure 4.3 shows the event tree while Table 4.3 shows a table form of the sample space. Note that the compound events are listed in the order {computer1, computer2 }. The sample space is { *WW*, *WD*, *DW*, *DD* }.

This type of event tree is a *binary* tree since only binary probabilities are involved. That is, either the computer works or it doesn't. Many types of problems have this type of tree. For example, the toss of a coin leads to a binary event tree since there are only two possible outcomes for every throw.

Probability and statistics are fields that make extensive use of each other's theories. Statistics is concerned with collecting and analyzing data about **populations**, a set from which samples are drawn. One goal of statistics is to make inferences about the parent population from which the sample population is drawn. A typical example of statistical inference is to infer what proportion of registered voters favors a certain candidate, based on a poll.

Figure 4.3 Event Tree for a Compound Event

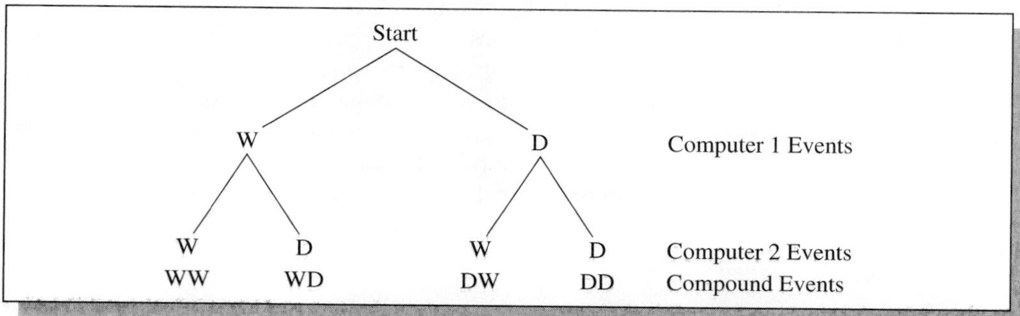

Table 4.3 Sample Space of Binary Events

		Computer 2	
		W	*D*
Computer 1	W	WW	WD
	D	DW	DD

One application of probability theory is to deduce whether the sample of voters is really representative of all voters, or whether it may be biased in favor of a certain party. Although this example relates to real objects such as people other populations such as the possible number of coin tosses is hypothetical. Every coin toss is a sample of the hypothetical population of all coin tosses.

Deduction and induction are the basis of reasoning about populations, as shown in Figure 4.4. Given a known population, deduction lets us make inferences about the unknown sample. Correspondingly, given a known sample, induction lets us make inferences about the unknown population.

Theory of Probability

A formal theory of probability can be made using three axioms:

axiom 1: $0 \leq P(E) \leq 1$

This axiom defines the range of probability to be the real numbers from 0 to 1. Negative probabilities are not allowed. A **certain event** is assigned probability 1 and an **impossible event** is assigned probability 0:

axiom 2: $\sum_i P(E_i) = 1$

Figure 4.4 Deductive and Inductive Reasoning about Populations and Samples

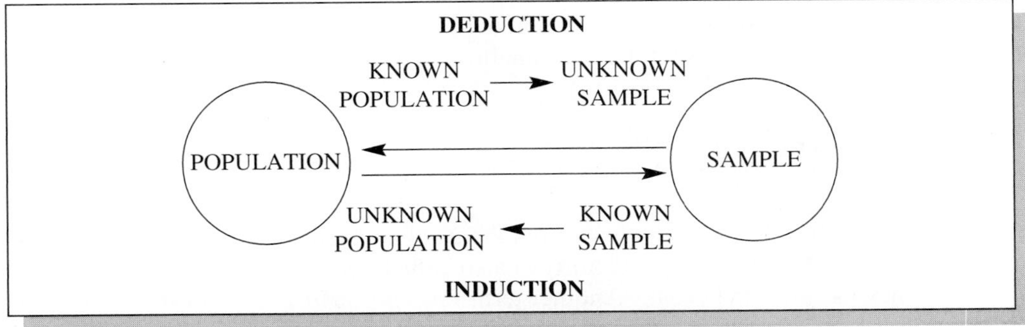

This axiom states that the sum of all events that do not affect each other, called **mutually exclusive events**, is 1. Mutually exclusive events have no sample point in common. For example, a computer cannot be both working correctly and not working correctly at the same time, unless it is a quantum computer.

As a corollary of this axiom:

$$P(E) + P(E') = 1$$

where E′ is the complement of event E. This corollary means that the probability of an event occurring plus the probability of it not occurring is 1. That is, the occurrence and nonoccurrence of an event is a mutually exclusive and complete sample space:

$$\textit{axiom 3:} \quad P(E_1 \cup E_2) = P(E_1) + P(E_2)$$

where E_1 and E_2 are mutually exclusive events. This axiom means that if E_1 and E_2 cannot both occur simultaneously (mutually exclusive events) then the probability of one or the other occurring is the sum of their probabilities.

From these axioms, theorems can be deduced concerning the calculation of probabilities under other situations, such as nonmutually exclusive events, as we shall see later. While these axioms form the basis for a theory of probability, notice that they *do not specify the basic probabilities P(E)*. The basic probabilities of events are determined by other methods such as a priori.

These axioms put probability on a sound theoretical basis. In fact, the axiomatic theory is also called the **objective theory of probability**. These particular axioms were devised by Kolmogorov. An equivalent theory using axioms of conditional probability was created by Renyi.

4.6 EXPERIMENTAL AND SUBJECTIVE PROBABILITIES

Other than ideal games with equal likelihood, classical probability cannot answer questions like what is the probability of your disk drive crashing tomorrow or what is the life expectancy of your spouse (unless you have a gun pointed at them.)

In contrast to the a priori approach, **experimental probability** defines the probability of an event, P(E), as the limit of a frequency distribution:

$$P(E) = \lim_{N \to \infty} \frac{f(E)}{N}$$

where f(E) is the frequency of outcomes of an event for N observed total outcomes. This type of probability is also called ***a posteriori* probability**, which means "after the event." Another term for *a posteriori* is the **posterior probability**. The idea of a posteriori is to measure the frequency that an event occurs for a large number of trials and from this induce the experimental probability.

For example, to determine the experimental probability of your disk drive crashing, you could take a poll of other people with your type of drive. The results of a hypothetical poll are shown in Table 4.4.

Table 4.4 Hypothetical Time for a Disk Drive to Crash

Total Percent Crashed	Hours Used
10	100
25	250
50	500
75	750
99	1,000

If your drive has been used 750 hours, then you could induce that there is a 75 percent probability of it crashing tomorrow. Notice that this 75 percent figure is an induction rather than a deduction. Unlike an ideal game, your disk drive is not exactly the same as others. There may be differences in the materials used, quality control, environmental conditions, and use that affect the drive and its longevity. It is much easier to produce simple devices such as dice or cards with much finer tolerances than a complex piece of equipment like a disk drive.

Another type of experimental probability can be induced from mortality tables used by life insurance companies that show the probability of a person dying, as a function of age and sex. Calculating the odds of *your* mortality based on these tables is an induction since you are unique. An analogous situation holds for house insurance. Unless your house is prefabricated and burns down frequently so that the individual experimental probability can be calculated, the experimental probabilities used will be based on similar types of houses. In fact you should show this book to your insurance company and demand a discount if you live in a trailer since their probability of its burning down is subject to classical probability and can be exactly calculated. (This is another example of the utility of this book to get an insurance discount as well as evading speeding tickets as discussed in a previous chapter.)

There is also a type of probability called **subjective probability**. Suppose you were asked the probability that automobiles using superconducting electric motors would cost $10,000 by the year 2020. Since there is no data on the cost of these cars, there is no way to extrapolate the costs to see if $10,000 is reasonable. On the other hand, hybrid gas/electric cars such as the Toyota Prius are already providing some data which may be extrapolated to all electric cars. And if the motor is superconducting and an order of magnitude more efficient, some reasonable extrapolation can be made.

Subjective probability deals with events that are not reproducible and have no historical basis on which to extrapolate, such as drilling an oil well at a new site. However, a subjective probability by an expert is better than no estimate at all and is usually very accurate (or the expert won't be an expert for long.)

A subjective probability is actually a belief or opinion expressed as a probability rather than a probability based on axioms or empirical measurement. Beliefs and opinions of an expert play important roles in expert systems, as we shall see later in this chapter. Table 4.5 summarizes the different types of probabilities.

Table 4.5 Types of Probabilities

Names	Formula	Characteristics
a priori (classical, theoretical, mathematical, symmetric, equiprobable, equal-likelihood)	$P(E) = \frac{W}{N}$ where W is the number of outcomes of event E for a total of N possible outcomes	Repeatable events Equally likely outcomes Exact math form known Not based on experiment All possible events and outcomes known
a posteriori (experimental, empirical, scientific, relative frequency, statistical) $P(E) \approx \frac{f(E)}{N}$	$P(E) = \lim_{N \to \infty} \frac{f(E)}{N}$ where f(E) is the frequency, f, that event, E, is observed for N total outcomes	Repeatable events based on experiments Approximated by a finite number of experiments Exact math form unknown
subjective (personal)	See Section 4.12	Nonrepeatable events Exact math form unknown Relative frequency method not possible Based on expert's opinion experience, judgment, belief

4.7 COMPOUND PROBABILITIES

The probabilities of compound events can be computed from their sample spaces. As a very simple example, consider the probability of rolling a die such that the outcome is an even number and a number divisible by three. This can be expressed in terms of a Venn diagram for the sets:

$$A = \{ 2, 4, 6 \} \quad B = \{ 3, 6 \}$$

in the sample space of the die, as shown in Figure 4.5.

Notice that the intersection of the sets A and B is:

$$A \cap B = \{ 6 \}$$

The compound probability of rolling an even number and a number divisible by three is:

$$P(A \cap B) = \frac{n(A \cap B)}{n(S)} = \frac{1}{6}$$

where n is the number of elements in the sets and S is the sample space.

Figure 4.5 Compound Probability of Rolling a Single Die to Give an Even Number and a Number Divisible by Three

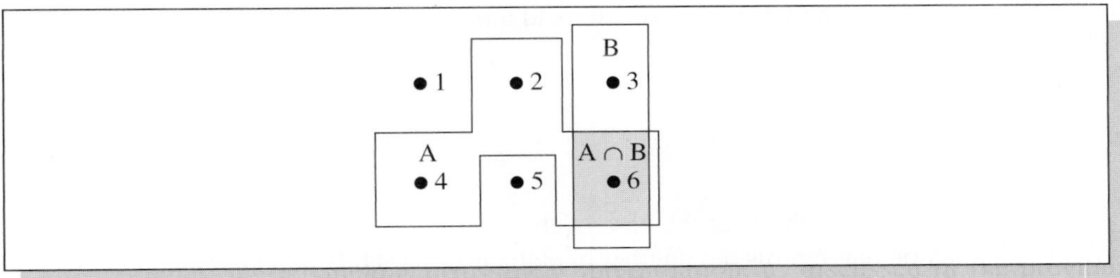

Events that do not affect each other in any way are called **independent events**. For two independent events A and B, the probability is simply the product of the individual probabilities. Events A and B are said to be **pairwise independent:**

$$P(A \cap B) = P(A)\ P(B)$$

Two events are called **stochastically independent** events if and only if the above formula is true. The term *stochastic* comes from the Greek and means "guess." It is commonly used as a synonym for probability. Thus a stochastic experiment has a probabilistic outcome, in contrast to the nonrandom outcome of a deterministic experiment. As a stochastic experiment, try marrying and divorcing 10 people one after another and you might wind up in a happy or unhappy state. On the other hand, if you marry all ten at once you will wind up in the deterministic state of prison.

For three events you might assume that independence is:

$$P(A \cap B \cap C) = P(A)\ P(B)\ P(C)$$

Unfortunately, life and probability are not that simple. The formula for the **mutual independence** of N events requires that 2^N equations be satisfied. This requirement is summarized by the following equation, where the asterisks mean that every combination of an event and its complement must be satisfied:

$$P(A^*_1 \cap A^*_2 \ldots \cap A^*_N) = P(A^*_1)\ P(A^*_2)\ \ldots\ P(A^*_N)$$

For three events, the above equation for mutual independence requires that *all* the following equations be satisfied:

$$\begin{aligned}
P(A \cap B \cap C) &= P(A)\ P(B)\ P(C) \\
P(A \cap B \cap C') &= P(A)\ P(B)\ P(C') \\
P(A \cap B' \cap C) &= P(A)\ P(B')\ P(C) \\
P(A \cap B' \cap C') &= P(A)\ P(B')\ P(C') \\
P(A' \cap B \cap C) &= P(A')\ P(B)\ P(C) \\
P(A' \cap B \cap C') &= P(A')\ P(B)\ P(C') \\
P(A' \cap B' \cap C) &= P(A')\ P(B')\ P(C) \\
P(A' \cap B' \cap C') &= P(A')\ P(B')\ P(C')
\end{aligned}$$

The pairwise independence of every two events is not enough to guarantee mutual independence as shown in Problem 4.6.

For our die, the events of an even number and a number divisible by three definitely affect each other and so is *not* a stochastic experiment. The probability of an even number on one die and a number divisible by three on another *is* stochastic,

$$P(A \cup B) = P(A)\ P(B) = \frac{3}{6} \cdot \frac{2}{6} = \frac{1}{6}$$

Now let's consider the case of the union of events, $P(A \cup B)$. Define n as a function that returns the number of elements of a set. If we add the number of elements in A to those in B and divide by the total elements in the sample space n(S),

$$(1)\quad P(A \cup B) = \frac{n(A) + n(B)}{n(S)} = P(A) + P(B)$$

then the result will be too big if the sets overlap. If you look at Figure 4.5, applying this formula gives:

$$P(A \cup B) = \frac{3 + 2}{6} = \frac{5}{6}$$

but you can easily see that there are only four elements in the union since:

$$A \cup B = \{ 2, 3, 4, 6 \}$$

The problem is that just adding n(A) to n(B) is counting the set intersection {6} twice since it belongs to both A and B.

The correct formula simply requires subtracting the extra probability of set intersection:

$$(2)\quad P(A \cup B) = P(A) + P(B) - P(A \cap B)$$

which for our die reduces to:

$$P(A \cup B) = \frac{3}{6} + \frac{2}{6} - \frac{1}{6} = \frac{4}{6} = \frac{2}{3}$$

Formula (1) holds when the sets are disjoint and so have no elements in common. It is a special case of formula (2), which is called the **Additive Law**. The Additive Law can also be derived as a theorem using the three axioms of probability discussed earlier. The Additive Law for three events is:

$$\begin{aligned} P(A \cup B \cup C) = {} & P(A) + P(B) + P(C) \\ & - P(A \cap B) - P(A \cap C) - P(B \cap C) \\ & + P(A \cap B \cap C) \end{aligned}$$

Other laws for neither A nor B and the exclusive-OR of A and B can also be derived from the axioms. The value of these laws for compound probabilities is that (1) experiments do not have to be made for each possible combination of probabilities and (2) the individual elements of large sample spaces do not have to be counted.

4.8 CONDITIONAL PROBABILITIES

Events that are not mutually exclusive influence one another. Knowing that one event has occurred may cause us to revise the probability that another event will occur.

Multiplicative Law

The probability of an event A, given that event B occurred, is called a **conditional probability** and is indicated by P (A | B). The conditional probability is defined as:

$$P(A \mid B) = \frac{P(A \cap B)}{P(B)} \quad \text{for } P(B) \neq 0$$

The probability P(B) is the a priori or prior probability before any information is known. When used in association with a conditional probability, the prior probability is sometimes called the **unconditional probability** or an **absolute probability**.

This definition of conditional probability can be intuitively explained if you look at the example of Figure 4.6, which is a sample space of eight events. From Figure 4.6 the probabilities can be calculated as the ratios of the number of events, n(A) or n(B), to the total number in the sample space n(S). That is,

$$P(A) = \frac{n(A)}{n(S)} = \frac{4}{8}$$

$$P(B) = \frac{n(B)}{n(S)} = \frac{6}{8}$$

Figure 4.6 Sample Space of Two Intersecting Events

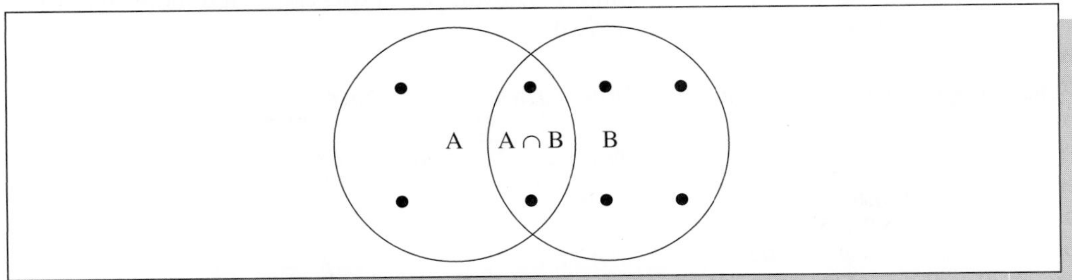

If we know that event B has occurred, the reduced sample space is just that of B:

$$n(S) = 6$$

Since B occurred, only the events in A that are associated with B are considered:

$$P(A \mid B) = \frac{n(A \cap B)}{n(B)} = \frac{2}{6}$$

To express the result in terms of probabilities, just divide the numerator and denominator of the above by n(S):

$$P(A \mid B) = \frac{\dfrac{n(A \cap B)}{n(S)}}{\dfrac{n(B)}{n(S)}}$$

$$= \frac{P(A \cap B)}{P(B)} \quad \text{for } P(B) \neq 0$$

The **Multiplicative Law** of probability for two events is then defined as:

$$P(A \cap B) = P(A \mid B)\ P(B)$$

which is equivalent to the following:

$$P(A \cap B) = P(B \mid A)\ P(A)$$

The Multiplicative Law for three events is the following:

$$P(A \cap B \cap C) = P(A \mid B \cap C)\ P(B \mid C)\ P(C)$$

and the Generalized Multiplicative Law is:

$$P(A_1 \cap A_2 \cap \ldots \cap A_N) = P(A_1 \mid A_2 \cap \ldots \cap A_N) \cdot P(A_2 \mid A_3 \cap \ldots \cap A_N) \cdot \ldots P(A_{N-1} \mid A_N)\ P(A_N)$$

As an example of probabilities, Table 4.6 shows hypothetical probabilities of a disk crash using a Brand X drive within one year.

Table 4.6 Hypothetical Probabilities of a Disk Crash Within One Year

	Brand X	Not Brand X′	Total of Rows
Crash C	0.6	0.1	0.7
No Crash C′	0.2	0.1	0.3
Total of Columns	0.8	0.2	1.0

The probabilities of 0.6, 0.1, 0.2, and 0.1 inside the middle region in the table are called **interior probabilities** and represent the intersections of events. The sum of the rows and columns are displayed as *Totals*, and are called **marginal probabilities** because they lie on the margin of the table.

Tables 4.7 and 4.8 show the set and probability meanings in more detail. Figure 4.7 shows the Venn diagram of the sample space intersection. From Table 4.8 you can see that the sum of total row probabilities and total column probabilities is 1.

Table 4.7 Set Interpretation

	X	X′	Total of Rows
C	$C \cap X$	$C \cap X'$	$C = (C \cap X) \cup (C \cap X')$
C′	$C' \cap X$	$C' \cap X'$	$C' = (C' \cap X) \cup (C' \cap X')$
Total of Columns	$X = (C' \cap X) \cup (C \cap X)$	$X' = (C' \cap X') \cup (C \cap X')$	*S* (Sample Space)

Table 4.8 Probability Interpretation of Two Sets

	X	X′	Total of Rows
C	$P(C \cap X)$	$P(C \cap X')$	P(C)
C′	$P(C' \cap X)$	$P(C' \cap X')$	P(C′)
Total of Columns	P(X)	P(X′)	1.0

Using Table 4.8, the probabilities of all events can be calculated. Some probabilities are:

(1) The probability of a crash for both Brand X and not Brand X (the sample space) is

```
P(C)  = 0.7
```

Figure 4.7 The Sample Space Interpretation of Two Sets

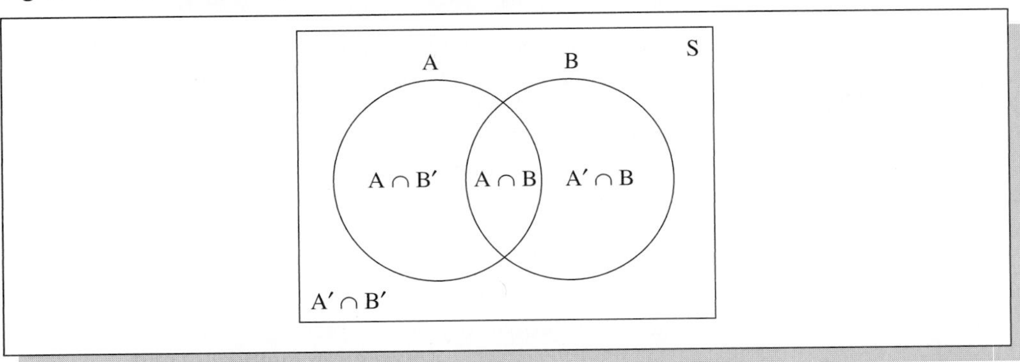

(2) The probability of no crash for the sample space is:

$$P(C') = 0.3$$

(3) The probability of using Brand X is:

$$P(X) = 0.8$$

(4) The probability of not using Brand X is:

$$P(X') = 0.2$$

(5) The probability of a crash and using Brand X is:

$$P(C \cap X) = 0.6$$

(6) The probability of a crash, given that Brand X is used, is:

$$P(C \mid X) = \frac{P(C \cap X)}{P(X)} = \frac{0.6}{0.8} = 0.75$$

(7) The probability of a crash, given that Brand X is not used, is:

$$P(C \mid X') = \frac{P(C \cap X')}{P(X')} = \frac{0.1}{0.2} = 0.50$$

Probabilities (5) and (6) may appear to have similar meanings when you read their descriptions. However, (5) is simply the intersection of two events, while (6) is a conditional probability. The meaning of the intersection, (5), is the following:

```
If a disk drive is picked randomly, then 0.6 of the
time it will be Brand X and have crashed.
```

In other words, we are just picking samples from the population of disk drives. Some of those drives are Brand X and have crashed (0.6), some are not Brand X and have crashed (0.1), some are Brand X and have not crashed (0.2), and some are not Brand X and have not crashed (0.1).

In contrast, the meaning of the conditional probability (6) is very different:

```
If a Brand X drive is picked, then 0.75 of the time
it will have crashed.
```

Notice that in the conditional probability we are picking those items (Brand X) of interest to us and considering them as the new sample space.

If any of the following equations are true, then events A and B are **independent**:

$$P(A \mid B) = P(A) \text{ or}$$
$$P(B \mid A) = P(B) \text{ or}$$
$$P(A \cap B) = P(A)\, P(B)$$

If any one of these equations are true, then so are the others.

Bayes' Theorem

The conditional probability, P(A | B), states the probability of event A given that event B occurred. The inverse problem is to find the **inverse probability,** which states the probability of an earlier event given that a later one occurred. This type of probability occurs often, as in the case of medical or equipment diagnosis where symptoms appear and the problem is to find the most likely cause. The solution to this problem is **Bayes' Theorem**, also sometimes called Bayes' Formula, Bayes' Rule, or Bayes' Law, named after the 18th Century British clergyman and mathematician, Thomas Bayes. Bayesian theory is extensively used today in many applications. In fact the familiar Office Assistant, and Technical Troubleshooter Help that is provided automatically in Microsoft Office and Windows use Bayesian logic to better try and help you rather than relying on simple decision trees (Gates 00).

As an example of Bayes' Theorem, let's see how it applies to the disk drive crashes. From the conditional probability (6), there is a 75% probability a Brand X drive will crash within one year, while based on (7), the probability of a non-Brand X drive crash within one year is 50%. The inverse question is, suppose you have a drive and don't know its brand, what is the probability that if it crashes, it is Brand X? Non-Brand X?

A situation like this, in which you don't really know the drive, occurs all the time since computer manufacturers seldom make their own drives. Instead many buy drives from an original equipment manufacturer (OEM) and repackage the drives to sell under their own label. Depending on what OEM offers the lowest cost, the drive may vary from year to year with only the computer manufacturer's label remaining the same.

Given that a drive crashed, the probability of it being Brand X can be stated using conditional probability and the results (1), (5):

$$P(X \mid C) = \frac{P(C \cap X)}{P(C)} = \frac{0.6}{0.7} = \frac{6}{7}$$

Alternatively, using the Multiplicative Law on the numerator, and (1), (3), (6):

$$P(X \mid C) = \frac{P(C|X)P(X)}{P(C)} = \frac{(0.75)(0.8)}{0.7} = \frac{0.6}{0.7} = \frac{6}{7}$$

The probability P(X | C) is the **inverse** or a posteriori probability, which states that if the drive crashed, it was Brand X. Figure 4.8 shows a decision tree

Figure 4.8 Decision Tree for the Disk Crashes

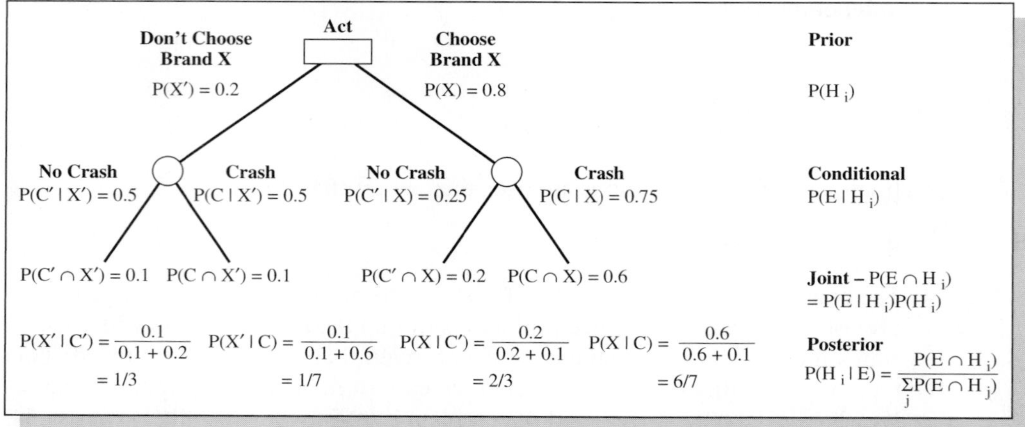

for the disk crashes. The square symbol indicates an **act** or decision, and the circle indicates an **event** or occurrence. The prior probabilities are those before the experiments of measuring crashes. The posterior or inverse probabilities are those determined after the completion of the experiments. The posterior probabilities allow us to revise the prior probabilities to obtain more accurate results.

The general form of Bayes' Theorem can be written in terms of events, E, and hypotheses (assumptions), H, in the following alternative forms:

$$P(H_i \mid E) = \frac{P(E \cap H_i)}{\sum_j P(E \cap H_j)}$$

$$= \frac{P(E \mid H_i)\, P(H_i)}{\sum_j P(E \mid H_j)\, P(H_j)}$$

$$= \frac{P(E \mid H_i)\, P(H_i)}{P(E)}$$

4.9 HYPOTHETICAL REASONING AND BACKWARD INDUCTION

Bayes' Theorem is commonly used for decision tree analysis of business and the social sciences. The method of **Bayesian decision making** is also used in the PROSPECTOR expert system to decide favorable sites for mineral exploration. PROSPECTOR achieved a great deal of fame as the first expert system to discover a valuable molybdenum deposit worth $100,000,000.

As an example of Bayesian decision making under uncertainty, let's look at the problem of oil exploration. Initially, the prospector must decide what the chances are of finding oil. If there is no evidence either for or against oil, the prospector may assign the subjective prior probabilities for oil, O, of:

```
P(O) = P(O') = 0.5
```

With no evidence, an assignment of probabilities that are equally weighted between possible outcomes is said to be made **in desperation**. The term *in desperation* does not mean that the prospector is (necessarily) in desperate need. It is a technical term for the unbiased prior assignment of probabilities. Naturally, the prospector believes that there is better than a 50-50 chance of finding oil, and so may assume the following:

```
P(O) = 0.6    P(O') = 0.4
```

A very important tool in oil and mineral exploration is the **seismic survey**. In this technique, dynamite or machinery creates sound pulses that travel through the earth. The sound waves are detected by microphones at various locations. By observing the arrival time of pulses and distortion of the sound waveform, it is possible to determine geologic structures and the possibility of oil and minerals. Unfortunately seismic tests are not 100 percent accurate. The sound waves may be affected by some types of geologic structures so the test reports the presence of oil when there really is none (false positive). Likewise, the test may report the absence of oil when there really is oil (false negative). Assume that the past history of the seismic test has given the following conditional probabilities, where + means a positive outcome and − is a negative outcome. Note that these are conditional probabilities because the cause (oil or no oil) must have occurred before the effect (test result). A posterior probability would be from an effect (test result) back to the cause (oil or no oil). Generally, a conditional probability is forward in time while a posterior probability is backward in time.

```
P(+ | O)  = 0.8                 P(− | O)  = 0.2 (false −)
P(+ | O') = 0.1 (false +)       P(− | O') = 0.9
```

Using the prior and conditional probabilities, we can construct the initial probability tree as shown in Figure 4.9. Also shown are the joint probabilities, which are calculated from the prior and conditional probabilities.

The Addition Law is then used to calculate the total probability of a + and a − test.

```
P(+) = P(+ ∩ O) + P(+ ∩ O') = 0.48 + 0.04 = 0.52
P(−) = P(− ∩ O) + P(− ∩ O') = 0.12 + 0.36 = 0.48
```

The P(+) and P(−) are unconditional probabilities that can now be used to calculate the posterior probabilities at the site, as shown in Figure 4.10. For example, the P(O′ | −) is the posterior probability for no oil at the site based on a negative test. The joint probabilities are then computed. Notice that the joint probabilities of Figure 4.10 are the same as in Figure 4.9. The revision of probabilities

Figure 4.9 Initial Probability Tree for Oil Exploration

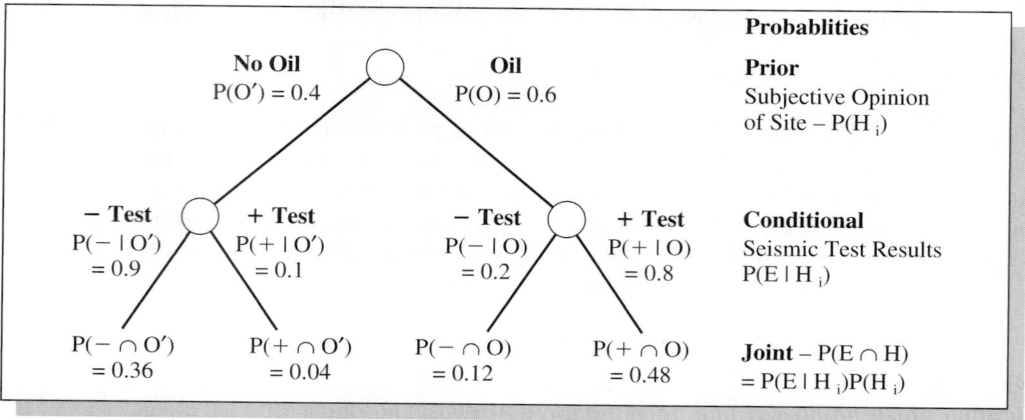

Figure 4.10 Revised Probability Tree for Oil Exploration

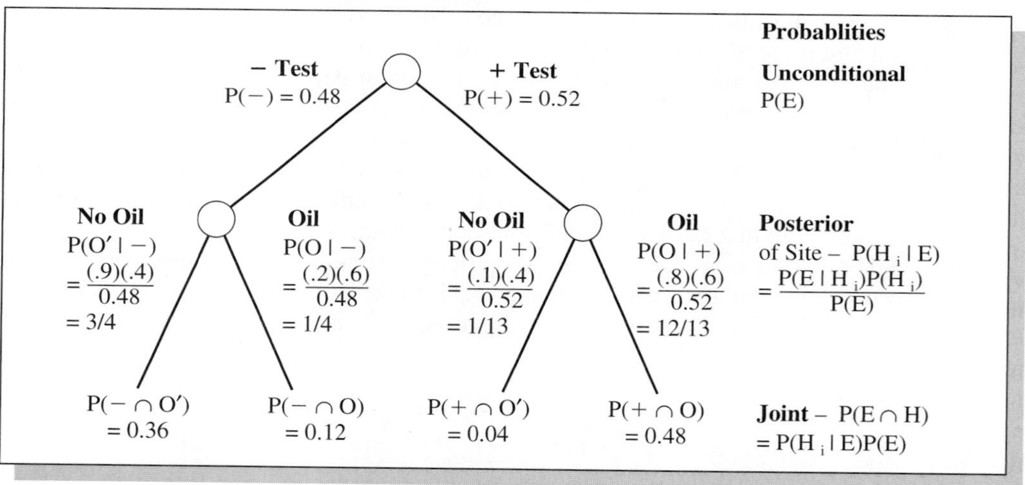

is necessary to give good results when experimental information, such as the seismic test results, occurs after the initial probability estimates (or guess).

Figure 4.11 shows the initial Bayesian decision tree using the data from Figure 4.10. The **payoffs** at the bottom of the tree are positive if money is made and negative if money is lost. The assumed amounts are shown in Table 4.9.

Thus, if oil is found, the payoff is \$1,000,000 − \$200,000 − \$50,000 = \$750,000 while a decision to quit after the seismic test result gives a payoff of −\$50,000, and the payoff for seismic testing and drilling but no oil is −\$200,000 − \$50,000 = −\$250,000. Note that this payoff is *not* −\$1,000,000 − \$ 200,000 − \$50,000 = −\$1,250,000 unless you can take advantage of a tax loophole (which is not impossible since many special tax riders are attached to bills in Congress if you have a good lobbyist).

Figure 4.11 Initial Bayesian Decision Tree for Oil Exploration

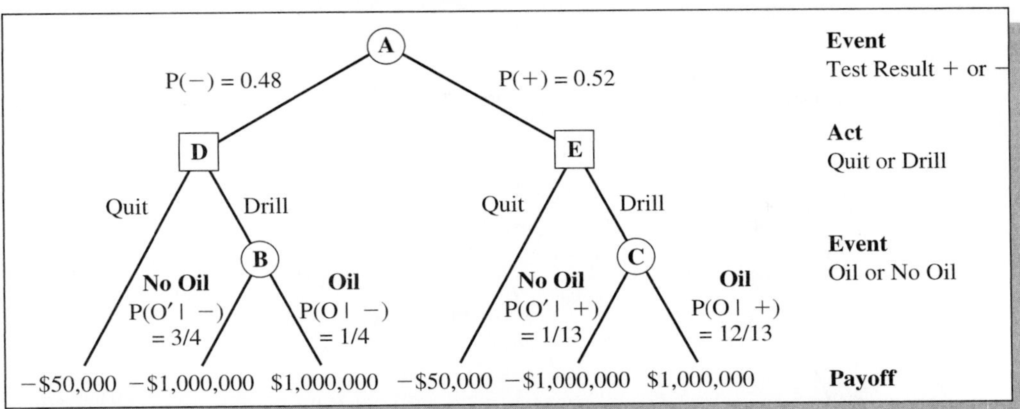

Table 4.9 Payoff Table for the Oil Exploration Problem

Oil lease, if successful	$1,000,000
Drilling expense	−$200,000
Seismic survey	−$50,000

In order for the prospector to make the best decision, the **expected payoff** must be calculated at event node A. The expected payoff is the amount the prospector can make by following the best course of action. To compute the expected payoff at the start, A, we must work backwards from the leaves. In probability theory, this process is called **backward induction**. That is, in order to achieve the expected payoff or goal that we want, we must reason backwards to find the causes that will lead us to the goal.

The expected payoff from an event node is the sum of the payoffs times the probabilities leading to the payoffs:

```
Expected payoff at node C
$673,077 = ($750,000) (12/13) – ($250,000) (1/13)

Expected payoff at node B
$0 = ($750,000) (1/4) – ($250,000) (3/4)
```

At the action node E, we must decide between an expected payoff of −$50,000 by quitting or $846,153 by drilling. Since $846,153 is greater than −$50,000, we will induce that this is the better action and write it over node E. The path to quitting will be **pruned** or **poisoned** by breaking it with a "=" symbol to indicate this path will not be followed, as in Figure 4.12. Likewise at action node D, the best choice between a payoff of −$50,000 and a payoff of −$500,000 is −$50,000 and so this is written at D.

Figure 4.12 Complete Bayesian Decision Tree for Oil Exploration Using Backward Induction

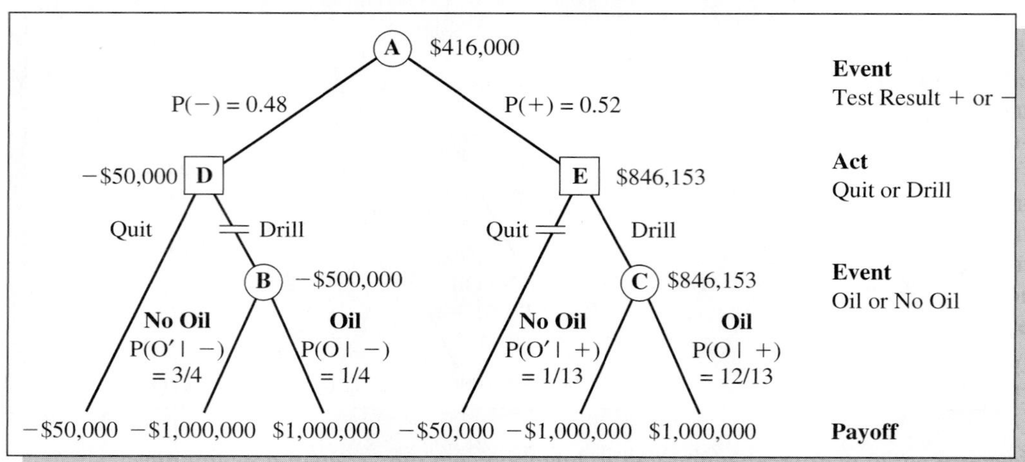

Finally, the expected payoff at the beginning is computed as follows:

```
Expected payoff at node A
$350,000 = ($673,077) (0.52) — ($0) (0.48)
```

and this value is written at node A. No path can be pruned at node A because we have already decided to do the seismic test. To decide on a seismic test, the decision tree would have to be extended backward before node A. Notice that in backward induction, we are reasoning back in time so that our actions in the future will be optimum.

For these particular choices in the Payoff Table, a prospector would have a no-brainer decision at Action node D since the expected payoff is $0. However this is where guts, luck, and experience enter into the gamble. A prospector may just trust his or her feelings and go with the drilling at D in spite of the negative seismic test and the chance of no oil. Sometimes they win, sometimes they lose. There is one important piece of wisdom to remember in situations like this: Always gamble with someone else's money! As the expected return on a successful oil well increases, so does the payoffs at nodes B and D. For example, if the expected oil well has a payoff of $1,250,000 instead of $1,000,000 the expected payoff at B and D is $62,500 which is still less than the $200,000 cost of deciding to drill but a lot better than the previous expected payoff of $0. This strengthens our commonsense that the more expensive an item, the greater is the payoff. Notice though that even if the price of the oil climbs to a billion dollars the risks of the probabilities remain the same. (The only thing that is different is the payoff but that overrides the risks, as people in prison know.)

The decision tree is an example of hypothetical reasoning or *What if* type situations. By exploring alternate paths of action, we can prune paths that do not lead to optimal payoffs. Some types of expert systems tools and Bayesian software have elaborate mechanisms for hypothetical reasoning and poisoning. For more details, see Appendix G on Software Resources.

In particular, the Bayesian tools available free or from commercial sources now make it easy to construct Bayesian and probability trees in graphical form and play around with different, "What if," scenarios. Spreadsheets like Microsoft Excel have very elaborate ways of dealing with uncertainty and many macros are available if you search the Web for more than the built-in functions of classical probability and statistics that come with Excel. The easy graphing capabilities of a spreadsheet also make it easy to visualize complex data.

The decision tree of Figure 4.12 shows the optimal strategy for the prospector. If the seismic test is positive, the site should be drilled. If the seismic test is negative, the site should be abandoned. Although this is a very simple example of Bayesian decision making, it does illustrate the type of reasoning involved in dealing with uncertainty. In more complex cases, such as deciding to use a seismic test, the decision trees may grow much larger.

4.10 TEMPORAL REASONING AND MARKOV CHAINS

Reasoning about events that depend on time is called **temporal reasoning** and is something that humans do fairly easily. However, it is difficult to formalize **temporal events** so that a computer can make temporal inferences. Yet expert systems that reason about temporal events such as aircraft traffic control could be very useful. Expert systems that reason over time have been developed in medicine. These include the VM system for ventilator management of patients on a respirator, to help them breathe. Other systems are CASNET for eye glaucoma treatment and the digitalis therapy advisor for heart patients.

Except for VM, the other medical systems mentioned above have a much easier problem of temporal reasoning compared to an aircraft control system that must operate in **real time**. Most expert systems cannot operate in real time because of the inference engine design and large amounts of processing required. An expert system that does a lot of temporal reasoning to explore multiple hypotheses in real time is very difficult to build. Different temporal logics have been developed based on different axioms. Different theories are based on the way that certain questions are answered. Does time have a first and last moment? Is time continuous or discrete? Is there only one past but many possible futures?

Depending on how these questions are answered, many different logics can be developed. Temporal logic is also useful in conventional programs, such as in the synthesis and the synchronization of processes in concurrent programs.

Another approach to temporal reasoning is with probabilities. We can think of a system moving from one state to another as evolving over time. The system can be anything that is probabilistic such as stocks, voters, weather, business, disease, equipment, genetics, and so forth. The system's progression through a sequence of states is called a **stochastic process** if it is probabilistic.

It is convenient to represent a stochastic process in the form of a transition matrix. For the simple case of two states, S_1 and S_2, the transition matrix is:

$$\begin{array}{ccc} & & \text{Future} \\ & & \begin{array}{cc} S_1 & S_2 \end{array} \\ \text{Present} & \begin{array}{c} S_1 \\ S_2 \end{array} & \begin{bmatrix} P_{11} & P_{12} \\ P_{21} & P_{22} \end{bmatrix} \end{array}$$

where P_{mn} is the probability of a transition from state *m* to state *n*.

As an example, assume that 10% of all people who now use Brand X drives will buy another Brand X drive when needed. Also, 60% of the people who don't use Brand X now will buy Brand X when they need a new drive (the only good thing about Brand X is their advertising). Over a long period of time, how many people will use Brand X?

The transition matrix, T, is:

$$T = \begin{array}{c} \\ X \\ X' \end{array} \begin{array}{c} \begin{array}{cc} X & X' \end{array} \\ \begin{bmatrix} 0.1 & 0.9 \\ 0.6 & 0.4 \end{bmatrix} \end{array}$$

where the sum of each row must add up to 1. A vector whose components are not negative and add up to 1 is called a **probability vector**. Each row of T is a probability vector. One way of interpreting the transition matrix is in terms of a state diagram as shown in Figure 4.13. Notice that there is a 0.1 probability of remaining in state X, a 0.4 probability of remaining in state X′, a 0.9 probability of going from X to X′, and a 0.6 probability of going from X′ to X.

Suppose initially that 80% of the people use Brand X. Figure 4.14(a) shows a probability tree for a few state transitions, where the states are labeled by state number and drive owned. Notice how the tree is starting to grow. If there were 10 transitions, the tree would have $2^{10} = 1024$ branches. An alternate way of drawing the tree as a lattice is shown in Figure 4.14b. The advantage of the lattice representation is that it doesn't need as many links connecting the states.

Figure 4.13 State Diagram Interpretation of a Transition Matrix

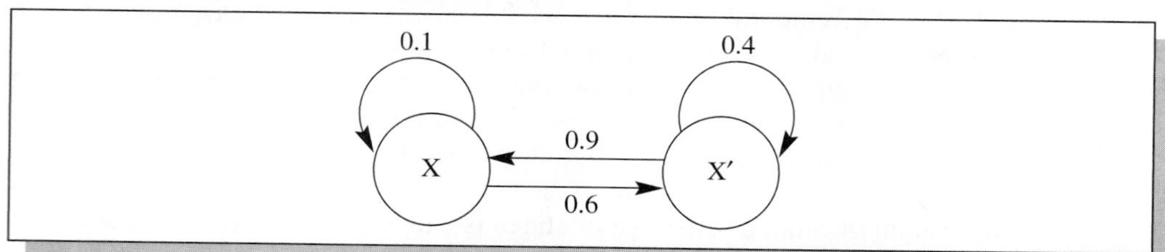

Figure 4.14 Tree and Lattice Diagrams of States Evolving Over Time

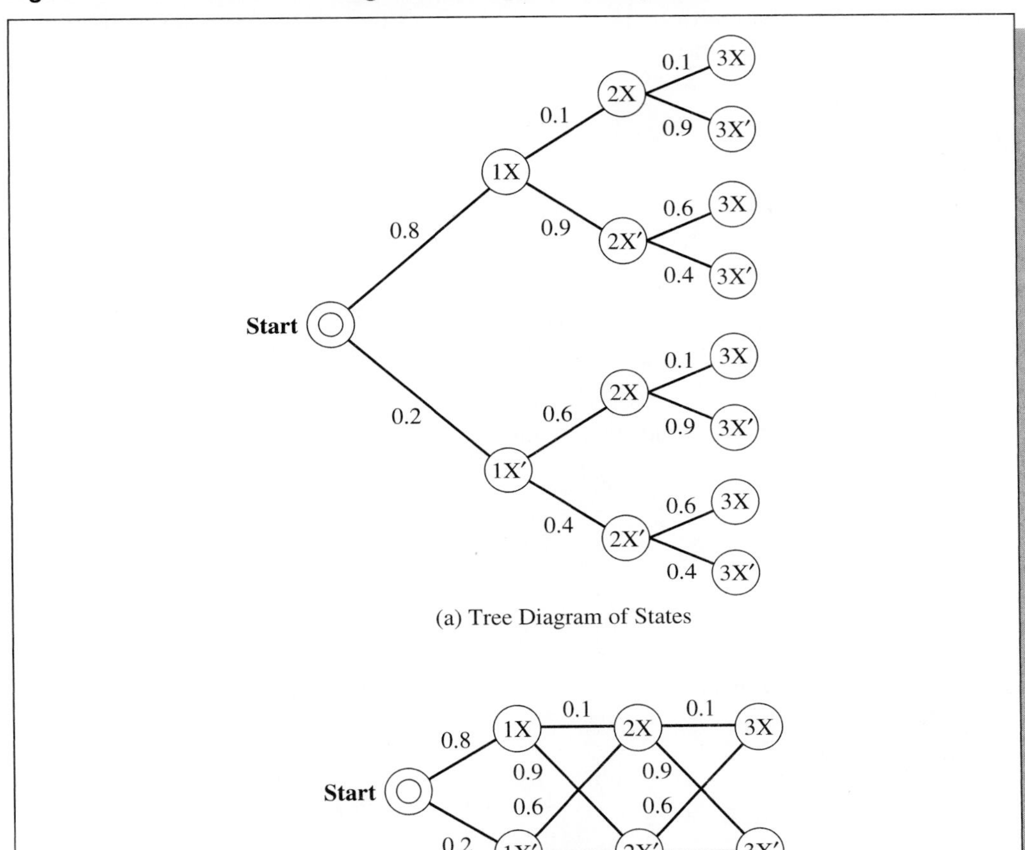

(a) Tree Diagram of States

(b) Lattice Diagram of States

The probability of the system being in a certain state can be represented as a row matrix called the **state matrix**:

$$S = [P_1 \quad P_2 \quad \ldots \quad P_N]$$

where $P_1 + P_2 + \ldots + P_N = 1$

Initially with 80% of the people owning Brand X, the state matrix is:

$$S_1 = [0.8 \quad 0.2]$$

As time goes on, these numbers will change depending on what drive people buy.

In order to calculate the number of people in state 2 having Brand X and not Brand X, just multiply the state matrix times the transition matrix using the ordinary laws of matrix multiplication:

$$S_2 = S_1 T$$

which gives:

$$S_2 = [0.8 \quad 0.2] \begin{bmatrix} 0.1 & 0.9 \\ 0.6 & 0.4 \end{bmatrix}$$

$$= [(0.8)(0.1) + (0.2)(0.6) \quad (0.8)(0.9) + (0.2)(0.4)]$$

$$= [0.2 \quad 0.8]$$

Multiplying this second state by the transition matrix gives:

$$S_3 = S_2 T$$

$$= [0.2 \quad 0.8] \begin{bmatrix} 0.1 & 0.9 \\ 0.6 & 0.4 \end{bmatrix}$$

$$S_3 = [0.5 \quad 0.5]$$

Multiplying this third state by the transition matrix gives:

$$S_4 = S_3 T$$

$$= [0.5 \quad 0.5] \begin{bmatrix} 0.1 & 0.9 \\ 0.6 & 0.4 \end{bmatrix}$$

$$S_4 = [0.35 \quad 0.65]$$

The next states are:

$$S_5 = [0.425 \quad 0.575]$$

$$S_6 = [0.3875 \quad 0.6125]$$

$$S_7 = [0.40625 \quad 0.59375]$$

$$S_8 = [0.396875 \quad 0.602125]$$

Notice that the states are converging on:

$$[0.4 \quad 0.6]$$

which is called a **steady-state matrix**. The system is said to be in equilibrium when it is in the steady-state since it does not change. It's interesting that the steady-state values do not depend on the initial state. If any initial probability vector had been used, the steady-state values would be the same.

A probability vector S is a steady-state matrix for the transition matrix T if:

$$(1) \quad S = S\,T$$

If T is a **regular transition matrix**, which has some power with only positive elements, then a unique steady-state S exists. The fact that the transition matrix elements are positive means that at some time, it is possible to be in any state no matter what the initial state had been. That is, every state is potentially accessible.

A **Markov chain process** is defined as having the following characteristics:

(1) The process has a finite number of possible states.
(2) The process can be in one and only one state at a time.
(3) The process moves or **steps** successively from one state to another over time.
(4) The probability of a move depends only on the immediately preceding state.

For example, given a finite set of states {A,B,C,D,E,F,G,H,I}, then if the next state that the process goes to after H is I, the conditional probability is the following:

$$P(I \mid H) = P(I \mid H \cap G \cap F \cap E \cap D \cap C \cap B \cap A)$$

Notice how the lattice diagram of Figure 4.14 (b) resembles a chain.

The disk drive case is a Markov chain process and the steady-state matrix can be found by applying equation (1). Assume some arbitrary vector S with components X and Y and apply equation (1) as follows:

$$[X \quad Y] \begin{bmatrix} 0.1 & 0.9 \\ 0.6 & 0.4 \end{bmatrix} = [X \quad Y]$$

Multiplying the left-hand side and setting its elements equal to the corresponding elements on the right-hand side gives:

$$0.1\,X + 0.6\,Y = X$$
$$0.9\,X + 0.4\,Y = Y$$

which is a dependent system of equations. Solving for X in terms of Y gives:

$$X = \frac{0.6}{0.9}\,Y = \frac{2}{3}\,Y$$

To completely solve for X and Y, we'll make use of the fact that the sum of the probabilities equals 1. That is,

$$X + Y = 1$$

and so:

$$X = 1 - Y = \frac{2}{3} Y$$

and therefore:

$$X = \frac{2}{5} \quad Y = \frac{3}{5}$$

so the steady-state matrix is:

$$[0.4 \quad 0.6]$$

which is what our trial values were indeed converging to.

4.11 THE ODDS OF BELIEF

So far we have been concerned with probabilities as measures of repeatable events of ideal systems. However, humans are experts at calculating the probabilities of many nonrepeatable events such as medical diagnosis and mineral exploration where each patient and site are unique. In order to make expert systems in areas like this, we must expand the scope of events to deal with **propositions**, which are statements that are true or false. For example, an event may be:

```
"The patient is covered with red spots"
```

and the proposition is:

```
"The patient has measles"
```

Given that A is a proposition, the conditional probability:

$$P(A \mid B)$$

is not necessarily a probability in the classical sense if the events and propositions cannot be repeated or have a mathematical basis. Instead, $P(A \mid B)$ can be interpreted as the **degree of belief** that A is true, given B.

If $P(A \mid B) = 1$, then we believe that A is certainly true. If $P(A \mid B) = 0$, then we believe A is certainly false while other values, $0 < P(A \mid B) < 1$, means that we are not entirely sure that A is true or false. From statistics, the term **hypothesis** is used for some proposition whose truth or falseness is not known for sure on the basis of some **evidence**. The conditional probability is then referred to as the **likelihood**, as in $P(H \mid E)$, which expresses the likelihood of a hypothesis, H, based on some evidence, E.

Although $P(H \mid E)$ has the form of a conditional probability, it actually means something different—the likelihood or degree of belief. Probability refers to repeatable events, while likelihood refers to our degree of belief in nonrepeatable events. Since expert systems are models of human experts, $P(H \mid E)$ is generally the expert's degree of belief that some hypothesis is true given some evidence, E. Of course, if the events are repeatable, then $P(H \mid E)$ is simply the probability.

If we agree that $P(H \mid E)$ means the likelihood or degree of belief, then what does a value such as 50% or 95% mean? For example, suppose you are 95% sure that your car will start the next time. One way of interpreting this likelihood is in terms of the **odds** of a bet. The odds on A against B given some event C is:

$$\text{odds} = \frac{P(A \mid C)}{P(B \mid C)}$$

If $B = A'$

$$\text{odds} = \frac{P(A \mid C)}{P(A' \mid C)} = \frac{P(A \mid C)}{1 - P(A \mid C)}$$

defining:

$$P = P(A \mid C)$$

gives:

$$\text{odds} = \frac{P}{1 - P} \text{ and } P = \frac{\text{odds}}{1 + \text{odds}}$$

In terms of gambling odds, we can interpret P as wins and $1 - P$ as losses, so:

$$\text{odds} = \frac{\text{wins}}{\text{losses}}$$

Knowing the odds allows the probability or likelihood to be calculated and vice versa.

The likelihood of $P = 95\%$ is thus equivalent to:

$$\text{odds} = \frac{.95}{1 - .95} = 19 \text{ to } 1$$

that you believe the car will start. That is, you should be **indifferent** to a bet of odds at 19 to 1 that the car will start. If someone offers a $1 bet that the car won't start, you will pay $19 if it doesn't start. Whenever a degree of belief is stated as a probability, you can interpret it in terms of a bet at equivalent odds. In other words, you should be indifferent to the real situation with its degree of belief or the equivalent odds of a bet.

Probabilities are generally used with deductive problems in which a number of different events, E_i, may occur given the same hypothesis. For example, given that a die rolls an even number, there are three possible events:

$$P(2 \mid even)$$
$$P(4 \mid even)$$
$$P(6 \mid even)$$

In probability, we are generally interested in $P(E_i \mid H)$ where E_i are the possible events from a common hypothesis. In statistics and inductive reasoning, we know the event that has occurred and want to find the likelihood of the hypothesis that can cause E, which is $P(E \mid H_i)$. Probability is naturally forward chaining or deductive while likelihood is backward chaining and inductive. Although we use the same symbolism, $P(X \mid Y)$, for probability and likelihood, the applications are different. Normally we refer to the likelihood of a hypothesis or the probability of an event.

One theory that has been developed using degrees of belief is **personal probability**. In personal probability, **states** are the possible hypotheses and the **consequences** are the results of actions based on the beliefs.

4.12 SUFFICIENCY AND NECESSITY

Bayes' Theorem is:

$$(1)\quad P(H \mid E) = \frac{P(E \mid H)P(H)}{P(E)}$$

and for the negation of H becomes:

$$(2)\quad P(H' \mid E) = \frac{P(E \mid H')P(H')}{P(E)}$$

Dividing (1) by (2) gives:

$$(3)\quad \frac{P(H \mid E)}{P(H' \mid E)} = \frac{P(E \mid H)P(H)}{P(E \mid H')P(H')}$$

Defining the prior odds on H as:

$$O(H) = \frac{P(H)}{P(H')}$$

and the posterior odds as:

$$O(H \mid E) = \frac{P(H \mid E)}{P(H' \mid E)}$$

and finally defining the likelihood ratio:

$$(4)\quad LS = \frac{P(E \mid H)}{P(E \mid H')}$$

then (3) becomes:

$$(5)\quad O(H \mid E) = LS\ O(H)$$

Equation (5) is known as the **odds-likelihood form** of Bayes' Theorem. It is a more convenient form of Bayes' Theorem to work with than equation (1).

The factor LS is also called the **likelihood of sufficiency** because if $LS = \infty$, then the evidence E is logically sufficient for concluding that H is true. If E is logically sufficient for concluding H, then $P(H \mid E) = 1$ and $P(H \mid E') = 0$. Equation (5) can be used to solve for LS as follows:

$$(6)\quad LS = \frac{O(H \mid E)}{O(H)} = \frac{\dfrac{P(H \mid E)}{P(H' \mid E)}}{\dfrac{P(H)}{P(H')}}$$

Now P(H) / P(H′) is some constant, C, and so equation (6) becomes:

$$LS = \frac{\dfrac{1}{0}}{C} = \infty$$

Equation (4) also shows in this case that H is sufficient for E. Table 4.10 summarizes the meaning of other values of LS.

The likelihood of necessity, LN, is defined similarly to LS as:

$$(7)\quad LN = \frac{O(H \mid E')}{O(H)} = \frac{P(E' \mid H)}{P(E' \mid H')} = \frac{\dfrac{P(H \mid E')}{P(H' \mid E')}}{\dfrac{P(H)}{P(H')}}$$

$$(8)\quad O(H \mid E') = LN\ O(H)$$

If $LN = 0$, then $P(H \mid E') = 0$. This means that H must be false when E′ is true. Thus if E is not present then H is false, which means that E is necessary for H.

Table 4.11 shows the relationship among LN, E, and H. Notice that it is the same as Table 4.10 with "evidence" replaced by "absence of evidence."

The likelihood values LS and LN must be provided by a human expert in order to compute the posterior odds. The form of equations (5) and (8) is simple for people to understand. The LS factor shows how much the prior odds are changed when the evidence is present. The LN factor shows how much the prior odds are changed when the evidence is absent. These forms make it easier for a human expert to then specify the LS and LN factors.

As an example, in the PROSPECTOR expert system, there is a rule which specifies how evidence of a certain mineral supports a hypothesis:

```
IF there are quartz-sulfide veinlets
THEN there is a favorable alteration
     for the potassic zone
```

This particular intermediate hypothesis provides support for other hypotheses leading to the top-level hypothesis that copper is present. The LS and LN values for this rule are:

```
LS = 300
LN = 0.2
```

which means that observation of quartz-sulfide veinlets is very favorable while not observing the veinlets is mildly unfavorable. If LN were $<< 1$, then the absence of quartz-sulfide veinlets would strongly suggest the hypothesis is false.

Table 4.10 Relationship Among Likelihood Ratio, Hypothesis, and Evidence

LS	Effect on Hypothesis
0	H is false when E is true or E′ is necessary for concluding H
small ($0 < LS << 1$)	E is unfavorable for concluding H
1	E has no effect on belief of H
large ($1 << LS$)	E is favorable for concluding H
∞	E is logically sufficient for H or Observing E means H must be true

Table 4.11 Relationship Among Likelihood of Necessity, Hypothesis, and Evidence

LN	Effect on Hypothesis
0	H is false when E is absent or E is necessary for H
small ($0 < LN << 1$)	Absence of E is unfavorable for concluding H
1	Absence of E has no effect on H
large ($1 << LN$)	Absence of E is favorable for H
∞	Absence of E is logically sufficient for H

An example is the rule:

```
IF glassy limonite
THEN best mineralization favorability
```

with:

```
LS = 1000000
LN = 0.01
```

4.13 UNCERTAINTY IN INFERENCE CHAINS

Uncertainty may be present in rules, evidence used by the rules, or both. In this section, you will see some real-world problems of uncertainty and how probability provides an answer.

Expert Inconsistency

From equation (4) of the preceding section,

$$\text{if LS} > 1 \text{ then } P(E \mid H') < P(E \mid H)$$

Subtracting each side from 1 reverses the inequality:

$$1 - P(E \mid H') > 1 - P(E \mid H)$$

Since $P(E' \mid H) = 1 - P(E \mid H)$, and $P(E' \mid H') = 1 - P(E \mid H')$, then (7) becomes:

$$LN = \frac{1 - P(E \mid H)}{1 - P(E \mid H')} < 1$$

The constraints on the values of LS and LN are summarized as the following:

```
Case 1: LS > 1 and LN < 1
```

From equations (4) and (7), the other cases are:

```
Case 2: LS < 1 and LN > 1
Case 3: LS = LN = 1
```

Although these three cases are mathematically rigorous constraints on the values of LS and LN, they don't always work out in the real world. For the expert system PROSPECTOR used for mineral exploration, it was not uncommon for experts to specify an LS > 1 and LN = 1, which is not one of these three cases. That is, the expert is saying that the observation of evidence is important but the absence of the evidence is unimportant.

This last case shows that the likelihood theory based on Bayesian probability theory is incomplete for the mineral exploration problem. That is, the Bayesian likelihood theory is only an approximation to a theory that can also deal with the case that LS > 1 and LN = 1. For domains in which experts' opinions satisfy one of the first three cases, the Bayesian likelihood theory is satisfactory.

Uncertain Evidence

In the real world we are seldom absolutely sure of anything except death and taxes and now with cloning and cryonics we're not even sure about death. Although so far we have concentrated on uncertain hypotheses, the more general and realistic situation is uncertain hypotheses *and* uncertain evidence.

For the general case, assume that the degree of belief in the **complete evidence**, E, is dependent on the **partial evidence**, e, by:

```
P(E | e)
```

The complete evidence is the total evidence which represents all possible evidence and hypotheses which compose E. The partial evidence, e, is the portion of E that we know. If we do know all the evidence, then E = e and:

```
P(E | e) = P(E)
```

where P(E) is the prior likelihood of the evidence E. The likelihood P(E | e) is our belief in E given our imperfect knowledge, e, of the complete evidence E.

For example, suppose that people in your neighborhood who started drilling for oil in their kitchens have become rich. You may consider a hypothesis and evidence:

```
H = I'm going to get rich
E = there is oil under my kitchen
```

as expressed in the rule:

```
IF there is oil under my kitchen
THEN I'm going to get rich          P(H | E) = 1
```

At this initial stage, you do not know for certain that there is oil under your kitchen. Conclusive evidence would be drilling a test well, but this is rather expensive. So you consider the partial evidence, e, in support of E as follows:

- Other people in the neighborhood have struck it rich.

- There is some black substance always seeping up around the kitchen stove (which your spouse has blamed on your cooking and cleaning until now).
- A stranger came to the door and offered $20,000,000 for your house because she said that she liked the view.

Based on this partial evidence, you may decide that the likelihood of oil under your kitchen is rather high, $P(E \mid e) = 0.98$.

In a probabilistic or likelihood type of inference chain, if H depends on E and E is based on some partial evidence e, then $P(H \mid e)$ is the likelihood that H depends on e. By the rule for conditional probability:

$$P(H \mid e) = \frac{P(H \cap e)}{P(e)}$$

Figure 4.15 illustrates how H can be considered to be made up of E and e. So the above becomes:

Figure 4.15 The Intersection of H and e

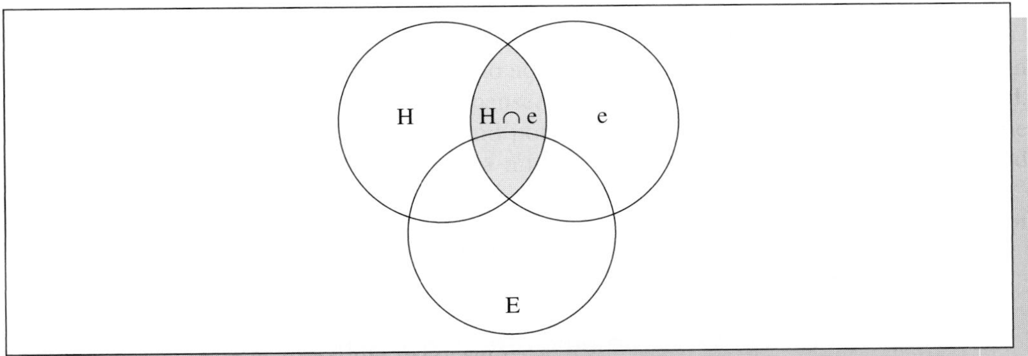

$$P(H \mid e) = \frac{P(H \cap E \cap e) + P(H \cap E' \cap e)}{P(e)}$$

Using the rule of conditional probability gives:

$$P(H \mid e) = \frac{P(H \cap E \mid e)P(e) + P(H \cap E' \mid e)\ P(e)}{P(e)}$$

$$(1)\quad P(H \mid e) = P(H \cap E \mid e) + P(H \cap E' \mid e)$$

Another way of expressing (1) follows since:

$$P(H \cap E \mid e) = \frac{P(H \cap E \cap e)}{P(e)}$$

$$(2)\quad P(H \cap E \mid e) = \frac{P(H \mid E \cap e)\ P(E \cap e)}{P(e)}$$

and since:

$$P(E \mid e) = \frac{P(E \cap e)}{P(e)}$$

then (2) becomes:

$$P(H \cap E \mid e) = P(H \mid E \cap e)\ P(E \mid e)$$

Likewise:

$$P(H \cap E' \mid e) = P(H \mid E' \cap e)\ P(E' \mid e)$$

and (1) becomes:

$$(3)\quad P(H \mid e) = P(H \mid E \cap e)\ P(E \mid e) + P(H \mid E' \cap e)\ P(E' \mid e)$$

Normally, we do not know the probabilities $P(H \mid E \cap e)$ and $P(H \mid E' \cap e)$. However, if we assume these can be approximated by $P(H \mid E)$ and $P(H \mid E')$, then (3) simplifies to:

$$(4)\quad P(H \mid e) = P(H \mid E)\ P(E \mid e) + P(H \mid E')\ P(E' \mid e)$$

Equation (4) is essentially a linear interpolation of $P(H \mid e)$ vs. $P(E \mid e)$. The endpoints are:

(i) E is true and so $P(H \mid e) = P(H \mid E)$.
(ii) E is false and so $P(H \mid e) = P(H \mid E')$.

The problem with equation (4) shows up when $P(E \mid e)$ equals the prior probability $P(E)$. If the system obeys pure Bayesian probability, then:

$$(5)\quad P(H \mid e) = P(H \mid E)\ P(E) + P(H \mid E')\ P(E')$$
$$(6)\quad P(H \mid e) = P(H)$$

which is correct.

However, in the real world, experience has shown that human experts give subjective probabilities that are almost certain to be inconsistent. For example, if the expert uses the inconsistent case of $LS > 1$ and $LN = 1$, then:

$$O(H \mid E') = LN\ O(H) = O(H)$$

and since:

$$O = \frac{P}{1 - P}$$

then:

$$(7)\quad P(H \mid E') = P(H)$$

Using (7) in (5) gives:

$$P(H \mid e) = P(H \mid E)\ P(E) + P(H)\ P(E')$$

$$= P(H \mid E)\ P(E) + P(H)\ (1 - P(E))$$

$$(8)\quad P(H \mid e) = P(H) + P(H \mid E)\ P(E) - P(H)\ P(E)$$

Now:

$$O(H \mid E) = LS\ O(H)$$

If LS = 1, then:

$$O(H \mid E) = O(H)$$
$$P(H \mid E) = P(H)$$

Since the human expert has specified LS > 1, then P(H | E) > P(H) and so the term:

$$P(H \mid E)\ P(E) - P(H)\ P(E)$$

in equation (8) will be > 0, where 0 is the lower bound when LS = 1. So from (8):

$$P(H \mid e) > P(H)$$

when LS > 1 and LN = 1. This contradicts the fact that P(H | e) should equal P(H) when P(E | e) = P(E). Since P(H | e) > P(H), the probability is greater than it should be and may become magnified further as the inference from one rule is used by another in an inference chain.

Correcting Uncertainty

One way of correcting this problem is to assume that P(H | e) is a piecewise linear function. This is an ad hoc assumption that worked well with PROSPECTOR but is not based on traditional probability theory. The function is chosen linear for simplicity in calculations.

The function matches the constraints at the three circled points in Figure 4.16. The formula for P(H | e) is calculated using linear interpolation as follows:

$$P(H \mid e) = \begin{cases} P(H \mid E') + \dfrac{P(H) - P(H \mid E')}{P(E)}\, P(E \mid e) \\ \quad \text{for } 0 \le P(E \mid e) < P(E) \\ \\ P(H) + \dfrac{P(H \mid E) - P(H)}{1 - P(E)}\, [P(E \mid e) - P(E)] \\ \quad \text{for } P(E) \le P(E \mid e) \le 1 \end{cases}$$

Figure 4.16 Piecewise Linear Interpolation Function for Partial Evidence in PROSPECTOR

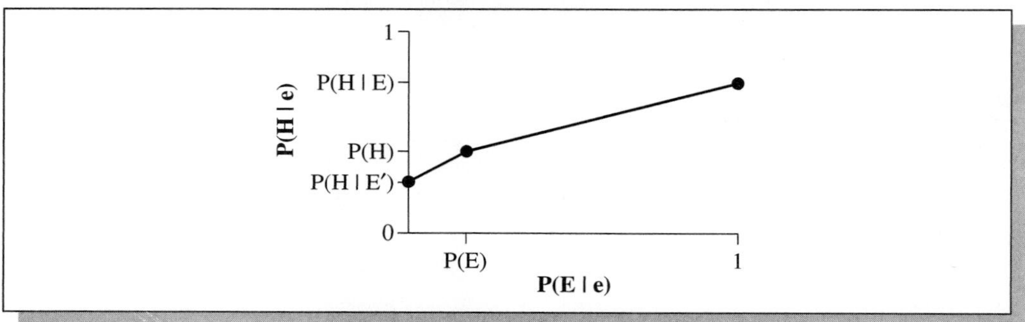

Using this formula, the inconsistent case discussed before of LS > 1 and LN = 1, can be satisfied. Now the value of P(H | e) remains the same if P(E | e) < P(E), and increases if P(E | e) ≥ P(E). The reason for choosing this piecewise rather than a single straight line, is to ensure that when P(E | e) = P(E), then P(H | e) = P(H).

4.14 THE COMBINATION OF EVIDENCE

The simplest type of rule is of the form:

```
IF E THEN H
```

where E is a single piece of known evidence from which we can conclude that H is true. Unfortunately, not all rules may be this simple so compensation for uncertainty is necessary.

Classifications of Uncertain Evidence

More complex situations arise if there is uncertainty about the rule. This uncertainty can be expressed as a probability or likelihood depending on whether we are dealing with reproducible events or subjective probabilities. For simplicity, we'll use the term *probability* for uncertainties.

The different situations can be classified on whether the evidence is certain or uncertain and whether there is **simple evidence** or **compound evidence**. Simple evidence consists of a single piece of evidence such as:

```
IF the transmission is bad
THEN repair the car
```

while compound evidence consists of multiple pieces of evidence usually linked by AND connections, as in:

```
IF the transmission is bad AND
   the engine is bad
THEN sell the car
```

or expressed formally:

IF E_1 and E_2 then H

We may assign a probability to this rule such as $P(H \mid E_1 \cap E_2) = 0.80$, which means we are 80% sure the car should be sold on the basis of this evidence.

A further refinement of the evidence is determining its probability. For example, the probability of the transmission being bad may depend on two symptoms:

(a) Transmission fluid is leaking
(b) The car jerks when changing gears

These observations lead to a probability of the transmission evidence. For example, on the basis of symptoms (a) and (b), we may decide:

$P(E \mid e) = 0.95$

```
where E = transmission is bad
      e = symptoms (a) and (b) above
```

Now let's examine in more detail the probabilities associated with the different situations.

Situation 1: One piece of known evidence concludes H.

This is the simplest case with rules of the form:

```
IF E THEN H
```

Before any evidence is known, the prior probability of H is P(H). After the evidence is known the probability of H changes by Bayes' Theorem:

$$P(H \mid E) = \frac{P(H \cap E)}{P(E)} = \frac{P(H \cap E)}{P(E \cap H) + P(E \cap H')}$$

$$P(H \mid E) = \frac{P(H \mid E)P(H)}{P(E \mid H)P(H) + P(E \mid H')P(H')}$$

where P(E) is the probability of observing E.

Situation 2: Two pieces of known evidence conclude H.

This is a more complex case than situation 1 and corresponds to rules of the form:

```
IF E1 and E2 then H
```

After E_1 and E_2 are observed, the probability of H changes from the prior P(H) to:

$$P(H \mid E_1 \cap E_2) = \frac{P(H \cap E_1 \cap E_2)}{P(E_1 \cap E_2)}$$

$$= \frac{P(H \cap E_1 \cap E_2)}{P(E_1 \cap E_2 \cap H) + P(E_1 \cap E_2 \cap H')}$$

(1) $P(H \mid E_1 \cap E_2)$

$$= \frac{P(E_1 \cap E_2 \mid H)\ P(H)}{P(E_1 \cap E_2 \mid H)\ P(H) + P(E_1 \cap E_2 \mid H')\ P(H')}$$

This formula cannot be reduced further unless a simplifying assumption is made. If the evidence E_1 and E_2 are assumed conditionally independent of each other, then:

$$P(E_1 \cap E_2 \mid H) = P(E_1 \mid H)\ P(E_2 \mid H)$$
$$P(E_1 \cap E_2 \mid H') = P(E_1 \mid H')\ P(E_2 \mid H')$$

and so (see Problem 4.12 for conditional independence):

(2) $P(H \mid E_1 \cap E_2)$

$$= \frac{P(E_1 \mid H)\ P(E_2 \mid H)}{P(E_1 \mid H)\ P(E_2 \mid H) + O(H')\ P(E_1 \mid H')P(E_2 \mid H')}$$

Equation (2) is a major simplification of equation (1) since the probabilities are now all expressed in terms of the individual probabilities rather than the joint ones such as $P(E_1 \cap E_2 \mid H')$. There are problems with this assumption of conditional independence that will be discussed later.

While (2) is a simplification, it still does require knowledge of the prior probabilities $P(E_1)$ and $P(E_2)$. It's usually difficult for experts to state prior probabilities because they don't reason that way. For example, if a person goes to see a doctor, the doctor does not assume that the person has a cold a priori, because that is the most common disease and so its probability is highest.

The major problem in assigning prior probabilities is the difficulty of determining them for likelihoods. For probabilities involving reproducible events such as throwing dice, it's easy to acquire the probabilities by empirical or theoretical studies. However, when dealing with events such as finding a major mineral deposit, it's impossible to determine the prior likelihoods exactly. For example, what's the prior likelihood that your house sits on land with a major gold deposit under it? Is it 1.0, 0.01, 0.00000001, or some other number? These are unique situations in which the prior probabilities cannot be determined.

Situation 3: N pieces of uncertain evidence conclude H.

This is the general case of uncertainty in the evidence and in the rule, which depends on the evidence. As the number of pieces of evidence increases, it becomes impossible to determine all the joint and prior probabilities or likelihoods. Different approximations have been used to account for the general case of N pieces of evidence.

Combining Evidence by Fuzzy Logic

Conjunction of Evidence

Suppose a rule:

```
IF E THEN H
```

has E as the conjunction of evidence, as in:

$$\text{IF } E_1 \text{ AND } E_2 \text{ AND } \ldots E_N \text{ THEN } H$$

All the E_i must be true with some probability for the antecedent to be true. In the general case, each piece of evidence is based on partial evidence e. The probability of the evidence is:

$$P(E \mid e) = P(E_1 \cap E_2 \cap \ldots E_N \mid e)$$

$$= \frac{P(E_1 \cap E_2 \cap \ldots E_N \cap e)}{P(e)}$$

If the evidence, E_i, are all conditionally independent, then the joint probability becomes the product of the individual probabilities. This follows from the Generalized Multiplicative Law. As an example, for two pieces of evidence:

$$P(E_1 \cap E_2 \mid e) = \frac{P(E_1 \cap E_2 \cap e)}{P(e)}$$

$$= \frac{P(E_2 \mid E_1 \cap e)\ P(E_1 \mid e)\ P(e)}{P(e)}$$

Using the assumption of independence,

$$P(E_2 \mid e) = P(E_2 \mid E_1 \cap e)$$

because the evidence E_1 does not contribute any knowledge toward E_2. So:

$$P(E_2 \cap E_1 \mid e) = P(E_2 \mid e)\ P(E_1 \mid e)$$

and in general:

$$P(E_1 \cap E_2 \cap \ldots E_N \mid e) = \prod_{i=1}^{N} P(E_i \mid e)$$

Although this formula is correct in a theoretical sense, there are two difficulties in applying it to real-world problems. First, the individual $P(E_i \mid e)$ are usually not independent in the real world. Second, the multiplication of many factors based on the first assumption leads to a product that is generally far too small for $P(E \mid e)$.

An approximate solution to this problem is use of **fuzzy logic** to calculate $P(E \mid e)$ as follows:

$$P(E \mid e) = \min\ [P(Ei \mid e)]$$

where the **min function** returns the minimum value of all the $P(E_i \mid e)$. In the PROSPECTOR system, this formula was satisfactory. Once $P(E \mid e)$ is determined, it can be used with the piecewise linear formula for $P(H \mid e)$.

The main problem with the fuzzy logic formula is that it makes $P(E \mid e)$ insensitive to any $P(E_i \mid e)$ except the minimum. This means that even if all the other probabilities increase and the minimum remains the same, no change in $P(E \mid e)$ will be affected. That is, the minimum $P(E_i \mid e)$ blocks other probability changes from propagating through the inference chain. An advantage of the fuzzy logic formula is that it is computationally simple.

Disjunction of Evidence

If the rule is a disjunction of evidence:

```
IF E1 OR E2 OR ... EN THEN H
```

then it can be shown (see Problem 4.13) that assuming independence of the evidence gives:

$$P(E \mid e) = 1 - \prod_{i=1}^{N} [1 - P(E_i \mid e)]$$

The problem with this formula is that the calculated probability is much too high. The formula used by PROSPECTOR as an alternative to this is based on fuzzy logic:

$$P(E \mid e) = \max [P(E_i \mid e)]$$

where the **max function** returns the maximum $P(E_i \mid e)$.

Logical Combination of Evidence

If the antecedent is a logical combination of evidence, then the fuzzy logic and negation rules can be used to combine evidence. For example,

```
IF E1 AND (E2 OR E3') THEN H
```

then:

$$E = E_1 \text{ AND } (E_2 \text{ OR } E_3')$$
$$E = \min \{P(E_1 \mid e), \max [P(E_2 \mid e), 1 - P(E_3 \mid e)]\}$$

Although these formulas from fuzzy logic have been successfully used by a number of systems, other functions for combining evidence may be defined. For example, the following is an alternative to the max function of disjunction:

$$P(E_1 \cup E_2 \mid H) = \min [1, P(E_1 \mid H) + P(E_2 \mid H)]$$

Effective Likelihoods

For the general case, multiple rules with uncertain evidence and inconsistent prior probabilities may conclude a specific hypothesis. Assuming conditional independence of the evidence and all the E_i contributing to H are true, then:

$$O(H \mid E_1 \cap E_2 \cap \ldots E_N) = \left[\prod_{i=1}^{N} LS_i\right] O(H)$$

where LS_i is defined as:

$$LS_i = \frac{P(E_i \mid H)}{P(E_i \mid H')}$$

and a similar formula holds if all the evidence contributing to H is false:

$$O(H \mid E_1' \cap E_2' \cap \ldots E_N') = \left[\prod_{i=1}^{N} LN_i\right] O(H)$$

where:

$$LN_i = \frac{P(E_i' \mid H)}{P(E_i' \mid H')}$$

In the general case of inconsistent prior probabilities and uncertain evidence, the **effective likelihood ratio**, LE, is defined as:

$$LE_i = \frac{O(H \mid e_i)}{O(H)}$$

where e_i is the i'th partial evidence contributing to H. The updating of H based on uncertain and inconsistent evidence is analogous to the previous case:

$$O(H \mid e_1 \cap e_2 \cap \ldots e_N) = \left[\prod_{i=1}^{N} LE_i\right] O(H)$$

For an expert system using uncertain evidence and inconsistent prior probabilities, this formula can be used in the following way:

(a) Store the prior odds of each rule and the LE from each contribution to the rule.
(b) Whenever $P(E_i \mid e_i)$ is updated, compute the new LE_i and posterior odds.

Difficulties with Conditional Independence

Although the assumption of conditional independence is useful in simplifying the Bayes' Theorem, there are a number of problems. The assumption is mainly useful in the initial phases of building up an expert system, when the general behavior of the system is more important than correct numerical results. Initially, a knowledge engineer may be more interested in developing correct inference chains than the correct numbers. That is, in some system, intermediate hypothesis 10 should be activated by evidence 23 and 34. Hypothesis 10 and evidence 8 should then activate hypotheses 52 and 96. Hypothesis 15 should *not* be activated by evidence 23 and 24, and so on.

As shown by equation (2) of this section, under conditional independence only five probabilities are required to compute $P(H \mid E_1 \cap E_2)$. These are:

$$P(E_1 \mid H),\ P(E_2 \mid H),\ P(E_1 \mid H'),\ P(E_2 \mid H'),\ P(H)$$

The other probability $P(H')$ needed to compute $O(H')$ is not independent of the others since:

$$P(H') = 1 - P(H)$$

Another formula for $P(H \mid E_1 \cap E_2)$ is shown in Problem 4.12 (b). This formula involves four other probabilities:

$$P(H \mid E_1),\ P(H \mid E_2),\ P(H' \mid E_1),\ P(H' \mid E_2)$$

Thus, there are a total of nine probabilities that can be used to calculate $P(H \mid E_1 \cap E_2)$ but only five are really needed to be specified. Given the five, the other four can be calculated.

This constraint on the number of independent probabilities becomes a real problem as the expert system matures. Once the inference chains function correctly, the knowledge engineer must ensure that the correct numbers are output. Because of the conditional independence assumption, the knowledge engineer does not have complete freedom to tune all nine probabilities by adjusting their values to yield the desired results.

The conditional independence assumption fixes the joint probability $P(E_1 \cap E_2)$ since:

$$P(E_1 \cap E_2) =$$

$$P(E_1)P(E_2)\left[\frac{P(H \mid E_1)P(H \mid E_2)}{P(H)} + \frac{P(H' \mid E_1)P(H' \mid E_2)}{P(H')}\right]$$

This means that the prior probabilities $P(E_1)$, $P(E_2)$, and $P(H)$ now constrain $P(E_1 \cap E_2)$. This runs contrary to the knowledge of the human expert who may know $P(E_1)$, $P(E_2)$, and $P(E_1 \cap E_2)$ separately. Conditional independence thus restricts applying the entire human expert's knowledge.

Although the assumption of conditional independence appears reasonable, it does depend on the real situation being modeled by the expert system and so may not hold in all cases. One theory claims that the conditional independence is usually false. Another theory claims that conditional independence implies strict independence and this proves that the evidence is irrelevant to updating hypotheses! However, this claim has been claims to be disproved by another theory. (The moral of all this is that fuzzy claims are not very clear.)

Another method of applying subjective Bayesian probabilities shows how the assumption of conditional independence can be weakened so that the strict independence is no longer implied (Pearl 00).

4.15 INFERENCE NETS

Up to this point, the examples of forward and backward chaining that you have seen have been very small, consisting of a few rules. For real-world problems, the number of inferences required to support a hypothesis or reach a conclusion is much larger. In addition, many or all of these inferences are made under uncertainty of the evidence and rules themselves. Probabilistic reasoning and Bayes' Theorem have been used successfully in real-world systems such as this.

An inference net is a good architecture for expert systems that rely on a taxonomy of knowledge. A **taxonomy** is a classification and is commonly used in the natural sciences such as geology and biology. You have already seen a simple taxonomy in the figure classifying the different kinds of blackberries in the Chapter 2 problems.

A taxonomy is useful for two purposes. First, it helps to organize knowledge about a subject by classifying objects and showing their relationships to other objects. Important features such as inheritance of properties are made clear by taxonomies.

A second reason that taxonomies are useful is that they can guide the search for proof of a hypothesis, such as "there is copper ore at this site." This aid in proving or disproving hypotheses is very important in areas such as mineral exploration since there is rarely any direct evidence of valuable ore at the surface. Before deciding to invest the time and money for drilling, a geologist tries to gather evidence to support this hypothesis.

PROSPECTOR

The classic expert system that uses probabilistic reasoning is PROSPECTOR. It is designed to aid exploration geologists in determining whether a site is favorable for ore deposits of certain types. The basic idea of PROSPECTOR is to encode the expert economic geologists' knowledge of different ore **models** in the PROSPECTOR expert system. A geologic model is a group of evidence and hypotheses that support a certain type of mineral being present at a site. Besides aiding in identifying minerals, PROSPECTOR could also recommend the best location to drill on the site. As more models are created, the capabilities of PROSPECTOR increase.

The data for each model is organized as an **inference net**. Figure 4.17 summarizes the types of nets discussed so far and shows a very simple inference net in Figure 4.17(d). Inference net nodes can represent evidence to support other nodes that represent the hypotheses such as the type of mineral present. A few of the 22 mineral models in PROSPECTOR are summarized in Table 4.12.

Figure 4.17 Some Types of Networks

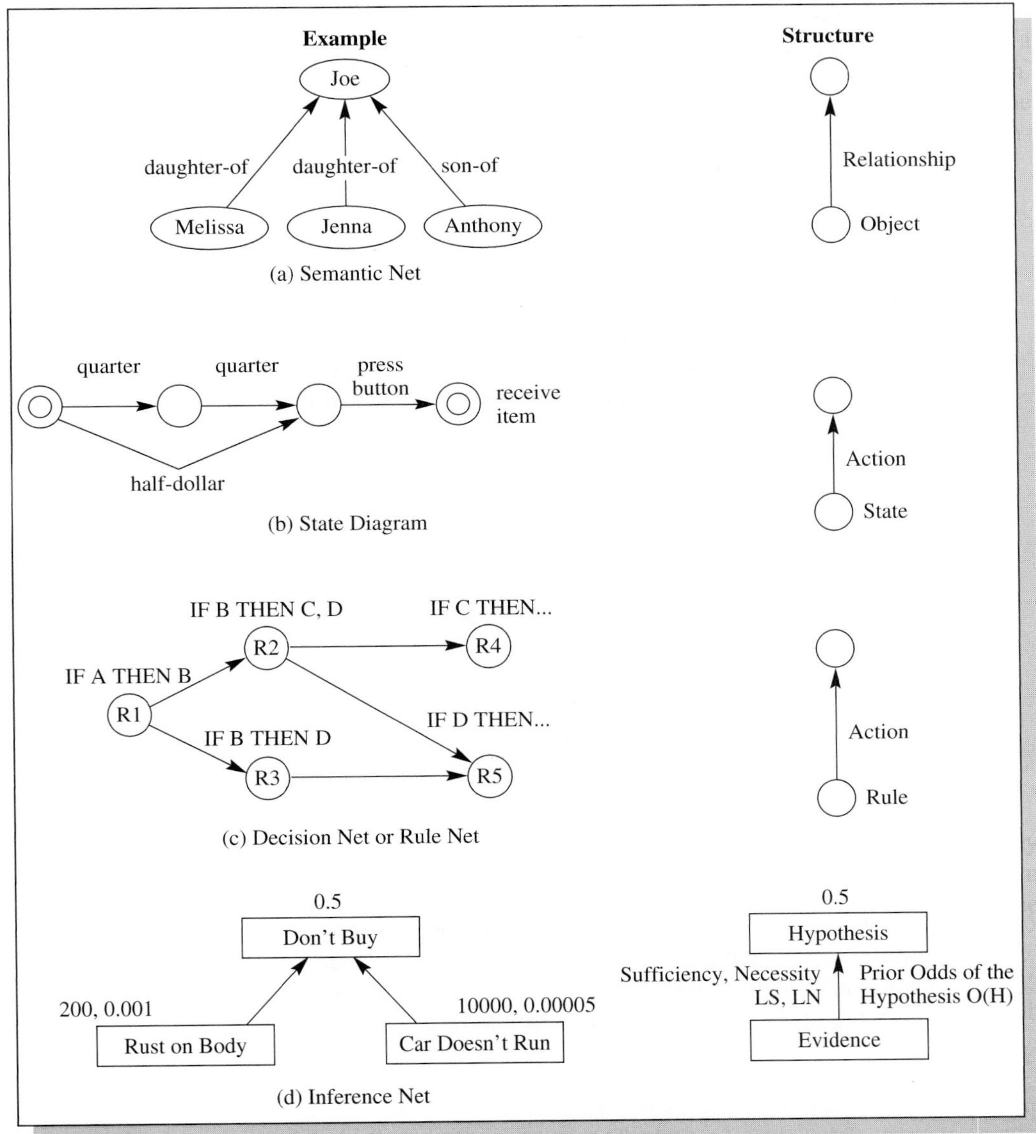

In Table 4.12, the number of nodes is the total number in the model. **Askable nodes** are those that ask questions of the user to obtain observable evidence. The number of rules in the table are probabilistic inference rules. As you can see, there is much uncertainty in the models, and probability is important in supporting hypotheses.

Table 4.12 Some PROSPECTOR Models

Model Name	Model Description	Number of Nodes	Number Askable	Number of Rules
PCD	Porphyry Copper	200	97	135
RFU	Roll-front Uranium	185	147	169
SPB	Sandstone-hosted Lead	35	21	32

Inference Networks

Each model for PROSPECTOR is encoded as a network of connections or relations between evidence and hypotheses. Thus, an inference net is a type of semantic net. Observable facts, such as the type of rock formations obtained from field exploration, compose the evidence to support the intermediate hypotheses. Groups of intermediate hypotheses are used to support the **top-level hypothesis**, which is what we want to prove. If it's not important to distinguish between evidence and hypotheses, the term **assertion** is used for either one. A small portion of the inference net for the top-level hypothesis of the porphyry copper model is shown in Figure 4.18.

The **certainty factors** CHE and CHNE in Figure 4.18 are used in PROSPECTOR because experience has shown that experts find it difficult to specify posterior probabilities or likelihood ratios. Similar experiences were found in the MYCIN system for diagnosing blood disease, where physicians did not like to specify probabilities, and certainty factors were used. As in MYCIN, certainty factors are ranked on an 11-point scale from −5 to +5 where −5 means "definitely not" and +5 means "definitely yes."

PROSPECTOR is not a pure probabilistic system because it uses fuzzy logic and certainty factors for combining evidence. Certainty factors and fuzzy logic will be discussed in more detail in Chapter 5.

Figure 4.19 shows the FRE node of Figure 4.18 expanded in more detail.

This particular diagram has two numbers above nodes which are the likelihood ratio, LS, and necessity measure, LN, separated by commas. For example the LS, LN values for the node labeled RCIB at the left bottom is 20,1. The acronym of each node stands for its description, such as RCIB for "the region contains intrusive breccias." Also shown at the top of each node is the single number of the prior probability, such as 0.001 for RCIB.

Figure 4.18 The Top-level Porphyry Copper Hypothesis of PROSPECTOR Expressed Using Certainty Factors

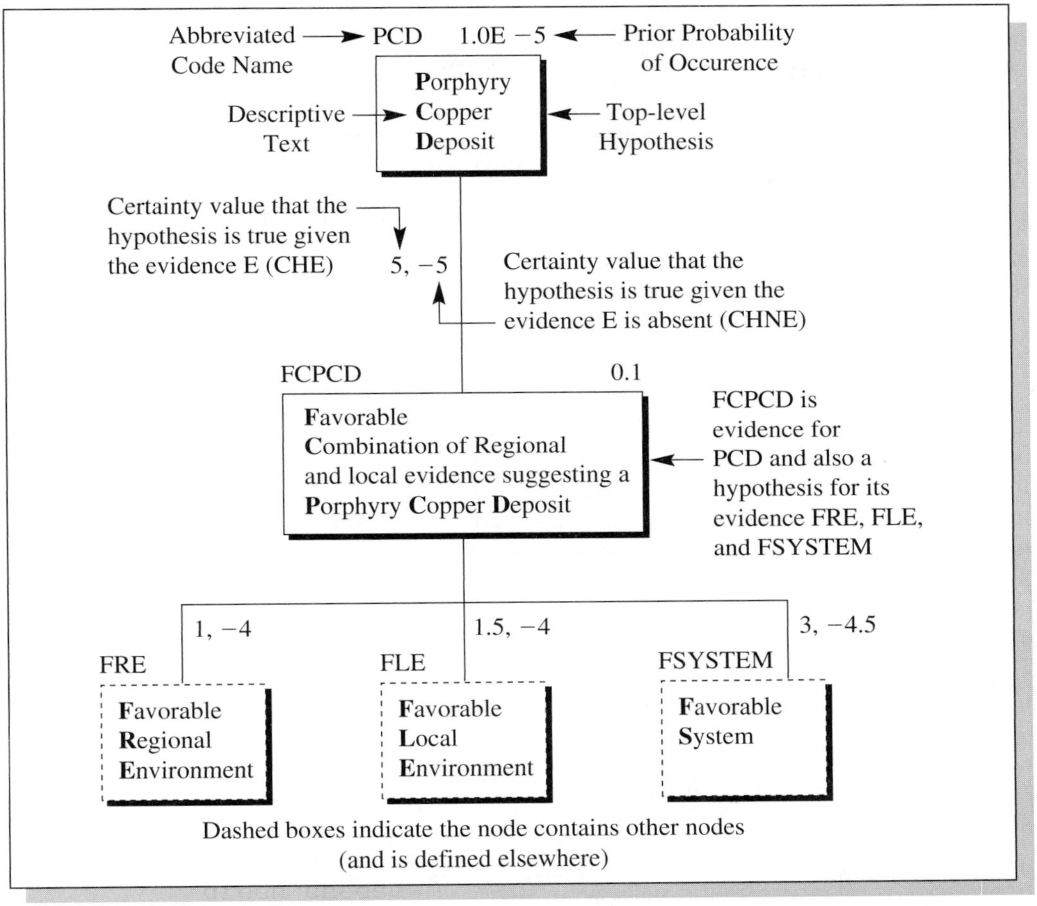

Abbreviated Code Name → PCD 1.0E −5 ← Prior Probability of Occurence

Descriptive Text → **P**orphyry **C**opper **D**eposit ← Top-level Hypothesis

Certainty value that the hypothesis is true given the evidence E (CHE) 5, −5

Certainty value that the hypothesis is true given the evidence E is absent (CHNE)

FCPCD 0.1

Favorable **C**ombination of Regional and local evidence suggesting a **P**orphyry **C**opper **D**eposit ← FCPCD is evidence for PCD and also a hypothesis for its evidence FRE, FLE, and FSYSTEM

1, −4 1.5, −4 3, −4.5

FRE: **F**avorable **R**egional **E**nvironment

FLE: **F**avorable **L**ocal **E**nvironment

FSYSTEM: **F**avorable **S**ystem

Dashed boxes indicate the node contains other nodes (and is defined elsewhere)

Inference Relations

Evidence supporting or disproving a hypothesis is directed up the inference net. For example, RCS, RCAD, RCIB, RCVP, and SMIRA all support or disprove the intermediate hypothesis SMIR. The intermediate hypothesis SMIR is also evidence for its hypothesis HYPE, which is evidence for FLE and so on.

Evidence can be combined in two general ways to yield the relationships desired by the geologist in the definition of the model:

- **logical combinations** such as by AND and OR nodes. As mentioned in the previous section, fuzzy logic can be used to calculate the result at these logical nodes.

Figure 4.19 A Small Part of the PROSPECTOR Inference Net for Porphyry Copper

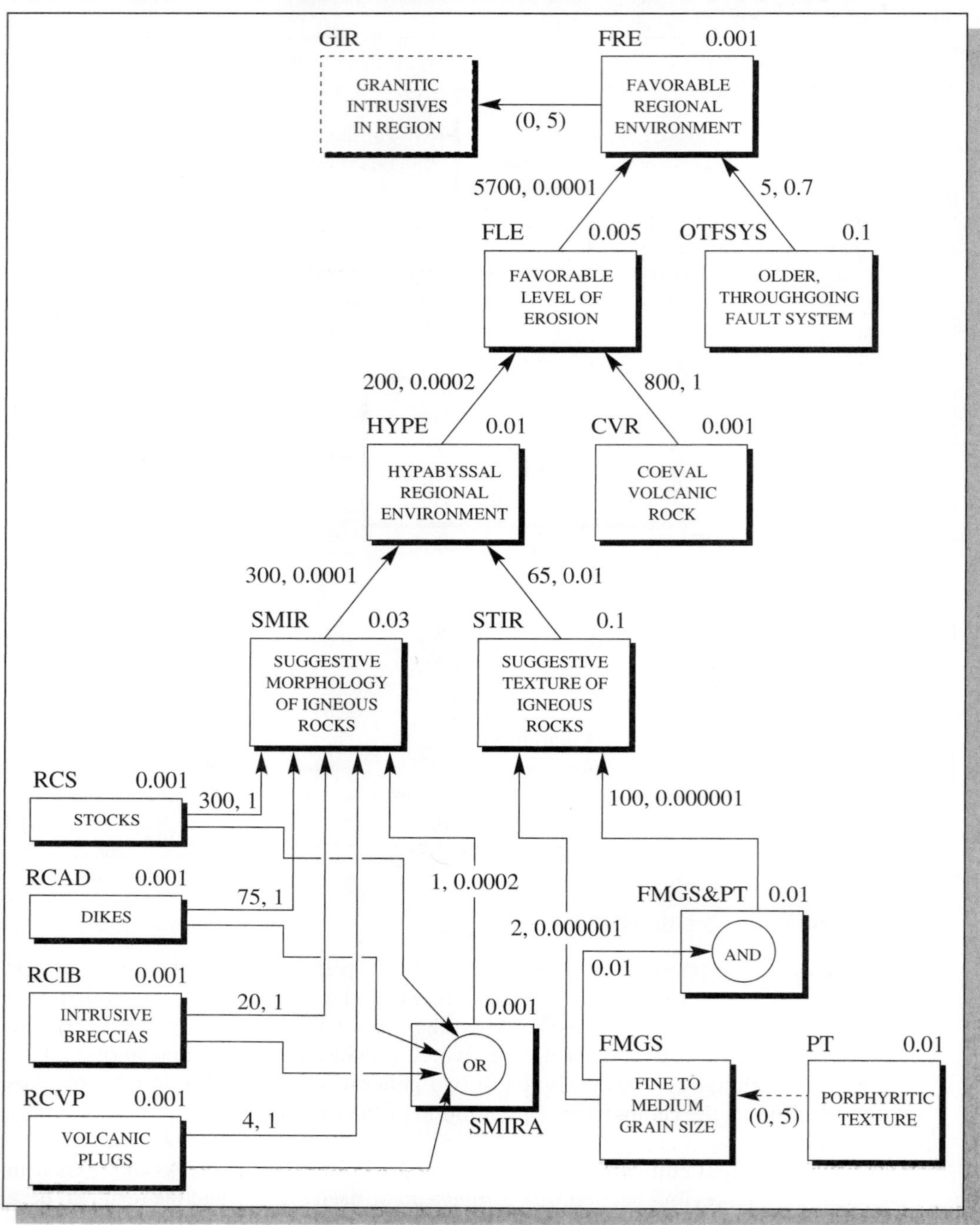

- **weighted combinations** using the likelihood ratios, LS, and necessity ratios, LN. The posterior odds are calculated from:

  $$O(H \mid E) = LS\ O(H)$$

  when the evidence E is known true and:

  $$O(H \mid E') = LN\ O(H)$$

  when E is known to be false. If E is not known for certain, then P(H | E) can be calculated by linear interpolation, as discussed in the previous section.

The term **weighted combination** arises because of the general case in which multiple pieces of evidence contribute to a hypothesis. As shown in the previous section:

$$O(H \mid E_1 \cap E_2 \cap \ldots E_N) = \left[\prod_{i=1}^{N} LS_i\right] O(H)$$

The log of this is:

$$\log O(H \mid E_1 \cap E_2 \cap \ldots E_N) = \log O(H) + \prod_{i=1}^{N} \log LS_i$$

which can be interpreted as each LS_i casting log LS_i "votes" for the hypothesis. Each log LS_i is a weight that affects the hypothesis.

Although PROSPECTOR is sometimes called a rule-based system because weighted combinations correspond to rules such as:

IF E_1 AND E_2 AND ... E_N THEN H

it is not as flexible as a true production system based on rules. One limitation is lack of a full mechanism to bind variables. PROSPECTOR is a custom-designed system that emphasizes efficiency and control for geological applications rather than the generality of a production system.

The weighted combinations are also an example of **plausible relations**. The term *plausible* means that there is some evidence for belief. PROSPECTOR is an example of a system that uses plausible inference for or against a hypothesis. The plausible inferences of PROSPECTOR are based on Bayesian probabilities with the LS and LN values supplied by human experts.

Plausible and other different degrees of belief are illustrated in the fuzzy graph of Figure 4.20. The terms have the following general meanings as shown in Table 4.13.

The graph of Figure 4.20 is purposely drawn fuzzy to illustrate the vague nature of these terms and the vagueness in progression from one to another. In

Figure 4.20 Relative Meaning of Some Terms Used to Describe Evidence

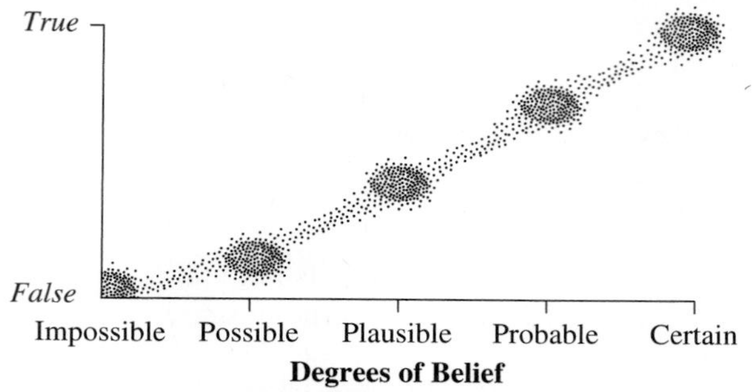

True
False
Impossible Possible Plausible Probable Certain
Degrees of Belief

Table 4.13 Some Terms Used with Evidence

Term	Evidence Relative to Hypothesis
impossible	definitely known against
possible	not definitely disproved
plausible	some evidence exists
probable	some evidence for
certain	definitely known supporting

Figure 4.20, notice how our belief in a hypothesis increases from "impossible" to "certain." A **certain** means that the belief is true while an **impossible belief** means that it is false. There is no uncertainty involved with certain and impossible beliefs. These beliefs are equivalent to logical true and logical false. The term **certain evidence** is sometimes used in an ambiguous way. Certain evidence is logically true or false. That is, there is no uncertainty associated with certain evidence. This means that certain evidence corresponds to either certain belief (logically true) or an impossible belief (logically false).

A **possible belief** means that no matter how remote, the hypothesis cannot be ruled out. For example, before scientific analysis of the Moon's surface, it was possible, but very, very, very remote, for the Moon to be made of white cheese. This possibility existed because no definite proof was available.

A **plausible belief** means that more than a possibility exists. The term *plausible* is often used in legal cases to mean reasonable, but without hard evidence to back up the belief. Thus, even before scientific studies, it was not plausible that the moon was made of green cheese.

A **probable belief** means that there is some evidence favoring the hypothesis but not enough to definitely prove it. For example, if you have been winning at dice and suddenly start losing when your friend offers to let you use their "lucky dice," you might have a probable belief that they are now receiving the luck.

Without field evidence, such as observation of RCIB, the relations in Figure 4.19 for a particular site are merely possible. As evidence accumulates, the possible relations may become plausible and then probable, and finally certain if a sample confirms the hypothesis. In the case of playing with someone else's dice, if you lose all your winnings, it's certainly plausible that you hit a streak of bad luck. If you lose all your winnings and all the money you started with as well, then it's definitely sure you have bad luck. However no matter how many times you roll the dice, even a million times, there is always a chance that it's statistical because it would take an infinite number of rolls to achieve 100% probability. The case of "0% probability" or "100% probability" is actually an **oxymoron**, which means a self-contradictory term. The cases of 0% and 100% are **certainty**. There is nothing probable about certainty because in the real world, certainty is a belief. When someone says, "I have seen the same evidence as others but am still certain there is a nonblack crow somewhere," they are expressing a belief, and true beliefs cannot be changed by facts.

This is an important consideration when you are building an expert system and trying to formally express the expert's knowledge in rules and facts. During the **knowledge acquisition** phase when you are interviewing an expert, you may hear something that sounds like knowledge but is actually belief. You must be very careful in putting beliefs into expert systems because they may yield invalid conclusions. On the other hand, if that's what the expert is paying you for, they will not be happy if the system does not perform as expected.

There is another oxymoron associated with probability that you will hear when the weather forecaster reports a "50% chance" of rain. A 50% chance means **total ignorance**. It either will rain or it won't. You don't need probability theory or a weather forecaster predicting that it will either rain or it will not rain. The fact that it will or will not rain is commonsense. Likewise you may hear a weather forecaster predict a 100% chance of rain while a thunderstorm is pouring down rain. That is not a probability; it is a certainty.

Besides the relationships in inference nets between decision nodes and their probabilistic actions, a desirable trait is **contexts**, which block the propagation of information until it is appropriate. The use of contexts enables or disables portions of the inference net until certain portions are known present, absent, or unknown. One purpose of contexts is to avoid having the system ask the user for questions about some evidence until it is established that the evidence is needed. This is very important because people get annoyed if they are asked questions which seem irrelevant. The goal of any system should be to acquire the minimum information to reach a valid, or at least acceptable conclusion. For example, if you go to a doctor, the first context is: "Do you have medical insurance?" It is expensive in terms of time and money to ask for more information than is needed such as, "What problem are you having? Are you in pain?" Do you have a mortuary picked out?

The basic idea of contexts is to control the order in which assertions are pursued by the system. Contexts state a required condition that must be proven before an assertion can be used. Contexts are indicated by a dashed arrow with a certainty range under it as in the case of FMGS and PT. The PT node is blocked unless there is evidence with certainty values in the range 0 to +5 that there are fine to medium grain sizes of **porphyritic** rocks. Porphyritic rocks are igneous rocks whose **texture** or appearance consists of small crystals embedded within the rock holding it, the **matrix**. Igneous rocks are those formed by the solidification of molten rock called magma from deep within the earth. Certain types of igneous rocks that extend above ground called **intrusive breccias**, are evidence of mineral formations such as porphyry copper.

Thus, porphyry copper consists of small copper crystals embedded within a rock matrix that holds the crystals. Porphyry copper is the most commonly occurring form of copper. Unless there are at least small crystals present of fine to medium grain size, it's not worth asking about porphyritic texture and so the expert system should be intelligent enough not to ask this question. An expert system that asks unnecessary questions is inefficient and will quickly annoy the user.

The certainty range of 0 to +5 for the context means that the PT node will not be pursued unless the user indicates absence of evidence corresponding to a certainty factor of 0 or some positive amount ranging up to +5 for definitely present.

All three methods of combining or permitting evidence are really relations between nodes. They all specify how a change in the probability of one assertion affects others.

Inference Net Architecture

Formally, an **inference net** can be defined as a directed, acyclic graph in which the nodes are assertions and the arcs are measures of uncertainty such as LS and LN. Figure 4.21 (a), (b), and (c) could be used as valid inference net architectures because they have no cycles. Note that in the inference tree, the arrows point toward the hypothesis in contrast to the arrows pointing away from the root in a data structure tree. As described in Chapter 3, in an acyclic graph, there is no way to return to the starting point by following the arrows. In Figure 4.21(d) there is a cycle involving four nodes. The reason for prohibiting cycles is to prevent circular reasoning in establishing a hypothesis. A valid exception in rule-based systems is to establish a loop by having two rules trigger each other until a terminating condition is satisfied. Another popular use of cycles is political logic.

Figure 4.21(c) is an undesirable type of graph for an inference net. The problem is that when many pieces of evidence contribute to a single hypothesis, there is a greater chance of undesirable interactions between the evidence. It is also more expensive to gather so much evidence. It's generally better to restructure this type into a more tree-like structure with intermediate hypotheses.

The PROSPECTOR inference net is also a **partitioned semantic net** to group portions of the net into meaningful units. Partitioned semantic nets were developed by Hendrix to allow power of predicate calculus such as quantification, implication, negation, disjunction, and conjunction. Recall from Chapter 2 that ordinary semantic nets are really designed for expressing descriptive knowledge through relations. While frames are better for causal knowledge, they are difficult to use in expressing logical relationships.

The basic idea of a partitioned semantic net is to group sets of nodes and arcs in abstract **spaces** that define the scope of their relationships. A familiar

Figure 4.21 Some Types of Graphs

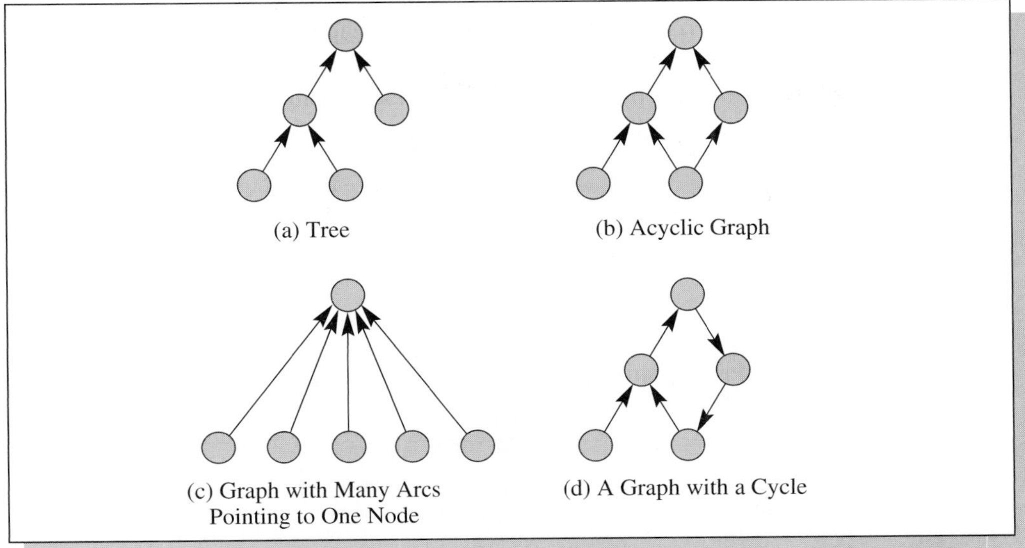

analogy to a space is the scope of a module or package in a structured language. For example, the Figure 4.18 FRE node can be considered a space with structure shown in Figure 4.19.

The power of semantic nets comes in modeling statements. In fact, Hendrix first developed them for expressing natural language in his Ph.D. dissertation. Statements are like the propositions of evidence and hypotheses that make up the nodes of inference nets. As a simple example of a partitioned semantic net for a statement, consider "there is a computer with a color screen." Notice that this is an existential statement because of the "there is" quantifier.

Figure 4.22 shows the partitioned semantic net expression of this statement using three spaces. SPACE-1 consists of some general related concepts about computers. SPACE-2 consists of the particular computer we are talking about, which has been given the identifier COMPUTER-1. SPACE-3 consists of the specific relation COMPONENTS-OF-1, which has as its object the specific COLOR-SCREEN-1 that we are concerned about. Each arc labeled *element* shows that one state is an element of another. The arc labeled *entity* shows which specific computer is the entity with the specific color screen.

The advantage of a partitioned semantic net is shown by a portion of a PROSPECTOR rule for STIR using FMGS evidence as shown in Figure 4.23. The rule can be stated as "If there is an entity named E-1 whose cardinality is ABUNDANT and is composed of INTRUSIVE ROCKS, then the consequent is the rule of Suggestive Texture of Igneous Rocks." Note that the diagram has been simplified by not including the requirement that the antecedent also have a fine to medium grain size.

Figure 4.22 A Simple Partitioned Semantic Net about a Computer

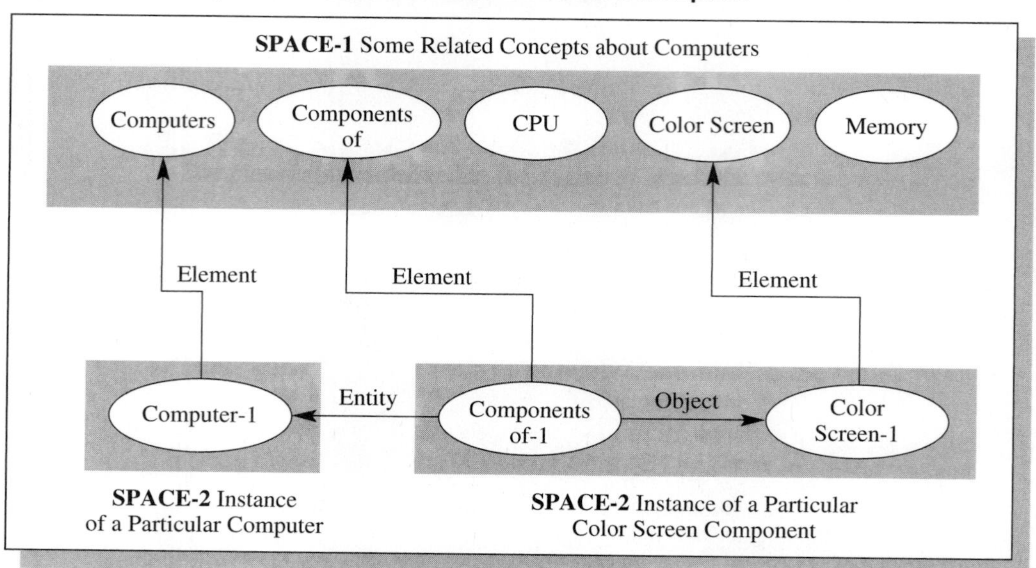

Notice that in Figure 4.23, one partitioned semantic net makes up the antecedent of the rule and one net makes up the consequent. Although the consequent of this rule is trivial, other rules will have a more complex structure. The advantage of the partitioned semantic nets is that the system can infer relationships between nodes that are indirectly linked. Thus the knowledge of the system is deeper than shallow knowledge.

4.16 THE PROPAGATION OF PROBABILITIES

Inference nets such as PROSPECTOR have a **static knowledge structure**. That is, the nodes and connections between them are fixed in order to retain the relationships between nodes in the knowledge structure. This contrasts with a rule-based system in which rules whose patterns match facts are put on the agenda, conflict resolution is performed, and then the top-priority rule is executed. Thus a common rule-based system is a **dynamic knowledge structure** because there are no fixed connections between rules as there are between nodes in an inference net.

While the structure of an inference net is static, the probabilities associated with each hypothesis node change as evidence is obtained. In fact, this change of probabilities is the *only* thing that does change in an inference net. The basic characteristic of an inference net is the change of probabilities from their prior probabilities to posterior probabilities as evidence is accumulated. This change of probabilities moves upwards to ultimately support or disprove a top-level hypothesis such as the existence of porphyritic copper, PCDA.

Let's examine some of the stages in the propagation of probabilities for PCDA on the basis of some evidence. This will serve as an explicit example of

Figure 4.23 Simplified Portion of the PROSPECTOR Partitioned Semantic Net for the STIR Rule Using FMGS Evidence

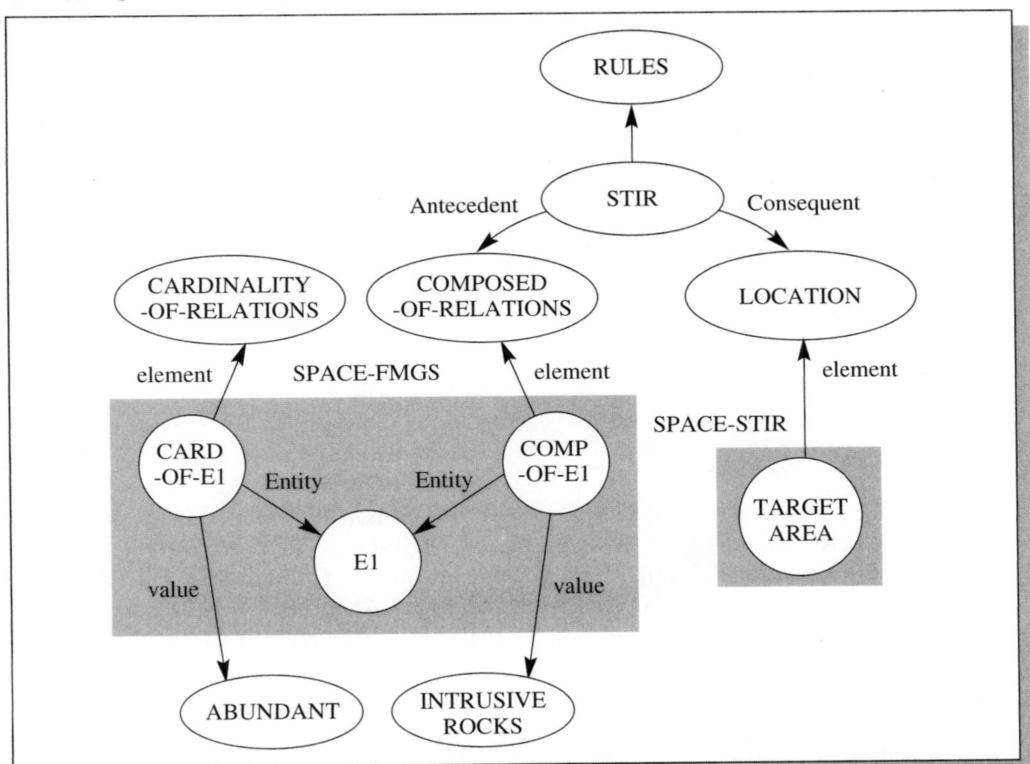

many of the formulas that you have seen. Referring back to Figure 4.19, we will follow the propagation of probabilities from the evidence node "the Region Contains Intrusive Breccias," with acronym RCIB.

If the user says that intrusive breccias are certainly present, then:

$$P(E \mid e) = P(RCIB \mid e) = 1$$

From Figure 4.19, notice that the LN values for the other evidence of SMIR are all 1. That is, if the user makes no comment about evidence for stocks, dikes, and volcanic plugs, these make no contribution to SMIR and so can be ignored in the propagation of probabilities.

The reason all this evidence can be ignored comes from the formula for compound evidence discussed in Section 4.14:

$$O(H \mid e) = \left[\prod_{i=1}^{N} L_i \right] O(H)$$

where the $L_i = LS_i$ for all evidence that is known true and $L_i = LN_i$ is used for known false evidence. If there is no evidence known, then $P(E_i \mid e)$ reduces to the prior odds of the evidence, $P(E_i)$ and so $P(H \mid E_i)$ reduces to the prior odds $P(H)$. Thus:

$$L_i = \frac{O(H \mid e_i)}{O(H)} = \frac{O(H)}{O(H)} = 1$$

and these L_i make no contribution to $O(H \mid E)$. For example, when only RCIB is known true, the odds of SMIR are:

$$O(H \mid E) = LS_{RCVP}\ LS_{RCAD}\ LS_{RCS}\ LS_{SMIRA}\ LS_{RCIB}$$

$$= 1 \cdot 1 \cdot 1 \cdot 1 \cdot 20$$

$$O(SMIR \mid RCIB) = 20$$

Another interesting feature of the SMIR evidence is the OR node called SMIRA. Notice that all the evidence for SMIR also goes to SMIRA. If there is any evidence contributing to SMIR such as RCS, RCAD, RCIB, or RCVP, then the OR node of SMIRA contributes nothing to SMIR since LS for SMIRA is 1. However, if there is no evidence of RCS, RCAD, RCIB, and RCVP, then the LN value of 0.0002 of SMIRA makes the probability of SMIR essentially zero. Basically, this means that while the absence of one or more of the evidences for SMIR is unimportant (LS = 1), the absence of all evidence is very important in ruling out SMIR.

The addition of OR nodes, AND nodes, LS and LN values lets the model designer manipulate the way in which evidence affects a hypothesis. However, in some complex cases, the addition of many OR and AND nodes to suit the evidence requirements will obscure the inference net so that it is difficult for a person to understand. The addition of these extra nodes also requires more testing of the model.

From Figure 4.20, LS = 20 for intrusive breccias, RCIB, and P(SMIR) = 0.03. Since :

$$\text{odds} = O = \frac{P}{1 - P}$$

then the prior odds of SMIR are:

$$O(SMIR) = \frac{0.03}{1 - 0.03} = 0.0309$$

If the evidence E is certain, then the posterior odds are:

$$O(H \mid E) = LS\ O(H)$$
$$O(SMIR \mid RCIB) = 20 \cdot 0.0309 = 0.618$$

and the posterior probability is calculated from the fundamental odds formula:

$$P = \frac{O}{1 + O}$$

$$P(H \mid E) = \frac{O(H|E)}{1 + O(H|E)}$$

$$P(H \mid E) = \frac{0.618}{1 + 0.618} = 0.382$$

and so the posterior probability of SMIR given certain evidence of RCIB is:

$$P(SMIR \mid RCIB) = 0.382$$

The HYPE prior odds are:

$$O(HYPE) = \frac{0.01}{1 - 0.01} = 0.0101$$

At this point it would be tempting to use:

$$O(H \mid E) = LS\ O(H)$$

$$O(HYPE \mid SMIR) = LS_{SMIR}\ O(SMIR)$$
$$= 300 \cdot \frac{0.0101}{1 + 0.0101} = 3.00$$

as the odds of HYPE due to SMIR, but it would be wrong. The formula:

$$O(H \mid E) = LS\ O(H)$$

is true when the evidence E is certain. This formula expresses the change in the hypothesis's probability assuming that the evidence is certain. However, SMIR is not known for certain. In fact, the probability of SMIR given certain intrusive breccias is:

$$P(SMIR \mid RCIB) = 0.382$$

which means that the likelihood of our belief is 38.2% that SMIR is true.

What we really need is the probability of the HYPE hypothesis based on the uncertain evidence of SMIR, which is P(HYPE | RCIB). One way of calculating this uses the formula for P(H | e) discussed in Section 4.14 as:

$$P(H \mid e) = \begin{cases} P(H \mid E') + \dfrac{P(H) - P(H \mid E')}{P(E)} \, P(E \mid e') \\ \quad \text{for } 0 \le P(E \mid e) < P(E) \\ \\ P(H) + \dfrac{P(H \mid E) - P(H)}{1 - P(E)} \, [P(E \mid e) - P(E)] \\ \quad \text{for } P(E) \le P(E \mid e) \le 1 \end{cases}$$

where the uncertainty in the SMIR evidence is:

$$P(E \mid e) = P(SMIR \mid RCIB) = 0.382$$

and the probability we want is:

$$P(H \mid e) = P(HYPE \mid SMIR)$$

where all we know is:

$$P(H \mid E) = \frac{O(H \mid E)}{1 + O(H \mid E)} = \frac{3.00}{1 + 3.00} = 0.75$$

and the prior odds from Figure 4.19 are:

$$P(H) = P(HYPE) = 0.01$$

$$P(E) = P(SMIR) = 0.03$$

Since P(E | e) > P(E), we will use the formula for P(E) ≤ P(E | e) ≤ 1 to compute P(H | E) as follows:

$$P(H \mid e) = 0.01 + \frac{(0.75 - 0.01)(0.382 - 0.03)}{1 - 0.03}$$

$$P(HYPE \mid RCIB) = 0.279$$

which is the posterior probability of HYPE.

This propagation of probabilities continues up the inference net. Now the probability P(HYPE | RCIB) is the uncertain evidence of FLE. The posterior probability P(FLE | RCIB) is calculated using the same formula with values adjusted for FLE:

$$P(E) = P(HYPE) = 0.01$$

$$P(E \mid e) = P(HYPE \mid RCIB) = 0.279$$

$$P(H) = P(FLE) = 0.005$$

$$O(H \mid E) = O(FLE \mid HYPE) = LS_{HYPE}\ O(FLE)$$

$$= 200 \cdot 0.005 = 1$$

$$P(H \mid E) = P(FLE \mid HYPE)$$

and since P = odds/(1 +odds),

$$P(H \mid E) = O(FLE|HYPE)/(1 + O(FLE|HYPE))$$

$$= 1/(1 +1)$$

$$= 0.5$$

$$P(H \mid e) = P(FLE \mid RCIB)$$

$$= 0.005 + \frac{(0.5 - 0.005)(0.279 - 0.01)}{1 - 0.01}$$

$$P(FLE \mid RCIB) = 0.140$$

4.17 SUMMARY

In this chapter we started by discussing the basic concepts of reasoning under uncertainty and the possible types of errors caused by uncertainty. The elements of classical probability theory were reviewed. The differences between classical theory and other theories of probability such as experimental and subjective probabilities were discussed. Methods of combining probabilities and Bayes' Theorem were covered. The relationship of belief to probability and the meaning of likelihood were described.

The classic expert system PROSPECTOR was analyzed in detail to illustrate how concepts of probability were used in a real system. The PROSPECTOR system was also used to introduce inference nets and partitioned semantic nets.

The main lesson you saw is that while classical probability is fine for ideal systems, it does not always work in real world problems such as mineral exploration in PROSPECTOR. Although probability was used as a starting point for dealing with uncertainty, the occurrence of certain minerals depends on playing around with probability theories to introduce confidence factors and fuzzy logic until the expert system correctly predicted known models .PROSPECTOR was then used on unknown features to successfully predict the molybdenum deposit worth $100,000,000.

Note that different models of geologic features, different certainty factors, and fuzzy logic would be needed to detect other types of minerals. There is nothing wrong with doing this because it simply reflects the fact that different minerals form in different ways in the real world and so the evidence and theories of detecting them are different. This is where the expert's knowledge of different domains is important. An expert who is good at locating molybdenum would not necessarily be good at locating oil.

The important thing to remember is that you must make your expert system fit the real world and not try to make the real world fit your expert system for that will lead to failure. All theories are ultimately based on axioms which are unproven truths, such as Euclid's axiom that straight lines only meet at infinity. While this is true on the flat Euclidean plane it does not hold in spherical geometry or other types that are not flat. Theories of uncertainty are also based on axioms. The fact that we have to introduce extra factors such as confidence factors and fuzzy logic simply means we don't know the correct axioms because of ignorance on how minerals really developed millions of years ago and the particular chemical composition of the earth at that location.

We also discussed the meaning of the terms impossible, possible, plausible, probable, and certain. It's important to understand these terms when interviewing an expert to separate probability from belief, which is a matter of "a pinion". In particular you need to be careful about things that are certain because this may be commonsense masquerading as reason. For example, commonsense would say that the conditional probability of a horse finishing a race is 100% if the horse is alive, P (Finish | Live) = 100%. Note that we are not stating that the horse will necessarily win but only that it will finish. Commonsense tell us that a contestant must be alive to win a race. That is a certainty. Right? So would you bet your grade in this course on that?

As mentioned before, political logic is not the same as any other type of logic. In October 2000, Missouri Governor Mel Carnahan died in a plane crash during a campaign trip. His opponent, Sen. John Ashcroft (R-Mo.), still lost his reelection bid in November. The voters elected a dead man Senator and the seat was filled by Gov. Carnahan's widow (http://www.specialednews.com/washwatch/washnews/election111000.html). This is further evidence that even death is not a certain factor these days in commonsense reasoning.

PROBLEMS

4.1 (a) Using only the three axioms of probability, prove the Additive Law of probability:

$$P(A \cup B) = P(A) + P(B) - P(A \cap B)$$

Hint: Any event $X \cup Y$ can be written in the form $X \cup (X' \cap Y)$ where X and $X' \cap Y$ are mutually exclusive. Also, write B as the union of two mutually exclusive sets.

(b) Given two computers that either work correctly or do not, what is the probability using the Additive Law that at least one works correctly?

4.2 Given events A and B that may overlap, derive the probability in terms of sets using the axioms of probability for:

(a) neither A nor B
(b) either A or B, not both (exclusive OR)

4.3 Three bins contain some good and defective components as follows:

Bin	Good	Bad
1	8	2
2	3	1
3	2	2

Over a long period of time, 20% of components are drawn from bin 1, 30% from bin 2, and 50% from bin 3.

(a) Draw a probability tree.
(b) If a defective part is drawn, what are the probabilities it came out of each bin? Write the probability table showing the outcomes, prior, conditional, joint, and posterior probabilities.

4.4 A person is considering the purchase of a disk drive and is trying to decide among three brands. The following table shows the person's preferences and probability of crashes within one year. (Preferences are a function of cost, speed, capacity, and reliability.)

Brand	Probability of Choosing	Probability of a Crash
X	0.3	0.1
Y	0.5	0.3
Z	0.2	0.6

(a) Make up a probability table showing outcomes, prior, conditional, joint, and posterior probabilities.
(b) What is the probability of each disk crashing within one year?
(c) What is the probability of any drive crashing within one year?
(d) For a crash within one year, what is the probability of Brand X, Y, or Z?

4.5 A screening test is a low-cost way of checking large groups of people for a disease. A more costly but accurate test shows that 1% of all people have the disease. The screening test indicates the disease (test positive) in 90% of those who have it, and in 20% of those who do not have the disease (false positive).

(a) Make a table showing the outcomes, prior, conditional, joint, and posterior probabilities.
(b) What percent of people who test positive don't have the disease (false +)?
(c) What percent of people who test negative do have the disease (false −)?

4.6 To show that pairwise independence does not necessarily mean mutual independence, define the following events for the toss of two dice:

A = even first die
B = even second die
C = even sum

(a) Draw the sample space of the two dice. Draw A, B, and $A \cap B$.
(b) Write the elements of $A \cap B$, C, $A \cap C$, and $B \cap C$.
(c) What is P(C)?
(d) Show the pairwise independence of the following:

$$P(A \cap B) = P(A)\ P(B)$$
$$P(A \cap C) = P(A)\ P(C)$$
$$P(B \cap C) = P(B)\ P(C)$$

(e) Show:

$$P(A \cap B \cap C) = P(A \cap B) \neq P(A\ B)\ P(C)$$

which proves that pairwise independence does not mean mutual independence.

4.7 For mutually exclusive sets A and B:

(a) What is $P(A \mid B')$ expressed in terms of A and B (not expressed in terms of A and B′)?
(b) What is the numeric value of $P(A' \mid B)$?
(c) What is the numeric value of $P(A \mid B)$?
(d) What is $P(A' \mid B')$ expressed in terms of A and B (not expressed in terms of A′ and B′)?
(e) What is

(i) $P(A \mid B) + P(A' \mid B)$
(ii) $P(A \mid B') + P(A' \mid B')$

4.8 (a) Prove that

$$P(A \cap B \cap C) = P(A \mid B \cap C)\ P(B \mid C)\ P(C).$$

(b) Prove that

$$P(A \cap B \mid C) = P(A \mid B \cap C)\ P(B \mid C).$$

4.9 A disk drive may malfunction with either fault F_1 or F_2, but not both. The possible symptoms are the following:

A = { bad writes, bad reads }
B = { bad reads }

and F_2 is three times as likely to occur as F_1. For this type of drive

$P(A \mid F_1) = 0.4 \quad P(B \mid F_1) = 0.6$
$P(A \mid F_2) = 0.2 \quad P(B \mid F_2) = 0.8$

What are the probabilities of a disk drive with fault F_1? F_2?

4.10 Given the transition matrix for switching brands of disk drives in a year:

		Next Year		
		X	X	Z
	X	.5	.5	0
This Year	Y	.25	.5	.25
	X	0	.5	.5

(a) Assuming that initially 50% of the people use drive X, 25% use drive Y, and 25% use drive Z, what percent will be using each drive in 1, 2, and 3 years?
(b) Determine the steady state matrix.

4.11 (a) Given N people selected at random, what is the probability that no two have the same birthday?
(b) What is the probability for 30 people?

4.12 Under conditional independence of E_1 and E_2, show that for a rule involving the conjunction of known evidence:

IF E1 AND E2 THEN H

that

(a) $$P(H \mid E_1 \cap E_2) = \frac{P(E_1 \mid H)P(E_2 \mid H)}{P(E_1 \mid H)P(E_2 \mid H') + O(H')P(E_1 \mid H')P(E_2 \mid H')}$$

(b) $$P(H \mid E_1 \cap E_2) = \frac{P(H \mid E_1)P(H \mid E_2)}{P(H \mid E_1)P(H \mid E_2) + O(H)P(H' \mid E_1)P(H' \mid E_2)}$$

4.13 Given a rule with a disjunction of evidence:

IF E_1 OR E_2 OR ... E_N THEN H

show that on the basis of probability theory and assuming conditional independence of the evidence:

$$P(E \mid e) = 1 - \prod_{i=1}^{N} (1 - P(E_i \mid e))$$

where E is the evidence and e is the relevant observations toward E.

4.14 Given the following evidence as the antecedent of:

IF E THEN H

write the fuzzy logic expressions for P(E | e):

(a) $E = E_1$ OR (E_2 AND E_3')
(b) $E =$ (E_1 AND E_2) OR (E_3 AND E_4)
(c) $E =$ (E_1' AND E_2') OR E_3
(d) $E = E_1'$ AND (E_2' OR E_3)
(e) $E = E_1'$ OR (E_2 AND E_3)

4.15 For the inference net of porphyritic copper, assume RCS is known true and RCAD is known false. What is the updated probability of FRE?

4.16 Consider the following problem of semantic induction to determine the next 3 numbers in the sequence 2, 8, 8, . . . In semantic induction a clue is needed to figure out the sequence hint: think "truck."

BIBLIOGRAPHY

Note: Many other references to probability, statistics and Bayesian software are given in Appendix G Software Resources.

(Castillo 97). Ed. by Enrique Castillo *et al., Expert Systems and Probabilistic Network Models,* Springer-Verlag New York, Inc., 1997.

(Gates 00). Bill Gates, *Business @ the Speed of Thought: Succeeding in the Digital Economy,* Warner Business Books, 2000. An excerpt from the book about Bayesian logic in Microsoft products is at: (http://www.microsoft.com/billgates/speedofthought/ additional/badnews.asp).

(Grinstead 97). Charles M. Grinstead and J. Laurie Snell, *Introduction to Probability,* American Mathematical Society, 2nd edition, 1997. NOTE: Besides including software, the book is also available GNU free from: (http://www.dartmouth.edu/~chance/teaching_aids/books_articles/probability_book/book-5-17-03.pdf)

(Jackson 99). Peter Jackson, *Introduction to Expert Systems*, Addison-Wesley, 3rd Edition, 1999.

(Neapolitan 03). Richard E. Neapolitan, *Learning Bayesian Networks*, Prentice-Hall, 2003.

(Pearl 00). Judea Pearl, *Causality: Models, Reasoning, and Inference*, Cambridge University Press, 2000.

(Ross 02). Sheldon M. Ross, *Introduction to Probability Models, Eighth Edition*, pp. 188-191, Academic Press, 2002.

CHAPTER 5
Inexact Reasoning

5.1 INTRODUCTION

This chapter continues the discussion of reasoning under uncertainty begun in Chapter 4. The main paradigm for reasoning under uncertainty in Chapter 4 was probabilistic reasoning and Bayes' Theorem. In this chapter we shall examine several other approaches to dealing with uncertainty. In particular, fuzzy logic has been extremely successful in many applications such as image processing and control, fuzzy rule-based machine learning classification, clustering, and function approximation (Ibrahim 03) (Chen 01).

Two versions of CLIPS have been created for developing expert systems that use a lot of fuzzy reasoning. The first is the NRC fuzzyCLIPS (http://ai.iit.nrc.ca/IR_public/fuzzy/). NRC also has a FuzzyJToolkit for the Java Platform and FuzzyJess (Java-based version of CLIPS). The second is the Togai InfraLogic Fuzzy CLIPS, with many links to other fuzzy resources (http://www.ortech-engr.com/fuzzy/togai.html). Fuzzy expert systems are now in common use as you can easily tell from searching the Web and books (Siller 04).

As described in Chapter 4, probability was originally developed for ideal games of chance in which the same experiment could be reproduced indefinitely. In fact, probability theory has been called by mathematicians a theory of **reproducible uncertainty**. At first reading, this sounds like an oxymoron, for if something is uncertain, how can we reproduce it over and over again? (Except for having kids, of course.) The term reproducible means in a statistical sense when there is a large population and the results are averaged over many trials. While it would be nice to predict exactly what would happen on the next roll of dice, we can only give the odds and not any statement of certainty.

While the subjective probability theory described in Chapter 4 has been successfully used with PROSPECTOR, there are many other applications that are better served by other theories. These alternative theories were specifically developed to deal with human belief rather than the classic frequency interpretation of probability. All these theories are examples of **inexact reasoning** in which the antecedent, the conclusion, and even the meaning of the rule itself are uncertain to some extent.

5.2 UNCERTAINTY AND RULES

This section provides an overview of rules and uncertainty. Later sections will cover other methods of dealing with uncertainty in rules and other **intelligent systems**. The term *intelligent system* is in wide use today and strictly speaking, is any application that uses AI. In practice, it is often used to describe any system that can operate with uncertain information.

Sources of Uncertainty in Rules

Figure 5.1 illustrates a high-level view of uncertainty in rule-based systems. This uncertainty may come from the individual rules, conflict resolution, and incompatibilities among the consequents of rules. The goal of the knowledge engineer is to minimize or eliminate these uncertainties, if possible.

Minimizing the uncertainties of individual rules is part of the **verification** of the rule. As mentioned in Section 3.15, verification is concerned with the correctness of the system's building blocks. For a rule-based system, the building blocks are the rules.

Just because the individual rules are correct doesn't mean the system will give a correct answer. Due to incompatibilities among rules, the inference chains may not be correct and so validation is necessary. For a rule-based system, part of validation is minimizing uncertainty in the inference chains. Verification can be viewed as minimizing the local uncertainties while validation minimizes the global uncertainty of the entire expert system. As a rough analogy to civil engineering, verification would ask if a bridge were being built properly in terms of good materials and assembly. Validation would ask if the bridge can handle the required traffic load and, most important, is the bridge being built at the right location? Both verification and validation are necessary to ensure a quality expert system, as discussed further in Chapter 6.

The top-level view of uncertainties in individual rules of Figure 5.1 is expanded in more detail in Figure 5.2. Besides the possible errors involved in the creation of rules, as described in Section 4.3, there are uncertainties associated

Figure 5.1 Major Uncertainties in a Rule-Based Expert System

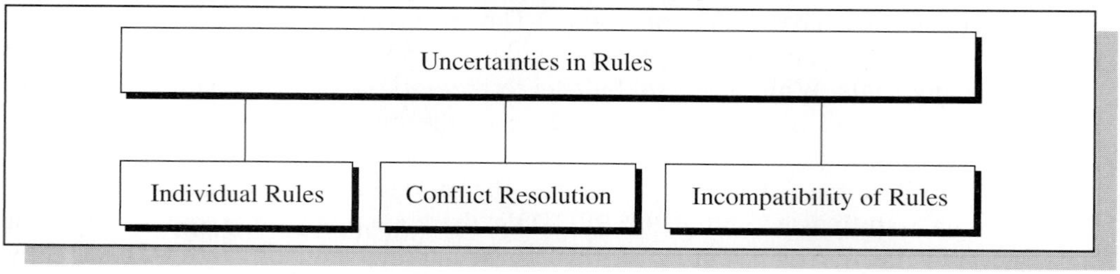

Figure 5.2 Uncertainties in Individual Rules

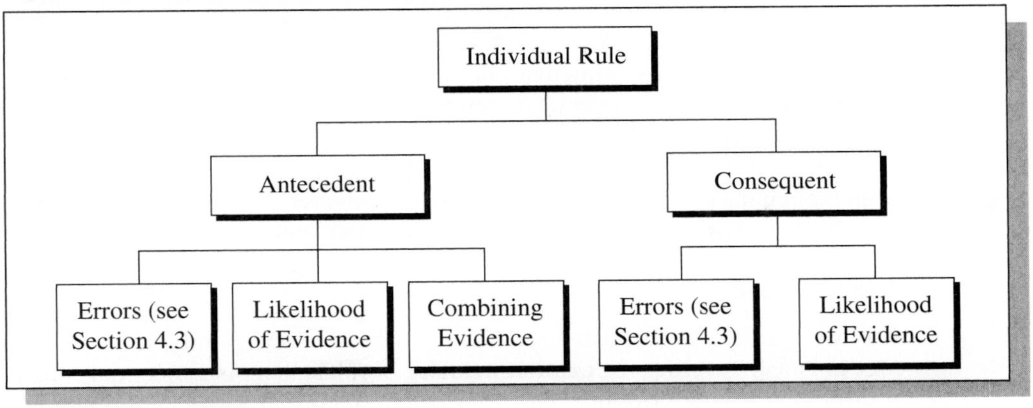

with the assignment of likelihood values. For probabilistic reasoning, as described in Chapter 4, these uncertainties are with the sufficiency, LS, and necessity, LN, values. Since the LS and LN values are based on estimates from humans, there is uncertainty with them. There is also an uncertainty with the likelihood of the consequent. For probabilistic reasoning, this was written as $P(H \mid E)$ for certain evidence and $P(H \mid e)$ for uncertain evidence.

Another source of uncertainty is the combining of the evidence. Should the evidence be combined, as in the following:

as E_1 AND E_2 AND E_3

or as E_1 AND E_2 OR E_3

or as E_1 AND NOT E_2 OR E_3

or some other possible way of logical combination using AND, OR, and NOT?

Lack of Theory

As mentioned in Chapter 4, the ad hoc introduction of formulas such as fuzzy logic to a probabilistic system introduces a problem. The expert system does not then have a sound theoretical foundation based on classical probability, and so represents an ad hoc method that works for a limited case. The danger of ad hoc methods is that there is no complete theory to guide the application or warn of inappropriate situations.

Another example of an ad hoc method that you have seen is the use of LS and LN factors with inference networks. Theoretically, an inference net with N nodes is a probabilistic system with an event space of N possible events. Thus, there are 2^N possible probabilities. In practice, for real-world situations, few of these probabilities are known. Rather than trying to enumerate all the probabilities, the LS and LN factors are used for significant (we hope) arcs between nodes. Use of LS and LN values for significant arcs greatly reduces the complexity of the net.

However, the LS and LN shortcut also has the detrimental effect that there is no theoretical guarantee that the sum of the conditional probabilities for each hypothesis in the net will be unity. This may not matter much to the user if the goal is simply to obtain a relative ranking of all the hypotheses in the net. For example, the user interested in the porphyry copper hypothesis may well be satisfied to know that the node indicating a favorable likelihood of copper is greatest, even if it is not 1. However, the absolute probability is important also. Even though the copper hypothesis is ranked number 1, is it worth drilling if the probability of finding copper is very low, say 0.00000001?

Rule Interactions

Another source of uncertainty is conflict resolution of uncertainty. If the knowledge engineer specifies the **explicit priority** of rules, there is a potential source of error since the priority may not be optimum or correct. Other problems with conflict resolution occur because of the **implicit priority** of rules.

Conflict resolution is part of a major source of uncertainty caused by the interactions between rules. The interaction of rules depends on conflict resolution, and the **compatibility of rules**, as shown in Figure 5.3. The compatibility of rules has uncertainty from five major causes.

One cause of uncertainty is the potential **contradiction of rules**. Rules may fire with contradictory consequents. This may happen if the antecedents are not specified properly. As a very simple example, assume two rules in the knowledge base:

```
(1) IF there is a fire THEN put water on it
(2) IF there is a fire THEN don't put water on it
```

Rule (1) is applicable for ordinary fires such as wood fires. Rule (2) is applicable for oil or grease fires. The problem is that the antecedents are not specified precisely enough for the type of fire. If a fact exists "there is a fire," then both rules will be executed with contradictory consequents and a resulting increase in uncertainty.

A second source of uncertainty is **subsumption of rules**. One rule is subsumed by another if a portion of its antecedent is a subset of another rule. For example, suppose there are two rules that both have the same conclusion:

Figure 5.3 Uncertainty Associated with the Compatibilities of Rules

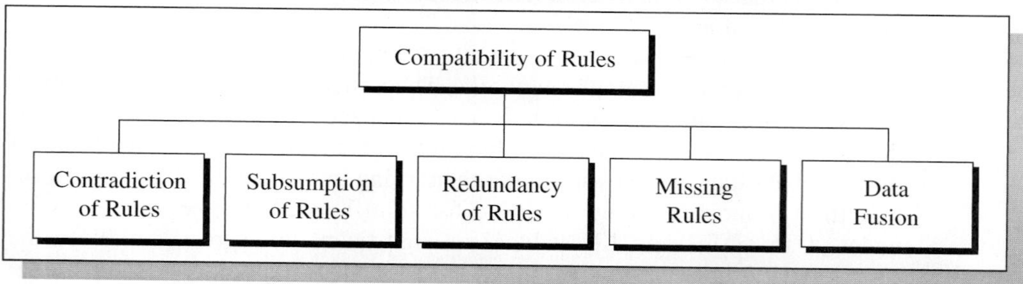

```
(3) IF E1 THEN H

(4) IF E1 AND E2 THEN H
```

If only E_1 is present, then there is no problem since only rule (3) will be activated. However if both E_1 and E_2 exist, then both rules (3) and (4) will be activated and conflict resolution on them is necessary.

Conflict Resolution

There is uncertainty in conflict resolution regarding priority for firing. This uncertainty depends on a number of factors, as illustrated in Figure 5.4.

Figure 5.4 Uncertainty Associated with Conflict Resolution

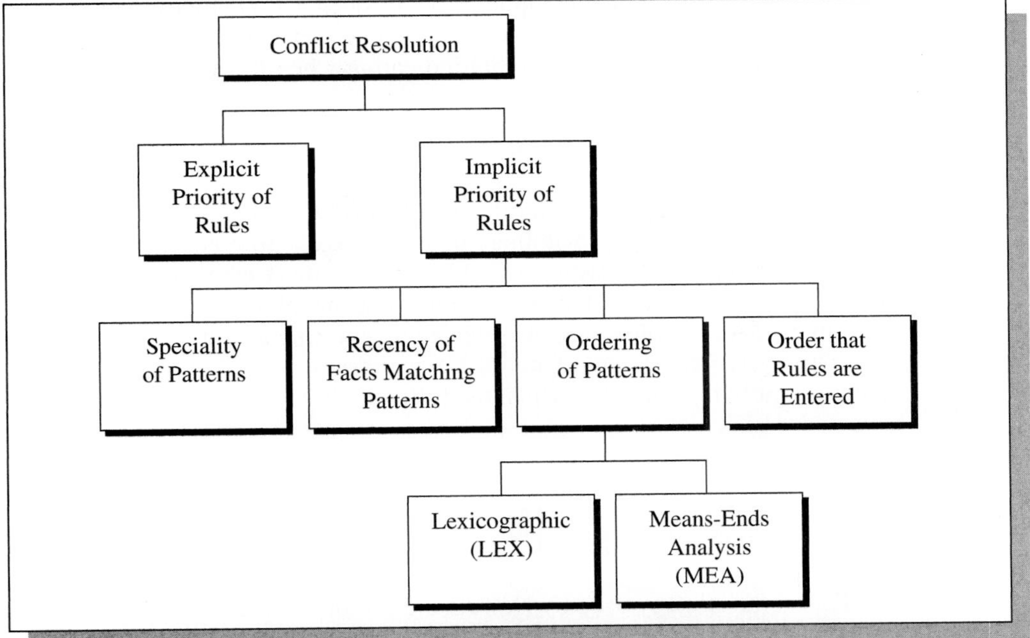

The first factor is the shell or tool used. In expert systems tools that use the Rete Algorithm, a rule with more specific patterns has a higher priority. This makes sense in that the more information that is available increases our confidence when multiple rules may be potentially triggered into firing.

For example, if someone says, "I feel hot," one rule might be IF hot THEN take an aspirin. On the other hand, a rule that says IF hot AND wearing a coat at the beach THEN take off coat, is more specific if more information is available that the person is at the beach wearing a coat. In general the amount of pattern matching on the left-hand-side of a rule is a measure of the confidence we have that the rule is more appropriate than one with fewer patterns, i.e., less information is available. The **specificity** of a CLIPS rule depends on the number of patterns and the internal complexity of each pattern. For example, the pattern:

```
(ball ellipsoidal)
```

is more specific than the pattern:

```
(ball)
```

The ellipsoidal ball is probably a football while just ball by itself could mean tennis ball, ping-pong ball, basketball, baseball, or any type of ball.

For our two rules, rule (4) is more specific because it has two patterns in its antecedent and thus has a higher implicit priority. In a CLIPS system, rule (4) is executed first.

However, there are other complications. Besides the specificity, there is also the consideration of **recency of facts**. Whenever a fact is entered in the working memory, it receives a unique **timetag** indicating when it was entered. Thus, a rule with the pattern:

(5) IF E_3 THEN H

would have a higher priority than rule (3) if fact E_3 was entered after E_1.

The ordering of patterns within a rule also makes a difference. OPS5 allows two different **control strategies** called **lexicographic (LEX)** and **means-ends analysis (MEA)**. These strategies determine how the inference engine interprets rule patterns. A control strategy is selected by entering a strategy command to the expert system interpreter. Under LEX, pattern order makes no difference, except possibly in efficiency. Thus, the following two rules are essentially the same under LEX:

IF E_1 AND E_2 THEN H

IF E_2 AND E_1 THEN H

MEA is the strategy used by Newell and Simon's General Problem Solver, discussed in Chapter 1. The basic idea of MEA is to keep reducing the difference between the starting state and the success state. In the OPS5 implementation of MEA, the first pattern is very important because it acts to control the pattern-matching process. The purpose of MEA is to help the system keep executing a certain task without becoming distracted by very recent facts that have entered working memory. MEA prioritizes rules on the basis of the first pattern, which follows the IF. If one of the rules dominates the others on the basis of the first pattern, then that rule is selected. This domination can be by specificity or recency. If there is more than one dominant rule-first pattern, then MEA orders the rules on the basis of the remaining patterns. Eventually, if there is no dominant rule, an arbitrary choice of a rule is made.

The order that rules are entered in the expert system may also be a factor in conflict resolution. If the inference engine cannot prioritize rules, an arbitrary choice should be made. However, unless the designers of the inference engine have been careful, the choice may be deterministic in a sense because it depends on the entry of the rule. This may come about because the designers of the inference engine used a stack or queue to store rules on the agenda. For an arbitrary choice of equally prioritized rules, there really should be a random choice from the stack or queue. Instead, the designers may simply take the easy way out and pop the stack or take the next rule from the queue. This selection method is easy but introduces a known artifact into the system because the choice of equally prioritized rules is not arbitrary.

Subsumption and Uncertainty

The problem of subsumption becomes more uncertain if there are likelihoods associated with the rules, as in:

(6) IF E_1 THEN H with LS_1

(7) IF E_1 AND E_2 THEN H with LS_2

For example, consider the following rules:

```
IF the starter motor doesn't work
THEN check the battery with LS1 = 5
IF the starter motor doesn't work AND
   the lights don't work
THEN check the battery with LS2 = 10
```

where LS_2 is greater than LS_1 because of more evidence supporting the conclusion.

From Chapter 4, the posterior odds formula:

$$(8)\quad O(H \mid E) = \left[\prod_{i=1}^{N} LS_i\right] O(H)$$

means that the product is $5 \cdot 10 = 50$, if both E_1 and E_2 are observed.

However, (8) was really meant to describe rules whose evidence combines independently. The antecedents of (6) and (7) are not really independent because they share evidence E_1 in common. Thus, E_1 AND E_2 subsume E_1 because E_1 alone is a special case of E_1 AND E_2. The product of the likelihood ratios LS_1 and LS_2 is thus erroneously high because the antecedents are not independent. A solution is to replace LS_2 by the ratio LS_2 / LS_1 so that when both E_1 and E_2 exist, the correct product LS_2 is computed. It may be hard to detect subsumption manually in a large knowledge base.

A third cause of uncertainty is **redundant rules**, which have the same consequent and evidence. Generally, these are accidentally entered by the knowledge engineer or accidentally occur when a rule is modified by pattern deletion. For example,

```
IF E1 AND E2 THEN H

IF E2 AND E1 AND E3 THEN H
```

are redundant rules if E_3 is deleted since the antecedents are the same pattern. Deciding which redundant rule to delete is not necessarily simple. One redundant rule may lead to greater system efficiency if a rare pattern is listed first. The inference engine may not need to check the second pattern for a match if the first pattern fails to match. A further complication arises in expert system shells such as OPS5, in which the order of activation depends on the user-selected control strategy. Like the case of subsumption, redundant rules also give an erroneously high product of the likelihood ratio.

The fourth cause of uncertainty in rule consequents arises from **missing rules**, which occurs if the human expert forgets or is unaware of a rule such as:

```
IF E4 THEN H
```

If evidence E_4 is ignored, then H is not concluded with the strength it deserves. One advantage of an inference network such as PROSPECTOR is the explicit nature of the network, which makes it easy to identify hypotheses that are impossible or difficult to achieve. If there are missing rules, the inference net may imply the need for these rules.

The fifth cause of uncertainty occurs because of problems with **data fusion**. This term refers to the uncertainty associated with fusing data from different types of information. For example, in making a diagnosis, a physician may consider evidence from widely different sources such as a physical exam, lab tests, patient history, socioeconomic environment, mental and emotional states, family and job problems, and so forth. These are all different types of evidence that must be fused to support a final hypothesis. The fusion of this evidence from so many different sources is much more difficult than evidence in one domain such as geology.

Likewise, a business decision may depend on the market for goods, economic conditions, foreign trade, takeover attempts, company politics, personal problems, unions, and many other factors. As with the medical problem, it is very difficult to assign likelihood ratios to all these factors and determine a reasonable combining function.

5.3 CERTAINTY FACTORS

Another method of dealing with uncertainty uses **certainty factors**, originally developed for the MYCIN expert system.

Difficulties with the Bayesian Method

Like the geological problem addressed by PROSPECTOR, medical diagnosis is almost always subject to uncertainty. The major difference is that there are a limited number of geologic hypotheses about minerals since there are only 92 natural elements. Possible disease hypotheses are much greater because there are many more pathogens.

While Bayes' Theorem is useful in medicine, its accurate use depends on knowing many probabilities. For example, Bayes' Theorem may be used to determine the probability of a specific disease, given certain symptoms as:

$$P(D_i \mid E) = \frac{P(E \mid D_i)\, P(D_i)}{P(E)} = \frac{P(E \mid D_i)\, P(D_i)}{\sum_j P(E \mid D_j)\, P(D_j)}$$

where the sum over j extends to all diseases, and:

D_i is the i'th disease,
E is the evidence,
$P(D_i)$ is the prior probability of the patient having the Disease_i before any evidence is known,
$P(E \mid D_i)$ is the conditional probability that the patient will exhibit evidence E, given that disease D_i is present.

It is usually impossible to determine consistent and complete values for all these probabilities for the general population.

In practice, evidence tends to accumulate piece by piece. This accumulation costs considerable time and expense, especially when medical tests are involved. These factors of time, cost, and potential risk to the patient usually limit the number of tests performed to a minimum required for a good diagnosis (and malpractice protection.).

A convenient form of Bayes' Theorem that expresses the accumulation of incremental evidence like this is (see Problem 5.1):

$$P(D_i \mid E) = \frac{P(E_2 \mid D_i \cap E_1)\, P(D_i \mid E_1)}{\sum_j P(E_2 \mid D_j \cap E_1)\, P(D_j \mid E_1)}$$

where E_2 is the new evidence added to the existing body of evidence, E_1, to yield the new augmented evidence:

$$E = E_1 \cap E_2$$

Although this formula is exact, all these probabilities are not generally known. Also, the situation grows much worse as more pieces of evidence accumulate and so more probabilities are required.

Belief and Disbelief

Besides the problem of amassing all the conditional probabilities for the Bayesian method, another major problem that appeared with medical experts was the relationship of belief and disbelief. At first sight this may appear trivial, since obviously disbelief is simply the opposite of belief. In fact, the theory of probability states that:

$$P(H) + P(H') = 1$$

and so:

$$P(H) = 1 - P(H')$$

For the case of a posterior hypothesis that relies on evidence, E:

$$(1)\quad P(H \mid E) = 1 - P(H' \mid E)$$

However, when the MYCIN knowledge engineers began interviewing medical experts, they found that physicians were extremely reluctant to state their knowledge in the form of equation (1).

For example, consider a MYCIN rule such as the following:

```
IF 1) The stain of the organism is gram positive,
   and
   2) The morphology of the organism is coccus,
   and
   3) The growth conformation of the organism is
   chains
THEN There is suggestive evidence (0.7) that the
     identity of the organism is streptococcus
```

In simple terms, this rule says that if a bacterial organism becomes colored when treated with Gram's stain and resembles chains of spheres, then there is a 70 percent likelihood that it is a type named *streptococcus.* This can be written in terms of posterior probability as:

$$(2)\quad P(H \mid E_1 \cap E_2 \cap E_3) = 0.7$$

where the E_i correspond to the three patterns of the antecedent.

The MYCIN knowledge engineers found that while an expert would agree to equation (2), they became uneasy and refused to agree with the probabilistic result:

$$(3)\quad P(H' \mid E_1 \cap E_2 \cap E_3) = 1 - 0.7 = 0.3$$

This reluctance by the experts to agree to equation (3) illustrates again that these numbers such as 0.7 and 0.3 are likelihoods of belief, not probabilities.

In order to fully appreciate this problem of inconsistent belief and disbelief, consider the following example. Suppose this is your last course required for a degree. Assume your grade point average (GPA) has not been too good and you need an "A" in this course to bring up your GPA. The following formula may express your belief in the likelihood of graduation:

```
(4) P(graduating | 'A' in this course) = 0.70
```

Notice that this likelihood is not 100 percent. The reason it's not 100 percent is that a final audit of your courses and grades will be made by the school. There could be problems due to a number of reasons that would still prevent your graduation, such as the following:

1. School catalog changes so that not all your courses counted toward the degree.
2. You forgot to take a required course.
3. Rejection of transfer courses.
4. Rejection of some elective courses you took.
5. Tuition and library fines that you owe and were hoping would be forgotten.
6. Your GPA was lower than you thought and an "A" still won't raise it up.
7. "They" are out to get you.

Assuming that you agree with (4) (or perhaps your own value for the likelihood) then by equation (1):

```
(5) P(not graduating | 'A' in this course) = 0.30
```

Although equation (5) is correct from a probabilistic viewpoint, it somehow seems intuitively wrong. It's just not right that if you really work hard and get an "A" in this course, then there is a 30 percent chance that you won't graduate. Equation (5) should make you as uneasy as the medical expert who believes:

$$P(H \mid E_1 \cap E_2 \cap E_3) = 0.70$$

but won't believe the probabilistic consequence:

$$P(H' \mid E_1 \cap E_2 \cap E_3) = 0.30$$

The fundamental problem is that while $P(H \mid E)$ implies a cause-and-effect relationship between E and H, there may be no cause-and-effect relationship between E and H′. Yet the equation:

$$P(H \mid E) = 1 - P(H' \mid E)$$

implies a cause-and-effect relationship between E and H′ if there is a cause-and-effect between E and H.

These problems with the theory of probability led Shortliffe to investigate other ways of representing uncertainty. The method that he used with MYCIN was based on **certainty factors** derived from Carnap's theory of confirmation. Carnap distinguished two types of probability.

One type of probability is **ordinary probability** associated with the frequency of reproducible events. The second type is called **epistemic probability** or the **degree of confirmation** because it confirms a hypothesis based on some evidence. This second type is another example of the degree of likelihood of a belief.

Measures of Belief and Disbelief

In MYCIN, the degree of confirmation was originally defined as the certainty factor, which is the difference between belief and disbelief:

$$\text{CF(H,E)} = \text{MB(H,E)} - \text{MD(H,E)}$$

where:

CF is the certainty factor in the hypothesis H due to evidence E
MB is the measure of increased belief in H due to E
MD is the measure of increased disbelief in H due to E

The certainty factor is a way of combining belief and disbelief into a single number.

Combining the measures of belief and disbelief into a single number has two uses. First, the certainty factor can be used to rank hypotheses in order of importance. For example, if a patient has certain symptoms that suggest several possible diseases, then the disease with the highest CF would be the one that is first investigated by ordering tests.

The measures of belief and disbelief were defined in terms of probabilities by:

$$\text{MB(H,E)} = \begin{cases} 1 & \text{if P(H)} = 1 \\ \dfrac{\max[\text{P(H} \mid \text{E), P(H)}] - \text{P(H)}}{\max[1,0] - \text{P(H)}} & \text{otherwise} \end{cases}$$

$$\text{MD(H,E)} = \begin{cases} 1 & \text{if P(H)} = 0 \\ \dfrac{\min[\text{P(H} \mid \text{E), P(H)}] - \text{P(H)}}{\min[1,0] - \text{P(H)}} & \text{otherwise} \end{cases}$$

Now max [1,0] is always 1 and min [1,0] is always 0. The reason for writing 1 and 0 in terms of max and min is to show the formal symmetry between MB and MD. The equations for MB and MD differ only in the replacement of max by min and vice versa.

Based on these definitions, some characteristics are shown in Table 5.1.

The certainty factor, CF, indicates the net belief in a hypothesis based on some evidence. A positive CF means the evidence supports the hypothesis since MB > MD. A CF = 1 means that the evidence definitely proves the hypothesis. A CF = 0 means one of two possibilities. First, a CF = MB − MD = 0 could mean that both MB and MD are 0. That is, there is no evidence. The second pos-

Table 5.1 Some Characteristics of MB, MD, and CF

Characteristics	Values
Ranges	$0 \leq$ MB ≤ 1 $0 \leq$ MD ≤ 1 $-1 \leq$ CF ≤ 1
Certain True Hypothesis P(H | E) = 1	MB = 1 MD = 0 CF = 1
Certain False Hypothesis P(H´ | E) = 1	MB = 0 MD = 1 CF = −1
Lack of Evidence P(H | E) = P(H)	MB = 0 MD = 0 CF = 0

sibility is that MB = MD and both are nonzero. The result is that the belief is cancelled out by the disbelief. Unfortunately the cancellation of strong belief by disbelief leads not to simple ignorance, but worse, to a state of confusion. For example, what is worse, coming to a street and not knowing which way to turn, or a passenger in your car saying "turn right" while pointing left?

A negative CF means that the evidence favors the negation of the hypothesis since MB < MD. Another way of stating this is that there is more reason to disbelieve a hypothesis than to believe it. For example, a CF = −70 percent means that the disbelief is 70 percent greater than the belief. A CF = 70 percent means that the belief is 70 percent greater than the disbelief. Notice that with certainty factors there are no constraints on the individual values of MB and MD. Only the difference is important. For example:

```
CF = 0.70 = 0.70 - 0
          = 0.80 - 0.10
```

and so forth.

Certainty factors allow an expert to express a belief without committing a value to the disbelief. As shown in Problem 5.2,

```
CF(H,E) + CF(H´,E) = 0
```

which means that if evidence confirms a hypothesis by some value CF(H | E) the confirmation of the negation of the hypothesis is not 1 − CF(H | E) which would be expected under probability theory. That is,

```
CF(H,E) + CF(H´,E) ≠ 1
```

The fact that CF(H | E) + CF(H´ | E) = 0 means that evidence supporting a hypothesis reduces support to the negation of the hypothesis by an equal amount so that the sum is always 0.

For the example of the student graduating if an "A" is given in the course,

```
CF(H,E) = 0.70      CF(H´,E) = −0.70
```

which means:

```
(6) I am 70 percent certain that I will graduate
    if I get an 'A' in this course.

(7) I am −70 percent certain that I will not
    graduate if I get an 'A' in this course.
```

Notice that the −70 percent comes about because certainty factors are defined on the interval:

$$-1 \le CF(H,E) \le +1$$

where 0 means no evidence. So certainty values greater than 0 favor the hypothesis while certainty factors less than 0 favor the negation of the hypothesis. Statements (6) and (7) are equivalent using certainty factors analogous to the fact that "yes = not no."

The above CF values might be elicited by asking:

```
How much do you believe that getting an 'A' will
help you graduate?
```

if the evidence is to confirm the hypothesis or:

```
How much do you disbelieve that getting an 'A'
will help you graduate?
```

An answer of 70 percent to each question will set CF(H | E) = 0.70 and CF (H´ | E) = −0.70. In MYCIN, rather than asking certainties on a percentage scale, the experts were asked to give certainty on a scale of 1 to 10, where 10 was definite. The user could answer UNK for unknown evidence corresponding to CF = 0.

Calculating with Certainty Factors

Although the original definition of CF was:

$$CF = MB - MD$$

there were difficulties with this definition because one piece of disconfirming evidence could control the confirmation of many other pieces of evidence. For example, 10 pieces of evidence might produce a MB = 0.999 and one disconfirming piece with MD = 0.799 could then give:

$$CF = 0.999 - 0.799 = 0.200$$

In MYCIN, a rule's antecedent CF must be > 0.2 for the antecedent to be considered true and activate the rule. This **threshold value** of 0.2 was not done as a fundamental axiom of CF theory, but rather as an ad hoc way of minimizing the activation of rules which only weakly suggest a hypothesis. Without a threshold, many rules may be activated of little or no value and greatly reduce the system's efficiency.

The definition of CF was changed in MYCIN in 1977 to be:

$$CF = \frac{MB - MD}{1 - \min(MB, MD)}$$

to soften the effects of a single piece of disconfirming evidence on many confirming pieces of evidence. Under this definition with MB = 0.999, MD = 0.799:

$$CF = \frac{0.999 - 0.799}{1 - \min(0.999, 0.799)} = \frac{0.200}{1 - 0.799} = 0.995$$

which is very different from the previous definition that gave 0.999 − 0.799 = 0.200 and so did not activate a rule since it was not greater than 0.2. Now the 0.995 will cause the rule to be activated.

The MYCIN methods for combining evidence in the antecedent of a rule are shown in Table 5.2. Notice that these are the same as the PROSPECTOR rules based on fuzzy logic.

Table 5.2 MYCIN Rules for Combining Antecedent Evidence of Elementary Expressions

Evidence, E	Antecedent Certainty
E_1 AND E_2	min [CF(H,E_1), CF(H,E_2)]
E_1 OR E_2	max [CF(H,E_1), CF(H,E_2)]
NOT E	– CF(H,E)

For example, given a logical expression for combining evidence such as:

$$E = (E_1 \text{ AND } E_2 \text{ AND } E_3) \text{ OR } (E_4 \text{ AND NOT } E_5)$$

the evidence E would be computed as:

$$E = \max[\min(E_1, E_2, E_3), \min(E_4, -E_5)]$$

For values:

$$E_1 = 0.9 \quad E_2 = 0.8 \quad E_3 = 0.3$$
$$E_4 = -0.5 \quad E_5 = -0.4$$

the result is:

```
E = max[min(0.9,0.8,0.3),min(−0.5,-(-0.4)]
  = max[0.3,−0.5]
  = 0.3
```

The fundamental formula for the CF of a rule:

```
IF E THEN H
```

is given by the formula:

```
(8) CF(H,e) = CF(E,e) CF(H,E)
```

where:

CF(E,e) is the certainty factor of the evidence E making up the antecedent of the rule based on uncertain evidence e.

CF(H,E) is the certainty factor of the hypothesis assuming that the evidence is known with certainty, when CF(E,e) = 1.

CF(H,e) is the certainty factor of the hypothesis based on uncertain evidence *e*.

Thus, if all the evidence in the antecedent is known with certainty, the formula for the certainty factor of the hypothesis is:

```
CF(H,e) = CF(H,E)
```

since CF(E,e) = 1.

As an example of these certainty factors, consider the CF for the streptococcus rule discussed before,

```
IF 1) The stain of the organism is gram positive,
   and
   2) The morphology of the organism is coccus,
   and
   3) The growth conformation of the organism is
   chains
THEN There is suggestive evidence (0.7) that the
identity of the organism is streptococcus
```

where the certainty factor of the hypothesis under certain evidence is:

$$CF(H,E) = CF(H,E_1 \cap E_2 \cap E_3) = 0.7$$

and is also called the **attenuation factor**.

The attenuation factor is based on the assumption that all the evidence—E_1, E_2 and E_3—is known with certainty. That is,

$$CF(E_1,e) = CF(E_2,e) = CF(E_3,e) = 1$$

where *e* is the observed evidence that leads to the conclusion that the E_i are known with certainty. These CF values are analogous to the conditional probabilities of the evidence of PROSPECTOR, P(E | e). The attenuation factor expresses the degree of certainty of the hypothesis, given certain evidence.

Just as with PROSPECTOR, a complication occurs if all the evidence is not known with certainty. With PROSPECTOR, the interpolation formula P(H | e) was used for uncertain evidence. In the case of MYCIN, the fundamental formula (8) must be used to determine the resulting CF value since $CF(H,E_1 \cap E_2 \cap E_3) = 0.7$ is no longer valid for uncertain evidence.

For example, assuming:

$$\begin{aligned} CF(E_1,e) &= 0.5 \\ CF(E_2,e) &= 0.6 \\ CF(E_3,e) &= 0.3 \end{aligned}$$

then:

$$\begin{aligned} CF(E,e) &= CF(E_1 \cap E_2 \cap E_3,e) \\ &= \min[CF(E_1,e),CF(E_2,e),CF(E_3,e)] \\ &= \min[0.5,0.6,0.3] \\ &= 0.3 \end{aligned}$$

Since the CF of the antecedent, CF(E,e) > 0.2, the antecedent is considered true and so the rule is activated. The certainty factor of the conclusion is:

$$\begin{aligned} CF(H,e) &= CF(E,e)\ CF(H,E) \\ &= 0.3 \cdot 0.7 \\ &= 0.21 \end{aligned}$$

Suppose another rule also concludes the same hypothesis, but with a different certainty factor. The certainty factors of rules concluding the same hypothesis are calculated from the **combining function** for certainty factors defined as:

$$(9) \quad CF_{COMBINE}(CF_1,CF_2,) = \begin{cases} CF_1 + CF_2\ (1 - CF_1) & \text{both} > 0 \\ \dfrac{CF_1 + CF_2}{1 - \min(|CF_1|,|CF_2|)} & \text{one} < 0 \\ CF_1 + CF_2\ (1 + CF_1) & \text{both} < 0 \end{cases}$$

where the formula for $CF_{COMBINE}$ used depends on whether the individual certainty factors are positive or negative. The combining function for more than two certainty factors is applied incrementally. That is, the $CF_{COMBINE}$ is calculated for two CF values, and then the $CF_{COMBINE}$ is combined using formula (9) with the third CF value, and so forth. Figure 5.5 summarizes the calculations with certainty factors for two rules based on uncertain evidence and concludes the

Figure 5.5 CF of Two Rules with the Same Hypothesis Based on Uncertain Evidence

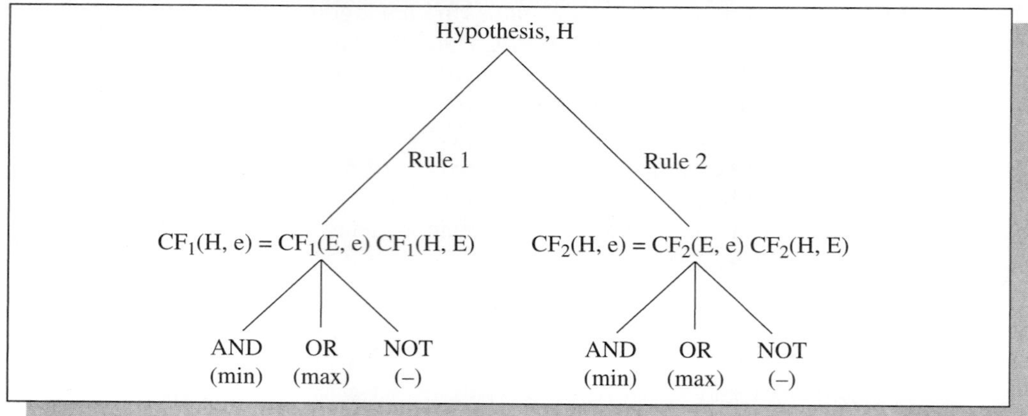

same hypothesis. Note that this is *not* an AND/OR tree because $CF_{COMBINE}$ has nothing to do with AND and OR goals.

In our example, if another rule concludes streptococcus with certainty factor $CF_2 = 0.5$, then the combined certainty using the first formula of (9) is:

$$CF_{COMBINE}(0.21, 0.5) = 0.21 + 0.5\ (1 - 0.21) = 0.605$$

Suppose a third rule also has the same conclusion, but with a $CF_3 = -0.4$. Then the second formula of (9) is used to give:

$$CF_{COMBINE}(0.605, -0.4) = \frac{0.605 - 0.4}{1 - \min(|0.605|, |-0.4|)}$$

$$= \frac{0.205}{1 - 0.4} = 0.34$$

The $CF_{COMBINE}$ formula preserves the commutativity of evidence. That is,

$$CF_{COMBINE}(X, Y) = CF_{COMBINE}(Y, X)$$

and so the order in which evidence is received does not affect the result.

Rather than storing separate MB and MD values for each hypothesis, MYCIN stored the current $CF_{COMBINE}$ with each hypothesis and combined it with new evidence as it became available.

$$CF_{COMBINE}(CF_1, CF_2) = \begin{cases} CF_1 + CF_2\ (1 - CF_1) & \text{both} > 0 \\ \dfrac{CF_1 + CF_2}{1 - \min(|CF_1|, |CF_2|)} & \text{one} < 0 \\ CF_1 + CF_2\ (1 + CF_1) & \text{both} < 0 \end{cases}$$

Difficulties with Certainty Factors

Although MYCIN was very successful in diagnosis, there were difficulties with the theoretical foundations of certainty factors. While certainty factors had some basis in both probability theory and confirmation theory, the CF were also partly ad hoc. The major advantage of CF was the simple computations by which uncertainty could be propagated in the system. The CF were also easy to understand and clearly separated belief from disbelief.

However, there were problems with CF. One problem was that the CF values could be the opposite of conditional probabilities. For example, if:

$$P(H_1) = 0.8 \qquad P(H_2) = 0.2$$
$$P(H_1 \mid E) = 0.9 \qquad P(H_2 \mid E) = 0.8$$

then:

$$CF(H_1,E) = 0.5 \text{ and } CF(H_2,E) = 0.75$$

Since one purpose of CF is to rank hypotheses in terms of likely diagnosis, it is a contradiction for a disease to have a higher conditional probability $P(H \mid E)$ and yet have a lower certainty factor, CF(H,E).

The second major problem with CF is that in general:

$$P(H \mid e) \neq P(H \mid i)\ P(i \mid e)$$

where *i* is some intermediate hypothesis based on evidence *e*, and yet the certainty factor of two rules in an inference chain is calculated as independent probabilities by:

$$CF(H,e) = CF(H,i)\ CF(i,e)$$

The above formula is only true in the special case that the statistical population with property H is contained in the population with property *i*, and that is contained in the population with property *e*. The success of MYCIN in spite of these problems is probably due to the short inference chains and simple hypotheses. There could be real problems in applying certainty factors to other domains that did not have short inference chains and simple hypotheses. In fact, Adams demonstrated that the theory of certainty factors is really an approximation to standard probability theory.

5.4 DEMPSTER-SHAFER THEORY

In this section, we will discuss a method of inexact reasoning called the **Dempster-Shafer theory** or Shafer-Dempster theory. It is based on work done originally by Dempster, who attempted to model uncertainty by a range of probabilities rather than as a single probabilistic number. Shafer later extended and refined Dempster's work in a book published in 1976 called *A*

Mathematical Theory of Evidence. A further extension called **evidential reasoning** deals with information that is expected to be uncertain, imprecise and occasionally inaccurate. The Dempster-Shafer theory has a good theoretical foundation. Certainty Factors can be shown to be a special case of Dempster-Shafer theory, which puts Certainty Factors on a theoretical rather than an ad hoc basis (Gardenfors 04). Dempster-Shafer theory is also used in intelligent databases where data mining is used to extract patterns (Bertino 01).

Frames of Discernment

The Dempster-Shafer theory assumes that there is a fixed set of mutually exclusive and exhaustive elements called the **environment** and symbolized by the Greek letter Θ:

$$\Theta = \{\theta_1, \theta_2, \ldots \theta_N\}$$

The environment is another term for the universe of discourse in set theory. That is, the environment is the set of objects that are of interest to us. Some examples of environments might be:

```
Θ = {airliner, bomber, fighter}
Θ = {red, green, blue, orange, yellow}
Θ = {barn, grass, person, cow, car}
```

Notice that the elements are all mutually exclusive. For example, an airliner is not a bomber or a fighter, red is not green, grass is not a cow, and so forth. Assume that all possible elements of the universe are in the set and so the set is exhaustive. For simplicity in our discussion, assume also that Θ is a finite set. However, work has been done on Dempster-Shafer environments whose elements are continuous variables such as time, distance, velocity, and so forth.

One way of thinking about Θ is in terms of questions and answers. Suppose:

```
Θ = {airliner, bomber, fighter}
```

and the question is "What are the military aircraft?" The answer is the subset of Θ:

$$\{\theta_2, \theta_3\} = \{\text{bomber}, \text{fighter}\}$$

Likewise, the question "What are the civilian aircraft?" is the set:

$$\{\theta_1\} = \{\text{airliner}\}$$

which is called a **singleton set** because it has only one element.

Each subset of Θ can be interpreted as a possible answer to a question. Since the elements are mutually exclusive and the environment is exhaustive, there can be only one correct answer subset to a question. Of course, not all possible questions may be meaningful nor interesting to ask. However, the important point to realize is that the subsets of the environment are all possible valid answers in this universe of discourse. Each subset can be considered an implied proposition, such as:

```
The correct answer is {θ1, θ2, θ3}
The correct answer is {θ1, θ2}
```

and so on for all subsets, where "The correct answer is" is implied with the subset.

All the possible subsets of the aircraft environment are shown in Figure 5.6, with lines drawn to indicate the relationships of the sets. The abbreviations A, B, and F are used for *airliner*, *bomber*, and *fighter*. This diagram is drawn as a hierarchical lattice with Θ at the top and the null set Ø = { } at the bottom. Usually, the null set is not explicitly shown because it always corresponds to the false answer. Since Ø has no elements, its choice as the answer below contradicts the assumption of environment as exhaustive:

```
The correct answer is no element
```

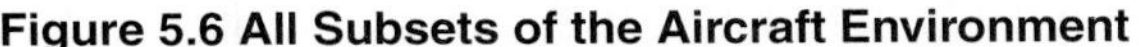

Figure 5.6 All Subsets of the Aircraft Environment

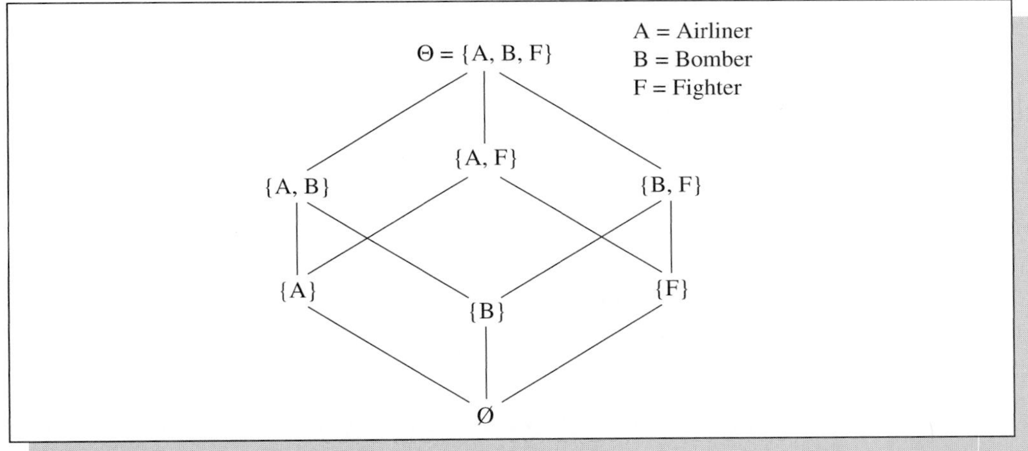

Notice that the figure is a lattice and not a tree because the subset nodes may have more than one parent. The lattice is hierarchical because it is drawn from larger sets to smaller sets. For example, one path from Θ to Ø expresses the hierarchical relation of subsets connecting parent to child, such as:

$$\emptyset \subset \{A\} \subset \{A,B\} \subset \{A,B,F\}$$

As discussed in Section 2.10, a relationship between two sets X and Y, such as:

$$X \subseteq Y$$

means that all elements of X are elements of Y, and is written more formally:

$$X \subseteq Y = \{x \mid x \in X \rightarrow x \in Y\}$$

This states that if x is an element of set X, then this implies x is also an element of set Y. If $X \subseteq Y$, but $X \neq Y$, there is at least one element of Y that is not an element of X, and X is called a *proper subset* of Y and is written:

$$X \subset Y$$

An environment is called a **frame of discernment** when its elements may be interpreted as possible answers, and only one answer is correct. The term *discern* means that it's possible to distinguish the one correct answer from all the other possible answers to a question. If the answer is not in the frame, then the frame must be enlarged to accommodate the additional knowledge of elements θ_{N+1}, θ_{N+2} and so forth. One correct answer requires that the set be exhaustive and that the subsets are disjointed.

A set of size N has exactly 2^N subsets, including itself, and these subsets define the power set (see problem 2.11), written as $P(\Theta)$. Thus, for the aircraft environment,

$$\mathscr{P}(\Theta) = \{\emptyset, \{A\}, \{B\}, \{F\}, \{A,B\}, \{A,F\}, \{B,F\}, \{A,B,F\}\}$$

The power set of the environment has as its elements all answers to the possible questions of the frame of discernment. This means that there is a one-to-one correspondence between the elements of $P(\Theta)$ and the subsets of Θ.

Mass Functions and Ignorance

In Bayesian theory the posterior probability changes as evidence is acquired. Likewise, in Dempster-Shafer theory the belief in evidence may vary. It's customary in Dempster-Shafer theory to think about the *degree of belief in evidence* as analogous to the **mass** of a physical object. That is, the mass of evidence supports a belief. The **evidence measure**, symbolized by the letter m, is analogous to the amount of mass. Another term for mass is the **basic probability assignment** (**bpa**) or sometimes simply **basic assignment**, because of an analogy in the form of the equations describing probability densities and mass. However, because of potential confusion with probability theory, we shall not use these terms and simply refer to *mass*. The reason for the analogy with an object of mass is to consider belief as a quantity that can move around, be split up, and combined. It may be helpful to think of the object as composed of clay so that pieces of it can be removed and stuck together again.

A fundamental difference between Dempster-Shafer theory and probability theory is the treatment of **ignorance**. As discussed in Chapter 4, probability theory must distribute an equal amount of probability even in ignorance. For example, if you have no prior knowledge, then you must assume the probability P of each possibility is:

$$P = \frac{1}{N}$$

where N is the number of possibilities. As mentioned in Chapter 4, this assignment of P is made *in desperation* or, using a more impressive-sounding term, by using the **principle of indifference**.

The extreme case of applying the principle of indifference occurs when there are only two possibilities, such as oil or no oil, symbolized by H and H´. In cases like this, P = 50 percent even when there is no knowledge at all since probability theory says that:

$$P(H) + P(H') = 1$$

That is, anything that does not support *must* refute, since ignorance is not allowed.

This can lead to some ridiculous consequences if applied without thinking. For example, either there is or is not oil under your house. By the principle of indifference, if you have *absolutely no other knowledge*, there is a 50 percent probability of having oil under your house. If you think about it, a 50 percent chance of oil is very impressive and offers a better chance at getting rich quick than any legal investment. Since there is a 50 percent chance of oil, should you immediately withdraw all your savings, hire a drilling rig, and start drilling in the kitchen?

Following this same line of reasoning, application of the principle of indifference and probability theory says there is a 50 percent chance of:

```
diamonds
a pirate's treasure
fur coats
green cheese
your next homework assignment
```

and anything else you can think of under your house. (In fact, you can probably become rich by just going on TV and telling everyone how *they* can become rich by sending in $9.95 for your book on probability theory. This is also the best reason for never cleaning. If you don't know what's there, it could be anything, and so there's a 50 percent chance of getting rich by discovering something valuable.)

Even if the principle of indifference is not used, the constraint:

$$P(H) + P(H') = 1$$

forces the assignment of probability to the negation of the hypothesis even if there is no evidence for this. As discussed in Section 5.3, this is not a good assumption with many types of belief such as medical knowledge. However, probability theory requires that evidence that does not support a hypothesis must refute it.

The Dempster-Shafer theory does not force belief to be assigned to ignorance or refutation of a hypothesis. Instead, the mass is assigned only to those subsets of the environment to which you wish to assign belief. Any belief that is not assigned to a specific subset is considered **no belief** or **nonbelief** and just associated with the environment Θ. Belief that refutes a hypothesis is disbelief, which is *not* nonbelief.

For example, suppose that a sensor such as an Identification Friend or Foe (IFF) obtains no response from the transponder of an aircraft. An IFF is a radio transmitter/receiver that transmits a radio message to an aircraft. If the aircraft is friendly, its transponder should respond by sending back its identification code. Aircraft that do not respond are assumed hostile by default. An aircraft may not respond to IFF for a variety of reasons, such as:

- Malfunction in the IFF
- Malfunction in the aircraft transponder
- No IFF on the aircraft
- Jamming of the IFF signal
- Orders to maintain radio silence

Assume that the failure of IFF to elicit a response indicates a belief in the evidence of 0.7 that the target aircraft is hostile, where hostile aircraft are only considered to be bombers and fighters. Thus, the mass assignment is to the subset {B,F}, and:

$$m_1(\{B,F\}) = 0.7$$

where m_1 refers to this first IFF sensor evidence.

The rest of the belief is left with the environment, Θ, as nonbelief:

$$m_1(\Theta) = 1 - 0.7 = 0.3$$

Every set in the power set of the environment which has a mass greater than 0 is a **focal element**. The term *focal element* is used because a set X such that $m(X) > 0$ is a power set element in which the available evidence is focused or concentrated.

The Dempster-Shafer theory has a major difference with probability theory, which would assume that:

```
P(hostile) = 0.7
P(non-hostile) = 1 - 0.7 = 0.3
```

In probability theory, if the belief in hostile is 0.7, then the disbelief in hostile must be 0.3. Instead, the 0.3 in Dempster-Shafer theory is held as nonbelief in the environment by m(Θ). This means *neither belief nor disbelief* in the evidence to a degree of 0.3. We believe that the target is hostile to a degree of 0.7 and are reserving judgment of 0.3 in disbelief and the additional belief in hostile. It's very important to realize that the assignment of 0.3 to the environment

Θ does not assign *any* value to the subsets of Θ, even though the subsets include the hostile subsets {B,F}, {B}, and {F}.

Going back to the student example of the last section,

```
m(getting an 'A' and graduating) = 0.7
```

would not automatically mean:

```
m(getting an 'A' and not graduating) = 0.3
```

unless both of these were assigned values.

A mass has considerably more freedom than probabilities, as Table 5.3 shows.

Table 5.3 Comparison of Dempster-Shafer Mass with Probability Theory

Dempster-Shafer Theory	Probability Theory
m(Θ) does not have to be 1	$\sum_i P_i = 1$
If $X \subseteq Y$, it is not necessary that $m(X) \le m(Y)$	$P(X) \le P(Y)$
No required relationship between m(X) and m(X´)	$P(X) + P(X') = 1$

Every mass can formally be expressed as a function that maps each element of the power set into a real number in the interval 0 to 1. This simply means that the belief in a subset may take any values from 0 to 1. This mapping is formally stated:

$$m: \mathscr{P}(\Theta) \rightarrow [0,1]$$

By convention, the mass of the empty set is usually defined as zero:

$$m(\emptyset) = 0$$

and the sum of all the masses for every subset, X, of the power set is 1:

$$\sum_{X \varepsilon \mathscr{P}(\Theta)} m(X) = 1$$

For example, in the aircraft environment:

$$\sum_{X \varepsilon \mathscr{P}(\Theta)} m(X) = m(\{B,F\}) + m(\theta) = 0.7 + 0.3 = 1$$

Combining Evidence

Now let's look at the case in which additional evidence becomes available. We would like to combine all the evidence to produce a better estimate of belief in the evidence. To show how this is done, let's first look at an example that is a special case of the general formula for combining evidence.

Suppose that a second type of sensor identifies the target as a bomber with a belief in the evidence of 0.9. The masses of evidence from the sensors are now the following:

$$m_1(\{B,F\}) = 0.7 \qquad m_1(\Theta) = 0.3$$

$$m_2(\{B\}) = 0.9 \qquad m_2(\Theta) = 0.1$$

where m_1 and m_2 refer to the first and second types of sensors.

This evidence can be combined using the following special form of **Dempster's Rule of Combination** to yield the **combined mass**:

$$m_1 \oplus m_2(Z) = \sum_{X \cap Y = Z} m_1(X)\, m_2(Y)$$

where the sum extends over all elements whose intersection $X \cap Y = Z$. The $\oplus$ **operator** denotes the **orthogonal sum** or **direct sum** which is defined by summing the mass product intersections on the right-hand side of the rule. Dempster's rule combines masses to produce a new mass that represents a **consensus** of the original, possibly conflicting evidence. The new mass is a *consensus* because it tends to favor agreement rather than disagreement by including only masses in the set intersections. The set intersections represent common elements of evidence. An important point is that the rule should be used to combine evidence having *independent errors*, which is *not* the same as independently gathered evidence.

Table 5.4 shows the masses and product intersections for the aircraft environment arranged in a table. Each set intersection is followed by its numeric mass product.

Table 5.4 Confirming Evidence

	m2({B}) = 0.9	**m2(Θ) = 0.1**
m1({B,F}) = 0.7	{B} 0.63	{B,F} 0.07
m1(Θ) = 0.3	{B} 0.27	Θ 0.03

The entries in the table are calculated by cross-multiplying mass products of rows and columns as follows, where T_{ij} denotes the ith row and jth column of the table:

$$T_{11}(\{B\}) = m_1(\{B,F\})\, m_2(\{B\}) = (0.7)\,(0.9) = 0.63$$

T_{21} ({B}) = $m_1(\Theta)$ m_2({B}) = (0.3) (0.9) = 0.27
T_{12} ({B,F}) = m_1({B,F}) $m_2(\Theta)$ = (0.7) (0.1) = 0.07
T_{22} (Θ) = $m_1(\Theta)$ $m_2(\Theta)$ = (0.3) (0.1) = 0.03.

Once the individual mass products have been calculated, as shown above, then according to Dempster's Rule the products over the common set intersections are added:

m_3({B}) = $m_1 \oplus m_2$({B}) = 0.63 + 0.27 = 0.90 bomber
m_3({B,F}) = $m_1 \oplus m_2$({B,F}) = 0.07 bomber or fighter
$m_3(\Theta)$ = $m_1 \oplus m_2(\Theta)$ = 0.03 nonbelief

The m_3({B}) represents the belief that the target is a bomber and *only* a bomber. However, m_3({B,F}) and $m_3(\Theta)$ imply additional information. Since their sets include a bomber, it's plausible that their orthogonal sums may contribute to a belief in the bomber. So their 0.07 + 0.03 = 0.1 may be added to the belief of 0.90 in the bomber set to yield the maximum belief that it could be a bomber—the plausible belief. Instead of restricting belief to a single value, there is a **range of belief** in the evidence. The belief ranges from a minimum 0.9 that is known for the bomber to the maximum plausible 0.90 + 0.1 = 1 that it *might* be a bomber. The true belief is assumed somewhere in the range 0.9 to 1.

In evidential reasoning the evidence is said to induce an **evidential interval**. The **lower bound** is called the **support** (**Spt**) in evidential reasoning and **Bel** in Dempster-Shafer theory. The **upper bound** is called the **plausibility** (**Pls**). For this example, the evidential interval is [0.90,1], the lower bound is 0.90, and the upper bound is 1. The support is the *minimum belief* based on the evidence, while the plausibility is the *maximum belief* we are willing to give. In general, the ranges of Bel and Pls are $0 \leq \text{Bel} \leq \text{Pls} \leq 1$. In Dempster-Shafer theory, the lower and upper bounds are sometimes called the lower and upper probabilities, based on Dempster's original paper. Table 5.5 shows some common evidential intervals.

Table 5.5 Some Common Evidential Intervals

Evidential Interval		Meaning
[1,1]		Completely true
[0,0]		Completely false
[0,1]		Completely ignorant
[Bel,1]	where 0 < Bel < 1 here	Tends to support
[0,Pls]	where 0 < Pls < 1 here	Tends to refute
[Bel,Pls]	where 0 < Bel ≤ Pls < 1 here	Tends to both support and refute

The support or **belief function, Bel**, is the *total belief* of a set and *all* its subsets. Bel is all the mass that supports a set, and is defined in terms of the mass:

$$\text{Bel}(X) = \sum_{Y \subseteq X} m(Y)$$

For example, in the aircraft environment for the first sensor:

$$\text{Bel}_1(\{B,F\}) = m_1(\{B,F\}) + m_1(\{B\}) + m_1(\{F\})$$

$$= 0.7 + 0 + 0 = 0.7$$

The Bel function is sometimes called the **belief measure,** or simply **belief**. However, note that the belief function is very different from the mass, which is the belief in the evidence assigned to a *single* set. For example, suppose that you own a Ford and hear that the police are looking for a Ford that was used as the getaway car in a bank robbery. There is a big difference between hearing that the police are looking for *a* Ford, and hearing that the police are looking for *your* Ford. Mass is the belief in a set and *not* any of its subsets, while a belief function applies to a set and *all* its subsets. Bel is the *total belief* and so is more global than the *local belief* of mass. Because of the interrelationship of mass and Bel, Dempster-Shafer theory is also called a **theory of belief functions**. In a general sense, Dempster's rule can then be interpreted as a way of combining belief functions. The mass and belief function are related by:

$$m(X) = \sum_{Y \subseteq X} (-1)^{|X - Y|} \text{Bel}(Y)$$

where $|X - Y|$ is the **cardinality** of the set,

$$X - Y = \{x \mid x \in X \text{ and } x \notin Y\}$$

That is, $|X - Y|$ is the number of elements in the set $X - Y$.

Since belief functions are defined in terms of masses, the combination of two belief functions also can be expressed in terms of orthogonal sums of the masses of a set and all its subsets. For example,

$$\text{Bel}_1 \oplus \text{Bel}_2(\{B\}) = m_1 \oplus m_2(\{B\}) + m_1 \oplus m_2(\emptyset)$$

$$= 0.90 + 0 = 0.90$$

Normally, the null set mass is not written since it's usually defined to be zero. The total belief for the bomber-fighter subset {B,F}, has more subsets than the above:

$$\text{Bel}_1 \oplus \text{Bel}_2(\{B,F\})$$

$$= m_1 \oplus m_2(\{B,F\}) + m_1 \oplus m_2(\{B\}) + m_1 \oplus m_2(\{F\})$$

$$= 0.07 + 0.90 + 0 = 0.97$$

The terms for {B} and {F} are included because they are subsets of {B,F}. From Figure 5.6 you can see that {B,F} has subsets {B} and {F}. Since no mass was given {F}, then m({F}) = 0 and so it does not contribute anything to the sum. In fact, m({F}) and the other masses of value zero never entered into Table 5.4 at all since the result of any cross products with them would be zero. If masses had been assigned to every subset of {A,B,F} except the null set, which is zero, then Table 5.4 would be a $(2^3 - 1)\ (2^3 - 1) = 7 \cdot 7 = 49$-cell table.

The combined belief function for Θ based on all evidence is the following:

$$\begin{aligned} Bel_1 \oplus Bel_2(\Theta) &= m_1 \oplus m_2(\Theta) + m_1 \oplus m_2(\{B,F\}) \\ &\quad + m_1 \oplus m_2(\{B\}) \\ &= 0.03 + 0.07 + 0.90 = 1 \end{aligned}$$

Actually, Bel(Θ) = 1 in all cases since the sum of masses must always equal 1. The combination of evidence just *redistributes* the masses in different subsets.

The **evidential interval** of a set S, EI(S), may be defined in terms of the belief:

$$EI(S) = [Bel(S), 1 - Bel(S')]$$

If S = {B}, then S´ = {A,F} and:

$$\begin{aligned} Bel(\{A,F\}) &= m_1 \oplus m_2(\{A,F\}) + m_1 \oplus m_2(\{A\}) \\ &\quad + m_1 \oplus m_2(\{F\}) \\ &= 0 + 0 + 0 = 0 \end{aligned}$$

since these are not focal elements and the mass is zero for nonfocal elements. Thus, the evidential interval for {B} is the following:

$$\begin{aligned} EI(\{B\}) &= [0.90, 1 - 0] \\ &= [0.90, 1] \end{aligned}$$

Likewise, if S = {B,F}, then S´ = {A} and:

$$Bel(\{A\}) = 0$$

since {A} is not a focal element. Also:

$$Bel(\{B,F\}) = Bel_1 \oplus Bel_2(\{B,F\}) = 0.97$$

$$EI(\{B,F\}) = [0.97, 1 - 0] = [0.97, 1]$$

$$EI(\{A\}) = [0, 1]$$

where the evidential interval [0, 1] reflects our *total ignorance* of {A}.

The evidential interval of [total belief, plausibility] can be expressed as:

[evidence for support, evidence for support + ignorance]

Under probability theory, this interval is the single point:

```
[evidence for support, evidence for support]
```

since ignorance is not allowed. That is, evidence which does not support must refute, e.g., "If the glove don't fit, you must acquit."

The plausibility is defined as the degree to which the evidence fails to refute X:

$$\text{Pls}(X) = 1 - \text{Bel}(X') = 1 - \sum_{Y \subseteq X} m(X')$$

The plausible belief, Pls, stretches belief to the absolute maximum in which the unassigned belief m(Θ) may possibly contribute to the belief. While the m(Θ) could be a bomber, fighter, or airliner, under the assumption of plausibility it is assumed to contribute belief to one of its subsets. Since {B} is a subset of Θ, it is plausible that the 0.3 belief of $m_1(\Theta)$ might be assigned to a bomber. Recall from Section 4.15 that a plausible belief is a little stronger than a possible belief, but not necessarily a belief supported by strong evidence. Another point is that Θ isn't the only type of set that stretches the belief of any set X. Any set that intersects X and its complement does it.

The **dubiety (Dbt)** or **doubt** represents the degree to which X is disbelieved or refuted. The **ignorance (Igr)** is the degree to which the mass supports X and X'. These are defined as follows:

$$\text{Dbt}(X) = \text{Bel}(X') = 1 - \text{Pls}(X)$$

$$\text{Igr}(X) = \text{Pls}(X) - \text{Bel}(X)$$

The Normalization of Belief

Suppose a third sensor now reports conflicting evidence of an airliner:

$$m_3(\{A\}) = 0.95 \qquad m(\Theta) = 0.05$$

Table 5.6 shows how the cross products are calculated.

Table 5.6 Combining Additional Evidence, m_3

	$m_1 \oplus m_2(\{B\})$ 0.90	$m_1 \oplus m_2(\{B,F\})$ 0.07	$m_1 \oplus m_2(\Theta)$ 0.03
$m_3(\{A\}) = 0.95$	Ø 0	Ø 0	{A} 0.0285
$m_3(\Theta) = 0.05$	{B} 0.045	{B,F} 0.0035	Θ 0.0015

The null set, Ø, occurs because {A} and {B} have no elements in common and neither does {A} and {B,F}, so their cross product is 0 rather than 0.855 and 0.0665. However we will see shortly these null values are useful in normalization. The cross product of rows times columns and:

$$m_1 \oplus m_2 \oplus m_3(\{A\}) = 0.0285$$
$$m_1 \oplus m_2 \oplus m_3(\{B\}) = 0.045$$
$$m_1 \oplus m_2 \oplus m_3(\{B,F\}) = 0.0035$$
$$m_1 \oplus m_2 \oplus m_3(\Theta) = 0.0015$$
$$m_1 \oplus m_2 \oplus m_3(\emptyset) = 0 \quad \text{(by definition of the null set)}$$

Note that for this example, the sum of all the masses is less than 1:

$$\sum m_1 \oplus m_2 \oplus m_3(X) = .0285 + .045 + .0035 + .0015$$
$$= .0785$$

where the sum ranges over all focal elements. However, a sum of 1 is required since the combined evidence, $m_1 \oplus m_2 \oplus m_3$, is a valid mass and the sum over all focal elements must be 1. The fact that the sum is less than 1 presents a problem.

The solution to this problem is a **normalization** of the focal elements by dividing each focal element by:

$$1 - k$$

where κ is defined for any sets X and Y as:

$$\kappa = \sum_{X \cap Y = \emptyset} m_1(X)\, m_2(Y)$$

In our example,

$$\kappa = 0.855 + 0.0665 = 0.9215$$

and so:

$$1 - \kappa = 1 - 0.9215 = 0.0785$$

Dividing each $m_1 \oplus m_2 \oplus m_3$ focal element by $1 - \kappa$ gives the normalized values:

$$m_1 \oplus m_2 \oplus m_3\{A\} = 0.363$$
$$m_1 \oplus m_2 \oplus m_3\{B\} = 0.573$$
$$m_1 \oplus m_2 \oplus m_3\{B,F\} = 0.045$$
$$m_1 \oplus m_2 \oplus m_3(\Theta) = 0.019$$

The total normalized belief in {B} is now:

$$\text{Bel}(\{B\}) = m_1 \oplus m_2(\{B\}) = 0.573$$

Notice that the one evidence of {A} has now considerably eroded the belief in {B} by almost ½ from 0.90 to 0.573 as would be expected.

$$\begin{aligned}\text{Bel}(\{B\}') &= \text{Bel}(\{A,F\}) \\ &= m_1 \oplus m_2 \oplus m_3(\{A,F\}) + \\ &\quad m_1 \oplus m_2 \oplus m_3(\{A\}) + \\ &\quad m_1 \oplus m_2 \oplus m_3(\{F\}) \\ &= 0 + 0.363 + 0 = 0.363\end{aligned}$$

and so the evidential interval is now:

$$\begin{aligned}\text{EI}(\{B\}) &= [\text{Bel}(\{B\}), 1 - \text{Bel}(\{B\}')] \\ &= [0.573, 1 - 0.363] \\ &= [0.573, 0.637]\end{aligned}$$

Notice that the support and plausibility of {B} has been greatly reduced by the conflicting evidence of {A}. The general form of Dempster's Rule of Combination is:

$$m_1 \oplus m_2(Z) = \frac{\sum_{X \cap Y = Z} m_1(X)\ m_2(Y)}{1 - \kappa}$$

where κ is defined again for convenience. No orthogonal sum is defined if $\kappa = 1$:

$$\kappa = \sum_{X \cap Y = \emptyset} m_1(X)\ m_2(Y)$$

κ indicates the amount of **evidential conflict**. $\kappa = 0$ for complete compatibility and 1 for complete contradiction. Values of $0 < \kappa < 1$ show partial compatibility.

Moving Masses and Sets

The moving mass analogy is helpful in understanding support and plausibility. The main concepts are the following:

- The support is the mass assigned to a set and all its subsets.
- Mass of a set can move freely into its subsets.
- Mass in a set cannot move into its supersets.
- Moving mass from a set into its subset can only contribute to the plausibility of the subset, not its support.
- Mass in the environment, Θ, can move into *any* subset since Θ is outside all.

In Figure 5.7 (a) all the mass is assumed inside set X and so:

$$m(X) = 1$$

which means that the support of X is 1. The plausibility of X is also 1 because all the mass is in X and there is no superset that can contribute mass. Thus:

```
EI(X) = [1,1]
```

If m(X) = 0.5 then EI(X) = [0.5,0.5] and in general, if m(X) = a, where *a* is any constant, then EI(X) = [a,a].

Figure 5.7 Sets Illustrating Support and Plausibility

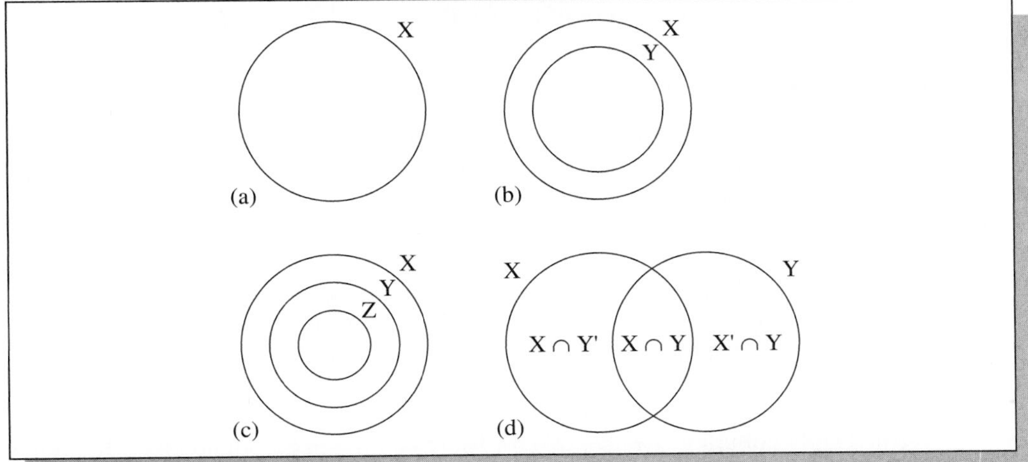

In Figure 5.7 (b), assume that m(X) = 0.6 and m(Y) = 0.4, which are also their supports. The plausibility of X is 0.6 since the mass of Y cannot move to X. However, the mass of X can move inside Y since Y is a subset of X and so the plausibility of Y is 0.4 + 0.6 = 1. Thus, the evidential intervals for X and Y are the following:

```
EI({X}) = [0.6,0.6]
EI({Y}) = [0.4,1]
```

Figures 5.7 (c) and (d) are used in Problem 5.4.

Difficulty with the Dempster-Shafer Theory

One difficulty with the Dempster-Shafer theory occurs with normalization and may lead to results that are contrary to our expectations. The problem with normalization is that it ignores the belief that the object being considered does not exist.

An example quoted by Zadeh is the belief by two doctors, A and B, in a patient's illness. The beliefs in the patient's problem are as follows:

m_A(meningitis) = 0.99
m_A(brain tumor) = 0.01

```
mB(concussion)  = 0.99
mB(brain tumor) = 0.01
```

Notice that both doctors think there is a very low chance, 0.01, of a brain tumor but greatly disagree on the major problem. The Dempster Rule of Combination gives a combined belief of 1 in the brain tumor. This result is unexpected and against our intuition since both doctors had agreed the brain tumor was very improbable. The same result of 1 for brain tumor would occur no matter what the other probabilities were. This is a good example of why just because you meet on common ground doesn't mean that ground is not quicksand.

5.5 APPROXIMATE REASONING

In this section we will discuss a theory of uncertainty based on **fuzzy logic**. This theory is primarily concerned with quantifying and reasoning using natural language in which many words have ambiguous meanings such as *tall*, *hot*, *dangerous*, *a little*, *very much*, and so on. People use fuzzy IF THEN rules all the time, as in "If my alarm clock goes off, then I can sleep a little longer." But as we all know, sleeping a little longer is a very inexact term that varies from person to person. Fuzzy rules are now used all the time in computers (Kerre 00), either built in to the tool or added to a basic tool such as CLIPS.

Fuzzy logic is a superset of conventional (Boolean) logic that has been extended to handle the concept of partial truth; truth values between "completely true" and "completely false." Fuzzy logic is not what it sounds like. It's not a nebulous, cloudy, vague way of thinking; in fact, it's quite the opposite. When anything becomes too complex to fully understand, then it becomes uncertain. The more complex something is, the more inexact or "fuzzier" it will be. Fuzzy logic provides a precise approach for dealing with uncertainty which grows out of the complexity of human behavior.

The concept was first articulated by Zadeh in a seminal paper published in 1965, which provided the theoretical basis for fuzzy computer systems and chips which appeared 20 years later. His theory has led to whole new branches of mathematics, engineering, and science. The term **soft computing** has come to mean computing that is not based on the classical two-valued logics (Roger 96). Soft computing includes fuzzy logic, neural networks, and probabilistic reasoning. Today the term *probabilistic* in AI means not just classical probability theory but also Bayesian belief networks, evolutionary computing including DNA computing, chaos theory, and quantum computing.

The theory has been extended and applied to many fields for a long time, such as automatic camera tracking of an object in space (Giarratano 91). Fuzzy logic has also been combined with neural networks in many applications (Liu 04). Many camcorders and cameras use fuzzy logic. Table 5.7 lists a few of the major applications of fuzzy logic. For a specific application, simply use a search engine and you will be deluged with a flood of information.

Fuzzy Sets and Natural Language

The traditional way of representing which objects are members of a set is in terms of a **characteristic function**, sometimes called a **discrimination function**. If an object is an element of a set, then its characteristic function is 1. If an object is not an element of a set, then its characteristic function is 0. This definition is summarized by the following characteristic function:

$$\mu_A(x) = \begin{cases} 1 & \text{if x is an element of set A} \\ 0 & \text{if x is not an element of set A} \end{cases}$$

where the objects x are elements of some universe X (Ross 04).

The characteristic function can also be defined in terms of a functional mapping (see Section 1.10 on *Functional Programming*):

$$\mu_A(x) \ : \ X \rightarrow \{0,1\}$$

which states that the characteristic function maps a universal set X to the set consisting of 0 and 1. This definition simply expresses the classical concept that an object is either in a set or not in a set. Sets to which this applies are called **crisp sets**, in contrast to fuzzy sets. This type of thinking dates from the Aristotelian view of **bivalent logic** or **two-valued logic**, in which true and false are the only possibilities.

Table 5.7 Some Applications of Fuzzy Theory

Control Algorithms
Medical Diagnosis
Decision Making
Economics
Engineering
Environmental
Literature
Operations Research
Pattern Recognition
Psychology
Reliability
Security
Science

Unlike traditional or classical logic which attempts to categorize information into binary patterns such as black / white, true / false, yes / no, or all / nothing, fuzzy logic pays attention to the "excluded middle" and tries to account for the "grays," the partially true and partially false situations which make up most human reasoning in everyday life. It builds upon the assumption that everything consists of degrees on a sliding scale—whether it be truth, age, beauty, wealth, color, race, or anything else that is affected by the dynamic nature of human behavior and perception.

The problem with this bivalent logic is that we live in an analog, not a digital world. In the real world, things are generally not in one state or another. It is only in conventional computer architecture using digital logic that bivalent logic holds. The development of analog theories of computation such as artificial neural systems and fuzzy theory more accurately represents the real world.

In fuzzy sets an object may belong partially to a set. The degree of membership in a fuzzy set is measured by a generalization of the characteristic function called the **membership function** or **compatibility function** defined as:

$$\mu_A(x) : X \rightarrow [0,1]$$

Although this definition looks superficially like the definition of the characteristic function, it is actually very different. The characteristic function maps all elements of X into one of exactly two elements: 0 or 1. In contrast, the membership function maps X into the codomain of real numbers defined in the **interval** from 0 to 1 inclusive and symbolized by [0,1]. That is, the membership function is a real number:

$$0 \leq \mu_A \leq 1$$

where 0 means no membership and 1 means full membership in the set. A particular value of the membership function, such as 0.5, is called a **grade of membership**.

Although it may seem strange at first to talk about an element being only partially in a set, it is actually more natural than the classical two-valued sets. Although many people wish it were, the real world is not just yes or no, black or white, right or wrong, on or off. Just as there are many shades of gray, not just black and white, so too there are many different gradations of meaning in the real world. Only debts and computer source code must be exact.

Using the membership function, real-world situations can be described. As a very simple example, consider cloudy days. A crisp set description requires an arbitrary decision as to what constitutes a cloudy day. Is a cloudy day one with a few clouds, many clouds, totally overcast, partially overcast, or some other definition? Is a rainy day one with 1" of precipitation, 2", 3", or is it a certain rate of precipitation?

Fuzzy sets and concepts are commonly used in natural language, such as:

"John is *tall*"
"The weather is *hot*"
"Turn the dial a *little higher*"
"*Most* tests are *hard*"
"If the dough is *much too thick*,
    add *a lot* of water"

where the words in italics refer to fuzzy sets and **quantifiers**. All these fuzzy sets and quantifiers can be represented and operated on in fuzzy theory. In particular, the "most" quantifier that was pointed out as a major limitation of predicate logic in Section 2.16 can be handled in fuzzy logic, as you will see shortly.

In natural language the terms *vague* and *fuzzy* are sometimes used synonymously. However, there is a major difference between the terms in the context of fuzzy theory. A **fuzzy proposition** contains words such as *tall,* which is the identifier of a fuzzy set TALL. Here we shall follow the convention of using all uppercase letters to label fuzzy sets such as this. In contrast to a classic proposition such as "John is exactly five feet tall," which represents a proposition that is either true or false, a fuzzy proposition may have degrees of truth. For example, the fuzzy proposition "John is tall," may be true to some degree: *A Little True*, *Somewhat True*, *Fairly True*, *Very True*, and so on. A fuzzy truth value is called a **fuzzy qualifier**, and may be used as a fuzzy set or to modify a fuzzy set. Unlike crisp propositions, which are not allowed to have quantifiers, fuzzy propositions may have **fuzzy quantifiers** such as *Most*, *Many*, *Usually*, and so on, with no distinction between statements and propositions as in the classical case.

The term *vague* is used in the sense of incomplete information. For example, "John is somewhere" is vague if it does not provide sufficient information for a decision. A fuzzy proposition such as "He is tall" may also be vague if we do not know to whom the pronoun refers. There are also degrees of vagueness. A proposition such as "John is tall" is less vague than "He is tall" but is still vague if we do not know which John.

Many fuzzy words are used in natural language, such as those shown in Table 5.8. The meanings of these words can be defined in terms of fuzzy sets, as you'll see shortly. Compound terms, such as those shown in Table 5.9, can also be defined and manipulated in fuzzy theory.

While it's difficult to think of an object as being only partially in a set, another way is to consider the membership function as representing the degree to which an object has some attribute. This concept of degree of attribute is expressed by the alternate meaning of the membership function as a compatibility

Table 5.8 Some Fuzzy Terms of Natural Language

tall
hot
low
medium
high
very
not
little
several
few
many
more
most
about
approximately
left-winger

Table 5.9 Compound Fuzzy Natural Language Terms

more or less low
approximately low
not low
not very low
more or less low
medium to sort of high
higher than slightly low
low to sort of medium
most high
liberal left-winger
ultra-liberal left-winger

function. The term **compatibility** means how well one object conforms to some attribute and is really better for describing fuzzy sets. However, the term *membership function* is most commonly used in the literature and so we will use it. In thinking about fuzzy sets, you may find it helpful to consider fuzzy elements as an object-attribute-value triplet, as described in Chapter 2. For crisp sets there is only the object-attribute since it is assumed the value is either 0 or 1. That is, in crisp sets, an element is either in a set or not in a set. For fuzzy sets the value may be anywhere in the range from 0 to 1.

To illustrate the concept of fuzzy sets, consider the previous example:

```
"John is tall"
```

If the person is an adult, then one possible membership function is shown in Figure 5.8. Anyone about 7 feet and taller is considered to have a membership function of 1.0. Anyone less than 5 feet is not considered to be in the fuzzy set TALL and so the membership function is 0. Between 5 and 7 feet, the membership function is monotonically increasing with height. Notice how adding the quantifies "very" gives a different membership function. What kind of curve would you have for average height?

This particular membership function is only one of many possible functions. The membership functions will be very different for the average person, basketball players, jockeys, and so on. For example, a five-foot-tall jockey is considered tall to some degree for a jockey even though the membership function for a five-foot-tall person in Figure 5.8 is 0.

Depending on the application, a membership function may be constructed from one person's opinions or from a group of people's opinions. In an expert system the membership function will be constructed from the expert's opinion that is being modeled by the system. Although the opinion of tallness is not likely to be modeled in an expert system, many other opinions may be modeled. Some examples might be credit risk for a loan, hostile intent of an unknown aircraft, quality of a product, suitability of a candidate for a job, and so on. Notice that opinions like these are not simple yes or no ones. Although it's possible to establish threshold values for a yes or no decision, there is a real question as to the validity of a crisp threshold. For example, should a person be turned down for a mortgage loan because his or her income is $29,999.99 and the threshold is $30,000.00?

Intuitively, the membership function for a group of people also may be thought of in terms of an opinion poll. Suppose a group of off-the-street people were asked to specify a minimum value for the word *tall*. No one would probably say that someone under 5 feet is tall. Likewise everyone would probably say someone 7 feet and over is tall. In between 5 feet and 7 feet the percentage of people agreeing as to what constitutes *tall* is analogous to the membership function curve shown in Figure 5.8. As the value for tall increases from 5 to 6 feet, more and more people might agree that someone is tall. For this particular membership function, the **crossover point** for tall is 6 feet. A crossover point is where $\mu = 0.5$. In terms of our opinion analogy, 50 percent of the people would agree that someone 6 feet and over is tall. At 6.5 feet, the percentage of people agreeing is 90 percent. From 7 feet up, everyone agrees on tallness, and so the membership function is flat at 1.

Figure 5.8 A Membership Function for the Fuzzy Set TALL

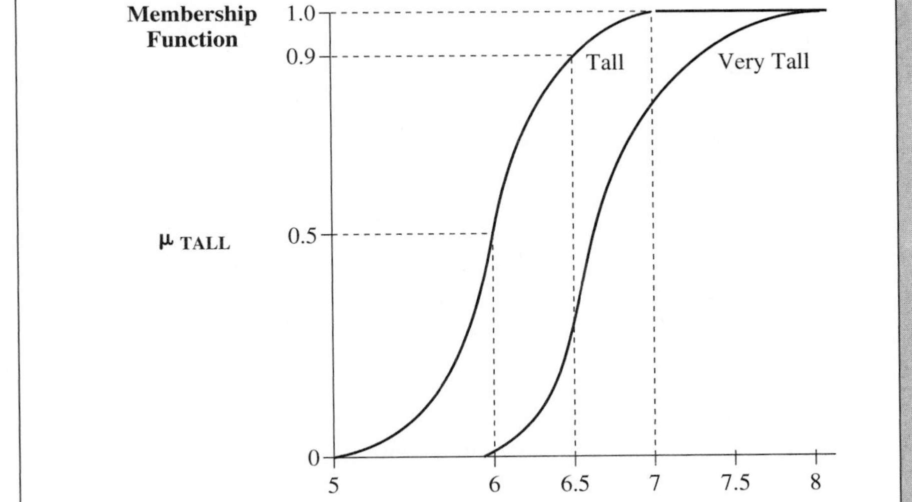

It's important to realize that although this example is given in terms of an opinion poll of a group, the membership function is really *not* a frequency distribution. As we discussed in Chapter 4, probabilities are used for repeatable observations of the same or identical objects. Although each person in the group might give a repeatable opinion when asked the question again, the opinions are likelihoods because they express a personal belief.

The **S-function** is a mathematical function that is often used in fuzzy sets as a membership function. It is defined as follows:

$$S(x;\ \alpha, \beta, \gamma) = \begin{cases} 0 & \text{for } x \le \alpha \\ 2\left(\dfrac{x-\alpha}{\gamma-\alpha}\right)^2 & \text{for } \alpha \le x \le \beta \\ 1 - 2\left(\dfrac{x-\gamma}{\gamma-\alpha}\right)^2 & \text{for } \beta \le x \le \gamma \\ 1 & \text{for } x \ge \gamma \end{cases}$$

A plot of the S-function is shown in Figure 5.9.

Figure 5.9 The S-Function

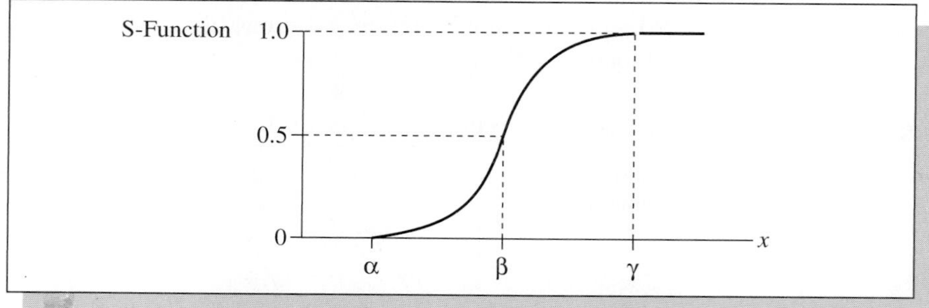

The S-function can be a valuable tool in defining fuzzy functions such as the word tall. Rather that maintaining a table of data defining the membership function, all the data may be compactly represented by a formula. In this definition, α, β, and γ are parameters that may be adjusted to fit the desired membership data. Depending on the given membership data, it may be possible to give an exact fit for some values of α, β, and γ, or the fit may be only approximate. Of course, the membership function may simply be defined as an S-function with no reference to any tabular data. Other functions, such as triangular ones, may also be defined depending on the application.

The S-function is flat at a value of 0 for $x \le \alpha$ and at 1 for $x \ge \gamma$. In between α and γ the S-function is a quadratic function of *x*. As you can see from Figure 5.9, the β parameter corresponds to the crossover point of 0.5 and is $(\alpha + \gamma) / 2$. For the TALL membership function of Figure 5.8, the S-function is the following:

$$
(1)\quad S(x;\ 5,\ 6,\ 7) = \begin{cases} 0 & \text{for } x \le 5 \\ 2\left(\dfrac{x-5}{7-5}\right)^2 = \dfrac{(x-5)^2}{2} & \text{for } 5 \le x \le 6 \\ 1 - 2\left(\dfrac{x-7}{7-5}\right)^2 = 1 - \dfrac{(x-7)^2}{2} & \text{for } 6 \le x \le 7 \\ 1 & \text{for } x \ge 7 \end{cases}
$$

A membership function for the fuzzy proposition "X is close to γ" is shown in Figure 5.10. For example, this membership function could represent all numbers close to a specified value γ, as in "X is close to 6," where X could be defined as {5.9,6,6.1}. The membership function may be expressed as:

$$
\mu_{CLOSE}(x) = \frac{1}{1 + \left(\dfrac{x-\gamma}{\beta}\right)^2}
$$

with crossover points:

$$
x = \gamma \pm \beta
$$

The parameter β is the **half-width** of the curve at the crossover point, as shown in Figure 5.10. Larger values of β correspond to a wider curve and smaller values correspond to a narrower curve. A larger β means that numbers must be more close to γ to have a significantly large membership value. Notice that in this definition the membership function only goes to zero at infinity.

A function that also gives a similar curve but does go to zero at specified points is the following:

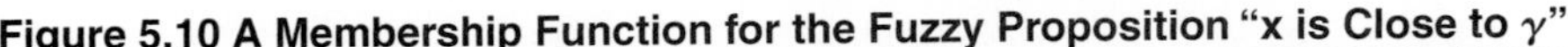

Figure 5.10 A Membership Function for the Fuzzy Proposition "x is Close to γ"

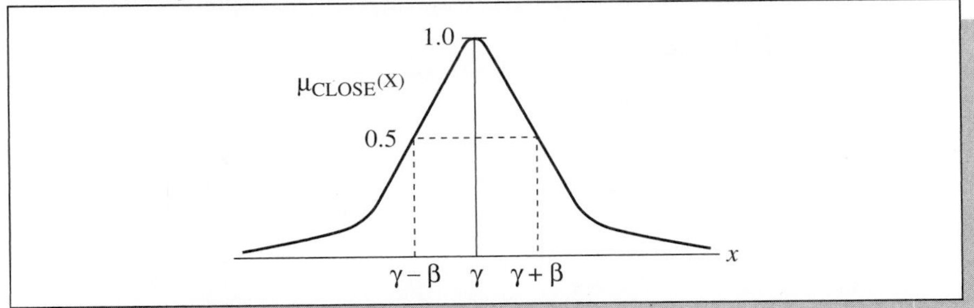

$$\Pi(x;\ \beta,\ \gamma) = \begin{cases} S(x;\ \gamma-\beta,\ \gamma-\beta/2,\ \gamma) & \text{for } x \le \gamma \\ 1 - S(x;\ \gamma,\ \gamma+\beta/2,\ \gamma+\beta) & \text{for } x \ge \gamma \end{cases}$$

This **Π-function** is plotted in Figure 5.11. Notice that the β parameter is now the **bandwidth** or **total width** at the crossover points. The Π-function goes to zero at the points:

$$x = \gamma \pm \beta$$

while the crossover points are at:

$$x = \gamma \pm \frac{\beta}{2}$$

Instead of a continuous function, the membership function can be a finite set of elements. For example, in the universe of heights defined as:

```
U = {5,5.5,6,6.5,7,7.5,8}
```

a fuzzy subset can be defined for a finite set of elements for TALL as follows:

```
TALL = {0/5,0.125/5.5,0.5/6,0.875/6.5,1/7,1/7.5,1/8}
```

In this fuzzy set the symbol "/" separates the membership grades from the numbers corresponding to the heights. Note that the "/" does not mean division in customary fuzzy set notation. The fuzzy set elements for which $\mu(x) > 0$ make up the **support** of the fuzzy set. For TALL, the support is all the elements except 0/5.

A finite fuzzy subset of N elements is represented in standard fuzzy notation as the union of fuzzy singletons μ_i/x_i, where the "+" signs are Boolean union:

$$(2)\quad F = \mu_1/x_1 + \mu_2/x_2 + \ldots\ \mu_N/x_N$$

Figure 5.11 The Π-Function

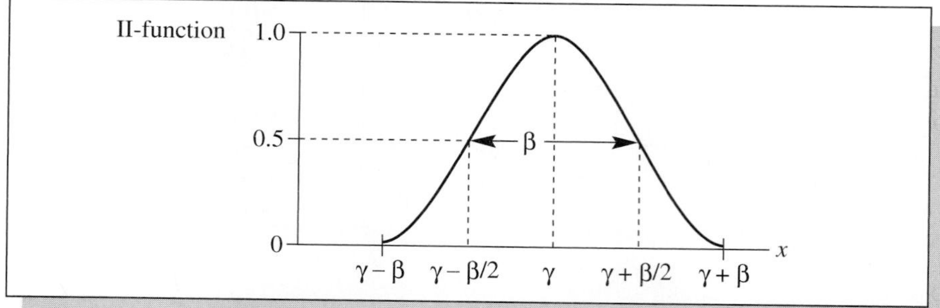

$$F = \sum_{i=1}^{N} \mu_i/x_i$$

$$F = \bigcup_{i=1}^{N} \mu_i/x_i$$

In some papers the "/" symbol is not written and so F can be written in the forms:

$$(3)\quad F = \mu_1 x_1 + \mu_2 x_2 + \ldots \mu_n x_N$$

$$F = \sum_{i=1}^{N} \mu_i x_i$$

$$F = \bigcup_{i=1}^{N} \mu_i x_i$$

Both equations (2) and (3) represent finite fuzzy subsets of N elements. Equation (3) is useful for writing fuzzy sets in a compact symbolic form. However, the forms of equation (3) are difficult for people to read when numbers are involved, such as in:

$$F = .127 + .385$$

Without the "/" separator, it is impossible to tell if the membership grades are .1 and .3 or .12 and .38, or something else. This is why the notation:

$$F = .1/27 + .38/5$$

is better when dealing with numbers.

More formally, the support of a fuzzy set, F, is a subset of the universe set, X, defined as:

$$\text{support}(F) = \{x \mid x \in X \text{ and } \mu_F(x) > 0\}$$

The support set is usually written with the abbreviation **supp**, as in:

$$\text{supp}(F)$$

for compactness. The advantage of the support is that a fuzzy set F can be written as:

$$F = \{\ \mu_F(x)/x \mid x \in \text{supp}(F)\ \}$$

which means that only those fuzzy elements whose membership function is greater than zero contribute to F. Thus the TALL set can be written without the 0/5 element since this element is not in the support set:

```
TALL = {0.125/5.5,0.5/6,0.875/6.5,1/7,1/7.5,1/8}
```

Although there is only a small savings of one element, the reduction in elements can be significant for fuzzy sets with many elements of membership zero. On the other hand, you may be interested in knowing which elements have a membership of zero.

A related concept to the support is **α–cuts**. The α-cut of a set is a nonfuzzy set of the universe whose elements have a membership function greater than or equal to some value α:

$$F_\alpha = \{ x \mid \mu_F(x) \geq \alpha \} \qquad \text{for } 0 < \alpha \leq 1$$

Some α-cuts of the TALL set are:

$$TALL_{0.1} = \{ 5.5, 6, 6.5, 7, 7.5, 8 \}$$

$$TALL_{0.5} = \{ 6, 6.5, 7, 7.5, 8 \}$$

$$TALL_{0.8} = \{ 6.5, 7, 7.5, 8 \}$$

$$TALL_{1} = \{ 7, 7.5, 8 \}$$

Notice that the α-cuts of a set are subsets of the support. The values of α can be chosen arbitrarily but are usually picked to select desired subsets of the universe.

Another term often used with fuzzy sets is the **height**, which is the maximum membership grade of an element. For our TALL set, the maximum membership grade is 1. If an element in a fuzzy set attains the maximum possible grade, then the set is called **normalized**. Usually the membership grades are defined in the closed interval [0,1] and so the maximum possible membership grade is 1. However, the grades may be defined in other intervals and so the membership grade may not necessarily be 1.

An arbitrary fuzzy subset of the universe over the **continuum** is written in the form of an integral. The term *continuum* refers to the set of real numbers. The integral represents the union of the fuzzy singletons, μ(x) / x. For example, we could define:

$$TALL = \int_X \mu_{TALL}(x)/x$$

$$= \int_5^8 \mu_{TALL}(x)/x$$

$$= \int_5^6 \frac{(x-5)^2}{2}/x + \int_6^7 \left[1 - \frac{(x-7)^2}{2}\right]/x + \int_7^8 1/x$$

using an S-function for TALL. In this formula the "+" signs separating the integrals stand for union, as in Boolean logic notation, rather than arithmetic addition.

There are different types of fuzzy sets. The elementary **type 1 fuzzy subset**, F, of a universe, X, is defined as follows:

$$\mu_F: X \rightarrow [0,1]$$

That is, a type 1 fuzzy subset is simply defined by giving numeric values for its membership function in the closed interval of real numbers from 0 to 1. For example,

```
TALL = .125/5.5 + .5/6 + .875/6.5 +
       1/7 + 1/7.5 + 1/8
```

is a type 1 set because its membership grades are all real numbers in [0,1]. Likewise, from equation (1):

$$\mu_{TALL}(x) = S(x;\ 5,\ 6,\ 7)$$

is a type 1 fuzzy subset.

In general, a **type N fuzzy subset** is defined by a mapping for μ_F from a universe to the set of fuzzy subsets of type N – 1. For example, a **type 2 fuzzy subset** is defined in terms of a type 1 subset. For heights, a type 2 fuzzy set can be:

$$\mu_{TALL}(5) = \text{LESS THAN AVERAGE}$$
$$\mu_{TALL}(6) = \text{AVERAGE}$$
$$\mu_{TALL}(7) = \text{GREATER THAN AVERAGE}$$

where LESS THAN AVERAGE, AVERAGE, and GREATER THAN AVERAGE are all fuzzy subsets of type 1. These might be defined as the following fuzzy subsets:

$$\mu_{\text{LESS THAN AVERAGE}}(x) = 1 - S(x;\ 4.5,\ 5,\ 5.5)$$
$$\mu_{\text{AVERAGE}}(x) = \Pi\ (x;\ 1,\ 5.5)$$
$$\mu_{\text{GREATER THAN AVERAGE}}(x) = S(x;\ 5.5,\ 6,\ 6.5)$$

Fuzzy Set Operations

An ordinary crisp set is a special case of a fuzzy set with membership function {0,1}. All the definitions, proofs, and theorems of fuzzy sets must be compatible in the limit as the fuzziness goes to 0 and the fuzzy sets become crisp sets. The theory of fuzzy sets thus has a wider range of applications than crisp sets and so can deal with situations involving subjective opinions. The basic idea of fuzzy sets is to specify fuzzy real-world concepts such as TALL by a set of fuzzy elements rather than demanding a sharp binary threshold. Following is a summary of some fuzzy set operators in a universe X:

- set equality:

$A = B$

$\mu_A(x) = \mu_B(x) \quad \text{for all } x \in X$

- set complement:

A'

$\mu_{A'}(x) = 1 - \mu_A(x) \quad \text{for all } x \in X$

Figure 5.12 illustrates the fuzzy complement of a set. This definition of complementation is justified by Bellman and Giertz.

Figure 5.12 Fuzzy Complement

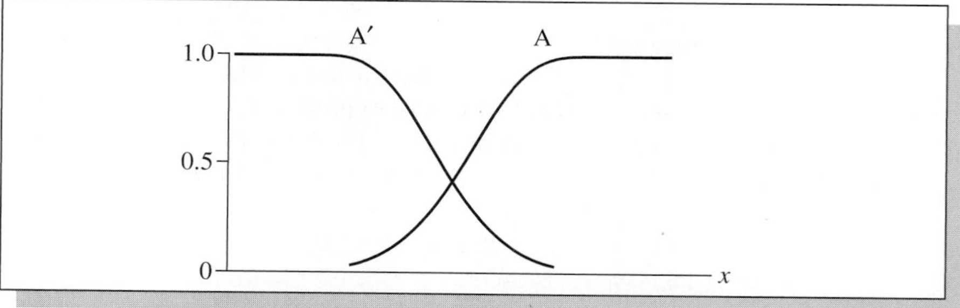

- set containment:

$A \subseteq B$

Fuzzy set A is contained in B or is a **subset** of B if and only if:

$\mu_A(x) \leq \mu_B(x) \quad \text{for all } x \in X$

Fuzzy set A is a **proper subset** of B if A is a subset of B and the two are unequal:

$\mu_A(x) \leq \mu_B(x)$ and $\mu_A(x) < \mu_B(x)$
for at least one $x \in X$

- set union:

$$A \cup B$$

$$\mu_{A \cup B}(x) = \vee(\mu_A(x), \mu_B(x)) \quad \text{for all } x \in X$$

where the **join operator**, $\vee$, means the maximum of the arguments.

- set intersection:

$$A \cap B$$

$$\mu_{A \cap B}(x) = \wedge(\mu_A(x), \mu_B(x)) \quad \text{for all } x \in X$$

where the **meet operator**, $\wedge$, means the minimum of the arguments.

You have already encountered the join and meet operators when discussing the application of fuzzy logic in combining antecedents in PROSPECTOR in Section 4.13, in the subsection "Combining Evidence by Fuzzy Logic." The justification for using the max and min functions for join and meet was given by Bellman.

With these definitions, the standard laws for crisp sets of commutativity, associativity, and so forth hold for fuzzy sets, with the exception of the Laws of the Excluded Middle and Contradiction. Thus it is possible that for a fuzzy set A:

$$A \cup A' \neq \mathcal{U} \text{ and } A \cap A' \neq \emptyset$$

where $\emptyset$ is the empty set and $\mathcal{U}$ is the universe. Since fuzzy sets may have no definite boundary, the only constraint on intersection is that:

$$A \cap A' = \min(\mu_A(x), \mu_{A'}(x)) \leq 0.5$$

if $\mu(x)$ is defined in the closed range [0,1] and $\mu_{A'}(x) = 1 - \mu_A(x)$.

Likewise, the only constraint on union is:

$$A \cup A' = \max(\mu_A(x), \mu_{A'}(x)) \geq 0.5$$

Because fuzzy sets A and A′ may overlap, they may not cover the universe completely.

If the Laws of the Excluded Middle and Contradiction are defined to hold for fuzzy sets, then idempotentcy and distribution may not be satisfied. For idempotentcy, this is:

$$A \cup A \neq A \qquad A \cap A \neq A$$

Because of the fuzzy nature of sets, it appears more reasonable to accept that the Laws of Excluded Middle and Contradiction do not hold so that idempotentcy will be satisfied. See Appendix C for useful set properties.

- set product:

$$A\ B$$

$$\mu_{AB}(x) = \mu_A(x)\mu_B(x)$$

- power of a set:

$$A^N$$

$$\mu_{A^N}(x) = (\mu_A(x))^N$$

- probabilistic sum:

$$A \hat{+} B$$

$$\mu_{A\hat{+}B}(x) = \mu_A(x) + \mu_B(x) - \mu_A(x)\mu_B(x)$$

$$= 1 - (1 - \mu_A(x))(1 - \mu_B(x))$$

where the "+" and "–" are ordinary arithmetic operators.

- bounded sum or bold union:

$$A \oplus B$$

$$\mu_{A\oplus B}(x) = \wedge(1, (\mu_A(x) + \mu_B(x)))$$

where the $\wedge$ is the min function and "+" is the ordinary arithmetic operator.

- bounded product or bold intersection:

$$A \odot B$$

$$\mu_{A\odot B}(x) = \vee(0, (\mu_A(x) + \mu_B(x) - 1))$$

where the $\vee$ is the max function and "+" is the arithmetic operator. The bounded sum and product operators do not satisfy idempotentcy, distributivity, and absorption, but do satisfy commutativity, associativity, de Morgan's laws, $A \oplus U = U$, $A \odot \emptyset = \emptyset$, and the Laws of Excluded Middle and Contradiction (see Appendix C for a summary).

- bounded difference:

$$A\ |-|\ B$$

$$\mu_{A|-|B}(x) = \vee(0, (\mu_A(x) - \mu_B(x)))$$

where the "–" separating μ_A and μ_B is the arithmetic minus operator. A |–| B represents those elements which are more in A than B. The complement can be written in terms of the universe set, $\mathcal{U}$, and bounded difference as:

$$A' = \mathcal{U} \; |-| \; A$$

- concentration:

CON(A)

$$\mu_{CON(A)}(x) = (\mu_A(x))^2$$

The CON operation concentrates fuzzy elements by reducing the membership grades more of elements that have smaller membership grades. Figure 5.13 illustrates the CON operation. This operation and the following ones of DIL, NORM, and INT have no counterpart in ordinary set operations. The CON operator can be used to roughly approximate the effect of the linguistic modifier

Figure 5.13 Concentration of a Fuzzy Set

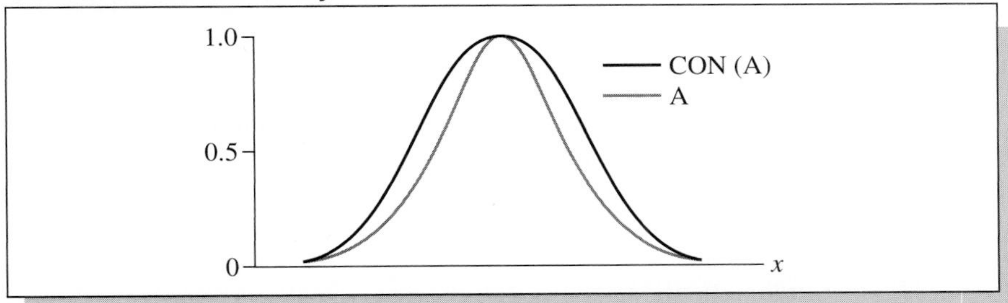

Very. That is, for some fuzzy set F,

$$\text{Very F} = F^2$$

For the example of the TALL set,

```
TALL = .125/5 + .5/6 + .875/6.5 + 1/7 + 1/7.5 + 1/8
```

then to two significant digits:

```
Very TALL = .016/5 + .25/6 + .76/6.5 +
            1/7 + 1/7.5 + 1/8
```

Notice how the membership grades have decreased for all except those of grade 1. The net effect is to make the Very TALL fuzzy set include fewer small grades.

- dilation:

DIL(A)

$$\mu_{DIL(A)}(x) = (\mu_A(x))^{0.5}$$

The DIL operation dilates fuzzy elements by increasing the membership grade more of elements with smaller membership grades. Figure 5.14 illustrates DIL.

Figure 5.14 Dilation of a Fuzzy Set

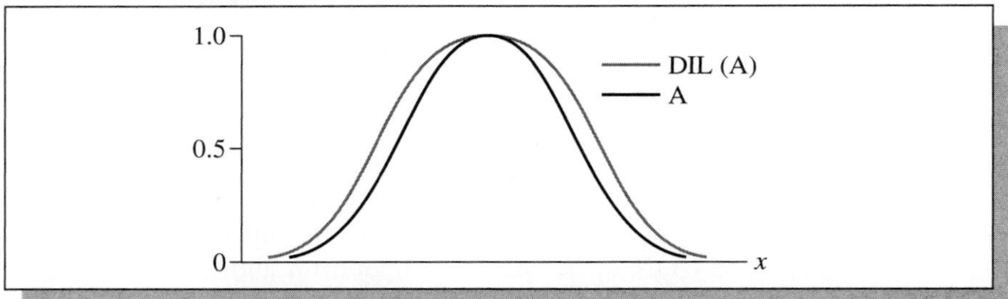

Notice that it performs the inverse operation to concentration for these choices of powers 2 and 0.5:

$$A = DIL(CON(A)) = CON(DIL(A))$$

The dilation operator is roughly approximated by the linguistic modifier *More Or Less*. Thus for any fuzzy set F:

$$\text{More Or Less } F = F^{0.5} = DIL(F)$$

- intensification:

INT(A)

$$\mu_{INT(A)}(x) = \begin{cases} 2(\mu_A(x))^2 & \text{for } 0 \le \mu_A(x) \le 0.5 \\ 1 - 2(1 - \mu_A(x))^2 & \text{for } 0.5 \le \mu_A(x) \le 1 \end{cases}$$

The INT operation is like contrast intensification of a picture. As illustrated in Figure 5.15, the intensification raises the membership grade of those elements within the crossover points and reduces the membership grade of those outside the crossover points. As an electronic analogy, consider the crossover points as defining the bandwidth of a signal. Intensification amplifies the signal within the bandwidth while reducing the "noise" outside the bandwidth. Intensification thus increases the contrast in grade between those elements within the crossover points compared to those outside the crossover points.

Figure 5.15 Intensification of a Fuzzy Set

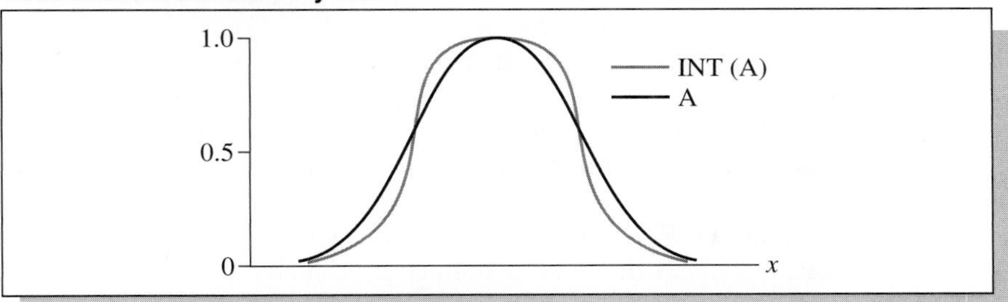

- normalization:

```
NORM(A)

μNORM(A)(x) = μA(x)/max{μA(x)}
```

where the max function returns the maximum membership grade for all elements x. If the maximum grade is < 1, then all membership grades will be increased. If the max = 1, then the membership grades are unchanged.

Fuzzy Relations

An important concept that can also be modeled by fuzzy sets is that of a **relation**. The intuitive idea of a relation is that of some association between elements. Some examples of relations are as follows:

```
Bob and Ellis are friends
Los Angeles and New York are very far apart
1, 2, 3, and 4 are much less than 100
1, 2, and 3 are small numbers
apples and oranges are sort of round fruits
```

where the italicized words are fuzzy.

The **Cartesian product** of N crisp sets is defined as the crisp set whose elements are ordered N-tuples $(x_1, x_2, x_3, \ldots x_N)$, where each x_i is an element of its crisp set X_i. For the two sets A and B:

```
A × B = {(a,b) | a ∈ A and b ∈ B}
```

Defining:

```
A = {chocolate, strawberry}
B = {pie, milk, candy}
```

then the Cartesian product is:

```
A × B = {(chocolate, pie), (chocolate, milk),
         (chocolate, candy), (strawberry, pie),
         (strawberry, milk), (strawberry, candy)}
```

Notice that B × A is generally unequal to A × B if A and B have different elements. That is, generally (a,b) ≠ (b,a). A × B is said to define a **binary variable**, (a,b).

A relation, R, is a subset of the Cartesian product. For example, the relation that R = LIKES PIE could be defined as a subset of A × B by:

```
R = {(chocolate, pie), (strawberry, pie)}
```

while the relation R = LIKES SWEETS could be defined as:

```
R = {(chocolate, pie), (chocolate, candy),
     (strawberry, pie), (strawberry, candy)}
```

A relation is also sometimes called a **mapping** because it associates elements from one domain to another. In A × B, the relation is a mapping from A → B, where the → means a mapping in this context. Chocolate in A is mapped or associated with pie and candy in B, and likewise for strawberry.

If X and Y are universe sets, then:

$$R = \{ \mu_R(x,y)/(x,y) \mid (x,y) \subseteq X \times Y\}$$

is a fuzzy relation on X × Y.

A fuzzy relation is fundamentally a fuzzy subset in the Cartesian product universe. Another definition of fuzzy sets is useful when dealing with fuzzy graphs.

The **fuzzy relation** for N sets is defined as an extension of the crisp relation to include the membership grade. That is,

$$R = \{\mu_R(x_1,\ x_2,\ \ldots\ x_N)/(x_1,\ x_2,\ \ldots\ x_N) \mid x_i \in X_i,\ i = 1,\ ..\ N)\}$$

which associates the membership grade of each N-tuple. For the binary relation of the pie example, another definition could be:

```
R = {.9/(chocolate, pie),.2/(strawberry,pie)}
```

as the fuzzy relation to indicate that a person is much more fond of chocolate pie than strawberry pie.

A convenient way of representing a relation is by a matrix. For the relation LIKES SWEETS,

$$M_R = \begin{array}{c} \\ \text{chocolate} \\ \text{strawberry} \end{array} \begin{array}{c} \text{pie} \quad \text{candy} \\ \begin{bmatrix} 0.9 & 0.7 \\ 0.2 & 0.1 \end{bmatrix} \end{array}$$

where M_R is the matrix representation of the fuzzy relation. Notice that for crisp sets, M_R would consist of only zeroes and ones expressing whether you totally like or totally dislike the ordered pairs (flavor, sweet). (This is probably the best proof that the world is truly fuzzy rather than crisp.)

The **composition** of relations is the net effect of applying one relation after another. For the case of two binary relations P and Q, the composition of their relations is the binary relation R:

$$R(A,C) = Q(A,B) \circ P(B,C)$$

where:

R(A,C) is a relation between A and C
Q(A,B) is a relation between A and B
P(B,C) is a relation between B and C
A, B, and C are sets

and o is the **composition operator**. The relation of R is the same as applying P first followed by Q. In terms of membership grades,

$$R = \{\mu_R(a,c)/(a,c) \mid a \in A,\ c \in C\}$$

where μR is defined as follows:

$$\mu_R(a,c) = \bigvee_{b \in B} [\mu_Q(a,b) \wedge \mu_P(b,c)]$$

$$= \max_{b \in B} [\min(\mu_Q(a,b), \mu_P(b,c))]$$

This composition is commonly defined by the **max-min matrix product** or simply **max-min**. The max and min functions can be used in place of addition and multiplication for matrix operations. As an example, define:

$$Q = \begin{bmatrix} 0.1 & 0.2 \\ 0.3 & 0.4 \end{bmatrix} \qquad P = \begin{bmatrix} 0.1 & 0.3 & 0.5 \\ 0.2 & 0.0 & 0.4 \end{bmatrix}$$

then the composition, R, is:

$$R = Q \circ P = \begin{bmatrix} 0.1 & 0.2 \\ 0.3 & 0.4 \end{bmatrix} \circ \begin{bmatrix} 0.1 & 0.3 & 0.5 \\ 0.2 & 0.0 & 0.4 \end{bmatrix}$$

$$R = Q \circ P = \begin{bmatrix} \max(0.1, 0.2) & \max(0.1, 0.0) & \max(0.1, 0.2) \\ \max(0.1, 0.2) & \max(0.3, 0.0) & \max(0.3, 0.4) \end{bmatrix}$$

$$= \begin{bmatrix} 0.2 & 0.1 & 0.2 \\ 0.2 & 0.3 & 0.4 \end{bmatrix}$$

Other common relational operator definitions are the **max-product** and **relational join**.

Fuzzy relations have important applications to approximate reasoning, as shown later. The **projection** of a relation is another useful fuzzy set concept. Basically, the projection eliminates specified elements. Before giving the formal definition, let's look at a simple example in Table 5.10.

Table 5.10 A Relation and Its Projections

	y_1	y_2	y_3	1st Projection	
x_1	0.2	0.1	0.2	0.2	
x_2	0.2	0.3	0.4	0.4	
2nd Projection	0.2	0.3	0.4	0.4	Total Projection

Table 5.10 shows the projections of the previous relation for R, where the rows and columns have been given identifiers of x_i and y_i for convenience. Notice that the column labeled *1st Projection* contains the maximum membership grade for the row. Likewise, the row labeled *2nd Projection* contains the maximum membership grade of each column. The cell of value 0.4 at the lower right labeled *Total Projection* is the maximum membership grade of the total relation.

The relation for R can be written in terms of the x_i and y_i as the following:

$$R = .2/x_1,y_1 + .1/x_1,y_2 + .2/x_1,y_3 + .2/x_2,y_1 + .3/x_2,y_2 + .4/x_2,y_3$$

The 1st Projection is denoted by R_1 and is obtained by dropping all except the first point, x_i, of the Cartesian pair, x_i, y_j, where the leftmost element is defined as first:

$$R_1 = .2/x_1 + .1/x_1 + .2/x_1 + .2/x_2 + .3/x_2 + .4/x_2$$

The equation for R_1 is further reduced after the projection because the "+" represents the union operator and so only the maximum fuzzy element is kept:

$$R_1 = .2/x_1 + .4/x_2$$

Likewise, the 2nd Projection retains only the second point, y_j, of each Cartesian pair:

$$R_2 = .2/y_1 + .1/y_2 + .2/y_3 + .2/y_1 + .3/y_2 + .4/y_3$$

which reduces to the following upon applying the union operator:

$$R_2 = .2/y_1 + .3/y_2 + .4/y_3$$

In the general case of a relation involving N Cartesian points, drop all components of the N-tuple except those points on which the projection is to be made. For example, if the relation is over N points, then R_{136} would drop all points except the first, third, and sixth.

For a relation over the universe $X \times Y$,

$$R = \{\mu_R(x,y)/(x,y)\} \text{ for all } (x,y) \in X \times Y$$

the 1st Projection is defined as:

$$proj(R;X) = R_1$$

where:

$$R_1 = \{\max_y \mu_R(x,y)/x \mid (x,y) \in X \times Y\}$$

and the max is taken over all y. Likewise,

$$proj(R;Y) = R_2$$

where:

$$R_2 = \{\max_x \mu_R(x,y)/y \mid (x,y) \in X \times Y\}$$

where the max is taken over all x values for R_2.

The **cylindrical extension** of the projection relation is defined as the largest fuzzy relation that is compatible with a projection. The cylindrical projection is somewhat analogous to projection since it expands the projected value (which is max) for all other elements, for example:

$$proj(R;X) = R_1 = .2/x_1 + .4/x2$$

so:

$$R_1 = .2/x_1,y_1 + .2/x_1,y_2 + .2/x_1,y_3 \\ + .4/x_2,y_1 + .4/x_2,y_2 + .4/x_2,y_3$$

$$R_2 = .2/y_1,x_1 + .2/y_1,x_2 + .3/y_2,x_1 \\ + .3/y_2,x_1 + .3/y_2,x_2 \\ + .4/y_2,x_1 + .4/y_3,x_2$$

that is, replace the second variable, $.2/x_1$,{all var} + $.4/x_2$, {all var}. Since the projection gives the max μ then the cylindrical extension is the greatest relation compatible with the projection.

For the previous example,

$$\overline{R_1} = \begin{bmatrix} 0.2 & 0.2 & 0.2 \\ 0.4 & 0.4 & 0.4 \end{bmatrix}$$

$$\overline{R_2} = \begin{bmatrix} 0.2 & 0.3 & 0.4 \\ 0.2 & 0.3 & 0.4 \end{bmatrix}$$

where a bar over a projection symbolizes the cylindrical extension of the projection.

The composition can be defined in terms of projections and cylindrical extensions. For the binary relation R defined on the universe set $\mathcal{U}_1 \times \mathcal{U}_2$, and S defined on $\mathcal{U}_2 \times \mathcal{U}_3$, the composition is:

$$R \circ S = \text{proj}\ (\overline{R} \cap \overline{S};\ U_1\ ¥\ U_3)$$

Linguistic Variables

One very important application of fuzzy sets is in **computational linguistics**. The goal is to calculate with natural language statements analogous to the way that logic calculates with logic statements. Fuzzy sets and **linguistic variables** can be used to quantify the meaning of natural language, which can then be manipulated. A linguistic variable is assigned values, which are expressions such as words, phrases, or sentences in a natural or artificial language. Table 5.11 shows some linguistic variables and typical values that might be assigned to them.

Table 5.11 Typical Values

Linguistic Variable	Typical Values
height	dwarf, short, average, tall, giant
number	almost none, several, few, many
stage of life	infant, toddler, child, teenager, adult
color	red, blue, green, yellow, orange
light	dim, faint, normal, bright, intense
dessert	pie, cake, ice cream, baked alaska

Although it's possible to define values such as the color red, corresponding to these linguistic values, they are very much subjective in nature. For example, the color red corresponds to a range in frequencies that the eye perceives as red, not just a single frequency. Other problems are colors such as aquamarine. Is it blue or green?

Linguistic variables are commonly used in heuristic rules. However, the variables may be implied, as illustrated in the first two rules of Table 5.12.

The implied linguistic variables are sound volume and water temperature.

Table 5.12 Some Heuristic Rules Involving Implied Linguistic Variables

IF the sound is too low THEN turn up the volume IF it's too hot THEN add some cold IF the pressure is too high THEN open the relief valve IF interest rates are going up THEN buy bonds IF interest rates are going down THEN buy stocks

Some linguistic variables like sound volume may be labels of fuzzy sets of order 2. For example, the values of sound volume could be bass, treble, and reverb,where each of these values may be linguistic variables that can take on values that are fuzzy sets. Thus linguistic variables may be arranged in a hierarchy corresponding to their fuzzy set order. Eventually a fuzzy set of order 1 is reached, such as TALL or BASS, which is defined as a mapping into the closed interval [0,1], and so the linguistic value becomes a numeric range.

The **term-set**, T(L), of a linguistic variable, L, is the set of values it may take. For example,

```
T(PIE) = CHOCOLATE + APPLE + STRAWBERRY + PECAN
```

where each of the terms in T(PIE) is a label of a fuzzy set. These sets may be the union of other sets consisting of subsets. For example,

```
CHOCOLATE = SEMI-SWEET CHOCOLATE + MILK CHOCOLATE
          + DUTCH CHOCOLATE + DARK CHOCOLATE + ...
```

Another definition for the CHOCOLATE fuzzy set may involve **hedges** or quantifiers to modify the meaning of a set. For example, a CHOCOLATE fuzzy set of one type of chocolate could be defined as follows:

```
CHOCOLATE = Very CHOCOLATE + Very Very CHOCOLATE +
            More Or Less CHOCOLATE +
            Slightly CHOCOLATE +
            Plus CHOCOLATE + Not Very CHOCOLATE + ...
```

Standard hedges can be defined in terms of some fuzzy set operators and a fuzzy set, F, as shown in Table 5.13.

Table 5.13 Some Linguistic Hedges and Operators

Hedge	Operator Definition
Very F	$CON(F) = F^2$
More or Less F	$DIL(F) = F^{0.5}$
Plus F	$F^{1.25}$
Not F	$1 - F$
Not Very F	$1 - CON(F)$
Slightly F	INT [NORM (PLUS F And NOT (VERY F))]

As shown by the "Not Very F" hedge, other compound hedges can be made by combining operators. Notice that the "And" in the "Slightly" hedge is the fuzzy set operator for intersection, $\cap$, acting on the fuzzy sets "Plus F" and "Not (Very F)."

The hierarchy of the linguistic variable Appetite is illustrated in Figure 5.16. The LIGHT and HEAVY fuzzy sets are assumed to be S-functions while the MODERATE set is taken as a Π-function.

Figure 5.16 The Linguistic Variable Appetite and Its Values

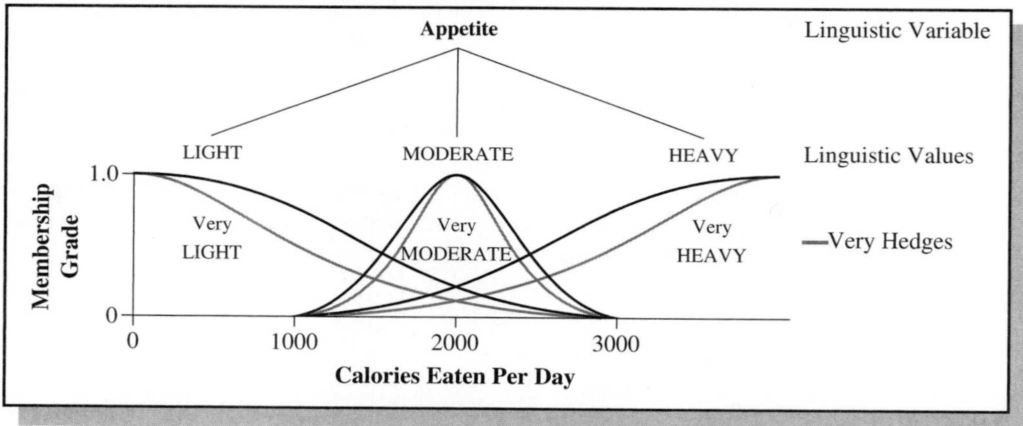

Notice that there is overlap of the fuzzy sets such as LIGHT and MODERATE and even LIGHT and HEAVY. In classical crisp sets there would be no overlap since all these sets would be disjoint. That is, a LIGHT appetite could not be a MODERATE or HEAVY appetite. However, in fuzzy sets there are usually not (unless defined) sharp boundaries between sets.

The hedged sets are shown as dashed curves within the borders of the fuzzy sets. The hedges, such as *Very*, act as modifiers to the linguistic values to yield the fuzzy sets Very LIGHT, Very MODERATE, and Very HEAVY.

A linguistic variable must have a valid syntax and semantics, which can be specified by fuzzy sets or rules. A **syntactic rule** defines the well-formed expressions in T(L). For example, the term-set:

T(Age) = {OLD, Very OLD, Very Very OLD, ...}

can be generated recursively using the following syntactic rule:

$$T^{i+1} = \{OLD\} \cup \{Very\ T^i\}$$

For example,

$T^0 = \emptyset$ (the null set)

$T^1 = \{OLD\}$

$T^2 = \{OLD, Very\ OLD\}$

$T^3 = \{OLD, Very\ OLD, Very\ Very\ OLD\}$

The **semantic rule** associated with T(L) defines the **meaning** of a term, L_i, in L, by a fuzzy set. For example, the semantic rule for Very OLD could be defined as:

$$Very\ OLD = \mu^2_{OLD}$$

where the membership function could be defined as the S-function following:

$$\mu_{OLD}(X) = S(x;\ 60,\ 70,\ 80)$$

A **primary term** is a term such as YOUNG, OLD, CHOCOLATE, STRAWBERRY, and so on, whose meaning must be defined before a hedge. Hedges modify the meaning of the primary terms to yield other terms in a term set, such as Very YOUNG, Very OLD, Very CHOCOLATE, Slightly CHOCOLATE, and so forth. The meaning of the hedged fuzzy sets is determined by applying the appropriate fuzzy set operators. For example,

$$\mu_{Very\ CHOCOLATE} = \mu^2_{CHOCOLATE}$$

$$\mu_{Not\ CHOCOLATE} = 1 - \mu_{CHOCOLATE}$$

$$\mu_{More\ Or\ Less\ CHOCOLATE} = \mu^{0.5}_{CHOCOLATE}$$

$$\mu_{Not\ Very\ CHOCOLATE} = 1 - \mu_{Very\ CHOCOLATE}$$

Just as conventional language grammars can be defined by BNF notation (see Section 2.2), so too can a **fuzzy grammar**. In fact, the grammar described in Section 2.2 used a fuzzy modifier, "heavy," as in:

```
<adjective> → heavy
```

to generate the fuzzy production:

```
an eater was the heavy man
```

In this production, *heavy* is a hedge on the fuzzy set *man*. At first you may not think *man* is a fuzzy set. However, when does a boy become a man? In some cultures a boy becomes a man at 12 or after a religious ceremony. Some governments define a man at 18 or 21. Newspaper articles appear to have a policy of referring to a male aged 17 to 19 as a man if he is accused of committing a crime, but refer to a 17- to 19-year-old as a youth if he has done something commendable. Males in the armed forces are sometimes referred to as boys and sometimes as men, especially in political speeches.

A fuzzy grammar can be specified in BNF notation by adding nonterminals such as:

```
<Range Phrase> ::= <Hedged Primary> TO
                   <Hedged Primary>
<Hedged Primary> ::= <Hedge> <Primary> | <Primary>
<Hedge> ::= Very | More Or Less | A Little
<Primary> ::= SHORT | MEDIUM | TALL
```

to generate productions such as:

```
Very SHORT TO Very TALL
A Little TALL TO Very SHORT
More Or Less MEDIUM TO TALL
```

The first application of the linguistic variable concept was the fuzzy car built by Sugeno at the Tokyo Institute of Technology. The Sugeno car uses a control system based on fuzzy logic that allows autonomous operation on a rectangular track. The car can park itself at a specified space and also learn from examples. Linguistic variables are used in rules that control the car's movement. Many other types of fuzzy logic control systems have also been built to control devices and industrial processes such as a cement kiln to manufacture cement.

Extension Principle

The **extension principle** is a very important concept in fuzzy theory. This principle defines how to extend the domain of a given crisp function to include fuzzy sets. By using the extension principle, any ordinary or crisp function from mathematics, science, engineering, business, and so forth can be extended to work in a fuzzy domain with fuzzy sets. This principle makes fuzzy sets applicable to all fields.

Let f be an ordinary function which maps from a universe X to Y. If F is a fuzzy subset of X such that:

$$F = \int_X \mu_F(x)/x$$

then the extension principle defines the image of the fuzzy set F under a mapping function *f(x)* as:

$$f(F) = \int_X \mu_F(x)/f(x)$$

For example, let *f(x)* be defined as a crisp function which squares its arguments:

$$f(x) = x^2$$

The extension principle states how to implement a squaring function of fuzzy sets:

$$f(F) = \int_X \mu_F(x)/f(x) = \int_X \mu_F(x)/x^2$$

For example, define the universes X and Y as the closed real interval [0,1000], and the fuzzy set:

$$F = .3/15 + .8/20 + 1/30$$

then the extension principle defines the mapping f(F) as:

$$f(F) = \int_X \mu_F(x)/f(x)$$

$$= .3/f(15) + .8/f(20) + 1/f(30)$$

$$f(F) = .3/225 + .8/400 + 1/900$$

Fuzzy Logic

Just as classical logic forms the basis of conventional expert systems, fuzzy logic forms the basis of **fuzzy expert systems**. Besides dealing with uncertainty, fuzzy expert systems are also capable of modeling **commonsense reasoning**, which is very difficult for conventional systems. However, the big problem with modeling common sense is the huge ontology of information that we take for granted. For more details, see www.OpenCyc.org.

The basic limitation of classical logic is its restriction to the two values of true and false. As we discussed in Chapters 2 and 3 this restriction has advantages and disadvantages. The main advantage is that systems based on two-valued logic are easy to model deductively and so the inferences can be exact. The main disadvantage is that very little in the real world is really two-valued. The real world is an analog—not a digital world (unless you believe in *The Matrix* movies).

The limitations of two-valued logic have been known since the time of Aristotle. Although Aristotle first formulated the syllogistic rules of inference and the Law of the Excluded Middle, he recognized that propositions about future events were neither actually true nor actually false until they occurred.

A number of different logic theories based on multiple values of truth have been formulated, such as those of Lukasiewicz, Bochvar, Kleene, Heyting, and Reichenbach. Some common types are those based on three values of truth representing TRUE, FALSE, and UNKNOWN. These **trivalent** or **three-valued logics** commonly represent the three truth values of TRUE, FALSE, and UNKNOWN by 1, 0, and 1/2, respectively.

Several generalized logics of N truth values, where N is an arbitrary integer number greater than or equal to two, have been developed. Lukasiewicz developed the first N-valued logic in the 1930s. In an N-valued logic, the set T_N of truth values are assumed evenly divided over the closed interval [0,1]:

$$T_N = \left\{\frac{i}{N-1}\right\} \text{ for } 0 \le i < N$$

For example,

$$T_2 = \{0,\ 1\} \qquad T_3 = \{0,\ 1/2,\ 1\}$$

Table 5.14 defines some **Lukasiewicz logic operators** for N-valued logic, where $N \geq 2$. As shown in Problem 5.13, these reduce to the standard logic values for $N = 2$. Notice that the minus, min, and max operators are the same as in fuzzy logic.

Table 5.14 Primitive Lukasiewicz N-Valued Logic Operators

x'	=	$1 - x$
$x \wedge y$	=	$\min(x, y)$
$x \vee y$	=	$\max(x, y)$
$x \to y$	=	$\min(1, 1 + y - x)$

Each N-valued Lukasiewicz logic, or **L-logic**, is written as $\mathbf{L_N}$, where N is the number of truth values. L_2 is the classical two-valued logic, while at the other extreme of $N = \infty$, the L_∞ defines an **infinite-valued logic** with truth values in the set T_∞. While T_∞ is defined on rational numbers, an alternative infinite-valued logic can be defined on the continuum, which is the set of all real numbers. The term *infinite-valued logic* is commonly taken for this alternative logic where the truth values are the real numbers in [0,1], and this logic is called $\mathbf{L_1}$.

However, L_1 is *not* the same as the **unary logic** with N = 1. Unary logic is not a Lukasiewicz logic at all since **L-logics** are defined only for N ≥ 2. The 1 in L_1 is actually an abbreviation for $\aleph_1$ (read "aleph 1"), the cardinality of the real numbers. $\aleph_1$ is not a finite but a **transfinite number**. This theory was first developed by Cantor as a way of computing with infinite numbers. Instead of one infinite number, Cantor defined different orders of infinity. For example, the smallest transfinite number is $\aleph_0$, which is the cardinality of the natural numbers. $\aleph_1$ is a higher order infinity than $\aleph_0$ since there are infinitely many real numbers for each natural number.

Fuzzy logic may be considered an extension of multivalued logic. However, the goals and applications of fuzzy logic are different because fuzzy logic is the logic of **approximate reasoning** rather than exact multivalued reasoning. Essentially, approximate or **fuzzy reasoning** is the inference of a possibly imprecise conclusion from a set of possibly imprecise premises. People are very familiar with approximate reasoning since it is the most common type of reasoning done in the real world and is the basis of many heuristic rules. Some examples of heuristic rules of approximate reasoning are the following:

```
IF the stereo sound is too low
THEN increase the volume some

IF the stereo sound is loud the neighbors complain
THEN turn up the volume more

IF the traffic is heavy
THEN turn start changing lanes a lot

IF you're getting too fat from eating banana
splits, pies, ice cream and cake
THEN reduce the number of bananas
```

Approximate reasoning is concerned with reasoning that is neither exact nor totally inexact such as a pure guess. Approximate reasoning is particularly concerned with reasoning about natural-language statements and the inferences that follow. Fuzzy logic is related to approximate reasoning in the same way that two-valued logic is related to precise reasoning. An example of precise or exact reasoning is deduction and theorem proving, as discussed in Chapter 3.

There are many different types of possible fuzzy set theory, fuzzy logic, and approximate reasoning. The type of fuzzy logic discussed from now on is Zadeh's theory of approximate reasoning, which uses a fuzzy logic whose base is Lukasiewicz L_1 logic. In this fuzzy logic, truth values are linguistic variables that are ultimately represented by fuzzy sets.

Fuzzy logic operators based on the Lukasiewicz operators of Table 5.14 are defined in Table 5.15. x(A) is a numeric truth value in the range [0,1] representing the truth of the proposition "x is A," which can be interpreted as the membership grade $\mu_A(x)$.

Table 5.15 Some Fuzzy Logic Operators

x(A')	= x(NOT A)	$= 1 - \mu_A(x)$
$x(A) \wedge x(B)$	= x(A AND B)	$= \min(\mu_A(x), \mu_B(x))$
$x(A) \vee x(B)$	= x(A OR B)	$= \max(\mu_A(x), \mu_B(x))$
$x(A) \rightarrow x(B)$	$= x(A \rightarrow B)$	$= x((\sim A) \vee B) = \max[(1 - \mu_A(x)), \mu_B(x)]$

As an example of fuzzy logic operators, assume a fuzzy set called TRUE defined as:

```
TRUE = .1/.1 + .3/.5 + 1/.8
```

Using the operators of Table 5.15 gives:

```
FALSE = 1 - TRUE

      = (1 - .1)/.1 + (1 - .3)/.5 + (1 - 1)/.8

      = .9/.1 + .7/.5
```

Using the CON operator for the hedge Very gives:

```
Very TRUE = .01/.1 + .09/.5 + 1/.8

Very FALSE = .81/.1 + .49/.5
```

Fuzzy Rules

As a simple example of fuzzy set operators, consider the problem of pattern recognition. The patterns might represent objects examined for quality control such as manufactured parts or fresh-picked fruit (Harris 00). Other types of important pattern recognition problems are medical image diagnosis, seismic data from mineral and oil exploration, and facial recognition.

Table 5.16 shows some hypothetical data representing the membership grade in fuzzy sets of missile, fighter, and airliner corresponding to some images. These images might be produced from a system at long range and contain uncertainty due to target motion and orientation, noise, and so forth.

The union of the fuzzy sets for each image represents the total uncertainty in the target identification. Figure 5.17 illustrates the fuzzy set unions for the ten target images of Table 5.16. Of course, in a real situation there would be many other possible images than these ten depending on the system resolution and distance to the target. Besides uncertainty in the system hardware, there is also uncertainty in the primitive fuzzy sets for missile, fighter, and airliner. The membership grades are assigned in a subjective way based on a knowledge of typical missile, fighter, and airliner configurations. In a real situation there are many types of each of these primitive sets, depending on the different types of aircraft.

Table 5.16 Membership Grades for Images

Image	Missile	Fighter	Airliner
	Membership Grade		
1	1.0	0.0	0.0
2	0.9	0.0	0.1
3	0.4	0.3	0.2
4	0.2	0.3	0.5
5	0.1	0.2	0.7
6	0.1	0.6	0.4
7	0.0	0.7	0.2
8	0.0	0.0	1.0
9	0.0	0.8	0.2
10	0.0	1.0	0.0

Figure 5.17 Fuzzy Sets for Aircraft Identification

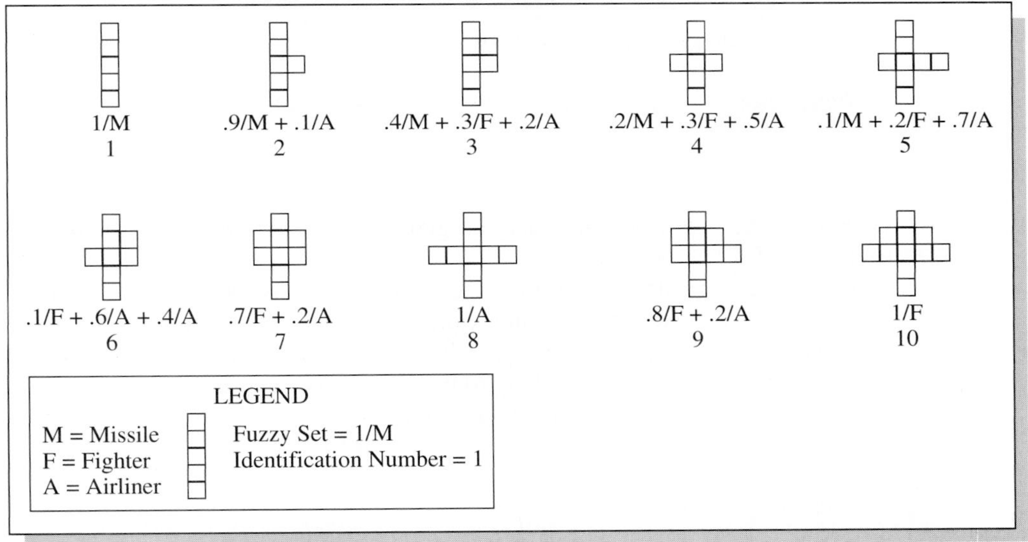

The fuzzy set unions shown in Figure 5.17 can be considered as representing rules such as:

```
IF E THEN H
```

where E is the observed image and H is the fuzzy set union. For example,

```
IF IMAGE4 THEN TARGET (.2/M + .3/F + .5/A)
```

where the expression in parentheses is the fuzzy set union of the target. Alternatively, the rule could be expressed:

```
IF IMAGE4 THEN TARGET4
```

where:

```
TARGET4 = .2/M + .3/F + .5/A
```

Suppose that there is additional time to make another observation of the target and that IMAGE6 is observed. This corresponds to a rule:

```
IF IMAGE6 THEN TARGET6
```

where:

```
TARGET6 = .1/M + .6/F + .4/A
```

The total elements that have been measured for the target are:

```
TARGET = TARGET4 + TARGET6
```

where the "+" denotes set union. Thus,

```
TARGET = .2/M + .3/F + .5/A + .1/M + .6/F + .4/A

TARGET = .2/M + .6/F + .5/A
```

where only the maximum membership grades for each element are retained in the TARGET fuzzy set.

If the element with maximum grade is interpreted as the most likely target, then the target is most likely a fighter, since it has the highest membership grade of 0.6. However, if the airliner membership grade was also 0.6, then all we could say is that the target is equally likely to be a fighter or an airliner.

In general, given N observations and rules,

$$\begin{array}{l} \text{IF } E_1 \text{ THEN } H_1 \\ \text{IF } E_2 \text{ THEN } H_2 \\ \quad\quad\vdots \\ \text{IF } E_N \text{ THEN } H_N \end{array}$$

where all the H_i bear on some common hypothesis H, then the union of the hypotheses determines the membership grade of H. That is,

$$\mu_H = \max(\mu_{H1}, \mu_{H2}, \ldots \mu_{HN})$$

Notice that this result differs from the Certainty Factors and Dempster-Shafer theories. The μ_H of the hypothesis H is called the **truth value** of H.

It is also a reasonable assumption (except in political logic) that the truth of a hypothesis can be no greater than the truth of its evidence. In terms of rules, the truth of the consequent can be no greater than the truth of its antecedent. Thus,

$$\mu_H = \max(\mu_{H1}, \mu_{H2}, \ldots \mu_{HN})$$

$$= \max[\min(\mu_{E1}), \min(\mu_{E2}), \ldots \min(\mu_{EN}))$$

where each E_i may be some fuzzy expression. For example, E_1 might be defined as:

$$E_1 = E_A \text{ AND } (E_B \text{ OR NOT } E_C)$$

and the fuzzy logic operators are used to evaluate the expression. That is,

$$\mu_{E1} = \min(\mu_{EA}, \max(\mu_{EB}, 1 - \mu_{EC}))$$

The combined membership grade of the antecedent is called the **truth value of the antecedent**. This is analogous to the partial evidence of the antecedent in PROSPECTOR rules. In fact, recall that the PROSPECTOR antecedent evidence was combined using fuzzy logic on an *ad hoc* basis. Now you can see that this combination is justified by the fuzzy theory compositional rule of inference.

Max-Min Composition

The equation for H above is the fuzzy logic **max-min compositional rule of inference**. In a simple case of two items of evidence per rule,

$$\text{IF } E_{11} \text{ AND } E_{12} \text{ THEN } H_1$$
$$\text{IF } E_{21} \text{ AND } E_{22} \text{ THEN } H_2$$
$$\vdots$$
$$\text{IF } E_{N1} \text{ AND } E_{N2} \text{ THEN } H_N$$

and so the max-min compositional inference rule is:

$$\mu_H = \max[\min(\mu_{E11}, \mu_{E12}), \min(\mu_{E21}, \mu_{E22}), \ldots \min(\mu_{EN1}, \mu_{EN2})]$$

with similar extensions for additional evidence E_{i3}, E_{i4}, and so on.

As another example of the compositional rule of inference, let's see how it is used with a relation. Define the fuzzy relation R(x,y) = APPROXIMATELY EQUAL on the binary relation of people's weights in the range of 120–160 pounds of Table 5.17.

In constructing this table, the membership grades were defined so that the difference from the mean of two values is a decrease of 0.075%. For example, if the *x* and *y* values are 150 and 130, then the average is 140. The absolute difference of 150 and 130 from the average is 10/140 = 7.1%. This value is multiplied

Table 5.17 The Relation APPROXIMATELY EQUAL Defined on People's Weights

x	Y 120	130	140	150	160
120	1.0	0.7	0.4	0.2	0.0
130	0.7	1.0	0.6	0.5	0.2
140	0.4	0.6	1.0	0.8	0.5
150	0.2	0.5	0.8	1.0	0.8
160	0.0	0.2	0.5	0.8	1.0

by the constant factor of −.075% to yield −0.5. Thus, the final membership grade for 150, 130 is 1 − .5 = 0.5 and this is the table entry. An alternative and computationally simpler definition would be to define any change of 10 as a fixed decrease in the membership grade, such as .3. However, this alternative definition does not yield reasonable results for small weights such as 10 and 20, which would be APPROXIMATELY EQUAL to grade 0.7.

Notice how the relation R(x,y) acts as a **fuzzy restriction** on any two values *x* and *y,* which have a nonzero membership grade R(x,y). A fuzzy relation acts as an **elastic constraint** by allowing a range of membership grades rather than demanding the rigid constraint of crisp relations. In fact the term APPROXIMATELY EQUAL could not even be defined in non-fuzzy logic. The rigid constraint of crisp relations would demand that values be either exactly equal or not. That is, either *x* exactly equals *y* or it does not.

As an example of a fuzzy restriction, consider the proposition, p, as follows:

```
p = X is F
```

where F is some fuzzy set that acts as a fuzzy restriction on the linguistic variable named X. The following are some examples of fuzzy propositions of the form above:

```
John is tall
Sue is over 21
The concrete mix is too thick
Target is friendly
x is a number approximately equal to 100
The pie is fruit
```

In the last example a fuzzy set could be defined as:

```
FRUIT = 1/apples + 1/oranges
```

to indicate the type of elements that are considered fruit. Notice that in fuzzy theory you *can* add apples and oranges in a meaningful way.

Let's now define a fuzzy restriction $R_1(x)$. For example, the fuzzy set HEAVY could be defined as:

$$R_1(x) = \text{HEAVY} = .6/140 + .8/150 + 1/160$$

The compositional rule of inference defines the fuzzy restriction on y values as:

$$R_3(y) = R_1(x) \text{ o } R_2(x,y)$$

where the composition operator, o, is the max-min operation:

$$\max_{x} \min(\mu_1(x), \mu_2(x,y))$$

Another way of viewing $R_3(y)$ is by interpreting it as the solution of the relational equations:

$$R_1(x)$$
$$R_2(x,y)$$

for $R_3(y)$. That is, given the fuzzy restriction of x and the fuzzy restriction on x and y, a fuzzy restriction on y can be deduced. Deductions like this comprise the **calculus of fuzzy restrictions**, which is the basis of approximate reasoning.

Using these definitions, $R_3(y)$ can be calculated as follows:

$$R_3(y) = R_1(x) \text{ o } R_2(x,y)$$

$$R_3(y) = \begin{bmatrix} 0.0 & 0.0 & 0.6 & 0.8 & 1.0 \end{bmatrix} \text{ o }$$

$$\begin{bmatrix} 1.0 & 0.7 & 0.4 & 0.2 & 0.0 \\ 0.7 & 1.0 & 0.6 & 0.5 & 0.2 \\ 0.4 & 0.6 & 1.0 & 0.8 & 0.5 \\ 0.2 & 0.5 & 0.8 & 1.0 & 0.8 \\ 0.0 & 0.2 & 0.5 & 0.8 & 1.0 \end{bmatrix}$$

where $R_1(x)$ is represented as a row vector. The nonzero elements of $R_3(y)$ are calculated as follows:

$$R_3(120) = \max \min[(.6,.4),(.8,.2)]$$

$$= \max(.4,.2) = .4$$

$$R_3(130) = \max \min[(.6,.6),(.8,.5),(1,.2)]$$

$$= \max(.6,.5,.2) = .6$$

```
R3(140) = max min[(.6,1),(.8,.8),(1,.5)]

        = max(.6,.8,.5) = .8

R3(150) = max min[(.6,.8),(.8,1),(1,.8)]

        = max(.6,.8,.8) = .8

R3(160) = max min[(.6,.5),(.8,.8),(1,1)]

        = max(.5,.8,1) = 1
```

and so if $R_1(x)$ is HEAVY, then:

```
R3(y) = .4/120 + .6/130 + .8/140 + .8/150 + 1/160
```

which has the rough linguistic approximation: $R_3(y)$ is MORE OR LESS HEAVY.

The relation $R_3(y)$ is a rough linguistic approximation since the DIL operation of $\mu^{0.5}$ acting on HEAVY actually yields:

```
DIL(HEAVY) = .8/140 + .9/150 + 1/160
```

and the terms for 120 and 130 are missing. However, the elements with large membership grades of $\mu \geq .8$ are represented well and this justifies the claim that MORE OR LESS HEAVY is a rough approximation. Thus the compositional inference by max-min has shown the fuzzy linguistic relation:

```
MORE OR LESS HEAVY = HEAVY o APPROXIMATELY EQUAL
```

Note that these relations depend on the fuzzy set definitions and the linguistic labels of the sets. Thus the above relation is not true in an absolute sense since it depends on the definitions of the fuzzy sets, relations, and labels. However, once these basic definitions are made, fuzzy theory provides a mechanism for manipulating these expressions in a formal and consistent way. This is very important since the linguistic manipulation and meanings of terms are then on a sound theoretical basis and do not depend on an *ad hoc* or intuitive understanding by a person.

Maximum and Moments Methods

The choice of the element with the maximum membership grade is called the **maximum method** for deciding the truth of rule consequents. An alternate method, called the **moments method**, assigns the truth of rule consequents in a way that is analogous to calculating the first moment of inertia of an object in physics. The basic idea of the moments method is to consider the consequents of all rules in a decision rather than just the one maximum. As mentioned before, even the maximum method may lead to ambiguity if the consequents of multiple rules all have the same maximum value.

As a simple example of the moments method, let's first consider the following set of fuzzy production rules for making concrete:

```
R1:   IF MIX IS TOO WET
      THEN ADD SAND AND COARSE AGGREGATE

R2:   IF MIX IS WORKABLE
      THEN LEAVE ALONE

R3:   IF MIX IS TOO STIFF
      THEN DECREASE SAND AND COARSE AGGREGATE
```

Concrete consists of cement, water, sand, and coarse aggregate such as small rocks, mixed in proper proportions. The **mix** is a trial amount of the concrete mixture, which is made to determine the optimum proportions for the desired application. General guidelines for the proportions are available depending on the desired concrete strength. However, there is variability due to the local materials used, aggregate sizes, environmental conditions, and other factors. It's a good idea to do a mix before starting a $10,000,000 building.

One common method of determining if the mix is correct or workable is the **slump test**. A trial batch of concrete is put into a cone and the cone is removed. The distance that the mix slumps after cone removal indicates the condition of the material. Concrete designed for ordinary slabs and beams should have a minimum and maximum slump of 4 and 8 inches, respectively. The fuzzy sets of Figure 5.18 illustrate possible definitions for the fuzzy concrete mix production rules antecedents. These fuzzy sets also may be defined in a table or as S-functions and Π-functions.

Figure 5.18 Fuzzy Production Rule Antecedents for Concrete Mixture Process Control

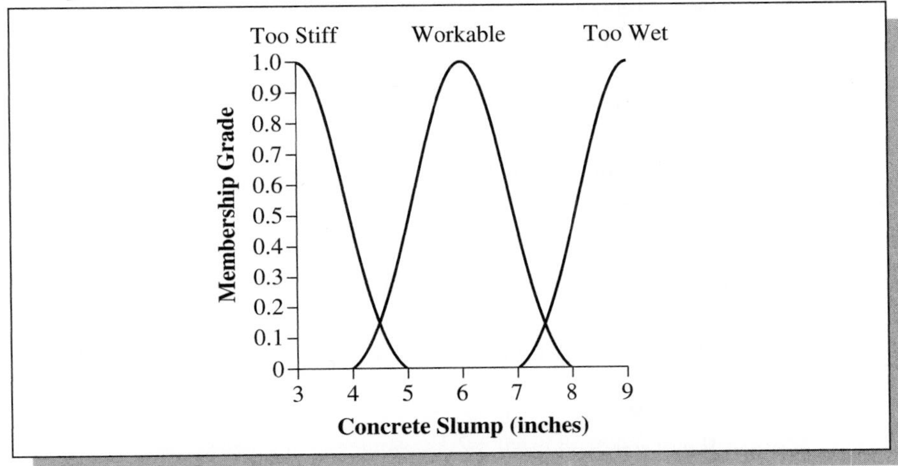

The fuzzy sets used for the fuzzy rule consequents are defined in Figure 5.19. As with the antecedents, there is overlap between these fuzzy consequent actions to provide a workable mix. Note that the limits of -20 and 20% for the change in sand and coarse aggregates are defined arbitrarily. Like the fuzzy set antecedents, the consequents may also be defined by S-functioons and Π-functions.

Figure 5.19 Fuzzy Production Rule Consequents for Concrete Mixture Process Control

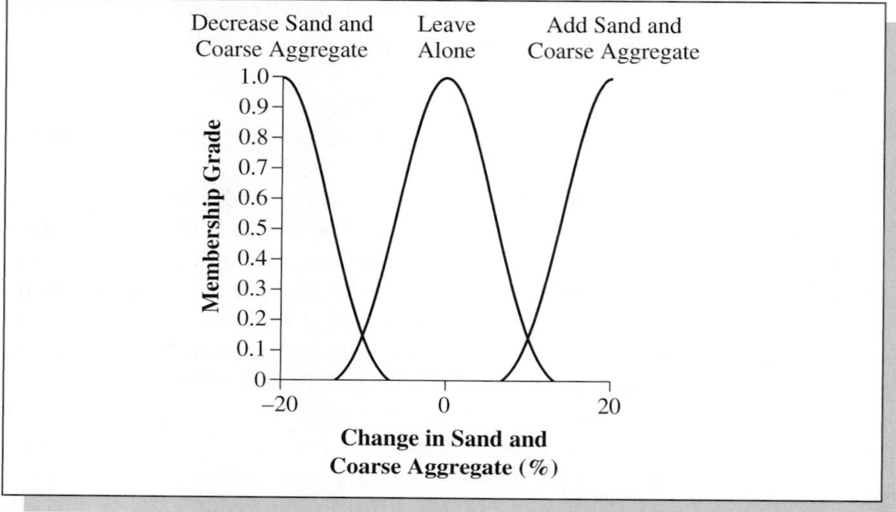

As an example of how this fuzzy production rule set works, assume that the concrete slump is 6 inches. From Figure 5.18, the membership grade or antecedent truth value for each rule is the following:

$$\mu_{\text{TOO STIFF}}(6) = 0$$
$$\mu_{\text{WORKABLE}}(6) = 1$$
$$\mu_{\text{TOO WET}}(6) = 0$$

and so the only rule whose antecedent is satisfied is R_2. This rule is activated and fires with the resulting fuzzy consequent LEAVE ALONE.

Applying the compositional rule of inference gives:

$$\mu_{\text{LEAVE ALONE}} = \max[\min(\mu_{\text{WORKABLE}}(6)] = \max[\min(1)] = 1$$

and from Figure 5.19, this translates into a 0% change in the sand and coarse aggregate.

Now suppose that the slump is 4.8 inches. From Figure 5.18,

$$\mu_{\text{TOO STIFF}}(4.8) = .05$$
$$\mu_{\text{WORKABLE}}(4.8) = .2$$
$$\mu_{\text{TOO WET}}(4.8) = 0$$

Rules R_1 and R_2 have antecedents that are partially satisfied analogous to the partial evidence satisfaction of probabilistic PROSPECTOR rule antecedents. Since there is some nonzero truth that the mix is too stiff or workable, then both rules R_1 and R_2 will become activated and fire. Notice that in a fuzzy production system, unless there is a threshold on antecedent truth, every rule will fire with a nonzero antecedent truth. Setting a threshold may be desirable to prevent inefficiencies due to many rules with low truth values from becoming activated and firing. Recall that in the MYCIN system, the minimum certainty level of a rule to fire must be greater than 0.2 to improve the expert system's efficiency. A similar threshold on the antecedent truth value of fuzzy sets can be defined.

For the slump of 4.8 inches, there are two rules that become activated. Applying the max-min composition rule gives:

$$\mu_{\text{DECREASE SAND AND COARSE AGGREGATE}} = \max\ [\min(\mu_{\text{TOO STIFF}}(4.8)]$$

$$= .05$$

$$\mu_{\text{LEAVE ALONE}} = \max\ [\min(\mu_{\text{WORKABLE}}(4.8)] = .2$$

As you can see for a single antecedent term the max and min functions are unnecessary.

Since there are now two rules with nonzero consequents, we must decide on a control action. The maximum method will simply pick the rule with the largest membership grade. In this case, the LEAVE ALONE action is chosen since its grade is .2 compared to .05 of the other rule.

The moments method basically calculates the **center of gravity** of the fuzzy consequent rules. The term *center of gravity* comes from physics, where it represents the point where, if all the mass of an object were concentrated, the point mass would act the same under the influence of an external force. The definition of the center of gravity, also called the **first moment of inertia**, I, is:

$$I = \frac{\int m(x)x\ d(x)}{\int m(x)\ d(x)}$$

where the integral sign denotes ordinary integration.

Figure 5.20 shows the fuzzy sets for the two rules R_2 and R_3. Notice that the fuzzy sets are truncated at the truth values of their antecedents. This reflects the compositional rule of inference. The truncation is done because, intuitively, it makes sense that the truth value of a consequent cannot exceed that of its antecedent.

Figure 5.20 Maximum and Moments Methods for the Concrete Process Control Fuzzy Rules

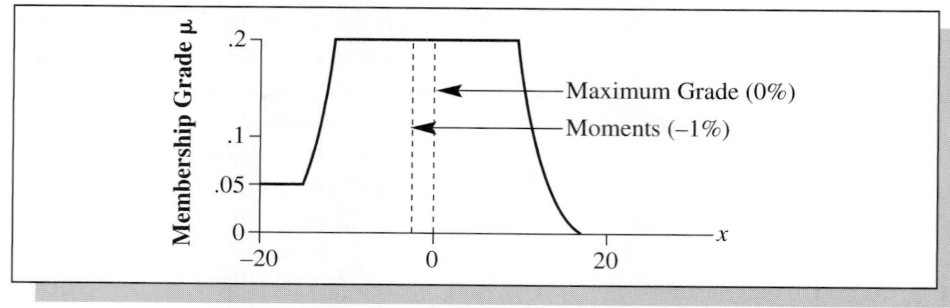

The moment of the consequents is calculated as:

$$I = \frac{\int \mu(x)\ x\ d(x)}{\int \mu(x)\ d(x)} \qquad \text{for continuous elements}$$

or:

$$I = \frac{\sum_i \mu_i x}{\sum_i \mu_i} \qquad \text{for discrete elements}$$

and is about -1% for Figure 5.20. While this is very close to 0% obtained from the maximum method, the difference may become significant for fuzzy sets that are defined with a considerable amount of overlap. Both the maximum and the moments methods have been used in a fuzzy controller for aircraft control. In this controller the maximum method calculated the arithmetic mean of all the maxima of the fuzzy consequents. Thus, if there were multiple elements with the same maximum value, one crisp control value would still be calculated.

Besides the maximum and moments methods, other approaches have been used to solve the **defuzzification problem** of translating a membership grade into a crisp control value, or a linguistic approximation describing the control variable. However, it is difficult to describe a set of values—the fuzzy set—by a single number or a linguistic phrase (except when someone cuts you off in traffic).

Possibility and Probability

The term **possibility** has a specific meaning in fuzzy theory. Essentially, possibility refers to allowed values. For example, suppose a proposition is defined regarding the throw of two dice in a universe $\mathcal{U}$ of their sum, as follows:

p = X is an integer in $\mathcal{U}$

$\mathcal{U}$ = {2,3,4,5,6,7,8,9,10,11,12}

In fuzzy terminology, for any integer i,

Poss {X = i} = 1   for $2 \le i \le 12$
Poss (X = i} = 0   otherwise

where **Poss** (X = i} is short for "The possibility that X may assume the value i." The possibility of the dice showing a value from 2 to 12 is very different from the probability of a value i. That is, the **possibility distribution** is not the same as the **probability distribution**. The probability distribution of the dice is the frequency of expected occurrence of the **random variable** X, the sum. For example, a 7 can occur due to 1 + 6, 2 + 5, and 3 + 4. So the probability of rolling a 7 is:

$$\frac{2 \cdot 3}{36} = \frac{1}{6}$$

while the probability of rolling a 2 is:

$$\frac{1}{36}$$

In contrast, the possibility distribution is a constant value of 1 for fair dice for all integers from 2 to 12. A proposition p is said to *induce a possibility distribution*, Π_X. That is, given a fuzzy proposition, p, based on a fuzzy set F and a linguistic variable X,

p = X is F

The proposition is said to be in **canonical form** when expressed this way, where the term *canonical* means a standard form. The fuzzy set, F, is a **fuzzy predicate**, in contrast to the predicates of ordinary logic. F can also be a fuzzy relation. The possibility distribution induced by p is equal to F, and is defined by the following **possibility assignment equation**:

$$\Pi_X = F$$

which means that for all values x in the universe, $\mathcal{U}$:

Poss (X = x} = $\mu_F(x)$ $x \in \mathcal{U}$

As an example, given the proposition:

p = John is tall

a linguistic variable, Height, can be defined with a value, John. The canonical form:

```
X is F
```

is represented in terms of the variable Height by:

```
Height(John) is TALL
```

and so:

$$\text{Poss}\ \{\text{Height(John)} = x\} = \mu_{\text{TALL}}(x)$$

The proposition, p, can be written as a possibility distribution as follows:

$$\text{John is tall} \rightarrow \Pi_{\text{Height(John)}} = \text{TALL}$$

where the arrow symbol means "translates into," Height is a linguistic variable, and TALL is a fuzzy set. Note that John is not a linguistic variable.

Although a fuzzy set can be assigned to a possibility distribution, as in $\Pi_X = F$, the two are not really the same. As an example to illustrate the difference, consider the fuzzy set defined for a roll of dice as follows:

```
ROLL(1) = 1/3 + 1/4
```

This set is defined to mean that a specific roll of the dice, Roll 1, gave a 3 on one die and a 4 on the other. In contrast, the possibility distribution,

$$\Pi_{\text{ROLL(1)}} = 1/3 + 1/4$$

means that the roll gave a 3 *or* a 4, where the "or" is the exclusive-or representing the uncertainty in our knowledge of the roll. There is a possibility of unity that it is a 3 and a possibility of unity that it is a 4. In the fuzzy set it is certain that the dice values were 3 *and* 4. The possibility distribution means that the dice are fair with regard to whether a 3 or a 4 can occur. The fuzzy set tells what values showed after a roll.

As another example, consider the proposition that "Hans ate X eggs for breakfast," where X is any value in the universe, X = {1, 2, ... 8}:

Table 5.17 The Relation APPROXIMATELY EQUAL Defined on People's Weights

X	1	2	3	4	5	6	7	8
$\Pi_{\text{ATE(Hans)}}(\text{X})$	1.0	1.0	1.0	1.0	0.8	0.6	0.4	0.2
P(X)	0.1	0.8	0.1	0.0	0.0	0.0	0.0	0.0

The possibility distribution $\prod_{\text{ATE(Hans)}}(X)$ is interpreted as how easily Hans can eat X eggs. The probability distribution, P(X), is determined empirically by asking Hans if you can join him for breakfast for a year to conduct a scientific study.

An important point to realize is that possibility is *nonstatistical* while probability is *statistical*. For example, although Hans can eat eight eggs, the empirical study shows that over the period of observation, he has never eaten more than three (and kept them down.) In this sense, possibility is capability or capacity. A high degree of possibility does not necessarily mean a high degree of probability. That is, there may be no correlation between possibility and probability. For example, the possibility of weapons of mass destruction does not mean there is a probability of weapons of mass destruction without some evidence.

The fuzzy extension to ordinary probability is **fuzzy probability**, which describes probabilities that are known only imprecisely. Some examples of fuzzy probabilities are the **fuzzy qualifiers** *Very Likely*, *Unlikely*, *Not Very Likely*, and so forth. An example of a fuzzy proposition with a fuzzy probability is the following:

```
the battery is BAD is Very Likely
```

Translation Rules

Fuzzy probability is incorporated into the fuzzy logic called **FL** based on Lukasiewicz's L_1 logic. One main component of FL is a group of **translation rules,** which specify how modified or composite propositions are generated from their elementary propositions.

The translation rules are divided in four categories:

- *Type I* : **modification rules**, such as:

```
X is very large

John is much taller than Mike
```

- *Type II* : **composition rules**, such as:

conditional composition

```
If X is TALL then Y is SHORT
```

conjunctive composition

```
X is TALL and Y is SHORT
```

disjunctive composition

```
X is TALL or Y is SHORT
```

conditional and conjunctive composition

```
If X is TALL then Y is SHORT
else Y is Rather SHORT
```

- *Type III* : **quantification rules**, such as:

  Most desserts are WONDERFUL

```
Too Much nutritious food is FATTENING
```

- *Type IV* : **qualification rules**, such as:

  truth qualification

```
chocolate pie is DELICIOUS is Very True
```

probability qualification

```
chocolate pie is served SOON is Very Likely
```

possibility qualification

```
chocolate pie is BAD for you is Impossible
```

The qualification rules are those pertaining to fuzzy probabilities. The quantification rules deal with fuzzy quantifiers such as *Most*, which is not capable of being defined using the classical universal and existential quantifiers.

The translation of a Type I rule is represented by:

$$X \text{ is } F \rightarrow \Pi_X = F$$

with translated proposition:

$$X \text{ is } mF \rightarrow \Pi_X = F^+$$

where m is a modifier such as *Not*, *Very*, *More Or Less*, and so on. F^+ represents the modification of F by m. Some default definitions for m and F^+ are shown in Table 5.18. These are defined the same as the linguistic hedges discussed previously. Other definitions for m and F^+ may also be used.

As an example, defining TALL,

```
TALL = .2/5 + .6/6 + 1/7
```

then the translations are as follows:

```
John is not tall → .8/5 + .4/6 + 0/7
John is very tall → .04/5 + .36/6 + 1/7
John is more or less tall → .45/5 + .77/6 + 1/7
```

Table 5.18 Translation Parameters Values for Some Type I Rules. Note that all integrals are over the universe.

m	F+
Not	$F' = \int [1 - \mu_F(x)]/x$
Very	$F^2 = \int \mu_{F^2}(x)/x$
More Or Less	$\sqrt{F} = \int \sqrt{\mu_F(x)}/x$

The variable X does not have to be a unary variable. Instead, X may be a binary or N-ary relation in general. For example, a proposition such as "Y and Z are F" is subsumed by "X is F." Defining CLOSE as a fuzzy binary relation in $\mathcal{U} \times \mathcal{U}$,

CLOSE = 1/(1,1) + .5/(1,2) + .5/(2,1)

then:

X and Y are close $\rightarrow \Pi_{(X,Y)}$ = CLOSE

X and Y are very close $\rightarrow \Pi_{(X,Y)}$
= CLOSE^2
= 1/(1,1) + .25/(1,2) + .25/(2,1)

An example of a type II rule is:

IF X is F then Y is G $\rightarrow \Pi_{(X,Y)} = \overline{F}' \oplus \overline{G}$

where $\overline{F}$ and $\overline{G}$ are the cylindrical extensions of F and G in their universes.

$\overline{F} = F \times V \quad \overline{G} = U \times G$

and $\oplus$ is the bounded sum. For this rule:

$\mu_{\overline{F}' \oplus \overline{G}}(x,y) = 1 \wedge [1 - \mu_F(x) + \mu_G(y)]$

and the min function is $\wedge$. This definition is consistent with implication in L_1 logic, while other definitions may not be consistent. As an example of a Type II rule, define:

```
U = V = {4, 5, 6, 7}

F = TALL = .2/5 + .6/6 + 1/7

G = SHORT = 1/4 + .2/5
```

IF X is tall then Y is short $\rightarrow \prod_{(X,Y)}$

```
  = 1/(5,4)  + 1/(5,5) + 1/(6,4) +
    .6/(6,5) + 1/(7,4) + .2(7,5)
```

where the membership grade of an element such as (5, 4) is calculated as follows:

$$\mu_{\overline{F'} \oplus \overline{G}}(5,4) = 1 \wedge [1 - .2 + 1] = 1 \wedge [1.8] = 1$$

Uncertainty in Fuzzy Expert Systems

When fuzzy probabilities are used in expert systems, there is a difference compared to ordinary probabilistic inference. Consider the canonical fuzzy rule:

```
If X is F then Y is G (with probability ß)
```

This rule can be written as a conditional probability:

$$P(Y \text{ is } G \mid X \text{ is } F) = ß$$

A conventional expert system using classical probability theory would then assume:

$$P(Y \text{ is not } G \mid X \text{ is } F) = 1 - ß$$

However, this is not correct in fuzzy theory if F is a fuzzy set. The valid fuzzy result is weaker:

$$P(Y \text{ is not } G \mid X \text{ is } F) + P(Y \text{ is } G \mid X \text{ is } F) \geq 1$$

because it only sets a lower limit on the probabilities, which may be fuzzy numbers. In general, for fuzzy systems,

P(H | E) is not necessarily equal to 1 – P(H′ | E)

In fuzzy expert systems there may be fuzziness in three areas:
(1) antecedents and/or consequents of rules such as:

```
If X is F then Y is G
If X is F then Y is G with CF = α
```

where CF is the certainty factor and α is a numeric value such as 0.5.

(2) partial match between the antecedent and facts which match the antecedent patterns. In nonfuzzy expert systems, a rule does not become activated unless the patterns match the facts exactly. However, in a fuzzy expert system everything is a matter of degree and all rules may be activated to some extent unless a threshold is set.

(3) fuzzy quantifiers such as *Most*, and fuzzy qualifiers such as *Very Likely*, *Quite True*, *Definitely Possible*, and so forth.

Propositions often contain implicit and/or explicit fuzzy quantifiers. As an example, consider the **disposition:**

```
d = desserts are WONDERFUL
```

The term *disposition* means a proposition that is usually true, with canonical form:

```
Usually(X is R)
```

where *Usually* is an implied fuzzy quantifier and R is a **constraining relation** acting on the constrained variable X to limit the values it may take. Many heuristic rules that people know about are dispositions. In fact, **commonsense knowledge** is basically a collection of dispositions about the real world.

The disposition may be translated into the explicit propositional forms:

```
p = Usually desserts are wonderful
p = Most desserts are wonderful
```

which may be expressed as a heuristic rule:

```
r = If x is a dessert
    then it is likely that x is wonderful
```

Some rules of inference in fuzzy systems are the following:

- **entailment principle**

```
X is F
F ⊂ G
X is G
```

- **dispositional entailment**: limiting cases where *Usually* becomes *Always:*

```
Usually (X is F)
F ⊂ G
Usually (X is G)
```

- compositional rule:

```
X is F
(X,Y) is R
Y is F o R
```

where R is a binary relation over the binary variable (X,Y) and:

$$\mu_{F \circ R}(y) = \sup_{x}[\mu_F(x) \wedge \mu_R(x,y)]$$

and the **supremum**, symbolized by **sup**, is the **least upper bound**. Generally the supremum is the same as the max function. The difference arises in cases where there is no maximum value, such as the real-number interval of numbers less than 0. Since there is no maximum real number less than 0, the supremum is used to take 0 as the least upper bound.

- generalized modus ponens:

```
X is F
Y is G if X is H
Y is F o (H´ ⊕ G)
```

where H´ is the fuzzy negation of H and the bounded sum is defined:

$$\mu_{H' \oplus G}(x,y) = 1 \wedge [1 - \mu_H(x) + \mu_G(y)]$$

The generalized *modus ponens* does not require that the antecedent "X is H" be identical with the premise "X is F." Notice that this is very different from classical logic, which requires that they match exactly. The generalized *modus ponens* is actually a special case of the compositional rule of inference. Unlike conventional expert systems, in which *modus ponens* is the basic rule of inference, the compositional rule of inference is the basic rule in fuzzy expert systems.

Expert systems using approximate reasoning may use a number of different methods such as truth value restriction, and compositional inference. In Whalen's survey of eleven fuzzy expert systems, nearly all used compositional inference. It's difficult to predict which method works best in advance so empirical modeling is used to see which best fits the data. This is not as bad as it sounds since in statistics, the use of linear regression is tried first because it's the simplest and people assume the population distribution is Gaussian. If that doesn't work, they will try a more complex model such as a polynomial fit and so forth until the errors are acceptable.

5.6 THE STATE OF UNCERTAINTY

Wow! If you have read every single word in the last five chapters and derived every equation and worked every problem, then you either have an unquenchable thirst for knowledge or suffer from insomnia. In either case reading the rest of the book will solve your problem. The big question is, after all the trees and forests of different, competing theories, can we see any mountains? Where is the certainty that we know the right way to build an expert system?

In the distance there are two mountains that stand out from all the trees and forests. One mountain rises very tall and appears very clear. This is the Mountain of Logic on which all expert systems *must* be built. An expert system *must* act like a human in reaching valid conclusions given valid premises. The expert system must come up with valid conclusions given that, (1) the rules were written correctly and, (2) the facts on which the inference engine generates valid conclusions are true facts. Notice that we did not say the facts are sound in the sense of being true in the in the real world. We do not expect that our inference engine will come to sound conclusions if the reasoning of our expert is not sound and the facts are invalid. The expert system is designed only to model the expertise of a human in a limited knowledge domain, and people do not always reason rationally. At the very least, our expert system *must* come to valid conclusions given valid facts. (If not, it will probably be a success as the first piece of software that gets elected to office.)

The second mountain that looms very high is the Mountain of Uncertainty. The peculiar thing is that no matter how close you get, it doesn't appear much more clear. In fact as you examine a particular theory, a new variation of it appears and that has a new variation in a fractal mountain of uncertainty. The best we can do on this mountain is model it on the expertise of our expert, or try to include more than one approach to uncertainty and let the different techniques fight it out. Such an evolutionary approach is based on the classic **blackboard architecture** in which different agents simultaneously work on a problem from different angles. All the agents post their pieces of the puzzle on a public blackboard for all to see in the hope that different pieces may suddenly come together. A supervisory program then looks at all the little pieces and tried to see the big picture. In the landscape of uncertainty, if there was a certain theory, there would be no uncertainty.

Today fuzzy logic and Bayesian theory are most often used for uncertainty. However there are many variations of these theories which are also tried in making an application work. It's important to choose software which gives a wide range of choices. As usual, commercial software offers the most choices but costs the most. In many cases, academic pricing is available or trial versions that will work for some time.

With the common availability of powerful desktop computers and now the linking of thousands or potentially millions of computers using the Grid, you can try out various models of uncertainty on very large datasets in a short time. The problem with all this massive multicomputing that you should be careful of is overfitting the data by using so many parameters that a 100% fit can be made to your test data set. A 100% fit is just as bad as a 0% fit (or good depending on how you look at it) because it means there is something wrong. From statistics we know there should be random fluctuations due to noise or the finite sample size.

For example, given N data points we can always draw a series of N-1 straight lines from the first to the last. Such a model would fit perfectly for interpolation between any two points, but be of perfectly no use in extrapolation beyond the data. What we really want in an expert system is the ability to predict and extrapolate from the known to new cases just as a human does.

Classical Bayesian, **convex set Bayesian**, Dempster-Shafer, **Kyburg**, and the possibility theory of fuzzy logic are among a few methods that are widely available as software tools today. It may take you far more time trying different models than the analysis itself. In the convex set approach to Bayes theory, the belief state is not a single function of the classical Bayes method. Instead, the belief state is characterized by a set of **convex functions**. This means that any function can be represented as a linear combination of two other functions.

Since the Dempster-Shafer theory was first introduced as a generalization of classical probability there have been rebuttals. For example, Kyburg's paper claims that Dempster-Shafer theory is not a generalization of classical probability, but is actually the other way around. Kyburg believes that Dempster-Shafer theory is included in classical probability and that the Dempster-Shafer intervals are included in the convex set Bayes approach. The Dempster-Shafer theory also seems to have difficulties in dealing with beliefs that are close to zero. Very different results are obtained when beliefs are zero compared to when the beliefs are very small. Another problem with the Dempster-Shafer theory is the exponential explosion in the number of computations as the possible answers to a diagnostic problem increase.

Although the Gordon and Shortliffe approximation avoids the exponential explosion, it may produce poor results in the case of highly conflicting evidence. An alternative approach that is not an approximation and gives good results for hierarchical evidence without the combinatorial explosion has been given. A number of other papers have attempted to overcome the exponential explosion problem by different generalizations to Dempster-Shafer theory.

The major benefit of all this work has been a reexamination of the foundations of probability theory and widespread interest in methods of dealing with uncertainty. In addition, a variety of hybrid approaches combining fuzzy logic with ANS have been developed and met with success (Mendel (00). The im≠portant thing to remember is that trying to decide on a particular model of uncertainty is analogous to deciding on a particular data structure in a conventional programming language, e.g., arrays, linked lists, trees, queues, stacks, etc. Choose the model that best fits the problem.

5.7 SOME COMMERCIAL APPLICATIONS OF FUZZY LOGIC

Many commercial applications of fuzzy logic are in everything from cameras to washing machines. Links to fuzzy resources are shown in Appendix G.

- Automatic control of dam gates for **hydroelectric-powerplants** (Tokyo Electric Power)
- Simplified control of **robots** (Hirota, Fuji Electric, Toshiba, Omron)
- **Camera aiming** for the telecast of sporting events *(Omron)*

- Substitution of an expert for the **assessment of stock exchange activities** *(Yamaichi, Hitachi)*
- Preventing unwanted temperature fluctuations in **air-conditioning systems** *(Mitsubishi, Sharp)*
- Efficient and stable control of **car-engines** *(Nissan)*
- Cruise-control for **automobiles** *(Nissan, Subaru)*
- Improved efficiency and optimized function of **industrial control applications** (Aptronix, Omron, Meiden, Sha, Micom, Mitsubishi, Nisshin-Denki, Oku-Electronics)
- Positioning of wafer-steppers in the **production of semiconductors** *(Canon)*
- Optimized planning of **bus time-tables** (Toshiba, Nippon-System, Keihan-Express)
- Archiving system for **documents** *(Mitsubishi Electric.)*
- **Prediction system** for early recognition of earthquakes *(Inst. of Seismology Bureau of Metrology, Japan)*
- **Medicine technology:** cancer diagnosis *(Kawasaki Medical School)*
- Combination of Fuzzy Logic and **Neural Nets** *(Matsushita)*
- Recognition of handwritten symbols with **pocket computers** *(Sony)*
- Compensation of motion in camcorders *(Canon, Minolta)*
- Automatic motor-control for **vacuum cleaners** with recognition of surface condition and degree of soiling *(Matsushita)*
- Back light control for **camcorders** *(Sanyo)*
- Compensation against vibrations in **camcorders** *(Matsushita)*
- Single button control for **washing-machines** *(Matsushita, Hitatchi)*
- **Recognition** of handwriting, objects, voice *(CSK, Hitachi, Hosai Univ., Ricoh)*
- Flight aid for **helicopters** *(Sugeno)*
- Simulation for **legal proceedings** *(Meihi Gakuin Univ, Nagoy Univ.)*
- **Software-design** for industrial processes (Aptronix, Harima, Ishikawajima-OC Engeneering)
- Controlling of machinery speed and temperature for **steel-works** *(Kawasaki Steel, New-Nippon Steel, NKK)*

- Controlling of **subway systems** in order to improve driving comfort, precision of halting and power economy
  (Hitachi)
- Improved fuel-consumption for **automobiles**
  (NOK, Nippon Denki Tools)
- Improved sensitiveness and efficiency for **elevator control**
  (Fujitec, Hitachi, Toshiba)
- Improved safety for **nuclear reactors**
  (Hitachi, Bernard, Nuclear Fuel Div.)

5.7 SUMMARY

In this chapter, nonclassical probability theories of uncertainty were discussed. Certainty factors, Dempster-Shafer theory, and fuzzy theory are all ways of dealing with uncertainty in expert systems. Certainty factors are simple to implement and have been used successfully in expert systems such as MYCIN, where the inference chains are short. However, the theory of certainty factors is an ad hoc theory that does not appear to be generally valid for longer inference chains.

Dempster-Shafer theory has a rigorous foundation and is used in expert systems.

Fuzzy theory is the most general theory of uncertainty that has been formulated. It has wide applicability because of the extension principle. Since the first classic paper by Zadeh in 1965, fuzzy theory has been applied to many fields. Many links are shown in Appendix G.

PROBLEMS

5.1 Given that evidence E2 adds to the original evidence E1 , show that:

$$P(D_i \mid E_1 \cap E_2) = \frac{P(E_2 \mid D_i \cap E_1) P(D_i \mid E_1)}{\sum_j P(E_2 \mid D_j \cap E_1) P(D_j \mid E_1)}$$

Hint: use the results of Problem 4.8 (b).

5.2 Prove that:

$$CF(H,E) + CF(H',E) = 0$$

5.3 Given rules:

```
IF E₁ AND E₂ AND E₃
            THEN H (CF₁)

IF E₄ OR E₅
            THEN H  (CF₂)
```

where:

$CF_1(E_1,e) = 1$ $CF_1(E_2,e) = 0.5$ $CF_1(E_3,e) = 0.3$
$CF_2(E_4,e) = 0.7$ $CF_2(E_5,e) = 0.2$
$CF_1(H,E) = 0.5$ $CF_2(H,E) = 0.9$

(a) Draw a tree illustrating how these rules support H.
(b) Calculate the certainty factors $CF_1(H,e)$ and $CF_2(H,e)$.
(c) Calculate CFCOMBINE $[CF_1(H,e),CF_2(H,e)]$.

5.4 (a) In Figure 5.7 (c) assuming:

$m(X) = 0.2$
$m(Y) = 0.3$
$m(Z) = 0.5$

find the evidential intervals of X, Y, and Z using the Dempster-Shafer theory.

(b) In Figure 5.7 (d) assuming:

$m(X) = 0.4$
$m(Y) = 0.6$

find the evidential intervals for:

X
$X \cap Y$
Y
$X \cap Y'$
$X' \cap Y$

5.5 Given the rules:

```
Rule 1: IF E THEN H
Rule 2: IF E THEN H´
```

and assuming:

$\Theta = \{H, H'\}$
$m_1(H) = 0.5$ $m_1(\Theta) = 0.5$ for Rule 1
$m_2(H') = 0.3$ $m_2(\Theta) = 0.7$ for Rule 2

(a) Write the Dempster-Shafer table showing the combination of evidence and calculate the combined belief functions.
(b) Calculate the plausibilities.
(c) Calculate the evidential intervals.
(d) Calculate the dubieties.
(e) Calculate the ignorances.

5.6 Based on reports from different types of sensors, the following table gives the degrees of belief in the aircraft environment of airliner (H), bomber (B), and fighter (F):

Focal elements	Sensor 1 (m_1)	Sensor 2 (m_2)
Q	0.15	0.2
A,B	0.3	0.1
A,F	0.1	0.05
B,F	0.1	0.1
A	0.05	0.3
B	0.2	0.05
F	0.1	0.2

(a) Calculate the initial belief functions, plausibility, evidential intervals, dubieties, and ignorances.

(b) Calculate these same parameters after the evidence is combined.

5.7 A policeman stops a motorist for speeding. Due to errors in the policeman's radar gun and the motorist's speedometer, the belief functions are as follows:

Policeman	Motorist
$m_1(57) = 0.3$	$m_2(56) = 0.2$
$m_1(56) = 0.5$	$m_2(55) = 0.6$
$m_1(55) = 0.2$	$m_2(54) = 0.2$

(a) Calculate the belief functions, plausibility, evidential intervals, dubieties, and ignorance of each person.

(b) Calculate these parameters after combining the evidences.

(c) Explain why you believe the motorist was or was not speeding, based on the parameters.

5.8 Given the fuzzy sets,

```
A = .1/1 + .2/2 + .3/3   B = .2/1 + .3/2 + .4/3
```

calculate/explain the following:

(a) Are the sets equal? Explain.

(b) Set complement

(c) Set union

(d) Set intersection

(e) Does the Law of Excluded Middle hold for each set? Explain.

(f) Set product

(g) Second power of each set

(h) Probabilistic sum

(i) Bounded sum

(j) Bounded product
(k) Bounded difference
(l) Concentration
(m) Dilation
(n) Intensification
(o) Normalization

5.9 Given the fuzzy sets:

$$Q = \begin{bmatrix} 0.2 & 0.3 \\ 0.4 & 1.0 \end{bmatrix} \text{ defined on } U1 \times U2$$

$$P = \begin{bmatrix} 0.1 & 0.5 & 0.3 \\ 0.2 & 0.0 & 0.4 \end{bmatrix} \text{ defined on } U2 \times U3$$

(a) Calculate the first, second, and total projections for each set.
(b) Calculate the cylindrical extensions of each set.
(c) Show that:

$$Q \circ P = \text{proj}(\overline{Q} \cap \overline{P};\ U_1 \times U_3)$$

5.10 Consider the linguistic variable Person as a fuzzy set of order 3.

(a) Define Person as three fuzzy sets of order 2.
(b) Define each of the order 2 sets in terms of three fuzzy sets of order 1.
(c) Define three of the fuzzy order 1 sets in terms of S- and/or Π-functions.

5.11 (a) Define five linguistic values for the linguistic variable Uncertainty.
(b) Draw appropriate functions for these values and explain your choices.
(c) Draw the fuzzy sets for:

```
Not TRUE
More Or Less TRUE
Sort Of TRUE
Pretty TRUE
Rather TRUE
TRUE
```

assuming TRUE is an S-function. What are the limits of TRUE? Explain.

5.12 (a) Define at least six values for the linguistic variable Water Temperature.
(b) Draw the appropriate functions for the fuzzy set values on one graph.
(c) Give three hedged fuzzy set functions based on FREEZING.

5.13 (a) Show by truth table for N = 2 and N = 3 the values of the primitive Llogic operators of Table 5.14.

(b) derive $x \leftrightarrow y$ in terms of the absolute values of x and y.

5.14 Given numeric truth values,

```
x(A)  =  .2/.1 + .6/.5 + 1/.9
x(B)  =  .1/.1 + .3/.5 + 1/.9
```

calculate the fuzzy logic truth of the following:

(a) NOT A
(b) A AND B
(c) A OR B
(d) $A \rightarrow B$
(e) $B \rightarrow A$

5.15 Define a fuzzy grammar using hedged primaries and range phrases to generate productions such as:

```
IF PRESSURE IS HIGH
THEN TURN VALVE LOWER

IF PRESSURE IS VERY HIGH
THEN TURN VALVE MUCH LOWER

IF PRESSURE IS VERY VERY HIGH
THEN TURN VALVE MUCH MUCH LOWER

IF PRESSURE IS LOW TO MEDIUM
THEN TURN VALVE HIGHER
```

Assume (1) that the primaries for PRESSURE are only LOW and HIGH, (2) the range phrases involving TO only occur in the antecedent, and (3) the primaries for VALVE in the conclusion are only LOWER and HIGHER.

BIBLIOGRAPHY

Note that many software resources and online material on fuzzy logic is shown in Appendix G Software Resources.

(Bertino 01). Elisa Bertino *et. al., Intelligent Database Systems,* ACM Press, 2001.

(Chen 01). Guanrong Chen and Trung Tat Pham, Introduction to Fuzzy Sets, Fuzzy Logic, and Fuzzy Control Systems, CRC Press, 2001.

(Constantin 95). Von Altrock Constantin, *Fuzzy Logic and Neuro Fuzzy Applications Explained,* Prentice- Hall, 1995.

(Cornelius 98). *Fuzzy Logic and Expert Systems Applications* ed. by Cornelius T. Leondes Academic Press, 1998.

(Kerre 00). Da Ruan and Etienne E. Kerre, *Fuzzy If-Then Rules in Computational Intelligence*, Kluwer Academic Publishers, 2000.

(Da Ruan 97). Intelligent Hybrid Systems: Fuzzy Logic, Neural Networks, and Genetic Algorithms, Kluwer Academic Publishers, 1997.

(Gardenfors 04). Peter Gardenfors, *Belief Revision,* Cambridge Tracts in Theoretical Computer Science, 2004. (Dempster 67). A. P. Dempster, "Upper and Lower Probabilities Induced by Multivalued Mappings," *Annals of Math. Stat.*, 38, pp. 325-329, 1967.

(Giarratano 91). Joseph Giarratano, *et al*.," Fuzzy Logic Control for Camera Tracking System," Fifth Annual Workshop on Space Operations Applications and Research (SOAR '91), pp. 94-99, 1991.

(Harris 00). John Harris, *An Introduction to Fuzzy Logic Applications*, Kluwer Academic Publishers, 2000.

(Ibrahim 03). Ahmed M. Ibrahim, *Fuzzy Logic for Embedded Systems Applications*, book with CDROM with lots of references, pub. by Newnes, 2003.

(Kosko 96). Bart Kosko, *Fuzzy Engineering,* Prentice Hall, 1996

(Liu 04). Puyin Liu, *Fuzzy Neural Network Theory and Application (Machine Perception and Artificial Intelligence*, World Scientific Publishing Company, 2004.

(Mendel 00). Uncertain Rule-Based Fuzzy Logic Systems: Introduction and New Directions, Prentice-Hall, 2000.

(Nguyen 99). Hung T. Nguyen and Elbert A. Walker *A First Course in Fuzzy Logic*, CRC Press, 1999.

(Roger 96). Jyh-Shing Roger Jang, Chuen-Tsai Sun, Eiji Mizutani, *Neuro-Fuzzy and Soft Computing: A Computational Approach to Learning and Machine Intelligence*, Prentice-Hall, 1996.

(Ross 04). Timothy J. Ross, *Fuzzy Logic with Engineering Applications*, John Wiley & Sons, 2004.

(Siller 04). William Siler and James J. Buckley , *Fuzzy Expert Systems: Theory and Applications*, Wiley-Interscience 2004.

CHAPTER 6
Design of Expert Systems

6.1 INTRODUCTION

In the previous chapters, we have discussed the general concepts and theory of expert systems and other intelligent decision making-systems. A number of papers have attempted to summarize the properties of intelligent systems. There are many pros and cons for each type (Begley 03). This chapter presents general guidelines for building practical expert systems designed for real-world applications, not research prototypes. A **software engineering methodology** is described so that an expert system can be a quality product developed in a cost-effective and timely manner.

Many books, papers, and software tools have been devoted to the design of expert systems, covering all aspects in great detail. So this one chapter will not make you an instant expert. (You'll have to read the chapter first). However by understanding the principles that explain why expert systems are designed the way they are, you'll be better able to take advantage of sophisticated tools and methodologies. In fact the design of expert systems is part of a more general field called **Knowledge Management** (KM) which deals with all the knowledge assets available to an organization (Becerra-Fernandez 03).

KM is connected to the Information Management (IM) which is connected to the Information Processing (IP) which is connected to the Information Systems (IS) which is connected to the Information Technology (IT). (On second thought, if you can say KM, IM, IP, IT, three times in a row without mispronouncing, you *are* an Instant Expert!) KM is a major problem considering all the different types of resources for many different types of audiences such as office, web, FAQs, Help Desk (human and automated), email, fax, phone, product, program, developer, manager, end-user, and publicity.

Large companies have their own very detailed methods, documents, books, and software they developed to create, manage, maintain, and sell knowledge assets because it is such a profitable field (Conway 02). This is especially true when intelligent tools are created that can greatly reduce human expenses because that's even cheaper than global outsourcing.

If you think how much time a typical person spends using computers, it's a tautology that we need computers to manage all the documents created by computers. Expert systems are widely used in business because they are so essential to the dramatically increasing amount of information and knowledge available on the web (Malhotra 01). As usual, links to software and other online resources for this chapter are listed in Appendix G.

6.2 SELECTING THE APPROPRIATE PROBLEM

There are many ways and resources by which you can build a knowledge-based or expert system. There are even more ways you can waste your time and money (for example, donating to the Starving Authors and Copyeditors Fund, a for-profit organization). However, the **Fourth Law of Wisdom** states that before you set out on a journey, you should know your destination.

Before you build an expert system, you should select an appropriate problem, as discussed in Section 1.6. Like any software project, there are a number of general considerations that should be made before a large commitment of people, resources, and time to a proposed expert system. These general considerations are typical of project management concerns in conventional programs, but must be customized for the special requirements of expert systems. A very high-level view of project development is shown in Figure 6.1. The three general stages of Activity, Product Configuration, and Resource Management have some more specific considerations, shown below. These more specific considerations will be discussed as questions and answers to serve as guidelines for expert systems projects.

Selecting the Appropriate Paradigm

Why are we building an expert system?

This is probably the most important question to be asked of *any* project. The most desirable answer is that the president of the company wants it built. If that's not the case, see if the general advantages of expert systems as described in Chapter 1, Section 2 apply. Most of all, remember only management can authorize the system and technical personnel needed. If you decide to build it on your own time to show the company you were right, and then realize what a great product it is, and decide to quit and form your own company, there is the small matter of that **Intellectual Property Agreement** you signed. Most IPAs state that whatever you come up with, whether related or not to your job duties, 24x7x52, belongs to the company. In particular, the answer to this question must eventually be given to the owners or stockholders funding development. Before starting, there should be a clear identification of the problem, expert, and users.

Note that the singular term *expert* is used, not plural *experts*. Just as the best way to guarantee trouble is to have multiple spouses at once, more than one expert will also guarantee trouble. Even the President only sees one doctor at a time, so it's not a matter of cost. Trying to model the expertise of multiple

Figure 6.1 Project Management Tasks

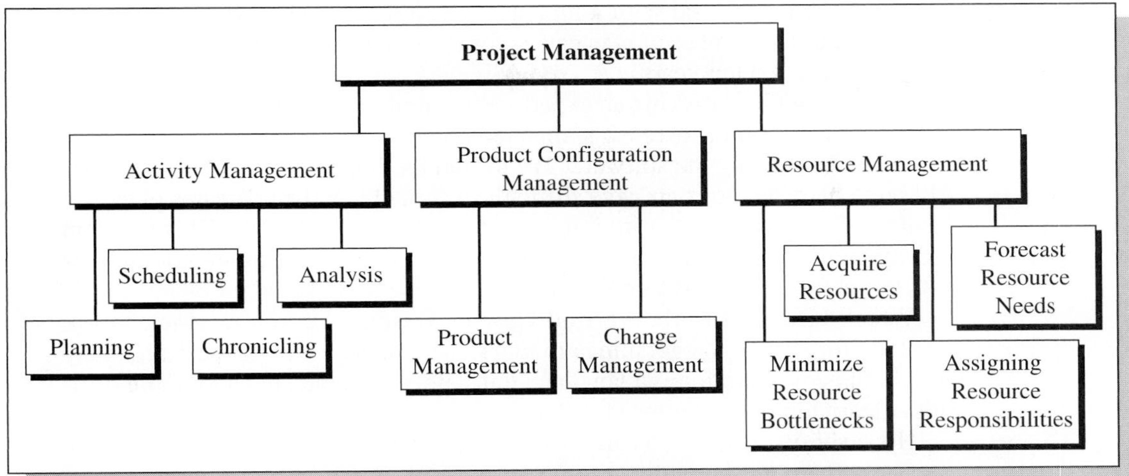

experts in one system is a bad idea. However, modeling the expertise of multiple experts in multiple systems using a blackboard architecture to reach at least a majority opinion is good. This does bring up what the fuzzy term *good* means. If nine out of ten doctors say the patient will die, the patient will inevitably choose the doctor that offers a treatment for life (unless the patient is really cheap and the treatment costs money). Trying to decide how to rank multiple expert opinions is a daunting task, usually more formidable than building a single expert system for a single expert. So we'll stick with the single-system-single-expert approach in this chapter and leave the multiple-experts-multiple-systems as a class project.

Payoff

What is the payoff?

This question is related to the first question. However, this question is more pragmatic by asking for a specific return on investment of people, resources, time, and money. The payoff may be in money, increased efficiency, or any of the other advantages of expert systems described in Chapter 1. It is also important to remember that if no one uses the system, there will be no payoff. Because expert systems is different from conventional programming it is more difficult to answer this question.

Tools

What tools are available to build the system?

There are many expert systems tools available today with advantages and disadvantages as discussed in Appendix G. However, this should be taken only as a guide since software tools develop so rapidly. Generally, you can count on an enhancement every couple years in each tool and a major revision every five years. Of course there's more money to be made in major bug fixes of old software that are introduced with a new name as a new version. If you have any doubts, count the number of new names for the same operating system you have been using the last ten years.

The best guide to picking an expert system tool follows from the **Third Law of Wisdom**: if you're lost, ask someone. Check the web for applications that have been built using the software. Try to find the failures, not just the success. Although hard statistics are very difficult to come by, most estimates place the number of successful software implementations at only 20-30%. This problem is compounded if you have to work with a busy expert and you are not familiar with terms from the expert's domain.

Which brings us to the **Second Law of Wisdom**: if you're going to ask someone for help, it's a good idea to know the language. While there are many human and computer foreign language translators available, it's a lot more difficult to learn terms in a knowledge domain.

However just learning terms or memorizing dictionary definitions of words does not create the semantic net of relationships on which a rule-based expert system is based. While each rule does represent a chunk of knowledge, there is both strong and weak coupling between rules in the knowledge base. If the firing of one rule is guaranteed to make another rule fire, that is **strong-coupling**, or to put it another way, a strong link in the inference chain that leads from valid facts to a valid conclusion. If one rule firing leads to multiple rules being available for triggering by the inference engine, that is **weak-coupling**. This means the inference chain is not as strong; we are not as sure which path to follow because there is more than one.

The more rules that can potentially fire indicate that the inference chain is not as strong as in strong coupling. However *this is not bad*. If every rule was strongly coupled to another rule, there would be no need for an inference engine or expert system because a procedural programming language is perfect for that. A procedural language is designed to operate sequentially, statement by statement, in the order entered unless there are control decisions such as IF tests. If there is an algorithm that can solve a problem efficaciously, then there is no need for an AI solution. Ideally, an expert system is a balanced mix of strong and weakly coupled rules, just as humans may use deductive, inductive, probabilistic, and other methods to reach a conclusion.

Consider the following **semantic list** of terms in a knowledge domain. The term *semantic list* is used here because no graph links these words together. Instead, one word naturally follows from the previous. (Note that the older you are, the more you'll understand the complete list!) Think how long it took to understand terms like: overdue movie, overdue notices, overdue fines, account delinquent, account closed, debt collection agency, phone calls ("Are you home? We know you're at home because you're not at work"), huge increase in spam email, bad credit, low credit, no credit, "we can finance you", in arrears, taxes due, taxes plus interest on taxes, attorney fees, foreclosure, sheriff's sale, lobbyist, campaign contribution, rider on appropriations bill, apology from sheriff, apology from company, huge cash award for mental pain and suffering, leveraged buyout of video rental company.

Semantic lists are often associated with other **signs**. The field of **semiotics** studies signs and their meanings. An example that is familiar to everyone is learning your "A, B, Cs" as a child. You should still remember the melody that goes along with children singing the "A, B, Cs" because there is a semiotic relationship between the song, i.e., lyrics and music. Semiotic relationships are used all the time by advertisers in famous TV jingles. Some jingle creators are so good at this art that you can't get a jingle out of your head for days; it just keeps repeating over and over in a loop.

When you are interviewing an expert, it's essential to also create a written transcript of the interview. By reading the transcript you can spot the semantic relationships between terms. That is what is important. Knowledge terms are not isolated words; they form semantic clusters that link to form the entire semantic net of knowledge in the expert's mind. The mind is a good example of an associative semiotic memory in which one word, smell, touch, sight, or sound may elicit all kinds of other memories.

The classic tool for eliciting knowledge the standard interview and much work has been done on this (Novak 98). In fact the interview technique is usually augmented by drawing diagrams to make sure the concepts and relationships. Visual metaphors are useful because the developers and experts can both see the relationships and meanings at the same time and agree on what is to be represented and how. Software tools are also available that can represent the entire ontology. Recall from Chapter 1 that an ontology is the complete description of a domain represented in a formal way.

One tool which has been used very successfully **is** Protégé, an ontology editor and knowledge-base editor. This is a very sophisticated tool is available free from Stanford University and well-supported on their website with tutorials on creating your first ontology and many other topics. Protégé is used with TixClips, an integrated development environment for CLIPS. Ontologies are essential when building very large systems having thousands of rules.

Cost

How much will it cost?

This is like asking how much a divorce will cost. It's not the up-front costs that you can see in email spam for do-it-yourself-divorce or do-your-own-brain-surgery kits. It's the costs that come later which keep adding up and up. The cost of building an expert system depends on the people, resources, and time devoted to its construction. Also, just like any other piece of software or hardware, you have to figure in the cost of maintenance. This brings us to the **First Law of Wisdom**: If you've bought a car and are not worried about the cost of gas, it's a good idea to own your own oil well. And the **Zero Law of Wisdom**: It's better to use someone else's car and gas. Maintenance of an expert system is also much more difficult if your expert is no longer available.

Bringing in another expert is not much help since experts are quite competitive. It's a lot easier to build a knowledge-based system where the knowledge comes from people, documents, and other sources that are publicly available. Many companies have done this because they have found these systems are useful screening tools that get rid of 90% of the problems with a few questions. This is a lot cheaper than funding a telephone call center.

Besides the hardware and software required to run an expert systems tool, there may also be considerable cost in training. If your personnel have little or no experience with a tool, it can be costly to train them. Professional training courses for any software often runs to $2500/week per person. Of course this is no longer the disadvantage it used to be. Now companies can make far more money providing for their products in classes and online courses, certification exams, preparing for certification exams, how to be an instructor for certification exams, books, seminars, workshops, and in-home support. Today, putting out a product that is powerful, easy to use, and bug free is a recipe for failure.

6.3 STAGES IN THE DEVELOPMENT OF AN EXPERT SYSTEM

How will the system be developed?
To a large extent, the development of an expert system will depend on the resources provided. However, like any other project, the development will also depend on how the process is organized and managed. A good reference based on an expert system developed for the Federal Highway Administration that used over 300 rules is (Wentworth 94). If you're familiar with a standard project planning tool like Microsoft Project, then stick to that tool. It will make it easier to explain to management what is going on and why the project is a little behind schedule (as you get your resume up-to-date).

Project Management

Standard project management techniques and software tools are expected to provide the following.

Activity Management

- planning
  - define activities
  - specify priority of activities
  - resource requirements
  - milestones
  - durations
  - responsibilities
- scheduling
  - assign starting and ending times
  - resolve conflicts in scheduling tasks of equal priority
- chronicling
  - monitor project performance
- analysis
  - analyze plans, schedules, and chronicled activities

Product Configuration Management

- product management
  - manage the different versions of the product

- change management
  - manage change proposals and impact evaluations
  - assign personnel to make changes
  - install new product versions

Resource Management

- forecast needs for resources
- acquire resources
  - identify expert or knowledge base
  - arrange *your* schedule for convenience of expert
- assign responsibilities for optimum use of resources
- provide critical resources to minimize bottlenecks

In particular, note that in the acquisition of resources, the point is made that you should adjust your schedule to that of the expert and not vice versa. Unless you are paying the expert full-time, there will be other duties and their time is very valuable.

Figure 6.2 shows the ideal high-level view of the activities required to produce a system in terms of the stages that a system goes through.

Figure 6.2 General Stages in the Development of an Expert System

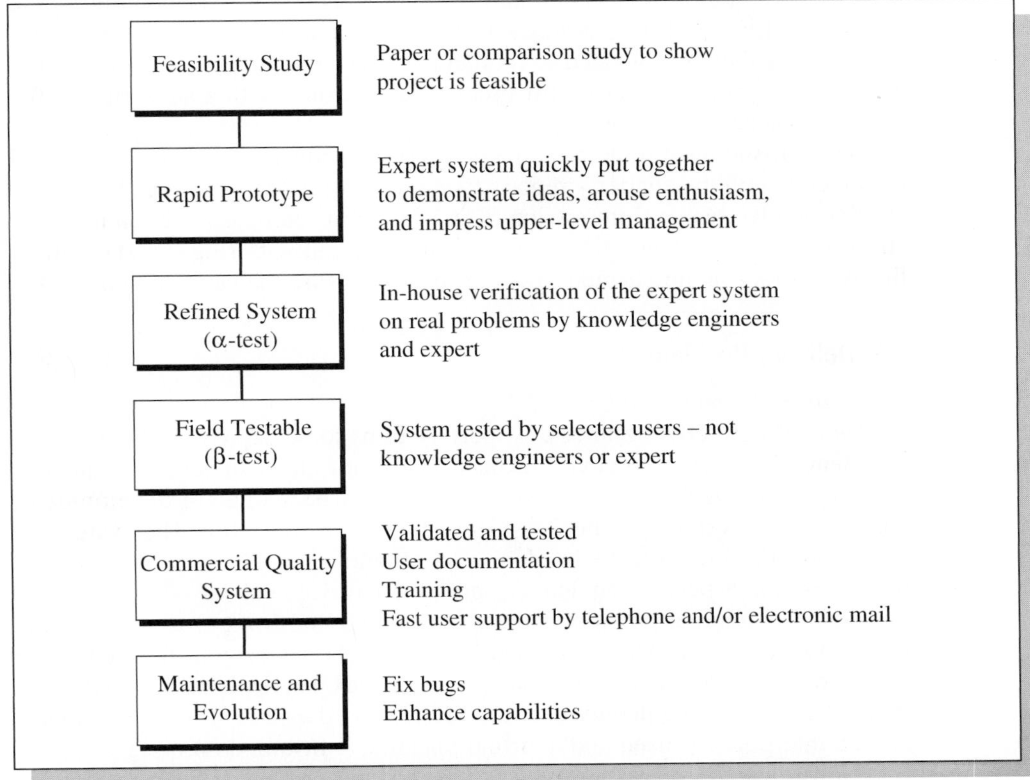
Feasibility Study
Paper or comparison study to show project is feasible
Rapid Prototype
Expert system quickly put together to demonstrate ideas, arouse enthusiasm, and impress upper-level management
Refined System (α-test)
In-house verification of the expert system on real problems by knowledge engineers and expert
Field Testable (β-test)
System tested by selected users – not knowledge engineers or expert
Commercial Quality System
Validated and tested
User documentation
Training
Fast user support by telephone and/or electronic mail
Maintenance and Evolution
Fix bugs
Enhance capabilities

In the ideal view, the product is not deployed for end users until all the bugs are worked out. In the case of military products, this is a really good idea since it's not that easy to recall a nuclear missile once it's been launched.

In contrast to government contracts, things are different in the commercial world since there are no guaranteed contracts that pay money on a regular basis, and cost overruns if the project is late. The commercial paradigm followed today is to spend a lot of money on publicity for the product every quarter until it is released several years later. This has two purposes. First, private developers who want to use your product in their products are willing to pay money for pre release versions even with known bugs. So this provides a continuing source of revenue as the product is being developed instead of your company having to fund all the development costs for several years. A secondary benefit is that you don't need to do much (if any) in-house testing.

Simply make sure that every time the product crashes, it asks the user if it can send an automatic bug report. When the user clicks OK, the message will be automatically sent with diagnostic information as to where the fault occurred. An automated email program at your company will store the bug report in a database. Standard data mining tools will then look for patterns to notify your particular developer team responsible for a particular aspect of the product. Different trigger levels will be set up so that only when the number of bugs has exceeds their particular trigger level will a notification be sent to the teams. Some teams work is more important than others so it is not necessary that the same trigger level be used. Depending on the number and severity of the bugs, resources may then be allocated to fix them for the next quarterly release. A special website should be set up for prerelease versions, with a subscription fee charged to access each new quarterly preview version.

Second, and most important, the quarterly announcements should be timed to coincide with the quarterly reports to public stockholders required by the Securities and Exchange Commission (SEC) for public companies. Even if you're still private and have not yet released an initial public offering (IPO) of stock, this will attract venture capital to your site and increase the value of your IPO.

The Delivery Problem

How will the system be delivered?

Depending on the number of expert systems to be deployed, the **delivery problem** of the developed systems may be a major factor in development. The delivery problem should be considered in the earliest stage of development. Development systems in the 20th Century cost far more than the system on which the product was to be deployed to end users. Now with low cost machines, that aspect of the delivery problem has been solved.

However, another problem is the wide range of hardware that your product is supposed to run on. This accounted for the initial popularity of Java with their "Write once, use anywhere," slogan and guarantees that applets could only play in the "sandbox." The deployment on different hardware is still a problem unless an interpreter is used and a virtual machine is installed on every different type of hardware. That has worked successfully since bytecode interpreters were introduced with Pascal in the 1970s so that it could run on any microcomputer. This same approach was used by Java.

Although CLIPS does not generate bytecodes, it is designed to produce a standard C version of the finished expert system. This can then be compiled using a standard C compiler for the specific hardware platform and the executable deployed for that particular platform. No "CLIPS Virtual Machine" is required. One of the original design goals of CLIPS was to produce an expert system that could easily be deployed on any new hardware that may arise. If this is not adequate, other versions of CLIPS such as Jess have been developed as mentioned in the Preface. Jess is written in Java and although it does not support multiple inheritance, it has all of the advantages of Java in being easily deployed to different hardware.

In many cases the expert system must be integrated with other existing programs. Consideration should be given to the communication and coordination of the expert system input/output with these programs. It may also be desirable to call the expert system as a procedure from a conventional programming language, and the system should support this. CLIPS is designed so that it can be called from a **host language** such as a C++ program, do its function, and then return control to the host program. Such a hybrid system was also one of the main design considerations of CLIPS since the performance of an expert system can decrease quickly depending on how many rules are in the system and how much pattern matching must be done. While the Rete Algorithm is good, an expert system is still not as fast as compiled code.

Although you could use CLIPS to simulate a calculator, spreadsheet, or even a word processor, its performance would be not as good as a program written in a third generation language such as C, C++, or C#. For example, you could create an intelligent data mining tool by calling CLIPS from a standard database such as Oracle or MySql and return recommendations to the database user. In Oracle, the cursor is designed to let other applications use data and then return control to Oracle. CLIPS follows this same principle of being a good host or a good guest. Another alternative is to use/modify the CLIPS source code and integrate it into your application, then compile the result into a new application for deployment.

Maintenance and Evolution

How will the system be maintained and evolve?

The maintenance and evolution of an expert system is more of an open-ended activity than with conventional programs. Because expert systems are not based on algorithms, their performance is dependent on knowledge and expertise. As new knowledge is acquired and old knowledge modified, the performance of the system should ideally remain constant.

However there is a problem in that conventional programs based on algorithms will not have rule conflicts like expert systems. A rule conflict is nothing to be afraid of. In fact that is why inference engines were developed. All a rule conflict means is that more than one rule has matched the pattern on its left-hand-side and can potentially be fired. People do thinking of this type all the time.

For example, consider the **Game Paradox**. If you're sitting on the couch watching a game on TV and have a beer in one hand and a handful of chips in the other hand, which do you put in your mouth? One rule is saying, "If food is available then eat." Another rule is saying, "If beer is available then drink." Since both food and drink are available you have a rule conflict.

Fortunately for those who have read this book, the **Minus One Law of Wisdom** states: If you don't have a specific destination, go everywhere because you never know what you're missing. The obvious solution to the Game Paradox is to dunk the chips in beer and then eat-drink. (After all, where would the world be if the Earl of Sandwich had not been so busy gambling he couldn't spare time to sit down for dinner so he just put some meat in between two slices of bread and became famous?)

The enhancement of an expert system after delivery is also more of a concern in a commercial-quality system. The developers of a commercial system want it to be a financial success. This means listening to what the users want and are willing to pay for in improvements. In the commercial world, it has been proven over and over again that people will continually pay for software upgrades in the desperate hope there will be fewer bugs.

Naturally this will never happen as long as new features are added. In fact it is accepted practice to release products with hundreds or thousands of known bugs. This is actually a way of fighting software piracy since legitimate users will be able to go to the manufacturer's website and download patches, and patches, and patches, until a service pak is available, then more patches until another service pak is available, until finally a company must release its new product or face stiff penalties from the SEC for stock price manipulation. Like all such software, an expert system may never really be finished—it only keeps getting better.

6.4 ERRORS IN DEVELOPMENT STAGES

The potential major errors of expert systems development can be classified by the most likely stages in which they occur, as illustrated in Figure 6.3. These errors include the following:

Expert's Errors. The expert is the **expertise source** of the expert system. If the expert's knowledge is erroneous, the results may be propagated through the entire development process. As mentioned in Chapter 1, a side benefit of building an expert system is the potential detection of erroneous knowledge when the expert's knowledge is made explicit. Just because someone is an expert does not mean they will never make a mistake. It is just that they are far less likely than an ordinary person in their domain of expertise. For example, you could perform brain surgery on someone. However unless you are a trained neurosurgeon, your patient is less likely to survive. On the other hand, we have all heard TV ads proclaiming that if you have been injured by an expert (or anyone with money), there are plenty of lawyers willing to help you receive compensation.

For **mission-critical** projects in which human life and property are at risk, it may be necessary to set up formal procedures to certify an expert's knowledge. One approach that NASA has successfully used for space flight is **Flight**

Figure 6.3 Major Errors in Expert Systems and Some Causes

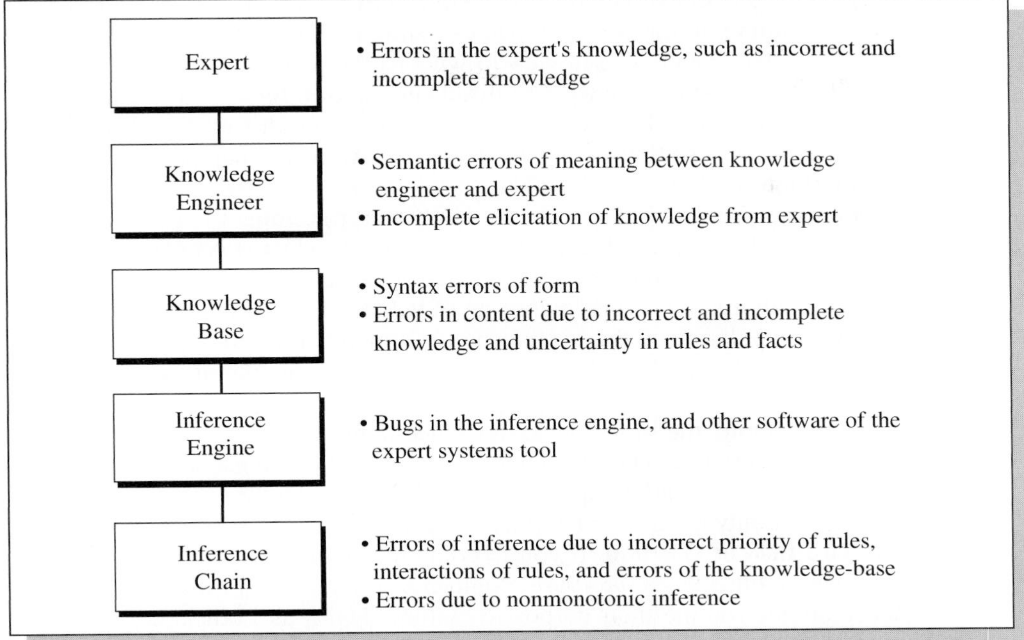

Expert
• Errors in the expert's knowledge, such as incorrect and incomplete knowledge
Knowledge Engineer
• Semantic errors of meaning between knowledge engineer and expert
• Incomplete elicitation of knowledge from expert
Knowledge Base
• Syntax errors of form
• Errors in content due to incorrect and incomplete knowledge and uncertainty in rules and facts
Inference Engine
• Bugs in the inference engine, and other software of the expert systems tool
Inference Chain
• Errors of inference due to incorrect priority of rules, interactions of rules, and errors of the knowledge-base
• Errors due to nonmonotonic inference

Technique Panels, which regularly review problem solutions and the analysis techniques used to develop the solutions. The panels consist of system users, independent domain experts, system developers, and managers to ensure coverage of all areas affecting development.

The advantage of a group panel approach is that the expert's knowledge is placed under close scrutiny at the beginning of the development process, when erroneous knowledge is easier to correct. The longer that erroneous knowledge goes undetected, the more expensive it is to correct. If the expert's knowledge is not initially verified, the ultimate test is the validation of the expert system. The final validation of the expert system demonstrates whether the system satisfies requirements, especially correctness and completeness of solutions.

Panels are used all the time in large companies. Sometimes they are called performance review teams or a more neutral term. During the 1970s and 80s, a variation of the panel review was tried in software development by allowing programmers to review each other's code. Unfortunately it quickly degenerated into a bad management review tool once manager's started equating a programmer's performance in terms of metrics like "correct lines of code per day," or "errors per 100 lines of code." Although management was not supposed to know the details of this peer review process so that programmers would be honest, some peers were not as **peerful** when promotions and raises were at stake. Panels can be a useful tool when there is appropriate oversight but the "peerful" factor should always be considered when it comes to the reliability of information.

Another useful aid is the **focus group**. A focus group is very helpful in attempting to find out what will really sell. Before starting new product development, it's common for large companies to hire people to discuss issues so that they can listen to an unbiased view of whether the product is really wanted and what features it should have. The disadvantage of a focus group approach is primarily the cost and extra time involved. However, this cost is offset by the greater efficiency of the development process. A focus group may save a company millions of dollars if the product is not desired at all by consumers.

Leaving marketing decisions to the system developers is generally not a good idea unless the developers are targeting the product at people of their own **culture**. The term *culture* is used in the technical sense of **corporate culture** or end-user culture; the common core set of values that distinguish a group. This has been popular since the 1980s when company's tried to define what made them separate from others. However with global outsourcing, it's now declining in use.

For example, the most successful video games are produced by programmers who love games and play them all the time. Thus, these developers really know their market and companies that have a game culture hire programmers who are not only good at programming but love games. This illustrates the **Minus Two Law of Wisdom**: If you're going to set out on a journey, it's good if you love to journey. In the 1990s, companies spent a lot of time and money on consultants to define their corporate culture, TQM, and other "trends of the decade." This still continues as companies evolve to meet changing times.

However once a company goes public, it becomes very difficult to maintain a distinct corporate culture because of the need to release good Quarterly Reports for the stock market. A company president who built a computer company from scratch may be replaced by the president of a soft drink company. (NOTE: For those who are wondering about using negative numbering of the Laws of Wisdom; it is valid in this application of Philosophical Engineering.)

Semantic Errors. An error of semantics occurs when the meaning of knowledge is not properly communicated. As a very simple example, suppose an expert says "You can extinguish a fire with water" and the knowledge engineer interprets this as "All fires can be extinguished by water." This is a good reason why all knowledge engineers should learn to cook and put out grease fires. Semantic errors occur if the knowledge engineer misinterprets the expert's answers, or the expert misinterprets the knowledge engineer's question, or both.

One reason misinterpretations occur is because of semiotic associations that trigger misunderstanding. For example, suppose a new worker is hired whose cubicle is next to yours and every day when he arrives for work you notice an unpleasant odor. Eventually you encounter him and are shocked when he says, "It's good to beat you," when he actually said (as recorded on the office security camera), "It's good to meet you." Although people are listening or reading words, our other senses are always at work and if you associate something unpleasant with someone, it spills over into communication.

This is very important when interviewing an expert. A special interview room should be set up with neutral-tone carpeting and walls, fresh air with *no fragrances*, comfortable but not too comfortable furniture, and QUIET is best. The expert will relax and start associating the special interview room with sharing domain knowledge. The worst place to conduct an interview is in your office. The expert will be uncomfortable on someone else's "turf." But it's also bad to do the interviews in the expert's office because of constant phone rings, email chimes, people stopping by "just for a minute," and the ever present reminder of work waiting as soon as the interview is over. Naturally they will want to hurry through the interview as soon as possible to get back to "real work."

Another common error in interviewing occurs because of cognitive illusions (Pohl 04). An illusion is something you know isn't there but it looks real, like a mirage in the desert. People have a difficult time letting go of cognitive illusions especially when coupled with perception. If you look at the classic Muller-Lyer figure, you know that the length of the line is the same for both arrows, yet your eyes claim they are not (it's OK, measure it with a ruler if you doubt this.)

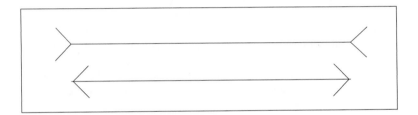

The reason this illusion occurs is that your visual perception system is separate from your thinking, cognitive part. Your brain operated on the Blackboard Architecture model where different activities are carried out by specialized portions of neural clusters. Think of these clusters as hardware agents wired in your brain in contrast to the common software agents. The visual system undoubtedly evolved earlier than the higher cognitive part as an important survival reflex mechanism.

Cognitive illusions occur all the time and are hard to dispel. For example, which is further west: Los Angeles, California or Reno, Nevada? Most people would immediately say Los Angeles since it borders on the Pacific Ocean and Reno is inland in the state of Nevada. This is a good example of commonsense reasoning. Unfortunately it's wrong. Reno is indeed to the west of Los Angeles as you can check on a globe or on the Web. As another example, which is further north: Rome or New York? We've all seen movies of sunny Italy and snow in New York so it's commonsense that New York is further north. Again that's not the case. New York is more south of Rome. It is a cognitive illusion that even knowing this, you find it hard to believe, like the arrow illusion before.

Such cognitive illusions are very tricky to spot, especially when interviewing an expert. Just because someone is an expert in one domain does not mean they are expert in others. As humans, they are as susceptible to cognitive illusions as anyone else. The danger is that you may assume that everything they say is correct outside of their domain of expertise. (Of course, this is true of your boss and you should tell them so every day, especially paydays.)

Syntax Errors. These are simple errors that occur when the incorrect form of a rule or fact is entered. The expert systems tools should flag these errors and issue an appropriate message. Other errors that occur in the knowledge-base building phase are due to knowledge source errors that were not detected in the previous stages.

Inference Engine Errors. Just as with any other piece of software, the inference engine may have bugs. By the time that an expert systems tool is released for general use, all of the common bugs should be fixed. However, there may be bugs that show up only in rare circumstances, such as having 159 rules on the agenda on April 1. Some bugs may be very subtle and show up only in certain pattern-matching operations.

In general, inference engine bugs may show up in pattern matching, conflict resolution, and execution of the actions. These bugs may be very difficult to detect if they are not consistent. If the expert systems tool is used for mission-critical applications, you should determine how the tool was validated. In general, a test suite should be run for every new version of the expert systems tool, as is done with CLIPS. The testing is automated so it delivers unbiased results; not hurried because management insists that the product be launched because of external pressures.

The simplest method of checking for tool errors is the classic method of asking other users and the tool vendor. The tool vendor should be willing to supply a list of customers, bug reports, and fixes, and how long the tool has been in use. A user's group is an excellent source of information.

Inference Chain Errors. These errors may be caused by erroneous knowledge, semantic errors, inference engine bugs, incorrect specification of rule priorities, and unplanned interactions between rules. More complex inference chain errors are due to uncertainty of rules and evidence, the propagation of uncertainty in the inference chain, and nonmonoticity where facts shown invalid should be retracted and all facts they generated be retracted. It's similar to your hearing that a meeting has been canceled. You don't go anyway and wait in an empty room but rather make other plans (like taking a nap since no one else is around.)

The choice of a method for dealing with uncertainty does not automatically resolve all issues dealing with uncertainty. For example, before choosing simple Bayesian inference, you should check to see if the assumption of conditional independence is warranted.

Limits of Ignorance Errors. A problem that is common to all development stages is specifying the limits of ignorance of the system. As mentioned in Chapter 1, human experts (hopefully) know the extent of their knowledge and their performance degrades (hopefully) gracefully at the boundaries of their ignorance. Human experts should be honest enough to admit more uncertainty in their conclusions near the boundaries. However, unless an expert system is specifically programmed to handle uncertainty, it may continue to supply answers even if the inference chain and evidence are very **brittle** and unreliable. The worse thing is that the human may believe the conclusions are reliable.

6.5 SOFTWARE ENGINEERING AND EXPERT SYSTEMS

In the previous sections we have discussed the general considerations in using the expert systems paradigm. Now let's examine the stages of expert systems development from the more technical perspective of the knowledge engineer who actually builds the system.

Since expert systems have moved out of the research stage, there is a real need to deliver quality software up to the standards of conventional software. The accepted methodology for developing quality software for commercial, industrial, and governmental standards is software engineering.

It is important to follow good standards in the development of a product or the product will probably not be of good quality. Expert systems are products just as any other software product such as a word processor, payroll program, or computer game.

However, there is a significant difference of **mission** between expert systems and typical consumer products such as word processors and video games. The term *mission* refers to the overall purpose of a project or a technology. Expert systems technology generally has a serious mission of supplying expertise in high-performance and possibly hazardous situations where human life and property are at stake. These are the mission-critical applications mentioned in the previous section. Knowledge-based systems do not have to meet such high standards.

Mission-critical applications are very different from the more relaxed mission of word processors and video games, which are developed to increase efficiency and provide recreation. Human life is not jeopardized by a bug in a word processor or a video game (or at least it shouldn't).

Expert systems are high-performance systems that must be of high quality or they will be prone to bugs. Software engineering provides methodologies for building quality software, as illustrated in Figure 6.4.

Quality is a difficult term to describe in a general sense because it means different things to different people. One way of defining **quality** is as the required or desirable attributes of an object determined on some scale. The term *object* is used here to mean any software or hardware, such as a software product. The attributes and their values are called **metrics** because they are used as measures of an object. For example, the measured reliability of a disk drive is a metric of its quality. One measure of this attribute is the **mean time between failures** (MTBF) of the drive. A reliable drive might have an MTBF of 50,000 hours of use between crashes, while a cheap drive might have a MTBF of 10,000 hours. In the 20th century, people might use their computers a few hours at work or at home. Now it's customary to leave the computer on 24x7x52 and the hours do

Figure 6.4 The Software Engineering Methodology

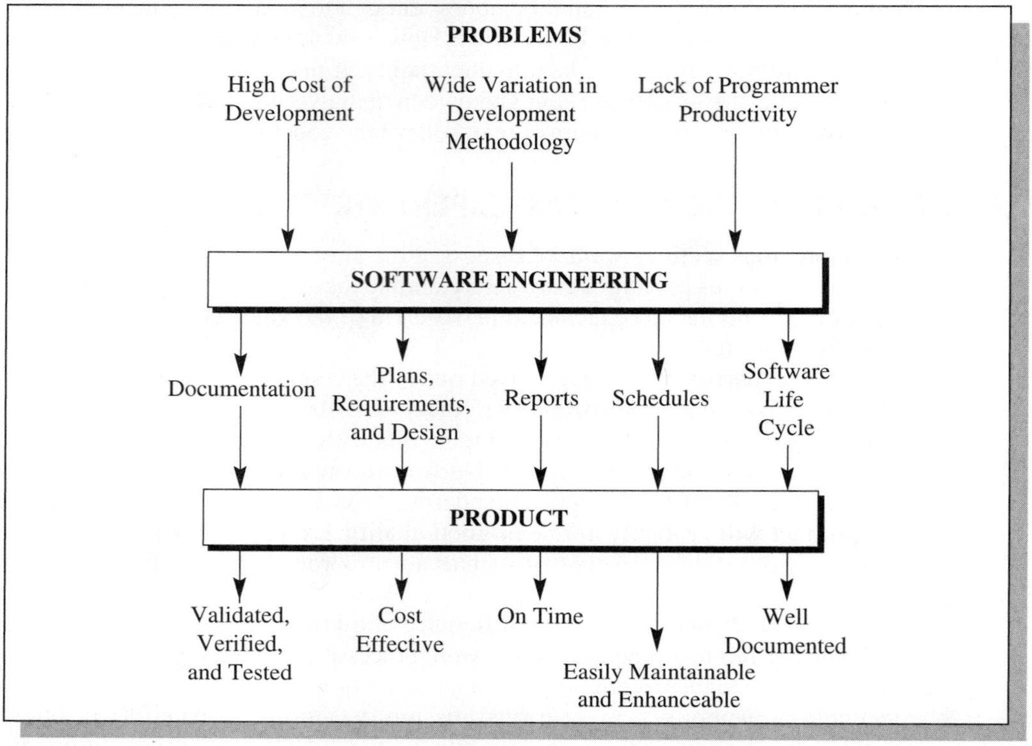

add up. Of course you can set your operating system to power down the drive just like the monitor screen. However turning these on and off a dozen times a day may introduce new risks.

What's important is not just the time, but the error rate in writing. Suppose a disk drive has a quoted error of one bit in every billion writes. In the 1990s when common disk drives were 20 Megabytes, that meant you could fill your drive 50 times over without a single write error. Now with drives in the 200 Gigabyte range, one write error in a billion means there may be 200 errors on your hard drive, assuming the same error rate.

If the error occurs in writing a compressed image such as a .jpg it will probably not be noticed. But if the error occurs in a line of code, a single bit error could turn a program statement like X=A to X=B, with potentially very bad results. Modern drives have a built-in sensor that continuously monitors disk health through a feature called Self-Monitoring, Analysis, and Reporting Technology (SMART). The **SMART** technology can be accessed by programs such as Norton System Utilities when the Disk Doctor Utility is run. This can give advance warning of most potential disk hardware failures. However you must heed the warning by backing up and replacing the drive before data is lost.

SMART is a tool that predicts your disk drive heath but cannot cure it if the problem is with deteriorating magnetic media, since nothing is perfect. The smaller a microscopic imperfection in the magnetic coating of the hard disk surface created during manufacturing or operation, the greater is the possibility of a write error, and thus an error in the software. As more data is read and written onto the magnetic surface of a hard disk, and the longer the drive runs, parts wear down. Newer drives may run down faster since they spin at higher speeds and the magnetic coating must be even more uniform and without imperfections.

In the 1990s the standard was 3600 RPM, then 5400 RPM, and now 7,200 RPM with premium drives available at 10,000 RPM. As an analogy, assume the tire of your car is 2 ft. in diameter and so is about 6 feet in circumference. If your tire turned 3,600 RPM, you'd be going about 250 mph, while a 10,000 RPM tire would make you go 700 MPH, thus breaking the sound barrier if your disk rotated as fast as a car tire! It used to be that the weakest spot in a computer system was the moving components because of the friction and heat they generate.

However a new point of failure has arisen with 64-bit processors available and generating a lot more heat than the old 32-bit ones. This is such a critical problem that new motherboards come with temperature sensors, a heat-sink fan right on top of the microprocessor, a case with 6 fans for cooling, and software to shut down the system if the temperature rises too high. It's also a good idea to physically locate the disk drive and memory as far away from the CPU as possible.

Table 6.1 gives a checklist of some metrics that may be used in assessing the quality of an expert system. These metrics should be taken only as a guide since a specific expert system may have more or fewer of these. However, the important concept is to have a required list of metrics that can be used in describing quality.

Table 6.1 Some Software Quality Metrics for Expert Systems

Software Metrics
Correct output given correct input
Complete output given correct input
Consistent output given the same input again
Reliable so that it does not crash (often) due to bugs
Usable for people and preferably user-friendly
Maintainable
Extensible
Validated to prove it satisfies the user's needs and requests
Tested to prove correctness and completeness
Cost effective
Reusable code for other applications
Portable to other hardware/software environments
Interfaceable with other software
Understandable code
Accurate
Precise
Graceful degradation at the boundaries of knowledge
Embedded capability with other languages
Validated knowledge base
Explanation facility

A list of metrics allows you to more easily prioritize metrics since many may be in conflict with others. For example, increasing the testing of an expert system to assure its validation will increase the cost. Deciding when testing ends is generally a complex decision involving the factors of schedules, cost, and requirements. Ideally, all three of these requirements should be satisfied. In practice, some may be judged more important than others and the constraints of satisfying all factors will be weakened.

6.6 THE EXPERT SYSTEM LIFE CYCLE

One of the key concepts of software engineering is the **life cycle**. The software life cycle is the period of time that starts with the initial concept of the software and ends with its retirement from use. Rather than thinking of development and maintenance separately, the life cycle concept provides a continuity that connects all stages. Planning for maintenance and evolution early in the life cycle reduces the cost of these stages later.

Maintenance Costs

For successful conventional software that keeps getting modified and enhanced every few years, maintenance can easily be ten times the initial development costs when the product was first released and grows with every new version. Even though this may seem a lot, as mentioned earlier there's a lot of money to be made in maintenance. However the **Minus Three Law of Wisdom** states: If you don't love to journey, then love what you've got. So if you keep coming out with bug fixes of your product, don't change the name to something entirely new. Stick with a variation of the old name, but don't say "Doors BugFix No.10," say "Doors 2010."

Expert systems tend to be more knowledge based these days than based on human expertise. There are significant exceptions such as intelligent trainers for special personnel such as doctors or pilots. Expert systems are used very successfully as training systems to reduce the amount of time experts spend teaching introductory material. However if enough time and resources are devoted to the expert system, it can teach a student to be ready for the real thing.

As technology changes, there is less demand to preserve a retiring person's knowledge. Expert systems require more maintenance because they are based on much knowledge that is heuristic and experiential. Expert systems that do a lot of inference under uncertainty are even more susceptible to high maintenance and evolution costs. With the availability of automatic tools for building and importing ontologies into expert systems, it is becoming easier to maintain the systems. However the systems also tend to become larger, just like all software, so it's always a running battle.

Waterfall Model

A number of different life cycle models have been developed for conventional software. The classic **waterfall model** was the original life cycle model and is illustrated in Figure 6.5.

Figure 6.5 The Waterfall Model of the Software Life Cycle

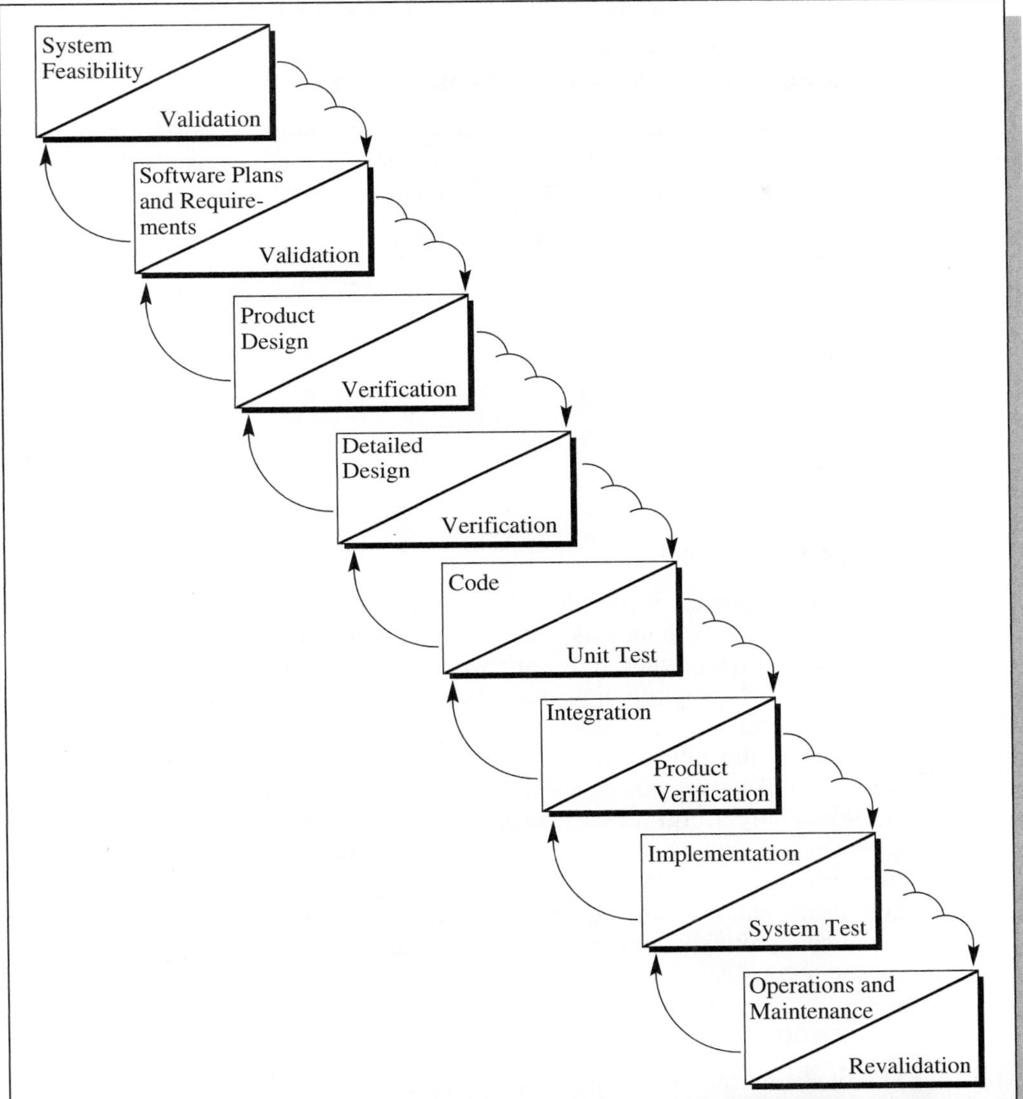

This model is familiar to programmers of conventional software. In the waterfall model each stage ends with a verification and validation (V & V) activity to minimize any problems in that stage. Also, notice that the arrows go back and forth only one stage at a time. This represents the iterative development between two adjacent stages in order to minimize the cost compared to the much higher cost of iterating development over several stages. The cost of going back stages is not a simple linear function but grows exponentially harder.

Another term for life cycle is **process model** because it is concerned with the following two fundamental issues of software development:

(1) What should be done next?
(2) How long should the next stage be performed?

The process model is actually a **metamethodology** because it determines the order and duration that the common software methods are applied. The common software development methods (or methodologies):

specific methods to accomplish a stage such as

- planning
- requirements
- knowledge acquisition
- testing

representation of stage products

- documentation
- code
- diagrams

Code-and-Fix Model

A number of process models have been used for software development. The earliest "model" is the infamous **code-and-fix model**, in which some code is written and then fixed when it doesn't work right. This is usually the method of choice for new programming students both in conventional programming and expert systems.

By 1970 the deficiencies in the code-and-fix approach were so obvious that the waterfall model was developed to provide a systematic methodology that was especially useful for large projects. However, there were difficulties with the waterfall model because it assumed that all the information necessary for a stage was known. In practice, it was often not possible to write the complete requirements until a prototype had been built. This led to the **do-it-twice** concept, in which a prototype was built, the requirements determined, and then the final system was built.

Incremental Model

The **incremental waterfall model** is a refinement of the waterfall and of the standard top-down approach. The basic idea of incremental development is to develop software in increments of functional capability. The incremental model has been used very successfully in large conventional software projects. The incremental model is also useful for expert systems development, in which the addition of rules increases the capabilities of the system from assistant to colleague and finally expert level. Thus in an expert system the **major increments** are from assistant, to colleague, and from colleague to expert.

The **minor increments** correspond to increments of expertise within each level that offer some significant increase. A **microincrement** is the change in expertise by adding or refining an individual rule.

Figure 6.6 A Spiral Model of Expert System Development

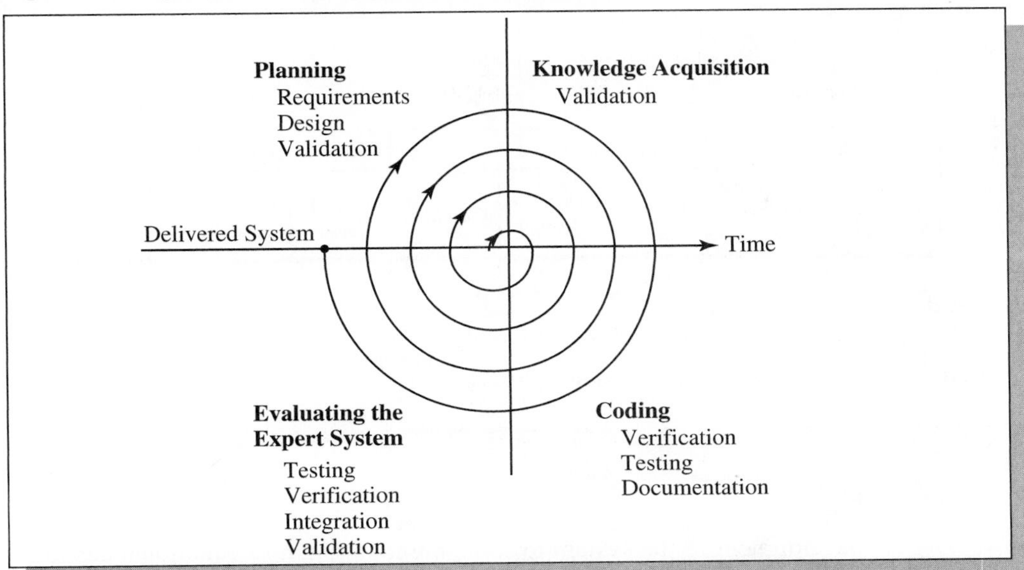

The primary advantage of the incremental model is that the increases in functional capability are easier to test, verify, and validate than the products of individual stages in the waterfall model. Each functional increment can be tested, verified, and validated immediately with the expert rather than waiting to do the entire validation at the end. This decreases the cost of incorporating corrections in the system. In essence, the incremental model is similar to a continuous rapid prototype that extends over the entire development. Rather than just a rapid prototype of the initial stages to determine requirements in the do-it-twice approach, the evolving prototype *is* the system.

Spiral Model

One way of visualizing the incremental model is an adaptation of the Barry Boem's standard **spiral model** for software engineering, as shown in Figure 6.6. Each circuit of the spiral adds some functional capability to the system. The ending point label "Delivered System" is actually not the end of the spiral. Instead, a new spiral begins with maintenance and evolution of the system. The spiral can be further refined to specify more precisely the general stages of Knowledge Acquisition, Coding, Evaluation, and Planning.

6.7 A DETAILED LIFE CYCLE MODEL

A life cycle model that has been successfully used in a number of expert systems projects is the **Linear Model,** illustrated in Figure 6.7. This life cycle consists of a number of stages from Planning to System Evaluation and describes

Figure 6.7 The Linear Model of Expert System Development Life Cycle

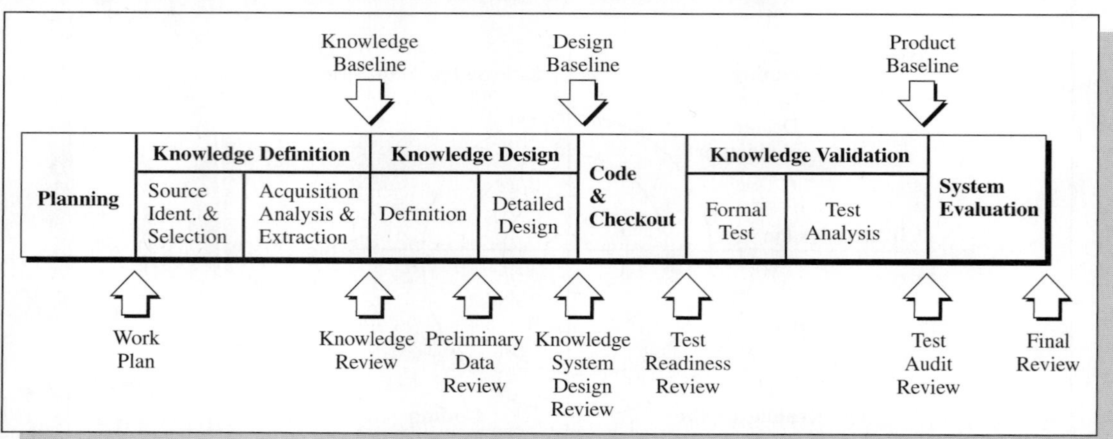

the development of the system to some point at which its functional capabilities will be evaluated. After this, the life cycle repeats this same sequence from Planning to System Evaluation until the system is delivered for routine use. The life cycle is then used for subsequent maintenance and evolution of the system. Although not explicitly shown, verification and validation proceed in parallel with the stages. Rather than just fixing up some bugs, it is important to follow through with the same sequence of stages to maintain the quality of the expert system. Skipping stages, even to fix one little bug, impairs the entire quality.

This life cycle shown may be considered one circuit of the spiral model. Each stage consists of **tasks**. Not all tasks may be necessary for a stage, especially once the system goes into maintenance and evolution. Instead, the tasks are meant to serve as a composite of all tasks for the entire life cycle, from initial concept to software retirement. The tasks will also depend on the exact type of application being built and so should be considered only as a guide, rather than absolute requirements that must be performed for each stage to be completed.

This life cycle model will be discussed in detail to illustrate the many factors that should be considered for a large quality expert system. For small research-type prototypes that are not intended for general use, not all tasks or even stages are necessary. However, it is amazing how much software that is developed for personal or research use gets released to associates and then into general use.

Planning

The purpose of the Planning Stage is to produce a formal **work plan** for the expert system development. The work plan is a set of documents that will be used to guide and evaluate development. Table 6.2 illustrates the tasks in this stage.

Table 6.2 Planning Stage Tasks

Task	Objective
Feasibility assessment	Determine if it is worthwhile to build the system and if so, whether expert systems technology should be used.
Resource management	Assess resources of people, time, money, software, and hardware required. Acquire and manage the required resources.
Task phasing	Specify the tasks and their order in the stages.
Schedules	Specify the starting and delivery dates of tasks in the stages.
Preliminary functional layout	Define what the system should accomplish by specifying the high-level functions of the system. This task specifies the purpose of the system.
High-level requirements	Describe in high-level terms how the functions of the system will be accomplished.

The feasibility assessment is the most important task in the life cycle. The assessment must answer the questions of whether the project is worthwhile and the related question of whether an expert system is the appropriate paradigm. The answers to these two questions determine if the project should proceed using an expert systems approach. Many factors are involved in feasibility assessment. As discussed in Section 6.1, these factors include selection of an appropriate expert systems domain, cost, payoff, and others.

Knowledge Definition

The object of the **knowledge definition stage** is to define the knowledge requirements of the expert system. The Knowledge Definition Stage consists of two main tasks, as follows:

- Knowledge source identification and selection
- Knowledge acquisition, analysis, and extraction

Each of these major tasks is composed of other tasks. Table 6.3 describes the tasks involved in source identification and selection.

Table 6.3 Knowledge Source Identification and Selection Tasks

Task	Objective
Source identification	Who and what are the knowledge sources, without regard to availability.
Source importance	Prioritized list of knowledge sources in order of importance to development.
Source availability	List of knowledge sources ranked in order of availability. The Web, books and other documents are generally much more available than human experts.
Source selection	Select the knowledge sources based on importance and availability.

Acquisition, analysis, and extraction tasks are described in Table 6.4.

Table 6.4 Knowledge Acquisition, Analysis, and Extraction Tasks

Task	Objective
Acquisition strategy	Specify how knowledge will be acquired by methods for interviewing experts, reading documents, rule induction, repertory grids, and so forth.
Knowledge element identification	Pick out the specific knowledge from sources that will be useful in this iteration of the life cycle.
Knowledge classification system	Classify and organize the knowledge to aid in knowledge verification and understanding by developers. Use hierarchical groups whenever possible.
Detailed functional layout	Specify the functional capabilities of the system in detail. This level is at a more technical level while the preliminary functional layout was at a managerial level.
Preliminary control flow	Describe general phases that the expert system will execute. Phases correspond to logical groups of rules that are activated/deactivated in groups to control execution flow.
Preliminary user's manual	Describes system from user's viewpoint. An often ignored, but essential part of the system. It is absolutely important to involve users as soon as possible for feedback. If they don't use the system, it's worthless.
Requirements specifications	Define exactly what the system is supposed to do. The expert system will be validated using these requirements.
Knowledge baseline	Baseline knowledge for the system. Any changes must now be done by a formal change request. The high-level knowledge is now adequate for the next stage of knowledge design.

The main objective of the knowledge acquisition task, the knowledge analysis task, and the knowledge extraction task is to produce and verify the knowledge required by the system. By the time that the knowledge is baselined, it should be correct and suitable for the next stage of knowledge design. In addition to the customary method of interviewing experts, many software tools may be used to perform automated knowledge acquisition. Often these tools are provided by the tool vendor. Knowledge acquisition by a knowledge engineer trying to elicit knowledge from an expert requires a great deal of skill and is discussed further in (Grzymala-Busse 91).

Knowledge Design

The objective of the **knowledge design stage** is to produce the detailed design for an expert system. There are two main tasks that comprise this stage:

- Knowledge definition
- Detailed design

Table 6.5 describes the tasks associated with knowledge definition.

Table 6.5 Knowledge Definition Tasks

Task	Objective
Knowledge representation	Specify how knowledge will be represented, such as rules, frames, or logic. Dependent upon what the expert systems tool will support.
Detailed control structure	Specify three general control structures: (1) if the system is embedded in procedural code, how it will be called; (2) control of related groups of rules within an executing system; (3) metalevel control structures for rules.
Internal fact structure	Specify the internal structure of facts in a consistent manner to aid in understanding and good style.
Preliminary user interface	Specify a preliminary user interface. Get feedback from users about the interface.
Initial test plan	Specify how code will be tested. Define test data, test drivers, and how test results will be analyzed.

The internal fact structures described in Table 6.5 are discussed in much more detail in the chapters on CLIPS. The basic idea of specifying fact structures is to adapt good style. For example, a fact such as "10" is not very meaningful by itself. What does the "10" represent? If additional information is included with the fact such as "price 10" or, better still, "gold price 10," then the gold price is meaningful. Notice that this form of the fact is in conventional object-attribute-value form and so is convenient for people to read and understand. CLIPS supports this through the deftemplate construct for rules, and also objects.

In some expert systems languages the fields may have **strong typing** so that only certain values are allowed. If a rule tries to specify a value that is not allowed, the inference engine flags this as an error. The **detailed design stage** of knowledge is shown in Table 6.6.

The product of the detailed design stage is the baselined design document from which coding can proceed. The baselined design document undergoes a knowledge system design review as a final check before coding begins.

Table 6.6 Detailed Design of Knowledge Tasks

Task	Objective
Design structure	Specify how knowledge is logically organized in the knowledge base and what is in the knowledge base.
Implementation strategy	Specify how the system is to be implemented.
Detailed user interface	Specify the detailed user interface after receiving user feedback from the preliminary user interface design.
Design specifications and report	Document the design.
Detailed test plan	Specify exactly how the code will be tested and verified.

Code and Checkout

Table 6.7 describes the **code and checkout stage,** which begins the actual code implementation.

Table 6.7 Code and Checkout Tasks

Task	Objective
Coding	Implement coding.
Tests	Test code using test data, test drivers, and test analysis procedures.
Source listings	Produce commented, documented source code.
User manual	Produce working user's manual so experts and users can provide feedback on system.
Installation/operations guide	Document installation/operation of system for users.
System description document	Document overall expert system functionality, limitations, and problems.

This stage terminates with the **test readiness review,** which determines if the expert system is ready for the next stage of knowledge verification.

Knowledge Verification

The **knowledge verification stage** has the objective of determining the correctness, completeness, and consistency of the system. This stage is divided into two main tasks:

- Formal tests
- Test analysis

Table 6.8 describes the **formal test task** of the knowledge verification stage.

Table 6.8 Formal Test Tasks of the Knowledge Verification Stage

Task	Objective
Test procedures	Implement formal test procedures.
Test reports	Document test results.

The **test analysis tasks** are shown in Table 6.9. The test analysis looks for the following major problems:

- incorrect answers
- incomplete answers
- inconsistent answers

and determines if the problem lies in rules, inference chains, uncertainty, or some combination of these three factors. If the problem cannot be pinned down to the expert system, then it is necessary to analyze the expert systems tool software for bugs, which should only be done as a last resort. Unlike other tools, CLIPS does provide all the source code and manuals so that you can do this.

Table 6.9 Test Analysis Tasks

Task	Objective
Results evaluations	Analyze test results.
Recommendations	Document recommendations and conclusions of tests.

System Evaluation

As described in Table 6.10, the final stage in the development life cycle is the **system evaluation stage**. The purpose of this stage is to summarize what has been learned with recommendations for improvements and corrections.

Table 6.10 System Evaluation Stage Tasks

Task	Objective
Results evaluation	Summarize the results of testing and verification.
Recommendations	Recommend any changes to the system.
Validation	Validate that the system is correct with respect to user needs and requirements.
Interim or final report	If the system is complete, then issue final report. If not, issue an interim report. Ask for more money.

Since an expert system is usually built up in iterations, the report from the System Evaluation Stage will usually be an interim report describing the increased functionality of the system as new knowledge is added. However, the new system capability must be verified by itself and also as part of the previous knowledge in the system. That is, the system verification must also be performed in conjunction with all the system knowledge, not just the new knowledge. Ideally the expert system should also be validated each time at this stage rather than waiting for the final iteration. However this runs the risk of irritating the expert.

6.8 SUMMARY

In this chapter we discussed a software engineering approach to the construction of expert systems. Principles were given about conducting a good interview with an expert. Now that expert systems technology are widely used for solving real-world problems, expert systems *must* be quality products, especially since so many are used in defense systems and by credit bureaus.

A number of factors must be considered in the design of an expert system such as problem selection, cost, and payoff. Both managerial and technical aspects have to be considered in building a successful system (Gonzalez 93).

One very useful concept of software engineering is the expert system life cycle. The life cycle views software development as a series of stages from initial concept to retirement of the software. However with the modern business paradigm of making more money off bug fixes/enhancements, it appears more profitable to never retire software. By consistently following a life cycle, it is possible to build quality software. Several different life cycle models were discussed for expert systems and one was shown in detail.

Efforts to make rules machine readable are underway in RuleXML and the Rule Markup Initiative, RuleML (http://www.ruleml.org).

PROBLEMS

6.1 Consider a simple knowledge-based system for diagnosing problems in an automobile. Describe this proposed system for each stage of the linear model. (It is not necessary to do this in terms of each task.) Assume there are many people working on the project and consider the coordination of their efforts. Explain any assumptions you make.

6.2 Write a report on a commercial automated tool for KM. Download a trial version by either searching in Appendix G or on the web. List the major problems it can detect and its cost.

6.3 Explain any changes or differences in the linear model for a large project development with many developers versus a small project with only one person.

BIBLIOGRAPHY

(Becerra-Fernandez 04). Irma Becerra-Fernandez, Avelino Gonzalez, and Rajiv Sabherwal, *Knowledge Management,* Prentice-Hall, 2003.

(Begley 03). Good explanation of developing knowledge acquisition in expert systems and summaries of decision making systems in convenient tables, "Adding Intelligence to Medical Devices An overview of decision support and expert system technology in the medical device industry." Ralph J. Begley, Mark Riege, John Rosenblum, and Daniel Tseng: (http://www.devicelink.com/mddi/archive/00/03/014.html).

(Chandler 01). Daniel Chandler, *Semiotics: The Basics*, Rutledge Press, 2001. Note, a shorter online version is at: (http://www.aber.ac.uk/media/Documents/S4B/).

(Conway 02). Susan Conway and Char Sligar, *Unlocking Knowledge Assets: Solutions from Microsoft*, Microsoft Press, 2002.

(Gonzalez 93). Avelino J. Gonzalez and Douglas D. Dankel, *The Engineering of Knowledge-based Systems: Theory and Practice*, Prentice-Hall, 1993. Excellent supplement to this book. Similar coverage with more details, and even includes an older version DOS version of CLIPS discussed in an appendix. It is recommended you use the latest version of CLIPS with this book. Lots of good problems from easy to hard.

(Grzymala-Busse 91). Jerzy W. Grzymala-Busse, *Managing Uncertainty in Expert Systems*, Kluwer Academic Publishers, 1991.

(Malhotra 01). Y. Malhotra, "Expert Systems for Knowledge Management: crossing the chasm between information processing and sense making," *Expert Systems with Applications* journal, (20) 2002 pp. 7–16, available online at: (http://www.brint.org/expertsystems.pdf).

(Pohl 04). Rudiger Pohl, Cognitive Illusions: A Handbook On Fallacies And Biases In Thinking, Judgement And Memory, pub. by Taylor & Francis, 2004.

(Tiwana 03). Book and CDROM with many case studies, lots of software resources, and many links. Amrit Tiwana, *Knowledge Management Toolkit : Orchestrating IT, Strategy, and Knowledge Platforms*, 2nd Edition, Prentice-Hall, 2003.

(Wentworth 94). Good online book based on Federal Highway Administration experience with "PAMEX: Expert System for Maintenance Management of Flexible Pavements," with 327 rules, by James A. Wentworth, Rodger Knaus, and Hamid Aougab, *Verification, Validation and Evaluation of Expert Systems*, (http://www.tfhrc.gov/advanc/vve/cover.htm).

CHAPTER 7
Introduction to CLIPS

7.1 INTRODUCTION

This chapter begins the introduction of the practical concepts necessary to build an expert system. Chapters 1 through 6 looked at the background, history, definitions, terminology, concepts, tools, and applications of expert systems. In short, they provided an understanding of what expert systems are and what they can do. This theoretical framework of concepts and algorithms is essential in building expert systems. However, there are many practical aspects to building expert systems that must be learned by doing. Building an expert system is much like writing a program in a procedural language. Knowing how an algorithm works is not the same as being able to write a procedural program to perform that algorithm. Similarly, capturing an expert's knowledge is not the same as building an expert system. For this reason, practical experience in using an expert system tool is invaluable in learning about expert systems.

The expert system language that will be used to demonstrate various concepts in the rest of this book is CLIPS. Three types of programming paradigms are supported by CLIPS: rule-based, object-oriented, and procedural. Chapters 7, 8, and 9 cover rule-based programming. Chapter 10 covers procedural programming. Chapter 11 covers object-oriented programming. Finally, Chapter 12 discusses several example problems that demonstrate the capabilities covered in the preceding chapters. Chapters 7 through 12 focus on this author's opinion of the most useful CLIPS features and the context in which they should be used. Although these chapters and associated appendices may be of use as a reference for the CLIPS programming language, they are primarily intended to teach you how to write a CLIPS program. They do not exhaustively document every detail of every feature provided by CLIPS. The *CLIPS Basic Programming Guide*, included in electronic format on the CD-ROM accompanying this book, is intended as the definitive reference for the CLIPS programming language. Befitting the purpose of a reference manual, it is most useful once you already know how to write a CLIPS program and need specific information on a particular feature.

This chapter describes the basic components of a rule-based expert system (as discussed in Chapter 1) that are found within CLIPS. These basic components are:

1. **fact list**: contains the data on which inferences are derived
2. **knowledge base**: contains all the rules
3. **inference engine**: controls overall execution

These three components of CLIPS will provide the focus of this chapter. The first component, facts, will be covered in detail. Adding, removing, modifying, duplicating, displaying, and tracing facts will be discussed, followed by an explanation of how the rules of a CLIPS program interact with facts to make a program execute. The use of variables and wildcards in pattern matching will be covered. Finally, the "blocks world" program will be used to demonstrate the interaction of multiple rules using the features introduced in this chapter.

7.2 CLIPS

CLIPS is a multiparadigm programming language that provides support for rule-based, object-oriented, and procedural programming. The inferencing and representation capabilities provided by the rule-based programming language of CLIPS are similar to, but more powerful than, those of OPS5. Syntactically, CLIPS rules very closely resemble rules in languages such as Eclipse, CLIPS/R2, and Jess. CLIPS supports only forward-chaining rules—it does not support backward chaining.

The object-oriented programming capabilities in CLIPS, collectively referred to as the CLIPS Object-Oriented Language (COOL), are a hybrid combination of features found in other object-oriented languages such as the Common Lisp Object System (CLOS) and SmallTalk, in addition to a number of new ideas. The procedural programming language provided by CLIPS has features similar to languages such as C, Ada, and Pascal and is syntactically similar to LISP.

CLIPS, an acronym for C Language Integrated Production System, was designed using the C programming language at NASA/Johnson Space Center with the specific purpose of providing high portability, low cost, and easy integration with external systems. Portions of the CLIPS acronym, however, can be misleading. Originally, CLIPS provided support only for rule-based programming (hence "Production System"). Version 5.0 of CLIPS introduced procedural and object-oriented programming support. The "C Language" portion of the acronym is also misleading since there is one version of CLIPS developed entirely in Ada. The CD-ROM included with this book contains CLIPS 6.2 executables for DOS, Windows 2000/XP, and MacOS, documentation in electronic format, and the C source code for CLIPS.

Because of its portability, CLIPS has been installed on a variety of computers ranging from PCs to CRAY supercomputers. The majority of examples shown in this and the following chapters should work on any computer on which CLIPS has been installed. It is recommended that CLIPS users have some knowledge of the operating system of the computer on which CLIPS is being used. For example, the method for specifying files tends to vary from one operating system to another. When commands may vary depending on the machine or the operating system, this will be noted.

7.3 NOTATION

This chapter and those following will use the same notation for describing the syntax of various commands and constructs that are introduced. This notation consists of three different types of text to be entered.

The first type of notation is for symbols and characters that are to be entered exactly as shown; this includes anything that is not enclosed by the character pairs <>, [ ], or { }. For example, consider the following syntax description:

```
(example)
```

This syntax description means that *(example)* should be entered as shown. To be exact, the character "(" should be entered first, followed by the character "e," then "x," "a," "m," "p," "l," "e," and finally the character ")."

Square brackets, [ ], indicate that the contents of the brackets are optional. For example, the syntax description:

```
(example [1])
```

indicates that the 1 found within the brackets is optional. So the following entry would be consistent with the above syntax:

```
(example)
```

as would this entry:

```
(example 1)
```

The less than and greater than characters together, <>, indicate that a replacement is to be made with a value of the type specified by the contents found within the < >. For example, the following within a syntax description:

```
<integer>
```

indicates that a substitution should be made with an actual integer value. Following the previous examples, the syntax description:

```
(example <integer>)
```

could be replaced with:

```
(example 1)
```

or:

```
(example 5)
```

or:

```
(example -20)
```

or many more entries that contained the characters "(example ," followed by an integer, followed by the character ")." It is important to note that spaces shown in the syntax description should also be included in the entry.

Another notation is indicated with an asterisk, "*," following a description. This indicates that the description can be replaced with *zero* or more occurrences of the value specified. Spaces should be placed after each occurrence of a value. For example, the syntax description:

```
<integer>*
```

could be replaced with:

```
1
```

or:

```
1 2
```

or:

```
1 2 3
```

or with any number of integers, or with nothing at all.

A description followed by a plus sign, "+," indicates that *one* or more of the values specified by the description should by used in place of the syntax description. Note that for this notation, the syntax description:

```
<integer>+
```

is equivalent to the syntax description:

```
<integer> <integer>*
```

A vertical bar, "|," indicates a choice among one or more of the items separated by the bars. For example, the syntax description:

```
all | none | some
```

could be replaced with:

```
all
```

or:

```
none
```

or:

```
some
```

7.4 FIELDS

As a knowledge base is constructed, CLIPS must read input from the keyboard and files in order to execute commands and load programs. As CLIPS reads characters from the keyboard or files, it groups them together into **tokens**. Tokens represent groups of characters that have special meaning to CLIPS. Some tokens such as left and right parentheses consist of only one character.

The group of tokens known as **fields** is of particular importance. There are eight types of fields, also called the CLIPS primitive data types: **float**, **integer**, **symbol**, **string**, **external address**, **fact address**, **instance name**, and **instance address**.

The first two types of fields, floats and integers, are called ***numeric fields*** or simply ***numbers***. A numeric field consists of three parts: the sign, the value, and the exponent. The sign and the exponent are optional. The sign is either + or –. The value contains one or more digits with a single optional decimal point contained with the digits. The exponent consists of the letter e or E followed by an optional + or – followed by one or more digits. Any number consisting of an optional sign followed by only digits is stored as an **integer**. All other numbers are stored as **floats**.

The following are examples of valid CLIPS floats:

```
1.5
1.0
0.7
9e+1
3.5e10
```

The following are examples of valid CLIPS integers:

```
1
+3
-1
65
```

A **symbol** is a field that starts with a printable ASCII character and is followed by zero or more characters. The end of a symbol is reached when a **delimiter** is encountered. Delimiters include any nonprintable ASCII character (including spaces, tabs, carriage returns, and line feeds), the **"** (double quotation mark) character, the **(** (opening parenthesis) character, the **)** (closing parenthesis) character, the **;** (semicolon) character, the **&** (ampersand) character, the **|** (vertical bar) character, the **~** (tilde) character, and the **<** (less than) character. Symbols cannot contain delimiters (with the exception of the **<** character, which may be the first in a symbol). Also, the **?** and **$?** (question mark and dollar sign/question mark) sequence of characters cannot be placed at the beginning of a symbol since they are used to denote variables (see Section 7.19). In addition, a sequence of characters that does not exactly follow the numeric field format is treated as a symbol.

The following are examples of valid symbols:

```
Space-Station
February
fire
activate_sprinkler_system
notify-fire-department
shut-down-electrical-junction-387
!?#$^*
345B
346-95-6156
```

Notice how the underscore and hyphen characters are used to tie symbols together to make them into a single field.

CLIPS will preserve the uppercase and lowercase letters it finds in tokens. Because it distinguishes between uppercase and lowercase letters, CLIPS is called ***case-sensitive***. For example, the following symbols are considered different by CLIPS:

```
case-sensitive
Case-Sensitive
CASE-SENSITIVE
```

The next type of field is a **string**. A string must begin and end with double quotation marks, which are part of the field. There can be zero or more characters of any kind between the double quotes, including characters normally used by CLIPS as delimiters. The following are examples of valid CLIPS strings:

```
"Activate the sprinkler system."
"Shut down electrical junction 387."
"!?#$^"
"John Q. Public"
```

Spaces normally act as delimiters in CLIPS to separate fields (such as symbols) and other tokens. Additional spaces used between tokens are discarded.

Spaces included as part of a string, however, are preserved. For example, CLIPS considers the following four strings distinct:

```
"spaces"
"spaces  "
"  spaces"
"  spaces  "
```

If the surrounding double quotes were removed, CLIPS would consider each of the lines as containing the same symbol since spaces other than those used as delimiters would be ignored.

Because double quotes are used to delimit strings, it is not possible to directly place a double quote within a string. For example, the line:

```
""three-tokens""
```

would be interpreted by CLIPS as the three separate tokens following since double quotes act as delimiters:

```
""
three-tokens
""
```

Within a string, double quotes can be included by using the backslash operator, \. For example, the line:

```
"\"single-token\""
```

will be interpreted by CLIPS as the string field:

```
""single-token""
```

Only a single field is created because the backslash character prevents the following double quotes from acting as a delimiter. The backslash character itself may be placed within a string by using two backslashes in succession. For example, the line:

```
"\\single-token\\"
```

will be interpreted by CLIPS as the string field:

```
"\single-token\"
```

The next field type, **external address**, is of limited interest in an introduction to the programming capabilities of CLIPS. External addresses represent the address of an external data structure returned by a **user-defined function** (a function written in a language such as C or Ada and linked with CLIPS to add additional functionality). Since the value of an external address cannot be specified by a sequence of characters that form a token and the basic unmodified version of CLIPS contains no functions that return external addresses, it is not possible to create this type of field in the basic unmodified version of CLIPS.

The remaining three types of fields are **fact address**, **instance address**, and **instance name**. Facts, as will be discussed shortly, are one of the complex data representations provided by CLIPS. A fact address is used to refer to a specific fact. Like an external address, a fact address can't be specified by a sequence of characters that form a token. Rules, however, are able to obtain fact addresses as part of the pattern-matching process. The syntax for accomplishing this will be discussed in Section 7.21.

Instances are the other complex data representation provided by CLIPS and will be discussed in greater detail in Chapter 11. Instances can be referred to using either an instance address or an instance name. An instance address is like a fact address, but it refers to an instance rather than a fact. An instance can also be referred to by name. An instance name is a special type of symbol that is enclosed within left and right square brackets. For example, [pump-1] is an instance name.

A series of zero or more fields contained together is referred to as a **multifield value**. Multifield values are usually created by calling a function (as will be shown in subsequent chapters) or when specifying a series of fields. When printed, a multifield value is enclosed by left and right parentheses. For example, the zero length multifield would be printed as follows:

```
()
```

and the multifield containing the symbols *this* and *that* would be printed as follows:

```
(this that)
```

7.5 ENTERING AND EXITING CLIPS

CLIPS can be entered by issuing the appropriate run command for the machine on which CLIPS has been installed. The CLIPS prompt should appear as follows:

```
CLIPS>
```

At this point commands can be entered directly to CLIPS; this mode is called the ***top level***.

The normal mode of leaving CLIPS is the **exit** command. The syntax of this command is:

```
(exit)
```

Notice that the symbol *exit* is enclosed within matching parentheses. Many rule-based languages draw their origins from LISP, which uses parentheses as delimiters. Since CLIPS is based on a language that was originally developed using LISP machines, it retains these delimiters. The symbol *exit* without enclosing parentheses has quite a different meaning than the symbol *exit* with enclosing parentheses. The parentheses around *exit* indicate that *exit* is a command to be executed and not just the symbol *exit*. We'll see later that parentheses serve as important delimiters for commands.

For now it is important to remember only that each CLIPS command must have a matching number of left and right parentheses.

The final step in executing a CLIPS command after it has been entered with properly balanced parentheses is to press the return key. The return key may also be pressed before or after any token has been entered. For example, pressing the return key after entering the characters "ex," but before entering the characters "it," would create two tokens: a token for the symbol *ex* and a token for the symbol *it*.

The following command sequence demonstrates a sample session of entering CLIPS, evaluating a constant field value, evaluating a function, and then exiting using the exit command. The example shown is for an IBM PC using MS-DOS in which the CLIPS executable is stored in a disk in drive A and the current drive is also A. The name of the CLIPS executable is assumed to be CLIPSDOS. Output displayed by MS-DOS or CLIPS is shown in regular type. All input that must be typed by the user is shown in bold type. The return key is indicated by the character ↵. Remember that CLIPS is case sensitive, so it is important to type upper- and lowercase letters exactly as they appear.

```
A:\>CLIPSDOS↵
            CLIPS (V6.22 06/15/04)
CLIPS> exit↵
exit
CLIPS> (+ 3 4)↵
7
CLIPS> (exit)↵
A:\>
```

While at the top level, CLIPS will accept input from the user and attempt to evaluate that input to determine the appropriate response. Fields entered by themselves are considered constants and the result of evaluating a constant is the constant itself. So when the symbol *exit* is typed by itself and followed by a carriage return, CLIPS evaluates this input and the symbol *exit* is displayed as the result. A symbol surrounded by parentheses is considered to be a command or function call. Thus the input (+ 3 4) is a call to the + function, which performs addition. Its arguments are the values 3 and 4. The return value of this function call is the value 7 (return values will be discussed in greater detail in Chapter 8). Finally, the input (exit) invokes the *exit* command, which exits CLIPS. The terms *function* and *command* should be thought of interchangeably. Throughout this text, *function* will be used to indicate that a value is returned and *command* will indicate either that no value is returned or that the action is normally performed at the top-level prompt.

7.6 FACTS

In order to solve a problem, a CLIPS program must have data or information with which it can reason. A "chunk" of information in CLIPS is called a ***fact***. Facts consist of a **relation name** (a symbolic field) followed by zero or more **slots** (also symbolic fields) and their associated values. The following is an example of a fact:

```
(person (name "John Q. Public")
        (age 23)
        (eye-color blue)
        (hair-color black))
```

The entire fact, as well as each slot, is delimited by an opening left parenthesis and a closing right parenthesis. The symbol *person* is the fact's relation name and the fact contains four slots: *name*, *age*, *eye-color*, and *hair-color*. The value of the *name* slot is "John Q. Public," the value of the *age* slot is 23, the value of the *eye-color* slot is *blue*, and the value of the *hair-color* slot is *black*. Note that the order in which slots are specified is irrelevant. The fact:

```
(person (hair-color black)
        (name "John Q. Public")
        (eye-color blue)
        (age 23))
```

is treated by CLIPS as identical to the first *person* fact shown.

The Deftemplate Construct

Before facts can be created, CLIPS must be informed of the list of valid slots for a given relation name. Groups of facts that share the same relation name and contain common information can be described using the **deftemplate** construct. **Constructs** form the core of a CLIPS program by adding the programmer's knowledge to the CLIPS environment and are different from functions and commands. The deftemplate construct is analogous to a record structure in a language such as Pascal. The general format of a deftemplate is:

```
(deftemplate <relation-name> [<optional-comment>]
   <slot-definition>*)
```

The syntax description <slot-definition> is defined as:

```
(slot <slot-name>) | (multislot <slot-name>)
```

Using this syntax, the *person* fact could be described with the following deftemplate:

```
(deftemplate person "An example deftemplate"
   (slot name)
   (slot age)
```

```
(slot eye-color)
(slot hair-color))
```

Multifield Slots

Slots of a fact that have been specified with the *slot* keyword in their corresponding deftemplates are allowed to contain only one value (these are referred to as *single-field slots*). It is often desirable to place zero or more fields into a given slot. Slots of a fact that have been specified with the **multislot** keyword in their corresponding deftemplates are allowed to contain zero or more values (these are referred to as *multifield slots*). For example, the *name* slot of the *person* deftemplate stores the person's name as a single string value. If the *name* slot were defined using the *multislot* keyword in place of the *slot* keyword, then any number of fields could be stored in it. Thus, the fact:

```
(person (name John Q. Public)
        (age 23)
        (eye-color blue)
        (hair-color brown))
```

is illegal if *name* is a single-field slot, but legal if *name* is a multifield slot. A deftemplate can have any combination of single and multifield slots.

Ordered Facts

Facts with a relation name that has a corresponding deftemplate are called ***deftemplate facts***. Facts with a relation name that does not have a corresponding deftemplate are called ***ordered facts***. Ordered facts have a single implied multifield slot that is used to store all values following the relation name. In fact, whenever CLIPS encounters an ordered fact it automatically creates an **implied deftemplate** for that fact (as opposed to an **explicit deftemplate**, created using the deftemplate construct). Since an ordered fact has only one slot, the slot name isn't required when defining a fact. For example, a list of numbers could be represented with the following fact:

```
(number-list 7 9 3 4 20)
```

Essentially this is equivalent to defining the following deftemplate:

```
(deftemplate number-list (multislot values))
```

and then defining the fact as follows:

```
(number-list (values 7 9 3 4 20))
```

Generally, deftemplate facts should be used whenever possible because the slot names make the facts more readable and easier to work with. There are two cases in which ordered facts are useful. First, facts consisting of just a relation name are useful as flags and look identical regardless of whether a deftemplate has been defined. For example, the ordered fact:

```
(all-orders-processed)
```

could be used as a flag to indicate when all orders have been processed.

Second, for facts containing a single slot, the slot name is usually synonymous with the relation name. For example, the facts:

```
(time 8:45)
(food-groups meat dairy bread
             fruits-and-vegetables)
```

are just as meaningful as:

```
(time (value 8:45))
(food-groups (values meat dairy bread
                     fruits-and-vegetables))
```

Figure 7.1 graphically depicts the relationships among the terms introduced in this section.

Figure 7.1 Deftemplate Overview

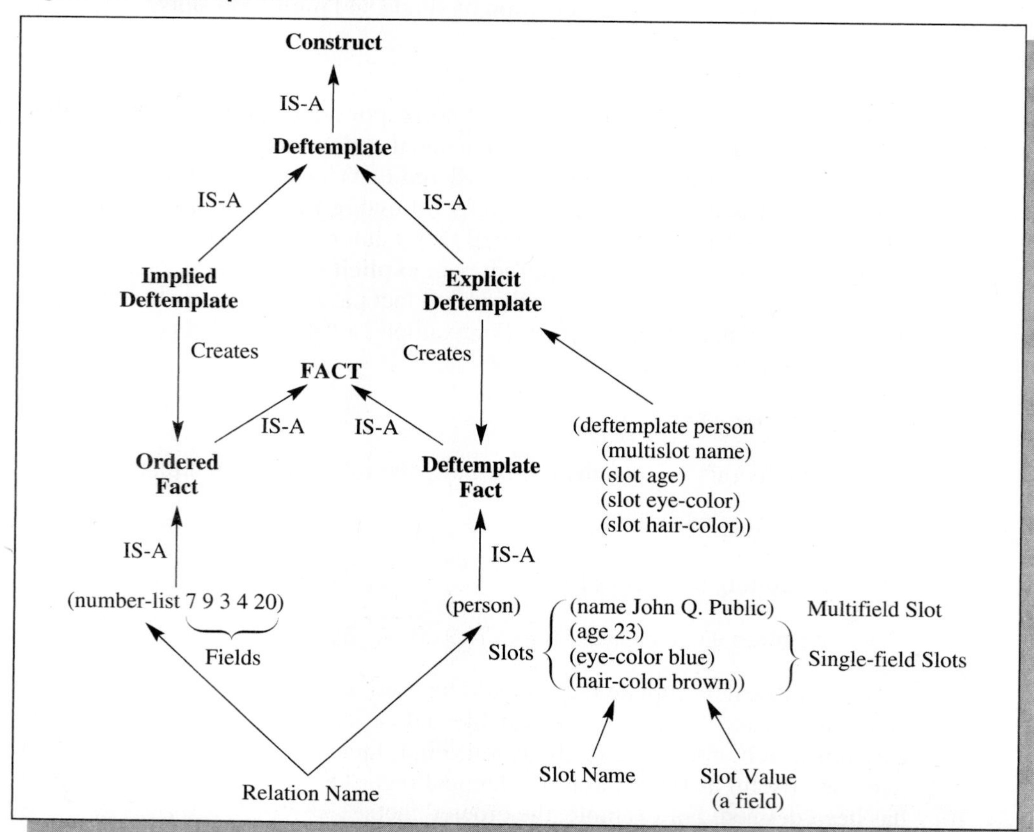

7.7 ADDING AND REMOVING FACTS

The group of all facts known to CLIPS is stored in the fact list. Facts representing information can be added and removed from the fact list. New facts can be added to the fact list using the **assert** command. The syntax of the *assert* command is:

```
(assert <fact>+)
```

As an example, let's use the *person* deftemplate to describe some people as facts. Information about John Q. Public can be added to the fact list by using the following commands:

```
CLIPS>
(deftemplate person
   (slot name)
   (slot age)
   (slot eye-color)
   (slot hair-color))↵
CLIPS>
(assert (person (name "John Q. Public")
                (age 23)
                (eye-color blue)
                (hair-color black)))↵
<Fact-0>
CLIPS>
```

Notice that the assert command returns a value, <Fact-0>. The use of return values will be discussed in Chapter 8.

The **facts** command can be used to display the facts in the fact list. The basic syntax of the *facts* command is:

```
(facts)
```

For example,

```
CLIPS> (facts)↵
f-0     (person (name "John Q. Public")
                (age 23)
                (eye-color blue)
                (hair-color black))
For a total of 1 fact.
CLIPS>
```

The term "*f*-0" is the **fact identifier** assigned to the fact by CLIPS. Every fact that is inserted into the fact list is assigned a unique fact identifier starting with the letter *f* and followed by an integer called the ***fact index***. The fact index

0 was also displayed in the return value, <Fact-0>, from the previous *assert* command. Note that, as shown in this book, extra spaces have been added in the output of the *facts* command between the *(age 23)* and the *(eye-color blue)* slots to improve readability. Normally CLIPS would put only one space between the slots and would wrap the output from the far-left column to the far-right column. In other CLIPS examples throughout this book, spaces will occasionally be added to CLIPS output to improve readability so long as the addition of spaces does not cause confusion.

Normally CLIPS does not accept duplicate entries of a fact (although this behavior can be changed, as shown in Section 12.2). Therefore, attempting to place a second "John Q. Public" fact with identical slot values into the fact list will have no result. Of course, other facts that do not duplicate existing facts can be easily added to the fact list. For example,

```
CLIPS>
(assert (person (name "Jane Q. Public")
                (age 36)
                (eye-color green)
                (hair-color red)))↵
<Fact-1>
CLIPS> (facts)↵
f-0    (person (name "John Q. Public")
               (age 23)
               (eye-color blue)
               (hair-color black))
f-1    (person (name "Jane Q. Public")
               (age 36)
               (eye-color green)
               (hair-color red))
For a total of 2 facts.
CLIPS>
```

As the syntax of the *assert* command indicates, more than one fact can be asserted using a single *assert* command. For example, the command:

```
(assert (person (name "John Q. Public")
                (age 23)
                (eye-color blue)
                (hair-color black))
        (person (name "Jane Q. Public")
                (age 36)
                (eye-color green)
                (hair-color red)))
```

will assert two facts into the fact list.

It is important to realize that identifiers in the fact list are not necessarily sequential. Just as facts can be added to the fact list, there is also a way to remove facts. As facts are removed from the fact list, the deleted fact identifiers will be missing in the fact list, so the fact identifiers may not be strictly sequential as a CLIPS program executes.

Since large numbers of facts can be contained in the fact list, it is often useful to be able to view only a portion of the fact list. This can be accomplished using additional arguments for the *facts* command. The complete syntax for the *facts* command is:

```
(facts [<start> [<end> [<maximum>]]])
```

where <start>, <end>, and <maximum> are positive integers. Notice that the syntax of the *facts* command allows from zero to three arguments. If no arguments are specified, all facts are displayed. If the <start> argument is specified, all facts with fact indexes greater than or equal to <start> are displayed. If <start> and <end> are specified, all facts with fact indexes greater than or equal to <start> and less than or equal to <end> are displayed. Finally, if <maximum> is specified along with <start> and <end>, no more than <maximum> facts will be displayed.

Just as facts can be added to the fact list, they can also be removed. Removing facts from the fact list is called ***retraction*** and is done with the **retract** command. The syntax of the *retract* command is:

```
(retract <fact-index>+)
```

The fact indices of one or more facts to be retracted are included as the arguments of the *retract* command. For example, John Q. Public can be removed from the fact list with the command:

```
(retract 0)
```

Similarly, the command:

```
(retract 1)
```

will retract the Jane Q. Public fact.

Attempting to retract a nonexistent fact will produce the following error message (where [PRNTUTIL1] is a key for finding the error message in the *CLIPS Reference Manual*):

```
[PRNTUTIL1] Unable to find fact <fact-identifier>.
```

For example,

```
CLIPS> (retract 1)↵
CLIPS> (retract 1)↵
[PRNTUTIL1] Unable to find fact f-1.
CLIPS>
```

A single *retract* command can be used to retract multiple facts at once. For example, the command:

```
(retract 0 1)
```

will retract facts f-0 and f-1.

7.8 MODIFYING AND DUPLICATING FACTS

Slot values of deftemplate facts can be modified using the **modify** command. The syntax of the *modify* command is:

```
(modify <fact-index> <slot-modifier>+)
```

where <slot-modifier> is:

```
(<slot-name> <slot-value>)
```

For example, if John Q. Public just had a birthday, his age could be changed from 23 to 24 using the modify command.

```
CLIPS> (modify 0 (age 24))↵
<Fact-2>
CLIPS> (facts)↵
f-2     (person (name "John Q. Public")
                (age 24)
                (eye-color blue)
                (hair-color black))
For a total of 1 fact.
CLIPS>
```

The modify command works by retracting the original fact and then asserting a new fact with the specified slot values modified. Because of this, a new fact index is generated for a modified fact.

The **duplicate** command works in the same way with the exception that it does not retract the original fact. Thus, if John's long lost twin brother Jack is found, he can be added to the fact list by duplicating John's fact and changing the name slot.

```
CLIPS> (duplicate 2 (name "Jack S. Public"))↵
<Fact-3>
CLIPS> (facts)↵
f-2     (person (name "John Q. Public")
                (age 24)
                (eye-color blue)
                (hair-color black))
```

```
f-3     (person (name "Jack S. Public")
                (age 24)
                (eye-color blue)
                (hair-color black))
For a total of 2 facts.
CLIPS>
```

The modify and duplicate commands cannot be used with ordered facts.

7.9 THE WATCH COMMAND

The **watch** command is useful for debugging programs. The effect of watching facts will be discussed in this section; the remaining watch items will be discussed in this and later chapters. The syntax of this command is:

```
(watch <watch-item>)
```

where <watch-item> is one of the symbols *facts*, *rules*, *activations*, *statistics*, *compilations*, *focus*, *deffunctions*, *globals*, *generic-functions*, *methods*, *instances*, *slots*, *messages*, *message-handlers*, or *all*.

These items may be watched in any combination to provide the appropriate amount of debugging information. The *watch* command can be used more than once to watch more than one feature of CLIPS execution. The word *all* can be used to enable all of the watch features. By default, when CLIPS is first started, compilations are watched and the remaining watch items are not watched.

If facts are being watched, CLIPS will automatically print a message indicating that an update has been made to the fact list whenever facts are asserted or retracted. The following command dialog illustrates the use of this debugging command:

```
CLIPS> (facts 3 3)↵
f-3     (person (name "Jack S. Public")
                (age 24)
                (eye-color blue)
                (hair-color black))
For a total of 1 fact.
CLIPS> (watch facts)↵
CLIPS> (modify 3 (age 25))↵
<== f-3      (person (name "Jack S. Public")
             (age 24)
             (eye-color blue)
             (hair-color black))
==> f-4      (person (name "Jack S. Public")
             (age 25)
             (eye-color blue)
             (hair-color black))

<Fact-4>
CLIPS>
```

The character sequence <== indicates that the fact is being retracted. The character sequence ==>> indicates that the fact is being asserted.

It's possible to watch specific facts by specifying one or more deftemplate names at the end of a watch command. For example, (watch facts person) would just display fact messages for the *person* facts.

The effects of a *watch* command may be turned off by using the corresponding **unwatch** command. The syntax of the *unwatch* command is:

```
(unwatch <watch-item>)
```

7.10 THE DEFFACTS CONSTRUCT

It is often convenient to be able to automatically assert a set of facts instead of typing in the same assertions from the top level. This is particularly true for facts that are known to be true before running a program (i.e., the initial knowledge). Running test cases to debug a program is another instance in which it is useful to automatically assert a group of facts. Groups of facts that represent initial knowledge can be defined using the **deffacts** construct. For example, the following deffacts statement provides initial information about some people we have already encountered:

```
(deffacts people "Some people we know"
   (person (name "John Q. Public") (age 24)
           (eye-color blue) (hair-color black))
   (person (name "Jack S. Public") (age 24)
           (eye-color blue) (hair-color black))
   (person (name "Jane Q. Public") (age 36)
           (eye-color green) (hair-color red)))
```

The general format of a deffacts is:

```
(deffacts <deffacts name> [<optional comment>]
   <facts>*)
```

Following the deffacts keyword is the required name of this deffacts construct. Any valid symbol can be used as the name. In this case the name chosen was *people*. Following the name is an optional comment in double quotes. Like the optional comment of a rule, this comment will be retained with the deffacts after it has been loaded by CLIPS. After the name or comment, are the facts that will be asserted in the fact list by this deffacts statement.

The facts in a deffacts statement are asserted using the CLIPS **reset** command. The *reset* command removes all facts from the fact list and then asserts the facts from existing deffacts statement. The syntax of the *reset* command is:

```
(reset)
```

Assuming that the *people* deffacts had been entered (after the *person* deftemplate), the following dialog shows how the *reset* command adds the facts to the fact list:

```
CLIPS> (unwatch facts)↵
CLIPS> (reset)↵
CLIPS> (facts)↵
f-0     (initial-fact)
f-1     (person (name "John Q. Public")
                (age 24)
                (eye-color blue)
                (hair-color black))
f-2     (person (name "Jack S. Public")
                (age 24)
                (eye-color blue)
                (hair-color black))
f-3     (person (name "Jane Q. Public")
                (age 36)
                (eye-color green)
                (hair-color red))
For a total of 4 facts.
CLIPS>
```

The output shows the facts from the deffacts statement and a new fact generated by the reset command called ***initial-fact***. Upon startup, CLIPS automatically defines the following two constructs:

```
(deftemplate initial-fact)

(deffacts initial-fact
   (initial-fact))
```

Thus, even if you have not defined any deffacts statements, a reset will assert the fact (initial-fact). The fact identifier of the initial-fact is always f-0. The utility of (initial-fact) lies in starting the execution of a program (as will be discussed in the next section).

7.11 THE COMPONENTS OF A RULE

In order to accomplish useful work, an expert system must have rules as well as facts. Now that fact assertions and retractions have been discussed, it's possible to see how rules work.

Rules can be typed directly into CLIPS or loaded in from a file of rules created by an editor (loading constructs from a file will be discussed in Section 7.17). For all but the smallest programs you'll probably want to use one of the integrated editors provided with CLIPS. Information about the editors for Windows 2000/XP and MacOS executables can be found in the *Interfaces Guide* that is in electronic format on the CD-ROM included with this book. Information about the EMACS editor, which can be used in environments such as UNIX, is described in the *Basic Programming Guide*. The integrated editors allow you to selectively redefine constructs during program development, which can be extremely useful. For example, if you have a typo in a construct that you entered at the top-level prompt, you have to retype the entire construct. If you first entered the construct in the editor, then you can correct the typo and redefine the construct with a few keystrokes from within the editor. Initially, the examples shown will be rules entered directly into CLIPS from the top level.

As an example, let's consider the types of facts and rules that might be used to monitor and respond to a range of possible emergencies. One such emergency would be a fire; another would be a flood. The pseudocode for one of the possible rules in the industrial plant monitoring expert system is shown as follows:

```
IF the emergency is a fire
THEN the response is to activate
     the sprinkler system
```

Before converting the pseudocode to a rule, the deftemplates for the types of facts referred to by the rule must be defined. An emergency can be represented by the following deftemplate:

```
(deftemplate emergency (slot type))
```

where the *type* field of the *emergency* fact would contain symbols such as fire, flood, and power outage. Similarly, the response can be represented by the following deftemplate:

```
(deftemplate response (slot action))
```

where the *action* field of the *response* fact indicates the response to be taken.

The rule expressed in CLIPS syntax is shown below. The rule can be entered by typing it in after the CLIPS prompt, but you'll have to enter the *emergency* and *response* deftemplates before you can enter the rule. However, before entering any of these constructs, type the command (clear) followed by a return at the top-level prompt. This will remove the deftemplates and deffacts created from the previous section. The *clear* command will be fully explained in Section 7.13.

```
(defrule fire-emergency "An example rule"
   (emergency (type fire))
   =>
   (assert (response
               (action activate-sprinkler-system))))
```

If the rule is entered correctly as shown, the CLIPS prompt reappears. Otherwise an error message, most likely indicating a misspelled keyword or misplaced parenthesis, will appear.

The following is the same rule with comments added to match the parts of the rule. Comments begin with a semicolon and continue until a carriage return. They are ignored by CLIPS and will be discussed in Section 7.18.

```
; Rule header
(defrule fire-emergency "An example rule"
   ; Patterns
   (emergency (type fire))
   ; THEN arrow
   =>
   ; Actions
   (assert (response
              (action activate-sprinkler-system))))
```

The general format of a rule is:

```
(defrule <rule name> [<comment>]
   <patterns>* ; Left-Hand Side (LHS) of the rule
   =>
   <actions>*) ; Right-Hand Side (RHS) of the rule
```

The entire rule must be surrounded by parentheses and each of the patterns and actions of the rule must be surrounded by parentheses. A rule may have multiple patterns and actions. The parentheses surrounding patterns and actions must be properly balanced if they are nested. In the *fire-emergency* rule there is one pattern and one action.

The header of the rule consists of three parts. The rule must start with the **defrule** keyword, followed by the name of the rule. The name can be any valid CLIPS symbol. If a rule is entered with a rule name that is the same as an existing rule, then the new rule replaces the old rule. In this rule the rule name is *fire-emergency*. Next comes an optional comment string. For this rule the comment is "An example rule". The comment is normally used to describe the purpose of the rule or any other information the programmer desires. Unlike comments beginning with a semicolon, the comment following the rule name is not ignored and can be displayed along with the rest of the rule (using the *ppdefrul*e command, which will be introduced in Section 7.13).

After the rule header are zero or more conditional elements (CEs). The simplest type of CE is a **pattern CE** or simply **pattern**. Each pattern consists of one or more constraints intended to match the fields of a deftemplate fact. In the *fire-emergency* rule the pattern is (emergency (type fire)). The constraint for the *type* field indicates that this rule will be satisfied only for *emergency* facts that contain the symbol *fire* in their *type* field. CLIPS attempts to match the patterns of rules against facts in the fact list. If all the patterns of a rule match facts, the rule is **activated** and put on the **agenda**, the collection of activated rules. There may be zero or more rules in the agenda.

The symbol **=>** that follows the patterns in a rule is called an **arrow**. It is formed by typing the equal sign and then the greater-than sign. The arrow is a symbol representing the beginning of the THEN part of an IF-THEN rule. The part of the rule before the arrow is called the left-hand side (**LHS**) and the part after the arrow is called the right-hand side (**RHS**).

If a rule has no patterns, the special pattern (initial-fact) will be added as a pattern for the rule. Since the *initial-fact* deffacts is automatically defined, any rules with no patterns on their LHSs will be activated when a *reset* command is performed since the (initial-fact) fact will automatically be asserted. Thus any rule without LHS patterns will be placed on the agenda when a reset is performed.

The last part of a rule is the list of actions that will be executed when the rule **fires**. A rule may have no actions. This is not particularly useful, but it can be done. In our example the one action is to assert the fact (response (action activate-sprinkler-system)). The term *fires* means that CLIPS executes the actions of a rule from the agenda. A program normally ceases execution when there are no rules on the agenda. When there are multiple rules on the agenda, CLIPS automatically determines which is the appropriate rule to fire. CLIPS orders the rules on the agenda in terms of increasing priority and fires the rule with the highest priority. The priority of a rule is an integer attribute called ***salience***. Salience will be discussed in more detail in Chapter 9.

7.12 THE AGENDA AND EXECUTION

A CLIPS program can be made to run with the **run** command. The syntax of the *run* command is:

```
(run [<limit>])
```

where the optional argument <limit> >is the maximum number of rules to be fired. If <limit> is not included or <limit> is –1, rules will be fired until none are left on the agenda. Otherwise, execution of rules will cease after <limit> number of rules have fired.

When a CLIPS program is run, the rule with the highest salience on the agenda is fired. If there is only one rule on the agenda, of course that rule will fire. Since the conditional element of the *fire-emergency* rule is satisfied by the fact (emergency (type fire)), the *fire-emergency* rule should fire when the program is run.

Rules become activated whenever all the patterns of the rule are matched by facts. The process of pattern matching is always kept current and occurs regardless of whether facts are asserted before or after a rule has been defined.

Because rules require facts to execute, the *reset* command is the key method for starting or restarting an expert system in CLIPS. Typically, the facts asserted by a reset satisfy the patterns of one or more rules and place activations of these rules on the agenda. Issuing the *run* command then begins execution of the program.

Displaying the Agenda

The list of rules on the agenda can be displayed with the **agenda** command. The syntax of the *agenda* command is:

```
(agenda)
```

If no activations are on the agenda, the CLIPS prompt will reappear after the *agenda* command is issued. If the *fire-emergency* rule had been activated by the (emergency (type fire)) fact with a fact index of 1, an *agenda* command would produce the following output:

```
CLIPS> (reset)↵
CLIPS> (assert (emergency (type fire)))↵
<Fact-1>
CLIPS> (agenda)↵
0       fire-emergency: f-1
For a total of 1 activation.
CLIPS>
```

The 0 indicates the salience of the rule on the agenda. Salience is followed by the name of the rule and then the fact identifiers that match the patterns of the rule. In this case there is only one fact identifier, f-1.

Rules and Refraction

With the *fire-emergency* rule on the agenda, the *run* command will now cause the rule to fire. The fact (response (action activate-sprinkler-system)) will be added to the fact list as the action of the rule, as the following output shows:

```
CLIPS> (run)↵
CLIPS> (facts)↵
f-0     (initial-fact)
f-1     (emergency (type fire))
f-2     (response
            (action activate-sprinkler-system))
For a total of 3 facts.
CLIPS>
```

An interesting question occurs at this point: What if the *run* command is issued again? There is a rule and there is a fact that satisfies the rule and so the rule should fire again. However, a *run* command if attempted now will produce no results. Checking the agenda will verify that no rules are fired because there were no rules on the agenda.

The rule didn't fire again because of the way CLIPS is designed. Rules in CLIPS exhibit a property called **refraction**, which means they won't fire more than once for a specific set of facts. Without refraction, expert systems would always be caught in trivial loops. That is, as soon as a rule fired, it would keep on firing on that same fact over and over again. In the real world the stimulus that caused the firing would eventually disappear. For example, the fire would eventually be put out by the sprinkler system or would burn out by itself. However, in the computer world, once a fact is entered in the fact list, it stays there until explicitly removed.

If necessary, the rule can be made to fire again by retracting the fact (emergency (type fire)) and asserting it again. Basically, CLIPS remembers the fact identifiers that triggered a rule into firing and will not activate that rule again with the exact same combination of fact identifiers. Identical sets of fact identifiers must match one-for-one in both order and fact indices. Examples later in this chapter will show how a single fact can match a pattern in more than one way. In this case, several activations with the same set of fact identifiers for a single rule can be placed on the agenda, one for each distinct match.

Alternatively, the **refresh** command can be used to make the rule fire again. The *refresh* command places all activations that have already fired for a rule back on the agenda (with the restriction that the facts that triggered the activation are still present in the fact list). The syntax of the *refresh* command is:

```
(refresh <rule-name>)
```

and the following commands show how the *refresh* command could be used to reactivate the *fire-emergency* rule:

```
CLIPS> (agenda)↵
CLIPS> (refresh fire-emergency)↵
CLIPS> (agenda)↵
0      fire-emergency: f-1
For a total of 1 activation.
CLIPS>
```

Watching Activations, Rules, and Statistics

If activations are being watched, CLIPS will automatically print a message whenever an activation has been added to or removed from the agenda. As with facts, the character sequence <== indicates that an activation is being removed from the agenda and the character sequence ==>> indicates that an activation is being added to the agenda. After the initial character sequence the activation is printed with the same format used by the *agenda* command. The following command sequence illustrates activations being watched:

```
CLIPS> (reset)↵
CLIPS> (watch activations)↵
CLIPS> (assert (emergency (type fire)))↵
==> Activation 0      fire-emergency: f-1
<Fact-1>
CLIPS> (agenda)↵
0      fire-emergency: f-1
For a total of 1 activation.
CLIPS> (retract 1)↵
<== Activation 0      fire-emergency: f-1
CLIPS> (agenda)↵
CLIPS>
```

If rules are being watched, CLIPS will print a message whenever a rule is fired. The following command sequence illustrates activations and rules being watched:

```
CLIPS> (reset)↵
CLIPS> (watch rules)↵
CLIPS> (assert (emergency (type fire)))↵
==> Activation 0        fire-emergency: f-1
<Fact-1>
CLIPS> (run)↵
FIRE    1 fire-emergency: f-1
CLIPS> (agenda)↵
CLIPS>
```

The number following the symbol *FIRE* indicates how many rules have fired since the *run* command was given. For example, if another rule were to fire after the *fire-emergency rule*, it would be preceded by "FIRE 2." After the firing order is printed the name of the rule is printed, followed by the fact indices that matched the patterns of the rule. Note that watching activations will not cause a message to be displayed when a rule is fired (and hence removed from the agenda).

It's possible to watch specific rules and activations by specifying one or more rule names at the end of a watch command. For example, (watch activations fire-emergency) would just display activation messages for the *fire-emergency* rule.

If statistics are being watched, CLIPS will print informational messages such as the following at the completion of a run:

```
CLIPS> (unwatch all)↵
CLIPS> (reset)↵
CLIPS> (watch statistics)↵
CLIPS> (assert (emergency (type fire)))↵
<Fact-1>
CLIPS> (run)↵
1 rules fired     Run time is 0.02 seconds
50.0 rules per second
3 mean number of facts (3 maximum)
1 mean number of instances (1 maximum)
1 mean number of activations (1 maximum)
CLIPS> (unwatch statistics)↵
CLIPS>
```

When statistics are watched, six statistics are printed out after a *run* command. First displayed are the total number of rules fired, the amount of time in seconds it took to fire the rules, and the average number of rules fired per second (the first statistic divided by the second statistic). In addition, for each cycle of execution, CLIPS keeps statistics on the number of facts, activations, and instances. The mean number of facts is the sum of the total number of facts in the fact list after each rule firing divided by the number of rules fired. The number contained within the parentheses followed by the word *maximum* indicates the largest number of facts contained in the fact list for any one rule firing. Similarly, the mean and maximum numbers of activations statistics indicate the average number of activations per rule firing and the largest number of activations on the agenda for any one rule firing. The mean and maximum numbers of instances display information associated with COOL.

7.13 COMMANDS FOR MANIPULATING CONSTRUCTS

Displaying the List of Members of a Specified Construct

The **list-defrules** command is used to display the current list of rules maintained by CLIPS. Similarly, the **list-deftemplates** and **list-deffacts** commands, respectively can be used to display the current list of deftemplates or the current list of deffacts. The syntax of these commands is:

```
(list-defrules)

(list-deftemplates)

(list-deffacts)
```

For example,

```
CLIPS> (list-defrules)↵
fire-emergency
For a total of 1 rule.
CLIPS> (list-deftemplates)↵
initial-fact
emergency
response
For a total of 3 deftemplates.
CLIPS> (list-deffacts)↵
initial-fact
For a total of 1 deffacts.
CLIPS>
```

Displaying the Text Representation of a Specified Construct Member

The **ppdefrule** (pretty print defrule), **ppdeftemplate** (pretty print deftemplate), and **ppdeffacts** (pretty print deffacts) commands are used to display the text representations of a defrule, a deftemplate, and a deffacts respectively. The syntax of these commands is:

```
(ppdefrule <defrule-name>)

(ppdeftemplate <deftemplate-name>)

(ppdeffacts <deffacts-name>)
```

The single argument for each command specifies the name of the defrule, deftemplate, or deffacts to be displayed. When displayed, CLIPS puts different parts of the constructs on different lines for the sake of readability. For example,

```
CLIPS> (ppdefrule fire-emergency)↵
(defrule MAIN::fire-emergency "An example rule"
   (emergency (type fire))
   =>
   (assert (response
              (action activate-sprinkler-system))))
CLIPS> (ppdeftemplate response)↵
(deftemplate MAIN::response
   (slot action))
CLIPS> (ppdeffacts initial-fact)↵
CLIPS> (deffacts start-fact (start-fact))↵
CLIPS> (ppdeffacts start-fact)↵
(deffacts MAIN::start-fact
   (start-fact))
CLIPS>
```

The symbol MAIN:: preceding each of the construct names indicates the module in which the constructs have been placed. Modules provide a mechanism for partitioning a knowledge base and will be discussed in greater detail in Chapter 9. Notice that the *initial-fact* deffacts has no text representation (since it is automatically created by CLIPS). However, the *start-fact* deffacts that was entered does have a text representation.

Deleting a Specified Construct Member

The **undefrule**, **undeftemplate**, and **undeffacts** commands are used to delete a defrule, a deftemplate, and a deffacts, respectively. The syntax of these commands is:

```
(undefrule <defrule-name>)

(undeftemplate <deftemplate-name>)

(undeffacts <deffacts-name>)
```

The single argument for each command specifies the name of the defrule, deftemplate, or deffacts to be deleted. For example,

```
CLIPS> (undeffacts start-fact)↵
CLIPS> (list-deffacts)↵
initial-fact
For a total of 1 deffacts.
CLIPS> (undefrule fire-emergency)↵
CLIPS> (list-defrules)↵
CLIPS>
```

Notice that the *initial-facts* deffacts and the *initial-facts* deftemplate can be deleted just like any other user-defined construct. If a *reset* command were performed now, the (initial-fact) fact would not be added to the fact list.

If the symbol * is given as an argument to any of the construct deletion commands, then all constructs of the appropriate type are deleted. For example, (undefrule *) would delete all defrule constructs. The symbol * can also be used with the *retract* command to remove all facts.

Constructs that are referred to by other constructs cannot be deleted until the referring constructs are deleted. As the following dialog shows, the *initial-fact* deftemplate cannot be deleted until the *initial-fact* deffacts is deleted, the fact (initial-fact) is deleted, and the *example* defrule is deleted (which uses the default *initial-fact* pattern):

```
CLIPS> (defrule example =>)↵
CLIPS> (undeftemplate initial-fact)↵
[PRNTUTIL4] Unable to delete deftemplate
initial-fact.
CLIPS> (undeffacts initial-fact)↵
CLIPS> (undeftemplate initial-fact)↵
[PRNTUTIL4] Unable to delete deftemplate
initial-fact.
CLIPS> (undefrule example)↵
CLIPS> (undeftemplate initial-fact)↵
[PRNTUTIL4] Unable to delete deftemplate
initial-fact.
CLIPS> (retract *)↵
CLIPS> (undeftemplate initial-fact)↵
CLIPS>
```

Clearing All Constructs from the CLIPS Environment

The **clear** command can be used to remove all information contained in the CLIPS environment. It removes all constructs currently contained in CLIPS and all facts in the fact list. The syntax of the *clear* command is:

```
(clear)
```

After *clearing* the CLIPS environment, the clear command adds the *initial-facts* deffacts to the CLIPS environment:

```
CLIPS> (list-deffacts)↵
CLIPS> (list-deftemplates)↵
emergency
response
start-fact
For a total of 3 deftemplates.
CLIPS> (clear)↵
CLIPS> (list-deffacts)↵
initial-fact
For a total of 1 deffacts.
```

```
CLIPS> (list-deftemplates)↵
initial-fact
For a total of 1 deftemplate.
CLIPS>
```

7.14 THE PRINTOUT COMMAND

Besides asserting facts in the RHS of rules, the RHS can also be used to print out information using the **printout** command. The syntax of the *printout* command is:

```
(printout <logical-name> <print-items>*)
```

where <logical-name> indicates the output destination of the *printout* command and <print-items>* are the zero or more items to be printed by this command.

The following rule demonstrates the use of the *printout* command:

```
(defrule fire-emergency
   (emergency (type fire))
   =>
   (printout t "Activate the sprinkler system"
                  crlf))
```

It is very important to include the letter *t* after the *printout* command because this argument indicates the destination of the output. This destination is also referred to as a ***logical name***. In this case, the logical name *t* tells CLIPS to send the output to the **standard output device** of the computer, usually the terminal. This may be redefined so that the standard output device is something else, such as a modem or a printer. The concept of logical names will be fully introduced in Section 8.6.

The arguments following the logical name are items to be printed by the *printout* command. The string:

```
"Activate the sprinkler system"
```

will be printed at the terminal without the enclosing quotation marks. The word **crlf** is treated specially by the *printout* command. It forces a carriage return/line feed, which improves the appearance of output by formatting it on different lines.

7.15 USING MULTIPLE RULES

Until now, only the simplest type of program consisting of just one rule has been shown. However, expert systems consisting of only one rule are not particularly useful. Practical expert systems may consist of hundreds or thousands of rules. In addition to the *fire-emergency* rule, the expert system monitoring the industrial plant might include a rule for emergencies in which flooding has occurred. The expanded set of rules now looks like this:

```
(defrule fire-emergency
   (emergency (type fire))
   =>
   (printout t "Activate the sprinkler system"
               crlf))

(defrule flood-emergency
   (emergency (type flood))
   =>
   (printout t "Shut down electrical equipment"
               crlf))
```

Once these rules have been entered into CLIPS, asserting the fact (emergency (type fire)) and then issuing a *run* command will produce the output "Activate the sprinkler system." Asserting the fact (emergency (type flood)) and issuing a *run* command will produce the output "Shut down the electrical equipment."

Capturing the Real World in a Rule

As long as the fires and floods are the only two emergencies that must be handled, the above rules are sufficient. However, the real world is not quite that simple. For instance, not all fires can be extinguished using water. Some may require chemical extinguishers. What should be done if a fire produces poisonous gases or an explosion occurs? Should an off-site fire department be notified in addition to the on-site firefighters? Does it matter which floor of the building the fire is on? Activating the water sprinklers on the second floor might cause water damage to both the first and the second floors. Electrical power to equipment might have to be shut off on both floors. A fire on the first floor may require that power be shut off to equipment only on the first floor. If the building is flooded, are there watertight doors that can be shut to prevent damage? What should be done in case a plant break-in is detected? If all of these situations are included as rules, have all possibilities now been covered?

Unfortunately, the answer is no. In the real world, things don't always operate perfectly. Capturing all pertinent knowledge in an expert system can be quite difficult. In the best case, it may be possible to recognize most major emergencies and to provide rules to allow the expert system to recognize when it can't handle an emergency.

Rules with Multiple Patterns

Most real-world heuristics are too complicated to be expressed as rules with just a single pattern. For example, activating the sprinkler system for any type of fire might not only be wrong, it could be dangerous. Fires involving ordinary combustibles such as paper, wood, and cloth (class A fires) can be extinguished using water or water-based extinguishers. Fires involving flammable and combustible liquids, greases, and similar materials (class B fires) must be extinguished using a different method, such as a carbon dioxide extinguisher. Rules with more than one pattern could be used to express these conditions. For example:

```
(deftemplate extinguisher-system
   (slot type)
   (slot status))

(defrule class-A-fire-emergency
   (emergency (type class-A-fire))
   (extinguisher-system (type water-sprinkler)
                        (status off))
   =>
   (printout t "Activate water sprinkler" crlf))

(defrule class-B-fire-emergency
   (emergency (type class-B-fire))
   (extinguisher-system (type carbon-dioxide)
                 (status off))
   =>
   (printout t "Use carbon dioxide extinguisher"
               crlf))
```

Both rules have two patterns. The first pattern would determine that a fire emergency exists and whether the fire was class A or class B. The second pattern determines whether the appropriate extinguisher has been turned on. More rules could be added to shut off the extinguishers (e.g., if the water sprinkler is already on and a class B fire occurs, then shut it off; or if the fire has been extinguished, shut off the extinguishers). Still more rules could be used to determine whether a specific burning material constituted a class A or class B fire.

Any number of patterns can be placed in a rule. The important point to realize is that the rule is placed on the agenda only if *all* the patterns are satisfied by facts. This type of restriction is called an ***and conditional element***. Because the patterns of all rules are implicitly contained within an *and* conditional element, the rule will not fire if only one of the patterns is satisfied. All the facts must be present before the LHS of a rule is satisfied and the rule is placed on the agenda.

7.16 THE SET-BREAK COMMAND

CLIPS has a debugging command called ***set-break*** that allows execution to be halted before any rule from a specified group of rules is fired. A rule that halts execution before being fired is called a ***breakpoint***. The syntax of the set-break command is:

```
(set-break <rule-name>)
```

where <rule-name> is the name of the rule for which the breakpoint is set. As an example, consider the following rules (note the use of ordered facts, as described in Section 7.6):

```
(defrule first
   =>
   (assert (fire second)))

(defrule second
   (fire second)
   =>
   (assert (fire third)))

(defrule third
   (fire third)
   =>)
```

The following command dialog shows execution of the rules without any breakpoints set:

```
CLIPS> (watch rules)↵
CLIPS> (reset)↵
CLIPS> (run)↵
FIRE    1 first: f-0
FIRE    2 second: f-1
FIRE    3 third: f-2
CLIPS>
```

All three rules fire in succession when the *run* command is issued. The following command dialog demonstrates the use of the *set-break* command to halt execution:

```
CLIPS> (set-break second)↵
CLIPS> (set-break third)↵
CLIPS> (reset)↵
CLIPS> (run)↵
FIRE    1 first: f-0
Breaking on rule second
CLIPS> (run)↵
FIRE    1 second: f-1
Breaking on rule third
CLIPS> (run)↵
FIRE    1 third: f-2
CLIPS>
```

In this case execution halts before the rules *second* and *third* are allowed to fire. Notice that at least one rule must be fired by the *run* command before a breakpoint will stop execution. For example, after the rule *second* has halted execution, it does not halt execution again when the *run* command is given.

The **show-breaks** command can be used to list all breakpoints. Its syntax is:

```
(show-breaks)
```

The **remove-break** command can be used to remove breakpoints. Its syntax is:

```
(remove-break [<rule-name>])
```

If <rule-name> is provided as an argument, only the breakpoint for that rule will be removed. Otherwise, all breakpoints will be removed.

7.17 LOADING AND SAVING CONSTRUCTS

Loading Constructs from a File

A file of constructs made with a text editor can be loaded into CLIPS using the **load** command. The syntax of the *load* command is:

```
(load <file-name>)
```

where <file-name> is a string or symbol containing the name of the file to be loaded.

Assuming that the emergency rules and deftemplates were stored in a file called fire.clp on drive B of an IBM PC, the following command would load the constructs into CLIPS:

```
(load "B:fire.clp")
```

Of course, the specification of a file name will be machine dependent, so this example should be taken only as a guide. A problem that may occur in loading is due to the backslash character used on some operating systems as a directory path separator. Since CLIPS interprets the backslash as an escape character, two backslashes must be used to create a single backslash in a string. For example, normally a pathname might be written as:

```
B:\usr\clips\fire.clp
```

To preserve the backslash characters, the pathname would have to be written as shown in the following command:

```
(load "B:\\usr\\clips\\fire.clp")
```

Constructs do not all have to be kept in a single file. They can be stored in more than one file and loaded using several load commands. If no errors occur when a file is loaded, the load command will return the symbol *TRUE* (Chapter 8 will go into detail about return values). Otherwise, it will return the symbol *FALSE*.

Watching Compilations

When compilations are watched (by default), an informational message including the construct name is printed for each construct loaded by the load command. For example, assume CLIPS has just been started and the following commands are entered:

```
CLIPS> (load "fire.clp")↵
Defining deftemplate: emergency
Defining deftemplate: response
Defining defrule: fire-emergency +j
TRUE
CLIPS>
```

The messages indicate that two deftemplates were loaded (*emergency* and *response*), followed by the *fire-emergency* rule. The "+j" string at the end of the "Defining defrule" message is information from CLIPS about the internal structure of the compiled rules. This information will be useful for tuning a program and will be discussed in Chapter 9, which deals with efficiency.

If compilations are not being watched, then CLIPS prints a single character for each construct loaded: * for defrules, % for deftemplates, and $ for deffacts. For example:

```
CLIPS> (clear)↵
CLIPS> (unwatch compilations)↵
CLIPS> (load fire.clp)↵
%%*
TRUE
CLIPS>
```

Saving Constructs to a File

CLIPS also provides the opposite of the *load* command. The **save** command allows the set of constructs stored in CLIPS to be saved to a disk file. The syntax of the *save* command is:

```
(save <file-name>)
```

For example, the following command will save the fire constructs to a file called *fire.clp* on drive B:

```
(save "B:fire.clp")
```

The *save* command will save all the constructs in CLIPS to the specified file. It is not possible to save specified constructs to a file. Normally if an editor is used to create and modify the constructs there is no need to use the *save* command, since the constructs will be saved while you are using the editor. However, sometimes it is convenient to enter constructs directly at the CLIPS prompt and then save the constructs to a file.

7.18 COMMENTING CONSTRUCTS

It's a good idea to include comments in a CLIPS program. Sometimes constructs can be difficult to understand, and comments can be used to explain to the reader what the constructs are doing. Comments are also used for good documentation of programs and will be helpful in lengthy programs.

A comment in CLIPS is any text that begins with a semicolon and ends with a carriage return. The following is an example of comments in the fire program:

```
;**********************************
;*                                 *
;* Programmer: G. D. Riley         *
;*                                 *
;* Title: The Fire Program         *
;*                                 *
;* Date: 05/17/04                  *
;*                                 *
;**********************************
; Deftemplates
 (deftemplate emergency "template #1"
  (slot type))        ; What type of emergency

 (deftemplate response  "template #2"
  (slot type))        ; How to respond
; The purpose of this rule is to activate
; the sprinkler system if there is a fire

 (defrule fire-emergency "An example rule" ; IF
  ; There is a fire emergency
  (emergency (type fire))
=>                                         ; THEN
  ; Activate the sprinkler system
 (assert (response
              (action activate-sprinkler-system))))
```

Loading these constructs into CLIPS and then pretty printing them will demonstrate that every comment starting with a semicolon is eliminated in the CLIPS program. The only comment that is retained is the one in quotes after the construct's name.

7.19 VARIABLES

Just as with other programming languages, CLIPS has **variables** available to store values. Variables in CLIPS are always written in the syntax of a question mark followed by a symbolic field name. Variable names follow the syntax of a symbol, with the exception that they must begin with a character. For good programming style, variables should be given meaningful names. Some examples of variables are:

```
?speed
?sensor
?value
?noun
?color
```

There should be no space between the question mark and the symbolic field name. As will be discussed later, a question mark by itself has its own use. Variables are used on the LHS of a rule to contain slot values that can later be compared to other values on the LHS of a rule or accessed on the RHS of a rule. The terms ***bound*** and ***bind*** are used to describe the assignment of a value to a variable.

One common use of variables is to bind a variable on the LHS of a rule and then use that value on the RHS of the rule. For example:

```
CLIPS> (clear)↵
CLIPS>
(deftemplate person
   (slot name)
   (slot eyes)
   (slot hair))↵
CLIPS>
(defrule find-blue-eyes
   (person (name ?name) (eyes blue))
   =>
   (printout t ?name " has blue eyes." crlf))↵
CLIPS>
(deffacts people
   (person (name Jane)
           (eyes blue) (hair red))
   (person (name Joe)
           (eyes green) (hair brown))
   (person (name Jack)
           (eyes blue) (hair black))
   (person (name Jeff)
           (eyes green) (hair brown)))↵
CLIPS> (reset)↵
CLIPS> (run)↵
Jack has blue eyes.
Jane has blue eyes.
CLIPS>
```

Both Jane and Jack have blue eyes, so the *find-blue-eyes* rule is activated twice, once each for the facts describing Jane and Jack. When the rule fires, it examines the *name* slot for the fact that activated the rule currently being fired and uses that value for the printout statement.

If a variable is referred to on the RHS of a rule but was not bound on the LHS of the rule, CLIPS will print the following error message (assuming the unbound variable was ?x):

```
[PRCCODE3] Undefined variable x referenced in
           RHS of defrule.
```

7.20 MULTIPLE USE OF VARIABLES

Variables with the same name that are used in multiple places on the LHS of a rule have an important and useful property. The first time a variable is bound to a value, it retains that value within the rule. Other occurrences of the same variable must match the same value that was first assigned to the variable.

Instead of writing a single rule that looks only for people with blue eyes, a fact can be asserted that indicates the specific color of eyes to look for. For example:

```
CLIPS> (undefrule *)↵
CLIPS> (deftemplate find (slot eyes))↵
CLIPS>
(defrule find-eyes
   (find (eyes ?eyes))
   (person (name ?name) (eyes ?eyes))
   =>
   (printout t ?name " has " ?eyes " eyes."
      crlf))↵
CLIPS>
```

The *find* deftemplate indicates the eye color; this is specified by the *eyes* slot. The *find-eyes* rule will then retrieve the value from the *eyes* slot in the *find* deftemplate and then look for all person facts for which the value of the *eyes* slot is the same as was bound to the ?eyes variable. The following dialog shows how this works:

```
CLIPS> (reset)↵
CLIPS> (assert (find (eyes blue)))↵
<Fact-5>
CLIPS> (run)↵
Jack has blue eyes.
Jane has blue eyes.
CLIPS> (assert (find (eyes green)))↵
<Fact-6>
CLIPS> (run)↵
Jeff has green eyes.
Joe has green eyes.
CLIPS> (assert (find (eyes purple)))↵
<Fact-7>
CLIPS> (run)
CLIPS>
```

Notice that no rules fire when the (find (eyes purple)) fact is asserted because there are no *person* facts with the value *purple* in the *eyes* slot.

7.21 FACT ADDRESSES

Retraction, modification, and duplication of facts are extremely common operations and are usually done on the RHS of a rule rather than at the top level. Performing these operations on facts at the top-level prompt using fact indices has already been demonstrated. Before a fact can be manipulated from the RHS of a rule, however, there must be some way to specify the fact that matched a particular pattern. To accomplish this, a variable can be bound to the **fact address** of the fact matching a pattern on the LHS of a rule by using the **pattern binding** operator, "<-". Once the variable is bound it can be used with the retract, modify, or duplicate commands in place of a fact index. For example, the following dialog shows how to update deftemplate slot values from the RHS of a rule:

```
CLIPS> (clear)↵
CLIPS>
(deftemplate person
   (slot name)
   (slot address))↵
CLIPS>
(deftemplate moved
   (slot name)
   (slot address))↵
CLIPS>
(defrule process-moved-information
   ?f1 <- (moved (name ?name)
                 (address ?address))
   ?f2 <- (person (name ?name))
   =>
   (retract ?f1)
   (modify ?f2 (address ?address)))↵
CLIPS>
(deffacts example
   (person (name "John Hill")
           (address "25 Mulberry Lane"))
   (moved  (name "John Hill")
           (address "37 Cherry Lane")))↵
CLIPS> (reset)↵
CLIPS> (watch rules)↵
CLIPS> (watch facts)↵
CLIPS> (run)↵
FIRE    1 process-moved-information: f-2,f-1
<== f-2    (moved (name "John Hill")
                  (address "37 Cherry Lane"))
```

```
<== f-1   (person (name "John Hill")
                  (address "25 Mulberry Lane"))
==> f-3   (person (name "John Hill")
                  (address "37 Cherry Lane"))
CLIPS>
```

Two deftemplates are used in this example. The *person* deftemplate is used to store information about a person, in this case just the name of the person and the person's address. Other information, such as age or eye color, could also be stored. The *moved* deftemplate is used to indicate that a person's address has changed. The new address is given in the *address* slot.

The first pattern in the *process-moved-information* rule determines whether an address change needs to be processed, and the second pattern finds the *person* fact for which the address information will need to be changed. The fact address of the *moved* fact is bound to the variable ?f1 so that this fact can be retracted once the change is processed. The fact address of the *person* fact is bound to the variable ?f2, which is later used on the RHS of the rule to modify the value of the *address* slot.

Note that variables bound to values within a fact and variables bound to the fact address of a fact can both be used. In addition, the value of the ?address variable can still be used on the RHS after the fact from which it received its value has been retracted.

Retracting the *moved* fact on the RHS of the *process-moved-information* rule is important for the rule to work correctly. Notice what happens when the *retract* command is removed:

```
CLIPS>
(defrule process-moved-information
   (moved (name ?name) (address ?address))
   ?f2 <- (person (name ?name))
   =>
   (modify ?f2 (address ?address)))↵
CLIPS> (unwatch facts)↵
CLIPS> (unwatch rules)↵
CLIPS> (reset)↵
CLIPS> (watch facts)↵
CLIPS> (watch rules)↵
CLIPS> (watch activations)↵
CLIPS> (run 3)↵
FIRE    1 process-moved-information: f-2,f-1
<== f-1   (person (name "John Hill")
                  (address "25 Mulberry Lane"))
==> f-3   (person (name "John Hill")
                  (address "37 Cherry Lane"))
==> Activation 0 process-moved-information: f-2,f-3
FIRE    2 process-moved-information: f-2,f-3
```

```
<== f-3    (person (name "John Hill")
                   (address "37 Cherry Lane"))
==> f-4    (person (name "John Hill")
                   (address "37 Cherry Lane"))
==> Activation 0  process-moved-information: f-2,f-4
FIRE  3 process-moved-information: f-2,f-4
<== f-4    (person (name "John Hill")
                   (address "37 Cherry Lane"))
==> f-5    (person (name "John Hill")
                   (address "37 Cherry Lane"))
==> Activation 0  process-moved-information: f-2,f-5
CLIPS>
```

The program executes an infinite loop since it asserts a new *person* fact after modifying the fact bound to ?f2, thus reactivating the *process-moved-information* rule. Remember that a *modify* command is treated as a *retract* command followed by an *assert* command. Since the *run* command was told to fire only three rules, that is when the program stopped. If no limit argument had been given to the *run* command, the program would have looped endlessly. The only way to stop an infinite loop like this is by interrupting CLIPS using Control-C, or another appropriate interrupt command for the computer on which CLIPS is running.

7.22 SINGLE-FIELD WILDCARDS

Sometimes it is useful to test for the existence of a field within a slot without actually assigning a value to a variable. This is particularly useful for multifield slots. For example, suppose we want to print the social security number of every person with a specified last name. The following shows the deftemplate used to describe each person, a deffacts with some predefined people, and a rule to print the social security numbers of every person with a specified last name:

```
(deftemplate person
   (multislot name)
   (slot social-security-number))

(deffacts some-people
   (person (name John Q. Public)
           (social-security-number 483-98-9083))
   (person (name Jack R. Public)
           (social-security-number 483-98-9084)))

(defrule print-social-security-numbers
   (print-ss-numbers-for ?last-name)
   (person (name ?first-name ?middle-name
                 ?last-name)
```

```
            (social-security-number ?ss-number))
   =>
   (printout t ?ss-number crlf))
```

The *print-social-security-numbers* rule binds the first and middle names of the person to the variables ?first-name and ?middle-name, respectively. These variables, however, are not referred to by actions on the RHS or other pattern or slots on the LHS of the rule. Instead of using a variable, a **single-field wildcard** can be used when a field is required, but the value is not important. A single-field wildcard is represented by a question mark. Using single-field wildcards, the *print-social-security-numbers* rule can be rewritten as follows:

```
(defrule print-social-security-numbers
   (print-ss-numbers-for ?last-name)
   (person (name ? ? ?last-name)
           (social-security-number ?ss-number))
   =>
   (printout t ?ss-number crlf))
```

Note that the *name* slot of a *person* fact must contain exactly three fields for the *print-social-security-numbers* rule to be activated. For example, the fact:

```
(person (name Joe Public)
        (social-security-number 345-89-3039))
```

would not satisfy the *print-social-security-numbers* rule.

Notice the importance of not including a space between the question mark and the symbolic name of a variable. The pattern:

```
(person (name ?first ?last))
```

expects two fields for the *name* slot, but the pattern:

```
(person (name ?first ? last))
```

expects three fields for the *name* slot, and the last field must be the symbol *last*.

When a single-field slot is left unspecified in a pattern, CLIPS automatically treats it as if there is a single-field wildcard check for that slot. For example, the pattern:

```
(person (name ?first ?last))
```

is equivalent to:

```
(person (name ?first ?last)
        (social-security-number ?))
```

7.23 BLOCKS WORLD

To demonstrate variable bindings, we will build a program to move blocks in a simple blocks world. This type of program is analogous to the classic blocks world program in which the knowledge domain is restricted to blocks (Firebaugh 88). This is a good example of planning and might be applied to automated manufacturing, where a robot arm manipulates parts.

The only things of interest in a blocks world are blocks. A single block may be stacked on another block. The goal of a complex blocks world program is to rearrange the stacks of blocks into a goal configuration with the minimum number of moves. For this example, a number of simplifying restrictions will be made. The first of these restrictions is that only one initial goal is allowed, and this goal can only be to move one block on top of another. With this restriction it is rather trivial to determine the optimal moves to achieve the goal. If the goal is to move block x on top of block y, then move all blocks (if any) on top of block x to the floor and all blocks (if any) on top of block y to the floor and then move block x on top of block y.

The second restriction will be that any goal must not already have been achieved. That is, the goal cannot be to move block x on top of block y if block x is already on top of block y. This is a rather simple condition to check; however, the appropriate syntax to test for this condition will not be introduced until Chapter 8.

To begin to solve this problem, it will be useful to set up a configuration of blocks that can be used for testing the program. Figure 7.2 shows the configuration that will be used. There are two stacks in this configuration. The first stack has block A on top of block B on top of block C. The second stack has block D on top of block E on top of block F.

Figure 7.2 Blocks World Initial Configuration

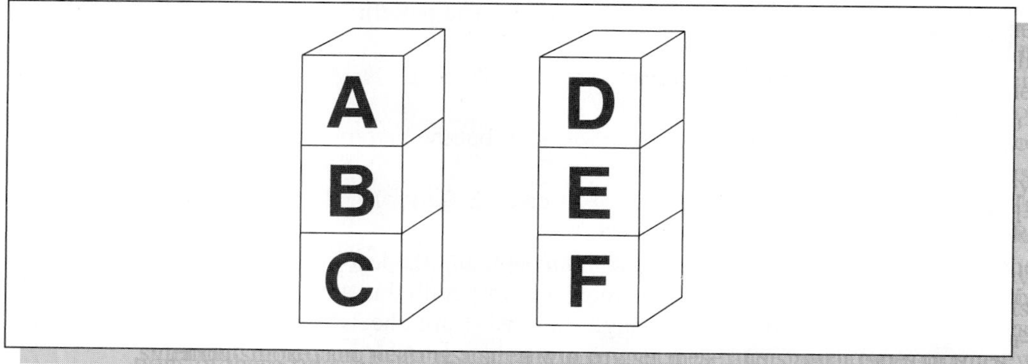

To determine which type of rules would be effective in solving the problem, a step-by-step completion of a blocks world goal is useful. What steps must be taken to move block C on top of block E? The easiest solution for this problem would be to directly move block C on top of block E. However, this rule could only be applied if both block C and block E had no blocks on top of them. The pseudocode for this rule would be:

```
RULE MOVE-DIRECTLY
IF   The goal is to move block ?upper on top of
       block ?lower and
     block ?upper is the top block in its stack and
     block ?lower is the top block in its stack,
THEN Move block ?upper on top of block ?lower.
```

The *move-directly* rule cannot be used in this case since blocks A and B are on top of block C, and block D is on top of block E. In order to allow the *move-directly* rule to move block C on top of block E, blocks A, B, and D must be moved to the floor. Since this is the easiest step to take to get them out of the way, that is what happens. The simple blocks world does not require that the blocks be restacked and only a single initial goal is allowed, so there is no need to stack blocks when they are moved out of the way. This rule can be expressed as two pseudocode rules: one rule to clear blocks off the block to be moved and one rule to clear blocks off the block to be stacked on.

```
RULE CLEAR-UPPER-BLOCK
IF   The goal is to move block ?x and
     block ?x is not the top block in its stack and
     block ?above is on top of block ?x,
THEN The goal is to move block ?above to the floor

RULE CLEAR-LOWER-BLOCK
IF   The goal is to move another block on top of
       block ?x and
     block ?x is not the top block in its stack and
     block ?above is on top of block ?x,
THEN The goal is to move block ?above to the floor
```

The *clear-upper-block* rule will work to clear the blocks off block C. It will first determine that block B needs to be moved to the floor. In order to move block B to the floor, this same rule will determine that block A needs to be moved to the floor. Similarly, the *clear-lower-block* rule will determine that block D needs to be moved to the floor in order to move something on top of block E.

Now there are subgoals: to move blocks A, B, and D to the floor. Blocks A and D can be moved directly to the floor. If written properly, the *move-directly* rule might be able to handle moving blocks on top of the floor as well as on other blocks. Since the floor is really not a block, it may be necessary to treat the floor differently. The following pseudocode rule will handle the special case of moving a block to the floor:

```
RULE MOVE-TO-FLOOR
IF   The goal is to move block ?upper on top of
       the floor and
     block ?upper is the top block in its stack,
THEN Move block ?upper on top of the floor.
```

The *move-to-floor* rule can now move blocks A and D to the floor. Once block A is moved to the floor, the *move-to-floor* rule can be activated to move block B to the floor. With blocks A, B, and D on the floor, blocks C and E are now the top blocks in their stacks and it is possible to use the *move-directly* rule to move block C on top of block E.

Now that the rules have been written using pseudocode, the facts to be used by the rules should be determined. The types of facts needed cannot always be determined without some prototyping. In this case, the pseudocode rules point out several types of facts that will be needed. For example, the information about which blocks are on top of other blocks is crucial. This information could be described with the following deftemplate:

```
(deftemplate on-top-of
   (slot upper)
   (slot lower))
```

and the facts described by this template would be:

```
(on-top-of (upper A) (lower B))
(on-top-of (upper B) (lower C))
(on-top-of (upper D) (lower E))
(on-top-of (upper E) (lower F))
```

Since it is also important to know which blocks are at the top and bottom of a stack, it would be useful to include the following facts:

```
(on-top-of (upper nothing) (lower A))
(on-top-of (upper C) (lower floor))
(on-top-of (upper nothing) (lower D))
(on-top-of (upper F) (lower floor))
```

The words *nothing* and *floor* have special meaning in these facts. The facts (on-top-of (upper nothing) (lower A)) and (on-top-of (upper nothing) (lower D)) indicate that A and D are the top blocks in their stacks. Similarly, the facts (on-top-of (upper C) (lower floor)) and (on-top-of (upper F) (lower floor)) indicate that blocks C and F are the bottom blocks in their stacks. Including these facts does not necessarily solve the problem of determining the top and bottom blocks in a stack. If the rules are not written correctly, the words *floor* and *nothing* might be mistaken as the names of blocks. Facts that indicate the names of the blocks might be useful. The following facts using the implied deftemplate *block* can be used to identify the blocks from the special words *nothing* and *floor*:

```
(block A)
(block B)
(block C)
(block D)
(block E)
(block F)
```

Finally, a fact is needed to describe the block-moving goals that are being processed. These goals could be described with the deftemplate:

```
(deftemplate goal (slot move) (slot on-top-of))
```

and the initial goal using this deftemplate would be:

```
(goal (move C) (on-top-of E))
```

With the facts and deftemplates now defined, the initial configuration of the blocks world can be described by the following deffacts:

```
(deffacts initial-state
   (block A)
   (block B)
   (block C)
   (block D)
   (block E)
   (block F)
   (on-top-of (upper nothing) (lower A))
   (on-top-of (upper A) (lower B))
   (on-top-of (upper B) (lower C))
   (on-top-of (upper C) (lower floor))
   (on-top-of (upper nothing) (lower D))
   (on-top-of (upper D) (lower E))
   (on-top-of (upper E) (lower F))
   (on-top-of (upper F) (lower floor))
   (goal (move C) (on-top-of E)))
```

The *move-directly* rule is written as follows:

```
(defrule move-directly
   ?goal <- (goal (move ?block1)
                  (on-top-of ?block2))
   (block ?block1)
   (block ?block2)
   (on-top-of (upper nothing) (lower ?block1))
   ?stack-1 <- (on-top-of (upper ?block1)
                          (lower ?block3))
```

```
   ?stack-2 <- (on-top-of (upper nothing)
                          (lower ?block2))
   =>
   (retract ?goal ?stack-1 ?stack-2)
   (assert (on-top-of (upper ?block1)
                      (lower ?block2))
           (on-top-of (upper nothing)
                      (lower ?block3)))
   (printout t ?block1 " moved on top of " ?block2
                "." crlf))
```

The first three patterns determine that there is a goal to move a block on top of another block. Patterns two and three ensure that a goal to move a block onto the floor will not be processed by this rule. The fourth and sixth patterns check that the blocks are the top blocks in their stacks. The fifth and sixth patterns match against information necessary to update the stacks that the moving block is being taken from and moved to. The actions of the rule update the stack information for the two stacks and print a message. The block beneath the moved block is now the top block in that stack, and the block being moved is now the top block in the stack to which it was moved.

The *move-to-floor* rule is implemented as follows:

```
(defrule move-to-floor
   ?goal <- (goal (move ?block1)
   (on-top-of floor))
   (block ?block1)
   (on-top-of (upper nothing) (lower ?block1))
   ?stack <- (on-top-of (upper ?block1)
                        (lower ?block2))
   =>
   (retract ?goal ?stack)
   (assert (on-top-of (upper ?block1)
                      (lower floor))
           (on-top-of (upper nothing)
                      (lower ?block2)))
   (printout t ?block1 " moved on top of floor."
                crlf))
```

This rule is similar to the *move-directly* rule with the exception that it is not necessary to update some information about the floor since it is not a block.

The *clear-upper-block* rule is implemented as follows:

```
(defrule clear-upper-block
   (goal (move ?block1))
   (block ?block1)
   (on-top-of (upper ?block2) (lower ?block1))
```

```
   (block ?block2)
   =>
   (assert (goal (move ?block2)
                 (on-top-of floor))))
```

The *clear-lower-block* rule is implemented as follows:

```
(defrule clear-lower-block
   (goal (on-top-of ?block1))
   (block ?block1)
   (on-top-of (upper ?block2) (lower ?block1))
   (block ?block2)
   =>
   (assert (goal (move ?block2)
                 (on-top-of floor))))
```

The program is now complete with the *move-directly*, *move-to-floor*, *clear-upper-block*, and *clear-lower-block* rules, the *goal* and *on-top-of* deftemplates, and the *initial-state* deffacts. The following output shows a sample run of this blocks world program:

```
CLIPS> (unwatch all)↵
CLIPS> (reset)↵
CLIPS> (run)↵
A moved on top of floor.
B moved on top of floor.
D moved on top of floor.
C moved on top of E.
CLIPS>
```

Blocks A and B are first moved to the floor to clear block C. Block D is then moved to the floor to clear block E. Finally, block C can be moved on top of block E to solve the initial goal.

This example has demonstrated how to build a program using a step-by-step method. First, pseudorules were written using English-like text. Second, the pseudorules were used to determine the types of facts that would be required. Deftemplates describing the facts were designed, and the initial knowledge for the program was coded using these deftemplates. Finally, the pseudorules were translated to CLIPS rules using the deftemplates as a guide for translation.

The development of an expert system typically requires a great deal more prototyping and iterative development than in this example. It is not always possible to determine the best method for representing facts or the types of rules that will be needed to build an expert system. Following a consistent methodology, however, can aid in the development of an expert system even when a great deal of prototyping and iteration need to be performed.

7.24 MULTIFIELD WILDCARDS AND VARIABLES

Multifield Wildcards

Multifield wildcards and variables can be used to match against zero or more fields of a pattern. The **multifield wildcard** is indicated by a dollar sign followed by a question mark, "**$?**," and represents zero or more occurrences of a field. Note that ordinary variables and wildcards match exactly one field. This is a slight but significant difference. To illustrate the use of multifield wildcards, recall the *print-social-security-numbers* rule described in Section 7.22:

```
(defrule print-social-security-numbers
   (print-ss-numbers-for ?last-name)
   (person (name ? ? ?last-name)
           (social-security-number ?ss-number))
   =>
   (printout t ?ss-number crlf))
```

This rule will only match a name slot that has exactly three fields. The fact:

```
(person (name Joe Public)
        (social-security-number 345-89-3039))
```

will not match the rule. However, if the two single-field wildcards are replaced with a single multifield wildcard (as shown below), then the *person* pattern will match any name slot that contains at least one field and has as its last field the specified name:

```
(defrule print-social-security-numbers
   (print-ss-numbers-for ?last-name)
   (person (name $? ?last-name)
           (social-security-number ?ss-number))
   =>
   (printout t ?ss-number crlf))
```

Likewise, when a multifield slot is left unspecified in a pattern, CLIPS automatically treats it as if there is a multifield wildcard check for that slot. For example, the pattern:

```
(person (social-security-number ?ss-number))
```

is equivalent to:

```
(person (name $?)
        (social-security-number ?ss-number))
```

Multifield Variables

Just as single-field variables are preceded by a "?," multifield variables are preceded by a "$?." The following constructs show how to print names of all the children of a specified person:

```
(deftemplate person
   (multislot name)
   (multislot children))

(deffacts some-people
   (person (name John Q. Public)
           (children Jane Paul Mary))
   (person (name Jack R. Public)
           (children Rick)))

(defrule print-children
   (print-children $?name)
   (person (name $?name)
           (children $?children))
   =>
   (printout t ?name " has children " ?children
              crlf))
```

The first pattern of the *print-children* rule binds the name of the person whose children will be printed to the variable $?name. The second pattern matches the *person* fact with the specified name contained in $?name and then binds the list of that person's children to the variable $?children. This value is then printed from the RHS of the rule.

Notice that when a multifield variable is referred to on the RHS of a rule, it is not necessary to include the $ as part of the variable name. The $ is only used on the LHS to indicate that zero or more fields can be bound to the variable.

The following dialog shows how the *print-children* rule works:

```
CLIPS> (reset)↵
CLIPS> (assert (print-children John Q. Public))↵
<Fact-3>
CLIPS> (run)↵
(John Q. Public) has children (Jane Paul Mary)
CLIPS>
```

Notice that the multifield values bound to the variables ?name and ?children are surrounded by parentheses when printed.

More than one multifield variable can be used in a single slot. Suppose, for example, that we want to find all the people who have a child with a specific name. The following rule accomplishes this task:

```
(defrule find-child
   (find-child ?child)
   (person (name $?name)
           (children $?before ?child $?after))
   =>
   (printout t ?name " has child " ?child crlf)
   (printout t "Other children are "
               ?before " " ?after crlf))
```

Generally, if we were interested only in the value of the ?child variable, the variables ?before and ?after would have been replaced with multifield wildcards (and the printout statement referring to these variables would be removed). The following dialog shows how the *find-child* rule works:

```
CLIPS> (reset)↵
CLIPS> (assert (find-child Paul))↵
<Fact-3>
CLIPS> (run)↵
(John Q. Public) has child Paul
Other children are (Jane) (Mary)
CLIPS> (assert (find-child Rick))
<Fact-4>
CLIPS> (run)↵
(Jack R. Public) has child Rick
Other children are () ()
CLIPS> (assert (find-child Bill))↵
<Fact-5>
CLIPS> (run)↵
CLIPS>
```

When Paul is the child bound to the variable ?child, the variable ?before is bound to (Jane) and the variable ?after is bound to (Mary). Similarly, when Rick is bound to the variable ?child, then the variable ?before is bound to (), a multifield containing zero fields, and the variable ?after is also bound to ().

Matching Patterns in More than One Way

So far we've dealt with situations in which a single fact can match a pattern in only one way. With multifield variables or wildcards, it is possible to match a pattern in more than one way. Suppose that a fact is entered for a person who has named all of his children after himself. For example:

```
CLIPS> (reset)↵
CLIPS> (assert (person (name Joe Fiveman)
                       (children Joe Joe Joe)))↵
<Fact-3>
CLIPS> (assert (find-child Joe))↵
<Fact-4>
```

```
CLIPS> (agenda)↵
0      find-child: f-4,f-3
0      find-child: f-4,f-3
0      find-child: f-4,f-3
For a total of 3 activations.
CLIPS> (run)↵
(Joe Fiveman) has child Joe
Other children are () (Joe Joe)
(Joe Fiveman) has child Joe
Other children are (Joe) (Joe)
(Joe Fiveman) has child Joe
Other children are (Joe Joe) ()
CLIPS>
```

As the rule firings show, there are three different ways in which the variables ?child, ?before, and ?after can be bound with the fact f-3. In the first case, ?before is bound to (), ?child is bound to *Joe*, and ?after is bound to (Joe Joe). In the second case, ?before is bound to (Joe), ?child is bound to *Joe*, and ?after is bound to (Joe). In the third case, ?before is bound to (Joe Joe), ?child is bound to *Joe*, and ?after is bound to ().

Implementing a Stack

A **stack** is an ordered data structure to which items can be added and removed. Items are added and removed to one "end" of the stack. A new item can be pushed (added) to the stack or the last item added can be popped (removed) from the stack. In a stack the first value added is the last item removed and the last item added is the first item removed.

A useful analogy for a stack is a set of cafeteria trays. New trays are added (pushed) on top of the trays already in the stack. The last trays added to the top of the stack will be the first trays removed (popped).

It is relatively easy to implement a stack capable of performing push and pop operations using multifield variables. First, an ordered *stack* fact that contains a list of items will be used. The following rule will push a value onto the *stack* fact:

```
(defrule push-value
   ?push-value <- (push-value ?value)
   ?stack <- (stack $?rest)
   =>
   (retract ?push-value ?stack)
   (assert (stack ?value $?rest))
   (printout t "Pushing value " ?value crlf))
```

Two rules are necessary to implement the pop action: one for an empty stack and another if the stack has a value to pop:

```
(defrule pop-value-valid
   ?pop-value <- (pop-value)
   ?stack <- (stack ?value $?rest)
   =>
   (retract ?pop-value ?stack)
   (assert (stack $?rest))
   (printout t "Popping value " ?value crlf))

(defrule pop-value-invalid
   ?pop-value <- (pop-value)
   (stack)
   =>
   (retract ?pop-value)
   (printout t "Popping from empty stack" crlf))
```

These rules could easily be changed to push and pop values to named stacks. For example, the patterns:

```
?push-value <- (push-value ?value)
?stack <- (stack $?rest)
```

could be replaced with:

```
?push-value <- (push-value ?name ?value)
?stack <- (stack ?name $?rest)
```

where ?name represents the name of the stack.

Blocks World Revisited

The blocks world problem can be reimplemented in a much easier fashion using multifield wildcards and variables. Each stack can be represented by a single fact, as shown below. The operations on moving the blocks are similar to those used in the push/pop example.

```
(deffacts initial-state
   (stack A B C)
   (stack D E F)
   (goal (move C) (on-top-of E))
   (stack))
```

The empty *stack* fact is included to prevent this fact from being added later; for example, when a stack has one block in it and that block is moved on top of another.

The rules for the blocks world program using multifield variables are:

```
(defrule move-directly
   ?goal <- (goal (move ?block1)
                  (on-top-of ?block2))
   ?stack-1 <- (stack ?block1 $?rest1)
   ?stack-2 <- (stack ?block2 $?rest2)
   =>
   (retract ?goal ?stack-1 ?stack-2)
   (assert (stack $?rest1))
   (assert (stack ?block1 ?block2 $?rest2))
   (printout t ?block1 " moved on top of "
             ?block2 "." crlf))

(defrule move-to-floor
   ?goal <- (goal (move ?block1) (on-top-of floor))
   ?stack-1 <- (stack ?block1 $?rest)
   =>
   (retract ?goal ?stack-1)
   (assert (stack ?block1))
   (assert (stack $?rest))
   (printout t ?block1 " moved on top of floor."
                crlf))

(defrule clear-upper-block
   (goal (move ?block1))
   (stack ?top $? ?block1 $?)
   =>
   (assert (goal (move ?top) (on-top-of floor))))

(defrule clear-lower-block
   (goal (on-top-of ?block1))
   (stack ?top $? ?block1 $?)
   =>
   (assert (goal (move ?top) (on-top-of floor))))
```

7.25 SUMMARY

This chapter introduced the fundamental components of CLIPS. Facts are the first component of a CLIPS system and are made up of fields, which are either a symbol, a string, an integer, or floats. The first field of a fact is normally used to indicate the type of information stored in the fact and is called a *relation name.* The deftemplate construct is used to assign slot names to specific fields of a fact beginning with a specified relation name. The deffacts construct is used to specify facts as initial knowledge.

Rules are the second component of a CLIPS system. A rule is divided into an LHS and an RHS. The LHS of a rule can be thought of as the IF portion and the RHS can be thought of as the THEN portion. Rules can have multiple patterns and actions.

The third component of CLIPS is the inference engine. Rules that have their patterns satisfied by facts produce an activation that is placed on the agenda. Refraction prevents rules from being constantly activated by old facts.

This chapter also introduced the concept of variables, which are used to retrieve information from facts and to constrain slot values when pattern matching on the LHS of a rule. Variables can store the fact addresses of patterns on the LHS of a rule so that the fact bound to the pattern can be retracted on the RHS of the rule. Single-field wildcards can be used in place of variables when the field to be matched against can be anything and its value is not needed later in the LHS or RHS of the rule. Multifield variables and wildcards allow matching against more than one field in a pattern.

PROBLEMS

7.1 Convert the following sentences to facts in a deffacts statement. For each group of related facts, define a deftemplate that describes a more general relationship.

```
The father of John is Tom.
The mother of John is Susan.
The parents of John are Tom and Susan.
Tom is a father.
Susan is a mother.
John is a son.
Tom is a male.
Susan is a female.
John is a male.
```

7.2 Define a deftemplate for a fact containing information about a set. The deftemplate should include information about the name or description of the set, the list of elements in the set, and whether it is a subset of another set. Represent the following sets as facts using the format specified by your deftemplate:

```
A = { 1, 2, 3 }
B = { 1, 2, 3, red, green }
C = { red, green, yellow, blue }
```

7.3 A sparsely populated array contains relatively few nonzero elements. It is more efficiently represented as a linked list or tree. How might a sparsely populated array be represented using facts? Describe the deftemplate used for the facts to represent the array. What are the possible disadvantages of representing an array using facts as opposed to using an array data structure in a procedural language?

7.4 Convert the general net representing airline routes as shown in Figure 2.4a on page 64 to a series of facts in a deffacts statement. Use a single deftemplate to describe the facts.

7.5 Convert the semantic net representing a family as shown in Figure 2.4b on page 64 as a series of facts in a deffacts statement. Use several deftemplates to describe the facts produced.

7.6 Convert the semantic net shown in Figure 2.5 on page 65 to a series of facts in a deffacts statement. Use several deftemplates to describe the facts. For example, the IS-A and AKO links should be relation names and each should have their own deftemplate.

7.7 Convert the binary decision tree representing animal classification information in Figure 3.3 on page 99 to a series of facts in a deffacts statement. Show how the links between the nodes can be represented. Do the leaves of the tree require a different representation from the other nodes of the tree?

7.8 Implement the semantic net of Problem 2.1 as a deffacts statement using AKO and IS-A deftemplates.

7.9 Plants require many different types of nutrients for proper growth. Three of the most important plant nutrients that are provided by fertilizer are nitrogen, phosphorus, and potassium. A deficiency in one of these nutrients will produce various symptoms. Translate the heuristics below to rules that determine nutrient deficiency. Assume that the plant is normally green.

```
A plant with stunted growth may have a nitrogen
   deficiency.
A plant that is pale yellow in color may have a
   nitrogen deficiency.
A plant that has reddish-brown leaf edges may have a
   nitrogen deficiency.
A plant with stunted root growth may have a
   phosphorus deficiency.
A plant with a spindly stalk may have a phosphorus
   deficiency.
A plant that is purplish in color may have a
   phosphorus deficiency.
A plant that has delayed in maturing may have a
   phosphorus deficiency.
A plant with leaf edges that appear scorched may have
   a potassium deficiency.
A plant with weakened stems may have a potassium
   deficiency.
A plant with shriveled seeds or fruits may have a
   potassium deficiency.
```

Use deftemplates to describe the facts used in the rules. The input to the program should be made by asserting symptoms as facts. The output should indicate which nutrient deficiencies exist by printing to the terminal. Implement a method so multiple printouts for a single deficiency caused by more than one symptom are avoided. Test your program with the following inputs:

```
The plant has stunted root growth.
The plant is purplish in color.
```

7.10 Fires are classified according to the principal burning material. Translate the following information to rules for determining fire class:

```
Type A fires involve ordinary combustibles such as
   paper, wood, and cloth.
Type B fires involve flammable and combustible
   liquids (such as oil and gas), greases,
   and similar materials.
Type C fires involve energized electrical equipment.
```

```
Type D fires involve combustible metals such as
   magnesium, sodium, and potassium.
```

The type of extinguisher that should be used on a fire depends on the fire class. Translate the following information to rules:

```
Class A fires should be extinguished with
   heat-absorbing or combustion-retarding
   extinguishers such as water or water-based liquids
   and dry chemicals.
Class B fires should be extinguished by excluding
   air, inhibiting the release of combustible vapors,
   or interrupting the combustion chain reaction.
   Extinguishers include dry chemicals, carbon
   dioxide, foam, and bromotrifluoromethane.
Class C fires should be extinguished with a
   nonconducting agent to prevent short circuits. If
   possible the power should be cut. Extinguishers
   include dry chemicals, carbon dioxide, and
   bromotrifluoromethane.
Class D fires should be extinguished with smothering
   and heat-absorbing chemicals that do not react
   with the burning metals. Such chemicals include
   trimethoxyboroxine and screened graphitized coke.
```

Describe the facts used in the rules. The input to the program should be made by asserting the type of burning material as a fact. The output should indicate which extinguishers may be used and other actions that should be taken, such as cutting off the power. Show that your program works for one material from each of the fire classes.

7.11 Low-altitude clouds, those at 6,000 feet or less, include stratus and stratocumulus clouds. Medium-altitude clouds, those between 6,000 and 20,000 feet, include altostratus, altocumulus, and nimbostratus clouds. High-altitude clouds, those at greater than 20,000 feet, include cirrus, cirrostratus, and cirrocumulus clouds. Cumulus and cumulonimbus clouds can extend from low to high altitudes. Cumulus, stratocumulus, altocumulus, cumulonimbus, and cirrocumulus clouds appear as large rounded piles. Stratus, altostratus, nimbostratus, and cirrostratus clouds appear as smooth even sheets. Cirrus clouds have a wispy appearance, like tufts of hair. Nimbostratus and cumulonimbus clouds are rain clouds and dark gray in color. Write a program to identify cloud types. The input to the program should be facts describing the attributes of the cloud. The program should then print the type of cloud identified.

7.12 Stars can be classified into color groups called *spectral classes*. The classes range from the blue class "O" stars to the yellow class "G" stars to the red class "M" stars. The star's spectral class correlates to its temperature: class "O" stars have a temperature of more than 37,000° F; class "B" temperatures range from 17,001° F to 37,000° F; class "A" temperatures range from 12,501° F to 17,000° F; class "F" temperatures range from 10,301° F to 12,500° F; class "G" temperatures range from 8,001° F to 10,300° F; class "K" temperatures range from 5,501° F to 8,000° F; and class "M" temperatures are 5,500° F or less. Stars can also be classified by their magnitude, which is a measure of their brightness. The lower the magnitude, the brighter the star. Assume that magnitudes can range from -7 to 15. The table below lists some common brightest stars with their spectral class and magnitude and also their distance from Earth in light-years. Write a program that takes as input two facts representing the spectral class and magnitude of a star. The program should then output the following information in this order: all stars having the specified spectral class, all stars having the specified magnitude, and finally all stars matching both the spectral class and magnitude along with their distance from Earth in light-years.

Star	Spectral Class	Magnitude	Distance
Sirius	A	1	8.8
Canopus	F	–3	98
Arcturus	K	0	36
Vega	A	1	26
Capella	G	–1	46
Rigel	B	–7	880
Procyon	F	3	11
Betelgeuse	M	–5	490
Altair	A	2	16
Aldebaran	K	–1	68
Spica	B	–3	300
Antares	M	–4	250
Pollux	K	1	35
Deneb	A	–7	1630

7.13 The table below lists characteristics of common gems including their hardness (resistance to external stresses as measured by Mohs' scale), density (weight per unit volume in grams per cubic centimeter), and colors. Given three facts representing the hardness, density, and color of a gem, write the rules necessary to determine if the gem is a Chyrsoberyl.

Gem	Hardness	Density	Colors
Diamond	10	3.52	yellow, brown, green, blue, white, colorless
Corundum	9	4	red, pink, yellow, brown, green, blue, violet, black, white, colorless
Chrysoberyl	8.5	3.72	yellow, brown, green
Spinel	8	3.6	red, pink, yellow, brown, green, blue, violet, white, colorless
Topaz	8	3.52–3.56	red, pink, yellow, brown, blue, violet, white, colorless
Beryl	7.5–8.0	2.7	red, pink, yellow, brown, green, blue, white, colorless
Zircon	6–7.5	4.7	yellow, brown, green, violet, white, colorless
Quartz	7	2.65	red, pink, green, blue, violet, white, black, colorless
Tourmaline	7	3.1	red, pink, yellow, brown, green, blue, white, black, colorless
Peridot	6.5–7	3.3	yellow, brown, green
Jadeite	6.5–7	3.3	red, pink, yellow, brown, green, blue, violet, white, black, colorless
Opal	5.5–6.5	2–2.2	red, pink, yellow, brown, white, black, colorless
Nephrite	5-6	2.9–3.4	green, white, black, colorless
Turquoise	5-6	2.7	blue

7.14 Write a CLIPS program that aids in the selection process of a suitable shrub for planting. The table below lists several shrubs and indicates whether each shrub possesses certain characteristics, which include tolerance to cold weather, tolerance to shade, tolerance to drought, tolerance to wet soil, tolerance to acidic soil, tolerance to city dwelling (high pollution), tolerance to growth in a container, whether the shrub is easy to care for, and whether the shrub is fast growing. A bullet indicates the shrub has the characteristic. Input to the program should be facts indicating a desired characteristic that the shrub must have, and the output should be a list of the plants having each specified characteristic.

Shrub	Cold	Shade	Dry	Wet Soil	Acid Soil	City	Pot	Easy Care	Grows Fast
French hydrangea		•				•	•		•
Oleander						•	•	•	•
Northern bayberry	•	•	•	•		•		•	•
Box honeysuckle						•	•	•	•
Gardenia		•			•		•		
Common juniper	•		•		•	•		•	
Sweet pepperbush	•	•		•	•			•	
Tartarian dogwood	•	•		•		•		•	
Japanese aucuba		•	•				•	•	
Swamp azalea		•		•	•		•		

7.15 In a stack the first value added is the last value removed and the last value added is the first value removed. A queue works in the opposite manner—the first value added is the first value removed and the last value added is the last value removed. Write rules that will add and remove values to a queue. Assume that only one queue exists.

7.16 Write one or more rules that will generate all the permutations of a base fact and print them out. For example, the fact:

```
(base-fact red green blue)
```

should generate the output:

```
Permutation is (red green blue)
Permutation is (red blue green)
Permutation is (green red blue)
Permutation is (green blue red)
Permutation is (blue red green)
Permutation is (blue green red)
```

7.17 Write rules that will take a finite state machine from its present state to its next state given a fact of the form:

```
(input <value>)
```

The state machine and its arcs should be represented as facts. The input fact should be retracted when the machine goes to its next state. Test your rules and fact representations on the finite state machines shown in Figures 3.5 and 3.6 on pages 101 and 102.

BIBLIOGRAPHY

(Firebaugh 88). Morris W. Firebaugh, *Artificial Intelligence: A Knowledge-Based Approach*, Boyd & Fraser Publishing Co., pp. 224–226, 1988.

CHAPTER 8
Advanced Pattern Matching

8.1 INTRODUCTION

The types of rules shown in Chapter 7 illustrate simple pattern matching of patterns to facts. This chapter will introduce several concepts that provide powerful capabilities for matching and manipulating facts. The first is field constraints. The use of functions in CLIPS will then be introduced including a number of functions for basic arithmetic and I/O operations. Various techniques for controlling the execution of rules will be discussed. Groups of rules are used to build more powerful and more complex programs than have been shown in the last chapter. Techniques for input, comparing values, and generating loops will be demonstrated, as will techniques for specifying control knowledge using rules. Several other types of conditional elements besides the pattern CE are introduced here. These conditional elements allow a single rule to perform the function of several rules and provide the capability to allow matching against the absence of facts.

8.2 FIELD CONSTRAINTS

The *Not* Field Constraint

In addition to the elementary pattern-matching capabilities of literal constants and variable bindings, CLIPS has more powerful pattern-matching operators. These additional pattern-matching capabilities will be introduced by reconsidering the problem of determining groups of people with certain hair and eye colors. For example, suppose it is necessary to find all people who do *not* have brown hair. One way to do this is to write rules for each type of hair color. For example, the following rule finds people with black hair (the *person* deftemplate from Section 7.19 is used for the examples in this section):

```
(defrule black-hair-is-not-brown-hair
   (person (name ?name) (hair black))
   =>
   (printout t ?name " does not have brown hair"
                  crlf))
```

Another rule finds people with blonde hair:

```
(defrule blonde-hair-is-not-brown-hair
   (person (name ?name) (hair blonde))
   =>
   (printout t ?name " does not have brown hair"
              crlf))
```

Yet another rule could be written to find people with red hair. The problem with writing the rules in this manner is that the condition being checked is that the hair is not brown. The previous rules attempt to test this condition in a roundabout manner—that is, they determine all the hair colors other than brown and write a rule for each one. If all the colors can be specified, then this technique will work. For this example it would be simpler to assume that hair color could be anything (even purple or green).

One way of handling this problem is to use a **field constraint** to restrict the values a field may have on the LHS. One type of field constraint is called a ***connective constraint*** (so called because it is used for connecting variables and other constraints). There are three types of connective constraints. The first is called a ***not* constraint**. Its symbol is the tilde, "~." The *not* constraint acts on the one constraint or variable that immediately follows it. If the constraint following matched a field, then the *not* constraint fails. If the constraint following failed to match, then the *not* constraint succeeds. Essentially the *not* constraint negates the result of the constraint following.

The rule that looks for people without brown hair can be written much more easily using the *not* constraint:

```
(defrule person-without-brown-hair
   (person (name ?name) (hair ~brown))
   =>
   (printout t ?name " does not have brown hair"
                  crlf))
```

By using the *not* constraint this one rule does the work of many others that required specifying each possible hair color.

The *Or* Field Constraint

The second connective constraint is the ***or* constraint**, represented by the bar, "|." The *or* constraint is used to allow one or more possible values to match a field of a pattern.

For example, the following rule finds all people with either black or brown hair using the *or* constraint:

```
(defrule black-or-brown-hair
   (person (name ?name) (hair brown | black))
   =>
   (printout t ?name " has dark hair" crlf))
```

Asserting the facts (person (name Joe) (eyes blue) (hair brown)) and (person (name Mark) (eyes brown) (hair black)) would place an activation of this rule for each of the facts on the agenda.

The *And* Field Constraint

The third type of connective constraint is the ***and* constraint**. The *and* constraint is different from the *and* conditional element discussed in Section 7.15. The symbol of the *and* constraint is the ampersand, "&." The *and* constraint is normally used only with the other constraints; otherwise it's not of much practical use.

One case in which the *and* constraint is useful is in placing additional constraints with the binding instance of a variable. Suppose, for example, that a rule is triggered by a *person* fact with the hair color brown or black. The pattern to find such a fact can be expressed easily using the *or* constraint, as shown in the previous example. However, how can the value of the hair color be identified? The solution is to bind a variable to the color that is matched using the *and* constraint and then print out the variable:

```
(defrule black-or-brown-hair
   (person (name ?name) (hair ?color&brown|black))
   =>
   (printout t ?name " has " ?color " hair" crlf))
```

The variable ?color will be bound to whatever color is matched by the brown|black constraint.

The *and* constraint is also useful with the *not* constraint. For example, the following rule triggers when a person's hair color is neither black nor brown:

```
(defrule black-or-brown-hair
   (person (name ?name)
           (hair ?color&~brown&~black))
   =>
   (printout t ?name " has " ?color " hair" crlf))
```

Combining Field Constraints

Field constraints can be used together with variables and other literal values to provide powerful pattern-matching capabilities. Suppose, for example, that a rule is needed to determine whether two people exist with the following descriptive conditions. The first person has either blue or green eyes and does not have black hair. The second person does not have the same color eyes as the first person and has either red hair or the same color hair as the first person. The following rule will match these constraints:

```
(defrule complex-eye-hair-match
   (person (name ?name1)
           (eyes ?eyes1&blue|green)
           (hair ?hair1&~black))
   (person (name ?name2&~?name1)
           (eyes ?eyes2&~?eyes1)
           (hair ?hair2&red|?hair1))
  =>
   (printout t ?name1 " has " ?eyes1 " eyes and "
               ?hair1 " hair" crlf)
   (printout t ?name2 " has " ?eyes2 " eyes and "
               ?hair2 " hair" crlf))
```

This example is worth studying in some detail. The constraint ?eyes1&blue|green in the first pattern's *eyes* slot binds the first person's eye color to the variable ?eyes1 if the eye color value of the fact being matched is either blue or green. The constraint ?hair1&~black in the first pattern's *hair* slot binds the variable ?hair1 if the hair color value of the fact being matched is not black.

The constraint ?name2&~?name1 in the second pattern's *name* slot performs a useful operation. It binds the value of the *name* slot of the *person* fact to the variable ?name2 if it is not the same as the value of ?name1. If names are unique identifiers (i.e., no two people in the database have the same name), this will ensure that both patterns do not match the same fact. This cannot happen for these two patterns, since the eye color of the second person must be different from the eye color of the first. However, it is a useful technique to understand and has many useful applications. Section 12.2 will show how this same technique can be accomplished using fact addresses to make sure the facts are different. This will allow the rule to work for people with the same names but different hair and eye colors.

The constraint ?eyes2&~?eyes1 in the second pattern's *eyes* slot performs much the same test as the previous constraint. The final constraint, ?hair2&red|?hair1, in the second pattern's *hair* slot binds the hair color value of the second person to the variable ?hair2 if the hair color is either red or the same value as the variable ?hair1. Note that a variable must already be bound if it is used as part of an *or* field constraint.

Variables will be bound only if they are the first condition in a field and only if they occur singly or are tied to the other conditions by an *and* connective constraint. For example, the rule:

```
(defrule bad-variable-use
   (person (name ?name) (hair red|?hair))
  =>
   (printout t ?name " has " ?hair " hair " crlf))
```

will produce an error since ?hair is not bound.

As a final note for combining constraints, keep in mind that there are combinations of constraints that perform no useful purpose. For example, using the *and* constraint to tie together literal constants (e.g., black&blue) will always cause the constraint to not be satisfied unless the literals are identical. Similarly, tying together negated literals using the *or* constraint (e.g., ~black|~blue) will always cause the constraint to be satisfied.

8.3 FUNCTIONS AND EXPRESSIONS

Elementary Math Functions

In addition to dealing with symbolic facts, CLIPS can perform calculations. Keep in mind, though, that an expert systems language like CLIPS is not designed for number crunching. Although the math functions of CLIPS are powerful, they are primarily meant for modification of numbers that are being used to make inferences by the application program. Other languages such as FORTRAN are better for number crunching in which little or no reasoning about the numbers is done. CLIPS provides the elementary arithmetic operators, shown in Table 8.1. (Appendix E contains a list of other mathematical functions provided by CLIPS. The *Basic Programming Guide*, provided in electronic format in the CD-ROM accompanying this book, offers additional details on all of the functions available in CLIPS.)

Table 8.1 CLIPS Elementary Arithmetic Operators

Arithmetic Operators	Meaning
+	Addition
–	Subtraction
*	Multiplication
/	Division

Numeric expressions are represented in CLIPS according to the style of LISP. In LISP and CLIPS, a numeric expression that would customarily be written as 2 + 3 must be written in **prefix form**, (+ 2 3). The customary way of writing numeric expressions is called **infix form** because the math operators are between the **operands** or **arguments**. In the prefix form of CLIPS the operator must go before the operands and parentheses must surround the numeric expression.

It is relatively easy to convert from infix to prefix format. For example, suppose two points are to be checked to see whether they have a positive slope. In the customary infix way, this can be written as:

```
(y2 - y1) / (x2 - x1)  >  0
```

Note that the greater than symbol, ">," is a CLIPS function that determines if the first argument is greater than the second argument. (The > function is described in Appendix E and in the *Basic Programming Guide*.) In order to write this expression in prefix form it will be useful to start by thinking of the numerator as (Y) and the denominator as (X). So the expression above can be written as:

```
(Y) / (X) > 0
```

The prefix form for division is then:

```
(/ (Y) (X))
```

since in prefix form the operator comes before the argument. Now the result of the division must be tested to determine whether it is greater than 0. Thus the prefix form is as follows:

```
(> (/ (Y) (X)) 0)
```

In infix form, Y = y2 – y1. But the prefix form needs to be used, since a prefix expression is being created. So (– y2 y1) will be used for (Y) and (– x2 x1) for (X). Replacing (Y) and (X) by their prefix forms will yield the final expression of whether the two points have a positive slope:

```
(> (/ (- y2 y1) (- x2 x1)) 0)
```

The simplest way to evaluate a numeric expression (as well as any other expression) in CLIPS is to evaluate the expression at the top-level prompt. For example, entering (+ 2 2) at the CLIPS prompt would produce the following output:

```
CLIPS> (+ 2 2)↵
4
CLIPS>
```

The output shows the correct response, 4. In general, any CLIPS expression to be evaluated can be entered at the top level. Most functions, such as the addition function, have a **return value**. This return value can be an integer, a float, a symbol, a string, or even a multifield value. Other functions, such as the *facts* and *agenda* commands, have no return value. Functions without a return value typically have what is called a **side effect**. The side effect of the *facts* command is to list the facts in the fact list.

The other arithmetic functions also work at the top level. The following output demonstrates the evaluation of some other expressions:

```
CLIPS> (+ 2 3)↵
5
CLIPS> (- 2 3)↵
-1
CLIPS> (* 2 3)↵
```

```
6
CLIPS> (/ 2 3)↵
0.66666667
CLIPS>
```

Note that the answer for division will probably show a round-off error in the last digit. This result may vary from machine to machine.

The return value of the +, –, and * functions is an integer if all of the arguments to the function are integers. If one of the arguments to the function is a floating-point number, then the return value is a floating-point number. The first argument to the / function is always converted to a float, so the return value of this function is always a float. For example,

```
CLIPS> (+ 2 3.0)↵
5.0
CLIPS> (+ 2.0 3)↵
5.0
CLIPS> (+ 2 3)↵
5
CLIPS>
```

Variable Numbers of Arguments

Prefix notation allows variable numbers of arguments to be represented quite simply. Many CLIPS functions accept a variable number of arguments. The arguments in a numeric expression can be extended beyond two for the +, –, /, and * functions. The same sequence of arithmetic calculations is performed for more than two arguments. The following examples, entered at the top level, show how three arguments are used. Evaluation proceeds from left to right:

```
CLIPS> (+ 2 3 4)↵
9
CLIPS> (- 2 3 4)↵
-5
CLIPS> (* 2 3 4)↵
24
CLIPS> (/ 2 3 4)↵
0.16666667
CLIPS>
```

Once again note that the answer for division may vary slightly depending on the machine being used.

Precedence and Nesting Expressions

One important fact about CLIPS and LISP calculations is that there is no built-in precedence of arithmetic operations. In other computer languages, multiplication and division rank higher than addition and subtraction and the computer does the higher–ranked operations first. In LISP and CLIPS everything is simply evaluated from left to right, with parentheses determining precedence.

Mixed calculations can be done in prefix notation. For example, suppose the following infix expression is to be evaluated:

```
2 + 3 * 4
```

The customary evaluation is to multiply 3 by 4 and then add the result to 2. However, in CLIPS the precedence must be explicitly written. The expression could be evaluated by entering the following at the top level:

```
CLIPS> (+ 2 (* 3 4))↵
14
CLIPS>
```

In this rule the expression in the innermost parentheses is evaluated first, so 3 is multiplied by 4. The result is then added to 2. If the desired evaluation is (2 + 3) * 4, where addition is done first, the top-level expression would be:

```
CLIPS> (* (+ 2 3) 4)↵
20
CLIPS>
```

In general, expressions may be freely embedded within other expressions. Thus it is possible to place an expression within an assert command, as the following example shows:

```
CLIPS> (clear)↵
CLIPS> (assert (answer (+ 2 2)))↵
<Fact-0>
CLIPS> (facts)↵
f-0    (answer 4)
For a total of 1 fact.
CLIPS>
```

Also, since function names are also symbols, you can use them as you would other symbols. For example, you could use them as fields in a fact:

```
CLIPS> (clear)↵
CLIPS> (assert (expression 2 + 3 * 4))↵
<Fact-0>
CLIPS> (facts)↵
f-0    (expression 2 + 3 * 4)
For a total of 1 fact.
CLIPS>
```

However, parentheses are used by CLIPS as delimiters, so it's not possible to use them as you would other symbols. In order to use them in facts or as an argument to a function, enclose them in quotation marks to make them strings.

8.4 SUMMING VALUES USING RULES

As a simple example of using functions to perform calculations, consider the problem of summing up the area of a group of rectangles. The heights and widths of the rectangles can be specified using the following deftemplate:

```
(deftemplate rectangle (slot height) (slot width))
```

and the sum of rectangle areas could be specified using an ordered fact such as the following:

```
(sum 20)
```

A deffacts containing sample information is:

```
(deffacts initial-information
   (rectangle (height 10) (width 6))
   (rectangle (height 7) (width 5))
   (rectangle (height 6) (width 8))
   (rectangle (height 2) (width 5))
   (sum 0))
```

An initial attempt to produce a rule to sum the rectangle might be:

```
(defrule sum-rectangles
   (rectangle (height ?height) (width ?width))
   ?sum <- (sum ?total)
   =>
   (retract ?sum)
   (assert (sum (+ ?total (* ?height ?width)))))
```

This rule, however, will loop endlessly. Retracting the *sum* fact and then reasserting it will produce a loop with a single *rectangle* fact. One solution to solve the problem would be to retract the *rectangle* fact after its area was added to the *sum* fact. This would prevent the rule from firing off the same *rectangle* fact with a different *sum* fact. If the *rectangle* fact needs to be preserved, a different approach is required. A temporary fact containing the area to be added to the sum is created for each *rectangle* fact. This temporary fact can then be retracted, preventing an endless loop. The modified program is as follows:

```
(defrule sum-rectangles
   (rectangle (height ?height) (width ?width))
   =>
   (assert (add-to-sum (* ?height ?width))))

(defrule sum-areas
   ?sum <- (sum ?total)
   ?new-area <- (add-to-sum ?area)
   =>
   (retract ?sum ?new-area)
   (assert (sum (+ ?total ?area))))
```

The following output shows how these two rules interact to sum the areas of the rectangles:

```
CLIPS> (unwatch all)↵
CLIPS> (watch rules)↵
CLIPS> (watch facts)↵
CLIPS> (watch activations)↵
CLIPS> (reset)↵
==> f-0       (initial-fact)
==> f-1       (rectangle (height 10) (width 6))
==> Activation 0        sum-rectangles: f-1
==> f-2       (rectangle (height 7) (width 5))
==> Activation 0        sum-rectangles: f-2
==> f-3       (rectangle (height 6) (width 8))
==> Activation 0        sum-rectangles: f-3
==> f-4       (rectangle (height 2) (width 5))
==> Activation 0        sum-rectangles: f-4
==> f-5       (sum 0)
CLIPS> (run)↵
FIRE    1 sum-rectangles: f-4
==> f-6       (add-to-sum 10)
==> Activation 0          sum-areas: f-5,f-6
FIRE    2 sum-areas: f-5,f-6
<== f-5       (sum 0)
<== f-6       (add-to-sum 10)
==> f-7       (sum 10)
FIRE    3 sum-rectangles: f-3
==> f-8       (add-to-sum 48)
==> Activation 0    sum-areas: f-7,f-8
FIRE    4 sum-areas: f-7,f-8
<== f-7       (sum 10)
<== f-8       (add-to-sum 48)
==> f-9       (sum 58)
FIRE    5 sum-rectangles: f-2
```

```
==> f-10       (add-to-sum 35)
==> Activation 0    sum-areas: f-9,f-10
FIRE    6 sum-areas: f-9,f-10
<== f-9       (sum 58)
<== f-10      (add-to-sum 35)
==> f-11      (sum 93)
FIRE    7 sum-rectangles: f-1
==> f-12      (add-to-sum 60)
==> Activation 0    sum-areas: f-11,f-12
FIRE    8 sum-areas: f-11,f-12
<== f-11      (sum 93)
<== f-12      (add-to-sum 60)
==> f-13      (sum 153)
CLIPS> (unwatch all)↵
CLIPS>
```

The *sum-rectangles* rule is activated four times when the *rectangle* facts are asserted as a result of the *reset* command. Each time the *sum-rectangles* rule is fired it asserts a fact that activates the *sum-areas* rule. The *sum-areas* rule adds the area to the running total and removes the *add-to-sum* fact. Since the *sum-rectangles* rule does not pattern match against the *sum* fact, it is not reactivated when a new *sum* fact is asserted.

8.5 THE *BIND* FUNCTION

It is often useful to store a value in a temporary variable to avoid recalculation, which is crucial when functions produce side effects. The **bind** function can be used to bind the value of a variable to the value of an expression. The syntax of the *bind* function is:

```
(bind <variable> <value>)
```

The bound variable, <variable>, uses the syntax of a single-field variable. The new value, <value>, should be an expression that evaluates to either a single-field or a multifield value. For example, the *sum-areas* rule could print out the total sum and the area being added to it for each rectangle:

```
(defrule sum-areas
   ?sum <- (sum ?total)
   ?new-area <- (add-to-sum ?area)
   =>
   (retract ?sum ?new-area)
   (printout t "Adding " ?area " to " ?total crlf)
   (printout t "New sum is " (+ ?total ?area) crlf)
   (assert (sum (+ ?total ?area))))
```

Notice that the expression (+ ?total ?area) is used twice in the RHS of the rule. Replacing the two separate evaluations with one *bind* function would eliminate unnecessary calculations. The rule rewritten with the *bind* function is:

```
(defrule sum-areas
   ?sum <- (sum ?total)
   ?new-area <- (add-to-sum ?area)
   =>
   (retract ?sum ?new-area)
   (printout t "Adding " ?area " to " ?total crlf)
   (bind ?new-total (+ ?total ?area))
   (printout t "New sum is " ?new-total crlf)
   (assert (sum ?new-total)))
```

In addition to creating new variables for use on the RHS of a rule, the *bind* function can be used to rebind the value of a variable used in the LHS of a rule.

8.6 I/O FUNCTIONS

The *Read* Function

Expert systems often require input from the user of the program. CLIPS allows information to be read from the keyboard using the **read** function. The basic syntax of the *read* function requires no arguments and the following example shows how it is used to input data:

```
CLIPS> (clear)↵
CLIPS>
(defrule get-first-name
   =>
   (printout t "What is your first name? ")
   (bind ?response (read))
   (assert (user's-name ?response)))
CLIPS> (reset)↵
CLIPS> (run)↵
What is your first name? Gary↵
CLIPS> (facts)↵
f-0     (initial-fact)
f-1     (user's-name Gary)
For a total of 2 facts.
CLIPS>
```

Notice that the *read* function requires a carriage return before it will read the token entered. The *read* function can be used to input only a single field at a time. All extra characters entered after the first field, up to the carriage return, are discarded. For example, if the *get-first-name* rule tried to read both the first name and the last name with the following input,

```
Gary Riley↵
```

only the first field, *Gary*, will be read. To read all of the input, both fields must be enclosed within double quotes. Of course, once the input is within double quotes, it is a single literal field. The individual fields, *Gary* and *Riley,* cannot easily be accessed.

The read function allows fields that are not symbols, strings, integers, or floats, such as parentheses, to be entered. Such fields are placed within double quotes and treated as strings. The following command-line dialog demonstrates this capability:

```
CLIPS> (read)↵
(↵
"("
CLIPS>
```

The *Open* Function

In addition to keyboard input and terminal output, CLIPS can also read from and write to files. Before a file can be accessed for reading or writing, it must be opened using the **open** function. The number of files that can be open simultaneously depends on the individual operating system and hardware.

The syntax of the *open* function is:

```
(open <file-name> <file-ID> [<file-access>])
```

As an example,

```
(open "input.dat" data "r")
```

The first argument of *open*, <file-name>, is a string representing the name of the file on your computer. In the example, the file name "input.dat" is used. The file name may also include path information (the directory in which the file is found). Path specifications typically vary from one operating system to another, so you will have to be somewhat familiar with your computer's operating system to specify a path.

The second argument, <file-ID>, is the **logical name** CLIPS associates with the file. The logical name is a global name by which CLIPS can access the file from any rule or the top-level prompt. Although the logical name could be the same as the file name, it is good idea to use a different name to avoid confusion. For the example shown, the logical name *data* was used to refer to the "input.dat" file. Other meaningful names, such as input or file-data, could have been used.

One advantage of using a logical name is that a different file name can easily be substituted without making major changes to the program. Since the file name is used only in the *open* function and is later referred to by its logical name, only the *open* function need be changed to read from a different file.

The third argument, <file-access>, is a string representing one of the four possible modes of file access. Table 8.2 lists the file access modes.

Table 8.2 File Access Modes

Mode	Action
"r"	Read access only
"w"	Write access only
"r+"	Read and write access
"a"	Append access only

If <file-access> is not included as an argument, the default value of "r" will be used. Some access modes may not be meaningful to certain operating systems. Most operating systems will support read access (for inputting data) and write access (for outputting data). Read and write access and append access (for appending output data to the end of a file) may not always be available.

It is important to remember that the consequences of opening a file may vary from one machine to another. For example, operating systems that do not support multiple file versions, such as MS-DOS on an IBM PC or UNIX, will replace an existing file if that file is opened using write access. In contrast, VMS on a VAX will create a new version of a file if it already exists and is opened using write access.

The *open* function acts as a predicate function (described in Section 8.8). It returns the symbol *TRUE* if a file was successfully opened; otherwise the symbol *FALSE* is returned. The return value can be used to perform error checking. For example, if the user supplies the name of a file that does not exist and an attempt is made to open the file using read access, the *open* function will return the symbol *FALSE*. The rule that opens the file could detect this and perform the appropriate actions to prompt the user for another file name.

The Close Function

Once access is no longer needed to a file, it should be closed. Unless a file is closed, there is no guarantee that the information written to it will be saved. Furthermore, the longer a file is open, the greater the chances that a power loss or other malfunction would prevent the information from being saved.

The general form of the **close** function is:

```
(close [<file-ID>])
```

where the optional argument <file-ID> specifies the logical name of the file to be closed. If <file-ID> is not specified, all open files will be closed. As an example,

```
(close data)
```

will close the file known to CLIPS by the logical file name *data*. The statements:

```
(close input)
(close output)
```

will close the files associated with the logical names *input* and *output*. Note that separate statements are necessary to close specific files.

It is important when using files to remember that each opened file should eventually be closed with the *close* function. In particular, if a command is not issued to close a file, the data written to it may be lost. CLIPS will not prompt you to close an open file. The only safeguard built into CLIPS for closing files that have been inadvertently left open is that all open files will be closed when an *exit* command is issued.

Reading and Writing to a File

In the examples thus far, all input has been read from the keyboard and all output has been sent to the terminal. The use of logical names allows input and output to and from other sources. In Chapter 7 the *printout* function used the logical name *t* to send output to the screen. Other logical names can be used with the *printout* function to send output to destinations other than the screen.

When used as a logical name for an output function, the logical name *t* writes output to the standard output device, usually the terminal. Similarly, when used as the logical name for an input function, the logical name *t* reads input from the **standard input device**, normally the keyboard.

The following example illustrates the use of logical names for writing to a file:

```
CLIPS> (open "example.dat" example "w")↵
TRUE
CLIPS> (printout example "green" crlf)↵
CLIPS> (printout example 7 crlf)↵
CLIPS> (close example)↵
TRUE
CLIPS>
```

First, the file "example.dat" is opened with write access so values may be written to it. The open function has now associated the logical name example with the "example.dat" file. The values *green* and 7 are then written to the file "example.dat" by using the logical name *example* as the first argument to the *printout* function. Once the values have been written to the file, the file is closed using the *close* command.

Now that the values have been written to the file, it can be opened with read access and the values can be retrieved using the *read* function. The general format of the *read* function is:

```
(read [<logical-name>])
```

The *read* function defaults to reading from the standard input device, *t*, if it is given no arguments. The previous example of the *read* function made use of this default logical name. The following example shows how a logical name can be used with the *read* function to retrieve the values from the "example.dat" file:

```
CLIPS> (open "example.dat" example "r")↵
TRUE
CLIPS> (read example)↵
green
CLIPS> (read example)↵
7
CLIPS> (read example)↵
EOF
CLIPS> (close example)↵
TRUE
CLIPS>
```

First the file "example.dat" is opened, but with read access this time. Note that the "r" option did not have to be used for opening the "example.dat" file with the second call to the *open* function since that is the default. Once the file is open, the *read* function is used to retrieve the values *green* and 7 from the file associated with the logical name *example*. Notice that the third call of the *read* function returns the symbol **EOF**. CLIPS returns this value for input functions when an attempt is made to read past the end of the file. By checking the return value of the *read* (or other input) function it is possible to determine when there are no more data left in the file.

The *Format* Function

There are times when it is desirable to format output from a CLIPS program, such as when arranging data in tables. Although the *printout* function is useful, there is a function specifically designed for formatting, called **format**, which provides a wide variety of formatting styles. The syntax of the *format* function is:

```
(format  <logical-name> <control-string>
         <parameters>*)
```

The *format* function has several parts. The <logical-name> is the logical name where the output is sent. The default standard output device can be specified with the logical name *t*. Next comes a **control string**, which must be contained within double quotes. The control string consists of **format flags**, which indicate how the parameters to the *format* function should be printed. Following the control string is a list of parameters. The number of format flags in the control string will determine how many parameters should be specified. Parameters can be either constant values or expressions. The return value of the *format* function is the formatted string. If the logical name *nil* is used with the format command, then no output is printed (either to the terminal or a file), but the formatted string is still returned.

An example of the *format* function is shown by the following dialog, which creates a formatted string containing a person's name (reserving 15 spaces for the name) followed by the person's age. In the example notice how the names and ages are aligned in columns. The *format* function is useful for displaying columns of data:

```
CLIPS> (format nil "Name: %-15s Age: %3d"
                   "Bob Green" 35)↲
"Name: Bob Green          Age: 35"
CLIPS> (format nil "Name: %-15s Age: %3d"
            "Ralph Heiden" 32)↲
"Name: Ralph Heiden       Age: 32"
CLIPS>
```

Format flags always begin with a percent sign, "%." Ordinary strings such as "Name:" can also be put in the control string and will be printed in the output. Some format flags do not format parameters. For example, "%n" is used to put a carriage return/line feed in the output much as the symbol *crlf* is used with the *printout* command.

In this example the format flag "%-15s" is used to print the name in a column that is 15 characters wide. The - sign indicates that the output is to be left justified and the character *s* indicates that a string or symbol is to be printed. The format flag "%3d" indicates that a number is to be printed right justified as an integer value in a three-character column. If the value 5.25 had been supplied as the parameter for the format flag, then the number 5 would have been printed since the fractional part of a number is not allowed in an integer format.

Note that when the *format* function is used on the RHS of a rule, its return value is usually ignored. In these cases the logical name will either be associated with a file or *t* to send output to the screen. The general specification of a format flag is:

```
%-M.Nx
```

where "-" is optional and means to **left justify**. The default is to **right justify**. Justification occurs when the amount of space provided to print a number exceeds the amount of space required to print it. If this situation occurs, left justification of the number will cause it to be printed on the left side of the space provided with unused space to the right filled with character spaces. Right justification causes the number to be printed on the right side of the space provided with unused space to the left filled with character spaces.

The letter M is a number specifying the field width in columns. At least M characters will be output. Spaces are normally used to pad the output to make up the M columns unless M starts with a 0, in which case zeros are used. If the output exceeds M columns, the format function will expand the field as needed.

The letter N is an optional number specifying the number of digits past the decimal point that will be printed. The default is six digits past the decimal point for floating-point numbers.

The letter x is a character specifying the display format specification. Table 8.3 gives the display format specifications.

Table 8.3 Display Format Specifications

Character	Meaning
d	Integer
f	Floating-point
e	Exponential (in power-of-ten format)
g	General (numeric); display in whatever format is shorter
o	Octal; unsigned number (N specifier not applicable)
x	Hexadecimal; unsigned number (N specifier not applicable)
s	String; quoted strings will be stripped of quotes
n	Carriage return/line feed
%	The "%" character itself

The Readline Function

The **readline** function can be used to read an entire line of input. Its syntax is:

```
(readline [<logical-name>])
```

As with the *read* function, the logical name is optional. If no logical name is provided or if the logical name *t* is used, input will be read from the standard input device. The *readline* function will return as a string the next line of input from the input source associated with the logical name up to and including the carriage return. The *readline* function will return the symbol *EOF* if the end of the file has been reached. This will only occur when the logical name used by *readline* is associated with a file. The following dialog illustrates the use of the *readline* function:

```
CLIPS> (clear)↵
CLIPS>
(defrule get-name
   =>
   (printout t "What is your name? ")
   (bind ?response (readline))
   (assert (user's-name ?response)))
CLIPS> (reset)↵
CLIPS> (run)↵
What is your name? Gary Riley↵
CLIPS> (facts)↵
f-0     (initial-fact)
f-1     (user's-name "Gary Riley")
For a total of 2 facts.
CLIPS>
```

In this example the name "Gary Riley" is stored in the *user's-name* fact as a single field. Because it is stored as a single field, it's not possible to directly retrieve the first and last names from the field using pattern variables. Using the **explode$** function, which accepts a single string argument and converts it to a multifield value, we can convert the string returned by the *readline* function to a multifield value, which will be asserted as a series of fields in the *user's-name* fact. The following dialog illustrates the use of the *readline* in conjunction with the *explode$* function:

```
CLIPS>
(defrule get-name
   =>
   (printout t "What is your name? ")
   (bind ?response (explode$ (readline)))
   (assert (user's-name ?response)))↵
CLIPS> (reset)↵
CLIPS> (run)↵
What is your name? Gary Riley
CLIPS> (facts)↵
f-0      (initial-fact)
f-1      (user's-name Gary Riley)
For a total of 2 facts.
CLIPS>$
```

Appendix E contains a list of other functions that are useful for creating and manipulating strings and multifield values. The *Basic Programming Guide* accompanying this book provides additional details on all of the functions available in CLIPS .

8.7 THE GAME OF STICKS

In the next few sections, a simple two-player game called Sticks will be used to demonstrate various techniques of control in a rule-based language. The object of Sticks is to avoid being forced to take the last one in a pile of sticks. Each player must take 1, 2, or 3 sticks in turn. The trick (or heuristic) to winning this game is in noticing that you can force your opponent to lose if it is your turn and there are 2, 3, or 4 sticks remaining. A player who has 5 sticks remaining on his or her move has lost. To force the other player to face 5 sticks, always leave 5 sticks plus some multiple of 4 at the end of your turn. That is, at the end of your turn, force the remaining pile of sticks to 5, 9, 13, and so on. If you move first and the pile is set to one of the "losing" numbers, you cannot win unless your opponent makes a mistake. If you move first and the pile is not set to a "losing" number, then you can always win.

Before it can begin to play Sticks, the program must determine some information. First, because the program will play against a human opponent, it must be determined who will get the first move. In addition, the starting size of the pile must be determined. This information could be placed in a deffacts construct. However, it is quite simple to ask the program's opponent for this information by input from the keyboard. The following example shows how the *read* function is used to input data:

```
(deffacts initial-phase
   (phase choose-player))

(defrule player-select
   (phase choose-player)
   =>
   (printout t "Who moves first (Computer: c "
          "Human: h)? ")
   (assert (player-select (read))))

(defrule good-player-choice
   ?phase <- (phase choose-player)
   ?choice <- (player-select ?player&c | h)
   =>
   (retract ?phase ?choice)
   (assert (player-move ?player)))
```

Both rules use the pattern (phase choose-player) to indicate their applicability only when a specific fact is in the fact list. This is called a **control pattern** because it is specifically used to control when the rule is applicable. A **control fact** is used to trigger a control pattern. Since the control pattern for these rules contains only literal fields, the control fact must match the pattern exactly. In this case the control fact to trigger these rules must be the fact (phase choose-player). This control fact will be useful for error correction when the input received by the read function does not match the expected values of "c" or "h," for "computer" and "human." By retracting and reasserting the control fact, the *player-select* rule can be retriggered.

The following output shows how the *player-select* and *good-player-choice* rules work to determine who should move first:

```
CLIPS> (unwatch all)↵
CLIPS> (watch facts)↵
CLIPS> (reset)↵
==> f-0     (initial-fact)
==> f-1     (phase choose-player)
CLIPS> (run)↵
Who moves first (Computer: c Human: h)? c↵
==> f-2     (player-select c)
<== f-1     (phase choose-player)
<== f-2     (player-select c)
==> f-3     (player-move c)
CLIPS>
```

These rules work properly if the correct response of *c* or *h* is entered, but if an incorrect response is entered no error checking is performed. There are many situations in which an input request should be repeated to correct faulty input. One way of programming an input request loop is shown in the next example. The following rule used in conjunction with the *player-select* and *good-player-choice* rules provides error checking:

```
(defrule bad-player-choice
   ?phase <- (phase choose-player)
   ?choice <- (player-select ?player&~c&~h)
   =>
   (retract ?phase ?choice)
   (assert (phase choose-player))
   (printout t "Choose c or h." crlf))
```

Once again, note the use of the control pattern (phase choose-player). It provides the basic control for the input loop and also prevents this group of rules from firing during other phases of execution in the program.

Notice how the two rules, *player-select* and *bad-player-choice*, work together in that each rule supplies the facts necessary to activate the other. If the response to the player question is incorrect, the *bad-player-choice* rule will retract the control fact (phase choose-player) and then reassert it, causing the *player-select* rule to be reactivated.

8.8 PREDICATE FUNCTIONS

A **predicate function** is defined to be any function that returns either the symbol *TRUE* or the symbol *FALSE*. Actually, when dealing with predicate logic, CLIPS treats any value other than the symbol FALSE as the symbol TRUE. A predicate function may also be thought of as having a Boolean return value. Predicate functions may be either **predefined** or **user-defined functions**. Predefined functions are those functions already provided by CLIPS. User-defined or **external functions** are functions other than predefined functions that are written in C or another language and linked with CLIPS. Appendix E contains a list of predefined CLIPS predicate functions for performing Boolean logic operations, comparing values, and testing for a specific type. Some of these functions are shown in the following dialog:

```
CLIPS> (and (> 4 3) (> 4 5))↵
FALSE
CLIPS> (or (> 4 3) (> 4 5))↵
TRUE
CLIPS> (> 4 3)↵
TRUE
CLIPS> (< 6 2)↵
FALSE
CLIPS> (integerp 3)↵
TRUE
```

```
CLIPS> (integerp 3.5)↵
FALSE
CLIPS>
```

8.9 THE TEST CONDITIONAL ELEMENT

There are many instances in which it is useful to repeat a calculation or other information processing. The common way of doing this is by setting up a loop. In the previous example a loop was set up to repeat until the user responded correctly to a question. However, there are many situations in which a loop needs to terminate automatically as the result of the evaluation of an arbitrary expression.

The **test conditional element** provides a powerful way to evaluate expressions on the LHS of the rule. Instead of pattern matching against a fact in the fact list, the test CE evaluates an expression. The outermost function of the expression must be a predicate function. If the expression evaluates to any value other than the symbol *FALSE*, the test CE is satisfied. If the expression evaluates to the symbol *FALSE*, the test CE is not satisfied. A rule will be triggered only if all its test CEs are satisfied along with other patterns. The syntax of the test CE is:

```
(test <predicate-function>)
```

As an example, suppose it is the human player's turn. If only one stick remains in the pile, the human player has lost. If there is more than one stick, the human player should be asked how many sticks are to be removed from the pile. The rule that asks the human player how many sticks should be removed from the pile needs to check that there is more than one stick remaining in the pile. The > predicate function can be used to express this constraint, as shown in the following test CE, where ?size is the number of sticks remaining in the pile:

```
(test (> ?size 1))
```

Once the human player has stated the number of sticks to be removed, the response must be checked to ensure that it is valid. The number of sticks taken must be an integer and it must be greater than or equal to one and less than or equal to three. A player cannot take more sticks than are in the pile and must be forced to take the last stick. The *and* predicate function can be used to express all of these constraints, as shown in the following test CE, where ?choice would contain the number of sticks to be taken and ?size is the number of sticks remaining in the pile:

```
(test (and (integerp ?choice)
           (>= ?choice 1)
           (<= ?choice 3)
           (< ?choice ?size)))
```

Likewise, an invalid number of sticks to take would be a value that is not an integer, less than one or greater than three, or greater than or equal to the number of sticks remaining. This can be expressed using the *or* predicate function, as shown in the following test CE, where ?choice would contain the number of sticks to be taken and ?size is the number of sticks remaining in the pile:

```
(test (or (not (integerp ?choice))
          (< ?choice 1)
          (> ?choice 3)
          (>= ?choice ?size)))
```

The following rules use the preceding test CEs to check that the human player has taken a valid number of sticks. The *pile-size* fact used in these rules stores the information about the number of sticks remaining in the pile:

```
(defrule get-human-move
   (player-move h)
   (pile-size ?size)
   ; Human player only has a choice when there is
   ; more than one stick remaining in the pile
   (test (> ?size 1))
   =>
   (printout t
          "How many sticks do you wish to take?")
   (assert (human-takes (read))))

(defrule good-human-move
   ?whose-turn <- (player-move h)
   (pile-size ?size)
   ?number-taken <- (human-takes ?choice)
   (test (and (integerp ?choice)
              (>= ?choice 1)
              (<= ?choice 3)
              (< ?choice ?size)))
=>
   (retract ?whose-turn ?number-taken)
   (printout t "Human made a valid move" crlf))

(defrule bad-human-move
   ?whose-turn <- (player-move h)
   (pile-size ?size)
   ?number-taken <- (human-takes ?choice)
   (test (or (not (integerp ?choice))
             (< ?choice 1)
             (> ?choice 3)
             (>= ?choice ?size)))
=>
   (printout t "Human made an invalid move" crlf)
   (retract ?whose-turn ?number-taken)
   (assert (player-move h)))
```

This program will end when a valid choice for the number of sticks taken has been entered. Once again, a control fact is used to retrigger a rule to allow invalid responses to be reentered. The *bad-human-move* rule will reassert the control fact (player-move h) to reactivate the *get-human-move* rule. The human player can then reenter the number of sticks to be taken from the pile.

8.10 THE PREDICATE FIELD CONSTRAINT

The **predicate field constraint**, :, is useful for performing predicate tests directly within patterns. In many ways it is similar to performing a test CE directly after a pattern, although in some cases, as will be discussed in Chapter 9, it is more efficient to use the predicate field constraint than it is to use a test CE. The predicate field constraint can be used just like a literal field constraint. It can stand by itself in a field or be used as one part of a more complex field using the ~, &, and | connective field constraints. The predicate field constraint is always followed by a function for evaluation. As with a test CE, this function should be a predicate function.

As an example, the *get-human-move* rule in the previous section used the following two patterns to check that the pile contained more than one stick:

```
(pile-size ?size)
(test (> ?size 1))
```

These two patterns could be replaced with the following single pattern:

```
(pile-size ?size&:(> ?size 1))
```

The predicate field constraint can be used by itself; however, there are few situations in which this is useful. Typically a variable is bound and then tested using the predicate field constraint. When reading a pattern it is useful to think of the predicate field constraint as meaning *such that*. For example, the field constraint shown previously,

```
?size&:(> ?size 1)
```

could be read as "bind ?size such that ?size is greater than 1."

One application of the predicate field constraint is error checking of data. For example, the following rule checks that a data item is numeric before adding it to a running total:

```
(defrule add-sum
   (data-item ?value&:(numberp ?value))
   ?old-total <- (total ?total)
   =>
   (retract ?old-total)
   (assert (total (+ ?total ?value))))
```

The second field of the first pattern can be read as "bind ?value such that ?value is a number." The following two rules both perform the same kind of error checking and demonstrate the use of the ~ and | connective field constraints with the predicate field constraint:

```
(defrule find-data-type-1
   (data ?item&:(stringp ?item)|:(symbolp ?item))
   =>
   (printout t ?item " is a string or symbol "
               crlf))

(defrule find-data-type-2
   (data ?item&~:(integerp ?item))
   =>
   (printout t ?item " is not an integer " crlf))
```

The rule *find-data-type-1* checks that a data item is either a string or a symbol by using the *stringp* and *symbolp* type predicate functions. The rule *find-data-type-2* checks that a data item is not an integer by using the *integerp* function and then using the ~ connective constraint to negate the value.

8.11 THE RETURN VALUE FIELD CONSTRAINT

The **return value field constraint**, =, allows the return value of a function to be used for comparison inside a pattern. The return value field constraint can be used in conjunction with the ~, &, and | connective field constraints, as well as the predicate field constraint. Like the predicate field constraint, the return value field constraint must be followed by a function. However, the function does not have to be a predicate function. The only restriction is that the function must have a single-field return value. The following rule shows how the return value constraint can be used in the Sticks program to determine the number of sticks the computer player should remove from the pile:

```
(deftemplate take-sticks
   (slot how-many)
   (slot for-remainder))

(deffacts take-sticks-information
   (take-sticks (how-many 1) (for-remainder 1))
   (take-sticks (how-many 1) (for-remainder 2))
   (take-sticks (how-many 2) (for-remainder 3))
   (take-sticks (how-many 3) (for-remainder 0)))
```

```
(defrule computer-move
   ?whose-turn <- (player-move c)
   ?pile <- (pile-size ?size)
   (test (> ?size 1))
   (take-sticks (how-many ?number)
                (for-remainder =(mod ?size 4)))
   =>
   (retract ?whose-turn ?pile)
   (assert (pile-size (- ?size ?number)))
   (assert (player-move h)))
```

The *computer-move* rule determines the appropriate number of sticks for the computer to take on its turn. The first pattern CE ensures that the rule is applicable only when it is the computer's move. The second and third CEs check to see that the remaining number of sticks is greater than one. If there had been only one remaining stick, the computer would be forced to take it and lose. The final pattern works in conjunction with the *take-sticks-information* deffacts to determine the appropriate number of sticks to take. The **mod** (short for *modulus*) function returns the integer remainder of its first argument divided by its second. When reading a pattern it is useful to think of the return value field constraint as meaning *is equal to*. For example, the field constraint:

```
=(mod ?size 4)
```

could be read as "The field is equal to ?size modulus 4."

The computer will try to take enough sticks to set the remainder to one when the total number of sticks is divided by four. If the remainder is one when the computer has begun its move, then it has lost unless its opponent makes a mistake. It takes only one stick in this case to make the game last longer (hoping that the human player will make a mistake). In all other cases the computer can take the appropriate number of sticks to cause its opponent to lose.

To demonstrate how the return value field constraint works in more detail, let's consider a specific example. Assume that the pile size is 7 and that it is the computer's move. The first three CEs of the *computer-move* rule will be satisfied with the last CE remaining. The function expression (mod ?size 4) will have the value 7 substituted for ?size, leaving the expression (mod 7 4), which evaluates to 3. There is only one take-sticks fact with a for-remainder slot value of 3. The how-many slot value for this fact is 2, so the computer will end up taking 2 sticks, leaving a pile size of 5. After the human player's next move, the computer can force a loss.

Note that the = field constraint, which can be used only within a pattern CE, is not the same as the = predicate function, which can be used within a : field constraint, test CE, RHS of rule, or at the top-level prompt. Again, as with the predicate field constraint, more complex field constraints can be generated by using the return value constraint with the ~, &, and | connective field constraints.

8.12 THE STICKS PROGRAM

All of the basic techniques needed for completing the Sticks program have been discussed. The complete listing of the Sticks program is in the file *sticks.clp*, found on the CD-ROM packaged with this book. A sample run of the program after it has been loaded is shown below:

```
CLIPS> (reset)↵
CLIPS> (run)↵
Who moves first (Computer: c Human: h)? c↵
How many sticks in the pile? 15↵
Computer takes 2 stick(s).
13 stick(s) left in the pile.
How many sticks do you wish to take? 3↵
10 stick(s) left in the pile.
Computer takes 1 stick(s).
9 stick(s) left in the pile.
How many sticks do you wish to take? 2↵
7 stick(s) left in the pile.
Computer takes 2 stick(s).
5 stick(s) left in the pile.
How many sticks do you wish to take? 1↵
4 stick(s) left in the pile.
Computer takes 3 stick(s).
1 stick(s) left in the pile.
You must take the last stick!
You lose!
CLIPS>
```

8.13 THE *OR* CONDITIONAL ELEMENT

Thus far all the rules shown have an **implicit *and* conditional element** between the patterns. That is, a rule will not be triggered unless all the patterns are true. CLIPS also provides the capability of specifying both an **explicit *and* conditional element** and an **explicit *or* conditional element** on the LHS.

As an example of an *or* CE, consider the following rules for use by the industrial plant monitoring system (as discussed in Chapter 7) that are first written without an *or* CE. Then you will see how to rewrite them with an *or* CE:

```
(defrule shut-off-electricity-1
   (emergency (type flood))
   =>
   (printout t "Shut off the electricity" crlf))
```

```
(defrule shut-off-electricity-2
   (extinguisher-system (type water-sprinkler)
                        (status on))
   =>
   (printout t "Shut off the electricity" crlf))
```

Rather than write two separate rules, they can all be combined into the following rule, using an *or* CE:

```
(defrule shut-off-electricity
  (or (emergency (type flood))
      (extinguisher-system (type water-sprinkler)
                           (status on)))
  =>
  (printout t "Shut off the electricity" crlf))
```

This one rule using the *or* CE is equivalent to the two previous rules. Asserting the two facts matching the patterns of this rule would cause the rule to be triggered twice, once for each of the facts.

Other CEs can be included outside the *or* CE and will be part of the implicit *and* CE for the entire LHS of the rule. For example, the rule:

```
(defrule shut-off-electricity
   (electrical-power (status on))
   (or (emergency (type flood))
       (extinguisher-system (type water-sprinkler)
                            (status on)))
   =>
   (printout t "Shut off the electricity" crlf))
```

is equivalent to these two rules:

```
(defrule shut-off-electricity-1
   (electrical-power (status on))
   (emergency (type flood))
   =>
   (printout t "Shut off the electricity" crlf))

(defrule shut-off-electricity-2
   (electrical-power (status on))
   (extinguisher-system (type water-sprinkler)
                        (status on))
   =>
   (printout t "Shut off the electricity" crlf))
```

Since an *or* CE generates the equivalent of multiple rules, it is possible for a rule to be activated more than once by patterns contained with the *or* CE. Thus a natural question to ask is how to prevent the problem of more than one triggering. For example, multiple printouts of "Shut off the electricity" appearing for multiple facts are unnecessary. After all, the power needs to be shut off only once, regardless of the number of reasons to do so.

Perhaps the most appropriate manner to prevent the other rules from firing is to change the rule to update the fact list, indicating that the electricity has been shut off. The modified rule is shown below. (Note that we've been assuming in writing these rules that we have an alert plant operator who's watching the output of the monitoring system and taking action. In the real world the expert system might have direct control to turn various systems on and off or the plant operator might have a mechanism for telling the monitoring system that various actions have been taken.)

```
(defrule shut-off-electricity
   ?power <- (electrical-power (status on))
   (or (emergency (type flood))
       (extinguisher-system (type water-sprinkler)
                            (status on)))
=>
   (modify ?power (status off)))
   (printout t "Shut off the electricity" crlf))
```

The rule now fires only once because the fact containing information about the electrical power is modified when the rule fires. This will remove other activations of the rule made by the other patterns. If it is also necessary to remove the supporting reason for shutting off the power from the fact list, then the rule would have to be written as follows:

```
(defrule shut-off-electricity
   ?power <- (electrical-power (status on))
   (or ?reason <- (emergency (type flood))
       ?reason <- (extinguisher-system
                      (type water-sprinkler)
                  (status on)))
   =>
   (retract ?reason)
   (modify ?power (status off))
   (printout t "Shut off the electricity" crlf))
```

Notice that all the pattern CEs within the *or* CE are bound to the same variable, ?reason. At first this may appear to be an error, since the same variables are not normally assigned to different patterns of an ordinary rule. But a rule using an *or* CE is different. Since an *or* CE will produce multiple rules, the above rule is equivalent to the following two rules:

```
(defrule shut-off-electricity-1
   ?power <- (electrical-power (status on))
   ?reason <- (emergency (type flood))
   =>
   (retract ?reason)
   (modify ?power (status off))
   (printout t "Shut off the electricity" crlf))

(defrule shut-off-electricity-2
   ?power <- (electrical-power (status on))
   ?reason <- (extinguisher-system
                  (type water-sprinkler)
                  (status on))
=>
  (retract ?reason)
   (modify ?power (status off))
    (printout t "Shut off the electricity" crlf))
```

By looking at the two rules we can see that the same variable name was necessary to match the (retract ?power ?reason) action on the RHS.

8.14 THE *AND* CONDITIONAL ELEMENT

The *and* CE is opposite in concept to the *or* CE. Instead of any one of several CEs triggering a rule, the *and* CE requires that all of the CEs be satisfied. CLIPS automatically places an implicit *and* CE around the LHS of a rule. A rule such as:

```
(defrule shut-off-electricity
   ?power <- (electrical-power (status on))
   (emergency (type flood))
   =>
   (modify ?power (status off))
   (printout t "Shut off the electricity" crlf))
```

could also be written with an explicit *and* CE as:

```
(defrule shut-off-electricity
   (and ?power <- (electrical-power (status on))
        (emergency(type flood)))
   =>
   (modify ?power (status off))
   (printout t "Shut off the electricity" crlf))
```

Of course there is no advantage to writing a rule with an explicit *and* CE around the entire LHS. The *and* CE is provided so it can be used with other CEs to make more complex patterns. For example, it can be used with an *or* CE to require groups of multiple conditions to be true, as shown in the following example:

```
(defrule use-carbon-dioxide-extinguisher
   ?system <- (extinguisher-system
                  (type carbon-dioxide)
                  (status off))
   (or (emergency (type class-B-fire))
       (and (emergency (type class-C-fire))
            (electrical-power (status off))))
   =>
   (modify ?system (status on))
   (printout t "Use carbon dioxide extinguisher"
               crlf))
```

This rule will be activated if there is a class B fire emergency (such as burning oil or grease) or if there is a class C fire emergency (involving electrical equipment) and the electrical power has already been shut off. In effect, always use the carbon dioxide extinguisher for a class B fire, but use it for a class C fire only if turning off the electricity didn't extinguish the fire. The *use-carbon-dioxide-extinguisher* is equivalent to the following two rules:

```
(defrule use-carbon-dioxide-extinguisher-1
   ?system <- (extinguisher-system
                  (type carbon-dioxide)
                  (status off))
   (emergency (type class-B-fire))
   =>
   (modify ?system (status on))
   (printout t "Use carbon dioxide extinguisher"
               crlf))

(defrule use-carbon-dioxide-extinguisher-2
   ?system <- (extinguisher-system
              (type carbon-dioxide)
              (status off))
   (emergency (type class-C-fire))
   (electrical-power (status off))
   =>
   (modify ?system (status on))
   (printout t "Use carbon dioxide extinguisher"
               crlf))
```

8.15 THE *NOT* CONDITIONAL ELEMENT

Sometimes it is useful to be able to activate rules based on the absence of a particular fact in the fact list. CLIPS allows the specification of the absence of a fact in the LHS of a rule using the ***not* conditional element**. As a simple example, the monitoring expert system might have two rules for reporting its status:

```
IF the monitoring status is to be reported and
   there is an emergency being handled
THEN report the type of the emergency

IF the monitoring status is to be reported and
   there is no emergency being handled
THEN report that no emergency is being handled
```

The *not* CE can be conveniently applied to the simple rules above as follows:

```
(defrule report-emergency
   (report-status)
   (emergency (type ?type))
   =>
   (printout t "Handling " ?type " emergency"
               crlf))

(defrule no-emergency
   (report-status)
   (not (emergency))
   =>
   (printout t "No emergency being handled" crlf))
```

Notice that these two rules are mutually exclusive. That is, they cannot be on the agenda at the same time because the second pattern in each rule cannot be satisfied simultaneously.

Variables can also be used within a negated pattern to produce some interesting effects. Consider the following rule, which looks for the largest number out of a group of facts representing numbers:

```
(defrule largest-number
   (number ?x)
   (not (number ?y&:(> ?y ?x)))
   =>
   (printout t "Largest number is " ?x crlf))
```

The first pattern will bind to all of the *number* facts, but the second pattern will not allow the rule to become activated for any but the fact with the largest value for ?x.

Note that variables first bound within a *not* CE retain their value only within the scope of the *not* CE. For example, the rule:

```
(defrule no-emergency
   (report-status)
   (not (emergency (type ?type)))
   =>
   (printout t "No emergency of type " ?type crlf))
```

will generate an error since the variable ?type is used in the RHS of the rule but is bound only within the *not* CE in the LHS of the rule.

The scope of variables also applies to the LHS of a rule. For example, the following rule determines that there are no known people who have a birthday on a given day:

```
(defrule no-birthdays-on-specific-date
   (check-for-no-birthdays (date ?date))
   (not (person (birthday ?date)))
   =>
   (printout t "No birthdays on " ?date crlf))
```

If the first two CEs are switched as follows,

```
(defrule no-birthdays-on-specific-date
   (not (person (birthday ?date)))
   (check-for-no-birthdays (date ?date))
   =>
   (printout t "No birthdays on " ?date crlf))
```

then the rule no longer works correctly. The first CE will be unsatisfied if there are *any person* facts at all. The value bound to the variable ?date in the first CE has no effect on the allowed values for the variable ?date in the second CE. This contrasts with the original version of the *no-birthdays-on-specific-date* rule, in which the value bound to the variable ?date in the first CE restricted the search for *person* facts in the second CE to those having a birthday on a specific date. Unlike pattern CEs, the order of placement of a *not* CE on the LHS of a rule can affect the activation of the rule.

The *not* CE can be used in conjunction with other CEs. For example, the following rule determines that there are no two people who have birthdays on the same date:

```
(defrule no-identical-birthdays
   (not (and (person (name ?name)
                     (birthday ?date))
             (person (name ~?name)
                     (birthday ?date))))
   =>
   (printout t
      "No two people have the same birthday"
      crlf)
```

The *and* CE is used within the *not* CE because the *not* CE can contain at most one CE. Notice that the variables ?name and ?date are reused within the *not* CE to correctly constrain the search for two people with the same birthday.

Because of the underlying algorithm used by CLIPS, the (initial-fact) pattern is added to the beginning of any *and* CE (implicit or explicit) whose first CE is a *not* CE or a *test* CE. Thus the rule:

```
(defrule no-emergencies
   (not (emergency))
   =>
   (printout t "No emergencies" crlf))
```

is converted to the following rule:

```
(defrule no-emergencies
   (initial-fact)
   (not (emergency))
=>
   (printout t "No emergencies" crlf))
```

Understanding this conversion is useful when examining the output from the *matches* command. Also note that fact indices for *not* CEs are not displayed in partial matches or activations for rules. Thus the activation "f-5,,f-3" indicates that the first CE was matched by the fact with fact index 5, the second CE was a *not* CE that was not matched by any facts and thus is satisfied, and the third CE was matched by the fact with fact index 3.

8.16 THE *EXISTS* CONDITIONAL ELEMENT

The ***exists* conditional element** allows you to pattern match based on the existence of at least one fact that matches a pattern without regard to the total number of facts that actually match the pattern. This allows a single partial match or activation for a rule to be generated based on the existence of one fact out of a class of facts. For example, suppose an informational message should be printed whenever an emergency occurs to indicate to the plant operators that they should be on alert. The rule could be written as follows:

```
(deftemplate emergency (slot type))

(defrule operator-alert-for-emergency
   (emergency)
   =>
   (printout t "Emergency: Operator Alert" crlf)
   (assert (operator-alert)))
```

Notice what happens when more than one *emergency fact* is asserted—the message to the operators is printed more than once:

```
CLIPS> (reset)↵
CLIPS> (assert (emergency (type fire)))↵
<Fact-1>
CLIPS> (assert (emergency (type flood)))↵
<Fact-2>
CLIPS> (run)↵
Emergency: Operator Alert
Emergency: Operator Alert
CLIPS>
```

The *operator-alert-for-emergency* rule could be modified in the following way to prevent the retriggering of the rule for an additional emergency:

```
(defrule operator-alert-for-emergency
   (emergency)
   (not (operator-alert))
   =>
   (printout t "Emergency: Operator Alert" crlf)
   (assert (operator-alert)))
```

The (not (operator-alert)) CE prevents the rule from being retriggered; however, changing the rule in this manner assumes that if there is already an operator alert, it was triggered by the *operator-alert-for-emergency* rule. It's possible that the operators could be placed on alert for an emergency drill, as the following rule shows:

```
(defrule operator-alert-for-drill
   (operator-drill)
   (not (operator-alert))
   =>
   (printout t "Drill: Operator Alert" crlf)
   (assert (operator-alert)))
```

Notice that if the drill alert rule fires first, the emergency alert rule will not be able to fire later since the *operator-alert* fact will have been asserted. To correct the problem the *operator-alert* fact could be modified to store the cause of the alert; however, excessive use of control facts to prevent rules from firing increases the complexity of rules and decreases the maintainability of rules by adding control dependencies between rules.

Fortunately, the *operator-alert-for-emergency* rule can be modified to use the *exists* CE, which will remove the need for control facts. Regardless of how many facts match the CEs inside the *exists* CE, the *exists* CE will generate only one partial match. Thus if an *exists* CE is the *Nth* CE of a rule and the previous $N - 1$ CEs have generated M partial matches, the largest number of partial matches that can be generated by the first N CEs is M. The *operator-alert-for-emergency* rule rewritten to use the *exists* CE is:

```
(defrule operator-alert-for-emergency
   (exists (emergency))
   =>
   (printout t "Emergency: Operator Alert" crlf)
   (assert (operator-alert)))
```

This rule will generate only one activation and thus the operator alert message will be printed only once, as the following dialog shows:

```
CLIPS> (reset)↵
CLIPS> (assert (emergency (type fire)))↵
<Fact-1>
CLIPS> (assert (emergency (type flood)))↵
<Fact-2>
CLIPS> (agenda)↵
0      operator-alert-for-emergency: f-0,
For a total of 1 activation.
CLIPS> (run)↵
Emergency: Operator Alert
CLIPS>
```

The *exists* CE is implemented by using a combination of *and* CEs and *not* CEs. The CEs within the *exists* CE are enclosed within an *and* CE and then within two *not* CEs. Thus the *operator-alert-for-emergency* rule is converted to the following by surrounding the entire LHS with an *and* CE and then replacing the *exists* CE as stated:

```
(defrule operator-alert-for-emergency
   (and (not (not (and (emergency)))))
   =>
   (printout t "Emergency: Operator Alert" crlf)
   (assert (operator-alert)))
```

Since the *and* CE surrounding the LHS of the rule has a *not* CE as its first CE, the (initial-fact) pattern CE is added to the beginning. Making this addition and removing the extraneous *and* CE around the emergency pattern produces the following rule:

```
(defrule operator-alert-for-emergency
   (and (initial-fact)
        (not (not (emergency))))
   =>
   (printout t "Emergency: Operator Alert" crlf)
   (assert (operator-alert)))
```

The (initial-fact) pattern at the beginning of the rule explains the f-0 fact index that was displayed for the rule when the *agenda* command was issued in the previous dialog. If there are no *emergency* facts, then the innermost *not* CE will be satisfied. If this CE is satisfied, then the outermost *not* CE will not be satisfied and the rule will not be activated. Conversely, if there are emergency facts, the innermost *not* CE will not be satisfied. Since this CE is not satisfied, the outermost *not* CE will be satisfied and the rule will be activated.

8.17 THE *FORALL* CONDITIONAL ELEMENT

The ***forall* conditional element** allows you to pattern match based on a set of CEs that are satisfied for *every* occurrence of another CE. For example, suppose there are a number of locations (such as buildings) at an industrial plant that could be on fire, and we want to determine if every building that's on fire has been evacuated and has a squad of firefighters attempting to extinguish the fire. The *forall* CE can be used to check this. The *emergency* fact will be modified as shown below to contain the location of the emergency in addition to the type of emergency. Two other deftemplates will be used to indicate the location of fire squads and whether a building has been evacuated. The *all-fires-being-handled* rule uses these deftemplates to determine whether the appropriate conditions have been satisfied.

```
(deftemplate emergency
   (slot type)
   (slot location))

(deftemplate fire-squad
   (slot name)
   (slot location))

(deftemplate evacuated
   (slot building))

(defrule all-fires-being-handled
   (forall (emergency (type fire)
                      (location ?where))
           (fire-squad (location ?where))
           (evacuated (building ?where)))
=>
  (printout t
            "All buildings that are on fire " crlf
            "have been evacuated and" crlf
            "have firefighters on location" crlf))
```

For every fact that matches the (emergency (type fire) (location ?where)) pattern, there must also be facts matching the (fire-squad (location ?where)) pattern and the (evacuated (building ?where)) pattern. When the deftemplates and defrule are initially loaded and the *reset* command is issued, the rule should be satisfied since there are no fire emergencies:

```
CLIPS> (watch activations)↵
CLIPS> (reset)↵
==> Activation 0       all-fires-being-handled:
  f-0,
CLIPS>
```

Once an *emergency* fact is asserted, the rule is deactivated until the appropriate *fire-squad* and *evacuated* facts are asserted:

```
CLIPS>
(assert (emergency (type fire)
                   (location building-11)))↵
<== Activation 0  all-fires-being-handled: f-0,
<Fact-1>
CLIPS>
(assert (evacuated (building building-11)))↵
<Fact-2>
CLIPS>
(assert (fire-squad (name A)
                    (location building-11)))↵
==> Activation 0  all-fires-being-handled: f-0,
<Fact-3>
CLIPS>
(assert (fire-squad (name B)
                    (location building-1)))↵
<Fact-4>
CLIPS>
(assert (emergency (type fire)
                   (location building-1)))↵
<== Activation 0  all-fires-being-handled: f-0,
<Fact-5>
CLIPS> (assert (evacuated (building building-1)))↵
==> Activation 0       all-fires-being-handled:
  f-0,
<Fact-6>
CLIPS>
```

If the *fire-squad* fact for building-1 is removed, then the rule is deactivated. Removing the *emergency* fact for this building will reactivate the rule:

```
CLIPS> (retract 4)↵
<== Activation 0  all-fires-being-handled: f-0,
CLIPS> (retract 5)↵
==> Activation 0  all-fires-being-handled: f-0,
CLIPS> (run)↵
All buildings that are on fire
have been evacuated and
```

```
have firefighters on location
CLIPS>
```

The general format of the *forall* CE is as follows:

```
(forall <first-CE>
        <remaining-CEs>+)
```

In order for the *forall* CE to be satisfied, each fact matching the <first-CE> must also have facts that match all of the <remaining-CEs>. The general format of the *forall* CE is replaced with combinations of the *and* and *not* CEs using the following format:

```
(not (and <first-CE>
          (not (and <remaining-CEs>+))))
```

8.18 THE *LOGICAL* CONDITIONAL ELEMENT

The ***logical* conditional element** allows you to specify that the existence of a fact depends on the existence of another fact or group of facts. The *logical* CE is the facility that CLIPS provides for truth maintenance. As an example, consider the following rule, which indicates that oxygen masks should be used by firefighters when a fire is giving off noxious fumes:

```
(defrule noxious-fumes-present
   (emergency (type fire))
   (noxious-fumes-present)
   =>
   (assert (use-oxygen-masks)))
```

As the following dialog shows, the preceding rule will assert the *use-oxygen-masks* fact whenever there is such a fire emergency:

```
CLIPS> (unwatch all)↵
CLIPS> (reset)↵
CLIPS> (watch facts)↵
CLIPS> (assert (emergency (type fire))
               (noxious-fumes-present))↵
==> f-1    (emergency (type fire))
==> f-2    (noxious-fumes-present)
<Fact-2>
CLIPS> (run)↵
==> f-3    (use-oxygen-masks)
CLIPS>
```

What happens when the fire is extinguished and there are no longer any noxious fumes? As the next dialog shows, retracting the *emergency* fact or *noxious-fumes-present* fact doesn't affect the *use-oxygen-masks* fact:

```
CLIPS> (retract 1 2)↵
<== f-1        (emergency (type fire))
<== f-2        (noxious-fumes-present)
CLIPS> (facts)↵
f-0      (initial-fact)
f-3      (use-oxygen-masks)
For a total of 2 facts.
CLIPS>
```

CLIPS provides a truth maintenance mechanism for creating dependencies between facts; that mechanism is the *logical* CE. Modifying the *noxious-fumes-present* rule as shown below allows a dependency to be created between the facts that match the patterns in the LHS of a rule and the facts that are asserted from the RHS of the rule:

```
(defrule noxious-fumes-present
   (logical (emergency (type fire))
            (noxious-fumes-present))
   =>
   (assert (use-oxygen-masks)))
```

When the *noxious-fumes-present* rule is executed, a link is created between the facts matching the patterns contained within the logical CE in the LHS of a rule and the facts asserted from the RHS of a rule. For this rule, if either the *emergency* fact or the *noxious-fumes-present* fact is retracted, then the *use-oxygen-masks* rule will also be retracted, as the following dialog shows:

```
CLIPS> (unwatch all)↵
CLIPS> (reset)↵
CLIPS> (watch facts)↵
CLIPS> (assert (emergency (type fire))
               (noxious-fumes-present)))↵
==> f-1        (emergency (type fire))
==> f-2        (noxious-fumes-present)
<Fact-2>
CLIPS> (run)↵
==> f-3        (use-oxygen-masks)
CLIPS> (retract 1)↵
<== f-1        (emergency (type fire))
<== f-3        (use-oxygen-masks)
CLIPS>
```

The *use-oxygen-masks* fact receives **logical support** from the *emergency* fact and the *noxious-fumes-present* fact. The *emergency* fact and the *noxious-fumes-present* fact provide logical support to the *use-oxygen-masks* fact. The *use-oxygen-masks* fact is a **dependent** of the *emergency* fact and the *noxious-fumes-present* fact. The *noxious-fumes-present* fact and the *emergency* fact are **dependencies** of the use-oxygen-masks fact.

The *logical* CE does not have to be included around all the patterns on the LHS of a rule. If it is used, however, it must enclose the first CE in the LHS of a rule, and there can be no gaps between CEs enclosed by the *logical* CE. For example, *logical* CEs could not be placed around the second and fourth CEs of a rule or even around the first and third CEs of a rule, since this would leave gaps. This restriction on the *logical* CE is the result of its underlying implementation. It's also possible to make facts dependent on the nonexistence of facts by using the *not* CE within the *logical* CE. Even more complex conditions using the *exists* and *forall* CEs or other combinations of CEs can be used within the logical CE. Other than creating dependencies between groups of facts, the *logical* CE acts in all other respects like an *and* CE.

In order to modify the *noxious-fumes-present* rule to make the *use-oxygen-masks* fact dependent on only the *noxious-fumes-present* fact it would be necessary to reorder the patterns as shown:

```
(defrule noxious-fumes-present
   (logical (noxious-fumes-present))
   (emergency (type fire))
   =>
   (assert (use-oxygen-masks)))
```

With the rule modified as shown, the *use-oxygen-masks* fact won't be retracted automatically if the *emergency* fact is retracted (which is a safer approach since there may still be noxious fumes even if the fire is extinguished).

Normally, asserting a fact that's already in the fact list has no effect. However, a logically dependent fact that is derived from more than one source is not automatically retracted until the logical support from all of its sources is removed. For example, suppose another rule is added to indicate that oxygen masks should be used if gas extinguishers are in use:

```
(defrule gas-extinguishers-in-use
   (logical (gas-extinguishers-in-use))
   (emergency (type fire))
   =>
   (assert (use-oxygen-masks)))
```

Running the system now causes two separate rules to assert the same fact based on different reasons:

```
CLIPS> (unwatch all)↵
CLIPS> (reset)↵
CLIPS> (watch facts)↵
CLIPS> (watch rules)↵
CLIPS> (assert (emergency (type fire))
               (noxious-fumes-present)
               (gas-extinguishers-in-use))↵
==> f-1     (emergency (type fire))
==> f-2     (noxious-fumes-present)
==> f-3     (gas-extinguishers-in-use)
<Fact-3>
CLIPS> (run)↵
FIRE    1 gas-extinguishers-in-use: f-3,f-1
==> f-4     (use-oxygen-masks)
FIRE  2 noxious-fumes-present: f-1,f-2
CLIPS>
```

Retracting the *noxious-fumes-present* fact isn't sufficient to cause the automatic retraction of the *use-oxygen-masks* fact since there is other logical support for the oxygen masks to be used. The *gas-extinguishers-in-use* fact must also be retracted before the *use-oxygen-masks* fact will be retracted:

```
CLIPS> (retract 2)↵
<== f-2     (noxious-fumes-present)
CLIPS> (retract 3)↵
<== f-3     (gas-extinguishers-in-use)
<== f-4     (use-oxygen-masks)
CLIPS>
```

A fact that is asserted from the top-level prompt or from the RHS of a rule that does not have any logical CEs in its LHS is **unconditionally supported**. A fact that is unconditionally supported will never be automatically retracted by the retraction of another fact. Any previous logical support for a fact is discarded once it receives unconditional support.

CLIPS provides two commands for viewing the **dependents** and the **dependencies** associated with a fact. The syntax for these commands is:

```
(dependents <fact-index-or-address>)

(dependencies <fact-index-or-address>)
```

For the last example, before the *noxious-fumes-present* and *gas-extinguishers-in-use* facts were retracted, these commands would have produced the following output:

```
CLIPS> (facts)↵
f-0     (initial-fact)
```

```
f-1       (emergency (type fire))
f-2       (noxious-fumes-present)
f-3       (gas-extinguishers-in-use)
f-4       (use-oxygen-masks)
For a total of 5 facts.
CLIPS> (dependents 1)↵
None
CLIPS> (dependents 2)↵
f-4
CLIPS> (dependents 3)↵
f-4
CLIPS> (dependents 4)↵
None
CLIPS> (dependencies 1)↵
None
CLIPS> (dependencies 2)↵
None
CLIPS> (dependencies 3)↵
None
CLIPS> (dependencies 4)↵
f-2
f-3
CLIPS>
```

8.19 SUMMARY

This chapter introduced the concept of field constraints, which allow the negation and combination of more than one constraint for a given field. The *not* field constraint is used to prevent matching against certain values. The *and* field constraint is used to guarantee that all of a series of matching conditions are true. The *or* field constraint is used to guarantee that at least one of a series of matching conditions is true.

Functions are entered into the CLIPS top-level command loop or are used on the LHS or RHS of a rule. Many functions, such as some of the arithmetic functions, can have a variable number of arguments. Function calls can be nested within other function calls. The bind command allows variables to be bound on the RHS of a rule.

CLIPS provides several I/O functions. The *open* and *close* functions can be used to open and close files. Opened files are associated with a logical name. Logical names can be used in most functions that perform input and output to more than one type of physical device. Both *printout* and *read* functions use logical names. The *printout* function can output to the terminal and files. The *read* function can input from the keyboard and files. The *format* and *readline* functions also accept logical names. The *format* function allows more control over the appearance of output. The *readline* function can be used to read an entire line of data. The *explode$* function converts a string to a multifield value.

Various concepts for controlling the flow of execution are available. The *read* function was used to demonstrate how a simple control loop for input could be created using control facts that are retracted and then asserted again. *Test* CEs along with predicate functions can be used on the LHS of a rule to provide more powerful pattern-matching capabilities. In addition, *test* CEs can be used to maintain a control loop. The predicate field constraint allows predicate tests to be placed directly within a pattern. The equality field constraint is used to compare a field to a value returned by a function. The Sticks program demonstrates several of these control techniques.

There are several other CEs besides the *test* CE. The *or* CE is used to express several rules as a single rule. The *not* CE allows pattern matching against the absence of a fact in the fact list. The *and* CE is used to group CEs together and, in conjunction with the *or* and *not* CEs, can be arbitrarily nested to express complex conditions needed to satisfy a rule. The *exists* CE is used to determine the existence of at least one group of facts that satisfies a CE or a combination of CEs. The *forall* CE is used to determine that a set of CEs is satisfied for *every* occurrence of another CE. The *logical* CE provides a truth maintenance mechanism. The existence of facts can be made dependent on the existence or nonexistence of other facts.

PROBLEMS

8.1 Given the following deftemplates for facts describing a family tree,

```
(deftemplate father-of (slot father) (slot child))
(deftemplate mother-of (slot mother) (slot child))
(deftemplate male (slot person))
(deftemplate female (slot person))
(deftemplate wife-of (slot wife) (slot husband))
(deftemplate husband-of (slot husband) (slot wife))
```

write rules that will infer the following relations. Describe the deftemplates you use to solve the problem.

(a) Uncle, aunt
(b) Cousin
(c) Grandparent
(d) Grandfather, grandmother
(e) Sister, brother
(f) Ancestor

8.2 An industrial plant has ten sensors with ID numbers 1 through 10. Each sensor has either "good" or "bad" status. Build a deftemplate for representing the sensors and write one or more rules that will print a warning message if three or more sensors have bad status. Test your rules with sensors 3 and 5 bad; sensors 2, 8, and 9 bad; and sensors 1, 3, 5, and 10 bad. What must be done to prevent the warning message from being displayed multiple times?

8.3 Build a CLIPS program based on the IF-THEN rules developed for Problem 3.5 on page 158. The program should ask for the traveler's payment method and travel interests and should output potential trips based on these two inputs.

8.4 Given a series of facts describing shapes using the following deftemplates:

```
(deftemplate square
   (slot id) (slot side-length))
(deftemplate rectangle
   (slot id) (slot width) (slot height))
(deftemplate circle
   (slot id) (slot radius))
```

write one or more rules that will compute the sum of:

(a) the areas of the shapes.

(b) the perimeters of the shapes.

Test the output of the rules with the following deffacts:

```
(deffacts test-8-8
   (square (id A) (side-length 3))
   (square (id B) (side-length 5))
   (rectangle (id C) (width 5) (height 7))
   (circle (id D) (radius 2))
   (circle (id E) (radius 6)))
```

8.5 Given information about the name, eye color, hair color, and nationality of a person from a group using the following deftemplate,

```
(deftemplate person (slot name)
                    (slot eye-color)
                    (slot hair-color)
                    (slot nationality))
```

write one rule that will identify:

(a) anyone with blue or green eyes who has brown hair and is from France.

(b) anyone who does not have blue eyes or black hair and does not have the same color hair and eyes.

(c) two people, the first having brown or blue eyes, not having blond hair, and a German nationality; the second having green eyes, the same hair color as the first person, and any nationality. The second person's eyes may be brown if the first person's hair is brown.

8.6 Convert the following infix expressions to prefix expressions:

(a) `(3 + 4) * (5 + 6) + 7`

(b) `(5 * (5 + 6 + 7)) - ((3 * (4 / 9) + 2) / 8)`

(c) `6 - 9 * 8 / 3 + 4 - (8 - 2 - 3) * 6 / 7`

8.7 Consider the following information about a baseball team. Andy dislikes the catcher. Ed's sister is engaged to the second baseman. The center fielder is taller than the right fielder. Harry and the third baseman live in the same building. Paul and Allen each won $20 from the pitcher at pinochle. Ed and the outfielders play poker during their free time. The pitcher's wife is the third baseman's sister. All the battery (the pitcher and catcher) and infield, except Allen, Harry, and Andy, are shorter than Sam. Paul, Andy, and the shortstop each lost $50 at the racetrack. Paul, Harry, Bill, and the catcher took a trouncing at pool from the second baseman. Sam is undergoing a divorce. The catcher and the third baseman each have two children. Ed, Paul, Jerry, the right fielder, and the center fielder are bachelors; the others are married. The shortstop, the third baseman, and Bill each cleaned up $100 betting on a fight. One of the outfielders is either Mike or Andy. Jerry is taller than Bill. Mike is shorter than Bill. Each of them is heavier than the third baseman. Sam, the catcher, and the third baseman are left-handed. Ed, Sam, and the shortstop went to high school together. Write a CLIPS program to determine who plays each position.

8.8 Convert the decision tree shown in Figure 3.3 on page 99 to a series of CLIPS rules. Create patterns to match facts using the following deftemplate:

```
(deftemplate question
   (slot query-string)
   (slot answer))
```

For example, if the answer to the question represented by the root node in the tree was "no," the fact representing this information would be:

```
(question (query-string "Is it very big?")
          (answer no))
```

Use the *printout* and *read* functions on the RHS of the rules to ask the questions shown in Figure 3.3 and assert *question* facts with the user's response.

8.9 Write a CLIPS program that will add two binary numbers without using any arithmetic functions. Represent the binary numbers using the following deftemplate:

```
(deftemplate binary-#
   (multislot name)
   (multislot digits))
```

Given a fact indicating which two named binary numbers are to be added, the program should create a new named binary number containing the sum. For example, the facts:

```
(binary-# (name A) (digits 1 0 1 1 1))
(binary-# (name B) (digits 1 1 1 0))
(add-binary-#s (name-1 A) (name-2 B))
```

should cause the following fact to be added to the fact list:

```
(binary-# (name { A + B }) (digits 1 0 0 1 0 1))
```

8.10 Write a CLIPS program that prompts for the blood types of a patient in need of a blood transfusion and a donor. The program should then determine whether the transfusion should proceed based on the blood types. Type O blood can be transfused only with type O blood. Type A blood can be transfused with either type A or type O blood. Type B blood can be transfused with either type B or type O blood. Type AB blood can be transfused with type AB, type A, type B, or type O blood.

8.11 Write a CLIPS program that gives information on either how a specified cut of beef can be cooked or the cuts of beef that can be cooked in a specific way. The program should first prompt whether a cut of beef or a method of cooking is to be selected and then it should prompt for the appropriate selection. Use the following guidelines to determine the appropriate cuts or methods of cooking: rump roast should be braised or roasted; sirloin steak should be broiled, pan-broiled, or pan-fried; T-bone steak should be broiled, pan-broiled, or pan-fried; rib roast should be roasted; ground beef should be roasted, broiled, pan-broiled, pan-fried, or braised; flank steak should be braised; and round steak should be braised.

8.12 Modify the program developed for Problem 7.14 on page 363 so that the input is determined by asking the user a series of questions regarding the necessary characteristics of the shrub. The output of the program should be the same.

8.13 Bacteria can be classified by several characteristics including their basic shape (spherical, rod, spiral, or filamentous), the results of a laboratory gram stain test (positive, negative, or none), and whether they require oxygen to survive (aerobic or anaerobic). Write a program that identifies the bacterial type based on the information stored in the table below. The program should ask the user for the shape, gram stain, and oxygen requirements of the bacteria. The user should be able to specify that any of the inputs is unknown. The output of the program should be all of the possible bacteria types based on the information from the user.

Type	Shape	Gram Stain	Oxygen Requirements
Actinomycete	rod or filamentous	positive	aerobic
Coccoid	spherical	positive	aerobic and anaerobic
Coryneform	rod	positive	aerobic
Endospore-forming	rod	positive or negative	aerobic and anaerobic
Enteric	rod	negative	aerobic
Gliding	rod	negative	aerobic
Mycobacterium	spherical	none	aerobic
Mycoplasma	spherical	none	aerobic
Pseudomonad	rod	negative	aerobic
Rickettsia	spherical or rod	negative	aerobic
Sheathed	filamentous	negative	aerobic
Spirillum	spiral	negative	aerobic
Spirochete	spiral	negative	anaerobic
Vibrio	rod	negative	aerobic

8.14 Acme Electronics makes a device called the Thingamabob 2000. This device is available in five different models distinguished by the chassis. Each chassis provides a number of bays for optional gizmos and is capable of generating a certain amount of power. The following table summarizes the chassis attributes:

Chassis	Gizmo Bays Provided	Power Provided	Price ($)
C100	1	4	2000.00
C200	2	5	2500.00
C300	3	7	3000.00
C400	2	8	3000.00
C500	4	9	3500.00

Each gizmo that can be installed in the chassis requires a certain amount of power to operate. The following table summarizes the gizmo attributes:

Gizmo	Power Used	Price ($)
Zaptron	2	100.00
Yatmizer	6	800.00
Phenerator	1	300.00
Malcifier	3	200.00
Zeta-shield	4	150.00
Warnosynchronizer	2	50.00
Dynoseparator	3	400.00

Given as input facts representing the chassis and any gizmos that have been selected, write a program that generates facts representing the number of gizmos used, the total amount of power required for the gizmo, and the total price of the chassis and all gizmos selected.

8.15 Using the gem table from Problem 7.13 on page 363, write rules for identifying the following gems: diamond, corundum, chrysoberyl, spinel, quartz, and tourmaline. Include rules to query the user for the hardness, density, and color of the gem. The user should be prompted until he or she responds with one of the colors listed in the table.

8.16 Add rules to the Sticks program that will ask if the human player wants to play again after the game has finished.

8.17 Modify the Sticks program to allow two human players to play the game against each other, in addition to the computer playing against a human.

8.18 Rewrite the following rules as a single rule using *and* and *or* CEs:

```
(defrule rule-1
   (fact-a)
   (fact-d)
   =>)

(defrule rule-2
   (fact-b)
   (fact-c)
   (fact-e)
   (fact-f)
   =>)

(defrule rule-3
   (fact-a)
   (fact-e)
   (fact-f)
   =>)

(defrule rule-4
   (fact-b)
   (fact-c)
   (fact-d)
   =>)
```

8.19 Write a program using *and* and *or* CEs for the AND/OR tree of getting to work shown in Figure 3.10 on page 107. Test it for all branches.

8.20 Determine whether the variable x is referenced properly for each of the following rules. Explain your answers.

(a)
```
(defrule example-1
   (not (fact ?x))
   (test (> ?x 4))
   =>)
```

(b)
```
(defrule example-2
   (not (fact ?x&:(> ?x 4)))
   =>)
```

(c)
```
(defrule example-3
    (not (fact ?x))
    (fact ?y&:(> ?y ?x)))
    =>)
```
(d)
```
(defrule example-4
    (not (fact ?x))
    (fact ?x&:(> ?x 4)))
    =>)
```

8.21 Rewrite the Blocks World program from Section 7.23 so it can rearrange the blocks from any initial state of stacked blocks to any goal state of stacked blocks. For example, if the initial state of the blocks was:

```
(stack A B C)
(stack D E F)
```

One possible goal state might be:

```
(stack D C B)
(stack A)
(stack F E)
```

8.22 Write a CLIPS program that will query a user for color values and then print a list of all countries with flags that contain all of the specified colors. The flag colors for various countries are listed below:

Country	Flag Colors
United States	Red, white, and blue
Belgium	Black, yellow, and red
Poland	White and red
Monaco	White and red
Sweden	Yellow and blue
Panama	Red, white, and blue
Jamaica	Black, yellow, and green
Colombia	Yellow, blue, and red
Italy	Green, white, and red
Ireland	Green, white, and orange
Greece	Blue and white
Botswana	Blue, white, and black

8.23 Given the following deftemplate describing a set,

```
(deftemplate set
   (multislot name)
   (multislot members))
```

write one or more rules that will:

(a) Compute the union of two specified sets given a fact using the following deftemplate:

```
(deftemplate union
   (multislot set-1-name)
   (multislot set-2-name))
```

(b) Compute the intersection of two specified sets given a fact using the following deftemplate:

```
(deftemplate intersection
   (multislot set-1-name)
   (multislot set-2-name))
```

Note that when computing the union and intersection, duplicate elements should not be allowed to appear in the union or the intersection of the sets. The final result for both (a) and (b) should be a new *set* fact containing the union or intersection of the two specified sets and the *union* and *intersection* facts should be retracted when the operations are complete.

8.24 Write a set of rules for classifying syllogistic forms by mood and figure. For example, the syllogistic form:

```
No M is P
Some M is not S
∴ Some S is P
```

is of type EOI-3. The input for the rules should be a single fact representing the major and minor premises and the conclusion. The output should be a printed statement of the mood and figure.

8.25 Write a program that will read a data file containing a list of people's names and ages and create a new file containing the list sorted in ascending order by age. The program should prompt for both input and output files. For example, input file:

```
Linda A. Martin 43
Phyllis Sebesta 40
Robert Delwood 38
Jack Kennedy 39
Glen Steele 37
```

should create the output file:

```
Glen Steele 37
Robert Delwood 38
Jack Kennedy 39
Phyllis Sebesta 40
Linda A. Martin 43
```

8.26 Write a program to compute the value of the 13 cards in a bridge player's hand using the point-count method. Aces count for four points; kings count for three points; queens count for two points; and jacks count for one point. A void suit (no cards of one suit) counts for three points; a singleton suit (one card of a suit) counts for two points; and a doubleton suit (two cards of a suit) counts for one point.

8.27 Write a program that will indicate the action to be taken when someone swallows poison. The program should have knowledge of the following poisons: acids (such as rust remover and iodine), alkalines (such as ammonia and bleach), and petroleum products (such as gasoline and turpentine). All other poisons should be grouped into the category *other*.

In the event of poisoning, a physician or poison control center should be called. For acids, alkalines, and other types of poison (but not petroleum products), dilute the poison by having the victim drink a liquid such as water or milk. Induce vomiting for other types of poison, but do not induce vomiting for acids, alkalines, or petroleum products. Do not give liquids or induce vomiting if the victim is unconscious or is having convulsions.

8.28 Write a program that, when given two points, computes the slope of the line formed by the two points. Your program should check to ensure that the points provided contain numbers and that one point is not specified twice. Treat vertical lines as having an infinite slope.

8.29 A scalene triangle has three unequal sides. An isosceles triangle has two sides of the same length. An equilateral triangle has three sides of the same length. Write a program that, when given the three points forming a triangle, will determine the type of triangle. The program should account for possible round-off error (assume two sides are equal if the difference between their lengths is less than .00001). Test your program with the following triangles:
(a) Points (0,0), (2,4), and (6,0).
(b) Points (1,2), (4,5), and (7,2).
(c) Points (0,0), (3,5.196152), and (6,0).

8.30 Write a program to solve the Towers of Hanoi problem in which you must move a set of rings from one peg to another peg without ever putting a larger ring on top of a smaller ring. There are three pegs for you to use. The number of rings should be an input to the program. In the initial configuration all the rings are on the first peg in descending size from bottom to top. The initial goal should be to move all of the rings from the first peg to the third peg.

8.31 Write a program to determine the values of the letters that make the following cryptoarithmetic problem correct. Each of the letters H, O, C, U, S, P, R, E, and T corresponds uniquely to a digit in the range 0 to 9.

```
  HOCUS
+ POCUS
= PRESTO
```

8.32 Write a program that gives advice on investing in mutual funds. The output of the program should indicate the percentage of money to be invested in fixed-income funds; funds mainly investing in bonds and preferred stocks; and stock funds, funds with a higher risk but greater potential returns. The percentages will be determined by "scoring" the amount of risk the investor is willing to take based on the responses to various questions. If the investor is 29 years old or younger, add 4 to the score; 30 to 39, add 3; 40 to 49, add 2; 50 to 59, add 1; and 60 or more, add 0. If the investor has 0 to 9 years until retirement, add 0; 10 to 14, add 1; 15 to 19, add 2; 20 to 24, add 3; and 25 or more, add 4. If the investor is willing to ride out losses of only 5% or less, add 0 to the score; 6% to 10%, add 1; 11% to 15%, add 2; and 16% or more, add 3. If the investor is very knowledgeable about investments and the stock market, add 4 to the score; if somewhat knowledgeable, add 2 to the score; if not knowledgeable, add 0 to the score. If the investor is willing to take significant risk for higher possible returns, add 4 to the score; if some risk, add 2; and if little risk, add 0. If the investor believes his or her retirement goals will be met given his or her current income and assets, add 4 to the score; if the goals might possibly be met, add 2; if the goals are unlikely to be met, add 0. If the final score is more than 20 points, then 100% of the investments should be in stock funds; if 16 to 20 points, 80% should be in stock funds and 20% in fixed-income funds; if 11 to 15 points, 60% should be in stock funds and 40% in fixed-income funds; if 6 to 10 points, then 40% should be in stock funds and 60% in fixed-income funds; if 0 to 5 points, then 20% should be in stock funds and 80% in fixed-income funds.

8.33 Modify the program developed for Problem 7.12 on page 362 so that the information about stars is represented using facts. The program output should be in the same order: all stars having the specified spectral class, all stars having the specified magnitude, and finally all stars matching both the spectral class and magnitude along with their distance from Earth in light-years.

CHAPTER 9
Modular Design, Execution Control, and Rule Efficiency

9.1 INTRODUCTION

This chapter introduces a number of CLIPS features useful for the development and maintenance of expert systems. Deftemplate attributes allow the enforcement of value constraints for deftemplate slot values. When a rule is loaded, deftemplate constraint attributes can detect semantics errors that prevent the LHS of that rule from being matched. Using salience, which provides a method for prioritizing rules, and facts representing flow of control knowledge, this chapter demonstrates techniques for controlling the execution of a CLIPS program. In addition, it looks at the defmodule construct, which allows a knowledge base to be partitioned and provides a more explicit method for controlling the execution of a system. This chapter also provides many techniques for increasing the efficiency of a rule-based expert system that uses the Rete Pattern Matching algorithm. The reasons for needing an efficient pattern-matching algorithm will be discussed before the Rete algorithm is explained. Several techniques for writing rules more efficiently will also be discussed.

9.2 DEFTEMPLATE ATTRIBUTES

CLIPS provides a number of slot attributes that can be specified when a deftemplate's slots are defined. These attributes aid in the development and maintenance of an expert system by providing strong typing and constraint checking. It is possible to define the allowed types and values that can be stored in a slot. For numeric values, the allowed range of numbers can be specified. Multislots can specify the minimum and maximum number of fields they can contain. Finally, the default attribute provides a default slot value to be used for slots that are not specified in an *assert* command.

The Type Attribute

The **type attribute** defines the data types that can be placed in a slot. The general format of the type attribute is (type <type-specification>) where <type-specification> is either ?VARIABLE or one or more of the symbols SYMBOL, STRING, LEXEME, INTEGER, FLOAT, NUMBER, INSTANCE-NAME, INSTANCE-ADDRESS, INSTANCE, FACT-ADDRESS, or EXTERNAL-ADDRESS. If ?VARIABLE is used, the slot may contain any data type (which is the default behavior for all slots). If one or more of the symbolic type specifications are used, the slot is restricted to one of the specified types. The type specification LEXEME is equivalent to specifying SYMBOL and STRING. The type specification NUMBER is equivalent to specifying INTEGER and FLOAT. The type specification INSTANCE is equivalent to specifying INSTANCE-NAME and INSTANCE-ADDRESS.

The following *person* deftemplate restricts the values stored in the *name* slot to symbols and the values stored in the *age* slot to integers:

```
(deftemplate person
   (multislot name (type SYMBOL))
   (slot age (type INTEGER)))
```

Once this deftemplate has been defined, CLIPS will automatically enforce the restrictions of any slot attributes. For example, assigning the symbol four to the age slot rather than the integer 4 will cause an error as shown:

```
CLIPS> (assert (person (name Fred Smith)
                       (age four)))↵

[CSTRNCHK1] A literal slot value found in the
assert command does not match the allowed types
for slot age.
CLIPS>
```

CLIPS will also check the consistency of variable bindings in the LHS and the RHS of a rule. For example, let's assume there is a rule that updates a person's age slot whenever he or she has a birthday. The deftemplate for the control fact that indicates that a person has just had a birthday is:

```
(deftemplate had-a-birthday
   (slot name (type STRING)))
```

The allowed types of the name slots for the two deftemplates are inconsistent. An attempt to directly compare the two slots will generate an error, as the following dialog illustrates:

```
CLIPS>
(defrule update-birthday
   ?f1 <- (had-a-birthday (name ?name))
```

```
   ?f2 <- (person (name ?name) (age ?age))
   =>
   (retract ?f1)
   (modify ?f2 (age (+ ?age 1))))↵

[RULECSTR1] Variable ?name in CE #2 slot name has
constraint conflicts which make the pattern
unmatchable.

ERROR:
(defrule MAIN::update-birthday
   ?f1 <- (had-a-birthday (name ?name))
   ?f2 <- (person (name ?name) (age ?age))
   =>
   (retract ?f1)
   (modify ?f2 (age (+ ?age 1))))
CLIPS>
```

The *name* slot for the *had-a-birthday* fact must be a string and the *name* slot for the *person* fact must be a symbol. It is not possible for the variable ?name to satisfy both of these constraints and thus the LHS of the rule can never be satisfied.

Static and Dynamic Constraint Checking

CLIPS provides two levels of constraint checking. The first level, **static constraint checking**, is performed by default when CLIPS parses an expression or a construct and is illustrated by the previous constraint violation examples using the type attribute. Static constraint checking can be disabled by calling the **set-static-constraint-checking** function and passing it the symbol *FALSE*. Conversely, calling this function with the symbol *TRUE* will activate static constraint checking. The value returned by the function is the previous status value (the symbol *FALSE* if it was previously disabled and the symbol *TRUE* otherwise). You can determine the current status of static constraint checking by calling the **get-static-constraint-checking** function (which returns the symbol *TRUE* if static constraint checking is enabled and the symbol *FALSE* otherwise).

It is not always possible to determine all constraint errors at parse time. For example, in the *create-person* rule shown here, the variables ?age and ?name can be bound to illegal values:

```
(defrule create-person
   =>
   (printout t "What is your name? ")
   (bind ?name (explode$ (readline)))
   (printout t "What is your age? ")
   (bind ?age (read))
   (assert (person (name ?name) (age ?age))))
```

The *readline* function is used to input a person's entire name as a string and the *explode$* function then converts it to a multifield value that can be placed in the *name* slot. The *read* function is used to input a person's age, which can be placed in the *age* slot. For both input values it is possible to receive invalid values. For example, the symbol *four* may be input for the person's age, as the following dialog shows:

```
CLIPS> (reset)↵
CLIPS> (run)↵
What is your name? Fred Smith↵
What is your age? four↵
CLIPS> (facts)↵
f-0     (initial-fact)
f-1     (person (name Fred Smith) (age four))
For a total of 2 facts.
CLIPS>
```

Notice that the same *person* fact for Fred Smith that caused a constraint violation before and was not added to the fact list has now been added to it. This is because the second level of constraint checking performed by CLIPS, **dynamic constraint checking,** is disabled by default. Dynamic constraint checking is performed on facts when they are actually asserted, thus catching errors that cannot be detected at parse time.

Dynamic constraint checking can be enabled or disabled using the function **set-dynamic-constraint-checking** and the current status of dynamic constraint checking can be determined with the **get-dynamic-constraint-checking function** function. With dynamic constraint checking enabled, the following dialog shows how the constraint violation is handled. The Fred Smith *person* fact is still added to the fact list, but the constraint violation is detected and the execution of rules is halted.

```
CLIPS> (set-dynamic-constraint-checking TRUE)↵
FALSE
CLIPS> (reset)↵
CLIPS> (run)↵
What is your name? Fred Smith↵
What is your age? four↵

[CSTRNCHK1] Slot value (Fred Smith) found in fact
f-1 does not match the allowed types for slot age.
[PRCCODE4] Execution halted during the actions of
defrule create-person.
CLIPS> (facts)↵
f-0     (initial-fact)
f-1     (person (name Fred Smith) (age four))
```

```
For a total of 2 facts.
CLIPS>
```

The Allowed Value Attributes

In addition to restricting allowed types with the type attribute, CLIPS also allows you to specify a list of allowed values for a specific type. For example, if a *gender* slot is added to the *person* deftemplate, the allowed symbols for that slot can be restricted to *male* and *female*:

```
(deftemplate person
   (multislot name (type SYMBOL))
   (slot age (type INTEGER))
   (slot gender (type SYMBOL)
                (allowed-symbols male female)))
```

There are eight different allowed value attributes provided by CLIPS: **allowed-symbols**, **allowed-strings**, **allowed-lexemes**, **allowed-integers**, **allowed-floats**, **allowed-numbers**, **allowed-instance-names**, and **allowed-values**. Each of these attributes should be followed either by ?VARIABLE (which indicates that any values of the specified type are legal) or by a list of values of the type following the *allowed-* prefix. For example, the *allowed-lexemes* attribute should by followed either by ?VARIABLE or by a list of symbols and/or strings. The default allowed value attribute for slots is (allowed-values ?VARIABLE).

Note that the allowed value attributes do not restrict the allowed types of a slot. For example, (allowed-symbols male female) does not restrict the type of the *gender* slot to being a symbol. It merely indicates that if the slot's value is a symbol, then it must be one of the two symbols: either *male* or *female*. Any string, integer, or float would be a legal value for the *gender* slot if the (type SYMBOL) attribute were removed.

The allowed-values attribute can be used to completely restrict the set of allowed values for a slot to a specified list. For example, changing the *person* deftemplate to the following effectively limits the allowed types for the *gender* slot to symbols:

```
(deftemplate person
   (multislot name (type SYMBOL))
   (slot age (type INTEGER))
   (slot gender (allowed-values male female)))
```

The Range Attribute

The **range attribute** allows the specification of minimum and maximum numeric values. The general format of the range attribute is (range <lower-limit> <upper-limit>), where <lower-limit> and <upper-limit> are either ?VARIABLE or a numeric value. The <lower-limit> term indicates the minimum value for the slot and the <upper-limit> term indicates the maximum value for the slot. ?VARIABLE indicates that there is either no minimum or no maximum value (depending on whether it is first or second). For example, the *age* slot in the *person* deftemplate can be modified to prevent negative values from being placed in the slot:

```
(deftemplate person
   (multislot name (type SYMBOL))
   (slot age (type INTEGER) (range 0 ?VARIABLE)))
```

If we're willing to assume that no one lives beyond 125 years, then the range attribute could be changed to (range 0 125). As with the allowed value attributes, the range attribute does not restrict the type of a slot value to being numeric. It restricts only the allowed numeric values of a slot to the specified range if the slot's value is numeric. The default range attribute for slots is (range ?VARIABLE ?VARIABLE).

The Cardinality Attribute

The **cardinality attribute** allows the specification of the minimum and maximum number of values that can be stored in a multislot. The general format of the cardinality attribute is (cardinality <lower-limit> <upper-limit>), where <lower-limit> and <upper-limit> are either ?VARIABLE or a positive integer. The <lower-limit> term indicates the minimum number of values the slot can contain and the <upper-limit> term indicates the maximum number of values the slot can contain. ?VARIABLE indicates that there is either no minimum or no maximum number of values the slot can contain (depending on whether it is first or second). The default cardinality attribute for a multislot is (cardinality ?VARIABLE ?VARIABLE). The following deftemplate could be used to represent company volleyball teams, which must have six players and may have up to two alternate players. Note that type, allowed value, and range attributes are applied to every value contained in a multislot.

```
(deftemplate volleyball-team
   (slot name (type STRING))
   (multislot players (type STRING)
                      (cardinality 6 6))
   (multislot alternates (type STRING)
                         (cardinality 0 2)))
```

The Default Attribute

In previous chapters each deftemplate fact that was asserted always had an explicit value stated for every slot. It is often convenient to automatically have a specified value stored in a slot if no value is explicitly stated in an *assert* command. The **default attribute** allows such a default value to be specified. The general format of the default attribute is (default <default-specification>), where <default-specification> is either ?DERIVE, ?NONE, a single expression (for a single-field slot), or zero or more expressions (for a multifield slot).

If ?DERIVE is specified in the default attribute, then a value is derived for the slot that satisfies all of the slot attributes. If the default attribute is not specified for a slot, then it is assumed to be (default ?DERIVE). For a single-field slot, this means that a value is selected that satisfies the type, range, and allowed values attributes for the slot. The derived default value for a multifield slot will be a list of identical values that are the minimum allowed cardinality for the slot (zero by default). If one or more values are contained in the default value for a multifield slot, then each value will satisfy the type, range, and allowed values attributes for the slot. An example of derived values is the following:

```
CLIPS> (clear)↵
CLIPS>
(deftemplate example
   (slot a)
   (slot b (type INTEGER))
   (slot c (allowed-values red green blue))
   (multislot d)
   (multislot e (cardinality 2 2)
                (type FLOAT)
                (range 3.5 10.0)))↵
CLIPS> (assert (example))↵
<Fact-0>
CLIPS> (facts)↵
f-0     (example (a nil)
                 (b 0)
                 (c red)
                 (d)
                 (e 3.5 3.5))
For a total of 1 fact.
CLIPS>
```

CLIPS guarantees only that the derived default value for a slot satisfies the constraint attributes for the slot. In other words, your programs should not depend on specific derived values (such as the symbol *nil* for slot *a* or the integer 0 for slot *b* in the previous example) being placed in slots. If your program depends upon a specific default value, you should use an expression with the default attribute (which will be explained shortly).

If ?NONE is specified in the default attribute, a value must be supplied for the slot when the fact is asserted. That is, there is no default value. For example,

```
CLIPS> (clear)↵
CLIPS>
(deftemplate example
   (slot a)
   (slot b (default ?NONE)))↵
CLIPS> (assert (example))↵
```

```
[TMPLTRHS1] Slot b requires a value because of its
(default ?NONE) attribute.
CLIPS> (assert (example (b 1)))↵
<Fact-0>
CLIPS> (facts)↵
f-0     (example (a nil) (b 1))
For a total of 1 fact.
CLIPS>
```

If one or more expressions are used with the default attribute, the expressions are evaluated when the slot is parsed and this value is stored in the slot whenever the value for the slot is left unspecified in an *assert* command. The default attribute for a single-field slot must contain exactly one expression. If no expressions are specified in the *default* attribute for a multifield slot, then a multifield of length zero is used for the default value. Otherwise, the return values of all of the expressions are grouped together to form one multifield value. The following is an example using expressions with the *default* attribute:

```
CLIPS> (clear)↵
CLIPS>
(deftemplate example
  (slot a (default 3))
  (slot b (default (+ 3 4)))
  (multislot c (default a b c))
  (multislot d (default (+ 1 2) (+ 3 4))))↵
CLIPS> (assert (example))↵
<Fact-0>
CLIPS> (facts)↵
f-0     (example (a 3) (b 7) (c a b c) (d 3 7))
For a total of 1 fact.
CLIPS>
```

The Default-Dynamic Attribute

When the default attribute is used, the default value for a slot is determined when the slot definition is parsed. It's also possible to have the default value generated when the fact that will use the default value is asserted. This is done with the **default-dynamic attribute**. When the value of a slot that uses the default-dynamic attribute is left unspecified in an *assert* command, the expression specified with the default-dynamic attribute is evaluated and used for the slot's value.

As an example, let's consider the problem of deleting facts after a certain amount of time has transpired. First, we'll need some way of knowing when our facts have been asserted. The **time** function provided by CLIPS will be used to tag the facts with time of creation. It returns the number of seconds that have elapsed since a system-dependent reference time. By itself, the return value of the time function is not meaningful. It is useful only when compared with other values returned by the function. The following deftemplate will be used for this example. It contains a *creation-time* slot, to store the time of creation, and a *value* slot, to store a value associated with the fact.

```
(deftemplate data
   (slot creation-time (default-dynamic (time)))
   (slot value))
```

Each time a *data* fact is created and the *creation-time* slot is unspecified, the *time* function is called and the value is stored in the *creation-time* slot:

```
CLIPS> (watch facts)↵
CLIPS> (assert (data (value 3)))↵
==> f-0       (data (creation-time 12002.45)
                    (value 3))
<Fact-0>
CLIPS> (assert (data (value b)))↵
==> f-1       (data (creation-time 12010.25)
                    (value b))
<Fact-1>
CLIPS> (assert (data (value c)))↵
==> f-2       (data (creation-time 12018.65)
                    (value c))
<Fact-2>
CLIPS>
```

Assuming that a *current-time* fact is asserted and updated by other rules to contain the current system time, the following rule will retract *data* facts that were asserted more than one minute ago:

```
(defrule retract-data-facts-after-one-minute
   ?f <- (data (creation-time ?t1))
   (current-time ?t2)
   (test (> (- ?t2 ?t1) 60))
   =>
   (retract ?f))
```

Note that changing the *retract-data-facts-after-one-minute* rule to the following does not produce the same results:

```
(defrule retract-data-facts-after-one-minute
   ?f <- (data (creation-time ?t1))
   (test (> (- (time) ?t1) 60))
   =>
   (retract ?f))
```

The *time* function in the *test* CE will be checked only when the first pattern is matched by a *data* fact. Since the value returned will be approximately the same time as the value in the *creation-time* slot, the rule will not be satisfied. CLIPS does not continually recheck *test* CEs to determine whether they evaluate to a different value; they are checked only when changes occur to preceding CEs. This is why the *current-time* fact in the original version of the rule must be updated so the *test* CE will be periodically rechecked.

Conflicting Slot Attributes

CLIPS does not allow you to specify conflicting attributes for a slot. For example, a slot's default value must satisfy the slot's type, allowed- . . . , range, and cardinality attributes. If an allowed- . . . attribute is specified, the type associated with the attribute must satisfy the slot's type attribute. The allowed-numbers, allowed-integers, and allowed-floats attributes may not be used with the range attribute.

9.3 SALIENCE

Up to this point, control facts have been used to indirectly control the execution of programs. CLIPS provides two explicit techniques for controlling the execution of rules: salience and modules. The control of rule execution using modules will be discussed later in this chapter. The use of the keyword ***salience*** allows the priority of rules to be explicitly specified. Normally the agenda acts like a stack. That is, the most recent activation placed on the agenda is the first to fire. Salience allows more important rules to stay at the top of the agenda, regardless of when the rules were added. Lower salience rules are pushed below higher salience rules on the agenda.

Salience is set using a numeric value ranging from the smallest value of –10,000 to the highest of 10,000. If a rule has no salience explicitly assigned by the programmer, CLIPS assumes a salience of 0. Notice that a salience of 0 is midway between the largest and the smallest salience values. A salience of 0 does not mean that the rule has no salience, but rather that it has an intermediate priority level. A newly activated rule is placed on the agenda before all rules with equal or lesser salience and after all rules with greater salience.

One use of salience is to force rules to fire in a sequential fashion. Consider the following set of rules, in which no salience values are declared:

```
(defrule fire-first
   (priority first)
   =>
   (printout t "Print first" crlf))

(defrule fire-second
   (priority second)
   =>
   (printout t "Print second" crlf))
```

```
(defrule fire-third
   (priority third)
   =>
   (printout t "Print third" crlf))
```

The order in which the rules fire depends on the order in which the facts that satisfy the CEs in the LHS of the rules are asserted. For example, if the rules are entered, the following commands will produce the output shown below:

```
CLIPS> (unwatch all)↵
CLIPS> (reset)↵
CLIPS> (assert (priority first))↵
<Fact-1>
CLIPS> (assert (priority second))↵
<Fact-2>
CLIPS> (assert (priority third))↵
<Fact-3>
CLIPS> (run)↵
Print third
Print second
Print first
CLIPS>
```

Notice the order of output statements. First "Print third" is printed, then "Print second," and finally "Print first." The first fact (priority first) activates the rule *fire-first*. When the second fact is asserted, it activates the rule *fire-second*, which is stacked on top of the activation for rule *fire-first*. Finally, the third fact is asserted and its activated rule, *fire-third*, is stacked on top of the activation for rule *fire-second*.

In CLIPS, rules of equal salience that are activated by different patterns are prioritized based on the stack order of facts. Rules are fired from the agenda from the top of the stack down. So rule *fire-third* is fired first because it's on the top of the stack, then rule *fire-second*, and finally rule *fire-first*. If the order in which the facts are asserted is reversed, then the order in which the rules are fired will also be reversed. This is seen in the following output:

```
CLIPS> (reset)↵
CLIPS> (assert (priority third))↵
<Fact-1>
CLIPS> (assert (priority second))↵
<Fact-2>
CLIPS> (assert (priority first))↵
<Fact-3>
CLIPS> (run)↵
Print first
Print second
Print third
CLIPS>
```

One important point is that if two or more rules with the same salience are activated by the same fact, there is no guarantee in which order the rules will be placed on the agenda.

Salience can be used to force the rules to fire in the order *fire-first*, *fire-second*, *fire-third*, despite the order in which the activating facts are asserted. This can be accomplished by declaring salience values:

```
(defrule fire-first
   (declare (salience 30))
   (priority first)
   =>
   (printout t "Print first" crlf))

(defrule fire-second
   (declare (salience 20))
   (priority second)
   =>
   (printout t "Print second" crlf))

(defrule fire-third
   (declare (salience 10))
   (priority third)
   =>
   (printout t "Print third" crlf))
```

Regardless of the order in which the priority facts are asserted, the agenda will always be ordered the same. Performing the *agenda* command after asserting the priority facts would produce the following output:

```
CLIPS> (reset)↵
CLIPS> (assert (priority second)
               (priority first)
               (priority third))↵
<Fact-3>
CLIPS> (agenda)↵
30     fire-first: f-2
20     fire-second: f-1
10     fire-third: f-3
For a total of 3 activations.
CLIPS>
```

Notice how the salience values have rearranged the priority of rules in the agenda. When the program is run, the order of rule firing will always be *fire-first*, *fire-second*, *fire-third*.

9.4 PHASES AND CONTROL FACTS

The purest concept of a rule-based expert system is one in which the rules act opportunistically whenever they are applicable. However, most expert systems have some procedural aspect to them. The Sticks program, for example, had different rules that were applicable depending on whether it was the human's or the computer's move. The control for this program was handled by facts that indicated whose turn it was. These control facts allow information about the control structure of the program to be embedded in the rules of domain knowledge. This does have a drawback: knowledge about the control of the rules is intermixed with knowledge about how to play the game. This is not a major drawback in the case of the Sticks program because it is small. However, for programs involving hundreds or thousands of rules, the intermixing of domain knowledge and control knowledge makes development and maintenance a major problem.

As an example, consider the problem of performing **fault detection**, **isolation**, and **recovery** of a system such as an electronic device. *Fault detection* is the process of recognizing that the electronic device is not working properly. *Isolation* is the process of determining the components of the device that have caused the fault. *Recovery* is the process of determining the steps necessary to correct the fault, if possible. Typically with this type of problem the expert system will have rules to determine whether a fault has occurred, other rules to isolate the cause of the fault, and still other rules to determine how to recover from the fault. The cycle will then loop back. Figure 9.1 shows an example of control flow in this type of system.

Figure 9.1 Different Phases for Fault Detection, Isolation, and Recovery Problem

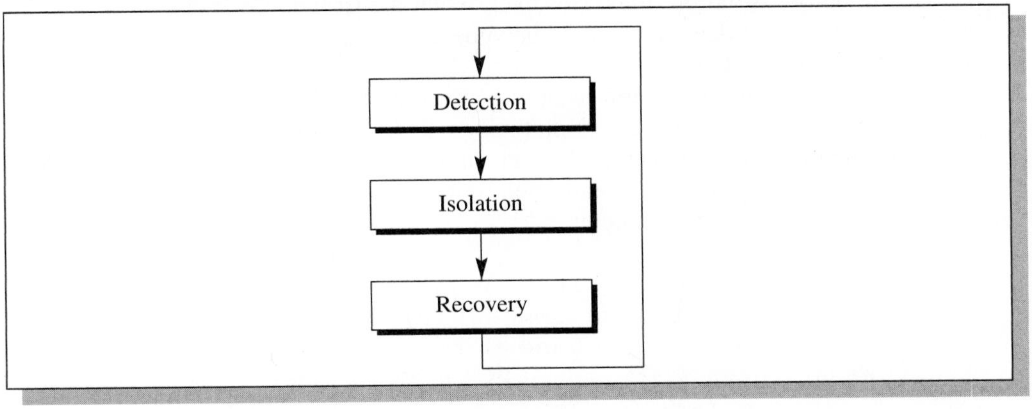

Implementing the flow of control in this system can be done in at least four ways. The first three approaches use salience and will be discussed in this section. The fourth approach uses modules and will be discussed later in the chapter.

The first approach to implementing the flow of control is to embed the control knowledge directly into the rules. For instance, the detection rules would include rules indicating when the isolation phase should be entered. Each group of rules would be given a pattern indicating in which phase it would be applicable. This technique has two drawbacks. First, as already mentioned, control knowledge is being embedded into the domain knowledge rules, which makes them more difficult to understand. Second, it is not always easy to determine when a phase is completed. This generally requires writing a rule that is applicable only when all the other rules have fired.

Figure 9.2 Assignment of Salience for Different Phases

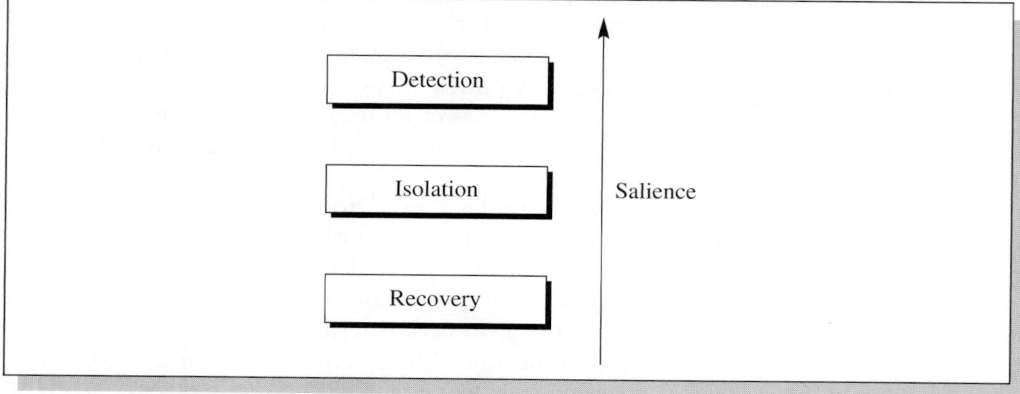

The second approach is to use salience to organize the rules, as shown in Figure 9.2. This approach also has two major drawbacks. First, control knowledge is still being embedded into the rules using salience. Second, this approach does not guarantee the correct order of execution. Detection rules will always fire before isolation rules. However, when the isolation rules begin firing they might cause a detection rule to become activated and immediately fire because of its higher salience.

A third and better approach in controlling the flow of execution is to separate the control knowledge from the domain knowledge, as shown in Figure 9.3. Using this approach, each rule is given a control pattern that indicates its applicable phase. Control rules are then written to transfer control between the different phases, as shown here:

```
(defrule detection-to-isolation
   (declare (salience -10))
   ?phase <- (phase detection)
   =>
   (retract ?phase)
   (assert (phase isolation)))

(defrule isolation-to-recovery
   (declare (salience -10))
   ?phase <- (phase isolation)
   =>
```

```
      (retract ?phase)
      (assert (phase recovery)))

   (defrule recovery-to-detection
      (declare (salience -10))
      ?phase <- (phase recovery)
      =>
      (retract ?phase)
      (assert (phase detection)))
```

Figure 9.3 Separation of Expert Knowledge from Control Knowledge

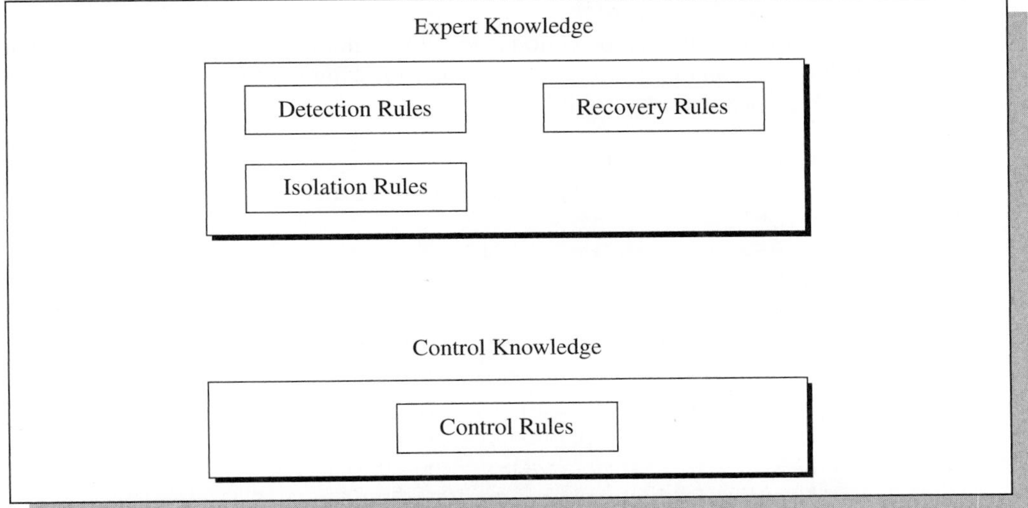

Each of the rules applicable for a particular phase is then given a control pattern that confirms that the appropriate control fact is present. For example, a recovery rule might look like this:

```
(defrule find-fault-location-and-recovery
   (phase recovery)
   (recovery-solution switch-device
                      ?replacement on)
   =>
   (printout t "Switch device" ?replacement "on"
               crlf))
```

A **salience hierarchy** is a description of the salience values used by an expert system. Each level in a salience hierarchy corresponds to a specific set of rules whose members are all given the same salience. If the rules for detection, isolation, and recovery are given a default salience of zero, then the salience hierarchy is as shown in Figure 9.4. Notice that while the fact (phase detection) is in the fact list, the *detection-to-isolation* rule will be on the agenda. Since it has

Figure 9.4 Salience Hierarchy Using Expert and Control Rules

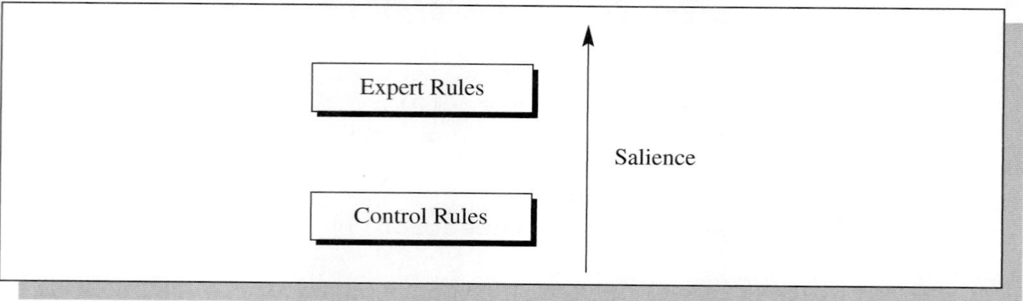

a lower salience than the detection rules, it will not fire until all of the detection rules have had an opportunity to fire. The following output shows a sample run of the three previous control rules:

```
CLIPS> (reset)↵
CLIPS> (assert (phase detection))↵
<Fact-1>
CLIPS> (watch rules)↵
CLIPS> (run 10)↵
FIRE    1 detection-to-isolation: f-1
FIRE    2 isolation-to-recovery: f-2
FIRE    3 recovery-to-detection: f-3
FIRE    4 detection-to-isolation: f-4
FIRE    5 isolation-to-recovery: f-5
FIRE    6 recovery-to-detection: f-6
FIRE    7 detection-to-isolation: f-7
FIRE    8 isolation-to-recovery: f-8
FIRE    9 recovery-to-detection: f-9
FIRE   10 detection-to-isolation: f-10
CLIPS>
```

Notice that the control rules just keep firing in sequence because there are no domain knowledge rules to be applied during any of the phases. If there were, then the domain knowledge rules would be applied for activated rules during the appropriate phases.

The previous control rules could be more generically written with a deffacts construct and a single rule as:

```
(deffacts control-information
   (phase detection)
   (phase-after detection isolation)
   (phase-after isolation recovery)
   (phase-after recovery detection))
```

```
(defrule change-phase
   (declare (salience -10))
   ?phase <- (phase ?current-phase)
   (phase-after ?current-phase ?next-phase)
   =>
   (retract ?phase)
   (assert (phase ?next-phase)))
```

or they could be written using a sequence of phases to be cycled through as:

```
(deffacts control-information
   (phase detection)
   (phase-sequence isolation recovery detection))

(defrule change-phase
   (declare (salience -10))
   ?phase <- (phase ?current-phase)
   ?list <- (phase-sequence ?next-phase
                            $?other-phases)
   =>
   (retract ?phase ?list)
   (assert (phase ?next-phase))
   (assert (phase-sequence ?other-phases
                           ?next-phase)))
```

Additional levels can easily be added to the salience hierarchy. Figure 9.5 shows a hierarchy with two additional levels. The constraint rules represent rules that detect illegal or unproductive states that may occur in the expert system. For example, an expert system scheduling people to various tasks may

Figure 9.5 Four-Level Salience Hierarchy

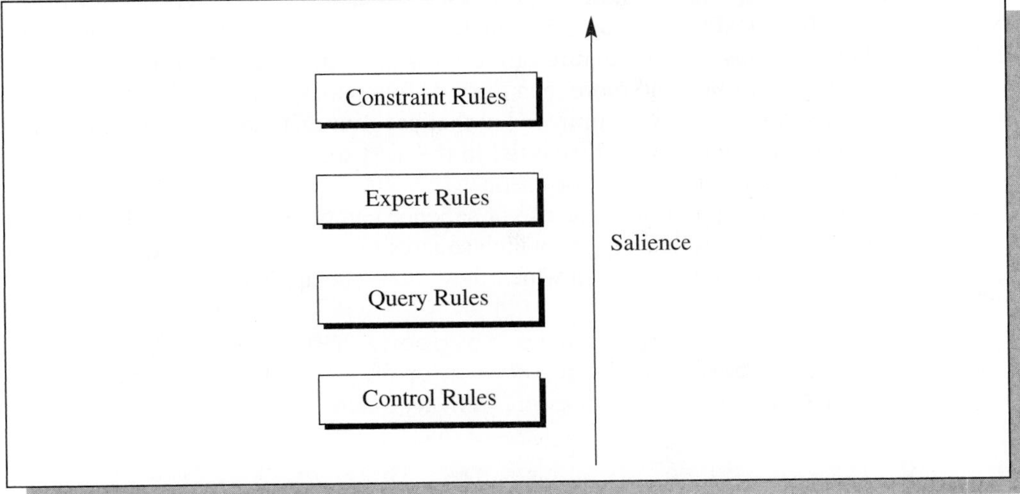

produce a schedule that violates a constraint. Instead of allowing the lower salience rules to continue working on the schedule, the constraint rules will immediately remove violations in the schedule. As another example, the user may enter in response to a series of questions a series of legal values that result in an illegal value being generated. The constraint rules could be used to detect such violations.

The query rules shown in Figure 9.5 represent rules that ask the user particular questions to aid the expert system in determining an answer. These rules have lower salience than the expert rules because it is undesirable to ask the user a question that can be determined by the expert rules. Thus the query rules are fired only when no more information can be derived by the expert rules.

9.5 MISUSE OF SALIENCE

Although salience is a powerful tool for controlling execution, it can easily be misused. In particular, people who are just learning rule-based programming tend to overuse salience because it gives them explicit control of execution. It is more like the procedural programming they are used to, in which statements execute sequentially.

Overuse of salience results in a poorly coded program. The main advantage of a rule-based program is that the programmer does not have to worry about controlling execution. A well-designed rule-based program has a natural mode of execution that permits the inference engine to guide rule firings in an optimal manner.

Salience should primarily be used as a mechanism for determining the order in which rules fire. This means that in general a rule that is placed on the agenda is eventually fired. Salience should not be used as a method for selecting a single rule from a group of rules when patterns can be used to express the criteria for selection, nor should salience be used as a "quick fix" to get rules to fire in the proper order.

In general, *any* salience value used in a rule should correspond to a level in the salience hierarchy of the expert system. The range of salience values from –10,000 to 10,000 is somewhat misleading. Rarely should more than seven salience values ever be required for coding an expert system; most well-coded expert systems need no more than three or four salience values. For large expert systems, it is strongly recommended that programmers use modules to control the flow of execution (as discussed in the next section) and that no more than two or three salience values be used.

As an example of how the use of salience can be avoided, the following is a simple set of rules that suggest which squares to mark in a tic-tac-toe game. The rules are listed in the order in which they should be applied.

```
IF a winning square is open, THEN take it.
IF a blocking square is open, THEN take it.
IF a square is open, THEN take it.
```

If the *choose-move* fact indicates that a move should be taken and the *open-square* facts indicate whether a winning, blocking, middle, corner, or side square is open, the following rules will select the appropriate move:

```
(defrule pick-to-win
   (declare (salience 10))
   ?phase <- (choose-move)
   (open-square win)
   =>
   (retract ?phase)
   (assert (move-to win)))

(defrule pick-to-block
   (declare (salience 5))
   ?phase <- (choose-move)
   (open-square block)
   =>
   (retract ?phase)
   (assert (move-to block)))

(defrule pick-any
   ?phase <- (choose-move)
   (open-square ?any&corner|middle|side)
   =>
   (retract ?phase)
   (assert (move-to ?any)))
```

Notice that if more than one type of square is available, all three rules will be placed on the agenda. When rule *pick-to-win*, *pick-to-block*, or *pick-any* is fired, the retraction of the control fact will remove the other rules from the agenda. All three rules are thus very closely interrelated. It is not possible to understand the intent of each of these rules without seeing all the rules together. This violates a basic concept of rule-based programming. As much as possible, a rule should represent a completely expressed heuristic. In this case, salience is used to express an implicit relationship among these rules that could be explicitly stated with additional patterns in the rules. The rules can be rewritten without salience as follows:

```
(defrule pick-to-win
   ?phase <- (choose-move)
   (open-square win)
   =>
   (retract ?phase)
   (assert (move-to win)))

(defrule pick-to-block
   ?phase <- (choose-move)
```

```
   (open-square block)
   (not (open-square win))
   =>
   (retract ?phase)
   (assert (move-to block)))

(defrule pick-any
   ?phase <- (choose-move)
   (open-square ?any&corner|middle|side)
   (not (open-square win))
   (not (open-square block))
   =>
   (retract ?phase)
   (assert (move-to ?any)))
```

Adding the additional patterns to the rules explicitly states the conditions under which the rules are applicable. The tight interaction between the rules is removed, allowing the rules to act opportunistically. Rewriting the rules also demonstrates that the original heuristics could have been expressed more clearly:

```
IF a winning square is open, THEN take it.
IF a blocking square is open, and
   a winning square is not open, THEN take it.
IF a corner, middle, or side square is open, and
   a winning square is not open, and
   a blocking square is not open, THEN take it.
```

9.6 THE DEFMODULE CONSTRUCT

Until now, all the defrules, deftemplates, and deffacts have been contained in a single work space. CLIPS uses the **defmodule** construct to partition a knowledge base by defining the various modules. The basic syntax for this construct is:

```
(defmodule <module-name> [<comment>])
```

By default CLIPS defines a module called the MAIN module. In previous examples we have seen that the MAIN module name appears with the pretty print representation of the constructs. For example:

```
CLIPS> (clear)↵
CLIPS> (deftemplate sensor (slot name))↵
CLIPS> (ppdeftemplate sensor)↵
(deftemplate MAIN::sensor
   (slot name))
CLIPS>
```

The :: symbol in the name MAIN::sensor is called the ***module separator***. To the right of the module separator is the name of the construct. To the left of the module separator is the name of the module in which the construct is contained. Since all the constructs that have been defined so far have been placed in the MAIN module by default, the MAIN module name appears with the pretty print representation of the constructs.

Now that we know the defmodule syntax, we can define new modules. Using the previous example of a fault detection system, we will define modules that correspond to the phases DETECTION, ISOLATION, and RECOVERY:

```
CLIPS> (defmodule DETECTION)↵
CLIPS> (defmodule ISOLATION)↵
CLIPS> (defmodule RECOVERY)↵
```

Once we've defined more than the MAIN module, the question arises: "In which module are new constructs placed?" By default, CLIPS places newly defined constructs in the current module. When CLIPS is initially started or cleared, the current module is automatically the MAIN module. Thus in our previous examples, since there was only one module and that was the current module, all defined constructs were placed in the MAIN module.

Whenever a new module is defined, CLIPS makes it the current module. Because the dialog above last defined the RECOVERY module, that is the current module and a newly defined rule will be placed in it:

```
CLIPS> (defrule example1 =>)↵
CLIPS> (ppdefrule example1)↵
(defrule RECOVERY::example1
   =>)
CLIPS>
```

The module in which a construct is placed can be specified in the construct's name. In the name, specify the module first, followed by the module separator, and then the construct's name:

```
CLIPS> (defrule ISOLATION::example2 =>)↵
CLIPS> (ppdefrule example2)↵
(defrule ISOLATION::example2
   =>)
CLIPS>
```

The current module is changed when the module name is specified in a construct's name. The current module can be determined with the **get-current-module** function. This function takes no arguments and returns the name of the current module. The function **set-current-module** is used to change the current module. It takes a single argument, the name of the new current module, and returns the name of the previous current module:

```
CLIPS> (get-current-module)↵
ISOLATION
CLIPS> (set-current-module DETECTION)↵
```

```
ISOLATION
CLIPS>
```

Specifying Modules in Commands

By default, most of the CLIPS commands that operate on constructs work only on the constructs contained in the current module. For example, the *list-defrules* command will produce no output if the current module is the DETECTION module because that module contains no rules:

```
CLIPS> (list-defrules)↵
CLIPS>
```

If we wanted to see the defrules contained in the ISOLATION module we could set the current module to the ISOLATION module and then execute another *list-defrules* command:

```
CLIPS> (set-current-module ISOLATION)↵
DETECTION
CLIPS> (list-defrules)↵
example2
For a total of 1 defrule.
CLIPS>
```

Alternatively, the *list-defrules* command accepts a module name as an optional argument. This argument specifies which module will have its rules listed:

```
CLIPS> (list-defrules RECOVERY)↵
example1
For a total of 1 defrule.
CLIPS>
```

If the symbol * is passed as an argument to *list-defrules*, then the rules in all of the modules are listed. Each list is preceded by the name of the module followed by the list of the rules contained in that module:

```
CLIPS> (list-defrules *)↵
MAIN:
DETECTION:
ISOLATION:
   example2
RECOVERY:
   example1
For a total of 2 defrules.
CLIPS>
```

The listing functions *list-deftemplates* and *list-deffacts* work similarly to the list-defrules command. The *show-breaks* command also allows you to specify which module will have its breakpoints displayed. The modified syntax for these functions is:

```
(list-defrules [<module-name>])
(list-deftemplates [<module-name>])
(list-deffacts [<module-name>])
(show-breaks [<module-name>])
```

Rules that operate on specific constructs also allow a module to be specified. For example, *ppdefrule* will search only the current module if no module name is specified:

```
CLIPS> (ppdefrule example2)↵
(defrule ISOLATION::example2
   =>)
CLIPS> (ppdefrule example1)↵
[PRNTUTIL1] Unable to find defrule example1.
CLIPS>
```

The rule *example2* has its pretty print form displayed since it is contained in the ISOLATION module, but because rule *example1* is not in the ISOLATION module, it is not found by the *ppdefrule* command.

The module in which to search for a construct can be specified by placing the module name, followed by the module separator, in front of the construct's name. For example:

```
CLIPS> (ppdefrule RECOVERY::example1)↵
(defrule RECOVERY::example1
   =>)
CLIPS>
```

It is possible to have two constructs with the same name in different modules. Using the module specifier before the construct's name allows you to distinguish between the two in a command:

```
CLIPS> (defrule DETECTION::example1 =>)↵
CLIPS> (list-defrules *)↵
MAIN:
DETECTION:
   example1
ISOLATION:
   example2
RECOVERY:
   example1
For a total of 3 defrules.
```

```
CLIPS> (ppdefrule RECOVERY::example1)↵
(defrule RECOVERY::example1
   =>)
CLIPS> (ppdefrule DETECTION::example1)↵
(defrule DETECTION::example1
   =>)
CLIPS>
```

The following commands allow the module to be specified as part of the construct name: *ppdefrule*, *undefrule*, *ppdeftemplate*, *undeftemplate*, *ppdeffacts*, *undeffacts*, *matches*, *refresh*, *remove-break*, and *set-break*.

9.7 IMPORTING AND EXPORTING FACTS

You have learned how to partition constructs by placing them in separate modules. Facts themselves can also be partitioned. Asserted facts are automatically associated with the module in which their corresponding deftemplates are defined. For example:

```
CLIPS>
(deftemplate DETECTION::fault
   (slot component))↵
CLIPS> (assert (fault (component A)))↵
<Fact-0>
CLIPS> (facts)↵
f-0      (fault (component A))
For a total of 1 fact.
CLIPS>
(deftemplate ISOLATION::possible-failure
   (slot component))↵
CLIPS> (assert (possible-failure (component B)))↵
<Fact-1>
CLIPS> (facts)↵
f-1      (possible-failure (component B))
For a total of 1 fact.
CLIPS> (set-current-module DETECTION)↵
ISOLATION
CLIPS> (facts)↵
f-0      (fault (component A))
For a total of 1 fact.
CLIPS>
```

Notice that in the ISOLATION module the only fact listed is the *possible-failure* fact, whose corresponding deftemplate is contained in the ISOLATION module. The same is true for the *fault* fact in the DETECTION module.

The *facts* command, like the *list-defrules* and similar commands, can accept a module name as an optional argument. The syntax for the *facts* command is:

```
(facts [<module-name>]
       [<start> [<end> [<maximum>]]])
```

As with the *list-defrules* command, specifying a module name lists only the facts contained in the specified module. If * is used for the module name, then all the facts are listed:

```
CLIPS> (facts DETECTION)↵
f-0     (fault (component A))
For a total of 1 fact.
CLIPS> (facts ISOLATION)↵
f-1     (possible-failure (component B))
For a total of 1 fact.
CLIPS> (facts RECOVERY)↵
CLIPS> (facts *)↵
f-0     (fault (component A))
f-1     (possible-failure (component B))
For a total of 2 facts.
CLIPS>
```

Unlike defrule and deffacts constructs, deftemplate constructs (and all facts using that deftemplate) can be shared with other modules. A fact is "owned" by the module in which its deftemplate is contained, but the owning module can **export** the deftemplate associated with the fact, thus making that fact and all other facts using that deftemplate visible to other modules. It is not sufficient just to export the deftemplate to make a fact visible to another module. In order to use a deftemplate defined in another module, a module must also **import** the deftemplate definition.

Modules that export deftemplates must use the export attribute in their defmodule definition. The export attribute must use one of the following formats:

```
(export ?ALL)
(export ?NONE)
(export deftemplate ?ALL)
(export deftemplate ?NONE)
(export deftemplate <deftemplate-name>+)
```

The first format will export all exportable constructs from a module. Of the constructs discussed so far in this book, only deftemplates are exportable. Some of the other procedural and object-oriented programming constructs in CLIPS can be exported and the syntax for exporting these will be discussed in Chapters 10 and 11. The second format indicates that no constructs are exported and is the default for a defmodule. The third format indicates that all deftemplates in a module are exported. For the constructs discussed in this book, this is the same as the first format. Similarly, the fourth format indicates that no deftemplate constructs are exported. The second and fourth formats are provided primarily so the constructs exported by a module can be explicitly stated. Finally, the fifth format gives a specific list of deftemplates exported by a module. The export attribute can be used more than once in a defmodule definition to specify different types of exported constructs, but since deftemplates are the only exportable construct that we have discussed there will be no need to use more than one export attribute statement.

The import attribute also has five possible formats:

```
(import <module-name> ?ALL)
(import <module-name> ?NONE)
(import <module-name> deftemplate ?ALL)
(import <module-name> deftemplate ?NONE)
(import <module-name> deftemplate
                      <deftemplate-name>+)
```

Each of the formats has the same meaning as its export counterpart except that the specified constructs are imported. In addition, the module from which the constructs are being imported must be specified. Like the export attribute, a defmodule definition can have more than one import attribute.

A construct must be defined before it can be specified in an import list, but it does not have to be defined before it can be specified in an export list (in order to place a construct in a module, the module must be defined, so in fact it is not possible to have a construct defined before the module that exports it is defined). Because of this restriction, it is not possible for two modules to mutually import from each other (i.e., if module A imports from module B, it isn't possible for module B to import from module A).

To illustrate importing and exporting facts, let's assume that the RECOVERY module wants to import the *fault* deftemplate from the DETECTION module and the *possible-failure* deftemplate from the ISOLATION module. Unlike other constructs, once defined, a defmodule cannot be redefined. Thus, in order to change the import and export attributes of a defmodule, a clear command must be issued first. There is one exception to the restriction: the MAIN module, which is predefined, may be redefined once to include different import and export attributes (by default the MAIN module exports and imports nothing). *Note* that the default definition of the MAIN module *does not* export the *initial-fact* deftemplate. Recall from Chapter 8 that the (initial-fact) pattern is added to the LHS of a rule under certain circumstances (such as when the first CE is a *not* CE). If such a rule is placed in a module that does not import the *initial-fact* deftemplate from the MAIN module, that rule cannot be activated. Also note that you will not get an error when the rule is defined since the (initial-fact) pattern will cause the creation of an implied *initial-fact* deftemplate in the current module.

The new definitions for the DETECTION, ISOLATION, and RECOVERY modules along with their deftemplates (which should all be entered after a *clear* command) are the following:

```
(defmodule DETECTION
   (export deftemplate fault))

(deftemplate DETECTION::fault
   (slot component))
```

```
(defmodule ISOLATION
   (export deftemplate possible-failure))

(deftemplate ISOLATION::possible-failure
   (slot component))

(defmodule RECOVERY
   (import DETECTION deftemplate fault)
   (import ISOLATION deftemplate possible-
   failure))
```

With the defmodules and deftemplates defined, it is now possible to assert *fault* facts in the DETECTION and RECOVERY modules and *possible-failure* facts in the ISOLATION and RECOVERY modules:

```
CLIPS>
 (deffacts DETECTION::start
 (fault (component A)))↵
CLIPS>
 (deffacts ISOLATION::start
 (possible-failure (component B)))↵
CLIPS>
 (deffacts RECOVERY::start
 (fault (component C))
 (possible-failure (component D)))↵
CLIPS> (reset)↵
CLIPS> (facts DETECTION)↵
f-0     (fault (component A))
f-2     (fault (component C))
For a total of 2 facts.
CLIPS> (facts ISOLATION)↵
f-1     (possible-failure (component B))
f-3     (possible-failure (component D))
For a total of 2 facts.
CLIPS> (facts RECOVERY)↵
f-0     (fault (component A))
f-1     (possible-failure (component B))
f-2     (fault (component C))
f-3     (possible-failure (component D))
For a total of 4 facts.
CLIPS>
```

Notice that both the DETECTION and the RECOVERY modules see the *fault* facts asserted by either module. The same holds true for the *possible-failure* facts asserted by the ISOLATION and RECOVERY modules.

9.8 MODULES AND EXECUTION CONTROL

In addition to controlling which deftemplates a module can import and export, the defmodule construct can be used to control the execution of rules. Instead of being part of just one overall agenda, each module defined in CLIPS has its own agenda. Execution can then be controlled by deciding which module's agenda is selected for executing rules. For example, the following defrules should all be activated by the fault and possible-failure facts asserted in the previous example:

```
(defrule DETECTION::rule-1
   (fault (component A | C))
   =>)

(defrule ISOLATION::rule-2
   (possible-failure (component B | D))
   =>)

(defrule RECOVERY::rule-3
   (fault (component A | C))
   (possible-failure (component B | D))
   =>)
```

If the *agenda* command is issued after these rules are loaded, the agenda of the RECOVERY module will be displayed because the last rule defined was placed in that module:

```
CLIPS> (get-current-module)↵
RECOVERY
CLIPS> (agenda)↵
0      rule-3: f-0,f-3
0      rule-3: f-0,f-1
0      rule-3: f-2,f-3
0      rule-3: f-2,f-1
For a total of 4 activations.
CLIPS>
```

Like the *list-defrules* and *facts* commands, the agenda command accepts an optional argument that, if specified, indicates the module whose agenda will be listed:

```
CLIPS> (agenda DETECTION)↵
0      rule-1: f-2
0      rule-1: f-0
For a total of 2 activations.
CLIPS> (agenda ISOLATION)↵
0      rule-2: f-3
```

```
0       rule-2: f-1
For a total of 2 activations.
CLIPS> (agenda RECOVERY)↵
0       rule-3: f-0,f-3
0       rule-3: f-0,f-1
0       rule-3: f-2,f-3
0       rule-3: f-2,f-1
For a total of 4 activations.
CLIPS> (agenda *)↵
MAIN:
DETECTION:
   0       rule-1: f-2
   0       rule-1: f-0
ISOLATION:
   0       rule-2: f-3
   0       rule-2: f-1
RECOVERY:
   0       rule-3: f-0,f-3
   0       rule-3: f-0,f-1
   0       rule-3: f-2,f-3
   0       rule-3: f-2,f-1
For a total of 8 activations.
CLIPS>
```

The Focus Command

Now that there are rules on three separate agendas, what happens when a *run* command is issued?

```
CLIPS> (unwatch all)↵
CLIPS> (watch rules)↵
CLIPS> (run)↵
CLIPS>
```

No rules fire! In addition to the current module, which CLIPS uses to determine where new constructs are added and which constructs are used or affected by commands, CLIPS also maintains a **current focus**, which determines which agenda the *run* command uses during execution. The *reset* and *clear* commands automatically set the current focus to the MAIN module. The current focus *does not* change when the current module is changed. Thus, in the current example, when the *run* command is issued, the agenda associated with the MAIN module is used to select rules to execute. Since this agenda is empty, no rules are fired.

The **focus** command is used to change the current focus. Its syntax is:

```
(focus <module-name>+)
```

In the simple case in which only one module name is specified, the current focus is set to the specified module. By setting the current focus to the DETECTION module and then issuing a *run* command, the rules on the DETECTION module's agenda will be fired:

```
CLIPS> (focus DETECTION)↵
TRUE
CLIPS> (run)↵
FIRE    1 rule-1: f-2
FIRE    2 rule-1: f-0
CLIPS>
```

Using the *focus* command not only changes the current focus but also recalls the previous value of the current focus. The current focus is really the top value of a stack data structure called the ***focus stack***. Whenever the *focus* command changes the current focus, it is actually pushing the new current focus onto the top of the focus stack, displacing the previous current focuses. As rules execute, when the agenda of the current focus becomes empty, the current focus is popped (removed) from the focus stack and the next module becomes the current focus. Rules are then executed from the agenda of the new current focus until a new module is focused on or until there are no rules left on the agenda of the current focus. Rules will continue to execute until there are no modules left on the focus stack or the *halt* command is issued.

Continuing the current example, focusing first on the ISOLATION module and then on the RECOVERY module will cause all of the rules on the RECOVERY module's agenda to fire, which will be followed by the firing of rules on the ISOLATION module's agenda. The **list-focus-stack** command (which takes no arguments) is used to display the modules on the focus stack:

```
CLIPS> (focus ISOLATION)↵
TRUE
CLIPS> (focus RECOVERY)↵
TRUE
CLIPS> (list-focus-stack)↵
RECOVERY
ISOLATION
CLIPS> (run)↵
FIRE    1 rule-3: f-1,f-4
FIRE    2 rule-3: f-1,f-2
FIRE    3 rule-3: f-3,f-4
FIRE    4 rule-3: f-3,f-2
FIRE    5 rule-2: f-4
FIRE    6 rule-2: f-2
CLIPS> (list-focus-stack)↵
CLIPS>
```

Using two focus commands to push the ISOLATION and RECOVERY modules causes the RECOVERY rules to execute before the ISOLATION rules. However, when more than one module is specified in a single *focus* command, the modules are pushed onto the focus stack from right to left. For example:

```
CLIPS> (focus ISOLATION RECOVERY)↵
TRUE
CLIPS> (list-focus-stack)↵
ISOLATION
RECOVERY
CLIPS> (focus ISOLATION)↵
TRUE
CLIPS> (list-focus-stack)↵
ISOLATION
RECOVERY
CLIPS> (focus RECOVERY)↵
TRUE
CLIPS> (list-focus-stack)↵
RECOVERY
ISOLATION
RECOVERY
CLIPS>
```

Notice that the same module can be on the focus stack more than once, but focusing on a module that is already the current focus has no effect.

Manipulating and Examining the Focus Stack

CLIPS provides several commands and functions for manipulating the current focus and the focus stack. The **clear-focus-stack** command removes all modules from the focus stack. The **get-focus** function returns the module name of the current focus or the symbol FALSE if the focus stack is empty. The **pop-focus** function removes the current focus from the focus stack (and returns the module name or the symbol FALSE if the focus stack is empty). The **get-focus-stack** function returns a multifield value containing the modules on the focus stack.

```
CLIPS> (get-focus-stack)↵
(RECOVERY ISOLATION RECOVERY)
CLIPS> (get-focus)↵
RECOVERY
CLIPS> (pop-focus)↵
RECOVERY
CLIPS> (clear-focus-stack)↵
CLIPS> (get-focus-stack)↵
()
CLIPS> (get-focus)↵
FALSE
CLIPS> (pop-focus)↵
```

```
FALSE
CLIPS>
```

The *watch* command can be used to see changes to the focus stack using the keyword *focus* as the command's argument:

```
CLIPS> (watch focus)↵
CLIPS> (focus DETECTION ISOLATION RECOVERY)↵
==> Focus RECOVERY
==> Focus ISOLATION from RECOVERY
==> Focus DETECTION from ISOLATION
TRUE
CLIPS> (run)↵
<== Focus DETECTION to ISOLATION
<== Focus ISOLATION to RECOVERY
<== Focus RECOVERY
CLIPS>
```

In the event that the *run* command is given and the focus stack is empty, the MAIN module is automatically pushed onto the focus stack. This feature is provided mainly as a convenience for the case in which new activations are added after the program has ended because there are no modules left on the focus stack. For example,

```
CLIPS> (clear)↵
CLIPS> (watch focus)↵
CLIPS> (watch rules)↵
CLIPS> (defrule example-1 =>)↵
CLIPS> (reset)
<== Focus MAIN
==> Focus MAIN
CLIPS> (run)↵
FIRE    1 example-1: f-0
<== Focus MAIN
CLIPS> (defrule example-2 =>)↵
CLIPS> (agenda)↵
0      example-2: f-0
For a total of 1 activation.
CLIPS> (list-focus-stack)↵
CLIPS>
```

The rule *example-2* is on the agenda, but there are no modules on the focus stack. Issuing a *run* command, however, places the MAIN module on the focus stack, so rule *example-2* is able to fire anyway:

```
CLIPS> (run)↵
==> Focus MAIN
FIRE    1 example-2: f-0
```

```
<== Focus MAIN
CLIPS>
```

The Return Command

One of the drawbacks of controlling the flow of execution by using control facts to represent phases, as discussed in Section 9.4, is that it is not possible to fire some activations in a particular phase, exit that phase, and then return later to the phase and execute the remaining activations on the agenda. This occurs because once the control fact representing the phase is retracted, all of the activations from that phase are removed from the agenda. When the control fact is later reasserted, *all* of the previous activations for that phase will be reactivated, not just those that didn't fire (this, of course, is assuming that only the control fact and not any other facts were asserted or retracted).

If modules are used to control the flow of execution, it is possible to stop executing the activations from a specific module's agenda prematurely (that is, before the module's agenda is empty). The ***return*** command can be used to immediately terminate the execution of a rule's RHS and remove the current focus from the focus stack (thus returning control of execution to the next module on the focus stack). When used from the RHS of a rule, the *return* command should be passed no arguments (the *return* command can also used by the procedural programming constructs provided with CLIPS). The following example illustrates the use of the *return* command:

```
CLIPS> (clear)↵
CLIPS>
(defmodule MAIN
   (export deftemplate initial-fact))↵
CLIPS>
(defmodule DETECTION
   (import MAIN deftemplate initial-fact))↵
CLIPS>
(defrule MAIN::start
   =>
   (focus DETECTION))↵
CLIPS>
(defrule DETECTION::example-1
 =>
  (return)
  (printout t "No printout!" crlf))↵
CLIPS>
(defrule DETECTION::example-2
 =>
  (return)
  (printout t "No printout!" crlf))↵
CLIPS> (watch rules)↵
CLIPS> (watch focus)↵
CLIPS> (reset)↵
```

```
<== Focus MAIN
==> Focus MAIN
CLIPS> (run)↵
FIRE    1 start: f-0
==> Focus DETECTION from MAIN
FIRE    2 example-1: f-0
<== Focus DETECTION to MAIN
<== Focus MAIN
CLIPS>
```

There are two points worth noting about this example. First, in order for the rules in the DETECTION module to be activated by using the default *initial-fact* pattern, the *initial-fact* deftemplate must be exported by the MAIN module and imported by the DETECTION module. Second, notice that the return command *immediately* halts execution of the rule's RHS. The *printout* command following the *return* command is not executed in the *example-1* rule (or in the *example-2* rule, since it didn't get the opportunity to fire). Note that the functionality of the *return* command is similar to, but not the same as, the *pop-focus* command, which removes the current focus from the focus stack but will allow the execution of the actions of the RHS of a rule to continue. If the *pop-focus* command had been used in place of the *return* command for this example, the string "No printout!" would have been printed when the actions of the *example-1* rule were executed.

The Auto-Focus Feature

In addition to being able to explicitly focus on modules using the *focus* command, it's also possible to automatically focus on a module when specific rules from that module are activated. By default, a rule's module is not automatically focused upon when that rule is activated. This can be changed by using the **auto-focus** attribute. The auto-focus attribute is specified in the declare statement along with the salience attribute. The keyword *auto-focus* is specified, followed by either TRUE (to enable the feature) or FALSE (to disable the feature). It's not necessary that all rules in a module have the auto-focus feature enabled in order for some rules in the module to make use of it. Similarly, it's not necessary to declare both the salience attribute and the auto-focus attribute if the declare statement is used for a rule. The following example illustrates the use of the auto-focus feature:

```
CLIPS> (clear)↵
CLIPS>
(defmodule MAIN
   (export deftemplate initial-fact))↵
CLIPS>
(defmodule DETECTION
   (import MAIN deftemplate initial-fact))↵
CLIPS>
(defrule DETECTION::example
   (declare (auto-focus TRUE))
   =>)↵
```

```
CLIPS> (watch focus)↵
CLIPS> (reset)↵
<== Focus MAIN
==> Focus MAIN
==> Focus DETECTION from MAIN
CLIPS>
```

When the *reset* command is issued, the MAIN module is automatically focused on because the focus stack is empty. The *example* rule is activated by the assertion of the *initial-fact* fact. Since the auto-focus attribute is enabled for this rule, its module, the DETECTION module, is automatically pushed onto the focus stack. The auto-focus feature is particularly useful for rules that detect constraint violations. Because the constraint rule's module immediately becomes the current focus, it is possible to take action when the violation occurs, rather than having an explicit phase in which violations are detected.

Replacing Phases and Control Facts

Through the use of defmodules, the *focus* and *return* commands, and the auto-focus feature it is now possible to replace the use of phases and control facts with a much more explicit mechanism for controlling the flow of execution of rules. The constructs described in Section 9.4 for controlling execution can be replaced with the following constructs:

```
(defmodule DETECTION)
(defmodule ISOLATION)
(defmodule RECOVERY)

(deffacts MAIN::control-information
   (phase-sequence DETECTION ISOLATION RECOVERY))

(defrule MAIN::change-phase
   ?list <- (phase-sequence ?next-phase
                            $?other-phases)
   =>
   (focus ?next-phase)
   (retract ?list)
   (assert (phase-sequence ?other-phases
                           ?next-phase)))
```

Control of execution will be cycled from the DETECTION module to the ISOLATION module to the RECOVERY module, and back again. All the rules in each module would fire before allowing the rules in the next module to fire (unless a *return* command was issued or a new module was focused on as a result of the auto-focus feature):

```
CLIPS> (unwatch all)↵
CLIPS> (reset)↵
```

```
CLIPS> (watch rules)↵
CLIPS> (watch focus)↵
CLIPS> (run 5)↵
FIRE    1 change-phase: f-1
==> Focus DETECTION from MAIN
<== Focus DETECTION to MAIN
FIRE    2 change-phase: f-2
==> Focus ISOLATION from MAIN
<== Focus ISOLATION to MAIN
FIRE    3 change-phase: f-3
==> Focus RECOVERY from MAIN
<== Focus RECOVERY to MAIN
FIRE    4 change-phase: f-4
==> Focus DETECTION from MAIN
<== Focus DETECTION to MAIN
FIRE    5 change-phase: f-5
==> Focus ISOLATION from MAIN
<== Focus ISOLATION to MAIN
CLIPS>
```

9.9 THE RETE PATTERN-MATCHING ALGORITHM

Rule-based languages such as CLIPS, Jess, Eclipse, and OPS5 use a very efficient algorithm for matching facts against the patterns in rules to determine which rules have had their conditions satisfied. This algorithm is called the ***Rete Pattern-Matching Algorithm*** (Forgy 79) (Forgy 85) (Brownston 85). Writing efficient CLIPS rules does not require an understanding of the Rete algorithm. However, an understanding of the underlying algorithm used in CLIPS and other rule-based languages makes it easier to understand why writing rules one way is more efficient than writing them another way.

To understand why the Rete algorithm is efficient, it is helpful to look at the problem of matching facts to rules in general and then to examine other algorithms that are not as efficient. Figure 9.6 shows the problem addressed by the Rete algorithm.

If the matching process has to occur only once, then the solution to the problem is straightforward. The inference engine can examine each rule and then search the set of facts to determine whether the rule's patterns have been satisfied. If the rule's patterns have been satisfied, then the rule can be placed on the agenda. Figure 9.7 shows this approach.

In rule-based languages, however, the matching process takes place repeatedly. Normally the fact list will be modified during each cycle of execution. New facts may be added to the fact list or old facts may be removed from it. These changes may cause previously unsatisfied patterns to be satisfied or vice versa. The problem of matching now becomes an ongoing process. During each cycle, as facts are added and removed the set of rules satisfied must be maintained and updated.

Figure 9.6 Pattern Matching: Rules and Facts

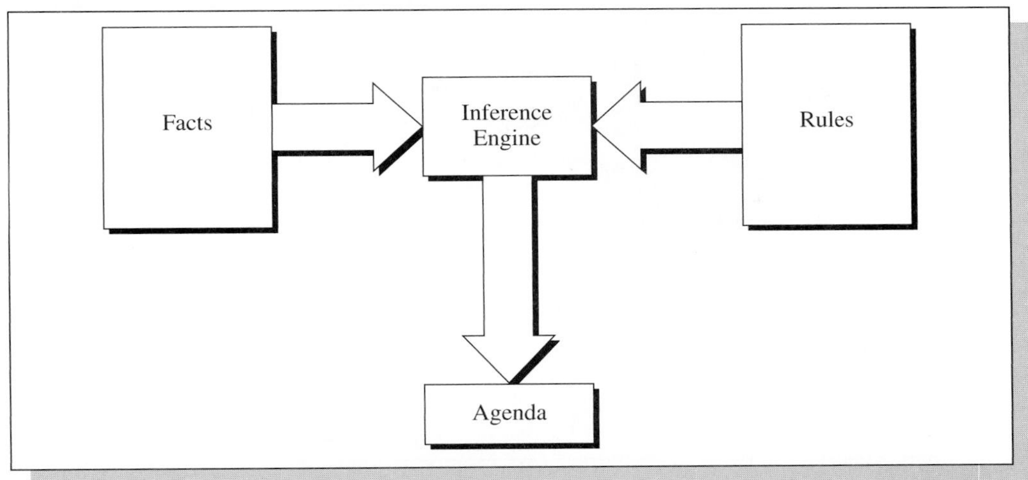

Having the inference engine check each rule to direct the search for facts after each cycle of execution provides a simple and straightforward technique for solving this problem. The primary disadvantage of such an approach is that it can be very slow. Most rule-based expert systems exhibit a property called ***temporal redundancy***. Typically, the actions of a rule will change only a few facts in the fact list. That is, the facts in the expert system change slowly over time. Each cycle of execution may see only a small percentage of facts either added or removed and so only a small percentage of rules are typically affected by the changes in the fact list. Thus, having the rules drive the search for needed facts requires a lot of unnecessary computation, since most of the rules are likely to find the same facts in the current cycle as were found in the last

Figure 9.7 Rules Searching for Facts

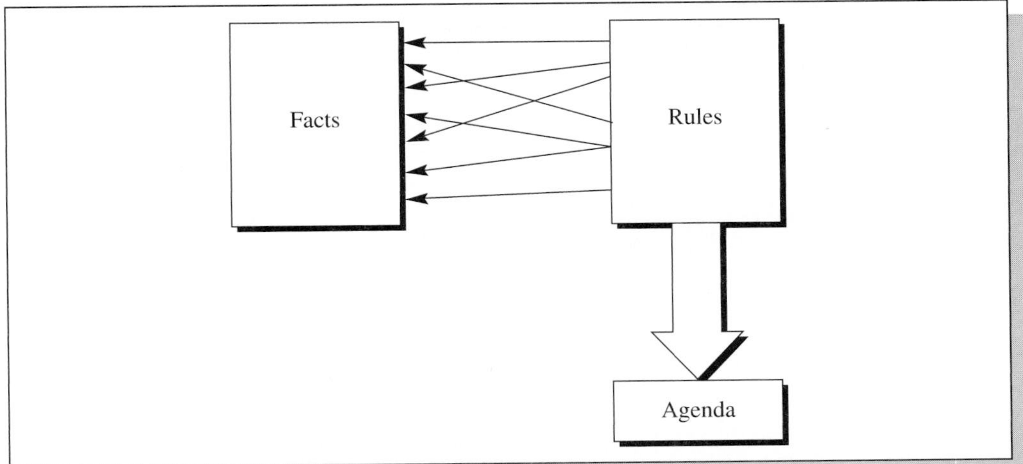

Figure 9.8 Unnecessary Computations When Rules Search for Facts

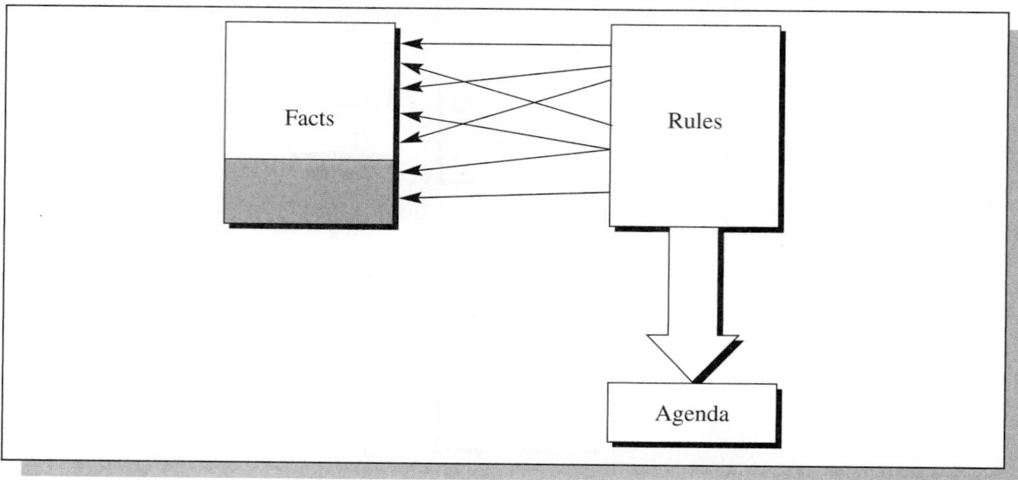

cycle. The inefficiency of this approach is shown in Figure 9.8. The shaded area represents the changes that have been made to the fact list. Unnecessary recomputation could be avoided by remembering what has already been matched from cycle to cycle and then computing only the changes necessary for the newly added or newly removed facts, as shown in Figure 9.9. The rules remain static and the facts change, so the facts should find the rules, and not the other way around.

The Rete Pattern-Matching Algorithm is designed to take advantage of the temporal redundancy exhibited by rule-based expert systems. It does so by saving the state of the matching process from cycle to cycle and recomputing the changes in this state only for the changes that occur in the fact list. That is, if a set of patterns finds two of three required facts in one cycle, it is not necessary

Figure 9.9 Facts Searching for Rules

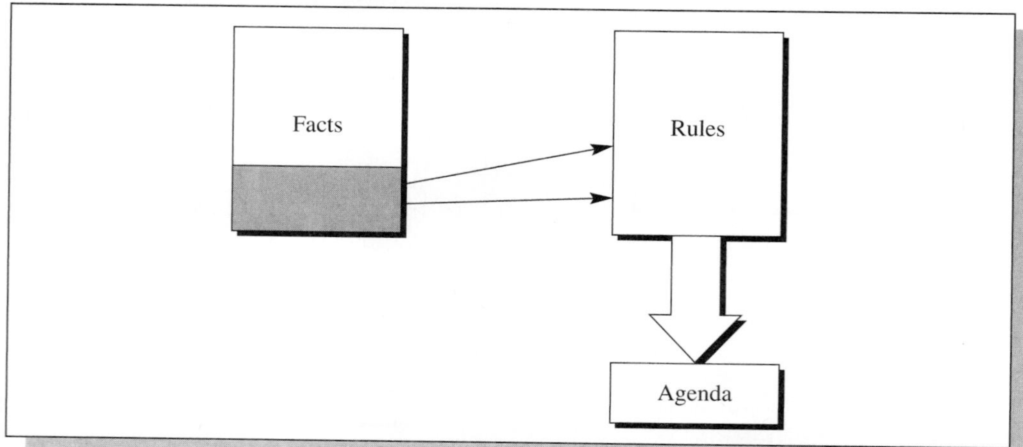

for a check to be made in the next cycle for the two facts that have already been found—only the third fact is of interest. The state of the matching process is updated only as facts are added and removed. If the number of facts added and removed is small compared to the total number of facts and patterns, the process of matching will proceed quickly. As a worst case, if all the facts were to be changed, then the matching process would work as if all the facts were to be compared against all the patterns.

If only updates to the fact list are processed, then each rule must remember what has already matched it. That is, if a new fact has matched the third pattern of a rule, information about the matches for the first two patterns must be available to finish the matching process. This type of state information indicating the facts that have matched previous patterns in a rule is called a ***partial match***. A partial match for a rule is any set of facts that satisfy the rule's patterns, beginning with the first pattern of the rule and ending with any pattern up to and including the last. Thus, a rule with three patterns would have partial matches for the first pattern, the first and second patterns, and the first, second, and third patterns. A partial match of all of the patterns of a rule will also be an activation. The other type of state information saved is called a ***pattern match***. A pattern match occurs when a fact has satisfied a single pattern in any rule without regard to variables in other patterns that may restrict the matching process.

The primary disadvantage of the Rete Pattern-Matching Algorithm is that it is memory intensive. Simply comparing all the facts to all the patterns requires no memory. Saving the state of the system using pattern matches and partial matches can consume considerable amounts of memory. In general, this tradeoff of memory for speed is worthwhile, however, it is important to remember that a poorly written rule can not only run slowly, it can use up considerable amounts of memory.

The Rete algorithm also improves the efficiency of rule-based systems by taking advantage of **structural similarity** in the rules. *Structural similarity* refers to the fact that many rules often contain similar patterns or groups of patterns. The Rete algorithm uses this feature to increase efficiency by pooling common components so they don't have to be computed more than once.

9.10 THE PATTERN NETWORK

The problem of matching facts to rules can be divided into two steps. First, when facts are added and removed, it must be determined which patterns have been matched. Second, comparison of variable bindings across patterns must be checked to determine the partial matches for a group of patterns.

The process of determining which facts have matched which patterns is performed in the **pattern network**. For brevity we will limit the explanation of pattern matching to single-field slots of deftemplate facts. All matching that does not involve comparison against variables bound in other patterns can be performed in the pattern network. The pattern network is structured like a tree, where the first slot constraint of all the patterns are the nodes connected to the root of the tree, the second slot constraints of all of the patterns are the nodes connected to those nodes, and so on. The last slot constraints in a pattern are the leaves of the tree. The nodes in the pattern network are called ***one-input nodes*** because each only receives information from the node above it. Nodes in the pattern network are sometimes referred to as ***pattern nodes***. The leaf nodes are also referred to as ***terminal nodes***. Each pattern node contains a specification used for determining whether the slot value of a fact has matched the slot constraint of a pattern. For example, the pattern:

```
(data (x 27))
```

would be represented by one node since there is only one slot constraint. The matching specification for the first node would then be the following:

```
The slot x value is equal to the constant 27
```

Actually, determining whether the fact has the appropriate relation name for the pattern also must be checked (e.g., you don't want *foobar* facts to be matching *data* patterns just because they have the same slot names). To perform this test CLIPS maintains separate pattern networks for each deftemplate so the relation name check is performed as the fact is created, but before pattern matching occurs.

Matching specifications include all the information for matching a single slot. Several tests can be performed together. For example, the pattern:

```
(data (x ~red&~green))
```

would generate the following matching specification for the *x* slot:

```
The slot x value is not equal to the constant red
                   and is not equal to the constant green
```

Normally variable bindings are not checked in the pattern network unless the variable is used more than once in the pattern. For example, the pattern:

```
(data (x ?x) (y ?y) (z ?x))
```

would not generate match specifications for either the *x* slot or the *y* slot since the first binding of a variable to a slot value has no effect on whether the pattern is matched by the fact. However, the *z* slot must have the same value as the *x* slot, so the match specification for the *z* slot would be the following:

```
The z slot value is equal to the x slot value
```

Expressions containing variables that are all found within the pattern can be checked within the pattern network. For example, the pattern:

```
(data (x ?x&:(> ?x ?y)))
```

would not generate a match specification for the *x* slot because the variable ?y is not contained within the pattern (assuming, of course, that the variable ?y is defined in a previous pattern). However, the *x* slot in the pattern:

```
(data (x ?x&:(> ?x 4)))
```

would have the match specification:

```
The x slot value is greater than the constant 4
```

since the only variable found in the expression, *?x*, is also contained within the pattern.

As stated previously, the pattern network is arranged hierarchically, with the pattern nodes corresponding to the first slot constraints of the patterns at the top. When a fact is asserted, the pattern nodes for the first slot constraints in the pattern network are checked. Any pattern node whose matching specification is satisfied will activate the pattern nodes directly below it. This process continues until a terminal node in the pattern network has been reached. The terminal nodes in the pattern network represent the end of a pattern and a successful pattern match. Each terminal node has an **alpha** or **right memory** associated with it. The alpha memory contains the set of all facts that have matched the pattern associated with the terminal node. In other words, the alpha memory stores the set of pattern matches for a particular pattern.

The pattern network takes advantage of structural similarity by sharing common pattern nodes among patterns. Since the pattern nodes are stored hierarchically, two patterns can share their first *N* pattern nodes if the match specifications for their first *N* slot constraints are identical. For example, the patterns:

```
(data (x red) (y green))
(data (x red) (y blue))
```

can share common pattern nodes for the *x* slot. Notice that it is the match specifications that must be identical, and not necessarily the slot constraints found in the pattern. For example, the patterns:

```
(data (x ?x) (y ?x))
(data (x ?y) (y ?y))
```

can share the pattern node for the *y* slot even though the variables used in the two patterns are different. The *x* slots don't generate a match specification and so are ignored for sharing purposes. However, switching the order of the slots to:

```
(data (x ?x) (y ?x))
(data (y ?y) (x ?y))
```

would prevent the patterns from sharing nodes since the first pattern would generate a match specification for the *y* slot and the second pattern would generate a match specification for the *x* slot.

Figure 9.10 Pattern Network for Two Rules

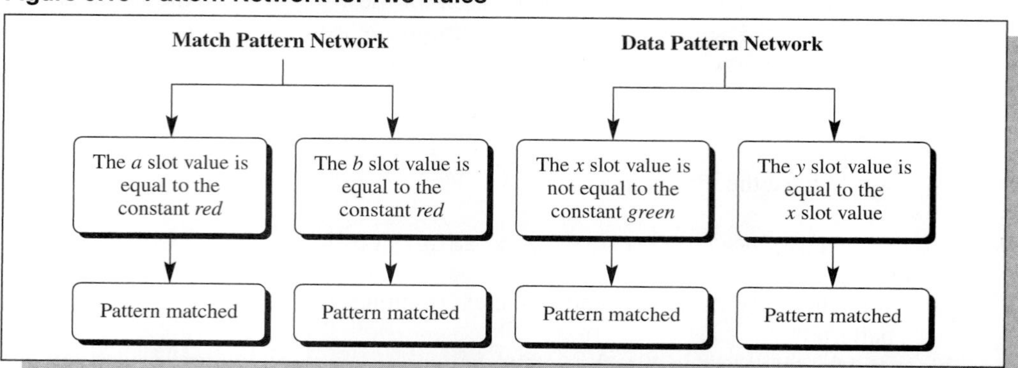

Figure 9.10 shows the pattern network generated by the following rules:

```
(defrule Rete-rule-1
   (match (a red))
   (data (x ?x) (y ?x))
   =>)

(defrule Rete-rule-2
   (match (a ?x) (b red))
   (data (x ~green) (y ?x))
   (data (x ?x) (y ?x))
   =>)
```

9.11 THE JOIN NETWORK

Once it has been determined which patterns have been matched by facts, comparison of variable bindings across patterns must be checked to ensure that variables used in more than one pattern have consistent values. This comparison is performed in the **join network**. Each terminal node in the pattern network acts as an input to a **join**, or **two-input node**, in the join network. Each join contains a matching specification for the matches of the alpha memory associated with its terminal node and for the set of partial matches that have matched previous patterns. The partial matches for previous patterns are stored in the **beta** or **left memory** of the join. A rule with *N* patterns would then have *N* – 1 joins (although CLIPS actually uses *N* joins to simplify the Rete algorithm, thus allowing each join to be entered by only one pattern).

The first join compares the first two patterns and the remaining joins compare an additional pattern to the partial matches of the previous join. For example, given the rule *Rete-rule-2* used in the previous example,

```
(defrule Rete-rule-2
   (match (a ?x) (b red))
```

```
(data (x ~green) (y ?x))
(data (x ?x) (y ?x))
=>)
```

the first join would contain the match specification:

```
The a slot value of the fact
    bound to the first pattern is equal to
the y slot value of the fact
    bound to the second pattern.
```

The second join would receive as input the set of partial matches from the first join and it would contain the following match specification:

```
The x slot value of the fact
    bound to the third pattern is equal to
the y slot value of the fact
    bound to the second pattern.
```

Notice that the variable *?x* in the third pattern could have its value compared to the variable *?x* in the first pattern instead of variable *?x* in the second pattern. The second occurrence of *?x* in the third pattern does not have to be checked in the join network since it can be checked in the pattern network. The pattern and join networks for rule *Rete-rule-2* are shown in Figure 9.11.

The join network takes advantage of structural similarity by sharing joins between rules. Joins in the join network can be shared by two rules if they have identical patterns and join comparisons for two or more patterns, starting with the first pattern. For example, these rules:

```
(defrule sharing-1
   (match (a ?x) (b red))
   (data (x ~green) (y ?x))
   (data (x ?x) (y ?x))
   (other (q ?z))
   =>)

(defrule sharing-2
   (match (a ?y) (b red))
   (data (x ~green) (y ?y))
   (data (x ?y) (y ?y))
   (other (q ?y))
   =>)
```

could share all of their patterns in the pattern network and the joins created for their first three patterns in the join network. The join for the fourth pattern cannot be shared in the join network because the match specifications for the

Figure 9.11 Pattern and Join Networks for Rule Rete-Rule-2

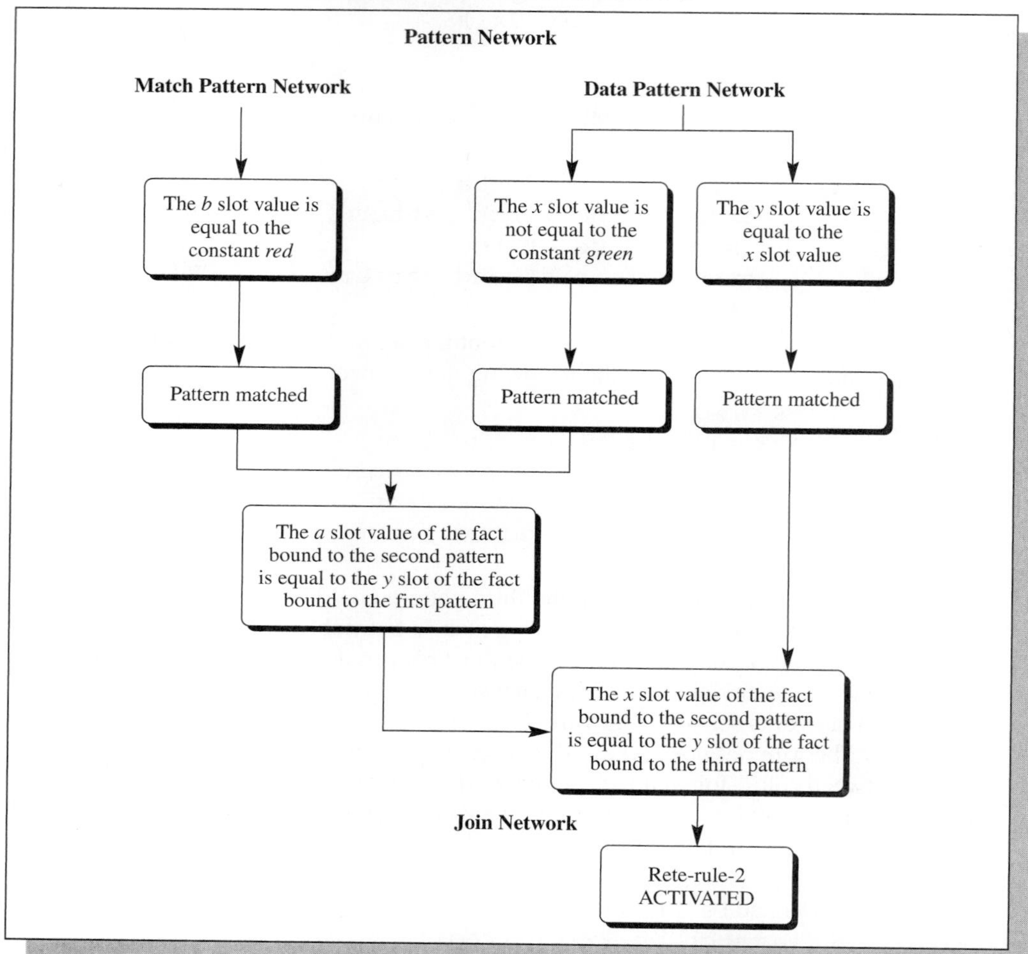

two rules are different. The match specification for the fourth pattern of rule *sharing-1* does not have to perform any comparisons because the variable *?z* is not used in other patterns. However, the match specification for the fourth pattern of rule *sharing-2* must compare the variable *?y* to the variable *?y* in another pattern to ensure that the variable bindings are consistent. Notice again that the variable names do not have to be identical to take advantage of structural similarity. All that matters is that the match specifications be identical.

CLIPS provides useful information about join sharing if the *watch compilations* command has been issued. For example, the following commands illustrate how information about sharing is displayed. Assume that rules *sharing-1* and *sharing-2* are in the file "rules.clp":

```
CLIPS> (watch compilations)↵
CLIPS> (load "rules.clp")↵
Defining defrule: sharing-1 +j+j+j+j
Defining defrule: sharing-2 =j=j=j+j
TRUE
CLIPS>
```

The *+j* in the output indicates that a join is being added, whereas *=j* indicates that a join is being shared. Thus when rule *sharing-1* is added four new joins are created. When rule *sharing-2* is added, it shares its first three joins with rule *sharing-1* and creates a new join for its last pattern. Notice that CLIPS has used four joins to represent the rule, as opposed to the three joins that would normally be required. For implementation reasons it is convenient to have only one pattern per join; so instead of using one join for the first two patterns, CLIPS uses two joins.

9.12 THE IMPORTANCE OF PATTERN ORDER

Programmers new to rule-based languages often have misconceptions about the importance of ordering the patterns in rules correctly for both speed and memory efficiency. Since the Rete algorithm saves the state from one cycle to the next, it is very important to make sure that rules do not generate large numbers of partial matches. For example, consider the following simple program:

```
(deffacts information
   (find-match a c e g)
   (item a)
   (item b)
   (item c)
   (item d)
   (item e)
   (item f)
   (item g))

(defrule match-1
   (find-match ?x ?y ?z ?w)
   (item ?x)
   (item ?y)
   (item ?z)
   (item ?w)
   =>
   (assert (found-match ?x ?y ?z ?w)))
```

This program will reset very quickly. A *watch facts* command followed by a *reset* command will verify this. Now consider the following program:

```
(deffacts information
   (find-match a c e g)
```

```
   (item a)
   (item b)
   (item c)
   (item d)
   (item e)
   (item f)
   (item g))

(defrule match-2
   (item ?x)
   (item ?y)
   (item ?z)
   (item ?w)
   (find-match ?x ?y ?z ?w)
   =>
   (assert (found-match ?x ?y ?z ?w)))
```

A *watch facts* command followed by a *reset* command for this program will demonstrate a considerably slower reset time. As the reset is performed, the first few facts in the deffacts construct will be asserted quickly. Subsequent facts will require an increasingly longer time to be asserted. Rules *match-1* and *match-2* each have the same patterns, but rule *match-2* takes much longer to reset. In fact, on some computers rule *match-2* may cause CLIPS to run out of memory. An even greater difference in speed can be demonstrated by adding more item facts to the *information* deffacts (in fact, on some computers it may be necessary to add additional *item* facts to the *information* deffacts in order to see a noticeable difference).

Counting for Rule *match-1*

Counting the pattern matches and partial matches for rule *match-1* provides useful information. The fact ids will be used instead of the entire fact in listing the pattern and partial matches. In addition, partial matches will be enclosed in braces. The fact IDs are as follows:

```
f-1 (find-match a c e g)
f-2 (item a)
f-3 (item b)
f-4 (item c)
f-5 (item d)
f-6 (item e)
f-7 (item f)
f-8 (item g)
```

Rule *match-1* has the following pattern matches:

```
Pattern 1: f-1
Pattern 2: f-2, f-3, f-4, f-5, f-6, f-7, f-8
```

```
Pattern 3: f-2, f-3, f-4, f-5, f-6, f-7, f-8
Pattern 4: f-2, f-3, f-4, f-5, f-6, f-7, f-8
Pattern 5: f-2, f-3, f-4, f-5, f-6, f-7, f-8
```

Rule *match-1* has the following partial matches:

```
Pattern  1:    [f-1]
Patterns 1-2: [f-1,f-2]
Patterns  1-3: [f-1,f-2,f-4]
Patterns  1-4: [f-1,f-2,f-4,f-6]
Patterns  1-5: [f-1,f-2,f-4,f-6,f-8]
```

In total rule *match-1* has 29 pattern matches and 5 partial matches.

Counting for Rule match-2

Rule *match-2* has the following pattern matches:

```
Pattern 1: f-2, f-3, f-4, f-5, f-6, f-7, f-8
Pattern 2: f-2, f-3, f-4, f-5, f-6, f-7, f-8
Pattern 3: f-2, f-3, f-4, f-5, f-6, f-7, f-8
Pattern 4: f-2, f-3, f-4, f-5, f-6, f-7, f-8
Pattern 5: f-1
```

Rules *match-1* and *match-2* have the same number of pattern matches. Now consider only the partial matches for pattern 1:

```
[f-2],[f-3],[f-4],[f-5],[f-6],[f-7],[f-8]
```

Pattern 1 has seven partial matches. This is no surprise since the partial and pattern matches will be the same for the first pattern. The partial matches for patterns 1 and 2, however, are numerous:

```
[f-2,f-2],[f-2,f-3],[f-2,f-4],[f-2,f-5],
          [f-2,f-6],[f-2,f-7],[f-2,f-8],
[f-3,f-2],[f-3,f-3],[f-3,f-4],[f-3,f-5],
          [f-3,f-6],[f-3,f-7],[f-3,f-8],
[f-4,f-2],[f-4,f-3],[f-4,f-4],[f-4,f-5],
          [f-4,f-6],[f-4,f-7],[f-4,f-8],
[f-5,f-2],[f-5,f-3],[f-5,f-4],[f-5,f-5],
          [f-5,f-6],[f-5,f-7],[f-5,f-8],
[f-6,f-2],[f-6,f-3],[f-6,f-4],[f-6,f-5],
          [f-6,f-6],[f-6,f-7],[f-6,f-8],
[f-7,f-2],[f-7,f-3],[f-7,f-4],[f-7,f-5],
          [f-7,f-6],[f-7,f-7],[f-7,f-8],
[f-8,f-2],[f-8,f-3],[f-8,f-4],[f-8,f-5],
          [f-8,f-6],[f-8,f-7],[f-8,f-8]
```

In all there are forty-nine partial matches for patterns 1 and 2 (seven pattern matches for pattern 1 multiplied by seven pattern matches for pattern 2). Space will quickly limit the partial matches that can be listed for the other patterns since there will be 343 partial matches for patterns 1 through 3 and 2,401 partial matches for patterns 1 through 4. Just as for rule *match-1*, only one partial match exists for patterns 1 through 5.

```
[f-2,f-4,f-6,f-8,f-1]
```

Notice that although the numbers of pattern matches and activations are the same for rules *match-1* and *match-2*, rule *match-1* has only five partial matches, whereas rule *match-2* has 2,801 partial matches, a difference that will continue to grow as more item facts are added. The fact (item h) will create no new partial matches for rule *match-1*; however, it will create 1,880 new partial matches for rule *match-2*. This example demonstrates that the number of partial matches created can drastically affect the performance of a program. An efficient set of rules should attempt to minimize not only the creation of new partial matches but the deletion of old partial matches as well. In effect, an attempt should be made to minimize the change of state of the system from one cycle to the next. Specific techniques for minimizing the change of state will be discussed later in this chapter.

The Matches Command

CLIPS has a debugging command called ***matches*** that will display the pattern matches, partial matches, and activations of a rule. This command is useful for finding rules that generate large numbers of partial matches and for debugging cases in which a rule appears to have all of its patterns satisfied but is nonetheless not activated. The syntax of the *matches* command is:

```
(matches <rule-name>)
```

The argument of the *matches* command is the name of the rule for which matches are displayed. The following dialog illustrates the output of the *matches* command:

```
CLIPS> (clear)↵
CLIPS>
(defrule match-3
   (find-match ?x ?y)
   (item ?x)
   (item ?y)
   =>
   (assert (found-match ?x ?y)))↵
CLIPS>
(assert (find-match a b)
        (find-match c d)
        (find-match e f)
        (item a)
```

```
        (item b)
        (item c)
        (item f))↵
<Fact-6>
CLIPS> (facts)↵
f-0     (find-match a b)
f-1     (find-match c d)
f-2     (find-match e f)
f-3     (item a)
f-4     (item b)
f-5     (item c)
f-6     (item f)
For a total of 7 facts.
CLIPS> (matches match-3)↵
Matches for Pattern 1
f-0
f-1
f-2
Matches for Pattern 2
f-3
f-4
f-5
f-6
Matches for Pattern 3
f-3
f-4
f-5
f-6
Partial matches for CEs 1 - 2
f-1,f-5
f-0,f-3
Partial matches for CEs 1 - 3
f-0,f-3,f-4
Activations
f-0,f-3,f-4
CLIPS>
```

The first pattern of rule *match-3* has three pattern matches, one for each *find-match* fact. Similarly, the second and third patterns both have four pattern matches, one for each *item* fact. The first two patterns have two partial matches: one for the facts (find-match c d) and (item c), and another for the facts (find-match c d) and (item c). There is no partial match associated with the fact (find-match e f) since the fact (item e) does not exist. There is only one partial match for all three patterns: the partial match for the facts (fact-match a b), (item a), and (item b). There is also an activation for this partial match. Once the *match-3* rule has fired for this activation it will no longer be displayed by the *matches* command.

Watching the Changing State

The *matches* command provides one useful way of examining partial matches for a rule. Another way to watch partial matches is to consider them partial activations of a rule. If rule *match-1* is considered several separate rules each trying to compute partial matches, the *watch activations* command can be used to see the partial matches as they are generated. The rule *match-1* can be split into several rules as follows:

```
(defrule m1-pm-1
         "Partial matches for pattern 1"
   (find-match ?x ?y ?z ?w)
   =>)

(defrule m1-pm-1-to-2
         "Partial matches for patterns 1 and 2"
   (find-match ?x ?y ?z ?w)
   (item ?x)
   =>)

(defrule m1-pm-1-to-3
         "Partial matches for patterns 1 to 3"
   (find-match ?x ?y ?z ?w)
   (item ?x)
   (item ?y)
   =>)

(defrule m1-pm-1-to-4
         "Partial matches for patterns 1 to 4"
   (find-match ?x ?y ?z ?w)
   (item ?x)
   (item ?y)
   (item ?z)
   =>)

(defrule match-1 "Activations for the match rule"
   (find-match ?x ?y ?z ?w)
   (item ?x)
   (item ?y)
   (item ?z)
   (item ?w)
   =>
   (assert (found-match ?x ?y ?z ?w)))
```

If the preceding rules and the *information* deffacts are loaded, the partial matches can be watched as they are created using the following command dialog:

```
CLIPS> (watch activations)↵
CLIPS> (watch facts)↵
CLIPS> (reset)↵
==> f-0      (initial-fact)
==> f-1      (find-match a c e g)
==> Activation 0      m1-pm-1: f-1
==> f-2      (item a)
==> Activation 0      m1-pm-1-to-2: f-1,f-2
==> f-3      (item b)
==> f-4      (item c)
==> Activation 0      m1-pm-1-to-3: f-1,f-2,f-4
==> f-5      (item d)
==> f-6      (item e)
==> Activation 0      m1-pm-1-to-4: f-1,f-2,f-4,f-6
==> f-7      (item f)
==> f-8      (item g)
==> Activation 0      match-1: f-1,f-2,f-4,f-6,f-8
CLIPS>
```

Using this same technique for rule *matches-2* would produce hundreds of partial activations. It should be clear by now that the LHS of a rule cannot be considered as a whole for purposes of efficiency. Each LHS of a rule should be considered several separate rules, each producing a set of partial matches for the rule as a whole. Writing an efficient rule becomes a matter of limiting not just the total number of activations for a rule, but also the partial matches for each of the separate subrules that make up the LHS of the rule.

9.13 ORDERING PATTERNS FOR EFFICIENCY

Several guidelines should be kept in mind when ordering patterns to limit the number of partial matches that are made. Finding the best way to order patterns can be difficult because some guidelines may conflict with others. In general, the guidelines for ordering are used to avoid gross inefficiencies that may appear in a rule-based system. Fine-tuning an expert system can require considerable trial and error in reordering patterns to determine which changes make the system run faster. Often, trying a completely different approach rather than attempting the fine-tuning of patterns may yield much better results.

Most Specific Patterns Go First

The most specific pattern should be placed toward the front of the LHS of a rule. A specific pattern will generally have the smallest number of matching facts in the fact list and will have the largest number of variable bindings that constrain other patterns. The pattern (match ?x ?y ?z ?w) shown in rules *match-1* and *match-2* is specific because it constrains the facts allowed to generate partial matches for the four other patterns of the rule.

Patterns Matching Volatile Facts Go Last

Patterns matching against facts that are frequently added and removed from the fact list should be placed toward the end of the LHS of a rule. This causes the smallest number of changes in the partial matches for the rule. It is important to note that patterns matching volatile facts are often the most specific patterns in the rule. This can create a dilemma in trying to arrange the patterns of the rule for greatest efficiency. For example, it is generally advantageous to place control facts as the beginning pattern of a rule. If the control fact is not present, no partial matches will be generated for the rule. However, if control facts are being asserted and retracted quite frequently and a larger number of partial matches are constantly being recomputed, then it can be more efficient to place the control fact toward the end of a rule.

Patterns Matching the Fewest Facts Go First

Placing patterns that will match very few facts in the fact list near the front of the rule will reduce the number of partial matches that can be generated. Once again, use of this guideline may conflict with other guidelines. A pattern matching that matches very few facts is not necessarily the most specific pattern, or the facts matched by the pattern might be volatile.

9.14 MULTIFIELD VARIABLES AND EFFICIENCY

Multifield wildcards and multifield variables provide powerful pattern-matching capabilities. When used improperly, however, they can lead to inefficiency. Two rules should be applied to the use of multifield wildcards and variables. First, they should not be used unless needed. Second, when they are used, care should be taken to limit the number of multifield wildcards and variables in a single slot of a pattern. The following rule demonstrates that multifield wildcards and variables can be useful, but are also quite expensive:

```
(defrule produce-twoplets
   (list (items $?b $?m $?e))
   =>
   (assert (front ?b))
   (assert (middle ?m))
   (assert (back ?e)))
```

Given a fact such as (list (items a 4 z 2)), this rule will produce facts representing the front, middle, and back parts of the list. The lengths of the various parts will vary from zero to the length of the list. This rule is easy to state using multifield variables; however, it is an extremely expensive pattern-matching operation. Table 9.1 shows all of the matches that were attempted and also that multifield wildcards and variables can perform a great deal of work as part of the pattern-matching process. In general, for N fields contained in the *items* fact, $(N^2 + 3N + 2) / 2$ matches for the *produce-twoplets* rule will occur.

Table 9.1 Matching Attempts for Three Multifield Variables

Match attempt	Fields matched by $?b	Fields matched by $?m	Fields matched by $?e
1			a 4 z 2
2		a	4 z 2
3		a 4	z 2
4		a 4 z	2
5		a 4 z 2	
6	a		4 z 2
7	a	4	z 2
8	a	4 z	2
9	a	4 z 2	
10	a 4		z 2
11	a 4	z	2
12	a 4	z 2	
13	a 4 z		2
14	a 4 z	2	
15	a 4 z 2		

9.15 THE TEST CE AND EFFICIENCY

Any test conditional elements within a rule should be placed as close to the top of the rule as possible. For example, the following rule tests to find three distinct points:

```
(defrule three-distinct-points
   ?point-1 <- (point (x ?x1) (y ?y1))
   ?point-2 <- (point (x ?x2) (y ?y2))
   ?point-3 <- (point (x ?x3) (y ?y3))
   (test (and (neq ?point-1 ?point-2)
              (neq ?point-2 ?point-3)
              (neq ?point-1 ?point-3)))
   =>
   (assert (distinct-points (x1 ?x1) (y1 ?y1)
                            (x2 ?x2) (y2 ?y2)
                            (x3 ?x3) (y3 ?y3))))
```

The test CE that determines that the fact address ?point-1 is not the same as the fact address ?point-2 can be placed immediately after the second pattern. Placing the test CE at this point will reduce the number of partial matches created:

```
(defrule three-distinct-points
   ?point-1 <- (point (x ?x1) (y ?y1))
   ?point-2 <- (point (x ?x2) (y ?y2))
   (test (neq ?point-1 ?point-2))
   ?point-3 <- (point (x ?x3) (y ?y3))
   (test (and (neq ?point-2 ?point-3)
              (neq ?point-1 ?point-3)))
```

```
   =>
   (assert (distinct-points (x1 ?x1) (y1 ?y1)
                            (x2 ?x2) (y2 ?y2)
                            (x3 ?x3) (y3 ?y3))))
```

Test CEs on the LHS of a rule are always evaluated when partial matches are being generated in the join network. Expressions used with the predicate or equality field constraint may be evaluated during the pattern-matching process if certain conditions are met. Expression evaluation during the pattern-matching process in the pattern network yields greater efficiency. An expression used by the predicate or return value field constraints will be evaluated during the pattern-matching process if all variables referenced in the expression can be found within the enclosing pattern.

The expression in the following rule will be evaluated during the generation of partial matches because it is within a test CE:

```
(defrule points-share-common-x-or-y-value
   (point (x ?x1) (y ?y1))
   (point (x ?x2) (y ?y2))
   (test (or (= ?x1 ?x2) (= ?y1 ?y2)))
   =>
   (assert (common-x-or-y-value
              (x1 ?x1) (y1 ?y1)
              (x2 ?x2) (y2 ?y2))))
```

Placing the expression within the pattern does not cause evaluation during pattern matching because the variables *?x1* and *?y1* are not contained within the second pattern:

```
(defrule points-share-common-x-or-y-value
   (point (x ?x1) (y ?y1))
   (point (x ?x2) (y ?y2&:(or (= ?x1 ?x2)
                              (= ?y1 ?y2))))
   =>
   (assert (common-x-or-y-value
              (x1 ?x1) (y1 ?y1)
              (x2 ?x2) (y2 ?y2))))
```

Once again, the expression in the following rule will be evaluated during the generation of partial matches because it is within a test CE:

```
(defrule point-not-on-x-y-diagonals ""
   (point (x ?x1) (y ?y1))
   (test (and (<> ?x1 ?y1) (<> ?x1 (- 0 ?y1))))
   =>
   (assert (non-diagonal-point (x ?x1) (y ?y1))))
```

This time, however, placing the expression within the pattern allows it to be evaluated during pattern matching because the two variables *?x1* and *?y1* are both contained within the enclosing pattern of the expression:

```
(defrule point-not-on-x-y-diagonals
   (point (x ?x1)
          (y ?y1&:(and (<> ?x1 ?y1)
                       (<> ?x1 (- 0 ?y1)))))
   =>
   (assert (non-diagonal-point (x ?x1) (y ?y1))))
```

9.16 BUILT-IN PATTERN-MATCHING CONSTRAINTS

The built-in pattern-matching constraints are always more efficient than an equivalent expression that must be evaluated. For example, a rule such as:

```
(defrule primary-color
   (color ?x&:(or (eq ?x red)
                  (eq ?x green)
                  (eq ?x blue)))
   =>
   (assert (primary-color ?x)))
```

should not be used when pattern-matching constraints can be used to accomplish the same results, as shown here:

```
(defrule primary-color
   (color ?x&red|green|blue)
   =>
   (assert (primary-color ?x)))
```

9.17 GENERAL RULES VERSUS SPECIFIC RULES

It is not always obvious whether many specific rules will perform more efficiently than fewer, more general rules. Specific rules tend to isolate much of the pattern-matching process in the pattern network, reducing the amount of work in the join network. General rules often provide more opportunity for sharing in the pattern and join networks. A single rule can also be more maintainable than a larger group of specific rules. General rules, though, need to be written carefully. Since they tend to perform the work of several rules, it is much easier to write an inefficient general rule than an inefficient specific rule. To illustrate the difference between the two techniques, consider the following deftemplate and four rules that will update a fact containing the grid coordinates of an object that can move north, south, east, or west. The location fact contains the *x* and *y* coordinates of the object. A move north increases the value of the *y* coordinate; a move east increases the value of the *x* coordinate.

```
(deftemplate location (slot x) (slot y))

(defrule move-north
   (move north)
   ?old-location <- (location (y ?old-y))
   =>
   (modify ?old-location (y (+ ?old-y 1))))

(defrule move-south
   (move south)
   ?old-location <- (location (y ?old-y))
   =>
   (modify ?old-location (y (- ?old-y 1))))

(defrule move-east
   (move east)
   ?old-location <- (location (x ?old-x))
   =>
   (modify ?old-location (x (+ ?old-x 1))))

(defrule move-west
   (move west)
   ?old-location <- (location (x ?old-x))
   =>
   (modify ?old-location (x (- ?old-x 1))))
```

The four previous rules can be replaced with a single more general rule, an additional deftemplate, and a deffacts construct:

```
(deftemplate direction
   (slot which-way)
   (slot delta-x)
   (slot delta-y))

(deffacts direction-information
   (direction (which-way north)
              (delta-x 0) (delta-y 1))
   (direction (which-way south)
              (delta-x 0) (delta-y -1))
   (direction (which-way east)
              (delta-x 1) (delta-y 0))
   (direction (which-way west)
              (delta-x -1) (delta-y 0)))

(defrule move-direction
   (move ?dir)
   (direction (which-way ?dir)
```

```
               (delta-x ?dx)
               (delta-y ?dy))
   ?old-location <- (location (x ?old-x)
                              (y ?old-y))
   =>
   (modify ?old-location (x (+ ?old-x ?dx))
                         (y (+ ?old-y ?dy))))
```

The variables *?dx* and *?dy* are the delta *x* and delta *y* values, which need to be added to the *x* and *y* values of the old location to obtain the *x* and *y* values for the new location.

This new rule requires more work in creating partial matches to determine the delta *x* and delta *y* values to be added to the current location. However, it provides a level of abstraction that makes it simple to add more directions. To move northeast, southeast, northwest, and southwest would require the addition of four new specific rules. The general example requires only the addition of four new facts in the deffacts construct, as follows:

```
(deffacts direction-information
   (direction (which-way north)
              (delta-x 0) (delta-y 1))
   (direction (which-way south)
              (delta-x 0) (delta-y -1))
   (direction (which-way east)
              (delta-x 1) (delta-y 0))
   (direction (which-way west)
              (delta-x -1) (delta-y 0))
   (direction (which-way northeast)
              (delta-x 1) (delta-y 1))
   (direction (which-way southeast)
              (delta-x 1) (delta-y -1))
   (direction (which-way northwest)
              (delta-x -1) (delta-y 1))
   (direction (which-way southwest)
              (delta-x -1) (delta-y -1)))
```

9.18 SIMPLE RULES VERSUS COMPLEX RULES

Rule-based languages allow many problems to be expressed in a simple yet elegant manner. Although not specifically designed for algorithmic or computational problems, CLIPS can easily be used to find the largest of a group of numbers. The following rule and associated deffacts will assert a group of sample numbers that will be used as test data by the rule that finds the largest number:

```
(deffacts max-num
   (loop-max 100))
```

```
(defrule loop-assert
   (loop-max ?n)
   =>
   (bind ?i 1)
   (while (<= ?i ?n) do
      (assert (number ?i))
      (bind ?i (+ ?i 1))))
```

The simplest way of finding the largest number was demonstrated in Chapter 8. As shown below, one rule can be used to find the largest number:

```
(defrule largest-number
   (number ?number1)
   (not (number ?number2&:(> ?number2 ?number1)))
   =>
   (printout t "Largest number is " ?number1 crlf))
```

This rule, although simple, is not the fastest method for finding the largest number. If N represents the number of facts with the *number* relation, then both the first and second patterns will have a number of pattern matches equal to N. Even though there will be only one partial match for the first two patterns, N-squared comparisons will have to be performed to find that partial match. Increasing the value of the *loop-max* fact to 200, 300, 400, and so on will demonstrate that the time to run the problem is proportional to the square of N.

This type of comparison is extremely inefficient because as each number is added it is compared to *all* other numbers to determine whether it is the largest. For example, if the facts representing the numbers 2 through 100 have already been asserted and the fact representing the number 1 is asserted, 199 comparisons will be made to determine whether 1 is the largest number. The fact (number 1) will match the first pattern, so it will be compared to the 99 facts matching the second pattern to determine whether it is the largest. The first comparison will fail (because any of the numbers between 2 and 100 will be larger), but the remaining numbers will still be compared. Similarly, the fact (number 1) will match the second pattern, so it will be compared to the 100 facts matching the first pattern (which now includes the (number 1) fact as well).

The key to speeding up the program is to prevent unnecessary comparisons from occurring. This can be accomplished by using an additional fact to keep track of the largest number and comparing the *number* facts with it. The following rules show how this is done:

```
(defrule try-number
   (number ?n)
   =>
   (assert (try-number ?n)))

(defrule largest-unknown
   ?attempt <- (try-number ?n)
```

```
   (not (largest ?))
   =>
   (retract ?attempt)
   (assert (largest ?n)))

(defrule largest-smaller
   ?old-largest <- (largest ?n1)
   ?attempt <- (try-number ?n2&:(> ?n2 ?n1))
   =>
   (retract ?old-largest ?attempt)
   (assert (largest ?n2)))

(defrule largest-bigger
   (largest ?n1)
   ?attempt <- (try-number ?n2&:(<= ?n2 ?n1))
   =>
   (retract ?attempt))

(defrule print-largest
   (declare (salience -1))
   (largest ?number)
   =>
   (printout t "Largest number is " ?number crlf))
```

Running this program for *max-loop* values of 100, 200, 300, 400, and so on will demonstrate that the time to run this program is proportional to *N*. This is even more interesting considering that the first program will fire only two rules whereas the second program will fire approximately *2N* rules. The second group of rules demonstrates that a rule should try to limit not only the number of partial matches it has, but also the number of comparisons needed for determining the partial matches. As demonstrated by the first rule, if the first pattern has *N* matches and the second pattern has *N* matches, then the rule will make *N*-squared comparisons in determining the partial matches for the first two patterns. Even if no partial matches are generated, the computational time spent will be roughly equivalent to having generated *N*-squared partial matches. The second group of rules limits the number of comparisons that will be made to *N*. Since only one *largest* and one *try-number* fact exist at a time, only one partial match can exist at any time for the *largest-unknown*, *largest-smaller*, and *largest-bigger* rules. Since *N* try-number facts are generated, this will limit the computational time to that of generating *N* partial matches. At first glance it may appear that it's possible to generate more than one *try-number* fact (thus causing *N*-squared partial matches). But recall from Section 9.3, that the agenda works like a stack—this means that all of the *try-number* activations placed on the agenda by the *loop-assert* rule will always fire after any activations of the *largest-unknown*, *largest-smaller*, and *largest-bigger* rules. Since these rules always remove the current *try-number* fact, there will never be more than one fact of this type.

This example demonstrates two important concepts. First, the easiest way to code a problem in a rule-based language is not necessarily the best. Second, the number of comparisons performed can often be reduced by using temporary facts to store data. The *largest* fact is used in this problem to store the value for later comparison so that not all the *number* facts have to be searched when comparing.

9.19 SUMMARY

This chapter introduced various CLIPS features to assist in the development of robust expert systems. Deftemplate attributes permit enforcement of type and value constraints, which can prevent typographic as well as semantic errors. Constraint checking can be performed statically (when expressions or constructs are defined) or dynamically (when expressions are evaluated). The type attribute allows the legal types allowed for a slot to be constrained. The allowed value attributes allow the legal values of a slot to be restricted to a specified list. The range attribute allows numeric values to be restricted to a specified range. The cardinality attribute allows the minimum and maximum number of fields stored in a multifield slot to be restricted. Two other deftemplate attributes, the default and default-dynamic attributes, don't constrain slot values but allow the initial value of a deftemplate slot to be specified.

Salience provides a mechanism for even more complex control structures. It is used to prioritize rules such that the activated rule with the highest salience is fired first. Salience can be combined with control facts in order to separate expert knowledge from control knowledge.

The defmodule construct allows a knowledge base to be partitioned. By explicitly stating which deftemplates are imported from and exported to other modules, a module can control which facts are visible to it. Using the *focus* command, the execution of a program can be controlled without the use of salience by partitioning rules into groups and placing them in separate modules.

This chapter demonstrates the importance of matching facts against rules in an efficient manner. The Rete algorithm is efficient for this matching process because it takes advantage of the temporal redundancy and structural similarity exhibited by rule-based expert systems.

Rules are converted into data structures in a rule network. This network consists of a pattern network and a join network. The pattern network matches facts against patterns and the join network ensures that variable bindings across patterns are consistent. The ordering of patterns can have a significant effect on the performance of a rule. Generally, the most specific patterns and patterns matching the fewest facts should be placed first in the LHS of a rule and volatile patterns should be placed last in the LHS of a rule. The *matches* command is used to display the pattern matches, partial matches, and activations of a rule.

There are several other techniques for improving rule efficiency, including proper use of multifield variables, the positioning of test patterns, and the use of built-in pattern matching constraints. There are also efficiency tradeoffs associated with writing general versus specific rules and simple versus complex rules.

PROBLEMS

9.1 Modify the Sticks program in Chapter 8 so the control rules are separated from the rules of playing the game. Use salience to give the control rules lower priority.

9.2 Add a rule to the Blocks World program in Section 7.23 that would remove a move goal if it has already been satisfied.

9.3 Create rules for implementing the decision procedure for determining whether a syllogism is valid. Test your program on the syllogism from Problem 8.24 on page 492.

9.4 Write a program to determine the prime factors of a number. For example, the prime factors of 15 are 3 and 5.

9.5 Given the following distances between cities in Texas, solve the Traveling Salesman problem (page 52 in Section 1.13) for the cities. Write a program that finds the shortest route that visits all the cities. The input to the program should be the starting city and the list of cities to be visited. To test your program, determine the shortest route, beginning in Houston.

	Houston	**Dallas**	**Austin**	**Abilene**	**Waco**
Houston	—	241	162	351	183
Dallas	241	—	202	186	97
Austin	162	202	—	216	106
Abilene	351	186	216	—	186
Waco	183	97	106	186	—

9.6 Given the following information, write a program that will ask for the type of clouds visible and the wind direction, and then give a forecast for the chances of rain. Cumulus clouds indicate good weather, but they may change to nimbostratus clouds if the wind blows from the northeast to the south. Cirrocumulus clouds indicate rain within a day if the wind direction is northeast to south. If the wind blows north to west, then overcast skies are predicted. Stratocumulus clouds may change to cumulonimbus clouds if the wind direction is northeast to south. Stratus clouds indicate a light drizzle. If the wind blows from the northeast to the south, then a long rain may occur. Nimbostratus clouds indicate a short rain if wind direction is southwest to north. A long rain is indicated if the wind blows from the northeast to the south. Cumulonimbus clouds indicate showers if they are visible before noon. Cirrostratus clouds indicate rain within 15 to 24 hours if the wind direction is northeast to south. Altostratus clouds indicate rain within a day if winds are northeast to south, otherwise the skies will be overcast. Altocumulus clouds indicate rain within 15 to 20 hours if winds are from northeast to south.

9.7 Write a program to convert a Morse code message to its equivalent series of alphabetic characters. The following is an example of input and output to the program (where the * and - are dots and dashes and the character / is used to delimit the Morse code characters):

```
Enter a message (<CR> to end): * * * / - - - /
   * * *↵
```

```
The message is S O S
Enter a message (<CR> to end): ↲
CLIPS>
```

The codes and their character equivalents are the following:

A	•-	H	••••	O	---	V	•••-
B	-•••	I	••	P	•--•	W	•--
C	-•-•	J	•---	Q	--•-	X	-••-
D	-••	K	-•-	R	•-•	Y	-•--
E	•	L	•-••	S	•••	Z	--••
F	••-•	M	--	T	-		
G	--•	N	-•	U	••-		

9.8 Write a program that when given an expression consisting of numbers and units, will convert the units in the expression into a set of base units (such as meters, seconds, kilograms, pennies, and amps). The following is an example of input and output to the program:

```
Enter an expression (<CR> to end): 30 meters /
  minute↲
Conversion is 0.5 m / s
Enter an expression (<CR> to end): ↲
CLIPS>
```

9.9 Write a program for playing Life (a common program that simulates cellular automata). Given a two-dimensional array of cells in which each cell is either dead or alive, the values for the next generation of cells are based on the following rules. Any living cell that is adjacent to exactly two or three other living cells continues to live. Any living cell that is adjacent to any less than two or any greater than three other living cells will die. Any dead cell that is adjacent to exactly three other living cells comes to life. For example, if the first generation was a five-by-five array with the live cells filled with dots as shown,

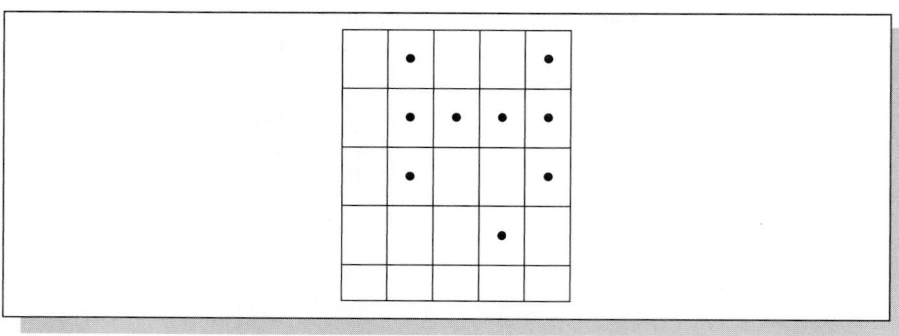

then the next generation would appear as follows:

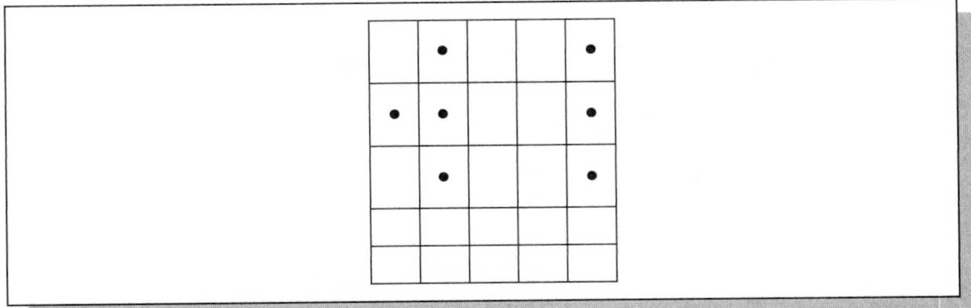

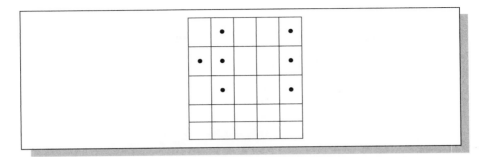

Using the initial configuration shown previously, compute the next four generations.

9.10 A quadrilateral is a four-sided figure. A quadrilateral is a kite if it has two distinct pairs of consecutive sides of the same length. A quadrilateral is a trapezoid if it has at least one pair of parallel sides. A quadrilateral is a parallelogram if both pairs of its opposite sides are parallel. A quadrilateral is a rhombus if its four sides are equal in length. A quadrilateral is a rectangle if it has four right angles. A quadrilateral is a square if it has four equal sides and four right angles. Note that a rhombus is a kite and a parallelogram, a parallelogram is a trapezoid, a rectangle is a parallelogram, and a square is a rhombus and a rectangle.

Write a program that, when given the four points forming a quadrilateral, will determine the type of quadrilateral. The program should account for possible round-off error (assume that two sides are equal if the difference between their lengths is less than .00001). Test your program with the following quadrilaterals:

(a) Points (0,0), (2,4), (6,0), and (3,2).
(b) Points (0,3), (2,5), (4,3), and (2,0).
(c) Points (0,0), (3,2), (4,2), and (9,0).
(d) Points (0,0), (1,3), (5,3), and (4,0).
(e) Points (0,0), (3,5.196152), (9,5.196152), and (6,0).
(f) Points (0,0), (0,4), (2,4), and (2,0).
(g) Points (0,2), (4,6), (6,4), and (2,0).
(h) Points (0,2), (2,4), (4,2), and (2,0).

Hint: If side 1 contains the points (x1,y1) and (x2,y2) and side 2 contains the points (x3,y3) and (x4,y4), then side 1 is parallel to side 2 if (x2 - x1) * (y4 - y3) is equal to (x4 - x3) * (y2 - y1).

9.11 Write a CLIPS program that can determine if a simple sentence is grammatically correct. The sentence should use the following BNF:

```
<sentence> ::= <verb> <direct-object>
                       [<indirect-object>]
<direct-object> ::= [<determiner>] <adjective>* <noun>
<indirect-object> ::= <preposition> <direct-object>
<determiner> ::= a | an | the
```

```
<adjective> ::= red | shiny | heavy
<noun> ::= ball | wrench | gun | pliers
<preposition> ::= with | in | at
<verb> ::= get | throw | shoot
```

For example:

```
Enter a sentence (<CR> to end): shoot the red
shiny gun at the pliers.↵
OK
Enter a sentence (<CR> to end): gun shoot↵
I don't understand.
Enter a sentence (<CR> to end):
CLIPS>
```

9.12 Modify the program developed for Problem 8.12 on page 488 so that only the shrubs having all of the necessary characteristics are listed. For example, if the user specifies that the plant must tolerate cold and drought, then only northern bayberry and common juniper should be listed. If none of the shrubs meet all requirements, then a message should be printed to indicate this.

9.13 Given a number of generators supplying power and a number of devices consuming power, write a program to attach devices to generators that minimizes the number of generators used and the amount of unused power for each generator used. For example, if there are four generators supplying 5, 6, 7, and 10 watts of power and four devices consuming 4, 5, 6, and 7 watts of power, attaching the 5-watt device to the 5-watt generator, the 7-watt device to the 7-watt generator, and the 4- and 6-watt devices to the 10-watt generator would minimize both the number of generators used and the unused power. The input and output of the program can be a series of facts. Test your program with the example above and also for the case using the same generators as above but with devices consuming 1, 3, 4, 5, and 9 watts of power.

9.14 Write a program that functions like the operating system of a computer and determines suitable locations in memory to load applications with fixed amounts of memory allocated to them. The input to the program will be a series of facts such as the following:

```
(launch (application word-processor)
(memory-needed 2))
(launch (application spreadsheet)
(memory-needed 6))
(launch (application game) (memory-needed 1))
(terminate (application word-processor))
(launch (application game) (memory-needed 1))
(terminate (application spreadsheet))
(terminate (application game))
```

Assume the computer has eight megabytes of memory and that the number of megabytes required by an application is an integer. If an exact fit in memory exists for an application, it should be used. For example, if there were two blocks of free memory, one of six megabytes and another of four megabytes, and an application was launched that required four megabytes, then the application should be placed in the four-megabyte free block rather than the six-megabyte free block. When a launch or terminate command is processed, a message should be printed. If there is not a large enough memory block to launch a program, then a message to this effect should be printed. Test your program by asserting the preceding facts and issuing a *run* command after each fact is asserted. The output should be similar to the following:

```
Application word-processor memory location is 1 to 2.
Application spreadsheet memory location is 3 to 8.
Unable to launch application game.
Terminating word-processor.
Application game memory location is 1 to 1.
Terminating spreadsheet.
Terminating game.
```

9.15 Develop a text menu interface that is self-contained within a module and is suitable for reuse in other programs. The menu items should be represented as facts. Two types of actions should be supported for menu items. One is to quit execution of the program. If this item type is selected, the program should halt execution. The other is to assert a fact and focus on a specific module. For this action, the menu-item facts should contain slots that specify the focus module and fact value to be asserted when the item is selected. For example, in the following dialog the result of selecting "Option A" would be to focus on module *A* and assert the fact (menu-select (value option-a)) where *A* and *option-a* are the values specified in the *menu-item* fact. Module *A* contains a rule that matches on the *menu-select* fact causing the "Executing Option A" message to be printed.

```
CLIPS> (run)

Select one of the following options:

 1 – Option A
 2 – Option B
 9 – Quit Program

Your choice: 1

Executing Option A

Select one of the following options:

 1 – Option A
 2 – Option B
 9 – Quit Program

Your choice: 9

CLIPS>
```

9.16 Modify the program developed for Problem 8.33 on page 493 so that the separate modules are used to print the information of all stars having the specified spectral class, all stars having the specified magnitude, and all stars matching both the spectral class and magnitude along with their distance from Earth in light-years.

9.17 Modify the program developed for Problem 8.15 on page 490 to include the remaining gems found in the gem table in Problem 7.13 on page 439. For gems having a single numerical value for their hardness or density, modify the rules so that any value within .01 of the specified value is acceptable. Include rules to verify and reprompt the user if the hardness is not between 1 and 10 inclusive and the density is not between 1 and 6 inclusive.

9.18 The table below lists available courses at a high school, the name of the instructor, and the class periods during which the course is available. Given as input a fact indicating a class to be scheduled and preferences indicating the instructors and periods that are preferred and not preferred, write a program that suggests an appropriate instructor and period in which to take the class. To determine the "best" instructor and period, score each possible candidate as follows: the starting score is zero; a preferred instructor or period each adds one point to the score; an instructor or period that is not preferred each subtracts one point from the score; no preference for an instructor or period leaves the score unchanged; the instructor and period with the highest score is the "best."

Course	Instructor	Periods Offered
Algebra	Jones	1, 2, 3
Algebra	Smith	3, 4, 5, 6
American History	Vale	5
American History	Hill	1, 2
Art	Jenkins	1, 3, 5
Biology	Dolby	1, 2, 5
Chemistry	Dolby	3, 6
Chemistry	Vinson	6
French	Blake	2, 4
Geology	Vinson	1
Geometry	Jones	5, 6
Geometry	Smith	1
German	Blake	5
Literature	Henning	2, 3, 4, 5, 6
Literature	Davis	1, 2, 3, 4, 5
Music	Jenkins	2, 4
Physical Education	Mack	1, 2, 3, 4, 5
Physical Education	King	1, 2,3, 4, 6
Physical Education	Simpson	2, 3, 4, 5, 6
Physics	Vinson	2, 3, 5
Spanish	Blake	1, 3
Texas History	Vale	2, 3, 4
Texas History	Hill	5, 6
World History	Vale	2, 3, 4
World History	Hill	4

9.19 Modify the program developed for Problem 8.14 on page 489 so that the total price of the configuration is printed. A warning message should be printed if more gizmos are selected than there are available bays or if the power required for the gizmos exceeds the power supplied by the chassis.

9.20 List the pattern node specifications generated for the slots of the following patterns:

(a) `(blip (altitude 100))`
(b) `(blip (altitude ?x&:(> ?x 100)))`
(c) `(stop-light (color ~red))`
(d) `(balloon (color blue|white))`

9.21 Draw the pattern network for the following group of patterns:

```
(data (x red) (y ?y) (z ?y))
(data (x ~red))
(item (b ?y) (c ?x&:(> ?x ?y)))
(item (a red) (b blue|yellow))
```

9.22 Draw the pattern and join network for the following rules. List the expressions evaluated at each node.

```
(defrule rule1
  (phase (name testing))
  (data (x ?x) (y ?y))
  (data (x ?y) (y ?x&:(> ?x ?y)))
  =>)

(defrule rule2
  (phase (name testing))
  (data (x ?x) (y ?y))
  (data (x ?y&~red) (y ?x&~green))
  =>)
```

9.23 Rewrite the following rule to make it more efficient:

```
(defrule bad-rule
  (items (x ?x1) (y ?y1) (z ?z1))
  (items (x ?x2) (y ?y2) (z ?z2))
  (items (x ?x3) (y ?y3) (z ?z3))
  (test (and (or (eq ?x3 green)
                 (eq ?x3 red))
             (eq ?z2 ?y3)
             (> ?y1 ?x1)
             (< ?z1 ?x1)
             (neq ?z3 ?x1)))
  =>)
```

9.24 The figure below shows a fault network for a hypothetical piece of equipment. The arrows indicate the direction in which faults will be propagated. For example, if component A has a fault, then components B and C will also have faults.

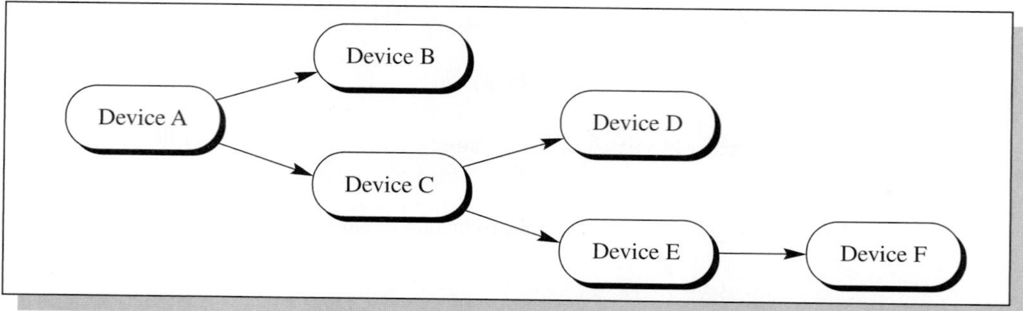

The following rules will propagate faults throughout the network:

```
(defrule propagate-device-A-fault
 (fault device-A)
=>
 (assert (fault device-B))
 (assert (fault device-C)))

(defrule propagate-device-C-fault
 (fault device-C)
=>
 (assert (fault device-D))
 (assert (fault device-E)))

(defrule propagate-device-E-fault
 (fault device-E)
=>
 (assert (fault device-F)))
```

Rewrite these three rules as one general rule and a deffacts construct that will propagate the faults as the three rules do. Explain the changes that must be made for each of these approaches when a new device is added to the fault network.

BIBLIOGRAPHY

(Brownston 85). Lee Brownston et al., *Programming Expert Systems in OPS5: An Introduction to Rule-Based Programming*, Addison-Wesley, 1985.

(Forgy 85). Charles L. Forgy, "Rete: A Fast Algorithm for the Many Pattern/Many Object Pattern Match Problem," *Artificial Intelligence*, 19, pp. 17–37, 1985.

(Forgy 79). Charles L. Forgy, "On the Efficient Implementation of Production Systems," Ph.D. thesis, Carnegie-Mellon University, 1979.

CHAPTER 10
Procedural Programming

10.1 INTRODUCTION

This chapter introduces the procedural-programming paradigms provided by CLIPS that are similar to those in languages such as C, Ada, and Pascal. Occasionally it is useful (and more efficient) to perform some operations using a procedural-programming paradigm rather than a rule-based programming paradigm. This chapter first introduces a number of procedural functions including some allowing looping and conditional behavior. The deffunction construct can be used to define new functions that can be called from rules or other functions. The defglobal construct allows the definition of global variables. Unlike local variables defined within a rule or function, these variables always retain their values. The defgeneric and defmethod constructs allow the definition of generic functions, which are similar to functions, except the specific code that is executed is dependent upon the number and types of arguments supplied to the function. Finally, this chapter introduces a number of useful utility functions.

10.2 PROCEDURAL FUNCTIONS

CLIPS provides several functions for controlling the flow of execution of actions. The ***while***, ***if***, **switch**, ***loop-for-count***, **progn$**, and **break** functions provide similar functionality to control structures found in modern high-level languages such as Ada, Pascal, and C. In addition, the ***halt*** function allows the execution of rules to be stopped from the RHS of a rule.

CLIPS is designed to be an efficient rule-based language. These procedural functions are intended for judicious use only. Writing a lengthy procedural program on the RHS of a rule defeats the entire purpose of using a rule-based language. In general, such functions should be used for performing simple tests and loops on the RHS of a rule. Complex nesting of these functions on the RHS of a rule should be avoided.

The *If* Function

The syntax of the *if* function is:

```
(if <predicate-expression>
   then <expression>+
   [else <expression>+])
```

where <predicate-expression> is a single expression (such as a predicate function or variable) and the <expression>+ following the *if* and *then* keywords are the one or more expressions to be evaluated based on the return value of evaluating <predicate-expression>. Notice that the *else* clause is optional.

When an *if* function is evaluated, the condition represented by <predicate-expression> is first evaluated to determine whether the actions of the *then* clause or the *else* clause are executed. If the condition evaluates to any symbol other than FALSE, the actions in the *then* clause of the function are executed. If the condition evaluates to the symbol FALSE, the actions in the *else* clause are executed. If the *else* clause has not been included, then no action is taken on a false condition. Once the *if* function completes execution, CLIPS continues with the next action, if any, on the RHS.

The *if* function can be useful for checking values on the RHS of a rule instead of having other rules perform a test. For example, the following rule could be used to determine whether a program should continue:

```
(defrule continue-check
   ?phase <- (phase check-continue)
   =>
   (retract ?phase)
   (printout t "Continue? ")
   (bind ?answer (read))
   (if (or (eq ?answer y) (eq ?answer yes))
      then (assert (phase continue))
      else (assert (phase halt))))
```

Notice that the *if* function is used to convert the user's yes or no response to a fact indicating the type of action to be taken. In this case the action is either to continue or to halt.

The return value of the *if* function is the last expression evaluated in either the *then* or the *else* portions of the function. If the <predicate-expression> evaluates to FALSE and there is no *then* portion, the symbol FALSE is returned.

The *While* Function

The syntax of the *while* function is:

```
(while <predicate-expression> [do]
   <expression>*)
```

where <predicate-expression> is a single expression (such as a predicate function or variable) and the <expression>* following the optional *do* keyword are the zero or more expressions to be evaluated based on the return value of evaluating <predicate-expression>. These expressions comprise the **body** of the loop.

The part of the *while* function represented by <predicate-expression> is evaluated before the actions in the body are executed. If the <predicate-expression> evaluates to any value other than the symbol FALSE, the expressions in the body will be executed. If the <predicate-expression> evaluates to the symbol FALSE, execution continues with the next statement after the *while* function, if any. The condition of the *while* function will be checked each time the body is executed to determine whether it should be executed again.

The *while* function can be used with the *if* function to implement input error checking on the RHS of a rule. The following modification to the rule *continue-check* uses the *while* function to continue looping until an appropriate answer is received:

```
(defrule continue-check
   ?phase <- (phase check-continue)
   =>
   (retract ?phase)
   (printout t "Continue? ")
   (bind ?answer (read))
   (while (and (neq ?answer yes) (neq ?answer no))
      do
      (printout t "Continue? ")
      (bind ?answer (read)))
   (if (eq ?answer yes)
      then (assert (phase continue))
      else (assert (phase halt))))
```

The *Switch* Function

The syntax of the *switch* function is:

```
(switch <test-expression>
    <case-statement>*
    [<default-statement>])
```

where <case-statement> is defined as:

```
(case <comparison-expression> then <expression>*)
```

and <default-statement> is defined as:

```
(default <expression>*)
```

The <expression>* portion following the *then* and *default* keywords are the one or more expressions to be evaluated based on the return value of <comparison-expression> matching the return value of <test-expression>. Note that the optional default case must come after all other cases.

When the *switch* function is executed, the portion represented by <test-expression> is evaluated first. Each <comparison-expression> is then evaluated in the order defined and if it matches the value of <comparison-expression>, the actions after the *then* keyword are executed and the *switch* function terminates. If no match is found and a <default-statement> is specified, then the actions of the <default-statement> are executed.

The following code uses the *switch* function to map a symbolic name to an arithmetic function:

```
(defrule perform-operation
   (operation ?type ?arg1 ?arg2)
   =>
   (switch ?type
      (case times then
         (printout t ?arg1 " times " ?arg2
                           " is " (* ?arg1 ?arg2)
                                  crlf))
      (case plus then
         (printout t ?arg1 " plus " ?arg2
                           " is " (+ ?arg1 ?arg2)
                                  crlf))
      (case minus then
         (printout t ?arg1 " minus " ?arg2
                           " is " (- ?arg1 ?arg2)
                                  crlf))
      (case divided-by then
         (printout t ?arg1 " divided by " ?arg2
                           " is " (/ ?arg1 ?arg2)
                                  crlf))))
```

For example:

```
CLIPS> (assert (operation plus 3 4))↵
<Fact-1>
CLIPS> (run)↵
3 plus 4 is 7
CLIPS>
```

The symbol *plus* in the *operation* fact triggers the *plus* case in the *switch* statement and the resultant sum of 3 and 4 is printed.

The *perform-operation* rule could be rewritten without using the *switch* function as four separate rules:

```
(defrule perform-operation-times
   (operation times ?arg1 ?arg2)
```

```
    =>
    (printout t ?arg1 " times " ?arg2
                      " is " (* ?arg1 ?arg2) crlf))

(defrule perform-operation-plus
    (operation plus ?arg1 ?arg2)
    =>
    (printout t ?arg1 " plus " ?arg2
                      " is " (+ ?arg1 ?arg2) crlf))

(defrule perform-operation-minus
    (operation minus ?arg1 ?arg2)
    =>
    (printout t ?arg1 " minus " ?arg2
                      " is " (- ?arg1 ?arg2) crlf))

(defrule perform-operation-divided-by
    (operation divided-by ?arg1 ?arg2)
    =>
    (printout t ?arg1 " divided by " ?arg2
                      " is " (/ ?arg1 ?arg2) crlf))
```

The *Loop-For-Count* Function

The syntax of the *loop-for-count* function is:

```
(loop-for-count <range-spec> [do] <expression>*)
```

where <range-spec> is defined as:

```
<end-index> |
(<loop-variable> <end-index>) |
(<loop-variable> <start-index> <end-index>)
```

and <end-index> and <start-index> are expressions that return integers. If just the <end–index> is specified, then the body of the function, <expression>*, is executed that number of iterations. If the <loop-variable> and <end-index> are specified, then the body of the function is executed that number of iterations and the current iteration ranging from 1 to <end-index> will be stored in <loop-variable> in each iteration. If in addition <start-index> is specified, the iteration count begins as <start-index> rather than 1 and the number of iterations performed will be the difference between <end-index> and <start-index> plus one. No iterations will be performed if <start-index> is greater than <end-index>.

The following is an example using all three variations of <range-spec> and nesting loop-for-count calls:

```
CLIPS>
(loop-for-count (?cnt1 2 4) do
   (loop-for-count (?cnt2 3) do
     (printout t ?cnt1 " ")
     (loop-for-count 3 do
        (printout t "."))
        (printout t " " ?cnt2 crlf)))↵
2 ... 1
2 ... 2
2 ... 3
3 ... 1
3 ... 2
3 ... 3
4 ... 1
4 ... 2
4 ... 3
FALSE
CLIPS>
```

A <loop-variable> will mask any variables declared outside a *loop-for-count* expression that have the same name. For example:

```
CLIPS>
(defrule masking-example
   =>
   (bind ?x 4)
   (loop-for-count (?x 2) do
      (printout t "inside ?x is " ?x crlf))
     (printout t "outside ?x is " ?x crlf))
CLIPS> (reset)↵
CLIPS> (run)↵
inside ?x is 1
inside ?x is 2
outside ?x is 4
CLIPS>
```

The *Progn$* Function

The syntax of the *progn$* function is:

```
(progn$ <list-spec> <expression>*)
```

where <list-spec> is defined as:

```
<multifield-expression> |
(<list-variable> <multifield-expression>)
```

If <list-spec> is specified just as <multifield-expression>, then the body of the function, <expression>*, is executed once for each field in the resultant multifield value generated by evaluating <multifield-expression>. Specifying <list-variable> with <multifield-expression> allows the field of the current iteration to be retrieved by referencing the variable. A special variable is also created by appending *–index* to <list-variable>. This variable contains the index of the current iteration. The return value of this function is the return value of the last <expression> evaluated for the last field of <multifield-expression>. Like *loop-for-count* calls, *progn$* calls can be nested and variables created for the *progn$* expression will mask variables declared outside the *progn$* expression that have the same name. The following are examples using both variations of <list-spec>:

```
CLIPS>
(progn$ (create$ 1 2 3)
   (printout t . crlf))↵
.
.
.
CLIPS>
(progn$ (?v (create$ a b c))
   (printout t ?v-index " " ?v crlf))↵
1 a
2 b
3 c
CLIPS>
```

The *Break* Function

The syntax of the *break* function is:

```
(break)
```

The *break* function terminates the execution of the *while*, *loop-for-count*, or *progn$* function in which it is immediately contained. It is typically used to cause early termination of a loop when a specific condition has been met. For example, the *print-list* rule shown in the following dialog prints the first five members of a list and then prints ... if there are any remaining members:

```
CLIPS>
(defrule print-list
   (print-list $?list)
   =>
   (progn$ (?v ?list)
      (if (<= ?v-index 5)
          then
```

```
                  (printout t ?v " ")
                  else
                  (printout t "...")
                  (break)))
         (printout t crlf))↵
CLIPS> (reset)↵
CLIPS> (assert (print-list a b c d e))↵
<Fact-1>
CLIPS> (run)↵
a b c d e
CLIPS> (assert (print-list a b c d e f g h))↵
<Fact-2>
CLIPS> (run)↵
a b c d e ...
CLIPS>
```

The *Halt* Function

The *halt* function can be used on the RHS of a rule to stop the execution of rules on the agenda. It requires no arguments. When called, no further actions will be executed from the RHS of the rule being fired and control will return to the top-level prompt. The agenda will contain any remaining rules that were activated when the *halt* function was called.

For example, the *continue-check* rule could replace the action:

```
(assert (phase halt))
```

with the following action:

```
(halt)
```

which would stop the execution of rules.

The *halt* function is particularly useful for halting execution when the user intends to restart execution later using the *run* command. Consider the following modification to the *continue-check* rule:

```
(defrule continue-check
   ?phase <- (phase check-continue)
   =>
   (retract ?phase)
   (printout t "Continue? ")
   (bind ?answer (read))
   (while (and (neq ?answer yes) (neq ?answer no))
      do
      (printout t "Continue? ")
      (bind ?answer (read)))
   (assert (phase continue))
   (if (neq ?answer yes)
    then (halt)))
```

Notice that the rule asserts the fact (phase continue) regardless of the user's response to the continue question. Asserting this fact will place the appropriate rules on the agenda to continue execution. If the reply to the continue question was not yes, execution will be stopped by the *halt* function. The user could then examine the rules and facts, later restarting execution where it had left off by issuing a *run* command.

10.3 THE DEFFUNCTION CONSTRUCT

CLIPS allows you to define new functions as you can in other procedural languages. With rules, this can help to reduce repeated expressions in both the LHS and RHS portions. New functions are defined using the **deffunction** construct. The general format of a deffunction is:

```
(deffunction <deffunction-name> [<optional-comment>]
   (<regular-parameter>* [<wildcard-parameter>])
   <expression>*)
```

where <regular-parameter> is a single-field variable and <wildcard-parameter> is a multifield variable. The name of the deffunction, <deffunction-name>, must be distinct. It cannot be the same as one of the existing predefined CLIPS functions. The body of the deffunction, represented by <expression>*, is a series of expressions similar to the RHS of a rule that are executed in order when the deffunction is called. User-defined deffunctions behave similarly to the predefined functions provided by CLIPS. Wherever you could call a predefined CLIPS system function, you can call a deffunction. Unlike predefined functions, deffunctions can be deleted and the *watch* command can be used to trace their execution.

The <regular-parameter> and <wildcard-parameter> declarations allow you to specify the arguments that will be passed into the deffunction when it is called. This is somewhat analogous to rules if you consider the variables bound on the LHS of the rule that are used in the RHS to be parameter declarations. Just as you can on the RHS of a rule, you can use the *bind* command in the body of a deffunction to create local variables.

Just as some predefined functions return values, a deffunction can return values as well. The return value of a deffunction is that value of the last expression evaluated within the body of the deffunction.

As an example, we'll write a deffunction that computes the length of the hypotenuse of a right triangle using the Pythagorean Theorem. If a and b are the sides forming the right angle and c is the hypotenuse, then the theorem states:

$$a^2 + b^2 = c^2$$

Rearranging the terms gives the length of the hypotenuse:

$$c = \sqrt{a^2 + b^2}$$

Converting this formula to a deffunction yields the following:

```
(deffunction hypotenuse-length (?a ?b)
   (** (+ (* ?a ?a) (* ?b ?b)) 0.5))
```

The two parameters of the function are ?a and ?b, which are used to pass in the lengths of the two right angle sides of the triangle. The ** function with its second argument of 0.5 is used to compute the square root because the value of (** <numeric-expression> <numeric-expression>) is the first argument raised to the power of the second argument. Once the *hypotenuse-length* function is defined it can be called from the command prompt:

```
CLIPS> (hypotenuse-length 3 4)↵
5.0
CLIPS>
```

Since the length of the right angle sides are 3 and 4, the length of the hypotenuse is correctly computed to be 5.

Since deffunctions can use local variables, the computation of the hypotenuse length could have been computed in a more readable format:

```
(deffunction hypotenuse-length (?a ?b)
   (bind ?temp (+ (* ?a ?a) (* ?b ?b)))
   (** ?temp 0.5))
```

The *Return* Function

In addition to terminating the execution of the RHS of a rule, the *return* function also allows the currently executing deffunction to be terminated. Its syntax for use with deffunctions is:

```
(return [<expression>])
```

If <expression> is specified, the result of its evaluation is used as the return value of the deffunction. The *hypotenuse-length* function could have explicitly used the *return* function to return the computed length of the hypotenuse in one of the following ways:

```
(deffunction hypotenuse-length (?a ?b)
   (bind ?temp (+ (* ?a ?a) (* ?b ?b)))
   (return (** ?temp 0.5)))
```

or:

```
(deffunction hypotenuse-length (?a ?b)
```

```
   (bind ?temp (+ (* ?a ?a) (* ?b ?b)))
   (bind ?c (** ?temp 0.5))
   (return ?c))
```

However, since the last expression evaluated is the return value of the deffunction and each expression in the *hypotenuse-length* deffunction is sequentially evaluated, there's no need for an explicit *return* statement. The *return* function is primarily useful when a condition is satisfied that should terminate the deffunction execution or when the return value is computed from an expression that is not the last expression to be evaluated. For example, the following deffunction determines if a specified number is a prime number:

```
(deffunction primep (?num)
   (loop-for-count (?i 2 (- ?num 1))
      (if (= ?num (* (div ?num ?i) ?i))
         then
         (return FALSE)))
   (return TRUE))
```

The *primep* deffunction returns TRUE if the ?num argument is a prime number; otherwise it returns FALSE. A number is prime if it has only 1 and itself as a factor, so if it is evenly divisible by any other number, it can't be prime. The *primep* deffunction uses the *loop-for-count* function to iterate over all the numbers between 2 and one less than the number being checked for prime status, ?num. If any of these numbers evenly divides ?num, then the function is terminated and FALSE is returned because the number is not prime. The *div* function is used in determining the prime status of ?num. The *div* function performs integer division yielding an integer return value. So (div 5 2) returns 2 rather than the value of 2.5, which would be returned by (/ 5 2). If the expression (* (div ?num ?i) ?i) returns the original value of ?num, then ?num is evenly divisible by ?i and ?num is thus not prime. In the event that none of the values ?i assumes in the *loop-for-count* function evenly divide ?num, then ?num is a prime number and the return value of the deffunction is TRUE.

Revisiting the Sticks Program

Recall from Section 8.7 the deffacts and three rules that determined whether the computer or human moved first:

```
(deffacts initial-phase
   (phase choose-player))

(defrule player-select
   (phase choose-player)
   =>
```

```
(printout t "Who moves first (Computer: c "
                    "Human: h)? ")
     (assert (player-select (read))))

(defrule good-player-choice
   ?phase <- (phase choose-player)
   ?choice <- (player-select ?player&c | h)
   =>
   (retract ?phase ?choice)
   (assert (player-move ?player)))

  (defrule bad-player-choice
  ?phase <- (phase choose-player)
  ?choice <- (player-select ?player&~c&~h)
  =>
  (retract ?phase ?choice)
  (assert (phase choose-player))
  (printout t "Choose c or h." crlf))
```

Since the need to validate input is common, let's take a look at a function that will eliminate the need in this case for three rules:

```
(deffunction check-input (?question ?values) ;; Line 1
   (printout t ?question " " ?values " ")    ;; Line 2
   (bind ?answer (read))    ;; Line 3
   (while (not (member$ ?answer ?values))    ;; Line 4
      (printout t ?question " " ?values " ") ;; Line 5
      (bind ?answer (read)))                 ;; Line 6
   (return ?answer))                        ;; Line 7
```

Line 1 begins the definition of the *check-input* deffunction. It accepts two arguments: ?question is the question prompt displayed to the user and ?values is the list of acceptable values in response to the question. Line 2 prints the question prompt along with the list of acceptable values. The user's response to the question is captured in line 3 by the *read* function. Line 4 begins a *while* loop that is executed until the user supplies a valid response. The *member$* function returns TRUE if its first argument is a member of the multifield value supplied as the second argument. In this case if the response supplied by the user, ?answer, is not a member of the list of acceptable values, ?values, then the body of the *while* loop is executed. Lines 5 and 6 form the body of the *while* loop, which queries the user repeatedly. Once the user supplies a valid response, the *while* loop terminates and line 7 is executed, which returns the valid response supplied by the user.

The following is an example usage of the *check-input* deffunction. The *create$* function is used to create a multifield value from its single-field arguments, which can be passed in as the second argument to the deffunction:

```
CLIPS>
(check-input "Who moves first, Computer or Human?"
             (create$ c h))↵
Who moves first, Computer or Human? (c h) x↵
Who moves first, Computer or Human? (c h) computer↵
Who moves first, Computer or Human? (c h) c↵
c
CLIPS>
```

Using the *check-input* function, the *player-select* rule can be rewritten as follows eliminating the need for the *good-player-choice* and *bad-player-choice* rules:

```
(defrule player-select
   ?f <- (phase choose-player)
   =>
   (retract ?f)
   (bind ?player
      (check-input
      "Who moves first, Computer or Human?"
      (create$ c h)))
  (assert (player-move ?player)))
```

Recursion

Deffunctions can call other deffunctions within their body, including themselves. For example, the factorial of a positive integer *n* is defined as:

$$\text{factorial}(\text{n}) = \begin{cases} n^*factorial(n-1) & \text{if } n \text{ is } > 1 \\ 1 & \text{if } n \text{ is } 0 \end{cases}$$

Notice that to compute the factorial of *n* it is necessary to compute the factorial of $n-1$. So the factorial of 3 (also denoted 3!) is 3 * 2!, which is 3 * 2 * 1!, which is 3 * 2 * 1 or 6. The following deffunction will compute the factorial of an integer:

```
(deffunction factorial (?n)
   (if (>= ?n 1)
      then (* ?n (factorial (- ?n 1)))
      else 1))
```

As above, (factorial 3) will be computed as 3 * (factorial 2), then 3 * 2 * (factorial 1), and then finally 3 * 2 * 1, which is 6. This can be verified with explicit calls to the factorial deffunction:

```
CLIPS> (factorial 3)↵
6
CLIPS> (factorial 2)↵
2
CLIPS> (factorial 1)↵
1
CLIPS>
```

Forward Declarations

Sometimes deffunctions make circular references to one another. For example, deffunction *A* might make a call to deffunction *B,* which makes a call to deffunction *C,* which makes a call to deffunction *A* as shown here:

```
(deffunction A (?n)
   (if (<= ?n 0)
      then 1
      else (+ 2 (B (- ?n 1)))))

(deffunction B (?n)
   (if (<= ?n 0)
      then 1
      else (* 2 (C (- ?n 1)))))

(deffunction C (?n)
   (if (<= ?n 0)
      then 1
      else (- 2 (A (- ?n 1)))))
```

In a more readable form, the values computed by these functions are as follows:

$$A(n) = \begin{cases} 1 & \text{if } n \text{ is } \leq 0 \\ 2 + B(n-1) & \text{otherwise} \end{cases}$$

$$B(n) = \begin{cases} 1 & \text{if } n \text{ is } \leq 0 \\ 2 * C(n-1) & \text{otherwise} \end{cases}$$

$$C(n) = \begin{cases} 1 & \text{if } n \text{ is } \leq 0 \\ 2 - A(n-1) & \text{otherwise} \end{cases}$$

Since referenced deffunctions must exist at the time they're referenced, there's a problem. It's not possible to compile any of the functions because they each depend on one another:

```
CLIPS>
(deffunction A (?n)
   (if (<= ?n 0)
      then 1
      else (+ 2 (B (- ?n 1)))))↵
[EXPRNPSR3] Missing function declaration for B.

ERROR:
(deffunction MAIN::A
   (?n)
   (if (<= ?n 0)
      then
      1
      else
      (+ 2 (B
CLIPS>
```

The way to solve this problem is to make forward declarations for some of the functions. In a forward declaration, the name and argument list of the function are declared but the body of the function is left empty. The function is declared and thus can be referenced, but since it has no body it doesn't reference other functions. The forward declaration can then be replaced later with a version that includes the body. For example:

```
CLIPS> (deffunction B (?n))↵
CLIPS>
(deffunction A (?n)
   (if (<= ?n 0)
      then 1
      else (+ 2 (B (- ?n 1)))))↵
CLIPS> (deffunction C (?n))↵
CLIPS>
(deffunction B (?n)
   (if (<= ?n 0)
      then 1
      else (* 2 (C (- ?n 1)))))↵
CLIPS>
(deffunction C (?n)
   (if (<= ?n 0)
      then 1
      else (- 2 (A (- ?n 1)))))↵
CLIPS>
```

In this example, the forward declarations have been entered just before the deffunction requiring the declaration. Usually if you're storing your rules in a text file to load, you'll want to put all of your forward declarations together near the top of the file to make the code easier to understand and maintain, but the only enforced requirement is that the declaration is made at some point before the deffunction requiring it is defined.

Watching Deffunctions

When *deffunctions* are watched using the *watch* command, an informational message is printed whenever a deffunction begins or ends execution. For example:

```
CLIPS> (watch deffunctions)↵
CLIPS> (factorial 2)↵
DFN >> factorial ED:1 (2)
DFN >> factorial ED:2 (1)
DFN >> factorial ED:3 (0)
DFN << factorial ED:3 (0)
DFN << factorial ED:2 (1)
DFN << factorial ED:1 (2)
2
CLIPS>
```

The *DFN* at the beginning of the information message indicates that it relates to deffunctions. The >> symbol indicates that a deffunction is being entered and the << symbol indicates that a deffunction is being exited. The next symbol is the name of the deffunction being entered or exited, in this case the *factorial* deffunction. The ED symbol is short for "Evaluation Depth" and is followed by a colon and then the current evaluation depth, an integer. The evaluation depth is an indication of the nesting of deffunction calls. It starts at zero and then each time a deffunction is entered it increases by one. Each time a deffunction exits, it decreases by one. Finally the last piece of information displayed is the actual arguments to the deffunction.

In this example, the *factorial* deffunction is initially called with an argument of 2. The evaluation depth for this call is 1. The *factorial* deffunction must be called again to compute the factorial of 1. This call has an evaluation depth of 2 and an argument of 1. The next call is to compute the factorial of 0. This call has an evaluation depth of 3 and an argument of 0. Since the *factorial* deffunction does not need to recurse to determine the factorial of 0, the deffunction does not have to be called again and the nested deffunction calls can be exited. Each exit decrements the evaluation depth by 1 until the original deffunction call is exited and the value of 2 is returned.

It's also possible to watch specific deffunctions by adding their names to the end of a *watch deffunctions* command. For example:

```
CLIPS> (unwatch deffunctions)↵
CLIPS> (watch deffunctions C)↵
CLIPS> (A 2)↵
DFN >> C ED:3 (0)
```

```
DFN << C ED:3 (0)
4
CLIPS> (watch deffunctions A B)↵
CLIPS> (A 2)↵
DFN >> A ED:1 (2)
DFN >> B ED:2 (1)
DFN >> C ED:3 (0)
DFN << C ED:3 (0)
DFN << B ED:2 (1)
DFN << A ED:1 (2)
4
CLIPS>
```

Note that the evaluation depth for a deffunction call is still computed even if the deffunction is not being watched.

Wildcard Parameter

If all of the arguments in the parameter list of a deffunction are single-field variables, then there is a one-to-one correspondence between these parameters and the number of arguments that must be passed in when the deffunction is called. In other words, if there are three parameter arguments, then three values must be passed into the deffunction when it is called.

If the last parameter declared in a deffunction is a multifield variable, which is referred to as a wildcard parameter, then the deffunction can be called with more arguments than are specified in the parameter list. If there are M arguments in the parameter list and N arguments are supplied in the deffunction call, then the first M−1 arguments in the deffunction call are mapped to the first M−1 arguments in the parameter list. Arguments M through N of the deffunction call are mapped to the Mth argument in the parameter list as a multifield value.

As an example, let's revisit the *check-input* deffunction and convert its last parameter, ?values, to a wildcard parameter:

```
(deffunction check-input (?question $?values)
   (printout t ?question " " ?values " ")
   (bind ?answer (read))
   (while (not (member$ ?answer ?values))
      (printout t ?question " " ?values " ")
      (bind ?answer (read)))
   (return ?answer))
```

With the last parameter converted to a wildcard parameter, it is no longer necessary to use the *create$* function to create a multifield value to pass into the deffunction:

```
CLIPS>
(check-input "Who moves first, Computer or Human?"
c h)↵
Who moves first, Computer or Human? (c h) computer↵
Who moves first, Computer or Human? (c h) human↵
Who moves first, Computer or Human? (c h) h↵
h
CLIPS>
```

When *check-input* is called in this example, the string "Who moves first, Computer or Human?" is bound to the parameter ?question. The remaining arguments, c and h, are converted to a multifield value and stored in the wildcard parameter $?values.

Deffunction Commands

The **ppdeffunction** (pretty print deffunction) command is used to display the text representations of a deffunction. The **undeffunction** command is used to delete a deffunction. The **list-deffunctions** command is used to display the list of deffunctions defined in CLIPS. The **get-deffunction-list** function returns a multifield value containing the list of deffunctions. The syntax of these commands is:

```
(ppdeffunction <deffunction-name>)

(undeffunction <deffunction-name>)

(list-deffunctions [<module-name>])

(get-deffunction-list [<module-name>])
```

The following examples show how to use these functions:

```
CLIPS> (list-deffunctions)↵
hypotenuse-length
primep
check-input
factorial
A
B
C
For a total of 7 deffunctions.
CLIPS> (get-deffunction-list)↵
(hypotenuse-length primep check-input factorial
A B C)
CLIPS> (undeffunction primep)↵
```

```
CLIPS> (get-deffunction-list)↵
(hypotenuse-length check-input factorial A B C)
CLIPS> (ppdeffunction factorial)↵
(deffunction MAIN::factorial
   (?n)
   (if (>= ?n 1)
      then
      (* ?n (factorial (- ?n 1)))
      else
      1))
CLIPS>
```

You can't delete a deffunction when other deffunctions or constructs reference the deffunction to be deleted. In this situation, the only way to delete the deffunction is to remove the other references or issue a *clear* command. For example:

```
CLIPS> (undeffunction A)↵
[PRNTUTIL4] Unable to delete deffunction A.
CLIPS> (deffunction C (?n))↵
CLIPS> (undeffunction A)↵
CLIPS> (undeffunction C)↵
[PRNTUTIL4] Unable to delete deffunction C.
CLIPS> (clear)↵
CLIPS>
```

User-Defined Functions

In addition to deffunctions, CLIPS also provides a method for calling functions written in the C programming language. Functions defined using this methodology are referred to as **user-defined functions**. This name dates back to the early days of CLIPS when the deffunction construct was not yet available and the only way to add new functions was by writing them in C. So although deffunctions are defined by the user and could be described by the term *user-defined functions*, we'll use this term only when referring to functions written in C.

The *Advanced Programming Guide*, which is included on the CD-ROM accompanying this book, describes how to create and add a user-defined function to CLIPS. Typically there are only two reasons for writing a user-defined function rather than using a deffunction. The first is if you have code already written in C that you want to integrate with CLIPS. Rewriting large amounts of code is undesirable so in many cases it's easier just to leave the code in C and have CLIPS call it through a user-defined function. The second reason is for speed. Especially for large pieces of code, execution of a C function compiled into native code will run match faster than a deffunction run in the interpretive environment that CLIPS provides. Fortunately, for most tasks, the convenience of being able to define deffunctions directly in the CLIPS environment compensates for the slower speed caused by running interpretive code. Adding user-defined functions to CLIPS requires creating a new CLIPS executable program and if you are not familiar with the use of compilers or programming in C, this may be more effort than you want to undertake. In addition to the examples of user-defined functions contained in the *Advanced Programming Guide*, you can also find numerous examples of user-defined functions by looking through the CLIPS source code, which is also included on the CD-ROM. All of the functions and commands described in Sections 7 through 12 were added to CLIPS using the user-defined functions methodology.

10.4 THE DEFGLOBAL CONSTRUCT

CLIPS allows you to define variables that retain their values outside the scope of a construct. These variables are known as **global variables**. Up to now, all the variables that have been used within constructs have been **local variables**. These variables are local to the construct that references them. For example, consider the variable ?x used in the following two rules:

```
(defrule example-1
   (data-1 ?x)
   =>
   (printout t "?x = " ?x crlf))

(defrule example-2
   (data-2 ?x)
   =>
   (printout t "?x = " ?x crlf))
```

The value of ?x in rule *example-1* does not constrain in any way the value of ?x in rule *example-2*. If the fact (data-1 3) is asserted, then the value of 3 will be assigned to ?x in the *example-1* rule. This won't restrict the pattern in the *example-2* rule to matching only a *data-2* fact with a value of 3 for ?x. Furthermore, additionally asserting the fact (data-1 4) doesn't restrict the value of ?x to be the same in the two activations of the *example-1* rule. Essentially each partial match or activation of a rule has its own set of local variables. The same is true for each call of a deffunction.

Global variables are defined using the **defglobal** construct. The general format of a defglobal is:

```
(defglobal [<defmodule-name>] <global-assignment>*)
```

where <global-assignment> is:

```
<global-variable> = <expression>
```

and <global-variable> is:

```
?*<symbol>*
```

The <defmodule-name> is the module in which the globals will be defined. If none is specified, the globals will be placed in the current module. Global variable names begin and end with the * character, so you can easily tell that ?x is a local variable, whereas ?*x* is a global variable. When a defglobal construct is defined, the initial value for each defglobal is determined by evaluating <expression> and assigning the resultant value to the defglobal. For example:

```
CLIPS>
(defglobal ?*x* = 3
           ?*y* = (+ ?*x* 1))↵
CLIPS> ?*x*↵
3
CLIPS> ?*y*↵
4
CLIPS>
```

Note that since the global ?*x* is defined before ?*y*, we can use its value to determine the initial value of ?*y*. Also, since globals retain their values outside of constructs, we can just enter a global variable name at the command prompt to determine its value. In addition to the command line, defglobal references can be used anywhere you could use an <expression>, which among other places means you can use them in the body of a deffunction or on the RHS of a rule. You can't use them as a parameter of a deffunction and can use them only on the LHS of a rule if they are contained within a function call. For example, the following constructs are all illegal:

```
(deffunction illegal-1 (?*x* ?y)
   (+ ?*x* y))

(defrule illegal-2
   (data-1 ?*x*)
   =>)

(defrule illegal-3
   (data-1 ?x&~?*x*)
   =>)
```

Defglobal Commands

The value of a defglobal can be changed using the *bind* command. Instead of specifying a local variable, just specify a global variable. Several commands are provided for manipulating defglobals. The **ppdefglobal** (pretty print defglobal) command is used to display the text representations of a defglobal. The **undefglobal** command is used to delete a defglobal. The **list-defglobals** command is used to display the list of defglobals defined in CLIPS. The **show-defglobals** command is used to display the names and values of defglobals defined in CLIPS. The **get-defglobal-list** function returns a multifield value containing the list of defglobals. The syntax of these commands is:

```
(ppdefglobal <defglobal-name>)

(undefglobal <defglobal-name>)

(list-defglobals [<module-name>])

(show-defglobals [<module-name>])

(get-defglobal-list [<module-name>])
```

The <defglobal-name> for the *ppdefglobal* and *undefglobal* commands should use the name of the global variable without the beginning and ending * character (for example, x rather than *x*). The following examples use these functions:

```
CLIPS> (ppdefglobal y)↵
(defglobal MAIN ?*y* = (+ ?*x* 1))
CLIPS> (list-defglobals)↵
x
y
For a total of 2 defglobals.
CLIPS> (get-defglobal-list)↵
(x y)
CLIPS> (show-defglobals)↵
?*x* = 3
?*y* = 4
CLIPS> (bind ?*y* 5)↵
5
CLIPS> (show-defglobals)↵
?*x* = 3
?*y* = 5
CLIPS> (undefglobal y)↵
CLIPS> (list-defglobals)↵
x
For a total of 1 defglobal.
CLIPS>
```

Defglobal Reset Behavior

The value of a defglobal is restored to its original definition value whenever a *reset* command is issued or when a bind command is used to change the value of the global and a new value is not supplied. For example:

```
CLIPS> (bind ?*x* some-value)↵
some-value
CLIPS> ?*x*↵
some-value
CLIPS> (reset)↵
CLIPS> ?*x*↵
3
CLIPS> (bind ?*x* another-value)↵
another-value
CLIPS> ?*x*↵
another-value
CLIPS> (bind ?*x*)↵
3
CLIPS> ?*x*↵
3
CLIPS>
```

The reset behavior of global variables can be disabled by calling the **set-reset-globals** function and supplying a value of FALSE. Supplying a value of TRUE will restore the behavior. When this behavior is disabled, the *reset* command will not restore the value of the defglobal to its original definition value. For example:

```
CLIPS> (bind ?*x* 5)↵
5
CLIPS> (set-reset-globals FALSE)↵
TRUE
CLIPS> (reset)↵
CLIPS> ?*x*↵
5
CLIPS> (set-reset-globals TRUE)↵
FALSE
CLIPS> (reset)↵
CLIPS> ?*x*↵
3
CLIPS>
```

Watching Defglobals

When defglobals are watched using the *watch* command, an informational message is printed whenever the value of a defglobal changes. For example:

```
CLIPS> (watch globals)↵
CLIPS> (bind ?*x* 6)↵
```

```
:== ?*x* ==> 6 <== 3
6
CLIPS> (bind ?*x* 7)↵
:== ?*x* ==> 7 <== 6
7
CLIPS> (reset)↵
:== ?*x* ==> 3 <== 7
CLIPS> (unwatch globals)↵
CLIPS> (bind ?*x* 8)↵
8
CLIPS>
```

The *:==* at the beginning of the information message indicates an assignment to a global variable is occurring. The next symbol is the name of the defglobal being changed. This is followed by ==> and then the new value of the global variable. Next comes <== followed by the old value of the global variable.

Defglobals and Pattern Matching

Defglobals can be used in expressions on the LHS of rules, but changes to defglobals don't trigger pattern matching. For example, consider the following defglobal and defrule:

```
(defglobal ?*z* = 4)

(defrule global-example
   (data ?z&:(> ?z ?*z*))
   =>)
```

Now consider what happens when *data* facts are asserted matching the single pattern in the *global-example* rule:

```
CLIPS> (reset)↵
CLIPS> ?*z*↵
4
CLIPS> (assert (data 5) (data 6))↵
<Fact-2>
CLIPS> (facts)↵
f-0     (initial-fact)
f-1     (data 5)
f-2     (data 6)
For a total of 3 facts.
CLIPS> (agenda)↵
0       global-example: f-1
0       global-example: f-2
```

```
For a total of 2 activations.
CLIPS>
```

When the fact (data 5) is asserted, the value 5 is bound to the local variable ?z and this value is then compared to the value of the global variable ?*z*, which is 4. Since 5 is greater than 4, the *global-example* rule is activated by fact f-1. Similarly, since 6 is greater than 4, the rule is also activated by fact f-2. At this point, pattern matching is complete and changing the value of ?*z* will not cause the pattern to be reevaluated for the activations generated for this rule:

```
CLIPS> (bind ?*z* 5)↵
5
CLIPS> (agenda)↵
0      global-example: f-1
0      global-example: f-2
For a total of 2 activations.
CLIPS>
```

Changing the value of ?*z* to 5 does not remove the activation caused by fact f-1, even though the value of 5 found in the *data* fact matching the global-example rule is no longer greater than the value stored in the global variable ?*z*. Retracting the fact and then reasserting it, however, will retrigger the pattern-matching process and use the new value of the global variable just as any newly asserted fact would:

```
CLIPS> (retract 1)↵
CLIPS> (assert (data 5))↵
<Fact-3>
CLIPS> (agenda)↵
0      global-example: f-2
For a total of 1 activation.
CLIPS> (assert (data 7))↵
<Fact-4>
CLIPS> (agenda)↵
0      global-example: f-2
0      global-example: f-4
For a total of 2 activations.
CLIPS>
```

When the (data 5) fact, f-1, is retracted and then reasserted, the *global-example* rule is no longer satisfied by this fact and so no activation is generated. Asserting the fact (data 7), however, will cause an activation since the value of ?z is 7 and this is greater than the new value of 5 for the global variable ?*z*.

Uses of Defglobals

Defglobals are most appropriately used in rules as either constants or to pass in information that is used only on the RHS of the rule and should not trigger pattern matching. Used as constants, defglobals can make your program easier to understand. Consider the following rule:

```
(defrule plant-advisory
   (temperature ?value Fahrenheit)
   (test (<= ?value 32))
   =>
   (printout t "It's freezing." crlf)
   (printout t "Bring your plants inside." crlf))
```

Certainly most people are aware that the freezing point of water is 32° Fahrenheit (or 0° Celsius), so the significance of the constant 32 in the *plant-advisory* rule should be easily deduced. But not all constants are common knowledge. By assigning the value of 32 to a global variable, we can use a meaningful symbolic name in the *plant-advisory* rule making it easier to understand:

```
(defglobal ?*water-freezing-point-Fahrenheit* = 32)

(defrule plant-advisory
   (temperature ?value Fahrenheit)
   (test (<= ?value
   ?*water-freezing-point-Fahrenheit*))
   =>
   (printout t "It's freezing." crlf)
   (printout t "Bring your plants inside." crlf))
```

One use of defglobals to avoid triggering pattern matching is for debugging. Suppose you want to print some additional information beyond what's provided by the *watch* command. One way to do that would be by adding printout or format commands to your rules like the following:

```
(defrule debug-example
   (data ?x)
   =>
   (printout t "Debug-example ?x = " ?x crlf))
```

The problem arises, however, that you may not want to see these debugging messages all the time so you would either have to delete them or convert them into comments when you don't want them active. One way to conveniently get around this problem is to store the logical name to which the debugging output is sent in a defglobal. If *nil* is used as the logical name argument to either the *printout* or the *format* command, then no output is produced (although the *format* command still returns the formatted string as its return value). You can take advantage of this fact to discard debugging information when you don't want to see it. Here's how you would modify the debug-example rule to use a defglobal:

```
(defglobal ?*debug-print* = nil)

(defrule debug-example
   (data ?x)
   =>
   (printout                                    ?*debug-print*
   "Debug-example ?x = " ?x crlf))
```

By default, the debugging information will be sent to the logical name *nil* so you won't see it printed to the screen. To send the output to the screen, all you need to do is set the value of the ?*debug-print* global to the symbol *t* as the following dialog shows:

```
CLIPS> (reset)↵
CLIPS> (assert (data a) (data b) (data c))↵
<Fact-3>
CLIPS> (agenda)↵
0       debug-example: f-1
0       debug-example: f-2
0       debug-example: f-3
For a total of 3 activations.
CLIPS> (run 1)↵
CLIPS> (bind ?*debug-print* t)↵
t
CLIPS> (run 2)↵
Debug-example ?x = b
Debug-example ?x = c
CLIPS>
```

Notice that we enabled the debugging information after one of the *debug-example* activations had been allowed to fire. If we had stored the debugging information in a fact, we wouldn't have been able to do that. The debug-example rule would be the following in this case:

```
(defrule debug-example
   (debug-print ?debug-print)
   (data ?x)
   =>
   (printout ?debug-print "Debug-example ?x = " ?x
   crlf))
```

Retracting the *debug-print* fact and then reasserting it with a new value would retrigger any *debug-example* activations that had already fired, which would be highly undesirable.

10.5 THE DEFGENERIC AND DEFMETHOD CONSTRUCTS

In addition to the functions defined using the deffunction construct, CLIPS also provides generic functions. A **generic function** is essentially a group of related functions (called *methods*) sharing a common name. In fact, a generic function that has more than one method is said to be **overloaded** (since the same name is being used to potentially reference more than one method). Each method in the group has its own signature: the number and types of arguments it expects. When a call is made to a generic function, the arguments are examined and the method with a signature matching the argument is the one that is executed. This process is known as the **generic dispatch**. The **defgeneric** construct is used to define the common generic function name used by a group of methods. The general format of a defgeneric is:

```
(defgeneric <defgeneric-name> [<optional-comment>])
```

The only reason that you ever have to explicitly define a defgeneric is to act as a forward declaration when you make a reference to a generic function before you have actually defined any methods of that generic function. If a method of a generic function is defined before a defgeneric construct has been specified, then a defgeneric is automatically generated for you.

Specific methods for a generic function are defined using the **defmethod** construct. The general format of a defmethod is:

```
(defmethod <defgeneric-name> [<index>]
    [<optional-comment>]
    (<regular-parameter-restriction>*
    [<wildcard-parameter-restriction>])
 <expression>*)
```

Specific defmethods don't have names. The same <defgeneric-name> is used for all methods comprising the generic function. Each specific method, however, is assigned a unique integer index that can be used to reference the method. You can assign a specific index to a method by specifying <index> when the method is defined. If <index> is not specified, CLIPS automatically creates one for you. For a given generic function, there can be only one method for a specific argument signature (the values supplied for <regular-parameter-restriction> and <wildcard-parameter-restriction>). If you define a method of a generic function that has the same argument signature as an existing method of that generic function and you didn't specify <index>, then the existing method is replaced by the new method and the same index is used. If you specify <index> when defining a method and there is a method of the generic function with the same argument signature, then <index> must be the same as the index of the existing method with the same signature, and if so the existing method is replaced with the new method.

Each <regular-parameter-restriction> can be one of two forms. It can either be a single-field variable (as in a deffunction) or it can be of the following form:

```
(<single-field-variable> <type>* [<query>])
```

In this second form, which is surrounded by parentheses, the single-field variable is followed by zero or more types and then an optional query. The allowed values for <type> are any valid class name. This will be covered in detail in Chapter 11, but for now examples will be limited to the values already used with the type attribute, which also happens to be class names: SYMBOL, STRING, LEXEME, INTEGER, FLOAT, NUMBER, INSTANCE-NAME, INSTANCE-ADDRESS, INSTANCE, FACT-ADDRESS, and EXTERNAL-ADDRESS. The <query> value that comes last if specified must either be a global variable or a function call.

The <wildcard-parameter-restriction> is similar to the <regular-parameter-restriction>, except that multifield variables are used in place of single-field variables. So its two forms are either a multifield variable or the following form:

```
(<multifield-variable> <type>* [<query>])
```

With the exception of using <multifield-variable> instead of <single-field-variable>, the values that can be substituted for <type> and <query> follow the same restrictions as the <regular-parameter-restriction>. When a method is invoked, the multifield variable specified for the <wildcard-parameter-restriction> behaves similarly to the wildcard parameter of a deffunction. Any remaining arguments in the method call that exceed the number of parameters for the method are grouped together as a single multifield value and are assigned to the wildcard parameter variable.

The final portion of the defmethod, represented by <expression>*, is the body of the method. Like the RHS of a defrule or the body of a deffunction, it's a series of expressions that are executed in order when the method is invoked.

Revisiting the Check-Input Deffunction

Let's revisit the check-input deffunction from Section 10.3. Its original definition was:

```
(deffunction check-input (?question $?values)
   (printout t ?question " " ?values " ")
   (bind ?answer (read))
   (while (not (member$ ?answer ?values))
      (printout t ?question " " ?values " ")
      (bind ?answer (read)))
   (return ?answer))
```

This deffunction can be directly converted to a defmethod simply by replacing the name of the construct:

```
(defmethod check-input (?question $?values)
   (printout t ?question " " ?values " ")
   (bind ?answer (read))
   (while (not (member$ ?answer ?values))
```

```
         (printout t ?question " " ?values " ")
         (bind ?answer (read)))
    (return ?answer))
```

Note that you can't replace a deffunction with a generic function of the same name and vice versa, so in order to define the *check-input* defmethod you'd have to delete the *check-input* deffunction. The *check-input* defmethod that we've just defined will work identically to our original deffunction. If we don't define any more methods, there's really no reason to use generic functions rather than the original deffunction. So let's examine another portion of the Stick program. Recall from Section 8.9 that three rules were used to determine the number of sticks removed by the human player:

```
(defrule get-human-move
   (player-move h)
   (pile-size ?size)
   (test (> ?size 1))
   =>
   (printout t
   "How many sticks do you wish to take? ")
   (assert (human-takes (read))))

(defrule good-human-move
   ?whose-turn <- (player-move h)
   (pile-size ?size)
   ?number-taken <- (human-takes ?choice)
   (test (and (integerp ?choice)
              (>= ?choice 1)
              (<= ?choice 3)
              (< ?choice ?size)))
   =>
   (retract ?whose-turn ?number-taken)
   (printout t "Human made a valid move" crlf))

(defrule bad-human-move
   ?whose-turn <- (player-move h)
   (pile-size ?size)
   ?number-taken <- (human-takes ?choice)
   (test (or (not (integerp ?choice))
                  (< ?choice 1)
                  (> ?choice 3)
                  (>= ?choice ?size)))
   =>
   (printout t "Human made an invalid move" crlf)
   (retract ?whose-turn ?number-taken)
   (assert (player-move h)))
```

Since the number of sticks you're allowed to take isn't always 1, 2, or 3, the user can't be prompted for the number of sticks with the following call:

```
(check-input " How many sticks do you wish to take?"
 1 2 3)
```

Instead the number of sticks would have to be dynamically computed, as the following update to the *get-human-move* rule demonstrates:

```
(defrule get-human-move
   (player-move h)
   (pile-size ?size)
   (test (> ?size 1))
   =>
   (bind ?responses (create$))
   (bind ?upper-choice (min (- ?size 1) 3))
   (loop-for-count (?i ?upper-choice)
      (bind ?responses (create$ ?responses ?i)))
      (bind ?answer
      (check-input "How many sticks do you wish to
      take?"
      ?responses))
   (assert (human-takes ?answer)))
```

The first four lines in the *get-human-move* rule dynamically create a multifield value containing the possible values that the user can select. The number taken can only be 1, 2, or 3, but it must also be less than the number of sticks remaining. It's inconvenient to have to compute the allowed responses and since all possible responses are displayed when the question is asked, there would be 100 values displayed if *check-input* were to ask the user for a number between 1 and 100. Adding an additional method can solve this problem. The following method uses type restrictions to provide special behavior when two integers are specified after the question in a check-input call:

```
(defmethod check-input ((?question STRING)
                        (?value1 INTEGER)
                        (?value2 INTEGER))
  (printout t ?question " (" ?value1 "-"
   ?value2 ") ")
  (bind ?answer (read))
  (while (or (not (integerp ?answer))
        (< ?answer ?value1)
        (> ?answer ?value2))
     (printout t ?question " (" ?value1 "-"
      ?value2 ") ")
      (bind ?answer (read)))
  (return ?answer))
```

This method shares some code with the original ask-user method, but there are significant differences, the most important of which is the argument list. Each of the arguments is enclosed with parentheses and also includes a type specification. The type specification for the variable ?question is STRING, for ?value1 it is INTEGER, and for ?value2 it is INTEGER. Because of these restrictions, this particular method will be invoked only when three arguments are supplied to *ask-user* and the first is a STRING, the second is an INTEGER, and the third is an INTEGER.

Another change in the method is that following the question, the range of allowed integers is printed instead of printing each allowed integer. The final change in the method is replacing the *member$* test in the *while* loop with three tests to ensure that the response is an integer and that it is in the allowed range. With both methods defined, a sample run demonstrates that both methods work properly:

```
CLIPS> (check-input "Pick a number" 1 3)↵
Pick a number (1-3) a↵
Pick a number (1-3) 34↵
Pick a number (1-3) 3↵
3
CLIPS> (check-input "Pick a number" 1 2 3)↵
Pick a number (1 2 3) a↵
Pick a number (1 2 3) 34↵
Pick a number (1 2 3) 3↵
3
CLIPS>
```

Note that the first method invoked displays the valid range (1–3) where the second method invoked displays the list of valid values (1 2 3).

Method Precedence

When you call a generic function, CLIPS executes only one of its methods. The process of determining which method to execute is called the **generic dispatch**. In our prior example, the *check-input* generic function provided different behavior when it was called with an integer range instead of a list of allowed values. The second expression in our prior example was the following:

```
(check-input "Pick a number" 1 2 3)
```

The two signatures for the methods that have been defined are the following:

```
(?question $?values)
(?question STRING) (?value1 INTEGER)
(?value2 INTEGER)
```

It's apparent that the first method signature can be used to evaluate the expression since it requires one or more arguments, but the second method signature can't be used to evaluate the expression since it requires exactly three arguments and there are four supplied. On the other hand, if we examine the first expression in our prior example:

```
(check-input "Pick a number" 1 3)
```

and compare it to the method signatures that have been defined, it's apparent that both method signatures can handle the expression. Again the first method signature just expects one or more arguments of any type. The second method signature expects exactly three arguments: the first a STRING, the second an INTEGER, and the third an INTEGER. Since the expression contains the exact number and types of arguments required, this method is also applicable. So how does CLIPS determine which method to execute if more than one is applicable?

The answer to this question is that CLIPS defines a precedence order to the methods defined for a particular method. If more than one method is applicable, the method with higher precedence is the one that is executed. The **preview-generic** command can be used to display the precedence order for the methods applicable to a specific set of arguments. The syntax of this command is:

```
(preview-generic <defgeneric-name> <expression>*)
```

The <defgeneric-name> argument is the name of the generic function and <expression>* is the zero or more arguments that are to be passed to the generic function. The generic function isn't actually executed when this function is called. All applicable methods are determined and then listed in precedence order. For example:

```
CLIPS>
(preview-generic check-input "Pick a number" 1 3)↵
check-input #2 (STRING) (INTEGER) (INTEGER)
check-input #1 () $?
CLIPS>
```

The output confirms what we have already determined empirically: the integer range check *check-input* method has a higher precedence than the *check-input* value check method using the wildcard parameter. Method #2, the integer range check method, is listed first, which means it has the highest precedence. The generic function name is listed followed by the method index. The allowed types for each argument are then listed enclosed within parentheses. The names of the variables in the parameter list of a defmethod have no effect on precedence, so there's no need to list them. The next method listed is #1. Since no type restrictions were placed on the first argument, an empty set of parentheses, (), is displayed. The remaining parameter to method #1 is the wildcard parameter. If no type restrictions have been specified for a wildcard parameter, then preview-generic just displays the symbol $? to represent it.

Given two methods of a generic function, CLIPS uses the following steps to determine which method has higher precedence:

1. Compare the left-most unexamined parameter restrictions of the two methods. If only one method has parameters left, proceed to step 6. If neither method has parameters remaining, proceed to step 7. Otherwise, proceed to step 2.
2. If one parameter is a regular parameter and the other parameter is a wildcard parameter, then the method with the regular parameter has precedence. Otherwise, proceed to step 3.
3. If one parameter has type restrictions and the other parameter does not, then the method with the types restrictions has precedence. Otherwise, proceed to step 4.
4. Compare the left-most unexamined type restriction of the two parameters. If the type restriction on one parameter is more specific than the type restriction on the other parameter, then the method with the more specific type restriction has precedence. For example, the type restriction INTEGER is more specific than NUMBER. If neither type restriction is more specific (for example, INTEGER is not more specific than LEXEME), and both parameters have remaining type restrictions, then repeat step 4. If one parameter has remaining type restrictions and the other parameter does not, then the method without additional type restrictions has precedence. Otherwise, proceed to step 5.
5. If one parameter has a query restriction and the other does not, then the method with the query restriction has precedence. Otherwise return to step 1 and compare the next set of parameters.
6. If the next parameter of the method with parameters remaining is a regular parameter, then this method has precedence. Otherwise, the other method has precedence.
7. The method that was defined first has precedence.

Figure 10.1 shows a flowchart that yields equivalent results to steps 1 through 7. Step 1 begins with the box in the upper-left corner of the figure. Figure 10.2 shows a flowchart that yields the equivalent results to steps 3 and 4 in determining whether one parameter has more specific type restrictions than another parameter.

Using these steps we can determine why the method #2 of generic function check-input has higher precedence than method #1. Starting with step 1, we compare the left-most unexamined parameters of both methods. The parameter restriction for method #1 is () and the parameter restriction for method #2 is (STRING). Since both methods have parameters, we proceed to step 2. Since both parameters are regular parameters, we proceed to step 3.

Figure 10.1 Method Precedence Determination

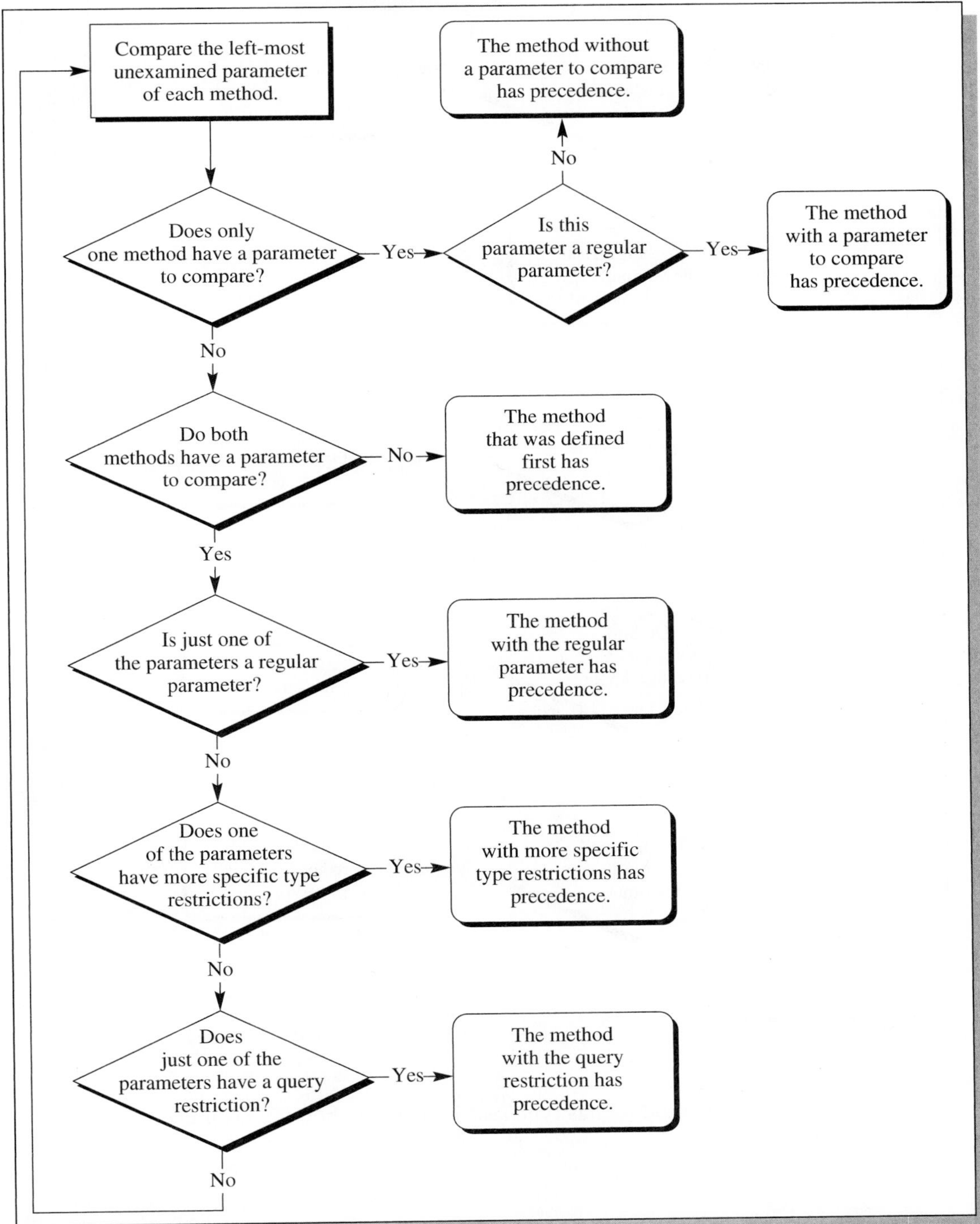

Figure 10.2 Method Type Specificity Determination

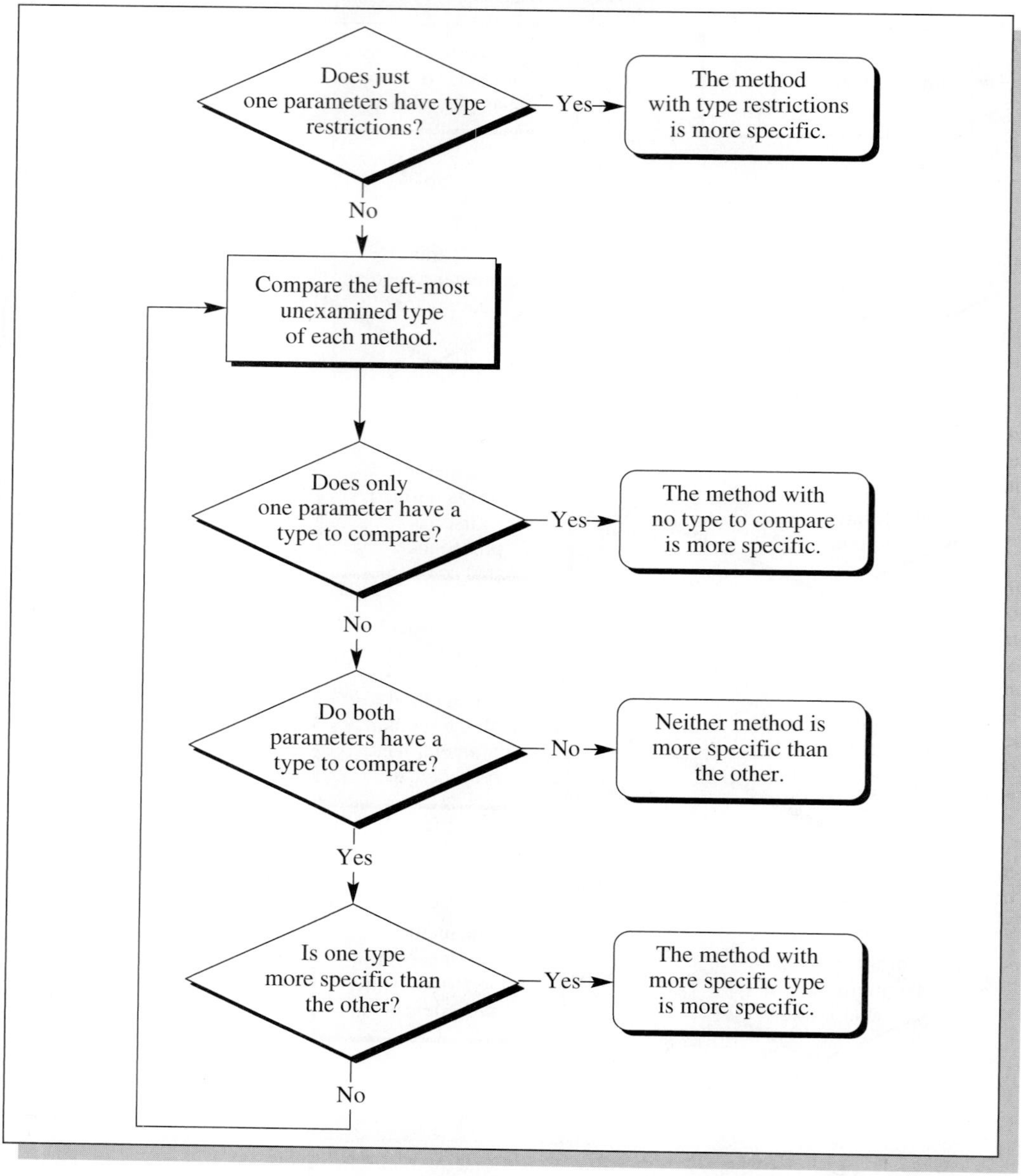

Since only method #2 has type restrictions, method #2 has precedence over method #1.

Since the check-input method #2 allows us to enter only integer values, let's create another method that will allow us to enter a floating-point value within a specified range:

```
(defmethod check-input ((?question STRING)
                        (?value1 NUMBER)
                        (?value2 NUMBER))
   (printout t ?question " (" (float ?value1)
                         "-" (float ?value2) ") ")
   (bind ?answer (read))
   (while (or (not (numberp ?answer))
      (< ?answer ?value1)
      (> ?answer ?value2))
       (printout t ?question " (" (float ?value1)
                             "-" (float ?value2)
                             ") ")
       (bind ?answer (read)))
   (return ?answer))
```

This method is similar to our prior integer range check method except it substitutes NUMBER for INTEGER in the parameter restrictions, it forces any integer range values to floats when displaying the valid range, and it uses *numberp* rather than *integerp* to check for non-valid types. With this additional method defined, a sample run demonstrates that both range check methods work properly:

```
CLIPS> (check-input "Pick a number" 1 3.5)↵
Pick a number (1.0-3.5) 6↵
Pick a number (1.0-3.5) 2.7↵
2.7
CLIPS> (check-input "Pick a number" 1 3)↵
Pick a number (1-3) 2.7↵
Pick a number (1-3) 2↵
2
CLIPS>
```

The *preview-generic* command shows that for the second *check-input* generic call all three methods are applicable:

```
CLIPS>
(preview-generic check-input "Pick a number" 1 3)↵
check-input #2 (STRING) (INTEGER) (INTEGER)
check-input #3 (STRING) (NUMBER) (NUMBER)
check-input #1 () $?
CLIPS>
```

The method with two INTEGER restrictions has higher precedence than the method with two NUMBER restrictions. Using the precedence determination steps we can determine why. Starting with step 1, we compare the left-most unexamined parameters of both methods. The parameter restriction for method #2 and method #3 is (STRING). Since both methods have parameters, we proceed to step 2. Since both parameters are regular parameters, we proceed to step 3. Since both parameters have type restrictions, we proceed to step 4. Since both type restrictions are the same, we proceed to step 5. Since neither parameter has a query restriction, we proceed back to step 1. The left-most unexamined parameter restriction for method #2 is (INTEGER) and the left-most unexamined parameter restriction for method #3 is (NUMBER). Since both methods have parameters, we proceed to step 2. Since both parameters are regular parameters, we proceed to step 3. Since both parameters have type restrictions, we proceed to step 4. Since the INTEGER type restriction on method #2 is more specific than the NUMBER type restriction on method #3, method #2 has precedence.

Let's take a look at one more example of precedence. In this case, we'll define a method that is essentially the same as the last method defined except instead of using NUMBER for the type restriction, we'll specify the two types INTEGER and FLOAT:

```
(defmethod check-input ((?question STRING)
                        (?value1 INTEGER FLOAT)
                        (?value2 INTEGER FLOAT))
   (printout t ?question " (" (float ?value1)
                   "-" (float ?value2) ") ")
   (bind ?answer (read))
   (while (or (not (numberp ?answer))
              (< ?answer ?value1)
              (> ?answer ?value2))
      (printout t ?question " (" (float ?value1)
                      "-" (float ?value2) ") ")
      (bind ?answer (read)))
   (return ?answer))
```

If we look at the results of a *preview-generic* call, we'll see that the new method #4 is sandwiched between method #2 and method #3:

```
CLIPS>
(preview-generic check-input "Pick a number" 1 3)↵
check-input #2 (STRING) (INTEGER) (INTEGER)
check-input #4 (STRING) (INTEGER FLOAT) (INTEGER FLOAT)
check-input #3 (STRING) (NUMBER) (NUMBER)
check-input #1 () $?
CLIPS>
```

This placement is a result of step #4 on the second parameter of the methods. When comparing methods #3 and #4, the first type restriction from method #4, INTEGER, is more specific than the first type restriction from method #3, NUMBER, so method #4 has higher precedence. When comparing methods #2 and #4, the first type restriction from method #2, INTEGER, is the same as the first type restriction from method #4, so we proceed to the second type restriction from each method. Since method #2 does not have a second type restriction, but method #4 does, method #2 has higher precedence.

Query Restrictions

In addition to placing type restrictions on a method parameter, it's also possible to place a query restriction on a parameter. A **query restriction** is a defglobal reference or function call that is evaluated to determine the applicability of a method when a generic function is called. If the query restriction evaluates to FALSE, then the method is not applicable. The query restriction for a parameter isn't evaluated unless the type restrictions for that parameter are satisfied. A method with multiple parameters can have multiple query restrictions and each must be satisfied in order for the method to be applicable.

Let's consider an example where a query restriction might be useful. If we call the *check-input* generic function, but don't supply any additional arguments beyond the question string, we get the following behavior:

```
CLIPS> (check-input "Pick a number")↵
Pick a number () 3
Pick a number () 2
Pick a number () 5
Pick a number () 0
  .
  .
  .
```

The applicable method for this situation is method #1, the method using the wildcard parameter. Since no additional arguments were supplied past the question string parameter, ?question, the wildcard parameter, $?values, is bound to a multifield of length zero. The *member$* test used by the method will always return FALSE because no value supplied by the user will be contained within the empty multifield and thus the method will never return. We can get around this problem by using a query restriction on the wildcard parameter:

```
(defmethod check-input
(?question ($?values (= (length$ ?values) 0)))
   (return FALSE))
```

In this method, the number of values stored in the $?values wildcard parameters is determined by calling the *length$* function and the return value is compared to zero using the = function. This ensures that the method will be applicable only for an empty multifield. Note that you're allowed to use the method parameters (in this case ?value) within the query restriction. All the method does is return the symbol *FALSE* since it's not possible for the user to return a legal value. With this method defined, our prior generic call no longer causes an endless loop:

```
CLIPS> (check-input "Pick a number")↵
FALSE
CLIPS>
```

Calling *preview-generic* with just the question string parameter shows that with all the parameters equal in other ways, the query restriction on method #2 gives it higher precedence than the other applicable method, #5:

```
CLIPS>
(preview-generic check-input "Pick a number")↵
check-input #5 () ($? <qry>)
check-input #1 () $?
CLIPS>
```

Let's look at another situation where an endless loop can occur with the *check-input* generic function:

```
CLIPS> (check-input "Pick a number" 3 1)↵
Pick a number (3-1) 3
Pick a number (3-1) 2
Pick a number (3-1) 5
Pick a number (3-1) 0
 .
 .
 .
```

In this situation, the applicable method is #2, the one with the question string parameter and two integer parameters. Since no integer exists that is greater or equal to 3 and less than or equal to 1, the user can never supply a value to satisfy the generic function. We could solve this problem by creating an additional method with a query restriction that detected the upper limit is less than the lower limit:

```
(defmethod check-input ((?question STRING)
                        (?value1 INTEGER)
                        (?value2 INTEGER
                                (< ?value2 ?value1)))
   (return FALSE))
```

This method just returns the symbol FALSE if it detects the ranges are reversed. We could go a step further and simply switch the values of the ranges. One way to do this would be to duplicate the code but switch the variables at the appropriate places:

```
(defmethod check-input ((?question STRING)
                        (?value1 INTEGER)
                        (?value2 INTEGER
                                (< ?value2 ?value1)))
```

```
(printout t ?question " (" ?value2 "-"
                  ?value1 ") ")
(bind ?answer (read))
(while (or (not (integerp ?answer))
       (< ?answer ?value2)
       (> ?answer ?value1))
   (printout t ?question " (" ?value2 "-"
                     ?value1 ") ")
   (bind ?answer (read)))
(return ?answer))
```

This approach works, but it duplicates more code than is necessary. A better way to do it is just call the generic function again but with the arguments switched:

```
(defmethod check-input
((?question STRING) (?value1 INTEGER)
   (?value2 INTEGER (< ?value2 ?value1)))
   (check-input ?question ?value2 ?value1))
```

With this method, an endless loop now won't occur when the arguments are in the wrong order:

```
CLIPS> (check-input "Pick a number" 3 1)↵
Pick a number (1-3) 3
3
CLIPS>
```

For completeness, we should add an additional method to handle the other method that uses the NUMBER type to specify the ranges:

```
(defmethod check-input
((?question STRING) (?value1 NUMBER)
   (?value2 NUMBER (< ?value2 ?value1)))
   (check-input ?question ?value2 ?value1))
```

A call to *preview-generic* with reversed ranges now shows a considerable number of applicable methods:

```
CLIPS>
(preview-generic check-input "Pick a number" 3 1)↵
check-input #6 (STRING) (INTEGER) (INTEGER <qry>)
check-input #2 (STRING) (INTEGER) (INTEGER)
```

```
check-input #4 (STRING) (INTEGER FLOAT)
        (INTEGER FLOAT)
check-input #7 (STRING) (NUMBER) (NUMBER <qry>)
check-input #3 (STRING) (NUMBER) (NUMBER)
check-input #1 () $?
CLIPS>
```

Watching Generic Functions and Methods

When generic functions are watched using the *watch* command, an informational message is printed whenever a generic function begins or ends execution. And when methods are watched using the *watch* command, an informational message is printed whenever a method begins or ends execution. For example:

```
CLIPS> (watch methods)↵
CLIPS> (watch generic-functions)↵
CLIPS> (check-input "Pick a number" 3 1)↵
GNC >> check-input ED:1 ("Pick a number" 3 1)
MTH >> check-input:#6 ED:1 ("Pick a number" 3 1)
GNC >> check-input ED:2 ("Pick a number" 1 3)
MTH >> check-input:#2 ED:2 ("Pick a number" 1 3)
Pick a number (1-3) 2↵
MTH << check-input:#2 ED:2 ("Pick a number" 1 3)
GNC << check-input ED:2 ("Pick a number" 1 3)
MTH << check-input:#6 ED:1 ("Pick a number" 3 1)
GNC << check-input ED:1 ("Pick a number" 3 1)
2
CLIPS>
```

The *GNC* at the beginning of the information message indicates that it relates to a generic function. The >> symbol indicates that the invocation of a generic function has begin and the << symbol indicates that the invocation of a generic function has ended. The next symbol is the name of the generic function, in this case the *check-input* generic function. The ED symbol is short for "Evaluation Depth" and is followed by a colon and then the current evaluation depth, an integer. The evaluation depth is an indication of the nesting of generic function and deffuction calls. It starts at zero and then each time a deffunction or generic function is entered, it increases by one. Each time a deffunction or generic function exits, it decreases by one. Finally the last piece of information displayed is the actual arguments to the generic function. The information messages for methods, denoted with *MTH* at the beginning, contain virtually the same information as those for generic functions. The main addition is the method index after the generic function name. This indicates the specific method that is executed.

In this example, you can see that two methods end up being executed. Method #6 is first entered because the end range argument of 1 is less than the begin range argument of 3. The *check-input* generic function is called again, this time with the arguments switched. With the arguments in the correct order, method #2 is now executed, the user enters the value 2, which is in the allowed range, and then both methods return. Generally it's more useful to watch *methods* instead of *generic-functions* since you want to know the specific method that's executed, but the option exists to watch either.

Defmethod Commands

Several commands are provided for manipulating defmethods. The **ppdefmethod** (pretty print defmethod) command is used to display the text representations of a defmethod. The **undefmethod** command is used to delete a defmethod. The **list-defmethods** command is used to display the list of defmethods defined in CLIPS. The **get-defmethod-list** function returns a multifield value containing the list of defmethods. The syntax of these commands is:

```
(ppdefmethod <defgeneric-name> <index>)

(undefmethod <defgeneric-name> <index>)

(list-defmethods [<defgeneric-name>])

(get-defmethod-list [<defgeneric-name>])
```

The *ppdefmethod* and *undefmethod* commands differ from those of other constructs in that you have to specify an index in addition to the name of the defgeneric. Also the *list-defmethods* and *get-defmethod-list* functions do not take an optional module name argument. Instead the optional argument is the name of a generic function. If this is specified, then the command applies only to methods of that generic function; otherwise it is applied to all methods of all generic functions. The following are examples showing the use of these functions:

```
CLIPS> (ppdefmethod check-input 5)↵
(defmethod MAIN::check-input
   (?question ($?values (= (length$ ?values) 0)))
   (return FALSE))
CLIPS> (undefmethod check-input 4)↵
CLIPS> (list-defmethods)↵
check-input #6 (STRING) (INTEGER) (INTEGER <qry>)
check-input #2 (STRING) (INTEGER) (INTEGER)
check-input #7 (STRING) (NUMBER) (NUMBER <qry>)
check-input #3 (STRING) (NUMBER) (NUMBER)
check-input #5 () ($? <qry>)
check-input #1 () $?
For a total of 6 methods.
CLIPS> (get-defmethod-list check-input)↵
(check-input 6 check-input 2 check-input 7
 check-input 3 check-input 5 check-input 1)
CLIPS>
```

Note that the methods listed by the *list-defmethods* command are listed in order of precedence. Also the return value of the *get-defmethod-list* function is pairs consisting of a generic function name and a method index.

Defgeneric Commands

Several commands are provided for manipulating defgenerics. The **ppdef-generic** (pretty print defgeneric) command is used to display the text representations of a defgeneric. The **undefgeneric** command is used to delete a defgeneric. The **list-defgenerics** command is used to display the list of defgenerics defined in CLIPS. The **get-defgeneric-list** function returns a multifield value containing the list of defgenerics. The syntax of these commands is:

```
(ppdefgeneric <defgeneric-name>)

(undefgeneric <defgeneric-name>)

(list-defgenerics [<module-name>])

(get-defgeneric-list [<defgeneric-name>])
```

The undefgeneric command deletes not only the specified defgeneric, but all the methods associated with it as the following commands show:

```
CLIPS> (list-defgenerics)↵
check-input
For a total of 1 defgeneric.
CLIPS> (undefgeneric check-input)↵
CLIPS> (list-defgenerics)↵
CLIPS> (list-defmethods)↵
CLIPS>
```

Overloading Functions and Commands

Deffunctions and generic functions can't share a common name, but a generic function can overload a user-defined function. Suppose, for example, you want to provide analagous operations for addition of data types other than numbers. Normally, CLIPS won't allow you to do this:

```
CLIPS> (+ 3 4)↵
7
CLIPS> (+ "red" "blue")↵
[ARGACCES5] Function + expected argument #1 to be
of type integer or float
CLIPS> (+ (create$ a b c) (create$ d e f))↵
[ARGACCES5] Function + expected argument #1 to be
of type integer or float
CLIPS>
```

Trying to add two strings or two multifield values together using the + function generates an error. If we want to implement addition for strings by concatenating them together and addition for multifield values by combining them, we can create this functionality by defining methods that use the *str-cat* and *create$* functions to do this:

```
(defmethod + ((?x LEXEME) (?y LEXEME))
   (str-cat ?x ?y))

(defmethod + ((?x MULTIFIELD) (?y MULTIFIELD))
   (create$ ?x ?y))
```

Once these methods have been defined, we can now add these new data types without generating an error:

```
CLIPS> (+ "red" "blue")↵
"redblue"
CLIPS> (+ (create$ a b c) (create$ d e f))↵
(a b c d e f)
CLIPS>
```

A *list-defmethods* call displays the two new methods that have been defined along with the original + function defined by CLIPS denoted with the SYS1 method index:

```
CLIPS> (list-defmethods +)↵
+ #SYS1 (NUMBER) (NUMBER) ($? NUMBER)
+ #2 (LEXEME) (LEXEME)
+ #3 (MULTIFIELD) (MULTIFIELD)
For a total of 3 methods.
CLIPS>
```

Notice that CLIPS is able to determine the argument types of the system-defined + function when it creates the method signature. In this case, the + function expects two or more numeric arguments.

If you intend to overload a user-defined function, you should do so before defining any constructs that reference that user-defined function. You can do this by either explicitly defining a defgeneric or implicitly defining a defgeneric by defining a defmethod before you make the function reference. Construct references to a user-defined function made before it is overloaded will not use the generic dispatch mechanism and the user-defined function will always be called. Construct references made to a user-defined function made after it is overloaded will use the generic dispatch mechanism.

10.6 PROCEDURAL CONSTRUCTS AND DEFMODULES

In a similar manner to deftemplate constructs, defglobal, deffunction, and defgeneric constructs can be imported and exported by modules. Four of the possible export and import statements discussed in Chapter 9 with relation to deftemplates apply the same behavior to the procedural constructs:

```
(export ?ALL)
(export ?NONE)
(import <module-name> ?ALL)
(import <module-name> ?NONE)
```

The first format will export all exportable constructs from a module; the second format indicates that no constructs are exported; the third format imports all exported constructs from the specified module; and the fourth format imports none of the exported constructs from the specified module.

Each of the defglobal, deffunction, and defgeneric constructs also has associated import/export statements that allow you to specify whether all, none, or a specified set of each construct should be imported/exported:

```
(export defglobal ?ALL)
(export defglobal ?NONE)
(export defglobal <defglobal-name>+)

(export deffunction ?ALL)
(export deffunction ?NONE)
(export deffunction <deffunction-name>+)

(export defgeneric ?ALL)
(export defgeneric ?NONE)
(export defgeneric <defgeneric-name>+)

(import <module-name> defglobal ?ALL)
(import <module-name> defglobal ?NONE)
(import <module-name> defglobal
                      <defglobal-name>+)

(import <module-name> deffunction ?ALL)
(import <module-name> deffunction ?NONE)
(import <module-name> deffunction
                      <deffunction-name>+)

(import <module-name> defgeneric ?ALL)
(import <module-name> defgeneric ?NONE)
(import <module-name> defgeneric
                      <defgeneric-name>+)
```

When importing/exporting specific defglobals, the * character at the beginning and end of the defglobal name should not be included. For example, *water-freezing-point-Fahrenheit* should be used rather than **water-freezing-point-Fahrenheit**. A module that imports a defgeneric construct imports all of its methods as well. It's not possible to import or export specific methods. A module that does not import a defglobal, deffunction, or defgeneric construct from another module can create its own definition of that construct using the same name. Referencing a construct that is not properly exported and imported results in an error. For example:

```
CLIPS> (clear)↵
CLIPS>
(defmodule MAIN
   (export deffunction function-1)
   (export defglobal global-1)
   (export defgeneric generic-1))↵
CLIPS>
(deffunction MAIN::function-1 (?x)
   (+ 1 ?x))↵
CLIPS>
(deffunction MAIN::function-2 (?x)
   (+ 2 ?x))↵
CLIPS>
(defglobal MAIN ?*global-1* = 1
  ?*global-2* = 2)↵
CLIPS>
(defmodule EXAMPLE
   (import MAIN deffunction ?ALL)
   (import MAIN defglobal global-1))↵
CLIPS>
(defglobal EXAMPLE ?*global-2* = 3)↵
CLIPS>
```

The *EXAMPLE* module implicitly imports defglobal *global-1* from the *MAIN* module by using the *?ALL* keyword and explicitly imports deffunction *function-1* from the *MAIN* module by specifying its name. The effects of the import and export statements can be seen by attempting to access each of the constructs from each module:

```
CLIPS> (get-current-module)↵
EXAMPLE
CLIPS> (function-1 1)↵
2
CLIPS> (function-2 1)↵
[EXPRNPSR3] Missing function declaration for
function-2.
CLIPS> ?*global-1*↵
```

```
1
CLIPS> ?*global-2*↵
3
CLIPS> (set-current-module MAIN)↵
EXAMPLE
CLIPS> (function-1 1)↵
2
CLIPS> (function-2 1)↵
3
CLIPS> ?*global-1*↵
1
CLIPS> ?*global-2*↵
2
CLIPS>
```

10.7 USEFUL COMMANDS AND FUNCTIONS

Loading and Saving Facts

The speed of a CLIPS program can be increased by reducing the number of facts in the fact list. One method for reducing the number of facts is to load facts into CLIPS only when they are needed. For example, a program for diagnosing problems with cars might first ask for the make and model of the car and then load information specific for that car. The **load-facts** and **save-facts** functions are provided by CLIPS to allow facts to be loaded from or saved to a file. The syntax of these two functions is:

```
(load-facts <file-name>)

(save-facts <file-name>
            [<save-scope> <deftemplate-names>*])
```

where <save-scope> is defined as:

```
visible | local
```

The *load-facts* function will load in a group of facts stored in the file specified by <file-name>. The facts in the file should be in the standard format of either an ordered or a deftemplate fact. For example, if the file "facts.dat" contained:

```
(data 34)
(data 89)
(data 64)
(data 34)
```

then the command:

```
(load-facts "facts.dat")
```

would load the facts contained in that file.

The *save-facts* function can be used to save facts in the fact list to the file specified by <file-name>. The facts are stored in the format required by the *load-facts* function. If <save-scope> is not specified or if it is specified as **local,** then only those facts corresponding to deftemplates defined in the current module would be saved to the file. If <save-scope> is specified as **visible,** then all facts corresponding to deftemplates that are visible to the current module would be saved to the file. If <save-scope> is specified, one or more deftemplate names may also be specified. In this case, only facts corresponding to the specified deftemplates will be saved (however, the deftemplate names must still satisfy the *local* or *visible* specification).

Both load-facts and save-facts return TRUE if the facts file is successfully opened and then loaded or saved; otherwise, FALSE is returned. It is the programmer's responsibility to ensure that the deftemplates corresponding to deftemplate facts in a facts file are visible to the current module in which the *load-facts* command is being executed.

The System Command

The **system** command allows the execution of operating-system commands from within CLIPS. The syntax of the system command is:

```
(system <expression>+)
```

For example, the following rule will give a directory listing for a specified directory on a machine using the UNIX operating system:

```
(defrule list-directory
(list-directory ?directory)
   =>
   (system "ls " ?directory))
```

For this example the first argument to the *system* command, "ls ", is the UNIX command for listing a directory. Notice that a space is included after the characters. The *system* command simply appends all its arguments together as strings before allowing the operating system to process the command. Any spaces needed for the operating-system command must be included as part of an argument in the *system* command call.

The effects of the *system* command may vary from one operating system to another. Not all operating systems provide the functionality for implementing the *system* command, so you cannot rely on this command being available in CLIPS. The *system* command does not return a value, so it is not possible to directly return a value to CLIPS after executing an operating-system command.

The Batch Command

The **batch** command allows commands and responses that would normally have to be entered at the top-level prompt to be read directly from a file. The syntax of the *batch* command is:

```
(batch <file-name>)
```

For example, suppose the following dialog shows the commands and responses that must be entered to run a CLIPS program (remember that the boldface letters indicate the keys that you enter):

```
CLIPS> (load "rules1.clp")↲
*************
CLIPS> (load "rules2.clp")↲
******************
CLIPS> (load "rules3.clp")↲
**********
CLIPS> (reset)↲
CLIPS> (run)↲
How many iterations? 10↲
Starting value? 1↲
End value? 20↲
Completed
CLIPS>
```

The commands and responses needed to run the program could be stored in a file as shown:

```
(load "rules1.clp")↲
(load "rules2.clp")↲
(load "rules3.clp")↲
(reset)↲
(run)↲
10↲
1↲
20↲
```

If the file with the commands and responses was named "commands.bat", the following dialog shows how the *batch* command can be used (notice again that the boldface letters indicate the keys that you enter):

```
CLIPS> (batch "commands.bat")↲
CLIPS> (load "rules1.clp")↲
*************
CLIPS> (load "rules2.clp")↲
******************
CLIPS> (load "rules3.clp")↲
**********
CLIPS> (reset)↲
CLIPS> (run)↲
How many iterations? 10↲
Starting value? 1↲
End value? 20↲
Completed
CLIPS>
```

Once all the commands and responses have been read from a batch file, keyboard interaction at the top-level prompt is returned to normal.

When run under operating systems that support command-line arguments for executables (such as UNIX), CLIPS can automatically execute commands from a batch file on startup. Assuming that the CLIPS executable can be executed by typing "clips," the syntax for executing a batch file on startup is:

```
clips -f <file-name>
```

Using the -f option is equivalent to entering the command (batch <file-name>) once CLIPS has been started. Calls to the *batch* command can be nested.

The Dribble-on and Dribble-off Commands

The **dribble-on** command can be used to store a record of all output to the terminal and all input from the keyboard. The syntax of the *dribble-on* command is:

```
(dribble-on <file-name>)
```

Once the dribble-on command has been executed, all output sent to the terminal and all input entered at the keyboard will be echoed to the file specified by <file-name>, as well as to the terminal.

The effects of the *dribble-on* command can be turned off with the **dribble-off** command. The syntax of the *dribble-off* command is:

```
(dribble-off)
```

Generating a Random Number

The **random** function generates a random integer value. The syntax of the *random* function is:

```
(random [<start-expression> <end-expression]])
```

where <start-expression> and <end-expression> if specified should be integer values and indicate the range of integers to which the randomly returned integer is limited. For example, the following *roll-die* deffunction uses the random function to simulate the roll of a six-sided die by generating an integer value between 1 and 6:

```
(deffunction roll-die ()
   (random 1 6))
```

Multiple calls to the roll-die deffunction return differing results:

```
CLIPS> (roll-die)↵
6
CLIPS> (roll-die)↵
1
CLIPS> (roll-die)↵
```

```
4
CLIPS> (roll-die)↵
1
CLIPS>
```

The **seed** function can be used to seed the random number generator allowing the values returned to be reproduced by using the same seed at a later point. The syntax of the *seed* function is:

```
(seed <integer-expression>)
```

where <integer-expression> is the seed value. The effect of the *seed* command in reproducing the same random values can be seen in the following series of commands:

```
CLIPS> (seed 30)↵
CLIPS> (roll-die)↵
4
CLIPS> (roll-die)↵
5
CLIPS> (roll-die)↵
3
CLIPS> (seed 30)↵
CLIPS> (roll-die)↵
4
CLIPS> (roll-die)↵
5
CLIPS> (roll-die)↵
3
CLIPS>
```

Converting a String to a Field

The **string-to-field** function can be used to convert a string-field value into a field. The syntax of the *string-to-field* function is:

```
(string-to-field <string-expression>)
```

where <string-expression> is the string field that will be parsed and converted to a field. For example:

```
CLIPS> (string-to-field "7")↵
7
CLIPS> (string-to-field " 3.4 2.1  3")↵
3.4
CLIPS>
```

The first example call to *string-to-field* takes the string field "7.3" and converts it to the integer field value of 7. The second example call to *string-to-field* has several fields contained in the string argument passed into it. The first field found, the floating-point field 3.4, is returned and the remaining fields in the string are discarded. Note that the extra spacing in the string has no effect on the returned value. Essentially calling *string-to-field* is identical to calling the *read* function where the string argument represents what the user types at the keyboard.

Finding a Symbol

The **apropos** command can be used to display all symbols defined in CLIPS that contain a specified substring. The syntax of the *apropos* command is:

```
(apropos <symbol-or-string-expression>)
```

where <symbol-or-string-expression> is the substring being sought. The apropos command is really useful when you want to display a list of functions or commands sharing a common substring or you can remember part but not all of a symbol used in a function, command, or construct. For example, suppose you want a list of all the functions and commands containing the symbol *deftemplate*:

```
CLIPS> (apropos deftemplate)↵
get-deftemplate-list
deftemplate
list-deftemplates
undeftemplate
ppdeftemplate
deftemplate-module
CLIPS>
```

Sorting a List of Fields

The **sort** function can be used for a list of fields. The syntax of the *sort* function is:

```
(sort <comparison-function-name> <expression>*)
```

where <comparison-function-name> is the name of the function, deffunction, or generic function that is used to determine whether two fields need to be swapped during sorting. The remaining arguments denoted by <expression>* can be either single- or multifield values. They are joined together into a single multifield value, which is then sorted. The return value of this function is a sorted multifield value. The following example sorts a list of integers:

```
CLIPS> (sort > 4 3 5 7 2 7)↵
(2 3 4 5 7 7)
CLIPS>
```

The *sort* function isn't limited to sorting numbers. For example, consider the following deffunction:

```
(deffunction string> (?a ?b)
   (> (str-compare ?a ?b) 0))
```

Any comparison function used with the *sort* function should accept two arguments and return TRUE if the first argument should come after the second argument in the sorted list; otherwise it should return FALSE. The *str-compare* function will return a positive integer if the first argument is lexicographically greater than the second argument, so by comparing the return value to 0 using the > function, the *string>* deffunction can be used to lexicographically sort a list of symbols or strings. For example:

```
CLIPS> (sort string> ax aa bk mn ft m)↵
(aa ax bk ft m mn)
CLIPS>
```

The *str-compare* function treats all uppercase letters as being less than all lowercase letters, so if you sort mixed combinations of the two, the result may not be what you expect:

```
CLIPS> (sort string> a C b A B c)↵
(A B C a b c)
CLIPS>
```

As you can see from the output all of the uppercase letters have been sorted before the lowercase letters. The *string>* function can be modified as follows to keep uppercase and lowercase letters together:

```
(deffunction string> (?a ?b)
   (bind ?rv (str-compare (lowcase ?a)
   (lowcase ?b)))
   (if (= ?rv 0)
       then
       (> (str-compare ?a ?b) 0)
       else
       (> ?rv 0)))
```

The strings are first converted to lowercase and then compared. Only if the strings are equal is case considered. This yields the more expected results shown following:

```
CLIPS> (sort string> a C b A B c)↵
(A a B b C c)
CLIPS>
```

One final consideration when using the *sort* function is that the comparison function should return TRUE only if two values need to be swapped. Consider the following call:

```
CLIPS> (sort <> 3 4 5 6)↵
...
```

In this situation the sort function calls the <> function to determine when fields need to be swapped. Since none of the fields are equal, the <> function will always return TRUE and the sort will never complete. Clearly this is a situation you want to avoid.

10.8 SUMMARY

The *if*, *while*, *switch*, *loop-for-count*, *progn$*, and *break* functions can be used for flow of control in a deffunction, generic function, or on the RHS of a rule. Overuse of these functions on the RHS of a rule is considered poor programming style. The *halt* function can be used to halt the execution of rules.

The deffunction construct allows you to define new functions as you can in other procedural languages, but without the need to use a C compiler to recompile the CLIPS source code. Alternatively, CLIPS provides a mechanism described in the *Advanced Programming Guide* that allows you to integrate functions written in C with CLIPS, but this requires using a C compiler to create a new CLIPS executable.

The defglobal construct allows you to define variables, called global variables, that retain their values outside of the scope of constructs. Generic functions, implemented using the defgeneric and defmethod constructs, provide more power and flexibility than deffunctions by allowing you to associate multiple procedural methods with a generic function name. When a generic function is called, the generic dispatch mechanism examines the types of arguments passed to the function and evaluates any associated query restrictions to determine the appropriate method to invoke.

Several utility commands were introduced. The *save-facts* and *load-facts* functions can be used to save facts to and load facts from a file. The *system* command allows operating-system commands to be executed from within CLIPS. The *batch* command allows a series of commands and responses stored in a file to replace normal keyboard input. The *dribble-on* and *dribble-off* commands allow a record of terminal output to be stored in a file. The *random* function can be used to generate a random integer value and the *seed* function is used to seed the random number generator. The *string-to-field* function can be used to parse a field contained within a string. The *apropos* command is used to display all symbols containing a specified substring. The *sort* function can be used to sort a list of fields.

PROBLEMS

10.1 Rewrite the following rule into one or more rules that do not use the *if* and *while* functions. Verify that your rules perform the same actions by comparing the output and final fact list of your rules with this rule.

```
(defrule continue-check
   ?phase <- (phase check-continue)
   =>
   (retract ?phase)
   (printout t "Continue? ")
   (bind ?answer (read))
   (while (and (neq ?answer yes) (neq ?answer no)) do
      (printout t "Continue? ")
      (bind ?answer (read)))
   (if (eq ?answer yes)
      then (assert (phase continue))
      else (assert (phase halt))))
```

10.2 Given an *N* x *N* chessboard, where *N* is an integer, write a program that will place *N* queens on the chessboard such that no queen can capture another. Hint: Develop your program using 4 as the number of rows and columns. This is the smallest number for which there is a solution (with the exception of the trivial case of a 1 x 1 board).

10.3 Modify the program developed for Problem 9.12 on page 558 so that if none of the shrubs meet all requirements, the shrubs meeting the most requirements are listed. The number of requirements satisfied should be printed.

10.4 Modify the program developed for Problem 9.17 on page 560 to use modules. If no matching gem can be found for the specified color, hardness, and density, the program should indicate this. After identifying a gem, the program should provide the user an opportunity to identify another gem.

10.5 Combine the programs developed for Problems 9.14 and 9.15 on pages 558 and 559. The resulting program should have a textual menu interface with menu items for launching an application, terminating an application, and quitting the program. When the launch menu item is selected, the user should be prompted for the name and memory requirements of the application. When the terminate menu item is selected, the user should be prompted for the name of the application to terminate.

10.6 Modify the program developed for Problem 9.15 on page 559 to support submenus. For example:

```
CLIPS> (run)

Select one of the following options:

 1 — Option A
 2 — Option B
 3 — Submenu 1
```

```
 9 — Quit Program
Your choice: 3

Select one of the following options:

 1 — Option C
 2 — Option D
 9 — Previous Menu

Your choice: 9

Select one of the following options:

 1 — Option A
 2 — Option B
 3 — Submenu 1
 9 — Quit Program

Your choice: 9
CLIPS>
```

10.7 Modify the program developed for Problem 9.18 on page 560 to schedule six courses for a single student. The program should attempt to maximize the overall score (as described in Problem 9.18) for all six courses. The input to the program should be six facts indicating the courses to be scheduled, and the output should be the list of scheduled courses in order from period one to six. Test your program with the following course selections:

Course	Instructors Preferred	Periods Preferred	Instructors Not Preferred	Periods Not Preferred
Texas History	Hill	2, 5	—	1, 3
Algebra	Smith	1, 2	Jones	6
Physical Education	—	—	Mack, King	1
Chemistry	Dolby	5, 6	—	—
Literature	—	3, 4	—	1, 6
German	—	—	—	—

10.8 A poker player has just been dealt five cards. Given as input facts representing these five cards, write a program that will print the type of the player's hand: royal flush, straight flush, four-of-a-kind, full house, flush, straight, three-of-a-kind, two pair, one pair, or nothing.

10.9 Write a program that will simplify an algebraic equation by moving all constants to the right side of the equation and all variables to the left side of the equation and then reducing common terms. For example, the equation:

```
2 x + y + 5 + 3 y - 2 z - 8 = 3 z - 4 y + 4
```

can be simplified to:

```
2 x + 8 y - 5 z = 7
```

Since the = symbol has special significance in patterns, you will probably want to represent the equation in a format where the = symbol is implied. For example:

```
(equation (LHS 2 x + y + 5 + 3 y - 2 z - 8)
          (RHS 3 z - 4 y + 4))
```

10.10 Combine the programs developed for Problems 9.19 on page 561 and Problem 10.6 to create a menu-driven interface for the configuration program. The main menu options should allow the user to select a chassis, add gizmos to the configuration, remove gizmos from the configuration, and print the cost of the configuration. Submenus should be used to allow the selection of the chassis and to add or remove gizmos to the configuration. After selecting a chassis or adding or removing a gizmo, warning messages should be printed indicating if there are conflicts between the gizmos and the number of bays and power supplied by the chassis. Control should then return to the main menu. Selecting the menu option to print the configuration should list the chassis and gizmos selected along with their individual prices and the total price of all added together.

10.11 Using the algorithm specified in Section 2.2, write a deffunction that will convert the string "137179766832525156430015" to "GOLD 438+".
Hint: Use the substring and string-to-field functions to extract the numbers from the string and then use the %c flag with the format function to convert the number to a character.

10.12 Write deffunctions that will compute the union and intersection of two multifield values. Note that when computing the union and intersection, duplicate fields should not appear in the return value of the functions.

10.13 Write a deffunction that will compute the experimental probability (as described in Section 4.6) of rolling a one on a six-sided die. The argument to the deffunction should be the number of rolls and the return value should be the empirically determined probability.

10.14 Write a deffunction that determines all of the primes between 1 and a specified integer and returns the primes as a multifield value.

10.15 Write a deffunction that determines the number of occurrences of one string within another string.

10.16 Write a deffunction that compares two files line by line and prints the differences to a specified logical name.

10.17 Write a deffunction that accepts zero or more arguments and returns a multifield value containing the argument values in reverse order.

10.18 Write a deffunction that does not use recursion to compute the factorial of an integer N.

10.19 Write a deffunction that converts a binary string consisting of zeroes and ones to a decimal number.

10.20 Without using the if or switch functions, write a series of methods that will convert measurements between inches, feet, and yards. For example, (convert 3 feet inches) should return 36. Write another series of methods thatwill convert measurements between centimeters, meters, and kilometers.

10.21 Using the methods developed for Problem 10.20, overload the + functions with methods that allow two measurements to be added. The result returned should be in the units of the first measurement to the + method. For example, (+ 3 feet 12 inches) should return 4. Addition between metric and English measurements does not need to be supported.

10.22 Overload the - function with a method that removes the fields contained in one multifield value from another multifield value. For example, (- (create$ a b c d) (create$ b d f)) should return the multifield value (a c).

10.23 Write a method for each of the four cases in the definition of the S-function described in Section 5.5.

10.24 Given the definition of a power set from Problem 2.11 on page 113, write a deffunction that prints each of the sets within the power set of a set represented by a multifield value.

10.25 The number of miles on Jack's car, N, is between 200,000 and 300,000. N has exactly one 0 in its decimal representation. N is a square. The sum of the squares of the decimal digits of N is also a square. Write one or more deffunctions that determine the value of N.

CHAPTER 11

Classes, Instances, and Message-Handlers

11.1 INTRODUCTION

In addition to facts, instances (or objects) are another data representation provided by CLIPS. Instances are created from classes, which are defined using the CLIPS Object-Oriented Language (COOL). Just as the structure of facts is specified using deftemplates, the structure of instances is specified using defclasses. There are several advantages to using instances and classes over using facts and deftemplates. The first is inheritance. A defclass can inherit information from one or more different classes. This allows a more modular definition of data. Second, objects can have procedural information attached to them through the use of message-handlers. Third, pattern matching on objects provides more flexibility than pattern matching on facts. Object patterns can make use of inheritance, can pattern match on slots belonging to multiple classes, can prevent changes to unspecified slots from retriggering a pattern, and can provide truth maintenance based on slots.

11.2 THE DEFCLASS CONSTRUCT

Before instances can be created, CLIPS must be informed of the list of valid slots for a given class. The **defclass** construct is used to do this. Its most basic form is very similar to a deftemplate:

```
(defclass <class-name> [<optional-comment>]
   (is-a <superclass-name>)
   <slot-definition>*)
```

where <superclass-name> is the class from which the newly defined class will inherit information. The system class USER is the class from which all user-defined classes ultimately inherit. A user-defined class will either inherit from another user-defined class or it will inherit from the USER class. The syntax description <slot-definition> is defined as:

```
(slot <slot-name> <slot-attribute>*) |
(multislot <slot-name> <slot-attribute>*)
```

Using this syntax, the *person* instance could be described with the following defclass:

```
(defclass PERSON "Person defclass"
   (is-a USER)
   (slot full-name)
   (slot age)
   (slot eye-color)
   (slot hair-color))
```

Note that unlike the *person* deftemplate used as an example in Section 7.6, the slot name *full-name* has been used rather than *name*. For object pattern matching, *name* is a reserved symbol that has special meaning, which will be discussed later.

The following deftemplate slot attributes can also be used when defining defclass slots: **type**, **range**, **cardinality**, **allowed-symbols**, **allowed-strings**, **allowed-lexemes**, **allowed-integers**, **allowed-floats**, **allowed-numbers**, **allowed-values**, **allowed-instance-names**, **default**, and **default-dynamic**. For example:

```
(defclass PERSON "Person defclass"
   (is-a USER)
   (slot full-name
      (type STRING))
   (slot age
      (type INTEGER)
      (range 0 120))
   (slot eye-color
      (type SYMBOL)
      (allowed-values brown blue green)
      (default brown))
   (slot hair-color
      (type SYMBOL)
      (allowed-values black brown red blonde)
      (default brown)))
```

Slot attributes for defclasses are also referred to as slot facets.

11.3 CREATING INSTANCES

Instances are created using the **make-instance** command. The syntax of the *make-instance* command is:

```
(make-instance [<instance-name-expression>]
               of <class-name-expression>
               <slot-override>*)
```

where <slot-override> is:

```
(<slot-name-expression> <expression>)
```

For example, here's how to create some instances using the *person* defclass:

```
CLIPS>
(make-instance [John] of PERSON
   (full-name "John Q. Public")
   (age 24)
   (eye-color blue)
   (hair-color black))↵
[John]
CLIPS> (make-instance of PERSON)↵
[gen1]
CLIPS> (make-instance Jack of PERSON)↵
[Jack]
CLIPS> (instances)↵
[John] of PERSON
[gen1] of PERSON
[Jack] of PERSON
For a total of 3 instances.
CLIPS>
```

Three instances were created with instance names [John], [gen1], and [Jack]. If you don't supply an instance name when creating an instance, the system will provide one for you (such as [gen1] in this example). It doesn't matter to *make-instance* whether you enclose the instance name with brackets [] or not as the [John] and Jack make-instance calls show. The **instances** command shown in the example is similar to the facts command except it displays the list of instances. Slot values are not displayed by the instances, but the next section shows how this can be done. The complete syntax for the *instances* command is:

```
(instances [<module-name> [<class-name> [inherit]]])
```

Similarly to facts and their corresponding deftemplate, instances belong to the module in which their corresponding defclass is defined (see Section 11.16). If the optional module name argument is specified, then only the instances contained in the specified module are listed. If * is used for the module name, then all instances are listed. If an optional class name is also specified, then only instances belonging to that class are listed. Finally, if the optional *inherit* keyword is also specified, then all instances belonging to subclasses (see Section 11.6) of the specified class name are also listed.

11.4 SYSTEM-DEFINED MESSAGE-HANDLERS

In addition to data, procedural information can also be attached to classes. Such procedures are called message-handlers. In addition to user-defined message-handlers, a number of system-defined message-handlers are automatically created for each class. These message-handlers can be invoked for an instance by using the **send** command. The syntax for the *send* command is:

```
(send <object-expression>
<message-name-expression> <expression>*)
```

For example, the **print** message displays slot information about an instance:

```
CLIPS> (send [John] print)↵
[John] of PERSON
(full-name "John Q. Public")
(age 24)
(eye-color blue)
(hair-color black)
CLIPS>
```

For each slot defined in a defclass, CLIPS automatically defines **get-** and **put-** slot message-handlers that are used to retrieve and set slot values. The actual message-handler names are appended with the name of the slot. So, for example, the PERSON defclass with slots full-name, age, eye–color, and hair-color will automatically have created for it eight message-handlers called get-full-name, put-full-name, get-age, put-age, get-eye-color, put-eye-color, get-hair-color, and put-hair-color. The get-message-handlers have no arguments and return the value of the slot. For example:

```
CLIPS> (send [John] get-full-name)↵
"John Q. Public"
CLIPS> (send [John] get-age)↵
24
CLIPS>
```

The put-message-handlers take zero or more arguments. If no arguments are supplied, the slot is restored to its original default value. One or more supplied arguments will set the slot value to those specified. Attempting to place more than one value in a single-field slot will result in an error. The return value of a put-message-handler is the new value of the slot. For example:

```
CLIPS> (send [Jack] get-age)↵
nil
```

```
CLIPS> (send [Jack] put-age 22)↵
22
CLIPS> (send [Jack] get-age)↵
22
CLIPS> (send [Jack] put-age)↵
nil
CLIPS> (send [Jack] get-age)↵
nil
CLIPS>
```

The *watch* command takes several instance-related watch items. One of these is **slots**. If slots are being watched, then an informational message is printed whenever the value of an instance slot is changed. Watching slot changes can be disabled using the **unwatch** command:

```
CLIPS> (watch slots)↵
CLIPS> (send [Jack] put-age 24)↵
::= local slot age in instance Jack <- 24
24
CLIPS> (unwatch slots)↵
CLIPS> (send [Jack] put-age 22)↵
22
CLIPS>
```

Another predefined message-handler is **delete**. As you might suspect, the delete message-handler is used to delete an instance. It returns the symbol TRUE if the instance was successfully deleted, otherwise the symbol FALSE:

```
CLIPS> (instances)↵
[John] of PERSON
[gen1] of PERSON
[Jack] of PERSON
For a total of 3 instances.
CLIPS> (send [gen1] delete)↵
TRUE
CLIPS> (instances)↵
[John] of PERSON
[Jack] of PERSON
For a total of 2 instances.
CLIPS>
```

Another watch item is **instances**. If instances are being watched, CLIPS will automatically print a message whenever an instance is created or deleted. Unlike modifying a fact slot value, changing an instance slot value does not create a new instance with the changed value and delete the original instance, so to see slot changes for instances you must use the *slots* watch item. The following command dialog illustrates the use of the instances watch item:

```
CLIPS> (watch instances)↵
CLIPS> (make-instance Jill of PERSON)↵
⇒ instance [Jill] of PERSON
[Jill]
CLIPS> (send [Jill] put-age 22)↵
22
CLIPS> (send [Jill] delete)↵
⇐ instance [Jill] of PERSON
TRUE
CLIPS> (unwatch instances)↵
CLIPS>
```

The character sequence ⇐ indicates that an instance is being deleted and the character sequence ⇒ indicates that an instance is being created.

11.5 THE DEFINSTANCES CONSTRUCT

The instance equivalent of the deffacts construct is the **definstances** construct. When a reset command is issued, all instances are sent a *delete* message and then all instances found in definstances constructs are created. The general format of a definstances is:

```
(definstances <definstances name> [active]
   [<optional comment>]
   <instance-definition>*)
```

where <instance-definition> is:

```
([<instance-name-expression>] of
   <class-name-expression>
   <slot-override>*)
```

The optional **active** keyword in the definstances construct is used to indicate that pattern matching should occur as the slot overrides are processed during instance creation. By default, pattern matching does not occur for definstance instances until all the slot overrides have been processed. Here is an example of definstances:

```
(definstances people
   (Jack of PERSON (full-name "Jack Q. Public")
               (age 23))
   (of PERSON (full-name "John Doe")
               (hair-color black)))
```

Several commands are provided for manipulating definstances. The **list-definstances** command is used to display the current list of definstances maintained by CLIPS. The **ppdefinstances** (pretty print definstances) command is used to display the text representations of a definstances. The **undefinstances** command is used to delete a definstances. The **get-definstances-list** function returns a multifield value containing the list of definstances. The syntax of these commands is:

```
(list-definstances [<module-name>])

(ppdefinstances <definstances-name>)

(undefrule <defrule-name>)

(get-definstances-list [<module-name>])
```

11.6 CLASSES AND INHERITANCE

One of the benefits of using COOL is that classes can inherit information from other classes, which allows information to be shared. Consider what must be done if we have a deftemplate that represents information about people:

```
(deftemplate person "Person deftemplate"
   (slot full-name)
   (slot age)
   (slot eye-color)
   (slot hair-color))
```

What must be done in order to represent additional information relevant to someone who is an employee of a company and someone who is a student at a university? One approach would be to extend the people deftemplate to include other information:

```
(deftemplate person "Person deftemplate"
   (slot full-name)
   (slot age)
   (slot eye-color)
   (slot hair-color)
   (slot job-position)
   (slot employer)
   (slot salary)
   (slot university)
   (slot major)
   (slot GPA))
```

Only four of the slots in this deftemplate would apply to all people: *full-name*, *age*, *eye-color*, and *hair–color*. The *job-position*, *employer*, and *salary* slots would apply only to employees. The *university*, *major*, and *GPA* slots would apply only to students. As we add more information about people, we would have to add more slots to the *person* deftemplate and many of these slots would be inapplicable for all people.

Another approach would be to create separate deftemplates for employees and students:

```
(deftemplate employee "Employee deftemplate"
   (slot full-name)
   (slot age)
   (slot eye-color)
   (slot hair-color)
   (slot job-position)
   (slot employer)
   (slot salary))

(deftemplate student "Student deftemplate"
   (slot full-name)
   (slot age)
   (slot eye-color)
   (slot hair-color)
   (slot university)
   (slot major)
   (slot GPA))
```

With this approach, each deftemplate contains only the necessary information, but we have to duplicate several of the slots. If we need to change the attributes of one of these duplicated slots, we have to change it in multiple locations if we want it to remain consistent. Also, if you want to write a rule that looks for anyone with blue eyes, you have to use two patterns instead of one (three if you also want to include *person* facts):

```
(defrule find-blue-eyes
   (or (employee (full-name ?name)
                 (eye-color blue))
       (student (full-name ?name)
                (eye-color blue)))
   =>
   (printout t ?full-name "has blue eyes." crlf))
```

Classes allow us to share common information among multiple classes without duplication of information or inclusion of unnecessary information. Let's return to our original PERSON defclass:

```
(defclass PERSON "Person defclass"
   (is-a USER)
   (slot full-name)
```

```
   (slot age)
   (slot eye-color)
   (slot hair-color))
```

To define new classes that extend the definition of the PERSON class, we just use the PERSON class in the is-a attribute of the new class. For example:

```
(defclass EMPLOYEE "Employee defclass"
   (is-a PERSON)
   (slot job-position)
   (slot employer)
   (slot salary))

(defclass STUDENT "Student defclass"
   (is-a PERSON)
   (slot university)
   (slot major)
   (slot GPA))
```

Both the EMPLOYEE and STUDENT classes inherit the attributes of the PERSON class. The following dialog illustrates the creation of instances for each of these three classes:

```
CLIPS> (make-instance [John] of PERSON)↵
[John]
CLIPS> (make-instance [Jack] of EMPLOYEE)↵
[Jack]
CLIPS> (make-instance [Jill] of STUDENT)↵
[Jill]
CLIPS> (send [John] print)↵
[John] of PERSON
(full-name nil)
(age nil)
(eye-color nil)
(hair-color nil)
CLIPS> (send [Jack] print)↵
[Jack] of EMPLOYEE
(full-name nil)
(age nil)
(eye-color nil)
(hair-color nil)
(job-position nil)
(employer nil)
(salary nil)
CLIPS> (send [Jill] print)↵
[Jill] of STUDENT
(full-name nil)
```

```
(age nil)
(eye-color nil)
(hair-color nil)
(university nil)
(major nil)
(GPA nil)
CLIPS>
```

Notice that each instance contains slots applicable only for its class. It's possible for a class to redefine a slot that was already defined by one of its superclasses as the next subsection discusses.

A class that inherits either directly or indirectly from another class is a **subclass** of the inherited class. The inherited class is referred to as the **superclass** of the inheriting class. PERSON, EMPLOYEE, and STUDENT are subclasses of USER. EMPLOYEE and STUDENT are subclasses of PERSON. USER is a superclass of PERSON, EMPLOYEE, and STUDENT. PERSON is a superclass of EMPLOYEE and STUDENT. A single-inheritance class hierarchy is one in which each class has only one direct superclass. A multiple-inheritance hierarchy is one in which a class may have more than one direct superclass. COOL supports multiple inheritance but we will limit ourselves to single-inheritance examples until Section 11.15 where multiple inheritance will be explained in further detail. The following is an example of a class using multiple inheritance (a student who also has a job):

```
(defclass WORKING-STUDENT
"Working Student defclass"
(is-a STUDENT EMPLOYEE))
```

Resolving Conflicting Slot Definitions

By default if a subclass redefines a slot, then instances of that class exclusively use the slot attributes from the new definition. For example, given the following classes,

```
(defclass A
   (is-a USER)
   (slot x (default 3))
   (slot y)
   (slot z (default 4)))

(defclass B
   (is-a A)
   (slot x)
   (slot y (default 5))
   (slot z (default 6)))
```

creating instances of classes *A* and *B* produces the following results:

```
CLIPS> (make-instance [a] of A)↵
[a]
```

```
CLIPS> (make-instance [b] of B)↵
[b]
CLIPS> (send [a] print)↵
[a] of A
(x 3)
(y nil)
(z 4)
CLIPS> (send [b] print)↵
[b] of B
(x nil)
(y 5)
(z 6)
CLIPS>
```

Note that slot *x* of instance *b* is given a default value of *nil* instead of 3. This is because the absence of a default value for slot *x* of class *B* completely overrides the default of 3 given to slot *x* in class *A*. The **source** slot attribute can be used to allow slot attributes to be inherited from superclasses. If this attribute is set to **exclusive**, which is the default, then attributes for a slot are determined by the most specific class defining the slot. In a single-inheritance hierarchy, this will be the class having the fewest superclasses. If the *source* attribute is set to **composite**, then attributes that are not explicitly defined in the most specific class defining the slot are taken from the next most specific class that defines the attribute. For example, if the prior A and B defclasses are redefined as follows:

```
(defclass A
   (is-a USER)
   (slot x (default 3))
   (slot y)
   (slot z (default 4)))

(defclass B
   (is-a A)
   (slot x (source composite))
   (slot y (default 5))
   (slot z (default 6)))
```

then creating an instance of classes *A* and *B* produces the following results:

```
CLIPS> (make-instance [a] of A)↵
[a]
CLIPS> (make-instance [b] of B)↵
[b]
CLIPS> (send [a] print)↵
[a] of A
(x 3)
```

```
(y nil)
(z 4)
CLIPS> (send [b] print)↵
[b] of B
(x 3)
(y 5)
(z 6)
CLIPS>
```

Now that slot *x* of class *B* is defined with the *source* attribute set to *composite*, it can inherit the default attribute of class *A* and the default resulting value for the *x* slot of the instance *b* is set to 3.

It's also possible to disable the inheritance of a slot using the **propagation** slot attribute. If this attribute is set to **inherit**, which is the default, then the slot will be inherited by subclasses. If this attribute is set to **no-inherit**, then the slot will not be inherited by subclasses. For example, defining classes *A* and *B* as follows:

```
(defclass A
   (is-a USER)
   (slot x (propagation no-inherit))
   (slot y))

(defclass B
   (is-a A)
   (slot z))
```

then creating an instance of classes *A* and *B* produces the following result:

```
CLIPS> (make-instance [a] of A)↵
[a]
CLIPS> (make-instance [b] of B)↵
[b]
CLIPS> (send [a] print)↵
[a] of A
(x nil)
(y nil)
CLIPS> (send [b] print)↵
[b] of B
(y nil)
(z nil)
CLIPS>
```

Instance *b* of class *B* inherits slot *y* from class *A*, but it does not inherit slot *x* from class *A* because its *propagation* attribute is *no-inherit*.

Abstract and Concrete Classes

It's possible to define classes that can be used only for inheritance. Such classes are called **abstract** classes. It's not possible to create instances of *abstract* classes. By default, classes are **concrete**. The **role** class attribute is used to specify whether a class is *abstract* or *concrete*. The *role* class attribute must be specified after the *is-a* class attribute but before any slot definitions. For example:

```
(defclass ANIMAL
   (is-a USER)
   (role abstract))

(defclass MAMMAL
   (is-a ANIMAL)
   (role abstract))

(defclass CAT
   (is-a MAMMAL)
   (role concrete))

(defclass DOG
   (is-a MAMMAL)
   (role concrete))
```

Classes *ANIMAL* and *MAMMAL* are abstract. Classes *CAT* and *DOG* are *concrete*. The *role* attribute is inherited, so while it was not necessary to declare *MAMMAL* as abstract because it inherits this attribute from *ANIMAL*, it was necessary to declare the *CAT* and *DOG* classes as *concrete* since they would otherwise be *abstract*. Attempting to create an instance of an *abstract* class will generate an error message:

```
CLIPS> (make-instance [animal-1] of ANIMAL)↵
[INSMNGR3] Cannot create instances of abstract
class ANIMAL.
CLIPS> (make-instance [cat-1] of CAT)↵
[cat-1]
CLIPS>
```

It's never necessary to declare a class *abstract*, but doing so when appropriate makes the code more maintainable and easier to reuse. You simply don't want someone using a class to create instances if the class was not intended for that purpose. If someone were to use that class, you would be prevented in future implementations from removing it without breaking existing code.

In our current example, the argument can be made either way as to whether the *ANIMAL* and *MAMMAL* classes should be *abstract*. If we're going to create an inventory of animals in a zoo, then these classes should probably be *abstract*. There are no existing animals or mammals that are just that and not a member of a more specific class. However, if we're trying to identify an animal it's conceivable that we might want to create instances of the *ANIMAL* or *MAMMAL* class, for example, to indicate what we've been able to determine about the animal.

Defclass Commands

Several commands are provided for manipulating defclasses. The **list-defclasses** command is used to display the current list of defclasses maintained by CLIPS. Its syntax is:

```
(list-defclasses [<module-name>])
```

It's worthwhile taking a look at the output from this function:

```
CLIPS> (list-defclasses)↵
FLOAT
INTEGER
SYMBOL
STRING
MULTIFIELD
EXTERNAL-ADDRESS
FACT-ADDRESS
INSTANCE-ADDRESS
INSTANCE-NAME
OBJECT
PRIMITIVE
NUMBER
LEXEME
ADDRESS
INSTANCE
USER
INITIAL-OBJECT
PERSON
EMPLOYEE
STUDENT
For a total of 20 defclasses.
CLIPS>
```

There are a number of predefined primitive classes: OBJECT, PRIMITIVE, NUMBER, LEXEME, FLOAT, INTEGER, SYMBOL, STRING, MULTIFIELD, ADDRESS, INSTANCE, EXTERNAL-ADDRESS, FACT-ADDRESS, INSTANCE-ADDRESS, and INSTANCE–NAME. You can't use these classes to create other classes. The primitive classes are primarily useful with generic functions, which were discussed in Chapter 10. The remaining predefined classes are USER and INITIAL-OBJECT. USER is the base for creating new classes. INITIAL-OBJECT is a subclass of USER and is used to create the initial-object instance (see Section 11.7). The classes we created (PERSON, EMPLOYEE, and STUDENT) complete the list. Figure 11.1 shows the predefined class hierarchy.

Figure 11.1 Predefined Classes Overview

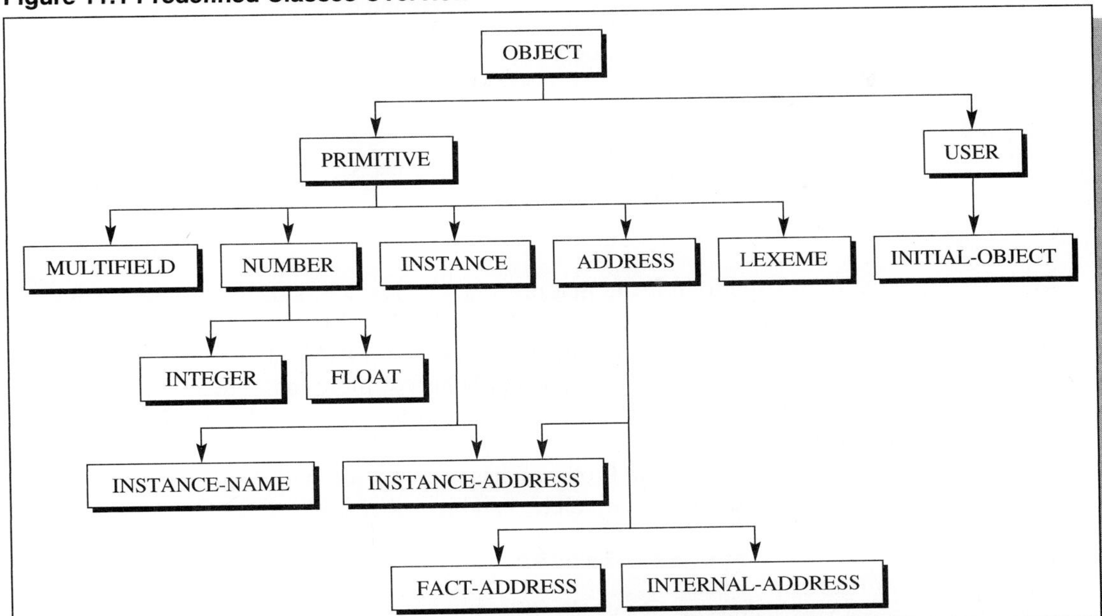

The **browse-classes** command is used to display the inheritance relationships between a class and its subclasses. Its syntax is:

```
(browse-classes [<class-name>])
```

If no class name is specified, the inheritance relationships for the root class OBJECT are displayed. For example, the following command displays the information contained in Figure 11.1 along with PERSON classes and subclasses used as examples:

```
CLIPS> (browse-classes)↵
OBJECT
  PRIMITIVE
    NUMBER
      INTEGER
      FLOAT
    LEXEME
      SYMBOL
      STRING
    MULTIFIELD
    ADDRESS
      EXTERNAL-ADDRESS
      FACT-ADDRESS
      INSTANCE-ADDRESS *
```

```
        INSTANCE
          INSTANCE-ADDRESS *
          INSTANCE-NAME
      USER
        INITIAL-OBJECT
        PERSON
          EMPLOYEE
          STUDENT
    CLIPS>
```

Indentation is used to indicate that one class is a subclass of the first preceding class with less indentation. For example, NUMBER, LEXEME, MULTIFIELD, ADDRESSS, and INSTANCE are all subclasses of PRIMITIVE. An asterisk before a class indicates that it is a direct subclass of more than one class. For example, INSTANCE-ADDRESS is a direct subclass of both ADDRESS and INSTANCE.

Specifying a class in the browse-classes command will display inheritance information only for the specified class and its subclasses:

```
CLIPS> (browse-classes PERSON)↵
PERSON
  EMPLOYEE
  STUDENT
CLIPS>
```

The **ppdefclass** (pretty print defclass) command is used to display the text representation of a defclass. The **undefclass** command is used to delete a defclass. The syntax of these commands is:

```
(ppdefclass <defclass-name>)

(undefclass <defclass-name>)
```

You can't delete a defclass while instances of that class exist. Any instance belonging to that class or any subclass of that class must be deleted before the class can be removed. For example:

```
CLIPS> (undefclass STUDENT)↵
[PRNTUTIL4] Unable to delete defclass STUDENT.
CLIPS> (send [Jill] delete)↵
TRUE
CLIPS> (undefclass STUDENT)↵
CLIPS>
```

11.7 OBJECT PATTERN MATCHING

Object patterns provide several capabilities that are not available with deftemplate or ordered fact patterns. First, a single object pattern can match instances from several classes. Second, changes to slot values that are not specified in an object pattern do not retrigger the rule to which the pattern belongs. Third, changes to slot values that are not specified in an object pattern within a *logical* conditional element do not remove logical support provided by the associated rule. The general form of an object pattern is:

```
(object <attribute-constraint>*)
```

where <attribute-constraint> is:

```
(is-a <constraint>) |
(name <constraint>) |
(<slot-name> <constraint>*)
```

and <constraint> is the same as the pattern slot constraints that are used in deftemplate patterns. The significance of the *is-a* and *name* keywords will be discussed shortly. Let's first start with a simple example of object pattern matching:

```
CLIPS> (clear)↵
CLIPS>
(defclass 1D-POINT
   (is-a USER)
   (slot x))↵
CLIPS>
(defrule Example-1
   (object (x ?x))
   =>
   (printout t "Value of x slot is " ?x crlf))↵
CLIPS> (make-instance p1 of 1D-POINT (x 3))↵
[p1]
CLIPS> (agenda)↵
0      Example-1: [p1]
For a total of 1 activation.
CLIPS> (run)↵
Value of x slot is 3
CLIPS>
```

First, we define the class *1D-POINT* with the single attribute *x*. The defrule *Example-1* is then defined. Note that this rule matches only on the slot *x*, it makes no mention of the *1D-POINT* class. When the rule is created, CLIPS automatically determines that the *1D-POINT* class is capable of matching the pattern. After creating an instance of the *1D-POINT* class, the *Example-1* rule has been appropriately activated and running the program provides the correct output of the value of the *x* slot of the instance.

Let's look at what happens if we define another class containing an *x* slot:

```
CLIPS>
(defclass 2D-POINT
```

```
      (is-a USER)
      (slot x)
      (slot y))↵
CLIPS> (make-instance p2 of 2D-POINT (x 4) (y 2))↵
[p2]
CLIPS> (agenda)↵
CLIPS>
```

Perhaps unexpectedly, the *Example-1* rule is not activated by the instance [p2]. This is because the determination of whether a class can match an object pattern is made when the rule is defined. Instances of classes defined after the rule is defined will not match object patterns used by the rule. If the *Example-1* rule is redefined, we'll see the behavior we were originally expecting:

```
CLIPS>
(defrule Example-1
   (object (x ?x))
   =>
   (printout t "Value of x slot is " ?x crlf))↵
CLIPS> (agenda)↵
0      Example-1: [p2]
0      Example-1: [p1]
For a total of 2 activations.
CLIPS> (run)↵
Value of x slot is 4
Value of x slot is 3
CLIPS>
```

Note that the Example-1 rule is now activated for both the [p1] and [p2] instances containing *x* slots from different classes.

Object Pattern Matching and Inheritance

Object patterns can also match on inherited slots:

```
CLIPS> (clear)↵
CLIPS>
(defclass 1D-POINT
   (is-a USER)
   (slot x))↵
CLIPS>
(defclass 2D-POINT
   (is-a 1D-POINT)
   (slot y))↵
CLIPS>
(defclass 3D-POINT
   (is-a 2D-POINT)
   (slot z))↵
```

```
CLIPS>
(defrule Example-2
   (object (y ?y))
   =>
   (printout t "Value of y slot is " ?y crlf))↵
CLIPS> (make-instance p1 of 1D-POINT (x 3))↵
[p1]
CLIPS> (make-instance p2 of 2D-POINT (x 1) (y 2))↵
[p2]
CLIPS> (make-instance p3 of 3D-POINT (x 2) (y 4) (z 3))↵
[p3]
CLIPS> (agenda)↵
0      Example-2: [p3]
0      Example-2: [p2]
For a total of 2 activations.
CLIPS> (run)↵
Value of y slot is 4
Value of y slot is 2
CLIPS>
```

Note that the *Example-2* rule is activated by instances [p2] and [p3], but not [p1]. Instances [p2] is an instance of class *2D–POINT,* which defines a *y* slot that is referenced by the rule. Instance [p3] is a member of class *3D-POINT,* which inherits the y slot from class *2D-POINT*. Instance [p1] of class *1D-POINT* has only an *x* slot, so it cannot match the object pattern from rule *Example-2*.

Is-a and Name Keywords

The **is-a** keyword when used like a slot name has special significance when used in an object pattern. It restricts the instances matching the pattern to those classes satisfying the *is-a* constraint. For example:

```
CLIPS>
(defrule Example-3
   (object (is-a 2D-POINT) (x ?x))
   =>
   (printout t "Value of x slot is " ?x crlf))↵
CLIPS> (agenda)↵
0      Example-3: [p3]
0      Example-3: [p2]
For a total of 2 activations.
CLIPS> (run)↵
Value of x slot is 2
Value of x slot is 1
CLIPS>
```

Note that only instances [p2] and [p3] activate the *Example-3* rule even though instance [p1] also has an *x* slot attribute. This is because [p1] is not an instance of or inherits from the *2D-POINT* class. Instance [p3], however, does satisfy the object pattern since it is a member of the 2D-POINT class through inheritance. Instance [p3] could be prevented from matching the object pattern by explicitly disallowing the *3D-POINT* class:

```
CLIPS>
(defrule example-4
   (object (is-a 2D-POINT&~3D-POINT) (x ?x))
   =>
   (printout t "Value of x slot is " ?x crlf))↵
CLIPS> (agenda)↵
0      example-4: [p2]
For a total of 1 activation.
CLIPS> (run)↵
Value of x slot is 1
CLIPS>
```

Any class referenced by the object pattern must already be defined; otherwise an error will result:

```
CLIPS>
(defrule example-5
   (object (is-a 4D-POINT) (x ?x))
   =>
   (printout t "Value of x slot is " ?x crlf))↵
[OBJRTBLD5] Undefined class in object pattern.

ERROR:
(defrule MAIN::example-5
   (object (is-a 4D-POINT)
CLIPS>
```

The same also holds true for slots referenced by an object pattern. There must be at least one class that contains all of the slot attributes referenced in the object pattern or an error will result:

```
CLIPS>
(defrule example-6
   (object (w ?w))
   =>
   (printout t "Value of w slot is " ?w crlf))↵
[OBJRTBLD2] No objects of existing classes can
satisfy w restriction in object pattern.
```

```
ERROR:
(defrule MAIN::example-6
   (object (w
CLIPS>
```

Since none of the existing classes (*1D-POINT*, *2D-POINT*, and *3D-POINT*) have a *w* slot attribute, the object pattern in rule *Example-6* cannot be satisfied and so an error is generated.

The **name** keyword can be used to match specific instances. For example:

```
CLIPS>
(defrule example-7
   (object (name [p1] | [p3]) (x ?x))
   =>
   (printout t "Value of x slot is " ?x crlf))↵
CLIPS> (agenda)↵
0      example-7: [p3]
0      example-7: [p1]
For a total of 2 activations.
CLIPS> (run)↵
Value of x slot is 2
Value of x slot is 3
CLIPS>
```

Rule *Example-7* uses the *name* keyword to restrict the instances that can match the object pattern to instances [p1] and [p3]. The instance [p2], which has an *x* slot value, will not match the pattern since its name will not satisfy the name restriction. Because of their special significance in an object pattern, the *is-a* and *name* keywords cannot be used as slot names in a defclass definition.

Triggering Object Patterns

One very important difference between object patterns and fact patterns is that only those object patterns that explicitly match on a slot are affected when the slot value of an instance is changed. To illustrate this point, let's revisit the initial-attempt of the sum-rectangles rule from Section 8.10:

```
(defrule sum-rectangles
   (rectangle (height ?height) (width ?width))
   ?sum <- (sum ?total)
   =>
   (retract ?sum)
   (assert (sum (+ ?total (* ?height ?width)))))
```

The problem with this rule is that any attempt to modify the *sum* fact causes the rule to be retriggered for the *rectangle* fact just processed, causing an infinite loop. Converting the *sum* fact from an ordered fact to a deftemplate fact and using the *modify* command will not solve the problem. The solution proposed in Section 8.4 uses multiple rules to compute the sum. A better solution is to make use of object patterns in an appropriate manner. Here's an initial attempt to rewrite the sum-rectangles code from Section 8.4 to use objects:

```
(defclass RECTANGLE
   (is-a USER)
   (slot height)
   (slot width))

(defclass SUM
   (is-a USER)
   (slot total))

(definstances initial-information
   (of RECTANGLE (height 10) (width 6))
   (of RECTANGLE (height 7) (width 5))
   (of RECTANGLE (height 6) (width 8))
   (of RECTANGLE (height 2) (width 5))
   ([sum] of SUM (total 0)))

(defrule sum-rectangles
(object (is-a RECTANGLE)
     (height ?height) (width ?width))
?sum <- (object (is-a SUM) (total ?total))
 =>
(send ?sum put-total
  (+ ?total (* ?height ?width))))
```

There are several things to note about the new *sum-rectangles* rule. First, just as with fact patterns we can bind the instance matching a pattern to a variable using the <- pattern-binding operator. In this case the instance address matching the SUM object pattern is bound to the ?sum variable. This variable can then be used as an argument to the *send* function to send messages to instances. Running this code, however, demonstrates the same problem that we had with fact patterns: an infinite loop. This is because changing the value of the *total* slot from the RHS of the rule using the *put-total* message retriggers the *SUM* object pattern because it matches on the *total* slot.

We don't have to match on the *total* slot on the LHS of the rule since the value bound to ?total is never referenced again in any LHS patterns. Retrieving the value by message passing on the RHS of the rule yields the following rule:

```
(defrule sum-rectangles
   (object (is-a RECTANGLE)
        (height ?height) (width ?width))
   ?sum <- (object (is-a SUM))
```

```
   =>
   (bind ?total (send ?sum get-total))
   (send ?sum put-total
      (+ ?total (* ?height ?width))))
```

This version of the rule won't infinitely loop like the initial version. If we know that there will be only one instance of the *SUM* class, we can take the process one step further to simplify the rule:

```
(defrule sum-rectangles
   (object (is-a RECTANGLE)
        (height ?height) (width ?width))
   =>
   (bind ?total (send [sum] get-total))
   (send [sum] put-total
     (+ ?total (* ?height ?width))))
```

Rather than pattern matching to retrieve the instance address of the [sum] instance in the ?sum variable, we can simply reference the instance by name on the RHS of the rule.

The Pattern-Matching Attribute

It's possible to indicate that either a slot or a class cannot participate in pattern matching using the **pattern-match** attribute. If this attribute is set to **reactive**, which is the default, then the specified slot or class will be able to trigger pattern matching on the LHS of a rule. If the attribute is set to **non-reactive**, then the specified slot or class will not trigger pattern matching on the LHS of a rule. For example, if the SUM class were redefined to use the *pattern-match* attribute and the original *sum-rectangles* rule were used as follows:

```
(defclass SUM
   (is-a USER)
   (slot total (pattern-match non-reactive)))

(defrule sum-rectangles
   (object (is-a RECTANGLE)
        (height ?height) (width ?width))
   ?sum <- (object (is-a SUM) (total ?total))
   =>
   (send ?sum put-total
     (+ ?total (* ?height ?width))))
```

then the following error message would occur when defining the *sum-rectangles* rule:

```
[OBJRTBLD2] No objects of existing classes can
satisfy total restriction in object pattern.
```

Basically, since the *is-a* condition in the second pattern restricts the possible classes to *SUM* and this class doesn't have a *total* slot available for pattern matching, it isn't possible to match this pattern and so the rule generates an error. It's possible to have multiple classes with a slot of the same name, some of which are reactive and others non-reactive. When the rule is defined it's determined which classes could possibly match and the classes having non-reactive slots that are referenced in the pattern are discarded from consideration.

It's also possible to use the pattern-match attribute at the class level. For example:

```
(defclass SUM
   (is-a USER)
   (pattern-match non-reactive)
   (slot total))
```

The *pattern-match* class attribute must be specified after the *is-a* and *role* class attributes but before any slot definitions. If a class is declared to be non-reactive, then instances of that class won't match any patterns (regardless of individual slot *pattern-match* attribute settings), but instances of subclasses can match patterns if the *pattern-match* class attribute is redefined to be *reactive*. Since the class *pattern-match* attribute doesn't explicitly affect the slot *pattern-match* attribute, a class can inherit *reactive* slots from a *non-reactive* class.

Object Patterns and the Logical Conditional Element

Object patterns and instance creation can be used in conjunction with the *logical* conditional element just as facts and fact patterns can. Changes in instance slots do not affect the logical support for a fact or instance if the slot was not referenced in an object pattern within the *logical* conditional element. For example, consider the following constructs using deftemplate patterns:

```
(deftemplate emergency
   (slot type)
   (slot location))

(deftemplate response-team
   (slot name)
   (slot location))

(defrule create-response-team
   (logical (emergency (location ?location)))
   =>
   (assert (response-team (name first-response)
                          (location ?location))))
```

If the constructs are loaded and an *emergency* fact is asserted, the *create-response-team* rule will create a *response-team* fact when the program is run:

```
CLIPS> (reset)↵
CLIPS> (watch facts)↵
CLIPS>
(assert (emergency (type unknown)
                   (location building-1)))↵
==> f-1     (emergency (type unknown)
                      (location building-1))
<Fact-1>
CLIPS> (run)↵
==> f-2     (response-team (name first-response)
                          (location building-1))
CLIPS>
```

Modifying the *emergency* fact causes the *response-team* fact to be retracted even though the *type* slot is not accessed by the *create-response-team* rule:

```
CLIPS> (modify 1 (type fire))↵
<== f-1     (emergency (type unknown)
               (location building-1))
<== f-2     (response-team (name first-response)
                          (location building-1))
==> f-3     (emergency (type fire)
                      (location building-1))
<Fact-3>
CLIPS>
```

The *create-response-team* rule needs to fire again in order to recreate the *response-team* fact:

```
CLIPS> (run)↵
==> f-4     (response-team (name first-response)
                          (location building-1))
CLIPS>
```

The following is the same program using defclasses and objects. Note that we removed the *name* slot used in *response-team* deftemplate since this has special significance to object patterns. The RESPONSE–TEAM instance is just given the name that would have been placed in the *response-team* deftemplate *name* slot:

```
(defclass EMERGENCY
   (is-a USER)
   (slot type)
   (slot location))
```

```
(defclass RESPONSE-TEAM
   (is-a USER)
   (slot location))

(defrule create-response-team
   (logical (object (is-a EMERGENCY)
                    (location ?location)))
   =>
   (make-instance first-response of RESPONSE-TEAM
      (location ?location)))
```

Interacting with these new constructs, we can see that the initial behavior is similar to using facts:

```
CLIPS> (reset)↵
CLIPS> (watch instances)↵
CLIPS>
(make-instance e1 of EMERGENCY
(type unknown) (location building-1))↵
==> instance [e1] of EMERGENCY
[e1]
CLIPS> (send [e1] print)↵
[e1] of EMERGENCY
(type unknown)
(location building-1)
CLIPS> (run)↵
==> instance [first-response] of RESPONSE-TEAM
CLIPS>
```

The [first-response] instance is created by running the program after the [e1] instance is created. These instances are analogous to the *emergency* and *response-team* deftemplates created in the fact example.

Changing the type of the [e1] instance from *unknown* to *fire*, however, does not cause the deletion and creation of another [first-response] instance:

```
CLIPS> (send [e1] put-type fire)↵
fire
CLIPS> (send [e1] print)↵
[e1] of EMERGENCY
(type fire)
(location building-1)
CLIPS>
```

Because the [first-response] instance isn't deleted and the *create–response-team* rule executed again to recreate it, the use of object patterns and instances is more efficient for this example that the use of facts and fact patterns.

Since the location slot is explicitly matched against in the *create–response-team* rule object pattern, changing this slot value will produce behavior analogous to using facts:

```
CLIPS> (send [e1] put-location building-2)↵
<== instance [first-response] of RESPONSE-TEAM
building-2
CLIPS> (run)↵
==> instance [first-response] of RESPONSE-TEAM
CLIPS>
```

The Initial-Object Pattern

As discussed in Sections 7.11 and 8.15, under some circumstances CLIPS will add an *initial-fact* pattern to the LHS of a rule. When using object pattern in a rule, however, CLIPS will under some circumstances use the *initial-object* pattern instead. The object equivalents of the *initial-fact* deftemplate and the *initial-fact* deffacts discussed in Section 7.10 are the INITIAL-OBJECT defclass and the *initial-object* definstances:

```
(defclass INITIAL-OBJECT
   (is-a USER))

(definstances initial-object
   (initial-object of INITIAL-OBJECT))
```

If an *initial-fact/initial-object* pattern needs to be added at some position in a rule, an *initial-fact* pattern is added if the pattern preceding the insertion position is a fact pattern, otherwise if the pattern preceding the insertion point is an object pattern, then an *initial-object* pattern is inserted. If there is no pattern preceding the insertion point, then the pattern succeeding the insertion point is used to determine the type of pattern being added. The following format is used for the *initial-object* pattern:

```
(object (is-a INITIAL-OBJECT)
    (name [initial-object]))
```

Using these new rules for pattern addition, the defrule:

```
(defrule no-emergencies
   (not (object (is-a EMERGENCY)))
   =>
   (printout t "No emergencies" crlf))
```

would be converted to:

```
(defrule no-emergencies
   (object (is-a INITIAL-OBJECT)
           (name [initial-object]))
```

```
(not (object (is-a EMERGENCY)))
=>
(printout t "No emergencies" crlf))
```

since there are no patterns preceding the *not* conditional element, but the pattern succeeding the *not* conditional element is an object pattern.

11.8 USER-DEFINED MESSAGE-HANDLERS

In addition to the *print*, *delete*, *put-*, and *get-* system-defined message-handlers COOL automatically defines for each class, you can also define your own message-handlers. The **defmessage-handler** construct is used to do this. The general syntax of this construct is:

```
(defmessage-handler <class-name> <message-name>
                    [<handler-type>]
                    [<optional-comment>]
   (<regular-parameter>*
[<wildcard-parameter>])
   <expression>*)
```

where <regular-parameter> is a single-field variable, <wildcard-parameter> is a multifield value, and <handler-type> is one of the symbols *around*, *before*, *primary*, or *after*. By default, a message-handler is a primary message-handler. The significance of the *around*, *before*, and *after* handler types will be discussed in Section 11.10. Each class has its own set of message-handlers so there is no need for <message-name> to be distinct from the message-handler names used by other classes. The <regular-parameter> and <wildcard-parameter> declarations are the arguments that will be passed into the message-handler when it is called. These function identically to the way parameters are used with deffunctions. The body of the message-handler, represented by <expression>*, also behaves like the body of a deffunction. You can use the *bind* function to bind local variables and the last expression evaluated in the body is the return value of the message-handler.

Let's take a look at an example:

```
(defclass RECTANGLE
   (is-a USER)
   (slot height)
   (slot width))

(defclass CIRCLE
   (is-a USER)
   (slot radius))

(defmessage-handler RECTANGLE compute-area
   ()
   (* (send ?self get-height)
      (send ?self get-width)))
```

```
(defmessage-handler CIRCLE compute-area
   ()
   (* (pi)
      (send ?self get-radius)
      (send ?self get-radius)))

(definstances figures
   (rectangle-1 of RECTANGLE (height 2) (width 4))
   (circle-1 of CIRCLE (radius 3)))
```

This example defines two classes, *RECTANGLE* and *CIRCLE*, with the appropriate slots for each. A message-handler, *compute-area*, is attached to each class. The purpose of this message-handler is to compute the area for each object. For the *RECTANGLE* class, the area of the RECTANGLE instance is the height of the instance multiplied by the width. For the CIRCLE class, the area of the RECTANGLE instance is the value of π returned by the *pi* function multiplied by the radius of the instance squared. Notice that the variable *?self* is used in both message-handlers. This is a special variable automatically defined for each message-handler. When the message-handler is called, the value of the *?self* variable is assigned the instance-address of the instance to which the message has been sent. You can use this variable to send messages to the instance as we do in this example to retrieve the values of the *height*, *width*, and *radius* slots.

Once the message-handlers are defined, we can send a *compute-area* message to instances of the RECTANGLE and CIRCLE classes to determine the area of the instance:

```
CLIPS> (reset)↵
CLIPS> (send [circle-1] compute-area)↵
28.2743338823081
CLIPS> (send [rectangle-1] compute-area)↵
8
CLIPS>
```

Notice that we send each instance the same message, but each responds differently in computing their area. This ability for different instances to respond to the same message in a manner specific to itself is known as **polymorphism**.

Slot Shorthand References

It's often inconvenient to always have to send a message to an instance in order to retrieve or set a slot value, so a shorthand mechanism is available that allows you to access the slots of the instance bound to the ?self variable. Instead of using the expression:

```
(send ?self get-<slot-name>)
```

the expression:

```
?self:<slot-name>
```

can be used to retrieve the value of a slot. For example, our *compute-area* message-handlers can be redefined as the following:

```
(defmessage-handler RECTANGLE compute-area
   ()
   (* ?self:height ?self:width))

(defmessage-handler CIRCLE compute-area
   ()
   (* (pi) ?self:radius ?self:radius))
```

A similar mechanism is available for setting slot values. Instead of the expression:

```
(send ?self put-<slot-name> <expression>*)
```

the expression:

```
(bind ?self:slot-name <expression>*)
```

can be used.

These alternate mechanisms both bypass message-passing and directly manipulate slots. This has some significance if you are defining *after*, *before*, or *around* message-handlers on *get-* and *put-* message-handlers of your classes (which will be discussed in Section 11.10).

By default, the message-handlers for a class can use shorthand references only for slots that are directly defined by the class (i.e., slots that are not inherited). For example, given the following two defclasses:

```
(defclass A
   (is-a USER)
   (slot x))

(defclass B
   (is-a A)
   (slot y))
```

the following dialog shows that you can use a shorthand reference only to refer to slot *y* and not slot *x* in a message-handler for class *B*:

```
CLIPS>
(defmessage-handler B bmh1 ()
   (* 2 ?self:x))↵
[MSGFUN6] Private slot x of class A cannot be
accessed directly by handlers attached to class B

[PRCCODE3] Undefined variable self:x referenced in
message-handler.
```

```
ERROR:
(defmessage-handler MAIN::B bmh1
   ()
   (* 2 ?self:x)
   )
CLIPS>
(defmessage-handler B bmh2 ()
   (* 2 ?self:y))↵
CLIPS>
```

The *bmh1* message-handler makes a reference to ?self:x, which is not allowed since the *x* slot is inherited from class *A*. The *bmh2* message-handler is allowed to make a reference to ?self:y since the *y* slot is defined by class *B*. COOL supports object **encapsulation**, which means that the implementation details of a class are hidden and that access to a class is limited to a well-defined interface: the message-handlers defined for the class. Since the *get-x* message-handler is the interface for retrieving the value of the *x* slot from instances of class *A*, this interface must be used by the *bmh1* message-handler. With this change, the *bmh1* message-handler can be defined without error:

```
CLIPS>
(defmessage-handler B bmh1 ()
   (* 2 (send ?self get-x)))↵
CLIPS>
```

It's possible to disable the encapsulation behavior of a slot using the **visibility** slot attribute. If this attribute is set to **private**, which is the default, then the slot can be directly accessed only in message-handlers of a class defining it. If this attribute is set to **public**, then the slot can be directly accessed by subclasses and superclasses of any class defining it. In the prior example, defining class *A* as follows:

```
(defclass A
   (is-a USER)
   (slot x (visibility public)))
```

would allow you to define the message-handler *bmh1* as follows:

```
(defmessage-handler B bmh1 ()
   (* 2 ?self:x))
```

Watching Messages and Message-Handlers

If *messages* or *message-handlers* are watched using the *watch* command, an informational message is printed whenever a message-handler begins or ends execution. For example:

```
CLIPS> (watch messages)↵
CLIPS> (watch message-handlers)↵
CLIPS> (send [circle-1] compute-area)↵
```

```
MSG >> compute-area ED:1 (<Instance-circle-1>)
HND >> compute-area primary in class CIRCLE
       ED:1 (<Instance-circle-1>)
HND << compute-area primary in class CIRCLE
       ED:1 (<Instance-circle-1>)
MSG << compute-area ED:1 (<Instance-circle-1>)
28.2743338823081
CLIPS> (send [rectangle-1] compute-area)↵
MSG >> compute-area ED:1 (<Instance-rectangle-1>)
HND >> compute-area primary in class RECTANGLE
       ED:1 (<Instance-rectangle-1>)
HND << compute-area primary in class RECTANGLE
       ED:1 (<Instance-rectangle-1>)
MSG << compute-area ED:1 (<Instance-rectangle-1>)
8
CLIPS>
```

Watching *messages* prints debugging information when a message is sent to an instance and when the execution of that message has been totally completed. Watching *message-handlers* prints debugging information when a specific message-handler begins and ends execution. Watching *message-handlers* provides all of the information provided by watching *messages,* along with additional information. In the preceding dialog, the information printed by watching *messages* is prefaced with MSG and the information printed by watching *message-handlers* is prefaced with HND. The >> symbol indicates message/message-handler initiation and the << symbol indicates message/message-handler completion. This is followed by the name of the message or message-handler. For message-handlers some additional information is now printed: the handle type (before, after, primary, or around) followed by the class associated with the specific message-handler being executed. A single message is capable of causing the execution of multiple message-handlers of different types or classes, so this information allows you to determine which one is actually executed. The final information printed is the evaluation depth denoted by the symbol ED followed by the arguments to the message-handler. As with deffunctions, the evaluation depth is an indication of the nesting of deffunction and message-handler calls. It starts at zero and then each time a deffunction/message-handler is entered it increases by one. Each time a deffunction/message-handler exits, it decreases by one. In the argument list, the first argument listed is always the value of the ?self variable. The explicit arguments of the message-handler are then listed next.

It's also possible to watch all of the message-handlers of a specific class by just specifying the class; to watch a specific message-handler by specifying just the class and message-handler name; or to watch a specific message-handler and a specific type by specifying the class, message-handler name, and then the type (before, after, primary, or around):

```
CLIPS> (unwatch all)↵
CLIPS> (watch message-handlers CIRCLE)↵
```

```
CLIPS> (watch message-handlers RECTANGLE
       compute-area)↵
CLIPS> (watch message-handlers RECTANGLE
       get-height primary)↵
CLIPS>
```

The first *watch* command will watch all of the user- and system-defined message-handlers for the *CIRCLE* class. The second *watch* command will watch the primary *compute-area* message-handler for the *RECTANGLE* class (and it would also watch the after, before, and around handlers if any of these were defined). The third *watch* command will watch just the primary *get-height* system-defined message-handler for the *RECTANGLE* class.

Defmessage-Handler Commands

Several commands are provided for manipulating defmessage-handlers. The **list-defmessage-handlers** command is used to display the current list of defmessage-handlers maintained by CLIPS. Its syntax is:

```
(list-defmessage-handlers
   [<defclass-name> [inherit]])
```

where the keyword **inherit** indicates that you want inherited message-handlers to be listed. For example:

```
CLIPS> (list-defmessage-handlers RECTANGLE)↵
get-height primary in class RECTANGLE
put-height primary in class RECTANGLE
get-width primary in class RECTANGLE
put-width primary in class RECTANGLE
compute-area primary in class RECTANGLE
For a total of 5 message-handlers.
CLIPS>
```

The **ppdefmessage-handler** (pretty print defmessage-handler) command is used to display the text representation of a defmessage-handler. The **undefmessage-handler** command is used to delete a defmessage-handler. The **get-defmesage-handler-list** function returns a multifield value containing the list of defmessage-handlers belonging to a specified class. The syntax of these commands is:

```
(ppdefmessage-handler <defclass-name>
                      <handler-name>
                      [<handler-type>])

(undefmessage-handler <defclass-name>
                      <handler-name>
                      [<handler-type>])
```

```
(get-defmessage-handler-list <defclass-name>
                              [inherit])
```

where <handler-type> is one of the symbols *around*, *before*, *primary*, or *after*. For example:

```
CLIPS>
 (ppdefmessage-handler RECTANGLE compute-area)↵
(defmessage-handler MAIN::RECTANGLE compute-area
   ()
   (* (send ?self get-height) (send ?self
                               get-width)))
CLIPS>
 (undefmessage-handler RECTANGLE get-height)↵
[MSGPSR3] System message-handlers may not be
modified.
CLIPS> (undefmessage-handler RECTANGLE
       compute-area before)↵
[MSGFUN8] Unable to delete message-handler(s) from
   class RECTANGLE.
CLIPS> (undefmessage-handler RECTANGLE
       compute-area primary)↵
CLIPS> (get-defmessage-handler-list CIRCLE)↵
(CIRCLE get-radius primary
CIRCLE put-radius primary
CIRCLE compute-area primary)
CLIPS>
```

Note that you can't delete system-defined message-handlers. The *RECTANGLE* class doesn't have a *before* message-handler for *compute-area* so it can't be deleted. It does have a primary *compute-area* message-handler that can be deleted although we didn't have to specify *primary* in the command since this is the one deleted by default. The *get-defmessage-handler-list* function returns three values for each message-handler: the class to which the handler is attached (which will only be different from the class name passed into the function if the *inherit* keyword was specified), the name of the message-handler, and the type of the message-handler.

11.9 SLOT ACCESS AND HANDLER CREATION

It's possible to control access to slots using the **access** and **create-accessor** slot attributes. The *access* attribute directly restricts the type of access allowed to slots. If this attribute is set to **read-write**, which is the default, then the slot can be directly read or written to by handlers of the class using the slot shorthand notation: ?self:<slot-name>. If this attribute is set to **read-only** then the value of the slot can be retrieved using the shorthand notation, but the *bind* function can't be used to change the value. The only way to supply a value to store in the slot is to use the default attribute. Setting the *access* attribute to **initialize-only** is similar to read-only, except the slot value can be set when the instance is created (using for example, *make-instance*).

The *create-accessor* attribute is used to control the automatic creation of the get- and put- handlers for class slots. If this attribute is set to **read-write**, which is the default, then both the get- and put- handlers are created. Similarly if this attribute is set to **read,** then only the get- handlers are generated and if set to **write,** then only the put- handlers are generated. Finally if set to **?NONE,** neither get- nor put- handlers are generated.

Some explicit combinations of the *access* and *create-accessor* attributes will cause errors; for example, setting *access* for a slot to *read-only* and *create-accessor* to *read-write*. Obviously you can't write to a slot you're allowed only to read from.

Let's look at an example to demonstrate these attributes. Let's say we've got an order from a customer that we want to generate a total price for. We want to tag each order with a unique ID, but once assigned we don't want this ID ever to be changed. The total price for an order will be computed from the price of the items in the order plus a sales tax, and further we don't want the total price computed or set by any code other than the handler code for our class. The code we'll use for our order class is as follows:

```
(defclass ORDER
    (is-a USER)
    (slot ID (access initialize-only)
          (default-dynamic (gensym)))
(slot total-price (create-accessor read)
      (default 0.0))
    (slot order-price (default 0.0))
    (slot sales-tax (default 0.0)))

(defmessage-handler ORDER compute-total-price ()
    (bind ?self:total-price
       (* ?self:order-price
          (+ 1 ?self:sales-tax))))
```

The *ID* slot can only be specified when the instance is defined. If we don't define a value for it, it will be dynamically generated by calling the *gensym* function. The *total-price* slot has its *create-accessor* attribute set to *read,* which means that a *get-total-price* handler will be generated, but a *put-total-price* handler will not. Finally a *compute-total-price* handler is defined, which computes the total price of the order by adding to the order price the appropriate tax for the indicated sales tax. For example if the *order-price* is 10.00 and the *sales-tax* is 0.05, then the *total-price* will be 10.50. The following interactions demonstrate the restrictions placed on the slots:

```
CLIPS>
(make-instance order1 of ORDER
```

```
   (ID #001)
   (order-price 10.00)
   (sales-tax 0.05))↵
[order1]
CLIPS> (send [order1] put-ID #002)↵
[MSGFUN3] ID slot in [order1] of ORDER: write
access denied.
[PRCCODE4] Execution halted during the actions of
message-handler put-ID primary in class ORDER
FALSE
CLIPS>
```

Note that the *ID* slot can be set when the *order1* instance is created, but not later using the *put-ID* handler. Similarly, the *total-price* can be retrieved using the *get-total-price* handler but not set using *put-total-price* handler:

```
CLIPS> (send [order1] get-total-price)↵
0.0
CLIPS> (send [order1] put-total-price 10.50)↵
[MSGFUN1] No applicable primary message-handlers
found for put-total-price.
FALSE
CLIPS>
```

The *compute-total-price* handler has to be called in order to set the correct price:

```
CLIPS> (send [order1] compute-total-price)↵
10.5
CLIPS> (send [order1] get-total-price)↵
10.5
CLIPS>
```

It's possible to manually define the *get-total-price* handler so that the *compute-total-price* handler doesn't have to be explicitly called in order to compute the correct value for the total price. When you use the *create-accessor* attribute to define a get- handler for a class it creates a message-handler of the following form:

```
(defmessage-handler <class> get-<slot-name>
            primary ()
?self:<slot-name>)
```

Similarly for put- handlers the following form is used:

```
(defmessage-handler <class> put-<slot-name>
            primary (?value)
(bind ?self:<slot-name> ?value))
```

In both cases, <class> is the name of the defclass and <slot-name> is the name of the slot in the class. If the *total-price create-accessor* attribute is modified to ?NONE in the ORDER class, then the get-total-price handler can be defined to compute the price whenever it is called:

```
(defclass ORDER
   (is-a USER)
   (slot ID (access initialize-only)
            (default-dynamic (gensym)))
   (slot total-price (create-accessor ?NONE)
                     (default 0.0))
   (slot order-price (default 0.0))
   (slot sales-tax (default 0.0)))

(defmessage-handler ORDER get-total-price ()
   (send ?self compute-total-price))

(defmessage-handler ORDER get-total-price ()
   (send ?self compute-total-price))
```

Creating an ORDER instance and then requesting the total price now returns an up-to-date value:

```
CLIPS>
(make-instance order2 of ORDER
   (ID #002)
   (order-price 20.00)
   (sales-tax 0.05))↵
[order2]
CLIPS> (send [order2] get-total-price)↵
21.0
CLIPS>
```

11.10 BEFORE, AFTER, AND AROUND MESSSAGE-HANDLERS

The behavior of a class may not always meet your needs and you may not be able to change the class to meet your needs. Other code may depend upon the class maintaining its behavior or you may not be familiar enough with the code to modify its behavior. In cases like this, you can define a new class that inherits the behavior you want from the parent class and then modify the class with the new behavior you want. Let's reexamine the code from the ORDER example and see how we can create a new class that will ensure that the total price information of an order is always up-to-date:

```
(defclass ORDER
   (is-a USER)
```

```
   (slot ID (access initialize-only))
   (slot total-price (create-accessor read)
                     (default 0.0))
   (slot order-price (default 0.0))
   (slot sales-tax (default 0.0)))

(defmessage-handler ORDER compute-total-price ()
   (bind ?self:total-price
      (* ?self:order-price
        (+ 1 ?self:sales-tax))))
```

Next we need to define a new class with which we'll implement the special behavior. We'll call the class *MY-ORDER*:

```
(defclass MY-ORDER
   (is-a ORDER))
```

One approach that we can take is to completely redefine the *get-total-price* message-handler incorporating both the new behavior and the old behavior:

```
(defmessage-handler MY-ORDER get-total-price ()
   (send ?self compute-total-price)
   ?self:total-price)
```

In this case we call the *compute-total-price* message-handler before returning the value of the *total-price* slot. There are a couple of problems with doing this. First, it simply won't work. The *total-price* slot is private, so we can't access it using the ?self reference outside of the *ORDER* class. You also can't replace the ?self:total-price reference with (send ?self get-total-price) because this will call the *MY-ORDER* handler instead of the *ORDER* handler.

The second problem with this approach comes from the duplication of code. In this case it's a very small, simple piece of code, ?self:total-price, but let's assume it's not. The smaller concern is the program space required to duplicate the code. The larger concern is the fact that if the original *ORDER* handler changes, the *MY-ORDER* handler will not inherit the new behavior. For this reason alone, you shouldn't try to redefine a handler this way.

It's possible to slightly redefine the handler to get the desired behavior:

```
(defmessage-handler MY-ORDER get-total-price ()
   (send ?self compute-total-price)
   (call-next-handler))
```

The **call-next-handler** function will call the next message-handler that the current message-handler has overridden. There's no need to supply any arguments. The argument used with the current handler will be passed to it. If you watch *message-handlers* when sending a *MY-ORDER* instance a *get-total-price* message, you can see that both the *MY-ORDER* and *ORDER get-total-price* message-handlers are called:

```
CLIPS>
(make-instance order3 of MY-ORDER
   (ID #003)
   (order-price 10.00)
   (sales-tax 0.05))↵
CLIPS> (watch message-handlers)↵
CLIPS> (send [order3] get-total-price)↵
HND >> get-total-price primary in class MY-ORDER
       ED:1 (<Instance-order3>)
HND >> compute-total-price primary in class ORDER
       ED:2 (<Instance-order3>)
HND << compute-total-price primary in class ORDER
       ED:2 (<Instance-order3>)
HND >> get-total-price primary in class ORDER
       ED:1 (<Instance-order3>)
HND << get-total-price primary in class ORDER
       ED:1 (<Instance-order3>)
HND << get-total-price primary in class MY-ORDER
       ED:1 (<Instance-order3>)
10.5
CLIPS>
```

Before and After Handlers

In addition to *primary* message-handlers, which are the default if no handler type is specified, CLIPS also provides *before*, *after*, and *around* handler types. The handler type is specified after the handler name and each class may have a handler of each type. The *before* message-handler type, not surprisingly, specifies a message-handler that is to be executed before the *primary* message-handler. The following is an example *before* message-handler on the *MY-ORDER* class:

```
(defmessage-handler MY-ORDER get-total-price
            before ()
(send ?self compute-total-price))
```

Unlike the previous *get-total-price primary* message-handler, in this handler we send only the *compute-total-price* message and we don't call the *call-next-handler* function. We don't have to call this function because the *MY-ORDER before* handler will first be called and then *ORDER primary* handle will be called. If you delete the previously defined *MY-ORDER primary* handler, you can see this by watching message-handlers:

```
CLIPS>
(make-instance order4 of MY-ORDER
```

```
      (ID #004)
      (order-price 10.00)
      (sales-tax 0.05))↵
[order4]
CLIPS> (watch message-handlers)↵
CLIPS> (send [order4] get-total-price)↵
HND >> get-total-price before in class MY-ORDER
       ED:1 (<Instance-order4>)
HND >> compute-total-price primary in class ORDER
       ED:2 (<Instance-order4>)
HND << compute-total-price primary in class ORDER
       ED:2 (<Instance-order4>)
HND << get-total-price before in class MY-ORDER
       ED:1 (<Instance-order4>)
HND >> get-total-price primary in class ORDER
       ED:1 (<Instance-order4>)
HND << get-total-price primary in class ORDER
       ED:1 (<Instance-order4>)
10.5
CLIPS>
```

The *MY-ORDER get-total-price before* message-handler is first called, which calls the *ORDER compute-total-price primary* message-handler, and then both of these handlers exit. Finally, the *ORDER get-total-price primary* message-handler is called, which returns the updated value of the total-price slot.

Instead of computing the correct *total-price* value before the *get-total-price* handler is called, we can also compute the *total-price* after we make changes to either the *sales-tax* or *order-price* slots. We'll accomplish this task by defining the following *after* message-handlers:

```
(defmessage-handler MY-ORDER put-sales-tax
                         after (?value)
   (if (numberp (send ?self get-order-price))
      then
      (send ?self compute-total-price)))

(defmessage-handler MY-ORDER put-order-price
                         after (?value)
   (if (numberp (send ?self get-sales-tax))
      then
      (send ?self compute-total-price)))
```

These handlers will call the *compute-total-price* handler after the *put-sales-tax* and *put-order-price primary* handlers are called. In each handler, we have to check that the other slot value used in the *compute-total-price* message-handler is appropriately defined as a number since these slots will not be set to their default value of 0.0 during the entire process of instance creation. If we delete the previous *get-total-price before* handler, we can see this if *message-handlers* are watched:

```
CLIPS>
(make-instance order5 of MY-ORDER
   (ID #005)
   (order-price 10.00)
   (sales-tax 0.05))↵
[order5]
CLIPS> (send [order5] get-total-price)↵
10.5
CLIPS> (watch message-handlers)↵
CLIPS> (send [order5] put-order-price 20.00)↵
HND >> put-order-price primary in class ORDER
       ED:1 (<Instance-order5> 20.0)
HND << put-order-price primary in class ORDER
       ED:1 (<Instance-order5> 20.0)
HND >> put-order-price after in class MY-ORDER
       ED:1 (<Instance-order5> 20.0)
HND >> get-sales-tax primary in class ORDER
       ED:2 (<Instance-order5>)
HND << get-sales-tax primary in class ORDER
       ED:2 (<Instance-order5>)
HND >> compute-total-price primary in class ORDER
       ED:2 (<Instance-order5>)
HND << compute-total-price primary in class ORDER
       ED:2 (<Instance-order5>)
HND << put-order-price after in class MY-ORDER
       ED:1 (<Instance-order5> 20.0)
20.0
CLIPS> (send [order5] get-total-price)↵
HND >> get-total-price primary in class ORDER
       ED:1 (<Instance-order5>)
HND << get-total-price primary in class ORDER
       ED:1 (<Instance-order5>)
21.0
CLIPS>
```

After we create the instance, we can see that the *total-price* slot value is up-to-date. We didn't watch *message-handler* at this point because there are several messages sent during the instance creation that we aren't interested in. If we change the *order-price* slot value by calling *put-order-price*, we can see that the *ORDER put-order-price primary* message-handler is first called and exited. Subsequently the *MY-ORDER put-order-price after* message-handler is called, which then calls the *ORDER get-sales-tax primary* message-handler to determine that *sales-tax* is set to an appropriate value. Since *sales-tax* has a valid value, the *ORDER compute-total-price primary* handler is called computing the correct price, and then the *compute-total-price primary* and *put-order-price after* handlers both exit. Sending the *get-total-price* message subsequently returns the correct value.

Around Handlers

Having to test that the order-price and sales-tax slots have numeric values in the *after* message-handlers is awkward, so let's look at a different way to do it. First, let's remove the value tests from the *after* message-handlers:

```
(defmessage-handler MY-ORDER put-sales-tax
                         after (?value)
   (send ?self compute-total-price))

(defmessage-handler MY-ORDER put-order-price
                         after (?value)
   (send ?self compute-total-price))
```

The fourth and final message-handler type provided by COOL is the *around* message-handler. This message-handler type is also referred to as a *wrapper* because it wraps around the other message-handler types executing both before and after them. The *around* message-handler is kind of a combination *before* and *after* handler that also allows you to abort the message during the message passing process. The following is an *around* handler for the *compute-total-price* message:

```
(defmessage-handler MY-ORDER compute-total-price
                         around ()
   (if (or (not (numberp
                 (send ?self get-order-price)))
           (not (numberp
                 (send ?self get-sales-tax))))
     then
     (return))
   (call-next-handler))
```

First, the *around* handler checks if the *order-price* and *sales-tax* slots are numbers. If they aren't, then the handler returns, doing nothing more. At this point, none of the *before*, *primary*, or *after* handlers for *compute-total-price* will be called. On the other hand if both *order-price* and *sales-tax* are numbers, the *call-next-handler* will be invoked and the other message-handlers will be called. In this case, just the *ORDER compute-total-price primary* message-handler will be called. The following dialog demonstrates this. Because the output is rather lengthy, comments have been inserted between portions of the message-handler trace:

```
CLIPS> (watch message-handlers)↵
CLIPS>
```

```
(make-instance order5 of MY-ORDER
   (ID #005)
   (order-price 10.00)
   (sales-tax 0.05))↵
HND >> create primary in class USER
       ED:1 (<Instance-order5>)
HND << create primary in class USER
       ED:1 (<Instance-order5>)
HND >> put-ID primary in class ORDER
       ED:1 (<Instance-order5> #005)
HND << put-ID primary in class ORDER
       ED:1 (<Instance-order5> #005)
```

The *order5* instance is created using the *make-instance* call. The *create* message-handler, another system-defined message-handler, is invoked right after the instance is created. Once the raw instance has been created, the values specified in the *make-instance* call are placed in the instance's slots. First the *put-ID* message-handler is called to store *#005* in the *ID* slot:

```
HND >> put-order-price primary in class ORDER
       ED:1 (<Instance-order5> 10.0)
HND << put-order-price primary in class ORDER
       ED:1 (<Instance-order5> 10.0)
HND >> put-order-price after in class MY-ORDER
       ED:1 (<Instance-order5> 10.0)
HND >> compute-total-price around in class MY-ORDER
       ED:2 (<Instance-order5>)
HND >> get-order-price primary in class ORDER
       ED:3 (<Instance-order5>)
HND << get-order-price primary in class ORDER
       ED:3 (<Instance-order5>)
HND >> get-sales-tax primary in class ORDER
       ED:3 (<Instance-order5>)
HND << get-sales-tax primary in class ORDER
       ED:3 (<Instance-order5>)
HND >> get-order-price primary in class ORDER
       ED:3 (<Instance-order5>)
HND << get-order-price primary in class ORDER
       ED:3 (<Instance-order5>)
HND << compute-total-price around in class MY-ORDER
       ED:2 (<Instance-order5>)
HND << put-order-price after in class MY-ORDER
       ED:1 (<Instance-order5> 10.0)
```

Next the *ORDER put-order-price primary* message-handler is called to store the value 10.0 in the *order-price* slot. Once this handler finishes, the *MY-ORDER put-order-price after* handler is called. This handler sends the *compute-total-price* message, which invokes the *MY-ORDER compute-total-price around* handler. Within the *around* handler, the *ORDER get-order-price primary* handler is called to determine if *order-price* is numeric (which it is since it was just set to 10.0). Next the *ORDER get-sales-tax primary* handler is called to determine if *sales-tax* is numeric. It isn't, since the slot hasn't been set to the value supplied by *make-instance*, so the *around* handler calls the *ORDER get-order-price primary* handler again and returns this value. In this case, the *computer-order-price around* handler terminates without calling the *primary* handler. Finally the *MY-ORDER put-order-price after* handler exists:

```
HND >> put-sales-tax primary in class ORDER
       ED:1 (<Instance-order5> 0.05)
HND << put-sales-tax primary in class ORDER
       ED:1 (<Instance-order5> 0.05)
HND >> put-sales-tax after in class MY-ORDER
       ED:1 (<Instance-order5> 0.05)
HND >> compute-total-price around in class MY-ORDER
       ED:2 (<Instance-order5>)
HND >> get-order-price primary in class ORDER
       ED:3 (<Instance-order5>)
HND << get-order-price primary in class ORDER
       ED:3 (<Instance-order5>)
HND >> get-sales-tax primary in class ORDER
       ED:3 (<Instance-order5>)
HND << get-sales-tax primary in class ORDER
       ED:3 (<Instance-order5>)
HND >> compute-total-price primary in class ORDER
       ED:2 (<Instance-order5>)
HND << compute-total-price primary in class ORDER
       ED:2 (<Instance-order5>)
HND << compute-total-price around in class MY-ORDER
       ED:2 (<Instance-order5>)
HND << put-sales-tax after in class MY-ORDER
       ED:1 (<Instance-order5> 0.05)
```

Next the *ORDER put-sales-tax primary* message-handler is called to store the value 0.05 in the *sales-tax* slot. Once this handler finishes, the *MY-ORDER put-sales-tax after* handler is called. This handler sends the *compute-total-price* message, which invokes the *MY-ORDER compute-total-price around* handler. Within the *around* handler, the *ORDER get-order-price primary* handler is called to determine if *order-price* is numeric. It is, so next the *ORDER get-sales-tax primary* handler is called to determine if *sales-tax* is numeric (which it is because it was just set to 0.05). The *around* handler now calls the *call-next-handler* function, which invokes the *ORDER compute-total-price primary* handler, which computes the updated value of the *total-price* slot. Finally the *ORDER compute-total-price primary* handler terminates, followed by the *MY-*

ORDER compute-total-price around handler, followed by the *MY-ORDER put-sales-tax after* handler:

```
HND >> init primary in class USER
       ED:1 (<Instance-order5>)
HND << init primary in class USER
       ED:1 (<Instance-order5>)
[order5]
CLIPS>
```

Finally the *init* message is sent to the newly created instance and then the instance name is returned. The *init* message-handler is another system-defined message-handler. It gets called at the end of instance creation after slot values have been initialized.

Overriding Message-Handler Arguments

It's possible to override the arguments passed to a message-handler by using the **override-next-handler** command. The syntax of this commands is:

```
(override-next-handler <expression>*)
```

where each <expression> is a replacement argument to be sent to the next message-handler. For an example use of this command, let's consider how we might handle orders in foreign currency. Again, let's assume that for various reasons we don't want to directly modify the *ORDER* class. If *order-price* value of an *ORDER* instance is in U.S. dollars, there might be special logic based on the price being in U.S. dollars. For example, shipping costs might be waved for orders over $100.

One approach we can take to handling different currency is to define a class that inherits from the ORDER class, but automatically converts between the foreign currency and U.S. dollars. The following FOREIGN-ORDER defclass and associated handlers implement this approach:

```
(defclass FOREIGN-ORDER
    (is-a ORDER)
    (slot exchange-rate (default 1.0)))

(defmessage-handler FOREIGN-ORDER get-order-price
                        around ()
    (* ?self:exchange-rate (call-next-handler)))

(defmessage-handler FOREIGN-ORDER put-order-price
                        around (?value)
(override-next-handler
    (/ ?value ?self:exchange-rate)))
```

The *FOREIGN-ORDER* class has an *exchange*-rate slot that is used to represent the exchange rate between the foreign currency and U.S. dollars. For example, if the exchange rate was 2, then 10 U.S. dollars would be equivalent to 20 units of the foreign currency. For actual use, we'd probably also provide a slot to indicate the units of the foreign currency (for example Euros), but for this example, it's not necessary.

The *FOREIGN-ORDER get-order-price around* handler invokes the *ORDER get-order-price primary* handler by using the *call-next-handler* command. The return value is then multiplied by the value of the *exchange-rate* slot and this value is returned. The *FOREIGN-ORDER put-order-price around* handler invokes the *ORDER put-order-price primary* handler using *override-next-handler*, but instead of passing in the value based in the foreign currency it divides this value by the exchange rate and passes this value instead, which is in U.S. dollars.

By watching message-handlers, we can observe the behavior of the *FOREIGN-CURRENCY* class. First, we create an instance of the class:

```
CLIPS> (unwatch all)↵
CLIPS>
(make-instance order6 of FOREIGN-ORDER
   (ID #006)
   (exchange-rate 2)
   (sales-tax .10))↵
[order6]
CLIPS>
```

Next, we change the *order-price* slot to the value of 20.00 in the foreign currency:

```
CLIPS> (watch message-handlers)↵
CLIPS> (send [order6] put-order-price 20.00)↵
HND >> put-order-price around in class FOREIGN-
ORDER
       ED:1 (<Instance-order6> 20.0)
HND >> put-order-price primary in class ORDER
       ED:1 (<Instance-order6> 10.0)
HND << put-order-price primary in class ORDER
       ED:1 (<Instance-order6> 10.0)
HND << put-order-price around in class FOREIGN-
ORDER
       ED:1 (<Instance-order6> 20.0)
10.0
CLIPS>
```

First the *FOREIGN-ORDER put-order-price around* handler is invoked with a value of 20. The *ORDER put-order-price primary* handle is then invoked with a value of 10 as a result of the *override-next-handler* call. This value in U.S. dollars is then passed back as the return value of the send command.

Retrieving the order-price slot works similarly:

```
CLIPS> (send [order6] get-order-price)↵
HND >> get-order-price around in class
       FOREIGN-ORDER
       ED:1 (<Instance-order6>)
HND >> get-order-price primary in class ORDER
       ED:1 (<Instance-order6>)
HND << get-order-price primary in class ORDER
       ED:1 (<Instance-order6>)
HND << get-order-price around in class
       FOREIGN-ORDER
       ED:1 (<Instance-order6>)
20.0
CLIPS>
```

The *FOREIGN-ORDER get-order-price around* handler is invoked first and calls the *ORDER get-order-price primary* handler using *call-next-handler*. The U.S. dollar value of 10 is returned by the primary handler which is then multiplied by the exchange rate in the *around* handler to return a final value of 20 in units of the foreign currency.

Sending a *print* message to the *FOREIGN-CURRENCY* instance shows that the currency value is actually stored in the U.S. dollar amount rather than the foreign currency amount:

```
CLIPS> (unwatch all)↵
CLIPS> (send [order6] print)↵
[order6] of FOREIGN-ORDER
(ID #006)
(total-price 0.0)
(order-price 10.0)
(sales-tax 0.1)
(exchange-rate 2)
CLIPS>
```

Handler Execution Order

We've used four different techniques to modify the behavior of the *ORDER* class by attaching handlers to the *MY-ORDER* class: overriding the *primary* handler, defining a *before* handler, defining *after* handlers, and defining *after* and *around* handlers. The obvious question at this point is which approach is the best. In this case using the *before* handler is probably the best solution. It uses the least amount of code and it has a key advantage compared to overriding the *primary* handler (which uses the second least amount of code): All inherited *before* and *after* message-handlers belonging to a class or its superclass are called unless an error occurs or an *around* handler terminates the message. This means that a class can slightly modify the behavior of a superclass using *before* and *after* handlers without overriding the *primary* handler and subclasses can't prevent the execution of a *before* or *after* handler unless they terminate the message, thus preventing the execution of all *before*, *after*, and *primary* handlers. If you modify the behavior of an existing class by redefining a new class and then overriding the *primary* handler, your *primary* handler is also subject to being overridden by a subclass. Unless the overriding class calls the *call-next-handler* function, your *primary* handler won't get executed. This is not to say that you should never override the *primary* handler, but if you have some special behavior that you don't want inheriting classes to be able to override, you should definitely consider placing this behavior in a *before* or *after* handler.

Given that you may have specialized behavior in multiple *before*, *after*, and *around* handlers inherited by a class, it's important to know the order in which the various message-handlers are called. When a message is sent to an instance using the *send* command, all the applicable message-handlers are determined and the following steps are taken:

1. If there are any uncalled *around* handlers, then invoke the most specific one; otherwise proceed to step 2. If the invoked *around* handler calls *call-next-handler* or *override-next-handler,* then repeat this step; otherwise proceed to step 6.
2. If there are any uncalled *before* handlers, then invoke the most specific one, wait for it to finish, then repeat this step. Otherwise, proceed to step 3. The return values of the *before* handlers are ignored. There is no way to directly return these values to another handler.
3. If there are any uncalled *primary* handlers, then invoke the most specific one; otherwise proceed to step 4. If an invoked *primary* handler calls *call-next-handler* or *override-next-handler*, then repeat this step; otherwise proceed to step 4. You can't send a message to an instance unless there is at least one applicable *primary* handler.
4. Allow each *primary* handler to finish and return, then remove it from the list of called *primary* handlers. If a *primary* handler calls *call-next-handler* or *override-next-handler* again, go back to step 3. Once all *primary* handlers have finished, remember the return value of the last *primary* handler executed and proceed to step 5.
5. If there are any uncalled *after* handlers, then invoke the least specific one, wait for it to finish, then repeat this step. Otherwise proceed to step 6. The return values of the *after* handlers are ignored. There is no way to directly return these values to another handler.
6. If no *around* handlers were called, proceed to step 7. Otherwise, allow each *around* handler to finish and return, then remove it from the list of called *around* handlers. If an *around* handler calls *call-next-handler* or *override-next-handler* again, proceed back to step 1. Once all *around* handlers have finished, remember the value of the last *around* handler executed and proceed to step 7.
7. The final return value of the *send* command is the return value of the most specific *around* handler from step 6. If there are no *around* handlers, then the return value of the most specific *primary* handler from step 4 is used.

The return value of the *call-next-handler* or *override-next-handler* function is the last action executed in the next *around* or *primary* handler called. A handler can either ignore this value or use it as its return value.

Figure 11.2 shows a flowchart that yields equivalent results to steps 1 through 7. Step 1 begins with the box in the upper-left corner of the figure. Figure 11.3 shows a flowchart that yields the equivalent results to steps 3 and 4 in executing the applicable primary handlers associated with a message sent to an instance. In cases where there are no applicable *around*, *before*, or *after* handlers (i.e., only *primary* handlers), the Figure 11.2 flowchart reduces equivalently to the Figure 11.3 flowchart.

The following constructs will be used to demonstrate the order of handler execution:

```
(defclass A
   (is-a USER))

(defmessage-handler A msg1 primary ()
 (return msg1-A))

(defmessage-handler A msg1 before ())

(defmessage-handler A msg1 after ())

(defmessage-handler A msg1 around ()
   (call-next-handler))

(defclass B
   (is-a A))

(defmessage-handler B msg1 primary ()
 (return msg1-B))

(defmessage-handler B msg1 before ())

(defmessage-handler B msg1 after ())

(defmessage-handler B msg1 around ()
   (call-next-handler))
```

Class *B* is a subclass of class *A*. Each class has its own *primary*, *before*, *after*, and *around* handlers. First, we'll create instances of both classes:

```
CLIPS> (make-instance [a1] of A)↵
[a1]
CLIPS> (make-instance [b1] of B)↵
[b1]
CLIPS>
```

Figure 11.2 Handler Execution Order Determination

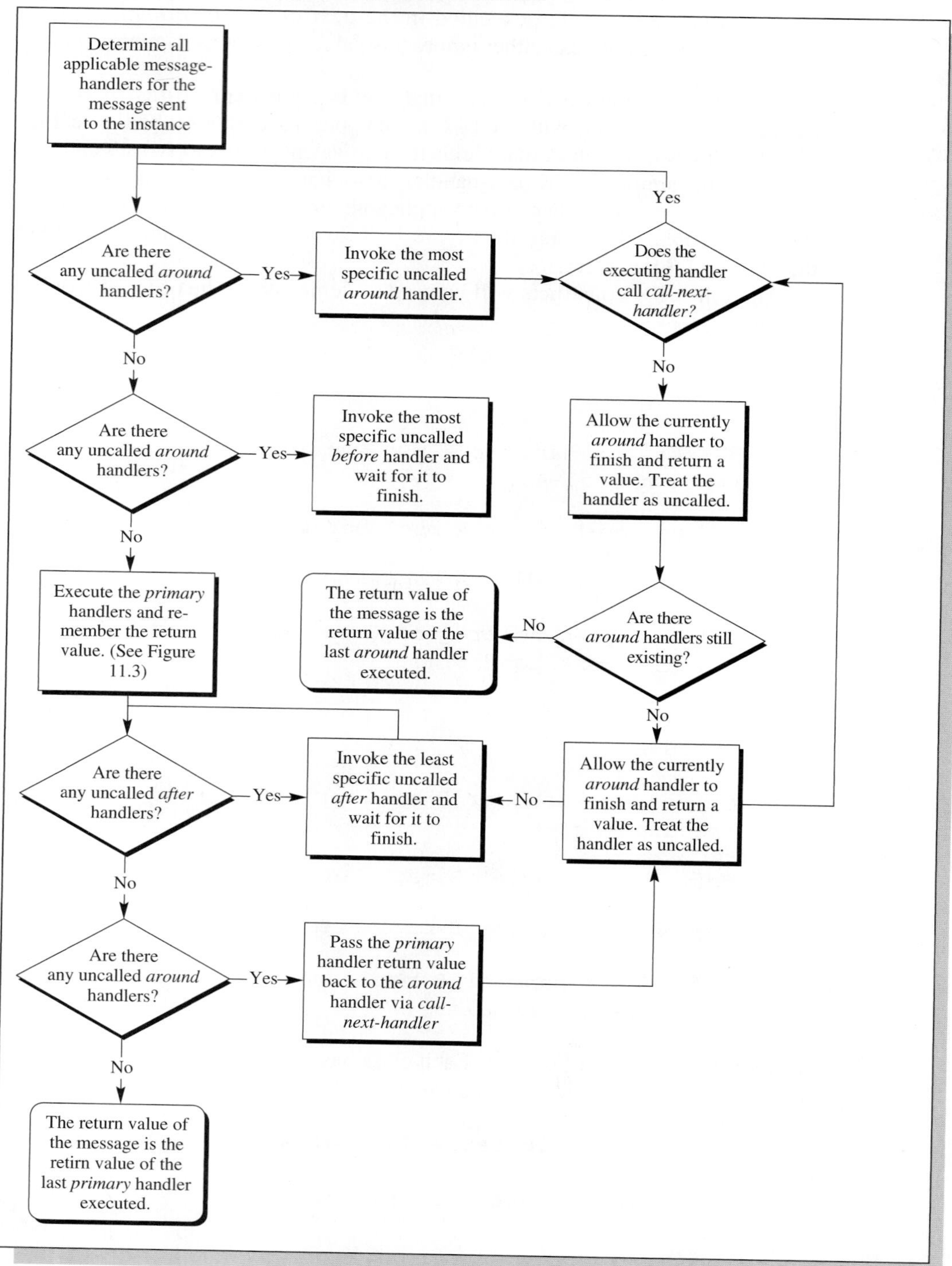

Figure 11.3 Primary Handler Execution Order Determination

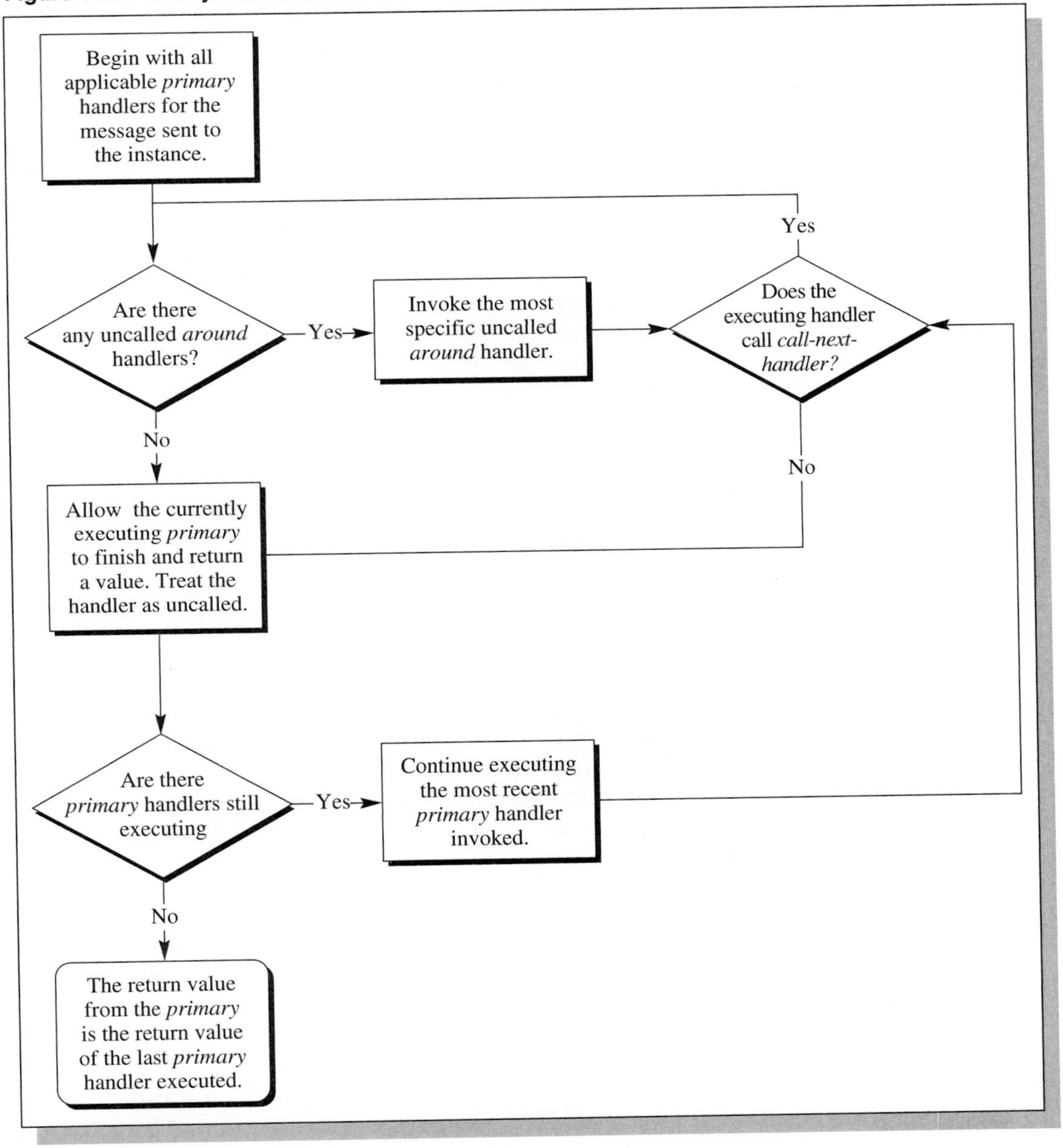

Now we'll watch *message-handlers* and send the instance *a1* the *msg1* message:

```
CLIPS> (watch message-handlers)↵
CLIPS> (send [a1] msg1)↵
HND >> msg1 around in class A
       ED:1 (<Instance-a1>)
HND >> msg1 before in class A
       ED:1 (<Instance-a1>)
HND << msg1 before in class A
       ED:1 (<Instance-a1>)
HND >> msg1 primary in class A
       ED:1 (<Instance-a1>)
HND << msg1 primary in class A
       ED:1 (<Instance-a1>)
HND >> msg1 after in class A
       ED:1 (<Instance-a1>)
HND << msg1 after in class A
       ED:1 (<Instance-a1>)
HND << msg1 around in class A
       ED:1 (<Instance-a1>)
msg1-A
CLIPS>
```

There are four applicable message-handlers for this message: the *msg1 primary*, *before*, *after*, and *around* handlers of class *A*. Beginning with step 1, the class *A msg1 around* handler is executed. This handler calls the *call-next-handler* function, so we repeat step 1. Since there are no remaining uncalled *around* handlers, we proceed to step 2. The class *A msg1 before* handler is allowed to execute and return. Since there are no other uncalled *before* handlers, we proceed to step 3. The class *A msg1 primary* message-handler is executed. It doesn't call *call-next-handler*, so we proceed to step 4. The class *A msg1 primary* message-handler is allowed to finish and it returns the symbol *msg1-A*. All *primary* handlers have finished execution, so we proceed to step 5. The class *A msg1 after* handler is allowed to execute and return. Since there are no other uncalled *after* handlers, we proceed to step 6. The class *A msg1 around* handler is allowed to finish. The last action executed by this handler is the *call-next-handler* function so the return value will be the return value of the next *around* or *primary* handler that was invoked. In this case it was the class *A msg1 primary* handler that had the return value *msg1-A*, so the return value of the *around* handler is the same. Since all *around* handlers have finished, we proceed with step 7. The final return value of the *send* command is the value *msg1-A* returned by the class *A msg1 around* handler.

Now let's send the *b1* instance the *msg1* message:

```
CLIPS> (send [b1] msg1)↵
HND >> msg1 around in class B
       ED:1 (<Instance-b1>)
```

```
HND >> msg1 around in class A
       ED:1 (<Instance-b1>)
HND >> msg1 before in class B
       ED:1 (<Instance-b1>)
HND << msg1 before in class B
       ED:1 (<Instance-b1>)
HND >> msg1 before in class A
       ED:1 (<Instance-b1>)
HND << msg1 before in class A
       ED:1 (<Instance-b1>)
HND >> msg1 primary in class B
       ED:1 (<Instance-b1>)
HND << msg1 primary in class B
       ED:1 (<Instance-b1>)
HND >> msg1 after in class A
       ED:1 (<Instance-b1>)
HND << msg1 after in class A
       ED:1 (<Instance-b1>)
HND >> msg1 after in class B
       ED:1 (<Instance-b1>)
HND << msg1 after in class B
       ED:1 (<Instance-b1>)
HND << msg1 around in class A
       ED:1 (<Instance-b1>)
HND << msg1 around in class B
       ED:1 (<Instance-b1>)
msg1-B
CLIPS>
```

There are eight applicable message-handlers for this message: the *msg1 primary*, *before*, *after*, and *around* handlers of class *A* and the *msg1 primary*, *before*, *after*, and *around* handlers of class *B*. Beginning with step 1, the class *B msg1 around* handler is executed since this is the most specific *around* handler. This handler calls the *call-next-handler* function, so we repeat step 1. The next most specific around handler is the class *A msg1 around* handler. This handler also calls the *call-next-handler* function, so we repeat step 1 again. Since there are no remaining uncalled *around* handlers, we proceed to step 2. The class *B msg1 before* handler is the most specific *before* handler since this one is executed first and then allowed to finish. The class *A msg1 before* handler is the next most specific so this one is allowed to execute and return. Since there are no other uncalled *before* handlers, we proceed to step 3. The class *B msg1 primary* message-handler is executed since this is the most specific *primary* handler. It doesn't call *call-next-handler*, so the class *A msg1 primary* handler isn't executed and we proceed to step 4. The class *B msg1 primary* message-handler is allowed to finish and it returns the symbol *msg1-B*. All *primary* handlers have finished execution, so we proceed to step 5. In reverse order from the *before* handlers, the class *A msg1 after* handler is allowed to execute first and return since it is the least specific *after* handler. Next the class *B msg1 after* handler is allowed to execute and return. Since there are no other uncalled *after* handlers, we proceed to step 6. The class *A msg1 around* handler is allowed to finish. The last action executed by this handler is the *call-next-handler* function so the return value will be the return value of the next *around* or *primary* handler that was invoked. In this case it was the class *B msg1 primary* handler that had the return value *msg1-B*, so the return value of the *around* handler is the same. Now the class *B msg1 around* handler is allowed to finish. Its last action was also a call to *call-next-handler* so its return value is the return value of the class *A msg1 around* handler that was *msg1-B*. Since all *around* handlers have finished, we proceed with step 7. The final return value of the *send* command is the value *msg1-B* returned by the class *B msg1 around* handler.

The **preview-send** command can be used to display the list of the applicable handlers for a message sent to an instance of a specified class. The syntax of this command is:

```
(preview-send <defclass-name> <message-name>)
```

For example, instead of watching *message-handlers* and sending a *msg1* message to instance *b1*, the following command could be executed:

```
CLIPS> (preview-send B msg1)↵
>> msg1 around in class B
| >> msg1 around in class A
| | >> msg1 before in class B
| | << msg1 before in class B
| | >> msg1 before in class A
| | << msg1 before in class A
| | >> msg1 primary in class B
| | | >> msg1 primary in class A
| | | << msg1 primary in class A
| | << msg1 primary in class B
| | >> msg1 after in class A
| | << msg1 after in class A
| | >> msg1 after in class B
| | << msg1 after in class B
| << msg1 around in class A
<< msg1 around in class B
CLIPS>
```

All of the applicable handlers are listed in the order they would be called if every *around* and *primary* handler called *call-next-handler*. The level of indentation indicates the nesting of handler calls. Similar to watching *message-handlers*, the >> and << symbols represent the beginning and end of handler execution. The vertical series of | characters link the beginning and end portion of execution of handlers that must call *call-next-handler* to allow the execution of superclass handlers. It's usually more convenient to call *preview-send* than it is to watch *message-handlers* and actually send an instance a message if you want to see the list of applicable handlers for a given message and instance class. The first method shows you what could be called, whereas the second method shows what was actually called.

11.11 INSTANCE CREATION, INITIALIZATION, AND DELETION MESSAGE-HANDLERS

As mentioned before, there are several predefined message-handlers that are inherited from the *USER* class including the **create**, **init**, and **delete** message-handlers. The *create* message-handler is called after an instance is created, but before any default values or slot overrides have been applied. The *init* message-handler is called after slot overrides have been processed to set any remaining slot values that were not overridden to their default values. The *delete* message-handler is either explicitly called to delete an instance or is automatically called when you call *make-instance* and specify an instance name of an already existing instance. Generally, when defining your own classes, you shouldn't override the primary handler for these message-handlers defined in the *USER* class, but it can be very useful to define your own *before* and *after* handlers to respond to these messages.

First let's look at a situation in which defining an *init after* handler is useful. Consider the following defclass:

```
(defclass PERSON
   (is-a USER)
   (slot first-name (type STRING)
   (access initialize-only))
   (slot middle-name (type STRING)
   (access initialize-only))
   (slot last-name (type STRING)
   (access initialize-only))
   (slot full-name (type STRING)
   (access initialize-only)))
```

We've made the restriction in defining the *PERSON* defclass that a person's name is specified when a *PERSON* instance is created and that it isn't changed afterwards. The *full-name* slot is intended to be the concatenation of the *first-name*, *middle-name*, and *last-name* slots with a space in between each name. Since the *full-name* slot can be specified only at initialization, we've got to provide a value for it along with the other names in order for it to be the appropriate value:

```
CLIPS>
(make-instance [p1] of PERSON
   (first-name "John")
   (middle-name "Quincy")
   (last-name "Public")
   (full-name "John Quincy Public"))↵
```

```
[p1]
CLIPS>
```

Instead of having to specify the *full-name* slot value, we can specify an *init after* message-handler that automatically constructs the full name from the other slot values:

```
(defmessage-handler PERSON init after ()
   (bind ?self:full-name
     (str-cat ?self:first-name " "
              ?self:middle-name " "
              ?self:last-name)))
```

By watching the appropriate *init* message-handlers, you can see that the *PERSON init after* message-handler is invoked after the *USER init* message-handler and that the value stored in the *full-name* slot is the expected value:

```
CLIPS> (watch message-handlers USER init)↵
CLIPS> (watch message-handlers PERSON init)↵
CLIPS>
(make-instance [p2] of PERSON
   (first-name "Jane")
   (middle-name "Paula")
   (last-name "Public"))↵
HND >> init primary in class USER
       ED:1 (<Instance-p2>)
HND << init primary in class USER
       ED:1 (<Instance-p2>)
HND >> init after in class PERSON
       ED:1 (<Instance-p2>)
HND << init after in class PERSON
       ED:1 (<Instance-p2>)
[p2]
CLIPS> (send [p2] get-full-name)↵
"Jane Paula Public"
CLIPS>
```

Note that it's usually not very useful to define an init before handler because all of the slot values of the instance have not yet been initialized.

The Storage Attribute

For an example using a *create after* handler and a *delete before* handler, we'll make use of the **storage** slot attribute. If this attribute is set to **local**, which is the default, then each instance that is created has its own storage in which to place the slot value. If the *storage* attribute is set to **shared**, then all instances of the class share the storage for the slot value. If the slot value is changed for one instance, then it is changed for all instances. For example, the following class has a *count* slot that uses shared storage:

```
(defclass INSTANCE-COUNTER
   (is-a USER)
   (slot count (storage shared) (default 1)))
```

If we create two instances and then change the *count* slot of one instance, it will change the *count* slot of the other instance as the following command sequence shows:

```
CLIPS> (make-instance i1 of INSTANCE-COUNTER)↵
[i1]
CLIPS> (make-instance i2 of INSTANCE-COUNTER)↵
[i2]
CLIPS> (send [i1] get-count)↵
1
CLIPS> (send [i2] get-count)↵
1
CLIPS> (send [i1] put-count 2)↵
2
CLIPS> (send [i1] get-count)↵
2
CLIPS> (send [i1] get-count)↵
2
CLIPS>
```

Given this behavior, we can define *create after* and *delete before* message-handlers that will increment the count slot each time an instance of this class is created and decrement the count slot each time an instance of this class is deleted:

```
(defmessage-handler INSTANCE-COUNTER create
                         after ()
   (if (integerp ?self:count)
      then
      (send ?self put-count (+ ?self:count 1))))

(defmessage-handler INSTANCE-COUNTER delete
                         before ()
   (bind ?self:count (- ?self:count 1)))
```

The *create after* message-handler requires some explanation. The *create* message is sent to an instance before any default values have been applied. In the case of the first *INSTANCE-COUNTER* instance created, the *count* slot value will be set to the symbol *nil* when the *create* message-handler is invoked. Attempting to add one to this value will result in an error since *nil* is non-numeric. The *if* function in the *create after* message-handler checks for this situation and prevents the addition from occurring. Since the default value of a shared slot is applied just once when the first instance is created, we've set the default value of the *count* slot to 1 so that the first instance automatically has the correct value. For subsequent invocations of the *create after* handler, the value of the *count* slot will be an integer so the *integerp* call in the *if* function will succeed and the value of the *count* slot will be incremented.

The following command sequence demonstrates that creating two new *INSTANCE-COUNTER* instances will appropriately increment the *count* slot to 4 and deleting one of the instances will appropriately decrement the *count* slot to 3:

```
CLIPS> (make-instance i3 of INSTANCE-COUNTER)↵
[i3]
CLIPS> (make-instance i4 of INSTANCE-COUNTER)↵
[i4]
CLIPS> (send [i1] get-count)↵
4
CLIPS> (send [i4] delete)↵
TRUE
CLIPS> (send [i1] get-count)↵
3
CLIPS>
```

11.12 MODIFYING AND DUPLICATING INSTANCES

CLIPS provides several instance commands that provide similar functionality to the *modify* and *duplicate* commands provided for facts. The syntax of these commands is:

```
(modify-instance
  <instance-expression> <slot-overrides>*)
(message-modify-instance
  <instance-expression> <slot-overrides>*)
(active-modify-instance
  <instance-expression> <slot-overrides>*)
(active-message-modify-instance
  <instance-expression> <slot-overrides>*)

(duplicate-instance <instance-expression>
                    [to <instance-name-expression>]
                    <slot-overrides>*)
(message-duplicate-instance <instance-expression>
                    [to <instance-name-expression>]
                    <slot-overrides>*)
(active-duplicate-instance <instance-expression>
                    [to <instance-name-expression>]
                    <slot-overrides>*)
```

```
(active-message-duplicate-instance
                        <instance-expression>
                        [to <instance-name-expression>]
                        <slot-overrides>*)
```

where <instance-expression> is the instance to be modified or duplicated, <slot-overrides> is the list of slot modifications, and for the duplicate commands, <instance-name-expression> is the optional new name for the duplicated instance.

The most basic instance-modification command is the **modify-instance** command. The following is an example of its use:

```
CLIPS> (unwatch all)↵
CLIPS> (clear)↵
CLIPS>
(defclass PERSON
   (is-a USER)
   (slot first-name)
   (slot last-name))
CLIPS>
(make-instance [p1] of PERSON
   (first-name "Jeff")
   (last-name "Public"))↵
[p1]
CLIPS> (watch messages)↵
CLIPS> (watch slots)↵
CLIPS>
(modify-instance [p1] (first-name "Jack")
                      (last-name "Private"))↵
MSG >> direct-modify ED:1 (<Instance-p1>
                           <Pointer-0x0062b200>)
::= local slot first-name in instance p1 <- "Jack"
::= local slot last-name in instance p1
<- "Private"
MSG << direct-modify ED:1 (<Instance-p1>
                           <Pointer-0x0062b200>)
TRUE
CLIPS> (unwatch all)↵
CLIPS> (send [p1] print)↵
[p1] of PERSON
(first-name "Jack")
(last-name "Private")
CLIPS>
```

Notice that a **direct-modify** message is sent to the instance [p1], but *put-first-name* and *put-last-name* messages are not sent. The *direct-modify* message-handler is another system-defined message-handler automatically created for you. When you use the *modify-instance* command, slot values are changed directly by the *direct-modify* message-handler without invoking message passing. The consequence of this is that *primary*, *after*, *before*, and *around put-* handlers associated with a slot will not be invoked.

The **message-modify-instance** command has the same argument syntax as the *modify-instance* command, but it uses message-passing to change slot values. For example:

```
CLIPS> (watch messages)↵
CLIPS> (message-modify-instance [p1]
                                (first-name "Jeff")
                                (last-name "Public"))↵
MSG >> message-modify ED:1 (<Instance-p1>
                            <Pointer-0x0062b1c0>)
MSG >> put-first-name ED:2 (<Instance-p1> "Jeff")
MSG << put-first-name ED:2 (<Instance-p1> "Jeff")
MSG >> put-last-name ED:2 (<Instance-p1> "Public")
MSG << put-last-name ED:2 (<Instance-p1> "Public")
MSG << message-modify ED:1 (<Instance-p1>
                            <Pointer-0x0062b1c0>)
TRUE
CLIPS>
```

In this case, because *message-modify-instance* was used, the *put-first-name* and *put-last-name* message-handlers are used to change the slot values. Instead of *direct-modify*, another system-defined message-handler, **message-modify**, is used to modify the instance.

Finally, two additional instance-modification commands are provided for additional control over object pattern matching: **active-modify-instance** and **active-message-modify-instance**. Again the argument syntax is the same as the other modification commands. With the *modify-instance* and *message-modify-instance* commands, object pattern matching does not occur until all of the slot changes have been processed. With the *active-modify-instance* and *active-message-modify-instance* commands, object pattern matching occurs after each slot change is made. Typically you will want to make all slot modifications on an instance before object pattern matching is invoked since this will typically improve performance, but the active modification commands are provided in case you have use for the alternate behavior.

Four counterpart commands for duplicating instances are also provided: **duplicate-instance**, **message-duplicate-instance**, **active-duplicate-instance**, and **active-message-modify-instance**. Each of these commands has similar behavior and arguments as its similarly named modification command; however, instead of modifying the instance passed as an argument, a duplicate of this instance is created and the slot overrides are applied to it. Optionally the name of the duplicated instance can be supplied; otherwise one is automatically generated. The return value of these commands is the duplicated instance. The following example shows how to use two of the duplicate commands:

```
CLIPS> (duplicate-instance [p1]
          (first-name "Jack"))↵
MSG >> direct-duplicate ED:1 (<Instance-p1> [gen2]
                               <Pointer-0x006b8840>)
MSG << direct-duplicate ED:1 (<Instance-p1> [gen2]
                               <Pointer-0x006b8840>)
[gen2]
CLIPS> (message-duplicate-instance [p1] to [p3]
          (first-name "Jill"))↵
MSG >> message-duplicate ED:1 (<Instance-p1> [p3]
                               <Pointer-0x006b8840>)
MSG >> create ED:2 (<Instance-p3>)682
MSG << create ED:2 (<Instance-p3>)
MSG >> put-first-name ED:2 (<Instance-p3> "Jill")
MSG << put-first-name ED:2 (<Instance-p3> "Jill")
MSG >> put-last-name ED:2 (<Instance-p3> "Public")
MSG << put-last-name ED:2 (<Instance-p3> "Public")
MSG >> init ED:2 (<Instance-p3>)
MSG << init ED:2 (<Instance-p3>)
MSG << message-duplicate ED:1 (<Instance-p1> [p3]
                               <Pointer-0x006b8840>)
[p3]
CLIPS> (instances)↵
[p1] of PERSON
[gen2] of PERSON
[p3] of PERSON
For a total of 3 instances.
CLIPS>
```

In the example use of *duplicate-instance*, since no instance name is specified, the generated name [gen2] is used. In the example use of *message-duplicate*, the specified name of [p3] is used for the duplicated instance. Two other system-defined message-handlers, **direct-duplicate** and **message-duplicate**, are sent messages depending upon which instance-duplication command is called. In this case of calling *message-duplicate* and *active-message-duplicate*, additional *create*, *init*, and *put-* messages will be sent to copy and override slot values in the newly created instance.

Finally, it's possible to define *around*, *before*, and *after* message-handlers for the system-defined message-handlers *direct-modify*, *message-modify*, *direct-duplicate*, and *message-duplicate*. However, since the slot overrides are passed in as type EXTERNAL-ADDRESS and you can decode such an argument only using external C code, there's not much you can accomplish by defining your own handlers.

11.13 CLASSES AND GENERIC FUNCTIONS

Parameter restrictions for generic functions aren't just limited to the predefined types provided by CLIPS. User-defined classes can also be used as a parameter restriction. For example, the following class could be used to represent a complex number:

```
(defclass COMPLEX
   (is-a USER)
   (slot real)
   (slot imaginary))
```

The *COMPLEX* class represents a complex number of the following format:

```
a + bi
```

where *a* and *b* are real numbers and *i* is the square root of –1. In the *COMPLEX* class, the value of *a* is stored in the *real* slot and the value of *b* is stored in the *imaginary* slot. Addition of complex numbers is simple:

```
(a + bi) + (c + di) = (a + c) + (b + d)i
```

The following method overloads the + function to implement addition of two complex numbers:

```
(defmethod + ((?c1 COMPLEX) (?c2 COMPLEX))
   (make-instance of COMPLEX
      (real (+ (send ?c1 get-real)
               (send ?c2 get-real)))
      (imaginary (+ (send ?c1 get-imaginary)
                    (send ?c2 get-imaginary)))))
```

All this method does is to add together first the real portions of the complex numbers and then the imaginary portions of the complex numbers and store them in a newly created *COMPLEX* instance. Creating instances of the COMPLEX class and adding them together demonstrates that the method works correctly:

```
CLIPS> (make-instance c1 of COMPLEX
       (real 3) (imaginary 4))↵
[c1]
CLIPS> (make-instance c2 of COMPLEX
       (real 5) (imaginary 6))↵
[c2]
CLIPS> (+ [c1] [c2])↵
[gen1]
```

```
CLIPS> (send [gen321] print)↵
[gen1] of COMPLEX
(real 8)
(imaginary 10)
CLIPS>
```

11.14 INSTANCE SET QUERY FUNCTIONS

In addition to pattern matching on objects, it's also possible to directly query COOL for sets of instances that satisfy a specified set of conditions. To illustrate the use of these functions, we'll use the following constructs that represent a small family tree:

```
(defclass PERSON
   (is-a USER)
   (slot full-name)
   (slot gender)
   (multislot children))

(defclass FEMALE
   (is-a PERSON)
   (slot gender (access read-only)
                (storage shared)
                (default female)))

(defclass MALE
   (is-a PERSON)
   (slot gender (access read-only)
                (storage shared)
                (default male)))

(definstances people
   ([p1] of MALE (full-name "John Smith")
            (children [p5]))
   ([p2] of FEMALE (full-name "Jan Smith")
            (children [p5]))
   ([p3] of MALE (full-name "Bob Jones")
            (children [p6]))
   ([p4] of FEMALE (full-name "Pam Jones")
            (children [p6]))
   ([p5] of MALE (full-name "Frank Smith")
            (children [p7]))
   ([p6] of FEMALE (full-name "Sue Jones")
            (children [p7]))
   ([p7] of MALE (full-name "Dave Smith")))
```

Determining if a Query Is Satisfied

The simplest of the query functions is **any-instancep**. The syntax of this function is:

```
(any-instancep <instance-set-template> <query>)
```

where <instance-set-template> is a specification of the classes to be searched and <query> is a boolean expression that the matching instances of those classes must satisfy. If a set of instances is found that satisfy the query, then the *any-instancep* function returns the symbol TRUE; otherwise the function returns the value false.

The syntax of <instance-set-template> is:

```
(<instance-set-member-template>+)
```

where <instance-set-member-template> is:

```
(<single-field-variable> <class-name-expression>+)
```

and <single-field-variable> is a variable to which an instance will be bound and the one or more occurrences of <class-name-expression> are the classes containing the instances that are to be individually bound to <single-field-variable>.

The simplest test that can be made with *any-instancep* is for the existence of any instance of a class:

```
CLIPS> (any-instancep ((?p PERSON)) TRUE)↵
FALSE
CLIPS> (reset)↵
CLIPS> (any-instancep ((?p PERSON)) TRUE)↵
TRUE
CLIPS>
```

In this example, there aren't any instances of the *PERSON* class until a *reset* is performed and the instances in the *people* definstances are created. The use of *TRUE* for the query means that any instance assigned to ?p will satisfy the query.

If we created only *MALE* and *FEMALE* instances, we could determine if there were any instances of the *PERSON* class by just specifying those two classes:

```
CLIPS> (any-instancep ((?p MALE FEMALE)) TRUE)↵
TRUE
CLIPS>
```

We could determine if there are any males using any of the following three queries:

```
CLIPS> (any-instancep ((?p MALE)) TRUE)↵
TRUE
CLIPS>
```

```
(any-instancep ((?p PERSON))
               (eq (send ?p get-gender) male))↵
TRUE
CLIPS>
(any-instancep ((?p PERSON)) (eq ?p:gender male))↵
TRUE
CLIPS>
```

In the first case we search for instances of the class *MALE* for which we know the *gender* slot will contain *male*. In the second case, we send the *PERSON* instance assigned to variable ?p the *get-gender* message and use the *eq* function to determine if the value is *male*. The third case demonstrates that slot shorthand notation can be used with variables bound in the instance set template.

It's also possible to specify more than one instance set member in the template:

```
CLIPS> (any-instancep ((?f FEMALE) (?p PERSON))
                      (member$ ?p ?f:children))↵
TRUE
CLIPS>
```

This example tests if there are any mothers. For every combination of instances of the *FEMALE* class with the instances of the *PERSON* class, the query is applied to determine if the PERSON ?p is one of the children of the FEMALE ?f.

Determining the Instances Satisfying a Query

The **find-instance** and **find-all-instances** query functions have syntax similar to that of the *any-instancep* function:

```
(find-instance <instance-set-template> <query>)
(find-all-instances
  <instance-set-template> <query>)
```

Instead of returning TRUE or FALSE, the *find-instance* query function returns a multifield value containing the first instance set satisfying the query. If no instance set was found satisfying the query, then the multifield value will be empty. Similarly, the *find-all-instances* function returns a multifield value containing all instance sets that satisfied the query. For example:

```
CLIPS> (find-instance ((?p MALE)) TRUE)↵
([p1])
CLIPS> (find-all-instances ((?p MALE)) TRUE)↵
([p1] [p3] [p5] [p7])
CLIPS>
```

```
(find-all-instances ((?p MALE))
                    (eq ?p:gender female))↵
()
CLIPS>
```

In the event that there is more than one set member specified in the template, you must programmatically group the members of the return-value together. For example:

```
CLIPS>
(find-all-instances ((?f FEMALE) (?p PERSON))
                    (member$ ?p ?f:children))↵
([p2] [p5] [p4] [p6] [p6] [p7])
CLIPS>
```

Instances [p2] and [p5] belong to the first instance set, [p4] and [p6] to the second instance set, and [p6] and [p7] to the third instance set. The following deffunction demonstrates how you can programmatically group the instance set members:

```
(deffunction print-mother-message (?query-result)
  (bind ?iterations
      (div (length$ ?query-result) 2))
(loop-for-count (?i ?iterations) do
   (bind ?mother (nth$
      (- (* 2 ?i) 1) ?query-result))
   (bind ?child (nth$ (* 2 ?i) ?query-result))
   (printout t (send ?mother get-full-name)
          " is the mother of "
          (send ?child get-full-name)
          "." crlf)))
```

The length of the query return value is divided by the number of instances per member set to determine the number of member set over which to iterate. The *loop-for-count* function is then used in conjunction with the *nth$* function to extract the value for each instance in the member set. Using the *print-mother-message* with the return value of the prior find-all-instances call produces the following results:

```
CLIPS>
(print-mother-message
   (find-all-instances ((?f FEMALE) (?p PERSON))
                       (member$ ?p ?f:children)))↵
Jan Smith is the mother of Frank Smith.
Pam Jones is the mother of Sue Jones.
Sue Jones is the mother of Dave Smith.
FALSE
CLIPS>
```

Performing an Action for the Instances Satisfying a Query

The **do-for-instance**, **do-for-all-instances**, and **delayed-do-for-all-instances** query functions allow you to perform actions on the instance sets satisfying a query. Their syntax is:

```
(do-for-instance
  <instance-set-template> <query> <expression>*)
(do-for-all-instances
  <instance-set-template> <query> <expression>*)
(delayed-do-for-all-instances
  <instance-set-template> <query> <expression>*)
```

The *do-for-instance* function evaluates the specified actions for the first instance set satisfying the query. For example:

```
CLIPS>
(do-for-instance ((?f FEMALE) (?p PERSON))
                 (member$ ?p ?f:children)
   (printout t ?f:full-name " is the mother of "
               ?p:full-name "." crlf))↵
Jan Smith is the mother of Frank Smith.
CLIPS>
```

The *do-for-all-instances* function evaluates the specified actions for all instance sets satisfying the query. For example:

```
CLIPS>
(do-for-all-instances ((?f FEMALE) (?p PERSON))
                      (member$ ?p ?f:children)
   (printout t ?f:full-name " is the mother of "
               ?p:full-name "." crlf))↵
Jan Smith is the mother of Frank Smith.
Pam Jones is the mother of Sue Jones.
Sue Jones is the mother of Dave Smith.
CLIPS>
```

Note that using *do-for-all-instances* is a simpler mechanism to achieve the same functionality in the prior example, which used the *find-all-instances* function with the *print-mother-message* deffunction.

The *delayed-do-for-all-instances* function is similar to the *do-for-all-instances* function except that it first finds all of the instance sets satisfying the query and then it executes the actions for each instance set. In contrast, the *do-for-all-instance* function applies the query to each instance set and if it succeeds executes the actions for that instance set. The only time these functions produce different results is when the executed actions change the query result of an instance set that hasn't yet been processed. Changing an instance slot value referenced by the query, for example, could cause different results for these two functions.

The return value of all the query functions that allow actions is the symbol *FALSE* if no instance sets satisfied the query. Otherwise it is the return value of the last action executed for the last instance set satisfying the query. In addition, the query functions that allow actions can also be prematurely terminated by using the *break* or *return* functions.

11.15 MULTIPLE INHERITANCE

All of the defclass examples so far have had a single class specified in the *is-a* attribute. These are all examples of **single inheritance**. It's possible to specify more than one class in the *is-a* attribute. When this occurs, it is called **multiple inheritance**. In the case where the specified classes have no slots or message-handlers in common, multiple inheritance is essentially equivalent to using single inheritance in the superclasses of the defined class. For example, in the following case, the *x*, *y*, and *z* slots are inherited directly by class *D* using multiple inheritance:

```
CLIPS> (clear)↵
CLIPS>
(defclass A
   (is-a USER)
   (slot x))↵
CLIPS>
(defclass B
   (is-a USER)
   (slot y))↵
CLIPS>
(defclass C
   (is-a USER)
   (slot z))↵
CLIPS>
(defclass D
   (is-a C B A))↵
CLIPS> (make-instance [d1] of D (x 3) (y 4) (z 5))↵
[d1]
CLIPS> (send [d1] print)↵
[d1] of D
(x 3)
(y 4)
(z 5)
CLIPS>
```

In the following case, classes *B* and *C* are used as intermediary classes to allow class *D* to indirectly inherit the slots *x* and *y* via single inheritance:

```
CLIPS> (clear)↵
CLIPS>
```

```
(defclass A
   (is-a USER)
   (slot x))↵
CLIPS>
(defclass B
   (is-a A)
   (slot y))↵
CLIPS>
(defclass C
   (is-a B)
   (slot z))↵
CLIPS>
(defclass D
   (is-a C))↵
CLIPS> (make-instance [d1] of D (x 3) (y 4) (z 5))↵
[d1]
CLIPS> (send [d1] print)↵
[d1] of D
(x 3)
(y 4)
(z 5)
CLIPS>
```

It is important to note that although class *D* inherits the same slots in both cases, classes *B* and *C* do not. Because we were able to redefine classes *B* and *C* in the second case, the same final results for class *D* could be achieved using single inheritance instead of multiple inheritance. Typical use of multiple inheritance, however, is for situations in which you have preexisting classes that you cannot change.

Multiple-Inheritance Conflicts

Most practical examples of multiple inheritance involve cases where the superclasses from which the class is inheriting do not share slots or message-handlers (other than the ones inherited from *USER*). In this situation, there are no conflicts between the superclasses that need to be resolved and slots and message-handlers of the class being defined that conflict with superclass slots and message-handlers override these definitions just as they would with single inheritance.

Let's look at a brief example in which multiple inheritance is used and there are conflicting superclass definitions of slots and message-handlers:

```
CLIPS> (clear)↵
CLIPS>
(defclass A
   (is-a USER)
   (slot x (default 3))
   (slot y (default 4)))↵
CLIPS>
```

```
(defmessage-handler A compute ()
   (* ?self:y 10))↵
CLIPS>
(defclass B
   (is-a USER)
   (slot y (default 1))
   (slot z (default 5)))↵
CLIPS>
(defmessage-handler B compute ()
   (+ ?self:y 3))↵
CLIPS> (defclass C (is-a A B))↵
CLIPS> (defclass D (is-a B A))↵
CLIPS>
```

In this example, both classes *C* and *D* directly inherit from classes *A* and *B*. Since both classes *A* and *B* have conflicting definitions of a *y* slot and a *compute* message-handler, let's examine how this is resolved:

```
CLIPS> (make-instance [c1] of C)↵
[c1]
CLIPS> (make-instance [d1] of D)↵
[d1]
CLIPS> (send [c1] print)↵
[c1] of C
(z 5)
(x 3)
(y 4)
CLIPS> (send [d1] print)↵
[d1] of D
(x 3)
(y 1)
(z 5)
CLIPS>
```

There are two things to note about the resulting slot values displayed for instances [c1] and [c2]. First is the order in which the slots are printed and second is the value for the *y* slot. The order in which the slots are printed is of little significance other than to indicate that the order in which the superclasses are listed in the *is-a* attribute has some effect on the resulting class definition. The significant difference between the two instances is that the default value of the *y* slot for instance [c1] is 4 whereas the default value of the *y* slot for instance [d1] is 1. Because class *C* inherits from class *A* first, it uses the default value in class *A* for slot *y* rather than the default value from class *B*. Similarly, because class *D* inherits from class *B* first, it uses the default value in class *B* for slot *y* rather than the default value from class *A*. Similar behavior occurs with the compute message-handler:

```
CLIPS> (send [c1] put-y 3)↵
3
```

```
CLIPS> (send [d1] put-y 3)↵
3
CLIPS> (send [c1] compute)↵
30
CLIPS> (send [d1] compute)↵
6
CLIPS>
```

Even though the value of 3 is assigned to the *y* slot for both instances, the result of the *compute* message for instance [c1] is 30 (3 * 10) where the result for instance [d1] is 6 (3 + 3). Again, this is because the *compute* message-handler for class *A* is used by instance [c1] and the *compute* message-handler for class *B* is used by instance [d1].

In simple cases where the classes specified in the *is-a* attribute do not share common user-defined superclasses, the order in which the classes are specified determines the precedence when there are multiple definitions of the same slot or message-handler. In this example, class *A* definitions take precedence over class *B* definitions in class *C* because *A* was specified before *B*. In class *D*, class *B* definitions take precedence over class *A* definitions because *B* was specified before *A*.

More complex cases of multiple inheritance are left up to the reader to investigate. The *Basic Programming Guide* included on the CD-ROM contains a complete explanation along with examples of how multiple inheritance is resolved for all situations. As a general rule, however, if you are creating classes using multiple inheritance and the order in which you specify the classes in the *is-a* attribute affects the behavior of the class being defined, then you should consider whether you are making the solution to your problem more complex than it needs to be.

Saving and Restoring Slot Values

Let's look at a practical example of multiple inheritance: defining a *RESTORABLE* class that can be used with other classes to save and restore the slot values of an instance. To implement this class, we'll need to define another class that we'll use to store the slot values:

```
(defclass SAVED-SLOT
   (is-a USER)
   (slot slot-name)
   (multislot slot-value))
```

The *SAVED-SLOT* class has *slot-name* and *slot-value* slots. The *slot-name* slot is used to store the name of a saved slot. The *slot-value* slot is used to store the value of the named slot. It's defined as a multifield slot since we'll need to be able to store slot values from both single-field and multifield slots.

The *RESTORABLE* class is defined as follows:

```
(defclass RESTORABLE
   (is-a USER)
   (multislot saved-slots))
```

The *saved-slots* multifield slot will hold zero or more references to *SAVED-SLOT* instances representing the slot values of the instance.

The *save* message-handler is used to save the slot values of a *RESTORABLE* instance:

```
(defmessage-handler RESTORABLE save ()
   ; Delete existing saved slots
   (progn$ (?si ?self:saved-slots)
      (send ?si delete))
   (bind ?self:saved-slots)
   ; Determine the list of slots
   (bind ?class (class ?self))
   (bind ?slots
     (delete-member$ (class-slots ?class inherit)
                     saved-slots))
   ; Create an empty list
   (bind ?list (create$))
   ; Iterate over each slot
   (progn$ (?slot ?slots)
      (bind ?value (send ?self
                      (sym-cat get- ?slot)))
      (bind ?ins (make-instance of SAVED-SLOT
                      (slot-name ?slot)
                      (slot-value ?value)))
      (bind ?list (create$ ?list ?ins)))
   ; Store the saved slots
   (bind ?self:saved-slots ?list))
```

The first action the *save* message-handler takes is to delete all *SAVED-SLOT* instances that have references stored in the *saved-slots* slot. The *saved-slots* slot is then bound to an empty multifield.

Next the list of slots to be saved is derived. The **class** function is called to determine the class name of the instance. The class name is then passed into the **class-slots** function along with the key word *inherit* to get a multifield list containing all the slot names associated with the class. Finally, the slot name *saved-slots* is removed from this list by calling the **delete-member$** function. We don't want to save the values in this slot because it is used as storage for the values of all other slots.

An empty list is then created to contain the *SAVED-SLOT* instances. The *progn$* function is used to iterate over each of the slots of the instance being saved. First, the slot value is retrieved. The slot name is appended to the symbol *get-* to create the appropriate message to send to the instance to retrieve the slot value. Once the slot value is retrieved, a *SAVED-SLOT* instance is created containing the slot name and value. The reference to this instance is added to the list of saved slots. Once all slots have been processed, the list of *SAVED-SLOT* instance references is stored in the *saved-slots* slot.

With the *save* message-handler now defined, the following *restore* message-handler can be used to restore an instance's slot values:

```
(defmessage-handler RESTORABLE restore ()
   (progn$ (?si ?self:saved-slots)
      (bind ?name (send ?si get-slot-name))
      (bind ?value (send ?si get-slot-value))
      (send ?self (sym-cat put- ?name) ?value)))
```

The *restore* message-handler iterates over all of the *SAVED-SLOT* instances stored in the *saved-slots* slot. First the name and value of each saved slot is retrieved from the SAVED-SLOT instance. The slot name is appended to the symbol *put-* to create the appropriate message to send to the instance to set the slot value. This message is then sent to the instance to restore the slot value to its save value.

Now that the RESTORABLE class is defined, let's examine how it would be used with an existing class to create a new class with save/restore functionality. We'll use a PERSON class similar to prior examples:

```
(defclass PERSON
   (is-a USER)
   (slot full-name)
   (slot gender)
   (multislot children))
```

The RESTORABLE-PERSON class will inherit from both the PERSON and RESTORABLE classes:

```
(defclass RESTORABLE-PERSON
   (is-a RESTORABLE PERSON))
```

To see how save/restore works, we first need to make an instance of the RESTORABLE-INSTANCE class:

```
CLIPS> (reset)↵
CLIPS>
(make-instance [p1] of RESTORABLE-PERSON
   (full-name "Sue Jones")
   (gender female)
   (children Bob Jan))↵
[p1]
CLIPS> (send [p1] print)↵
[p1] of RESTORABLE-PERSON
(full-name "Sue Jones")
(gender female)
(children Bob Jan)
(saved-slots)
CLIPS>
```

Sending instance [p1] a *save* message will save the current values of its slots:

```
CLIPS> (send [p1] save)↵
([gen1] [gen2] [gen3])
CLIPS> (send [p1] print)↵
[p1] of RESTORABLE-PERSON
(full-name "Sue Jones")
(gender female)
(children Bob Jan)
(saved-slots [gen1] [gen2] [gen3])
CLIPS>
```

Instances [gen1], [gen2], and [gen3] are instances of the *SAVED-SLOT* class created to store the slot values of [p1]. We can examine these instances to see the individual slot values saved:

```
CLIPS> (send [gen1] print)↵
[gen1] of SAVED-SLOT
(slot-name full-name)
(slot-value "Sue Jones")
CLIPS> (send [gen2] print)↵
[gen2] of SAVED-SLOT
(slot-name gender)
(slot-value female)
CLIPS> (send [gen3] print)↵
[gen3] of SAVED-SLOT
(slot-name children)
(slot-value Bob Jan)
CLIPS>
```

Next we'll change some of the slot values of instance [p1]:

```
CLIPS> (send [p1] put-full-name "Sue Smith")↵
"Sue Smith"
CLIPS> (send [p1] put-children Bob Jan Paul)↵
(Bob Jan Paul)
CLIPS> (send [p1] print)↵
[p1] of RESTORABLE-PERSON
(full-name "Sue Smith")
(gender female)
(children Bob Jan Paul)
(saved-slots [gen1] [gen2] [gen3])
CLIPS>
```

When we send the instance a *restore* message, the original slot values are restored:

```
CLIPS> (send [p1] restore)↵
(Bob Jan)
```

```
CLIPS> (send [p1] print)↵
[p1] of RESTORABLE-PERSON
(full-name "Sue Jones")
(gender female)
(children Bob Jan)
(saved-slots [gen1] [gen2] [gen3])
CLIPS>
```

11.16 DEFCLASSES AND DEFMODULES

In a similar manner to other constructs, defclass constructs can be imported and exported by modules. The export and import statements previously discussed, which export or import all constructs, also apply to defclasses. In addition, it's possible to explicitly specify which defclasses are exported or imported using one of the following statements:

```
(export defclass ?ALL)
(export defclass ?NONE)
(export defclass <deffunction-name>+)

(import <module-name> defclass ?ALL)
(import <module-name> defclass ?NONE)
(import <module-name> defclass <defclass-name>+)
```

If a class is imported or exported, then all of its associated defmessage-handler constructs are also imported or exported. It's not possible to import or export specific message-handlers. A module that does not import a defclass construct from another module can create its own definition of that class using the same name. The exceptions to this rule are the predefined system classes, such as the *USER* class, which are visible to all modules and cannot be redefined.

Just as facts are associated with the module in which their associated deftemplate is defined, instances are associated with the module in which their associated defclass is defined. Each module, however, has its own "name-space" for keeping instance names unique. What this means is that while a single module cannot have two instances sharing the same instance name, two separate modules can have instances sharing the same instance name. For example:

```
CLIPS> (defmodule A)↵
CLIPS>
(defclass A::ACLASS (is-a USER)
  (export defclass ?ALL))↵
CLIPS> (make-instance [same] of ACLASS)↵
[same]
CLIPS> (send [same] print)↵
[same] of A::ACLASS
CLIPS> (defmodule B)↵
```

```
CLIPS>
(defclass B::BCLASS (is-a USER)
  (export defclass ?ALL))↵
CLIPS> (make-instance [same] of BCLASS)↵
[same]
CLIPS> (send [same] print)↵
[same] of B::BCLASS
CLIPS> (set-current-module A)↵
B
CLIPS> (send [same] print)↵
[same] of A::ACLASS
CLIPS>
```

Note that defining the instance *[same]* in module *B* does not cause the deletion of the instance *[same]* in module *A* as it normally would if an instance with the same name were created in module *A*.

The instance namespace of an exporting module is not automatically visible to an importing module as the following example demonstrates:

```
CLIPS> (defmodule C (import A defclass ?ALL)
                    (import B defclass ?ALL))↵
CLIPS> (send [same] print)↵
[MSGPASS2] No such instance same in function send.
FALSE
CLIPS>
```

In this case, even though there is a *[same]* instance in both modules *A* and *B*, module *C* searches only its own instance namespace for the specified instance and thus does not find it. One way to refer to an instance name in another module is to include the module name and module separator as part of the instance name. For example:

```
CLIPS> (send [A::same] print)↵
[same] of A::ACLASS
CLIPS> (send [B::same] print)↵
[same] of B::BCLASS
CLIPS>
```

In this case, since a module was specified as part of the instance name, CLIPS knows which namespace to use to find the instance specified by the instance name. The module separator by itself can also be used to locate the instance referred to by an instance name:

```
CLIPS> (send [::same] print)↵
[same] of B::BCLASS
CLIPS>
```

In this case, CLIPS searches the current module first for the instance and then checks each module from which defclasses have been imported for the instance. Generally, you'll want to use only the module specifier if you know the instance is defined either in the current module or a single imported module. In this example, the instance *[B::same]* was found first, but if the order of the import statements had been switched, then *[A::same]* would have been found first.

The conventions for referring to instances in other modules may seem complicated, but in practice you need only general familiarity with how it works. Typically your programs will refer to instances using instance addresses rather than instance names. With instance addresses, there is no ambiguity of which instance is being referred to as there is with instance names. Instance names are typically used when you send a message to an instance from the command prompt and usually the names are unique so you can use just the module separator if the current module imports the defclass associated with the instance.

11.17 LOADING AND SAVING INSTANCES

Similarly to facts, there are several commands available for saving and loading instances to and from files. These commands are **save-instances**, **bsave-instances**, **load-instances**, **restore-instances**, and **bload-instances**. The syntax of these commands is:

```
(save-instances <file-name>
   [<save-scope> [[inherit] <class-names>+])

(bsave-instances <file-name>
   [<save-scope> [[inherit] <class-names>+])

(load-instances <file-name>)

(restore-instances <file-name>)

(bload-instances <file-name>)
```

where <save-scope> is defined as:

```
visible | local
```

The *load-instances* command will load in a group of instances stored in the file specified by <file-name>. The instances in the file should be in the standard format used by the definstances construct for specifying instances. For example, if the file "instances.dat" contained:

```
(Jack of PERSON (full-name "Jack Q. Public")
                (age 23))
(of PERSON (full-name "John Doe")
                (hair-color black))
```

then the command:

```
(load-instances "instances.dat")
```

would load the instances contained in that file. Calling *load-instances* is equivalent to making a series of *make-instance* calls. The *restore-instances* command is similar to the *load-instances* command; however, it does not use message-passing when deleting, initializing, or setting the slot values of the instances it is loading. The return value of both of these commands is the number or instances loaded or –1 if the command was unable to access the instance file.

The *save-instances* command can be used to save instances to the file specified by <file-name>. The instances are stored in the format required by the *load-instances* and *restore-instances* commands. If <save-scope> is not specified or if it is specified as **local**, then only those instances corresponding to defclasses defined in the current module would be saved to the file. If <save-scope> is specified as **visible**, then all instances corresponding to defclasses that are visible to the current module would be saved to the file. If <save-scope> is specified, one or more defclass names may also be specified. In this case, only instances corresponding to the specified defclasses will be saved (however, the defclass names must still satisfy the *local* or *visible* specification). If the **inherit** keyword is specified, then instances of subclasses of the specified classes will also be saved if the subclasses also satisfy the *local* or *visible* specification. The return value of this command is the number of instances saved.

The *bsave-instances* and *bload-instances* commands are similar to the *save-instances* and *load-instances* commands except a binary format is used to store instances rather than a text format. Because of this, you can use *bload-instances* only with files created using the *bsave-instances* command. The benefit of using these commands is that for large numbers of instances, it is faster to load the binary format than it is to load the text format. The drawback is that the binary files are usually not portable from one platform to another.

11.18 SUMMARY

This chapter introduced the CLIPS Object-Oriented Language (COOL). Instances (or objects) are another data representation provided by CLIPS. The attributes of an instance are specified using the *defclass* construct. Procedural code, called message-handlers, can be associated with classes using the *defmessage-handler* construct. Inheritance allows a class to make use of the slots and message-handlers associated with another class. COOL supports both single and multiple inheritance. A class that inherits from another class is a subclass of the other class. The class from which it inherits is called the superclass of that class. A subclass inherits attributes and message-handlers from its superclasses, but when duplicate definitions are found in both classes, the subclass overrides the superclass definition. Using the *role* attribute, *abstract* classes can be created that can be used only for inheritance. No instances of these classes can be created. In contrast, concrete classes can be used for inheritance and instances of these classes can be created. COOL predefines a number of primitive classes. Most user-created classes inherit from the system class USER. The *definstances* construct allows a set of specified instances to be created when a *reset* command is issued.

In addition to the slot attributes provided with deftemplates, several additional slot attributes are also supported by defclasses. The *source* attribute allows slot attributes to be inherited from superclasses. The *propagation* attribute allows the inheritance of a slot to be disabled. The pattern-match attribute allows you to specify whether a slot or class can participate in pattern matching. The *visibility* attribute allows you to specify whether a slot can be directly accessed by the message-handlers of subclasses. The *access* attribute directly restricts the type of access allowed to slots. The *create-accessor* attribute is used to control the automatic creation of the get- and put- handlers for class slots. The *storage* attribute allows you to specify whether a slot value is shared by all instances of a class or if each instance has its own value.

Several predefined system message-handlers for creating, initializing, printing, and deleting instances are available. In addition, user-defined message-handlers can also be created. Message-handlers are invoked by sending an instance a message name along with associated arguments via the *send* command. A message-handler can be one of four types: *primary*, *around*, *before*, or *after*. The *primary* handler is typically the main handler for responding to a message. The *before* and *after* handlers are invoked respectively before and after the primary handler. The *around* handler is also called a wrapper handler because it wraps around the *before*, *after*, and *primary* handlers executing code both before and after they are executed. *Around* handlers must explicitly invoke the other handler types. Primary message-handlers override or shadow the primary message-handler for the same message inherited from a superclass, although it is possible to invoke shadowed handlers. The *around*, *before*, and *after* message-handlers of superclasses, however, are not shadowed by subclass definition.

Object pattern matching provides several capabilities not found with fact pattern matching. First, a single object pattern can match instances from several classes. Second, changes to slot values that are not specified in an object pattern do not retrigger the rule to which the pattern belongs. Third, changes to slot values that are not specified in an object pattern within a *logical* conditional element do not remove logical support provided by the associated rule.

COOL provides several instance set query functions that allow direct queries on sets of instances satisfying a specified set of conditions. Several of these functions also allow actions to be performed on the query results. Parameter restrictions for generic functions can use user-defined classes in addition to the predefined types provided by CLIPS. The *save-instances*, *bsave-instances*, *load-instances*, *restore-instances*, and *bload-instances* functions can be used to save instances to, and load instances from, a file.

PROBLEMS

11.1 Modify the program developed for Problem 10.3 on page 618 to provide explanation capabilities. After the output for the best matching shrub is printed, the program should prompt the user to determine whether he or she wants an explanation for a specified shrub. If the return key is pressed, the program should stop. If the name of a shrub is entered, the program should list the requirements it satisfied, the requirements it did not satisfy, and other requirements that it could satisfy. Once the explanation is printed, the user should be prompted again to determine whether he or she wants another explanation.

11.2 Modify the program developed for Problem 10.7 on page 619 so that it can schedule several students. The input to the program should be read from a file. You are free to determine the format of the input data; however, it should contain at least the name of each student, the courses to be scheduled, and the student's preferences for instructors and periods. The output of the program should be written to a file. The output file should contain the name of each student followed by the courses scheduled for that student.

11.3 Modify the program developed for Problem 10.6 on page 618 to demonstrate dynamically reconfigurable menus. For example, selecting menu item 1 in submenu 1 causes two menu items to be displayed in submenu 2, but selecting menu item 2 in submenu 1 causes four menu items to be displayed in submenu 2.

11.4 For the following defclass, write a *before* handler for the *get-side* handler that will prompt the user for the value of the *side* slot if it's current value is the default value *unspecified*:

```
(defclass SQUARE
   (is-a USER)
   (slot side (default unspecified)))
```

11.5 Create an *ARRAY* defclass and associated message-handlers that allow a multi-dimensional array to be represented. Message-handlers for getting and setting array values should be provided. It should be possible to specify a default value for the array elements as well as specify an initial set of array values in the *make-instance* call used to create an *ARRAY* instance. Finally, a message-handler for displaying the contents of the array should be provided. Single-dimension arrays should be displayed as a row of values. Two-dimensional arrays should be displayed by row and column. Other multi-dimensional arrays should be displayed by listing one value per line with the value preceded by its indices.

11.6 Using the *ARRAY* defclass and message-handlers developed for Problem 11.5, overload the * function with a method that multiplies two two-dimensional arrays. Use additional methods to check for error conditions such as the rows and columns of the two arrays not being compatible for multiplication.

11.7 Create a *LINKED-LIST* defclass and associated message-handlers that allow a linked listed to be created. The defclass should be designed such that existing classes inherit from it to obtain the linked list functionality. Message-handlers for retrieving the next and previous objects in the list, inserting an object in the list, removing an object from the list, and printing the list should be provided. Write a program that demonstrates use of the *LINKED-LIST* defclass with a defclass that inherits from it as well as another class.

11.8 Create an *ITERATOR* defclass and associated message-handlers that allow iteration over the fields of a multifield value. The values over which to iterate can be read and also set as part of the make-instance call used to create an instance of this class, but otherwise no slots of the class should be accessible except to the message-handlers of the class. A *first* message-handler should be provided to initiate iteration and return the first value in the iteration list. *Next* and *previous* message-handlers should be provided to respectively retrieve the next or previous value in the iteration list.

11.9 Create a *MEASUREMENT* defclass that stores both the amount and units of a length. Using the methods developed for problems 10.20 and 10.21, create a new method that will add two *MEASUREMENT* instances and return a new instance storing the computed sum.

11.10 Create a *STACK* defclass along with message-handlers supporting push and pop operations on the stack.

11.11 Create a *SHUFFLER* defclass that implements a *shuffle* message-handler that randomly reorders a list of values stored in a *SHUFFLER* instance.

11.12 Create a *CARD* defclass to represent a playing card. Create a *DECK* defclass that is initialized to contain the 52 playing cards of a deck. Provide a *shuffle* message-handler that uses the *SHUFFLER* defclass from problem 10.11 to shuffle the deck.

11.13 Override the -, *, and / functions with methods that perform subtraction, multiplication, and division on instances of the *COMPLEX* class.

11.14 Write a deffunction that counts all of the occurrences of each character within a string and prints a summary of the counts.

11.15 Create a *DIRECTORY* defclass that stores names and telephone numbers. Message-handlers should be provided that allow you to add and remove listings from the directory and to search the directory either by name or number and print all matching listings.

CHAPTER 12
Expert System Design Examples

12.1 INTRODUCTION

This chapter provides several examples of CLIPS programs. The first example demonstrates how uncertainty can be represented in CLIPS. The next two examples demonstrate how other knowledge representation paradigms can be emulated using CLIPS. One shows how decision trees can be represented in CLIPS and the other shows how backward-chaining rules can be represented in CLIPS. The fourth and final example builds the framework of a simple expert system that monitors a group of sensors.

12.2 CERTAINTY FACTORS

CLIPS has no built-in capabilities for handling uncertainty. However, it is possible to incorporate uncertainty into CLIPS by placing information dealing with uncertainty directly into facts and rules. As an example, the MYCIN uncertainty mechanism will be emulated using CLIPS. This section will demonstrate how the following MYCIN rule (Firebaugh 88) can be rewritten in CLIPS:

```
IF
   The stain of the organism is gramneg and
   The morphology of the organism is rod and
   The patient is a compromised host
THEN
   There is suggestive evidence (0.6) that the
     identity of the organism is pseudomonas
```

MYCIN represents factual information as object–attribute–value triples. These OAV triples can be represented in CLIPS using the following deftemplate construct (which will be placed in its own module to create a reusable software component):

```
(defmodule OAV (export deftemplate oav))

(deftemplate OAV::oav
   (multislot object (type SYMBOL))
   (multislot attribute (type SYMBOL))
   (multislot value))
```

Using this deftemplate, some of the facts required by the IF portion of the preceding MYCIN rule would be:

```
(oav (object organism)
     (attribute stain)
     (value gramneg))

(oav (object organism)
     (attribute morphology)
     (value rod))

(oav (object patient)
     (attribute is a)
     (value compromised host))
```

MYCIN also associates with each fact a certainty factor (CF) that represents a degree of belief in the fact. The certainty factor ranges from -1 to 1; -1 means the fact is known to be false, 0 means no information is known about the fact (complete uncertainty), and 1 means the fact is known to be true.

Since CLIPS does not handle certainty factors automatically, this information must also be maintained. To do this, an additional slot in each fact will be used to represent the certainty factor. The *oav* deftemplate for each fact now becomes:

```
(deftemplate OAV::oav
   (multislot object (type SYMBOL))
   (multislot attribute (type SYMBOL))
   (multislot value)
   (slot CF (type FLOAT) (range -1.0 +1.0)))
```

and the examples facts might be:

```
(oav (object organism)
     (attribute stain)
     (value gramneg)
     (CF 0.3))
```

```
(oav (object organism)
     (attribute morphology)
     (value rod)
     (CF 0.7))

(oav (object patient)
     (attribute is a)
     (value compromised host)
     (CF 0.8))
```

One further modification to CLIPS must be made in order for the *oav* facts to work properly. MYCIN allows the same OAV triple to be derived by separate rules. The OAV triples are then combined to produce a single OAV triple that combines the certainty factors of the two. The current *oav* deftemplate will allow two identical OAV triples to be asserted only if they have different certainty factors (since CLIPS normally does not allow two duplicate facts to be asserted). In order to allow identical OAV triples to be asserted with the same certainty factors, the **set-fact-duplication** command can be used to disable the CLIPS behavior that prevents duplicate facts from being asserted. The command:

```
(set-fact-duplication TRUE)
```

will disable the behavior. Similarly, the command:

```
(set-fact-duplication FALSE)
```

will prevent duplicate facts from being asserted.

As stated, MYCIN will combine two identical OAV triples into a single OAV triple with a combined certainty. If the certainty factors of the two facts (represented by CF_1 and CF_2) are both greater than or equal to zero, MYCIN uses the following formula to compute the new certainty factor:

$$\text{New Certainty} = (CF_1 + CF_2) - (CF_1 * CF_2)$$

For example, assume that the following facts are in the fact list:

```
(oav (object organism)
     (attribute morphology)
     (value rod)
     (CF 0.7))

(oav (object organism)
     (attribute morphology)
     (value rod)
     (CF 0.5))
```

Let CF_1 be 0.7 and CF_2 be 0.5; then the new certainty for the combination of the two facts is computed as:

```
New Certainty = (0.7 + 0.5) - (0.7 * 0.5)
              = 1.2 - 0.35
              = 0.85
```

and the new fact to replace the two original facts would then be:

```
(oav (object organism)
     (attribute morphology)
     (value rod)
     (CF 0.85))
```

Since CLIPS does not automatically handle certainty factors for facts, it follows that it also does not automatically combine two OAV triples derived from different rules. The combination of OAV triples can easily be handled by a rule that searches the fact list for identical OAV triples to be combined. The following method and rule demonstrate how this can be accomplished when the certainty factors of both OAV triples are greater than or equal to zero:

```
(defmethod OAV::combine-certainties
   ((?C1 NUMBER (> ?C1 0))(?C2 NUMBER (> ?C2 0)))
    (- (+ ?C1 ?C2)(* ?C1 ?C2)))

(defrule OAV::combine-certainties
   (declare (auto-focus TRUE))
   ?fact1 <- (oav (object $?o)
                  (attribute $?a)
                  (value $?v)
                  (CF ?C1))
   ?fact2 <- (oav (object $?o)
                  (attribute $?a)
                  (value $?v)
                  (CF ?C2))
   (test (neq ?fact1 ?fact2))
   =>
   (retract ?fact1)
   (modify ?fact2
(CF (combine-certainties ?C1 ?C2))))
```

Notice that the fact identifiers *?fact1* and *?fact2* are compared to each other in the *test* CE. This is to ensure that the rule does not match using the exact same fact for the first two patterns. The functions *eq* and *neq* are able to compare fact addresses. Also note that the auto-focus attribute for the rule has been enabled. This will ensure that two OAV triples are combined before other rules satisfied by both of the triples are allowed to fire.

The next step in implementing certainty factors is to link the certainty factors of the facts that match the LHS of the rule to the certainty factors of the facts asserted by the RHS of the rule. In MYCIN the certainty factor associated with the LHS of a rule is derived using the following formulas:

```
CF(P1 or P2)  = max { CF(P1), CF(P2) }
CF(P1 and P2)  = min { CF(P1), CF(P2) }
CF(not P)  = - CF(P)
```

where P, P_1, and P_2 represent patterns from the LHS. Additionally, if the certainty factor of the LHS is less than 0.2 the rule is considered inapplicable and will not be fired.

The certainty factor of a fact asserted from the RHS of a rule is derived by multiplying the certainty factor of the assertion by the certainty factor of the LHS of the rule. The following CLIPS rule translation of the MYCIN rule introduced at the beginning of this section demonstrates the computation of LHS and RHS certainty factors. The rule is placed in the *IDENTIFY* module, which imports the *oav* deftemplate from the *OAV* module:

```
defmodule IDENTIFY (import OAV deftemplate oav))

(defrule IDENTIFY::MYCIN-to-CLIPS-translation
   (oav (object organism)
        (attribute stain)
        (value gramneg)
        (CF ?C1))
   (oav (object organism)
        (attribute morphology)
        (value rod)
        (CF ?C2))
   (oav (object patient)
        (attribute is a)
        (value compromised host)
        (CF ?C3))
   (test (> (min ?C1 ?C2 ?C3) 0.2))
   =>
   (bind ?C4 (* (min ?C1 ?C2 ?C3) 0.6))
   (assert (oav (object organism)
                (attribute identity)
                (value pseudomonas)
                (CF ?C4))))
```

One final step is required for completing the MYCIN certainty factor emulation. The single *combine-certainties* method used by the *combine-certainties* rule handles only the case where both certainty factors are positive. By adding additional methods the other cases of certainty combination can be handled. The remaining combination cases are the following:

$$\text{New Certainty} = (CF_1 + CF_2) + (CF_1 * CF_2)$$

$$\text{if} \quad CF_1 \le 0 \text{ and } CF_2 \le 0$$

$$\text{New Certainty} = \frac{CF_1 + CF_2}{1 - \min\{|CF_1|, |CF_2|\}}$$

$$\text{if} \quad -1 < CF_1 * CF_2 < 0$$

12.3 DECISION TREES

Recall from Chapter 3 that decision trees provide a useful paradigm for solving certain types of classification problems. Decision trees derive solutions by reducing the set of possible solutions with a series of decisions or questions that prune their search space. Problems that are suitable for solution by decision trees are typified by the characteristic that they provide the answer to a problem from a predetermined set of possible answers. For example, a taxonomy problem might require the identification of a gem from the set of all known gems or a diagnosis problem might require the selection of a possible remedy from a set of remedies or the selection of the cause of a failure from a set of possible causes. Because the answer set must be predetermined, in general decision trees do not work well for scheduling, planning, or synthesis problems—problems that must generate solutions in addition to selecting among them.

Remember that a decision tree is composed of nodes and branches. Nodes represent locations in the tree. Branches connect parent nodes to child nodes when moving from top to bottom and connect child nodes to parent nodes when moving from bottom to top. The node at the top of the tree that has no parent is called the root node. Note that in a tree, every node has only one parent, with the exception of the root node, which has none. Nodes with no children are called leaves.

The leaf nodes of a decision tree represent all the possible solutions that can be derived from the tree. These nodes are referred to as *answer nodes*, and all other nodes in the tree are referred to as *decision nodes*. Each decision node represents a question or decision that when answered or decided, determines the appropriate branch of the decision tree to follow. In simple decision trees this question could be a yes or no question such as "Is the animal warm-blooded?" The left branch of the node would represent the path to follow if the answer is yes and the right branch of the node would represent the path to follow if the answer is no. In general, a decision node may use any criteria to select which branch to follow, provided that the selection process always yields only a single branch. Thus, decision nodes may select a branch corresponding to a set or range of values, a series of cases, or functions mapping from the state at the decision node to the branches of the decision node. Sophisticated decision nodes might even allow backtracking or probabilistic reasoning.

To illustrate the operation of a decision tree, consider the following heuristics in selecting the appropriate wine to serve with a meal:

```
IF the main course is red meat
THEN serve red wine

IF the main course is poultry and it is turkey
THEN serve red wine

IF the main course is poultry and it is not turkey
THEN serve white wine

IF the main course is fish
THEN serve white wine.
```

The representation of the wine heuristics as a binary decision tree is shown in Figure 12.1. The decision nodes assume that each question can be answered only yes or no. A default answer node containing the answer "The best color is unknown" has been added to the set of heuristics in the event that the main course is neither red meat, nor poultry, nor fish.

The procedure for traversing the tree to reach an answer node is quite simple. The inferencing process is started by setting the current location in the decision tree to the root node. If the current location is a decision node, then the question associated with the decision node must be answered in some manner (typically by the person consulting the decision tree). If the answer is yes, then the current location is set to the child node connected to the yes (or left) branch of the current location.

Figure 12.1 Binary Decision Tree

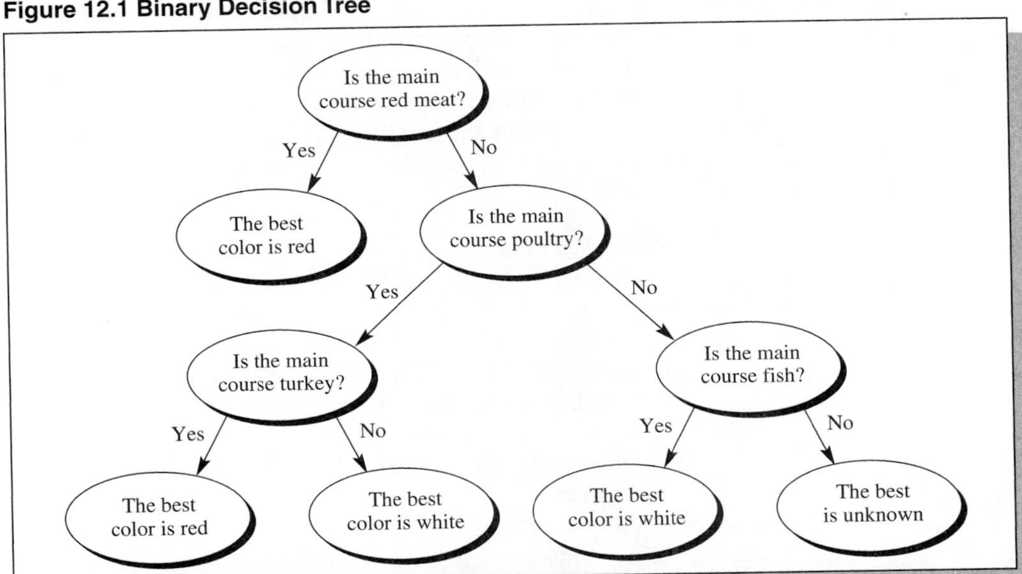

If the answer is no, then the current location is set to the child node connected to the no (or right) branch of the current location. If at any point an answer node becomes the current location, then the value of the answer node is the answer derived through consultation with the decision tree. Otherwise the procedure for handling a decision node is repeated until an answer node is reached. The pseudocode for this algorithm is:

```
procedure Solve_Binary_Tree
    Set the current location in the tree
        to the root node.
    while the current location is a decision node do
        Ask the question at the current node.
        if the reply to the question is yes
            Set the current node to the yes branch.
        else
            Set the current node to the no branch.
        end if
    end do
    Return the answer at the current node.
end procedure
```

Decision Trees with Multiple Branches

Decision trees that allow only binary branches from a decision node make it difficult to represent a decision that allows for a set of responses or a series of cases. The binary decision tree constructed for the wine example provides a good example of this inefficiency. In the event that the main course is fish, three decisions must be made before it can be determined that the best color is white: the questions "Is the main course red meat?", "Is the main course poultry?", and "Is the main course fish?" must all be asked. A much more direct question that would allow the decision node to be expressed succinctly is "What is the main course?" A decision node capable of handling this question must allow multiple branches, given a series of possible decisions (in this case red meat, poultry, fish, and other). Figure 12.2 shows the modified decision tree of Figure 12.1 now allowing multiple branches achieved through a simple modification in the *Solve_Binary_Tree* algorithm:

```
procedure Solve_Tree
    Set the current tree location to the root node.
    while the current location is a decision node do
        Ask the question at the current node until
            an answer in the set of valid choices
            for this node has been provided.
        Set the current node to the child node of
            the branch associated with the choice
            selected.
    end do
    Return the answer at the current node.
end procedure
```

Figure 12.2 Decision Tree with Multiple Branches

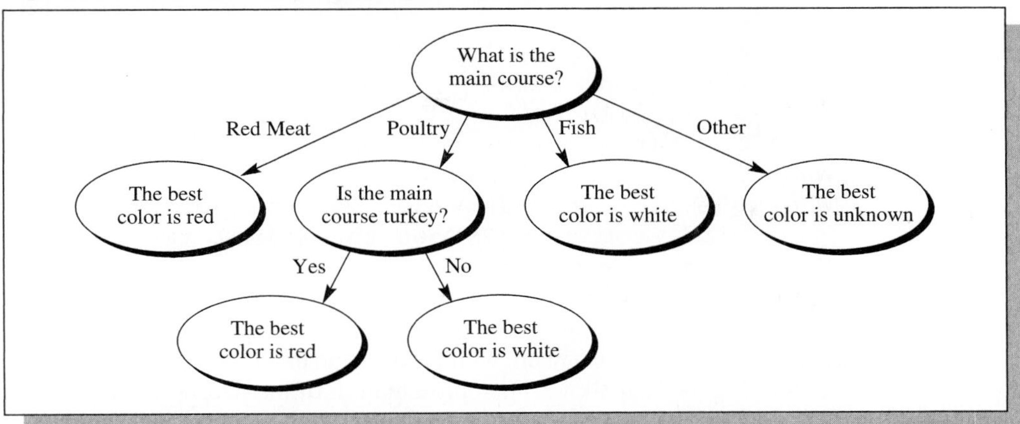

Decision Trees That Learn

Occasionally it is useful to add new knowledge to a decision tree as it is learned, as in the commonly used example of the animal identification decision tree. Once the decision tree has reached an answer, it asks whether the answer is correct, and if so, then nothing more is done. If the answer is incorrect, however, the decision tree is modified to accommodate the correct answer. The answer node is replaced with a decision node that contains a question that will differentiate between the old answer that was at the node and the answer that was not correctly guessed. Figure 12.3 shows a decision tree that will classify an animal by characteristics. This decision tree is somewhat naive (it knows only three animals) and is in need of learning.

Figure 12.3 Animal Identification Decision Tree

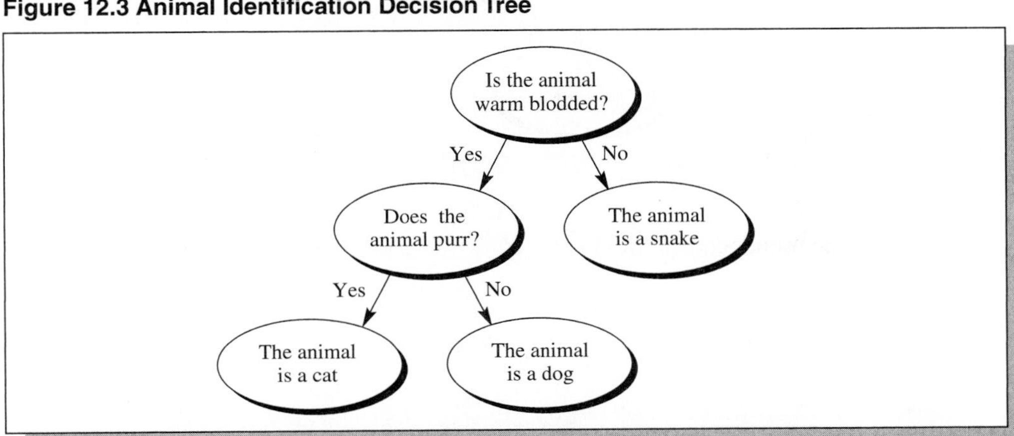

An example guessing session with the tree might proceed as follows:

```
Is the animal warm-blooded? (yes or no) yes↵
Does the animal purr? (yes or no) no↵
I guess it is a dog
Am I correct? (yes or no) no↵
What is the animal? bird↵
What question when answered yes will distinguish
   a bird from a dog? Does the animal fly?↵
Now I can guess bird
Try again? (yes or no) no↵
```

The session can continue on and on, with the decision tree learning more and more information. Figure 12.4 shows the representation of the decision tree after the above session. One drawback to learning in this manner is that the decision tree may not end up being either very hierarchically structured or very efficient in guessing the appropriate animal. An efficient decision tree should have approximately the same number of branches from root to answer nodes for all paths.

Figure 12.4 Animal Identification Decision Tree after Learning *Bird*

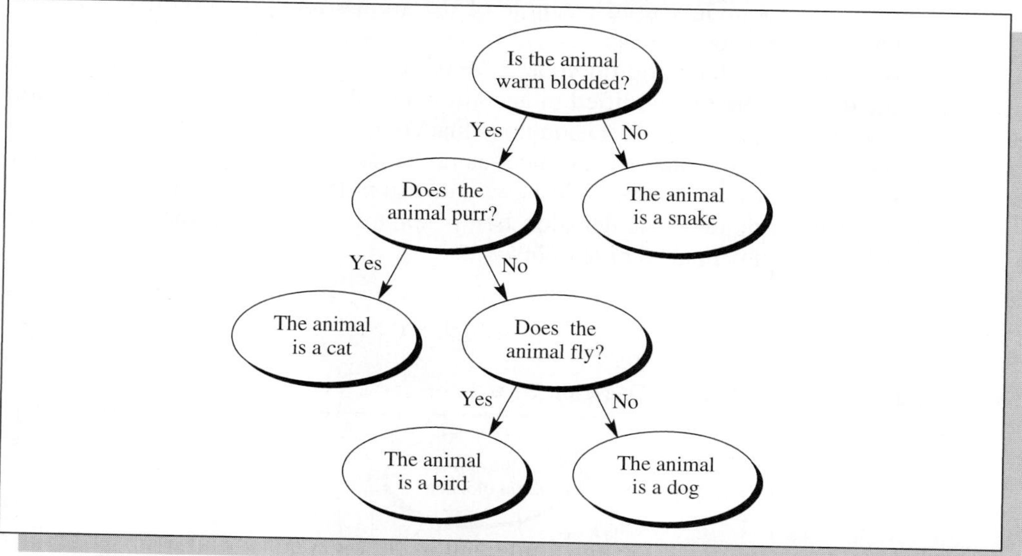

The pseudocode to modify the *Solve_Tree* algorithm to incorporate learning is:

```
procedure Solve_Tree_and_Learn
   Set the current location in the tree
```

```
      to the root node
   while the current location is a decision node do
      Ask the question at the current node.
      if the reply to the question is yes
         Set the current node to the yes branch.
      else
         Set the current node to the no branch.
      end if
   end do
   Ask if the answer at the current node is
   correct.
   if the answer is correct
      Return the correct answer.
   else
      Determine the correct answer.
      Determine a question which when answered yes
         will distinguish the answer at the current
         node from the correct answer.
      Replace the answer node with a decision node
         that has as its no branch the current
         answer node and as its yes branch an
         answer node with the correct answer.
         The decision node's question should be
         the question which distinguishes the
         two answer nodes.
   end if
end procedure
```

A Rule-Based Decision Tree Program

The first step in determining how a learning decision tree can be implemented in CLIPS is to decide how the knowledge should be represented. Since the decision tree must learn, it will probably be worthwhile to represent the tree as facts instead of rules because facts can easily be added and removed to update the tree as it learns. A set of CLIPS rules can be used to traverse the decision tree by implementing the *Solve_Tree_and_Learn* algorithm using a rule-based approach.

Each node of the decision tree will be represented by a fact. The following deftemplate will be used to represent both answer and decision nodes:

```
(deftemplate node
   (slot name)
   (slot type)
   (slot question)
   (slot yes-node)
   (slot no-node)
   (slot answer))
```

where the *name* slot is the unique name for the node and the *type* slot is the type of the node and contains the value *answer* or *decision*. The *question*, *yes-node*, and *no-node* slots are used only for decision nodes. The *question* slot is the question that is asked when a question node is traversed. The *yes-node* slot is the node to proceed to if the question is answered affirmatively, and the *no-node* slot is the node to proceed to if the question is answered negatively. The *answer* slot is used only by answer nodes and is the answer to the decision tree when an answer node is traversed.

Because the animal program will learn, it will be necessary to store information about what has been learned from one run of the program to the next. Since the decision tree will be structured as a collection of facts, it will be useful to store them in a file in the *load-facts* command format and assert them using the *load-facts* command when the program begins and save them using the *save-facts* command when the program finishes. For this program the facts will be stored in a file called animal.dat. If Figure 12.3 is used for the initial decision tree the file animal.dat should contain the text below. Notice that the root node has been labeled as such and that each of the other nodes has been given a unique name. Also note that some slots (such as the *decision*, *yes-node*, and *no-node* slots for the answer nodes) remain unspecified, since these will be assigned default values (and our program won't care what values are placed in the slots):

```
(node (name root) (type decision)
      (question "Is the animal warm-blooded?")
      (yes-node node1) (no-node node2))
(node (name node1) (type decision)
      (question "Does the animal purr?")
      (yes-node node3) (no-node node4))
(node (name node2) (type answer) (answer snake))
(node (name node3) (type answer) (answer cat))
(node (name node4) (type answer) (answer dog))
```

Now the rules to traverse the decision tree must be written. The following rule will initialize the learning decision tree program:

```
(defrule initialize
   (not (node (name root)))
   =>
   (load-facts "animal.dat")
   (assert (current-node root)))
```

This *initialize* rule will fire if the root node is not present in the fact list. The actions of the *initialize* rule load the decision tree representation into the fact list and assert a fact indicating that the current node of interest is the root node.

The next deffunction and rule asks the question associated with a decision node and then asserts a fact containing the answer to the question:

```
(deffunction ask-yes-or-no (?question)
   (printout t ?question " (yes or no) ")
```

```
   (bind ?answer (read))
   (while (and (neq ?answer yes) (neq ?answer no))
      (printout t ?question " (yes or no) ")
      (bind ?answer (read)))
   (return ?answer))

(defrule ask-decision-node-question
   ?node <- (current-node ?name)
   (node (name ?name)
         (type decision)
         (question ?question))
   (not (answer ?))
   =>
   (assert (answer (ask-yes-or-no ?question))))
```

The second pattern matches against the current node only if it is a decision node. The third pattern checks that the question hasn't already been answered. In the RHS of the rule, the *ask-yes-or-no* deffunction repeatedly asks the question until an answer of either *yes* or *no* is supplied. One of the following two rules will be fired in response to the answer:

```
(defrule proceed-to-yes-branch
   ?node <- (current-node ?name)
   (node (name ?name)
         (type decision)
         (yes-node ?yes-branch))
   ?answer <- (answer yes)
   =>
   (retract ?node ?answer)
   (assert (current-node ?yes-branch)))

(defrule proceed-to-no-branch
   ?node <- (current-node ?name)
   (node (name ?name)
         (type decision)
         (no-node ?no-branch))
   ?answer <- (answer no)
   =>
   (retract ?node ?answer)
   (assert (current-node ?no-branch)))
```

In both rules, the *current-node* fact is retracted and then updated with a new assertion that depends on the answer to the question. The answer fact will be retracted so that the *ask-decision-node-question* rule will be activated again.

The next rule asks whether an answer node has made the correct guess. It acts similarly to the *ask-decision-node-question* rule:

```
(defrule ask-if-answer-node-is-correct
   ?node <- (current-node ?name)
```

```
   (node (name ?name) (type answer)
         (answer ?value))
   (not (answer ?))
   =>
   (printout t "I guess it is a " ?value crlf)
   (assert
(answer (ask-yes-or-no "Am I correct?"))))
```

If the answer is something other than yes or no, then the bad-answer rule will cause another activation of the *ask-if-answer-node-is-correct* rule. If the answer is yes or no, then one of the two rules below will be fired. If the value of the answer node is verified, then the *ask-try-again* fact is asserted to indicate the user should be asked to continue. If the answer is wrong, then learning will occur and the *replace-answer-node* fact is asserted to indicate the name of the node to be replaced. In either case the *current-node* and *answer* facts are retracted:

```
(defrule answer-node-guess-is-correct
   ?node <- (current-node ?name)
   (node (name ?name) (type answer))
   ?answer <- (answer yes)
   =>
   (assert (ask-try-again))
   (retract ?node ?answer))

(defrule answer-node-guess-is-incorrect
   ?node <- (current-node ?name)
   (node (name ?name) (type answer))
   ?answer <- (answer no)
   =>
   (assert (replace-answer-node ?name))
   (retract ?node ?answer))
```

The following three rules are used to determine whether the user wants to continue. The *ask-try-again* rule asks the “Try again?” question. Once again, the bad-answer rule will fire if other than a yes or no answer is given. If the answer is yes, the *one-more-time* rule will reset the current-node fact to the root node to begin the guessing process again. If the answer is no, the facts representing the decision tree are saved to the animal.dat file using the *save-facts* command:

```
(defrule ask-try-again
   (ask-try-again)
   (not (answer ?))
   =>
   (assert (answer (ask-yes-or-no "Try again?"))))

(defrule one-more-time
   ?phase <- (ask-try-again)
```

```
   ?answer <- (answer yes)
   =>
   (retract ?phase ?answer)
   (assert (current-node root)))

(defrule no-more
   ?phase <- (ask-try-again)
   ?answer <- (answer no)
   =>
   (retract ?phase ?answer)
   (save-facts "animal.dat" local node))
```

Finally, if the answer is wrong the following rule will add a new decision node that allows the decision tree to learn:

```
(defrule replace-answer-node
   ?phase <- (replace-answer-node ?name)
   ?data <- (node (name ?name)
                  (type answer)
                  (answer ?value))
   =>
   (retract ?phase)
   ; Determine what the guess should have been
   (printout t "What is the animal? ")
   (bind ?new-animal (read))
   ; Get the question for the guess
   (printout t "What question when answered yes ")
   (printout t "will distinguish " crlf "   a ")
   (printout t ?new-animal " from a " ?value "? ")
   (bind ?question (readline))
   (printout t "Now I can guess " ?new-animal crlf)
   ; Create the new learned nodes
   (bind ?newnode1 (gensym*))
   (bind ?newnode2 (gensym*))
   (modify ?data (type decision)
                 (question ?question)
                 (yes-node ?newnode1)
                 (no-node ?newnode2))
   (assert (node (name ?newnode1)
                 (type answer)
                 (answer ?new-animal)))
   (assert (node (name ?newnode1)
                 (type answer)
                 (answer ?value)))
   ; Determine if the player wants to try again
   (assert (ask-try-again)))
```

The *replace-answer node* rule asks for the correct identification of the animal and for a question that will distinguish this animal from the animal the decision tree had identified as the correct answer. The old answer node is replaced by a decision node and two answer nodes are created as the answers for the newly learned question. The **gensym*** function (which generates a unique symbol each time it is called) is used to provide a name for each of the two new answer nodes. The *ask-try-again* fact is then asserted to determine whether another run of the program should be made.

A Step-by-Step Trace of the Decision Tree Program

The behavior of the decision tree program can be observed by watching its execution. Assuming that decision tree rules have been loaded and the file animal.dat containing the facts representing the initial decision tree has been created, the following dialog shows the state of the system after a *reset* command has been performed:

```
CLIPS> (watch facts)↵
CLIPS> (watch rules)↵
CLIPS> (reset)↵
==> f-0      (initial-fact)
CLIPS> (agenda)↵
0      initialize: f-0,
For a total of 1 activation.
CLIPS>
```

The *initialize* rule has been activated by the absence of the *root node* fact. Allowing the *initialize* rule to fire will load in the decision tree. Note that some of the output in the following traces is indented to improve its readability:

```
CLIPS> (run 1)↵
FIRE    1 initialize: f-0,
==> f-1      (node (name root) (type decision)
           (question "Is the animal warm-blooded?")
              (yes-node node1) (no-node node2)
              (answer nil))
==> f-2      (node (name node1) (type decision)
              (question "Does the animal purr?")
              (yes-node node3) (no-node node4)
              (answer nil))
==> f-3      (node (name node2) (type answer)
              (question nil) (yes-node nil)
              (no-node nil) (answer snake))
==> f-4      (node (name node3) (type answer)
              (question nil) (yes-node nil)
              (no-node nil) (answer cat))
==> f-5      (node (name node4) (type answer)
```

```
                (question nil) (yes-node nil)
                (no-node nil) (answer dog))
==> f-6        (current-node root)
CLIPS> (agenda)↵
0       ask-decision-node-question: f-6,f-1,
For a total of 1 activation.
CLIPS>
```

The *initialize* rule uses the load-facts function to load in the decision tree. The *current-node* fact is set to the *root node* fact. Since the root node is a decision node, the *ask-decision-node-question* rule is activated. Allowing this rule and the associated *proceed-to-yes-branch* rule to fire produces the following dialog:

```
CLIPS> (run 2)↵
FIRE    1 ask-decision-node-question: f-6,f-1,
Is the animal warm-blooded? (yes or no) yes↵
==> f-7        (answer yes)
FIRE    2 proceed-to-yes-branch: f-6,f-1,f-7
<== f-6        (current-node root)
<== f-7        (answer yes)
==> f-8        (current-node node1)
CLIPS> (agenda)↵
0       ask-decision-node-question: f-8,f-2,
For a total of 1 activation.
CLIPS>
```

The question associated with the root decision node is "Is the animal warm-blooded?" Since the reply to the question is yes, the left node of the decision node (node1) is made the current node by the *proceed-to-yes-branch* rule. Since node1 is also a decision node, the rule *ask-decision-node-question* is activated again. Allowing the next two rules to fire again produces the following dialog:

```
CLIPS> (run 2)↵
FIRE    1 ask-decision-node-question: f-8,f-2,
Does the animal purr? (yes or no) no↵
==> f-9        (answer no)
FIRE    2 proceed-to-no-branch: f-8,f-2,f-9
<== f-8        (current-node node1)
<== f-9        (answer no)
==> f-10       (current-node node4)
CLIPS> (agenda)↵
0       ask-if-answer-node-is-correct: f-10,f-5,
For a total of 1 activation.
CLIPS>
```

The question associated with the node1 decision node is "Does the animal purr?" Since the reply to the question is no, the right node of the decision node, node4, is made the current node by the *proceed-to-no-branch* rule. Since node4 is an answer node, the rule *ask-if-answer-node-is-correct* is activated. Allowing this rule and the next to fire produces the following dialog:

```
CLIPS> (run 2)↵
FIRE    1 ask-if-answer-node-is-correct: f-10,f-5,
I guess it is a dog
Am I correct? (yes or no) no↵
==> f-11     (answer no)
FIRE   2 answer-node-guess-is-incorrect: f-10,f-5,
                                         f-11
==> f-12     (replace-answer-node node4)
<== f-10     (current-node node4)
<== f-11     (answer no)
CLIPS> (agenda)↵
0       replace-answer-node: f-12,f-5
For a total of 1 activation.
CLIPS>
```

The guess associated with this answer node is dog. Since the guess is incorrect, the *replace-answer-node* rule is activated to determine the correct answer. Allowing this rule to fire produces the following dialog:

```
CLIPS> (run 1)↵
FIRE    1 replace-answer-node: f-12,f-5
<== f-12     (replace-answer-node node4)
What is the animal? bird↵
What question when answered yes will distinguish
   a bird from a dog? Does the animal fly?↵
Now I can guess bird
<== f-5      (node (name node4) (type answer)
                   (question nil)
                   (yes-node nil) (no-node nil)
                   (answer dog))
==> f-13     (node (name node4) (type decision)
                   (question
                   "Does the animal fly?")
                   (yes-node gen1) (no-node gen2)
                   (answer dog))
==> f-14     (node (name gen1) (type answer)
                   (question nil)
                   (yes-node nil) (no-node nil)
                   (answer bird))
==> f-15     (node (name gen2) (type answer)
                   (question nil)
                   (yes-node nil) (no-node nil)
```

```
                    (answer dog))
==> f-16     (ask-try-again)
CLIPS> (agenda)↵
0       ask-try-again: f-16,
For a total of 1 activation.
CLIPS>
```

First, the control fact (*replace-answer-node* node4) is retracted. The correct guess is then determined along with the question that will determine the correct guess. The incorrect answer node is modified to be a question node and then two answer nodes for the new question node are generated. Finally, the *ask-try-again* control fact is asserted to determine whether another identification is to be made. Allowing the *ask-try-again* rule and then the *no-more* rule to fire produces the following dialog:

```
CLIPS> (run 2)↵
FIRE    1 ask-try-again: f-16,
Try again? (yes or no) no↵
==> f-17     (answer no)
FIRE    2 no-more: f-16,f-17
<== f-16     (ask-try-again)
<== f-17     (answer no)
CLIPS> (agenda)↵
CLIPS>
```

The user is asked by the *ask-try-again* rule whether another identification is to be made. Since the reply is no, the *no-more* rule saves the decision tree back to the animal.dat file. After this session the final form of the animal.dat file is:

```
(node (name root) (type decision)
      (question "Is the animal warm-blooded?")
      (yes-node node1) (no-node node2)
      (answer nil))
(node (name node1) (type decision)
      (question "Does the animal purr?")
      (yes-node node3) (no-node node4)
      (answer nil))
(node (name node2) (type answer)
      (question nil)
      (yes-node nil) (no-node nil) (answer snake))
(node (name node3) (type answer)
      (question nil)
      (yes-node nil) (no-node nil) (answer cat))
(node (name node4) (type decision)
      (question "Does the animal fly?")
      (yes-node gen1) (no-node gen2) (answer dog))
```

```
(node (name gen1) (type answer)
      (question nil)
      (yes-node nil) (no-node nil) (answer bird))
(node (name gen2) (type answer)
      (question nil)
      (yes-node nil) (no-node nil) (answer dog))
```

The node4 answer node has been replaced with a decision node that refers to two new answer nodes. In addition, the default value *nil*, automatically assigned to some of the deftemplate slots, is now explicitly stated when the facts are saved.

12.4 BACKWARD CHAINING

CLIPS does not directly implement backward chaining as part of its inference engine. However, backward chaining can be emulated using forward-chaining CLIPS rules. This section will demonstrate how a simple backward-chaining system can be built in CLIPS. It should be noted that CLIPS is designed to be used as a forward-chaining language; if a backward-chaining approach is most suitable for solving a problem, then a language that directly implements backward chaining within its inference engine, such as PROLOG, should be used.

The CLIPS backward-chaining system will be built with the following capabilities and limitations:

- Facts will be represented as Attribute-Value pairs.
- Backward chaining will be started with the assertion of a single initial goal attribute.
- Only the equality of an attribute to a specific value will be tested as a condition in the antecedent of a rule.
- The only action of the antecedent of a rule will be to assign the value of a single attribute.
- If the value of a goal attribute cannot be determined using rules, the backward chainer will ask for the value of the attribute to be supplied. Attributes cannot be assigned an unknown value.
- An attribute may have only a single value. Hypothetical reasoning about different attribute values from different rules will not be supported.
- Uncertainty will not be represented.

An Algorithm for the Backward Chainer

Before writing a backward-chaining inference engine and attempting a rule-based approach using CLIPS, we should consider a procedural algorithm. The following pseudocode procedure can be used to determine the value of a goal attribute using a backward-chaining approach with the capabilities and limitations discussed previously:

```
procedure Solve_Goal(goal)
  goal: the current goal to be solved
```

```
if value of the goal attribute is known
   Return the value of the goal attribute.
end if

for each rule whose consequent is the goal
attribute do
   call Attempt_Rule with the rule
   if Attempt_Rule succeeds then
      Assign the goal attribute the value
      indicated by the consequent of the rule.
      Return the value of the goal attribute.
   end if
end do

Ask the user for the value of the goal
attribute.
Set the goal attribute to the value supplied
by the user.
Return the value of the goal attribute.

end procedure
```

A goal attribute is passed to procedure *Solve_Goal* as an argument. This procedure will determine the value of the goal attribute and return it. Procedure *Solve_Goal* first checks to determine whether the value of the goal attribute is already known. The value may already have been assigned as the consequent of another rule or supplied by the user of the backward chainer. If the value is indeed known, it is returned.

If the attribute value is not known, procedure *Solve_Goal* will attempt to determine the value by finding a rule that assigns the attribute a value as its consequent. Procedure *Solve_Goal* will attempt each rule that assigns a value to the goal attribute as its consequent until one of the rules succeeds. Procedure *Attempt_Rule* (which will be discussed in more detail shortly) is given each of the rules with the desired goal attribute to attempt. If the antecedent of the attempted rule is satisfied, the rule will succeed; otherwise it will fail. If the rule succeeds, the attribute value in the consequent of the rule is assigned to the goal attribute and this value is returned by procedure *Solve_Goal*. If the rule does not succeed, then the next rule that assigns a value to the goal attribute as its consequent is attempted.

If none of the rules succeed, the user must be queried to determine the value of the goal attribute. The value supplied by the user is returned by procedure *Solve_Goal*.

Procedure *Attempt_Rule* is used to determine whether the antecedent of a rule is satisfied. If the antecedent is satisfied, the consequent can be used to assign the value of a goal attribute. The pseudocode for this procedure is:

```
procedure Attempt_Rule(rule)
   rule: rule to be attempted to solve goal
```

```
        for each condition in the antecedent
        of the rule do
           call Solve_Goal with condition attribute
           if the value returned by solve_goal is not
           equal to the value required by the condition
           then
              Return unsuccessful.
           end if
        end for

        Return successful

    end procedure
```

Procedure *Attempt_Rule* will start at the first condition of a rule and attempt to prove it before attempting the subsequent conditions of the rule. In order to determine whether a condition is satisfied, procedure *Attempt_Rule* must know the value of the attribute being tested in the condition. To determine the value, procedure *Solve_Goal* is called recursively. If the value returned by procedure *Solve_Goal* is not equal to the value required by the condition, procedure *Attempt_Rule* exits with the return value unsuccessful (remember that only equality is being tested in conditions). Otherwise the next condition of the rule is tested. If all conditions of the rule are satisfied, procedure *Attempt_Rule* exits with the return value successful.

Representing Backward-Chaining Rules in CLIPS

Once again, the first step in solving this problem is determining how the knowledge should be represented. Since CLIPS does not automatically perform backward chaining, it will be useful to represent backward-chaining rules as facts so the antecedents and consequents can be examined by rules that will act as a backward-chaining inference engine. The deftemplate for representing backward-chaining rules is shown below. It will be stored in the defmodule *BC* (which will be defined at the end of this subsection once all the deftemplates needed for the backward-chaining engine have been identified):

```
(deftemplate BC::rule
   (multislot if)
   (multislot then))
```

The *if* and *then* slots will store the antecedent and the consequent, respectively, of each rule. Each antecedent will contain either a single attribute-value pair of the format:

```
<attribute> is <value>
```

or a series of such attribute-value pairs connected by the symbol *and*. The consequent of each rule will be allowed to contain only a single attribute-value pair.

As an example of representing rules using this format, consider the decision tree in Figure 12.2. This tree can easily be converted to rules using AV pairs, as described previously. The pseudocode for the converted rules is:

```
IF main-course is red-meat
THEN best-color is red

IF main-course is poultry and
   meal-is-turkey is yes
THEN best-color is red

IF main-course is poultry and
   meal-is-turkey is no
THEN best-color is white

IF main-course is fish
THEN best-color is white
```

The attributes used in the rules are *main-course*, *meal-is-turkey*, and *best-color*. The *main-course* attribute corresponds to the answer determined by the decision tree question "What is the main course?" *The meal-is-turkey* attri– bute corresponds to the answer determined by the question "Is the main course turkey?" Notice that the branch of the decision tree that determines that the best color is unknown is not represented as a rule, since one of the limitations of our backward chainer is that unknown values are not represented. If the main course is not one of these that produce an answer, in this case the user will be asked the value of the *best-color* attribute.

The following deffacts show how the wine rules can be represented using the backward-chaining rule format. Since these *rule* facts are not an intrinsic part of the backward-chaining mechanism, they'll be placed in the *MAIN* module (recall that the *MAIN* module imports from all other modules, so the *rule* deftemplate will be visible to it):

```
(deffacts MAIN::wine-rules
   (rule (if main-course is red-meat)
         (then best-color is red))

   (rule (if main-course is fish)
         (then best-color is white))

   (rule (if main-course is poultry and
             meal-is-turkey is yes)
         (then best-color is red))

   (rule (if main-course is poultry and
             meal-is-turkey is no)
         (then best-color is white)))
```

This representation provides a great deal of flexibility when manipulating the backward-chaining rules. For example, if the attribute *main-course* is determined to have the value *poultry*, the facts:

```
(rule (if main-course is red-meat)
      (then best-color is red))
```

and:

```
(rule (if main-course is fish)
      (then best-color is white))
```

can be removed from the fact list to indicate that these rules are not applicable, and the facts:

```
(rule (if main-course is poultry and
          meal-is-turkey is yes)
      (then best-color is red))
```

and:

```
(rule (if main-course is poultry and
          meal-is-turkey is no)
      (then best-color is white))
```

can respectively be modified to the facts:

```
(rule (if meal-is-turkey is yes)
      (then best-color is red))
```

and:

```
(rule (if meal-is-turkey is no)
      (then best-color is white))
```

to indicate that the first condition of these two rules has been satisfied.

As backward chaining proceeds, subgoals will be generated to determine the value of attributes. A fact will be needed to represent information about goal attributes. Ordered facts will be used to represent goal attributes and their format will be:

```
(deftemplate BC::goal
   (slot attribute))
```

Initially the goal attribute is *best-color*. This can be represented using a deffacts as shown here:

```
(deffacts MAIN::initial-goal
   (goal (attribute best-color)))
```

When values for attributes are determined, they will be need to be stored, which can be done with the following deftemplate:

```
(deftemplate BC::attribute
   (slot name)
   (slot value))
```

Now that all of the deftemplates have been identified we can provide the definition of the *BC* module. Remember that when you are loading a file of constructs the defmodule that will contain other constructs must be defined before the constructs it contains are defined:

```
(defmodule BC
   (export deftemplate rule goal attribute))
```

The CLIPS Backward-Chaining Inference Engine

The backward-chaining inference engine can be implemented with two sets of rules. The first group will generate goals for attributes and ask the user to supply attribute values when these values cannot be determined by rules. The second group of rules will perform update operations. Update operations include modifying rules when their conditions have been satisfied and removing goals when they have been satisfied. The first set of rules is the following:

```
(defrule BC::attempt-rule
   (goal (attribute ?g-name))
   (rule (if ?a-name $?)
         (then ?g-name $?))
   (not (attribute (name ?a-name)))
   (not (goal (attribute ?a-name)))
   =>
   (assert (goal (attribute ?a-name))))

(defrule BC::ask-attribute-value
   ?goal <- (goal (attribute ?g-name))
   (not (attribute (name ?g-name)))
   (not (rule (then ?g-name $?)))
   =>
   (retract ?goal)
   (printout t "What is the value of "
               ?g-name "? ")
   (assert (attribute (name ?g-name)
                      (value (read)))))
```

The *attempt-rule* rule searches for rules whose antecedents will supply the attribute value for a goal attribute. The first pattern matches against a *goal* fact. The second pattern searches for all rules whose antecedent assigns a value to the goal attribute. The third pattern checks to see that the value of the goal attribute has not already been determined. The fourth pattern confirms that there is not already a goal to determine the attribute's value. For each rule found, the RHS of the *attempt-rule* rule will assert a goal to determine the value of the attribute tested by the first condition of the rule.

The *ask-attribute-value* rule is quite similar to the *attempt-rule* rule. Its first two patterns are identical. Its third pattern checks that there are no remaining rules that can be used to determine the value of the goal attribute. In this case the user is asked to supply the value of the attribute. A fact representing the attribute's value is asserted and the *goal* fact for the attribute is retracted.

The next four rules are used to update the backward-chaining rules and goals that are represented as facts. These rules are given a salience of 100 so that updates will occur before any attempts are made to generate new goals or ask the user for attribute values:

```
(defrule BC::goal-satisfied
   (declare (salience 100))
   ?goal <- (goal (attribute ?g-name))
   (attribute (name ?g-name))
   =>
   (retract ?goal))

(defrule BC::rule-satisfied
   (declare (salience 100))
   (goal (attribute ?g-name))
   (attribute (name ?a-name)
              (value ?a-value))
   ?rule <- (rule (if ?a-name is ?a-value)
                  (then ?g-name is ?g-value))
   =>
   (retract ?rule)
   (assert (attribute (name ?g-name)
                      (value ?g-value))))

(defrule BC::remove-rule-no-match
   (declare (salience 100))
   (goal (attribute ?g-name))
   (attribute (name ?a-name) (value ?a-value))
   ?rule <- (rule (if ?a-name is ~?a-value)
                  (then ?g-name is ?g-value))
   =>
   (retract ?rule))

(defrule BC::modify-rule-match
   (declare (salience 100))
   (goal (attribute ?g-name))
   (attribute (name ?a-name) (value ?a-value))
   ?rule <- (rule (if ?a-name is ?a-value and
                      $?rest-if)
                  (then ?g-name is ?g-value))
```

```
   =>
   (retract ?rule)
   (modify ?rule (if $?rest-if)))
```

The *goal-satisfied* rule removes any goals for which the attribute value has been determined.

The *rule-satisfied* rule searches for any rules that have a single remaining condition. If an attribute exists that satisfies this remaining condition and there is a goal to determine the value of this attribute, then the attribute value of the consequent of the rule is added to the fact list.

The *remove-rule-no-match* rule searches for rules whose antecedents can supply the attribute value for a goal attribute and contain one or more conditions of which the first conflicts with a value assigned to an attribute. If this is the case, then the rule is removed from the fact list since it is not applicable.

The *modify-rule-match* rule searches for rules whose antecedents can supply the attribute value for a goal attribute and contain two or more conditions of which the first is satisfied by a value assigned to an attribute. If such a rule is found, the first condition is removed from the rule to leave the remaining conditions, which must be tested.

Now that all of the backward-chaining rules have been provided, all that is required to start the backward-chaining process is to focus on the *BC* module. This can be accomplished by adding the following rule to the *MAIN* module:

```
(defrule MAIN::start-BC
   =>
   (focus BC))
```

A Step-by-Step Trace of the Backward Chainer

The behavior of the CLIPS backward-chaining inference engine implemented using rules can be observed by watching its execution. Assuming that the *wine-rules* and *initial-goal* deffacts have been loaded along with the backward-chaining inference engine rules, the initial state of the system after a *reset* command is as below (once again, some output has been indented to improve readability):

```
CLIPS> (unwatch all)↵
CLIPS> (reset)↵
CLIPS> (facts)↵
f-0     (initial-fact)
f-1     (goal (attribute best-color))
f-2     (rule (if main-course is red-meat)
              (then best-color is red))
f-3     (rule (if main-course is fish)
              (then best-color is white))
f-4     (rule (if main-course is poultry and
                  meal-is-turkey is yes)
              (then best-color is red))
```

```
f-5      (rule (if main-course is poultry and
                   meal-is-turkey is no)
               (then best-color is white))
For a total of 6 facts.
CLIPS> (agenda)↵
0       start-BC: f-0
For a total of 1 activation.
CLIPS>
```

The *start-BC* rule merely focuses on the *BC* module. Once this rule fires the *BC* module becomes the current focus:

```
CLIPS> (run 1)↵
CLIPS> (agenda)↵
0       attempt-rule: f-1,f-5,,
0       attempt-rule: f-1,f-4,,
0       attempt-rule: f-1,f-3,,
0       attempt-rule: f-1,f-2,,
For a total of 4 activations.
CLIPS>
```

Notice that the agenda contains four activations of the *attempt-rule* rule. The starting goal is to determine the value of the *best-color* attribute as specified by fact f-1. Since the consequents of the *rule* facts f-2, f-3, f-4, and f-5 each assign a value to the *best-color* attribute, each of these rules should be attempted to satisfy the *best-color* attribute goal.

The next step in execution is to fire the first activation of the *attempt-rule* rule. The rules and facts watch items are activated before the rule is fired:

```
CLIPS> (watch rules)↵
CLIPS> (watch facts)↵
CLIPS> (run 1)↵
FIRE    1 attempt-rule: f-1,f-5,,
==> f-6       (goal (attribute main-course))
CLIPS> (agenda)↵
0       ask-attribute-value: f-6,,
For a total of 1 activation.
CLIPS>
```

The *attempt-rule* rule fires based in part on fact f-5, which represents the backward-chaining rule shown here:

```
IF main-course is poultry and
   meal-is-turkey is no
THEN best-color is white
```

Before this rule can be applied to assign the value of the *best-color* attribute, the CEs in its antecedents must be satisfied. The first condition requires the value of the attribute main-course. Since this attribute is unknown, a goal is created for it, and is represented by fact f-6. Because there are no rules that assign the value of the *main-course* attribute, the rule *ask-attribute-value* rule is activated.

Proceeding with execution, the *ask-attribute-value* rule fires to determine the value of the attribute *main-course*:

```
CLIPS> (run 1)↵
FIRE    1 ask-attribute-value: f-6,,
<== f-6      (goal (attribute main-course))
What is the value of main-course? poultry↵
==> f-7      (attribute (name main-course)
                        (value poultry))
CLIPS> (agenda)↵
100     remove-rule-no-match: f-1,f-7,f-3
100     remove-rule-no-match: f-1,f-7,f-2
100     modify-rule-match: f-1,f-7,f-5
100     modify-rule-match: f-1,f-7,f-4
For a total of 4 activations.
CLIPS>
```

Since the user is being asked to supply the value of the *main-course* attribute, the goal for this attribute f-6 is removed. The value supplied by the user is asserted as the *attribute* fact f-7. The assertion of this fact causes four new activations to be placed on the agenda. The rules represented by facts f-4 and f-5 each require as the first condition that the *main-course* attribute be *poultry*. Since the value of the *main-course* attribute is *poultry*, both of these *rule* facts must be modified to represent that the first condition has been satisfied. Thus both facts cause activations of the *modify-rule-match* rule. The rules represented by facts f-2 and f-3 both require as the first condition that the *main-course* attribute be something other than *poultry*. Thus neither of these facts is applicable any longer. The rule *remove-rule-no-match* is activated to cause both of them to be removed.

Allowing the two *remove-rule-no-match* activations to fire produces the following output:

```
CLIPS> (run 2)↵
FIRE    1 remove-rule-no-match: f-1,f-7,f-3
<== f-3      (rule (if main-course is fish)
                   (then best-color is white))
FIRE    2 remove-rule-no-match: f-1,f-7,f-2
<== f-2      (rule (if main-course is red-meat)
                   (then best-color is red))
CLIPS> (agenda)↵
100     modify-rule-match: f-1,f-7,f-5
100     modify-rule-match: f-1,f-7,f-4
For a total of 2 activations.
CLIPS>
```

The facts f-2 and f-3 are removed from the fact list, indicating that the rules represented by these facts are no longer applicable. The *attempt-rule* activations for these facts are removed from the agenda when the facts are removed.

Moving now to the execution of the two *modify-rule-match* activations produces the following output:

```
CLIPS> (run 2)↵
FIRE    1 modify-rule-match: f-1,f-7,f-5
<== f-5      (rule (if main-course is poultry and
                       meal-is-turkey is no)
                   (then best-color is white))
==> f-8      (rule (if meal-is-turkey is no)
                   (then best-color is white))
FIRE    2 modify-rule-match: f-7,f-4
<== f-4      (rule (if main-course is poultry and
                       meal-is-turkey is yes)
                   (then best-color is red))
==> f-9      (rule (if meal-is-turkey is yes)
                   (then best-color is red))
CLIPS> (agenda)↵
0      attempt-rule: f-1,f-9,,
0      attempt-rule: f-1,f-8,,
For a total of 2 activations.
CLIPS>
```

The first firing of the *modify-rule-match* rule is based in part on fact f-5, which represents the following backward-chaining rule:

```
IF main-course is poultry and
   meal-is-turkey is no
THEN best-color is white
```

The actions of the *modify-match-rule* rule modify this backward-chaining rule as:

```
IF meal-is-turkey is no
THEN best-color is white
```

The new fact representing the modified rule is f-8. This new fact represents the conditions of the initial rule that remain after the first condition has been satisfied and causes another activation of the *attempt-rule* rule for this backward-chaining rule. This new activation will assert a new goal to determine the value of the meal-is-turkey so the consequent of the rule can be applied to assign the value of the best-color attribute.

The second firing of the modify-rule-match rule is similar to the first. The fact representing the rule:

```
IF main-course is poultry and
   meal-is-turkey is red
THEN best-color is red
```

is modified to the following rule:

```
IF meal-is-turkey is yes
THEN best-color is red
```

which is represented by fact f-9. Similarly, this new fact causes an activation of the *attempt-rule* rule to replace the activation lost when the fact representing the rule was retracted.

Allowing the first *attempt-rule* activation to fire produces the following output:

```
CLIPS> (run 1)↵
FIRE    1 attempt-rule: f-1,f-9,,
==> f-10     (goal (attribute meal-is-turkey))
CLIPS> (agenda)↵
0       ask-attribute-value: f-10,,
For a total of 1 activation.
CLIPS>
```

The fact f-10 is asserted representing a goal to determine the value of the *meal-is-turkey* attribute. Since no rule assigns the value of this attribute, the *ask-attribute-value* rule is activated to determine the value.

Allowing the *ask-attribute-value* rule to fire produces the following output:

```
CLIPS> (run 1)↵
FIRE    1 ask-attribute-value: f-10,,
<== f-10     (goal (attribute meal-is-turkey))
What is the value of meal-is-turkey? yes↵
==> f-11     (attribute (name meal-is-turkey)
                        (value yes))
CLIPS> (agenda)↵
100     rule-satisfied: f-1,f-11,f-9
100     remove-rule-no-match: f-1,f-11,f-8
For a total of 2 activations.
CLIPS>
```

An *attribute* fact representing the value of the *meal-is-turkey* attribute is asserted as a result of this rule firing. In addition, the *goal* fact to determine the value of this attribute is removed. The new *attribute* fact causes two activations. The first activation is for the *remove-rule-no-match* rule. Since fact f-8's first condition is inconsistent with the value of the new attribute and the rule represented by the fact is no longer applicable, this fact needs to be removed. The second activation is for the *rule-satisfied* rule. Since fact f-8's remaining condition is satisfied by the new *attribute* fact, the consequent of this fact can be applied.

The remaining rules left to fire finish the backward-chaining process:

```
CLIPS> (run)↵
FIRE    1 rule-satisfied: f-1,f-11,f-9
<== f-9      (rule (if meal-is-turkey is yes)
                   (then best-color is red))
==> f-12     (attribute (name best-color)
                        (value red))
FIRE    2 goal-satisfied: f-1,f-12
<== f-1      (goal (attribute best-color))
CLIPS> (agenda)↵
CLIPS> (facts)↵
f-0      (initial-fact)
f-7      (attribute (name main-course)
                    (value poultry))
f-8      (rule (if meal-is-turkey is no)
               (then best-color is white))
f-11     (attribute (name meal-is-turkey)
                    (value yes))
f-12     (attribute (name best-color) (value red))
For a total of 5 facts.
CLIPS>
```

The rule *rule-satisfied* is fired to assign the value of the *best-color* attribute as part of the consequent of the rule represented by fact f-9. The *attribute* fact asserted by this rule satisfies the remaining *goal* fact in the fact list. The rule *goal-satisfied* is activated and then fired to remove the remaining *goal* fact.

The *agenda* command shows that there are no rules remaining to fire. The *facts* command shows the attributes that have been assigned values. Fact f-12 shows that the initial goal attribute *best-color* was assigned the value *red*.

12.5 A MONITORING PROBLEM

This section presents the step-by-step development of a CLIPS program as the solution of a simple problem. The development steps include the initial description of the problem, assumptions made about the nature of the problem, and the initial definitions for representation of problem knowledge, followed by an incremental buildup of the rules to solve the problem.

Problem Statement

The problem to be solved in this section is an example of a simple monitoring system. Monitoring problems tend to be well suited for forward-chaining rule-based languages because of their data-driven nature. Typically a set of input or sensor values are read during each program cycle. Inferencing occurs until all possible conclusions that can be derived from the input data are reached. This is consistent with a data-driven approach, in which reasoning occurs from data to the conclusions that can be derived from the data.

For this example the type of monitoring to be performed will be generic in nature. A hypothetical processing plant contains several devices that have to be monitored. Some devices will depend on others for their operation. Each device will have one or more sensors attached to it to provide numeric readings indicating the general health of the device. Each sensor will have low guard line (LGL), low red line (LRL), high guard line (HGL), and high red line (HRL) values. A reading between the low and high guard lines will be considered normal. A reading above the high guard line but below the high red line or below the low guard line but above the low red line will be considered acceptable, although it is an indication that the device may soon become unhealthy. A reading above the high red line or below the low red line will indicate an unhealthy device, which should be shut down. Any device in the guard region should have warnings issued. In addition, any device that remains in a guard region for an excessively long time should be shut down. Table 12.1 summarizes the actions to be taken for given sensor values.

Table 12.1 Actions for Sensor Values

Sensor Value	Action
Less than or equal to low red line	Shut down device
Greater than low red line and less than or equal to low guard line	Issue warning or shut down device
Greater than low guard line and less than high guard line	None
Greater than or equal to high guard line and less than high red line	Issue warning or shut down device
Greater than or equal to high red line	Shut down device

The monitoring program should be able to read in sensor data, evaluate the sensor readings, and issue warnings and shut down devices based on sensor evaluations and trends. Sample output from the monitoring program might look like the following:

```
Cycle 20 - Sensor 4 in high guard line
Cycle 25 - Sensor 4 in high red line
   Shutting down device 4
Cycle 32 - Sensor 3 in low guard line
Cycle 38 - Sensor 1 in high guard line for 6 cycles
   Shutting down device 1
```

For this example Figure 12.5 shows the connections between the devices and sensors to be monitored and Table 12.2 lists the attributes of each of the sensors.

Part of the solution of this problem involves using the general description of the problem to determine specific details that must be resolved before the implementation of the solution. Typically this process would include iterative

Figure 12.5 Devices and Sensors in a Monitored System

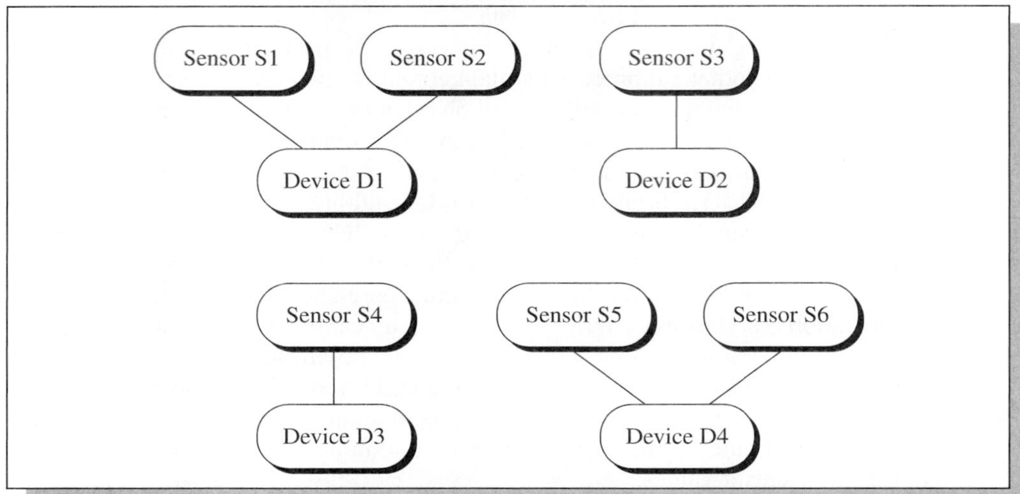

Table 12.2 Sensor Attributes

Sensor	Low Red Low	Low Guard Line	High Guard Line	High Red Line
S1	60	70	120	130
S2	20	40	160	180
S3	60	70	120	130
S4	60	70	120	130
S5	65	70	120	125
S6	110	115	125	130

consultation with experts knowledgeable about the problem domain but not necessarily able to completely specify the task intended to be captured by an expert system. Prototypes of the problem would be developed to point out details missing in the problem specification. These details would be determined through consultations with experts and another prototype would be developed that may reveal further missing details in the problem specification. Eventually the problem specification would be completely captured through this iterative development programming philosophy.

Many specification details of this problem remain unanswered: How will the information about the sensors and devices be represented? How general or specific should the facts and rules be made? How will the sensor data be retrieved? How long should a sensor be in a guard region before its associated device is shut down? What actions are to be taken when the monitor detects unhealthy devices?

The Details Needed to Begin

One of the major problems encountered in building an expert system is that more often than not the problem is poorly specified. The idea is to emulate an expert, but no one except the expert is sufficiently knowledgeable to specify the details. Typically the expected behavior of the system is known, but the manner in which this behavior is to be generated is not. An expert may have difficulty communicating the exact steps taken in coming to a solution. Because of the iterative development techniques the expert system paradigm naturally supports, it is relatively easy to build expert systems that solve poorly specified problems. This does not mean, however, that the expert systems can solve problems that have never been solved before, or that problems that are not understood can be solved.

Several problem specifications are necessary before an expert system for this monitoring example can be built. First, the expected behavior of the expert system should be specified, including the initial information and the information that the system is to produce. This does not mean that this specification cannot change. Development of the program may indicate that the scope of the problem should be narrowed or perhaps widened, and this would affect the initial inputs and final outputs. Some assumptions must be made and initial details about how the expert system should perform its tasks must be decided. Again, these types of decisions are not permanent. Experts often can demonstrate how they went about solving a problem, but then cannot easily formulate the rules they used. In describing the rules they use, experts may leave out details that are obvious to them or may forget exceptions.

The monitoring problem requires the making of many initial decisions. The first of these is in implementation. Should the solution be specifically geared to the exact details of the problem specification or should it incorporate enough generality to allow it to be easily upgraded or modified? Specific rules could be written for each of the devices to be monitored, or a general rule could be written to monitor all of the devices. For this problem writing general rules appears to be more appropriate because the individual devices and sensors to be modeled have no unique characteristics. This type of generality should allow the easy addition of more devices and sensors.

Details about the flow of control for the system are also missing. For this problem a simple monitoring cycle will be used. Each monitoring cycle will have three phases. During the first phase values will be read from the sensors. During the second phase an analysis will be made of the sensor values. During the third phase any appropriate actions will be taken.

Assumptions must also be made about how the sensor data are to be retrieved. Will they be read directly from sensors? Will it be necessary to handle the simulation of sensor data? Will sensor data always be available when requested? Are the sensor data reliable or are they subject to error? Under normal prototyping situations the experts could be interviewed to determine this information, but for the purposes of this problem assumptions will be made to fill in details.

All of these questions point out gaps that may be encountered in a poorly defined problem. During development a list of assumptions, questions, and possible inconsistencies relating to the problem specification should be maintained. In the iterative development of the program this list should be the focal point of discussion, with experts to ensure that the problem specification matches the expert's view of how the problem is to be solved. The following assumptions begin this list for the monitoring problem:

- Sensor data are always reliable and always available on request.
- Sensor values should be readable directly from sensors. Simulated sensor values should also be supported.
- Sensor values will not be monitored for a machine that has been shut down.
- Actions specified by the monitoring system are assumed to be carried out (i.e., we're assuming either that we have an alert operator or that control of the devices is directly handled by the program).
- The problem will be split into three phases: reading of sensor values, analysis of sensor values, and taking of appropriate actions such as shutting down a device.

In addition to details of problem specification, details of problem implementation must also be decided. These details include how to represent the available information, flow of control, and testing of the expert system.

Knowledge Definitions

Once again, we start solving the problem by determining how the knowledge should be represented. A good start for this problem is to encode the knowledge in Figure 12.5 and Table 12.2. The following deftemplate will be used to describe each of the devices:

```
(defmodule MAIN (export ?ALL))

(deftemplate MAIN::device
   (slot name (type SYMBOL))
   (slot status (allowed-values on off)))
```

where the *name* slot is the name of the device and the *status* slot indicates whether the device is on or off. Using Figure 12.5 and assuming that all devices are initially turned on, we describe the initial state of the devices using the following deffacts:

```
(deffacts MAIN::device-information
(device (name D1) (status on))
(device (name D2) (status on))
(device (name D3) (status on))
(device (name D4) (status on)))
```

Figure 12.5 also indicates which sensors are associated with which devices. The following deftemplate will be used to represent this relation:

```
(deftemplate MAIN::sensor
(slot name (type SYMBOL))
(slot device (type SYMBOL))
(slot raw-value (type SYMBOL NUMBER)
                 (allowed-symbols none)
                 (default none))
```

```
   (slot state (allowed-values low-red-line
                                low-guard-line
                                normal
                                high-red-line
                                high-guard-line)
               (default normal))
   (slot low-red-line (type NUMBER))
   (slot low-guard-line (type NUMBER))
   (slot high-guard-line (type NUMBER))
   (slot high-red-line (type NUMBER)))
```

where the *name* slot is the name of the sensor and the *device* slot is the name of the device with which the sensor is associated. The *raw-value* slot contains the data value read directly from the sensor before it has been processed. The state slot indicates the current state of the sensor (e.g., normal, low guard line, high red line, etc.). The *low-red-line*, *low-guard-line*, *expected-average-value*, *high-guard-line*, and *high-red-line* slots are used to contain the information described in Table 12.2. The following deffacts can be used to describe the sensors in Figure 12.5:

```
(deffacts MAIN::sensor-information
  (sensor (name S1) (device D1)
          (low-red-line 60) (low-guard-line 70)
          (high-guard-line 120)
          (high-red-line 130))
  (sensor (name S2) (device D1)
          (low-red-line 20) (low-guard-line 40)
          (high-guard-line 160)
          (high-red-line 180))
  (sensor (name S3) (device D2)
          (low-red-line 60) (low-guard-line 70)
          (high-guard-line 120)
          (high-red-line 130))
  (sensor (name S4) (device D3)
          (low-red-line 60) (low-guard-line 70)
          (high-guard-line 120)
          (high-red-line 130))
  (sensor (name S5) (device D4)
          (low-red-line 65) (low-guard-line 70)
          (high-guard-line 120)
          (high-red-line 125))
  (sensor (name S6) (device D4)
          (low-red-line 110) (low-guard-line 115)
          (high-guard-line 125)
          (high-red-line 130)))
```

Since the monitoring system will be cyclic, a fact will be needed to represent the current cycle. The first cycle can be started at one and then be incremented by one with each new cycle. The ordered fact format for this information will be:

```
(cycle <number>)
```

where <number> is the value of the current cycle. In addition, since sensor values might be read from more than one source (e.g., one source for simulation and another for actual operation), it will be useful to have a fact indicating the sensor data source. This fact can be represented with the following format:

```
(data-source <source>)
```

where <source> is an instance name representing the source from which data is read. The <source> instance will be a member of the *DATA-SOURCE* class which will be described shortly. Potential sources could be the sensors, a simulator, a text file, a set of facts, or user input.

A deffacts containing this initial information is:

```
(deffacts MAIN::cycle-start
(data-source [user])
(cycle 0))
```

Notice that the user will supply data for the sensors. For this example entering data from the keyboard will be more convenient than reading data from a file.

Control of Execution

The statement of problem assumptions indicates that there will be three specific phases to the monitoring process. The first phase will read in either user-supplied, simulated, or actual values from the sensors. The second phase will associate guard line and red line conditions for the sensor values and determine any developing trends. Once trends have been established the monitoring system will issue any appropriate warnings, shut down malfunctioning equipment, and restart equipment that can be brought back on line. After appropriate actions have been taken a new cycle will begin by reading new sensor values.

Control of the monitoring expert system will be handled using the techniques similar to those described in Chapter 9. Three separate modules will be created: *INPUT*, *TRENDS*, and *WARNINGS*. Each cycle, the value of the *cycle* fact will be updated and the proceeding modules will be focused on in the appropriate order. The following rule will perform these actions:

```
(defrule MAIN::Begin-Next-Cycle
   ?f <- (cycle ?current-cycle)
   (exists (device (status on)))
   =>
   (retract ?f)
   (assert (cycle (+ ?current-cycle 1)))
   (focus INPUT TRENDS WARNINGS))
```

The *Begin-Next-Cycle* rule reactivates itself as long as there are devices that are still on. The following rule ensures that the system is halted when there are no longer any devices still on:

```
(defrule MAIN::End-Cycles
   (not (device (status on)))
   =>
   (printout t "All devices are off" crlf)
   (printout t "Halting monitoring system" crlf)
   (halt))
```

Reading the Raw Sensor Values

The next step in building the monitoring system is to read in the sensor values from the sensors. The logical place to read the values is when the current focus is the *INPUT* module. For debugging and testing purposes it will be convenient to be able to read sensor values from several sources. This section will demonstrate how to read values directly from the sensors, from instances, from a file, and from the user. The data-source fact described previously is used to indicate the source of data for the monitoring system. Sensor values read as "raw" data will be stored directly in the *raw-value* slot of the *sensor* facts and processing and analysis of this raw value will be performed in the analysis phase.

To allow the flexibility for adding new input sources later, we'll make all of the input sources instances of the *DATA-SOURCE* defclass defined as follows:

```
(defclass INPUT::DATA-SOURCE
   (is-a USER))

(defmessage-handler INPUT::DATA-SOURCE
get-data (?name)
   (printout t "Input value for sensor "
   ?name ": ")
   (read))

(defmessage-handler INPUT::DATA-SOURCE
next-cycle (?cycle))

(definstances INPUT::user-data-source
   ([user] of DATA-SOURCE))
```

The *DATA-SOURCE* defclass has two message-handlers: *get-data* and *next-cycle*. The *get-data* message-handler is used to retrieve the raw value for the sensor specified by the ?name parameter. By default, this handler will simply query the user for the value. The *next-cycle* message-handler is used to handle any processing needed by a data source at the beginning of a new cycle. By default, this handler does nothing. The *user-data-source* definstances defines the [user] instance that if used as the data source will query the user for the sensor values.

Under actual operating conditions the sensor values would probably be extracted directly from the sensors rather than the user, requiring external functions to do this work. Let's assume that the function *get-sensor-value* will return the current sensor value, given an argument representing the sensor id for which the value is desired. (In order to call a function written in C, Ada, FORTRAN, or some other programming language, it's necessary to recompile the CLIPS source code.) By creating a subclass of *DATA-SOURCE* and referring to an instance of this class, the sensor values could be read directly from the sensors rather than the user:

```
(defclass INPUT::SENSOR-DATA-SOURCE
   (is-a DATA-SOURCE))

(defmessage-handler INPUT::SENSOR-DATA-SOURCE
            get-data (?name)
(get-sensor-value ?name))

(definstances INPUT::sensor-data-source
   ([sensor] of SENSOR-DATA-SOURCE))
```

Note that the only change of any significance is to override the *get-data* handler so that it calls the *get-sensor-value* function.

For test cases or to avoid a great deal of user input, it might be more desirable to read data from a "script" rather than actually reading from a sensor or questioning the user for every value. One technique for accomplishing this would store the data in instances that the rules could then access. The following defclass describes an instance used to store data values:

```
(defclass INPUT::SENSOR-DATA
   (is-a USER)
   (multislot data))
```

where the *data* slot is the actual list of data values for a sensor.

Using this defclass, a definstances containing test values might look like the following:

```
(definstances INPUT::sensor-instance-data-values
  ([S1-DATA-SOURCE] of SENSOR-DATA
    (data 100 100 110 110 115 120))
  ([S2-DATA-SOURCE] of SENSOR-DATA
    (data 110 120 125 130 130 135))
  ([S3-DATA-SOURCE] of SENSOR-DATA
    (data 100 120 125 130 130 125))
  ([S4-DATA-SOURCE] of SENSOR-DATA
    (data 120 120 120 125 130 135))
  ([S5-DATA-SOURCE] of SENSOR-DATA
    (data 110 120 125 130 135 135))
  ([S6-DATA-SOURCE] of SENSOR-DATA
    (data 115 120 125 135 130 135)))
```

Notice that the sensor name for which the data is intended is included as part of the instance name. For example, instance [S1-DATA-SOURCE] contains the data for sensor S1.

The *INSTANCE-DATA-SOURCE* class is used to read the sensor values from the *SENSOR-DATA* instances:

```
(defclass INPUT::INSTANCE-DATA-SOURCE
   (is-a DATA-SOURCE))

(defmessage-handler INPUT::INSTANCE-DATA-SOURCE
            get-data (?name)
   ;; Locate the SENSOR-DATA instance.
   (bind ?sensor-data
      (instance-name
         (sym-cat ?name -DATA-SOURCE)))
   (if (not (instance-existp ?sensor-data))
      then (return nil))
   ;; Verify there are remaining data values.
   (bind ?data (send ?sensor-data get-data))
   (if (= (length$ ?data) 0)
      then
      (return nil))
   ;; Remove the first value in the list and
   ;; return it.
   (send ?sensor-data put-data (rest$ ?data))
   (nth$ 1 ?data))

(definstances INPUT::instance-data-source
   ([instance] of INSTANCE-DATA-SOURCE))
```

The *INSTANCE-DATA-SOURCE get-data* message-handler is slightly more complicated than the prior two *get-data* handlers. First it appends the sensor name with the symbol *–DATA-SOURCE* to construct the name of the desired SENSOR-DATA instance and then verifies that it exists. Next it verifies that there are still raw data values remaining. If there are remaining values, it removes the first one from the list and returns it. If at any point it encounters an error, it returns the symbol *nil*.

The final input technique to be discussed involves reading the information from a data file. This is more complicated than the previous examples because issues must be handled. The data file must initially be opened and the data must be read sequentially from the file. The previous input techniques were not dependent on reading the data sequentially, but rather could access the new data values for the sensors in any order. It is also not necessarily known how many sensor values have to be read, and it is desirable to prevent hard-coding of such information. To add more complexity, an assumption will be made that sensor data values may be left unspecified, in which case they will assume the raw data value of the sensor from the previous cycle. The file data source will be implemented by the following defclass:

```
(defclass INPUT::FILE-DATA-SOURCE
   (is-a DATA-SOURCE)
   (slot file-logical-name (default FALSE))
   (multislot sensor)
   (multislot value))
```

The *file-logical-name* slot will be used to store the logical name associated with the opened file. As values are read from the file, the sensor name will be stored in the *sensor* slot and the raw value will be stored in the corresponding position in the *value* slot.

The first issue that must be handled is to open the data file initially. The *get-file* handler will be used to query the user for a file name and then open the file:

```
(defmessage-handler INPUT::FILE-DATA-SOURCE
            get-file ()
   (bind ?logical-name (gensym*))
   (while TRUE
     (printout t
     "What is the name of the data file? ")
     (bind ?file-name (readline))
     (if (open ?file-name ?logical-name "r")
        then
        (bind ?self:file-logical-name
        ?logical-name)
        (return))))
```

First, a unique logical name to associate with the opened file is created by calling the *gensym** function. A specific name could be hard-coded into the handler since only one file data source is going to be used for this example, but it's conceivable that you might want to read sensor values from multiple different files so automatically generating a unique logical name makes it easier to add this enhancement. The *while* loop in the handler repeatedly queries the user for a data file to open. If the file can be successfully opened, the *file-logical-name* slot is set to the value of the generated logical name and the handler is exited. Otherwise the user is repeatedly queried for the name of a source data file as long as the *open* function is unsuccessful in opening the file name supplied.

The next decision involves the file format for storing the sensor data. It is desirable to be able to specify only those sensor values that have changed since the last cycle. Therefore, for a given cycle it is not known how many sensor values are to be read. Also, the order in which sensor values are to be read cannot necessarily be determined beforehand. These assumptions dictate a data format in which the name of the sensor is kept alongside the raw sensor value to be read. Since the number of data values to be read is unknown, the end-of-data values for a cycle will be indicated by the keyword *end-of-cycle*. The data format will look like this:

```
S1 100
S2 110
S3 100
```

```
S4 120
S5 110
S6 115
end-of-cycle
S2 120
S3 120
S5 120
S6 120
end-of-cycle
S1 110
S2 125
S3 125
S5 125
S6 125
end-of-cycle
...
```

The *put-sensor-value* message-handler will be used to store values retrieved from the file into the *FILE-DATA-SOURCE* instance:

```
(defmessage-handler INPUT::FILE-DATA-SOURCE
            put-sensor-value (?sensor ?value)
   (bind ?position (member$ ?sensor ?self:sensor))
   (if ?position
      then
      (bind ?self:value
        (replace$ ?self:value ?position
             ?position ?value))
      else
      (bind ?self:sensor ?self:sensor ?sensor)
   (bind ?self:value ?self:value ?value)))
```

First, the message-handler looks for the position of the sensor name within the *sensor* slot value. If the name is contained in this *sensor* slot, it replaces the corresponding value in the *value* slot with the new raw value. Otherwise, it adds the sensor name and value at the end of the values contained in the *sensor* and *value* slots. Because values are only added or replaced, if a sensor value isn't specified for a given cycle the prior value will still be available when the data source is queried.

The *close-data-source* message-handler will be used to close the file when there are no sensor values left in the file:

```
(defmessage-handler INPUT::FILE-DATA-SOURCE
            close-data-source ()
   (close ?self:file-logical-name)
   (bind ?self:sensor (create$))
   (bind ?self:value (create$)))
```

The *close* function is called to close the file associated with the *file-logical-name* slot. The contents of the *sensor* and *value* slots are also emptied so that no further sensor values are retrieved from them.

Unlike the prior subclasses of *DATA-SOURCE*, the *FILE-DATA-SOURCE* class will override the *next-cycle* message-handler to retrieve the sensor values for the next cycle all together from the file:

```
(defmessage-handler INPUT::FILE-DATA-SOURCE
            next-cycle (?cycle)
   (if (not ?self:file-logical-name)
      then (send ?self get-file))
   (bind ?name (read ?self:file-logical-name))
   (if (eq ?name EOF)
      then
      (send ?self close-data-source)
      (return))
   (while (and (neq ?name end-of-cycle)
               (neq ?name EOF))
      (bind ?raw-value
         (read ?self:file-logical-name))
      (if (eq ?raw-value EOF)
         then
         (send ?self close-data-source)
         (return))
      (send ?self put-sensor-value
         ?name ?raw-value)
      (bind ?name (read ?self:file-logical-name))
      (if (eq ?name EOF)
         then
         (send ?self close-data-source)
         (return))))
```

First, if the *file-logical-name* slot hasn't been changed from its original default value of *FALSE*, the *get-file* message is sent to the instance to retrieve the file name and open the file. This handler then reads all of the data values from the data file until the keyword *end-of-cycle* has been reached. If the end of file is reached, then the *close-data-source* message is sent to the instance to close the file and remove any existing sensor values. Otherwise, as the data values are read they are stored in the instance for later retrieval by sending the *put- sensor-value* message.

The *get-data* message-handler must also be overridden:

```
(defmessage-handler INPUT::FILE-DATA-SOURCE
            get-data (?name)
   (bind ?position (member$ ?name ?self:sensor))
```

```
   (if ?position
      then
      (nth$ ?position ?self:value)
      else
      (return nil)))
```

It searches for the position of the specified sensor in the *sensor* slot and then if it exists, it returns the corresponding value stored in the *value* slot. Finally, a definstances containing an instance of the *FILE-DATA-SOURCE* class must also be added:

```
(definstances INPUT::file-data-source
   ([file] of FILE-DATA-SOURCE))
```

With four different sources of data sharing a common set of message-handlers, we can use two rules and a deffacts to read data from any of them:

```
(deffacts local-cycle
   (local-cycle 0))

(defrule INPUT::next-cycle
(cycle ?cycle)
  ?f <- (local-cycle ~?cycle)
  (data-source ?source)
  (object (is-a DATA-SOURCE) (name ?source))
=>
  (send ?source next-cycle ?cycle)
  (retract ?f)
  (assert (local-cycle ?cycle)))

(defrule INPUT::Get-Sensor-Value-From-Data-Source
(cycle ?cycle)
(local-cycle ?cycle)
(data-source ?source)
(object (is-a DATA-SOURCE) (name ?source))
  ?s <- (sensor (name ?name)
                (raw-value none)
                (device ?device))
  (device (name ?device) (status on))
=>
  (bind ?raw-value (send ?source get-data ?name))
  (if (not (numberp ?raw-value))
      then
      (printout t "No data for sensor "
                  ?name crlf)
      (printout  t  "Halting  monitoring  system"
           crlf)
```

```
          (halt)
          else
          (modify ?s (raw-value ?raw-value))))
```

The *local-cycle* fact is used to indicate whether the *next-cycle* message has been processed for the current cycle of monitoring. The *next-cycle* rule checks to see if the cycle specified by the *cycle* fact differs from the cycle specified by the *local-cycle* fact. If this situation exists, the *DATA-SOURCE* instance matched on the LHS of the rule is sent the *next-cycle* message and the *local-cycle* fact is updated with the same value as the *cycle* fact. For *DATA-SOURCE*, *SENSOR-DATA-SOURCE*, and *INSTANCE-DATA-SOURCE* instances, the *next-cycle* message-handler does nothing. For a *FILE-DATA-SOURCE* instance, the *next-cycle* handler reads all of the data values for the current cycle into the instance.

Once the *cycle* and *local-cycle* facts match, the *Get-Sensor-Value-From-Data-Source* rule is used to retrieve the raw values for each sensor connected to a device that is on. The *get-data* message is sent to the *DATA-SOURCE* instance matched on the LHS of the rule to get the raw value for a specific sensor. If a non-numeric value is returned, the monitoring system is halted because non-numeric values are used to indicate there is no more data. Otherwise, the raw sensor value is stored in the *raw-value* slot of the *sensor* fact.

Detecting a Trend

The next phase of activity, the *trends* phase, determines the current state of the sensors and calculates trends that may be developing. The current state of the sensor (normal, low or high guard line, or low or high red line) must be determined from the raw sensor value asserted during the *input* phase. The current state of the sensor is stored in the *state* slot of the *sensor* deftemplate. The following rule determines whether a sensor is in the normal state:

```
(defrule TRENDS::Normal-State
  ?s <- (sensor (raw-value ?raw-value&~none)
          (low-guard-line ?lgl)
          (high-guard-line ?hgl))
  (test (and (> ?raw-value ?lgl)
          (< ?raw-value ?hgl)))
  =>
  (modify ?s (state normal) (raw-value none)))
```

The first pattern and following test CE look for any sensors that are in the normal state. The *raw-value* slot in the *sensor* pattern is compared against the value *none* to ensure that a symbol is not compared to numeric values in the test CE of the rule. The range needed for testing whether a sensor is in a normal state is between the low and high guard line values. The test CE constrains the rule to situations in which the raw sensor value is in the normal state range. The only action of this rule is to assert the derived state of the sensor. The *raw-value* slot is also set to the literal *none* so it will be read in the next *input* phase.

Four more rules are necessary to analyze the remaining four possible states of a sensor. Each of the rules will be similar to the rule *Normal-State*, with the exception of the values retrieved from the *sensor* fact and the test CE used to determine the current state. All five of the state rules could be written as a single rule with an *if* expression on the RHS of the rule to determine the appropriate state of the sensor. This type of coding, however, defeats the purpose of a data-driven system. In addition, further modifications involving actions or conditions or both of a subset of the possible states would be made much more difficult by a single unwieldy rule. The remaining four state analysis rules are as follows:

```
(defrule TRENDS::High-Guard-Line-State
  ?s <- (sensor (raw-value ?raw-value&~none)
          (high-guard-line ?hgl)
          (high-red-line ?hrl))
  (test (and (>= ?raw-value ?hgl)
          (< ?raw-value ?hrl)))
  =>
  (modify ?s (state high-guard-line)
          (raw-value none)))

(defrule TRENDS::High-Red-Line-State
  ?s <- (sensor (raw-value ?raw-value&~none)
          (high-red-line ?hrl))
  (test (>= ?raw-value ?hrl))
  =>
  (modify ?s (state high-red-line)
          (raw-value none)))

(defrule TRENDS::Low-Guard-Line-State
  ?s <- (sensor (raw-value ?raw-value&~none)
          (low-guard-line ?lgl)
          (low-red-line ?lrl))
  (test (and (> ?raw-value ?lrl)
          (<= ?raw-value ?lgl)))
  =>
  (modify ?s (state low-guard-line)
          (raw-value none)))

(defrule TRENDS::Low-Red-Line-State
  ?s <- (sensor (raw-value ?raw-value&~none)
          (low-red-line ?lrl))
  (test (<= ?raw-value ?lrl))
  =>
  (modify ?s (state low-red-line)
          (raw-value none)))
```

The five previous rules determine the state of a sensor for the current cycle. Since detecting trends in the sensors is one of the objectives of the *TRENDS* module, it will be necessary to maintain information about the past state of a sensor. The following deftemplate will be used to store this information. Since both the *TRENDS* and the *WARNINGS* module will use this deftemplate, it will be placed in the MAIN module.

```
(deftemplate MAIN::sensor-trend
   (slot name)
   (slot state (default normal))
   (slot start (default 0))
   (slot end (default 0))
   (slot shutdown-duration (default 3)))
```

The *name* slot is the name of the sensor, the *state* slot corresponds to the most current state of the sensor, the *start* slot is the first cycle during which the sensor was in its current state, the *end* slot is the current cycle, and the *shutdown-duration* slot is the amount of time a sensor must be in a guard line region before its associated device must be shut down.

The rules that update the trend information will depend on a *sensor-trend* fact existing in the fact list for each sensor. For this reason the initial sensor trends will be defined in a deffacts construct:

```
(deffacts MAIN::start-trends
(sensor-trend (name S1) (shutdown-duration 3))
(sensor-trend (name S2) (shutdown-duration 5))
(sensor-trend (name S3) (shutdown-duration 4))
(sensor-trend (name S4) (shutdown-duration 4))
(sensor-trend (name S5) (shutdown-duration 4))
(sensor-trend (name S6) (shutdown-duration 2)))
```

With this information, two rules may be defined to monitor the trends for a sensor. One rule will monitor a trend that has *not* changed since the last cycle and the other will monitor a trend that *has* changed since the last cycle:

```
(defrule TRENDS::State-Has-Not-Changed
  (cycle ?time)
  ?trend <- (sensor-trend
(name ?sensor) (state ?state)
         (end ?end-cycle&~?time))
  (sensor (name ?sensor) (state ?state)
          (raw-value none))
  =>
  (modify ?trend (end ?time)))

(defrule TRENDS::State-Has-Changed
  (cycle ?time)
```

```
  ?trend <- (sensor-trend
(name ?sensor) (state ?state)
               (end ?end-cycle&~?time))
  (sensor (name ?sensor)
          (state ?new-state&~?state)
          (raw-value none))
  =>
  (modify ?trend (start ?time)
            (end ?time)
            (state ?new-state)))
```

The first pattern of both rules establishes the cycle. The next pattern finds the *sensor-trend* fact for the previous cycle. The constraint on the *end* slot ensures that the rules do not endlessly loop. For the rule *State-Has-Not-Changed*, the next pattern checks that the state from the previous cycle is the same as the state for the current cycle. The constraint ?new-state&~?state in the rule *State-Has-Changed* performs exactly the opposite test, making sure that the state has changed from the last cycle. Checking that the *raw-value* slot is the literal *none* prevents the trend from being determined before the present state of the sensor is determined. In both rules the end cycle time is updated. If the state has changed, then the state value and start cycle time must be updated as well.

Issuing Warnings

The final phase of the cycle is the *warnings* phase. Three types of actions must be handled during this phase: sensors that have entered a red line region will have their associated devices shut off, sensors that have stayed in the guard line region for a specified number of cycles will have their associated devices shut off, and sensors that are in the guard line region and did not have their associated devices shut off will have a warning issued.

The following rule shuts off sensors that have entered a red line region:

```
(defrule WARNINGS::Shutdown-In-Red-Region
  (cycle ?time)
  (sensor-trend
     (name ?sensor)
     (state ?state&high-red-line | low-red-line))
  (sensor (name ?sensor) (device ?device))
  ?on <- (device (name ?device) (status on))
  =>
  (printout t "Cycle " ?time " - ")
  (printout t "Sensor " ?sensor " in "
?state crlf)
  (printout t "   Shutting down device "
?device crlf)
  (modify ?on (status off)))
```

The state of a sensor is checked using the *sensor-trend* fact. If the sensor is in a red line region, the associated device is turned off. Devices are immediately shut off once one of their sensors enters a red line region, so it serves little purpose to check how long a sensor has been in this state.

The rule *Shutdown-In-Guard-Region* is similar to the previous rule, with the difference that the sensor must have been in the guard line region for a period of time (specified by the shutdown-duration slot of the sensor-trend fact) before it is shut down. The length of time a sensor has been in a particular state can be determined by subtracting the *start* slot from the *end* slot of the *sensor-trend* fact:

```
(defrule WARNINGS::Shutdown-In-Guard-Region
  (cycle ?time)
  (sensor-trend
       (name ?sensor)
       (state ?state&high-guard-line |
                 low-guard-line)
       (shutdown-duration ?length)
       (start ?start) (end ?end))
  (test (>= (+ (- ?end ?start) 1)  ?length))
  (sensor (name ?sensor) (device ?device))
  ?on <- (device (name ?device) (status on))
  =>
  (printout t "Cycle " ?time " - ")
  (printout t "Sensor " ?sensor " in " ?state " ")
  (printout t "for " ?length " cycles " crlf)
  (printout t "   Shutting down device " ?device
              crlf)
  (modify ?on (status off)))
```

The addition of the *shutdown-duration* slot in the *sensor-trend* pattern and the associated test CE is the only major difference between this rule and the *Shutdown-In-Red-Region* rule. These two patterns determine whether a sensor has been in a guard region long enough to shut down the device associated with the sensor.

The final rule for the monitoring system will issue a warning for sensors that are in a guard region but that have not been in the region long enough to warrant shutting off their associated devices:

```
(defrule WARNINGS::Sensor-In-Guard-Region
  (cycle ?time)
  (sensor-trend
       (name ?sensor)
       (state ?state&high-guard-line |
                 low-guard-line)
       (shutdown-duration ?length)
```

```
    (start ?start) (end ?end))
(test (< (+ (- ?end ?start) 1) ?length))
=>
(printout t "Cycle " ?time " - ")
(printout t "Sensor " ?sensor " in "
            ?state crlf))
```

This rule acts as the complement of the *Shutdown-In-Guard-Region* rule. The test CE has been modified to check that the sensor has been in the guard line region less than the number of cycles required to shut down its associated device. Since the sensor's associated device does not need to be shut down, the patterns to determine the associated device are not included.

This final rule completes the basis of a very simple monitoring system. Additional rules could cover specific situations that should be monitored or provide a generic model for handling complex monitoring situations and representing sensor/device relationships.

12.6 SUMMARY

This chapter demonstrated a technique for representing MYCIN-style certainty factors in CLIPS. Facts are used to represent Object–Attribute–Value triples. An additional slot in each fact represents the certainty factor of the fact. Rules are used to compute certainty values for newly asserted facts on the RHS of a rule by using the certainty values bound in the LHS of the rule. A rule is then used to combine two occurrences of an OAV triple into a single occurrence with a new certainty factor computed from the certainty factors of the original pair.

Decision trees can also be represented using the forward-chaining paradigm of CLIPS. There are several algorithms for traversing decision trees including binary decision trees, multiple-branch decision trees, and learning multiple-branch decision trees. The algorithm for a multiple-branch decision tree that learns is implemented in CLIPS.

CLIPS can also emulate a backward-chaining inferencing strategy. A backward-chaining inference engine is built using CLIPS rules and is based in part on an algorithm for accomplishing backward chaining in a procedural language. Backward-chaining rules are represented as facts and acted on by the CLIPS backward-chaining inference rules. A step-by-step trace of a sample backward-chaining session demonstrates how this paradigm is represented in CLIPS.

The final example in this chapter is a simple monitoring expert system. An initial statement of the monitoring problem is used to begin the process of writing the expert system. Assumptions are made and additional details are added as more rules are added to the monitoring system. The execution of the monitoring system is split into three phases. The *input* phase gathers raw data values for the sensors. Several different methods for supplying data values are demonstrated. The *trends* phase analyzes the raw sensor values and checks for developing trends. Finally, the *warnings* phase issues warnings and performs appropriate actions based on the analysis of the *trends* phase.

PROBLEMS

12.1 Write CLIPS rules to combine MYCIN certainty factors as shown in Section 12.2 for the following two cases:

$$\text{New Certainty} = (CF_1 + CF_2) + (CF_1 * CF_2)$$

$$\text{if} \quad CF_1 \leq 0 \text{ and } CF_2 \leq 0$$

$$\text{New Certainty} = \frac{CF_1 + CF_2}{1 - \min\{|CF_1|, |CF_2|\}}$$

$$\text{if} \quad -1 < CF_1 * CF_2 < 0$$

12.2 Show how classical probability could be incorporated into CLIPS using the types of techniques demonstrated in Section 12.2. List possible advantages and disadvantages of using classical probability in rules.

12.3 Implement the *Solve_Tree_and_Learn* algorithm described in Section 12.3 using a procedural language such as LISP, C, or PASCAL. Test your implementation using the animal identification example.

12.4 Implement the *Solve_Goal* and *Attempt_Rule* algorithms described in Section 12.4 using a procedural language such as LISP, C, or PASCAL. Test your implementation using the wine selection example.

12.5 Modify the *DATA-SOURCE get-data* message-handler so it will allow only numeric input from the user. The handler should return only a non-numeric value if the word *halt* is entered during input.

12.6 Create a subclass of the *DATA-SOURCE* defclass that allows the user to use a carriage return to indicate that the previous value of each sensor should be retained. For example, if the previous values for sensors 1 and 2 were 100 and 120, then the following responses:

```
What is the value for sensor 1? ↵
What is the value for sensor 2? 130↵
```

should set the raw data value of sensor 1 to 100 and the raw data value of sensor 2 to 130. What assumptions should be made and what actions should be taken if the previous sensor value is unknown?

12.7 Modify the program so a device that has been shut off will continue to have its sensors monitored. If all sensors for the device return to a normal state, then the device should be turned back on.

12.8 The rule *Sensor-In-Guard-Region* will issue a warning for a sensor even if another rule is on the agenda, after which it would shut off its associated device. What change should be made to this rule to prevent it from issuing a warning if another rule in the *WARNINGS* module would turn off its associated device?

12.9 Add rules to print a message in the *warnings* phase to indicate that a sensor has had normal status for at least *n* cycles, where the number *n* is specified in a fact. Print the message only every *n*th cycle.

12.10 How could the backward-chaining rules in Section 12.4 be modified to allow forward chaining?

12.11 Modify the program developed for Problem 11.1 on page 702 so that the facts representing the shrubs are loaded from a file using the load-facts function. After explanations are provided, the user should be queried to determine whether another shrub selection is desired, and, if so, the program should be run again.

12.12 Using the program developed for Problem 11.3, modify the program developed for Problem 10.10 on page 620 so that only the gizmos that have not been selected are listed in the "Add Gizmo" submenu and only the gizmos that have been selected are listed in the "Remove Gizmo" submenu. In the main menu, the "Add Gizmo" menu choice should appear only if there are unselected gizmos, and the "Remove Gizmo" menu choice should appear only if there are selected gizmos.

12.13 Using the program developed for Problem 11.3 on page 702, modify the program developed for Problem 10.4 on page 618 to use a menu-driven interface. The user should be provided with separate menu options for specifying the color, hardness, and density of the gem being identified. Specification of the color should be done using a submenu containing the valid colors. A menu option should be provided that lists the gems satisfying the currently specified criterion. For example, if the user has only specified that the gem is black, the selection of this menu option will list only gems that can be black. Two other menu options should be provided, one that lists the current values specified for the criterion and another that resets all of the criteria to an unspecified state.

BIBLIOGRAPHY

(Firebaugh 88). Morris W. Firebaugh, *Artificial Intelligence: A Knowledge-Based Approach*, Boyd & Fraser Publishing, p. 309, 1988.

APPENDIX A
Some Useful Equivalences

$$\sim\sim p \equiv dp$$

$$p \rightarrow q \equiv \sim p \vee q \equiv \sim q \rightarrow \sim p$$

$$\sim(p \wedge q) \equiv \sim p \vee \sim q$$
$$\sim(p \vee q) \equiv \sim p \wedge \sim q$$

$$p \wedge (q \vee r) \equiv (p \wedge q) \vee (p \wedge r)$$
$$p \vee (q \wedge r) \equiv (p \vee q) \wedge (p \vee r)$$

$$(p \wedge q) \wedge r \equiv p \wedge (q \wedge r)$$
$$(p \vee q) \vee r \equiv p \vee (q \vee r)$$

$$p \wedge q \equiv q \wedge p$$
$$p \vee q \equiv q \vee p$$

$$\sim(\forall x)\ P(x) \equiv (\exists x)\ \sim P(x)$$
$$\sim(\exists x)\ P(x) \equiv (\forall x)\ \sim P(x)$$

$$(\forall x)\ P(x) \wedge (\forall x)\ Q(x) \equiv (\forall x)\ (P(x) \wedge Q(x))$$
$$(\exists x)\ P(x) \vee (\exists x)\ Q(x) \equiv (\exists x)\ (P(x) \vee Q(x))$$

Note: The $\forall$ does not distribute over an $\vee$, and $\exists$ does not distribute over $\wedge$, so a new dummy variable, *z*, is needed in the following two equivalences.

$$(\forall x)\ P(x) \vee (\forall x)\ Q(x) \equiv (\forall x)\ P(x) \vee (\forall z)\ Q(z)$$
$$\equiv (\forall x)\ (\forall z)\ (P(x) \vee Q(z))$$

$$(\exists x)\ P(x) \wedge (\exists x)\ Q(x) \equiv (\exists x)\ P(x) \wedge (\exists z)\ Q(z)$$
$$\equiv (\exists x)\ (\exists z)\ (P(x) \wedge Q(z))$$

APPENDIX B

Some Elementary Quantifiers and Their Meanings

Formula	Meaning
$(\forall x)\ (P(x) \rightarrow Q(x))$	For all x, all P are Q
$(\forall x)\ (P(x) \rightarrow \sim Q(x))$	For all x, no P are Q
$(\exists x)\ (P(x) \wedge Q(x))$	For some x, x are P and Q
$(\exists x)\ (P(x) \wedge \sim Q(x))$	For some x, x are P and not Q
$(\forall x)\ P(x)$	For all x, x is P
$(\exists x)\ P(x)$	Some x is P (or there are P)
$\sim(\forall x)\ P(x)$	Not all x are P (or some x are P)
$(\forall x) \sim P(x)$	All x are not P
$(\forall x)\ (\exists y)\ P(x,y)$	For all x, there is a y such that P
$(\exists x) \sim P(x)$	Some x is not P

APPENDIX C
Some Set Properties

Commutativity	$A \cup B = B \cup A$ $A \cap B = B \cap A$
Associativity	$A \cup (B \cup C) = (A \cup B) \cup C$ $A \cap (B \cap C) = (A \cap B) \cap C$
Idempotence	$A \cup A = A$ $A \cap A = A$
Distributivity	$A \cup (B \cap C) = (A \cup B) \cap (A \cup C)$ $A \cap (B \cup C) = (A \cap B) \cup (A \cap C)$
Law of the Excluded Middle	$A \cup A' = U$
Law of Contradiction	$A \cap A' = \emptyset$
Identity	$A \cup \emptyset = A$ $A \cap U = A$
Absorption	$A \cup (A \cap B) = A$ $A \cap (A \cup B) = A$
de Morgan's Laws	$(A \cap B)' = A' \cup B'$ $(A \cup B)' = A' \cap B'$
Involution	$(A')' = A$
Equivalence	$(A' \cup B) \cap (A \cup B') = (A' \cap B') \cup (A \cap B)$
Symmetrical Difference	$(A' \cap B) \cup (A \cap B') = (A' \cup B') \cap (A \cup B)$

Appendix D
CLIPS Support Information

The CD-ROM included with this book contains CLIPS 6.22 executables for MS-DOS, Windows 2000/XP, and MacOS X. Also included on the CD-ROM are all of the CLIPS source code, the three-volume *CLIPS Reference Manual*, and the *CLIPS User's Guide*. Volume I of the *CLIPS Reference Manual*, *The Basic Programming Guide*, provides the definitive description of CLIPS syntax and examples of usage. Volume II, *The Advanced Programming Guide*, provides details on customizing CLIPS, adding new functions to CLIPS, embedding CLIPS, and other advanced features. Volume III, *The Interfaces Guide*, provides information on the environment-specific interfaces for CLIPS. An X Windows version of CLIPS can be created by compiling the X Windows interface and CLIPS source code found on the CD-ROM.

Bug fixes, updates, and other information related to CLIPS can be found at the CLIPS home page at http://www.ghg.net/clips/CLIPS.html. Questions regarding CLIPS can be sent via electronic mail to clipsYYYY@ghg.net where YYYY is the current year (for example, 2004). Usenet users can find information and post questions about CLIPS at the comp.ai.shells news group.

The CLIPS Developers' Forum, located at http://www.cpbinc.com/clips, is a thread-based message board that provides a site for discussion of research, development, and implementation of the CLIPS Expert System and related technologies.

An electronic conferencing facility is also available to CLIPS users. Subscribers to this facility may send questions, observations, answers, editorials, and so forth in the form of electronic mail to the conference. All subscribers will have a copy of these messages reflected back to them at their respective email addresses. To subscribe, send a single line message to clips-request@discomsys.com containing the word "subscribe". The subject field is ignored but the address found in the 'Reply:', 'Reply to:', or 'From:' field will be entered in the distribution list. Upon subscription you will receive a mail message instructing you how to participate in the conference from that point forward.

APPENDIX E
CLIPS Commands and Functions Summary

Agenda

`(agenda [<module-name>])`
Lists the activations on the agenda of the specified module (or in the current module if <module-name> is unspecified).

`(clear-focus-stack)`
Returns all the module names from the focus stack.

`(focus <module-name>+)`
Pushes one or more modules onto the focus stack. The specified modules are pushed onto the focus stack in the reverse order from the argument list.

`(get-focus)`
Returns the module name of the current focus.

`(get-focus-stack)`
Returns all the module names in the focus stack as a multifield value.

`(get-salience-evaluation)`
Returns the current salience evaluation behavior.

`(get-strategy)`
Returns the current conflict resolution strategy.

`(halt)`
Stops the execution of rules.

`(list-focus-stack)`
Lists all the module names on the focus stack.

`(pop-focus)`
Returns the module name of the current focus and removes the current focus from the focus stack.

`(refresh-agenda [<module-name>])`
Forces reevaluation of the salience of rules on the agenda of the specified module (or in the current module if <module-name> is unspecified).

```
(run [<integer-expression>])
```
Starts the execution of rules in the current focus. If <integer-expression> is specified then only that number of rules is executed, otherwise execution halts when the agenda is empty.

```
(set-salience-evaluation <behavior>)
<behavior> ::= when-defined | when-activated |
                    every-cycle
```
Sets the salience evaluation behavior.

```
(set-strategy <strategy>)
<strategy> ::= depth | breadth | simplicity |
               complexity | lex | mea | random
```
Sets the current conflict resolution strategy.

Basic Math

```
(abs <numeric-expression>)
```
Returns the absolute value of its only argument.

```
(div <numeric-expression> <numeric-expression>+)
```
Returns the value of the first argument divided by each of the subsequent arguments. Division is performed using integer arithmetic.

```
(float <numeric-expression>)
```
Returns its only argument converted to type float.

```
(integer <numeric-expression>)
```
Returns its only argument converted to type integer.

```
(max <numeric-expression> <numeric-expression>+)
```
Returns the value of its largest argument.

```
(min <numeric-expression> <numeric-expression>+)
```
Returns the value of its smallest argument.

```
(+ <numeric-expression> <numeric-expression>+)
```
Returns the sum of its arguments.

```
(- <numeric-expression> <numeric-expression>+)
```
Returns the value of the first argument minus the sum of all subsequent arguments.

```
(* <numeric-expression> <numeric-expression>+)
```
Returns the product of its arguments.

```
(/ <numeric-expression> <numeric-expression>+)
```
Returns the value of the first argument divided by each of the subsequent arguments.

Conversion

```
(deg-grad <numeric-expression>)
```
Returns the value of its argument converted from units of degrees to units of gradients.

```
(deg-rad <numeric-expression>)
```
Returns the value of its argument converted from units of degrees to units of radians.

```
(exp <numeric-expression>)
```
Returns the value of *e* raised to the power of its only argument.

```
(grad-deg <numeric-expression>)
```
Returns the value of its argument converted from units of gradients to units of degrees.

`(log <numeric-expression>)`
Returns the logarithm base *e* of its argument.

`(log10 <numeric-expression>)`
Returns the logarithm base 10 of its argument.

`(mod <numeric-expression> <numeric-expression>)`
Returns the remainder of the result of dividing its first argument by its second argument.

`(pi)`
Returns the value of π.

`(rad-deg <numeric-expression>)`
Returns the value of its argument converted from units of radians to units of degrees.

`(round <numeric-expression>)`
Returns the value of its argument rounded to the closest integer.

`(sqrt <numeric-expression>)`
Returns the square root of its argument.

`(** <numeric-expression> <numeric-expression>)`
Returns the value of its first argument raised to the power of its second argument.

Debugging

`(dribble-off)`
Stops sending output to the trace file opened with the *dribble-on* function. Returns TRUE if the trace file was successfully closed, otherwise FALSE.

`(dribble-on <file-name>)`
Sends all output that normally goes to the screen to the trace file <file-name>. Returns TRUE if the trace file was successfully opened, otherwise FALSE.

`(list-watch-items)`
Displays the current state of watch items.

`(unwatch <watch-item>)`
Disables the display of informational messages when certain CLIPS operations occur.

```
(watch <watch-item>)
<watch-item> ::= activations | all | compilations |
                 deffunctions | facts | focus |
                 generic-functions | globals |
                 instances | messages |
                 message-handlers | methods |
                 rules | slots | statistics
```
Enables the display of informational messages when certain CLIPS operations occur.

Defclass

`(browse-classes [<class-name>])`
Displays the inheritance relationships between the specified class and its subclasses. If no class is specified, <class-name> defaults to OBJECT.

`(class-abstractp <class-name>)`
Returns TRUE if the specified class is abstract, otherwise FALSE.

`(class-existp <class-name>)`
Returns TRUE if the specified class is defined, otherwise FALSE.

(class-reactivep <class-name>)
Returns TRUE if the specified class is reactive, otherwise FALSE.

(class-slots <class-name> [inherit])
Returns the names of the explicitly defined slots of a class in a multifield value. If the optional inherit keyword is used, inherited slots are also included.

(class-subclasses <class-name> [inherit])
Returns the names of the direct subclasses of a class in a multifield value. If the optional inherit keyword is used, indirect superclasses are also included.

(class-superclasses <class-name> [inherit])
Returns the names of the direct superclasses of a class in a multifield value. If the optional inherit keyword is used, indirect superclasses are also included.

(defclass-module [<class-name>])
Returns the module in which the specified defclass is defined.

(describe-classes [<class-name>])
Provides a verbose description of a class.

(get-class-defaults-mode)
Returns the current defaults mode used when classes are defined.

(get-defclass-list [<module-name>])
Returns a multifield value containing the list of classes in the specified module (or in the current module if <module-name> is unspecified).

(list-defclasses [<module-name>])
Lists the classes in the specified module (or in the current module if <module-name> is unspecified).

(ppdefclass <class-name>)
Displays the text of the specified definstances.

(set-class-defaults-mode convenience | conservation)
Sets the defaults mode used when classes are defined.

(slot-allowed-values <class-name> <slot-name>)
Returns the allowed values for a slot in a multifield value.

(slot-cardinality <class-name> <slot-name>)
Returns the minimum and maximum number of fields allowed for a multislot in a multifield value.

(slot-default-value <class-name> <slot-name>)
Returns the default value associated with a slot.

(slot-direct-accessp <class-name> <slot-name>)
Returns TRUE if the specified slot can be accessed directly, otherwise FALSE.

(slot-existp <class-name> <slot-name> [inherit])
Returns TRUE if the specified slot is present in the class, otherwise FALSE. If the inherit keyword is specified, then the slot may be inherited.

(slot-facets <class-name> <slot-name>)
Returns the facet values for the specified slot of a class in a multifield value.

(slot-initablep <class-name> <slot-name>)
Returns TRUE if the specified slot is initializable, otherwise FALSE.

(slot-publicp <class-name> <slot-name>)
Returns TRUE if the specified slot is public, otherwise FALSE.

(slot-range <class-name> <slot-name>)
Returns the minimum and maximum numeric values allowed for a slot in a multifield value.

(slot-sources <class-name> <slot-name>)
Returns the names of the classes which provide facets for the specified slot of the specified class in a multifield value.

(slot-types <class-name> <slot-name>)
Returns the names of the primitive types allowed for the specified slot of the specified class in a multifield value.

(slot-writeablep <class-name> <slot-name>)
Returns TRUE if the specified slot is writable, otherwise FALSE.

(subclassp <class1-name> <class2-name>)
Returns TRUE if the first class is a subclass of the second class.

(superclassp <class1-name> <class2-name>)
Returns TRUE if the first class is a superclass of the second class.

(undefclass <class-name>)
Deletes the specified class.

Deffacts

(deffacts-module <deffacts-name>)
Returns the module in which the specified deffacts is defined.

(get-deffacts-list [<module-name>])
Returns the list of all deffacts in the specified module (or in the current module if <module-name> is unspecified).

(list-deffacts [<module-name>])
Lists the deffacts in the specified module (or in the current module if <module-name> is unspecified).

(ppdeffacts <deffacts-name>)
Displays the text of the specified deffacts.

(undeffacts <deffacts-name>)
Deletes the specified deffacts.

Deffunction

(deffunction-module <deffunction-name>)
Returns the module in which the specified deffunction is defined.

(get-deffunction-list [<module-name>])
Returns a multifield value containing the list of deffunctions in the specified module (or in the current module if <module-name> is unspecified).

(list-deffunctions [<module-name>])
Lists the deffunctions in the specified module (or in the current module if <module-name> is unspecified).

(ppdeffunction <deffunction-name>)
Displays the text of the specified deffunction.

(undeffunction <deffunction-name>)
Deletes the specified deffunction.

Defgeneric

`(defgeneric-module <defgeneric-name>)`
Returns the module in which the specified defgeneric is defined.

`(get-defgeneric-list [<module-name>])`
Returns a multifield value containing the list of defgenerics in the specified module (or in the current module if <module-name> is unspecified).

`(list-defgenerics [<module-name>])`
Lists the defgenerics in the specified module (or in the current module if <module-name> is unspecified).

`(ppdefgeneric <defgeneric-name>)`
Displays the text of the specified defgeneric.

`(preview-generic <generic-function-name> <expression>*)`
Lists all applicable methods for a particular generic function call in order of decreasing precedence, but does not execute them.

`(type <expression>)`
Returns a symbol which is the name of the type (or class) of its argument.

`(undefgeneric <defgeneric-name>)`
Deletes the specified defgeneric and all its methods.

Defglobal

`(defglobal-module <defglobal-name>)`
Returns the module in which the specified defglobal is defined.

`(get-defglobal-list [<module-name>])`
Returns a multifield value containing the list of defglobals in the specified module (or in the current module if <module-name> is unspecified).

`(get-reset-globals)`
Returns the current value of the reset global variables behavior (TRUE or FALSE).

`(list-defglobals [<module-name>])`
Lists the defglobals in the specified module (or in the current module if <module-name> is unspecified).

`(ppdefglobal <defglobal-name>)`
Displays the text of the specified defglobal.

`(set-reset-globals <boolean-expression>)`
Sets the reset global variables behavior. When this behavior is enabled (TRUE by default) global variables are reset to their original values when the *reset* command is performed.

`(show-defglobals [<module-name>])`
Lists the defglobals and their current values in the specified module (or in the current module if <module-name> is unspecified).

`(undefglobal <defglobal-name>)`
Deletes the specified defglobal.

Definstances

`(definstances-module <definstances-name>)`
Returns the module in which the specified definstances is defined.

`(get-definstances-list [<module-name>])`
Returns a multifield value containing the list of definstances in the specified module (or in the current module if <module-name> is unspecified).

`(list-definstances [<module-name>])`
Lists the definstances in the specified module (or in the current module if <module-name> is unspecified).

`(ppdefinstances <definstances-name>)`
Displays the text of the specified definstances.

`(undefinstances <definstances-name>)`
Deletes the specified definstances.

Defmessage-handler

`(call-next-handler)`
When called from within a message-handler, calls the next message-handler that is overridden or shadowed by the executing message-handler.

`(get-defmessage-handler-list <class-name> [inherit])`
Returns a multifield value containing triples of class names, handler names, and handler types for the specified class. If inherit is specified, then inherited message-handlers are also included in the multifield value.

`(list-defmessage-handlers [<class-name> [inherit]])`
Lists the defmessage-handlers for the specified class in the current module. If no class is specified, the message-handlers for all classes in the current module will be listed. If inherit is specified, then inherited message-handlers will also be displayed.

```
(message-handler-existp <class-name><handler-name>
                        [<handler-type>])
<handler-type> ::= around | before |
                   primary | after
```

Returns TRUE if the specified message-handler is defined directly (not by inheritance) for the specified class, otherwise FALSE.

`(next-handlerp)`
Returns TRUE if there is another message-handler available for execution, otherwise FALSE.

`(override-next-handler <expression>*)`
Calls the next shadowed handler and allows the arguments to be changed.

```
(ppdefmessage-handler <class-name> <handler-name>
                      [<handler-type>])
<handler-type> ::= around | before |
                   primary | after
```

Displays the text of the specified defmessage-handler. If <handler-type> is unspecified, it is assumed to be primary.

`(preview-send <class-name> <message-name>)`
Displays the list of the applicable handlers for a message sent to an instance of the specified class.

```
(undefmessage-handler <class-name> <handler-name>
                      [<handler-type>])
<handler-type> ::= around | before |
                   primary | after
```

Deletes the specified defmessage-handler. If <handler-type> is unspecified, it is assumed to be primary.

Defmethod

`(call-next-method)`

Calls the next shadowed method.

```
(call-specific-method <defgeneric-name> <method-index>
                      <expression>*)
```

Calls a particular method of a generic function without regards to method precedence.

`(get-defmethod-list [<defgeneric-name>])`

Returns a multifield value containing pairs of defgeneric names and methods indices for all methods in the current module. If a defgeneric name is specified, then only methods belonging to that defgeneric will be included in the return value.

```
(get-method-restrictions <defgeneric-name>
                         <method-index>)
```

Returns a multifield value containing information about the restrictions for the specified method.

`(list-defmethods [<defgeneric-name>])`

Lists all defmethods in the current module in order of precedence. If a defgeneric name is specified, then only methods belonging to that defgeneric are listed.

`(next-methodp)`

If called from a method for a generic function, the function next-methodp will return the symbol TRUE if there is another method shadowed by the current one. Otherwise, the function will return the symbol FALSE.

`(override-next-method <expression>*)`

Calls the next shadowed method allowing new arguments to be provided.

`(ppdefmethod <defgeneric-name> <index>)`

Displays the text of the defmethod associated with the specified generic function and method index.

```
(preview-generic <generic-function-name>
                 <expression>*)
```

Lists all applicable methods for a particular generic function call in order of decreasing precedence, but does not execute them.

`(undefmethod <defgeneric-name> <index>)`

Deletes the defmethod associated with the specified generic function and method index.

Defmodule

`(get-current-module)`

Returns the current module.

`(get-defmodule-list)`

Returns the list of all defmodules.

(list-defmodules)
Lists all defmodules in the CLIPS environment.

(ppdefmodule <defmodule-name>)
Displays the text of the specified defmodule.

(set-current-module <defmodule-name>)
Sets the current module to the specified module and returns the previous current module.

Defrule

(defrule-module <defrule-name>)
Returns the module in which the specified defrule is defined.

(get-defrule-list [<module-name>])
Returns the list of all defrules in the specified module (or in the current module if <module-name> is unspecified).

(get-incremental-reset)
Returns the current value of the incremental reset behavior.

(list-defrules [<module-name>])
Lists the defrules in the specified module (or in the current module if <module-name> is unspecified).

(matches <defrule-name>)
Displays the list of facts and partial matches that match the patterns of the specified rule.

(ppdefrule <defrule-name>)
Displays the text of the specified defrule.

(refresh <defrule-name>)
Refreshes the specified defrule. Activations for the rule that have already fired but are still valid are placed on the agenda.

(remove-break [<defrule-name>])
Removes a breakpoint for the specified rule. If no rule is specified, all breakpoints are removed.

(set-break <defrule-name>)
Sets a breakpoint for the specified rule. This will cause rule execution to halt before the rule is fired.

(set-incremental-reset <boolean-expression>)
Sets the incremental reset behavior.

(show-breaks [<module-name>])
Lists the rules in the specified module that have breakpoints set (or in the current module if <module-name> is unspecified).

(undefrule <defrule-name>)
Deletes the specified defrule.

Deftemplate

(deftemplate-module <deftemplate-name>)
Returns the module in which the specified deftemplate is defined.

(get-deftemplate-list [<module-name>])
Returns the list of all deftemplates in the specified module (or in the current module if <module-name> is unspecified).

`(list-deftemplates [<module-name>])`
Lists the deftemplates in the specified module (or in the current module if <module-name> is unspecified).

`(ppdeftemplate <deftemplate-name>)`
Displays the text of the specified deftemplate.

`(undeftemplate <deftemplate-name>)`
Deletes the specified deftemplate.

Environment

`(apropos <lexeme>)`
Displays all symbols currently defined in the CLIPS environment that contain the specified substring <lexeme>.

`(batch <file-name>)`
Allows "batch" processing of CLIPS interactive commands by replacing standard input with the contents of the file <file-name>. Returns TRUE if the file was successfully executed, otherwise FALSE.

`(batch* <file-name>)`
Executes commands from a file. Unlike the *batch* command, evaluates all of the commands in the specified file before returning rather than replacing standard input.

`(bload <file-name>)`
Loads a binary image from a file. Returns TRUE if the file was successfully loaded, otherwise FALSE.

`(bsave <file-name>)`
Saves a binary image to a file.

`(clear)`
Removes all constructs from the CLIPS environment.

`(exit)`
Exits from the CLIPS environment.

`(get-auto-float-dividend)`
Returns the current value of the auto-float dividend behavior.

`(get-dynamic-constraint-checking)`
Returns the current value of the dynamic constraint checking behavior.

`(get-static-constraint-checking)`
Returns the current value of the static constraint checking behavior.

`(load <file-name>)`
Loads the constructs stored in the file specified by <file-name> into the CLIPS environment. Returns TRUE if the file was successfully loaded, otherwise FALSE.

`(load* <file-name>)`
Loads the constructs stored in the file specified by <file-name> into the CLIPS environment with displaying informational messages. Returns TRUE if the file was successfully loaded, otherwise FALSE.

`(options)`
Lists the settings of CLIPS compiler flags.

`(reset)`
Resets the CLIPS environment.

(save <file-name>)

Saves all of the constructs in the CLIPS environment to the file specified by <file-name>.

(set-auto-float-dividend <boolean-expression>)

Disables the auto-float dividend behavior if <boolean-expression> is FALSE, otherwise enables auto-float dividend behavior. The old value of the auto-float dividend behavior is returned.

(set-dynamic-constraint-checking <boolean-expression>)

Disables dynamic constraint checking if <boolean-expression> is FALSE, otherwise enables dynamic constraint checking. The old value of the constraint checking behavior is returned.

(set-static-constraint-checking <boolean-expression>)

Disables static constraint checking if <boolean-expression> is FALSE, otherwise enables static constraint checking. The old value of the constraint checking behavior is returned.

(system <lexeme-expression>*)

Concatenates its arguments together as a string and passes the string as a command to be executed by the operating system.

Fact

(assert <RHS-pattern>)

Adds one or more facts to the fact list. The fact address of the last fact added is returned.

(assert-string <string-expression>)

Converts a string to a fact and asserts it. The fact address of the newly asserted fact is returned.

(dependencies <fact-index-or-fact-address>)

Lists all the partial matches from which the specified fact receives logical support.

(dependents <fact-index-or-fact-address>)

Lists all facts that receive logical support from the specified fact.

(duplicate <fact-index-or-fact-address> <RHS-slot>*)

Asserts a duplicated copy of a deftemplate fact with one or more slot values changed.

```
(facts [<module-name>]
       [<start-integer-expression>
          [<end-integer-expression>
             [<max-integer-expression>]]]])
```

Displays the facts in the fact list. If <module-name> is specified, only those facts visible to the specified module are listed, otherwise facts visible to the current module are listed. Facts with fact indices less than <start-integer-expression> or greater than <end-integer-expression> are not listed. If <max-integer-expression> is specified, then no more facts than that value will be listed.

(fact-existp <fact-address-expression>)

Returns TRUE if the fact specified by its fact-index or fact-address argument exists, otherwise FALSE.

(fact-index <fact-address-expression>)

Returns the fact index associated with a fact address.

(fact-relation <fact-address-expression>)

Returns the deftemplate (relation) name associated with the fact.

```
(fact-slot-names <fact-address-expression>)
```

Returns the slot names associated with the fact.

```
(fact-slot-value <fact-address-expression>
                 <slot-name>)
```

Returns the value of the specified slot from the specified fact.

```
(get-fact-duplication)
```

Returns the current value of the fact duplication behavior.

```
(get-fact-list [<module-name>])
```

Returns the list of all facts in the specified module (or in the current module if <module-name> is unspecified).

```
(load-facts <file-name>)
```

Asserts the facts contained in the file <file-name> in the current module. Returns TRUE if successful, otherwise FALSE.

```
(modify <fact-index-or-fact-address> <RHS-slot>*)
```

Changes one or more slot values of a deftemplate fact.

```
(retract <fact-index-or-fact-address>+)
```

Removes one or more facts from the fact list.

```
(save-facts <file-name>
            [visible | local <deftemplate-names>*])
```

Saves the specified facts to the file <file-name>. Returns TRUE if successful, otherwise FALSE.

```
(set-fact-duplication <boolean-expression>)
```

Allows identical facts to be asserted if <boolean-expression> is FALSE, otherwise prevents duplicate facts from being added to the fact list. The old value of the duplication behavior is returned.

Instance

```
(any-instancep <instance-set-template> <query>)

<instance-set-template> ::=
                           (<instance-set-member-template>+)
<instance-set-member-template ::=
        (<single-field-variable>    <class-name-expression>+)
<query> ::= <boolean-expression>
```

Returns TRUE if any instance set is found satisfying the specified query, otherwise FALSE is returned.

```
(class <object-expression>)
```

Returns a symbol which is the name of the class of its argument.

```
(delayed-do-for-all-instances <instance-set-template>
                              <query> <expression>*)
```

First determines all instance sets satisfying the specified query and then evaluates the specified expressions for each of the satisfying instance sets.

```
(delete-instance)
```

Deletes the active instance when called from within the body of a message-handler.

```
(direct-slot-delete$ <mv-slot-name>
                     <range-begin> <range-end>)
```

Allows the deletion of a range of fields in a multifield slot value of the active instance from within a message-handler.

```
(direct-slot-insert$ <mv-slot-name> <index>
                     <expression>+)
```

Allows the insertion of one or more values in a multifield slot value of the active instance from within a message-handler.

```
(direct-slot-replace$ <mv-slot-name> <range-begin>
                      <range-end> <expression>+)
```

Allows the replacement of a range of fields in a multifield slot value of the active instance within a message-handler.

```
(do-for-instance <instance-set-template> <query>
                 <expression>*)
```

Evaluates the specified expressions for the first instance set satisfying the specified query.

```
(do-for-all-instances <instance-set-template> <query>
                      <expression>*)
```

Evaluates the specified expressions for all instance sets satisfying the specified query.

```
(dynamic-get <slot-name-expression>)
```

Returns the value of the specified slot of the active instance.

```
(dynamic-put <slot-name-expression> <expression>*)
```

Sets the value of the specified slot of the active instance.

```
(find-instance <instance-set-template> <query>)
```

Returns a multifield value containing the first instance set found satisfying the specified query.

```
(find-all-instances <instance-set-template> <query>)
```

Returns a multifield value containing the all instance sets found satisfying the specified query.

```
(init-slots)
```

Implements the init message-handler attached to the class USER. This function should never be called directly unless an init message-handler is being defined such that the one attached to USER will never be called.

```
(instance-address <instance-expression>)
```

Converts an instance to an instance address.

```
(instance-addressp <expression>)
```

Returns TRUE if its argument is an instance address, otherwise FALSE.

```
(instance-existp <instance-expression>)
```

Returns TRUE if the specified instance exists, otherwise FALSE.

```
(instance-name <instance-expression>)
```

Converts an instance address to an instance name.

```
(instance-namep <expression>)
```

Returns TRUE if its argument is an instance name, otherwise FALSE.

```
(instance-name-to-symbol <instance-name-expression>)
```

Converts an instance name to a symbol.

```
(instancep <expression>)
```
Returns TRUE if its argument is an instance name or instance address, otherwise FALSE.

```
(instances [<module-name> [<class-name> [inherit]]])
```
Returns TRUE if its argument is an instance name or instance address, otherwise FALSE.

```
(load-instances <file-name>)
```
Loads instances from the specified file.

```
(make-instance [<instance-name-expression>]
    of <class-name-expression> <slot-override>*)
<slot-override> ::= (<slot-name-expression>
                    <expression>)
```
Creates and initializes an instance with the specified slot values.

```
(ppinstance )
```
Prints the slots of the active instance when called from within the body of a message-handler.

```
(restore-instances <file-name>)
```
Loads instances from the specified file.

```
(save-instances <file-name>)
```
Saves instances to the specified file.

```
(send <object-expression> <message-name-expression>
    <expression>*)
```
Sends a message to the specified object with the specified arguments.

```
(slot-delete$ <instance-expression> <mv-slot-name>
              <range-begin> <range-end>)
```
Allows the deletion of a range of fields in a multifield slot value.

```
(slot-insert$ <instance-expression> <mv-slot-name>
              <index> <expression>+)
```
Allows the insertion of one or more values in a multifield slot value.

```
(slot-replace$ <instance-expression> <mv-slot-name>
               <range-begin> <range-end>
               <expression>+)
```
Allows the replacement of a range of fields in a multifield slot value.

```
(symbol-to-instance-name <symbol-expression>)
```
Converts a symbol to an instance name.

```
(unmake-instance <instance-expression> | *)
```
Deletes the specified instance (or all instances if * is specified) by sending it the delete message.

I/O

```
(close [<logical-name>])
```
Closes the file associated with the logical name <logical-name> (or all files if unspecified). Returns TRUE if the file was successfully closed, otherwise FALSE.

```
(format <logical-name> <string-expression>
        <expression>*)
```

Evaluates and prints as formatted output to the logical name <logical-name> zero or more expressions formatted by <string-expression>. See Section 8.12 for details on formatting flags.

```
(open <file-name> <logical-name> [<mode>])
```

Opens the file <file-name> in the specified mode (either "r," "w," "r+," or "a") and associates the logical name <logical-name> with the file. Returns TRUE if the file was successfully opened, otherwise FALSE.

```
(printout <logical-name> <expression>*)
```

Evaluates and prints as unformatted output to the logical name <logical-name> zero or more expressions.

```
(read [<logical-name>])
```

Reads a single field from the specified logical name (*stdin* if unspecified). Returns the field if successful or EOF if no input available.

```
(readline [<logical-name>])
```

Reads an entire line from the specified logical name (*stdin* if unspecified). Returns a string if successful or EOF if no input available.

```
(remove <file-name>)
```

Deletes the file <file-name>.

```
(rename <old-file-name> <new-file-name>)
```

Renames the file <old-file-name> to <new-file-name>.

Memory

```
(conserve-mem  on | off)
```

Turns on or off the storage of information used for the save and pretty-print commands.

```
(mem-used)
```

Returns the number of bytes of memory CLIPS has requested from the operating system.

```
(mem-requests)
```

Returns the number of times CLIPS has requested memory from the operating system.

```
(release-mem)
```

Releases all free memory held internally by CLIPS to the operating system. The return value is the amount of memory freed.

Miscellaneous

```
(funcall <function-name-expression> <expression>*)
```

Constructs a function call from its arguments and then evaluates the function call.

```
(gensym)
```

Returns a sequenced symbol of the form genX where *X* is an integer.

```
(gensym*)
```

Returns a sequenced symbol of the form genX where *X* is an integer. Unlike the gensym function, gensym* produces a unique symbol that does not currently exist within the CLIPS environment.

```
(get-function-restrictions <function-name-expression>)
```

Returns the restriction string associated with a CLIPS or user defined function.

```
(length <lexeme-or-multifield-expression>)
```
Returns an integer for the number of fields in a multifield value or the length of a string or symbol.

```
(random [<start-integer-expression>
         <end-integer-expression>])
```
Returns a "random" integer value (optionally between the start and end integer values specified).

```
(seed <integer-expression>)
```
Sets the seed used by the random number generator for the *random* function.

```
(setgen <integer-expression>)
```
Sets the sequence index used by *gensym* and *gensym**.

```
(sort <comparison-function-name> <expression>*)
```
Sorts the list of fields specified by <expression>* using the comparison function to determine if any two fields need to be swapped.

```
(time)
```
Returns a floating-point value representing the number of elapsed seconds since a system reference time.

```
(timer <expression>*)
```
Returns the number of seconds elapsed evaluating a series of expressions.

Multifield

```
(create$ <expression>*)
```
Appends zero or more expressions together to create a multifield value.

```
(delete$ <multifield-expression>
         <begin-integer-expression>
         <end-integer-expression>)
```
Deletes all fields in the specified range (<begin-integer-expression> to <end-integer-expression>) from <multifield-expression> and returns the result.

```
(delete-member$ <multifield-expression> <expression>+)
```
Deletes specified values contained within a multifield value and returns the modified multifield value.

```
(explode$ <string-expression>)
```
Returns a multifield value created from the fields contained in a string.

```
(first$ <multifield-expression>)
```
Returns the first field of <multifield-expression>.

```
(implode$ <multifield-expression>)
```
Returns a string containing the fields from a multifield value.

```
(insert$ <multifield-expression>
         <integer-expression>
         <single-or-multifield-expression>+)
```
Inserts all the <single-or-multifield-expression> values in the <multifield-expression> before the *n*th value (<integer-expression>) of <multifield-expression>.

```
(length$ <multifield-expression>)
```
Returns the number of fields in a multifield value.

```
(member$ <single-field-expression>
         <multifield-expression>)
```

Returns the position of the first argument in the second argument or FALSE if the first argument is not contained in the second argument.

```
(nth$ <integer-expression> <multifield-expression>)
```

Returns the *n*th field (<integer-expression>) contained in <multifield-expression>.

```
(replace$ <multifield-expression>
          <begin-integer-expression>
          <end-integer-expression>
          <single-or-multifield-expression>+)
```

Replaces the fields in the specified range (<begin-integer-expression> to <end-integer-expression>) in <multifield-expression> with all of the <single-or-multifield-expression> values and returns the result.

```
(replace-member$ <multifield-expression>
                 <substitute-expression>
                 <search -expression>+)
```

Replaces specific values contained within a multifield value and returns the modified multifield value.

```
(rest$ <multifield-expression>)
```

Returns a multifield value containing all but the first field of <multifield-expression>.

```
(subseq$ <multifield-expression>
         <begin-integer-expression>
         <end-integer-expression>)
```

Extracts the fields in the specified range (<begin-integer-expression> to <end-integer-expression>) from <multifield-expression> and returns them in a multifield value.

```
(subsetp <expression>)
```

Returns TRUE if the first argument is a subset of the second argument, otherwise FALSE.

Predicate

```
(and <expression>+)
```

Returns TRUE if each of its arguments evaluates to TRUE, otherwise FALSE.

```
(eq <expression> <expression>+)
```

Returns TRUE if its first argument is equal in type and value to all its subsequent arguments, otherwise FALSE.

```
(evenp <expression>)
```

Returns TRUE if <expression> is an even integer, otherwise FALSE.

```
(floatp <expression>)
```

Returns TRUE if <expression> is a float, otherwise FALSE.

```
(integerp <expression>)
```

Returns TRUE if <expression> is an integer, otherwise FALSE.

```
(lexemep <expression>)
```

Returns TRUE if <expression> is a string or symbol, otherwise FALSE.

`(multifieldp <expression>)`
Returns TRUE if <expression> is a multifield value, otherwise FALSE.

`(neq <expression> <expression>+)`
Returns TRUE if its first argument is not equal in type and value to all its subsequent arguments, otherwise FALSE.

`(not <expression>)`
Returns TRUE if its argument evaluates to FALSE, otherwise TRUE.

`(numberp <expression>)`
Returns TRUE if <expression> is a float or an integer, otherwise FALSE.

`(oddp <expression>)`
Returns TRUE if <expression> is an odd integer, otherwise FALSE.

`(or <expression>+)`
Returns TRUE if any of its arguments evaluate to TRUE, otherwise FALSE.

`(pointerp <expression>)`
Returns TRUE for an external address, otherwise FALSE.

`(stringp <expression>)`
Returns TRUE if <expression> is a string, otherwise FALSE.

`(symbolp <expression>)`
Returns TRUE if <expression> is a symbol, otherwise FALSE.

`(= <numeric-expression> <numeric-expression>+)`
Returns TRUE if its first argument is equal in numeric value to all its subsequent arguments, otherwise FALSE.

`(<> <numeric-expression> <numeric-expression>+)`
Returns TRUE if its first argument is not equal in numeric value to all its subsequent arguments, otherwise FALSE.

`(> <numeric-expression> <numeric-expression>+)`
Returns TRUE if, for all its arguments, argument $n - 1$ is greater than argument n, otherwise FALSE.

`(>= <numeric-expression> <numeric-expression>+)`
Returns TRUE if, for all its arguments, argument $n - 1$ is greater than or equal to argument n, otherwise FALSE.

`(< <numeric-expression> <numeric-expression>+)`
Returns TRUE if, for all its arguments, argument $n - 1$ is less than argument n, otherwise FALSE.

`(<= <numeric-expression> <numeric-expression>+)`
Returns TRUE if, for all its arguments, argument $n - 1$ is less than or equal to argument n, otherwise FALSE.

Procedural

`(bind <variable> <value>)`
Binds a variable to a specified value.

`(break)`
Terminates the execution of the *while*, *loop-for-count*, *progn$*, *do-for-instance*, *do-for-all-instances*, or *delayed-do-for-all-instances* function in which it is immediately contained.

```
(if <predicate-expression> then <expression>+
                            [else <expression>+])
```

Evaluates the expressions contained in the *else* portion of the function if the <predicate-expression> evaluates to the symbol FALSE, otherwise evaluates the expressions contained in the *then* portion of the function.

```
(loop-for-count <range-spec> [do] <expression>*)
<range-spec> ::= <end-index> |
                 (<loop-variable> <end-index>) |
                 (<loop-variable> <start-index>
                                  <end-index>)
```

Evaluates <expression>* the number of times specified by <range-spec>. If <start-index> is not given, it is assumed to be one. If <start-index> is greater than <end-index>, then the body of the loop is never executed. The integer value of the current iteration can be examined with the variable <loop-variable> if specified.

```
(progn <expression>*)
```

Evaluates all arguments and returns the value of the last argument evaluated.

```
(progn$ <list-spec> <expression>*)
<list-spec> ::= <multifield-expression> |
                (<list-variable>
                 <multifield-expression>)
```

Evaluates <expression>* for each field contained in <list-spec>. The value of the field in the current iteration can be examined with the variable <list-variable> if specified. In addition, the integer index value of the current iteration can be examined with the variable <list-variable>-index.

```
(return [<expression>])
```

Terminates the execution of the currently executing deffunction, generic function method, message-handler, or defrule RHS. Without any arguments, there is no return value. However, if an argument is included, its evaluation is given as the return value of the deffunction , method or message-handler.

```
(switch <test-expression> <case-statement>*
                          [<default-statement>])

<case-statement> ::=
   (case <comparison-expression> then <expression>*)
<default-statement> ::= (default <expression>*)
```

Evaluates <test-expression> and compares to the result of the <comparison-expression> for each case in order. If a matching case is found, <expression>* is evaluated for that case and the function returns. If no match is found and a <default-statement> exists, then <expression>* for the default statement is executed.

```
(while <predicate-expression> [do] <expression>*)
```

Evaluates <expression>* as long as the <predicate-expression> does not evaluate to the symbol FALSE.

Profiling

```
(get-profile-percent-threshold )
```

Returns the current value of the profile percent threshold.

(profile constructs | user-functions | off)
Enables/disables profiling of constructs and user functions.

(profile-info)
Displays profiling information currently collected for constructs or user functions.

(profile-reset)
Resets all profiling information currently collected for constructs and user functions.

(set-profile-percent-threshold
<number-in-range-of-0-to-100>)
Sets the minimum percentage of time that must be spent executing a construct or user function for it to be displayed by the profile-info command.

Sequence Expansion

(expand$ <multifield-expression>*)
When used inside of a function call, expands its arguments as separate arguments to the function. The $ operator is merely a shorthand notation for the expand$ function call.

(get-sequence-operator-recognition)
Returns the current value of the sequence operator recognition behavior.

(aet-sequence-operator-recognition
<boolean-expression>)
Sets the sequence operator recognition behavior.

String

(build <string-or-symbol-expression>)
Evaluates a string as though it were entered at the command prompt. Only allows constructs to be evaluated.

(check-syntax <string-expression>)
Allows the text representation of a construct or function call to be checked for syntax and semantic errors. Returns FALSE if no errors or warnings detected.

(eval <string-or-symbol-expression>)
Evaluates a string as though it were entered at the command prompt. Only allows functions to be evaluated.

(lowcase <string-or-symbol-expression>)
Returns its argument with all uppercase letters replaced with lowercase letters.

(str-cat <expression>*)
Returns all of its arguments concatenated as a string.

(str-compare <string-or-symbol-expression>
<string-or-symbol-expression>)
Returns zero if both arguments are equal, a positive integer if the first argument is lexicographically greater than the second argument, and a negative integer if the first argument is lexicographically less than the second argument.

(str-index <lexeme-expression> <lexeme-expression>)
Returns the integer position of the first argument within the second argument if the first argument is a substring of the second argument, otherwise FALSE.

(str-length <string-or-symbol-expression>)
Returns the length of a string in characters.

```
(string-to-field <string-or-symbol-expression>)
```
Converts a string into a field.

```
(sub-string <begin-integer-expression>
            <end-integer-expression>
            <string-expression>)
```
Returns the substring from <string-expression> of the specified range (<begin-integer-expression> to <end-integer-expression>).

```
(sym-cat <expression>*)
```
Returns all of its arguments concatenated as a symbol.

```
(upcase <string-or-symbol-expression>)
```
Returns its argument with all lowercase letters replaced with uppercase letters.

Text Processing

```
(fetch  <file-name>)
```
Loads the named file into the internal lookup table.

```
(print-region <logical-name> <lookup-file>
              <topic-field>*)
```
Looks up the specified entry in a particular file which has been previously loaded into the lookup table and prints the contents of that entry to the specified logical name.

```
(toss <file-name>)
```
Unloads the named file from the internal lookup table.

Trigonometric

```
(acos <numeric-expression>)
```
Returns the arccosine of its argument (in radians).

```
(acosh <numeric-expression>)
```
Returns the hyperbolic arccosine of its argument (in radians).

```
(acot <numeric-expression>)
```
Returns the arccotangent of its argument (in radians).

```
(acoth <numeric-expression>)
```
Returns the hyperbolic arccotangent of its argument (in radians).

```
(acsc <numeric-expression>)
```
Returns the arccosecant of its argument (in radians).

```
(acsch <numeric-expression>)
```
Returns the hyperbolic arccosecant of its argument (in radians).

```
(asec <numeric-expression>)
```
Returns the arcsecant of its argument (in radians).

```
(asech <numeric-expression>)
```
Returns the hyperbolic arcsecant of its argument (in radians).

```
(asin <numeric-expression>)
```
Returns the arcsine of its argument (in radians).

```
(asinh <numeric-expression>)
```
Returns the hyperbolic arcsine of its argument (in radians).

`(atan <numeric-expression>)`
Returns the arctangent of its argument (in radians).

`(atanh <numeric-expression>)`
Returns the hyperbolic arctangent of its argument (in radians).

`(cos <numeric-expression>)`
Returns the cosine of its argument (in radians).

`(cosh <numeric-expression>)`
Returns the hyperbolic cosine of its argument (in radians).

`(cot <numeric-expression>)`
Returns the cotangent of its argument (in radians).

`(coth <numeric-expression>)`
Returns the hyperbolic cotangent of its argument (in radians).

`(csc <numeric-expression>)`
Returns the cosecant of its argument (in radians).

`(csch <numeric-expression>)`
Returns the hyperbolic cosecant of its argument (in radians).

`(sec <numeric-expression>)`
Returns the secant of its argument (in radians).

`(sech <numeric-expression>)`
Returns the hyperbolic secant of its argument (in radians).

`(sin <numeric-expression>)`
Returns the sine of its argument (in radians).

`(sinh <numeric-expression>)`
Returns the hyperbolic sine of its argument (in radians).

`(tan <numeric-expression>)`
Returns the tangent of its argument (in radians).

`(tanh <numeric-expression>)`
Returns the hyperbolic tangent of its argument (in radians).

Appendix F
CLIPS BNF

CLIPS Program

```
<CLIPS-program> ::= <construct>*

<construct>     ::= <deffacts-construct> |
                    <deftemplate-construct> |
                    <defglobal-construct> |
                    <defrule-construct> |
                    <deffunction-construct> |
                    <defgeneric-construct> |
                    <defmethod-construct> |
                    <defclass-construct> |
                    <definstance-construct> |
                    <defmessage-handler-construct> |
                    <defmodule-construct>
```

Deffacts Construct

```
<deffacts-construct> ::= (deffacts <name> [<comment>]
                             <RHS-pattern>*)
```

Deftemplate Construct

```
<deftemplate-construct>  ::= (deftemplate <name>
                                 [<comment>]
                                 <slot-definition>*)

<slot-definition>
   ::= <single-slot-definition> |
       <multislot-definition>

<single-slot-definition> ::= (slot <name>
                                   <slot-attribute>*)

<multislot-definition>   ::= (multislot <name>
                                 <template-attribute>*)

<template-attribute>     ::= <default-attribute> |
                             <constraint-attribute>
```

```
<default-attribute>
   ::= (default ?DERIVE | ?NONE | <expression>*) |
       (default-dynamic <expression>*)
```

Fact Specification

```
<RHS-pattern>             ::= <ordered-RHS-pattern> |
                              <template-RHS-pattern>
<ordered-RHS-pattern>     ::= (<symbol> <RHS-field>+)
<template-RHS-pattern>    ::= (<deftemplate-name>
                               <RHS-slot>*)
<RHS-slot>                ::= <single-field-RHS-slot> |
                              <multifield-RHS-slot>
<single-field-RHS-slot>   ::= (<slot-name> <RHS-field>)
<multifield-RHS-slot>     ::= (<slot-name> <RHS-field>*)
<RHS-field>               ::= <variable> |
                              <constant> |
                              <function-call>
```

Defrule Construct

```
<defrule-construct>     ::= (defrule <name> [<comment>]
                                 [<declaration>]
                                 <conditional-element>*
                                 =>
                                 <expression>*)
<declaration>           ::= (declare <rule-property>+)
<rule-property>
   ::= (salience <integer-expression>) |
       (auto-focus <boolean-symbol>)
<boolean-symbol>        ::= TRUE | FALSE
<conditional-element> ::= <pattern-CE> |
                          <assigned-pattern-CE> |
                          <not-CE> |
                          <and-CE> |
                          <or-CE> |
                          <logical-CE> |
                          <test-CE> |
                          <exists-CE> |
                          <forall-CE>
<pattern-CE>           ::= <ordered-pattern-CE> |
                           <template-pattern-CE> |
                           <object-pattern-CE)
<assigned-pattern-CE>
   ::= <single-field-variable> <- <pattern-CE>
<not-CE>           ::= (not <conditional-element>)
<and-CE>           ::= (and <conditional-element>+)
```

```
<or-CE>              ::= (or <conditional-element>+)

<logical-CE>         ::= (logical <conditional-element>+)

<test-CE>            ::= (test <function-call>)

<exists-CE>          ::= (exists <conditional-element>+)

<forall-CE>          ::= (forall <conditional-element>
                                 <conditional-element>+)

<ordered-pattern-CE>  ::= (<symbol> <constraint>+)

<template-pattern-CE>
   ::= (<deftemplate-name <LHS-slot>*)

<object-pattern-CE>
   ::= (object <attribute-constraint>*)

<attribute-constraint>  ::= (is-a <constraint>) |
                            (name <constraint>) |
                            (<slot-name> <constraint>*)

<LHS-slot>              ::= <single-field-LHS-slot> |
                            <multifield-LHS-slot>

<single-field-LHS-slot> ::= (<slot-name> <constraint>)

<multifield-LHS-slot> ::= (<slot-name> <constraint>*)

<constraint>       ::= ? | $? | <connected-constraint>

<connected-constraint>
   ::= <single-constraint> |
       <single-constraint> & <connected-constraint> |
       <single-constraint> | <connected-constraint>

<single-constraint>   ::= <term> | ~<term>

<term>                ::= <constant> |
                          <single-field-variable> |
                          <multifield-variable> |
                          :<function-call> |
                          =<function-call>
```

Defglobal Construct

```
<defglobal-construct>
   ::= (defglobal [<defmodule-name>]
           <global-assignment>*)

<global-assignment>
   ::= <global-variable> = <expression>

<global-variable>        ::= ?*<symbol>*
```

Deffunction Construct

```
<deffunction-construct>
   ::= (deffunction <name> [<comment>]
           (<regular-parameter>* [<wildcard-parameter>])
           <expression>*)
```

```
<regular-parameter>  ::= <single-field-variable>

<wildcard-parameter> ::= <multifield-variable>
```

Defgeneric Construct

```
<defgeneric-construct>
   ::= (defgeneric <name> [<comment>])
```

Defmethod Construct

```
<defmethod-construct>
   ::= (defmethod <name> [<index>] [<comment>]
          (<parameter-restriction>*
           [<wildcard-parameter-restriction>])
          <expression>*)

<parameter-restriction>
   ::=  <single-field-variable> |
        (<single-field-variable> <type>* [<query>])

<wildcard-parameter-restriction>
   ::= <multifield-variable> |
       (<multifield-variable> <type>* [<query>])

<type>          ::= <class-name>

<query>         ::= <global-variable> | <function-call>
```

Defclass Construct

```
<defclass-construct> ::= (defclass <name> [<comment>]
                            (is-a <superclass-name>+)
                            [<role>]
                            [<pattern-match-role>]
                            <slot>*
                            <handler-documentation>*)

<role>  ::= (role concrete | abstract)

<pattern-match-role>
   ::= (pattern-match reactive | non-reactive)

<slot>  ::= (slot <name> <facet>*) |
            (single-slot <name> <facet>*) |
            (multislot <name> <facet>*)

<facet> ::=  <default-facet> | <storage-facet> |
             <access-facet> | <propagation-facet> |
             <source-facet> | <pattern-match-facet> |
             <visibility-facet> |
             <create-accessor-facet> |
             <override-message-facet> |
             <constraint-attribute>

<default-facet>
   ::= (default ?DERIVE | ?NONE | <expression>*) |
       (default-dynamic <expression>*)
```

```
<storage-facet> ::= (storage local | shared)

<access-facet>  ::= (access read-write |
                            read-only |
                            initialize-only)

<propagation-facet>
   ::= (propagation inherit | no-inherit)

<source-facet> ::= (source exclusive | composite)

<pattern-match-facet>
   ::= (pattern-match reactive | non-reactive)

<visibility-facet> ::= (visibility private | public)

<create-accessor-facet>
   ::= (create-accessor ?NONE | read |
                        write | read-write)

<override-message-facet>
   ::= (override-message ?DEFAULT | <message-name>)

<handler-documentation>
   ::= (message-handler <name> [<handler-type>])

<handler-type> ::= primary | around | before | after
```

Defmessage-handler Construct

```
<defmessage-handler-construct>
   ::= (defmessage-handler <class-name>
          <message-name> [<handler-type>] [<comment>]
          (<parameter>* [<wildcard-parameter>])
          <action>*)

<handler-type>   ::= around | before | primary | after

<parameter>      ::= <single-field-variable>

<wildcard-parameter> ::= <multifield-variable>
```

Definstances Construct

```
<definstances-construct> ::= (definstances <name>
                               [active] [<comment>]
                               <instance-template>*)

<instance-template>   ::= (<instance-definition>)

<instance-definition>
   ::= <instance-name-expression> of
          <class-name-expression> <slot-override>*

<slot-override>
   ::= (<slot-name-expression> <expression>*)
```

Defmodule Construct

```
<defmodule-construct>
   ::= (defmodule <name> [<comment>])
          <port-specification>*)

<port-specification>
   ::= (export <port-item>) |
       (import <module-name> <port-item>)

<port-item>     ::= ?ALL |
                    ?NONE |
                    <port-construct> ?ALL |
                    <port-construct> ?NONE |
                    <port-construct> <construct-name>+

<port-construct> ::= deftemplate | defclass |
                     defglobal | deffunction |
                     defgeneric
```

Constraint Attributes

```
<constraint-attribute>
                    ::= <type-attribute> |
                        <allowed-constant-attribute> |
                        <range-attribute> |
                        <cardinality-attribute>

<type-attribute>    ::= (type <type-specification>)

<type-specification> ::= <allowed-type>+ | ?VARIABLE

<allowed-type>       ::= SYMBOL | STRING | LEXEME |
                         INTEGER | FLOAT | NUMBER |
                         INSTANCE-NAME |
                         INSTANCE-ADDRESS |
                         INSTANCE | EXTERNAL-ADDRESS |
                         FACT-ADDRESS

<allowed-constant-attribute>
   ::= (allowed-symbols <symbol-list>) |
       (allowed-strings <string-list>) |
       (allowed-lexemes <lexeme-list> |
       (allowed-integers <integer-list>) |
       (allowed-floats <float-list>) |
       (allowed-numbers <number-list>) |
       (allowed-instance-names <instance-list>) |
       (allowed-values <value-list>)

<symbol-list>     ::= <symbol>+ | ?VARIABLE

<string-list>     ::= <string>+ | ?VARIABLE

<lexeme-list>     ::= <lexeme>+ | ?VARIABLE

<integer-list>    ::= <integer>+ | ?VARIABLE

<float-list>      ::= <float>+ | ?VARIABLE

<number-list>     ::= <number>+ | ?VARIABLE
```

```
<instance-name-list> ::= <instance-name>+ | ?VARIABLE

<value-list>       ::= <constant>+ | ?VARIABLE

<range-attribute> ::= (range <range-specification>
                             <range-specification>)

<range-specification> ::= <number> | ?VARIABLE

<cardinality-attribute>
   ::= (cardinality <cardinality-specification>
                    <cardinality-specification>)

<cardinality-specification> ::= <integer> | ?VARIABLE
```

Variables and Expressions

```
<single-field-variable> ::= ?<variable-symbol>

<multifield-variable>   ::= $?<variable-symbol>

<global-variable>       ::= ?*<symbol>*

<variable>              ::= <single-field-variable> |
                            <multifield-variable> |
                            <global-variable>

<function-call>
   ::= (<function-name> <expression>*) |
       (<special-function-name>
        <special-function-arguments>)

<special-function-name>
   ::= The name of a function such as assert or
       make-instance that does not parse its
       arguments in the default manner that standard
       functions use.

<special-function-arguments>
   ::= Argument parsing for special functions varies.
       Refer to the documentation of each special
       function for its valid syntax. For example,
       in the function call (assert (value 3)), the
       argument (value 3) is not a call to the value
       function with an argument of 3, it is the
       fact to be asserted.

<expression>            ::= <constant> |
                            <variable> |
                            <function-call>
```

Data Types

```
<symbol> ::= A valid symbol as specified in Section 7.4

<string> ::= A valid string as defined in Section 7.4

<float>  ::= A valid float as defined in Section 7.4

<integer>
   ::= A valid integer as specified in Section 7.4
```

```
<instance-name>
   ::= A valid instance-name as specified in section 7.4

<number>          ::= <float> | <integer>

<lexeme>          ::= <symbol> | <string>

<constant>        ::= <number> | <lexeme>

<comment>         ::= <string>

<variable-symbol> ::= A <symbol> beginning with an
                      alphabetic character
<function-name>   ::= <symbol>

<name>            ::= <symbol>

<...-name>
   ::= A <symbol> where the ellipsis indicate what
       the symbol represents. For example,
       <deftemplate-name> is a symbol which
       represents the name of a deftemplate.
```

APPENDIX G
Software Resources

The primary purpose of this appendix is to provide current Web resources for topics discussed in each chapter of the book. However this material can also be used in the classroom to enrich the book's content by assigning students to investigate software and prepare class presentations and demos. While conventional classroom teaching using a textbook is good, students gain additional benefits by learning through knowledge discovery on their own.

Many of the commercial software products can be downloaded on a trial basis and come with examples to illustrate the capabilities of the product. Even better is to have students make up original examples and compare results. For example, comparisons can be made on the efficiency of solving the Traveling Salesman Problem discussed in Chapter 1 by the standard Greedy algorithm discussion in data structure courses, artificial neural networks (and deciding which is best out of the many types), Genetic algorithms, the Ant Evolutionary algorithm, and others as shown in this appendix.

In particular, it is interesting to see how the AI solutions compare to standard algorithms as the problems scale up from a few cities to hundreds. Relating the example to a real world case, such as the cities that Southwest Airlines flies, makes the comparison even more meaningful. Data for all the cities that Southwest Airlines serves, as well as their geographic location in terms of latitude and longitude, can easily be looked up on the Web and used as a data set.

JOBS

In addition to the many general job search engines, there are job sites specifically designed to recruit people with computer background in artificial intelligence and expert systems to work in defense, medicine, business, industry, and video games, which are the five greatest growth areas in computers these days. These jobs utilize many of the topics discussed in this book. For more experience, download the software demos and run the examples in the Resources for each chapter.

- Data analyst (Chapters 1–12)
- System designers (Chapters 1–12)
- Developers (Chapters 1–12)
- Knowledge domain experts (While you can't become a knowledge domain expert from reading this book, you *can* become a knowledge engineer. In particular, Chapter 6 gives practical tips for interviewing knowledge domain experts, an essential task for knowledge engineers.)
- Search techniques (Chapters 1 and 2)
- Rule based systems (finite state machines, decision trees, and production rule systems.) (Chapters 1–3, 6–12)

- Game theory and game trees (another term for finite state machines and decision trees, Chapter 1)
- Artificial life and flocking techniques (Chapter 1)
- Planning techniques (Chapter 2)
- Fuzzy logic (Chapters 4 and 5)
- Artificial neural networks, genetic algorithms, belief networks (Chapters 1 and 4)

Following is a list of links to some jobs. Other opportunities may be found by going to the homepages of companies that advertise in online magazines such as *PCAI.com* and others listed below. The magazines journals usually list jobs in the back and all are now available online. Your school library should have an electronic subscription to allow you free online access to the journals. Jobs are often posted in the Newsgroups section listed below. If fact it would make an interesting project to create an AI agent that would scan selected newsgroups for job postings and report back to you.

One word of caution: If you post or send your resume, be careful not to include any personal information such as a social security number that may lead to identity theft. This is a growing problem. In fact, do not send out any personal information that could be used for identity theft on the basis of email correspondence alone, no matter how good the job offer appears.

Don't worry if you don't meet all the qualifications. The **Fifth Rule of Wisdom** states that if you are the only person who completes the journey, you win the prize. This means that you need only to have the most qualifications and be willing to accept the maximum salary the company can afford to spend. While a company may want someone with 10 years experience in 20 different languages, they may not have the budget to pay for that person's salary requirements, and so you may be the best choice. Getting a job is like getting married. You marry the best person you can get at the time and find out their faults later.

JOB LINKS

http://www.aaai.org/Magazine/Jobs
http://www.mary-margaret.com/
http://www.blizzard.com/jobopp/
http://www.aktor-kt.com/jobs.htm
http://www.cdacindia.com/html/aai/aaidx.asp
http://www.lplizard.com/lounge/jobs_programmer.htm
http://corporate.infogrames.com/corp_hrmain.php?action=jobdetails&jobID=218&locationID=7
http://www.insomniacgames.com/html/about/jobs.html
http://www.alifemedical.com/careers.html
http://www.hirehealth.com/ci/servlet/com.ci.jobseeker.JobDetails;jsessionid=79FDF0992C80EB299B6B5778CBB6EB1D?JOB_ID=48179
http://www.shrinershq.org/cgi-bin/classifieds/classifieds.cgi
http://www.genesciences.com/DNAjobsNews/12June04.htm
http://www.business.com/search/rslt_default.asp?query=medical+field&bdct=&bdcf=&vt=all&type=jobs&search=Next+Search
http://www.aegiss.com/html/jobs.html
http://www.gamedev.net/directory/careers/
http://www.capcom.com/jobs/job.xpml?jobid=400016
http://www.gamerecruiter.com/
http://www.3drealms.com/gethired.html

ONLINE ENCYCLOPEDIAS

Online encyclopedias give quick and concise explanations of terms, some with examples and additional links. It is highly recommend that students read about new terms introduced in the book for further explanations and examples (unless you are an 'A' student and think the book is perfect as is).

Wikipedia: An excellent large open-content encyclopedia in many languages which offers clear explanations of many terms with links for further reading: http://en.wikipedia.org/wiki/Main_Page

Webopedia. A good general online encyclopedia devoted to Computer Science: http://www.webopedia.com/

Platonic Realms. A very student-friendly online math encyclopedia with other resources. Highly recommended: http://www.mathacademy.com/pr/

Math encyclopedia from Wolfram, makers of Mathematica: http://mathworld.wolfram.com/

The Internet Encyclopedia of Philosophy. Good online encyclopedia of philosophy and logic, mainly for Chapters 2–5: http://www.iep.utm.edu/

General definitions and explanations of Philosophy and Logic. See the online encyclopedia at http://plato.stanford.edu/

Interesting online lectures on a variety of topics from famous speakers through Microsoft Multi-University Research Laboratory: http://murl.microsoft.com/ContentMap.asp

Google. For those of you with insomnia, Google's claim to the most resources on Logic in the world at: http://www.uni-bonn.de/logic/world.html

NEWSGROUPS

Newsgroups have many postings, FAQs, resources, conferences, and other news about AI, expert systems, and thousands of other subjects. Newsgroups and journals also list job openings in their specific domain, such as expert systems and AI. Places to look for expert systems jobs on the Web are the newsgroup http://mailgate.supereva.it/comp/comp.ai.shells/ and its parent newsgroup for AI jobs at http://mailgate.supereva.it/comp/comp.ai/. You will need to know more Italian than "pizza" and more geography than "pepperoni" if you go there to register!

General questions about expert systems such as CLIPS may be answered if you post them to the comp.ai.shells newsgroup or to the official CLIPS site described in Appendix D. There are three ways to access AI newsgroups. One way is to find out the name of your news server from your internet service provider (ISP) and enter that in your browser. In Internet Explorer you select the *Tools* menu, then the *Mail* and *News* submenu, then the *Read Mail* submenu at the bottom. A new window opens and you'll see a link that says, *Set up a newsgroups account*, then follow the *Internet Connection Wizard*.

If you have better things to do with your time, a much easier way is to go to http://www.google.com and click on the red *Groups* link located above the search window where you type in keywords to search. A list of the general types of newsgroups appear. Click on the *comp.* link. Notice that there are some newsgroups that may be of interest to you:

comp.job.* (1 group)
comp.jobs.* (6 groups)
comp.jobsoffered

where the asterisk means multiple subgroups. Other newsgroups for specific languages may also have job postings in those groups. Be VERY careful these days in giving out any personal identification that can be used by identity thieves in *phishing* for information. Once you're in the general *comp.* set, you can then click on *comp.ai* to see all the AI newsgroups.

As for the third way, just enter:
http://groups.google.com/groups?hl=en&lr=&ie=UTF-8&group=comp.ai into the address window of your browser and you'll go directly there. You should see:

comp.ai
comp.ai.alife
comp.ai.doc-analysis.misc
comp.ai.analysis.ocr
comp.ai.edu
comp.ai.fuzzy
comp.ai.games
comp.ai.gentic
comp.ai.jair.announce
comp.ai.jair.papers
comp.ai.nat-lang
comp.ai.neural-nets
comp.ai.nlang-know-rep
comp.ai.philospohy
comp.ai.shells
comp.ai.vision

Note that *jair* is the Journal of AI Research, a refereed online journal. The nice thing about newsgroups is that you can post and reply to questions. There are also many newsgroups which list jobs by government, state, and some cities. A search with keyword *job* will find those.

One of the best ways to start research on a particular topic such as AI, neural nets, genetic algorithms, etc., as well as get an overview of many resources, is the list of Frequently Asked Questions (FAQs). A FAQ is a good starting point for someone new to a particular field, written by a knowledgeable volunteer, and it is commercial-free. Although commercial products are often mentioned, they are discussed in an objective way. While you can subscribe to every newsgroup that looks promising and then be able to read its FAQ, there is a better way. The FAQs for all the thousands of newsgroups are located in a searchable page that can be searched by keyword or browsed by category or alphabetically at: http://www.faqs.org/faqs/. In particular, the FAQs for AI and its subgroups are conveniently located at: http://www.faqs.org/faqs/ai-faq/. A large list of all computer-related FAQs is at: http://www.faqs.org/faqs/by-newsgroup/comp/.

JOURNALS AND ONLINE MAGAZINES

Journals and magazines, both on paper and online, provide the latest news and articles on a particular subject, and are good sources to look for jobs, conference announcements, workshops, and conventions. The main difference between a journal and a magazine is that journals are primarily supported by their subscribers, while magazines get most of their money through advertisements. Journals have long adopted this policy in order to emphasize unbiased reporting. Journal articles are subject to review by several referees, so a true journal, rather than one which simply has the name "Journal" in its title, has articles that are refereed.

It is not uncommon in magazines to see articles written by authors whose companies also place ads in the magazines. On the other hand, it is not uncommon to see articles in journals written by members of the editorial board and people from their institutions. You should be especially careful of articles that have a footnote such as "Research sponsored in part by XYZ Group," since naturally if the authors want to keep getting funding, they will take the "glass half-full" attitude towards their work rather than the "glass half-empty" view. In addition, the XYZ Group will also show their grants and contracts have yielded measurable work based on the numbers of articles produced or the funding their agency gets.

Conference papers should be viewed with the greatest scrutiny since work may be accepted to allow people to get travel funds, or they may be "works in progress" that represents a student's work towards a graduate degree and give an acknowledgment to the XYZ Group. That is why no conference proceedings are quoted in the bibliography of this book.

AI Case-Based Reasoning Journal: http://www.ai-cbr.org/theindex.htm

BusinessWeek Online: http://www.businessweek.com. Although not a journal, this online magazine has a good search engine for keywords like *artificial intelligence* and often carries stories about high-tech news in business, government, and the military because all three spend a lot of money. BusinessWeek is well worth checking out for commercial applications of the latest computer technology. This is where you find out that Wal-Mart uses **data mining** at all 3,000 of its stores to predict sales of every product with uncanny accuracy at a store-by-store basis, and how AI is used everywhere these days: http://www.businessweek.com/bw50/content/mar2003/a3826072.htm

American Association for Artificial Intelligence: http://www.aaai.org/

Expert Systems International Journal: http://www.blackwellpublishing. com/journal.asp?ref

Expert Systems Journal: http://www.aaai.org/AITopics/html/expert.html

Fuzzy Optimization and Decision Making: A journal of modeling and computation under uncertainty: http://www.kluweronline.com/issn/1568-4539

IEEE Intelligent Systems Journal: http://www.computer.org/intelligent/

IEEE Transactions on Fuzzy Systems: http://www.ieee.org/portal/index.jsp?pageID=corp_level1&path=pubs/transactions&file=tfs.xml&xsl=generic.xsl

IEEE Transactions on Neural Networks: http://www.ieee.org/portal/index.jsp?pageID=corp_level1&path=pubs/transactions&file=tnn.xml&xsl=generic.xsl

Journal of Artificial Intelligence Research: http://www.cs.washington.edu/ research/jair/home.html

Neural Computation by the MIT Press: http://mitpress.mit.edu/catalog/ item/default.asp?sid=B395B969-A0A5-4F6E-A566-AF7B2EDCE494&ttype=4&tid=31

Neural Computing & Applications by Springer-Verlag. Enter : http://springerlink.metapress.com. The click on Browse Publications. Then click Jump to N and then click on Neural Computing and Applications.

North American Fuzzy Information Processing Society. Click on their online resources links for many fuzzy resources: http://morden.csee.usf. edu/Nafipsf/

PCAI.com. An excellent online magazine with a good search engine. PCAI has been in publication since the 1980s with a vast repository of information about AI with links to software, articles and other resources grouped as follows: C++, Blackboard Technology, Client/Server, Dylan, Creative Thinking, Data Mining, Forth, Distributed Computing, Expert Systems, LISP, Fuzzy Logic, General AI Sites, Logo, Genetic Algorithms, OPS, Intelligent Agents, Intelligent Applications, Prolog, Internet, Logic Programming, Scheme, Machine Learning, Modeling and Simulation, Smalltalk, Multimedia, Natural Language Processing, Neural Networks, Object Oriented Development, Optical, Character, Recognition, Robotics, Speech Recognition, Virtual Reality: http://PCAI.com

Generation5.com. A good comprehensive AI site with news and information on all aspects of AI including games. Includes many links to the following general areas of AI: Aerospace and Military, Agents, Artificial Intelligence, Artificial Life, Biometrics, Constraint Satisfaction Programming, Creativity (Artificial), Fractals, Chaos, Complexity, Non-linear Dynamics, Gaming, Genetic Algorithms, Gesture Recognition, Home Automation, Commercial, Image Analysis/Recognition, Commercial, Knowledge-based Systems, LISP (Programming Language), Natural Language Processing, Neural Networks, Commercial, Neuroscience, Pattern Recognition, Personal, Philosophy, Prolog, Robotics, Commercial, Furby, LEGO Mindstorms, Scheme (Programming Language), Speech Recognition and Synthesis, Commercial, VoiceXML: http://www.generation5.org/

SourceForge.Net. A major source of software and other resources. Billed as the largest website of open source software with over 90,000 project, including resources for all the topics discussed in this book and much more: http://sourceforge.net/

AI@HOME. A good online AI site which publishes all open-source code for neural networks, evolutionary algorithms, meta-learning, and distributed computing. Meta-learning is using learning algorithms to create new learning algorithms: http://www.aiathome.com/

Dr Dobbs Portal AI Links. A great collection of papers, tutorials, links, and software from Dr. Dobbs Journal, a general magazine for many programming languages:
http://www.ddj.com/documents/s=7730/ddj0212ai/0212ai001.html#egyptian_cu

Adaptive Behavior. An international journal for research on adaptive behavior in animals and autonomous artificial systems such as robots. Topics include perception and motor control, learning, evolution, action selection and behavioral sequences, motivation and emotion, characterization of environments, collective and social behavior, navigation, communication and signaling:
http://www.isab.org/journal/

Artificial Life. A great site for AI research with many commercial applications. The movie industry generates $20 billion a year, video games generate even more, and AI offers many possible military applications as well. The site investigates the scientific, engineering, philosophical, and social issues to synthesize lifelike behaviors from scratch in computers, machines, molecules, and other alternative media, studies of the origin of life, self-assembly, growth and development, evolutionary and ecological dynamics, animal and robot behavior, social organization, and cultural evolution. Artificial life is an important topic in video games, movies such as the *Lord of the Rings* series, and *I, Robot*, in which the artificial lifeforms learned to fight and engage in huge battle scenes involving thousands of AI lifeforms.

Coordinating thousands of computer animated characters is much too massive a task for traditional computer animators and a human movie director. So the AI lifeforms were evolved to learn fighting skills and complex battle strategies that the director then selected as the most interesting. This is a revolutionary change from the way movies were once made with the director supervising individual actors or animations. Where in Star Wars 2: Attack of the Clones, movie makers used colored Q-tips to stimulate the crowd watching the podraces, now huge, dynamic crowd scenes are possible using AI lifeforms. (The scary thing is that the *Matrix* movies may be true of our "life," except the movie assumed there were real people trapped in a virtual environment; and now we know no real people are needed at all) http://www-mitpress.mit.edu/catalog/item/default.asp?ttype=4&tid=41

Computational Linguistics. Discusses the design and analysis of natural language processing systems. AI, cognitive science, speech, and the psychology of language processing and performance: http://www-mitpress.mit.edu/catalog/item/default.asp?ttype=4&tid=10

Computer-Mediated Communication Magazine. An online magazine provides the latest news including information technology, knowledge management, and e-business, people, events, technology, public policy, culture, practices, study, and applications related to human communication and interaction in online environments. Good survey of current events and technologies: http://www.december.com/cmc/mag/meta/

Decision Support Systems and Electronic Commerce. A journal of techniques for implementing and evaluating DSS in artificial intelligence, cognitive science, computer-supported cooperative work, database management, decision theory, economics, linguistics, management science, mathematical modeling, operations management psychology, user interface management systems, and other areas. http://www.elsevier.com/wps/find/journaldescription.cws_home/505540/description#description

Electronic Journals and Periodicals in Psychology. Although not a journal, this is an extensive list that attempts to provide links to all psychologically related electronic journals, conference proceedings, and other periodicals. One great feature includes an email alert that sends you new information about items of interest to you. The field of AI draws much of its inspiration from Psychology since people have evolved some pretty good (and pretty bad) techniques for solving problems over millions of years. If you want to get seriously into AI, you need to read psychology, biology, neuroscience, philosophy, and many other fields to enlarge your cognition (a term from psychology.) http://psych.hanover.edu/Krantz/journal.html

AI Events. Although not a journal, it is a very useful search database of upcoming AI conferences, workshops, summer schools, and similar events. A great way to plan your summer vacation: http://www.drc.ntu.edu.sg/users/mgeorg/enter.epl

Evolutionary Computation. A journal on computational systems drawing their inspiration from nature, with particular emphasis on evolutionary algorithms (EA), genetic algorithms (GA), evolution strategies (ES), evolutionary programming (EP), genetic programming (GP), classifier systems (CS), and other natural computation techniques drawn from biological systems: http://www-mitpress.mit.edu/catalog/ item/default.asp?ttype=4&tid=25

International Journal of Human-Computer Studies/Knowledge Acquisition. A;so useful for Chapter 6. Covers a wide range of topics: http://repgrid.com/IJHCS/

- intelligent user interfaces
- natural language interaction
- human factors of multimedia systems
- human and social factors of virtual reality
- human and social factors of the World Wide Web
- human and social factors of software engineering
- computer-supported collaborative work
- speech interaction
- graphic interaction
- knowledge acquisition
- knowledge-based systems
- hypertext and hypermedia
- user modeling
- empirical studies of user behavior
- the psychology of programming
- systems theory and foundations of human-computer interaction
- user interface management systems
- information and decision-support systems
- requirements engineering
- innovative designs and applications of interactive systems

Journal of Artificial Intelligence Research. A very comprehensive online journal on all topics in AI. http://www-mitpress.mit.edu/catalog/item/default.asp?ttype=4&tid=12

Journal of Cognitive Neuroscience. Discusses brain-behavior interaction, function and underlying brain events, neuroscience, neuropsychology, cognitive psychology, neurobiology, linguistics, computer science, and philosophy: (http://www-mitpress.mit.edu/catalog/item/default.asp?ttype=4&tid=12

Journal of Constructivist Psychology. Constructivism is also a popular branch of education and how people learn. http://www.tandf.co.uk/journals/titles/10720537.asp

Journal of Mind and Behavior. A theoretical journal trying to link mind and behavior: http://kramer.ume.maine.edu/~jmb/welcome.html

Noetica: A Cognitive Science Forum, An online refereed journal about cognitive science, machine learning, and many other topics related to AI: http://www.drc.ntu.edu.sg/users/ mgeorg/enter.epl

PRESENCE: **Teleoperators and Virtual Environments:** A fascinating journal with important applications in telesurgery and military applications, such as unmanned aerial vehicles used to conduct reconnaissance with no pilot aboard. UAVs are commonly used by the military because they are cheaper than a manned aircraft, harder to detect, and can fly and stay longer over a target than a manned vehicle. Best of all, one telepresence operator can control multiple UAVs with no bad press if a manned plane is shot down, as happened in the famous incident with Francis Gary Powers in 1962.

The intelligent brother of the UAV, the X-45 Unmanned Combat Air Vehicle (UCAV) is expected to be in military use by 2010 http://www.fas.org/man/dod-101/sys/ ac/ucav.htm. It will be a bomber/surveillance aircraft that can fly to a preprogrammed destination without a human in the loop. Many intelligent weapons systems costing billions of dollars are under development, as you can see by watching more TV. Cable shows such as *Mail Call* on the History Channel, *Tactics to Practice* on the Discovery Channel, and *Future Fighting Machines* on G4TechTV show how millions are being spent on AI-based military systems.

What's really disturbing is how much the X-45 looks like the AI aircraft under the control of the rogue AI program Skynet in the *Terminator* series of movies (in which a military AI tries to take over the world from humans.) The same theme was echoed in the movie *I, Robot* of 2004, and goes back to the classic 1970 movie, *Colossus: The Forbin Project*, in which the American and Russian supercomputers band together to save humans from destroying the world.

Public E-print Archive. Cognitive psychology papers by Stevan Harnad covering lots of interesting topics such as induction, cognitions, machine learning, robotics, and many others. Very readable papers: http://www.ecs.soton.ac.uk/~harnad/genpub.html

PSYCHE. An interdisciplinary journal of research on consciousness, featuring many interesting articles: http://psyche.cs.monash.edu.au/

Shufflebrain. Explorations of how a physical object, the brain, can store the mind and many other interesting questions such as the following at: http://www.indiana. edu/~pietsch/home.html

- Shuffle Brain — can a scrambled brain remember?
- The Beast's IQ — hidden facets of intelligence
- Hologramic Mind —what's really real, anyway?
- Microminds — can bacteria think? hurt? enjoy?
- Human Brain Shrinks, Yet Human Being Thinks
- Brain Swapping — excerpts from the book, Shufflebrain
- Hologic — an **Asa Zook** dialog on the nature of holograms
- Split Human Brain — our divided selves
- Musical Brain — the gentler side
- Optics of Memory — heck of an engineer!

The Journal of Computer-Mediated Communication. This site is not specifically AI, but it touches on many areas that may lead to new developments in AI. It makes interesting reading that may stimulate new directions in AI: http://www.ascusc.org/jcmc/

The Journal of Mind and Behavior. More for psychologists, but may provide clues to interesting new research areas in AI: http://kramer.ume.maine.edu/~jmb/welcome.html

CHAPTER 1

AI Resources

DARPA, the Defense Advanced Research Projects Agency of the Department of Defense, has always been a main source of funding for AI. In addition, DARPA also provided the funds to start ARPANET, which has evolved since the 1990s into the commercial Internet. DARPA claimed that the use of AI in planning the logistics of Desert Storm in Oil War I in 1990 repaid many times over all the money it had put into AI research since the 1950s: http://www.au.af.mil/au/aul/school/acsc/ai02.htm

American Association for Artificial Intelligence. A good starting point for learning about AI and expert systems: http://www.aaai.org/AITopics/html/welcome.html. For many expert systems papers and resources, see the link to: http://www.aaai.org/AITopics/html/expert.html#good

Out of Control: The New Biology of Machines by Kevin Kelly is a fascinating book you can read online about how AI will affect society and the economy. Well worth reading: http://www.kk.org/outofcontrol/

Metaxiotis K. and Psarras, J. "**Expert Systems in Business: Applications and future directions for the operations researcher**," *Industrial Management & Data Systems*, Vol. 103, No. 5, pp. 361-368, 2003.

Hugh McKellar, "**Artificial intelligence: Past and future**," KMWorld Magazine, Vol. 12, Issue 4, 2004. An article which surveys the growth of AI and projects the worldwide market in the top five AI market areas of expert systems, belief networks, decision support systems, neural networks and agents to be $21 billion by 2007. This free online magazine is aimed at keeping management up with the latest trends in knowledge management. Very readable articles for overviews.http://www.kmworld.com/publications/magazine/index.cfm?action=readarticle&article_id=1504&publication_id=1

Alexander Nareyek, "**AI in Computer Games.**" ACMQueue.com. ACM Queue Vol. 1, No.10, February 2004. Good discussion of practical use of finite state machines, decision trees and other AI techniques in games. Applicable to AI in general: http://acmqueue.com/modules.php?name=Content&pa=showpage& pid=117&page=1

AI on the Web. Huge collection to over 850 links on all areas of AI from Stuart Russell http://www.cs.berkeley.edu/~russell/ai.html. These and other resources from the book, Artificial Intelligence: A Modern Approach (Second Edition) by Stuart Russell and Peter Norvig, 2002. Highly recommended as a good introductory textbook on AI with lots of other support materials at http://aima.cs.berkeley.edu/

Browse and search **Google's Directory of AI links** at: http://directory.google.com/Top/Computers/Artificial_Intelligence/

Browse and search **Yahoo's Directory of AI links** at: http://dir.yahoo.com/Science/Computer_Science/Artificial_Intelligence/

The AI Center: http://www.ai-center.com/sitemap.html. A good starting portal for getting started in AI. Lots of resources organized if you click on Links: http://www.ai-center.com/links/

Dr. Mark Humphrey's Homepage with fascinating reading on how you can tell if there's royalty in your ancestry! Of course the other major reason for quoting his page is the extensive links to teaching, AI, and many other resources at his Homepage: http://www.compapp.dcu.ie/%7Ehumphrys/index.html

AI Links. Humphrey's huge list covering the following general topics with many links to each at http://www.compapp.dcu.ie/%7Ehumphrys/ai.links.html

- Architectures of Mind (Adaptive Behavior including robotics)
- Learning (Reinforcement Learning) (Neural Networks)
- Evolution (Computational Evolution) (Natural Evolution)

Teaching Links with Humphrey's gigantic online resources for AI. Really worth looking at if you've never taught an AI course before or are seeking some new ideas: http://www.compapp.dcu.ie/%7Ehumphrys/teaching.html

And, a nice Search Engines Collection for searching his site as well as the world, all from his one page at: http://www.compapp.dcu.ie/%7Ehumphrys/computers.internet.html

His Royal Descent Search really works. For example, you can see **Walt Disney's genealogy tree** all the way back to the King of England, Henry I Beauclerc (1070—1135 AD) at: http://members.aol.com/dwidad/disney.html#wd. Now you know why a castle is the symbol of Disneyland!

Virtual Environments including over 40 highly accurate 3D cities have been created by Planet 9 Studios. These datasets can be used for a variety of purposes, including the ultimate test of an autonomous robot that can successfully traverse city streets. If you've seen the 3D city in the *Matrix* movies, these will look eerily familiar and make you feel completely innocent the next time you eat a steak. Download their demo WMV and you'll see at: http://www. planet9.com/demos_dwnlds.html

Online Robotics and Cameras archive: http://ford.ieor.berkeley.edu/ir/

Huge collection of over 350 hyperlinked papers on AI by Stuart Reynolds: http://ford.ieor.berkeley.edu/ir/

Reinforcement Learning: An Introduction by Richard S. Sutton and Andrew G. Barto. An online book, also available in paper from the MIT Press (1998), that considers how software agents and robots can learn to respond to an environment. Discussion of many techniques including Markov Decision Process, Planning and Learning, and some sophisticated case studies. Well worth looking at: http://www-anw.cs.umass.edu/%7Erich/book/the-book.html

Complexity Papers Online A huge collection of papers on many subjects including **AI**, complexity theory, **chaos,** and hundreds of others including classic papers by the original founders of AI: http://www.calresco.org/papers.htm

EvoWeb. Entire European Web dealing with all aspects of evolutionary computing including genetic algorithms, robotics, intelligent systems, much software articles, books and links. See this site for all the latest news and technology. The European Union is making government-assisted grants to help small businesses create websites to provide global marketing of their products and services. The creation of EvoWeb shows their commitment to use advanced AI technologies such as evolutionary computation because they are not afraid of the term "evolutionary": http://evonet.lri.fr/

Other major European webs have been created to aggressively pursue specific areas of AI. These are linked to the main EvoWeb page above.

EvoBIO. Bioinformatics web which focuses on algorithms based on evolutionary computation that address important problems in molecular biology, genomics, and genetics.

EvoELEC. Evolutionary electronics European web covering digital and analog evolvable hardware, bio-inspired computing, evolving machines, and evolutionary electronics.

EvoGP. Genetic programming web for difficult design, pattern recognition, and control problems, and applications to financial data mining, signal and image processing, bio-informatics, engineering design, music, and art.

EvoIASP. Image analysis and signal processing European web. Evolutionary Algorithms (EAs) have been shown to be an efficient tool for the automatic design and optimization of systems with hundreds of papers published on EAs applied to image analysis and signal processing.

EvoROB. Evolutionary robotics European web focuses on EAs to automatically design autonomous robots. It takes a bottom-up approach to robotic learning, synthesizing controllers through interaction with the environment rather than design by humans.

EvoSTIM. Scheduling and timetabling European web using EAs have been shown to be highly successful.

Tom Lloyd, "**When swarm intelligence beats brainpower**." Article about complexity tools such as **swarm intelligence** that solves problems that are so complex, such as the Traveling Salesman Problem, that no efficient algorithm exists beyond a certain size. Even Grid computing will become too slow as the number of cities becomes large enough since the number of possible routes for N cities is (N-1)! Swarm intelligence uses techniques like the **Ant Algorithm** (mentioned elsewhere in this Appendix) to provide a good solution in a reasonable amount of time for large N. This article is a good survey of businesses actively pursuing swarm technologies to solve complex problems: http://money.telegraph.co.uk/money/main.jhtml?xml=%2Fmoney%2F2001%2F06%2F06%2Fcnantz06.xml

SwarmWiki. A major portal with information, software and many links all dealing with swarm intelligence and their applications to AI. http://wiki.swarm.org/wiki/ Main_Page

Good online lectures on a variety of topics including AI through Microsoft Multi-University Research Laboratory from famous speakers: http://murl.microsoft.com/ContentMap.asp.

Nice series of **online slides for teaching AI and expert systems from a PROLOG point of view** by Alison Cawsey covering most of the topics in the theory section of the book. PROLOG and Lisp are still the standard languages used in textbooks on AI in spite of competition from newer languages like Python: http://www.cee.hw.ac.uk/~alison/ai3/

Huge **collection of slides on many AI topics** Aaron Sloman, well worth a look: http://www.cs.bham.ac.uk/%7Eaxs/misc/talks/

Neural networks are not just for research but are in practical use to save millions of dollars in detecting debit-credit card fraud for credit union service organizations (CUSO). PSCU Financial Services, the country's largest CUSO, announced that out of 74,000 cases of suspected card fraud in 2002, it recovered $12.8 million, or 99.9% of its recoverable losses using neural networks. http:// www.cuna.org/newsnow/archive/list.php?date=041003.

The particular tool used by PSCU Financial Services is the **Falcon neural net tool** which detects credit card fraud in real-time, http://www.pscufs.com/falcon.htm. So if you're ever standing in a checkout line wondering what's taking so long, it's because a neural net is checking up on you for suspicious activities. For unusually large purchases, the transaction may be declined and you must then call your debit/credit card company to verify it's really you. (Fortunately they don't call your home to ask your spouse about the transaction or some people might be in real trouble.)

The **Credit Union National Association actually requires their credit union clients to use the neural net technology** as a way of reducing fraud and keeping costs low. Other business applications are described at the BusinessWeek online site which has a good search engine, which makes it easy to search for the latest applications of artificial intelligence:
http://www.businessweek.com/bw50/content/mar2003/a3826072.htm.

CorMac Technologies has a very comprehensive set of commercial AI tools and examples about the success of AI including:

- cancer diagnosis using a neural net
- cancer diagnosis using inductive rule extraction
- inductive rule extraction from mitochondrial DNA
- cluster identification from mitochondrial DNA

Their website is at http://www.cormactech.com. A trial version of the artificial neural net software is at: http://cormactech.com/neunet/index.html and other products can be accessed from their home page. Many complete examples with all data sets are at:
http://cormactech.com/neunet/download.html#DATA.

Lots of interesting AI Demos and Projects: http://www.cs.wisc.edu/ ~dyer/cs540/demos.html

Artificial life links: http://www.alcyone.com/max/links/alife.html

Simple online explanation called "Fuzzy logic for Just Plain Folks":
http://www.fuzzy-logic.com/

Fuzzy online book and fuzzy expert system FLOPS: http://members.aol.com/wsiler/

Advantages of Genetic Programming: http://murl.microsoft.com/LectureDetails.asp?785

Genetics and Evolutionary Algorithm Archive. A tremendous resource of links to GA and Evolutionary algorithms and applications: http://www.aic.nrl.navy.mil/galist/

GAUL™ - the Genetic Algorithm Utility Library. a leading open-source programming library for evolutionary computation: http://sourceforge.net/forum/forum.php?forum_id=386667

PMSI has an excellent site with a number of tutorials and tools that can be downloaded free along with working examples: http://www.pmsi.fr/home-gb.htm. The following applications of **Genetic Algorithms** are at: http://www.pmsi.fr/gafxmpa.htm

- FOOD: robots learning to look for food
- GAFUNC: various function optimization problems
- TSPSA: simulated annealing neural network to solve the **Traveling Salesman Problem**

Neural Net demos are at: http://www.pmsi.fr/sxcxmpa.htm

- Parabola: practical use of neural nets
- FUNCTION: illustrating the neural nets' ability to learn to model a function
- OCR: a simple Optical Character Recognition example
- VEHICLE.EXE: vehicle guiding, behavior modeling and model inversion where a vehicle (or robot) tried to find a path to a destination from some arbitrary starting point.

Evolutionary growth of a Neural Network using Genetic Algorithms and Simulated Annealing, many interesting examples you can download at: http://www.pmsi.fr/grnxmpa.htm

Inductive decision tree growth using classic ID3 and C4.5 methods that automatically build decision trees at: http://www.pmsi.fr/padxmpa.htm

Ant Colony Evolutionary Software from the book *Ant Colony Optimization* by Marco Dorigo and Thomas Stützle, MIT Press, 2004. One of the applications is solving the important **Traveling Salesman Problem**. The software is available at:
http://iridia.ulb.ac.be/~mdorigo/ACO/aco-code/public-software.html

The History of Computer Science. Many links on the progress of computer science over the years with many topics about important historical figures such as Alan Turing:
http://www.eingang.org/Lecture/toc.html

The Turing Test Page. Good overall starting point to Alan Turing, his life and many contributions with information on Turing test references online, background reading, the Grand $100,000 Loebner Prize created by Dr. Hugh Loebner in 1991 to the author of the first computer program to pass an unrestricted Turing test. You can interact with some programs, see links to people doing interesting work on the philosophy of the mind, intelligent robots, and many other topics suitable for class presentations and advanced work: http://cogsci.ucsd. edu/%7Easaygin/tt/ttest.html#people

The Alan Turing Home Page. Who was Alan Turing? Find out here. Provides a timeline, a complete bibliography of Turing's works, an online biography, an archive, photographs and professional papers: http://www.turing. org.uk/turing/

The Turing Test Is Not a Trick. Turing test to distinguish a computer from a real person is discussed as a valid scientific criteria, not just a game as some have contended. On the other hand, when people win over a million dollars on a TV game show like Jeopardy, or on a Survivor show, is it really just a game? That's like saying major league baseball is just a game when some players make $10,000,000 a year! http://www.ecs.soton.ac.uk/%7Eharnad/Papers/Harnad/harnad92.turing.html

The 2003 Loebner Prize Winner. Although it did not pass the full unrestricted version of the Turing Test in 2003, Jabberwock did win $2,000 for his creator. OK, so it wasn't $100K, but how many of your programs have won you $2,000? http://www.surrey.ac.uk/dwrc/loebner/

Botspot. Users can try out some of the many popular chatterbots on the web. Chatterbots are programs designed to carry on a conversation just like a person. Some are serious and designed for the Turing Test while others are meant for entertainment of all kinds! They are getting very sophisticated and while still not quite good enough to win the Loebner Prize, may make you wonder if your boss uses one to answer questions about your project assignment. The ultimate goal of course, is to replace humans in telephone call centers. That's even cheaper than global outsourcing, which at least pays human beings: http://www.botspot.com

The LISA project is a platform for the development of **L**isp-based **I**ntelligent **S**oftware **A**gents. It is a production-rule system implemented in the Common Lisp Object System (CLOS), and heavily influenced by CLIPS and Jess. Intelligent agents are used in many applications today. http://lisa.sourceforge.net/

New Directions Magazine has many articles and links to Quantum computers and other topics. Good place to start learning, articles written at an introductory level. The homepage is also a great place to see the latest information about the latest developments in science and computing. It also has an extensive Jobs section although most of the jobs are in Europe since New Scientist is published in England: http://www.newscientist.com/hottopics/quantum/

Quantum Information Science. Short Course in Innsbruck, Austria. Lots of state-of-the art presentations on quantum computing, quantum cryptography and many other topics. Some of the presentations are the fanciest I've ever seen, well worth a look: http://wtec.org/qis/Awschalom.PDF

Committee on Standards for Artificial Intelligence Interfaces. This is a subgroup of the International Game Developers Association. The subgroup's purpose is "… to promote interfaces for basic AI functionality, enabling code recycling and outsourcing thereby, and freeing programmers from low-level AI programming as to assign more resources to sophisticated AI." If you want to get into the game industry or are looking for ways to standardize AI development for your company so as not to "reinvent the wheel" every time a new project requires AI, this is a good site to check: http://www.igda.org/ai/

Grid Computing harnesses the background, unused power of many computers over a network or the Internet. It is being used to simulate the most massive Virtual Grid Computer capable of enormous power limited only by the bandwidth and number of computers; theoretically every computer in the world. Grid computing is being actively explored by companies such as IBM: http://www-1.ibm.com/grid/.

New Grid service providers are now providing supercomputer performance without the cost and expense of a real supercomputer. In fact the Grid may be much faster than any single supercomputer depending on how the particular task can be apportioned to all the linked machines. Special-purpose grids such as BioGrid are being utilized for biological and medical research since sharing software makes analysis much more efficient when running on all machines, although this is not a necessity. The Grid can also be used to explore new AI techniques and algorithms that have not been practical before because of limited computer power. Following are some references and links:

Madhu Chetty and Rajkumar Buyya. "**Weaving Computational Grids: How Analogous are they with Electrical Grids**," *Computing in Science & Engineering*, pp. 61-71, August 2002.

Sergio Rajsbaum. "**Distributed Computing Research Issues in Grid Computing**," *ACM SIGACT News Distributed Computing Column 8*, 50-70, July 2002.

More links on Grid Computing:

http://www.gridcomputing.com
http://www.globus.org/
http://www.gpds.org/
http://www.ncbiogrid.org/
http://www.biogrid.jp
http://www.biogrid.icm.edu.pl
http://www.ncbi.nih.gov/BLAST/
http://www.nbirn.net
http://www.eu-datagrid.org -
http://www.bioinformaticsworld.info/feature3b.html
http://www-1.ibm.com/grid
http://www.sbml.org
http://biocomp.ece.utk.edu
http://www.grid.org
http://gridcafe.web.cern.ch

APPLICATIONS OF EXPERT SYSTEMS

Expert Systems applications, papers, software, and companies. Huge list from PCAI online magazine: http://www.pcai.com/web/ai_info/ expert_systems.html

Medical expert systems, huge list: http://www.computer.privateweb.at/judith/name_3.htm

AI and Expert Systems, many links: http://www.dmaier.net/teaching/ cis386/links.htm

Agricultural Expert Systems, many links: http://potato.claes.sci.eg/Home/wes.htm

CLIPS Quick Overview slides from Peter Jackson, author of Introduction to Expert Systems, a book which describes CLIPS and other expert systems: http://www.geocities.com/jacksonpe/clips/clips.htm

Judith Lamont, "**Innovative Applications Make Government More Responsive**," KMWorld Magazine, Vol. 12, Issue 6. Good introduction about how different government agencies are using expert systems for better response to questions by the public. This is an online magazine with many interesting articles about knowledge management and intelligent systems in business and government. Well worth a look. Browse articles by issue or their search engine: http://www.kmworld.com/publications/magazine/index.cfm?action=readarticle&Article_ID=1541&Publication_ID=93

Online medical diagnostic expert system. Try their free sample diagnosis if you haven't been eating as much fiber as you should: http://easydiagnosis.com/

U.S. Department of Safety & Labor provides many expert systems about Federal employment laws with regards to compliance issues, workplace laws, rights, and responsibilities at the elaws Advisors site: http://www.dol.govelaws/ see_adv.asp?Subset=ID>0

OSHA government expert systems at eTools and Electronic Products for Compliance Assistance: http://www.osha.gov/dts/osta/oshasoft/eTools.

OSHA Emergency Action Plan expert systems. Designed to determine if your company needs an emergency action plan, and if so, helps you create one at: http://www.osha-slc.gov/SLTC/etools/evacuation/experts.html

National Science Foundation—Environmental Monitoring and Measurement Advisor: http://www.emma-expertsystem.com/

U.S. Geological Survey—Decision Support Systems for Trumpeter Swan Management: http://swan.msu.montana.edu/cygnet/

Department of Natural Resources and Environment expert systems for Dairy Farmers. Australia—Seven "Online Consultants": http://www.nre.vic.gov.au/web/root/Domino/Target10/T10Frame.nsf

BusinessLaw.gov has a huge amount of information for businesses as well as expert systems at: http://www.businesslaw.gov/tools/business-wizards.htm

Shyster, a case-based legal expert system developed by James Popple. Details of the design, implementation, operation, and testing of Shyster are given in his book, *A Pragmatic Legal Expert System*, Applied Legal Philosophy Series, Dartmouth, Aldershot, 1996. Shyster is at: http://cs.anu.edu.au/software/shyster/

Knowledge acquisition and expert system shell Acquire®. A trial version of their software is available at their website: http://www.aiinc.ca. They have a number of examples at http://www.aiinc.ca/demos/index.html:

- The Whale Watcher
- The Graduate Admissions Screening System
- The Spa Advisor
- The Stock Demo
- Petroleum Advisor for the Geochemical and Environmental Sciences
- The Job Coach
- Douglas-Fir Cone and Seed Insects System

XpertRule Knowledge Builder, and a tool for data mining called XpertRule Miner are available from Attar Software Limited. A list of expert systems created using their tool can be seen at: http://www.attar. com/deploy/demos.htm, and their affiliated company

- Expenses web demo
- Savings and Investments web demo
- PC support web demo
- Pension web demo
- Direct PC Sales
- PC support web demo

Other applications by Attar Software Limited at: http://www.intellicrafters.com/cases.htm

- **Rockwell Aerospace and NASA.** Expert system built for NASA by Rockwell International to advise on contamination control.
- **Channel 4 TVResource Optimization using XpertRule®** is used to sequence commercial breaks using genetic algorithms.
- **Tokyo Nissan.** Intelligent "Car Selection System" using XpertRule®.
- **Australian Taxation Office.** Expert Taxation System.

- **Work and Income New Zealand.** 3000 staff use an XpertRule® Expert Calculator to deal with questions of eligibility, allowances, and benefit amounts.
- **Hosokawa MicronData.** Mining for powder and particle processing.
- **GE Capital Global Consumer Finance.** Data mining for financial use.
- **The Gas Research and Technology Centre.** Data mining reduces the cost of gas drilling at BG plc.
- **Department of Industry and Fisheries, Tasmania.** Tasmanian Government Agency Expert Systems to assist farmers
- **Department of Industry and Fisheries, Tasmania.** Threatened Fauna Adviser for forestry companies and contractors.
- **Misselbrook and Weston stores.** Knowledge-Based System to detect in-store fraud.
- **Hibernian (Ireland).** Data Mining and Knowledge-Based System to achieve Business Process Re-engineering by Hibernian Life & Pensions (Ireland).
- **United Distillers.** Resource Opimization using XpertRule® to optimize the movements of whisky casks required to produce quality blends at United Distillers in Scotland.
- **ICI and Carlsberg Tetley.** ICI's Thornton Power Station and the Carlsberg Tetley brewery use data mining to reduce levels of energy consumption.
- **Elf-Atochem North America.** Produced Rilsan® Advisor, an expert system product guide for their technical sales and marketing people.
- **The Leeds Building Society.** Leeds Building Society (now part of HBOS plc) used data mining for mortgage arrears.
- **Swedish Marines.** Swedish Marines fitness expert system.
- **Heureka.** Swedish Board for Industrial Development expert system for evaluating product ideas
- **VAT in Sweden.** A Swedish VAT (Value Added Tax) tax advisor and training system.
- **Meiji Mutual Life Insurance.** Knowledge-Based System for the Meiji Mutual Life Insurance Plan Selection.
- **Ebara Manufacturing.** Allows a Japanese company to match their 3,000 wind and water pumps to customer needs.
- **Traversum AB.** Data Mining and Knowledge-Based System to advise on stocks and shares in Europe.
- **Sun Direct Insurance.** Knowledge-Based System for Home and Car insurance quotes.

LPA (Logic Programming Associates) has software tools based on an enhanced version of PROLOG called PROLOG++. Another tool called **Flint** is designed for fuzzy logic applications and PROLOG in a Windows environment. A free version of **PROLOG** is also available. Interesting demos are at http://www. lpa.co.uk/pws_dem.htm

- Moon Phase
- Choose Meal
- Salesman
- Eliza
- Chat-80
- Network
- Expert
- E-Forms
- Insurance

Exsys, Inc. has a large list of modern expert systems developed with their commercial expert systems tool. A demo version can also be downloaded http://www.exsys.com/case2.html. The following list shows the wide range of applications created by their expert systems tool and copyrighted on their website, reproduced with permission.

Financial Services - Fraud Detection - Insurance
- Commercial Loan Approval Predictor and Fund Selector
- Detecting Insider Trading
- Expert Credit Analysis & Analytical Report Support
- System Prevents $Millions in Costs Due to Compromised International Assignments
- EXPERTAX Handles Complex Tax and Legislative Auditing and Reporting
- Private Online Pension "Consultant" Helps with Financial Planning Decisions
- Expert Assistance and Database Analysis for Examiners Available Over a Network
- Online Business Structure Recommendations from SBA
- Bad Check Legal Assistant
- Web-based system provides financial services to Navajo Nation

Legal - Court Procedures - Law Enforcement
- Electronic Arrest Warrant and Bad Check Legal Assistance for Judges
- System Handles Many Requirements of Loans
- BusinessLaw.gov Provides Online Legal Business Structure Advisor
- Detecting Insider Trading on Stock Exchange
- Public School Online Advisor Helps Select Appropriate Disciplinary Actions
- Handling Legal Issues of Environmental Compliance
- System Provides Quick Determination for Claimants
- Tax and Legislative Auditing & Reporting
- Making Relevant Sense of Fire Code Standards
- The Expert on Security Classification Guidance
- Over 20 Advisory Systems (and Growing) from Dept. of Labor
- System Provides Federal and State Accounting and Reporting Capabilities

Agriculture - Agriforestry - Earth Sciences
- Best Seed Selection for Best Yield and Profit
- Cross Breeding System Increases Margins by up to 50%
- Forest Inventory - Quality and Quantity
- Lynx Population Management System
- Irrigation and Pest Management
- Planning and Design of Agroforestry Systems
- Tree Selection Application

Transportation - Shipping - Highway
- Rockwell's Aircraft Systems Material and Design Expertise
- Railroad, Navy and Air Force Engine Component Failure Prediction
- American Association of State Highway and Transportation Officials System
- Improved Nautical Chart Cartography
- Highway Construction Equipment Selection
- Better Weather Prediction for Safer Seas and Skies
- Federal Highway Administration and Transportation Research Council System
- System Identifies Problems with Overseas Assignments

Electronics - Telecommunications - Internet/Intranet
- System Runs on Same Hardware as Machine Vision Programmer
- Expertise for Rockwell's Autonetics Sensors and Aircraft Systems
- Analysis of Spectrum Analyzer Data Saves Millions

- Pacific Gas & Electric Field Assistant Helps Service Revenue Meters
- EPRI Prevents Power Outage Due to Bearing Failures
- GE Identification of Common Metals
- HP's Recommendations for Warehouse Implementations
- CIM Cell Re-Configuration in Minutes, Not a Full Day
- Rotating Equipment Vibration Advisor
- Pacific Bells' Monitoring, Prediction, and Repair Network Assistance
- AUDEX Provides Electrophysiological Expertise
- U.S. Postal Service Electronic Performance Support Systems
- Voice Driven Diagnostic System

Sales & Marketing - Online Product Selection - Publishing

- Online Product Configuration Drives HP's E-Business Strategy
- Sales Support System Provides Pricing, Quotations and Reports
- Multimillion$ Loan Approval System Saves Study Time and Costs
- Profiling System Helps Businesses Successfully Penetrate Foreign Markets
- Cost, Labor & Productivity Analysis and Estimating
- Credit Analysis Advisor and Report System
- Selecting the Right Equipment, Then the Right Model
- Power Generation Unit Commitment Advisor Customized for Each Client

Chemical - Natural Resources - Mining

- Compliance for Asbestos Contamination
- Texas Eastman Connects Over 400 Systems with External Programs
- System Identifies Impurities from Analysis of Spectrum Analyzer Data
- Know What to Do When Working with Fuel
- GE Identification of Common Metals
- Vibration Advisor Uses Patterns and Symptoms in Diagnosis
- Nestle's Real-Time Process Control
- EXNUT Reduces Fungicide Use in Farm Management Operations

Medical - Diagnostics - Healthcare Orgs.

- Respiratory & Anesthesia Monitoring
- Cedars-Sinai Information Management for Lung Cancer Patients
- System Determines Adjustment/Stress Issues Before Overseas Assignments
- Experts Agree with Pediatric Auditory Diagnostics System 100%
- Keeping People Safe From the Hazards of Asbestos
- In-Vitro Fertilization Cycle Stimulation
- Urodynamic Diagnosis Rates Diagnosis in Order of Probability
- Hematology Support with Voice Driven System for Accurate Diagnosis

Construction - Equipment Selection - Cost Estimating

- Advisors Help Contractors Interpret Complex Compliance Information
- Labor Cost Diagnostics for Steel Construction and Welding Selection
- Major Commercial Construction Loan Approval Predictor
- System Provides Front-End Analysis for Construction Simulation
- Equipment Selection for Highway Construction
- Fast Fire Code Interpretation for Architects, Engineers and Designers
- Control Panel Layout Design Aid
- In-the-Field Procedural Assistant
- Confined Spaces Work Place Advice
- Economic, Crew and Maintenance Optimization for Scheduling
- Construction Specialists Systems Help Project Supervisors at Field Sites
- Work Zone Interactive Video Trainer & Advisor

Computer Hardware & Software
- Complex Configuration of Computer Integrated Manufactured Cells
- Financial Analysis Support Techniques (FAST)
- Customized Diagnostic System
- Eastman Implements Knowledge Automation Systems Enterprise Wide
- EASE System for Dept. of Labor Running on LAN
- Langton Clarke's EXPERTAX in Use Since 1986
- HP's Interactive Hardware and Network Configuration
- A Blend of Knowledge Automation Systems and 3-D Design
- Nestle's Real-Time Process Control with IBM Cooperative Effort
- Systems Monitor Pacific Bell's Front-End Computers
- EXSYS Streamlines ANVIL's Tapes That Control Selection Process
- U.S. Postal Service Electronic Performance Support Systems
- Multimedia Integration Aids User in Analyzing and Diagnosing Problems

Training - Repairs - Troubleshooting
- System Keeps Compliance Support Up to Date for Businesses and Consultants
- Troubleshooting System Prevents Power Outages
- Tutorial Tool for Inexperienced Personnel
- 13 Years Running - Component Failure Prediction System Saves $Millions
- Profiling System Works in Tandem with Cross-Cultural Training
- Interactive System Helps Train New Auditors
- Troubleshooting Problems in Complex Equipment
- System Brings Less Experienced Case Workers Quickly Up To Speed
- System Assists New Judges
- No Electricity? No Problem - Laptop Systems Provide Support in the Field
- Training Tool Explains Recommendations and Brings in External Graphics
- Classification System Makes Determination in Minutes
- OSHA Helps Businesses Help Themselves
- NetHELP Provides 24-Hour Network Repair Assistance
- Diagnostics System Helps in Training Programs
- Portable Self-Paced Training Covers Operations Processing and Repairs
- System Chooses Testing by Considering all Relevant Factors
- Interactive Video/Trainer/Advisor

Research & Development - Identification
- Land Management System Assists Research Scientists
- Agronomy Systems Combine "Expert Intuition" and Hard Data
- Effective Cross Breeding Strategies via Genetic, Environmental Management
- System Runs on Same Hardware as Machine Vision Programmer
- Stratified Line Plot and Point Sampling Used in Forest Inventory System
- GE's System Identifies Metals in Non-Laboratory Setting
- System for Invitro Program Speeds-Up Critical Decision Making
- Improved Design Process Without Expensive Iterative Analyses
- Diagnose and Locate Problems in Electrical, Mechanical or Fluid Systems
- System Provides Relevant Staging, Prognostic and Therapeutic Information
- Improved Accuracy for Charting and Geodetic Service
- EXSYS Customized Interface Key to Real-Time System Success
- Years of Experience Codified into Classification System
- Turn Here When You Have to Work In Confined Spaces
- Pacific Bell Monitoring, Repair and Prediction Systems
- National Research Lab Systems Provide New Concepts
- Diagnostic System Challenge Results in 100% Domain Expert Agreement
- Scheduling System Combines Traditional Numeric Methods with Heuristic Rules
- Rubber Research Institute Fields Systems in the "Field"

- Sandia National Laboratory System Greatly Reduces Information Gathering Time
- National Oceanic and Atmospheric Administration Prediction System
- Support System in Latest Portable PC and Digital Technology
- Voice Driven Interactive Diagnostic System Frees Eyes and Hands for Other Work

Energy - Utilities - Oil & Gas

- Unit Commitment Advisor for Power Generation Scheduling
- Power Plant Outage Prevention and Maintenance Procedures
- Invisibly Embedded System Handles Failure Prevention with Extreme Accuracy
- Advisor for Fuel Delivery Systems
- Nuclear Power Plant Automates Emergency Contingency Plan
- Problem-Solving and Maintenance System Distributed to over 400 Client Installations
- Pacific Gas & Electric Personnel Assistance
- U.S. Department of Energy Classification Automation
- Work Place Confined Spaces Compliance Systems
- National Lab Numerically Controlled Machine Tool Selection

Engineering - Planning - Scheduling

- Human-Factors Engineering Reduces Costly Operator Errors
- Material and Process Design Expertise From the "Get-Go"
- Complex Configuration of Computer Integrated Manufactured Cells
- Construction Simulation & Analysis
- Customized Diagnostics for Machine Vision System
- Eastman Distributes Top Engineering Expertise Enterprise
- EPRI System Prevents Bearing Failures
- Highway Engineering Support for Earth-Moving Projects
- Oil Analysis Saves $Millions By Predicting Component Failure
- Fast and Specific Standards Interpretation for Engineers
- GE Identifies Common Metals
- Mechanical Equipment Diagnosis in Electrical, Mechanical or Fluid Systems
- Real-Time Analysis Increases Power and Enables Multi-Tasking
- Interactive Online and Downloadable Systems Help with Confined Spaces Permits
- Monitoring, Repair and Prediction Handled Through Network System
- Power Generation Scheduling Incorporating Numeric and Qualitative Aspects
- Numerically Controlled Machine Tool Selection
- Total Productivity Support for U.S. Postal Service Mail Sorter
- Major Oil Company Reduces Cost with Weld Procedure and Test Selection Systems
- Traffic Control and Management Strategies for Construction

Safety - Quality Control - Human Resources

- Asbestos Advisor System Honored in Vice President's "Best Practices" Award
- Disaster Manager's Emergency Management System
- Interactive Corporate Family Support for Overseas Assignments
- Career Goal Advisor Assists Supervisors with Development Planning
- Unemployment Eligibility Determination with Data Access and Automated Reports
- Tremendous Time Savings, Nothing Overlooked and Site-Specific Report
- Better Human-Factors Design Provides Safer Plant Operation
- Case Worker Advisor Provides Equitable, Effective Welfare Administration
- In-the-Field System Provides Quick Indexing and Reference to Safety Precautions
- Nestle Pension Fund Advisor Distributed to all Personnel Departments
- Public School Disciplinary Action Advisor
- Nuclear Weapons Security Classification
- Thousands Access System Which Provides Safer, Healthier Work Place
- Automated Student Advising System Provides Individualized Assistance

- Advisors Help Farm Operations Management
- Fast Storm Forecasting in Limited Time Frame
- Work Zone Planning, Safety and Design Aid

Regulatory / Environmental / Policy Compliance
- Interactive Regulatory Compliance Assistance
- Environmental Compliance Support System
- Public School Disciplinary Action Advisor
- Counter Measures for Nuclear Power Station Emergencies
- System Handles More than 400 Questions a Week
- Wildlife Population Protection and Trapping Regulations System
- System Detects Situations and Concerns in Overseas Relocations
- Online Help for Choosing a Legal Business Structure
- National Fire Code and Environmental Permit Advisor
- System Facilitates Transition of Welfare Program to Navajo Nation
- Organizational Policy on Development Goals
- Incorporating Environmental and Management Constraints
- Increasing Quality and Uniformity of Legal Procedures
- EPRI Reduces Forced Plant Outages with Maintenance Procedures System
- In the Field Procedural Assistant
- Consistency & Reduced Subjectivity for Marine Service Organization
- Pension Fund Advisor Conforms with Standards
- System Interprets over 100 Classification Guides
- Environmental Conditions Factor into Tree Selection
- Severe Thunderstorm Prediction
- Major Oil Company Reduces Costs with Selection of Qualification Tests

Manufacturing - Process Control - Predictive Maintenance
- Increased Performance, Productivity, Optimization and Overall Quality
- Nestle Foods Install Real-Time Applications
- Set of Systems Handle Monitoring, Repair and Prediction
- Bidding, Control and Productivity Analysis for Total Cost Evaluation
- Customized Port for Diagnostics for Machine Vision System
- Eastman Distributes "Know-How" Enterprise-Wide
- Fast Prediction Using External Calls and Complex Mathematical Calculations
- Complex Product Configuration of Computer Integrated Manufactured Cells
- GE Identifies Common Metals
- Optimized Control Panel Layout Reduces Costly Operator Errors
- Linear Programming Interface Optimizes Management Modules
- Numerical and Qualitative Rules Solve Scheduling Problems
- System Automates Appropriate Tool Selection
- Multimedia Electronic Repair Support Systems
- Voice Driven Diagnostics and Frees Hands for Other Work
- Procedure Selection System with Time Estimates and Material Requirements
- Selecting Appropriate Control and Management Strategies

Government - Military - Aerospace
- OSHA Compliance Advisor Helps Thousands
- SBA Legal Business Structure Recommendation Wizard
- System Identifies Potential Problems Before Overseas Assignments
- Federal Money Approval System for Major Construction
- Assistance for State Magistrate Court Judges
- Los Alamos National Laboratory Support System
- Public School Disciplinary Action Advisor

- Emergency Support System for Security Bureau
- American Association of State Highway and Transportation Equipment Selector
- Claimants Unemployment Compensation Determination
- Oil Analysis Saves U.S. Air Force over $100 Million
- U.S. Dept. of Commerce - 40% Higher Accuracy for U.S. Nautical Charts
- U.S. Dept. of Energy Security Classification
- Case Worker Advisor
- U.S. Dept. of Labor Saves Time, Resources and Taxpayer Money
- U.S. Dept. of Agriculture Planning Modules - Higher Yield/Less Water & Pesticides
- Sandia National Laboratories Machine Tool Selection
- Alaska Department of Fish and Game System
- National Oceanic and Atmospheric Admin. Severe Thunderstorm Prediction
- U.S. Postal Service Total Organization Productivity Support
- Federal Highway Administration Work Zone Safety Manager

CHAPTER 2

Ulf Nilsson and Jan Mahuszynski, Logic Programming and PROLOG, 2nd Edition, 2000. A free online book you can download. **PROLOG** is the language designed for backward chaining and it and LISP are the classic AI languages that are still used: http://www.ida.liu.se/~ulfni/lpp/. Many additional teaching resources are available from Nilsson's site at: http://www.ida.liu.se/~ulfni/teaching.shtml. Nilsson's book provides much more detail about knowledge representation, logic programming, and examples than covered in Chapters 2-3.

Special languages such as **KQML have been developed for knowledge representation** and query: http://www.cs.umbc.edu/kqml/

Dave Hannay's website allows you to try out Finite State Machines and other types of parsers to recognize tokens from his teaching materials at: http://scoter3.union.edu/~hannayd/csc140/simulators/

Doug Lenat online lecture on commonsense and AI: http://murl.microsoft.com/LectureDetails.asp?1032. He is famous for developing OpenCyc, the open source version of the Cyc technology (http://www.cyc.com/cyc/technology/whatiscyc), the world's largest and most complete general knowledge base and commonsense reasoning engine. He is also famous for his pioneering work in automated mathematics discovery with the Automated Mathematician (AM) and Eurisko, as mentioned in the book.

Formal Methods. Major site with many resources for logic: http://archive.comlab.ox.ac.uk/comp/formal-methods.html

Software for learning rules by induction. VisiRex 2.0 for Windows, including a trial version, is available from CorMac Technologies, Inc. Two other methods, the classic backprop and neural net SFAM, are also available. Nice examples with the software at: http://cormactech.com/visirex/faq.html.

DATA MINING RESOURCES AND SOFTWARE

Data mining success stories from the company Complexica®, which also provides data mining tools and services: http://internet.cybermesa.com/~rfrye/complexica/dm_em.htm

Classic software for inductive machine learning was Ross Quinlan's ID3, later enhanced to **C4.5**, available at his personal webpage as well as other papers and slides: http://www.cse.unsw.edu.au/~quinlan/. His latest data mining tools **See3** and **C5** offer significant advantages over C4.5, and are available commercially from his company at: http://www.rulequest.com/

Huge collection of programs for data mining, constructing decision trees, data analysis using neural nets, statistics, fuzzy technologies: http://www.the-data-mine.com/bin/view/Software/WebIndex

Large collection of databases, domain theories and data generators available for testing machine learning algorithms: http://www.ics.uci.edu/~mlearn/MLRepository.html

Large library of C++ classes for general machine learning algorithms to develop data mining and visualization tools. http://www.sgi.com/tech/mlc/. Since this code is written in C++, you can easily write CLIPS functions for these tasks and then recompile CLIPS for optimum performance. The complete C++ code of CLIPS is provided on the CDROM at the back of the book.

Collection of very large data sets in a variety of fields for testing data mining tools. You may find this useful if you develop your own data mining version of CLIPS as mentioned above: http://kdd.ics.uci.edu/

alphaWorks: a product for data mining and many other applications: http://www.alphaworks.ibm.com/Home/

Great software tool for making hyperlinked semantic nets, free and very powerful. Can also be used for expressing knowledge and expertise in a visual format. A good tool for knowledge acquisition, a topic discussed in Chapter 6. Lots of examples from users around the world. If you sign up for their email list, be prepared to get a lot of email in Spanish!: http://cmap.ihmc.us/

TAP is a knowledge-base designed to aid in the construction of the Semantic Web (http://www.w3.org/2001/sw/) which is a machine readable upgrade to the present World Wide Web. Many other links are available from: http://www.iturls.com/English/TechHotspot/TH_SemanticWeb.asp

Currently the Web is only searchable by humans using primitive Boolean operations using keyword search. Although websites are converting to XML languages for specific domains such as **MusicXML, RuleXML, MathXML**, etc., that is machine readable, TAP will know more about the real world and current events in a semantic context.

TAP is a shallow but broad knowledge base containing basic lexical and taxonomic information about a wide range of popular objects such as music, movies, authors, sports, autos, companies, home appliances, toys, baby products, places, consumer electronics, and health. It can be downloaded for testing many different types of expert systems. It's basically a shallow ontology that is meant to complement rather than replace Cyc, which has a deep ontology about commonsense phenomena but not about current events, like who is Yo-Yo Ma? Good student research projects can be made from TAP: http://tap.stanford.edu/tap/tapkb.html

The Classic Family of Knowledge Representation Systems for applications where only limited expressive power is necessary, but rapid responses to questions are essential. Most of the features available in **semantic networks** are available in Classic. It allows users to represent descriptions, concepts, roles, individuals, rules, frames of other knowledge representation systems and object-oriented programming languages. What is really interesting is that concepts are automatically organized into a taxonomy and objects are automatically inherited as appropriate.

Classic can also detect inconsistencies in information that it is told (which is probably why it should answer your phone when a telemarketer calls, or email spam arrives announcing how you can make $10 million by helping a foreign diplomat deposit money in a bank account. On the other hand, it should *not* be used by your spouse when you explain why you didn't come home last night.)

There are three members of the Classic family. They are (1) the **LISP version** that was developed for research purposes, (2) the **C version** and, (3) **NeoClassic** written in C++. Classic has been used for the PROSE and QUESTAR configuration products used to configure over $4 billion worth of AT&T and Lucent products. For more details on Classic see: http://www.bell-labs.com/project/classic/

The **Rule Markup Initiative, RuleML,** is a project to come up with a standard for forward and backward inference style for marking up rules so that they are universally machine readable by different expert systems. Another related project is the **RuleXML** language. Efforts are underway to achieve compatibility. The **RuleML** site is: http://www.ruleml.org/.

Rather than coding in different styles, a single uniform format for rules would be created. This would facilitate the exchange of knowledge between different expert systems. Currently there is no standard way for different expert systems to transfer knowledge since each expert system tool uses its own syntax. This is a major project and offers great research potential with huge payoffs if it works. Basically it's analogous to reusing software rather than starting from scratch each time a new expert system is constructed. The closest thing to a practical implementation is objects in CLIPS since objects are well defined and can be exchanged between different CLIPS expert systems. Although Jess is written in Java, an object-oriented language, as of 2004 Jess did not support objects in rules, i.e., COOL. The main advantage of Jess is embedding it in a host Java language.

Also because objects contain data and methods and a well-defined interface, it is easier to build large scale expert systems. The challenges involved in building a hybrid rule object-oriented system were enormous and CLIPS has been continually refined and rigorously debugged in every release since 1986. While there has been a great temptation to add new features like backward chaining, fuzzy logic, Bayesian capability, and many others, we have always restricted this temptation in favor of a simpler, robust tool that others can build on a stable software base. This philosophy has worked very well as you can see by the many and growing number of CLIPS-descended languages with extra features (which we don't have to support!).

SOFTWARE RESOURCES FOR LOGIC

A great deal of AI has been used to automate the reasoning processes by which people did logic. In fact this was the earliest challenge of AI, to duplicate the symbolic reasoning processes of mathematicians rather than being a number-crunching machine. While machines had been used for thousands of years to multiply the power of human muscles, or simple devices like the abacus used for arithmetic; now for the first time in history the intellectual ability of the human mind for proving symbolic mathematical theorems was being challenged.

FALLACIES

The study of Fallacies is important in expert systems when interviewing an expert for domain knowledge. Sometimes even the expert falls prey to logical fallacies or you may misinterpret what the expert says and so construct a fallacy. You need to validate the expert's knowledge before it is placed in the database. A more complete list of fallacies in the Chapter 6 section of this Appendix. (If you get really good at fallacies, you can always quit artificial intelligence and become a successful lawyer or politician. Fallacies are not only logically wrong, but are very seductive arguments that people want to believe, so it's a good method of persuading people your argument is the correct one.)

Good general descriptions and examples of logical fallacies in deduction: http://webpages.shepherd.edu/maustin/rhetoric/deductiv.htm

Induction fallacies: http://webpages.shepherd.edu/maustin/rhetoric/inductiv.htm

A list of many other logical fallacies: http://webpages.shepherd.edu/maustin/rhetoric/fallacies.htm

Critical Thinking on the Web with many links to logic, online tutorials, and a very comprehensive list of fallacies: http://www.austhink.org/critical/

SOFTWARE FOR LOGIC

The following selection of software available on the internet comprises a wide variety of topics about logic and may be used so that you can check your answers to logic problems and see how automated reasoning works. This information about educational software for logic and other references has been adapted by kind permission of Hans van Ditmarsch, hans@cs.otago.ac.nz, at his webpage: http:/www.cs.otago.ac.nz/staffpriv/hans/logiccourseware. html. Please see his webpage for further updates.

Akka, http://turing.wins.uva.nl/~lhendrik/AkkaStart.html
functions: provability of formulas in several logics, validity of formulas in a model, drawing and editing Kripke models and models for dynamic logic
platforms: web
developer: Lex Hendriks, ILLC, University of Amsterdam, the Netherlands
email: lhendrik@illc.uva.nl

Alfie, http://www.cs.chalmers.se/~sydow/alfie/index.html
functions: natural deduction for propositional logic
platforms: web
developers: Björn von Sydow, Department of Computing Science, Chalmers University, Göteborg, Sweden
email: sydow@cs.chalmers.se
comments: ASCII interface

Aristotle, http://www.utexas.edu/courses/plato/aristotle.html
functions: formalizing English sentences into symbolic logic

platforms: Windows95/98/NT
developers:
email: marcow@cs.utexas.edu, Robert C. Koons: rkoons@mail.utexas.edu
Athena Software, http://www.athenasoft.org/
functions: hierarchically structuring arguments and their support, in a graphical interface using a tree format; similar tools for negotation
platforms: Windows
developers: Bertil Rolf, Blekinge Institute of Technology, Sweden, and others
email: info@athenasoft.org, bertil.rolf@bth.se
book: various online documentation, PowerPoint, etc.
comments: also for use on high schools, teacher support, added to list in 2003
Bertie3, http://137.99.26.4/~wwwphil/SOFTWARE.HTML
functions: natural deduction in propositional and predicate logic
platforms: DOS, Windows
developer: Austen Clark, University of Connecticut, USA
email: austen.clark@uconn.edu
book: Merrie Bergmann, Jim Moor, and Jack Nelson, *The Logic Book,* 2nd edition. McGraw Hill, 1992.
comments: available as GNU Public Domain License software
Bertrand, http://www.uwosh.edu/faculty_staff/herzberg/Bertrand.html
functions: tableau-like validity testing of predicate logic formulas
platforms: Apple
developers: Larry A. Herzberg, University of Wisconsin - Oshkosh, USA
email: herzberg@vaxa.cis.uwosh.edu
comments: updated 2003
blobLogic, http://users.ox.ac.uk/~univ0675/blob/
functions: semantic tableaux for propositional and predicate logics
platforms: web (requires downloading Shockwave), Mac, PC
developers: Corin Howitt, Oxford University, U.K.
email: corin.howitt@philosophy.ox.ac.uk
book: no (particularly suitable for use with either Jeffrey or Hodges)
comments: online proof demonstrations; save/load to web servers; interactive tutorials; modal logic version to be released later; added to list in 2003
blogic, http://www.umich.edu/~velleman/Logic/
functions: Boolean search, logic circuits, truth-tables, semantics of modal logic with possible-worlds diagrams, quantification
platforms: web
developers: David Velleman, University of Michigan, USA
email: velleman@umich.edu
book: this is an interactive textbook
comments: added to list in 2003
Boole, http://www-csli.stanford.edu/LPL/
functions: truth tables
platforms: Windows, Apple
developers: John Etchemendy, Stanford University, USA, Jon Barwise, Indiana University, USA
email: Dave Barker-Plummer, dbp@csli.stanford.edu, or User Support, LPLbugs@csli.stanford.edu
book: John Etchemendy & Jon Barwise, *Language, Proof a*nd Logic. CSLI Publications, 2000. Note: This publisher publishes a huge number of books on logic at their website: http://www-csli.stanford.edu/
comments: The book comes with the software: Fitch, Boole, and Tarski's World, a widely used first order logic software to supplement any logic textbook. It represents logical propositions in visual graphical worlds.
Expression Evaluator, http://www.cc.utah.edu/~nahaj/logic/evaluate/
functions: semantic (interpreted) evaluation of propositional and predicate logic formulas
platforms: web
developers: John Halleck, University of Utah, USA

email: John.Halleck@utah.edu
book: no
comments: links to other web resources (modal logics)
Fitch, http://www-csli.stanford.edu/LPL/
functions: natural deduction for predicate logic
platforms: Windows, Apple
developers: John Etchemendy, Stanford University USA, Jon Barwise, Indiana University USA
email: Dave Barker-Plummer, dbp@csli.stanford.edu, or User Support, LPLbugs@ csli.stanford.edu
book: John Etchemendy & Jon Barwise, *Language, Proof and Logic*. CSLI Publications, 2000.
comments: The book comes with the software: Fitch, Boole, and Tarski's World.
Gateway to logic, http://logik.phl.univie.ac.at/~chris/formular-uk.html
functions: natural deduction for predicate logic (Lemmon- and Fitch-style), truth tables, ...
platforms: web
developers: Christian Gottschall (University of Vienna, Austria)
email: gottschall@gmx.de
book: no
comments: both in English and German
Hexagon, http://www.science.uva.nl/projects/opencollege/cognitie/hexagon/
functions: public updates in epistemic logic
platforms: web
developers: Jan Jaspars, Free-lance logician & University of Amsterdam, the Netherlands
email: jaspars@science.uva.nl
book: no
comments: in Dutch (courseware additional to University of Amsterdam lectures)
Hyperproof, http://csli-www.stanford.edu/hp/
functions: natural deduction for predicate logic, visual reasoning
platforms: Apple
developers: John Etchemendy, Stanford University USA, Jon Barwise, Indiana University USA
email: dbp@csli.stanford.edu (Dave Barker-Plummer)
book: Hyperproof, John Etchemendy and Jon Barwise, CSLI publications, 1994
comments:
Inference Engine, http://blue.butler.edu/~sglennan/InferenceEngine.html
functions:
platforms: Mac, PC
developers: Stuart Glennan
email: sglennan@butler.edu
book: Joseph Bessie and Stuart Glennan, *Elements of Deductive Inference*
http://blue.butler.edu/~sglennan/Elements.html, Wadsworth 2000
comments:
Interactive Logic Programs, http://www.thoralf.uwaterloo.ca/htdocs/LOGIC/st_ilp.html
functions: truth tables in propositional logic, unification of terms
platforms: web
developers: Stanley N. Burris, University of Waterloo, Canada
email: snburris@thoralf.uwaterloo.ca
book: Logic for Mathematics and Computer Science, Prentice-Hall, 1998
comments: added to list in 2003
Jape, http://www.jape.org.uk/
functions: natural deduction and sequent proof in classical predicate logic; plus various other logics and formal systems; plus user-defined logics
platforms: MacOSX, Unix, Linux, Solaris
developers: Bernard Sufrin, Oxford University, U.K. & Richard Bornat, QMW London, U.K.
email: Bernard.Sufrin@comlab.ox.ac.uk, richard@dcs.qmw.ac.uk
book: coming
comments: Jape is acronym for "just another proof editor"; updated in 2003
JOJ-logics: The Propositional Proof Generator,
http://pgs.twi.tudelft.nl/~tonino/teaching/JOJ-logics/JOJ-Logics.html

functions: truth tables and natural deduction for propositional logic
platforms: web
developers: Jonne Zutt and Joost Broekens, Delft University, the Netherlands
email: j.zutt@twi.tudelft.nl, d.j.broekens@twi.tudelft.nl or supervisor Hans Tonino: J.F.M.Tonino@its.tudelft.nl
book: no
comments: M.Sc. students project, no proof editing
LICS web tutor, http://www.cis.ksu.edu/~huth/lics/tutor/
functions: MC questions and answers about various logical topics, including modal
platforms: web
developers: Michael Huth and Marc Ryan, School of Computer Science, University of Birmingham, U.K.
email: M.Huth@doc.ic.ac.uk, M.D.Ryan@cs.bham.ac.uk
book : Logic in Computer Science, 2nd Edition, Cambridge University Press, 2004
comments:
Logic Animations, http://turing.wins.uva.nl/~jaspars/animations/
functions: semantic computations in propositional, predicate, dynamic, modal logic
platforms: web
developers: Jan Jaspars, Free-lance logician & University of Amsterdam, the Netherlands
email: jaspars@science.uva.nl
book: no
comments: mainly in Dutch
Logic Cafe, http://www.oakland.edu/phil/cafe/
functions: truth tables, predicate logic arguments, MC questions
platforms: web (Linux, Mac public domain versions)
developers: John Halpin, Oakland University, USA
email: halpin@oakland.edu
book: online
comments: online logic textbook with integrated web-based exercises, public domain
Logic Daemon, http://logic.tamu.edu/
functions: natural deduction for predicate logic
platforms: web
developers: Colin Allen, Texas A&M University USA
email: colin-allen@tamu.edu
book: Colin Allen and Michael Hand, *Logic Primer* (2nd ed.),MIT Press, 2001.
comments: ASCII interface
Logic for Fun, http://csl.anu.edu.au/~jks/puzzlesite/
functions: expressing puzzles and other problems in first order logic
platforms: web
developer: John Slaney, Australian National University
email: John.Slaney@anu.edu.au
Logic Toolbox, http://philosophy.lander.edu/~jsaetti/Welcome.html
functions: syllogisms, truth tables, natural deduction for propositional logic
platforms: web, windows
developers: John Saetti
email: john.saetti@gcccd.net
LogicCoach III and IV, http://academic.csuohio.edu/polen/
functions: Very comprehensive software to aid in teaching logic for several different logic books listed on the website. Covers Argument Diagrams, Definitions, Fallacies, Analogies, Mill's Methods, Probability, Categorical Propositions, Standardization, Syllogisms, Enthymemes, Sorites, Venn Diagrams, Symbolic Logic, Translation: English to Symbols, Translation: Symbols to English, Logical Form, Truth Tables, Indirect Truth Tables, Quantification, Identity, Proofs, Trees
platforms: Windows, Apple
developers: Nelson Pole, Cleveland State University, Ohio, USA
email: n.pole@csuohio.edu
book: Patrick Hurley, *A Concise Introduction to Logic*, 8th edition, Wadsworth, 2003

comments: instructor's package available; updated 2003
Logics Workbench, http://www.lwb.unibe.ch/
functions: proof and computation in propositional logics (minimal, intuitionist, classical, modal, non-monotonic)
platforms: web, Apple, Linux, Solaris
developers: Gerhard Jäger (project leader), Peter Balsiger, Alain Heuerding, Stefan Schwendimann, University of Bern, Switzerland
email: lwb@iam.unibe.ch
book: extensive online manual
comments: no proof editing
LogicWorks, http://www.pdcnet.org/logicwo.html
functions: truth tables, argument analysis (by example), fallacies (by example)
platforms: PC, Apple ("year 2000 compliant")
developers: Rob R. Brady, Stetson University, USA
email: (orders) order@pdcnet.org
comments: published by the Philosophy Documentation Center, http://www.pdcnet.org, instructor's package available
MacLogic, http://www-theory.dcs.st-and.ac.uk/~rd/logic/soft.html
functions: predicate logic (minimal, intuitionistic, classical), natural deduction, and sequent calculus
platforms: Apple
developers: Roy Dyckhoff, St Andrews University, Scotland, U.K.
email: rd@dcs.st-andrews.ac.uk
book: optional: G. Forbes, *Modern Logic,* Oxford University Press, 1993
comments: no longer updated to current versions of MacOS
New Pandora, http://www.doc.ic.ac.uk/~kb/NewPandora.html
functions: natural deduction for predicate logic
platforms: web
developers: Krysia Broda, Department of Computing, Imperial College, London, U.K.
email: kb@doc.ic.ac.uk
comments: based on 'Pandora'
Paul Tomassi, Logic, http://www.oxford-virtual.com/Philosophy/Tomassi/
functions: propositional and predicate logic
platforms: web
developers: Oxford Virtual Technology
book: Paul Tomassi, *Logic,* Routledge, 1999
comments: web tutor accompanying textbook
Pier, http://gentzen.math.hc.keio.ac.jp/
functions: interactive proof editor, natural deduction
platforms: web
developers: Masaru Shirahata, Keio University, Japan
email: sirahata@math.hc.keio.ac.jp
comments: written as a Java applet and application
Plato, http://www.utexas.edu/courses/plato/
functions: proofs in propositional and predicate calculus
platforms: PC, Mac
developers:
email: marcow@cs.utexas.edu, Robert C. Koons: rkoons@mail.utexas.edu
book: Robert C. Koons, A Logical Toolbox, 2000.
comments:
Power of Logic, http://www.poweroflogic.com/
functions: various logical topics, proof checking
platforms: web
developers:
email: webmaster@poweroflogic.com
book: C. Stephen Layman, The Power of Logic (2nd ed.), McGraw Hill.
comments:

Program to learn Natural Deduction in Gentzen-Kleene's style, http://193.51.78.161/dnfn/deductioneng.html
functions: sequent-style natural deduction for predicate logic, computation of normal forms
platforms: DOS
developers: Patrice Bailhache, University of Nantes, France
email: patrice.bailhache@humana.univ-nantes.fr
comments: used by Nantes (France) philosophy students
Reason!Able, http://www.goreason.com
functions: visually representing arguments
platforms: Windows 95 and up
developers: Tim van Gelder, University of Melbourne, Australia
email: info@goreason.com
comments: teachers' resources
Socrates, http://www.utexas.edu/courses/socrates/
functions: semantic tableaux
platforms: PC
developers:
email: marcow@cs.utexas.edu, Robert C. Koons: rkoons@mail.utexas.edu
book: Robert C. Koons, A Logical Toolbox, 2000
comments:
Tarski's World, http://csli-www.stanford.edu/hp/
functions: interpreted semantics of predicate logic
platforms: Windows, Apple
developers: John Etchemendy, Stanford University, USA, Jon Barwise, Indiana University USA
email: dbp@csli.stanford.edu (Dave Barker-Plummer)
book: The Language of First-order Logic (3rd edition), John Etchemendy and Jon Barwise, CSLI publications, 1994 (Also: Tarski "Lite," same authors; also: Language, Proof and Logic)
comments: Famous example. Includes the Hintikka game (semantic tableaux)
TPS and ETPS, http://gtps.math.cmu.edu/tps.html
functions: interactive proof of theorems of first-order logic or higher-order logic (type theory)
platforms: Unix, Windows, web
developers: Peter B. Andrews, Carnegie Mellon University; and others
email: andrews@cmu.edu
book: Peter B. Andrews, An Introduction to Mathematical Logic and Type Theory: To Truth Through Proof, 2nd. Edition, Kluwer Academic Publishers, 2002
comments: see also "ETPS: A System to Help Students Write Formal Proofs," at: http://gtps.math.cmu.edu/tps-papers.html; added to list in 2003
Twootie, http://137.99.26.4/~wwwphil/SOFTWARE.HTML
functions: computing truth (trees) in propositional and predicate logic
platforms: DOS, Windows
developer: Austen Clark, University of Connecticut, USA
email: austen.clark@uconn.edu
books: Merrie Bergmann, Jim Moor, and Jack Nelson, *The Logic Book,* 2nd edition. McGraw-Hill, 1992. Richard Jeffrey, *Formal Logic: Its Scope and Limits,* 3rd edition, McGraw-Hill, 1991
comments: available as GNU Public Domain License software

THEOREM PROVERS

More sophisticated software called Theorem Provers, Automated Reasoning, or Mechanized Reasoning are used for advanced work in Logic.

Mechanized Reasoning Home Page http://www-formal.stanford.edu/clt/ ARS/ars-db.html

World Wide Web Virtual Library: Formal Methods. A huge collection of logic tools and language verifiers: http://vl.fmnet.info/

Formal Methods Education Resources http://www.cs.indiana.edu/formal-methods-education/

Logik Software für Unterrichtszwecke (in German): http://www.phil-fak.uni-duesseldorf.de/logik/software.html)

Database of Existing Mechanized Reasoning Systems. A large resource of descriptions and links http://www-formal.stanford.edu/clt/ARS/systems.html)

Logic programs and teaching aids, theorem provers and languages, http://home.clara.net/ghrow/subjects/logic_software.html)

Newsletter on Philosophy and Computers: http://www.apa.udel.edu/apa/ publications/newsletters/computers.html)

A landmark Turing Test was performed in Spring 2000 marking the 50th anniversary of Turing's prediction that within 50 years a computer would pass his test. Although the humans did manage to soon figure out which was the computer, it's interesting to note that some humans thought other humans were computers for much longer. Thus, it will be some time yet before computers are replaced by humans: http://www.apa.udel.edu/apa/publications/newsletters/v99n2/computers/ chair.asp

Linear Logic Prover Naoyuki Tamura's web-based Linear Logic Prover also contains many references to other logic provers, programs including PROLOG and software lists: http://bach.cs.kobe-u.ac.jp/llprover/

LOGIC EDUCATION PROJECTS AND RESEARCH

Association of Symbolic Logic: Committee on Logic Education. Many links to a huge number of logic software and resources for teaching logic.http://www.math.ufl.edu/~jal/asl/logic_education.html

Taller de Didáctica de la Lógica. (in Spanish) Logic education pages in Mexico: http://www.filosoficas.unam.mx/~Tdl/TDL.htm

Aracne (in Spanish). Logic resources for Spain and Latin America: http://aracne.usal.es/

David Gries' website, http://www.cs.cornell.edu/gries/, with many links to logic and especially the new calculational logic. Also includes material from one of his many books, *A Logical Approach to Discrete Math*, Springer-Verlag, 1993 http://www.cs.cornell.edu/gries/Logic/intro.html

List to discuss logic education is maintained at Bucknell University, USA; to subscribe to the list send a message to: listserv@bucknell.edu containing the message subscribe logic-l@bucknell.edu

Carnegie Mellon Curriculum on Causal and Statistical reasoning, provides online courseware in causal reasoning. Their free Causality Lab download and examples teach students critical thinking of not accepting anything without real evidence. This is particularly important in these days when people believe everything they see on TV, even a year later when it's been proven wrong.

This brings up the important topic of **Truth Maintenance** in expert systems. CLIPS has a facility for Truth Maintenance where if a fact is proven incorrect, all succeeding facts or rules which were asserted, modified or deleted are retracted and the system restored to the state it was in before the incorrect fact was asserted. This allows the conclusions of CLIPS to be validated, which is more than most people can do: http://www.phil.cmu.edu/projects/csr/

The Self-Paced Logic Project, provides and develops software to create and manage a test bank of logic questions for a large self-paced logic course. The test bank of questions is automatically created by the program to cover the goals while not being the same every semester. While the course content is not included, the author does have a very comprehensive study guide for what he considers a student of logic should know. The list of topics is quite comprehensive and will probably make a student never again ask the question, "Exactly what do I need to know to pass the test?": http://www.sp.uconn.edu/~py102vc/selfpace.htm

CHAPTER 3

Probability Web. A large collection of resources on probability covering links to: Abstract, Books, Centers, groups and societies, Conferences, Jobs, Journals, The Mathematics Survey, Miscellaneous, Newsgroups and List servers, People, Probability pages by subject area, Publishers and Bookstores, Quotes, Software, Teaching Resources, What's New: http://www.mathcs.carleton.edu/ probweb/probweb.html

Chance: Materials to help teach a Chance course—a quantitative literacy course. The goal of Chance is to make students more informed, critical readers of current news stories that use probability and statistics. An excellent free GNU book on Probability and Statistics is available from the site by Grinstead and Snell listed below. The computer programs and answers to odd numbered exercises are also available from the Chance site. Other topics on the site include Chance News, Chance Course, Video and Audio, Teaching Aids, What's New?, Related Links: http://www.dartmouth.edu/~chance/

Probability Computer Projects with Mathematica:
http://www.wku.edu/~neal/probability/prob.html

Many links to Probability, Abstracts, Listservers, Newsgroups, People, Jobs, Journals, Software, Books, Conferences, Publishers and Miscellaneous:
http://www.maths.uq.oz.au/~pkp/probweb/probweb.html

Software for Probability and Statistics:
http://forum.swarthmore.edu/probstat/probstat.software.html

Publicly available software and online publishers for probability and statistics Internet project: http://forum.swarthmore.edu/probstat/probstat.projects.html

Many software tools for decision making under uncertainty are reviewed by the Decision Systems Laboratory of the University of Pittsburgh: http://www.sis.pitt.edu/~dsl/software.htm

CHAPTER 4

Statistics, Probability, and Data Mining

Large general collection of software for probability, statistics and Bayesian. Some are in DOS but still run: http://archives.math.utk.edu/software/msdos/probability/.html

Large collection of datasets for testing data mining software: http://lib.stat.cmu.edu/datasets/

Many datasets associated with books on statistics. A number are designed for use with Excel including Markov models:
http://www.duxbury.com/cgi-brookscole/course_products_bc.pl?fid=M67&discipline_number=17

Wide variety of probability calculators:
http://softsia.com/re.php?kw= Probability+Distribution+Calculator

Good variety of interesting videos you can download about probability, statistics, and applications to real life problems: http://www.dartmouth.edu/~chance/ChanceLecture/download.html

Huge Archive of Math Resources. Software, documents, tutorials, teaching aids including PowerPoint, and lists of books with associated software:
http://bayes.stat.washington.edu/almond/belief.html

Large list of links to all kinds of math software:
http://www.math.fsu.edu/Virtual/index.php?f=21

Huge list of international resources on statistics:
http://gsociology.icaap. org/methods/statontheweb.html

Very comprehensive list of links to all kinds of statistical resources:
http://gsociology.icaap.org/methods/statontheweb.html

Large collection of free statistical software: http://members.aol.com/johnp71/javasta2.html

Markov chains: http://www.saliu.com/Markov_Chains.html

BAYESIAN RESOURCES

(Korb 04). Kevin B. Korb and Ann E. Nicholson, ***Bayesian Artificial Intelligence***, CRC Press, 2004. The book includes a very extensive comparison of different Bayesian tools available in an online appendix at: http://www.csse.monash.edu.au/bai/book/appendix_b.pdf

Links to major sources of information on Bayesian Networks are available from Kevin Patrick Murphy's homepage. In particular his links to Tutorials and Software contain many other links to resources, and comparisons of Bayesian products and software: http://www.ai.mit.edu/~murphyk/

Microsoft's Free Bayesian analysis tool, Bayesian Network Editor and Toolkit for creating, assessing, and evaluating Bayesian Networks. MSBNx is used for Office Assistant, their Technical Support Troubleshooters, and antispam filters: http://research.microsoft.com/adapt/MSBNx/
Bayes Net Toolbox v5 for MATLAB. Cambridge, MA: MIT Computer Science and Artificial Intelligence Laboratory: http://www.ai.mit.edu/~murphyk/Software/BNT/bnt.html
Bayesian Knowledge Discoverer. Software able to learn Bayesian Belief Networks. A free student version of the commercial software is available: http://kmi.open.ac.uk/projects/bkd/
Java tools for Bayesian networks and AI: http://bndev.sourceforge.net/
Very sophisticated Bayesian tool for data mining and other problems, including a free trial version: http://www.bayesia.com/
Software for Manipulating Belief Networks: many resources for graphical belief function models, and related modes such as Bayesian networks, influence diagrams, and probabilistic graphical models: http://archives.math.utk.edu/
Bayesian and Dependency Networks Software: Large collection of Bayesian software and resources: http://www.kdnuggets.com/software/bayesian.html
Large collection of Bayesian and Markov software and resources:
http://www.cs.toronto.edu/~radford/fbm.software.html
Bayesian networks and influence diagrams. Great site with many resources on probabilistic, Bayesian theories and much software: http://www.ia. uned.es/~fjdiez/bayes/
Commercial tool for constructing Bayesian Belief and Influence Networks at: http://norsys.com. Excellent online tutorial on Bayes Networks with examples from automated diagnosis, prediction, financial risk management, portfolio allocation, insurance, modeling ecosystems, and sensor fusion: http://norsys.com/tutorials/netica/nt_toc_A.htm

(Das 99). Balaram Das, "**Representing Uncertainties Using Bayesian Networks**." Very detailed report of a mission-critical application of Bayesian networks for modeling and reasoning about uncertainties in a realistic naval anti-surface warfare scenario. Much more complex than the Prospector example in the book: http://www.dsto.defence.gov.au/corporate/reports/DSTO-TR-0918.pdf

CHAPTER 5

Dempster-Shafer Theory Homepage of Glenn Shafer. Many resources such as articles on his work: http://www.glennshafer.com/ In particular, a very short and clear explanation of the theory:
http://www.glennshafer.com/assets/ downloads/article48.pdf
Free MatLab Software on Belief Functions and Pattern Recognition. Software for different models such as Dempter-Shafer, Neural Nets, and Fuzzy logic: http://www.hds.utc.fr/~tdenoeux/software.htm
Good online teaching materials by Dave Marshall including Probability, Bayes theorem, Belief Models, Certainty Factors, Dempster-Shafer,Bayesian networks, and Fuzzy Logic:
http://www.cs.cf.ac.uk/Dave/AI2/node84.html
Good online teaching materials by Allan Ramsay. See links to why Predicate Logic is inadequate for the real world theory with coverage of fuzzy, Dempster-Shafer, and other alternatives:
http://www.ccl.umist.ac.uk/teaching/material/5005/
Dempster-Shafer Methods for Object Classification: Not light reading, but how Dempster-Shafter Theory may be used in anti-missile defense. http://www.stormingmedia.us/28/2812/A281293.html
What is Dempster-Shafer's model? Online introduction to the method:
http://iridia.ulb.ac.be/~psmets/WhatIsDS.pdf
International Fuzzy Systems Association home. Click on their Links to find many resources to fuzzy logic: http://www.pa.info.mie-u.ac.jp/~furu/ifsa/
University of Magdeburg has much neuro-fuzzy software and resources:
http://fuzzy.cs.uni-magdeburg.de/software.html

- Software on Neuro-Fuzzy Control
- Software on Neuro-Fuzzy Data Analysis (NEFCLASS now in JAVA!)
- Software on Neuro-Fuzzy Function Approximation
- Software on Fuzzy Clustering

- Teaching Software: Multilayer Perceptron Training Demonstration
- Teaching Software: Learning Vector Quantization Demonstration
- Teaching Software: Self-Organizing Map Training Demonstration
- Teaching Software: Hopfield Networks as Associative Memory

Christian Borgelt from the University of Magdeburg has a very extensive collection of free GNU software at: http://fuzzy.cs.uni-magdeburg.de/ ~borgelt/software.html. All programs are free GNU software which is distributed under the following terms: "All programs are free software; you can redistribute them and/or modify them under the terms of the GNU General Public License or the GNU Lesser (Library) General Public License as published by the Free Software Foundation (which license applies depends on the program)."

The following list is from his page:

Name	Lang.	Description
Apriori	C	Association Rule Induction/Frequent Item Set Mining
Eclat	C	Frequent Item Set Mining
MoSS/MoFa	Java	Molecular Substructure Miner
MPR	C/Java	Multivariate Polynomial Regression
Dtree	C	Decision and Regression Tree Induction
DTView	Java	Decision and Regression Tree Visualization
Bayes	C	Naive and Full Bayes Classifier Induction
BCView	C	Bayes Classifier Visualization
NPoss	C	Naive Possibilistic Classifier Induction
INeS	C	Induction of Network Structures (Graphical Models)
MLP	C	Multilayer Perceptron
LVQ	C	Learning Vector Quantization
Cluster	C	Fuzzy and Probabilistic Clustering Table C Table Utilities
Matrix	C	Matrix Utilities
CHull	C	Convex Hull Construction
MLP Demo	C	Multilayer Perceptron Demonstration
LVQ Demo	C	Learning Vector Quantization Demonstration
SOM Demo	C	Self-Organizing Map Demonstration
Hopf Demo	C	Hopfield Network Demonstration
Hamster	C	Programming Contest Environment
Bridgit	C	Simple Two Player Game

Data Generators

- The BAYES PACKAGE contains the program bcdb, with which a random database of sample cases can be generated from a probability distribution described by a naive or full Bayes classifier.
- The INES PACKAGE contains the program gendb, with which a random database of sample cases can be generated from a probability distribution described by a Bayesian network (over attributes with finite domains).

Fuzzy Logic Resources

Good page of links to many fuzzy logic resources from Ortec Engineering, a company that makes fuzzy logic hardware: http://www.ortech-engr.com/ fuzzy/reservoir.html#sharks

Fuzzy Logic Laboratorium has been having seminars each year on Fuzzy logic and math: http://www.flll.uni-linz.ac.at/navigation/main_navigation/frame_ research.html

Fuzzy Sets & Systems: A journal published by Elsevier Science Inc.
http://www.elsevier.com/wps/find/journaldescription.cws_home/505545/description

Fuzzy logic with CLIPS. NRC version:
http://ai.iit.nrc.ca/IR_public/fuzzy/fuzzyClips/fuzzyCLIPSIndex.html

James Mathews, "An Introduction to Fuzzy Logic." Brief tutorial on fuzzy logic and example of how fuzzy logic can be implemented in C++ with code and documentation:
http://www.genera ion5.org/content/1999/fuzzyintro.asp

CHAPTER 6

Microsoft has a huge Catalog on Knowledge Management available at:
http://www.microsoft.com/windows/catalog/

Example of a very sophisticated tool, KnowledgeBase.net 4.0, which attempts to manage all KM. Interesting reading about current concepts in the world of IT: http://www.knowledgebase.net/

Personal Construct Psychology. A popular theory dealing with the concept of people as being personal scientists, continually making hypothesis and theories about the world. This has been used as a basis for knowledge acquisition through Personal Repertory Grids. Many resources and links available at: http://repgrid.com/pcp/

Information and Knowledge Management Society has many conferences, papers, case studies, and software resources at: http://www.ikms.org.sg/resources/ index.html

Large international portal for Knowledge Management with many documents available for easy search: http://www.kmtool.net/

Brint Institute: The Knowledge Creating Company. Many excellent papers on a wide set of topics on Knowledge Management are on this site. Very nice abstracts of papers help you read those of interest: http://www.kmbook.com/

Course on Information Management in Organizations: models and platforms. Many resources on case studies and types of KM by Chun Wei Choo at:
http://choo.fis.utoronto.ca/FIS/Courses/LIS2102/LIS2102.slides.html

Soumeya L. Achour, et. al., "A UMLS-based Knowledge Acquisition Tool for Rule-based Clinical Decision Support System Development":
http://www.pubmedcentral.gov/articlerender.fcgi?tool=pmcentrez&artid=130080

Knowledge acquisition and expert system shell Acquire®. Although mentioned earlier in Applications of Expert Systems, this tool is mentioned again since it has knowledge acquisition abilities. While a tool is not as general purpose as a human knowledge engineer, it may be appropriate in certain domains where the knowledge is structured, like decision trees, so that it can be elicited by asking questions and rules automatically built. A trial version of their software is available at their website: http://www.aiinc.ca

Listen closely to the domain expert in coding the rules lest you write a fallacious rule. On the other hand, if it's for a legal expert system, that's OK since legal arguments do not have to be valid, only persuade the jury who has the better lawyer. The main thing about fallacious arguments is that people want to believe them. The best fallacies sound more convincing than the truth. The following have all been used successfully in persuasive arguments to convince someone that you're right and they're wrong even if you're wrong and they're right. Like Fallacies, **rhetoric** is about persuasive arguments and is also a very useful skill to know before getting married. Following is a **Partial list of Fallacies**: Note that even if you're not a lawyer or married, these are good techniques to convince your teacher you deserve an A, or your boss that you deserve a raise. http://www.iep.utm.edu/f/fallacies.htm

- Abusive Ad Hominem
- Accent
- Accident
- Ad Baculum
- Ad Consequentiam
- Ad Crumenum
- Ad Hoc Rescue
- Ad Hominem
- Ad Ignorantiam
- Ad Misericordiam
- Ad Novitatem
- Ad Numerum
- Ad Populum
- Ad Verecundiam
- Affirming the Consequent
- Amphiboly
- Anecdotal Evidence
- Anthropomorphism
- Appeal to Authority
- Appeal to Emotions
- Appeal to Force
- Appeal to Ignorance
- Appeal to the Masses
- Appeal to Money
- Appeal to the People
- Appeal to Pity
- Appeal to Consequence
- Argument from Outrage
- Argument from Popularity
- Argumentum Ad
- Avoiding the Issue
- Avoiding the Question
- Bald Man
- Bandwagon
- Begging the Question
- Biased Sample
- Biased Statistics
- Bifurcation
- Black-or-White
- Circular Reasoning
- Circumstantial Ad Hominem
- Clouding the Issue
- Common Belief
- Common Cause
- Common Practice
- Complex Question
- Composition
- Consensus Gentium
- Consequence
- Converse Accident
- Cover-up
- Cum Hoc, Ergo Propter Hoc
- Definist
- Denying the Antecedent
- Digression
- Distraction
- Division
- Domino
- Double Standard
- Either/Or
- Equivocation
- Etymological
- Every and All
- Excluded Middle
- False Analogy
- False Cause
- False Dichotomy
- False Dilemma
- Far-Fetched Hypothesis
- Faulty Comparison
- Formal
- Four Terms
- Gambler's
- Genetic
- Group Think
- Guilt by Association
- Hasty Conclusion
- Hasty Generalization
- Heap
- Hooded Man
- Ignoratio Elenchi
- Ignoring a Common Cause
- Incomplete Evidence
- Inconsistency
- Intensional
- Invalid Inference
- Irrelevant Conclusion
- Irrelevant Reason
- Is-Ought
- Jumping to Conclusions
- Line-Drawing
- Loaded Language
- Logical
- Lying
- Many Questions
- Misconditionalization
- Misleading Vividness
- Misrepresentation
- Missing the Point
- Modal
- Monte Carlo
- Name Calling
- Naturalistic
- Neglecting a Common Cause
- No Middle Ground
- No True Scotsman
- Non Causa Pro Causa
- Non Sequitur
- One-Sidedness
- Outrage, Argument from
- Oversimplification
- Past Practice
- Pathetic
- Perfectionist
- Petitio Principii
- Poisoning the Well
- Popularity, Argument from
- Post Hoc
- Prejudicial Language
- Questionable Analogy
- Questionable Cause
- Questionable Premise
- Quibbling
- Quoting out of Context
- Rationalization
- Red Herring
- Refutation by Caricature
- Regression
- Reversing Causation
- Scapegoating
- Scare Tactic
- Scope
- Secundum Quid
- Self-Fulfilling Prophecy
- Slanting
- Slippery Slope
- Small Sample
- Smear Tactic
- Smokescreen
- Sorites
- Special Pleading
- Specificity
- Stacking the Deck
- Stereotyping
- Straw Man
- Style Over Substance
- Subjectivist
- Superstitious Thinking
- Suppressed Evidence
- Sweeping Generalization
- Syllogistic
- Tokenism
- Traditional Wisdom
- Tu Quoque
- Two Wrongs Make a Right
- Undistributed Middle
- Unfalsifiability
- Unrepresentative Sample
- Untestability
- Weak Analogy
- Willed ignorance
- Wishful Thinking

CHAPTER 7

CLIPS has been used at hundreds of universities around the world to teach Expert Systems. The best way to find how typical courses are organized as well as teaching materials is by a search engine. Following are a few sample sites.

http://www.ghgcorp.com/clips/CLIPS.html Homepage of CLIPS. Links to many resources.
http://www.cs.unc.edu/Admin/Courses/descriptions/275.html
http://www.cs.wpi.edu/~dcb/courses/CS538/

INDEX